Lecture Notes in Computer Science   **13940**

The series Lecture Notes in Computer Science (LNCS), including its subseries Lecture Notes in Artificial Intelligence (LNAI) and Lecture Notes in Bioinformatics (LNBI), has established itself as a medium for the publication of new developments in computer science and information technology research, teaching, and education.

LNCS enjoys close cooperation with the computer science R & D community, the series counts many renowned academics among its volume editors and paper authors, and collaborates with prestigious societies. Its mission is to serve this international community by providing an invaluable service, mainly focused on the publication of conference and workshop proceedings and postproceedings. LNCS commenced publication in 1973.

Alexandra Boldyreva · Vladimir Kolesnikov
Editors

Public-Key Cryptography – PKC 2023

26th IACR International Conference
on Practice and Theory of Public-Key Cryptography
Atlanta, GA, USA, May 7–10, 2023
Proceedings, Part I

 Springer

Editors
Alexandra Boldyreva
Georgia Institute of Technology
Atlanta, GA, USA

Vladimir Kolesnikov ⓘ
Georgia Institute of Technology
Atlanta, GA, USA

ISSN 0302-9743   ISSN 1611-3349 (electronic)
Lecture Notes in Computer Science
ISBN 978-3-031-31367-7   ISBN 978-3-031-31368-4 (eBook)
https://doi.org/10.1007/978-3-031-31368-4

This Springer imprint is published by the registered company Springer Nature Switzerland AG
The registered company address is: Gewerbestrasse 11, 6330 Cham, Switzerland

Preface

The 26th International Conference on Practice and Theory of Public-Key Cryptography (PKC 2023) was held in Atlanta, Georgia, USA on May 7–10, 2023. It was sponsored by the International Association for Cryptologic Research (IACR).

The conference received 183 submissions, reviewed by the Program Committee of 49 cryptography experts working with 142 external reviewers. The reviewing process took 2.5 months and resulted in selecting 50 papers to appear in PKC 2023.

Papers were reviewed in the usual double-blind fashion. Program committee members were limited to two submissions, and their submissions were scrutinized more closely. The two program chairs were not allowed to submit papers.

The Program Committee recognized two papers and their authors. "The Hidden Number Problem with Small Unknown Multipliers: Cryptanalyzing MEGA in Six Queries and Other Applications," by Nadia Heninger and Keegan Ryan, and "Post-Quantum Anonymity of Kyber", by Varun Maram and Keita Xagawa, were selected Best Papers of the conference.

PKC 2023 welcomed Chris Peikert (University of Michigan) as the invited speaker.

The PKC Test-of-Time Award (ToT) recognizes outstanding and influential papers published in PKC about 15 years prior. The inaugural PKC Test of Time Award was given in PKC 2019 for papers published in the conference's initial years of the early 2000s and late 1990s. In 2023, the ToT committee, consisting of Alexandra Boldyreva, Goichiro Hanaoka, Vlad Kolesnikov, Moti Yung, and Yuliang Zheng, considered papers published in PKC 2006–2008 for the award. The committee selected the PKC 2008 paper "Unidirectional Chosen-Ciphertext Secure Proxy Re-encryption" by Benoît Libert and Damien Vergnaud for the Test-of-Time award.

PKC is the main IACR-sponsored conference with an explicit focus on public-key cryptography. It is a remarkable undertaking, only possible due to the hard work and significant contributions of many people. We would like to express our sincere gratitude to the authors of all submitted works, as well as to the PC and external reviewers, session chairs and presenters. Additionally, we would like to thank the following people and organizations for helping make PKC 2023 a success:

- Joseph Jaeger and Daniel Genkin – PKC 2023 General Chairs,
- Chris Peikert – invited speaker,
- Kay McKelly and Kevin McCurley – all things technical behind the scenes,
- Ellen Kolesnikova – design of the PKC 2023 logo,
- the team at Springer,
- Georgia Tech Hotel and Conference Center,
- Georgia Aquarium,
- School of Cybersecurity and Privacy at Georgia Tech - the academic home of the PKC 2023 Program and General Chairs.

We would also like to thank our sponsors: Google (platinum), Starkware (silver), Amazon AWS (silver), and Algorand (bronze). 2022 and 2023 were difficult years in the tech industry, making sponsors' contributions ever more valued. Their generous support covered several student travel stipends and helped minimize registration fees, including half-priced registration for all students.

Lastly, a big thanks to everyone who attended PKC 2023 in Atlanta. We hope you enjoyed the conference and the warm welcome of our city and university.

May 2023

Alexandra Boldyreva
Vlad Kolesnikov

Organization

General Chairs

Daniel Genkin   Georgia Tech, USA
Joseph Jaeger   Georgia Tech, USA

Program Committee Chairs

Alexandra Boldyreva   Georgia Tech, USA
Vladimir Kolesnikov   Georgia Tech, USA

Steering Committee

Masayuki Abe   NTT, Japan
Jung Hee Cheon   Seoul National University, Korea
Yvo Desmedt   University of Texas at Dallas, USA
Goichiro Hanaoka   AIST, Japan
Aggelos Kiayias   University of Edinburgh, UK
Tanja Lange   Eindhoven University of Technology, Netherlands
David Pointcheval   École Normale Supérieure, France
Moti Yung (Secretary)   Google Inc. & Columbia University, USA
Yuliang Zheng (Chair)   University of Alabama at Birmingham, USA

Program Committee

Ghada Almashaqbeh   University of Connecticut, USA
Nuttapong Attrapadung   AIST, Japan
Carlo Blundo   Università degli Studi di Salerno, Italy
Katharina Boudgoust   Aarhus University, Denmark
Dario Catalano   Università di Catania, Italy
Suvradip Chakraborty   ETH Zurich, Switzerland
Shan Chen   Southern University of Science & Technology, China
Jean Paul Degabriele   Technology Innovation Institute, UAE
Chaya Ganesh   Indian Institute of Science, India

Sean Hallgren	Penn State University, USA
David Heath	University of Illinois Urbana-Champaign, USA
Kristina Hostakova	ETH Zürich, Switzerland
Sorina Ionica	Université de Picardie Jules Verne, France
Stanislaw Jarecki	University of California, Irvine, USA
Shuichi Katsumata	AIST and PQShield Ltd., Japan
Kaoru Kurosawa	AIST, Japan
Tancrède Lepoint	Amazon, USA
Christian Majenz	Technical University of Denmark, Denmark
Daniel Masny	Meta, USA
Ryo Nishimaki	NTT Social Informatics Laboratories, Japan
Adam O'Neill	UMass Amherst, USA
Charalampos Papamanthou	Yale University, USA
Alain Passelègue	Inria and ENS Lyon, France
Sikhar Patranabis	IBM Research India, India
Alice Pellet-Mary	CNRS and Université de Bordeaux, France
Edoardo Persichetti	Florida Atlantic University, USA
Rachel Player	Royal Holloway, University of London, UK
David Pointcheval	ENS, Paris, France
Antigoni Polychroniadou	JPMorgan AI Research, USA
Willy Quach	Northeastern University, USA
Elizabeth Quaglia	Royal Holloway, University of London, UK
Adeline Roux-Langlois	Normandie Univ, GREYC, France
John Schanck	Mozilla, USA
Peter Scholl	Aarhus University, Denmark
Dominique Schröder	FAU Erlangen-Nürnberg, Germany
Peter Schwabe	MPI-SP & Radboud University, Netherlands
Jae Hong Seo	Hanyang University, Korea
Abhi Shelat	Northeastern University, USA
Akira Takahashi	University of Edinburgh, UK
Keisuke Tanaka	Tokyo Institute of Technology, Japan
Jean-Pierre Tillich	Inria, France
Frederik Vercauteren	KU Leuven, Belgium
Damien Vergnaud	Sorbonne Université, France
Ivan Visconti	University of Salerno, Italy
Benjamin Wesolowski	CNRS and University of Bordeaux, France
David Wu	UT Austin, USA
Kevin Yeo	Google and Columbia University, USA
Mark Zhandry	NTT Research & Princeton University, USA
Vassilis Zikas	Purdue University, USA

Additional Reviewers

Behzad Abdolmaleki
Calvin Abou Haidar
Ojaswi Acharya
Gorjan Alagic
Gennaro Avitabile
Arnab Bag
Shi Bai
Magali Bardet
Hugo Beguinet
Fabrice Benhamouda
Loris Bergerat
Ward Beullens
Olivier Blazy
Maxime Bombar
Cecilia Boschini
Vincenzo Botta
Samuel Bouaziz-Ermann
Charles Bouillaguet
Nicholas Brandt
Lennart Braun
Matteo Campanelli
André Chailloux
Rohit Chatterjee
Jesus-Javier Chi-Dominguez
Hien Chu
Heewon Chung
Michele Ciampi
Jean-Sébastien Coron
Anamaria Costache
Baptiste Cottier
Jan-Pieter D'Anvers
Pratish Datta
Gareth T. Davies
Paola De Perthuis
Jean-Christophe Deneuville
Julien Devevey
Mario Di Raimondo
Javad Doliskani
Keita Emura
Andreas Erwig
Daniel Escudero
Andre Esser
Pouria Fallahpour

Antonio Faonio
Joël Felderhoff
Weiqi Feng
Rune Fiedler
Georgios Fotiadis
Tako Boris Fouotsa
Georg Fuchsbauer
Clemente Galdi
Romain Gay
Robin Geelen
Paul Gerhart
Lenaïck Gouriou
Mohammad Hajiabadi
Erin Hales
Mickaël Hamdad
Patrick Harasser
Keitaro Hashimoto
Sorina Ionica
Vincenzo Iovino
Aayush Jain
Christian Janson
Corentin Jeudy
Saqib Kakvi
Daniel Kales
Harish Karthikeyan
Julia Kastner
Mojtaba Khalili
Hamidreza Khoshakhlagh
Ryo Kikuchi
Dongwoo Kim
Elena Kirshanova
Fuyuki Kitagawa
David Kohel
Sebastian Kolby
Walter Krawec
Mikhail Kudinov
Péter Kutas
Roman Langrehr
Mario Larangeira
Changmin Lee
Antonin Leroux
Andrea Lesavourey
Varun Madathil

Lorenzo Magliocco
Jules Maire
Monosij Maitra
Takahiro Matsuda
Liam Medley
Kelsey Melissaris
Hart Montgomery
Ngoc Khanh Nguyen
Ky Nguyen
Thi Thu Quyen Nguyen
Phong Nguyen
Ruben Niederhagen
Koji Nuida
Tapas Pal
Kunjal Panchal
Mahak Pancholi
Lorenz Panny
Robi Pedersen
Lucas Prabel
Thomas Prest
Sihang Pu
Krijn Reijnders
Mahshid Riahinia
Doreen Riepel
Felix Rohrbach
Mélissa Rossi
Olga Sanina
Paolo Santini

André Schrottenloher
Robert Schädlich
Yixin Shen
Mark Simkin
Animesh Singh
Sayani Sinha
Luisa Siniscalchi
Christoph Striecks
Atsushi Takayasu
Debadrita Talapatra
Aravind Thyagarajan
Junichi Tomida
Toi Tomita
Monika Trimoska
Damien Vidal
Chenkai Wang
Yohei Watanabe
Christian Weinert
Weiqiang Wen
Keita Xagawa
Shota Yamada
Takashi Yamakawa
Yibin Yang
Kazuki Yoneyama
Yusuke Yoshida
Bor de Kock
Rafael del Pino
Wessel van Woerden

Contents – Part I

Isogenies

Crypto for Crypto

Contents – Part II

Encryption

ZK I

IO and ZK II

Post-quantum Cryptography

Post-quantum Anonymity of Kyber

Varun Maram[1]([✉]) and Keita Xagawa[2]

[1] Department of Computer Science, ETH Zurich, Zürich, Switzerland
vmaram@inf.ethz.ch
[2] NTT Social Informatics Laboratories, Musashino, Japan
keita.xagawa.zv@hco.ntt.co.jp

Abstract. Kyber is a key-encapsulation mechanism (KEM) that was recently selected by NIST in its PQC standardization process; it is also the *only* scheme to be selected in the context of public-key encryption (PKE) and key establishment. The main security target for KEMs, and their associated PKE schemes, in the NIST PQC context has been IND-CCA security. However, some important modern applications also require their underlying KEMs/PKE schemes to provide *anonymity* (Bellare *et al.*, ASIACRYPT 2001). Examples of such applications include anonymous credential systems, cryptocurrencies, broadcast encryption schemes, authenticated key exchange, and auction protocols. It is hence important to analyze the compatibility of NIST's new PQC standard in such "beyond IND-CCA" applications.

Some starting steps were taken by Grubbs *et al.* (EUROCRYPT 2022) and Xagawa (EUROCRYPT 2022) wherein they studied the anonymity properties of most NIST PQC third round candidate KEMs. Unfortunately, they were unable to show the anonymity of Kyber because of certain technical barriers.

In this paper, we overcome said barriers and resolve the open problems posed by Grubbs *et al.* (EUROCRYPT 2022) and Xagawa (EUROCRYPT 2022) by establishing the anonymity of Kyber, and the (hybrid) PKE schemes derived from it, in a post-quantum setting. Along the way, we also provide an approach to obtain tight IND-CCA security proofs for Kyber with *concrete* bounds; this resolves another issue identified by the aforementioned works related to the post-quantum IND-CCA security claims of Kyber from a provable security point-of-view. Our results also extend to Saber, a NIST PQC third round finalist, in a similar fashion.

Keywords: anonymity · post-quantum cryptography · NIST PQC standardization · KEM · hybrid PKE · quantum random oracle model

1 Introduction

Roughly six years after kicking-off its post-quantum cryptography (PQC) standardization process, the US National Institute of Standards and Technology (NIST) has finally announced the first set of cryptographic algorithms that will be standardized (along with a set of alternate algorithms that will be considered

© International Association for Cryptologic Research 2023
A. Boldyreva and V. Kolesnikov (Eds.): PKC 2023, LNCS 13940, pp. 3–35, 2023.
https://doi.org/10.1007/978-3-031-31368-4_1

for future standardization) [2]. Among this first set of algorithms, CRYSTALS-Kyber [41] (or Kyber, for short) is the *only* key-encapsulation mechanism (KEM) selected by NIST for standardization, in the context of public-key encryption (PKE) and key-establishment. One of NIST's main criteria for evaluating and selecting PQC standards in the PKE/KEM category was on the algorithms' ability to offer semantic security with respect to adaptive chosen ciphertext attacks (a.k.a. IND-CCA security). IND-CCA security is widely accepted as a standard notion of security for PKE schemes and KEMs since the property suffices for many important use cases. However, as a NIST PQC standard, since Kyber is intended to be widely used for decades to come, it is also important to study the scheme's compatibility with emerging modern applications that require security properties beyond IND-CCA.

One such important security property is *anonymity* (or key privacy). Roughly speaking, a PKE scheme is said to be anonymous [6] if a ciphertext hides the receiver's information by not leaking anything about the public key used for encryption; anonymous KEMs are defined analogously [28,46]. Such anonymous cryptographic primitives are fundamental in several deployed privacy-enhancing systems, such as anonymous cryptocurrencies like Zcash [8], anonymous broadcast encryption schemes [5,37], anonymous credential systems [14], anonymous authenticated key exchange [12,24,25,42], auction protocols [40], and so on. The recent works of [28,46] have hence looked into anonymity properties of the NIST PQC third round candidate KEMs, and the hybrid PKE schemes derived from them via the "KEM-DEM" paradigm [16]. Collectively, both those works have established the post-quantum anonymity of all nine candidate KEMs except for three, which unfortunately includes the current standard Kyber (the other two KEMs being Saber [19] and Streamlined NTRU Prime [9]).

To see why the works of [28,46] could not establish the anonymity of Kyber, it helps to first look at how the NIST PQC candidate KEMs are constructed. The KEM candidates first specify a weakly secure (e.g., IND-CPA secure) "base" PKE scheme and then apply some variant of the *Fujisaki-Okamoto (FO) transform* [20,26,27,29] to obtain their respective KEMs. The "original" FO transforms of [20,26,27,29] were heavily analyzed in the idealized *Random Oracle Model (ROM)* [7], and later, in the *Quantum ROM (QROM)* [11] which is relevant for studying post-quantum security; it was shown in a long sequence of works (e.g., [10,22,31,32,35,39]) that such original transforms boost an IND-CPA secure PKE scheme to an IND-CCA secure KEM in the QROM. In the context of anonymity, it was shown in [28,46] that the FO transforms also elevate a weakly anonymous (i.e., ANO-CPA secure) base PKE scheme to a strongly anonymous (i.e., ANO-CCA secure) KEM in the QROM.

However, the specific variant of FO transform used in Kyber deviates quite significantly from the original transforms above. At a high-level, Kyber hashes more "intermediate" values in its internal computations than is the case in FO transforms in the literature. At the same time, this additional hashing is done in a way which creates barriers in applying the proof strategies used in [28,46] to show the anonymity boosting properties of the original FO transforms in the QROM. Hence, this raises the following question:

Is Kyber (provably) ANO-CCA secure in the QROM?

At the same time, as observed in [28,46], the additional hashing in Kyber also acts as a barrier in proving even the scheme's IND-CCA security in the QROM with the concrete bounds claimed in its specification document [4]. Given the importance placed on IND-CCA security in the NIST PQC standardization process, this raises another question:

Can we obtain a (tight) proof of IND-CCA security for Kyber in the QROM with concrete bounds?

1.1 Our Contributions

We answer the above questions in the affirmative by presenting the following results, thereby resolving the corresponding open problems posed in [28,46]:

- We show that Kyber and the hybrid PKE schemes derived from it are ANO-CCA secure in the QROM, under the standard hardness assumption of solving the *module learning-with-error (MLWE) problem* [13,36].
- We describe an approach to obtain tight IND-CCA security with *concrete* bounds for Kyber in the QROM, under the MLWE hardness assumption.

It is worth mentioning that the NIST PQC third round finalist Saber [19] implements the *same* variant of FO transform as Kyber in its KEM construction. Hence, our above results on anonymity and tight IND-CCA security also apply to Saber in a similar fashion, where we would instead need to rely on the hardness of solving the *module learning-with-rounding (MLWR) problem* [18].

We hope that our above results provide further confidence to cryptographic scheme designers in using the new PQC standard Kyber not only in general-purpose applications that need IND-CCA security but also in emerging modern applications that require anonymity.

1.2 Technical Overview

Here we give a high-level description of our approach to obtain proofs of anonymity (i.e., ANO-CCA security) and (tight) IND-CCA security for Kyber in the QROM. We first focus on the familiar setting of IND-CCA security and later consider ANO-CCA security.

IND-CCA Security of Kyber. We begin by first describing an *alternative* – and *"simpler"* – approach to prove IND-CCA security of Kyber in the QROM, and then contrasting it with our approach. As noted above, virtually all NIST PQC candidate KEMs, including Kyber, use variants of the FO transformation in their respective KEM constructions. Before discussing the specific variant

KGen′	Encap(pk)	Decap(sk′, c)
1 : (pk, sk) ← KGen	1 : $m \leftarrow_\$ \mathcal{M}$	1 : Parse sk′ = (sk, s)
2 : $s \leftarrow \perp$	2 : $r \leftarrow G_r(m)$	2 : $m' \leftarrow \mathsf{Dec}(\mathsf{sk}, c)$
3 : $\boxed{s \leftarrow_\$ \mathcal{M}}$	3 : $c \leftarrow \mathsf{Enc}(\mathsf{pk}, m; r)$	3 : $r' \leftarrow G_r(m')$
4 : sk′ ← (sk, s)	4 : $\overline{k} \leftarrow G_k(m)$	4 : $c' \leftarrow \mathsf{Enc}(\mathsf{pk}, m'; r')$
5 : **return** (pk, sk′)	5 : **return** $(c, \overline{k})$	5 : if $c' = c$ then
		6 : **return** $G_k(m')$
		7 : $\boxed{\textbf{else return } G_k(s, c)}$
		8 : **else return** $\perp$

Fig. 1. The KEMs $\mathsf{FO}_m^\perp[\mathsf{PKE}, G_r, G_k]$ and $\boxed{\mathsf{FO}_m^{\not\perp}[\mathsf{PKE}, G_r, G_k]}$. Here $\mathcal{M}$ is the message space of $\mathsf{PKE} = (\mathsf{KGen}, \mathsf{Enc}, \mathsf{Dec})$ and G_r, G_k are hash functions with appropriate domain and co-domain. For notational simplicity, we set $s \leftarrow \perp$ for $\mathsf{FO}_m^\perp$.

used by Kyber, let us first consider the *standard* FO transforms introduced by Dent [20] and Hofheinz et al. [29], namely the *explicitly-rejecting* $\mathsf{FO}_m^\perp$ and the *implicitly-rejecting* $\mathsf{FO}_m^{\not\perp}$, described in Fig. 1.

For ease of exposition, we consider a simplified version of Kyber's FO variant where the only main difference compared to $\mathsf{FO}_m^\perp$ is that, instead of stopping at "$\overline{k} \leftarrow G_k(m)$" (Line 4 in $\mathsf{Encap}(\mathsf{pk})$, Fig. 1) during encapsulation, there is an extra layer of hashing to compute the final encapsulated key. Namely, Kyber outputs keys of the form "$k \leftarrow H'(\overline{k}, H(c))$" where H, H' are two additional hash functions; decapsulation proceeds analogously where instead of returning a $\perp$ when rejecting a ciphertext, Kyber *implicitly* rejects by returning $H'(s, H(c))$. Hence, (this simplified version of) Kyber can be seen as a "wrapper" scheme w.r.t. the $\mathsf{FO}_m^\perp$ KEM with appropriate modifications to the encapsulation and decapsulation steps. As a result, the IND-CCA security of Kyber can be easily shown by relying on the IND-CCA security of the underlying $\mathsf{FO}_m^\perp$ KEM.

To sketch out the proof, we start with the IND-CCA security game w.r.t. (the simplified) Kyber where the adversary gets a challenge ciphertext c^* and the *real* encapsulated key "$H'(\overline{k}^*, H(c^*))$" (refer to Subsect. 2.2 for a precise description of the IND-CCA security games for KEMs). We then modify the game via the following "hybrids":

1. In the first hybrid, we provide the adversary with a new encapsulated key "$H'(\overline{k}', H(c^*))$", where $\overline{k}'$ is an independent and uniformly random value. This modification is justified by relying on IND-CCA security of the underlying $\mathsf{FO}_m^\perp$ KEM. Because note that $\overline{k}^*$ can be seen as the "real" encapsulated key of the $\mathsf{FO}_m^\perp$ KEM and $\overline{k}'$ a "random" key, and IND-CCA security of $\mathsf{FO}_m^\perp$ implies (computational) indistinguishability of both these keys. One important thing worth noting here is that in the reduction to IND-CCA security of $\mathsf{FO}_m^\perp$, we can simulate the decapsulation oracle of Kyber as follows. We

first sample the secret $s \leftarrow_{\$} \mathcal{M}$. Then to simulate the "Kyber-decapsulation" of a ciphertext c, we first perform the "$\mathsf{FO}_m^{\perp}$-decapsulation" of c: if the result is a key $\bar{k}$, we return the "Kyber-key" as $H'(\bar{k}, H(c))$; if the result is $\perp$, we return the "Kyber-key" as $H'(s, H(c))$. Note that for this reduction to work, it is crucial that the underlying FO transform, $\mathsf{FO}_m^{\perp}$, is explicitly rejecting, in order to perfectly simulate the rejection of ciphertexts during decapsulation.

2. In the second and final hybrid, we again switch back to the IND-CCA security game w.r.t. Kyber where the adversary gets a uniformly *random* encapsulated key "$\hat{k}$" which is independent of c^*. This modification is again justified by relying on the *pseudorandomness* provided by the quantum random oracle $H'(\bar{k}', \cdot)$: i.e., since the "PRF key" $\bar{k}'$ is independent of c^*, one can argue the (statistical) indistinguishability of the keys "$H'(\bar{k}', H(c^*))$" and "$\hat{k}$".

The IND-CCA security of (the simplified) Kyber in the QROM hence follows since the adversary cannot efficiently distinguish between the real and random encapsulated keys "$H'(\bar{k}^*, H(c^*))$" and "$\hat{k}$" respectively in the above hybrids.

However, a major issue with the above approach to prove *concrete* (and *tight*) IND-CCA security of Kyber is related to our dependence on the IND-CCA security of $\mathsf{FO}_m^{\perp}$ *in the QROM* in the first place. IND-CCA security of the $\mathsf{FO}_m^{\perp}$ transform, with concrete bounds, has been notoriously hard to prove in the QROM. To put things in context, let us first consider $\mathsf{FO}_m^{\not\perp}$, the *implicitly-rejecting* variant of $\mathsf{FO}_m^{\perp}$. A long sequence of prior works [10,30,32,35,39] provided concrete IND-CCA security proofs for $\mathsf{FO}_m^{\not\perp}$ in the QROM, with each follow-up improving the tightness of the corresponding reduction. For example, Kuchta *et al.* [35] were the first to provide a security proof that avoided a square-root advantage loss w.r.t. the weak (IND-CPA/OW-CPA) security of the underlying PKE scheme; this loss seemed inherent with previous reductions for the FO transforms in the QROM. To also showcase the relative simplicity of analyzing the IND-CCA security of $\mathsf{FO}_m^{\not\perp}$ in the QROM, Unruh [45] showed a framework for *formally verifying* the corresponding post-quantum security proof of the implicitly-rejecting transform provided in [30].

When it comes to the *explicitly-rejecting* $\mathsf{FO}_m^{\perp}$ transform, the story is arguably more complicated. Looking at prior work, some starting steps were taken in [3, 29,33,43] in this regard wherein concrete IND-CCA security proofs for *modified* versions of the $\mathsf{FO}_m^{\perp}$ transform – which include an additional "key confirmation" hash in the ciphertext – were provided (however, security proofs in [3,43] were later found to have bugs in them [3]). The *unmodified* $\mathsf{FO}_m^{\perp}$ transform was later analyzed in [34,48] in the QROM; however, the provided security proofs had some subtle gaps [22]. Quite recently, these gaps were resolved in [22,31] resulting in the first IND-CCA security proofs for the original $\mathsf{FO}_m^{\perp}$ transform in the QROM with concrete bounds. However, there are a couple of issues:

- The IND-CCA security analyses of $\mathsf{FO}_m^{\perp}$ by Don et al. [22] and Hövelmanns et al. [31] assume certain computational and statistical properties of the underlying PKE scheme which are not well-studied w.r.t. the NIST PQC candidates – *especially Kyber*. These properties include γ-*spreadness*, so-called *Find Failing Plaintext (FFP) security* (as introduced in [31]), etc.

– Even if the above properties are properly analyzed, the resulting IND-CCA security bounds for the final $FO_m^\perp$-based KEM are non-tight when compared to the corresponding state-of-the-art bounds for the implicitly-rejecting $FO_m^{\not\perp}$. E.g., all known IND-CCA security proofs for $FO_m^\perp$ transform in the QROM incur a square-root advantage loss w.r.t. passive security of the underlying PKE scheme. This is in contrast to the tight proof of IND-CCA security for $FO_m^{\not\perp}$ shown in [35]. In other words, we would also incur these non-tight bounds in our "wrapper-based" IND-CCA security analysis of Kyber in the QROM, when relying on the corresponding post-quantum security of $FO_m^\perp$.

This brings us to one of the main technical contributions of this paper. In essence, we provide a way to obtain tight proofs of IND-CCA security for Kyber in the QROM by salvaging the above "wrapper-based" approach – *even when the underlying FO transform is implicitly-rejecting*. As noted in the above reduction, we crucially relied on the explicit-rejection of $FO_m^\perp$ in order to perfectly simulate decapsulation oracles. But if we start with the $FO_m^{\not\perp}$ transform, it is not so straightforward how to simulate the "Kyber-decapsulation" oracle using the "$FO_m^{\not\perp}$-decapsulation" oracle especially when the latter oracle rejects ciphertexts; as described in Fig. 1 (Line 9), the rejection output $G_k(s, c)$ still "looks" like a valid key.

To resolve the above simulation issue, we start with the $FO_m^{\not\perp}$ transform and modify its decapsulation algorithm in a way such that the overall IND-CCA security of the transform in the QROM is affected negligibly (in a statistical sense). Similarly, we also modify the decapsulation procedure used in the actual Kyber scheme such that (i) the IND-CCA security of the original and modified schemes are statistically equivalent, and (ii) the IND-CCA security of the modified scheme can be reduced to the IND-CCA security of the modified $FO_m^{\not\perp}$ transform wherein we can now simulate the "modified-Kyber-decapsulation" oracle using the "modified-$FO_m^{\not\perp}$-decapsulation" oracle perfectly in the corresponding reduction. It is then not hard to see that this *indirectly* allows us to base IND-CCA security of the actual Kyber scheme on that of the unmodified $FO_m^{\not\perp}$ transform, with a negligible loss in tightness; full details of our security proof can be found in Sect. 4.

But one thing we would like to stress is that our current IND-CCA security proof for Kyber in Sect. 4 is non-tight in the sense that we still incur a square-root advantage loss w.r.t. passive security of the underlying PKE scheme mentioned above. This is because we are currently basing the IND-CCA security of Kyber on the (non-tight) IND-CCA security of $FO_m^{\not\perp}$ proven in [32,39] in the QROM, which incurs a similar square-root loss. The reason we are not relying on the tighter proof of IND-CCA security for $FO_m^{\not\perp}$ shown in [35] – which avoids such a loss – is that their tight proof makes an additional assumption on the underlying PKE scheme: namely, that the scheme satisfies a property called *injectivity* (as defined in [10]). However a detailed analysis of Kyber's injectivity is lacking, particularly in the context of NIST's PQC standardization process, and we also consider it out of the scope of our work. At the same time, this showcases an advantage of our "wrapper-based" approach w.r.t. the implicitly-rejecting $FO_m^{\not\perp}$

in that, if the injectivity of Kyber is well established in the future, then one can simply "plug in" [35]'s tight IND-CCA security result for $FO_m^{\not\perp}$ in our analysis in Sect. 4 as a *drop-in replacement* to essentially obtain a tight proof of IND-CCA security for Kyber in the QROM.

ANO-CCA Security of Kyber. Now when it comes to the main focus of this paper, i.e., the anonymity of Kyber in the QROM, we follow the framework of [46]. Namely, we instead show that Kyber satisfies a stronger security notion called *strong pseudorandomness (or, SPR-CCA security)*. A KEM is said to be SPR-CCA secure if, roughly speaking, an adversary cannot distinguish a *real* ciphertext/encapsulated-key pair (c^*, k^*) from a *random* pair (c', k') where c' is a random ciphertext and k' is a random key (see Subsect. 2.2 for a formal definition of SPR-CCA security where we also need to consider a *simulator* to specify what we mean by a "random" ciphertext c').

It was shown in [46] that SPR-CCA security straightforwardly implies ANO-CCA security. The key insight used in [46] is that since SPR-CCA security is a "single key-pair notion" like IND-CCA security (i.e., the corresponding security game involves a single KEM key-pair), it is easier to extend the IND-CCA security analysis of a KEM to also show its SPR-CCA security than trying to directly prove its ANO-CCA security; note that ANO-CCA security is a "double key-pair notion" and hence would involve simulating *two* different decapsulation oracles in the security analysis.

Following our above discussion on IND-CCA security of Kyber in the QROM, it is straightforward to show its SPR-CCA security by relying on the same strong pseudorandomness of $FO_m^{\perp}$-based KEMs by adopting the "wrapper-based" approach. But as noted above, since proving IND-CCA security of $FO_m^{\perp}$ has been a complicated affair, one can expect the same when it comes to proving "beyond IND-CCA" security properties (e.g., SPR-CCA) of the explicitly-rejecting transform. In fact, we consider extending the IND-CCA security analysis of $FO_m^{\perp}$ in [22,31] to other important properties, such as SPR-CCA security, in the QROM beyond the scope of this paper, and leave it as an open problem.

In contrast, SPR-CCA security of the implicitly-rejecting $FO_m^{\not\perp}$ in the QROM was already shown in [46], further indicating the simplicity of analyzing $FO_m^{\not\perp}$ in the QROM – when compared to its explicitly-rejecting counterpart – even w.r.t. security properties beyond IND-CCA. Hence, our above "wrapper-based" approach w.r.t. the underlying $FO_m^{\not\perp}$ transform can be used to also show SPR-CCA security – and hence, ANO-CCA security – of Kyber in the QROM; in such an approach (which is presented in detail in Sect. 5), we need to introduce additional hybrids to replace the real ciphertext c^* with a random ciphertext c'. This showcases yet another advantage of using our approach: *quantitatively*, not only does Kyber inherit existing tight (IND-CCA) security bounds for $FO_m^{\not\perp}$ in the QROM as seen above, but also *qualitatively*, Kyber inherits "beyond IND-CCA" security properties (such as SPR-CCA) of $FO_m^{\not\perp}$ in the post-quantum setting.

1.3 Related Work

In concurrent work, Ding *et al.* [21] established the injectivity of Kyber by providing both theoretical and numerical bounds. As mentioned above, this means that we can obtain tight IND-CCA security bounds for Kyber in the QROM (tighter than our current bounds in Sect. 4) by using our aforementioned "wrapper-based" approach in conjunction with [35]'s tight security analysis of $\mathsf{FO}_m^{\not\perp}$-based KEMs in the QROM.

Recently, Chen *et al.* [15] analyzed the concrete IND-CCA security of Kyber in the QROM using an alternative approach; more specifically, it involves using a well-known indistinguishability result between random functions and random permutations in the quantum setting [47]. However, since their reduction algorithm needs to efficiently simulate a random *permutation* in the QROM, their resulting IND-CCA security bounds include an additive term $O(\sqrt{q^3/2^{128}})$ which significantly restricts the number of quantum random oracle queries q an adversary can make – this is in contrast to the "collision-resistance" term $O(q^3/2^{256})$ in our obtained bounds in Sect. 4 (also see Remark 1 for some more related discussion).

2 Preliminaries

Notations. We denote $\lambda \in \mathbb{N}$ to be the security parameter. We sometimes omit writing λ when describing cryptosystems if it is clear from the context. PPT and QPT stand for probabilistic polynomial time and quantum polynomial time respectively. We use the standard O-notations. A function $f(\lambda)$ is said to be *negligible* if $f(\lambda) = \lambda^{-\omega(1)}$. For a finite set S, we write "$x \leftarrow_s S$" to denote that x is sampled uniformly at random from S. The value $[x = y]$ is defined to be 1 if $x = y$ and 0 otherwise. For probabilistic algorithms we use $y \leftarrow \mathcal{A}(x)$ to denote a (randomized) output of $\mathcal{A}$ on input x; we also sometimes specify the randomness r used in $\mathcal{A}$ as $y \leftarrow \mathcal{A}(x;r)$. We use "$\mathcal{A}^O$" to denote that the algorithm $\mathcal{A}$ has access to the oracle O; we'll also make it clear whether $\mathcal{A}$ has *classical* or *quantum* access to O in the description of our setting.

2.1 Quantum Random Oracle Model

Roughly speaking, the quantum random oracle model (QROM) is an idealized model where a hash function is modeled as a publicly and quantumly accessible random oracle. In this paper, we model a quantum oracle $O \colon \{0,1\}^n \to \{0,1\}^m$ as a mapping $|x\rangle|y\rangle \mapsto |x\rangle|y \oplus O(x)\rangle$, where $x \in \{0,1\}^n$ and $y \in \{0,1\}^m$. Refer to [11] for a more detailed description of the model.

We now review some useful lemmas in the QROM. The first lemma describes the collision resistance of quantum random oracles.

Lemma 1 ([47, Theorem 3.1]). *There is a universal constant C (< 648) such that the following holds: Let $\mathcal{X}$ and $\mathcal{Y}$ be finite sets. Let $H \colon \mathcal{X} \to \mathcal{Y}$ be a random oracle. If an unbounded-time quantum adversary $\mathcal{A}$ makes a query to H at most*

q times, then we have $\Pr[H(x_0) = H(x_1) \wedge x_0 \neq x_1 : (x_0, x_1) \leftarrow \mathcal{A}^H] \leq \frac{C(q+1)^3}{|\mathcal{Y}|}$, where all oracle accesses of $\mathcal{A}$ can be quantum.

The second lemma intuitively states that a quantum random oracle can be used as a *quantum-accessible* pseudorandom function, even if the distinguisher is given full access to the quantum random oracle in addition to the PRF oracle.

Lemma 2 ([32, Lemma 4]). *Let $H \colon \mathcal{K} \times \mathcal{X} \to \mathcal{Y}$ and $R \colon \mathcal{X} \to \mathcal{Y}$ be two independent quantum random oracles. Define the oracles $F_0 = H(k, \cdot)$, where we have the "PRF key" $k \leftarrow_\$ \mathcal{K}$, and $F_1 = R(\cdot)$. Consider an oracle algorithm/distinguisher A^{H,F_i} ($i \in \{0,1\}$) that makes at most q queries to H. Then we have $|\Pr[1 \leftarrow A^{H,F_0}] - \Pr[1 \leftarrow A^{H,F_1}]| \leq \frac{2q}{\sqrt{|\mathcal{K}|}}$.*

The lemmas below provide a generic reduction from a hiding-style property (indistinguishability) to a one-wayness-style property (unpredictability) in the QROM. It is also popularly known as the *One-Way To Hiding (OW2H) lemma* in the literature, originally appearing in [44]. We first state the original OW2H lemma of [44] and later state a generalized version of the OW2H lemma from [3]. As will be seen in Sect. 4, different parts of our security analysis of Kyber use different versions of the OW2H lemma for the sake of convenience.

Lemma 3 (Original OW2H [44]). *Let $H \colon \mathcal{X} \to \mathcal{Y}$ be a quantum random oracle. Consider an oracle algorithm A^H that makes at most q queries to H. Let B^H be an oracle algorithm that on input x does the following: picks $i \leftarrow_\$ \{1, \dots, q\}$ and $y \leftarrow_\$ \mathcal{Y}$, runs $A^H(x, y)$ until (just before) the i-th query, measures the argument of the query in the computational basis and outputs the measurement outcome (if A makes less than i queries, B outputs $\perp \notin \mathcal{X}$). Let*

$$P_A^1 = \Pr[1 \leftarrow A^H(x, H(x)) : x \leftarrow_\$ \mathcal{X}]$$
$$P_A^2 = \Pr[1 \leftarrow A^H(x, y) : x \leftarrow_\$ \mathcal{X}, y \leftarrow_\$ \mathcal{Y}]$$
$$P_B = \Pr[x \leftarrow B^H(x) : x \leftarrow_\$ \mathcal{X}].$$

Then, we have $|P_A^1 - P_A^2| \leq 2q\sqrt{P_B}$.

Lemma 4 (Generalized OW2H [3, Theorem 3]). *Let $\mathcal{S} \subseteq \mathcal{X}$ be random. Let $G, H \colon \mathcal{X} \to \mathcal{Y}$ be random functions satisfying $G(x) = H(x)$ for every $x \notin \mathcal{S}$. Let z be a random bit string. ($\mathcal{S}, G, H, z$ may have arbitrary joint distribution.) Let A be a quantum oracle algorithm making q queries to its corresponding oracle (either G or H).[1] Let B^H be an oracle algorithm that on input z does the following: picks $i \leftarrow_\$ \{1, \dots, q\}$, runs $A^H(z)$ until (just before) the i-th query,*

---

[1] Strictly speaking, the generalized OW2H lemma of [3] takes into account the *parallel* oracle queries made by A by having q to be the so-called *query depth* of A. In this paper, we won't consider parallel queries of A for the sake of simplicity and denote q to be the *query number* of A. But our subsequent analysis of Kyber can be modified to also consider parallel oracle queries in a straightforward way.

measures all query input registers in the computational basis, and outputs the set $\mathcal{T} = \{t_1, \ldots, t_{|\mathcal{T}|}\}$ *of measurement outcomes. Let*

$$P_{\text{left}} = \Pr[1 \leftarrow A^H(z)]$$
$$P_{\text{right}} = \Pr[1 \leftarrow A^G(z)]$$
$$P_{\text{guess}} = \Pr[\mathcal{S} \cap \mathcal{T} \neq \emptyset : \mathcal{T} \leftarrow B^H(x)].$$

Then, $|P_{\text{left}} - P_{\text{right}}| \leq 2q\sqrt{P_{\text{guess}}}$. *The same result also holds with* B^G *instead of* B^H *in the definition of* P_B.

2.2 Cryptographic Primitives

Public Key Encryption (PKE): The model for PKE schemes is summarized as follows:

Definition 1. *A PKE scheme* PKE *consists of the following triple of PPT algorithms* (KGen, Enc, Dec):

- KGen$(1^\lambda; r_g) \to (\mathsf{pk}, \mathsf{sk})$: *a key-generation algorithm that on input* 1^λ, *where* λ *is the security parameter, and randomness* $r_g \in \mathcal{R}_{\mathsf{KGen}}$, *outputs a pair of keys* $(\mathsf{pk}, \mathsf{sk})$. pk *and* sk *are called the public/encryption key and private/decryption key, respectively.*
- Enc$(\mathsf{pk}, m; r_e) \to c$: *an encryption algorithm that takes as input encryption key* pk, *message* $m \in \mathcal{M}$, *and randomness* $r_e \in \mathcal{R}_{\mathsf{Enc}}$, *and outputs ciphertext* $c \in \mathcal{C}$.
- Dec$(\mathsf{sk}, c) \to m/\bot$: *a decryption algorithm that takes as input decryption key* sk *and ciphertext* c *and outputs message* $m \in \mathcal{M}$ *or a rejection symbol* $\bot \notin \mathcal{M}$.

Definition 2 (PKE Correctness [29]). *We say that* PKE $=$ (KGen, Enc, Dec) *is* δ-*correct if*

$$\underset{(\mathsf{pk},\mathsf{sk}) \leftarrow \mathsf{KGen}(1^\lambda)}{\mathrm{Exp}} \left[\max_{m \in \mathcal{M}} \Pr[\mathsf{Dec}(\mathsf{sk}, c) \neq m : c \leftarrow \mathsf{Enc}(\mathsf{pk}, m)] \right] \leq \delta.$$

If $\delta = 0$, *then we just say that* PKE *is perfectly correct.*

Definition 3 (PKE Security). *Let* PKE $=$ (KGen, Enc, Dec) *be a PKE scheme. For any adversary* $\mathcal{A}$ *and* GOAL $\in$ {IND, SPR, ANO}, *we define* $\mathcal{A}$'s GOAL-CCA *advantage against* PKE *(w.r.t. a simulator* $\mathcal{S}$ *when* GOAL = SPR*) as follows:*

$$\mathbf{Adv}_{\mathsf{PKE}[,\mathcal{S}]}^{\mathrm{GOAL\text{-}CCA}}(\mathcal{A}) := \left| \Pr[\mathbf{Expt}_{\mathsf{PKE}[,\mathcal{S}],\mathcal{A}}^{\mathrm{GOAL\text{-}CCA}}(\lambda) = 1] - \frac{1}{2} \right|,$$

where $\mathbf{Expt}_{\mathsf{PKE}[,\mathcal{S}],\mathcal{A}}^{\mathrm{GOAL\text{-}CCA}}(\lambda)$ *is an experiment described in Fig. 2. For* GOAL $\in$ {IND, SPR, ANO}, *we say that* PKE *is* GOAL-CCA-*secure if (there exists a QPT simulator* $\mathcal{S}$ *when* GOAL = SPR *such that)* $\mathbf{Adv}_{\mathsf{PKE}[,\mathcal{S}]}^{\mathrm{GOAL\text{-}CCA}}(\mathcal{A})$ *is negligible (in* λ) *for any QPT adversary* $\mathcal{A}$. *We say that* PKE *is* GOAL-CPA-*secure if it is* GOAL-CCA-*secure without giving* $\mathcal{A}$ *access to decryption oracle.*

$\mathbf{Expt}_{\mathsf{PKE},\mathcal{A}}^{\text{IND-CCA}}(\lambda)$	$\mathbf{Expt}_{\mathsf{PKE},\mathcal{S},\mathcal{A}}^{\text{SPR-CCA}}(\lambda)$	$\mathbf{Expt}_{\mathsf{PKE},\mathcal{S},\mathcal{A}}^{\text{SDS-IND}}(\lambda)$
$(\mathsf{pk},\mathsf{sk}) \leftarrow \mathsf{KGen}(1^\lambda)$	$(\mathsf{pk},\mathsf{sk}) \leftarrow \mathsf{KGen}(1^\lambda)$	$(\mathsf{pk},\mathsf{sk}) \leftarrow \mathsf{KGen}(1^\lambda)$
$(m_0, m_1, \text{state}) \leftarrow \mathcal{A}^{\text{DEC}\perp(\cdot)}(\mathsf{pk})$	$(m, \text{state}) \leftarrow \mathcal{A}^{\text{DEC}\perp(\cdot)}(\mathsf{pk})$	$b \leftarrow\!\!{\scriptstyle\$} \{0,1\}$
$b \leftarrow\!\!{\scriptstyle\$} \{0,1\}$	$b \leftarrow\!\!{\scriptstyle\$} \{0,1\}$	$m \leftarrow\!\!{\scriptstyle\$} \mathcal{M};\ c_0^* \leftarrow \mathsf{Enc}(\mathsf{pk}, m)$
$c^* \leftarrow \mathsf{Enc}(\mathsf{pk}, m_b)$	$c_0^* \leftarrow \mathsf{Enc}(\mathsf{pk}, m)$	$c_1^* \leftarrow \mathcal{S}(1^\lambda)$
$b' \leftarrow \mathcal{A}^{\text{DEC}c^*(\cdot)}(c^*, \text{state})$	$c_1^* \leftarrow \mathcal{S}(1^\lambda)$	$b' \leftarrow \mathcal{A}(\mathsf{pk}, c_b^*)$
$\mathbf{return}\ [b' = b]$	$b' \leftarrow \mathcal{A}^{\text{DEC}c_b^*(\cdot)}(c_b^*, \text{state})$	$\mathbf{return}\ [b' = b]$
	$\mathbf{return}\ [b' = b]$	

$\text{DEC}_a(c)$	$\text{DEC}_a(\beta, c)$	$\mathbf{Expt}_{\mathsf{PKE},\mathcal{A}}^{\text{ANO-CCA}}(\lambda)$
$\mathbf{if}\ c = a\ \mathbf{then\ return}\ \perp$	$\mathbf{if}\ c = a\ \mathbf{then\ return}\ \perp$	$(\mathsf{pk}_0, \mathsf{sk}_0) \leftarrow \mathsf{KGen}(1^\lambda)$
$m \leftarrow \mathsf{Dec}(\mathsf{sk}, c)$	$m \leftarrow \mathsf{Dec}(\mathsf{sk}_\beta, c)$	$(\mathsf{pk}_1, \mathsf{sk}_1) \leftarrow \mathsf{KGen}(1^\lambda)$
$\mathbf{return}\ m$	$\mathbf{return}\ m$	$(m, \text{state}) \leftarrow \mathcal{A}^{\text{DEC}\perp(\cdot,\cdot)}(\mathsf{pk}_0, \mathsf{pk}_1)$
		$b \leftarrow\!\!{\scriptstyle\$} \{0,1\}$
		$c^* \leftarrow \mathsf{Enc}(\mathsf{pk}_b, m)$
		$b' \leftarrow \mathcal{A}^{\text{DEC}c^*(\cdot,\cdot)}(c^*, \text{state})$
		$\mathbf{return}\ [b' = b]$

Fig. 2. Games for PKE schemes

Definition 4 (Strong Disjoint Simulatablity [38,39,46]). *Let* $\mathsf{PKE} = (\mathsf{KGen}, \mathsf{Enc}, \mathsf{Dec})$ *be a PKE scheme and* $\mathcal{S}$ *be a QPT algorithm/simulator. For any adversary* $\mathcal{A}$, *we define* $\mathcal{A}$'s *SDS-IND advantage against* PKE, *w.r.t.* $\mathcal{S}$, *as follows:*

$$\mathbf{Adv}_{\mathsf{PKE},\mathcal{S}}^{\text{SDS-IND}}(\mathcal{A}) := \left| \Pr[\mathbf{Expt}_{\mathsf{PKE},\mathcal{S},\mathcal{A}}^{\text{SDS-IND}}(\lambda) = 1] - \frac{1}{2} \right|,$$

where $\mathbf{Expt}_{\mathsf{PKE},\mathcal{S},\mathcal{A}}^{\text{SDS-IND}}(\lambda)$ *is an experiment described in Fig. 2. In addition, we define disjointness as*

$$\mathsf{Disj}_{\mathsf{PKE},\mathcal{S}} = \Pr[c \in \mathsf{Enc}(\mathsf{pk}, \mathcal{M}) : (\mathsf{pk}, \mathsf{sk}) \leftarrow \mathsf{KGen}, c \leftarrow \mathcal{S}(1^\lambda)].$$

We say that PKE *is* strongly disjoint-simulatable *if there exists a QPT simulator* $\mathcal{S}$ *such that* $\mathbf{Adv}_{\mathsf{PKE},\mathcal{S}}^{\text{SDS-IND}}(\mathcal{A})$ *is negligible for any QPT adversary* $\mathcal{A}$ *and* $\mathsf{Disj}_{\mathsf{PKE},\mathcal{S}}$ *is negligible in* λ.

Key Encapsulation Mechanism (KEM): The model for KEM schemes is summarized as follows:

Definition 5. *A KEM scheme* KEM *consists of the following triple of polynomial-time algorithms* $(\mathsf{KGen}, \mathsf{Encap}, \mathsf{Decap})$:

– $\mathsf{KGen}(1^\lambda; r_g) \to (\mathsf{pk}, \mathsf{sk})$: *a key-generation algorithm that on input 1^λ, where λ is the security parameter, and randomness $r_g \in \mathcal{R}_{\mathsf{KGen}}$, outputs a pair of keys $(\mathsf{pk}, \mathsf{sk})$. pk and sk are called the public/encapsulation key and private/decapsulation key, respectively.*

– $\mathsf{Encap}(\mathsf{pk}; r_e) \to (c, k)$: *an encapsulation algorithm that takes as input encapsulation key pk, and randomness $r_e \in \mathcal{R}_{\mathsf{Encap}}$, and outputs ciphertext $c \in \mathcal{C}$ and encapsulated key $k \in \mathcal{K}$.*

– $\mathsf{Decap}(\mathsf{sk}, c) \to k/\bot$: *a decapsulation algorithm that takes as input decapsulation key sk and ciphertext c and outputs key $k \in \mathcal{K}$ or a rejection symbol $\bot \notin \mathcal{K}$.*

Definition 6 (KEM Correctness). *We say that* $\mathsf{KEM} = (\mathsf{KGen}, \mathsf{Encap}, \mathsf{Decap})$ *is δ-correct if*

$$\Pr[\mathsf{Decap}(\mathsf{sk}, c) \neq k : (\mathsf{pk}, \mathsf{sk}) \leftarrow \mathsf{KGen}(1^\lambda), (c, k) \leftarrow \mathsf{Encap}(\mathsf{pk})] \leq \delta.$$

In particular, we say that KEM *is* perfectly correct *if $\delta = 0$.*

Definition 7 (KEM Security). *Let $\mathsf{KEM} = (\mathsf{KGen}, \mathsf{Encap}, \mathsf{Decap})$ be a KEM scheme. For any adversary $\mathcal{A}$ and $\mathrm{GOAL} \in \{\mathrm{IND}, \mathrm{SPR}, \mathrm{ANO}, \mathrm{SSMT}\}$, we define $\mathcal{A}$'s GOAL-CCA advantage against KEM (w.r.t. a simulator $\mathcal{S}$ when $\mathrm{GOAL} \in \{\mathrm{SPR}, \mathrm{SSMT}\}$) as follows:*

$$\mathbf{Adv}_{\mathsf{KEM}[,\mathcal{S}]}^{\mathrm{GOAL\text{-}CCA}}(\mathcal{A}) := \left| \Pr[\mathbf{Expt}_{\mathsf{KEM}[,\mathcal{S}],\mathcal{A}}^{\mathrm{GOAL\text{-}CCA}}(\lambda) = 1] - \frac{1}{2} \right|,$$

where $\mathbf{Expt}_{\mathsf{KEM}[,\mathcal{S}],\mathcal{A}}^{\mathrm{GOAL\text{-}CCA}}(\lambda)$ is an experiment described in Fig. 3. For $\mathrm{GOAL} \in \{\mathrm{IND}, \mathrm{SPR}, \mathrm{ANO}, \mathrm{SSMT}\}$, we say KEM is GOAL-CCA-secure if (there exists a QPT simulator $\mathcal{S}$ when $\mathrm{GOAL} \in \{\mathrm{SPR}, \mathrm{SSMT}\}$ such that) $\mathbf{Adv}_{\mathsf{KEM}[,\mathcal{S}]}^{\mathrm{GOAL\text{-}CCA}}(\mathcal{A})$ is negligible for any QPT adversary $\mathcal{A}$.

We also define the above security properties for PKE schemes (in Definition 3) and KEMs (in Definition 7) in the QROM where the corresponding schemes have classical access and the adversary $\mathcal{A}$ has *quantum* access to a random oracle O. Following [29,32], we make the convention that the number q_O of queries made by $\mathcal{A}$ to O counts the total number of times O is executed in the corresponding security game/experiment; i.e., the number of $\mathcal{A}$'s explicit queries to O plus the number of implicit queries to O made by the experiment.

Data Encapsulation Mechanism (DEM): The model for DEM schemes is summarized as follows:

Definition 8. *A DEM scheme* DEM *consists of the following pair of polynomial-time algorithms* (E, D):

– $\mathsf{E}(k, m) \to c$: *an encapsulation algorithm that takes as input key $k \in \mathcal{K}$ and data $m \in \mathcal{M}$, and outputs ciphertext $c \in \mathcal{C}$.*

$\text{Expt}_{\text{KEM},\mathcal{A}}^{\text{IND-CCA}}(\lambda)$

$(\text{pk}, \text{sk}) \leftarrow \text{KGen}(1^\lambda)$
$b \leftarrow_\$ \{0, 1\}$
$(c^*, k_0^*) \leftarrow \text{Encap}(\text{pk})$
$k_1^* \leftarrow_\$ \mathcal{K}$
$b' \leftarrow \mathcal{A}^{\text{DECAPS}_{c^*}(\cdot)}(\text{pk}, c^*, k_b^*)$
return $[b' = b]$

$\text{Expt}_{\text{KEM},\mathcal{S},\mathcal{A}}^{\text{SPR-CCA}}(\lambda)$

$(\text{pk}, \text{sk}) \leftarrow \text{KGen}(1^\lambda)$
$b \leftarrow_\$ \{0, 1\}$
$(c_0^*, k_0^*) \leftarrow \text{Encap}(\text{pk})$
$(c_1^*, k_1^*) \leftarrow_\$ \mathcal{S}(1^\lambda) \times \mathcal{K}$
$b' \leftarrow \mathcal{A}^{\text{DECAPS}_{c_b^*}(\cdot)}(\text{pk}, c_b^*, k_b^*)$
return $[b' = b]$

$\text{Expt}_{\text{KEM},\mathcal{S},\mathcal{A}}^{\text{SSMT-CCA}}(\lambda)$

$(\text{pk}, \text{sk}) \leftarrow \text{KGen}(1^\lambda)$
$b \leftarrow_\$ \{0, 1\}$
$(c^*, k_0^*) \leftarrow \mathcal{S}(1^\lambda) \times \mathcal{K}$
$k_1^* \leftarrow \text{Decap}(\text{sk}, c^*)$
$b' \leftarrow \mathcal{A}^{\text{DECAPS}_{c^*}(\cdot)}(\text{pk}, c^*, k_b^*)$
return $[b' = b]$

$\text{DECAPS}_a(c)$

if $c = a$ then return $\perp$
$k \leftarrow \text{Decap}(\text{sk}, c)$
return k

$\text{DECAPS}_a(\beta, c)$

if $c = a$ then return $\perp$
$k \leftarrow \text{Decap}(\text{sk}_\beta, c)$
return k

$\text{Expt}_{\text{KEM},\mathcal{A}}^{\text{ANO-CCA}}(\lambda)$

$(\text{pk}_0, \text{sk}_0) \leftarrow \text{KGen}(1^\lambda)$
$(\text{pk}_1, \text{sk}_1) \leftarrow \text{KGen}(1^\lambda)$
$b \leftarrow_\$ \{0, 1\}$
$(c^*, k^*) \leftarrow \text{Encap}(\text{pk}_b)$
$b' \leftarrow \mathcal{A}^{\text{DECAPS}_{c^*}(\cdot, \cdot)}(\text{pk}_0, \text{pk}_1, c^*, k^*)$
return $[b' = b]$

Fig. 3. Games for KEM schemes

– $\mathsf{D}(k, c) \rightarrow m/\perp$: a decapsulation algorithm that takes as input key k and ciphertext c, and outputs data $m \in \mathcal{M}$ or a rejection symbol $\perp \notin \mathcal{M}$.

Definition 9 (DEM Correctness). *We say* $\mathsf{DEM} = (\mathsf{E}, \mathsf{D})$ *has* perfect cor-rectness *if for any* $k \in \mathcal{K}$ *and any* $m \in \mathcal{M}$, *we have*

$$\Pr[\mathsf{D}(k, c) = m : c \leftarrow \mathsf{E}(k, m)] = 1.$$

Definition 10 (One-time Strong Pseudorandomness of DEM). *Let the scheme* $\mathsf{DEM} = (\mathsf{E}, \mathsf{D})$ *be a DEM. For* $m \in \mathcal{M}$, *let* $\mathcal{C}_{|m|} (\subseteq \mathcal{C})$ *be the cipher-text space defined by the length of data* m. *For any adversary* $\mathcal{A}$, *we define* $\mathcal{A}$'s SPR-otCCA *advantage against* DEM *as follows:*

$$\mathbf{Adv}_{\mathsf{DEM}}^{\text{SPR-otCCA}}(\mathcal{A}) := \left| \Pr[\mathbf{Expt}_{\mathsf{DEM},\mathcal{A}}^{\text{SPR-otCCA}}(\lambda) = 1] - \frac{1}{2} \right|,$$

where $\mathbf{Expt}_{\mathsf{DEM},\mathcal{A}}^{\text{SPR-otCCA}}(\lambda)$ *is an experiment described in Fig. 4. We say that* DEM *is* strongly pseudorandom under one-time chosen-ciphertext attack *(SPR-otCCA* secure*) if* $\mathbf{Adv}_{\mathsf{DEM}}^{\text{SPR-otCCA}}(\mathcal{A})$ *is negligible for any QPT adversary* $\mathcal{A}$.

3 Specification of Kyber

As described in [4], Kyber is a KEM whose claimed IND-CCA security relies on hardness of the module learning-with-error problem (MLWE problem [36]). Kyber–or more formally, Kyber.KEM–is constructed by first starting with a *base*

$$
\begin{array}{l|l}
\textbf{Expt}_{\mathsf{DEM},\mathcal{A}}^{\mathrm{SPR\text{-}otCCA}}(\lambda) & \mathrm{DEC}_a(c) \\
\hline
k \leftarrow_\$ \mathcal{K} & \textbf{if } c = a \textbf{ then return } \bot \\
b \leftarrow_\$ \{0,1\} & m \leftarrow \mathsf{D}(k,c) \\
(m,\mathrm{state}) \leftarrow \mathcal{A}(1^\lambda) & \textbf{return } m \\
c_0^* \leftarrow \mathsf{E}(k,m) & \\
c_1^* \leftarrow_\$ \mathcal{C}_{|m|} & \\
b' \leftarrow \mathcal{A}^{\mathrm{DEC}_{c_b^*}(\cdot)}(c_b^*,\mathrm{state}) & \\
\textbf{return } [b' = b] &
\end{array}
$$

Fig. 4. SPR-otCCA game for DEM schemes.

PKE scheme Kyber.PKE and then applying a tweaked Fujisaki-Okamoto (FO) transform to it in order to obtain the final KEM. The tweaked FO transform is described in detail in Fig. 5; we also refer the reader to [4, Section 1.2] for a detailed specification of Kyber.PKE.

KGen′	Encap(pk)	Decap(sk′, c)
1 : (pk, sk) ← KGen	1 : $m \leftarrow_\$ \{0,1\}^{256}$	1 : Parse sk′ = (sk, pk, h, s)
2 : $s \leftarrow_\$ \{0,1\}^{256}$	2 : $m \leftarrow H(m)$	2 : $m' \leftarrow \mathsf{Dec}(\mathsf{sk}, c)$
3 : pk′ ← (pk, H(pk))	3 : $h \leftarrow H(\mathsf{pk})$	3 : $(\overline{k}', r') \leftarrow G(m', h)$
4 : sk′ ← (sk, pk′, s)	4 : $(\overline{k}, r) \leftarrow G(m, h)$	4 : $c' \leftarrow \mathsf{Enc}(\mathsf{pk}, m'; r')$
5 : return (pk, sk′)	5 : $c \leftarrow \mathsf{Enc}(\mathsf{pk}, m; r)$	5 : if $c' = c$ then
	6 : $k \leftarrow H'(\overline{k}, H(c))$	6 : return $H'(\overline{k}', H(c))$
	7 : return (c, k)	7 : else return $H'(s, H(c))$

Fig. 5. The tweaked FO transform, namely $\mathsf{FO}^{\not\perp'}$ (as described in [28,46]), used in Kyber. Here (KGen, Enc, Dec) is the base PKE scheme and (KGen′, Encap, Decap) is the final KEM. Also $H, H' : \{0,1\}^* \to \{0,1\}^{256}$ and $G : \{0,1\}^* \to \{0,1\}^{512}$ are hash functions. Technically, Kyber instantiates H' with the extendable-output function SHAKE-256 which can return outputs of arbitrary length. In this paper, we have H' to only return outputs of bit-length 256 for the sake of simplicity. But our subsequent analysis of Kyber can be modified in a straightforward manner to account for encapsulated keys (derived from H') with arbitrary length.

3.1 Security Properties of Kyber.PKE

In our IND-CCA security analysis of Kyber.KEM in Sect. 4, we rely on the IND-CPA security of Kyber.PKE. Similarly, in our ANO-CCA security analysis (cf. Sect. 5) of Kyber.KEM and the hybrid PKE schemes derived from it, we rely on the *strong disjoint simulatability* (i.e., *SDS-IND security* plus *statistical disjointness*) [38,39,46] of the base Kyber.PKE scheme.

It was argued in [4, Theorem 1] that (in the (quantum) random oracle model) Kyber.PKE is tightly IND-CPA secure under the MLWE hardness assumption, since under the MLWE assumption, the public-key and ciphertexts of Kyber.PKE are pseudorandom. Hence, we have:

Lemma 5 (informal). Kyber.PKE *is tightly* IND-CPA *secure under the MLWE hardness assumption, in the QROM.*

Regarding the strong disjoint simulatability of Kyber.PKE, we have:

Lemma 6 (informal). Kyber.PKE = (KGen, Enc, Dec) *is tightly* strong disjoint simulatable *under the MLWE hardness assumption, in the QROM.*

Proof (Sketch). Let $\mathcal{S}$ be a QPT simulator algorithm which simply outputs a uniformly random value from the ciphertext space $\mathcal{C}$ of Kyber.PKE. (Note that $\mathcal{C}$ is a set of bit strings with a *fixed pre-specified* length [4, Section 1.2], and hence, is *efficiently samplable.*) The above observation of Kyber.PKE's public-keys and ciphertexts being pseudorandom under the MLWE assumption can be used in a straightforward manner to show that Kyber.PKE is tightly SDS-IND secure w.r.t. $\mathcal{S}$ (cf. Definition 4) under the MLWE hardness assumption – as also noted in [4, Section 4.3.2].

Coming to the statistical disjointness of Kyber.PKE w.r.t. $\mathcal{S}$ (cf. Definition 4), we have $\mathsf{Disj}_{\mathsf{Kyber.PKE},\mathcal{S}} \leq \frac{|\mathsf{Enc}(\mathsf{pk},\mathcal{M})|}{|\mathcal{C}|} \leq \frac{\leq |\mathcal{M}||\mathcal{R}_{\mathsf{Enc}}|}{|\mathcal{C}|}$. Note that across all parameter sets of Kyber [4, Section 1], we have $|\mathcal{C}| \geq 2^{6144}$ and $|\mathcal{M} \times \mathcal{R}_{\mathsf{Enc}}| = 2^{512}$. Hence, for all intents and purposes, $\mathsf{Disj}_{\mathsf{Kyber.PKE},\mathcal{S}}$ can be considered to be negligible.

Finally, our IND-CCA and ANO-CCA security analyses of Kyber.KEM accounts for the δ-correctness of Kyber.PKE (cf. Definition 2). This particular correctness property of the base Kyber.PKE scheme has been rigorously analyzed in [4, Section 1.4].

4   IND-CCA Security of Kyber in the QROM

In this section, we prove the IND-CCA security of Kyber in the QROM with *concrete* bounds, before proceeding to show the scheme's anonymity (i.e., ANO-CCA security) later in Sect. 5.

Theorem 1 (IND-CCA security of Kyber.KEM). *Given the base PKE scheme* Kyber.PKE = (KGen, Enc, Dec) *is δ-correct, for any IND-CCA adversary $\mathcal{A}$ against* Kyber.KEM = (KGen', Encap, Decap) *issuing at most q_D classical queries to the decapsulation oracles, and at most q_G, q_H and $q_{H'}$ queries to the quantum random oracles G, H, and H', respectively, there exists an IND-CPA* *adversary $\mathcal{B}$ against* Kyber.PKE *such that*

$$\mathbf{Adv}^{\text{IND-CCA}}_{\text{Kyber.KEM}}(\mathcal{A}) \leq 2(q_G + q_{H'})\sqrt{\mathbf{Adv}^{\text{IND-CPA}}_{\text{Kyber.PKE}}(\mathcal{B}) + \frac{1}{2^{256}}} + \frac{9q_{H'} + 2q_H}{2^{128}}$$
$$+ 4q_G\sqrt{\delta} + \frac{C(q_H + 1)^3}{2^{256}},$$

where C (< 648) is the constant from Lemma 1, and the running time of $\mathcal{B}$ is about the same as that of $\mathcal{A}$.

The proof essentially follows the "wrapper-based" approach described in Subsect. 1.2 above but with respect to the *implicitly-rejecting* $\text{FO}^{\not\perp}_m$ transform. Formal details follow.

Proof. Towards proving the *concrete* IND-CCA security of Kyber in the QROM, we first consider an intermediate PKE $\rightarrow$ KEM transform $\text{FO}^{\not\perp'}_{\text{pre}}$, described in Fig. 6. Let $\overline{\text{Kyber.KEM}}$ be the KEM obtained by applying the $\text{FO}^{\not\perp'}_{\text{pre}}$ transform on Kyber.PKE, i.e., $\overline{\text{Kyber.KEM}} = \text{FO}^{\not\perp'}_{\text{pre}}[\text{Kyber.PKE}, G, H, H']$. We now consider the IND-CCA security of $\overline{\text{Kyber.KEM}}$ in the QROM.

KGen$'$	Encap(pk)	Decap(sk$'$, c)
1: $(\text{pk}, \text{sk}) \leftarrow$ KGen	1: $m \leftarrow_\$ \{0,1\}^{256}$	1: Parse sk$' = (\text{sk}, \text{pk}, h, s)$
2: $s \leftarrow_\$ \{0,1\}^{256}$	2: $h \leftarrow H(\text{pk})$	2: $m' \leftarrow \text{Dec}(\text{sk}, c)$
3: $\text{pk}' \leftarrow (\text{pk}, H(\text{pk}))$	3: $(\overline{k}, r) \leftarrow G(m, h)$	3: $(\overline{k}', r') \leftarrow G(m', h)$
4: $\text{sk}' \leftarrow (\text{sk}, \text{pk}', s)$	4: $c \leftarrow \text{Enc}(\text{pk}, m; r)$	4: $c' \leftarrow \text{Enc}(\text{pk}, m'; r')$
5: **return** (pk, sk')	5: **return** $(c, \overline{k})$	5: **if** $c' = c$ **then**
		6: **return** $\overline{k}'$
		7: **else return** $H'(s, c)$

Fig. 6. The PKE $\rightarrow$ KEM transform $\text{FO}^{\not\perp'}_{\text{pre}}$.

Let $\overline{\mathcal{A}}$ be an IND-CCA adversary against $\overline{\text{Kyber.KEM}}$ issuing at most q'_D classical queries to the decapsulation oracles, and q'_H and $q'_{H'}$ queries to the quantum random oracles H and H' respectively. Consider the sequence of games $\overline{\text{G}}_0$ – $\overline{\text{G}}_2$ described in Fig. 7 which only differ in the way their corresponding decapsulation oracles Decap(sk$'$, ·) reject invalid ciphertexts.

Game $\overline{\text{G}}_0$: This game is exactly the IND-CCA game for $\overline{\text{Kyber.KEM}}$. Hence,

$$\left| \Pr[\overline{\text{G}}_0 = 1] - \frac{1}{2} \right| = \mathbf{Adv}^{\text{IND-CCA}}_{\overline{\text{Kyber.KEM}}}(\overline{\mathcal{A}}). \qquad (1)$$

Game $\overline{\text{G}}_1$: In this game, the Decap(sk$'$, ·) oracle is modified such that $H''(c)$ is returned instead of $H'(s, c)$ for an invalid ciphertext c, where H'' is a fresh

Games $\overline{\mathsf{G}}_0 - \overline{\mathsf{G}}_2$	Decap(sk$'$, c)
1 : $(\mathsf{pk}, \mathsf{sk}) \leftarrow \mathsf{KGen}'$	1 : Parse $\mathsf{sk}' = (\mathsf{sk}, \mathsf{pk}, h, s)$
2 : $(c^*, \overline{k}_0^*) \leftarrow \mathsf{Encap}(\mathsf{pk})$	2 : $m' \leftarrow \mathsf{Dec}(\mathsf{sk}, c)$
3 : $\overline{k}_1^* \leftarrow_\$ \{0,1\}^{256}$	3 : $(\overline{k}', r') \leftarrow G(m', h)$
4 : $b \leftarrow_\$ \{0,1\}$	4 : $c' \leftarrow \mathsf{Enc}(\mathsf{pk}, m'; r')$
5 : $b' \leftarrow \overline{\mathcal{A}}^{G, H, H', \mathsf{Decap}(\mathsf{sk}', \cdot)}(\mathsf{pk}, c^*, \overline{k}_b^*)$	5 : if $c' = c$ then
6 : return $[b' = b]$	6 : return $\overline{k}'$
	7 : else return $H'(s, c) /\!\!/ \ \overline{\mathsf{G}}_0$
	8 : else return $H''(c) /\!\!/ \ \overline{\mathsf{G}}_1$
	9 : else return $\overline{H}(H(c)) /\!\!/ \ \overline{\mathsf{G}}_2$

Fig. 7. Games $\overline{\mathsf{G}}_0 - \overline{\mathsf{G}}_2$. Here $H'' : \{0,1\}^* \to \{0,1\}^{256}$ and $\overline{H} : \{0,1\}^{256} \to \{0,1\}^{256}$ are fresh *internal* random oracles, i.e., not directly accessible to $\overline{\mathcal{A}}$.

internal random oracle not directly accessible to $\overline{\mathcal{A}}$. Using Lemma 2 w.r.t. the pseudorandomness of $H'(s, \cdot)$ during decapsulation, where we have the "PRF key" $s \leftarrow_\$ \{0,1\}^{256}$, it is not hard to obtain the following via a straightforward reduction:

$$\left| \Pr[\overline{\mathsf{G}}_1 = 1] - \Pr[\overline{\mathsf{G}}_0 = 1] \right| \leq \frac{2q'_{H'}}{2^{128}}. \tag{2}$$

Game $\overline{\mathsf{G}}_2$: In this game, we again modify the $\mathsf{Decap}(\mathsf{sk}', \cdot)$ oracle such that $\overline{H}(H(c))$ is returned instead of $H''(c)$ for an invalid ciphertext c, where $\overline{H}$ is another fresh internal random oracle not directly accessible to $\overline{\mathcal{A}}$. Note that the oracles H'' and $\overline{H}$ are only accessible to $\overline{\mathcal{A}}$ *indirectly* via the $\mathsf{Decap}(\mathsf{sk}', \cdot)$ oracle. Now in the view of adversary $\overline{\mathcal{A}}$, the output distributions of the $\mathsf{Decap}(\mathsf{sk}', \cdot)$ oracle in games $\overline{\mathsf{G}}_1$ and $\overline{\mathsf{G}}_2$ with regards to invalid ciphertexts c are identical *unless* $\overline{\mathcal{A}}$ queries the decapsulations of two invalid ciphertexts c_1 and c_2 such that $H(c_1) = H(c_2)$ (and $c_1 \neq c_2$). Since decapsulation queries are considered to be classical in the QROM, we can bound the probability of such an event by collision-resistance of the QRO H – as described in Lemma 1 – again via a straightforward reduction. Hence, we have[2],

$$\left| \Pr[\overline{\mathsf{G}}_2 = 1] - \Pr[\overline{\mathsf{G}}_1 = 1] \right| \leq \frac{C(q'_H + q'_D + 1)^3}{2^{256}}, \tag{3}$$

where C (< 648) is the constant from Lemma 1.

---

[2] Recall from our convention (described in Subsect. 2.2) that q'_H counts the total number of times H is invoked in the game $\overline{\mathsf{G}}_0$. However in $\overline{\mathsf{G}}_2$, H is *additionally* invoked when $\overline{\mathcal{A}}$ queries the decapsulation of an invalid ciphertext. Hence, H is queried at most $(q'_H + q'_D)$ many times in $\overline{\mathsf{G}}_2$ in the context of applying Lemma 1.

Hence by collecting the above bounds (1) – (3), we obtain

$$\left| \Pr[\overline{\mathsf{G}}_2 = 1] - \frac{1}{2} \right| \leq \mathbf{Adv}^{\mathsf{IND\text{-}CCA}}_{\mathsf{Kyber.KEM}}(\overline{\mathcal{A}}) + \frac{2q'_{H'}}{2^{128}} + \frac{C(q'_H + q'_D + 1)^3}{2^{256}}, \quad (4)$$

which will be useful shortly when we now focus on proving concrete IND-CCA security of the *actual* scheme of Kyber.

Let $\mathcal{A}$ be an IND-CCA adversary against Kyber.KEM issuing at most q_D classical queries to the decapsulation oracles, and at most q_G, q_H and $q_{H'}$ queries to the quantum random oracles G, H and H' respectively. Consider the sequence of games G_0 – G_8 described in Fig. 8.

Games G_0 – G_8		$\mathsf{Decap}(\mathsf{sk}', c)$	
1 :	$(\mathsf{pk}, \mathsf{sk}) \leftarrow \mathsf{KGen}'$	1 :	Parse $\mathsf{sk}' = (\mathsf{sk}, \mathsf{pk}, h, s)$
2 :	$m^* \leftarrow_\$ \{0,1\}^{256}$	2 :	$m' \leftarrow \mathsf{Dec}(\mathsf{sk}, c)$
3 :	$m^* \leftarrow H(m^*) /\!\!/ \ \mathsf{G}_0, \mathsf{G}_8$	3 :	$(\overline{k}', r') \leftarrow G(m', h)$
4 :	$(\overline{k}^*_0, r^*) \leftarrow_\$ G(m^*, H(\mathsf{pk}))$	4 :	$c' \leftarrow \mathsf{Enc}(\mathsf{pk}, m'; r')$
5 :	$\overline{k}^*_1 \leftarrow_\$ \{0,1\}^{256}$	5 :	if $c' = c$ then
6 :	$c^* \leftarrow \mathsf{Enc}(\mathsf{pk}, m^*; r^*)$	6 :	return $H'(\overline{k}', H(c))$
7 :	$k^* \leftarrow H'(\overline{k}^*_0, H(c^*)) /\!\!/ \ \mathsf{G}_0 - \mathsf{G}_3$	7 :	else
8 :	$k^* \leftarrow H'(\overline{k}^*_1, H(c^*)) /\!\!/ \ \mathsf{G}_4$	8 :	return $H'(s, H(c)) /\!\!/ \ \mathsf{G}_0\text{-}\mathsf{G}_1, \mathsf{G}_7\text{-}\mathsf{G}_8$
9 :	$k^* \leftarrow_\$ \{0,1\}^{256} /\!\!/ \ \mathsf{G}_5 - \mathsf{G}_8$	9 :	return $H''(H(c)) /\!\!/ \ \mathsf{G}_2, \mathsf{G}_6$
10 :	$b' \leftarrow \mathcal{A}^{G,H,H',\mathsf{Decap}(\mathsf{sk}',\cdot)}(\mathsf{pk}, c^*, k^*)$	10 :	return $H'(\overline{H}(H(c)), H(c)) /\!\!/ \ \mathsf{G}_3\text{-}\mathsf{G}_5$
11 :	return b'		

Fig. 8. Games G_0 – G_8. Here $H'' \colon \{0,1\}^* \to \{0,1\}^{256}$ and $\overline{H} \colon \{0,1\}^{256} \to \{0,1\}^{256}$ are fresh *internal* random oracles, i.e., not directly accessible to $\mathcal{A}$.

Game G_0: This game is basically the IND-CCA game for Kyber.KEM where the adversary $\mathcal{A}$ gets the "real" encapsulated key k^*, i.e., $(c^*, k^*) \leftarrow \mathsf{Encap}(\mathsf{pk})$.

Game G_1: Here we essentially do not execute the "$m \leftarrow H(m)$" step during encapsulation (Line 2 in "$\mathsf{Encap}(\mathsf{pk})$", Fig. 5) in this game's setup. We now use the original OW2H lemma (Lemma 3) to bound the difference in $\mathcal{A}$'s "behavior" in games G_0 and G_1. In the context of applying Lemma 3, let $x := m^*_0 \leftarrow_\$ \{0,1\}^{256}$ and $y := m^*_1 \leftarrow_\$ \{0,1\}^{256}$, and consider an oracle algorithm A^H making at-most q_H queries to H such that $A^H(m^*_0, H(m^*_0))$ simulates the game G_0 towards $\mathcal{A}$ and $A^H(m^*_0, m^*_1)$ simulates G_1 towards $\mathcal{A}$. To be more specific, A^H sets "m^*" in Line 4, Fig. 8, to be its second input (either $H(m^*_0)$ or m^*_1) when simulating the appropriate game (G_0 or G_1, respectively) towards $\mathcal{A}$.

Again in the context of Lemma 3, it is not hard to see that $\Pr[\mathsf{G}_0 = 1] = P^1_A$ and $\Pr[\mathsf{G}_1 = 1] = P^2_A$. Regarding the probability P_B, note that during $A^H(m^*_0, m^*_1)$'s simulation of game G_1 towards $\mathcal{A}$, the view of $\mathcal{A}$ is completely independent of the value $m_0^* \; (= x) \leftarrow_\$ \{0,1\}^{256}$. Hence, we have $P_B = \frac{1}{2^{256}}$ which leads to

$$|\Pr[\mathsf{G}_1 = 1] - \Pr[\mathsf{G}_0 = 1]| \leq \frac{2q_H}{2^{128}} \; (= 2q_H \sqrt{P_B}). \tag{5}$$

Game G_2: In this game, the $\mathsf{Decap}(\mathsf{sk}', \cdot)$ oracle is modified such that $H''(H(c))$ is returned instead of $H'(s, H(c))$ for an invalid ciphertext c, where H'' is a fresh *internal* random oracle not directly accessible to $\overline{\mathcal{A}}$. Similar to the $\overline{\mathsf{G}}_0 \to \overline{\mathsf{G}}_1$ "hop" above, by using Lemma 2 w.r.t. the pseudorandomness of $H'(s, \cdot)$–this time on inputs of the form "$H(c)$"–during decapsulation, it is not hard to obtain:

$$|\Pr[\mathsf{G}_2 = 1] - \Pr[\mathsf{G}_1 = 1]| \leq \frac{2q_{H'}}{2^{128}}. \tag{6}$$

Game G_3: In this game, we again modify the $\mathsf{Decap}(\mathsf{sk}', \cdot)$ oracle such that $H'(\overline{H}(H(c)), H(c))$ is returned instead of $H''(H(c))$ for an invalid ciphertext c, where $\overline{H}$ is another fresh internal random oracle not directly accessible to $\overline{\mathcal{A}}$. Here we use the generalized OW2H lemma (Lemma 4) to bound the difference in $\mathcal{A}$'s behavior in games G_2 and G_3.

In the context of Lemma 4, note that the oracle algorithm needs to distinguish the pair of random functions $(H''(\cdot), H')$ in G_2 from the pair $(H'(\overline{H}(\cdot), \cdot), H')$ in G_3. But it is not hard to see that this is the same as distinguishing (H'', H') in G_2 from (H'', G') in G_3, where the oracle G' is obtained by *reprogramming* H' on inputs of the form "$(\overline{H}(x), x)$" with $x \in \{0,1\}^{256}$; namely, we have

$$G'(y) = \begin{cases} H''(x) & \text{if } y \text{ is of the form } (\overline{H}(x), x) \text{ with } x \in \{0,1\}^{256} \\ H'(y) & \text{otherwise.} \end{cases}$$

So again in the context of applying Lemma 4, consider an oracle algorithm A which has quantum access to either (H'', H') or (H'', G') such that $A^{H'', H'}$ and $A^{H'', G'}$ simulate G_2 and G_3 respectively towards $\mathcal{A}$, while making $q_{H'}$ oracle queries.[3] Note that the set of differences between the H' and G' oracles is $\mathcal{S} = \{(\overline{H}(x), x) \mid x \in \{0,1\}^{256}\}$. If we then set $\Pr[\mathsf{G}_2 = 1] = P_{\text{left}}$ and $\Pr[\mathsf{G}_3 = 1] = P_{\text{right}}$, from Lemma 4 we have $|\Pr[\mathsf{G}_3 = 1] - \Pr[\mathsf{G}_2 = 1]| \leq 2q_{H'} \sqrt{P_{\text{guess}}}$. Regarding P_{guess}, note that during $A^{H'', H'}$'s simulation of G_2 towards the adversary $\mathcal{A}$, the view of $\mathcal{A}$ is completely independent of the (internal) random oracle $\overline{H}$. Hence the probability that measurement of a random H'-oracle query in G_2 will be of the form $(\overline{H}(x), x)$ (with $x \in \{0,1\}^{256}$) is at-most $\frac{1}{2^{256}}$, i.e., $P_{\text{guess}} \leq \frac{1}{2^{256}}$, since $\overline{H}(x)$ will be a fresh uniformly random value in $\{0,1\}^{256}$. Therefore,

$$|\Pr[\mathsf{G}_3 = 1] - \Pr[\mathsf{G}_2 = 1]| \leq \frac{2q_{H'}}{2^{128}}. \tag{7}$$

---

[3] For example, A uses the first oracle H'' to simulate $\mathsf{Decap}(\mathsf{sk}', \cdot)$ in Fig. 8 w.r.t. invalid ciphertexts c; given such a decapsulation query c from $\mathcal{A}$, the algorithm A returns $H''(H(c))$, where the oracle H is sampled independently by A at the games' setup.

Game G_4: In this game, we generate the encapsulated key k^* in the setup as "$k^* \leftarrow H'(\overline{k}_1^*, H(c^*))$" instead of "$k^* \leftarrow H'(\overline{k}_0^*, H(c^*))$" where we have $(\overline{k}_0^*, r^*) \leftarrow_\$ G(m^*, H(pk))$ and $\overline{k}_1^* \leftarrow_\$ \{0,1\}^{256}$. Here we make use of our analysis of the $\mathsf{FO}_{\mathsf{pre}}^{\perp'}$ transform above.

Consider the game $\overline{G}_2$ "played" by adversary $\overline{\mathcal{A}}$ in Fig. 7 w.r.t. $\overline{\mathsf{Kyber.KEM}}$. Depending on whether $\overline{\mathcal{A}}$ gets the "real pre-key" $\overline{k}_0^*$ or the "random pre-key" $\overline{k}_1^*$ from its challenger, it can simulate the game G_3 or G_4 respectively towards $\mathcal{A}$. Namely, $\overline{\mathcal{A}}^{H,H'}(c^*, \overline{k}_b^*)$ computes the encapsulated key k^* as $k^* \leftarrow H'(\overline{k}_b^*, H(c^*))$ (where b is the bit sampled by $\overline{\mathcal{A}}$'s challenger in Fig. 7) and sends it to $\mathcal{A}$ during the games' setup. $\overline{\mathcal{A}}^{H,H',\mathsf{Decap}(\mathsf{sk}',\cdot)}$ also simulates the decapsulation oracle in games G_3 and G_4 (cf. Fig. 8) as follows: given a decapsulation query c from $\mathcal{A}$, $\overline{\mathcal{A}}$ queries its *own* $\mathsf{Decap}(\mathsf{sk}',\cdot)$ oracle in $\overline{G}_2$ on c to obtain a key $\overline{k}'$–which can also be the value "$\overline{H}(H(c))$" if c is invalid (cf. Line 9 in "$\mathsf{Decap}(\mathsf{sk}',c)$", Fig. 7)–and returns $H'(\overline{k}', H(c))$ to $\mathcal{A}$. Hence, it is not hard to see from this reduction that

$$|\Pr[G_4 = 1] - \Pr[G_3 = 1]| = \left|\Pr[1 \leftarrow \overline{\mathcal{A}} \mid b = 1] - \Pr[1 \leftarrow \overline{\mathcal{A}} \mid b = 0]\right|$$

$$= 2 \cdot \left|\Pr[\overline{G}_2 = 1] - \frac{1}{2}\right|.$$

By using Inequality (4) above w.r.t. our analysis of $\overline{\mathsf{Kyber.KEM}}$, we obtain[4]

$$|\Pr[G_4 = 1] - \Pr[G_3 = 1]| \le 2\mathbf{Adv}_{\overline{\mathsf{Kyber.KEM}}}^{\mathsf{IND\text{-}CCA}}(\overline{\mathcal{A}}) + \frac{4q_{H'}}{2^{128}} + \frac{2C(q_H + 1)^3}{2^{256}}. \quad (8)$$

Game G_5: Here we have the encapsulated key k^* in the setup to be an independent and uniformly random value, i.e., "$k^* \leftarrow_\$ \{0,1\}^{256}$", instead of deriving it from H' as "$k^* \leftarrow H'(\overline{k}_1^*, H(c^*))$". Similar to the $\overline{G}_0 \to \overline{G}_1$ hop above, by using Lemma 2 w.r.t. the pseudorandomness of $H'(\overline{k}_1^*, \cdot)$–with "PRF key" $\overline{k}_1^* \leftarrow_\$ \{0,1\}^{256}$–during setup, it is not hard to obtain:

$$|\Pr[G_5 = 1] - \Pr[G_4 = 1]| \le \frac{2q_{H'}}{2^{128}}. \quad (9)$$

Game G_6: In this game, we modify the $\mathsf{Decap}(\mathsf{sk}',\cdot)$ oracle such that $H''(H(c))$ is returned instead of $H'(\overline{H}(H(c)), H(c))$ for an invalid ciphertext c. In essence, we are reverting the changes introduced in the "$G_2 \to G_3$" hop. Hence, by applying a similar reasoning as that hop, we get

$$|\Pr[G_6 = 1] - \Pr[G_5 = 1]| \le \frac{2q_{H'}}{2^{128}}. \quad (10)$$

---

[4] Here we replace the term "$q_H' + q_D'$" in Inequality (4) with "q_H". Recall from Footnote 3 that $(q_H' + q_D')$ is the maximum number of times oracle H is queried in $\overline{G}_2$. But since the decapsulation algorithm of $\mathsf{Kyber.KEM}$ involves a single invocation of $H(\cdot)$ for each input ciphertext c (see "$\mathsf{Decap}(\mathsf{sk}',c)$", Fig. 5), the quantity "q_H" *includes* the number of times H is queried by $\overline{\mathcal{A}}$ to answer decapsulation queries from $\mathcal{A}$ – following our convention w.r.t. counting the number of random oracle queries in security games (cf. Subsect. 2.2).

Game G_7: In this game, $\mathsf{Decap}(\mathsf{sk}', \cdot)$ oracle is modified such that $H'(s, H(c))$ is returned instead of $H''(H(c))$ for an invalid ciphertext c. Again in essence, we are reverting the changes introduced in the "$G_1 \to G_2$" hop. Hence, by using a similar reasoning as that hop–namely, pseudorandomness of the oracle $H'(s, \cdot)$ on inputs of the form "$H(c)$"–we obtain

$$|\Pr[G_7 = 1] - \Pr[G_6 = 1]| \leq \frac{2q_{H'}}{2^{128}}. \tag{11}$$

Game G_8: Here we re-introduce the "$m \leftarrow H(m)$" step during encapsulation (Line 2 in "$\mathsf{Encap}(\mathsf{pk})$", Fig. 5) in this game's setup, thereby reverting the changes introduced in the "$G_0 \to G_1$" hop. By applying Lemma 3 in a similar way as that hop, we get

$$|\Pr[G_8 = 1] - \Pr[G_7 = 1]| \leq \frac{2q_H}{2^{128}}. \tag{12}$$

Now note that G_8 is the IND-CCA game for Kyber.KEM where the adversary $\mathcal{A}$ gets a "random" encapsulated key k^*, i.e., $k^* \leftarrow_\$ \{0,1\}^{256}$ (in contrast to getting the "real" encapsulated key in G_0). Hence, we have

$$2 \cdot \mathbf{Adv}_{\mathsf{Kyber.KEM}}^{\mathrm{IND\text{-}CCA}}(\mathcal{A}) = |\Pr[G_8 = 1] - \Pr[G_0 = 1]|.$$

By collecting the above bounds (5) – (12), we obtain

$$\mathbf{Adv}_{\mathsf{Kyber.KEM}}^{\mathrm{IND\text{-}CCA}}(\mathcal{A}) \leq \mathbf{Adv}_{\mathsf{Kyber.KEM}}^{\mathrm{IND\text{-}CCA}}(\overline{\mathcal{A}}) + \frac{7q_{H'} + 2q_H}{2^{128}} + \frac{C(q_H + 1)^3}{2^{256}}. \tag{13}$$

Coming to the term "$\mathbf{Adv}_{\mathsf{Kyber.KEM}}^{\mathrm{IND\text{-}CCA}}(\overline{\mathcal{A}})$", note that the $\mathsf{FO}_{\mathrm{pre}}^{\not\perp'}$ transform is essentially identical to the $\mathsf{FO}_m^{\not\perp}$ transform of [29] (also described in Fig. 1) in the context of proving IND-CCA security of the obtained KEM. That is, the existing IND-CCA security theorems w.r.t. $\mathsf{FO}_m^{\not\perp}$ in the QROM derived in the literature (e.g., in [10,32,35,39]) apply to $\mathsf{FO}_{\mathrm{pre}}^{\not\perp'}$ *as-it-is* because of the following reasons:

– Note that $\mathsf{FO}_{\mathrm{pre}}^{\not\perp'}$ uses a single hash function G to compute both the encapsulated key $\overline{k}$ and the random coins r for the deterministic encryption of m during encapsulation, whereas $\mathsf{FO}_m^{\not\perp}$ uses two separate hash functions for the same. However, these two computations are equivalent when the corresponding hash functions are modeled as independent random oracles with appropriate output lengths.
– Similarly, $\mathsf{FO}_{\mathrm{pre}}^{\not\perp'}$ uses the hash $H(\mathsf{pk})$ to compute $\overline{k}$ and r during encapsulation (and $H(\mathsf{pk})$ is also included in the KEM's secret key sk'), in contrast to $\mathsf{FO}_m^{\not\perp}$. But this change preserves the relevant IND-CCA theorems from $\mathsf{FO}_m^{\not\perp}$ to $\mathsf{FO}_{\mathrm{pre}}^{\not\perp'}$ with trivial changes to the corresponding proofs, to accommodate the inclusion of $H(\mathsf{pk})$, because the IND-CCA security notion only involves a *single* user's public-key pk (as opposed to multi-user security notions, such as ANO-CCA which involves *two* public-keys).

Hence, by applying [32, Theorem 2][5] regarding the IND-CCA security of "$\mathsf{FO}_m^{\not\perp}$-derived" KEMs in the QROM to $\overline{\mathsf{Kyber.KEM}}$, we have that there exists an IND-CPA adversary $\mathcal{B}$ against $\mathsf{Kyber.PKE}$, with its running time about the same as that of $\overline{\mathcal{A}}$ (and hence, that of $\mathcal{A}$ as well), such that[6]

$$\mathbf{Adv}_{\mathsf{Kyber.KEM}}^{\mathsf{IND\text{-}CCA}}(\overline{\mathcal{A}}) \leq 2(q_G + q_{H'})\sqrt{\mathbf{Adv}_{\mathsf{Kyber.PKE}}^{\mathsf{IND\text{-}CPA}}(\mathcal{B}) + \frac{1}{2^{256}}} + \frac{2q_{H'}}{2^{128}} + 4q_G\sqrt{\delta}.$$

$$(14)$$

Combining the inequalities (13) and (14) finishes the proof.

Remark 1. An alternative approach to prove IND-CCA security of Kyber in the QROM was suggested in [17], involving the *compressed oracle* technique introduced in [48]. More specifically, given two random oracles $H_1 : \{0,1\}^m \to \{0,1\}^n$, $H_2 : \{0,1\}^n \times \{0,1\}^\ell \to \{0,1\}^n$, and a polynomial-sized stateless classical circuit C which has quantum access to H_1, H_2, it was shown in [48, Section 5] that the "domain extender" $C^{H_1,H_2}(x,y) = H_2(H_1(x), y)$ is *indifferentiable* from a quantum random oracle $H : \{0,1\}^{m+\ell} \to \{0,1\}^n$. Informally, indifferentiability guarantees that any efficient adversary cannot distinguish $\langle (H_1, H_2), C^{H_1,H_2} \rangle$ from $\langle \mathcal{S}^H, H \rangle$ where the simulator $\mathcal{S}$ queries H and simulates the oracles H_1, H_2.

Now note that in Kyber (Fig. 5, Line. 6 of "$\mathsf{Encap(pk)}$"), the encapsulated keys are generated as "$k \leftarrow H'(\overline{k}, H(c))$" by hashing the "*pre-key*" $\overline{k}$ and a "nested hash" of the ciphertext, i.e., $H(c)$. And as noted in [28,46], this nested hash $H(c)$ creates problems when extending prior QROM security analysis of (implicitly-rejecting) FO transforms in the literature to Kyber. However, since [48, Section 5] essentially shows that $H'(\overline{k}, H(c))$ is indifferentiable from $H''(\overline{k}, c)$, for a fresh random oracle H'', we can "ignore" the nested hash $H(c)$ in our analysis of Kyber; in fact, [28, Appendix E] already proved the IND-CCA security of a variant of the FO transform where keys are derived as "$k \leftarrow H''(\overline{k}, c)$". However, we make a couple of remarks regarding this matter:

- At a conceptual level, our IND-CCA security analysis of Kyber above (Theorem 1) relies on arguably simpler proof techniques than the ones introduced in [48]. Specifically, our analysis of Kyber in the QROM is based on that of the $\mathsf{FO}_m^{\not\perp}$ transform in the literature, which in turn is based on the well-known

---

[5] As mentioned in Subsect. 1.2, the reason we are not applying the *tighter* QROM IND-CCA security theorems of [10,35] w.r.t. $\mathsf{FO}_m^{\not\perp}$-derived KEMs is that they make an additional assumption on the base PKE scheme being *injective* [10]. However, we leave a detailed analysis of $\mathsf{Kyber.PKE}$'s injectivity as an open question.

[6] Technically, [32, Theorem 2] reduces the IND-CCA security of the KEM to the OW-CPA security of the underlying PKE scheme. But it is well-known that IND-CPA security of a PKE scheme with a sufficiently large message space also implies its OW-CPA security; namely, for any OW-CPA adversary $\mathcal{B}_{ow}$ against a PKE scheme PKE with message space $\mathcal{M}$, there exists an IND-CPA adversary $\mathcal{B}_{ind}$ against PKE with the same running time as that of $\mathcal{B}_{ow}$ such that $\mathbf{Adv}_{\mathsf{PKE}}^{\mathsf{OW\text{-}CPA}}(\mathcal{B}_{ow}) \leq \mathbf{Adv}_{\mathsf{PKE}}^{\mathsf{IND\text{-}CPA}}(\mathcal{B}_{ind}) + \frac{1}{|\mathcal{M}|}$.

"One-Way To Hiding (OW2H) lemma" [3, 44] proof technique. And as mentioned in Sect. 1, [45] provided a framework for *formally* verifying security proofs that involve applications of the OW2H lemma in the QROM. Hence, this should make our security proofs for Kyber amenable to formal verification, thereby providing further confidence in our analysis of the new NIST PQC standard.

– Quantitatively, if we rely on the above indifferentiability argument to analyze Kyber instead, then when switching from "$H'(\overline{k}, H(c))$" to "$H''(\overline{k}, c)$" we would incur an additive "indifferentiability" term $O(q^2/2^{n/2})$ (as specified in [48, Section 5]) in our IND-CCA security bounds, where q is the number of adversarial quantum random oracle queries made to H, H', and $n = 256$ for Kyber. In contrast, our concrete bounds in Theorem 1 includes an additive "collision-resistance (of H)" term $O(q^3/2^n)$. Hence, our concrete IND-CCA security theorem for Kyber allows for strictly more number of random oracle queries q when compared to the indifferentiability-based argument, especially w.r.t. higher security level parameter sets for Kyber when the "correctness" term $O(q\sqrt{\delta})$ is no longer a limiting factor on q (e.g., $\delta = 2^{-164}, 2^{-174}$).

At the same time, there does not seem to be a straightforward *matching* attack on the IND-CCA security of Kyber that exploits finding collisions in H. Hence, we leave it as an open question to provide a concrete proof of IND-CCA security for Kyber in the QROM which does not rely on the collision-resistance of quantum random oracles, while ensuring tightness w.r.t. the passive IND-CPA security of the base PKE scheme as in the case with implicitly-rejecting FO transforms.

5   ANO-CCA Security of Kyber in the QROM

In this section, we prove the concrete ANO-CCA security of Kyber, and the hybrid PKE schemes derived from it, in the QROM. As mentioned in Subsect. 1.2 above, we first prove that the aforementioned schemes are *strongly pseudorandom* (or, *SPR-CCA secure*; cf. Definitions 3, 7) in the QROM, which in turn implies their ANO-CCA security [46, Thm. 2.5 of ePrint version].

5.1   SPR-CCA Security of Kyber.KEM

Here we prove the concrete SPR-CCA security of Kyber.KEM in the QROM while relying on the *strong disjoint simulatability* (i.e., *SDS-IND security* and *statistical disjointness*; cf. Lemma 6) of the base Kyber.PKE scheme.

Theorem 2 (SPR-CCA security of Kyber.KEM). *Let the base PKE scheme* Kyber.PKE $=$ (KGen, Enc, Dec) *be δ-correct, and $\mathcal{S}$ be a QPT simulator algorithm which simply outputs a uniformly random value from the ciphertext space of* Kyber.PKE. *Then for any* SPR-CCA *adversary $\mathcal{A}$ against* Kyber.KEM $=$ (KGen$'$, Encap, Decap) *w.r.t. $\mathcal{S}$ issuing at most q_D classical queries to the decapsulation oracles, and at most q_G, q_H and $q_{H'}$ queries to the quantum random* *oracles G, H and H' respectively, there exists an* IND-CPA *adversary $\mathcal{B}$ and a* SDS-IND *adversary $\mathcal{D}$ against* Kyber.PKE *w.r.t. $\mathcal{S}$ such that*

$$\mathbf{Adv}^{\text{SPR-CCA}}_{\text{Kyber.KEM},\mathcal{S}}(\mathcal{A}) \leq q_G \sqrt{\mathbf{Adv}^{\text{IND-CPA}}_{\text{Kyber.PKE}}(\mathcal{B}) + \frac{1}{2^{256}}} + \frac{1}{2}\mathsf{Disj}_{\text{Kyber.PKE},\mathcal{S}}(\lambda)$$

$$+ \mathbf{Adv}^{\text{SDS-IND}}_{\text{Kyber.PKE},\mathcal{S}}(\mathcal{D}) + (2 + 8(q_G + q_D + 2)^2 + 8(2q_G + 2)^2)\delta$$

$$+ \frac{2(q_{H'} + q_D)}{2^{128}} + \frac{C(q_H + 1)^3}{2^{256}} + \frac{q_H + 7q_{H'}}{2^{128}},$$

where C (< 648) is the constant from Lemma 1, and the running time of $\mathcal{B}$ and $\mathcal{D}$ is about the same as that of $\mathcal{A}$.

The proof follows quite closely to that of IND-CCA security of Kyber.KEM in the QROM above (Theorem 1). We will be focusing on the main differences in our SPR-CCA security analysis below.

Proof. Same as in our proof of IND-CCA security for Kyber.KEM (Theorem 1), we first consider SPR-CCA security of the "intermediate" scheme $\overline{\text{Kyber.KEM}} = \mathsf{FO}^{\nmid'}_{\text{pre}}[\text{Kyber.PKE}, G, H, H']$ (see Fig. 6) in the QROM.

Games $\overline{\mathsf{G}}_0 - \overline{\mathsf{G}}_2$	Decap(sk', c)
1 : $(\mathsf{pk}, \mathsf{sk}) \leftarrow \mathsf{KGen}'$	1 : Parse $\mathsf{sk}' = (\mathsf{sk}, \mathsf{pk}, h, s)$
2 : $(c_0^*, \overline{k}_0^*) \leftarrow \mathsf{Encap}(\mathsf{pk})$	2 : $m' \leftarrow \mathsf{Dec}(\mathsf{sk}, c)$
3 : $c_1^* \leftarrow \mathcal{S}()$	3 : $(\overline{k}', r') \leftarrow G(m', h)$
4 : $\overline{k}_1^* \leftarrow_{\$} \{0, 1\}^{256}$	4 : $c' \leftarrow \mathsf{Enc}(\mathsf{pk}, m'; r')$
5 : $b \leftarrow_{\$} \{0, 1\}$	5 : **if** $c' = c$ **then**
6 : $b' \leftarrow \overline{\mathcal{A}}^{G,H,H',\text{Decap}(\mathsf{sk}', \cdot)}(\mathsf{pk}, c_b^*, \overline{k}_b^*)$	6 : **return** $\overline{k}'$
7 : **return** $[b' = b]$	7 : **else return** $H'(s, c) /\!\!/ \ \overline{\mathsf{G}}_0$
	8 : **else return** $H''(c) /\!\!/ \ \overline{\mathsf{G}}_1$
	9 : **else return** $\overline{H}(H(c)) /\!\!/ \ \overline{\mathsf{G}}_2$

Fig. 9. Games $\overline{\mathsf{G}}_0 - \overline{\mathsf{G}}_2$. Here $H'': \{0, 1\}^* \to \{0, 1\}^{256}$ and $\overline{H}: \{0, 1\}^{256} \to \{0, 1\}^{256}$ are fresh *internal* random oracles, i.e., not directly accessible to $\overline{\mathcal{A}}$. Also, $\mathcal{S}$ is the simulator described above which simply outputs a uniformly random Kyber.PKE ciphertext.

Let $\overline{\mathcal{A}}$ be an SPR-CCA adversary against $\overline{\text{Kyber.KEM}}$ w.r.t. simulator $\mathcal{S}$ (described above) issuing at most q'_D classical queries to the decapsulation oracles, and q'_H and $q'_{H'}$ queries to the quantum random oracles H and H' respectively. Consider the sequence of games $\overline{\mathsf{G}}_0 - \overline{\mathsf{G}}_2$ described in Fig. 9. It is straightforward to obtain the following based on our IND-CCA security analysis of $\overline{\text{Kyber.KEM}}$ (Inequality (4)) in the proof of Theorem 1 above.

$$\left| \Pr[\overline{\mathsf{G}}_2 = 1] - \frac{1}{2} \right| \leq \mathbf{Adv}^{\text{SPR-CCA}}_{\overline{\text{Kyber.KEM}},\mathcal{S}}(\overline{\mathcal{A}}) + \frac{2q'_{H'}}{2^{128}} + \frac{C(q'_H + q'_D + 1)^3}{2^{256}}, \qquad (15)$$

Now, we return to proving SPR-CCA security of the *actual* Kyber.KEM. Let $\mathcal{A}$ be an SPR-CCA adversary against Kyber.KEM w.r.t. $\mathcal{S}$ issuing at most q_D classical queries to the decapsulation oracles, and at most q_G, q_H and $q_{H'}$ queries to the quantum random oracles G, H and H' respectively. Consider the sequence of games $G_0 - G_7$ described in Fig. 10. These games are quite similar to the ones described in Fig. 8 in our IND-CCA security proof.

Games $G_0 - G_7$	Decap(sk$'$, c)
1 : (pk, sk) $\leftarrow$ KGen$'$	1 : Parse sk$' = ($sk, pk, h, $s)$
2 : $m^* \leftarrow\!\!\!_\$ \{0,1\}^{256}$	2 : $m' \leftarrow$ Dec(sk, c)
3 : $m^* \leftarrow H(m^*) /\!\!/$ G$_0$	3 : $(\overline{k}', r') \leftarrow G(m', h)$
4 : $(\overline{k}_0^*, r^*) \leftarrow\!\!\!_\$ G(m^*, H(pk))$	4 : $c' \leftarrow$ Enc(pk, $m'; r'$)
5 : $\overline{k}_1^* \leftarrow\!\!\!_\$ \{0,1\}^{256}$	5 : **if** $c' = c$ **then**
6 : $c^* \leftarrow$ Enc(pk, $m^*; r^*) /\!\!/$ G$_0$ – G$_3$	6 : **return** $H'(\overline{k}', H(c))$
7 : $c^* \leftarrow \mathcal{S}() /\!\!/$ G$_4$ – G$_7$	7 : **else**
8 : $k^* \leftarrow H'(\overline{k}_0^*, H(c^*)) /\!\!/$ G$_0$ – G$_3$	8 : **return** $H'(s, H(c)) /\!\!/$ G$_0$ – G$_1$, G$_7$
9 : $k^* \leftarrow H'(\overline{k}_1^*, H(c^*)) /\!\!/$ G$_4$	9 : **return** $H''(H(c)) /\!\!/$ G$_2$, G$_6$
10 : $k^* \leftarrow\!\!\!_\$ \{0,1\}^{256} /\!\!/$ G$_5$ – G$_7$	10 : **return** $H'(\overline{H}(H(c)), H(c)) /\!\!/$ G$_3$–G$_5$
11 : $b' \leftarrow \mathcal{A}^{G,H,H',\text{Decap(sk}',\cdot)}(pk, c^*, k^*)$	
12 : **return** b'	

Fig. 10. Games $G_0 - G_7$. Here $H'' : \{0,1\}^* \rightarrow \{0,1\}^{256}$ and $\overline{H} : \{0,1\}^{256} \rightarrow \{0,1\}^{256}$ are fresh *internal* random oracles, i.e., not directly accessible to $\mathcal{A}$.

Game G_0: This game is the SPR-CCA game for Kyber.KEM with the "real" ciphertext c^* and "real" encapsulated key k^* where $(c^*, k^*) \leftarrow$ Encap(pk).

Now note that the games $G_0 - G_3$ in Fig. 10 are essentially *identical* to the games "$G_0 - G_3$" defined in Fig. 8. Hence, from our analysis of these game hops (i.e., Inequalities (5)–(7)) in the above IND-CCA security proof, it is not hard to obtain:

$$|\Pr[G_0 = 1] - \Pr[G_3 = 1]| \leq \frac{2q_H}{2^{128}} + \frac{4q_{H'}}{2^{128}}. \tag{16}$$

Game G_4: Relative to G_3 (and G_0), we modify how the challenge ciphertext c^* and corresponding encapsulated key k^* are generated. In this game, we generate (c^*, k^*) as $c^* \leftarrow \mathcal{S}()$ and $k^* \leftarrow H'(\overline{k}_1^*, H(c^*))$ instead, where $\mathcal{S}$ is the simulator described above and $\overline{k}_1^* \leftarrow\!\!\!_\$ \{0,1\}^{256}$. Here we use our SPR-CCA security analysis of the intermediate $\overline{\text{Kyber}}$.KEM.

To be specific, recall that in the corresponding "$G_3 \rightarrow G_4$" hop (Inequality (8)) in our above IND-CCA security proof of Kyber.KEM, we showed a reduction to IND-CCA security of the underlying $\overline{\text{Kyber}}$.KEM. In a similar way, it is straightforward to construct an SPR-CCA adversary $\overline{\mathcal{A}}$ against $\overline{\text{Kyber.KEM}}$ w.r.t. the same $\mathcal{S}$ above such that

$$|\Pr[\mathsf{G}_3 = 1] - \Pr[\mathsf{G}_4 = 1]| = 2 \cdot |\Pr[\overline{\mathsf{G}}_2 = 1] - 1/2|$$
$$\leq 2\mathbf{Adv}^{\text{SPR-CCA}}_{\overline{\text{Kyber.KEM}},\mathcal{S}}(\overline{\mathcal{A}}) + \frac{4q_{H'}}{2^{128}} + \frac{2C(q_H + 1)^3}{2^{256}}, \quad (17)$$

where we used Inequality (15) w.r.t. our analysis of $\overline{\text{Kyber.KEM}}$.

Game G_5: We further modify how k^* is generated. In this game, k^* is chosen from $\{0,1\}^{256}$ uniformly at random. Similar to our analysis of the "$\mathsf{G}_4 \to \mathsf{G}_5$" hop (Inequality (9)) in the proof of Theorem 1, we obtain the following by applying Lemma 2.

$$|\Pr[\mathsf{G}_4 = 1] - \Pr[\mathsf{G}_5 = 1]| \leq \frac{2q_{H'}}{2^{128}}. \quad (18)$$

Game G_6: We modify the decapsulation oracle such that the oracle rejects an invalid ciphertext c by returning $H''(H(c))$. In a sense, we are reverting the changes introduced in the "$\mathsf{G}_2 \to \mathsf{G}_3$" hop above (cf. Inequality (7) in the proof of Theorem 1). Hence, it is not hard to obtain

$$|\Pr[\mathsf{G}_5 = 1] - \Pr[\mathsf{G}_6 = 1]| \leq \frac{2q_{H'}}{2^{128}}. \quad (19)$$

Game G_7: We again modify the decapsulation oracle such that the oracle returns $H'(s, H(c))$ for an invalid ciphertext c. From our analysis of the "$\mathsf{G}_1 \to \mathsf{G}_2$" hop above (cf. Inequality (6) in the proof of Theorem 1), we have

$$|\Pr[\mathsf{G}_6 = 1] - \Pr[\mathsf{G}_7 = 1]| \leq \frac{2q_{H'}}{2^{128}}. \quad (20)$$

Note that G_7 is the SPR-CCA game for Kyber.KEM where $\mathcal{A}$ gets a "random" ciphertext $c^* \leftarrow \mathcal{S}()$ and "random" encapsulated key $k^* \leftarrow_\$ \{0,1\}^{256}$. Hence, by summing up the bounds (16)–(20), we obtain

$$2\mathbf{Adv}^{\text{SPR-CCA}}_{\text{Kyber.KEM},\mathcal{S}}(\mathcal{A}) = |\Pr[\mathsf{G}_0 = 1] - \Pr[\mathsf{G}_7 = 1]|$$
$$\leq 2\mathbf{Adv}^{\text{SPR-CCA}}_{\overline{\text{Kyber.KEM}},\mathcal{S}}(\overline{\mathcal{A}}) + \frac{2C(q_H + 1)^3}{2^{256}} + \frac{2q_H + 14q_{H'}}{2^{128}}.(21)$$

Finally, we replace the term "$\mathbf{Adv}^{\text{SPR-CCA}}_{\overline{\text{Kyber.KEM}},\mathcal{S}}(\overline{\mathcal{A}})$" with the existing SPR-CCA security bounds on the $\text{FO}_m^{\not\perp}$ transform in the QROM derived in [46]. Because as previously noted in our proof of Theorem 1 above, the intermediate $\text{FO}_{\text{pre}}^{\not\perp'}$ transform is essentially identical to $\text{FO}_m^{\not\perp}$ in the context of "single key-pair notions" such as IND-CCA security *and* SPR-CCA security. Hence, by applying [46, Thms. D.1 and 4.1 of ePrint][7] w.r.t. the SPR-CCA security of

---

[7] $\text{FO}_m^{\not\perp}$ is composed of two *modular* FO transforms: namely, the "T" and "$\mathsf{U}_m^{\not\perp}$" transforms defined in [29]; [46, Thm. D.1 of ePrint] considers the T transform and [46, Thm. 4.1 of ePrint] considers the $\mathsf{U}_m^{\not\perp}$ transform respectively.

"FO$_m^{\not\perp}$-derived" KEMs in the QROM to $\overline{\text{Kyber}}$.KEM, we have that there exists an IND-CPA adversary $\mathcal{B}$ and a SDS-IND adversary $\mathcal{D}$ w.r.t. $\mathcal{S}$ against Kyber.PKE, running in about the same time as that of $\overline{\mathcal{A}}$ (and $\mathcal{A}$), such that[8]

$$\mathbf{Adv}_{\text{Kyber.KEM},\mathcal{S}}^{\text{SPR-CCA}}(\overline{\mathcal{A}}) \leq q_G\sqrt{\mathbf{Adv}_{\text{Kyber.PKE}}^{\text{IND-CPA}}(\mathcal{B}) + \frac{1}{2^{256}}} + \frac{1}{2}\mathsf{Disj}_{\text{Kyber.PKE},\mathcal{S}}(\lambda)$$

$$+ \mathbf{Adv}_{\text{Kyber.PKE},\mathcal{S}}^{\text{SDS-IND}}(\mathcal{D}) + \frac{2(q_{H'} + q_D)}{2^{128}} + (2 + 8(q_G + q_D + 2)^2 + 8(2q_G + 2)^2)\delta. \tag{22}$$

Combining inequalities (21) and (22) finishes the proof.

Corollary 1 (ANO-CCA security of Kyber.KEM). *Given* Kyber.PKE *is* IND-CPA *secure and* strongly *disjoint-simulatable, then* Kyber.KEM *is* ANO-CCA *secure in the QROM.*

This follows from [46, Thm. 2.5 of ePrint] which states that the SPR-CCA security of a KEM implies its ANO-CCA security.

5.2   SPR-CCA Security of Hybrid PKE Derived from Kyber.KEM

We now focus on anonymity, or more specifically, SPR-CCA security of hybrid PKE schemes obtained from Kyber.KEM via the well-known "KEM-DEM" framework of [16]. It was shown in [46, Thm. 3.2 of ePrint] that composing a *one-time strongly pseudorandom* (or, *SPR-otCCA secure*; cf. Definition 10) DEM with an implicitly-rejecting KEM which is both SPR-CCA secure *and* strongly smooth (or, *SSMT-CCA secure*; cf. Definition 7) results in an SPR-CCA secure hybrid PKE scheme. Hence, we establish concrete SSMT-CCA security of Kyber.KEM in the QROM below while relying on statistical disjointness of the base Kyber.PKE scheme.

Theorem 3 (SSMT-CCA security of Kyber.KEM). *Let $\mathcal{S}$ be a QPT simulator which outputs a uniformly random value from the ciphertext space of* Kyber.PKE $=$ (KGen, Enc, Dec)*. For any* SSMT-CCA *adversary $\mathcal{A}$ against the scheme* Kyber.KEM $=$ (KGen', Encap, Decap) *w.r.t. $\mathcal{S}$ issuing at most q_D classical queries to the decapsulation oracles, and at most q_G, q_H and $q_{H'}$ queries to the quantum random oracles G, H and H' respectively. Consider the sequence of games G_0 – G_6 described in Fig. 11.*

---

[8] Technically, [46, Thm. 4.1 of ePrint] includes statistical disjointness (cf. Definition 4) of a *derandomized* version of the base PKE scheme in its SPR-CCA security bounds on the final KEM. Roughly speaking, in such a derandomized PKE, the random coins used to encrypt a message m is obtained by first hashing m. But from our proof sketch of Lemma 6, it is not hard to see that statistical disjointness of the derandomized Kyber.PKE is trivially upper-bounded by disjointness of the *original* Kyber.PKE, i.e., $\mathsf{Disj}_{\text{Kyber.PKE},\mathcal{S}}$. This is because our simulator $\mathcal{S}$ just outputs a uniformly random Kyber.PKE ciphertext.

$$\mathbf{Adv}^{\text{SSMT-CCA}}_{\text{Kyber.KEM},\mathcal{S}}(\mathcal{A}) \leq \text{Disj}_{\text{Kyber.PKE},\mathcal{S}}(\lambda) + \frac{2q_{H'}+1}{2^{128}} + \frac{C(q_H+1)^3}{2 \cdot 2^{256}},$$

where C (< 648) is the constant from Lemma 1.

Games G_0 – G_6	Decap(sk', c)
1 : $(\text{pk}, \text{sk}) \leftarrow \text{KGen}'$	1 : Parse $\text{sk}' = (\text{sk}, \text{pk}, h, s)$
2 : $c^* \leftarrow \mathcal{S}() /\!\!/ \; G_0, G_6$	2 : if $c = c^*$ then return $\perp$
3 : $c^* \leftarrow \mathcal{S}() \setminus \text{Enc}(\text{pk}, \mathcal{M}) /\!\!/ \; G_1 - G_5$	3 : $m' \leftarrow \text{Dec}(\text{sk}, c)$
4 : $k^* \leftarrow_\$ \{0,1\}^{256} /\!\!/ \; G_0 - G_2$	4 : $(\overline{k}', r') \leftarrow G(m', h)$
5 : $k^* \leftarrow H''(H(c^*)) /\!\!/ \; G_3$	5 : $c' \leftarrow \text{Enc}(\text{pk}, m'; r')$
6 : $k^* \leftarrow H'(s, H(c^*)) /\!\!/ \; G_4$	6 : if $c' = c$ then
7 : $k^* \leftarrow \text{Decap}(\text{sk}', c^*) /\!\!/ \; G_5 - G_6$	7 : return $H'(\overline{k}', H(c))$
8 : $b' \leftarrow \mathcal{A}^{G,H,H',\text{Decap}(\text{sk}',\cdot)}(\text{pk}, c^*, k^*)$	8 : else
9 : return b'	9 : return $H'(s, H(c)) /\!\!/ \; G_0\text{–}G_1, G_4\text{–}G_6$
	10 : return $H''(H(c)) /\!\!/ \; G_2 - G_3$

Fig. 11. Games G_0 – G_6. Here $H'' : \{0,1\}^* \rightarrow \{0,1\}^{256}$ is a fresh *internal* random oracle not directly accessible to $\mathcal{A}$. Also, $\mathcal{S}$ is the simulator described above which simply outputs a uniformly random Kyber.PKE ciphertext.

Proof. **Game** G_0: This game is the SSMT-CCA game for Kyber.KEM with the random encapsulated key $k^* \leftarrow_\$ \{0,1\}^{256}$ and simulated ciphertext $c^* \leftarrow \mathcal{S}()$.

Game G_1: We then modify how c^* is generated. In this game, c^* is generated by $\mathcal{S}()$ conditioned on that c^* is outside of $\text{Enc}(\text{pk}, \mathcal{M})$. More specifically, the game does a (potentially inefficient) check on whether $c^* \in \text{Enc}(\text{pk}, \mathcal{M})$ and aborts if it is the case. Note that this potential inefficiency does not really matter in our analysis since we will be bounding the difference between subsequent games using *statistical* bounds anyway.

Coming to the difference between games G_0 and G_1, it is bounded by the value $\text{Disj}_{\text{Kyber.PKE},\mathcal{S}}(\lambda)$, and we have

$$|\Pr[G_0 = 1] - \Pr[G_1 = 1]| \leq \text{Disj}_{\text{Kyber.PKE},\mathcal{S}}(\lambda). \tag{23}$$

Game G_2: We next modify the "implicit rejection" of the decapsulation oracle. In this game, the oracle rejects by outputting $H''(H(c))$ instead of $H'(s, H(c))$, where H'' is an independent random oracle. From the "$G_1 \rightarrow G_2$" hop (Inequality (6)) in the proof of Theorem 1 above, we obtain the following via Lemma 2:

$$|\Pr[G_1 = 1] - \Pr[G_2 = 1]| \leq \frac{2q_{H'}}{2^{128}}. \tag{24}$$

Game G_3: We next modify how k^* is generated. In this game, k^* is computed as $H''(H(c^*))$ instead of being chosen uniformly at random.

Notice that the adversary can only access H'' via the decapsulation oracle. Thus, if the adversary cannot query $c \neq c^*$ such that $H(c) = H(c^*)$, then the adversary cannot obtain any information on $H''(H(c^*))$ and this value looks completely random. Similar to the "$\overline{G}_1 \rightarrow \overline{G}_2$" hop (Inequality (3)) above in our IND-CCA security proof of Kyber.KEM, we can bound the difference between G_2 and G_3 via a straightforward reduction to the collision resistance of H. Hence, we have from Lemma 1

$$|\Pr[G_2 = 1] - \Pr[G_3 = 1]| \leq \frac{C(q_H + 1)^3}{2^{256}}. \tag{25}$$

Game G_4: We next replace all invocations of $H''(H(\cdot))$ in this game – particularly, during generation of k^* and decapsulation of ciphertexts – with $H'(s, H(\cdot))$. Again from the "$G_1 \rightarrow G_2$" hop above (Inequality 24), we can use the pseudorandomness of H' (Lemma 2) to obtain

$$|\Pr[G_3 = 1] - \Pr[G_4 = 1]| \leq \frac{2(q_{H'} + 1)}{2^{128}}. \tag{26}$$

Game G_5: In this game, we compute k^* as $k^* \leftarrow \mathsf{Decap}(\mathsf{sk}', c^*)$ instead of $k^* \leftarrow H'(s, H(c^*))$. Anyways the result of $\mathsf{Decap}(\mathsf{sk}', c^*)$ in G_5 will be equal to $H'(s, H(c^*))$ as in G_4. Because note that c^* is an invalid ciphertext since it is outside of $\mathsf{Enc}(\mathsf{pk}, \mathcal{M})$. Thus, even if the decryption of c^* yields some plaintext m', the re-encrypted ciphertext $c' = \mathsf{Enc}(\mathsf{pk}, m'; r')$ cannot be equivalent to c^*. Hence, we have $\Pr[G_4 = 1] = \Pr[G_5 = 1]$.

Game G_6: We finally modify how c^* is generated. In this game, c^* is generated by $\mathcal{S}()$ (and there is no check by the game on whether $c^* \in \mathsf{Enc}(\mathsf{pk}, \mathcal{M})$). We note that this game is the SSMT-CCA game for Kyber.KEM with simulated ciphertext $c^* \leftarrow \mathcal{S}()$ and decapsulated key $k^* \leftarrow \mathsf{Decap}(\mathsf{sk}, c^*)$.

The difference is again bounded by $\mathsf{Disj}_{\mathsf{Kyber.PKE}, \mathcal{S}}(\lambda)$, and we have

$$|\Pr[G_5 = 1] - \Pr[G_6 = 1]| \leq \mathsf{Disj}_{\mathsf{Kyber.PKE}, \mathcal{S}}(\lambda). \tag{27}$$

Summing up the above differences (23)–(27), we have

$$2\mathbf{Adv}_{\mathsf{Kyber.KEM}}^{\mathrm{SSMT\text{-}CCA}}(\mathcal{A}) = |\Pr[G_0 = 1] - \Pr[G_6 = 1]|$$

$$\leq 2\mathsf{Disj}_{\mathsf{Kyber.PKE}, \mathcal{S}}(\lambda) + \frac{4q_{H'} + 2}{2^{128}} + \frac{C(q_H + 1)^3}{2^{256}}.$$

Corollary 2 (ANO-CCA security of hybrid PKE from Kyber.KEM). *Given* Kyber.KEM *is SPR-CCA secure, SSMT-CCA secure, and δ-correct, and a* DEM *that is SPR-otCCA secure, then the hybrid PKE scheme obtained by composing* Kyber.KEM *and* DEM *is SPR-CCA secure, and hence, ANO-CCA secure.*

This follows from [46, Thm. 3.2 of ePrint].

Robustness of Kyber. The notion of *"robustness"* for PKE was defined in [1], and there it was argued that robustness is an essential conjunct of anonymous encryption. Roughly speaking, robustness guarantees that it is hard to produce a ciphertext which decrypts validly under two different private keys. Fortunately, it was shown in [28] that composing Kyber.KEM with an appropriately "robust" DEM (as defined in [23]) will result in a robust hybrid PKE scheme. In other words, composing Kyber with a one-time strongly pseudorandom and robust DEM will result in a post-quantum strongly anonymous *and* robust PKE scheme.

Acknowledgements. The first author is grateful to Kenny Paterson for helpful discussions on the "wrapper" approach. The authors also thank the anonymous reviewers of PKC 2023 for their constructive comments and suggestions.

References

1. Abdalla, M., Bellare, M., Neven, G.: Robust encryption. In: Micciancio, D. (ed.) TCC 2010. LNCS, vol. 5978, pp. 480–497. Springer, Heidelberg (2010). https://doi.org/10.1007/978-3-642-11799-2_28
2. Alagic, G., Apon, D., Cooper, D., Dang, Q., Dang, T., Kelsey, J., Lichtinger, J., Liu, Y.-K., Miller, C., Moody, D., Peralta, R., Perlner, R., Robinson, A., Smith-Tone, D.: Status report on the third round of the nist post-quantum cryptography standardization process. US Department of Commerce, NIST (2022)
3. Ambainis, A., Hamburg, M., Unruh, D.: Quantum security proofs using semi-classical Oracles. In: Boldyreva, A., Micciancio, D. (eds.) CRYPTO 2019. LNCS, vol. 11693, pp. 269–295. Springer, Cham (2019). https://doi.org/10.1007/978-3-030-26951-7_10
4. Avanzi, R., et al.: CRYSTALS-Kyber: NIST Round 3 Submission, Algorithm Specifications and Supporting Documentation (v3.02) (2021)
5. Barth, A., Boneh, D., Waters, B.: Privacy in encrypted content distribution using private broadcast encryption. In: FC 2006, pp. 52–64 (2006)
6. Bellare, M., Boldyreva, A., Desai, A., Pointcheval, D.: Key-privacy in public-key encryption. In: Boyd, C. (ed.) ASIACRYPT 2001. LNCS, vol. 2248, pp. 566–582. Springer, Heidelberg (2001). https://doi.org/10.1007/3-540-45682-1_33
7. Bellare, M., Rogaway, P.: Random oracles are practical: a paradigm for designing efficient protocols. In ACM CCS **93**, 62–73 (1993)
8. Ben-Sasson, E., Chiesa, A., Garman, C., Green, M., Miers, I., Tromer, E., Virza, M.: Zerocash: decentralized anonymous payments from bitcoin. In: 2014 IEEE Symposium on Security and Privacy, pp. 459–474 (2014)
9. Bernstein, D.J., et al.: NTRU Prime. Technical report, National Institute of Standards and Technology (2020). https://csrc.nist.gov/projects/post-quantum-cryptography/round-3-submissions
10. Bindel, N., Hamburg, M., Hövelmanns, K., Hülsing, A., Persichetti, E.: Tighter proofs of CCA security in the quantum random oracle model. In: TCC 2019, Part II, pp. 61–90 (2019)
11. Boneh, D., Dagdelen, Ö., Fischlin, M., Lehmann, A., Schaffner, C., Zhandry, M.: Random Oracles in a quantum world. In: Lee, D.H., Wang, X. (eds.) ASIACRYPT 2011. LNCS, vol. 7073, pp. 41–69. Springer, Heidelberg (2011). https://doi.org/10.1007/978-3-642-25385-0_3

12. Boyd, C., Cliff, Y., Nieto, J.M.G., Paterson, K.G.: One-round key exchange in the standard model. Int. J. Appl. Cryptogr. **1**(3), 181–199 (2009)
13. Brakerski, Z., Gentry, C., Vaikuntanathan, V.: (Leveled) fully homomorphic encryption without bootstrapping. In: ITCS 2012, pp. 309–325 (2012)
14. Camenisch, J., Lysyanskaya, A.: An efficient system for non-transferable anonymous credentials with optional anonymity revocation. In: Pfitzmann, B. (ed.) EUROCRYPT 2001. LNCS, vol. 2045, pp. 93–118. Springer, Heidelberg (2001). https://doi.org/10.1007/3-540-44987-6_7
15. Chen, Z., Lu, X., Jia, D., Li, B.: Ind-cca security of kyber in the quantum random Oracle model, revisited. In: Information Security and Cryptology - 18th International Conference, Inscrypt 2022, Beijing, 11–13 December 2022, Revised Selected Papers, 2022 (to appear)
16. Cramer, R., Shoup, V.: Design and analysis of practical public-key encryption schemes secure against adaptive chosen ciphertext attack. SIAM J. Comput. **33**(1), 167–226 (2003)
17. Bernstein, D.J.: Subject: Anonymity of KEMs in the QROM. NIST PQC Forum. https://groups.google.com/a/list.nist.gov/g/pqc-forum/c/8k3MhD_5stk/m/TWGKtuL4BgAJ
18. D'Anvers, J.-P., Karmakar, A., Roy, S.S., Vercauteren, F.: Saber: module-LWR based key exchange, CPA-secure encryption and CCA-secure KEM. In: AFRICACRYPT 18, pp. 282–305 (2018)
19. D'Anvers, J.-P.: SABER. Technical report, National Institute of Standards and Technology (2020). https://csrc.nist.gov/projects/post-quantum-cryptography/round-3-submissions
20. Dent, A.W.: A designer's guide to KEMs. In 9th IMA International Conference on Cryptography and Coding, pp. 133–151 (2003)
21. Ding, X., Esgin, M.F., Sakzad, A., Steinfeld, R.: An injectivity analysis of crystals-kyber and implications on quantum security. In: Information Security and Privacy - 27th Australasian Conference, ACISP 2022, Wollongong, NSW, Australia, November 28–30, 2022, Proceedings, pp. 332–351 (2022)
22. Don, J., Fehr, S., Majenz, C., Schaffner, C.: Online-extractability in the quantum random-oracle model. In: Dunkelman, O., Dziembowski, S. (eds.) EUROCRYPT 2022, Part III. LNCS, vol. 13277, pp. 677–706. Springer, Cham (2022). https://doi.org/10.1007/978-3-031-07082-2_24
23. Farshim, P., Orlandi, C., Roşie, R.: Security of symmetric primitives under incorrect usage of keys. IACR Trans. Symm. Cryptol. **2017**(1), 449–473 (2017)
24. Fujioka, A., Suzuki, K., Xagawa, K., Yoneyama, K.: Practical and post-quantum authenticated key exchange from one-way secure key encapsulation mechanism. In: ASIACCS 13, pp. 83–94 (2013)
25. Fujioka, A., Suzuki, K., Xagawa, K., Yoneyama, K.: Strongly secure authenticated key exchange from factoring, codes, and lattices. Des. Codes Cryptogr. **76**(3), 469–504 (2015)
26. Fujisaki, E., Okamoto, T.: Secure integration of asymmetric and symmetric encryption schemes. In: Wiener, M. (ed.) CRYPTO 1999. LNCS, vol. 1666, pp. 537–554. Springer, Heidelberg (1999). https://doi.org/10.1007/3-540-48405-1_34
27. Fujisaki, E., Okamoto, T.: Secure integration of asymmetric and symmetric encryption schemes. J. Cryptol. **26**(1), 80–101 (2013)
28. Grubbs, P., Maram, V., Paterson, K.G.: (2022). Anonymous, Robust Post-quantum Public Key Encryption. In: Dunkelman, O., Dziembowski, S. (eds) EUROCRYPT 2022. EUROCRYPT 2022. LNCS, vol. 13277, pp. 402–432. Springer, Cham (2022). https://doi.org/10.1007/978-3-031-07082-2_15

29. Hofheinz, D., Hövelmanns, K., Kiltz, E.: A modular analysis of the Fujisaki-Okamoto transformation. In: Kalai, Y., Reyzin, L. (eds.) TCC 2017. LNCS, vol. 10677, pp. 341–371. Springer, Cham (2017). https://doi.org/10.1007/978-3-319-70500-2_12

30. Hövelmanns, K., Kiltz, E., Schäge, S., Unruh, D.: Generic authenticated key exchange in the quantum random oracle model. In: Kiayias, A., Kohlweiss, M., Wallden, P., Zikas, V. (eds.) PKC 2020. LNCS, vol. 12111, pp. 389–422. Springer, Cham (2020). https://doi.org/10.1007/978-3-030-45388-6_14

31. Hövelmanns, K., Hülsing, A., Majenz, C.: Failing gracefully: Decryption failures and the Fujisaki-Okamoto transform. In: ASIACRYPT 2022 (to appear) (2022)

32. Jiang, H., Zhang, Z., Chen, L., Wang, H., Ma, Z.: IND-CCA-secure key encapsulation mechanism in the quantum random oracle model, revisited. In: Shacham, H., Boldyreva, A. (eds.) CRYPTO 2018, Part III. LNCS, vol. 10993, pp. 96–125. Springer, Cham (2018). https://doi.org/10.1007/978-3-319-96878-0_4

33. Jiang, H., Zhang, Z., Ma, Z.: Key encapsulation mechanism with explicit rejection in the quantum random oracle model. In: Lin, D., Sako, K. (eds.) PKC 2019. LNCS, vol. 11443, pp. 618–645. Springer, Cham (2019). https://doi.org/10.1007/978-3-030-17259-6_21

34. Katsumata, S., Kwiatkowski, K., Pintore, F., Prest, T.: Scalable ciphertext compression techniques for post-quantum KEMs and their applications. In: Moriai, S., Wang, H. (eds.) ASIACRYPT 2020. LNCS, vol. 12491, pp. 289–320. Springer, Cham (2020). https://doi.org/10.1007/978-3-030-64837-4_10

35. Kuchta, V., Sakzad, A., Stehlé, D., Steinfeld, R., Sun, S.-F.: Measure-rewind-measure: tighter quantum random oracle model proofs for one-way to hiding and CCA security. In: Canteaut, A., Ishai, Y. (eds.) EUROCRYPT 2020. LNCS, vol. 12107, pp. 703–728. Springer, Cham (2020). https://doi.org/10.1007/978-3-030-45727-3_24

36. Langlois, A., Stehlé, D.: Worst-case to average-case reductions for module lattices. Des. Codes Cryptogr. **75**(3), 565–599 (2015)

37. Libert, B., Paterson, K.G., Quaglia, E.A.: Anonymous broadcast encryption: Adaptive security and efficient constructions in the standard model. In: PKC 2012, pp. 206–224 (2012)

38. Liu, X., Wang, M.: QCCA-secure generic key encapsulation mechanism with tighter security in the quantum random oracle model. In: Garay, J.A. (ed.) PKC 2021. LNCS, vol. 12710, pp. 3–26. Springer, Cham (2021). https://doi.org/10.1007/978-3-030-75245-3_1

39. Saito, T., Xagawa, K., Yamakawa, T.: Tightly-secure key-encapsulation mechanism in the quantum random oracle model. In: Nielsen, J.B., Rijmen, V. (eds.) EUROCRYPT 2018. LNCS, vol. 10822, pp. 520–551. Springer, Cham (2018). https://doi.org/10.1007/978-3-319-78372-7_17

40. Sako, K.: An auction protocol which hides bids of losers. In: Imai, H., Zheng, Y. (eds.) PKC 2000. LNCS, vol. 1751, pp. 422–432. Springer, Heidelberg (2000). https://doi.org/10.1007/978-3-540-46588-1_28

41. Schwabe, P., et al.: CRYSTALS-KYBER. Technical report, National Institute of Standards and Technology (2020). https://csrc.nist.gov/projects/post-quantum-cryptography/round-3-submissions

42. Schwabe, P., Stebila, D., Wiggers, T.: Post-quantum TLS without handshake signatures. In: ACM CCS 2020, pp. 1461–1480 (2020)

43. Targhi, E.E., Unruh, D.: Post-quantum security of the Fujisaki-Okamoto and OAEP transforms. In: Hirt, M., Smith, A. (eds.) TCC 2016. LNCS, vol. 9986, pp.

192–216. Springer, Heidelberg (2016). https://doi.org/10.1007/978-3-662-53644-5_8

44. Unruh, D.: Revocable quantum timed-release encryption. In: Nguyen, P.Q., Oswald, E. (eds.) EUROCRYPT 2014. LNCS, vol. 8441, pp. 129–146. Springer, Heidelberg (2014). https://doi.org/10.1007/978-3-642-55220-5_8

45. Unruh, D.: Post-quantum verification of Fujisaki-Okamoto. In: Moriai, S., Wang, H. (eds.) ASIACRYPT 2020. LNCS, vol. 12491, pp. 321–352. Springer, Cham (2020). https://doi.org/10.1007/978-3-030-64837-4_11

46. Xagawa, K.: Anonymity of NIST PQC Round 3 KEMs. In: Dunkelman, O., Dziembowski, S. (eds.) EUROCRYPT 2022. LNCS, Part III, vol. 13277, pp. 551–581. Springer, Cham (2022). https://doi.org/10.1007/978-3-031-07082-2_20

47. Zhandry, M.: A note on the quantum collision and set equality problems. Quantum Inf. Comput. 15(7–8) (2015)

48. Zhandry, M.: How to record quantum queries, and applications to quantum indifferentiability. In: Boldyreva, A., Micciancio, D. (eds.) CRYPTO 2019. LNCS, vol. 11693, pp. 239–268. Springer, Cham (2019). https://doi.org/10.1007/978-3-030-26951-7_9

QCCA-Secure Generic Transformations in the Quantum Random Oracle Model

Tianshu Shan[1,2]($\boxtimes$) (iD), Jiangxia Ge[1,2] (iD), and Rui Xue[1,2] (iD)

[1] State Key Laboratory of Information Security, Institute of Information Engineering, Chinese Academy of Sciences, Beijing 100093, China
{shantianshu,gejiangxia,xuerui}@iie.ac.cn
[2] School of Cyber Security, University of Chinese Academy of Sciences, Beijing 100049, China

Abstract. The post-quantum security of cryptographic schemes assumes that the quantum adversary only receives the classical result of computations with the secret key. Further, it is unknown whether the post-quantum secure schemes still remain secure if the adversary can obtain a superposition state of the results.

In this paper, we formalize one class of public-key encryption schemes named oracle-masked schemes. Then we define the plaintext extraction procedure for those schemes and this procedure simulates the quantum-accessible decryption oracle with a certain loss.

The construction of the plaintext extraction procedure does not need to take the secret key as input. Based on this property, we prove the IND-qCCA security of the Fujisaki-Okamoto (FO) transformation in the quantum random oracle model (QROM) and our security proof is tighter than the proof given by Zhandry (Crypto 2019). We also give the first IND-qCCA security proof of the REACT transformation in the QROM. Furthermore, our formalization can be applied to prove the IND-qCCA security of key encapsulation mechanisms with explicit rejection. As an example, we present the IND-qCCA security proof of T_{CH} transformation, proposed by Huguenin-Dumittan and Vaudenay (Eurocrypt 2022), in the QROM.

Keywords: FO transformation · REACT transformation · quantum random oracle model · quantum chosen ciphertext attack

1 Introduction

There are two criteria for a practical encryption scheme: security and efficiency. Many generic transformations are proposed to enhance the security of public-key encryption schemes (PKEs) to achieve the indistinguishable under chosen ciphertext attacks (IND-CCA) security [2,8,11,23]. As for efficiency, Cramer and Shoup proposed the KEM-DEM hybrid construction that combines an IND-CCA key encapsulation mechanism (KEM) with a one-time chosen ciphertext secure secret-key encryption scheme (SKE) to obtain an IND-CCA PKE [9].

© International Association for Cryptologic Research 2023
A. Boldyreva and V. Kolesnikov (Eds.): PKC 2023, LNCS 13940, pp. 36–64, 2023.
https://doi.org/10.1007/978-3-031-31368-4_2

Cryptographic schemes often have efficient constructions in the random oracle model (ROM) [2], in which schemes are proven to be secure assuming the existence of the publicly accessible random oracle. Many generic transforms are relative to random oracles. For instance, the Fujisaki-Okamoto (FO) transformation turns an arbitrary PKE that is one-way under chosen plaintext attacks (OW-CPA) into an IND-CCA PKE in the ROM [11], and the REACT transformation turns an arbitrary PKE that is one-way under plaintext checking attacks (OW-PCA) into an IND-CCA PKE in the ROM [23].

Typically, the random oracle is instantiated with a cryptographic hash function. Thus in the real world attack, a quantum attacker can evaluate the hash function in superposition. To capture this issue, Boneh et al. [4] proposed the quantum random oracle model (QROM) where the quantum adversary can query the random oracle with superposition states. Further, classical schemes may be implemented on quantum computers, which potentially gives quantum attackers more power. For this case, Boneh and Zhandry [5] introduced the indistinguishability under quantum chosen ciphertext attacks (IND-qCCA) for encryption schemes, where the adversary can make quantum queries to the decryption oracle. Following it, Gagliardoni et al. [13] focused on SKE and proposed new notions of indistinguishability and semantic security in the quantum world, e.g. quantum semantic security under chosen plaintext attacks (qSEM-qCPA). On the other hand, Xagawa and Yamakawa [27] presented the IND-qCCA security of KEMs, where the adversary can query the decapsulation oracle in superposition.

Boneh et al. [4] summarized four proof techniques that are commonly used in the ROM but not appropriate to the quantum setting straightforwardly. "Extractability", as one of them, is that the simulator learns the preimages the adversary takes interest in when simulating the random oracle for the adversary.

Extractability is the core to simulate answers to decryption queries in the IND-CCA security proof for both FO and REACT in the ROM. However, in the quantum setting, the non-existence of this technique had been an obstacle to their security proofs in QROM. To circumvent it, Targhi and Unruh [26] and the follow-up work by Ambainis et al. [1] modified the FO transformation by appending an extra hash function to the ciphertext, then applied the One-way to Hiding (O2H) Theorem and its variant to prove the IND-CCA security of the modified FO in the QROM.

Hofheinz et al. [14] divided KEMs into two types: explicit rejection and implicit rejection. The explicit rejection (resp. implicit rejection) type returns a symbol ⊥ (resp. a pseudorandom value) if the ciphertext is invalid. For both two types, they presented the IND-CCA security proof of transformations with additional hash in the QROM. Later, transformations with implicit rejection had been free from the additional hash and proved to be IND-CCA and even IND-qCCA in the QROM [3,17,19–21,24,27]. Nonetheless, for explicit rejection type, the IND-CCA security proofs in the QROM were only given for those transformations either with additional hash [18] or with non-standard security assumptions [19]. It seemed infeasible to give post-quantum security proof of unmodified transformations due to the non-existence of extractability.

In his seminal paper [29], Zhandry proposed the compressed oracle technique, with which the simulator can "record" quantum queries to the random oracle while simulating it efficiently. This enables to use extractability technique in the quantum setting and thus makes it possible to give security proofs of the unmodified FO and those transformations with explicit rejection in QROM.

Indeed in the full version of [29], Zhandry gave a proof that the unmodified FO turns any OW-CPA PKE into an IND-qCCA PKE in the QROM. However, in this proof, as was pointed out by Don et al. [10], the answers to decryption queries in Hybrids 2 to 4 are simulated by applying (purified) measurements on the internal state of the compressed oracle, yet these measurements are hard to be determined explicitly from their respective descriptions. Until now, this is considered as the gap that prevents the analysis of the disturbance caused by those measurements.

As for transformations with explicit rejection, Don et al. [10] presented the first IND-CCA security proof of $\mathsf{FO}_m^\perp$, a variant of FO transformation, in the QROM, as well as its concrete security bound. Based on their work, Hövelmanns et al. [15] improved the proof in [10] resulting in a tighter bound. However, as far as we know, there are only a few results on the IND-qCCA security proof of any transformations with explicit rejection [27].

1.1 Our Results

In this paper, we improve the IND-qCCA security proof in [29] and avoid the gap mentioned in [10]. Especially, we simplify that proof with our tool and present a tighter proof. We also give the first IND-qCCA security proof for transformation REACT and $\mathsf{T_{CH}}$ in the QROM, where $\mathsf{T_{CH}}$ is a KEM variant of REACT with explicit rejection proposed in [16]. The concrete security bounds for these three transformations are shown in Table 1.

Table 1. Concrete security bounds for FO, REACT and $\mathsf{T_{CH}}$ in the QROM. The "Underlying security" column omits the one-time security of the underlying SKE for both FO and REACT. ϵ^{asy} is the advantage of the reduced adversary against the security of the underlying PKE. ϵ^{sy} is the advantage against the security of the underlying SKE. d is the number of decryption or decapsulation queries. q is the total number of random oracle queries. γ is from the γ-spreadness of the underlying PKE. n is the length of the hash value being one part of the ciphertext of the achieved PKE or KEM.

Transform	Underlying security	Achieved security	Security bound($\approx$)
FO	OW-CPA	IND-qCCA	$d/\sqrt{2^\gamma} + (q + d) \cdot \sqrt{\epsilon^{asy}} + \epsilon^{sy}$
REACT	OW-qPCA	IND-qCCA	$d/\sqrt{2^n} + q \cdot d \cdot \sqrt{\epsilon^{asy}} + \epsilon^{sy}$
$\mathsf{T_{CH}}$	OW-qPCA	IND-qCCA	$d/\sqrt{2^n} + (q + d) \cdot \sqrt{\epsilon^{asy}}$

Our main tool to prove our results is a unitary $\mathsf{U_{Ext}}$ named the plaintext extraction procedure for a class of PKE called oracle-masked schemes. Informally, the oracle-masked scheme is defined as follows.

Definition 1 (Oracle-Masked Scheme, Informal). *For random oracle* $\mathcal{O}$ *with codomain* $\mathcal{Y}$, *we call* $\Pi = (Gen, Enc^{\mathcal{O}}, Dec^{\mathcal{O}})$ *an oracle-masked scheme if* $Enc^{\mathcal{O}}$ *and* $Dec^{\mathcal{O}}$ *are constructed as in Fig. 1. Parameter* η *of* Π *is defined to be*

$$\eta := \max_{(pk,sk),\,c} |\{y \in \mathcal{Y} : c = A_2(pk, A_3(sk, c), y)\}|/|\mathcal{Y}|,$$

where (pk, sk) *is generated by* Gen *and* $c \in \mathcal{C}$ *is such that* $A_3(sk, c) \neq \perp$.

$\text{Enc}^{\mathcal{O}}(pk, m; r)$	$\text{Dec}^{\mathcal{O}}(sk, c)$	
$x := A_1(pk, m, r)$	$x := A_3(sk, c)$	**if** $c \neq c'$, **return** $\perp$
$y := \mathcal{O}(x)$	**if** $x = \perp$, **return** $\perp$	$m := A_4(x)$
$c := A_2(pk, x, y)$	$y := \mathcal{O}(x)$	**return** m
return c	$c' := A_2(pk, x, y)$	

Fig. 1. Algorithm $\text{Enc}^{\mathcal{O}}$ and $\text{Dec}^{\mathcal{O}}$ of an oracle-masked scheme Π, and the tuple of algorithm A_1, A_2, A_3 and A_4 is called the decomposition of Π.

According to the above definition, oracle-masked schemes contains PKEs obtained by several transformations, including FO transformation, REACT transformation and T in the modular FO toolkit [14]. We then present the plaintext extraction procedure U_{Ext} for oracle-masked scheme Π as below.

Definition 2 (Plaintext Extraction Procedure, informal). *Suppose that* $\mathcal{O}$ *is simulated by the compressed standard oracle* CStO *with database register* D. *Then the plaintext extraction procedure* U_{Ext} *of oracle-masked scheme* Π *applied on register* C, Z, D *is that* $U_{Ext}|c, z, D\rangle = |c, z \oplus f(c, D), D\rangle$, *where*

$$f(c, D) := \begin{cases} A_4(x) & \textit{if } c \neq c^* \textit{ and } \exists\, x \textit{ s.t. } A_2(pk, x, D(x)) = c,\ A_3(sk, c) = x \\ \perp & \textit{otherwise.} \end{cases}$$

Plaintext extraction procedure U_{Ext} is to apply extractability technique to simulate the quantum-accessible decryption oracle in the IND-qCCA security proof of Π. When random oracle $\mathcal{O}$ is simulated by CStO, the random oracle queries is recorded on the database register D. Note that the queries is not recorded perfectly, but the simulator can still learn some information from the state on D by quantum measurements or computing functions defined on database [7,10]. Following this fact, U_{Ext} extracts plaintext $m(:= A_4(x))$ for ciphertext c by computing a classical function $f(c, D)$ defined as above. Moreover, U_{Ext} is performed efficiently if f can be computed efficiently.

With the notions defined as above, we then prove the IND-qCCA security of transformation FO, REACT and T_{CH}. Our proofs can be outlined as the following three steps.

Firstly, we represent the schemes obtained by transformations as oracle-masked schemes relative to $\mathcal{O}$ and specify their decomposition (A_1, A_2, A_3, A_4). In the IND-qCCA security games of these schemes, random oracle $\mathcal{O}$ is simulated by CStO and accordingly, the quantum decryption oracle $\text{Dec}^{\mathcal{O}}$ is simulated by unitary U_{Sim}.

Next, we replace unitary U_{Sim} with the plaintext extraction procedure U_{Ext}. We also present the detailed construction of U_{Ext} without the secret key.

Finally, we apply the semi-classical O2H theorem to reprogram the compressed oracle at some points, which results in a new game. We then connect it to the security game of the underlying schemes.

Here we analyze the security loss introduced by the second and third step.

For the second step, we need to bound the security loss caused by the replacement of the simulation of the decryption oracle $\text{Dec}^{\mathcal{O}}$. Since CStO perfectly simulates the random oracle, U_{Sim} and $\text{Dec}^{\mathcal{O}}$ are perfectly indistinguishable for any adversary. Then we analyze the loss introduced by performing unitary U_{Ext}. For one type of state $|\psi\rangle$, we compute the difference between $U_{\text{Ext}}|\psi\rangle$ and $U_{\text{Sim}}|\psi\rangle$ and obtain the following lemma.

Lemma 1 (Informal). *Let $|\psi\rangle$ be a quantum state on register C, Z, D that is orthogonal to $\sum_{c,z,D,x} \alpha_{c,z,D,x}|c,z,D\cup(x,\beta_0)\rangle$. Then $\|(U_{Sim}-U_{Ext})|\psi\rangle\| \leq 5\sqrt{\eta}$.*

As is argued in [10], there are at least two requirements of refining the proof in [29]: To rigorously specify the quantum measurements in Hybrid 3 and 4, respectively; To analyze the disturbance of the state of CStO caused by quantum measurements.

Our proofs meet the first requirement by providing the plaintext extraction procedure U_{Ext} of oracle-masked schemes. Indeed, U_{Ext} and the scan operation in Hybrid 4 act similarly. They both learns the information from the database. But our U_{Ext} is represented in a more specific form and can also be viewed as a formalization of the scan operation. As for the second requirement, we apply Lemma 1 to bound the disturbance caused by performing U_{Ext}. If the adversary makes at most q decryption queries, then by the hybrid argument, the loss caused by U_{Ext} is upper bounded by $5q\sqrt{\eta}$.

For the third step, we stress that we can not reprogram CStO only by applying the semi-classical O2H theorem. As an explanation, suppose that we puncture CStO on point x via the semi-classical oracle $\mathcal{O}_{\{x\}}^{SC}$, which forbids the adversary from querying CStO by x if event Find does not occur. However, the performance of U_{Ext} disturbs the database state on register D, which disturbs the simulation of random oracle $\mathcal{O}$. Thus, it can not be concluded that CStO on x is uniformly random even if the adversary never queries CStO on point x (i.e., Find does not occur).

To fix it, before reprogramming the compressed oracle on x, we change U_{Ext} into $\text{StdDecomp}_x \circ U_{\text{Ext}} \circ \text{StdDecomp}_x$, where StdDecomp_x, the local decompression procedure defined in [29], is an involution performed on the database register D. Then by the definition of U_{Ext}, $\text{StdDecomp}_x \circ U_{\text{Ext}} \circ \text{StdDecomp}_x$ does not disturb any database state in the form of $|D\cup\text{StdDecomp}_x(x,y)\rangle$, which in contrast to the disturbance made by U_{Ext}. Then we apply the following lemma to bound the difference between U_{Ext} and $\text{StdDecomp}_x \circ U_{\text{Ext}} \circ \text{StdDecomp}_x$.

Lemma 2 (Informal). *For any x and state $|\psi\rangle$ on register C, Z, D,*

$$\left\| (U_{Ext} \circ \mathsf{StdDecomp}_x - \mathsf{StdDecomp}_x \circ U_{Ext}) |\psi\rangle \right\| \leq 7\sqrt{\eta}.$$

Overall, we propose the notion of oracle-masked schemes and define plaintext extraction procedure U_{Ext} for these schemes. They can be used to avoid the gap in the FO proof in [29]. And our proof outline can also be applied to the IND-qCCA security proofs of other transformations in the QROM.

1.2 Related Work

Abstract frameworks were proposed to simplify the application of the compressed oracle technique in different situations [6,7,10]. They formalized properties that are satisfied in the presence of random oracle, and lifted them to the quantum setting.

Existing proofs from [29] already implicitly were using compressed oracles for some sort of extractability. Don et al. [10] then considered extractability in a general form. Specifically, they define a simulator $\mathcal{S}$ that simulates the random oracle and also allows the extraction query that is replied with a guess of the plaintext of the query. They then prove that this simulation of the random oracle is statistically indistinguishable from the real one if some properties are satisfied. In their security proof, the extraction query is restricted to be classical in the simulation. Therefore, their result seems to be tailored for post-quantum security proofs, yet are not sufficient to prove the IND-qCCA security.

Based on [10], Hövelmanns et al. [15] proposed a variant of semi-classical O2H theorem as the core to prove the post-quantum security of $\mathsf{FO}_m^{\perp}$. Roughly speaking, this theorem states that the probabilities of classical event EXT and $FIND$ can bound the loss caused by the reprogramming of the oracle simulated by $\mathcal{S}$. Different from their work, our argument allows the adversary to make quantum extraction query, which makes event EXT no longer make sense.

2   Preliminaries

2.1   Notation

Denote $\mathcal{M}$, $\mathcal{C}$ and $\mathcal{R}$ as key space, message space and ciphertext space, respectively. A function $f(\lambda)$ is negligible if $f(\lambda) = \lambda^{-\omega(1)}$. Algorithms take as input a security parameter λ, and we omit it for convenience. Time(A) is denoted as the running time of algorithm A.

For a finite set $\mathcal{X}$, denote $|\mathcal{X}|$ as the number of elements $\mathcal{X}$ contains, and denote $x \xleftarrow{\$} \mathcal{X}$ as uniformly choose a random element x from $\mathcal{X}$. $[b = b']$ is an integer, that is 1 if $b = b'$ and 0 otherwise. $\Pr[P : Q]$ is the probability that predicate P keeps true where all the variables in P are assigned according to the program in Q.

2.2   Quantum Random Oracle Model

We refer to [22] for basics of quantum computation and quantum information.

In the ROM, we assume the existence of the random oracle $\mathcal{O} : \mathcal{X} \to \mathcal{Y}$, and $\mathcal{O}$ is publicly accessible to all parties. For concreteness, let $\mathcal{Y} = \{0,1\}^n$. $\mathcal{O}$ is initialized by choosing $H \xleftarrow{\$} \Omega_H$, where Ω_H is the set of all functions from $\mathcal{X}$ to $\mathcal{Y}$. In the QROM, quantum algorithms can query $\mathcal{O}$ with superposition states, and the oracle performs the unitary mapping $|x, y\rangle \mapsto |x, y \oplus H(x)\rangle$ on the query state. Oracle $\mathcal{O}$ also allows making classical queries. To query x, set the input and output state to be $|x, 0\rangle$ and measure it after querying $\mathcal{O}$ to obtain $H(x)$.

Below, we introduce several tools for QROM, that are used in this paper. We begin with two ways for the simulation of the quantum random oracle.

Theorem 1 ([28, Theorem 6.1]). *Let H be a function chosen from the set of $2q$-wise independent functions uniformly at random. Then for any quantum algorithm A with at most q queries,*

$$\Pr[b = 1 : b \leftarrow A^H()] = \Pr[b = 1 : b \leftarrow A^{\mathcal{O}}()].$$

The Compressed Oracle. Here we briefly introduce the compressed oracle technique, and we only consider the Compressed Standard Oracles(CStO), one version of the compressed oracle, with query number at most q. We refer to the full version of [29] for more details of the compressed oracle.

The core idea of the compressed oracle technique is the purification of the quantum random oracle, and the purified oracle imperfectly records quantum queries to the random oracle. In the QROM, random oracle $\mathcal{O}$ is initialized by uniformly sampling a function H from Ω_H. If $\mathcal{O}$ is queried with a quantum state $|x, y\rangle$, then the replied state is a mixed state and can be represented as $\{p_i, |x, y \oplus H_i(x)\rangle\}$, where $p_i = 1/|\Omega_H|$, $i = 1, \ldots, |\Omega_H|$. This mixed state can be purified to state $1/|\Omega_H| \sum_H |x, y \oplus H(x), H\rangle$, where $|H\rangle$ is the internal state of oracle $\mathcal{O}$ and H of $|H\rangle$ is a truth table of function H.

Instead of a superposition state of H, CStO takes a superposition of database as its internal state and simulates random oracle $\mathcal{O}$. We denote this simulated oracle by CStO directly, and database by D. Here D is an element of set $\mathbf{D}_l := (\mathcal{X} \times \bar{\mathcal{Y}})^l$ where $\bar{\mathcal{Y}} = \mathcal{Y} \cup \{\perp\}$, l is the length of D. For any $x \in \mathcal{X}$, if (x, y) exists as an entry of D, then $(x, y) \in D$ and $D(x) = y$. Otherwise, $D(x) = \perp$. Denote $|D|$ as the total number of $x \in \mathcal{X}$ such that $D(x) \neq \perp$. Then for any $y \in \mathcal{Y}$ and D that $D(x) = \perp$, $|D| < l$, define $D \cup (x, y)$ to be the database that $D \cup (x, y)(x') = D(x')$ for any $x' \neq x$ and $D \cup (x, y)(x) = y$. Moreover, any D is written in the form of $((x_1, y_1), \ldots, (x_s, y_s), (0, \perp), \ldots, (0, \perp))$ such that $|D| = s \leq l$, $x_1 < x_2 < \cdots < x_s$.

For any $x \in \mathcal{X}$, define the local decompression procedure $\mathsf{StdDecomp}_x$ applied on the database state $|D\rangle \in \mathbb{C}[\mathbf{D}_l]$ as below:

– For D that $D(x) = \perp$ and $|D| = l$, $\mathsf{StdDecomp}_x|D\rangle = |D\rangle$.

– For D that $D(x) = \perp$ and $|D| < l$, $\mathsf{StdDecomp}_x|D \cup (x, \beta_r)\rangle = |D \cup (x, \beta_r)\rangle$ for any $r \neq 0$, $\mathsf{StdDecomp}_x|D \cup (x, \beta_0)\rangle = |D\rangle$, $\mathsf{StdDecomp}_x|D\rangle = |D \cup (x, \beta_0)\rangle$, where state $|D \cup (x, \beta_r)\rangle = 1/\sqrt{2^n} \sum_{y \in \mathcal{Y}} (-1)^{y \cdot r} |D \cup (x, y)\rangle$ for any $r \in \mathcal{Y}$.

CStO initializes a database state $|(0, \perp)^q\rangle$ with length q. For any query $|x, y\rangle$ to random oracle $\mathcal{O}$, CStO does three steps: First, perform the unitary $|x, y, D\rangle \mapsto |x, y\rangle \mathsf{StdDecomp}_x|D\rangle$ in superposition. Next, apply the map $|x, y, D\rangle \mapsto |x, y \oplus D(x), D\rangle$. Finally, repeat the first step.

Theorem 2 ([29, **Lemma 4**]). CStO *and random oracle $\mathcal{O}$ are indistinguishable for any quantum algorithm A, i.e.,*

$$\Pr[b = 1 : b \leftarrow A^{\mathsf{CStO}}()] = \Pr[b = 1 : b \leftarrow A^{\mathcal{O}}()].$$

It is also observed that any quantum state on the database register is orthogonal to state $|D \cup (x, \beta_0)\rangle$ in the simulation of CStO. Therefore, the database state should be the superposition state of $|D \cup (x, \beta_r)\rangle$ for $r \neq 0$. This fact will be used later.

Semi-classical Oracle. For set $\mathcal{X}$ and $\mathcal{S}$, define $f_{\mathcal{S}} : \mathcal{X} \to \{0, 1\}$ to be an indicator function such that $f_{\mathcal{S}}(x) = 1$ if $x \in \mathcal{S}$ and 0 otherwise. Then we define the semi-classical oracle $\mathcal{O}_{\mathcal{S}}^{SC} : \mathcal{X} \to \{0, 1\}$. For any quantum query, $\mathcal{O}_{\mathcal{S}}^{SC}$ does the following steps. First, initialize a qubit T to be $|0\rangle$. Then evaluate the mapping $|x, 0\rangle \mapsto |x, f_{\mathcal{S}}(x)\rangle$ in superposition. Finally, measure T in the computational basis and obtain a bit $b \in \{0, 1\}$ as its output.

Theorem 3 (Semi-classical O2H [1, **Theorem 1**]**).** *Let $\mathcal{S}$ be a random subset of $\mathcal{X}$, $H : \mathcal{X} \to \mathcal{Y}$ a random function, z a random bitstring. And $H, \mathcal{S}, z$ may have arbitrary joint distribution. Let $H \setminus \mathcal{S}$ be an oracle that first queries $\mathcal{O}_{\mathcal{S}}^{SC}$ and then queries H. Let A be a quantum oracle algorithm with query depth d. In the execution of $A^{H \setminus \mathcal{S}}(z)$, let Find be the event that $\mathcal{O}_{\mathcal{S}}^{SC}$ ever outputs 1. Then*

$$\left| \Pr[b = 1 : b \leftarrow A^H(z)] - \Pr[b = 1 : b \leftarrow A^{H \setminus \mathcal{S}}(z)] \right| \leq \sqrt{(d+1) \cdot \Pr[\text{ Find }]}.$$

The following theorem gives an upper bound for the probability that Find occurs.

Theorem 4 ([1, **Theorem 2**]). *Let $\mathcal{S} \subseteq \mathcal{X}$ and $z \in \{0, 1\}^*$. And $\mathcal{S}, z$ may have arbitrary joint distribution. Let A be a quantum oracle algorithm making at most d queries to $\mathcal{O}_{\mathcal{S}}^{SC}$ with domain $\mathcal{X}$. Let B be an algorithm that on input z, chooses $i \xleftarrow{\$} \{1, \ldots, d\}$, runs $A^{\mathcal{O}_{\varnothing}^{SC}}(z)$ until (just before) the i-th query, and then measures all query input registers in the computational basis. Denote by $\mathcal{T}$ the set of measurement outcomes. Then*

$$\Pr\left[\text{Find} : A^{\mathcal{O}_{\mathcal{S}}^{SC}}(z)\right] \leq 4d \cdot \Pr[\mathcal{S} \cap \mathcal{T} \neq \varnothing : \mathcal{T} \leftarrow B(z)].$$

3   Plaintext Extraction of the Oracle-Masked Scheme

In this section, we start by the formalization of the class of PKE Π named the oracle-masked scheme. Then we will introduce plaintext extraction game $\text{Game}_{A,\Pi}^{\text{Ext}}$ for adversary A, and end this section with a theorem that bounds the difference of the output distributions of $\text{Game}_{A,\Pi}^{\text{IND-qCCA}}$ and $\text{Game}_{A,\Pi}^{\text{Ext}}$. The definition of the IND-qCCA security game $\text{Game}_{A,\Pi}^{\text{IND-qCCA}}$ is shown in the Appendix B.2.

Definition 3 (Oracle-Masked Scheme). *Let* $\Pi = (Gen, Enc^{\mathcal{O}}, Dec^{\mathcal{O}})$ *be a PKE relative to random oracle* $\mathcal{O}$ *with codomain* $\mathcal{Y}$. *We say that* Π *is an oracle-masked scheme if there exist deterministic polynomial time algorithm* A_1, A_2, A_3, A_4 *such that for any* (pk, sk) *generated by Gen,* $Enc^{\mathcal{O}}$ *and* $Dec^{\mathcal{O}}$ *are written as in Fig. 2. Tuple* (A_1, A_2, A_3, A_4) *is called the decomposition of* Π.

$\text{Enc}^{\mathcal{O}}(pk, m; r)$	$\text{Dec}^{\mathcal{O}}(sk, c)$	
$x := A_1(pk, m, r)$	$x := A_3(sk, c)$	**if** $c \neq c'$, **return** $\perp$
$y := \mathcal{O}(x)$	**if** $x = \perp$, **return** $\perp$	$m := A_4(x)$
$c := A_2(pk, x, y)$	$y := \mathcal{O}(x)$	**return** m
return c	$c' := A_2(pk, x, y)$	

Fig. 2. Algorithm $\text{Enc}^{\mathcal{O}}$ and $\text{Dec}^{\mathcal{O}}$ of an oracle-masked scheme Π

For an oracle-masked scheme Π, parameter η of Π is defined to be

$$\eta := \max_{(pk,sk),\, c} \left|\{y \in \mathcal{Y} : c = A_2\left(pk, A_3(sk, c), y\right)\}\right|/|\mathcal{Y}|,$$

where (pk, sk) is generated by Gen and $c \in C$ is such that $A_3(sk, c) \neq \perp$.

Let Π be an oracle-masked scheme. For quantum adversary A in the security game $\text{Game}_{A,\Pi}^{\text{IND-qCCA}}$ in the QROM, it can query random oracle $\mathcal{O}$ and decryption oracle $\text{Dec}^{\mathcal{O}}$ both in superposition. Write C and Z to denote the input and output register of the decryption query of A, respectively. The decryption oracle $\text{Dec}^{\mathcal{O}}$ in $\text{Game}_{A,\Pi}^{\text{IND-qCCA}}$ can be simulated by a unitary operator U_{Dec} applied on register C and Z, i.e., for any computational basis state $|c, z\rangle$, U_{Dec} acts as follows:

$$\text{U}_{\text{Dec}}|c, z\rangle = \begin{cases} |c, z \oplus \perp\rangle & \text{if } c^* \text{ is defined and } c = c^* \\ |c, z \oplus \text{Dec}^{\mathcal{O}}(c)\rangle & \text{else.} \end{cases}$$

where c^* is the challenge ciphertext in $\text{Game}_{A,\Pi}^{\text{IND-qCCA}}$.

Then we introduce a new game $\text{Game}_{A,\Pi}^{\text{Sim}}$, that is identical with $\text{Game}_{A\Pi}^{\text{IND-qCCA}}$ except that random oracle $\mathcal{O}$ is simulated by CStO. In this game, quantum queries to oracle $\mathcal{O}$ are recorded in the database register D imperfectly. The decryption oracle answers queries in the same process as in Fig. 2 and it can be simulated by a unitary operator on register C, Z, D. We denote this operator by $\mathsf{U}_{\mathsf{Sim}}$. Then by Theorem 2, $\mathsf{U}_{\mathsf{Dec}}$ and $\mathsf{U}_{\mathsf{Sim}}$, these two simulations of the decryption oracle are perfectly indistinguishable for any quantum adversary.

Notice that in the process of the decryption algorithm $\mathsf{Dec}^{\mathcal{O}}$, A_3 is computed first to obtain x and then A_2 is applied to check if $c = A_2(pk, x, \mathcal{O}(x))$. Then the query x to oracle $\mathcal{O}$ is recorded in the database D imperfectly if the decryption oracle is simulated by $\mathsf{U}_{\mathsf{Sim}}$. With this property, we design a new unitary to reply decryption queries, and it is defined as follows.

Definition 4 (Plaintext Extraction Procedure). *Let Π be an oracle-masked scheme and (A_1, A_2, A_3, A_4) be its decomposition. For any (pk, sk) of Π, define unitary operation U_{Ext}, as the plaintext extraction procedure of Π, applied on register C, Z, D as follows.*
$\underline{U_{Ext}|c, z, D\rangle}$:

1. *If the challenge ciphertext c^* is defined and $c = c^*$, return $|c, z \oplus \bot, D\rangle$.*
2. *Else if database D contains no pair $(x, D(x))$ such that $A_2(pk, x, D(x)) = c$, return $|c, z \oplus \bot, D\rangle$.*
3. *Else, for each tuple $(x, D(x))$ that $A_2(pk, x, D(x)) = c$, check if $A_3(sk, c) = x$ and do the following procedure:*
   (a) If a tuple $(x, D(x))$ passes this test,[1] compute $m := A_4(x)$ and return $|c, z \oplus m, D\rangle$.
   (b) Otherwise, return $|c, z \oplus \bot, D\rangle$.

In addition, the detailed construction of U_{Ext} is shown in Appendix A.

Compared with $\mathsf{U}_{\mathsf{Sim}}$, $\mathsf{U}_{\mathsf{Ext}}$ does not follow the decryption algorithm to produce the plaintext $m(:= \mathsf{Dec}^{\mathcal{O}}(sk, c))$, but just searches $(x, D(x))$ on D to obtain m. Therefore, we call $\mathsf{U}_{\mathsf{Ext}}$ the plaintext extraction procedure.

By the definition of $\mathsf{U}_{\mathsf{Ext}}$, for any computational basis state $|c, z, D\rangle$, $\mathsf{U}_{\mathsf{Ext}}$ has no effect on $|D\rangle$, and does not need to query oracle $\mathcal{O}$. And for any oracle-masked scheme, such a plaintext extraction procedure $\mathsf{U}_{\mathsf{Ext}}$ exists, and it can be used to answer quantum decryption queries. Then we introduce two properties of $\mathsf{U}_{\mathsf{Ext}}$ by the following two lemmas. Except register C, Z and D, we abbreviate other registers (e.g. other registers of adversary A) into W and the detailed proofs of these lemmas are shown in the full version [25].

Lemma 3. *Let $|\psi\rangle$ be a quantum state on register W, C, Z and D such that $|\psi\rangle$ is orthogonal to any state in the form of $\sum_{w,c,z,D,x} \alpha_{w,c,z,D,x}|w, c, z, D \cup (x, \beta_0)\rangle$. Then*

$$\|(U_{Sim} - U_{Ext})|\psi\rangle\| \leq 5\sqrt{\eta}.$$

Lemma 4. *Given any $x \in \{0, 1\}^*$, unitary $\mathsf{StdDecomp}_x$ is performed on register D. For any quantum state $|\psi\rangle$ on register W, C, Z and D,*

$$\|(U_{Ext} \circ \mathsf{StdDecomp}_x - \mathsf{StdDecomp}_x \circ U_{Ext})|\psi\rangle\| \leq 7\sqrt{\eta}.$$

---

[1] Such a tuple is unique, since c and sk determines the value of $A_3(sk, c)$.

Here we define a new game $\text{Game}_{A,\Pi}^{\text{Ext}}$ named plaintext extraction game that differs from $\text{Game}_{A,\Pi}^{\text{Sim}}$ in the way of answering decryption queries: In $\text{Game}_{A,\Pi}^{\text{Ext}}$, the decryption oracle is simulated by unitary U_{Ext} while that in $\text{Game}_{A,\Pi}^{\text{Sim}}$ is simulated by unitary U_{Sim}. With Lemma 3, we obtain Theorem 5 as follows to bound the output difference of $\text{Game}_{A,\Pi}^{\text{IND-qCCA}}$ and $\text{Game}_{A,\Pi}^{\text{Ext}}$.

Theorem 5. *Let Π be an oracle-masked scheme. For any quantum adversary A against the IND-qCCA security of Π in the QROM, if A makes at most q decryption queries, then*

$$\left|\Pr[Game_{A,\Pi}^{IND\text{-}qCCA} \to 1] - \Pr[Game_{A,\Pi}^{Ext} \to 1]\right| \leq 5q \cdot \sqrt{\eta}.$$

Proof. Given Π and A, recall that $\text{Game}_{A,\Pi}^{\text{Sim}}$ is identical with $\text{Game}_{A,\Pi}^{\text{IND-qCCA}}$ except that the random oracle is simulated by CStO. By Theorem 2,

$$\Pr[\text{Game}_{A,\Pi}^{\text{IND-qCCA}} \to 1] = \Pr[\text{Game}_{A,\Pi}^{\text{Sim}} \to 1].$$

In the following, we prove that

$$\left|\Pr[\text{Game}_{A,\Pi}^{\text{Sim}} \to 1] - \Pr[\text{Game}_{A,\Pi}^{\text{Ext}} \to 1]\right| \leq 5q \cdot \sqrt{\eta}.$$

For any fixed (pk, sk), the decryption oracle in $\text{Game}_{A,\Pi}^{\text{Sim}}$ and that in $\text{Game}_{A,\Pi}^{\text{Ext}}$ are simulated by unitary U_{Sim} and U_{Ext}, respectively.

For any $i = 1, \ldots, q$, define G_i to be a game that is the same as $\text{Game}_{A,\Pi}^{\text{Sim}}$ until just before the i-th decryption query of A, then simulates the decryption oracle with unitary U_{Ext} instead of U_{Sim}. Then G_1 is exactly $\text{Game}_{A,\Pi}^{\text{Ext}}$. We also denote $\text{Game}_{A,\Pi}^{\text{Sim}}$ by G_{q+1}.

For $i = 1, \ldots, q + 1$, denote by σ_i the final joint state of the registers of G_i including the register of A and the database register. By the triangle inequality of the trace distance,

$$\text{TD}(\sigma_1, \sigma_{q+1}) \leq \text{TD}(\sigma_1, \sigma_2) + \ldots + \text{TD}(\sigma_q, \sigma_{q+1}),$$

where $\text{TD}(\rho, \tau)$ is the trace distance of state ρ and τ.

Fix $1 \leq i \leq q$. Since game G_i and G_{i+1} only differ in the i-th decryption query, we denote by ρ the joint state of A and the database register just before the i-th decryption query. All the operations after the i-th decryption query can be represented by a trace-preserving operation, that is denoted by $\mathcal{E}$. Then σ_i and σ_{i+1} can be represented by $\sigma_i = \mathcal{E}(\text{U}_{\text{Sim}} \rho \text{U}_{\text{Sim}}^\dagger)$ and $\sigma_{i+1} = \mathcal{E}(\text{U}_{\text{Ext}} \rho \text{U}_{\text{Ext}}^\dagger)$, respectively. And we have

$$\text{TD}(\sigma_i, \sigma_{i+1}) \leq \text{TD}(\text{U}_{\text{Sim}} \rho \text{U}_{\text{Sim}}^\dagger, \text{U}_{\text{Ext}} \rho \text{U}_{\text{Ext}}^\dagger).$$

Let $\rho = \sum_j p_j |\psi_j\rangle\langle\psi_j|$ be a spectral decomposition of ρ, where $\sum_j p_j = 1$. Then by the convexity of the trace distance,

$$
\begin{aligned}
&\mathrm{TD}(\mathrm{U}_{\mathrm{Sim}}\, \rho \mathrm{U}_{\mathrm{Sim}}^{\dagger}, \mathrm{U}_{\mathrm{Ext}}\, \rho \mathrm{U}_{\mathrm{Ext}}^{\dagger}) \\
&= \mathrm{TD}\Big(\sum_j p_j \mathrm{U}_{\mathrm{Sim}} |\psi_j\rangle\langle\psi_j| \mathrm{U}_{\mathrm{Sim}}^{\dagger}, \sum_j p_j \mathrm{U}_{\mathrm{Ext}} |\psi_j\rangle\langle\psi_j| \mathrm{U}_{\mathrm{Ext}}^{\dagger} \Big) \\
&\leq \sum_j p_j \mathrm{TD}(\mathrm{U}_{\mathrm{Sim}} |\psi_j\rangle\langle\psi_j| \mathrm{U}_{\mathrm{Sim}}^{\dagger}, \mathrm{U}_{\mathrm{Ext}} |\psi_j\rangle\langle\psi_j| \mathrm{U}_{\mathrm{Ext}}^{\dagger}) \\
&\leq \sum_j p_j \| (\mathrm{U}_{\mathrm{Sim}} - \mathrm{U}_{\mathrm{Ext}}) |\psi_j\rangle \| .
\end{aligned}
$$

Note that before the i-th decryption query, the decryption procedure is $\mathrm{U}_{\mathrm{Sim}}$ and A can be considered as being in $\mathrm{Game}_{A,\Pi}^{\mathrm{Sim}}$. Thus, any state $|\psi_j\rangle$ in the spectral decomposition of ρ is in the form of the superposition state in Lemma 3. By Lemma 3, $\|(\mathrm{U}_{\mathrm{Sim}} - \mathrm{U}_{\mathrm{Ext}})|\psi_j\rangle\| \leq 5\sqrt{\eta}$. Then for every $1 \leq i \leq q$,

$$
\mathrm{TD}(\sigma_i, \sigma_{i+1}) \leq \sum_j p_j \cdot \|(\mathrm{U}_{\mathrm{Sim}} - \mathrm{U}_{\mathrm{Ext}})|\psi_j\rangle\| \leq \sum_j p_j \cdot 5\sqrt{\eta} = 5\sqrt{\eta} .
$$

Thus, $\mathrm{TD}(\sigma_1, \sigma_{q+1}) \leq 5q \cdot \sqrt{\eta}$. Further, the output difference of $\mathrm{Game}_{A,\Pi}^{\mathrm{Sim}}$ and $\mathrm{Game}_{A,\Pi}^{\mathrm{Ext}}$ is upper bounded by the trace distance of σ_1 and σ_{q+1}, the states of these two games. This completes the proof. $\square$

4   Application in the Quantum Security Proof

In this section, we apply Theorem 5 of oracle-masked schemes to provide the IND-qCCA security proof for transformation FO, REACT and T_{CH} in the QROM.

4.1   FO: From OW-CPA to IND-qCCA in the QROM

Let $\Pi^{asy} = (\mathrm{Gen}^{asy}, \mathrm{Enc}^{asy}, \mathrm{Dec}^{asy})$ be a PKE with message space $\mathcal{M}^{asy}$, randomness space $\mathcal{R}^{asy}(= \{0,1\}^n)$ and ciphertext space $\mathcal{C}^{asy}$. Let $\Pi^{sy} = (\mathrm{Enc}^{sy}, \mathrm{Dec}^{sy})$ be a SKE with key space $\mathcal{K}^{sy}$, message space $\mathcal{M}^{sy}$ and ciphertext space $\mathcal{C}^{sy}$. Let $H : \{0,1\}^* \to \mathcal{R}^{asy}$ and $G : \{0,1\}^* \to \mathcal{K}^{sy}$ be hash functions. We review the FO transformation in the following definition, and then provide its IND-qCCA security proof in the QROM.

Definition 5. FO$[\Pi^{asy}, \Pi^{sy}, H, G] = (Gen, Enc, Dec)$ *obtained from the FO transformation is constructed as shown in Fig. 3.*

Lemma 5. *Assume that H is the random oracle and Π^{asy} is γ-spread, then* FO$[\Pi^{asy}, \Pi^{sy}, H, G]$ *is an oracle-masked scheme relative to H, and its parameter η is such that $\eta \leq 1/2^{\gamma}$.*

Proof. We define deterministic polynomial-time algorithm $\mathrm{A}_1, \mathrm{A}_2, \mathrm{A}_3$ and A_4:

Gen	$\text{Enc}(pk, m; \delta)$	$\text{Dec}(sk, (c, d))$
$(pk, sk) \leftarrow \text{Gen}^{asy}$	$d := \text{Enc}^{sy}(G(\delta), m)$	$\delta' := \text{Dec}^{asy}(sk, c)$
return (pk, sk)	$c := \text{Enc}^{asy}(pk, \delta; H(\delta, d))$	**if** $\delta' = \bot$, **return** $\bot$
	return (c, d)	$c' := \text{Enc}^{asy}(pk, \delta'; H(\delta', d))$
		if $c' \neq c$, **return** $\bot$
		$m := \text{Dec}^{sy}(G(\delta'), d)$
		return m

Fig. 3. PKE $\text{FO}[\Pi^{asy}, \Pi^{sy}, H, G]$ obtained from FO transformation

- A_1 on input δ and m, evaluates $k := G(\delta)$ and $d := \text{Enc}^{sy}(k, m)$, then outputs (δ, d).
- A_2 takes pk, (δ, d) and $y \in \mathcal{R}^{asy}$ as input, computes $c := \text{Enc}^{asy}(pk, \delta; y)$, then outputs (c, d).
- A_3 takes sk and (c, d) as input, evaluates $\delta := \text{Dec}^{asy}(sk, c)$. If $\delta \neq \bot$, output (δ, d). Otherwise, output $\bot$.
- A_4 on input (δ, d), computes $k := G(\delta)$ and $m := \text{Dec}^{sy}(k, d)$, outputs m.

It can be verified that with these four algorithms, algorithm Enc and Dec given in Fig. 3 are written as $\text{Enc}^{\mathcal{O}}$ and $\text{Dec}^{\mathcal{O}}$ in Definition 3 with $\mathcal{O} = H$, respectively. Thus, $\text{FO}[\Pi^{asy}, \Pi^{sy}, H, G]$ is an oracle-masked scheme, and its parameter η is

$$\eta = \max_{(pk, sk),\, c} \left|\{r \in \mathcal{R}^{asy} : c = \text{Enc}^{asy}(pk, \text{Dec}^{asy}(sk, c); r)\}\right| / |\mathcal{R}^{asy}|,$$

where (pk, sk) and $c \in \mathcal{C}^{asy}$ are such that $\text{Dec}^{asy}(sk, c) \in \mathcal{M}^{asy}$.

Since Π^{asy} is γ-spread, for any (pk, sk) and $m \in \mathcal{M}^{asy}$,

$$\max_{c \in \mathcal{C}^{asy}} \left|\{r \in \mathcal{R}^{asy} : c = \text{Enc}^{asy}(pk, m; r)\}\right| / |\mathcal{R}^{asy}| \leq 1/2^\gamma.$$

Therefore, $\eta \leq 1/2^\gamma$. $\qquad\qquad\qquad\qquad\qquad\qquad\qquad\qquad\qquad\qquad\qquad\square$

Note that the above evaluation of function G can be replaced by querying an oracle that computes G. Then algorithm A_1 and A_4 become oracle algorithms denoted by A_1^G and A_4^G, respectively. In this case, the notions in Definition 3 still work, and Theorem 5 holds. Then we apply Theorem 5 to prove the IND-qCCA security of oracle-masked scheme $\text{FO}[\Pi^{asy}, \Pi^{sy}, H, G]$ in the QROM.

Theorem 6. *Let Π^{asy} be γ-spread, for any adversary against the IND-qCCA security of scheme $\Pi = \text{FO}[\Pi^{asy}, \Pi^{sy}, H, G]$, making at most q_D queries to the decryption oracle, at most q_H queries to random oracle H and at most q_G queries to random oracle G, there exist an adversary A_{asy} against the OW-CPA security of Π^{asy} and an adversary A_{sy} against the OT security of Π^{sy} such that*

$$\text{Adv}_{A,\Pi}^{IND\text{-}qCCA} \leq q_D \cdot \frac{12}{\sqrt{2^\gamma}} + 2(d+1)\sqrt{\text{Adv}_{A_{asy}, \Pi^{asy}}^{OW\text{-}CPA}} + 4d \cdot \text{Adv}_{A_{asy}, \Pi^{asy}}^{OW\text{-}CPA} + \text{Adv}_{A_{sy}, \Pi^{sy}}^{OT},$$

where $d = q_D + q_H + 2q_G$, $Time(A_{sy}) \approx Time(A) + O(d^2 + q_H \cdot q_D \cdot Time(\text{Enc}^{asy}))$ and $Time(A_{asy}) \approx Time(A_{sy})$.

Proof. Define **Game 0** to be $\mathrm{Game}_{A,\Pi}^{\mathrm{IND\text{-}qCCA}}$ as in Fig. 4. Then we obtain

$$\left| \Pr[\textbf{Game 0} \to 1] - \frac{1}{2} \right| = \mathrm{Adv}_{A,\Pi}^{\mathrm{IND\text{-}qCCA}} . \tag{1}$$

In the following, we will introduce a sequence of games to bound $\mathrm{Adv}_{A,\Pi}^{\mathrm{IND\text{-}qCCA}}$.

$\mathrm{Game}_{A,\Pi}^{\mathrm{IND\text{-}qCCA}}$	$\mathrm{Dec}_a(sk,(c,d))$
$G \xleftarrow{\$} \Omega_G, H \xleftarrow{\$} \Omega_H$	if $(c,d) = a$, **return** $\perp$
$(pk, sk) \leftarrow \mathrm{Gen}$	$\delta' := \mathrm{Dec}^{asy}(sk, c)$
$(m_0, m_1) \leftarrow A^{H,G,\mathrm{Dec}_\perp}(pk)$	if $\delta' = \perp$, **return** $\perp$
$b \xleftarrow{\$} \{0,1\}, \delta^* \xleftarrow{\$} \mathcal{M}^{asy}$	$c' := \mathrm{Enc}^{asy}(pk, \delta'; H(\delta', d))$
$d^* := \mathrm{Enc}^{sy}(G(\delta^*), m_b)$	if $c' \neq c$, **return** $\perp$
$c^* := \mathrm{Enc}^{asy}(pk, \delta^*; H(\delta^*, d^*))$	$m' := \mathrm{Dec}^{sy}(G(\delta'), d)$
$b' \leftarrow A^{H,G,\mathrm{Dec}_{(c^*,d^*)}}(pk, (c^*, d^*))$	**return** m'
return $[b = b']$	

Fig. 4. $\mathrm{Game}_{A,\Pi}^{\mathrm{IND\text{-}qCCA}}$ for FO transformation in the QROM, where oracle H, G and Dec_a are all quantum-accessible.

Starting from **Game 1**, random oracle H is simulated with CStO and its database register is denoted as D. This change is undetectable for A by Theorem 2. Moreover, δ^* is sampled uniformly at the beginning of the game, which is also undetectable for any adversary.

Game 1: In this game, the decryption oracle is simulated by the plaintext extraction procedure $\mathsf{U}_{\mathrm{Ext}}$ of Π. We refer to Appendix A for the detailed construction of $\mathsf{U}_{\mathrm{Ext}}$ of Π without sk.

Omitting the $(c,d) = (c^*, d^*)$ case, $\mathsf{U}_{\mathrm{Ext}}$ can also be rephrased as $\mathsf{U}_{\mathrm{Ext}} = \mathsf{U}_{\mathrm{E}}^\dagger \circ \mathsf{U}_{\mathrm{C}} \circ \mathsf{U}_{\mathrm{E}}$, based on Lemma 5. Here unitary U_{E} is used to extract (δ', d) corresponding to (c,d) from database and unitary U_{C} is used to compute plaintext m' from (δ', d). And U_{E} acts as follows.

$$\mathsf{U}_{\mathrm{E}}|(c,d), z_1, D\rangle = \begin{cases} |(c,d), z_1 \oplus (1, (\delta', d)), D\rangle & \text{if } \mathrm{Enc}^{asy}(pk, \delta'; D(\delta', d)) = c \\ |(c,d), z_1 \oplus (0, 0^n), D\rangle & \text{otherwise.} \end{cases}$$

It is obvious that **Game 1** is the plaintext extraction game $\mathrm{Game}_{A,\Pi}^{\mathrm{Ext}}$. Then by Theorem 5, we obtain $\left| \Pr[\textbf{Game 0} \to 1] - \Pr[\textbf{Game 1} \to 1] \right| \leq 5q_D \cdot \sqrt{\eta}$ for any fixed $G \in \Omega_G$. Therefore,

$$\left| \Pr[\textbf{Game 0} \to 1] - \Pr[\textbf{Game 1} \to 1] \right| \leq 5q_D \cdot \sqrt{\eta} \leq q_D \cdot \frac{5}{\sqrt{2^\gamma}}, \tag{2}$$

where variable G, both in **Game 0** and **Game 1**, is sampled from Ω_G uniformly.

Game 2: This game is identical with **Game 1** except that the decryption oracle is simulated by the following steps after the challenge query.

1. Perform unitary $\mathsf{StdDecomp}_{(\delta^*,d^*)}$ to register D.
2. Apply $\mathsf{U}_{\mathrm{Ext}}$ on register C, Z and D.
3. Perform $\mathsf{StdDecomp}_{(\delta^*,d^*)}$ to register D a second time.

We define unitary $\mathsf{SU}_{\mathrm{Ext}} := \mathsf{StdDecomp}_{(\delta^*,d^*)} \circ \mathsf{U}_{\mathrm{Ext}} \circ \mathsf{StdDecomp}_{(\delta^*,d^*)}$. If we flip the order of the last two steps of $\mathsf{SU}_{\mathrm{Ext}}$, then $\mathsf{StdDecomp}_{(\delta^*,d^*)} \circ \mathsf{StdDecomp}_{(\delta^*,d^*)}$ is an identity operator and in this way, $\mathsf{SU}_{\mathrm{Ext}}$ performs identically as $\mathsf{U}_{\mathrm{Ext}}$. Since Lemma 4 states that $\mathsf{U}_{\mathrm{Ext}}$ commutes with $\mathsf{StdDecomp}_{(\delta^*,d^*)}$ by a loss, we have

$$\mathrm{TD}(\mathsf{U}_{\mathrm{Ext}}\rho\mathsf{U}_{\mathrm{Ext}}^\dagger, \mathsf{SU}_{\mathrm{Ext}}\rho\,\mathsf{SU}_{\mathrm{Ext}}^\dagger) \leq 7\sqrt{\eta} \leq \frac{7}{\sqrt{2^\gamma}}$$

for any joint state ρ on registers in **Game 2**. At most q_D decryption queries are made after the challenge query, and then by the hybrid argument,

$$|\Pr[\textbf{Game 1} \rightarrow 1] - \Pr[\textbf{Game 2} \rightarrow 1]| \leq q_D \cdot \frac{7}{\sqrt{2^\gamma}}. \tag{3}$$

Game 3: Differing from **Game 2**, we change the way to answer random oracle queries in some cases: when random oracle H or G is queried by A or G is applied in the decryption process, we query E and then query the random oracle, where E is a constant zero function with quantum access.

Since E is a constant zero function, the random oracle query does not change after querying E, and we have

$$\Pr[\textbf{Game 2} \rightarrow 1] = \Pr[\textbf{Game 3} \rightarrow 1]. \tag{4}$$

Game 4: The only difference between **Game 3** and **Game 4** is that the semi-classical oracle $O_{\mathcal{S}}^{SC}$ is applied before each query to E, and set $\mathcal{S} := \{\delta^*, \delta^*\|\cdot\}$.

Let $z := \delta^*$, and $B^E(\delta^*)$ be the algorithm that runs A and simulates **Game 3**. Then we have

$$\Pr[\textbf{Game 3} \rightarrow 1] = \Pr[b = 1 : b \leftarrow B^E(\delta^*), \delta^* \overset{\$}{\leftarrow} \mathcal{M}^{asy}],$$

$$\Pr[\textbf{Game 4} \rightarrow 1] = \Pr[b = 1 : b \leftarrow B^{E\backslash\mathcal{S}}(\delta^*), \delta^* \overset{\$}{\leftarrow} \mathcal{M}^{asy}],$$

$$\Pr[\mathrm{Find} : \textbf{Game 4}] = \Pr[\mathrm{Find} : B^{E\backslash\mathcal{S}}(\delta^*), \delta^* \overset{\$}{\leftarrow} \mathcal{M}^{asy}].$$

It can be verified that B makes at most $q_H + q_G + 2q_D$ queries to E. We let $d = q_H + q_G + 2q_D$ and apply Theorem 3 to obtain

$$|\Pr[\textbf{Game 3} \rightarrow 1] - \Pr[\textbf{Game 4} \rightarrow 1]| \leq \sqrt{(d+1)\Pr[\mathrm{Find} : \textbf{Game 4}]}. \tag{5}$$

Notice that by A_4 defined in Lemma 5, G is queried in the process of U_C when performing $\mathsf{U}_{\mathrm{Ext}}$. Then oracle $O_{\mathcal{S}}^{SC}$ should be queried in the process of U_C in **Game 4**. We denote by U_C' the modified U_C. Accordingly, before the challenge query, the decryption oracle in **Game 4** is simulated by $U_E \circ U'_C \circ U_E^\dagger$, that is denoted by U'_{Ext}. After that, the decryption oracle is simulated by $StdDecomp_{(\delta^*, d^*)} \circ U'_{Ext} \circ StdDecomp_{(\delta^*, d^*)}$, that is denoted by SU'_{Ext}.

We assume that Find does not occur in **Game 4**. In this case, A never queries H by (δ^*, d^*), and the database D is such that $D(\delta^*, d^*) = \bot$ until the challenge query. To produce the challenge ciphertext, $r^* := H(\delta^*, d^*)$ is computed and then the joint state is in a superposition of $StdDecomp_{(\delta^*, d^*)}|w, D \cup ((\delta^*, d^*), r^*)\rangle$, here w is other registers of this game and $D(\delta^*, d^*) = \bot$. Then by the definition of U_E, we can conclude that for any ciphertext $(c, d) \neq (c^*, d^*)$,

$$U_E|(c, d), z_1, D \cup ((\delta^*, d^*), r^*)\rangle = |(c, d), z_1 \oplus (b, x), D \cup ((\delta^*, d^*), r^*)\rangle$$

if and only if $U_E|(c, d), z_1, D\rangle = |(c, d), z_1 \oplus (b, x), D\rangle$.

Furthermore, observe that $StdDecomp_{(\delta^*, d^*)}$ commutes with U'_C of U'_{Ext}. Then for any ciphertext $(c, d) \neq (c^*, d^*)$,

$$SU'_{Ext} \circ StdDecomp_{(\delta^*, d^*)}|(c, d), z, D \cup ((\delta^*, d^*), r^*)\rangle$$
$$= StdDecomp_{(\delta^*, d^*)}|c, z \oplus m', D \cup ((\delta^*, d^*), r^*)\rangle$$

if and only if $U'_{Ext}|(c, d), z, D\rangle = |(c, d), z \oplus m', D\rangle$. This means that the database state on (δ^*, d^*) is not involved in the decryption process of **Game 4**. Therefore, if Find does not occur, then random oracle H and G are never queried by (δ^*, d) and δ^* by the adversary. Meanwhile, the adversary A can not get information on $H(\delta^*, d^*)$ either by making decryption queries. Therefore, it is undetectable for adversary A to produce the challenge ciphertext with uniformly chosen $k^* \in \mathcal{K}^{sy}$ and $r^* \in \mathcal{R}^{say}$, which is the difference between **Game 4** and **Game 5**.

Game 5: In this game, we pick $k^* \in \mathcal{K}^{sy}$ and $r^* \in \mathcal{R}^{asy}$ uniformly and use them to produce the challenge ciphertext (c^*, d^*). And we replace SU'_{Ext} with U'_{Ext}.

As analysis in **Game 4**, the view of A in **Game 4** and that in **Game 5** are identical until Find occurs. Therefore,

$$\Pr[\text{Find} : \textbf{Game 4}] = \Pr[\text{Find} : \textbf{Game 5}], \tag{6}$$

$$\Pr[\neg\text{Find} \wedge \textbf{Game 4} \rightarrow 1] = \Pr[\neg\text{Find} \wedge \textbf{Game 5} \rightarrow 1]. \tag{7}$$

Lemma 6. *There exists a quantum adversary A_{sy} invoking A such that*

$$\left| \Pr[\textbf{Game 5} \rightarrow 1] - \frac{1}{2} \right| = Adv^{OT}_{A_{sy}, \Pi^{sy}} \tag{8}$$

and $Time(A_{sy}) \approx Time(A) + O((q_H + q_G + 2q_D)^2 + q_H \cdot q_D \cdot Time(Enc^{asy}))$.

Proof. A quantum algorithm A_{sy} that runs A and breaks the one-time security of Π^{sy} is constructed as follows.

A_{sy} generates $(pk, sk) \leftarrow Gen$, picks $\delta^* \xleftarrow{\$} \mathcal{M}^{asy}$ and simulates **Game 5** for A. Random oracle G is simulated by a $2(q_G + 2q_D)$-wise independent function, and other oracles used in **Game 5** can be implemented efficiently by A_{sy}. For A's challenge query (m_0, m_1), A_{sy} sends it to the challenger in $\text{Game}^{\text{OT}}_{A_{sy}, \Pi^{sy}}$. After receiving d^*, A_{sy} picks $r \in \mathcal{R}^{asy}$ uniformly, then computes $c^* := \text{Enc}^{asy}(pk, \delta^*; r)$ and sends (c^*, d^*) back to A. After receiving b' from A, A_{sy} output b'.

From the construction of A_{sy}, the output of A_{sy} is correct if and only if A guesses correctly. Moreover, the view of A invoked by A_{sy} is identical with that in **Game 5**. Therefore,

$$\left| \Pr[\textbf{Game 5} \to 1] - \frac{1}{2} \right| = \left| \Pr[\text{Game}^{\text{OT}}_{A_{sy}, \Pi^{sy}} \to 1] - \frac{1}{2} \right| = \text{Adv}^{\text{OT}}_{A_{sy}, \Pi^{sy}}.$$

Denote by $\text{T}_{\mathcal{O}}$ the time needed to simulate oracle $\mathcal{O}$, then the running time of B is given by $\text{Time}(B) = \text{Time}(A) + \text{T}_G + \text{T}_H + \text{Time}(\text{U}_{\text{Ext}})$, where $\text{T}_G = O\left((q_G + 2q_D)^2\right)$, $\text{T}_H = O(q_H^2)$, $\text{Time}(\text{U}_{\text{Ext}}) = O(q_D \cdot q_H \cdot \text{Time}(\text{Enc}^{asy}))$ by Appendix A.1. □

Lemma 7. *There is a quantum adversary A_{asy} invoking A such that*

$$\Pr[Find : \textbf{Game 5}] \leq 4d \cdot \text{Adv}^{OW\text{-}CPA}_{A_{asy}, \Pi^{asy}} \tag{9}$$

and $Time(A_{asy}) \approx Time(A) + O((q_H + q_G + 2q_D)^2 + q_H \cdot q_D \cdot Time(Enc^{asy}))$.

Proof. Define $B^{\mathcal{O}^{SC}_S}$ as a quantum oracle algorithm that on input pk, c^*, runs A and simulates **Game 5** for it. Then we have $\Pr[\text{Find} : \textbf{Game 5}] = \Pr[\text{Find} : B^{\mathcal{O}^{SC}_S}(pk, c^*)]$, where $c^* \leftarrow \text{Enc}^{asy}(pk, \delta^*)$, δ^* is sampled uniformly from $\mathcal{M}^{asy}$. As analyzed in **Game 4**, B makes at most $d = q_H + q_G + 2q_D$ queries, then by Theorem 4,

$$\Pr[\text{Find} : B^{\mathcal{O}^{SC}_S}(pk, c^*)] \leq 4d \cdot \Pr[(\delta, d) \in \mathcal{S} : (\delta, d) \leftarrow D(pk, c^*)].$$

Here D is a quantum algorithm invoking B. On input (pk, c^*), D chooses $i \xleftarrow{\$} \{1, \ldots, d\}$, runs $B^{\mathcal{O}^{SC}_\emptyset}(pk, c^*)$ until (just before) i-th query of B, and then measures the state on the input register of $\mathcal{O}^{SC}_\emptyset$ to obtain (δ, d). Note that the running time of D and that of B are almost the same.

Because $\mathcal{S} = \{\delta^*, \delta^* \| \cdot\}$, $(\delta, d) \in \mathcal{S}$ is equivalent to $\delta = \delta^*$. Then D can be considered as a quantum algorithm A_{asy} that breaks the OW-CPA security of Π^{asy}. Therefore,

$$\Pr[(\delta, d) \in \mathcal{S} : (\delta, d) \leftarrow D(pk, c^*)] = \text{Adv}^{OW\text{-}CPA}_{A_{asy}, \Pi^{asy}}.$$

The running time of B is $\text{Time}(B) = \text{Time}(A) + \text{T}_G + \text{T}_H + \text{Time}(\text{U}_{\text{Ext}})$, where $\text{T}_G = O\left((q_G + 2q_D)^2\right)$, $\text{T}_H = O(q_H^2)$, $\text{Time}(\text{U}_{\text{Ext}}) = O(q_D \cdot q_H \cdot \text{Time}(\text{Enc}^{asy}))$. □

Summarizing Eq. (1) to (9), we have

$$\text{Adv}^{\text{IND-qCCA}}_{A, \Pi} \leq q_D \cdot \frac{12}{\sqrt{2^\gamma}} + 2(d+1)\sqrt{\text{Adv}^{OW\text{-}CPA}_{A_{asy}, \Pi^{asy}}} + 4d \cdot \text{Adv}^{OW\text{-}CPA}_{A_{asy}, \Pi^{asy}} + \text{Adv}^{\text{OT}}_{A_{sy}, \Pi^{sy}}.$$

□

Furthermore, compared with Zhandry's proof for FO transformation, we notice that the plaintext extraction procedure in this proof acts the same as the decryption procedure defined in Hybrid 4 in his proof on input (c, d) such that $c \neq c^*$. With Theorem 5, we can prove that any polynomial time quantum adversary distinguishes Hybrid 1 from Hybrid 4 with a negligible probability. On the other hand, by Eq. (2), it seems unnecessary to restrict that the decryption oracle outputs $\perp$ directly for query (c, d) such that $c = c^*$.

4.2 REACT: From OW-qPCA to IND-qCCA in the QROM

Let $\Pi^{asy} = (\text{Gen}^{asy}, \text{Enc}^{asy}, \text{Dec}^{asy})$ be a PKE with key space $\mathcal{K}^{asy}$, message space $\mathcal{M}^{asy}$, randomness space $\mathcal{R}^{asy}$ and ciphertext space $\mathcal{C}^{asy}$. Let $\Pi^{sy} = (\text{Enc}^{sy}, \text{Dec}^{sy})$ be a SKE with message space $\mathcal{M}^{sy}$, ciphertext space $\mathcal{C}^{sy}$, key space $\mathcal{K}^{sy}$. Let $H : \{0,1\}^* \to \{0,1\}^n$ and $G : \{0,1\}^* \to \mathcal{R}^{sy}$ be hash functions. We recall the REACT transformation in the following definition, and then provide its IND-qCCA security proof.

Definition 6. REACT$[\Pi^{asy}, \Pi^{sy}, H, G] = (Gen, Enc, Dec)$ *obtained from the REACT transformation is constructed as in Fig. 5.*

Gen	Enc$(pk, m; (R, r))$	Dec$(sk, (c_1, c_2, c_3))$
$(pk, sk) \leftarrow \text{Gen}^{asy}$	$c_1 := \text{Enc}^{asy}(pk, R; r)$	$R := \text{Dec}^{asy}(sk, c_1)$
return (pk, sk)	$c_2 := \text{Enc}^{sy}(G(R), m)$	$m := \text{Dec}^{sy}(G(R), c_2)$
	$c_3 := H(R, m, c_1, c_2)$	**if** $R = \perp$ **or** $m = \perp$
	return (c_1, c_2, c_3)	**return** $\perp$
		$c_3' := H(R, m, c_1, c_2)$
		if $c_3' \neq c_3$, **return** $\perp$
		return m

Fig. 5. PKE REACT$[\Pi^{asy}, \Pi^{sy}, H, G]$ obtained from REACT transformation

Lemma 8. *Let H be the random oracle, then* REACT$[\Pi^{asy}, \Pi^{sy}, H, G]$ *is an oracle-masked scheme relative to H, and its parameter η is $1/2^n$.*

Proof. We define deterministic polynomial time algorithm A_1, A_2, A_3 and A_4:

- A_1 takes pk, (R, r) and m as input, evaluates $c_1 := \text{Enc}^{asy}(pk, R; r)$, $k := G(R)$, $c_2 := \text{Enc}^{sy}(k, m)$, and then outputs (R, m, c_1, c_2).
- A_2 on input (R, m, c_1, c_2) and $y \in \{0,1\}^n$, lets $c_3 := y$ and outputs (c_1, c_2, c_3).
- A_3 takes sk and (c_1, c_2, c_3) as input, computes $R := \text{Dec}^{asy}(sk, c_1)$. If $R = \perp$, output $\perp$. Else, compute $k := G(R)$ and $m := \text{Dec}^{sy}(k, c_2)$. If $m = \perp$, output $\perp$. Otherwise, output (R, m, c_1, c_2).
- A_4 on input (R, m, c_1, c_2), outputs m directly.

We can verify that with four algorithms defined as above, algorithm Enc and Dec given in Fig. 5 are written as $\mathrm{Enc}^{\mathcal{O}}$ and $\mathrm{Dec}^{\mathcal{O}}$ in Definition 3 with $\mathcal{O} = H$. And thus Π is an oracle-masked scheme, and its η is

$$\eta = \max_{(pk,sk),(c_1,c_2,c_3)} 1/2^n |\{y \in \{0,1\}^n : (c_1,c_2,c_3) = A_2(pk, A_3(sk,(c_1,c_2,c_3)),y)\}|$$

$$= \max_{(pk,sk),(c_1,c_2,c_3)} 1/2^n |\{y \in \{0,1\}^n : c_3 = y\}| = 1/2^n,$$

where (pk, sk) is generated by Gen, $(c_1, c_2, c_3) \in \mathcal{C}^{asy} \times \mathcal{C}^{sy} \times \{0,1\}^n$ is such that $A_3(sk,(c_1,c_2,c_3)) \neq \perp$. $\qquad \square$

Theorem 7. *For any adversary A against the IND-qCCA security of $\Pi =$ REACT$[\Pi^{asy}, \Pi^{sy}, H, G]$ in the QROM, making at most q_D queries to the decryption oracle, at most q_G queries to random oracle G and at most q_H queries to random oracle H, there exist an adversary A_{asy} against the OW-qPCA security of Π^{asy} and an adversary A_{sy} against the OT security of Π^{sy} such that*

$$Adv_{A,\Pi}^{IND\text{-}qCCA} \leq q_D \cdot \frac{12}{\sqrt{2^n}} + 2(d+1)\sqrt{Adv_{A_{asy},\Pi^{asy}}^{OW\text{-}qPCA}} + 4d \cdot Adv_{A_{asy},\Pi^{asy}}^{OW\text{-}qPCA} + Adv_{A_{sy},\Pi^{sy}}^{OT},$$

where $d = q_H + q_G + 2q_H \cdot q_D$, $Time(A_{sy}) \approx Time(A_{asy}) \approx Time(A) + O(d^2)$.

The IND-qCCA security proof of REACT transformation essentially follows the proof outline for FO transformation, which is presented in the proof of Theorem 6. Thus, we present the proof of Theorem 7 in the full version [25].

4.3 $\mathsf{T_{CH}}$: From OW-qPCA to IND-qCCA in the QROM

Transformation $\mathsf{T_{CH}}$ transforms a OW-PCA secure PKE to a q-IND-CCA[2] secure KEM in the quantum random oracle model [16].

Let $\Pi^{asy} = (\mathrm{Gen}^{asy}, \mathrm{Enc}^{asy}, \mathrm{Dec}^{asy})$ be a PKE with message space $\mathcal{M}^{asy}$. Let $H, G : \{0,1\}^* \rightarrow \{0,1\}^n$ be hash functions. We then introduce $\mathsf{T_{CH}}$ and a new transformation $\widetilde{\mathsf{T}}$ to prove the IND-qCCA security of $\mathsf{T_{CH}}$.

Definition 7. *PKE $\widetilde{\mathsf{T}}[\Pi^{asy}, H] = (Gen, Enc, Dec)$ and KEM $\mathsf{T_{CH}}[\Pi^{asy}, H, G] = (Gen, Encaps, Decaps)$ are as shown in Fig. 6, respectively. Particularly, $\mathsf{T_{CH}}$ is composed of transformation $\widetilde{\mathsf{T}}$ and modular FO transformation $\mathsf{U}_m^\perp$, i.e., $\mathsf{T_{CH}}[\Pi^{asy}, H, G] = \mathsf{U}_m^\perp[\widetilde{\mathsf{T}}[\Pi^{asy}, H], G]$.*

Lemma 9. *$\widetilde{\mathsf{T}}[\Pi^{asy}, H]$ is an oracle-masked scheme relative to random oracle H, and its parameter η is $1/2^n$.*

Proof. Tuple (A_1, A_2, A_3, A_4), as the decomposition of scheme $\widetilde{\mathsf{T}}[\Pi^{asy}, H]$, is defined as follows.

- A_1 takes pk, m and r as input, computes $c_1 := \mathrm{Enc}^{asy}(pk, m; r)$, then outputs (m, c_1).

---
[2] Here q is a constant and indicates q classical decryption queries.

Gen	Enc$(pk, m; r)$	Dec$(sk, (c_1, c_2))$
$(pk, sk) \leftarrow \text{Gen}^{asy}$	$c_1 := \text{Enc}^{asy}(pk, m; r)$	$m' := \text{Dec}^{asy}(sk, c_1)$
return (pk, sk)	$c_2 := H(m, c_1)$	**if** $H(m', c_1) \neq c_2$
	return (c_1, c_2)	**return** $\perp$
		return m'

Gen	Encaps(pk)	Decaps$(sk, (c_1, c_2))$
$(pk, sk) \leftarrow \text{Gen}^{asy}$	$m \xleftarrow{\$} \mathcal{M}^{asy}$	$m' := \text{Dec}^{asy}(sk, c_1)$
return (pk, sk)	$c_1 \leftarrow \text{Enc}^{asy}(pk, m)$	**if** $H(m', c_1) \neq c_2$
	$c_2 := H(m, c_1)$	**return** $\perp$
	$K := G(m)$	**return** $G(m')$
	return $(K, (c_1, c_2))$	

Fig. 6. PKE $\widetilde{\mathsf{T}}[\Pi^{asy}, H]$ and KEM $\mathsf{T_{CH}}[\Pi^{asy}, H, G]$

- A_2 takes (m, c_1) and $c_2 \in \{0, 1\}^n$ as input, then outputs (c_1, c_2).
- A_3 takes (c_1, c_2) as input, evaluates $m := \text{Dec}^{asy}(sk, c_1)$. If $m = \perp$, output $\perp$. Otherwise, output (m, c_1).
- A_4 on input (m, c_1), outputs m.

Then its parameter η is calculated by

$$\eta = \max_{(pk,sk),(c_1,c_2)} 1/2^n \cdot |\{y \in \{0, 1\}^n : (c_1, c_2) = A_2(pk, A_3(sk, (c_1, c_2)), y)\}|$$

$$= \max_{(pk,sk),(c_1,c_2)} 1/2^n \cdot |\{y \in \{0, 1\}^n : c_2 = y\}| = 1/2^n,$$

where (pk, sk) and $(c_1, c_2) \in \mathcal{C}^{asy} \times \{0, 1\}^n$ are such that $A_3(sk, (c_1, c_2)) \neq \perp$. $\square$

Theorem 8. *If Π^{asy} is δ-correct, for any adversary A against the IND-qCCA security of $\Pi = \mathsf{T_{CH}}[\Pi^{asy}, H, G]$ in the QROM, making at most q_D queries to decapsulation oracle* Decaps*, at most q_H queries to random oracle H and at most q_G queries to random oracle G, there exists an adversary A_{asy} against the OW-qPCA security of Π^{asy} such that*

$$\text{Adv}_{A,\Pi}^{IND\text{-}qCCA} \leq q_D \cdot \frac{24}{\sqrt{2^n}} + 4(d + 1)\sqrt{\text{Adv}_{A_{asy},\Pi^{asy}}^{OW\text{-}qPCA}} + 4d \cdot \text{Adv}_{A_{asy},\Pi^{asy}}^{OW\text{-}qPCA},$$

where $d = q_D + q_H + q_G$, $Time(A_{asy}) \approx Time(A) + O(d^2)$.

Proof. **Game 0**: This game is exactly $\text{Game}_{A,\Pi}^{IND\text{-}qCCA}$, that is given in Fig. 7. Then we have

$$\left| \Pr[\textbf{Game 0} \rightarrow 1] - \frac{1}{2} \right| = \text{Adv}_{A,\Pi}^{IND\text{-}qCCA}.$$

Starting from **Game 1**, random oracle H is simulated with CStO and its database register is denoted by D.

Game 1: In this game, we replace decapsulation oracle Decaps with oracle Decaps$_1$. Decaps$_1$ replies quantum query $|(c_1, c_2), z\rangle$ in three steps:

$\text{Game}_{A,\Pi}^{\text{IND-qCCA}}$

$H \xleftarrow{\$} \Omega_H, G \xleftarrow{\$} \Omega_G$

$(pk, sk) \leftarrow \text{Gen}$

$b \xleftarrow{\$} \{0,1\}, m^* \xleftarrow{\$} \mathcal{M}^{asy}$

$c_1^* \leftarrow \text{Enc}^{asy}(pk, m^*), c_2^* := H(m^*, c_1^*)$

$K_0^* := G(m^*), K_1^* \xleftarrow{\$} \{0,1\}^n$

$b' \leftarrow A^{H,G,\text{Decaps}_{(c_1^*, c_2^*)}}(pk, K_b^*, (c_1^*, c_2^*))$

return $[b = b']$

$\text{Decaps}_a(sk, (c_1, c_2))$

if $(c_1, c_2) = a$, **return** $\perp$

$m' := \text{Dec}^{asy}(sk, c_1)$

if $H(m', c_1) \neq c_2$, **return** $\perp$

return $G(m')$

Fig. 7. $\text{Game}_{A,\Pi}^{\text{IND-qCCA}}$ for T_{CH} transformation, where oracle H, G and Decaps are all quantum-accessible

1. Perform the plaintext extraction procedure U_{Ext} of $\widetilde{\mathsf{T}}[\Pi^{asy}, H]$ to obtain m.
2. If $m = \perp$, return $|(c_1, c_2), z \oplus \perp\rangle$. Otherwise, return $|(c_1, c_2), z \oplus G(m)\rangle$.
3. Perform U_{Ext} a second time to uncompute m.

Note that the construction of U_{Ext} of $\widetilde{\mathsf{T}}[\Pi^{asy}, H]$ is presented in Appendix A. We then can construct Decaps_1 by invoking plaintext checking oracle Pco, instead of using sk directly.

That Decaps_1 answers q_D decapsulation queries requires performing plaintext extraction procedure $2q_D$ times. By applying Theorem 5,

$$|\Pr[\textbf{Game 0} \rightarrow 1] - \Pr[\textbf{Game 1} \rightarrow 1]| \leq 10 q_D \cdot \sqrt{\eta} = q_D \cdot \frac{10}{\sqrt{2^n}}.$$

Game 2: In this game, we change oracle Decaps_1 by Decaps_2. Decaps_2 differs from Decaps_1 only after the challenge query: Decaps_2 performs $\text{StdDecomp}_{(m^*, c_1^*)}$ on register D before and after applying Decaps_1.

To consider the commutativity of $\text{StdDecomp}_{(m^*, c_1^*)}$ and Decaps_1, note that the second step of Decaps_1 commutes with $\text{StdDecomp}_{(m^*, c_1^*)}$. Then by Lemma 4, the first and last step commute with $\text{StdDecomp}_{(m^*, c_1^*)}$ by a loss. Therefore,

$$|\Pr[\textbf{Game 1} \rightarrow 1] - \Pr[\textbf{Game 2} \rightarrow 1]| \leq 14 q_D \cdot \sqrt{\eta} = q_D \cdot \frac{14}{\sqrt{2^n}}.$$

Game 3: In this game, we change the process of replying random oracle queries: When random oracles are queried in the execution of A, we query a constant zero function E and then query these random oracles. Then we have

$$\Pr[\textbf{Game 2} \rightarrow 1] = \Pr[\textbf{Game 3} \rightarrow 1].$$

Game 4: In this game, the only change is that the semi-classical oracle $\mathcal{O}_{\mathcal{S}}^{SC}$ is applied before querying E, where set $\mathcal{S} = \{m^*, m^* \| \cdot\}$.

E is queried at most $q_D + q_H + q_G$ times. We let $d = q_D + q_H + q_G$, and apply Theorem 3 to obtain

$$|\Pr[\textbf{Game 3} \rightarrow 1] - \Pr[\textbf{Game 4} \rightarrow 1]| \leq \sqrt{(d+1)\Pr[\text{Find} : \textbf{Game 4}]}.$$

Game 5: In this game, we pick $c_2^* \in \{0,1\}^n$ and $K_0^* \in \{0,1\}^n$ uniformly to produce (c_1^*, c_2^*) and K^*. And we replace Decaps_2 with Decaps_1.

By similar analysis in the proof of Theorem 6, the process of oracle Decaps_2 in **Game 4** does not disturb the database state on (m^*, c_1^*) if Find does not occur. Moreover, **Game 4** and **Game 5** are indistinguishable for adversary A until Find occurs. Thus,

$$\Pr[\text{Find} : \textbf{Game 4}] = \Pr[\text{Find} : \textbf{Game 5}],$$
$$\Pr[\neg\text{Find} \wedge \textbf{Game 4} \to 1] = \Pr[\neg\text{Find} \wedge \textbf{Game 5} \to 1].$$

Furthermore,

$$\Pr[\text{Find} : \textbf{Game 5}] \leq 4d \cdot \mathrm{Adv}_{A_{asy}, \Pi^{asy}}^{\mathrm{OW\text{-}qPCA}},$$

where adversary A_{asy} invokes A and breaks the OW-qPCA security of Π^{asy}. The running time of A_{asy} is $\mathrm{Time}(A_{asy}) \approx \mathrm{Time}(A) + O(d^2)$.

Game 6: In this game, $\mathcal{O}_S^{SC}$ is removed from the process of E.

The output difference of **Game 5** and **Game 6** is bounded by Theorem 3. And in **Game 6**, K_0^* and K_1^* are both chosen from $\{0,1\}^n$ uniformly, which means that **Game 6** outputs 1 with probability $1/2$.

Summarizing the above arguments, we obtain

$$\mathrm{Adv}_{A,\Pi}^{\mathrm{IND\text{-}qCCA}} \leq q_D \cdot \frac{12}{\sqrt{2^n}} + 4(d+1)\sqrt{\mathrm{Adv}_{A_{asy}, \Pi^{asy}}^{\mathrm{OW\text{-}qPCA}}} + 4d \cdot \mathrm{Adv}_{A_{asy}, \Pi^{asy}}^{\mathrm{OW\text{-}qPCA}}.$$

$\square$

Acknowledgments. We thank the anonymous reviewers of PKC 2023, and Shujiao Cao for their insightful comments and suggestions. This work is supported by National Natural Science Foundation of China (Grants No. 62172405).

A   The Construction of $\mathbf{U}_{\mathrm{Ext}}$

To implement $\mathrm{U}_{\mathrm{Ext}}$, we first give some notations, then introduce algorithm **Extract**, as a primitive of $\mathrm{U}_{\mathrm{Ext}}$, and finally present the construction of $\mathrm{U}_{\mathrm{Ext}}$.

As is shown in definition 4, $\mathcal{O}$ is simulated by CStO and we introduce two definitions related to database D: For any $c \in \mathcal{C}$, a completion in D is defined to be a pair $(x, y) \in D$ such that $\mathrm{A}_2(pk, x, y) = c$ and $\mathrm{A}_3(sk, c) = x$. Define D_c to be the subset of D such that $\mathrm{A}_2(pk, x, y) = c$ for any (x, y) in D_c. Then any completion of c in set D is necessarily in set D_c. Note that D contains at most one completion of c, since c determines $\mathrm{A}_3(sk, c)$.

Define relation $\mathcal{R}_1(pk, sk)$ and $\mathcal{R}_2(pk, sk)$ for any (pk, sk) of Π as below.

$$\mathcal{R}_1(pk, sk) := \{(x, c) \in \mathcal{X} \times \mathcal{C} : \exists y \in \mathcal{Y} \text{ s.t. } \mathrm{A}_2(pk, x, y) = c\},$$

$$\mathcal{R}_2(pk, sk) := \{(x, c) \in \mathcal{X} \times \mathcal{C} : \mathrm{A}_3(sk, c) = x\},$$

where $\mathcal{X}$ is the output space of algorithm A_1. And we give the definition of the verification oracle $\mathbf{V}(pk, sk, \cdot, \cdot)$ of Π. $\mathbf{V}(pk, sk, \cdot, \cdot)$ takes input $(x, c) \in \mathcal{X} \times \mathcal{C}$

and outputs a bit $b \in \{0,1\}$. For any $(x,c) \in \mathcal{R}_1(pk, sk)$, $\mathbf{V}(pk, sk, x, c) = 1$ if and only if $(x,c) \in \mathcal{R}_2(pk, sk)$.

Next, we define a classical algorithm **Extract**. **Extract** takes pk, sk, c and D as input. It looks for a completion of c in D. If a completion $(x,y) \in D$ is found, **Extract** outputs $(1,x)$. Otherwise, it outputs $(0,0)$.

Then we give a construction of **Extract** relative to oracle $\mathbf{V}$. **Extract** on input c and D, finds a completion in two steps: For each pair (x,y) in D, it computes $c' = \mathrm{A}_2(pk, x, y)$ and compares c' with c for equality to check whether $(x,y) \in D_c$. Then to extract a completion from D_c, it invokes $\mathbf{V}$ and computes $\mathbf{V}(pk, sk, x, y)$ for each pair $(x,y) \in D_c$. If $(x,y) \in D$ exists such that $\mathbf{V}(pk, sk, x, y) = 1$, **Extract** outputs $(1,x)$. Otherwise, it outputs $(0,0)$.

Then we construct $\mathrm{U}_{\mathrm{Ext}}$ with **Extract**, and we start with the case when the challenge query does not happen.

1. Evaluate $(b, x) = \mathbf{Extract}(pk, sk, c, D)$ in superposition and xor the output into a newly created register.
2. Apply the following conditional procedures in superposition:
3. Condition on $b = 0$, evaluate the map $|c, z, D, b, x\rangle \mapsto |c, z \oplus \bot, D, b, x\rangle$.
4. Condition on $b = 1$, evaluate the map $|c, z, D, b, x\rangle \mapsto |c, z \oplus \mathrm{A}_4(x), D, b, x\rangle$.
5. Uncompute (b, x) by evaluating $\mathbf{Extract}(pk, sk, c, D)$ in superposition again. Then discord the new register.

After the challenge query, the challenge ciphertext c^* is produced and $\mathrm{U}_{\mathrm{Ext}}$ is implemented below.

1. Apply the following conditional procedures in superposition:
2. Condition on $c = c^*$, evaluate the map $|c, z, D\rangle \mapsto |c, z \oplus \bot, D\rangle$.
3. Condition on $c \neq c^*$, apply the procedure in the case when c^* is undefined.

In addition, the running time of $\mathrm{U}_{\mathrm{Ext}}$ is upper bounded as follows. Denote the length of database by l. For each database D, $|D| \leq l$ and **Extract** invokes A_2 and $\mathbf{V}$ at most l times during the execution. Thus $O(l \cdot \mathrm{Time}(\mathrm{A}_2) + l \cdot \mathrm{Time}(\mathbf{V}))$ is an upper bound of the running time of $\mathrm{U}_{\mathrm{Ext}}$.

Then we will give respective constructions of $\mathrm{U}_{\mathrm{Ext}}$ for $\mathrm{FO}[\Pi^{asy}, \Pi^{sy}, H, G]$, $\mathrm{REACT}[\Pi^{asy}, \Pi^{sy}, H, G]$ and $\widetilde{\mathrm{T}}[\Pi^{asy}, H]$. Since the implementation of $\mathbf{V}$ is sufficient to determine the construction of $\mathrm{U}_{\mathrm{Ext}}$ for an oracle-masked scheme Π, we only give constructions of the verification oracle $\mathbf{V}$ for these three schemes.

A.1   The Construction of $\mathrm{U}_{\mathrm{Ext}}$ for FO

For scheme $\Pi = \mathrm{FO}[\Pi^{asy}, \Pi^{sy}, H, G]$, we first present relation $\mathcal{R}_1(pk, sk)$ and $\mathcal{R}_2(pk, sk)$ to determine the input form of the verification oracle $\mathbf{V}$, then give an implementation of $\mathbf{V}$.

By Lemma 5, relation $\mathcal{R}_1(pk, sk)$ and $\mathcal{R}_2(pk, sk)$ are subsets of $\mathcal{M}^{asy} \times \mathcal{C}^{sy} \times \mathcal{C}^{asy} \times \mathcal{C}^{sy}$ for any (pk, sk) of Π. Tuple $(\delta, d_1, c, d_2) \in \mathcal{R}_1(pk, sk)$ if $d_1 = d_2$ and $r \in \mathcal{R}^{asy}$ exists such that $c := \mathrm{Enc}^{asy}(pk, \delta; r)$. Tuple $(\delta, d_1, c, d_2) \in \mathcal{R}_2(pk, sk)$ if $d_1 = d_2$ and $\mathrm{Dec}^{asy}(sk, c) = \delta$.

Further, tuple $(\delta, d_1, c, d_2) \in \mathcal{R}_1(pk, sk)$ also satisfies $\mathrm{Dec}^{asy}(sk, c) = \delta$ by the correctness of Π^{asy}, and thus $(\delta, d_1, c, d_2) \in \mathcal{R}_2(pk, sk)$. Then $\mathcal{R}_1(pk, sk)$ is a subset of $\mathcal{R}_2(pk, sk)$. By similar arguments, we also conclude that $(\delta, d_1, c, d_2) \notin \mathcal{R}_1(pk, sk)$ implies $(\delta, d_1, c, d_2) \notin \mathcal{R}_2(pk, sk)$ for any (pk, sk). Thus for any (pk, sk) of Π, $\mathcal{R}_1(pk, sk) = \mathcal{R}_2(pk, sk)$ and

$$\mathcal{R}_2(pk, sk) = \left\{ (\delta, d, c, d) : c \in \mathcal{C}^{asy}, \delta = \mathrm{Dec}^{asy}(sk, c), d \in \mathcal{C}^{sy} \right\}.$$

By the definition of the verification oracle, $\mathbf{V}$ for Π can be simply simulated by an algorithm that takes as input tuple (δ, d_1, c, d_2) and trivially outputs 1. Moreover, notice that sk is not used in the construction of $\mathrm{U}_{\mathrm{Ext}}$ except for the verification oracle. Therefore, $\mathrm{U}_{\mathrm{Ext}}$ for Π can be implemented without sk.

Finally, the running time of $\mathrm{U}_{\mathrm{Ext}}$ is given by $O(l \cdot \mathrm{Time}(\mathrm{Enc}^{asy}))$.

A.2   The Construction of $\mathrm{U}_{\mathrm{Ext}}$ for REACT

For scheme $\Pi = \mathrm{REACT}[\Pi^{asy}, \Pi^{sy}, H, G]$, we only give an implementation of oracle $\mathbf{V}$ here.

By Lemma 8, $\mathcal{R}_1(pk, sk)$ and $\mathcal{R}_2(pk, sk)$ are subsets of $\mathcal{M}^{asy} \times \mathcal{M}^{sy} \times \mathcal{C}^{asy} \times \mathcal{C}^{sy} \times \mathcal{C}^{asy} \times \mathcal{C}^{sy} \times \{0, 1\}^n$ for any (pk, sk). Any tuple $(R, m, c_1, c_2, c_1', c_2', c_3') \in \mathcal{R}_1(pk, sk)$ if $c_1 = c_1'$, $c_2 = c_2'$. And this tuple is an element of $\mathcal{R}_2(pk, sk)$ if $R = \mathrm{Dec}^{asy}(sk, c_1')$, $m = \mathrm{Dec}^{sy}(G(R), c_2')$, $c_1 = c_1'$, $c_2 = c_2'$. Thus, we have $\mathcal{R}_1(pk, sk) = \{(R, m, c_1, c_2, c_1, c_2, c_3) : R \in \mathcal{M}^{asy}, m \in \mathcal{M}^{sy}, c_1 \in \mathcal{C}^{asy}, c_2 \in \mathcal{C}^{sy}, c_3 \in \{0, 1\}^n\}$ and $\mathcal{R}_2(pk, sk) = \{(R, m, c_1, c_2, c_1, c_2, c_3) : c_1 \in \mathcal{C}^{asy}, c_2 \in \mathcal{C}^{sy}, c_3 \in \{0, 1\}^n, R = \mathrm{Dec}^{asy}(sk, c_1), m = \mathrm{Dec}^{sy}(G(R), c_2)\}$. Then we assume the input form of $\mathbf{V}$ to be $(R, m, c_1, c_2, c_1, c_2, c_3)$ according to $\mathcal{R}_1(pk, sk)$ of Π.

We present an algorithm $\mathbf{V}_{\mathrm{Sim}}$ relative to plaintext checking oracle Pco. $\mathbf{V}_{\mathrm{Sim}}$ takes as input tuple $(R, m, c_1, c_2, c_1, c_2, c_3)$. It first invokes Pco and obtain $b := \mathrm{Pco}(R, c_1)$. If $b = 0$, $\mathbf{V}_{\mathrm{Sim}}$ outputs 0. Else, it computes $m' := \mathrm{Dec}^{sy}(G(R), c_2)$. If $m \neq m'$, output 0. Else, output 1. Then by the definition of Pco in Appendix B.2, it is easily verified that $\mathbf{V}$ can be simulated by $\mathbf{V}_{\mathrm{Sim}}$. In this way, $\mathrm{U}_{\mathrm{Ext}}$ for Π is implemented by invoking Pco instead of using sk directly. Moreover, the running time of $\mathrm{U}_{\mathrm{Ext}}$ is given by $O(l)$.

A.3   The Construction of $\mathrm{U}_{\mathrm{Ext}}$ for $\widetilde{\mathsf{T}}$

For scheme $\widetilde{\mathsf{T}}[\Pi^{asy}, H]$, we give a straightforward way to simulate oracle $\mathbf{V}$ here.

According to Lemma 9, tuple $((m, c_1), (c_1', c_2')) \in \mathcal{R}_1(pk, sk)$ if $c_1 = c_1'$, while tuple $((m, c_1), (c_1', c_2')) \in \mathcal{R}_2(pk, sk)$ if $c_1 = c_1'$ and $m = \mathrm{Dec}^{asy}(sk, c_1)$. Then we can assume the input form of $\mathbf{V}$ to be (m, c_1, c_1, c_2).

We construct an oracle $\mathbf{V}_{\mathrm{Sim}}$ relative to plaintext-checking oracle Pco and use it to simulate $\mathbf{V}$. On input (m, c_1, c_1, c_2), $\mathbf{V}_{\mathrm{Sim}}$ first invokes Pco and obtains $b := \mathrm{Pco}(m, c_1)$. If $b = 0$, it outputs 0. Otherwise, it outputs 1. Then $\mathrm{U}_{\mathrm{Ext}}$ can be implemented without sk, and its running time is $O(l)$.

B   Cryptographic Primitives

Here we introduce secret-key encryption schemes (SKE), public-key encryption schemes (PKE), key encapsulation mechanisms (KEM) and their security notions.

B.1   Secret-Key Encryption

Definition 8. *A SKE Π^{sy} consists of a pair of polynomial-time algorithms (E, D) as follows.*

1. *E, the encryption algorithm, takes as input a message m and a key k, and outputs a ciphertext c.*
2. *D, the decryption algorithm, on input a ciphertext c and a key k outputs either a message m or a special symbol $\perp$ if c is invalid.*

Let $\Pi^{sy} = (E, D)$ be a SKE and define one-time (OT) security for it.

Definition 9 (OT). *Define the advantage of adversary A against the OT security of Π^{sy} as $\mathrm{Adv}_{A,\Pi^{sy}}^{OT} := \left| \Pr[Game_{A,\Pi^{sy}}^{OT} \to 1] - 1/2 \right|$ and $\Pr[Game_{A,\Pi^{sy}}^{OT} \to 1]$ is written by $\Pr[b' = b : (m_0, m_1) \leftarrow A, b \xleftarrow{\$} \{0, 1\}, c^* \leftarrow E(k, m_b), b' \leftarrow A(c^*)]$. Then Π^{sy} is OT secure if $\mathrm{Adv}_{A,\Pi^{sy}}^{OT}$ is negligible for any polynomial-time adversary A.*

B.2   Public-Key Encryption

Definition 10. *A PKE Π^{asy} consists of a triple of polynomial-time algorithms (Gen, Enc, Dec) as follows.*

1. *Gen, the key generation algorithm, on input 1^λ outputs a public/secret key-pair (pk, sk).*
2. *Enc, the encryption algorithm, on input a public key pk and a message m outputs a ciphertext c.*
3. *Dec, the decryption algorithm, on input a secret key sk and a ciphertext c outputs either a message m or a special symbol $\perp$ if c is invalid.*

Let $\Pi^{asy} = (Gen, Enc, Dec)$ be a PKE with message space $\mathcal{M}$. Then we introduce γ-spread and δ-correct property for it.

Definition 11 (γ-spread [12]). *Π^{asy} is γ-spread if for any pk produced by $Gen(1^\lambda)$ and any message $m \in \mathcal{M}$,*

$$\max_{c \in \{0,1\}^*} \Pr[c' = c : c' \leftarrow Enc(pk, m)] \leq 1/2^\gamma.$$

And Π^{asy} is called well-spread in λ if $\gamma = \omega(\log(\lambda))$.

Definition 12 (δ-**correct** [14]). Π^{asy} *is* δ-*correct if*

$$\mathop{E}_{(pk,sk)\leftarrow Gen}\left[\max_{m\in\mathcal{M}}\Pr[Dec(sk,c)\neq m : c\leftarrow Enc(pk,m)]\right]\leq\delta.$$

And Π^{asy} *is called perfectly correct if* $\delta=0$.

In the following, we define one-wayness under chosen plaintext attacks (OW-CPA), one-wayness under quantum plaintext checking attacks (OW-qPCA) and indistinguishability under quantum chosen ciphertext attacks (IND-qCCA) these three security notions for Π^{asy}.

Definition 13 (OW-CPA). *The OW-CPA game for* Π^{asy} *is defined in Fig. 8. The advantage of an adversary A against the OW-CPA security of Π is defined to be* $\mathrm{Adv}_{A,\Pi^{asy}}^{OW\text{-}CPA} := \Pr[Game_{A,\Pi^{asy}}^{OW\text{-}CPA} \to 1]$. *Then* Π^{asy} *is OW-CPA secure if* $\mathrm{Adv}_{A,\Pi^{asy}}^{OW\text{-}CPA}$ *is negligible for any polynomial-time adversary A.*

Definition 14 (OW-qPCA [17]). *The OW-qPCA game for* Π^{asy} *is defined in Fig. 8. The advantage of an adversary A against the OW-qPCA security of* Π^{asy} *is defined as* $\mathrm{Adv}_{A,\Pi^{asy}}^{OW\text{-}qPCA} := \Pr[Game_{A,\Pi^{asy}}^{OW\text{-}qPCA} \to 1]$. Π^{asy} *is OW-qPCA secure if* $\mathrm{Adv}_{A,\Pi^{asy}}^{OW\text{-}qPCA}$ *is negligible for any polynomial-time adversary A.*

$\mathrm{Game}_{A,\Pi^{asy}}^{OW\text{-}ATK}$	$\mathrm{Pco}(m,c)$			
$(pk,sk)\leftarrow\mathrm{Gen}$	$m':=Dec(sk,c)$			
$m^*\xleftarrow{\$}\mathcal{M}$	**return** $[m=m']$	ATK	CPA	qPCA
$c^*\leftarrow Enc(pk,m^*)$		$\mathcal{O}_{ATK}$	$\perp$	Pco
$m'\leftarrow A^{\mathcal{O}_{ATK}}(pk,c^*)$				
return $[m=m']$				

Fig. 8. Game OW-ATK for Π^{asy} (ATK $\in$ {CPA, qPCA}), where oracle $\mathcal{O}_{ATK}$ is quantum-accessible.

Definition 15 (IND-qCCA [5]). *The IND-qCCA game for* Π^{asy} *is defined in Fig. 9. The advantage of an adversary A against the IND-qCCA security of* Π^{asy} *is defined as* $\mathrm{Adv}_{A,\Pi^{asy}}^{IND\text{-}qCCA} := |\Pr[Game_{A,\Pi^{asy}}^{IND\text{-}qCCA} \to 1] - 1/2|$. *Then* Π^{asy} *is IND-qCCA secure if* $\mathrm{Adv}_{A,\Pi^{asy}}^{IND\text{-}qCCA}$ *is negligible for any polynomial-time adversary A.*

B.3 Key Encapsulation

Definition 16. *A KEM* Π^{kem} *consists of a triple of polynomial-time algorithms (Gen, Encaps, Decaps) as follows.*

$$\begin{array}{lll}
\underline{\text{Game}^{\text{IND-qCCA}}_{A,\Pi^{asy}}} & \underline{\text{Game}^{\text{IND-qCCA}}_{A,\Pi^{kem}}} & \underline{\text{Dec}_a(sk,c)} \\
(pk,sk) \leftarrow \text{Gen} & (pk,sk) \leftarrow \text{Gen} & \text{if } c = a, \textbf{return } \bot \\
(m_0,m_1) \leftarrow A^{\text{Dec}_\bot}(pk) & b \xleftarrow{\$} \{0,1\} & m' := \text{Dec}(sk,c) \\
b \xleftarrow{\$} \{0,1\} & (K_0^*,c^*) \leftarrow \text{Encaps}(pk) & \textbf{return } m' \\
c^* \leftarrow \text{Enc}(pk,m_b) & K_1 \xleftarrow{\$} \mathcal{K} & \underline{\text{Decaps}_a(sk,c)} \\
b' \leftarrow A^{\text{Dec}_{c^*}}(pk,c^*) & b' \leftarrow A^{\text{Decaps}_{c^*}}(pk,K_b^*,c^*) & \textbf{if } c = a, \textbf{return } \bot \\
\textbf{return } [m = m'] & \textbf{return } [b = b'] & K := \text{Decaps}(sk,c) \\
& & \textbf{return } K
\end{array}$$

Fig. 9. Game IND-qCCA for Π^{asy} and Π^{kem}, where oracle Dec_a and Decaps_a are both quantum-accessible.

1. *Gen, the key generation algorithm, on input 1^λ outputs a public/secret key-pair (pk,sk).*
2. *Encaps, the encapsulation algorithm, takes as input a public key pk and outputs a ciphertext c and a key k.*
3. *Decaps, the decapsulation algorithm, on input a secret key sk and a ciphertext c outputs either a key k or a special symbol $\bot$ if c is invalid.*

Let $\Pi^{kem} = (\text{Gen}, \text{Encaps}, \text{Decaps})$ be a KEM and define IND-qCCA security for it.

Definition 17 (IND-qCCA [27]). *The IND-qCCA game for Π^{kem} is defined in Fig. 9. The advantage of an adversary A against the IND-qCCA security of Π^{kem} is defined as $\text{Adv}^{IND\text{-}qCCA}_{A,\Pi^{kem}} := |\Pr[Game^{IND\text{-}qCCA}_{A,\Pi^{kem}} \to 1] - 1/2|$. Then Π^{kem} is IND-qCCA secure if $\text{Adv}^{IND\text{-}qCCA}_{A,\Pi^{kem}}$ is negligible for any polynomial-time adversary A.*

References

1. Ambainis, A., Hamburg, M., Unruh, D.: Quantum security proofs using semi-classical oracles. In: Boldyreva, A., Micciancio, D. (eds.) CRYPTO 2019. LNCS, vol. 11693, pp. 269–295. Springer, Cham (2019). https://doi.org/10.1007/978-3-030-26951-7_10
2. Bellare, M., Rogaway, P.: Random oracles are practical: a paradigm for designing efficient protocols. In: Proceedings of the 1st ACM Conference on Computer and Communications Security, pp. 62–73 (1993). https://doi.org/10.1145/168588.168596
3. Bindel, N., Hamburg, M., Hövelmanns, K., Hülsing, A., Persichetti, E.: Tighter proofs of CCA security in the quantum random oracle model. In: Hofheinz, D., Rosen, A. (eds.) TCC 2019. LNCS, vol. 11892, pp. 61–90. Springer, Cham (2019). https://doi.org/10.1007/978-3-030-36033-7_3
4. Boneh, D., Dagdelen, Ö., Fischlin, M., Lehmann, A., Schaffner, C., Zhandry, M.: Random oracles in a quantum world. In: Lee, D.H., Wang, X. (eds.) ASIACRYPT 2011. LNCS, vol. 7073, pp. 41–69. Springer, Heidelberg (2011). https://doi.org/10.1007/978-3-642-25385-0_3

5. Boneh, D., Zhandry, M.: Secure signatures and chosen ciphertext security in a quantum computing world. In: Canetti, R., Garay, J.A. (eds.) CRYPTO 2013. LNCS, vol. 8043, pp. 361–379. Springer, Heidelberg (2013). https://doi.org/10.1007/978-3-642-40084-1_21
6. Chiesa, A., Manohar, P., Spooner, N.: Succinct arguments in the quantum random oracle model. In: Hofheinz, D., Rosen, A. (eds.) TCC 2019. LNCS, vol. 11892, pp. 1–29. Springer, Cham (2019). https://doi.org/10.1007/978-3-030-36033-7_1
7. Chung, K.-M., Fehr, S., Huang, Y.-H., Liao, T.-N.: On the compressed-oracle technique, and post-quantum security of proofs of sequential work. In: Canteaut, A., Standaert, F.-X. (eds.) EUROCRYPT 2021. LNCS, vol. 12697, pp. 598–629. Springer, Cham (2021). https://doi.org/10.1007/978-3-030-77886-6_21
8. Coron, J.S., Handschuh, H., Joye, M., Paillier, P., Pointcheval, D., Tymen, C.: GEM: a generic chosen-ciphertext secure encryption method. In: Preneel, B. (eds.) Topics in Cryptology–CT-RSA 2002. CT-RSA 2002. Lecture Notes in Computer Science, vol. 2271, pp. 263–276. Springer, Berlin (2002). https://doi.org/10.1007/3-540-45760-7_18
9. Cramer, R., Shoup, V.: Design and analysis of practical public-key encryption schemes secure against adaptive chosen ciphertext attack. SIAM J. Comput. **33**(1), 167–226 (2003). https://doi.org/10.1137/S0097539702403773
10. Don, J., Fehr, S., Majenz, C., Schaffner, C.: Online-extractability in the quantum random-oracle model. In: Dunkelman, O., Dziembowski, S. (eds.) Advances in Cryptology–EUROCRYPT 2022. EUROCRYPT 2022. Lecture Notes in Computer Science, vol. 13277, pp. 677–706. Springer, Cham (2022). https://doi.org/10.1007/978-3-031-07082-2_24
11. Fujisaki, E., Okamoto, T.: Secure integration of asymmetric and symmetric encryption schemes. In: Wiener, M. (ed.) CRYPTO 1999. LNCS, vol. 1666, pp. 537–554. Springer, Heidelberg (1999). https://doi.org/10.1007/3-540-48405-1_34
12. Fujisaki, E., Okamoto, T.: Secure integration of asymmetric and symmetric encryption schemes. J. Cryptol. **26**(1), 80–101 (2011). https://doi.org/10.1007/s00145-011-9114-1
13. Gagliardoni, T., Hülsing, A., Schaffner, C.: Semantic security and indistinguishability in the quantum world. In: Robshaw, M., Katz, J. (eds.) CRYPTO 2016. LNCS, vol. 9816, pp. 60–89. Springer, Heidelberg (2016). https://doi.org/10.1007/978-3-662-53015-3_3
14. Hofheinz, D., Hövelmanns, K., Kiltz, E.: A modular analysis of the fujisaki-okamoto transformation. In: Kalai, Y., Reyzin, L. (eds.) TCC 2017. LNCS, vol. 10677, pp. 341–371. Springer, Cham (2017). https://doi.org/10.1007/978-3-319-70500-2_12
15. Hövelmanns, K., Hülsing, A., Majenz, C.: Failing gracefully: decryption failures and the Fujisaki-Okamoto transform. In: Agrawal, S., Lin, D. (eds.) Advances in Cryptology–ASIACRYPT 2022. ASIACRYPT 2022. Lecture Notes in Computer Science, vol. 13794, pp. 414–443. Springer, Cham (2022). https://doi.org/10.1007/978-3-031-22972-5_15
16. Huguenin-Dumittan, L., Vaudenay, S.: On ind-qcca security in the ROM and its applications - CPA security is sufficient for TLS 1.3. In: Dunkelman, O., Dziembowski, S. (eds.) Advances in Cryptology– EUROCRYPT 2022. EUROCRYPT 2022. Lecture Notes in Computer Science, vol. 13277, pp. 613–642. Springer, Cham (2022). https://doi.org/10.1007/978-3-031-07082-2_22
17. Jiang, H., Zhang, Z., Chen, L., Wang, H., Ma, Z.: IND-CCA-Secure key encapsulation mechanism in the quantum random oracle model, revisited. In: Shacham, H., Boldyreva, A. (eds.) CRYPTO 2018. LNCS, vol. 10993, pp. 96–125. Springer, Cham (2018). https://doi.org/10.1007/978-3-319-96878-0_4

18. Jiang, H., Zhang, Z., Ma, Z.: Key encapsulation mechanism with explicit rejection in the quantum random oracle model. In: Lin, D., Sako, K. (eds.) PKC 2019. LNCS, vol. 11443, pp. 618–645. Springer, Cham (2019). https://doi.org/10.1007/978-3-030-17259-6_21

19. Jiang, H., Zhang, Z., Ma, Z.: Tighter security proofs for generic key encapsulation mechanism in the quantum random oracle model. In: Ding, J., Steinwandt, R. (eds.) PQCrypto 2019. LNCS, vol. 11505, pp. 227–248. Springer, Cham (2019). https://doi.org/10.1007/978-3-030-25510-7_13

20. Kuchta, V., Sakzad, A., Stehlé, D., Steinfeld, R., Sun, S.-F.: Measure-rewind-measure: tighter quantum random oracle model proofs for one-way to hiding and CCA security. In: Canteaut, A., Ishai, Y. (eds.) EUROCRYPT 2020. LNCS, vol. 12107, pp. 703–728. Springer, Cham (2020). https://doi.org/10.1007/978-3-030-45727-3_24

21. Liu, X., Wang, M.: QCCA-secure generic key encapsulation mechanism with tighter security in the quantum random oracle model. In: Garay, J.A. (ed.) PKC 2021. LNCS, vol. 12710, pp. 3–26. Springer, Cham (2021). https://doi.org/10.1007/978-3-030-75245-3_1

22. Nielsen, M.A., Chuang, I.: Quantum computation and quantum information (2002)

23. Okamoto, T., Pointcheval, D.: REACT: rapid enhanced-security asymmetric cryptosystem transform. In: Naccache, D. (ed.) CT-RSA 2001. LNCS, vol. 2020, pp. 159–174. Springer, Heidelberg (2000). https://doi.org/10.1007/3-540-45353-9_13

24. Saito, T., Xagawa, K., Yamakawa, T.: Tightly-secure key-encapsulation mechanism in the quantum random oracle model. In: Nielsen, J.B., Rijmen, V. (eds.) EUROCRYPT 2018. LNCS, vol. 10822, pp. 520–551. Springer, Cham (2018). https://doi.org/10.1007/978-3-319-78372-7_17

25. Shan, T., Ge, J., Xue, R.: QCCA-secure generic transformations in the quantum random oracle model. IACR Cryptology ePrint Archive, p. 1235 (2022). https://eprint.iacr.org/2022/1235

26. Targhi, E.E., Unruh, D.: Post-quantum security of the Fujisaki-Okamoto and OAEP transforms. In: Hirt, M., Smith, A. (eds.) TCC 2016. LNCS, vol. 9986, pp. 192–216. Springer, Heidelberg (2016). https://doi.org/10.1007/978-3-662-53644-5_8

27. Xagawa, K., Yamakawa, T.: (Tightly) QCCA-secure key-encapsulation mechanism in the quantum random oracle model. In: Ding, J., Steinwandt, R. (eds.) PQCrypto 2019. LNCS, vol. 11505, pp. 249–268. Springer, Cham (2019). https://doi.org/10.1007/978-3-030-25510-7_14

28. Zhandry, M.: Secure identity-based encryption in the quantum random oracle model. In: Safavi-Naini, R., Canetti, R. (eds.) CRYPTO 2012. LNCS, vol. 7417, pp. 758–775. Springer, Heidelberg (2012). https://doi.org/10.1007/978-3-642-32009-5_44

29. Zhandry, M.: How to record quantum queries, and applications to quantum indifferentiability. In: Boldyreva, A., Micciancio, D. (eds.) CRYPTO 2019. LNCS, vol. 11693, pp. 239–268. Springer, Cham (2019). https://doi.org/10.1007/978-3-030-26951-7_9

A Thorough Treatment
of Highly-Efficient NTRU Instantiations

Julien Duman[1], Kathrin Hövelmanns[2], Eike Kiltz[1]($\boxtimes$),
Vadim Lyubashevsky[3], Gregor Seiler[3], and Dominique Unruh[4]

[1] Ruhr-Universität Bochum, Bochum, Germany
eike.kiltz@rub.de
[2] TU Eindhoven, Eindhoven, The Netherlands
[3] IBM Research Europe, Zurich, Switzerland
[4] University of Tartu, Tartu, Estonia

Abstract. Cryptography based on the hardness of lattice problems over polynomial rings currently provides the most practical solution for public key encryption in the quantum era. Indeed, three of the four schemes chosen by NIST in the recently-concluded post-quantum standardization effort for encryption and signature schemes are based on the hardness of these problems. While the first encryption scheme utilizing properties of polynomial rings was NTRU (ANTS '98), the scheme that NIST chose for public key encryption (CRYSTALS-Kyber) is based on the hardness of the somewhat-related Module-LWE problem. One of the reasons for Kyber's selection was the fact that it is noticeably faster than NTRU and a little more compact. And indeed, the practical NTRU encryption schemes in the literature generally lag their Ring/Module-LWE counterparts in either compactness or speed, or both.

In this paper, we put the efficiency of NTRU-based schemes on equal (even slightly better, actually) footing with their Ring/Module-LWE counterparts. We provide several instantiations and transformations, with security given in the ROM and the QROM, that are on par, compactness-wise, with their counterparts based on Ring/Module-LWE. Performance-wise, the NTRU schemes instantiated in this paper over NTT-friendly rings of the form $\mathbb{Z}_q[X]/(X^d - X^{d/2} + 1)$ are the fastest of all public key encryption schemes, whether quantum-safe or not. When compared to the NIST finalist NTRU-HRSS-701, our scheme is 15% more compact and has a 15X improvement in the round-trip time of ephemeral key exchange, with key generation being 35X faster, encapsulation being 6X faster, and decapsulation enjoying a 9X speedup.

1 Introduction

The NTRU encryption scheme [19] was the first truly practical scheme based on the hardness of lattice problems over polynomial rings and, in many ways, the first really practical quantum-safe encryption scheme. The hardness of NTRU was originally stated as its own assumption, but as lattice cryptography evolved

A. Boldyreva and V. Kolesnikov (Eds.): PKC 2023, LNCS 13940, pp. 65–94, 2023.
https://doi.org/10.1007/978-3-031-31368-4_3

over the next few decades, the most natural way to view the hardness behind the NTRU encryption scheme was as a combination of two assumptions over a polynomial ring $R = \mathbb{Z}_q[X]/(f(X))$. The first assumption, which we call the NTRU assumption, is that the quotient of two polynomials $\mathbf{f}$ and $\mathbf{g}$, with coefficients chosen from some narrow distribution, looks uniform in R. The second assumption, which later became known as the Ring-LWE assumption [25,30] states that given a uniformly random $\mathbf{h} \in R$, and $\mathbf{hr} + \mathbf{e}$, for polynomials $\mathbf{e}$ and $\mathbf{r}$ with coefficients from a narrow distribution, it is difficult to recover $\mathbf{e}$. One could eliminate the need for the first assumption by choosing a relatively wide distribution for $\mathbf{f}$ and $\mathbf{g}$ [29], but the resulting scheme becomes very inefficient; thus all practical instantiations of NTRU were based on these two assumptions.

Since Regev's seminal work constructing an encryption scheme based on the LWE problem over general lattices [28], and its subsequent porting to lattices over polynomial rings [23,25,30], most of the community effort of shifted to building encryption schemes that do not require the NTRU assumption, and are just based on the decisional version (which was shown to be equivalent to the search one in [25], and for which no faster practical algorithm is known) of the Ring/Module-LWE problems. Indeed, in the first round of the NIST call for quantum-safe encryption, only 3 out of 17 proposals for lattice-based encryption schemes over polynomial rings relied on the NTRU assumption, while the rest used just an LWE-type assumption.

There are a few reasons for avoiding the NTRU assumption. The first is that the additional NTRU assumption is known to be false in the regime where the modulus q of the ring is noticeably larger than the dimension [1,8,15,22] (for the same parameters, the Ring-LWE problem is still believed to be hard). While the attacks against this parameter regime have not been extended to the one used for public key encryption, it does give some reason for concern. Secondly, in many rings, the division operation is significantly more expensive than multiplication, and so the assumption was also avoided for efficiency considerations. And third is that the NTRU assumption does not naturally lend itself to more flexible instantiations, such as Module-LWE. That is, it naturally operates over a module of dimension 1 (again, due to the division operation), whereas LWE-based schemes can be extended to work over modules of a larger dimension. This has the advantage that the underlying ring operations do not need to change as one increases the security parameter. In fact, all of the non-NTRU finalists in the NIST post-quantum standardization process use the module structure [5,10]. These schemes are also significantly more efficient than the finalist NTRU-based proposal [21].[1]

There are, however, also several advantages to NTRU-based schemes. One real-world advantage that NTRU has is that all patents on it have expired, while there may still conceivably be some (possibly still hidden) intellectual property claims on the Ring/Module-LWE schemes. Also, NTRU may have practical advantages when used in certain scenarios involving zero-knowledge proofs, since

---

[1] The schemes [5,10] can be made even more efficient by eliminating an unnecessary input to the random oracle (see [17]) which did not exist in [21].

the ciphertext has a simpler form and thus may require shorter proofs that it was correctly formed. In this paper, our goal is to put NTRU-based constructions on equal footing, performance-wise, as schemes based on Ring/Module-LWE.

1.1 Speed

The most efficient lattice-based schemes are those that natively work over rings $\mathbb{Z}_q[X]/(f(X))$ that support the Number Theory Transform (NTT). When the polynomial $f(X)$ factors into components having small degree, one can perform multiplication (and division) in the ring using the Chinese Remainder Theorem. That is, one evaluates the multiplicands modulo these factors, performs component-wise multiplication, and finally converts the product back into the original form. The process of efficiently doing these computations is the NTT and the inverse NTT.

The most commonly used NTT-friendly ring is of the form $\mathbb{Z}_q[X]/(X^d + 1)$, where d is a power-of-2. For well-chosen q, the polynomial $X^d + 1 = (X^{d/2} - r)(X^{d/2} + r) \bmod q$, and the respective factors similarly split as $(X^{d/2} - r) = (X^{d/4} - \sqrt{r})(X^{d/4} + \sqrt{r}) \bmod q$, etc. until one reaches an irreducible polynomial of a small (usually 1 or 2) degree. Because of this very nice factorization (the "niceness" mainly rests in the fact that all factors have 2 non-zero coefficients, making reduction modulo them linear-time), evaluation of any polynomial modulo the irreducible factors can be done using approximately $2d \log d$ operations over $\mathbb{Z}_q$. These rings also have some very nice algebraic properties – in particular the expansion factor [24] controlling the growth of polynomial products in the ring is the minimal of all rings. The one disadvantage of these rings is that they are sparse and so one cannot always find one for an appropriate security level. The hardness of the NTRU and Ring-LWE problem directly depends on the degree of the polynomial $f(X)$. Based on the current state of knowledge, obtaining 128-256 bit hardness requires taking dimensions somewhere between 512 and 1024. Since there are no powers of 2 in between, and because one may need to go beyond 1024 in case somewhat better algorithms are discovered, the sparsity of these rings is an inconvenience. The Module-LWE problem overcomes this inconvenience because the problem instance can be made up of a matrix of smaller rings, but this does not work for NTRU because this approach would significantly increase the size of the public key.

One can overcome this issue in NTRU by using "NTT-friendly" rings $f(X) = X^d - X^{d/2} + 1$ where $d = 2^i 3^j$.[2] The rings $\mathbb{Z}_q[X]/(X^d - X^{d/2} + 1)$, for appropriately-chosen primes, also support efficient NTT because $X^d - X^{d/2} + 1 = (X^{d/2} + \zeta)(X^{d/2} - (\zeta + 1)) \bmod q$, where ζ is a third root of unity in $\mathbb{Z}_q$ (not equal to 1). And after that, every term $(X^k - r)$ factors into either $(X^{k/2} - \sqrt{r})(X^{k/2} + \sqrt{r})$ or into $(X^{k/3} - \sqrt[3]{r})(X^{k/3} - \zeta \sqrt[3]{r})(X^{k/3} - \zeta^2 \sqrt[3]{r})$ modulo q. In both cases, one can efficiently proceed with the very efficient NTT because all factors have two non-zero coefficients. As can be seen from Table 1, there are

---

[2] The polynomial $f(X)$ is therefore the $3d$-th cyclotomic polynomial.

many such polynomials of degree between 512 and 1024. In the work of [26], a version of NTRU was implemented over the ring $\mathbb{Z}_{7681}[X]/(X^{768} - X^{384} + 1)$, but due to the structure of the ring, no factorization into three terms was necessary. In this work we show that there aren't any efficiency issues when the latter does happen, and give an instantiation of a scheme over the ring $\mathbb{Z}_{2917}[X]/(X^{648} - X^{324} + 1)$. The conclusion is that all of the schemes in Table 1 should have almost equally good instantiations.

One should also mention that Module and Ring-LWE schemes can be used in non-NTT-friendly rings [9], and the inefficiency of multiplication in these rings can be partially overcome by doing multiplication in a ring with a larger modulus and/or degree of $f(X)$ which supports NTT, and then reducing back into the original ring. This is, however not possible for NTRU-based schemes because NTRU requires polynomial *division*, and it is not known how to map this operation between rings. On the other hand, if a ring supports NTT, then division is essentially as fast as multiplication, with only the operation in the base ring (which is of a very low degree) being different. Thus any hope of having NTRU-based schemes being competitive with Ring/Module-LWE schemes seems to require defining the NTRU encryption scheme directly over NTT-friendly rings.

A reason that NTRU was traditionally not defined over NTT-friendly-rings was presumably due to an attack of Gentry [18] against a version of NTRU over the ring $\mathbb{Z}_q[X]/(X^d - 1)$, where the polynomial $X^d - 1$ could be factored as $(X^{d/2} - 1)(X^{d/2} + 1)$. The observation was that instead of working over the ring $\mathbb{Z}_q[X]/(X^d - 1)$, one can reduce everything modulo $X^{d/2} - 1$ and work over the ring $\mathbb{Z}_q[X]/(X^{d/2} - 1)$. What makes the attack work is that reduction modulo $X^{d/2} - 1$ is a ring homomorphism and that this reduction increases the size of the maximum coefficient by at most a factor of 2. Thus one can solve a shortest vector problem (upon which NTRU is based) in a lattice with a significantly smaller dimension, but whose norm increased by only a factor of 2. From this attack, one might infer that it's important to have the polynomial $f(X)$ be irreducible (or have a large component of it be irreducible). Interestingly, however, the theoretical works of [23–25] showed that in the reductions from worst-case lattice problems to average-case problems over polynomial rings (e.g. Ring/Module-SIS, Ring/Module-LWE), one needs the polynomial $f(X)$ to be *irreducible* in $\mathbb{Z}[X]$, but the polynomial $f(X)$ splitting in $\mathbb{Z}_q[X]$ does not seem to make the average-case problem easier.[3] And in fact, most practical lattice-based constructions work over the ring $\mathbb{Z}_q[X]/(X^d + 1)$, where d is a power of 2. While polynomials $X^d + 1$ are irreducible in $\mathbb{Z}[X]$, they are *always* reducible

---

[3] As a sanity check, one can see that the attack in [18] does not work because it is impossible for a polynomial $f(X)$ that's irreducible over the integers to split modulo q into polynomials of large degree (e.g. $d/2$) whose coefficients are small. For example, it's trivial to see that $X^d + 1$ cannot have factors $X^{d/2} \pm \beta$ with $\beta < \sqrt{q}$. For a more general result, one needs a little algebraic number theory (e.g. implicit in the proof of [27, Lemma 3.1] is that any factor of degree d/k of $X^d + 1$ has ℓ_2-norm at least $p^{1/k}$, and this result extends in a similar way to other polynomials).

in $\mathbb{Z}_q[X]$; and consistent with the theoretical intuition, there have not been any attacks exploiting the factorization of $X^d + 1$ modulo q. We therefore don't see any danger of using NTRU over NTT-friendly rings.

1.2   Decryption Error and Compactness

To make NTRU encryption work efficiently over NTT-friendly rings, one creates the public key as $\mathbf{h} = p\mathbf{g}/(p\mathbf{f} + 1)$, for a small prime p, and then the encryption function (which is one-way CPA secure – meaning that it is hard to decrypt for a random message) outputs $\mathbf{c} = \mathbf{hr} + \mathbf{m}$, where $\mathbf{r}, \mathbf{m}$ are polynomials with coefficients coming from a narrow distribution. The decryption algorithm computes $(p\mathbf{f} + 1)\mathbf{c} = p(\mathbf{gr} + \mathbf{fm}) + \mathbf{m}$. If the coefficients of the product $p(\mathbf{gr} + \mathbf{fm})$ are smaller than $q/2$, then one can recover $\mathbf{m}$ by taking the above value modulo p.

One important area of optimization (and what was already recognized in the original NTRU scheme [19]) is that the product $p(\mathbf{gr}+\mathbf{fm})$ does not *always* need to be less than $q/2$, but only with very high probability. On the one hand, this probability should be negligible, as obtaining decryption failures on honestly-generated ciphertexts is the folklore way of recovering the secret key in LWE-based schemes. On the other hand, the decryption error can be defined as an *information-theoretic* quantity. Unlike the security parameter, there is therefore no safety margin needed as there is no danger of a better algorithm being found to lower this quantity.

To make the decryption error an information-theoretic quantity, one should define it as being worst-case when the adversary is even given the secret key [20]. In LWE-based schemes, the message is an *additive* term in the decryption proce-dure, and since the message's coefficients are generally small (normally in $\{0, 1\}$), there is no difference between a worst-case and an "average-case" (or even best-case) message. In NTRU, however, as we saw from the decryption equation, we need the quantity $p(\mathbf{gr} + \mathbf{fm})$ to be smaller than $q/2$, and $\mathbf{m}$ is multiplied by $\mathbf{f}$. Purposefully choosing a "bad" $\mathbf{m}$ can, therefore, make a large difference (increasing the decryption error by factors larger than 2^{100} is normal for stan-dard parameter choices). The naive way to keep the worst-case decryption error small is to increase the modulus q so that encryption errors do not occur. But increasing q weakens the security of the scheme by making the lattice-reduction algorithms more effective.

In this paper, we demonstrate three different ways of handling the decryption error. The first way is a generic transformation ACWC_0 from any scheme into one in which the message does not affect the decryption error. Hence the worst-case correctness error of the transformed scheme equals the average-case correctness error of the original scheme. This transformation is most likely folklore, and it is presented in Fig. 5 on page 16. The downside of this transformation is that it increases the ciphertext size by the message length.

The two next manners in which a worst-case decryption error is handled pre-serves the ciphertext size of the underlying scheme. The transformation ACWC (Fig. 6 on page 18) requires some specific properties of the distribution from which the message is generated. A natural distribution that satisfies this prop-erty is having coefficients uniformly-random modulo p. When p is not a power of 2, this distribution is not particularly pleasant to sample with AVX2 optimizations (due to the branching caused by rejection sampling), and so it was proposed in [21] to sample the distribution as a binomial distribution modulo p. Since the binomial distribution is very easy to sample by summing up and subtracting random bits, and because this value modulo p is pretty close to the uniform distribution, this is a more preferable way of sampling the secret coefficients. Still, being required to only sample the message $\mathbf{m}$ according to the uniform distribution could be an acceptable compromise. It is an interesting open problem as to whether our transformation can still be proved secure under the same assumptions for a different, more easily sampled, distribution of the message.

Our final way of handling adversarial-generated messages does not involve any transformation, but rather shows how for certain distributions of $\mathbf{m}$, the worst-case decryption error is not much worse than the average-case (or best-case), as in LWE-based schemes. Consider the coefficients of $\mathbf{m}$ as consisting of a message part μ and an error part ϵ. One has this implicit split by defining a function $f(\mu, \epsilon) = \mathbf{m}$ in a particular way where ϵ and μ are sampled independently. A property that we need from f is that $f(\mu, \epsilon) \bmod 2 = \mu$. Thus if one recovers $\mathbf{m}$, one can also recover μ. If we want to choose $\mathbf{m}$ according to the binomial distribution (as in e.g. NewHope [3], Kyber [5], or Saber [10]), then f can be a very simple function as described in Lemma 4.1. And of course, we also want the decryption error of this function to be approximately the same for all adversarially-chosen μ. It turns out that because the adversary only gets to set the residue modulo 2 in the binomial distribution, he has no control over the sign of the final output, nor the variance of the conditional distribution. And for this reason, the worst-case error distribution is close to the random one.

A further observation is that if we only need to recover $\mu = \mathbf{m} \bmod 2$, then there is no need to set the parameter p large enough so as to be able to recover the entire $\mathbf{m}$. In particular, we could just set $p = 2$ and the decryption procedure would still work. By decoupling the magnitude of p from the magnitude of the coefficients of $\mathbf{m}$, we can set $\mathbf{m}$ to be large (which increases the hardness of Ring-LWE), while keeping $p = 2$. The value of p has no effect on the hardness of any version of Ring-LWE (since $p\mathbf{h}$ is as uniform as just $\mathbf{h}$), and based on the state of affairs regarding solving Ring-LWE problems, finding $\mathbf{m} \bmod 2$ is as hard as finding $\mathbf{m}$. We discuss the complexity of this problem in Sect. 4.3 and present the scheme in Sect. 4.4.

1.3 Proofs in the (Q)ROM

Our two transformations ACWC_0 and ACWC are defined relative to random oracles, and have proofs in the ROM that are conceptually very simple. We show that ACWC_0 transforms any one-way secure (OW-CPA) encryption scheme into one that is IND-CPA secure, and that ACWC transforms any OW-CPA secure encryption scheme into one that is also OW-CPA secure. Note that we cannot prove IND-CPA security of ACWC since there exist instantiations for which application of ACWC yields a scheme that simply isn't IND-CPA secure.[4] By working with q-OW-CPA security,[5] a slight generalisation of OW-CPA security, we can combine the aforementioned transformations with the well-known Fujisaki-Okamoto transformation $FO^\perp$ in a way such that we obtain a tight proof for the resulting KEMs.

Since post-quantum security is a central goal of the constructions in this paper, we also prove all our results in the quantum random oracle model (QROM). That is, we show the security even if the adversary can perform queries to the random oracle in superposition between different inputs. The two constructions involving the random oracle are $ACWC_0$ and ACWC. We show that $ACWC_0$ transforms a one-way secure (OW-CPA) encryption scheme into an IND-CPA secure one. This proof is a reasonably straightforward application of the one-way to hiding theorem, O2H [31] in the variant from [4]. (O2H is a common technique used in random oracle proofs for encryption schemes.) The drawback of the use of O2H is that it introduces a square-root in the adversary's advantage. (That is, if the adversary has ε advantage against the underlying scheme and it makes q random oracle queries, then it has advantage $O(\sqrt{q^2 \varepsilon})$ against the result of the transformation.)

In contrast, security of ACWC does not have an obvious proof using O2H. Instead, we use the measure-and-reprogram technique (M&R) from [11,13]. This technique was developed for proving the security of the Fiat-Shamir transform. The fact that this technique works here is unexpected for two reasons: First, it was designed specifically with transformations of sigma-protocols (or related structures) into signatures or non-interactive proof systems in mind; transformations of encryption schemes such as ACWC have a very different structure. Second, M&R is a technique for adaptive reprogramming of the random oracle: Its core feature is, on a high level, that we can measure a query that the adversary will use later for its attack (e.g., as part of a forged signature), and sneak in a value of interest Θ into the answer to exactly that query (e.g., the challenge in a sigma-protocol). But in our setting, there is no such value of interest Θ. (We use a random value Θ when invoking the M&R theorem because that is technically required, but we would be perfectly happy if the random oracle was not reprogrammed at all.) We thus "misuse" the M&R for a situation where reprogramming is not required in the first place. This raises the interesting open question whether there could be variants of the M&R theorem that only cover the measurement-part of it (without reprogramming) but have tighter parameters and could be used in situations such as ours to produce a tighter reduction.

---

[4] Say that PKE has message space $\mathcal{M} = \mathcal{M}_1 \times \mathcal{M}_2$, and say that PKE's encryptions of messages $M_1 \| M_2$ leak M_1 and the first bit of M_2. When instantiated with the classical one-time-pad, ACWC encrypts a message m by sampling a message $M_1 \leftarrow \mathcal{M}_1$ and encrypting $M_1 \| m \oplus F(M_1)$, thereby leaking the first bit of m.

[5] In q-OW-CPA security the adversary is given an encryption of a random plaintext and wins if it returns a set of cardinality at most q containing the plaintext. For $q = 1$ this is OW-CPA security.

$$
\begin{array}{ccc}
\text{NTRU-A (§4.4)} & \xdashrightarrow[\text{L. 2.1, Th. 2.3}]{\text{FO}^\perp} & \text{CCA-NTRU-A} \\
\text{OW-CPA} & & \\[2mm]
\text{GenNTRU}[U_3^d] & \xrightarrow[\text{L. 2.2, Th. 3.9}]{\text{ACWC (§3.2)}} & \text{NTRU-B (§4.5)} & \xrightarrow[\text{Th. 2.3}]{\text{FO}^\perp} & \text{CCA-NTRU-B} \\
\text{PRE-CPA} & & q\text{-OW-CPA} & & \\[2mm]
\text{GenNTRU}[\bar{\psi}_2^d] & \xrightarrow[\text{L. 2.2, Th. 3.3}]{\text{ACWC}_0 \text{ (§3.1)}} & \text{NTRU-C (§4.5)} & \xrightarrow[\text{[20]}]{\text{FO}^\perp} & \text{CCA-NTRU-C} \\
\text{PRE-CPA} & & \text{IND-CPA} & &
\end{array}
$$

$\underbrace{\hspace{4cm}}$ average-case correctness error $\underbrace{\hspace{4cm}}$ worst-case correctness error $\underbrace{\hspace{3cm}}$ CCA-secure KEM

Fig. 1. Overview: How to obtain efficient IND-CCA-secure KEMs from our NTRU-based PKE schemes. Solid arrows indicate tight reductions in the ROM, dashed arrows indicate non-tight reductions. q-OW-CPA is a strengthening of standard OW-CPA security, where the adversary is allowed to return q many guesses (instead of just one). PRE-CPA security stands preimage resistance which in the setting of NTRU is essentially equivalent to OW-CPA security.

Furthermore, the use of M&R also leads to better parameters than we got using O2H: The advantage of the adversary against the result of the transformation ACWC is $O(q^2\varepsilon)$, i.e., no square-root is involved. (However, in contrast to ACWC$_0$, we only get one-way security. This is not a limitation of the proof technique, though, but stems from the fact that ACWC does not achieve IND-CPA security. But note that in a setting were we only need one-way security, we still do not have a better bound than $\sqrt{q^2\varepsilon}$ for ACWC$_0$; in this case, ACWC gives strictly better security.)

1.4 Concrete Results and Comparison to the State of the Art

We now describe the various ways that one can instantiate NTRU using the techniques described in this paper and compare it to other lattice-based schemes. We defined three different ways to instantiate NTRU, with all three approaches being in the same ring and only differing in the secret distributions and the manner in which it is transformed into a scheme with a small "worst-case" decryption error. When working over the ring $\mathbb{Z}_q[X]/(X^d - X^{d/2}+1)$, we will write NTRU-A$_q^d$ to be the scheme in Fig. 7 which did not require any transformation. By NTRU-B$_q^d$, we denote the scheme presented in Fig. 9 which is derived from the generic NTRU scheme GenNTRU (Fig. 8) by utilizing the size-preserving transformation from Fig. 6. And by NTRU-C$_q^d$, we refer to the scheme in Fig. 10 derived from the folklore transformation of the generic NTRU scheme GenNTRU (Fig. 8) in Fig. 5. All of the aforementioned schemes are CPA-secure, and we use the standard FO-transformation from Fig. 4 to create a CCA-KEM. The above is summarized in the overview Fig. 1.

In Table 1, we summarize the "interesting" instantiations of the schemes described in this paper having between 150 and 350 bits of security. We also compare these to other instantiations of NTRU and Module-LWE based schemes in Fig. 2. For a consistent evaluation of security, we used the online LWE hardness estimator [2]. This estimator has undergone some updates since its initial release, but still does not (as of this writing) include some recent cryptanalytic techniques (e.g. [14]) which could lower the security a little bit. Nevertheless, it still provides very meaningful results for comparing between various schemes.

In comparison to NTRU-HRSS, which was a finalist in the NIST standardization process, NTRU-C$_{2917}^{648}$ is based on an NTRU problem with the same error distribution, and has an approximately equal security level. But due to the fact that we show how to control the worst-case decryption error, the ciphertext/public key sizes are 15% smaller. If one looks at NTRU-C$_{3457}^{768}$, which has a similar public key/ciphertext size as NTRU-HRSS-701, one sees that the tradeoff for no error vs. 2^{-252} error is 30 bits of security, and the difference in security is even larger if one considers the NTRU-A version. In our opinion, exchanging such a large security margin in return for reducing 2^{-250} to 0 in the information-theoretic decryption error term, is not a sensible trade-off. The comparison of our NTRU instantiations to Kyber shows that the two schemes are essentially on the same size/security curve.

We produced a sample implementation of NTRU-A$_{2917}^{648}$, as it is most similar in security to NTRU-HRSS-701. In Table 3, we compare this scheme to NTRU-HRSS and other highly-efficient lattice-based schemes such as Kyber and NTTRU. The efficiency of our implementation is similar to that of Kyber-512, even though the NTRU variant has about 30 extra bits of security. The efficiency improvement is due to the fact that there is no matrix sampling required in NTRU-based schemes. When compared to NTRU-HRSS-701, there is a clear difference in efficiency, with NTRU-A being over 15X faster for round-trip ephemeral key exchange. The running time of NTRU-C should be quite similar, and NTRU-B will be a little hampered by the more complicated (uniform vs. binomial) error distribution, but should also be close.

While all the parameters in Table 1 are over rings of the form $\mathbb{Z}_q[X]/(X^d - X^{d/2}+1)$, we mention that another interesting instantiation would be a version of NTRU-A from Fig. 7 with $\eta = \psi_3^d$ over the ring $\mathbb{Z}_{3329}[X]/(X^{512} + 1)$. This would have exactly the security of Level 1 Kyber, a decryption error of 2^{-197}, and public key/ciphertext sizes of 768 bytes. The parameters make it an attractive NIST level 1 candidate. The one difference is that the inertia degree would be 4, which requires one to do inversions and multiplications in degree 4 rings, but we don't believe that this should cause a noticeable slowdown.

2 Preliminaries

2.1 Notation

If $\mathcal{M}$ is a finite set and $\psi_{\mathcal{M}}$ is a distribution on $\mathcal{M}$, then $m \leftarrow \psi_{\mathcal{M}}$ samples m from $\mathcal{M}$ according to $\psi_{\mathcal{M}}$. We write $m \leftarrow \mathcal{M}$ to denote sampling according to the uniform distribution. For a random variable X, $H_\infty(X)$ denotes its min-entropy.

Table 1. Parameters for the NTRU schemes CCA-NTRU-A, CCA-NTRU-B, and CCA-NTRU-C from this paper. All of the variants of the NTRU schemes work over the same ring, with the only difference being the underlying distributions of the secrets and messages, as well as the transformation (if one is necessary) from an instance with worst-case decryption error to one with average-case. The public key and ciphertext are of the same length (except for the ciphertext of CCA-NTRU-C, which is 32 bytes larger) and it is reported in bytes. The inertia degree is the smallest degree of the polynomial ring over which one has to perform operations at the bottom of the NTT tree (for efficiency, one may not always want to split down to the smallest possible degree, though). The parameter δ is the decryption error for a worst-case message (computed via a Pari script), and the security (in the ROM) is obtained using the LWE estimator script [2].

d (dim.)	q (mod.)	inertia degree	pk & ct (B)^a	$\log_2(\delta)$ CCA-NTRU-A	security	$\log_2(\delta)$ CCA-NTRU-B	security	$\log_2(\delta)$ CCA-NTRU-C	security
576	2593	2	864	-150	162	-165	155	-187	153
576	3457	1	864	-257	157	-297	150	-333	149
648	2917	2	972	-170	180	-187	172	-211	171
648	3889	1	972	-289	175	-335	166	-376	165
768	3457	2	1152	-202	210	-222	201	-252	199
864	3457	3	1296	-182	238	-197	227	-224	225
972	3889	3	1458	-206	265	-223	253	-253	251
1152	3457	1	1728	-140	321	-147	306	-167	304
1296	3889	1	1944	-158	358	-166	342	-189	339
1296	6481	3	2106	-420	339	-471	324	-530	322

^{a} The ciphertext size for NTRU-C is 32 bytes larger.

Table 2. Comparison to Existing Work. The Kyber parameters are taken from the Round 3 submission to the NIST PQC Standardization Process. The NTTRU parameters are from [26], and the NTRU-HRSS-701 parameters are from [21], and the NTRU-HRSS-1373 instantiation is from the comments to the NIST PQC mailing list. For consistency of comparing these schemes to those in Table 1, the security of the schemes are computed using the LWE estimator script [2].

	dimension	modulus	pk (B)	ct (B)	$\log_2(\delta)$	security
Kyber-512	512	3329	800	768	-139	148
Kyber-768	768	3329	1184	1088	-164	212
Kyber-1024	1024	3329	1568	1568	-174	286
NTTRU	768	7681	1248	1248	-1217	183
NTRU-HRSS-701	701	8192	1138	1138	$-\infty$	166
NTRU-HRSS-1373	1373	16384	2401	2401	$-\infty$	314

Table 3. Number of cycles (on a Skylake machine) for various operations of a CCA-secure KEM. The numbers for Kyber-512 and Kyber-768 are taken from [17, Table 3], which shows an improved implementation of Kyber90's (i.e. the version using AES and SHA-256 instead of SHAKE) when using prefix hashing and employing an explicit reject in the decapsulation procedure.

Scheme	Key Gen	Encaps	Decaps	Total Round-Trip
CCA-NTRU-A$_{2917}^{648}$ (This Paper)	6.2K	5.6K	7.3K	19.1K
NTRU-HRSS-701	220.3K	34.6K	65K	319.9K
NTTRU	6.4K	6.1K	7.9K	20.4K
Kyber-512 (90's)	6.2K	7.9K	9.2K	23.3K
Kyber-768 (90's)	11K	13.1K	14.8K	38.9K

For the sake of completeness, we summarise all relevant quantum preliminaries in the full version [16].

2.2   Cryptographic Definitions

PUBLIC-KEY ENCRYPTION. A public-key encryption scheme PKE = (Gen, Enc, Dec) consists of three algorithms, a probability distribution $\psi_\mathcal{M}$ on a finite message space $\mathcal{M}$. If no probability distribution is specified we assume $\psi_\mathcal{M}$ to be the uniform distribution. The key generation algorithm KeyGen outputs a key pair (pk, sk), where pk also defines a finite randomness space $\mathcal{R} = \mathcal{R}(pk)$. The encryption algorithm Enc, on input pk and a message $m \in \mathcal{M}$, outputs an encryption $c \leftarrow \mathsf{Enc}(pk, m)$ of m under the public key pk. If necessary, we make the used randomness of encryption explicit by writing $c := \mathsf{Enc}(pk, m; r)$, where $r \in \mathcal{R}$. By $\psi_\mathcal{R}$ we denote be the distribution of r in Enc, which we require to be independent of m. The decryption algorithm Dec, on input sk and a ciphertext c, outputs either a message $m = \mathsf{Dec}(sk, c) \in \mathcal{M}$ or a special symbol $\perp \notin \mathcal{M}$ to indicate that c is not a valid ciphertext.

RANDOMNESS RECOVERABILITY. PKE is randomness recoverable (RR) if there exists an algorithm Recover such that for all $(pk, sk) \in \mathsf{supp}(\mathsf{Gen})$ and $m \in \mathcal{M}$, we have that

$$\Pr\left[\forall m' \in \mathsf{Preimg}(pk, c)\colon \mathsf{Enc}(pk, m'; \mathsf{Recover}(pk, m', c)) \neq c \mid c \leftarrow \mathsf{Enc}(pk, m)\right] = 0,$$

where the probability is taken over $c \leftarrow \mathsf{Enc}(pk, m)$ and $\mathsf{Preimg}(pk, c) := \{m \in \mathcal{M} \mid \exists r \in \mathcal{R}\colon \mathsf{Enc}(pk, m; r) = c\}$. Additionally, we will require that Recover returns $\perp$ if it is run with input $m \notin \mathsf{Preimg}(pk, c)$.

CORRECTNESS ERROR. PKE has (worst-case) correctness error δ [20] if

$$\mathbb{E}\left[\max_{m \in \mathcal{M}} \Pr\left[\mathsf{Dec}(sk, \mathsf{Enc}(pk, m)) \neq m\right]\right] \leq \delta,$$

where the expectation is taken over $(pk, sk) \leftarrow$ Gen and the choice of the random oracles involved (if any). PKE has average-case correctness error δ relative to distribution $\psi_{\mathcal{M}}$ over $\mathcal{M}$ if

$$\Pr[\mathsf{Dec}(sk, \mathsf{Enc}(pk, m)) \neq m] \leq \delta,$$

where the probability is taken over $(pk, sk) \leftarrow$ Gen, $m \leftarrow \psi_{\mathcal{M}}$ and the randomness of Enc. This condition is equivalent to

$$\mathbb{E}\left[\Pr[\mathsf{Dec}(sk, \mathsf{Enc}(pk, m)) \neq m]\right] \leq \delta,$$

where the expectation is taken over $(pk, sk) \leftarrow$ Gen, the choice of the random oracles involved (if any), and $m \leftarrow \psi_{\mathcal{M}}$.

SPREADNESS. PKE is weakly γ-spread [12] if

$$\mathbb{E}\left[\max_{m \in \mathcal{M}, c \in \mathcal{C}} \Pr[\mathsf{Enc}(pk, m) = c]\right] \leq 2^{-\gamma},$$

where the probability is taken over the random coins of encryptions and the expectation is taken over $(pk, sk) \leftarrow$ Gen.

SECURITY. In the usual one-way game OW-CPA for PKE, the adversary has to decrypt a ciphertext c^* of a random plaintext $m^* \leftarrow \psi_{\mathcal{M}}$ by sending *one* candidate m' back to the challenger, and wins if $m' = m^*$. In the generalized q-OW-CPA game, the adversary gets to send a set $\mathcal{Q}$ of size at most q and wins if $m^* \in \mathcal{Q}$. The formal definition of q-OW-CPA is given in Fig. 2 and the advantage function of an adversary $\mathcal{A}$ is

$$\mathsf{Adv}_{\mathsf{PKE}}^{q\text{-OW-CPA}}(\mathcal{A}) := \Pr\left[q\text{-OW-CPA}_{\mathsf{PKE}}^{\mathcal{A}} \Rightarrow 1\right].$$

For $q = 1$ one recovers standard OW-CPA security, i.e., OW-CPA := 1-OW-CPA. We also introduce preimage resistance of PKE by the defining the advantage function of an adversary $\mathcal{A}$ as

$$\mathsf{Adv}_{\mathsf{PKE}}^{\mathsf{PRE\text{-}CPA}}(\mathcal{A}) := \Pr\left[\mathsf{PRE\text{-}CPA}_{\mathsf{PKE}}^{\mathcal{A}} \Rightarrow 1\right],$$

Game q-OW-CPA	Game PRE-CPA	Game IND-CPA
$(pk, sk) \leftarrow$ KeyGen	$(pk, sk) \leftarrow$ KeyGen	$(pk, sk) \leftarrow$ Gen
$m^* \leftarrow \psi_{\mathcal{M}}$	$m^* \leftarrow \psi_{\mathcal{M}}$	$(m_0, m_1) \leftarrow \mathcal{A}_1(pk)$
$c^* \leftarrow \mathsf{Enc}(pk, m^*)$	$c^* \leftarrow \mathsf{Enc}(pk, m^*)$	$b \leftarrow \{0, 1\}$
$\mathcal{Q} \leftarrow \mathcal{A}(pk, c^*)$	$(m, r) \leftarrow \mathcal{A}(pk, c^*)$	$c^* \leftarrow \mathsf{Enc}(pk, m_b)$
$\mathbf{return}\ [\![m^* \in \mathcal{Q} \wedge \vert\mathcal{Q}\vert \leq q]\!]$	$\mathbf{return}\ [\![\mathsf{Enc}(pk, m; r) = c^*]\!]$	$b' \leftarrow \mathcal{A}_2(pk, c^*)$
		$\mathbf{return}\ [\![b = b']\!]$

Fig. 2. Left: q-Set One-Wayness game q-OW-CPA for PKE, where $q = 1$ is standard OW-CPA. Middle: Preimage resistance game PRE-CPA for PKE. Right: game IND-CPA for PKE and adversary $\mathcal{A} = (\mathcal{A}_1, \mathcal{A}_2)$.

where game PRE-CPA is given in Fig. 2.

Finally, we define the IND-CPA advantage for an adversary $\mathcal{A}$ as

$$\mathsf{Adv}_{\mathsf{PKE}}^{\mathsf{IND\text{-}CPA}}(\mathcal{A}) := \left| \Pr\left[\mathsf{IND\text{-}CPA}_{\mathsf{PKE}}^{\mathcal{A}} \Rightarrow 1\right] - \frac{1}{2} \right| ,$$

where the game $\mathsf{IND\text{-}CPA}_{\mathsf{PKE}}^{\mathcal{A}}$ is defined in Fig. 2.

Lemma 2.1 (PKE OW-CPA $\implies$ PKE q-OW-CPA). *For any adversary $\mathcal{A}$ against the q-OW-CPA security of PKE, there exists an OW-CPA adversary against PKE with*

$$\mathsf{Adv}_{\mathsf{PKE}}^{q\text{-}\mathsf{OW\text{-}CPA}}(\mathcal{A}) \leq q \cdot \mathsf{Adv}_{\mathsf{PKE}}^{\mathsf{OW\text{-}CPA}}(\mathcal{B}) .$$

where the running time of $\mathcal{B}$ is about that of $\mathcal{A}$.

Proof. Sketch. The reduction $\mathcal{B}$ runs the adversary $\mathcal{A}$ on the inputs it got from its OW-CPA challenger and obtains the set $\mathcal{Q}$ of size q. It samples $m \leftarrow \mathcal{Q}$ uniformly at random and forwards m to the OW-CPA challenger, with probability $1/q$ it guessed the right one when the solution is contained in $\mathcal{Q}$, thus, the claim follows.

Lemma 2.2 (PKE PRE-CPA and RR $\overset{\mathsf{tightly}}{\implies}$ PKE q-OW-CPA). *If PKE is randomness recoverable, then for any adversary $\mathcal{A}$ against the q-OW-CPA security of PKE, there exists an PRE-CPA adversary $\mathcal{B}$ against PKE with*

$$\mathsf{Adv}_{\mathsf{PKE}}^{q\text{-}\mathsf{OW\text{-}CPA}}(\mathcal{A}) \leq \mathsf{Adv}_{\mathsf{PKE}}^{\mathsf{PRE\text{-}CPA}}(\mathcal{B}) .$$

where the running time of $\mathcal{B}$ is about $\mathbf{Time}\,(\mathcal{A}) + q \cdot (\mathbf{Time}\,(\mathsf{Recover}) + \mathbf{Time}\,(\mathsf{Enc}))$.

Proof. The reduction $\mathcal{B}$ forwards to $\mathcal{A}$ the challenge public-key and ciphertext c^* and obtains a set $\mathcal{Q}$. For every $m \in \mathcal{Q}$ it runs $r := \mathsf{Recover}(pk, m, c)$ and then runs $\mathsf{Enc}(pk, m; r)$ to obtain c. If c equals c^* it returns (m, r) as the solution, otherwise it continues with the search. If no element is found it can return a random $m \leftarrow \mathcal{M}$. Clearly, if $\mathcal{A}$ wins, then so does $\mathcal{B}$. Since the reduction $\mathcal{B}$ runs $\mathcal{A}$ once, and algorithms Recover and Enc at most q many times, the claim follows.

KEY-ENCAPSULATION MECHANISM. A key encapsulation mechanism KEM = (Gen, Encaps, Decaps) consists of three algorithms and a finite key space $\mathcal{K}$ similar to a PKE scheme, but Encaps does not take a message as input. The key generation algorithm Gen outputs a key pair (pk, sk), where pk also defines a finite randomness space $\mathcal{R} = \mathcal{R}(pk)$ as well as a ciphertext space $\mathcal{C}$. The encapsulation algorithm Encaps takes as input a public-key pk and outputs a key encapsulation ciphertext c and a key K, that is $(c, K) \leftarrow \mathsf{Encaps}(pk)$. The decapsulation algorithm Decaps, on input sk and a ciphertext c, outputs either a key $K = \mathsf{Decaps}(sk, c) \in \mathcal{K}$ or a special symbol $\perp \notin \mathcal{K}$ to indicate that c is not a valid ciphertext. We say KEM has correctness error δ if

$$\Pr\left[\mathsf{Decaps}(sk, c) = K \mid (c, K) \leftarrow \mathsf{Encaps}(pk)\right] \leq \delta ,$$

where the probability is taken over the randomness in Encaps and $(pk, sk) \leftarrow$ Gen. In terms of KEM's security, we consider the IND-CCA advantage function of an adversary $\mathcal{A}$:

$$\mathsf{Adv}_{\mathsf{KEM}}^{\mathsf{IND\text{-}CCA}}(\mathcal{A}) := \Pr\left[\mathsf{IND\text{-}CCA}_{\mathsf{KEM}}^{\mathcal{A}} \Rightarrow 1\right] - \frac{1}{2}$$

where game IND-CCA is defined in Fig. 3.

IND-CCA	Decaps($c \neq c^*$)
01 $(pk, sk) \leftarrow$ Gen	06 **return** Decaps(sk, c)
02 $(K_0, c^*) \leftarrow$ Encaps(pk)	
03 $K_1 \leftarrow \mathcal{K}, b \leftarrow \{0, 1\}$	
04 $b' \leftarrow \mathcal{A}^{\mathsf{Decaps}}(pk, c^*, K_b)$	
05 **return** $[\![b = b']\!]$	

Fig. 3. Game IND-CCA for KEM

THE FUJISAKI-OKAMOTO TRANSFORMATION WITH EXPLICIT REJECT. To a public-key encryption scheme PKE = (KeyGen, Enc, Dec) with message space $\mathcal{M}$ and associated uniform distribution over $\mathcal{M}$, randomness space $\mathcal{R}$, and hash functions H : $\{0,1\}^* \to \mathcal{R} \times \mathcal{K}$, we associate KEM := $\mathsf{FO}^{\perp}[\mathsf{PKE}, \mathsf{H}]$:= (KeyGen, Encaps, Decaps). Its constituting algorithms are given in Fig. 4. In [17] it was formally shown that including a *short prefix* of the public-key into the hash function provably improves the multi-user security of the Fujisaki-Okamoto transform. In this work, for simplicity, we will omit this inclusion and analyze the security in the single-user setting.

Theorem 2.3 (q_H-OW-CPA of PKE $\overset{\mathsf{ROM}}{\Longrightarrow}$ IND-CCA of KEM). *For any adversary* $\mathcal{A}$, *making at most* q_D *decapsulation,* q_H *hash queries, against the* IND-CCA *security of* KEM, *there exists an adversary* $\mathcal{B}$ *against the* q_H-OW-CPA *security of* PKE *with*

$$\mathsf{Adv}_{\mathsf{KEM}}^{\mathsf{IND\text{-}CCA}}(\mathcal{A}) \leq \mathsf{Adv}_{\mathsf{PKE}}^{q_H\text{-}\mathsf{OW\text{-}CPA}}(\mathcal{B}) + q_D 2^{-\gamma} + q_H \delta,$$

where the running time of $\mathcal{B}$ *is about that of* $\mathcal{A}$.

The proof is very similar to formerly known proofs for FO - after showing how to simulate oracle Decaps, we argue that the challenge key cannot be distinguished from random unless the adversary $\mathcal{A}$ queries H on the challenge plaintext. When reducing to plain OW-CPA security, a reduction would have to guess, but a reduction to q_H-OW-CPA security can simply keep a list of all of $\mathcal{A}$ queries to H and return this list as the list of plaintext guesses. For the sake of completeness, a full proof is given in the full version [16].

Theorem 2.4 (IND-CPA of PKE $\overset{\mathsf{ROM}}{\Longrightarrow}$ IND-CCA of KEM [20]). *For any adversary* $\mathcal{A}$, *making at most* q_D *decapsulation,* q_H *hash queries, against the* IND-CCA

Encaps(pk)	Decaps$^\perp$(sk, c)
01 $m \leftarrow \mathcal{M}$	05 $m' := \mathsf{Dec}(sk, c)$
02 $(r, K) := \mathsf{H}(m)$	06 $(r', K') := \mathsf{H}(m')$
03 $c := \mathsf{Enc}(pk, m; r)$	07 **if** $m' = \perp$ **or** $c \neq \mathsf{Enc}(pk, m'; r')$
04 **return** (K, c)	08 **return** $\perp$
	09 **return** K'

Fig. 4. Key encapsulation mechanism $\mathsf{KEM} = \mathsf{FO}^\perp[\mathsf{PKE}, \mathsf{H}]$, obtained from $\mathsf{PKE} = (\mathsf{KeyGen}, \mathsf{Enc}, \mathsf{Dec})$ with worst-case correctness error.

security of KEM, *there exists an adversary* $\mathcal{B}$ *against the* IND-CPA *security of* PKE *with*

$$\mathsf{Adv}^{\mathsf{IND}\text{-}\mathsf{CCA}}_{\mathsf{KEM}}(\mathcal{A}) \leq 2\big(\mathsf{Adv}^{\mathsf{IND}\text{-}\mathsf{CPA}}_{\mathsf{PKE}}(\mathcal{B}) + q_\mathsf{H}/|\mathcal{M}|\big) + q_\mathsf{D}2^{-\gamma} + q_\mathsf{H}\delta,$$

where the running time of $\mathcal{B}$ *is about that of* $\mathcal{A}$.

Theorem 2.5 (OW-CPA of $\mathsf{PKE} \stackrel{\mathsf{QROM}}{\Longrightarrow} \mathsf{IND}$-$\mathsf{CCA}$ of KEM [12]). *For any quantum adversary* $\mathcal{A}$, *making at most* q_D *decapsulation,* q_H *(quantum) hash queries, against the* IND-CCA *security of* KEM, *there exists a quantum adversary* $\mathcal{B}$ *against the* OW-CPA *security of* PKE *with*

$$\mathsf{Adv}^{\mathsf{IND}\text{-}\mathsf{CCA}}_{\mathsf{KEM}}(\mathcal{A}) \leq 2q\sqrt{\mathsf{Adv}^{\mathsf{OW}\text{-}\mathsf{CPA}}_{\mathsf{PKE}}(\mathcal{B})} + 24q^2\sqrt{\delta} + 24q\sqrt{qq_\mathsf{D}} \cdot 2^{-\gamma/4}.$$

where $q := 2(q_\mathsf{H} + q_\mathsf{D})$ *and* $\mathbf{Time}(\mathcal{B}) \approx \mathbf{Time}(\mathcal{A}) + O(q_\mathsf{H} \cdot q_\mathsf{D} \cdot \mathbf{Time}(\mathsf{Enc}) + q^2)$.

3   Worst-Case to Average-Case Decryption Error

In this section we introduce two worst-case to average case correctness transform for public-key encryption.

3.1   Simple Transformation $\mathsf{ACWC_0}$ with Redundancy

Let PKE be an encryption scheme with small average-case correctness error and F be a random oracle. We first introduce a simple transformation $\mathsf{ACWC_0}$ by describing $\mathsf{ACWC_0}[\mathsf{PKE}, \mathsf{F}]$ in Fig. 5 which adds λ bits of redundancy to the ciphertexts, where λ is the size of the message space. The resulting scheme has small worst-case correctness error.

Lemma 3.1. *If* PKE *is* δ-*average-case-correct, then* $\mathsf{PKE'} := \mathsf{ACWC_0}[\mathsf{PKE}, \mathsf{F}]$ *is* δ-*worst-case-correct.*

$\mathsf{Enc}'(pk, m \in \{0,1\}^\lambda)$	$\mathsf{Dec}'(sk, (c, u))$
01 $r \leftarrow \psi_{\mathcal{R}}$	03 $r := \mathsf{Dec}(sk, c)$
02 **return** $(\mathsf{Enc}(pk, r), \mathsf{F}(r) \oplus m)$	04 **return** $\mathsf{F}(r) \oplus u$

Fig. 5. $\mathsf{ACWC}_0[\mathsf{PKE}, \mathsf{F}]$ transforms PKE with small average-case correctness error, with message space $\mathcal{R}$ and associated distribution $\psi_{\mathcal{R}}$, into PKE' with small worst-case correctness error. The resulting scheme is λ bits longer.

Proof. We need to upper bound $\delta' = \mathbb{E} \max_{m \in \{0,1\}^\lambda} \Pr[\mathsf{Dec}'(\mathsf{Enc}'(m)) \neq m]$, where the expectation is taken over the internal randomness of KeyGen and the choice of random oracle F, and the probability is taken over the internal randomness of Enc'. Since a ciphertext $(\mathsf{Enc}(pk, r), \mathsf{F}(r) \oplus m)$ fails to decrypt iff $\mathsf{Enc}(pk, r)$ fails to decrypt, and since message r is drawn according to the distribution $\psi_{\mathcal{R}}$ on the message space of PKE,

$$\mathbb{E} \max_{m \in \{0,1\}^\lambda} \Pr[\mathsf{Dec}'(sk, \mathsf{Enc}'(pk, m)) \neq m] = \mathbb{E} \Pr_{r \leftarrow \psi_{\mathcal{R}}} [\mathsf{Dec}(sk, \mathsf{Enc}(pk, r)) \neq r] = \delta .$$

Lemma 3.2. *If* PKE *is weakly* γ*-spread, then so is* $\mathsf{ACWC}_0[\mathsf{PKE}, \mathsf{F}]$.

Proof. Follows directly by how PKE is used, since the ciphertext of $\mathsf{ACWC}_0[\mathsf{PKE}, \mathsf{F}]$ consists of the ciphertext of PKE, plus the message blinding part.

Theorem 3.3 (q_F-OW-CPA *of* $\mathsf{PKE} \overset{\mathrm{ROM}}{\Longrightarrow}$ IND-CPA *of* $\mathsf{ACWC}_0[\mathsf{PKE}, \mathsf{F}]$). *For any adversary* $\mathcal{A}$ *against the* IND-CPA *security of* $\mathsf{ACWC}_0[\mathsf{PKE}, \mathsf{F}]$, *issuing at most* q_F *queries to* F, *there exists an adversary* $\mathcal{B}$ *against the* OW-CPA *security of* PKE *with*

$$\mathsf{Adv}^{\mathsf{IND\text{-}CPA}}_{\mathsf{ACWC}[\mathsf{PKE},\mathsf{F}]}(\mathcal{A}) \leq \mathsf{Adv}^{q_\mathsf{F}\text{-}\mathsf{OW\text{-}CPA}}_{\mathsf{PKE}}(\mathcal{B}) ,$$

and the running time of $\mathcal{B}$ *is about that of* $\mathcal{A}$.

In the IND-CPA game for $\mathsf{ACWC}_0[\mathsf{PKE}, \mathsf{F}]$, the challenge ciphertext $c^* \leftarrow (\mathsf{Enc}(pk, r), \mathsf{F}(r) \oplus m_b)$ perfectly hides m_b unless the adversary queries F on r, thus breaking OW-CPA security of PKE. A reduction to q_F-OW-CPA security can simply keep a list of all of $\mathcal{A}$ queries to F and return this list as the list of plaintext guesses. For the sake of completeness, a full proof of Theorem 3.3 is given in the full version [16].

Theorem 3.4 (p_F-OW-CPA *of* $\mathsf{PKE} \overset{\mathrm{QROM}}{\Longrightarrow}$ IND-CPA *of* $\mathsf{ACWC}_0[\mathsf{PKE}, \mathsf{F}]$). *For any quantum adversary* $\mathcal{A}$ *against the* IND-CPA *security of* $\mathsf{ACWC}_0[\mathsf{PKE}, \mathsf{F}]$, *with query depth at most* d_F *and query parallelism at most* p_F, *there exists a quantum adversary* $\mathcal{B}$ *against the* OW-CPA *security of* PKE *with*

$$\mathsf{Adv}^{\mathsf{IND\text{-}CPA}}_{\mathsf{ACWC}[\mathsf{PKE},\mathsf{F}]}(\mathcal{A}) \leq 2d_\mathsf{F} \sqrt{\mathsf{Adv}^{p_\mathsf{F}\text{-}\mathsf{OW\text{-}CPA}}_{\mathsf{PKE}}(\mathcal{B})}.$$

and the running time of $\mathcal{B}$ *is about that of* $\mathcal{A}$.

Since the random oracle is now quantum-accessible, we will use the O2H lemma to argue that we can reprogramm F on r, again with the consequence that c^* now perfectly hides b. In accordance with the definition of the O2H extractor, our reduction will pick one of $\mathcal{A}$'s queries at random, measure this query, and return the measured plaintexts as its guess list. Since the query has query parallelism at most p_F, the list has at most p_F many elements. For the sake of completeness, a full proof of Theorem 3.4 is given in the full version [16].

3.2   Transformation **ACWC** Without Redundancy

Let PKE be an encryption scheme with small average-case correctness error, and let F be a random oracle. We will now introduce our second transformation ACWC by describing $\mathsf{ACWC}[\mathsf{PKE}, \mathsf{GOTP}, \mathsf{F}]$ in Fig. 6. Again, the resulting scheme has a small worst-case correctness error. Instead of adding redundancy to the ciphertexts, however, the scheme makes use of a generalised One-Time Pad GOTP.

Definition 3.5. *Function* $\mathsf{GOTP} : \mathcal{X} \times \mathcal{U} \to \mathcal{Y}$ *is called generalized one-time pad (for distributions* $\psi_\mathcal{X}, \psi_\mathcal{Y}, \psi_\mathcal{U}$*) if*

1. Decoding: *There exists an efficient inversion algorithm* Inv *such that for all* $x \in \mathcal{X}$, $u \in \mathcal{U}$, $\mathsf{Inv}(\mathsf{GOTP}(x, u), u) = x$.
2. Message-hiding: *For all* $x \in \mathcal{X}$, *the random variable* $\mathsf{GOTP}(x, u)$, *for* $u \leftarrow \psi_\mathcal{U}$, *has the same distribution as* $\psi_\mathcal{Y}$
3. Randomness-hiding: *For all* $u \in \mathcal{U}$, *the random variable* $\mathsf{GOTP}(x, u)$, *for* $x \leftarrow \psi_\mathcal{X}$, *has the same distribution as* $\psi_\mathcal{Y}$

A simple example of the generalized one-time pad $\mathsf{GOTP} : \{0,1\}^n \times \{0,1\}^n \to \{0,1\}^n$ for the uniform distributions is $\mathsf{GOTP}(x, u) := x \oplus u$ with inversion algorithm $\mathsf{Inv}(y, u) := y \oplus u$. The second and third properties are obviously satisfied since the XOR operation is a one-time pad.

Let PKE be a public-key encryption scheme with $\mathcal{M} = \mathcal{M}_1 \times \mathcal{M}_2$, where $\psi_\mathcal{M} = \psi_{\mathcal{M}_1} \times \psi_{\mathcal{M}_2}$ is a product distribution. Let $\mathsf{GOTP} : \mathcal{M}' \times \mathcal{U} \to \mathcal{M}_2$ be a generalized one-time pad for distribution $\psi_{\mathcal{M}_2}$ and $\mathsf{F} : \mathcal{M}_1 \to \mathcal{U}$ be a random oracle. The associated distributions $\psi_{\mathcal{M}_1}, \psi_{\mathcal{M}_2}, \psi_{\mathcal{M}'}, \psi_\mathcal{U}$ do not necessarily have to be uniform. (If $\psi_\mathcal{U}$ is not uniform, then the distribution of the random oracle F is such that every output is independently $\psi_\mathcal{U}$-distributed.) PKE$'$ obtained by transformation $\mathsf{ACWC}[\mathsf{PKE}, \mathsf{GOTP}, \mathsf{F}]$ is described in Fig. 6.

Our first theorem relates the average-case correctness of PKE to the worst-case correctness of $\mathsf{ACWC}[\mathsf{PKE}, \mathsf{GOTP}, \mathsf{F}]$.

Lemma 3.6. *Let* PKE *be a public-key encryption scheme with* $\mathcal{M} = \mathcal{M}_1 \times \mathcal{M}_2$, *where* $\psi_\mathcal{M} = \psi_{\mathcal{M}_1} \times \psi_{\mathcal{M}_2}$ *is a product distribution, and let* $\|\psi_{\mathcal{M}_1}\| := \sqrt{\sum_{\mathcal{M}_1} \psi_1(M_1)^2}$. *Let* $\mathsf{GOTP} : \mathcal{M}' \times \mathcal{U} \to \mathcal{M}_2$ *be a generalized one-time pad (for*

$\mathsf{Enc}'(pk, m \in \mathcal{M}')$	$\mathsf{Dec}'(sk, c)$
01 $M_1 \leftarrow \psi_{\mathcal{M}_1}$	04 $M_1 \| M_2 := \mathsf{Dec}(sk, c)$
02 $M_2 := \mathsf{GOTP}(m, \mathsf{F}(M_1))$	05 $m := \mathsf{Inv}(M_2, \mathsf{F}(M_1))$
03 **return** $\mathsf{Enc}(pk, M_1 \| M_2)$	06 **return** m

Fig. 6. $\mathsf{ACWC}[\mathsf{PKE}, \mathsf{GOTP}, \mathsf{F}]$ transforms PKE with small average-case correctness error into PKE' with small worst-case correctness error. The output length of the two schemes is the same.

distributions $\psi_{\mathcal{M}'}, \psi_{\mathcal{U}}, \psi_{\mathcal{M}_2}$) *and* $\mathsf{F} : \mathcal{M}_1 \to \mathcal{U}$ *be a random oracle. If* PKE *is* δ-*average-case-correct then* $\mathsf{PKE}' := \mathsf{ACWC}[\mathsf{PKE}, \mathsf{GOTP}, \mathsf{F}]$ *is* δ' *worst-case-correct for*

$$\delta' = \delta + \|\psi_{\mathcal{M}_1}\| \cdot \left(1 + \sqrt{(\ln |\mathcal{M}'| - \ln \|\psi_{\mathcal{M}_1}\|)/2}\right).$$

Proof. For any fixed[6] key pair, $\delta'(pk, sk)$ can be bounded by an arbitrary $t \in \mathbb{R}^+$, plus the probability that $\delta'(pk, sk)$ exceeds t. To bound the latter, we set as t fixed-pair average-case correctness $\delta(pk, sk)$, plus $\|\psi_{\mathcal{M}_1}\| \cdot \sqrt{(c + \ln |\mathcal{M}'|)/2}$, and use helper Lemma 3.7 below. A full proof is given in the full version [16]. $\qed$

Lemma 3.7. *Let* g *be some function and* B *be some set such that*

$$\forall m \in \mathcal{M}, \quad \Pr_{r_1 \leftarrow \psi_1, r_2 \leftarrow \psi_2, u \leftarrow U}[g(m, r_1, r_2, u) \in B] \leq \mu, \tag{1}$$

where ψ_1 *and* ψ_2 *are independent. Let* F *be a random function mapping onto* U. *Define* $\|\psi_1\| = \sqrt{\sum_{r_1} \psi_1(r_1)^2}$. *Then for all but an* e^{-c} *fraction of random functions* F, *we have that* $\forall m \in \mathcal{M}$,

$$\Pr_{r_1 \leftarrow \psi_1, r_2 \leftarrow \psi_2}[g(m, r_1, r_2, \mathsf{F}(r_1)) \in B] \leq \mu + \|\psi_1\| \cdot \sqrt{(c + \ln |\mathcal{M}|)/2} \tag{2}$$

Proof. We show that for any fixed $m \in \mathcal{M}$, the probability in (2) holds for all but a $e^{-c} \cdot |\mathcal{M}|^{-1}$-fraction of random functions F. The claim then follows by the union bound. The full proof is provided in the full version [16]. $\qed$

Lemma 3.8. *If* PKE *is weakly* γ-*spread, then so is* $\mathsf{ACWC}[\mathsf{PKE}, \mathsf{GOTP}, \mathsf{F}]$.

Proof. Follows directly, since the ciphertext consists of the ciphertext of PKE. $\qed$

Theorem 3.9 (($q \cdot q_\mathsf{F}$)-**OW-CPA** *of* PKE $\overset{\mathrm{ROM}}{\Longrightarrow}$ q-OW-CPA *of* $\mathsf{ACWC}[\mathsf{PKE},$ $\mathsf{GOTP}, \mathsf{F}]$). *Let* $q \in \mathbb{N}$. *For any adversary* $\mathcal{A}$ *against the* q-OW-CPA *security of* $\mathsf{ACWC}[\mathsf{PKE}, \mathsf{GOTP}, \mathsf{F}]$, *making at most* q_F *random oracle queries, there exists an adversary* $\mathcal{B}$ *against the* ($q \cdot q_\mathsf{F}$)-*OW-CPA security of* $\mathsf{ACWC}[\mathsf{PKE}, \mathsf{GOTP}, \mathsf{F}]$ *with*

$$\mathsf{Adv}^{q\text{-OW-CPA}}_{\mathsf{ACWC}[\mathsf{PKE}, \mathsf{GOTP}, \mathsf{F}]}(\mathcal{A}) \leq \mathsf{Adv}^{(q \cdot q_\mathsf{F})\text{-OW-CPA}}_{\mathsf{PKE}}(\mathcal{B}) + q \cdot 2^{-H_\infty(\psi_{\mathcal{M}'})},$$

where the running time of $\mathcal{B}$ *is about* $\mathbf{Time}(\mathcal{A}) + \mathcal{O}(q \cdot q_\mathsf{F})$.

---

[6] In cases where the support of $\psi_{\mathcal{M}_1}$ is some finite set R, it may be sometimes convenient to upper bound $\|\psi_{\mathcal{M}_1}\|$ by $\|\psi_{\mathcal{M}_1}\|_\infty \cdot \sqrt{|R|}$, where $\|\psi_{\mathcal{M}_1}\|_\infty$ is the maximum probability for any element in R.

In the q-OW-CPA game for $\mathsf{ACWC}[\mathsf{PKE}, \mathsf{GOTP}, \mathsf{F}]$, the adversary is presented with an encryption $c^* \leftarrow \mathsf{Enc}(pk, M_1^* \| \mathsf{GOTP}(m^*, \mathsf{F}(M_1^*)))$ of a message pair $(M_1^*, m^*) \leftarrow \psi_{\mathcal{M}_1} \times \psi_{\mathcal{M}'}$, and has to return a list $\mathcal{Q}$ such that $m^* \in \mathcal{Q}$. Unless $\mathcal{A}$ queries F on M_1^*, m^* is perfectly hidden from $\mathcal{A}$ and $\mathcal{A}$ cannot win with probability better than $q \cdot 2^{-H_\infty(\psi_{\mathcal{M}'})}$. If $\mathcal{A}$ queries F on M_1^* and wins, a reduction can again record $\mathcal{A}$'s oracle queries, and then use the query list $\mathcal{L}_\mathsf{F}$ and $\mathcal{A}$'s one-way guessing list $\mathcal{Q}_\mathcal{A}$ to construct its set $\mathcal{Q}$ by going over all possible combinations $M' = M_1' \| M_2'$, where $M_1' \in \mathcal{L}_\mathsf{F}$ and $M_2' := \mathsf{GOTP}(m', \mathsf{F}(M_1'))$ for $m' \in \mathcal{Q}_\mathcal{A}$. If $\mathcal{A}$ queries F on M_1^* and wins, then $\mathcal{L}_\mathsf{F}$ will contain the right M_1^*, meaning that $\mathcal{B}$'s list $\mathcal{Q}$ will contain the challenge plaintext. Note that the ciphertext for $\mathcal{B}$ would be defined relative to $M_2^* \leftarrow \psi_{\mathcal{M}_2}$, but due to the properties of GOTP, $\mathcal{A}$'s one-way game can be conceptually changed such that its ciphertext is also defined relative to $M_2^* \leftarrow \psi_{\mathcal{M}_2}$, and $\mathcal{A}$ wins if it returns a list $\mathcal{Q}$ containing $m := \mathsf{Inv}(M_2^*, \mathsf{F}(M_1^*))$. For the sake of completeness, a full proof of Theorem 3.9 is given in the full version [16].

Theorem 3.10 (OW-CPA of PKE $\overset{\mathsf{QROM}}{\Longrightarrow}$ OW-CPA of $\mathsf{ACWC}[\mathsf{PKE}, \mathsf{GOTP}, \mathsf{F}]$). *For any quantum adversary $\mathcal{A}$ against the OW-CPA security of $\mathsf{ACWC}[\mathsf{PKE}, \mathsf{GOTP}, \mathsf{F}]$, making at most q_F random oracle queries, there exists a quantum adversary $\mathcal{B}$ against the OW-CPA security of PKE with*

$$\mathsf{Adv}_{\mathsf{ACWC}[\mathsf{PKE},\mathsf{GOTP},\mathsf{F}]}^{\mathsf{OW\text{-}CPA}}(\mathcal{A}) \leq (2q_\mathsf{F} + 1)^2 \, \mathsf{Adv}_{\mathsf{PKE}}^{\mathsf{OW\text{-}CPA}}(\mathcal{B}),$$

where the running time of $\mathcal{B}$ is about that of $\mathcal{A}$.

Intuitively, the proof follows the same idea as its classical counterpart. In contrast to the security proof for ACWC_0, however, we can not simply apply the O2H lemma, as a reduction needs both a query to F from which it can extract M_1^* *and* its final output m, and an O2H extractor would simply abort $\mathcal{A}$ once that $\mathcal{A}$ has issued the query to be extracted. We will therefore use the measure-and-reprogram technique (M&R) from [11,13], arguing that we can run the adversary, measure a random query, and continue running it afterwards to obtain its final output m. For the sake of completeness, a full proof of Theorem 3.10 is given in the full version [16].

4   NTRU Encryption over NTT Friendly Rings

In this section we present three instantiations of the NTRU encryption scheme in polynomial rings of the form $\mathbb{Z}_q[X]/(X^d - X^{d/2} + 1)$, where $d = 2^i 3^j$, where the parameters are set such that multiplication and inversion can be performed very efficiently using the NTT.

4.1   Notation

We denote by $\mathcal{R}$ the polynomial ring $\mathbb{Z}_q[X]/(X^d - X^{d/2} + 1)$, where the positive integer d (of the form $2^i 3^j$) and the prime q are implicit from context. Elements in $\mathcal{R}$ will be represented by polynomials of degree less than d, and we will denote these polynomials by bold lower-case letters. That is, all elements of $\mathcal{R}$ are of the form $\mathbf{h} = \sum_{i=0}^{d-1} \mathbf{h}_i X^i \in R$, where $\mathbf{h}_i \in \mathbb{Z}_q$. There is a natural correspondence between elements in $\mathcal{R}$ and vectors in $\mathbb{Z}_q^d$, where one simply writes the coefficients of a polynomial in vector form. As additive groups, the two are trivially isomorphic. We will thus sometimes abuse notation and for a vector $\vec{v}$, write $\mathbf{r} := \vec{v}$ to mean that the coefficients of the polynomial $\mathbf{r}$ are assigned the coefficients of the vector $\vec{v}$.

For an integer $h \in \mathbb{Z}_q$, we write $h \bmod {}^{\pm}q$ to mean the integer from the set $\{-\frac{q-1}{2}, \ldots, \frac{q-1}{2}\}$ which is congruent to h modulo q. Reducing an integer modulo 2 always maps it to a bit. These functions naturally extend to vectors and polynomials, where one applies the function individually to each coefficient. For a set S, the function $\mathsf{H}_S : \{0,1\}^* \to S$ denotes a hash function modeled as a random oracle that outputs a uniform distribution on S. Similarly, for a distribution ψ (over some implicit set S), we will write $\mathsf{H}_\psi : \{0,1\}^* \to S$ to denote a hash function modeled as a random oracle that outputs a distribution ψ. The function $\mathsf{pref}(\cdot)$ extracts a short (around 32-64 byte) prefix from an element of $\mathcal{R}$.

4.2   The Binomial Distribution

For an even k, we define the distribution ψ_k^d over $\mathbb{Z}^d$ to be the distribution

$$\sum_{i=1}^{k} \vec{a}_i - \sum_{i=1}^{k} \vec{b}_i, \quad \vec{a}_i, \vec{b}_i \leftarrow \{0,1\}^d. \tag{3}$$

The distribution $\bar{\psi}_k^d$ is the distribution over the set $\{-1,0,1\}^d$ defined as ψ_k^d reduced modulo 3. We will mostly be working with $\bar{\psi}_k^d$ and ψ_k^d for $k = 2$, which are, by definition, generated as $\vec{b} = \vec{b}_1 + \vec{b}_2 - \vec{b}_3 - \vec{b}_4$ and $\vec{b} \bmod {}^{\pm} 3$, where $\vec{b}_i \leftarrow \{0,1\}^d$. Each coefficient of $\vec{b}$ and $\vec{b} \bmod {}^{\pm} 3$ is distributed as

$$\psi_2 = \begin{array}{|c||c|c|c|c|c|} \hline \text{Output} & \text{-2} & \text{-1} & 0 & 1 & 2 \\ \hline \text{Prob} & 1/16 & 4/16 & 6/16 & 4/16 & 1/16 \\ \hline \end{array} \tag{4}$$

$$\bar{\psi}_2 = \begin{array}{|c||c|c|c|} \hline \text{Output} & \text{-1} & 0 & 1 \\ \hline \text{Prob} & 5/16 & 6/16 & 5/16 \\ \hline \end{array} \tag{5}$$

We now state a lemma, which is used for the construction of NTRU-A in Fig. 7 that shows that by creating the distribution ψ_2 in a special way, one of the components of the distribution can be completely recovered when having access to whole sample. Note that this cannot be done if each coefficient is generated as $b = b_1 + b_2 - b_3 - b_4$. For example, if $b = 0$, then every b_i has conditional probability of $1/2$ of being 0 or 1. If, on the other hand, we generate the distribution as $b = (b_1 - 2b_2b_3)(1 - 2b_4)$, where $b_i \leftarrow \{0,1\}$, then one can see that b_1 can be recovered by computing $b \bmod 2$.

Lemma 4.1. *The distribution* ψ_2^d *can be generated as*

$$\vec{b} = (\vec{b}_1 - 2\vec{b}_2 \odot \vec{b}_3) \odot (1 - 2\vec{b}_4),$$

where $\vec{b}_i \leftarrow \{0, 1\}^d$ *and* $\odot$ *denotes component-wise multiplication. Furthermore,* $\vec{b} \bmod 2 = \vec{b}_1$.

4.3   The NTRU Problem and Variants

In the framework for the NTRU trap-door function [19], the secret key consists of two polynomials $\mathbf{f}$ and $\mathbf{g}$ with small coefficients in a polynomial ring (e.g. $\mathcal{R}$) and the public key if the quotient $\mathbf{h} = \mathbf{g}\mathbf{f}^{-1}$. The hardness assumption states that given $(\mathbf{h}, \mathbf{hr} + \mathbf{e})$, where $\mathbf{r}, \mathbf{e}$ are sampled from some distribution with support of elements in $\mathcal{R}$ with small coefficients, it is hard to recover $\mathbf{e}$. For appropriately-set parameters, one can recover $\mathbf{e}$ when knowing $\mathbf{f}$, and we will discuss this when presenting the full encryption scheme later in the section. For now, we are mainly interested in the security of NTRU.

The security of the NTRU function described above is naturally broken down into two assumptions. The first is that the distribution of $\mathbf{h} = \mathbf{g}\mathbf{f}^{-1}$ is indistinguishable from a random element in $\mathcal{R}$. And the second assumption is essentially the Ring-LWE assumption which states that given $(\mathbf{h}, \mathbf{hr} + \mathbf{e})$, where $\mathbf{h}$ is uniform in $\mathcal{R}$ and $\mathbf{r}, \mathbf{e}$ are chosen from some distribution with small coefficients, it is hard to find $\mathbf{e}$ (and thus also $\mathbf{r}$). We point out that one can eliminate the need for the first assumption by choosing polynomials with coefficients that are small, but large enough, so that the quotient is statistically-close to uniform [29], but the resulting scheme ends up being significantly less efficient because the coefficients in the polynomials of the second (Ring-LWE) problem need to be rather small to compensate; and this in turn requires the dimension of the ring to be increased in order for the Ring-LWE problem to remain hard. The below definition formally states the first assumption for the distributions used in this paper.

Definition 4.2 (The $\mathcal{R}$-NTRU$_\eta$ assumption). *For a distribution η over the ring $\mathcal{R}$ and an integer p relatively-prime to q, the $\mathcal{R}$-NTRU$_\eta$ assumption states that $\mathbf{g} \cdot (p\mathbf{f} + 1)^{-1}$ is indistinguishable from a uniformly-random element in $\mathcal{R}$ when $\mathbf{g}$ and $\mathbf{f}$ are chosen from the distribution η, and $p\mathbf{f} + 1$ is invertible in $\mathcal{R}$.*

Another common version of the assumption simply states that $\mathbf{g} \cdot \mathbf{f}^{-1}$ is indistinguishable from random, and it doesn't appear that there is any difference in the hardness between the two. The reason that multiplication of $\mathbf{f}$ by p is useful is because it eliminates the need for an inversion (which cannot be done using NTT) during the decryption process; and so we use this version of the problem in the paper. The downside of this multiplication by p is that half of the "noise terms" in the decrypted ciphertext increase by a factor of p. We now define the Ring-LWE problem that is specific to our instantiation, and which forms the second assumption needed for the NTRU cryptosystem.

Definition 4.3 ($\mathcal{R}$-LWE$_\eta$). *Let η be some distribution over $\mathcal{R}$. In the $\mathcal{R}$-LWE problem, one is given $(\mathbf{h}, \mathbf{hr} + \mathbf{e})$, where $\mathbf{h} \leftarrow \mathcal{R}$ and $\mathbf{r}, \mathbf{e} \leftarrow \eta$, and is asked to recover $\mathbf{e}$.*

One can also define the decision version of the above assumption as

Definition 4.4 (Decision $\mathcal{R}$-LWE$_\eta$). *Let η be a distribution over $\mathcal{R}$. The decision $\mathcal{R}$-LWE assumption states that $(\mathbf{h}, \mathbf{hr} + \mathbf{e})$, where $\mathbf{h} \leftarrow \mathcal{R}$ and $\mathbf{r}, \mathbf{e} \leftarrow \eta$, is indistinguishable from $(\mathbf{h}, \mathbf{u})$, where $\mathbf{h}, \mathbf{u} \leftarrow \mathcal{R}$.*

In the original LWE definition of Regev [28], the distribution η was a rounded continuous Gaussian, as this was the distribution most convenient for achieving a worst-case to average-case reduction from certain lattice problems over solving $\mathcal{R}$-LWE$_\eta$. When implementing cryptographic primitives based on the hardness of $\mathcal{R}$-LWE$_\eta$, it is more convenient to take η to be a distribution that can be easily sampled. Some common distributions include uniform (although sometimes it is not that simple to sample) and those that can be generated as sums of Bernoulli random variables such as ψ_k and $\bar{\psi}_k$ from (4) and (5).

The most efficient known attack against the $\mathcal{R}$-NTRU and $\mathcal{R}$-LWE problems are lattice attacks. They work by defining a set

$$\mathcal{L}_{\mathbf{c}}^{\perp}(\mathbf{h}) = \{(\mathbf{v}, \mathbf{w}) \in \mathbb{Z}[X]/(X^d - X^{d/2} + 1) \; : \; \mathbf{hv} + \mathbf{w} \equiv \mathbf{c} \pmod{q}\}.$$

When $\mathbf{c} = \mathbf{0}$, the above set is closed under addition, and therefore forms a lattice. To distinguish the quotient $\mathbf{h} = \mathbf{g}/\mathbf{f}$, where $\mathbf{f}, \mathbf{g}$ have small coefficients, from a uniformly-random $\mathbf{h} \in \mathcal{R}$, one can try to find the shortest vector in $\mathcal{L}_{\mathbf{0}}^{\perp}(\mathbf{h})$. If $\mathbf{h}$ is random, then a vector of ℓ_2-norm less than $\Omega(\sqrt{qd})$ is very unlikely to exist in $\mathcal{L}_{\mathbf{c}}^{\perp}(\mathbf{h})$. On the other hand, if the coefficients of $\mathbf{f}, \mathbf{g}$ are noticeably less than $\sqrt{q}$, then $(\mathbf{f}, -\mathbf{g}) \in \mathcal{L}_{\mathbf{c}}^{\perp}(\mathbf{h})$, and so an algorithm that can find a good approximation to the shortest vector should find something of length significantly less than $\Omega(\sqrt{qd})$.

When $\mathbf{c} \neq 0$, $\mathcal{L}_{\mathbf{c}}^{\perp}(\mathbf{h})$ is a *shifted lattice* and finding the shortest vector in it is known as the Bounded Distance Decoding (BDD) problem. For practical parameters, the complexity of the two problems is identical. Interestingly, when q is very large with respect to the size of the secret coefficients, finding a short vector in $\mathcal{L}_{\mathbf{c}}^{\perp}(\mathbf{h})$ is significantly easier when $\mathbf{c} = 0$, as opposed to when $\mathbf{c}$ is random [1,8,15,22]. This phenomenon prevents the NTRU assumption from being used in scenarios requiring such a large gap (and so one uses Ring-LWE and Module-LWE schemes in those scenarios), such as in Fully-Homomorphic Encryption schemes. This security issue, however, does not seem to extend to the NTRU parameters that are used in practice for public key encryption and signature schemes.

We now define a version of the $\mathcal{R}$-LWE problem in which the adversary is not asked to recover the entire vector $\mathbf{e}$, but just $\mathbf{e} \bmod 2$.

Definition 4.5 ($\mathcal{R}$-LWE2$_\eta$). *Let η be a distribution over $\mathcal{R}$. In the $\mathcal{R}$-LWE problem, one is given $(\mathbf{h}, \mathbf{hr} + \mathbf{e})$, where $\mathbf{h} \leftarrow \mathcal{R}$ and $\mathbf{r}, \mathbf{e} \leftarrow \eta$, and is asked to recover $\mathbf{e} \bmod 2$.*

While we do not have a formal reduction from $\mathcal{R}$-LWE to $\mathcal{R}$-LWE2, based on the state of the art of how Ring-LWE problems are solved, the two are essentially equivalent. We now present two heuristic arguments for the equivalence of $\mathcal{R}$-LWE and $\mathcal{R}$-LWE2.

Suppose that there is an algorithm that solves $\mathcal{R}$-LWE2$_\eta$ and we feed it an instance $(\mathbf{h}, \mathbf{hr} + \mathbf{e})$ of $\mathcal{R}$-LWE$_\eta$. If the $\mathcal{R}$-LWE2$_\eta$ solver returns a correct $\mathbf{f} \equiv \mathbf{e}$ (mod 2), then we can create another instance

$$(2^{-1} \cdot \mathbf{h}, 2^{-1}\mathbf{hr} + 2^{-1}(\mathbf{e} - \mathbf{f})) = (\mathbf{h'r} + \mathbf{e'}).$$

Note that $\mathbf{h'}$ is still uniformly random and the distribution of $\mathbf{e'}$ is now "narrower" than that of the original $\mathbf{e}$ – if the coefficients of $\mathbf{e}$ were distributed as ψ_2, then each coefficient of $\mathbf{e'}$ has a probability $3/16$ of being ± 1 and $10/16$ of being 0. Based on the state of the art, a $\mathcal{R}$-LWE-type problem should be easier with this narrower distribution. So one should be able to call the $\mathcal{R}$-LWE2$_\eta$ oracle again, even though the distribution of $\mathbf{e'}$ is now different. It's easy to see now that this procedure will eventually recover the entire polynomial $\mathbf{e}$.

Another heuristic argument is based on a slightly-modified version of decision $\mathcal{R}$-LWE. In particular, if we assume that the decision $\mathcal{R}$-LWE problem, in which just the first polynomial coefficient in $\mathbb{Z}_q$ is noiseless, then there is a simple reduction from this problem to $\mathcal{R}$-LWE2$_\eta$. In the reduction, we simply add a noise with distribution η to the first coefficient, and we decide whether the decision $\mathcal{R}$-LWE instance is real or random based on whether or not the answer returned by the $\mathcal{R}$-LWE2$_\eta$ oracle matches our added error modulo 2. While the version of the decision $\mathcal{R}$-LWE problem where the first integer coefficient has no error is slightly different than usual, the current best-known algorithms would solve the decision problem by solving the search version. And in the search case, the two versions of the problem are equally hard.

The work of Brakerski et al. [7] considers this "First-is-Errorless" version of LWE and shows that it is essentially as hard as the usual version. Boudgoust et al. [6] extend this problem to it's Module-LWE variant and showed that an even stronger assumption has a (non-tight) reduction from the usual Module-LWE problem. In short, it is very reasonable to assume that the concrete hardness of the $\mathcal{R}$-LWE2$_\eta$ problem is the same as that of $\mathcal{R}$-LWE$_\eta$.

4.4   NTRU-A: Encryption Based on $\mathcal{R}$-NTRU + $\mathcal{R}$-LWE2 for $\eta = \psi_2^d$

We now give a construction of our first OW-CPA-secure encryption scheme, NTRU-A, whose hardness is based on the combination of the $\mathcal{R}$-NTRU$_\eta$ + $\mathcal{R}$-LWE2$_\eta$ problems for $\eta = \psi_2$. The way that this scheme differs from the more usual NTRU constructions is that the secret key does let one recover the entire $\mathbf{e}$. This can pose a problem because generally $\mathbf{e}$ the message in the OW-CPA NTRU scheme, and yet we can only recover a part of it. This is not a OW-CPA scheme and we will not be able to obtain a CCA-secure KEM using generic transformations.

We remedy this issue by only making the value $\mathbf{e}$ mod 2 be the message. This requires that for a given random message $\mathbf{m}$, the $\mathbf{e}$ is generated from the correct distribution (i.e. ψ_2) with the additional restriction that $\mathbf{m} = \mathbf{e} \bmod 2$. An interesting aspect of this scheme is that because the message is not the entire $\mathbf{e}$, the adversary does not have as much freedom to pick it so as to maximize the decryption error. If the adversary can only pick $\mathbf{e} \bmod 2$, it turns out that the worst-case decryption error is quite close to the "best case". We now proceed to describe the OW-CPA scheme in Fig. 7.

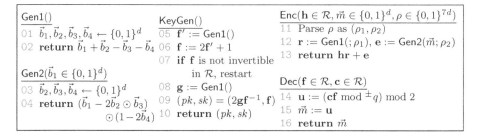

Fig. 7. OW-CPA Encryption Scheme NTRU-A based on the $\mathcal{R}\text{-NTRU}_{\psi_2} + \mathcal{R}\text{-LWE2}_{\psi_2}$ problems. Only the procedures Gen1 and Gen2 are randomized. We include the coins ρ as input for the Encryption algorithm (which will be passed to Gen1 and Gen2) because these are explicitly used in the CCA transformation. The coins used in the key generation are implicit.

OW-CPA Scheme. The distribution of the coefficients of the secret polynomials used in key generation and encryption ψ_2 (see (4)) and is produced by the Gen1() algorithm in Fig. 7. As per Lemma 4.1, this distribution can be generated as $b_1 + b_2 - b_3 - b_4$ or, equivalently, as $(b_1 - 2b_2b_3)(1 - 2b_4)$, where all the b_i are Bernoulli random variables. The reason the latter distribution is interesting to us is that modulo 2, it is one of the variables that creates it $- b_1$.

The secret key is generated by choosing polynomials $\mathbf{f}', \mathbf{g} \leftarrow \psi_2^d$ and computing $\mathbf{f} = 2\mathbf{f}' + 1$. If $\mathbf{f}$ is not invertible in $\mathcal{R}$, we restart. Otherwise, the public key is $\mathbf{h} = 2\mathbf{g}\mathbf{f}^{-1}$ and the secret key is $\mathbf{f}$.

To encrypt a message $\vec{m} \in \{0,1\}^d$, the encryptor first generates a random polynomial $\mathbf{r} \leftarrow \psi_2^d$ using the Gen1() procedure. He then needs to choose a polynomial $\mathbf{e}$ such that $\mathbf{e} \bmod 2$ (as a vector) is $\vec{m}$. Furthermore, when $\vec{m}$ is chosen uniformly at random from $\{0,1\}^d$, the distribution of $\mathbf{e}$ should be ψ_2^d. To create such a distribution, we define $\mathbf{e} = \text{Gen2}(\vec{m})$. By Lemma 4.1, $\mathbf{e}$ is distributed according to ψ_2^d. The ciphertext is $\mathbf{c} = \mathbf{hr} + \mathbf{e}$.

To decrypt the ciphertext $\mathbf{c} = \mathbf{hr} + \mathbf{e} = 2\mathbf{gr}/\mathbf{f} + \mathbf{e}$, we multiply it by $\mathbf{f}$, centralize it mod q, and then reduce modulo 2 to obtain

$$(\mathbf{cf} \bmod {}^\pm q) \bmod 2 = 2\mathbf{gr} + \mathbf{ef} \bmod 2 = 2\mathbf{gr} + 2\mathbf{ef}' + \mathbf{e} \bmod 2 \qquad (6)$$

If all the coefficients of $2\mathbf{gr} + 2\mathbf{ef'} + \mathbf{e}$ (as integers) are smaller than $q/2$, then modulo 2, this value will be exactly $\mathbf{e} \bmod 2$, which is $\bar{m}$. Since the coefficients of $\mathbf{e}$ have absolute value at most 2, in order to have decryption be correct, we need the coefficients of $\mathbf{gr} + \mathbf{ef'}$ to be less than $q/4 - 1$. We will now move on to show how to compute this probability.

Decryption Error for a Worst-Case Message. The decryption error of NTRU-A can be computed following the template given in [26, Section 3.2]. As discussed above, if a coefficient of $\mathbf{gr} + \mathbf{ef'}$ (as an integer) has absolute value less than $q/4 - 1$, then the output of that coefficient in (6) will be $\mathbf{e} \bmod 2$, as desired. So we now need to understand what each coefficient of $\mathbf{gr} + \mathbf{ef'}$ looks like. This is easiest to see via an example of how polynomial multiplication in the ring $\mathcal{R}$ can be represented by a matrix-vector product. If we, for example, want to multiply two polynomials $\mathbf{ab}$ in the ring $\mathbb{Z}_q[X]/(X^6 - X^3 + 1)$, where $\mathbf{a} = \sum_{i=0}^{5} \mathbf{a}_i$ and $\mathbf{b} = \sum_{i=0}^{5} \mathbf{b}_i$ then their product $\mathbf{c} = \sum_{i=0}^{5} \mathbf{c}_i$ can be written as in (7).

$$\begin{bmatrix} \mathbf{a}_0 & -\mathbf{a}_5 & -\mathbf{a}_4 & -\mathbf{a}_3 & -\mathbf{a}_2 - \mathbf{a}_5 & -\mathbf{a}_1 - \mathbf{a}_4 \\ \mathbf{a}_1 & \mathbf{a}_0 & -\mathbf{a}_5 & -\mathbf{a}_4 & -\mathbf{a}_3 & -\mathbf{a}_2 - \mathbf{a}_5 \\ \mathbf{a}_2 & \mathbf{a}_1 & \mathbf{a}_0 & -\mathbf{a}_5 & -\mathbf{a}_4 & -\mathbf{a}_3 \\ \mathbf{a}_3 & \mathbf{a}_2 + \mathbf{a}_5 & \mathbf{a}_1 + \mathbf{a}_4 & \mathbf{a}_0 + \mathbf{a}_3 & \mathbf{a}_2 & \mathbf{a}_1 \\ \mathbf{a}_4 & \mathbf{a}_3 & \mathbf{a}_2 + \mathbf{a}_5 & \mathbf{a}_1 + \mathbf{a}_4 & \mathbf{a}_0 + \mathbf{a}_3 & \mathbf{a}_2 \\ \mathbf{a}_5 & \mathbf{a}_4 & \mathbf{a}_3 & \mathbf{a}_2 + \mathbf{a}_5 & \mathbf{a}_1 + \mathbf{a}_4 & \mathbf{a}_0 + \mathbf{a}_3 \end{bmatrix} \cdot \begin{bmatrix} \mathbf{b}_0 \\ \mathbf{b}_1 \\ \mathbf{b}_2 \\ \mathbf{b}_3 \\ \mathbf{b}_4 \\ \mathbf{b}_5 \end{bmatrix} = \begin{bmatrix} \mathbf{c}_0 \\ \mathbf{c}_1 \\ \mathbf{c}_2 \\ \mathbf{c}_3 \\ \mathbf{c}_4 \\ \mathbf{c}_5 \end{bmatrix} \quad (7)$$

Notice that $\mathbf{c}_3, \mathbf{c}_4$, and $\mathbf{c}_5$ are a sum of three independently-generated integers of the form

$$c = ba + b'(a + a'). \quad (8)$$

The coefficient $\mathbf{c}_2$, however, is simply a sum of 6 independent random variables of the form ab. Or to make it look similar to (8), we can think of it as the sum of three random variables of the form

$$c = ba + b'a'. \quad (9)$$

It should be clear that the distribution of (8) is wider than that of (9), and so the probability that the coefficients which follow the former distribution will be outside of the "safe zone" is larger. The coefficients $\mathbf{c}_0$ and $\mathbf{c}_1$ are a hybrid of these two distributions. For example, $\mathbf{c}_1$ is the sum of one coefficient from (8) and two from (9); while $\mathbf{c}_2$ is the sum of two from (8) and one from (9).

To bound the probability that decryption will be correct, we should therefore bound the distribution of $\mathbf{c}_3, \mathbf{c}_4, \mathbf{c}_5$, or in the general case, a coefficient in the bottom half of $\mathbf{c}$ and then apply the union bound. So the widest distribution will consist of sums of $d/2$ random variables having the distribution as in (8). The term $\mathbf{gr}$ in (6) has this exact distribution, where each coefficient of $\mathbf{g}, \mathbf{r}$ is distributed according to Gen1().

The term $\mathbf{f}'\mathbf{e}$ is distributed differently because in our security proof we need to consider an adversarially-chosen message $\vec{m}$, after the adversary sees the public key. Because the adversary does not get to choose the whole message, but just the modulo 2 residue, it turns out that the failure probability for a worst-case message is not too different than for a uniformly random one. In (10), we give the distribution of a particular coefficient of $\mathbf{e}_i$ conditioned on the message bit being either 0 or 1.

$$\text{Gen2}(0) = \begin{array}{|c|c|c|c|} \hline \text{Output} & \text{-2} & 0 & 2 \\ \hline \text{Probability} & 0.125 & 0.75 & 0.125 \\ \hline \end{array} \quad \text{Gen2}(1) = \begin{array}{|c|c|c|} \hline \text{Output} & \text{-1} & 1 \\ \hline \text{Probability} & 0.5 & 0.5 \\ \hline \end{array} \quad (10)$$

One can see that in both cases the distribution is centered around 0 and has variance 1, and so one should not expect a very large difference in the decryption error. Experimentally, it turns out that the worst-case messages occur when choosing $\vec{m} = \vec{0}$. Furthermore, the worst-case message is the same for any secret key.[7] This implies that the worst-case correctness error is the average-case one where the distribution over the coefficients of $\mathbf{e}$ is as in Gen2(0) of (10). As in [3,5,26], the error probability reported in Table 1 is computed via polynomial multiplications which represent convolutions of random variables.

IND-CCA-Secure KEM. One can apply the Fujisaki-Okamoto transformation $\mathsf{FO}^\perp$ from Fig. 4 to obtain the IND-CCA secure version CCA-NTRU-A $:=$ $\mathsf{FO}^\perp[\mathsf{NTRU\text{-}A}, \mathsf{H}]$ of NTRU-A. The concrete security bounds on the IND-CCA security of CCA-NTRU-A from Table 4 can be derived in the ROM using Lemma 2.1 and Theorem 2.3 and in the QROM using Theorem 2.5.

Table 4. Bounds on the IND-CCA secure NTRU-variants CCA-NTRU-A, CCA-NTRU-B, and CCA-NTRU-C. Constants and negligible terms are suppressed for simplicity. The value q is the sum of all adversarial (random oracle and decryption) queries, i.e., $q = q_\mathsf{H} + q_\mathsf{D} + q_\mathsf{F}$. The ε values are the advantage functions of the underlying NTRU assumptions: $\varepsilon_A = \mathsf{Adv}^{\mathcal{R}\text{-NTRU}_\eta} + \mathsf{Adv}^{\mathcal{R}\text{-LWE2}_\eta}$ for $\eta = \psi_2^d$; $\varepsilon_B = \mathsf{Adv}^{\mathcal{R}\text{-NTRU}_\eta} + \mathsf{Adv}^{\mathcal{R}\text{-LWE}_\eta}$ for $\eta = U_3^d$ and $\varepsilon_C = \mathsf{Adv}^{\mathcal{R}\text{-NTRU}_\eta} + \mathsf{Adv}^{\mathcal{R}\text{-LWE}_\eta}$ for $\eta = \bar{\psi}_2^d$.

IND-CCA secure KEM	ROM	QROM
CCA-NTRU-A	$q(\varepsilon_A + \delta)$	$q\sqrt{\varepsilon_A} + q^2\sqrt{\delta}$
CCA-NTRU-B	$\varepsilon_B + q(3^{-\lambda} + \delta)$	$q^2(\sqrt{\varepsilon_B} + \sqrt{\delta})$
CCA-NTRU-C	$\varepsilon_C + q(2^{-\lambda} + \delta)$	$q^{1.5}(\sqrt[4]{\varepsilon_C} + q^{0.5}\sqrt{\delta})$

4.5 Generic NTRU Encryption and Error-Reducing Transformations

Figure 8 defines $\mathsf{GenNTRU}[\eta]$ relative to distribution η over $\mathcal{R}$. Note that $\mathsf{GenNTRU}[\eta]$ is randomness-recoverable (RR) because once we have $\mathbf{e}$ and

---

[7] This was verified experimentally by fixing the a, a' in (8) to all valid values and computing the probability of failure assuming that all the secret keys have this value.

$\mathbf{c} = \mathbf{hr} + \mathbf{e}$, we can compute $\mathbf{r} = (\mathbf{c} - \mathbf{e}) \cdot \mathbf{h}^{-1}$. Because we checked that $\mathbf{g}$ is invertible, it holds that $\mathbf{h} = 3\mathbf{gf}^{-1}$ also has an inverse.

KeyGen()

01 $\mathbf{f}', \mathbf{g} \leftarrow \eta$
02 $\mathbf{f} := 3\mathbf{f}' + 1$
03 **if** $\mathbf{f}$ or $\mathbf{g}$ is not invertible in $\mathcal{R}$, restart
04 **return** $(pk, sk) = (3\mathbf{gf}^{-1}, \mathbf{f})$

Enc($\mathbf{h} \in \mathcal{R}, \vec{m} \in \{-1, 0, 1\}^d$)

05 $\mathbf{r} \leftarrow \eta$
06 **return** $\mathbf{c} := \mathbf{hr} + \vec{m}$

Dec($\mathbf{f} \in \mathcal{R}, \mathbf{c} \in \mathcal{R}$)

07 **return** $\vec{m} := (\mathbf{cf} \bmod {}^{\pm}q) \bmod {}^{\pm} 3$

Fig. 8. Generic NTRU GenNTRU[η] relative to distribution ψ over ring $\mathcal{R}$ with average-case correctness error. During key-generation, we need to check that $\mathbf{g}$ is invertible in order to have the randomness recovery property. It seems doubtful that this check adds any actual security in practice, but for all parameter sets, it only adds less than 0.01% chance to a restart, so it does not make much difference either way.

By the definition, the OW-CPA security of GenNTRU[η] is implied by the $\mathcal{R}$-NTRU$_\eta$+$\mathcal{R}$-LWE$_\eta$ assumptions. In this subsection, we will consider two concrete instantiations of GenNTRU, namely GenNTRU[U_3], where U_3 is the uniform distribution over $\{-1, 0, 1\}^d$, and GenNTRU[$\bar{\psi}_2^d$], where $\bar{\psi}_2^d$ was defined in Sect. 4.2. Both schemes do not have sufficiently small worst-case correctness error, which is the reason why we will first apply one of our average-case to worst-case correctness error transformations from the last section.

NTRU-B: Encryption Based on $\mathcal{R}$-NTRU$_\eta$+$\mathcal{R}$-LWE$_\eta$ for $\eta = U_3^d$. We define the generalized one-time pad GOTP $: \mathcal{R} \times \mathcal{R} \rightarrow \mathcal{R}$ relative to distributions U_3^d as GOTP($\vec{m}, u$) $:= \vec{m} + u \bmod {}^{\pm} 3$. Then NTRU-B $:=$ ACWC[GenNTRU[U_3^d], GOTP, F], obtained by applying the ACWC transformation from Sect. 3.2 to GenNTRU[U_3^d], is described in Fig. 9. Its message space is $\mathcal{M}' = \{-1, 0, 1\}^\lambda$ with distribution U_3^d, where $\mathcal{M}_1 = \{-1, 0, 1\}^{d-\lambda}$ and $\mathcal{M}_2 = \{-1, 0, 1\}^\lambda$.

By Lemma 3.6, the average-case correctness error of GenNTRU[U_3^d] and the worst-case correctness error of NTRU-B are off by an additive factor of

$$\Delta = \|U_3^{d-\lambda}\| \cdot \left(1 + \sqrt{(\ln |\mathcal{M}'| - \ln \|U_3^{d-\lambda}\|)/2}\right) \approx \|U_3^{d-\lambda}\| = 3^{-(d-\lambda)/2} \approx 2^{-0.8 \times (d-\lambda)}$$

which can be neglected for $\lambda = 256$ and $d \geq 576$. Hence, for all practical parameters considered in Table 1, worst-case and average-case correctness errors are equal. Using the techniques Sect. 4.4 it can be verified that the error probabilities reported in Table 1 are correct for NTRU-B.

Finally, one can apply the Fujisaki-Okamoto transformation FO$^\perp$ from Fig. 4 to obtain the IND-CCA secure version CCA-NTRU-B $:=$ FO$^\perp$[NTRU-B, H] of NTRU-B. In the ROM, the concrete security bound on the IND-CCA security of CCA-NTRU-B from Table 4 can be derived by combining Lemma 2.2 with

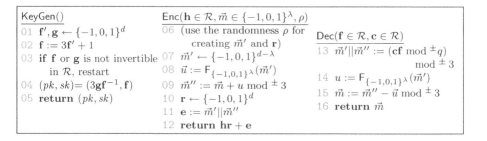

Fig. 9. Randomness-recoverable OW-CPA encryption scheme NTRU-B with worst-case correctness error based on the $\mathcal{R}$-NTRU$_{U_3^d}$ + $\mathcal{R}$-LWE$_{U_3^d}$ problems for U_3^d being uniform over $\{-1, 0, 1\}^d$.

Theorems 3.9 and 2.3. We refer to Fig. 1 for an overview of the implications. In the QROM, the bound can be derived by combining Theorem 3.10 with Theorem 2.5.

NTRU-C: Encryption Based on $\mathcal{R}$-NTRU$_\eta$+$\mathcal{R}$-LWE$_\eta$ for $\eta = \bar{\psi}_2^d$. We define NTRU-C := ACWC$_0$[GenNTRU[$\bar{\psi}_2^d$], F] with uniform message space $\mathcal{M}' = \{0,1\}^\lambda$, obtained by applying the ACWC$_0$ transformation with redundancy from Sect. 3.1 to GenNTRU[$\bar{\psi}_2^d$] is described in Fig. 10. By Lemma 3.1, the average-case correctness error of GenNTRU[$\bar{\psi}_2^d$] and the worst-case correctness error of NTRU-C are identical. Using the techniques Sect. 4.4 it can be verified that the error probabilities reported in Table 1 are correct for NTRU-C. Finally, one can apply the Fujisaki-Okamoto transformation FO$^\perp$ from Fig. 4 to obtain the IND-CCA secure version CCA-NTRU-C := FO$^\perp$[NTRU-C, H] of NTRU-C. In the ROM, the concrete security bound on the IND-CCA security of CCA-NTRU-C from Table 4 can be derived by combining Lemma 2.2 with Theorems 3.3 and 2.4. In the QROM, the bound can be derived by combining Lemma 2.2 with Theorem 3.4 and Theorem 2.5.

KeyGen()	Enc($\mathbf{h} \in \mathcal{R}, \vec{m} \in \{0,1\}^\lambda, \rho \in \{0,1\}^{8d}$)	Dec($\mathbf{f} \in \mathcal{R}, (\mathbf{c} \in \mathcal{R}, \vec{u} \in \{0,1\}^\lambda)$)
01 $\mathbf{f}', \mathbf{g} \leftarrow \bar{\psi}_2^d$	05 (use the randomness ρ for	09 $\mathbf{e} := (\mathbf{cf} \bmod \pm q) \bmod \pm 3$
02 $\mathbf{f} := 3\mathbf{f}' + 1$	creating $\mathbf{e}$ and $\mathbf{r}$)	10 $\vec{m} := \vec{u} \oplus \mathsf{F}_{\{0,1\}^\lambda}(\mathbf{e})$
03 if $\mathbf{f}$ or $\mathbf{g}$ is not invertible	06 $\mathbf{e}, \mathbf{r} \leftarrow \bar{\psi}_2^d$	11 **return** $\vec{m}$
in $\mathcal{R}$, restart	07 $\vec{u} := \vec{m} \oplus \mathsf{F}_{\{0,1\}^\lambda}(\mathbf{e})$	
04 **return** (pk, sk)= $(3\mathbf{gf}^{-1}, \mathbf{f})$	08 **return** $(\mathbf{hr} + \mathbf{e}, \vec{u})$	

Fig. 10. NTRU-C: a randomness-recoverable OW-CPA encryption scheme with worst-case correctness error based on the $\mathcal{R}$-NTRU$_\eta$ + $\mathcal{R}$-LWE$_\eta$ problems for $\eta = \bar{\psi}_2^d$.

Acknowledgements. The work of Julien Duman was supported by the German Federal Ministry of Education and Research (BMBF) in the course of the 6GEM Research Hub under Grant 16KISK037. Eike Kiltz was supported by the Deutsche Forschungsgemeinschaft (DFG, German research Foundation) as part of the Excellence Strategy of the German Federal and State Governments - EXC 2092 CASA - 390781972, and by the European Union (ERC AdG REWORC - 101054911). Dominique Unruh was supported by the ERC consolidator grant CerQuS (819317), by the Estonian Centre of Excellence in IT (EXCITE) funded by ERDF, by PUT team grant PRG946 from the Estonian Research Council. Vadim Lyubashevsky and Gregor Seiler were supported by the ERC Consolidator grant PLAZA (101002845).

References

1. Albrecht, M., Bai, S., Ducas, L.: A subfield lattice attack on overstretched NTRU assumptions. In: Robshaw, M., Katz, J. (eds.) CRYPTO 2016. LNCS, vol. 9814, pp. 153–178. Springer, Heidelberg (2016). https://doi.org/10.1007/978-3-662-53018-4_6
2. Albrecht, M.R., Player, R., Scott, S.: On the concrete hardness of Learning with Errors. J. Math. Cryptol. **9**(3), 169–203 (2015)
3. Alkim, E., et al.: Post-quantum key exchange - a new hope. In: USENIX Security Symposium. USENIX Association, pp. 327–343 (2016)
4. Ambainis, A., Hamburg, M., Unruh, D.: Quantum security proofs using semi-classical oracles. In: Boldyreva, A., Micciancio, D. (eds.) CRYPTO 2019. LNCS, vol. 11693, pp. 269–295. Springer, Cham (2019). https://doi.org/10.1007/978-3-030-26951-7_10
5. Bos, J.W., et al.: CRYSTALS - kyber: a CCA-secure module-lattice- based KEM. In: EuroS&P, pp. 353–367. IEEE (2018)
6. Boudgoust, K., Jeudy, C., Roux-Langlois, A., Wen, W.: On the hardness of module-LWE with binary secret. In: Paterson, K.G. (ed.) CT-RSA 2021. LNCS, vol. 12704, pp. 503–526. Springer, Cham (2021). https://doi.org/10.1007/978-3-030-75539-3_21
7. Brakerski, Z., et al.: Classical hardness of learning with errors. In: STOC, pp. 575–584 (2013)
8. Cheon, J.H., Jeong, J., Lee, C.: An algorithm for NTRU problems and cryptanalysis of the GGH multilinear map without a low-level encoding of zero. LMS J. Comput. Math. **19**(A), 255–266 (2016)
9. Chung, C.M., et al.: NTT multiplication for NTT-unfriendly rings new speed records for saber and NTRU on cortex-M4 and AVX2. IACR Trans. Cryptogr. Hardw. Embed. Syst. **2021**(2), 159–188 (2021)
10. D'Anvers, J.-P., Karmakar, A., Sinha Roy, S., Vercauteren, F.: Saber: module-LWR based key exchange, CPA-secure encryption and CCA-secure KEM. In: Joux, A., Nitaj, A., Rachidi, T. (eds.) AFRICACRYPT 2018. LNCS, vol. 10831, pp. 282–305. Springer, Cham (2018). https://doi.org/10.1007/978-3-319-89339-6_16
11. Don, J., Fehr, S., Majenz, C.: The measure-and-reprogram technique 2.0: multi-round fiat-shamir and more. In: Micciancio, D., Ristenpart, T. (eds.) CRYPTO 2020. LNCS, vol. 12172, pp. 602–631. Springer, Cham (2020). https://doi.org/10.1007/978-3-030-56877-1_21
12. Don, J., et al.: Online-extractability in the quantum random-oracle model. In: Dunkelman, O., Dziembowski, S. (eds.) EUROCRYPT 2022. LNCS, vol. 13277, pp. 677–706. Springer, Cham. (2022). https://doi.org/10.1007/978-3-031-07082-2_24
13. Don, J., Fehr, S., Majenz, C., Schaffner, C.: Security of the Fiat-Shamir transformation in the quantum random-oracle model. In: Boldyreva, A., Micciancio, D. (eds.) CRYPTO 2019. LNCS, vol. 11693, pp. 356–383. Springer, Cham (2019). https://doi.org/10.1007/978-3-030-26951-7_13

14. Ducas, L.: Shortest vector from lattice sieving: a few dimensions for free. In: Nielsen, J.B., Rijmen, V. (eds.) EUROCRYPT 2018. LNCS, vol. 10820, pp. 125–145. Springer, Cham (2018). https://doi.org/10.1007/978-3-319-78381-9_5

15. Ducas, L., van Woerden, W.: NTRU fatigue: how stretched is overstretched? In: Tibouchi, M., Wang, H. (eds.) ASIACRYPT 2021. LNCS, vol. 13093, pp. 3–32. Springer, Cham (2021). https://doi.org/10.1007/978-3-030-92068-5_1

16. Duman, J., et al.: A thorough treatment of highly-efficient NTRU instantiations. In: Cryptology ePrint Archive (2021)

17. Duman, J., et al.: Faster lattice-based KEMs via a generic Fujisaki-Okamoto transform using prefix hashing. In: CCS (2021)

18. Gentry, C.: Key recovery and message attacks on NTRU-composite. In: Pfitzmann, B. (ed.) EUROCRYPT 2001. LNCS, vol. 2045, pp. 182–194. Springer, Heidelberg (2001). https://doi.org/10.1007/3-540-44987-6_12

19. Hoffstein, J., Pipher, J., Silverman, J.H.: NTRU: a ring-based public key cryptosystem. In: ANTS, pp. 267–288 (1998)

20. Hofheinz, D., Hövelmanns, K., Kiltz, E.: A modular analysis of the Fujisaki-Okamoto transformation. In: TCC, pp. 341–371 (2017)

21. Hülsing, A., Rijneveld, J., Schanck, J., Schwabe, P.: High-speed key encapsulation from NTRU. In: Fischer, W., Homma, N. (eds.) CHES 2017. LNCS, vol. 10529, pp. 232–252. Springer, Cham (2017). https://doi.org/10.1007/978-3-319-66787-4_12

22. Kirchner, P., Fouque, P.-A.: Revisiting lattice attacks on overstretched NTRU parameters. In: Coron, J.-S., Nielsen, J.B. (eds.) EUROCRYPT 2017. LNCS, vol. 10210, pp. 3–26. Springer, Cham (2017). https://doi.org/10.1007/978-3-319-56620-7_1

23. Langlois, A., Stehlé, D.: Worst-case to average-case reductions for module lattices. Des. Codes Cryptography **75**(3), 565–599 (2015)

24. Lyubashevsky, V., Micciancio, D.: Generalized compact knapsacks are collision resistant. In: ICALP (2), pp. 144–155 (2006)

25. Lyubashevsky, V., Peikert, C., Regev, O.: On ideal lattices and learning with errors over rings. In: Gilbert, H. (ed.) EUROCRYPT 2010. LNCS, vol. 6110, pp. 1–23. Springer, Heidelberg (2010). https://doi.org/10.1007/978-3-642-13190-5_1

26. Lyubashevsky, V., Seiler, G.: NTTRU: truly fast NTRU using NTT. IACR Trans. Cryptogr. Hardw. Embed. Syst. **2019**(3), 180–201 (2019)

27. Lyubashevsky, V., Seiler, G.: Short, invertible elements in partially splitting cyclotomic rings and applications to lattice-based zero-knowledge proofs. In: Nielsen, J.B., Rijmen, V. (eds.) EUROCRYPT 2018. LNCS, vol. 10820, pp. 204–224. Springer, Cham (2018). https://doi.org/10.1007/978-3-319-78381-9_8

28. Regev, O.: On lattices, learning with errors, random linear codes, and cryptography. In: J. ACM 56.6 (2009)

29. Stehlé, D., Steinfeld, R.: Making NTRU as secure as worst-case problems over ideal lattices. In: Paterson, K.G. (ed.) EUROCRYPT 2011. LNCS, vol. 6632, pp. 27–47. Springer, Heidelberg (2011). https://doi.org/10.1007/978-3-642-20465-4_4

30. Stehlé, D., Steinfeld, R., Tanaka, K., Xagawa, K.: Efficient public key encryption based on ideal lattices. In: Matsui, M. (ed.) ASIACRYPT 2009. LNCS, vol. 5912, pp. 617–635. Springer, Heidelberg (2009). https://doi.org/10.1007/978-3-642-10366-7_36

31. Unruh, D.: Revocable quantum timed-release encryption. J. ACM **62**(6), 49, 1–49:76 (2015)

A Lightweight Identification Protocol Based on Lattices

Samed Düzlü[1], Juliane Krämer[1], Thomas Pöppelmann[2],
and Patrick Struck[1(✉)]

[1] Universität Regensburg, Regensburg, Germany
{samed.duzlu,juliane.kraemer,patrick.struck}@ur.de
[2] Infineon Technologies AG, Neubiberg, Germany
thomas.poeppelmann@infineon.com

Abstract. In this work we present a lightweight lattice-based identification protocol based on the CPA-secured public key encryption scheme Kyber. It is designed as a replacement for existing classical ECC- or RSA-based identification protocols in IoT, smart card applications, or for device authentication. The proposed protocol is simple, efficient, and implementations are supposed to be easy to harden against side-channel attacks. Compared to standard constructions for identification protocols based on lattice-based KEMs, our construction achieves this by avoiding the Fujisaki-Okamoto transform and its impact on implementation security.

Moreover, contrary to prior lattice-based identification protocols or standard constructions using signatures, our work does not require rejection sampling and can use more efficient parameters than signature schemes.

We provide a generic construction from CPA-secured public key encryption schemes to identification protocols and give a security proof of the protocol in the ROM. Moreover, we instantiate the generic construction with Kyber, for which we use the proposed parameter sets for NIST security levels I, III, and V. To show that the protocol is suitable for constrained devices, we implemented one selected parameter set on an ARM Cortex-M4 microcontroller. As the protocol is based on existing algorithms for Kyber, we make use of existing SW components (e.g., fast NTT implementations) for our implementation.

Keywords: Lattice-Based Cryptography · Identification Protocol · Post-Quantum Cryptography · LWE

1 Introduction

It is currently expected that large-scale quantum computers will be able to break classical cryptographic hardness assumptions in the future. This expectation has led to a standardization process by the National Institute of Standards and Technology (NIST). NIST aims to standardize digital signature schemes as well as key encapsulation mechanisms (KEMs) and public key encryption

© International Association for Cryptologic Research 2023
A. Boldyreva and V. Kolesnikov (Eds.): PKC 2023, LNCS 13940, pp. 95–113, 2023.
https://doi.org/10.1007/978-3-031-31368-4_4

(PKE) schemes that are supposed to be secured against attacks by quantum computers. From the pool for third round candidates, NIST recently selected three signature schemes (Dilithium, Falcon, SPHINCS$^+$) and one KEM (Kyber) for standardization.

While KEMs/PKEs and digital signature schemes are fundamental constructions that are in focus of the NIST process, further post-quantum cryptographic schemes will also be required in the future. For instance, instead of more advanced functionality, in some applications it may be sufficient to just verify that a communicating party is indeed the claimed identity, a property that is known as *authenticity*. This can be achieved by using an identification protocol that allows one party to prove its identity to another party. Such protocols enable one party (the prover) to convince another party (the verifier) that it knows some secret without revealing it.

Identification protocols can be based on a specific underlying problem, e.g., the hardness of lattice problems as shown in [37]. Another approach is to construct them from KEMs [3] or digital signature schemes. However, the resulting protocols may carry the overhead of the inherent security requirements of those schemes. In particular, simple constructions like [3] often require a KEM secured against chosen ciphertext attacks (CCA), which entails overhead from the Fujisaki-Okamoto (FO) transform. In such protocols, which we will refer to as generic 2-pass protocols, the verifier sends a ciphertext as a challenge and the prover authenticates by sending back the underlying message. In these protocols, the prover acts as a decryption oracle, which results in the necessity of CCA security for the underlying encryption scheme. However, it could be beneficial to remove the need for CCA security of the KEM by modifying the protocol for better efficiency or implementation security [4,7,43]. This may be required when establishing the authenticity of devices in a cost-effective manner on very constrained devices. Practical examples are standards like USB Type-C Authentication [49] or Qi 1.3 for wireless device charging [15] that now specify or even require ECDSA-based device authentication to test that parts are manufactured by trusted vendors and according to the necessary safety standardization. In the long term, such standards will have to be moved to schemes that offer sufficient quantum resistance.

1.1 Contribution

In this work we present a novel 4-pass identification protocol based on lattices that is efficient, lightweight, and easy to be securely implemented. The protocol is based on Kyber, however, by moving from a 2-pass protocol to a 4-pass protocol, we only need the CPA-secured variant of Kyber rather than the more costly CCA-secured variant. As a disadvantage, one might argue that we can only prove security assuming random oracles, whereas the 2-pass protocol does not require random oracles. We note, however, that achieving CCA-secured encryption via the FO transform also requires random oracles. The 2-pass protocol therefore inherits this assumption from the underlying encryption scheme. While our protocol requires more communication, it avoids the costly FO transform *without* adding costs in form of additional assumptions. In light of several works which indicate that side-channel security for the FO transform is a delicate matter [4, 7, 43], our new protocol provides an interesting alternative, despite the slightly extra cost in communication. Our idea avoids the need for CCA security and therefore the FO transform, by separating the challenge and a challenge verification, which is implicit in the CCA case. This separation allows the verification to be independent of the secret key including all data that is derived from it, so that the verification step on the prover side does not need to be secured against side-channel leakage. In particular for lattice-based cryptography, hardening the challenge verification against side-channels is expensive due to sampling procedures.

Furthermore, we provide a set of parameters following Kyber and an implementation targeting ARM Cortex-M4 based microcontrollers.

Our 4-pass identification protocol is, in fact, generic, using only a CPA-secured PKE. This allows to easily instantiate the generic version with different PKEs. In particular, the generic approach enables crypto-agile implementations using post-quantum assumptions other than lattice problems.

1.2 Related Work

In [3, 22] it is shown that KEMs can be used to construct identification schemes. The constructions require a OW-CCA and OW-ftCCA secured encryption scheme, respectively, whereas our construction only requires IND-CPA security. Additionally, the instantiations in [3, 22] are based on the Diffie-Hellman assumption and, hence, do not achieve post-quantum security. Similarly, using digital signature schemes allows to construct lattice-based identification protocols. Conversely, signature schemes like Dilithium [39] make use of the Fiat-Shamir transform with aborts [38]. However, the usage of rejection sampling results in a scheme that is less efficient than lattice-based KEM constructions and challenging to be secured against implementation attacks [41].

Note that in contrast to works like [1, 37, 38] our scheme has 4 steps of communication instead of 2. However, all three schemes have built-in aborts with significantly lower success ratio. Moreover, the additional communication step in the present case allows the honest generation of challenges, which is not the case in [1].

The authors of [10, 11] also proposed identification protocols specifically for smart cards and embedded devices. They measure the performance of GLP signatures [26] and BLISS signatures [19] in an ID-scheme setting and also evaluate a commitment protocol proposed in [18]. These identification protocols did not receive much attention and in contrast to our work, they do not consider side-channel attacks explicitly.

Aside from lattice-based cryptography, there are other assumptions on which quantum-secured cryptography can be based. Among those, there have been attempts to construct identification protocols based on multivariate polynomials [44], codes [47], and isogenies [16, 24, 29], where [29] is based on the SIDH problem and may be vulnerable due to the recent attack [14].

The symmetric counterpart of identification schemes is the notion of authentication schemes, where the prover and verifier have a shared secret. An instantiation using lattices has been developed in [28,34] based on the learning parity with noise (LPN) problem.

1.3   Outline

In Sect. 2, we give a brief discussion on the required technical background for the presentation of the identification protocol. In Sect. 3, we give a description of the identification protocol and provide a formal security reduction. In Sect. 4 we present an instantiation with the lattice-based PKE scheme Kyber and give design rationales of our construction. We further provide a choice of parameters for the instantiation and give details on the implementation.

2   Background

In this section, we explain the notation and basic concepts that are required for the description and analysis of the identification protocol.

2.1   Cyptographic Primitives

We will make use of cryptographic hash functions. The hash functions will be denoted F, H, and G_i, for i in some index set I. The family $(G_i)_{i \in I}$ of hash functions is denoted $\mathcal{G}$ for short. The hash functions are separated according to their use in the identification protocol, i.e., F is used to generate a random message (challenge), while $\mathcal{G}$ is used to generate the internal randomness of the underlying encryption algorithm, and H is used for the commitment computation.

In the instantiation, the distinct hash functions will be implemented from a single hash function using domain separation [5]. In the security proof, we will model the hash functions as random oracles [6].

IND-CPA *Security of* PKEs. As the identification protocol is based on IND-CPA secured public-key encryption scheme, we briefly recall its definition, cf. [33].

The security experiment for the IND-CPA security of a PKE scheme PKE = (KGen, Enc, Dec) is given as

1. KGen is run with output (pk, sk),
2. The adversary $\mathcal{A}$ receives the public key pk and outputs two messages m_0 and m_1 of the same length
3. A random bit $b \in \{0, 1\}$ is chosen and $\mathcal{A}$ receives $c_b := \mathrm{Enc}_{\mathsf{pk}}(m_b)$,
4. $\mathcal{A}$ outputs $b' \in \{0, 1\}$,
5. Finally, $\mathcal{A}$ wins, if $b' = b$ and loses otherwise.

The *advantage of* $\mathcal{A}$ *against the* IND-CPA *security of* PKE is then defined as

$$\mathbf{Adv}_{\mathsf{PKE}}^{\mathrm{IND\text{-}CPA}}(\mathcal{A}) = \mathbb{P}\left(\mathcal{A} \text{ wins game IND-CPA}\right).$$

2.2   Protocol Security

There are three distinct security notions for identification protocols, namely *passive* and *active* (*attack*) security, and the security against *man-in-the-middle* attacks. We will focus on active attack security, which is described in terms of three phases, the *setup phase*, the *probing phase*, and the *impersonation phase*.

In the setup phase, the keys are generated and the adversary receives the public key. In the probing phase, the adversary takes the role of the verifier and can interact with an honest prover. The adversary is allowed to invoke the honest prover multiple times. After the probing phase, the adversary proceeds to the impersonation phase. Here, the adversary takes the role of the prover, interacting with an honest verifier. The adversary wins, i.e., breaks the identification protocol, if the honest verifier accepts at the end.

Setup Phase: A key pair $(\mathsf{pk}, \mathsf{sk}) \leftarrow_\$ \mathsf{KGen}()$ is generated. The adversary $\mathcal{A}$ receives pk and the probing phase starts.

Probing Phase: In this phase, the adversary $\mathcal{A}$ can interact with an honest prover, knowing the secret key sk. At the end of the phase, the impersonation phase starts.

Impersonation Phase: In this phase, the adversary interacts with an honest verifier, knowing the public key pk. The adversary wins if the prover accepts, i.e., outputs 1 at the end.

For an adversary $\mathcal{A}$ against the active security AS, we denote by $\mathbf{Adv}^{\mathsf{AS}}(\mathcal{A})$ the probability that the honest verifier outputs 1 at the end of the security experiment above, i.e., that the adversary successfully impersonates an honest prover.

3   The Identification Protocol

In this section, we present an identification protocol (Fig. 1) based on an IND-CPA secured PKE scheme and prove its active security. The security of the identification protocol is independent of the underlying security assumptions on the PKE scheme. In Sect. 4, we provide an instantiation with the lattice-based Kyber PKE scheme, a collection of parameters, and a comparison of the implementation with other identification protocol constructions.

3.1   Description of the Identification Protocol

Before giving details, we want to briefly describe the identification on a high-level. See also Sect. 4.1 for more details on design rationales.

The protocol is executed between a verifier V who knows the public key and a prover P who knows the corresponding secret key. The protocol starts with a *challenge computation*, where the underlying encryption algorithm is made deterministic by generating message and random coins from a seed. The resulting ciphertext is send to the prover as the challenge. In the following *response computation*, the prover decrypts the ciphertext to receive a message. This is the only step, where the secret key is used. The resulting message is hashed together with a random value and the hash is send to the verifier. The verifier sends the seed used to generate the message and random coins to the prover. During the *challenge verification*, the prover can use this seed to check that the challenge was honestly generated. In this step, the prover does not make use of its secret (indeed, not even results of any computations using the secret key are required in this step). Only then, the prover sends its random value chosen in the response computation. Finally, in the *response verification*, the verifier checks that the hash value it received is compatible with the hash of the random response it received after the challenge verification with the original message it generated in the challenge computation.

The Underlying PKE Scheme and Public Parameters. Let $\mathsf{PKE} = (\mathsf{KGen}, \mathsf{Enc}, \mathsf{Dec})$ be a PKE scheme. Further, let F, G_i, H be hash functions, with $\mathcal{G} = (G_i)_{i \in I}$ is a (finite) family I of hash functions. We assume that PKE is instantiated with the hash functions $\mathcal{G}$. Lastly, α is a security parameter.

The identification protocol will be denoted Π_{PKE} and is depicted in Fig. 1. In what follows, we give a description of the steps.

Key Generation. The public and secret keys of Π_{PKE} are the same as the key pairs of PKE. Thus, the key generation is done by running the KGen algorithm, resulting in a key pair $(\mathsf{pk}, \mathsf{sk})$.

Identification. Given the key pair $(\mathsf{pk}, \mathsf{sk})$ as above, the 4-pass identification procedure of Π_{PKE} is as follows.

Verifier: Challenge Computation. In the first step, the verifier V picks a random value $\lambda \in \{0,1\}^\alpha$. Then, λ is used to compute a challenge message $m \leftarrow F(\lambda)$. We let $\mathsf{coins} = \mathcal{G}(\lambda)$ be the random coins used during the encryption and set $c = \mathsf{Enc}(\mathsf{pk}, m, \mathsf{coins})$.
1st Transmission: V→P. The verifier sends c to the prover P.
Prover: Response Computation. The prover decrypts c to get a message $\tilde{m} = \mathsf{Dec}(\mathsf{sk}, c)$. This is the only step where the secret key sk is used. Then, the prover samples a random value $r \leftarrow_s \{0,1\}^\alpha$ and computes $h := H(r, \tilde{m})$. Note that r is independent of the challenge c and the secret s.
2nd Transmission: P→V. The prover sends the hash digest h of $(r, \tilde{m})$ to the verifier. With h, the prover commits on its random value r.
Verifier. The verifier stores h.
3rd Transmission: V→P. The verifier sends λ to the prover.
Prover: Challenge Verification. The prover uses λ to re-generate $m' \leftarrow F(\lambda)$ and the random values $\mathsf{coins}' = \mathcal{G}(\lambda)$, with which it computes $c' = \mathsf{Enc}(\mathsf{pk}, m', \mathsf{coins}')$. Then, the prover checks whether $c = c'$ and aborts if not. Note that the prover uses m' instead of $\tilde{m}$ to re-compute the ciphertext, making this step independent of its secret s.
4th Transmission: P→V. The prover sends its commitment r to the verifier.
Verifier: Response Verification. The verifier checks, if $h = H(r, m)$ and outputs 1 if it holds. Otherwise, the verifier outputs 0.

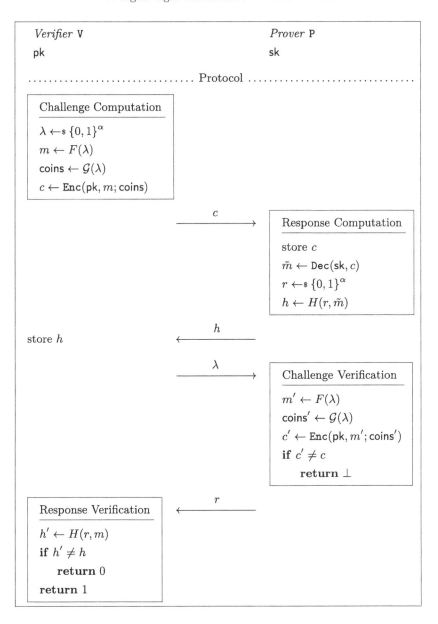

Fig. 1. The generalized identification protocol Π with hash functions F and H, and a family of hash functions $\mathcal{G} = (G_i)$ depending on the size of coins for the given PKE.

3.2   Security Analysis of the Identification Protocol

We proceed with the security analysis of the identification protocol described above. We show that its active attack security AS reduces to the IND-CPA security of the underlying PKE scheme. As a consequence, the identification protocol instantiated with Kyber.CPAPKE is secured, see Corollary 4.1. The security reduction is proved in the random oracle model and an extension to the quantum random oracle model is discussed in Sect. 3.3.

Theorem 3.1. *Let Π be the identification protocol described in Fig. 1 based on a PKE scheme* PKE $= (\mathsf{KGen}, \mathsf{Enc}, \mathsf{Dec})$. *Then, in the random oracle model, for any adversary $\mathcal{A}$ against Π, making q queries to $\mathcal{G}$, there exists an adversary $\mathcal{B}$ against* PKE *such that*

$$\mathbf{Adv}_{\Pi}^{\mathsf{AS}}(\mathcal{A}) \leq \mathbf{Adv}_{\mathsf{PKE}}^{\mathsf{IND\text{-}CPA}}(\mathcal{B}) + \frac{q}{2^{\alpha}},$$

where the hash functions are modeled as random oracles.

Proof. Let $\mathcal{A}$ be an adversary against Π instantiated with PKE. We construct an adversary $\mathcal{B}$ against PKE that makes use of $\mathcal{A}$ and breaks the IND-CPA security of PKE.

Let $\mathcal{B}$ be given a public key pk which is part of a key pair $(\mathsf{pk}, \mathsf{sk})$. Then by definition of IND-CPA, $\mathcal{B}$ picks two messages, receives the encryption of one of the messages, and has to distinguishing which one was encrypted. To achieve this, $\mathcal{B}$ runs $\mathcal{A}$ with its own challenge public key pk.

Probing Phase. To make $\mathcal{A}$ run the attack, $\mathcal{B}$ needs to simulate the probing phase of the active attack with the public key pk, in which $\mathcal{A}$ plays the role of a verifier and can submit challenges to the prover, which is played by $\mathcal{B}$. In the random oracle model, $\mathcal{B}$ can simulate a prover without knowledge of the secret key as follows. In the response computation, $\mathcal{B}$ samples a random value h, and returns h to the verifier, in this case $\mathcal{A}$. After receiving λ, $\mathcal{B}$ checks, whether the challenge of $\mathcal{A}$ was generated honestly. If the check holds, $\mathcal{B}$ is now in possession of the message $m = F(\lambda)$. Then $\mathcal{B}$ picks a random value r and programs the random oracle H to take (r, m) to h. It is impossible for $\mathcal{A}$ to detect this reprogramming, unless it requested the value $H(r, m)$ earlier. However, $\mathcal{B}$ has access to all random oracle calls of $\mathcal{A}$ and can check which values of the form (r, m) have been queried by $\mathcal{A}$. As even for a fixed m, there are exponentially many pairs (r, m), $\mathcal{B}$ can always find a pair which has not been queried before.

Impersonation Phase. The idea for the impersonation phase is that $\mathcal{B}$ will send its own challenge ciphertext (from the IND-CPA game) to the adversary. During the response computation, $\mathcal{A}$ has to commit to a message $\tilde{m}$ in form of sending $h = H(r, \tilde{m})$. This enables $\mathcal{B}$ to extract the message $\tilde{m}$ from the random oracle queries by $\mathcal{A}$; note that in the random oracle model that any (successful) adversary has to send r that was used to compute h. This enables $\mathcal{B}$ to run the impersonation phase up to the point where $\mathcal{A}$ has sent its commitment h and extracts the message from this.

However, simply injecting the ciphertext from the IND-CPA game does not correspond to challenge ciphertexts in the protocol as they are generated independently of the random oracles $F, \mathcal{G}$. Since the IND-CPA game allows $\mathcal{B}$ to choose arbitrary messages, it can simply compute those as outputs of F. But coins are chosen by the IND-CPA challenger, independently of any random oracle. This means, that $\mathcal{B}$ simulates the impersonation phase (up to the point where $\mathcal{A}$ sends h) for independently chosen coins. Detecting this simulation boils down to querying the random oracle $\mathcal{G}$ on λ, however, $\mathcal{A}$ does not have any information about it; even recovering m from c does not help due to the one-wayness of F. Since $\mathcal{A}$ makes q queries to $\mathcal{G}$, its probability of detecting the simulation is at most $\frac{q}{2^\alpha}$.

Now we can give the reduction $\mathcal{B}$. It picks λ_0, λ_1 uniformly at random from $\{0,1\}^\alpha$ to compute messages $m_b = F(\lambda_b)$, for $b \in \{0,1\}$. The messages m_0, m_1 are sent to the IND-CPA challenger which responds with $c_b = \mathtt{Enc}(\mathsf{pk}, m_b; \mathsf{coins})$ for coins chosen uniformly at random. Then $\mathcal{B}$ sends c_b to $\mathcal{A}$. When $\mathcal{A}$ outputs h, $\mathcal{B}$ will check for a query (r^*, m^*) to H. If $m^* = m_0$, $\mathcal{B}$ outputs 0, if $m^* = m_1$, $\mathcal{B}$ outputs 1. If neither check passes, i.e., $\mathcal{A}$ is not successful, $\mathcal{B}$ outputs a uniformly random bit. □

3.3   Extension to the Quantum Random Oracle Model

We briefly argue how the proof can be translated to the quantum random oracle model (QROM) [9]. In the probing phase, the reduction can no longer look up the queries that the adversary has made to the random oracle. This thwarts to simply choose a value r such that the adversary has not queries (r, m) to the random oracle. Instead the reduction will simply pick r at random and reprogram the random oracle on (r, m) to h, where m is the message it obtains after receiving the seed λ and h is the uniformly random value which the reduction send to the adversary after receiving the challenge ciphertext. The O2H lemma [2] allows to upper bound the chance that the adversary can detect this reprogramming where it still holds that the adversary has no knowledge of the value r, which was chosen uniformly at random and independent of everything else. This step, however, induces another term into the bound since the reprogramming cannot be made certain to happen at a point the adversary has not queried.

For the impersonation phase, the reduction extracts the query (r, m) from the hash value h it receives from the adversary; this does not work in the QROM, when the adversary makes its queries in superposition. Luckily, the technique by Targhi and Unruh [48] allows to circumvent the problem. The reduction simulates the random oracle using a $2q$-wise independent function (e.g., a polynomial of degree $2q$) which was shown to be indistinguishable up to q superposition queries by Zhandry [50]. Upon receiving the classical value h, the reduction can extract candidates for (r, m) by computing the roots of the polynomial and, if one of the candidates equals either of the messages, the reduction outputs the corresponding bit. Additionally, the adversary might be able to notice the simulation via the IND-CPA security game, where coins are generated independently of the random oracle $\mathcal{G}$. This step also boils down to applying the O2H lemma [2] and the fact that the adversary has no knowledge about λ. More recent variants of the O2H lemma [2,8,36] and other QROM extraction techniques [17] allow to achieve better bounds.

4   An Identification Protocol Based on Kyber

In this section we analyze an instantiation of the identification protocol with Kyber.CPAPKE from various perspectives. First, we deduce the security of the identification protocol from the general result in Sect. 3. We then provide design rationales that we used as orientation to create an appropriately protected and lightweight lattice-based identification protocol. Finally, we describe an implementation on a Cortex-M4 32-bit microcontroller, and compare our identification protocol with various other constructions based on lattices, including a discussion on side-channel protection.

4.1   Security and Design Rationales

The security of the protocol is given in the corollary below, which is a direct consequence of Theorem 3.1.

Corollary 4.1. *Let Π be the identification protocol described in Fig. 1 instantiated with* Kyber.CPAPKE. *Then, in the random oracle model, for any adversary $\mathcal{A}$ against Π, making q queries to the random oracles, there exists an adversary $\mathcal{C}$ against* Kyber.CPAPKE *such that*

$$\mathbf{Adv}_{\Pi}^{\mathsf{AS}}(\mathcal{A}) \leq 2\,\mathbf{Adv}_{\mathsf{Kyber.CPAPKE}}^{\mathsf{IND\text{-}CPA}}(\mathcal{C}) + \frac{q}{2^{\alpha}},$$

where the hash functions are modeled as random oracles.

Design Rationales. In what follows, we describe our approach with the view on highlighting the main design features. Specifically we compare the given ID protocol to the one constructed from CCA-secured encryption schemes when the CCA security is a result of the Fujisaki-Okamoto transform [23].

Indeed, given an encryption scheme, there is a simple construction of an identification protocol. In such a protocol, the verifier encrypts a random message, sends the ciphertext to the prover, the prover decrypts the ciphertext with the secret key and provides the message to the verifier. However, due to ciphertext malleability [21] an attacker could break such a scheme when it is based on common lattice-based CPA-secured KEMs and PKEs. During the probing phase, the honest prover acts as a decryption oracle for the adversary, as it decrypts any ciphertext it receives as a challenge. This entails that the used encryption scheme has to achieve CCA security for the protocol to be sufficiently secure; any scheme achieving only CPA security can be broken by performing a CCA attack against the underlying encryption during the probing phase of the protocol. The typical way of achieving CCA security is to design a CPA-secured encryption scheme and applying the FO transform to it. However, the FO transform adds overhead and—more importantly—is very hard to secure against side-channel attacks [4, 7, 43].

The fundamental idea of the FO transform is to avoid maliciously generated ciphertexts by re-encrypting the decrypted message and comparing it with the received ciphertext. The decrypted message is only outputted if the re-encryption results in the given ciphertext, otherwise, the ciphertext is rejected as an invalid one. The re-encryption procedure comes with a huge overload when used with lattice constructions. For example, it requires the sampling from a noise distribution, which is notoriously hard to secure against side-channels [13, 35, 40, 43, 45, 51].

Our approach mimics the idea to check that the challenge ciphertext is generated honestly. However, instead of using the decrypted message, we achieve this check independently of the secret key. In fact, an honest challenge in the present identification protocol is generated by means of a seed. This seed is provided to the prover only after the prover commits to its response by sending the hash value of its response. Then the seed can be used to check whether the ciphertext received after the first communication is indeed generated with the presented seed.

Note that the commitment to the response does not reveal any information about the secret unless either the hash function is broken, or the response computation leaked information. Thus, the CPA decryption still needs to be secured against side-channel attacks.

The benefit comes into play in the challenge verification step. As the computation uses the seed only and is independent of the secret key or any result of the response computation, the verification does not need to be secured against side channels. As will be discussed below (see Table 2), the challenge verification takes the greater computational costs of the prover, but in contrast to the CCA version, does not need to be side-channel secured. Also note that after the commitment in terms of the hash of the message with a random value, there is no need for the verifier to keep the message secret. Thus, the verifier can send the seed to the prover, who can check whether the challenge was generated honestly. This seed allows the prover to verify the challenge, without using the secret key or any values derived from the secret key.

The described benefits are achieved by adding a marginally larger communication cost given in terms of an additional hash value and the seed being transmitted in the intermediate steps.

Note that we are only interested in side-channel leakage on the prover side, which possesses a long-term secret. One could, of course, consider side-channel leakage on the verifier side, but the relevance is questionable. Assume that an adversary can obtain the challenge message m via some side-channel from the challenge computation. This would immediately allow to identify. However, it would only enable a single identification and be useless afterwards. It would also require to obtain this side-channel information from a single trace.

Table 1. Parameter sets and NIST security level for Kyber and the implementation of the identification protocol with Kyber.

Reference Kyber	Security	
	Bit	Level
Kyber512 $(k = 2, \eta_1 = 3, \eta_2 = 2)$	118	I
Kyber768 $(k = 3, \eta_1 = 2, \eta_2 = 2)$	183	III
Kyber1024 $(k = 4, \eta_1 = 2, \eta_2 = 2)$	256	V

4.2 Parameter Sets

The instantiation of our identification protocol with Kyber.CPAPKE comes with the NIST security levels I, III, and V corresponding to the Kyber parameter sets Kyber512, Kyber768, and Kyber1024, see Table 1. All parameter sets share the common MLWE structure instantiated with $n = 256$ and $q = 3329$. For our security analysis we rely on the core-SVP classical hardness that is also used by Kyber [46] version 3.02.

4.3 Implementation

In general, performance measurements for common PQC schemes can be performed with a portable and easier to maintain implementation (e.g., pq-clean [32]) or an implementation that is optimized for the target platform (e.g., pqm4 [31]) and that uses assembly instructions or CPU-specific operations. We evaluate our implementation using both approaches on an ARM Cortex-M4 32-bit microcontroller and use ARM GCC version 6.3.1. Our target device is an STM32F407 that is mounted on the popular STM32F4-DISCOVERY board[1]. For the evaluation, we set the clock frequency to 24 MHz and do not use the maximum frequency of 168 MHz to reduce the impact of caches or delays caused by wait states stemming from the particular non-volatile memory (NVM) technology.

For key generation we use the Kyber.CPAPKE key generation as is. For challenge computation, response computation, challenge verification, and response verification we call the Kyber.CPAPKE routines from either pq-clean or pqm4 and also use the hashing routines provided by these libraries.

The security analysis of the protocol makes use of different, independent random oracles. For the implementation, we make use of SHAKE and instantiate the different random oracles via domain separation, using different prefixes. This was shown in [5] to provide a sound method of instantiating multiple random oracles from a single one.

---

[1] The source code of our implementations is available at https://github.com/tpoeppelmann/id_protocol.

To measure the cycle counts we rely on the system timer (SysTick) and confirmed that we obtain the same cycle counts for Kyber768.CPAPKE with our compiler and setup as given in [30] for Kyber768.CPAPKE. In Table 2, we provide measured cycle counts of our implementation for the cryptographic processing (cf. Sect. 3). Cycles for communication and protocol state handling are excluded as they are highly application specific and depend on the used interface (e.g., contactless, IC2, SPI, CAN).

Table 2. Cycle counts of our implementation on an ARM Cortex-M4 using either pq-clean [32] or pqm4 [31] using the m4fspeed implementation.

Function	Cycles (pqclean)	Cycles (pqm4; m4fspeed)
Key generation	927412	607652
Challenge Computation (verifier)	1097362	637251
Response Computation (prover)	244264	62497
Challenge Verification (prover)	1099267	644945
Response Verification (verifier)	42089	38569

In Table 3 we compare our implementation with standard constructions for the realization of identification protocols based on Kyber.CCA and Dilithium when using different implementations. For Kyber.CCA we assume that the verifier runs encapsulation while the prover runs decapsulation and then provides the encapsulated secret back to the verifier. For the Dilithium instance we assume that the verifier sends a random number (not accounted in cycle counts) and that the prover executes a signing operation and the verifier a signature verification. The average cycle counts for Kyber and Dilithium are obtained from [30] in October 2022. We also provide cycle counts for an insecure instantiation of CPA-secured Kyber768.CPAPKE as ID scheme. The large difference in cycles to the CCA-secured version Kyber.CCA shows the overhead attributed to the FO transform. Another important metric for an ID scheme is the amount of data that has to be transferred. For our approach it is required to transmit 1088 bytes for c, 32 bytes for r, 32 bytes for h and 32 bytes for r, which results in 1184 bytes. When Kyber.CCA is used as ID scheme, it requires $1088 + 32 = 1120$ bytes and Dilithium3 needs $32 + 3293 = 3325$ bytes.

Table 3. Comparison of cycle counts for cryptographic operations when excluding communication.

Library	Function	Cycles verifier	Cycles prover
pq-clean	Our protocol ARM Cortex-M4	1 139 451	1 343 531
	Kyber768.CCA as ID scheme	1 352 393	1 470 514
	Dilithium3 as ID scheme	3 499 388	11 722 059
	Kyber768.CPAKEM as ID scheme (*insecure*)	1068 876	229 451
pqm4; m4fspeed	Our protocol ARM Cortex-M4	675 820	707 442
	Kyber768.CCA as ID scheme	869 974	795 161
	Dilithium3 as ID scheme	2691 469	6610 160
	Kyber768.CPAKEM as ID scheme (*insecure*)	611 076	49 021

4.4   Side-Channel Protection

Some implementations of identification schemes on embedded devices may require protection against physical attacks. For our protocol, we see the benefit that only the Response Computation by the prover is sensitive to side-channel attacks. This is a big advantage compared to KEMs that are using the FO transform where the decapsulation procedure is sensitive [42] and requires costly masking or other countermeasures [4,7,43]. The challenge verification routine is not sensitive as all inputs and the resulting ciphertexts c and c' are known by the prover and verifier. The only added operation on top of a masked Kyber.CPAPKE decryption is the masked computation of $h \leftarrow H(r, \tilde{m})$. This operation needs to be masked as well to prevent leakage of information on the decrypted message $\tilde{m}$. The value h itself is not critical anymore as it is randomized via r. Note that to obtain the cycle counts for the full computation of the prover, one has to add also the non-sensitive cycles for challenge verification.

As shown in Table 4, the overhead of a 1st-order masked Kyber decryption (including masked FO transform) is already roughly a factor of 3 (≈ 2200000 cycles) but increases massively for second or higher orders protection. And it is important to note that a first order masked scheme is not sufficient in practice, as practical attacks have already been shown that exploit in particular properties of the FO transform. Such a scheme would at least need to be combined with hiding measures to counter known attacks.

In Table 4, we also provide measurements for an implementation of the Response Computation using the open-source first-order masked implementation of Kyber presented in [27]. In addition, we do performance estimations of our scheme based on results reported in [12]. Such an approach using an estimation is necessary as the source code of [12] is not available but sufficient to reach a general impression about the benefits of our proposal as we mainly call Kyber as a subroutine.

The Response Computation of the prover is a masked Kyber.CPAPKE decapsulation (indcpa_dec in [12]) and a masked hashing operation (e.g., hashg in [12]). Therefore, the 1st-order Response Computation of the prover is estimated to be roughly 174 000 + 118 000 + 62 497 = 354 497 cycles, which fits to the results obtained via [27]. A 2nd-order protection implementation can be estimated with 2 916 000 + 1 543 000 + 62 497 = 4521497 cycles. This is roughly 8.5 times better than the approach of using Kyber768.CCA as ID scheme with 2nd-order protection (when also accounting for the non-sensitive 644 945 cycles for challenge verification the prover has to perform in our approach as well).

For a fair comparison, Table 4 also provides the full cycle count of the Prover. For the identification protocol based on Kyber768.CCA, there is no difference to the cycle count of the response computation. This is because the validity is already been checked by the Kyber768.CCA decryption algorithm. For our protocol, the full cycle count of the prover consists of the cycle count for the (masked) response computation plus the fixed cycle count of 644 945 (cf. Table 1) for the challenge verification, which does not need to be protected.

Table 4. Comparison of cycle counts.

Masking	Scheme	Cycles (Prover)		Speedup
		Resp. Comp.	Full Comp.	
none	Our protocol	62 497	707 442	≈ 1.12
	Kyber768.CCA as ID scheme	795 168	795 168	
1st-order [27]	Our protocol	241 887	886 832	≈ 3.35
	Kyber768.CCA as ID scheme	297 8441	2 978 441	
1st-order [12]	Our protocol	≈ 354497	≈ 999442	≈ 3.12
	Kyber768.CCA as ID scheme	3 116 000	3 116 000	
2nd-order [12]	Our protocol	≈ 4521497	≈ 5166442	≈ 8.58
	Kyber768.CCA as ID scheme	44347000	44 347 000	
3rd-order [12]	Our protocol	≈ 12009497	≈ 12654442	≈ 9.12
	Kyber768.CCA as ID scheme	115 481 000	115 481 000	

Comparison of cycle counts for response computation and the full computation performed by the prover between our protocol and the identification protocol based on Kyber768.CCA. For our protocol, only the response computation, as shown in the Resp. Comp. column, is required to be secured against side channels. The full computation cycles result from the cycles for the response computation and the (non-sensitive) 644 945 cycles for the challenge verification. For Kyber768.CCA as ID scheme, the response calculation is equivalent to decryption; the full computation is the same as there is no separate challenge verification. The listed speedup is based on the cycle count for the full computation. The comparison is based on the implementation using pqm4; m4fspeed.

5 Conclusion

This article presents a novel lattice-based identification protocol using an interactive challenge-response protocol. It is lightweight, efficient, and simple to implement, making it well-suited for use in IoT devices, microcontrollers, and constrained devices. The protocol is designed in a way that supposedly allows easier protection against side-channel attacks than generic constructions using KEMs as it avoids rejection sampling and the FO transform.

It might be of interest to investigate possible variations of the proposed protocol that may be able to realize identity-based identification [20]. As lattice-based constructions allow identity-based encryption schemes as shown in [25,50], a natural question is whether it is possible to extend the present scheme to develop an identity-based identification scheme.

Acknowledgments. We thank the anonymous reviewers for valuable comments. This work has been supported by the German Ministry of Education and Research in the context of the project Aquorypt (grant number 16KIS1022 and 16KIS1020), the Deutsche Forschungsgemeinschaft (DFG) – SFB 1119 – 236615297, and the Bavarian State Ministry of Science and the Arts in the framework of the bidt Graduate Center for Postdocs.

References

1. Abdalla, M., Fouque, P.-A., Lyubashevsky, V., Tibouchi, M.: Tightly-secure signatures from lossy identification schemes. In: Pointcheval, D., Johansson, T. (eds.) EUROCRYPT 2012. LNCS, vol. 7237, pp. 572–590. Springer, Heidelberg (2012). https://doi.org/10.1007/978-3-642-29011-4_34
2. Ambainis, A., Hamburg, M., Unruh, D.: Quantum security proofs using semi-classical oracles. In: Boldyreva, A., Micciancio, D. (eds.) CRYPTO 2019. LNCS, vol. 11693, pp. 269–295. Springer, Cham (2019). https://doi.org/10.1007/978-3-030-26951-7_10
3. Anada, H., Arita, S.: Identification schemes from key encapsulation mechanisms. In: Nitaj, A., Pointcheval, D. (eds.) AFRICACRYPT 2011. LNCS, vol. 6737, pp. 59–76. Springer, Heidelberg (2011). https://doi.org/10.1007/978-3-642-21969-6_4
4. Azouaoui, M., et al.: Surviving the FO-calypse: Securing PQC implementations in practice (2022). https://iacr.org/submit/files/slides/2022/rwc/rwc2022/48/slides.pdf
5. Bellare, M., Davis, H., Günther, F.: Separate your domains: NIST PQC KEMs, Oracle cloning and read-only indifferentiability. In: Canteaut, A., Ishai, Y. (eds.) EUROCRYPT 2020. LNCS, vol. 12106, pp. 3–32. Springer, Cham (2020). https://doi.org/10.1007/978-3-030-45724-2_1
6. Bellare, M., Rogaway, P.: Random oracles are practical: A paradigm for designing efficient protocols. In: Denning, D.E., Pyle, R., Ganesan, R., Sandhu, R.S., Ashby, V. (eds.) ACM CCS 93, pp. 62–73. ACM Press, November 1993
7. Bhasin, S., D'Anvers, J.-P., Heinz, D., Pöppelmann, T., Van Beirendonck, M.: Attacking and defending masked polynomial comparison. IACR TCHES **2021**(3), 334–359 (2021). https://tches.iacr.org/index.php/TCHES/article/view/8977

8. Bindel, N., Hamburg, M., Hövelmanns, K., Hülsing, A., Persichetti, E.: Tighter proofs of CCA security in the quantum random oracle model. In: Hofheinz, D., Rosen, A. (eds.) TCC 2019. LNCS, vol. 11892, pp. 61–90. Springer, Cham (2019). https://doi.org/10.1007/978-3-030-36033-7_3

9. Boneh, D., Dagdelen, Ö., Fischlin, M., Lehmann, A., Schaffner, C., Zhandry, M.: Random oracles in a quantum world. In: Lee, D.H., Wang, X. (eds.) ASIACRYPT 2011. LNCS, vol. 7073, pp. 41–69. Springer, Heidelberg (2011). https://doi.org/10.1007/978-3-642-25385-0_3

10. Boorghany, A., Jalili, R.: Implementation and comparison of lattice-based identification protocols on smart cards and microcontrollers. Cryptology ePrint Archive, Report 2014/078 (2014). https://eprint.iacr.org/2014/078

11. Boorghany, A., Sarmadi, S.B., Jalili, R.: On constrained implementation of lattice-based cryptographic primitives and schemes on smart cards. Cryptology ePrint Archive, Report 2014/514 (2014). https://eprint.iacr.org/2014/514

12. Bos, J.W., Gourjon, M., Renes, J., Schneider, T., van Vredendaal, C.: Masking kyber: first- and higher-order implementations. IACR TCHES **2021**(4), 173–214 (2021). https://tches.iacr.org/index.php/TCHES/article/view/9064

13. Groot Bruinderink, L., Hülsing, A., Lange, T., Yarom, Y.: Flush, gauss, and reload – a cache attack on the BLISS lattice-based signature scheme. In: Gierlichs, B., Poschmann, A.Y. (eds.) CHES 2016. LNCS, vol. 9813, pp. 323–345. Springer, Heidelberg (2016). https://doi.org/10.1007/978-3-662-53140-2_16

14. Castryck, W., Decru, T.: An efficient key recovery attack on SIDH (preliminary version). Cryptology ePrint Archive, Report 2022/975 (2022). https://eprint.iacr.org/2022/975

15. W. P. Consortium. The QI authentication system (2021). https://www.wirelesspowerconsortium.com/qi-authentication/

16. De Feo, L., Kohel, D., Leroux, A., Petit, C., Wesolowski, B.: SQISign: compact post-quantum signatures from quaternions and isogenies. In: Moriai, S., Wang, H. (eds.) ASIACRYPT 2020. LNCS, vol. 12491, pp. 64–93. Springer, Cham (2020). https://doi.org/10.1007/978-3-030-64837-4_3

17. Don, J., Fehr, S., Majenz, C., Schaffner, C.: Online-extractability in the quantum random-oracle model. In: EUROCRYPT 2022. Part III, LNCS, pp. 677–706. Springer, Heidelberg (2022). https://doi.org/10.1007/978-3-031-07082-2_24

18. Dousti, M.S., Jalili, R.: Efficient statistical zero-knowledge authentication protocols for smart cards secure against active & concurrent attacks. Cryptology ePrint Archive, Report 2013/709 (2013). https://eprint.iacr.org/2013/709

19. Ducas, L., Durmus, A., Lepoint, T., Lyubashevsky, V.: Lattice signatures and bimodal gaussians. In: Canetti, R., Garay, J.A. (eds.) CRYPTO 2013. LNCS, vol. 8042, pp. 40–56. Springer, Heidelberg (2013). https://doi.org/10.1007/978-3-642-40041-4_3

20. Fiat, A., Shamir, A.: How to prove yourself: practical solutions to identification and signature problems. In: Odlyzko, A.M. (ed.) CRYPTO 1986. LNCS, vol. 263, pp. 186–194. Springer, Heidelberg (1987). https://doi.org/10.1007/3-540-47721-7_12

21. S. Fluhrer. Cryptanalysis of ring-LWE based key exchange with key share reuse. Cryptology ePrint Archive, Report 2016/085, 2016. https://eprint.iacr.org/2016/085

22. Fujisaki, E.: New constructions of efficient simulation-sound commitments using encryption and their applications. In: Dunkelman, O. (ed.) CT-RSA 2012, volume 7178 of LNCS, pp. 136–155. Springer, Heidelberg, Feb. / (2012)

23. Fujisaki, E., Okamoto, T.: Secure integration of asymmetric and symmetric encryption schemes. In: Wiener, M.J. (ed.) CRYPTO'99. LNCS, vol. 1666, pp. 537–554. Springer, Heidelberg (1999)
24. Galbraith, S.D., Petit, C., Silva, J.: Identification protocols and signature schemes based on supersingular isogeny problems. In: Takagi, T., Peyrin, T. (eds.) ASIACRYPT 2017. Part I, volume 10624 of LNCS, pp. 3–33. Springer, Heidelberg (2017)
25. Gentry, C., Peikert, C., Vaikuntanathan, V.: Trapdoors for hard lattices and new cryptographic constructions. In: Ladner, R.E., Dwork, C. (eds.) 40th ACM STOC, pp. 197–206. ACM Press, May 2008
26. Güneysu, T., Lyubashevsky, V., Pöppelmann, T.: Practical lattice-based cryptography: a signature scheme for embedded systems. In: Prouff, E., Schaumont, P. (eds.) CHES 2012. LNCS, vol. 7428, pp. 530–547. Springer, Heidelberg (2012). https://doi.org/10.1007/978-3-642-33027-8_31
27. Heinz, D., Kannwischer, M.J., Land, G., Pöppelmann, T., Schwabe, P., Sprenkels, D.: First-order masked kyber on ARM cortex-M4. Cryptology ePrint Archive, Report 2022/058 (2022). https://eprint.iacr.org/2022/058
28. Heyse, S., Kiltz, E., Lyubashevsky, V., Paar, C., Pietrzak, K.: Lapin: an efficient authentication protocol based on ring-LPN. In: Canteaut, A. (ed.) FSE 2012. LNCS, vol. 7549, pp. 346–365. Springer, Heidelberg (2012). https://doi.org/10.1007/978-3-642-34047-5_20
29. Jao, D., De Feo, L.: Towards quantum-resistant cryptosystems from supersingular elliptic curve isogenies. In: Yang, B.-Y. (ed.) PQCrypto 2011. LNCS, vol. 7071, pp. 19–34. Springer, Heidelberg (2011). https://doi.org/10.1007/978-3-642-25405-5_2
30. Kannwischer, M.J., Rijneveld, J., Schwabe, P., Stoffelen, K.: PQM4: Post-quantum crypto library for the ARM Cortex-M4. https://github.com/mupq/pqm4
31. Kannwischer, M.J., Rijneveld, J., Schwabe, P., Stoffelen, K.: pqm4: testing and benchmarking NIST PQC on ARM cortex-M4. Cryptology ePrint Archive, Report 2019/844 (2019). https://eprint.iacr.org/2019/844
32. Kannwischer, M.J., Schwabe, P., Stebila, D., Wiggers, T.: Improving software quality in cryptography standardization projects. In: IEEE European Symposium on Security and Privacy, EuroS&P 2022 - Workshops, pp. 19–30. IEEE Computer Society, 2022. Cited for PQClean: Clean, portable, tested implementations of post-quantum cryptography, see https://github.com/PQClean/PQClean
33. Katz, J., Lindell, Y.: Introduction to Modern Cryptography, 2nd edn. CRC Press (2014)
34. Kiltz, E., Pietrzak, K., Cash, D., Jain, A., Venturi, D.: Efficient authentication from hard learning problems. In: Paterson, K.G. (ed.) EUROCRYPT 2011. LNCS, vol. 6632, pp. 7–26. Springer, Heidelberg (2011). https://doi.org/10.1007/978-3-642-20465-4_3
35. Kim, S., Hong, S.: Single trace analysis on constant time CDT sampler and its countermeasure. Appl. Sci. **8**(10), 1809 (2018)
36. Kuchta, V., Sakzad, A., Stehlé, D., Steinfeld, R., Sun, S.-F.: Measure-rewind-measure: tighter quantum random oracle model proofs for one-way to hiding and CCA security. In: Canteaut, A., Ishai, Y. (eds.) EUROCRYPT 2020. LNCS, vol. 12107, pp. 703–728. Springer, Cham (2020). https://doi.org/10.1007/978-3-030-45727-3_24
37. Lyubashevsky, V.: Lattice-based identification schemes secure under active attacks. In: Cramer, R. (ed.) PKC 2008. LNCS, vol. 4939, pp. 162–179. Springer, Heidelberg (2008)

38. Lyubashevsky, V.: Fiat-shamir with aborts: applications to lattice and factoring-based signatures. In: Matsui, M. (ed.) ASIACRYPT 2009. LNCS, vol. 5912, pp. 598–616. Springer, Heidelberg (2009). https://doi.org/10.1007/978-3-642-10366-7_35

39. Lyubashevsky, V., et al.: CRYSTALS-DILITHIUM. Technical report, National Institute of Standards and Technology (2020). https://csrc.nist.gov/projects/post-quantum-cryptography/round-3-submissions

40. Marzougui, S., Wisiol, N., Gersch, P., Krämer, J., Seifert, J.-P.: Machine-learning side-channel attacks on the GALACTICS constant-time implementation of BLISS. In: Proceedings of the 17th International Conference on Availability, Reliability and Security, pp. 1–11 (2022)

41. Migliore, V., Gérard, B., Tibouchi, M., Fouque, P.-A.: Masking Dilithium - efficient implementation and side-channel evaluation. In: Deng, R.H., Gauthier-Umaña, V., Ochoa, M., Yung, M. (eds.) ACNS 2019. LNCS, vol. 11464, pp. 344–362. Springer, Cham (2019). https://doi.org/10.1007/978-3-030-21568-2_17

42. Oder, T., Schneider, T., Pöppelmann, T., Güneysu, T.: Practical CCA2-secure masked Ring-LWE implementations. IACR TCHES 2018(1), 142–174 (2018). https://tches.iacr.org/index.php/TCHES/article/view/836

43. Ravi, P., Roy, S.S., Chattopadhyay, A., Bhasin, S.: Generic side-channel attacks on CCA-secure lattice-based PKE and KEMs. IACR TCHES 2020(3), 307–335 (2020). https://tches.iacr.org/index.php/TCHES/article/view/8592

44. Sakumoto, K., Shirai, T., Hiwatari, H.: Public-key identification schemes based on multivariate quadratic polynomials. In: Rogaway, P. (ed.) CRYPTO 2011. LNCS, vol. 6841, pp. 706–723. Springer, Heidelberg (2011). https://doi.org/10.1007/978-3-642-22792-9_40

45. Schneider, T., Paglialonga, C., Oder, T., Güneysu, T.: Efficiently masking binomial sampling at arbitrary orders for lattice-based crypto. In: Lin, D., Sako, K. (eds.) PKC 2019. LNCS, vol. 11443, pp. 534–564. Springer, Cham (2019). https://doi.org/10.1007/978-3-030-17259-6_18

46. Schwabe, P., et al.: CRYSTALS-KYBER. Technical report, National Institute of Standards and Technology (2020). https://csrc.nist.gov/projects/post-quantum-cryptography/round-3-submissions

47. Stern, J.: A new identification scheme based on syndrome decoding. In: Stinson, D.R. (ed.) CRYPTO 1993. LNCS, vol. 773, pp. 13–21. Springer, Heidelberg (1994). https://doi.org/10.1007/3-540-48329-2_2

48. Targhi, E.E., Unruh, D.: Post-quantum security of the Fujisaki-Okamoto and OAEP transforms. In: Hirt, M., Smith, A. (eds.) TCC 2016. LNCS, vol. 9986, pp. 192–216. Springer, Heidelberg (2016). https://doi.org/10.1007/978-3-662-53644-5_8

49. USB 3.0 Promoter Group. Universal serial bus security foundation specification, 2019. https://www.usb.org/document-library/usb-authentication-specification-rev-10-ecn-and-errata-through-january-7-2019

50. Zhandry, M.: Secure identity-based encryption in the quantum random oracle model. In: Safavi-Naini, R., Canetti, R. (eds.) CRYPTO 2012. LNCS, vol. 7417, pp. 758–775. Springer, Heidelberg (2012). https://doi.org/10.1007/978-3-642-32009-5_44

51. Zhao, R.K., Steinfeld, R., Sakzad, A.: FACCT: fast, compact, and constant-time discrete Gaussian sampler over integers. IEEE Trans. Comput. 69(1), 126–137 (2019)

POLKA: Towards Leakage-Resistant Post-quantum CCA-Secure Public Key Encryption

Clément Hoffmann[1(✉)], Benoît Libert[2], Charles Momin[1], Thomas Peters[1], and François-Xavier Standaert[1]

[1] Crypto Group, ICTEAM Institute, UCLouvain, Louvain-la-Neuve, Belgium
charlotte.hoffmann@ist.ac.at, fstandae@uclouvain.be
[2] Zama, Annecy, France

Abstract. As for any cryptographic algorithm, the deployment of post-quantum CCA-secure public key encryption schemes may come with the need to be protected against side-channel attacks. For existing post-quantum schemes that have not been developed with leakage in mind, recent results showed that the cost of these protections can make their implementations more expensive by orders of magnitude. In this paper, we describe a new design, coined POLKA, that is specifically tailored to reduce this cost. It leverages various ingredients in order to enable efficient side-channel protected implementations such as: (i) the rigidity property (which intuitively means that the de-randomized encryption and decryption are injective functions) to avoid the very leaky re-encryption step of the Fujisaki-Okamoto transform, (ii) the randomization of the decryption thanks to the incorporation of a dummy ciphertext, removing the adversary's control of its intermediate computations and making these computations ephemeral, (iii) key-homomorphic computations that can be masked against side-channel attacks with overheads that scale linearly in the number of shares, (iv) hard physical learning problems to argue about the security of some critical unmasked operations. Furthermore, we use an explicit rejection mechanism (returning an error symbol for invalid ciphertexts) to avoid the additional leakage caused by implicit rejection. As a result, the operations of POLKA can be protected against leakage in a cheaper way than state-of-the-art designs, opening the way towards schemes that are both quantum-safe and leakage-resistant.

1 Introduction

Recent research efforts showed that designing post-quantum chosen-ciphertext-secure public-key encryption (PKE) schemes that allow efficient implementations offering side-channel security guarantees is extremely challenging with existing techniques. One well-documented issue arises from the Fujisaki-Okamoto

---

B. Libert—This work was done when this author was a CNRS researcher at Laboratoire LIP (UMR CNRS - ENS Lyon - UCB Lyon 1 - INRIA 5668), Lyon, France.

A. Boldyreva and V. Kolesnikov (Eds.): PKC 2023, LNCS 13940, pp. 114–144, 2023.
https://doi.org/10.1007/978-3-031-31368-4_5

(FO) transform that is frequently used for building key encapsulation mechanisms (KEMs) with chosen-ciphertext (IND-CCA) security from PKE schemes or KEMs that only provide weak security notions like one-wayness under passive attacks (OW-CPA security) [42,43]. The FO transformation and its variants are, for example, used in the NIST post-quantum finalists KYBER [4,20] and SABER [10,31], where the CCA-secure KEM is combined with a secret-key (authenticated) encryption scheme into a hybrid PKE system.

Recall that a KEM system (Keygen, Encaps, Decaps) is a PKE scheme that does not take any plaintext as input, but rather computes an encryption of a random symmetric key K. To encrypt a plaintext M via the hybrid KEM/DEM framework [63], the Encaps algorithm often samples a random m, which is used to derive a symmetric key K and random coins r from a random oracle $(K, r) \leftarrow H(m)$ before deterministically encapsulating K as $c_{kem} = \mathsf{Encaps}_{pk}(m, r)$. Next, a secret-key scheme (E, D) (a.k.a. data encapsulation mechanism, or DEM) is used to compute $c_{sym} = \mathsf{E}_K(M)$ in order to obtain a hybrid PKE ciphertext $c = (c_{kem}, c_{sym})$. The receiver can then recover $m = \mathsf{Decaps}_{sk}(c_{kem})$ and $(K, r) \leftarrow H(m)$ before obtaining $M = \mathsf{D}_K(c_{sym})$. It is known that the hybrid construction provides IND-CCA security if the underlying KEM is itself IND-CCA-secure and if the DEM satisfies a similar security notion in the secret-key setting [63]. In order to secure the KEM part against chosen-ciphertext attacks, the FO transform usually checks the validity of the incoming c_{kem} by testing if $c_{kem} = \mathsf{Encaps}_{pk}(m, r)$ (a step known as "re-encryption") after having recovered the random coins r from $(K, r) \leftarrow H(m)$ upon decryption.

In the FO transform, the first computation during a decryption attempt is $\mathsf{Decaps}_{sk}(c_{kem})$, where Decaps is the underlying decapsulation of the OW-CPA secure KEM. While this has no impact in a black-box security analysis, in the context of side-channel chosen-ciphertext attacks the adversary remains able to target this component using many c_{kem} values of its choice [57,60,64], leaving an important source of vulnerabilities. Indeed, the adversary is free to adaptively feed Decaps_{sk} with (invalid) ciphertexts and craft c_{kem} in such a way that an internal message m with only few unknown bits is re-encrypted via the FO transform. This allows side-channel attacks to directly exploit the leakage of these bits obtained during the re-encryption test $c_{kem} \stackrel{?}{=} \mathsf{Encaps}_{pk}(m, r)$ to infer information about sk. This task is surprisingly easy since all the leakage samples of the deterministic re-encryption can be exploited for this purpose (i.e., much more than the few rounds of leakage that are typically exploited in divide-and-conquer side-channel attacks against symmetric encryption schemes) [53].

In parallel, several pieces of work started to analyze masked implementations of KYBER and SABER [11,17,21,22,41]. These works typically indicate large overheads when high security levels are required, which can be directly connected to a large amount of leaking intermediate computations [5]. In particular, these implementations all consider a uniform protection level for all their operations, that is in contrast with the situation of symmetric cryptography where so-called leveled implementations, in which different (more or less sensitive) parts of a mode of operation are protected with different (more or less expensive) side-channel countermeasures, can lead to important performance gains [14].

In this paper, we therefore initiate the study of quantum-safe CCA-secure public-key encryption schemes that have good features for leakage-resistant (LR) implementations. For this purpose, we propose to combine the different seed ingredients. First, we leverage the *rigidity* property introduced by Bernstein and Persichetti [15], as it allows building CCA-secure encryption schemes without relying on re-encryption nor on the FO transform. Despite removing an important source of leakage, getting rid of the FO transform is not yet sufficient to enable leveled implementations for KYBER (or SABER), since the rest of their operations remains expensive to protect [5]. Therefore, we also propose to randomize the decryption process by incorporating a "dummy ciphertext". It brings the direct benefit of removing the adversary's control on all intermediate computations that are dummied, while making these computations ephemeral, which is in general helpful against leakage. This second step already allows an interesting leveling between computations that require security against simple power analysis (SPA) and differential power analysis (DPA) attacks.[1] Eventually, we observe that the structure of the KEM's remaining DPA target shares similarities with the key-homomorphic re-keying schemes used in symmetric cryptography to prevent side-channel attacks [36,40,55]. Building on this observation, we propose to implement this DPA target such that only its key-homomorphic parts are (efficiently) protected thanks to masking, by relying on the recently introduced Learning With Physical Rounding (LWPR) assumption [39]. In short, the LWPR assumption is a physical version of the crypto dark matter introduced by Boneh *et al.* [19]. The latter assumes that low-complexity PRFs can be obtained by mixing linear mappings over different small moduli. LWPR further leverages the possibility that one of these mappings is computed by a leakage function.

We additionally observe that by carefully instantiating the symmetric authenticated encryption of the DEM as an Encrypt-then-MAC scheme with a one-time key-homomorphic MAC, the overheads due to the side-channel countermeasures can be reduced to linear in the number of shares used for masking for this part of the computation as well. And we finally combine these different ingredients into a new efficient post-quantum CCA-secure public-key encryption scheme, called POLKA (standing for POst-quantum Leakage-resistant public Key encryption Algorithm), that *simultaneously* provides excellent features against leakage and a proof of IND-CCA security (in the sense of the standard definition without leakage) under the standard RLWE assumption.

Without leakage, we show that POLKA provides CCA security in the quantum random oracle model (QROM) [18]. Our construction is a hybrid KEM-DEM encryption scheme built upon a variant of a public-key encryption scheme due to Lyubashevsky, Peikert and Regev (LPR) [52], which is well-known to provide IND-CPA security under the ring learning-with-errors (RLWE) assumption. In order to obtain a KEM, we modify the LPR system so as to recover the sender's random coins upon decryption. In contrast with the FO transformation and

---

[1] Informally, SPAs are side-channel attacks where the adversary can only observe the leakage of a few inputs to the target operation for a given secret. DPAs are attacks where the adversary can observe the leakage of many such inputs.

its variants, this is achieved without de-randomizing an IND-CPA system, by deriving the sender's random coins. Instead of encrypting a random message m to derive our symmetric key K, we always "encrypt" 0 and hash the random coins consisting of a tuple $(r, e_1, e_2) \in R$ of small-norm ring elements sampled from the noise distribution. These elements (r, e_1, e_2) are then encoded into a pair $c_{kem} = (a \cdot r + e_1, b \cdot r + e_2) \in R_q^2$, where $a, b \in R_q$ are random-looking elements included in the public key. Using its secret key, the decryptor can extract (r, e_1, e_2) from c_{kem} and check their smallness. This verification/extraction step is designed in such a way that decapsulation natively provides rigidity [15] without relying on re-encryption. Namely, due to the way to recover (r, e_1, e_2) from c_{kem}, we are guaranteed that deterministically re-computing $c_{kem} = (a \cdot r + e_1, b \cdot r + e_2)$ would yield the incoming ciphertext. This allows dispensing with the need to explicitly re-compute c_{kem} in the real scheme, thus eliminating an important source of side-channel vulnerability that affects KYBER and SABER.

In a black-box security analysis, our KEM can be seen as an injective trap-door function that maps $(r, e_1, e_2) \in R^3$ to $(a \cdot r + e_1, b \cdot r + e_2)$. As long as we sample (r, e_1, e_2) from a suitable distribution, c_{kem} is pseudorandom under the RLWE assumption. However, to ease the use of efficient side-channel counter-measures upon decryption, we also leverage the fact that our injection satisfies a (bounded) form of additive homomorphism for appropriate parameters. That is, if we generate what we call a *dummy* ciphertext c'_{kem} by having the decryp-tor honestly run the basic encapsulation step using its own random coins, the decapsulation of $\bar{c}_{kem} = c_{kem} + c'_{kem}$ should give the sum of the random coins chosen by the sender and the receiver. Then, we can easily remove the addi-tional *dummy* random coins after some additional tests. Introducing $\bar{c}_{kem}$ in the decryption process removes the adversary's freedom of forcing the computation of $\mathsf{Decaps}_{sk}(c_{kem})$ to take place on a c_{kem} under its control, which helps us pro-tecting the secret key. Moreover, the underlying coins of c_{kem} are now split into two shares upon decryption and they are only recombined in a step where we can safely derive K. To implement this idea, we prove the CCA security of our scheme in its variant endowed with a probabilistic decryption algorithm.

With leakage, we argue that POLKA offers a natural path towards efficient leveled implementations secured against side-channel attacks. For this purpose, we first use a methodology inspired from [14] to identify the level of security required for all its intermediate computations. We then focus on how to secure the polynomial multiplication used in POLKA against DPA, by combining mask-ing for its key-homomorphic parts and a variant of the aforementioned LWPR assumption after the shares recombination. Our contributions in this respect are twofold. On the one hand, we define the LWPR variant on which POLKA relies and discuss its difference from the original one. Given that LWPR is an admittedly recent assumption and in view of the important performance gains it can lead to, we additionally specify instances to serve as cryptanalysis targets. On the other hand, we describe a hardware architecture for these masked operations, which confirms these excellent features (e.g., simplicity to implement them securely, performance overheads that are linear in the number of shares). Overall, protect-ing the long-term secret of our leveled implementation only needs to combine the masking of key-homomorphic computations (which has linear overheads in the number of shares) with SPA security for other computations, which is directly obtained thanks to parallelism in hardware. Protecting the message confidentiality additionally requires protecting its symmetric cryptographic components (i.e., hash function and authenticated encryption) against DPA.

As a last result to confirm the generality of our findings, we also show in the ePrint report [46] that they apply to an LR variant of the NTRU cryptosystem [27], which satisfies the rigidity property, can be enhanced with a dummy mechanism and has internal computations that also generate LWPR samples.

2   Technical Overview and Cautionary Note

TECHNICAL OVERVIEW. Our construction can be seen as a rigid and randomness-recovering version of the RLWE-based encryption scheme described in [52]. By "randomness-recovering," we mean that the decryption procedure recovers the message *and* the sender's random coins. A randomness-recovering encryption scheme is rigid [15] if, when the decryptor obtains a message m and randomness r, running the encryption algorithm on input of (m, r) necessarily yields the incoming ciphertext. While rigidity can always be achieved by adding a re-encryption step (as pointed out in [47]), this generally introduces one-more place of potential side-channel vulnerabilities, which is precisely exploited in [57,60,64]. In order to eliminate the need for an explicit re-encryption step, it is thus desirable to have a decryption algorithm which is natively injective (when seen as a deterministic function). The first difficulty is thus to build a rigid, randomness-recovering PKE/KEM under the standard RLWE assumption. Our goal is to achieve this without sacrificing the efficiency of the original LPR system in order to remain reasonably competitive with NIST finalists.

The LPR cryptosystem is not randomness-recovering. In a cyclotomic ring $R = \mathbb{Z}[X]/(X^n + 1)$, it involves a public key containing a pair $(a, b = a \cdot s + e)$, where $a \in R/(qR)$ is uniform, $s \in R$ is the secret key and e is a noise. To encrypt $m \in R/(pR)$ (for some moduli $p < q$), the sender chooses small-norm randomness $r, e_1, e_2 \in R$ and computes $(c_1, c_2) = (a \cdot r + e_1, b \cdot r + e_2 + m \cdot \lfloor q/p \rceil)$, so that the receiver can obtain $c_2 - c_1 \cdot s \bmod q = m \cdot \lfloor q/p \rceil + \mathsf{small}$. While m is then computable, there is no way to recover (r, e_1, e_2) from the "decryption error" term small. To address this problem, a folklore solution is to introduce distinct powers of p. Suppose we want to build a randomness-recovering encryption of 0 (which is sufficient to build a KEM). The sender can then compute $(c_1, c_2) = (p^2 \cdot a \cdot r + p \cdot e_1, p^2 \cdot b \cdot r + e_2)$, which allows the receiver to obtain $\mu = c_2 - c_1 \cdot s \bmod q = p^2 e r - p e_1 s + e_2$. Since the right-hand-side member is small, the receiver can efficiently decode $(r, e_1, e_2) \in R^3$ from μ. Unfortunately, the latter construction is not rigid. Suppose that an adversary can somehow compute a non-trivial pair $(u, u \cdot s) \in R^2$ given $(a, a \cdot s + e)$. It can then faithfully compute $(c_1, c_2) = (p^2 \cdot a \cdot r + p \cdot e_1, p^2 \cdot b \cdot r + e_2)$ and turn it into $(c_1', c_2') = (c_1 + u, c_2 + u \cdot s)$, which yields a "decryption collision" $\mu = c_2 - c_1 \cdot s = c_2' - c_1' \cdot s$. Besides, as shown in [32], computing a pair $(u, u \cdot s)$

(for an arbitrary, possibly non-invertible $u \neq 0$) given $(a, a \cdot s + e)$ can only be hard in rings $R/(qR) \cong \mathbb{Z}_q[X]/(\Phi_1(X)) \times \cdots \times \mathbb{Z}_q[X]/(\Phi_t(X))$ that have no small-degree factors, which rules out NTT-friendly rings. Even for rings where $\Phi(X) = X^n + 1$ splits into degree-$n/2$ factors, the problem (called SIP-LWE in [32]) is non-standard and its hardness is not known to be implied by RLWE.[2] Here, we take a different approach since we aim at rigidity without relying on stronger assumptions than RLWE and without forbidding fully splitting rings.

We modify the original LPR system in the following way. The public key contains a random $a \in R/(qR)$ and a pseudorandom $b \in R/(qR)$, which is now of the form $b = p \cdot (a \cdot s + e)$, for small secrets $s, e \in R$ and a public integer p such that $\|e\|_\infty < p/2$. We also require b to be invertible over $R/(qR)$, so that the key generation phase must be repeated with new candidates (s, e) until b is a unit. To compute an encapsulation, we sample Gaussian ring elements $r, e_1, e_2 \in R$ and compute $c_{kem} = (c_1, c_2) = (a \cdot r + e_1, b \cdot r + e_2)$, where $K = H(r, e_1, e_2)$ is the encapsulated key. Decapsulation is performed by using $s \in R$ to compute $\mu = c_2 - p \cdot c_1 \cdot s \bmod q$, which is a small-norm element $\mu = e_2 + p \cdot \mathsf{small} \in R$ that reveals $e_2 = \mu \bmod p$. Given e_2, the receiver then obtains $r = (c_2 - e_2) \cdot b^{-1}$ and $e_1 = c_1 - a \cdot r$, and checks the smallness of (r, e_1, e_2). The decapsulation phase is natively *rigid* (without re-encryption) as it outputs small-norm $(r, e_1, e_2) \in R^3$ *if and only if* $(c_1, c_2) = (a \cdot r + e_1, b \cdot r + e_2)$.

Our hybrid encryption scheme builds on a variant of the above KEM with *explicit rejection*, where the decapsulation phase returns an error symbol $\perp$ on input of an invalid c_{kem}. It thus departs from NIST finalists that all rely on KEMs with implicit rejection, where the decapsulation algorithm never outputs $\perp$, but rather handles invalid encapsulations c_{kem} by outputting a random key $K' \leftarrow H(z, c_{kem})$ derived from an independent long-term secret z.[3] While our scheme could have relied on implicit rejection in a similar way, we chose to avoid additional computations involving an extra long-term secret z. The reason is that, if we were to introduce additional key material z, it should be DPA-protected with possibly heavy side-channel countermeasures (cf. Section 5.1).

When it comes to proving security in the QROM, the use of an explicit-rejection KEM introduces some difficulty as it is not clear how to deal with invalid ciphertexts. While the classical ROM allows inspecting all random oracle queries and determining if one of them explains a given ciphertext, we cannot use this approach in the QROM because RO-queries are made on superpositions of inputs. Our solution is to use an implicit-rejection KEM only in the security proof. In a sequence of games, we first modify the decryption oracle so as to make the rejection process implicit. Then, we argue that, as long as the DEM component is realized using an authenticated symmetric encryption scheme, the

---

[2] D'Anvers *et al.* [32] defined a homogeneous variant of SIP-LWE which is unconditionally hard, even in fully splitting rings. Still, relying on this variant incurs a partial re-encryption to enforce the equality $c_2 = c_2'$.

[3] When the hybrid KEM-DEM framework is instantiated with an implicit rejection KEM, invalid ciphertexts are usually rejected during the symmetric decryption step as decrypting c_{sym} with a random key K' yields $\perp$.

modified decryption oracle is indistinguishable from the real one. After having modified the decryption oracle, we can adapt ideas from Saito *et al.* [62] in order to tightly relate the security of the hybrid scheme to the RLWE assumption.

As mentioned earlier, avoiding re-encryption does not suffice to ensure side-channel resistance. As another improvement, we modify the decapsulation step and add a dummy ciphertext $(c_1', c_2') = (a \cdot r' + e_1', b \cdot r' + e_2')$ for fresh receiver-chosen randomness r', e_1', e_2' to (c_1, c_2) before proceeding with the decapsulation of $(\bar{c}_1, \bar{c}_2) = (c_1 + c_1', c_2 + c_2')$. This simple trick prevents the adversary from controlling the ring elements that multiply the secret key s at the only step where it is involved. We even show in Sect. 5 how this computation can be protected against DPA with minimum overheads by combination the masking countermeasure and a LWPR assumption. Additionally, the choice of (c_1', c_2') as an honestly generated encapsulation allows continuing the decryption process as if $(\bar{c}_1, \bar{c}_2)$ was the ciphertext computed from the (still) small-norm coins $(\bar{r}, \bar{e}_1, \bar{e}_2) = (r + r', e_1 + e_1', e_2 + e_2')$. That is, we do not have to remove the noise terms as we can retrieve $\bar{r}$, $\bar{e}_1$ and $\bar{e}_2$ and test their smallness. Since r', e_1' and e_2' do have small norm, if the decryption succeeds until this step, then r, e_1 and e_2 must be small as well (with a small constant slackness factor 3). Therefore, the dummy ciphertext/KEM makes it possible to eliminate an exponential amount of invalid ciphertexts without having ever tried to re-compute the correct (r, e_1, e_2). In case of an early rejection, and because the secret key s is now protected with a hidden and pseudorandom $(\bar{c}_1, \bar{c}_2)$, the leakage only provides limited information related to the ephemeral values in (r', e_1', e_2') which were sampled independently of the adversary's view. If no rejection occurs, (r', e_1', e_2') has components of (small but) sufficiently large norm to hide (at least most of the bits of) (r, e_1, e_2) if the adversary gets the full leakage of $(\bar{r}, \bar{e}_1, \bar{e}_2)$. At that time, we can safely recover (r, e_1, e_2) and check their norm (to eliminate the slackness) for technical reasons. This computation can only be repeated through many decryption queries on fixed inputs, and therefore only require SPA security (with averaging), which is cheaper to ensure than DPA security. As for the DEM, the general solutions outlined in [14] are a natural option. But we show an even cheaper one that leverages a key-homomorphic MAC.

CAUTIONARY NOTE. Advances in leakage-resistant cryptography usually combine progresses following two main movements. On the one hand, theoretical works aim to specify sufficient conditions of security in abstract models. On the other hand, practical works rather aim to study heuristic countermeasures against concrete attacks (i.e., necessary security conditions). The long-term goal of such researches is therefore to "meet in the middle", which can occur either by making sufficient security conditions empirically falsifiable or by making the heuristic study of countermeasures more and more general. Reaching this goal is challenging due to the continuous and device-specific nature of physical leakages. In the case of symmetric cryptography, such movements are for example witnessed by definitional efforts like [45] and instances of (initially) more heuristic designs like ISAP [34] or Ascon [35], while their match has been recently discussed in [14]. In the case of asymmetric post-quantum cryptography, it is expected to be even more challenging since algorithms come with more versatile building blocks that will in turn require a finer-grain analysis (than just relying on block ciphers or permutations, for example). Given the amplitude of the challenge, the approach we follow is a bottom-up one. That is, we aim to show that considering the need for side-channel countermeasures as a design criterion can lead to encryption schemes that are easier to protect. For this purpose, we focus our analysis on intuitive design tweaks (for which we can explain how they avoid certain attack vectors) and on their necessary security conditions. We hope the design of POLKA can serve as a trigger for more formal analyses leading to identify sufficient security conditions for (part of) its design or improvements thereof, and that this formal analysis will be easier than for encryption schemes that did not consider leakage to guide their design, like KYBER or SABER.

In this context, one can naturally wonder why we do not provide a comprehensive comparison of POLKA with KYBER or SABER. The short answer is that the current state-of-the-art does not allow such comparisons yet. That is, a sound comparison between post-quantum encryption schemes against side-channel attacks would require assessing their cost vs. security tradeoff. But while there are several works that evaluate the (high) cost of masking KYBER or SABER, none of them come with a quantitative security evaluation against worst-case adversaries (e.g., as done in [24] for the AES). Therefore, we are for now left with the more quantitative analysis of Sect. 5.1, where we identify the parts of POLKA that must be protected against DPA and the ones that only require protections against SPA, together with the observation of Sect. 5.2 and 5.3 that the DPA security of some critical operations in POLKA can be obtained with overheads that scale linearly in the number of shares (vs. quadratic for KYBER or SABER). As in the context of symmetric cryptography, it is naturally expected that POLKA comes with overheads in case leakage is not a concern. However, considering for simplicity that they are dominated by the cost of the NTTs and multiplications, the larger polynomials (e.g., $n = 1024$ vs. $n = 512$ for KYBER) and modulus (e.g., 16-bit vs. 12-bit for KYBER) of POLKA should not decrease performances by large factors. For example, assuming NTTs have complexity in $\mathcal{O}(n \log(n))$ and multiplications have complexity in $\mathcal{O}(\log(q)^2)$, while taking into account the number of such operations, the factor of overheads of POLKA over KYBER would be around two. Besides, POLKA makes a sparser use of symmetric cryptography and its design (without FO transform) should require less shares for its masked implementations to provide the same security level. We informally illustrate the cycle counts of POLKA and KYBER in function of the number of shares of their masked implementation in Fig. 1, where the black (quadratic) curve is from [22] and the red (linear) ones assume POLKA is from twice to (a conservative) five times more expensive than KYBER without countermeasures. Turning this qualitative analysis into a quantitative one in order to determine the target security level (and number of shares) that makes POLKA or improvements thereof a relevant alternative to existing schemes is an interesting scope for further investigations. As for the aforementioned quest towards analyzing sufficient security conditions for leakage-resistant post-quantum encryption schemes, we therefore hope our results can serve as a trigger towards evaluating the worst-case side-channel security level of masked post-quantum encryption schemes.

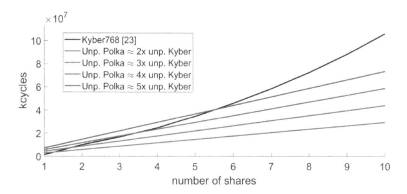

Fig. 1. Informal comparison between masked `POLKA` (n=1024, 16-bit modulus, $\approx$191 bits of security – see Sect. 4.3) and `KYBER768` (196 bits of security).

Additional related works are discussed in the ePrint report [46].

3 Background

3.1 Lattices and Discrete Gaussian Distributions

An n-dimensional lattice $\Lambda \subseteq \mathbb{R}^n$ is the set $\Lambda = \{\sum_{i=1}^{n} z_i \cdot \mathbf{b}_i \mid \mathbf{z} \in \mathbb{Z}^n\}$ of all integer linear combinations of a set of linearly independent basis vectors $\mathbf{B} = \{\mathbf{b}_1, \ldots, \mathbf{b}_n\} \subseteq \mathbb{R}^n$. Let $\mathbf{\Sigma} \in \mathbb{R}^{n \times n}$ be a symmetric positive definite matrix, and $\mathbf{c} \in \mathbb{R}^n$. The n-dimensional Gaussian function on $\mathbb{R}^n$ is defined as $\rho_{\sqrt{\mathbf{\Sigma}}, \mathbf{c}}(\mathbf{x}) = \exp(-\pi(\mathbf{x} - \mathbf{c})^\top \mathbf{\Sigma}^{-1}(\mathbf{x} - \mathbf{c}))$. In the special case where $\mathbf{\Sigma} = \sigma^2 \cdot \mathbf{I}_n$ and $\mathbf{c} = \mathbf{0}$, we denote it by ρ_σ. For any lattice $\Lambda \subset \mathbb{R}^n$, the discrete Gaussian distribution $D_{\Lambda, \sqrt{\mathbf{\Sigma}}, \mathbf{c}}$ has probability mass $\Pr_{X \sim D_{\Lambda, \sqrt{\mathbf{\Sigma}}, \mathbf{c}}}[X = \mathbf{x}] = \frac{\rho_{\sqrt{\mathbf{\Sigma}}, \mathbf{c}}(\mathbf{x})}{\rho_{\sqrt{\mathbf{\Sigma}}, \mathbf{c}}(\Lambda)}$ for any $\mathbf{x} \in \Lambda$. When $\mathbf{c} = \mathbf{0}$ and $\mathbf{\Sigma} = \sigma^2 \cdot \mathbf{I}_n$ we denote it by $D_{\Lambda, \sigma}$.

Lemma 1 (*[56]*, **Lemma 4.4**). *For $\sigma = \omega(\sqrt{\log n})$ there is a negligible function $\varepsilon = \varepsilon(n)$ such that $\Pr_{\mathbf{x} \sim D_{\mathbb{Z}^n, \sigma}}[\|\mathbf{x}\| > \sigma\sqrt{n}] \leq \frac{1+\varepsilon}{1-\varepsilon} \cdot 2^{-n}$.*

3.2 Rings and Ideal Lattices

Let n a power of 2 and define the rings $R = \mathbb{Z}[X]/(X^n + 1)$ and $R_q = R/qR$. Each element of R is a $(n-1)$-degree polynomial in $\mathbb{Z}[X]$ and can be interpreted as an element of $\mathbb{Z}[X]$ via the natural coefficient embedding that maps the polynomial $a = \sum_{i=0}^{n-1} a_i X^i \in R$ to $(a_0, a_1, \ldots, a_{n-1}) \in \mathbb{Z}^n$. An element of R_q can similarly be viewed as a degree-$(n-1)$ polynomial over $\mathbb{Z}_q[X]$ and represented as an n-dimensional vector with coefficients in the range $\{-(q-1)/2, \ldots, (q-1)/2\}$.

The Euclidean and infinity norms of an element of $a \in R$ are defined by viewing elements of R as elements of $\mathbb{Z}^n$ via the coefficient embedding.

The ring R can also be identified as the subring of anti-circulant matrices in $\mathbb{Z}^{n \times n}$ by viewing each $a \in R$ as a linear transformation $r \to a \cdot r$. This implies that, for any $a, b \in R$, $\|a \cdot b\|_\infty \leq \|a\| \cdot \|b\|$ by the Cauchy-Schwartz inequality.

As in [50], for any lattice Λ, $D_{\Lambda,\sigma}^{\mathsf{coeff}}$ denotes the distribution of a ring element $a = \sum_{i=0}^{n-1} a_i X^i \in R$ of which the coefficient vector $(a_0, \ldots, a_{n-1})^\top \in \mathbb{Z}^n$ is sampled from the discrete Gaussian distribution $D_{\Lambda,\sigma}$.

We now recall the ring variant of the Learning-With-Errors assumption [61]. The ring LWE (RLWE) problem is to distinguish between a polynomial number of pairs of the form $(a_i, a_i \cdot s + e_i)$, where $a_i \sim U(R_q)$ and $s, e_i \in R$ are sampled from some distribution χ of bounded-magnitude ring elements, and random pairs $(a_i, b_i) \sim U(R_q^2)$. In Definition 1, the number of samples k is made explicit.

Definition 1. *Let $\lambda \in \mathbb{N}$ a security parameter. Let positive integers $n = n(\lambda)$, $k = k(\lambda)$, and a prime $q = q(n) > 2$. Let an error distribution $\chi = \chi(n)$ over R. The $\mathsf{RLWE}_{n,k,q,\chi}$ assumption says that the following distance is a negligible function for any PPT algorithm $\mathcal{A}$,*

$$\mathbf{Adv}_{n,k,q,\chi}^{\mathcal{A},\mathsf{RLWE}}(\lambda) := \big| \Pr[\mathcal{A}(1^\lambda, \{(a_i, v_i)\}_{i=1}^k) = 1]$$
$$- \Pr[\mathcal{A}(1^\lambda, \{(a_i, a_i s + e_i)\}_{i=1}^k) = 1]\big|,$$

where $a_1, \ldots, a_i, v_1, \ldots, v_k \hookleftarrow U(R_q)$, $s \hookleftarrow \chi$, $e_1, \ldots, e_i \hookleftarrow \chi$.

For suitable parameters, the RLWE assumption is implied by the hardness of worst-case instances of the approximate shortest vector problem in ideal lattices.

Lemma 2 (*[52]*). *Let n a power of 2. Let $\Phi_m(X) = X^n + 1$ the m-th cyclotomic polynomial where $m = 2n$, and $R = \mathbb{Z}[X]/(\Phi_m(X))$. Let $q = 1 \bmod 2n$. Let also $r = \omega(\sqrt{\log n})$ Then, there is a randomized reduction from $2^{\omega(\log n)} \cdot (q/r)$-approximate R-SVP to $\mathsf{RLWE}_{n,\mathsf{poly}(n),q,\chi}$ where $\chi = D_{\mathbb{Z}^n,r}^{\mathsf{coeff}}$.*

4   POLKA: Rationale and Specifications

Our starting point is a variant of the LPR cryptosystem [52], which builds on a rigid randomness-recovering KEM. As in [52], the public key contains a random ring element $a \in R_q$ and a pseudorandom $b \in R_q$. Here, b is of the form $b = p \cdot (a \cdot s + e)$ (instead of $b = a \cdot s + e$ as in [52]), for secret $s, e \in R$ sampled from the noise distribution and where p is an integer such that $\|e\|_\infty < p$. Another difference with [52] is that decryption requires b to be invertible over R_q.

The encryptor samples ring elements $r, e_1, e_2 \in R$ from a Gaussian distribution and uses them to derive a symmetric key $K = H(r, e_1, e_2)$. The latter is then encapsulated by computing a pair $(c_1, c_2) = (a \cdot r + e_1, b \cdot r + e_2)$. The decryption algorithm uses $s \in R$ to compute $\mu = c_2 - p \cdot c_1 \cdot s \in R_q$, which is a small-norm ring element $\mu = e_2 + p \cdot (er - e_1 s) \in R$. This allows recovering $e_2 = \mu \bmod p$, which in turn reveals $r = (c_2 - e_2) \cdot b^{-1} \in R_q$ and $e_1 = c_1 - a \cdot r \in R_q$. After having checked the smallness of (r, e_1, e_2), the decryption procedure obtains $K = H(r, e_1, e_2)$. The scheme provides the *rigidity* property of [15] as the decryptor obtains $(r, e_1, e_2) \in R^3$ such that $\|r\|, \|e_1\|, \|e_2\| \le B$, for some norm bound B, if and only if $(c_1, c_2) = (a \cdot r + e_1, b \cdot r + e_2)$. This ensures that no re-encryption is necessary to check the validity of the input pair (c_1, c_2).

Our hybrid encryption scheme builds on a KEM with *explicit rejection* (as per [47,59]), meaning that invalid encapsulations are rejected as soon as they are noticed in decryption. In the security proof, we will switch to an implicit rejection mechanism (as defined [59, Section 5.3]), where the decapsulation algorithm outputs a random key on input of an invalid encapsulation. The rejection of malformed encapsulations is then deferred to the symmetric decryption.

4.1   The Scheme with an Additive Mask

We now describe a version of the scheme that has good features for side-channel resistant implementation, where the decryption algorithm first adds a "dummy ciphertext" to (c_1, c_2) before proceeding with the actual decryption.

Keygen(1^λ): Given a security parameter $\lambda \in \mathbb{N}$,

1. Choose a dimension $n \in \mathbb{N}$, a prime modulus $q = 1 \bmod 2n$. Let the rings $R = \mathbb{Z}[X]/(X^n + 1)$ and $R_q = R/(qR)$ such that $\Phi(X) = X^n + 1$ splits into linear factors over R_q. Let $R_q^\times$ the set of units in R_q.
2. Choose a noise parameter $\alpha \in (0, 1)$, and let a norm bound $B = \alpha q \sqrt{n}$. Choose an integer $p \in \mathbb{N}$ such that $4B < p < \frac{q}{8(B^2+1)}$.
3. Sample $a \hookleftarrow U(R_q)$ and $s, e \hookleftarrow D^{\text{coeff}}_{\mathbb{Z}^n, \alpha q}$ and compute $b = p \cdot (a \cdot s + e)$. If $b \notin R_q^\times$, restart step 3.
4. Choose an authenticated symmetric encryption scheme $\Pi^{sym} = (\mathsf{K}, \mathsf{E}, \mathsf{D})$ with key length $\kappa \in \mathsf{poly}(\lambda)$ and message space $\{0,1\}^{\ell_m}$.
5. Let a domain $D_E := \{(r, e_1, e_2) \in R^3 : \|r\|, \|e_1\|, \|e_2\| \le B\}$. Choose a hash function $H : D_E \to \{0,1\}^\kappa$ modeled as a random oracle.

Return the key pair (PK, SK) where

$$PK := \big(n,\ q,\ p,\ \alpha,\ a \in R_q,\ b \in R_q^\times,\ \Pi^{sym},\ H,\ B\big) \ \text{ and } \ SK := s \in R.$$

Optionally, one can add b^{-1} in PK (to avoid computing an inverse in decryption).

Encrypt(PK, M): Given a public key PK and a message $M \in \{0,1\}^{\ell_m}$:

1. Sample $r, e_1, e_2 \hookleftarrow D^{\text{coeff}}_{\mathbb{Z}^n, \alpha q}$ and compute

$$c_1 = a \cdot r + e_1 \in R_q, \qquad c_2 = b \cdot r + e_2 \in R_q$$

together with $K = H(r, e_1, e_2) \in \{0,1\}^\kappa$.
2. Compute $c_0 = \mathsf{E}_K(M)$.

Output the ciphertext $C = (c_0, c_1, c_2)$.

Decrypt(SK, C): Given $SK = s \in R$ and $C = (c_0, c_1, c_2)$, do the following:

1. Sample $r', e_1', e_2' \hookleftarrow D^{\text{coeff}}_{\mathbb{Z}^n, \alpha q}$ and return $\perp$ if $\|r'\| > B$, or $\|e_1'\| > B$, or $\|e_2'\| > B$. Otherwise, compute $c_1' = a \cdot r' + e_1'$ and $c_2' = b \cdot r' + e_2'$.
2. Compute $\bar{c}_1 = c_1 + c_1'$ and $\bar{c}_2 = c_2 + c_2'$.

3. Compute $\bar{\mu} = \bar{c}_2 - p \cdot \bar{c}_1 \cdot s$ over R_q.
4. Compute $\bar{e}_2 = \bar{\mu} \bmod p$. If $\|\bar{e}_2\| > 2B$, return $\perp$.
5. Compute $\bar{r} = (\bar{c}_2 - \bar{e}_2) \cdot b^{-1} \in R_q$. If $\|\bar{r}\| > 2B$, return $\perp$.
6. Compute $\bar{e}_1 = \bar{c}_1 - a \cdot \bar{r} \in R_q$. If $\|\bar{e}_1\| > 2B$, return $\perp$.
7. Compute $r = \bar{r} - r'$, $e_1 = \bar{e}_1 - e_1'$ and $e_2 = \bar{e}_2 - e_2'$. If $\|r\| > B$, or $\|e_1\| > B$, or $\|e_2\| > B$, then return $\perp$.
8. Compute $K = H(r, e_1, e_2) \in \{0,1\}^\kappa$ and return

$$M = \mathsf{D}_K(c_0) \in \{0,1\}^{\ell_m} \cup \{\perp\}.$$

The use of fully splitting rings may require multiple attempts to find an invertible $b \in R_q^\times$ as step 3 of Keygen. The proof of Lemma 7 shows that, unless the RLWE assumption is false, a suitable b can be found after at most $\lceil \lambda / \log n \rceil$ iterations, except with negligible probability $2^{-\lambda}$. In practice, a small number of attempts suffices since a random ring element is invertible with probability $1 - n/q$, which is larger than $1 - 1/n$ with our choice of parameters.

CORRECTNESS. Let $\bar{r} = r + r'$, $\bar{e}_1 = e_1 + e_1'$ and $\bar{e}_2 = e_2 + e_2'$ over R. At step 2, Decrypt computes $\bar{c}_1 = a \cdot \bar{r} + \bar{e}_1$, $\bar{c}_2 = b \cdot \bar{r} + \bar{e}_2$ over R_q, where $\|\bar{r}\|, \|\bar{e}_1\|, \|\bar{e}_2\| \le 2B$ with probability $1 - 2^{-\Omega(n)}$ over the randomness of Encrypt and Decrypt (by Lemma 1). At step 3, the decryptor obtains

$$\begin{aligned}
\bar{\mu} &= \bar{c}_2 - p \cdot \bar{c}_1 \cdot s \bmod q \\
&= (b \cdot \bar{r} + \bar{e}_2) - p \cdot (a \cdot \bar{r} + \bar{e}_1) \cdot s \bmod q \\
&= p \cdot (as + e) \cdot \bar{r} + \bar{e}_2 - p \cdot a\bar{r}s - p \cdot \bar{e}_1 s \bmod q \\
&= \bar{e}_2 + p \cdot e\bar{r} - p \cdot \bar{e}_1 s,
\end{aligned}$$

where the last equality holds over R with overwhelming probability over the randomness of Keygen, Encrypt and Decrypt. Indeed, Lemma 1 implies that $\|s\|, \|e\| \le \alpha q \sqrt{n}$ with probability $1 - 2^{-\Omega(n)}$ over the randomness of Keygen. With probability $1 - 2^{-\Omega(n)}$ over the randomness of Encrypt and Decrypt, we also have $\|\bar{r}\|, \|\bar{e}_1\|, \|\bar{e}_2\| \le 2\alpha q \sqrt{n}$. Then, the Cauchy-Schwartz inequality implies

$$\|\bar{e}_2 + p \cdot e\bar{r} - p \cdot \bar{e}_1 s\|_\infty < 2\alpha q \sqrt{n} + 4p \cdot (\alpha q)^2 n \qquad (1)$$
$$< 4p(B^2 + 1) < q/2.$$

Since $p/2 > 2\alpha q \sqrt{n}$, step 4 recovers $\bar{e}_2$ with overwhelming probability. Since $b \in R_q^\times$, Decrypt obtains $\bar{r}$ at step 5 and $\bar{e}_1$ at step 6. Therefore, it also recovers (r, e_1, e_2) at step 7 and the correct symmetric key $K = H(r, e_1, e_2)$ at step 8. Correctness thus follows from the correctness of Π^{sym}.

Remark 1. We note that correctness is guaranteed whenever $\|s\|, \|e\| \le B$ and $\|\bar{r}\|, \|\bar{e}_1\|, \|\bar{e}_2\| \le 2B$, as it is a sufficient condition to have inequalities (1).

RIGIDITY. By direct inspection of the decryption algorithm, given the KEM part (c_1, c_2), if it can extract a triple (r, e_1, e_2) in the domain, later called D_E, where each component has Euclidean norm bounded by B, the decapsulation is valid. If the decapsulation is valid we have $r = (c_2 - e_2)/b$ and $e_1 = c_1 - a \cdot r$ by definition (after removing the masks r', e_1', e_2'). Hence, $c_1 = a \cdot r + e_1$ and $c_2 = b \cdot r + e_2$, which is the public encapsulation part on input (r, e_1, e_2).

ON DECRYPTION FAILURES. Due to the rigidity and randomness recovery properties of the scheme, the probability of decryption failure does not depend on the specific secret key s in use as long as $\|s\| \le B$. If $(r, e_1, e_2) \in D_E$ and $\|s\| \le B$, we always have $\|\bar{\mu}\|_\infty \le q/2$, where $\bar{\mu} = \bar{c}_2 - p \cdot \bar{c}_1 \cdot s \bmod q = p \cdot (e \cdot \bar{r} - \bar{e}_1 \cdot s) + \bar{e}_2$ unless the ciphertext is rejected at step 1 (which does not depend on s). If $(r, e_1, e_2) \notin D_E$, then either: (i) we still have $\|\bar{\mu}\|_\infty \le q/2$ and Decrypt obtains (r, e_1, e_2), which are necessarily rejected; or (ii) $\|\bar{\mu}\|_\infty > q/2$ but the extracted $(r^\dagger, e_1^\dagger, e_2^\dagger)$ cannot land in D_E since, otherwise, the rigidity property would imply $(c_1, c_2) = (a \cdot r^\dagger + e_1^\dagger, b \cdot r^\dagger + e_2^\dagger)$, in which case we would have $\|\bar{\mu}\|_\infty \le q/2$ unless the ciphertext is rejected at step 1. Hence, if Decrypt does not return $\perp$ at step 1, it computes $(r, e_1, e_2) \in D_E$ if and only if $(c_1, c_2) = (a \cdot r + e_1, b \cdot r + e_2)$ no matter which s of norm $\|s\| \le B$ is used at step 2.

In contrast, when $m = 0$ is encrypted in the LPR cryptosystem, we have $\mu = c_2 - c_1 \cdot s \bmod q = e \cdot r - e_1 \cdot s + e_2$. An adversary can then fix a small (r, e_2) and play with many e_1's until it triggers a decryption failure when $\|\mu\|_\infty > q/2$. The probability that this happens depends on the secret s (as a different s' may not cause rejection for a fixed (r, e_1, e_2)). In KYBER and SABER, the FO transform allows restricting the adversary's control over e_1 (which is derived from a random message m using a random oracle and re-computed for verification upon decryption) so as to make such attacks impractical. The FO transform is thus crucial to offer a sufficient security margin against attacks like [30,33].

4.2 Black-Box Security Analysis

Our security proof uses ideas from Saito *et al.* [62, Section 4] to prove (tight) security in the QROM. Their approach exploits the implicit rejection mechanism of their KEM. Namely, when the incoming encapsulation (c_1, c_2) is found invalid upon decryption in [62], the decapsulated symmetric key K is replaced by a random-looking $K = H'(u, (c_1, c_2))$, where u is a random string included in the secret key and H' is an independent random oracle.

Here, in order to simplify the analysis of side-channel leakages in the real scheme, it is desirable to minimize the amount of secret key operations in the decryption algorithm and the amount of key material to protect against leakage. Therefore we refrain from introducing an additional secret key component u (cf. Section 5.1). Instead, our security proof will first switch (in Game$_2$) to a modified decryption algorithm where the rejection mechanism goes implicit and the decapsulation procedure computes K as a random function of (c_1, c_2). At this point, we will be able to apply the techniques from [62].

Since the implicit/explicit decapsulation mechanisms are used as part of a hybrid encryption system, we can argue that they are indistinguishable by relying on the ciphertext integrity of the symmetric encryption scheme. This is the reason why we are considering the CCA security of the hybrid combination as a whole, rather than that of its KEM component.[4] We note that similar ideas were previously used in the security proofs of hybrid PKE schemes [1,48], but usually in the opposite direction (to go from implicit rejection to explicit rejection).

For the rest, the proof in the ROM carries over to the QROM since it avoids ROM techniques that do not work in the QROM: we do not rely on the extraction of encryption randomness by inspecting the list of RO queries to answer decryption queries, which is not possible when queries are made on superpositions of inputs, and the RO is programmed identically for all queries.

Theorem 1. *If Π^{sym} is a symmetric authenticated encryption scheme, the construction specified in Sect. 4.1 provides IND-CCA security in the QROM under the ring learning-with-errors (RLWE) assumption.*

Proof. The proof considers a sequence of hybrid games, which is similar to that of [62, Theorem 4.2] from Game_3 to Game_5. For each i, we denote by W_i the event that the adversary wins (i.e., $d' = d$) in Game_i. We also denote by $\mathsf{Encaps}(PK, (r, e_1, e_2))$ the deterministic algorithm that takes as inputs PK and explicit randomness $(r, e_1, e_2) \in R^3$, and outputs $(c_1, c_2) = (a \cdot r + e_1, b \cdot r + e_2)$.

Game_0: This is the real IND-CCA game. The challenger faithfully answers (quantum) random oracle queries. All (classical) decryption queries are answered by running the real decryption algorithm. Note that a decryption query triggers a random oracle query at step 8 of $\mathsf{Decrypt}$. In the challenge phase, the adversary $\mathcal{A}$ outputs messages M_0, M_1 and obtains a challenge $C^\star = (c_0^\star, c_1^\star, c_2^\star)$, where $c_1^\star = a \cdot r^\star + e_1^\star$, $c_2^\star = b \cdot r^\star + e_2^\star$, with $r^\star, e_1^\star, e_2^\star \hookleftarrow D_{\mathbb{Z}^n, \alpha q}^{\mathsf{coeff}}$, and $c_0^\star = \mathsf{E}_{K^\star}(M_d)$ for some $d \hookleftarrow U(\{0, 1\})$. Eventually, $\mathcal{A}$ outputs $b' \in \{0, 1\}$ and its advantage is $\mathbf{Adv}(\mathcal{A}) := |\Pr[W_0] - 1/2|$.

Game_1: In this game, the challenger aborts and replaces $\mathcal{A}$'s output by a random bit $d' \in \{0, 1\}$ in the event that $\|s\| > B$ or $\|e\| > B$ at step 3 of Keygen. By Lemma 1, we have $|\Pr[W_1] - \Pr[W_0]| \leq 2^{-\Omega(n)}$.

Game_2: We modify the decryption algorithm. Throughout the game, the challenger uses an independent random oracle $H_Q : R_q^2 \to \{0, 1\}^\kappa$ that is only accessible to $\mathcal{A}$ via decryption queries (i.e., $\mathcal{A}$ has no direct access to H_Q). This random oracle is used to run the following decryption algorithm.

$\mathsf{Decrypt}_2$: Given $SK = s$ and $C = (c_0, c_1, c_2)$, initialize a Boolean variable flag $= 0$. Then, do the following.

1. Sample $r', e_1', e_2' \hookleftarrow D_{\mathbb{Z}^n, \alpha q}^{\mathsf{coeff}}$. If $\|r'\| > B$, or $\|e_1'\| > B$, or $\|e_2'\| > B$, then set flag $= 1$ and return $\perp$.[5] Otherwise, compute $c_1' = a \cdot r' + e_1'$ and $c_2' = b \cdot r' + e_2'$.

---

[4] The underlying explicit rejection KEM can be proven CCA-secure secure in the ROM but we do not prove it CCA-secure in the QROM as we only consider the CCA security of the hybrid PKE scheme.

[5] $\mathsf{Decrypt}_2$ still uses explicit rejection at step 1 because the secret key is not needed at this step and the goal of implicit rejection is to handle validity checks that depend on the secret key and the ciphertext.

2. Compute $\bar{c}_1 = c_1 + c_1'$ and $\bar{c}_2 = c_2 + c_2'$.
3. Compute $\bar{\mu} = \bar{c}_2 - p \cdot \bar{c}_1 \cdot s$ over R_q.
4. Compute $\bar{e}_2 = \bar{\mu} \bmod p$. If $\|\bar{e}_2\| > 2B$, set flag $= 1$.
5. Compute $\bar{r} = (\bar{c}_2 - \bar{e}_2) \cdot b^{-1} \in R_q$. If $\|\bar{r}\| > 2B$, set flag $= 1$.
6. Compute $\bar{e}_1 = \bar{c}_1 - a \cdot \bar{r} \in R_q$. If $\|\bar{e}_1\| > 2B$, set flag $= 1$.
7. Compute $r = \bar{r} - r'$, $e_1 = \bar{e}_1 - e_1'$ and $e_2 = \bar{e}_2 - e_2'$. If $\|r\| > B$, or $\|e_1\| > B$, or $\|e_2\| > B$, then set flag $= 1$.
8. If flag $= 0$, compute $K = H(r, e_1, e_2) \in \{0,1\}^\kappa$. Otherwise, compute $K = H_Q(c_1, c_2)$.
9. Compute and return $M = D_K(c_0) \in \{0,1\}^{\ell_m} \cup \{\bot\}$.

Lemma 3 shows that, if the adversary can distinguish Game_2 from Game_1, we can turn it into an adversary against the ciphertext integrity of Π^{sym} (of which the definition is recalled in the ePrint report [46]).

Game_3: We now simulate the random oracle[6] $H : D_E \to \{0,1\}^\kappa$ as

$$H(r, e_1, e_2) = H_Q'\big(\mathsf{Encaps}(PK, (r, e_1, e_2))\big) \tag{2}$$

where $H_Q' : R_q^2 \to \{0,1\}^\kappa$ is another random oracle to which $\mathcal{A}$ has no direct access. At each decryption query, $\mathsf{Decrypt}_2$ consistently computes K as per (2) when flag $= 0$. In the computation of $C^\star = (c_0^\star, c_1^\star, c_2^\star)$, the symmetric key $K^\star$ is similarly obtained as $K^\star = H_Q'\big(c_1^\star, c_2^\star\big)$, where $(c_1^\star, c_2^\star) = \mathsf{Encaps}(PK, (r^\star, e_1^\star, e_2^\star))$. Lemma 4 shows that, from $\mathcal{A}$'s view, Game_3 is identical to Game_2, so that we have $\Pr[W_3] = \Pr[W_2]$.

Game_4: This game is like Game_3 except that the random oracle H is now simulated as $H(r, e_1, e_2) = H_Q\big(\mathsf{Encaps}(PK, (r, e_1, e_2))\big)$, where $H_Q : R_q^2 \to \{0,1\}^\kappa$ is the random oracle introduced in Game_2. In the computation of the challenge ciphertext $C^\star = (c_0^\star, c_1^\star, c_2^\star)$, the symmetric key $K^\star$ is similarly obtained as $K^\star = H_Q\big(c_1^\star, c_2^\star\big)$, where $(c_1^\star, c_2^\star) = \mathsf{Encaps}(PK, (r^\star, e_1^\star, e_2^\star))$, and K is computed in the same way when flag $= 0$ at step 8 of $\mathsf{Decrypt}_2$. That is, Game_4 is identical to Game_3 except that H_Q' has been replaced by H_Q in the simulation of H. Lemma 5 shows that $\Pr[W_4] = \Pr[W_3]$ as the two games are perfectly indistinguishable.

Game_5: This game is like Game_4 except that we modify the decryption oracle. At each query $C = (c_0, c_1, c_2)$, if flag $= 0$ at the end of step 1, then the decryption oracle computes $K = H_Q(c_1, c_2)$ and returns $M = D_K(c_0) \in \{0,1\}^{\ell_m} \cup \{\bot\}$ (i.e., it ignores steps 2–7 of $\mathsf{Decrypt}_2$ and jumps to step 8 after having set flag $= 1$). Lemma 6 shows that $\Pr[W_5] = \Pr[W_4]$.

Game_6: We now remove the change introduced in Game_1. Namely, Game_6 is like Game_5, but we no longer replace $\mathcal{A}$'s output by a random bit if $\|s\| > B$ or $\|e\| > B$ at the end of Keygen. By Lemma 1, $|\Pr[W_6] - \Pr[W_5]| \leq 2^{-\Omega(n)}$.

In Game_6, we note that the decryption oracle does not use the secret s anymore.

---

[6] We may assume that H outputs $\bot$ on input of a triple $(r, e_1, e_2) \notin D_E$. A hash function can always check domain membership before any computation.

Game$_7$: We modify the generation of PK. The challenger initially samples $a_1, \ldots, a_k \hookleftarrow U(R_q)$, $e_1, \ldots, e_k \hookleftarrow D_{\mathbb{Z}^n, \alpha q}^{\text{coeff}}$, where $k = \lceil \lambda / \log n \rceil$, and computes $b_i = a_i \cdot s + e_i$ for each $i \in [k]$. If none of the obtained $\{b_i\}_{i=1}^k$ is invertible, the challenger aborts and replaces $\mathcal{B}$'s output by a random bit. Otherwise, it determines the first index $i \in [k]$ such that $b_i \in R_q^\times$ and defines the public key by setting $a = a_i$ and $b = p \cdot b_i$. Lemma 7 shows that, under the RLWE assumption, this modified key generation procedure does not affect $\mathcal{A}$'s view and we have $|\Pr[W_7] - \Pr[W_6]| \leq \mathbf{Adv}^{\mathsf{RLWE}}(\lambda) + 2^{-\lambda}$.

Game$_8$: We change again the generation of the public key. We replace the pseudorandom ring elements $\{b_i = a_i \cdot s + e_i\}_{i=1}^k$ of Game$_7$ by truly random $b_1, \ldots, b_k \hookleftarrow U(R_q)$ at the beginning of the game. Under the RLWE assumption, this change goes unnoticed and a straightforward reduction shows that $|\Pr[W_8] - \Pr[W_7]| \leq \mathbf{Adv}^{\mathsf{RLWE}}(\lambda)$. As a result, since $\gcd(p, q) = 1$, the public key is now distributed so that $a \sim U(R_q)$ and $b \sim U(R_q^\times)$.

Game$_9$: We change the generation of the challenge $C^\star = (c_0^\star, c_1^\star, c_2^\star)$. In this game, instead of computing $c_1^\star = a \cdot r^\star + e_1^\star$, $c_2^\star = b \cdot r^\star + e_2^\star$ with $r^\star, e_1^\star, e_2^\star \hookleftarrow D_{\mathbb{Z}^n, \alpha q}^{\text{coeff}}$, we now sample $c_1^\star, c_2^\star \hookleftarrow U(R_q)$ uniformly. Then, we compute $c_0^\star$ as a symmetric encryption of M_d under the key $K^\star = H_Q(c_1^\star, c_2^\star)$. Lemma 8 shows that Game$_9$ is indistinguishable from Game$_8$ under the RLWE assumption.

In Game$_9$, $\mathcal{A}$ can no longer query H on short ring elements $(r^\star, e_1^\star, e_2^\star)$ that underlie $(c_1^\star, c_2^\star)$ (in which case we would have $H_Q(c_1^\star, c_2^\star) = H(r^\star, e_1^\star, e_2^\star)$). With overwhelming probability $1 - 2^{-\Omega(n)}$, there exist no $r^\star, e_1^\star, e_2^\star \in R$ of norm $\leq B$ such that $c_1^\star = a \cdot r^\star + e_1^\star$ and $c_2^\star = b \cdot r^\star + e_2^\star$. Since $\mathcal{A}$ has no direct access to $H_Q(\cdot)$, this means that $H_Q(c_1^\star, c_2^\star)$ is now independent of $\mathcal{A}$'s view.

Game$_{10}$: In this game, we modify the decryption oracle that now rejects all ciphertexts of the form $C = (c_0, c_1^\star, c_2^\star)$ with $c_0 \neq c_0^\star$ after the challenge phase. Game$_{10}$ is identical to Game$_9$ until the event E_{10} that $\mathcal{A}$ queries the decryption of a ciphertext $C = (c_0, c_1^\star, c_2^\star)$ that would not have been rejected in Game$_9$. Since $c_0^\star = \mathsf{E}_{K^\star}(M_d)$ is encrypted under a random key $K^\star = H_Q(c_1^\star, c_2^\star)$ that is independent of $\mathcal{A}$'s view, E_{10} would imply an attack against the ciphertext integrity of Π^{sym} (as defined in the ePrint report [46]). We have $|\Pr[W_{10}] - \Pr[W_9]| \leq \Pr[E_{10}] \leq 2^{-\Omega(n)} + \mathbf{Adv}^{\mathsf{AE\text{-}INT}}(\lambda)$, where Q is the number of decryption queries.

In Game$_{10}$, the challenge $C^\star = (c_0^\star, c_1^\star, c_2^\star)$ is obtained by encrypting $c_0^\star$ under a random key $K^\star$ which is never used anywhere but in the computation of $c_0^\star = \mathsf{E}_{K^\star}(M_d)$. At this point, the adversary is essentially an adversary against the indistinguishability (under passive attacks) of the authenticated encryption scheme Π^{sym}. We have $|\Pr[W_{10}] - 1/2| \leq \mathbf{Adv}^{\mathsf{AE\text{-}IND}}(\lambda)$.

Putting the above altogether, we can bound the advantage of an IND-CCA adversary as

$$\mathbf{Adv}^{\text{cca}}(\mathcal{A}) \leq \frac{3}{1 - 2^{-\lambda}} \cdot \mathbf{Adv}_{n, \lceil \lambda / \log n \rceil, q, \chi}^{\mathcal{B}, \mathsf{RLWE}}(\lambda) + Q(Q+1) \cdot \mathbf{Adv}^{\mathsf{AE\text{-}INT}}(\lambda) \qquad (3)$$

$$+ \mathbf{Adv}^{\mathsf{AE\text{-}IND}}(\lambda) + \frac{1}{2^{\Omega(n)}},$$

where Q is the number of decryption queries.   □

Lemma 3. Game$_2$ *is indistinguishable from* Game$_1$ *as long as the authenticated encryption scheme* Π^{sym} *provides ciphertext integrity. Concretely, we have the inequality* $|\Pr[W_2] - \Pr[W_1]| \leq \frac{Q \cdot (Q+1)}{2} \cdot \mathbf{Adv}^{\mathsf{AE\text{-}INT}}(\lambda)$.

Proof. See the ePrint report [46].

Lemma 4. *If* $q > 8p(\alpha q)^2 n$ *and* $p > 4\alpha q \sqrt{n}$, Game$_3$ *is perfectly indistinguishable from* Game$_2$.

Proof. See the ePrint report [46].

Lemma 5. Game$_4$ *is perfectly indistinguishable from* Game$_3$.

Proof. See the ePrint report [46].

Lemma 6. Game$_5$ *is perfectly indistinguishable from* Game$_4$.

Proof. See the ePrint report [46].

Lemma 7. *Under the* $\mathsf{RLWE}_{n,k,q,\chi}$ *assumption where* $\chi = D^{\mathsf{coeff}}_{\mathbb{Z}^n,\alpha q}$ *and* $k = \lceil \lambda / \log n \rceil$, Game$_7$ *is indistinguishable from* Game$_6$ *if* $q > n^2$. *Concretely, there is a PPT algorithm* $\mathcal{B}$ *such that* $|\Pr[W_7] - \Pr[W_6]| \leq \mathbf{Adv}^{\mathcal{B},\mathsf{RLWE}}_{n,k,q,\chi}(\lambda) + 2^{-\lambda}$.

Proof. the ePrint report [46].

Lemma 8. *Under the* RLWE *assumption,* Game$_9$ *is indistinguishable from* Game$_8$. *We have* $|\Pr[W_9] - \Pr[W_8]| \leq (1 - 2^{-\lambda})^{-1} \cdot \mathbf{Adv}^{\mathcal{B},\mathsf{RLWE}}_{n,k,q,\chi}(\lambda)$, *where* $\chi = D^{\mathsf{coeff}}_{\mathbb{Z}^n,\alpha q}$ *and* $k = 2\lceil \lambda / \log n \rceil$ *is the number of samples.*

Proof. See the ePrint report [46].

We note that bound (3) tightly relates the security of the scheme to the RLWE assumption. On the other hand, it loses a quadratic factor $O(Q^2)$ with respect to the ciphertext integrity of the symmetric authenticated encryption scheme. However, the term $Q(Q+1) \cdot \mathbf{Adv}^{\mathsf{AE\text{-}INT}}(\lambda)$ becomes statistically negligible if Π^{sym} is realized using an information-theoretically secure one-time MAC, as we discuss in the following instantiation section.

4.3   Parameters and Instantiations

PARAMETERS. In an instantiation in fully splitting rings R_q (which allows faster multiplications using the NTT in Encrypt), we use $\Phi(X) = X^n + 1$, where n is a power of 2, with a modulus $q = 1 \bmod 2n$.

For correctness, we need to choose $\alpha \in (0, 1)$, q and p such that $p/2 > 2B$ and $4p(B^2 + 1) < q/2$, which satisfy the requirements of Lemma 4. To apply Lemma 2, we can set $\alpha \in (0, 1)$ so that $\alpha q = \Omega(\sqrt{n})$. To satisfy all conditions, we may thus set $p = \Theta(n)$, $q = \Theta(n^3)$ and $\alpha^{-1} = \Theta(n^{2.5})$.

CONCRETE PROPOSALS. Around the 128-bit security level, n has to be somewhere between 512 and 1024. In order to get a more efficient implementation, we sample s, e, r, e_1, e_2 from a centered binomial distributions as previously suggested in [3,20,38] and set the parameters according to the concrete hardness against known attacks via the heuristic LWE estimator [2]. Precisely, we consider the noise distribution ψ_k^n defined over $\mathbb{Z}^n$ as $\{\sum_{i=1}^k (a_i - b_i) \mid a_i, b_i \leftarrow U(\{0,1\}^n)\}$ instead of a Gaussian distribution. As in [38], we use the distribution $\bar{\psi}_2^n$ obtained by reducing $\psi_2^n \bmod 3$. We then obtain ciphertexts of 4Kb by setting $n = 1024$, $p = 5$ and $q = 59393$, and an estimated security level of 191 bits. This modification of POLKA only entails minor modifications in the security proof, which are detailed in the ePrint report [46] and is next used as our main instance.

In order to push optimizations even further, we could use rings where n does not have to be a power of 2, as suggested in [38]. For example, the cyclotomic polynomial $\Phi_{3n} = X^n - X^{n/2} + 1$ with $q = 1 \bmod 3n$ and $n = 2^i 3^j$ still gives a fully splitting $R_q = \mathbb{Z}_q[X]/(\Phi_{3n})$. This allows choosing $n = 768$, $p = 5$ (so that $\|\bar{e}_2\|_\infty \leq (p-1)/2)$, and $q = 28 \cdot 3n + 1 = 64513$. Correctness is ensured since we have $\|a \cdot b\|_\infty \leq 2\|a\|\|b\|$ for any $a, b \in R = \mathbb{Z}[X]/(\Phi_{3n})$, so that $\|\bar{e}_2 + p \cdot (e \cdot \bar{r} - \bar{e}_1 \cdot s)\|_\infty \leq (p-1)/2 + 8 \cdot p \cdot n \leq (q-1)/2$. We would then obtain a ciphertext (c_1, c_2) that only takes 3Kb to represent.

In all instantiations, the public key can compressed down to roughly 50% of the ciphertext size if we derive the random $a \in R_q$ from a hash function modeled as a random oracle (as considered by many NIST candidates).

INSTANTIATING THE DEM COMPONENT. The symmetric authenticated encryption scheme Π^{sym} can be instantiated with a a leakage-resistant Enc-then-MAC mode of operation. Candidates for this purpose that rely on a masked block cipher or permutation can be found in [14]. Yet, POLKA encourages the following more efficient solution based on a key-homomorphic one-time MAC. If ℓ_m is the message length, we can use a key length $\kappa = \lambda + 2\ell_m$ and a pseudo-random generator $G : \{0,1\}^\lambda \to \{0,1\}^{\ell_m}$. To encrypt $M \in \{0,1\}^{\ell_m}$, we parse $K = H(r, e_1, e_2) \in \{0,1\}^\kappa$ as a triple $K = (K_0, K_1, K_2) \in \{0,1\}^\lambda \times (\{0,1\}^{\ell_m})^2$. Then, we compute a ciphertext $c = (\bar{c}, \tau) = (M \oplus G(K_0), K_1 \cdot \bar{c} + K_2)$, where the one-time MAC $\tau = K_1 \cdot \bar{c} + K_2$ is computed over $\mathrm{GF}(2^{\ell_m})$. This specific MAC "annihilates" the quadratic term $O(Q^2)$ in the security bound (3). In the ciphertext integrity experiment (defined in the ePrint report [46]), the adversary's advantage can then be bounded as $(Q + 1)/2^{\ell_m}$ if Q is the number of decryption queries. To make the term $Q(Q + 1) \cdot \mathbf{Adv}^{\mathsf{AE\text{-}INT}}(\lambda)$ statistically negligible in (3), we can assume that $\ell_m \geq \lambda + 3\log^2 \lambda$ in order to have $(Q + 1)^2 Q/2^{\ell_m} < 2^{3\log^2 \lambda}/2^{\ell_m} < 2^{-\lambda}$. Concretely, if we set $\lambda = 128$ and assume $Q < 2^{60}$, we can choose $\ell_m \geq 308$. In terms of leakage, the computation $K_1 \cdot \bar{c} + K_2$ is linear in the key and can therefore be masked with overheads that are linear in the number of shares (rather than quadratic for a block cipher or permutation). The constraint on the message length could be relaxed by hashing the message at the cost of an additional idealized assumption, which we leave as a scope for further research.

5   Side-Channel Security Analysis

We now discuss the leakage properties of POLKA. In Sect. 5.1 we introduce the general ideas supporting its leveled implementation and explain how its security requirements can be efficiently fulfilled. In Sect. 5.2, we focus on its most novel part, namely the variant of the LWPR assumption on which this implementation relies. We also provide cryptanalysis challenges to motivate further research on hard physical learning problems. In Sect. 5.3 we describe a hardware architecture for the most sensitive DPA target of POLKA. Our descriptions borrow the terminology introduced in [45] for symmetric cryptography. Namely, we denote as leakage-resilient implementations of which confidentiality guarantees may vanish in the presence of leakage, but are restored once leakage is removed from the adversary's view; and we denote as leakage-resistant implementations that preserve confidentiality against leakage even for the challenge encryption.

5.1   Leveled Implementation and Design Goals

The high-level idea behind leveled implementations is that it may not be necessary to protect all the parts of implementation with equally strong (and therefore expensive) side-channel countermeasures. In the following, we describe how POLKA could be implemented in such a leveled manner. For this purpose, and as a first step, we follow the heuristic methodology introduced in [14] and identify its SPA and DPA targets in decryption. The resulting leveled implementation of POLKA is represented in Fig. 2. The lighter green-colored (dummied) operations need to be protected against SPA. The darker green-colored operations need to be protected against SPA with averaging (avg-SPA), which is a SPA where the adversary can repeat the measurement of a fixed target intermediate computation in order to remove the leakage noise. The lighter blue-colored operations need to be protected against DPA with unknown (dummied) inputs (UP-DPA). The darker blue-colored operations must be protected against DPA. Operations become generically more difficult to protect against side-channel attacks when moving from the left to the right of the figure. Eventually, securing the first four steps in the figure is needed to protect the long-term secret of POLKA, and therefore to ensure leakage-resilience. By contrast, securing the fifth step is only needed to ensure leakage-resistance (i.e., the key K can leak in full in case only leakage-resilience is needed). Next, we first explain how these security requirements can be efficiently satisfied by hardware designers. We then discuss the advantages of this implementation over a uniformly protected one.

SPA and DPA Protections. All the operations requiring SPA protection (with or without averaging) can be efficiently implemented thanks to parallelism in hardware. Typically, we expect that an implementation manipulating 128 bits or more in parallel is currently difficult to attack via SPA, even when leveraging advanced analytical strategies [65].[7] A bit more concretely, this reference

---

[7] As will be clear in conclusions, software implementations are left as an interesting open problem. In this case, the typical option to obtain security against SPA would be to emulate parallelism thanks to the shuffling countermeasure [66].

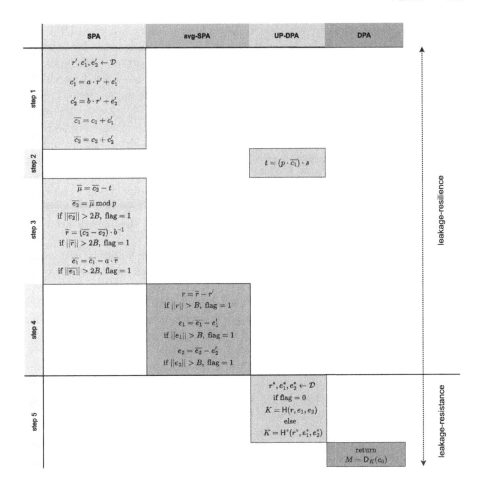

Fig. 2. Leveled implementation of POLKA.

shows that single-trace attacks are possible for Signal-to-Noise Ratios (SNRs) higher than one. Adversaries targeting a 128-bit secret based on 8-bit (resp., 32-bit) hypotheses would face an SNR of $\frac{1}{16}$ (resp., $\frac{1}{4}$). Securing the computations in steps 1, 3 and 4 of Fig. 2 against side-channel attacks should therefore lead to limited overheads. Note that the dependency on a dummy ciphertext in step 3 prevents the adversary to control the intermediate computations (and for example to try canceling the algorithmic noise for those sensitive operations).

Security against DPA is in general expected to be significantly more expensive to reach. The standard approach for this purpose is to mask all the operations that can be targeted, which leads to (roughly) quadratic performance overheads [49]. Furthermore, implementing masking securely is a sensitive process, which requires dealing with composition issues [8,29], physical defaults such as glitches [54,58] or transitions [6,28] or even their combination [25,26].

The main observation we leverage in POLKA is that its most critical DPA sensitive operation shares similarities with the key-homomorphic re-keying schemes used in symmetric cryptography to prevent side-channel attacks [36,39,40,55]. Namely, the operation $t = (p \cdot \overline{c_1}) \cdot s$ in step 2 of Fig. 2 can indeed be viewed as the product between a long-term secret s and an ephemeral (secret) value $(p \cdot \overline{c_1})$. As a result, it can be directly computed as $t = \sum_{i=1}^{d}(p \cdot \overline{c_1}) \cdot s^i$, where $s = s^1 + s^2 + \ldots s^d$ and the s^i's are the additive shares of the long-term secret s. Besides the linear (rather than quadratic) overheads that such a solution enables, key-homomorphic primitives have two important advantages for masking. First, their long-term secret can be refreshed with linear randomness requirements [9]. Second, their natural implementation offers strong immunity against composition issues and physical defaults [23]. On top of this, the fact that the variable input of $(p \cdot \overline{c_1}) \cdot s^i$ is dummied (hence unknown) implies that it will need one less share than in a known input attack setting [16].

Even more importantly, and as discussed in the aforementioned papers on fresh re-keying, it is then possible to re-combine the shares and to perform the rest of the computations on unshared values, hence extending the interest of a leveled approach. Various models have been introduced for this purpose in the literature, depending on the type of multiplication to perform. The first re-keying schemes considered multiplications in binary fields that require a sufficient level of noise to be secure [12,13]. Dziembowski et al. proposed a (more expensive) wPRF-based re-keying that is secure even if its output is leaked in full [40]. Duval et al. proposed an intermediate solution that only requires the (possibly noise-free) leakage function to be surjective and "incompatible" with the field multiplication: they for example show that this happens when combining multiplications in prime fields with the Hamming weight leakage function, which they formalized as the LWPR assumption [39]. Given that the multiplication of POLKA is based on prime moduli, we next focus on this last model, which provides a nice intermediate between efficiency and weak physical assumptions.

As for the operations of step 5 of Fig. 2, we first observe that despite the inputs of H being ephemeral, it is possible that an adversary obtains a certain level of control over them by incrementally increasing c_1 or c_2. This explains why it must be secure against DPA (with unknown plaintexts since r, e_1 and e_2 are unknown as long as steps 3 and 4 are secure against SPA). Finally, the protection of the authenticated encryption is somewhat orthogonal to POLKA since it is needed for any DEM. The standard option for this purpose would be to use a leakage-resistant mode of operation that ensures side-channel security with decryption leakage. As discussed in [14], state-of-the-art modes allow the authenticated encryption scheme to be leveled (i.e., to mix SPA-secure operations with DPA-secure ones), like the rest of POLKA. But as mentioned in Sect. 4.3, an even more efficient solution is to use an Enc-then-MAC scheme with a one-time key-homomorphic MAC that is linear in the key and therefore easy to mask.

Discussion. The main advantage of POLKA is that its structure allows avoiding the costly implementation of uniformly protected operations based on masking. In this respect, it is worth recalling that: (i) the removal of the dummy ciphertext takes place as late as possible in the process (i.e., just before the hashing and symmetric decryption), and (ii) if only the long-term secret s must be protected (i.e., if only leakage-resilience is required), step 5 of Fig. 2 does not need countermeasures. Overall, these design tweaks strongly limit the side-channel attack surface and the need to mask non-linear operations compared to algorithms like KYBER or SABER, at the cost of an admittedly provocative LWPR assumption.

We also remind that the implicit rejection used in schemes like KYBER or SABER generates a pseudorandom "garbage key" in case of invalid ciphertext, which implies the manipulation of additional long-term key material that must be secure against DPA. We avoid such a need by relying on an explicit rejection. Yet, it is an interesting open question to find out whether the same result could be obtained with other (implicit) rejection mechanisms or proof techniques.

Overall, Fig. 2 highlights that the novelty of POLKA mostly lies in its leakage-resilient parts (i.e., steps 1 to 4). In order to help their understanding, we provide an open source piece of code (for now without SPA and DPA countermeasures that require lower level programming languages, neither ensuring the leakage-resistance of the authenticated encryption in step 5).[8] In general, further improving the leakage-resistance of POLKA so that it can be ensured with weaker side-channel security requirements is another interesting research direction.

We finally note that ensuring a constant-time implementation of POLKA requires running a dummy hash function when flag $= 1$. Without such a dummy hash, the same granular increase of c_1 or c_2 as mentioned to justify the DPA security requirements of H could leak information on e_1, e_2 and r, by using a timing channel to detect whether a $\perp$ message is generated during step 4 or step 5 (by the authenticated encryption scheme). This also means that in order to avoid such a leakage on e_1, e_2 and r, it should be hard to distinguish whether the flag is 0 or 1 with SPA. We conjecture the latter is simpler/cheaper than protecting another long-term secret against DPA (as required with current implicit rejections), but as mentioned in introduction, POLKA could be adapted with an implicit rejection as well (in which case, it should also be hard to distinguish whether the key used to decrypt is a garbage one or not thanks to SPA).

5.2   Learning with Physical Rounding Assumption

We now move to the main assumption that allows an efficient leveling of POLKA. Namely, we study the security of step 2 in Fig. 2 after the recombination of the shares. In other words, we study the security of the long-term secret s assuming that the adversary can observe the leakage of the (unmasked) output t.[9] We start by recalling the LWPR problem introduced at CHES 2021 [39], then discuss its adaptation to polynomial multiplications used in POLKA. We finally propose security parameters together with cryptanalysis challenges.

---

[8] https://github.com/cmomin/polka_implem.

[9] As mentioned in Subsect. 5.1, the security of the internal computations of $t = \sum_{i=1}^{d}(p \cdot \overline{c_1}) \cdot s^i$ is obtained thanks to masking. So here, we only need to argue that the leakage of the recombined t does not lead to strong attacks.

A. The Original LWPR Problem can be viewed as an adaptation of the crypto dark matter proposed by Boneh et al. in [19], which showed that low-complexity PRFs can be obtained by mixing linear functions over different small moduli. Duval et al. observed that letting one of these functions being implicitly computed by a leakage function can lead to strong benefits for masking against side-channel attacks. Intuitively, it implies that a designer only has to implement a key-homomorphic function securely (i.e., the first crypto dark matter mapping), since the second (physical) mapping never has to be explicitly computed: it is rather the leakage function that provides its output to the adversary. The formal definition of the resulting LWPR problem is given next.

Definition 2 (Learning with physical rounding *[39]*). *Let* $q, x, y \in \mathbb{N}^*$, q *prime, for a secret* $\kappa \in \mathbb{F}_q^{x \times y}$. *The* $\mathsf{LWPR}_{\mathsf{L}_\mathsf{g}, q}^{x,y}$ *sample distribution is given by:*

$$\mathcal{D}_{\mathsf{LWPR}_{\mathsf{L}_\mathsf{g}, q}^{x,y}} := (r, \mathsf{L}_\mathsf{g}(\kappa \cdot r)) \text{ for } r \in \mathbb{F}_q^y \text{ uniformly random,}$$

where $\mathsf{L}_\mathsf{g} : \mathbb{F}_q^x \to \mathbb{R}^d$ *is the physical rounding function. Given query access to* $\mathcal{D}_{\mathsf{LWPR}_{\mathsf{L}_\mathsf{g}, q}^{x,y}}$ *for a uniformly random* κ, *the* $\mathsf{LWPR}_{\mathsf{L}_\mathsf{g}, q}^{x,y}$ *problem is* $(\chi, \tau, \mu, \epsilon)$-*hard to solve if after the observation of* χ LWPR *samples, no adversary can recover the key* κ *with time complexity* τ , *memory complexity* μ *and probability* $\geq \epsilon$.

Concretely, the LWPR problem consists in trying to retrieve a secret key matrix κ using the information leakage emitted on its product with a random vector r. It corresponds to a learning problem similar to LWR [7], with the rounding function instantiated with a leakage function. Its security depends on the dimensions (q, x, y) and the leakage function considered. In [39], it is argued that this problem is hard in the case of the Hamming weight leakage function that is frequently encountered in practice (with a binary representation) if the product is implemented in parallel. By this, we mean that $x \times \log_2(q)$ bits are produced per cycle by the implementation computing the LWPR samples. This problem can then be used as the basis of a fresh re-keying mechanism, producing an ephemeral key $\in \mathbb{F}_q^x$. The security analysis of Duval et al. shows that the complexity of various (algebraic and statistical) attacks against such a fresh re-keying scheme grows exponentially with the (main) security parameter y. The first instance they propose uses a 31-bit prime modulus $p = 2^{31} - 1$ with parameters $x = 4$ and $y = 4$ (i.e., it assumes that four $\log_2(p)$-bit multiplications can be performed in parallel). As can be seen in Fig. 2, step 2 of POLKA shares strong similarities with the aforementioned fresh-re-keying scheme based on LWPR, by simply viewing the intermediate value t as an ephemeral key. We next discuss the differences between the original LWPR assumption and the one needed for POLKA.

B. Ring-LWPR. Leveraging the fact that ring variants of learning problems are common [52], we now describe a ring version of the LWPR problem. Let us define $r := p \cdot \overline{c_1}$. Seeing s as a long-term secret (similar to κ in the original LWPR problem), the t value can be re-written as $t = r \cdot s$. Further denoting s_i (resp., r_i) the coefficients of s (resp., r), we can write:

$$r \cdot s = \left(\sum_{i=0}^{n-1} s_i X^i \right) \cdot \left(\sum_{i=0}^{n-1} r_i X^i \right) = \sum_{i=0}^{2n-2} \left(\sum_{j=max(0,i-n+1)}^{min(i,n-1)} s_j r_{i-j} \right) X^i,$$

$$= \sum_{i=0}^{n-2} \left(\sum_{j=0}^{i} s_j r_{i-j} \right) X^i + \left(\sum_{j=0}^{n-1} s_j r_{i-j} \right) X^{n-1} + \sum_{i=n}^{2n-2} \left(\sum_{j=i-n+1}^{n-1} s_j r_{i-j} \right) X^i,$$

$$= \sum_{i=0}^{n-2} \left(\sum_{j=0}^{i} s_j r_{i-j} \right) X^i + \left(\sum_{j=0}^{n-1} s_j r_{i-j} \right) X^{n-1} + \sum_{i=0}^{n-2} \left(\sum_{j=i+1}^{n-1} s_j r_{n+i-j} \right) X^{n+i},$$

$$= \sum_{i=0}^{n-2} \left(\sum_{j=i+1}^{n-1} s_j r_{i-j} - \sum_{j=0}^{i} s_j r_{n+i-j} \right) X^i + \left(\sum_{j=0}^{n-1} s_j r_{i-j} \right) X^{n-1}.$$

The above equation highlights the matrix representation of the polynomial multiplication carried out in POLKA. If we represent polynomials as n-dimension vectors, where the i-th coefficient is the polynomial's i-th coefficient, the product $r \cdot s$ can be represented as the following matrix-vector product:

The key is represented as the vector (rather than the matrix) in order to optimize memory usage when splitting it into shares. This product can therefore be seen as a large LWPR instance, with two significant differences. First, a circulant matrix is used instead of one having independent coefficients (which we will discuss when selecting parameters in the next subsection). Second, the size of the matrix is (much) larger than the one in the original LWPR. Concretely, this second difference implies that in practice, these products are unlikely to be performed in one step: they will rather be decomposed into several submatrix-subvector products. For this purpose, let $x \in \mathbb{N}$ be a divider of n, the s matrix can then be split in $\frac{n}{x}$ $(x \times n)$-submatrices, denoted $(B_u)_{0 \le u < \frac{n}{x}}$. The product can then be decomposed into $\frac{n}{x}$ subproducts (illustrated in blue) with x serving as a parameter to adapt the security vs. performance tradeoff, as in the original LWPR. For a given k, one can explicitly obtain the coefficient i, j of B_u. For a proposition $\mathcal{P}$, denote $\mathbb{1}_{\mathcal{P}} := \begin{cases} 1 \text{ if } \mathcal{P} \\ 0 \text{ else} \end{cases}$. Then, $B_u^{i,j} = (2\mathbb{1}_{(ux+i-j)<0} - 1) \cdot r_{ux+i-j \pmod n}$ and the $(x \times n)$-submatrices are therefore Toeplitz, determined by their first line and first column, each other value being equal to their top-left neighbor. Concretely, the x parameter sets the number of coefficients that are computed in parallel so that in practice, an adversary will be granted access to $\frac{n}{x}$ samples given by the leakage function applied to $x \log_2(q)$ bit-values.

Definition 3 (Ring learning with Physical rounding). *Let* $q, x, n \in \mathbb{N}$, q *prime, for a secret* $s \in R_q$. *The* $RLWPR_{L_g,q}^{n,x}(s)$ *sample distribution is given as:*

$$\mathcal{D}_{RLWPR_{L_g,q}^{n,x}(s)} := \left(r, (L_g(B_u \cdot s))_{0 \leq u < \frac{n}{x}} \right),$$

where L_g *is the physical rounding function and the* (B_u) *are submatrices made of elements of* r *as defined above. Given query access to* $\mathcal{D}_{RLWPR_{L_g,q}^{n,x}(s)}$ *for a uniformly random* s, *the* $RLWPR_{L_g,q}^{n,x}(s)$ *problem is* $(\chi, \tau, \mu, \epsilon)$*-hard to solve if after the observation of* χ $RLWPR$ *samples, no adversary can recover the key* s *with time complexity* τ, *memory complexity* μ *and probability higher than* ϵ.

Note that an implementer can also split each $(x \times n)$ submatrice into $\frac{n}{y}$ pieces (e.g., to further trade circuit size for cycles in hardware) but this has no impact on the security of the RLWPR assumption, since the internal computations are assumed to be secure thanks to masking, as per Footnote 9. By contrast, more parallel implementations (reflected by a large y) may increase the level of noise in the measurements and therefore the security of the masked computations [37]. So overall, the security of the above RLWPR problem only depends on n and x. For a similar reason, the polynomial multiplication can be implemented naively or in the NTT domain, as long as the inverse NTT is applied on every share before recombination. A more efficient solution for the NTT case would be to recombine the shares in the NTT domain (so that the inverse NTT is computed only once). This would provide the adversary with leakages having a slightly different structure than in the above RLWPR problem. We leave the security analysis of this variant as an interesting scope for further research.

C. Choice of Parameters and Cryptanalysis Challenges.

Applying the security analysis of LWPR described in Part A of this subsection to RLWPR, we could choose instances based on the main security parameter n using the parallelism parameter x to obtain security margins (a necessary condition to reach λ bits of security is that $(n+1) \log_2 q + 3 \log_2 n \geq \lambda$). However, as mentioned in Part B of this subsection, the RLWPR problem is not exactly the same as the LWPR one. Negatively, the $(x \times n)$ submatrices are Toeplitz and they are not independent. While using structured matrices is not unusual in the context of hard learning problems (see for example [52] for RLWE or [44,51] for LPN variants) and we could not identify parts of the analyses in [39] that become easy in this case, the corresponding problems are less studied, justifying additional security margins to cover possible cryptanalysis improvements. As for the non-independence issue, considering that the security of the full RLWPR is at least as strong as the security of one of its subproducts, we can conservatively assume that one RLWPR sample will generate at most $\frac{n}{x}$ leakages about this subsecret. So parameters' choices covering that the data complexity of attacks against RLWPR is reduced by this factor compared to attacks against LWPR should be safe. Positively, the secret s in the leveled implementation of POLKA is not multiplied with a public r since this r value is dummied. So concretely, the side-channel adversary will only be provided with the leakage of this ephemeral value.

Putting things together, and considering the instances proposed in Subsect. 4.3, we propose the sets of parameters in Table 1 as interesting targets for cryptanalysis with a time complexity of less than 2^{128} and at most 2^{64} queries to a $\mathsf{RLWPR} - b_{\mathsf{HW_g},q}^{n,x,y}$ (s), assuming a Hamming weight leakage function.

Table 1. Proposed sets of parameters.

	$\log_2(q)$	n	x
Set 1	16	1024	16
Set 2	16	1024	8

5.3   Hardware Performance Evaluation

We complete our results with a hardware prototype for the masked computation of t (i.e., step 2 in Fig. 2), which is the most sensitive operation in POLKA. Due to place constraints, we defer the description of the hardware architecture we use and its FPGA implementation results in the ePrint report [46]. They confirm overheads that are linear in the number of shares d. Since based on similar or larger levels of parallelism as [39], these implementations are expected to provide similar or larger levels of security against higher-order DPA.

6   Conclusions

The uniform protection of all the operations in recent post-quantum CCA-secure public key encryption schemes against side-channel attacks is known to be very expensive. To the best of our knowledge, POLKA is the first scheme for which a protected implementation can be leveled, mixing operations that only require SPA security with a few operations that require DPA security, some of them being easy to mask. We reach this goal by mixing various ideas which we believe of independent interest. We also believe these techniques are quite generic and could be exploited for other schemes. For example, a leakage-resistant variant of the NTRU cryptosystem is discussed in the ePrint report [46].

Our results lead to a number of interesting research challenges. First, the RLWPR assumption on which a part of POLKA's physical security relies is an admittedly recent one. So further cryptanalysis (e.g., generalized to wide classes of realistic leakage functions) is an important direction for further investigations. The study of such hard physical learning problems in increasingly serial implementations is another promising direction, as it could lead to their exploitation in a software context. As hinted in [39], this context may require additional countermeasures like shuffling [66], in order to emulate the leakage of a parallel implementation. The same holds for a NTT-LWPR variant of RLWPR that would allow re-combining shares in the NTT domain, therefore leading to more efficient multiplications and, in general, for efforts towards a more unified/less specialized view of hard physical learning problems. More related to the high-level design of POLKA, it would be interesting to study options to further improve its potential for leveling (e.g., by removing the possibility of DPA against the hash function of step 5). From a theoretical viewpoint, evaluating whether post-quantum and leakage-resistant schemes could take advantage of ciphertext compression would be relevant as well. Eventually, the first leakage analysis we provide in this work is based on the heuristic (attack-based) approach of [14]. So formalizing and proving the leakage security of POLKA with an appropriate set of physical assumptions and comparing the concrete security level of its implementations against the one of KYBER or SABER are necessary long-term goals.

Acknowledgments. The authors thank Tobias Schneider for useful feedback on the design of POLKA. Thomas Peters and François-Xavier Standaert are respectively research associate and senior research associate of the Belgian Fund for Scientific Research (F.R.S.-FNRS). This work has been funded in parts by the European Union through the ERC project 724725 (acronym SWORD) and the PROMETHEUS project (Horizon 2020 Research and Innovation Program, grant 780701), and by the Walloon Region Win2Wal project PIRATE.

References

1. Abe, M., Gennaro, R., Kurosawa, K., Shoup, V.: Tag-KEM/DEM: a new framework for hybrid encryption and a new analysis of Kurosawa-Desmedt KEM. In: Cramer, R. (ed.) EUROCRYPT 2005. LNCS, vol. 3494, pp. 128–146. Springer, Heidelberg (2005). https://doi.org/10.1007/11426639_8
2. Albrecht, M., Player, R., Scott, S.: On the concrete hardness of learning with errors. J. Math. Cryptol. **9**(3), 169–203 (2015)
3. Alkim, E., Ducas, L., Pöppelmann, T., Schwabe, P.: Post-quantum key exchange - a new hope. In: USENIX Security Symposium (2016)
4. Avanzi, R., et al.: CRYSTALS-KYBER algorithm specifications and supporting documentation. NIST PQC Round **3**, 42 (2020)
5. Azouaoui, M., Bronchain, O., Hoffmann, C., Kuzovkova, Y. , Schneider, T., Standaert, F.: Systematic study of decryption and re-encryption leakage: the case of kyber. In: COSADE (2022)
6. Balasch, J., Gierlichs, B., Grosso, V., Reparaz, O., Standaert, F.: On the cost of lazy engineering for masked software implementations. In: CARDIS (2014)
7. Banerjee, A., Peikert, C., Rosen, A.: Pseudorandom functions and lattices. In: Pointcheval, D., Johansson, T. (eds.) EUROCRYPT 2012. LNCS, vol. 7237, pp. 719–737. Springer, Heidelberg (2012). https://doi.org/10.1007/978-3-642-29011-4_42
8. Barthe, G., et al.: Strong non-interference and type-directed higher-order masking. In: CCS (2016)
9. Barthe, G., Dupressoir, F., Faust, S., Grégoire, B., Standaert, F.-X., Strub, P.-Y.: Parallel implementations of masking schemes and the bounded moment leakage model. In: Coron, J.-S., Nielsen, J.B. (eds.) EUROCRYPT 2017. LNCS, vol. 10210, pp. 535–566. Springer, Cham (2017). https://doi.org/10.1007/978-3-319-56620-7_19

10. Basso, A., et al.: SABER algorithm specifications and supporting documentation. NIST PQC Round **3**, 44 (2020)
11. Beirendonck, M.V., D'Anvers, J., Karmakar, A., Balasch, J., Verbauwhede, I.: A side-channel-resistant implementation of SABER. ACM J. Emerg. Technol. Comput. Syst. **17**(2), 1–26 (2021)
12. Belaïd, S., Coron, J., Fouque, P., Gérard, B., Kammerer, J., Prouff, E.: Improved side-channel analysis of finite-field multiplication. In: CHES (2015)
13. Belaïd, S., Fouque, P.-A., Gérard, B.: Side-channel analysis of multiplications in $GF(2^{128})$. In: Sarkar, P., Iwata, T. (eds.) ASIACRYPT 2014. LNCS, vol. 8874, pp. 306–325. Springer, Heidelberg (2014). https://doi.org/10.1007/978-3-662-45608-8_17
14. Bellizia, D., et al.: Mode-level vs. implementation-level physical security in symmetric cryptography. In: Micciancio, D., Ristenpart, T. (eds.) CRYPTO 2020. LNCS, vol. 12170, pp. 369–400. Springer, Cham (2020). https://doi.org/10.1007/978-3-030-56784-2_13
15. Bernstein, D.J., Persichetti, E.: Towards KEM unification. Cryptology ePrint Archive, Report 2018/526 (2018)
16. Berti, F., Bhasin, S., Breier, J., Hou, X., Poussier, R., Standaert, F., Udvarhelyi, B.: A finer-grain analysis of the leakage (non) resilience of OCB. IACR Trans. Cryptogr. Hardw. Embed. Syst. **1**, 2022 (2022)
17. Bhasin, S., D'Anvers, J., Heinz, D., Pöppelmann, T., Beirendonck, M.V.: Attacking and defending masked polynomial comparison for lattice-based cryptography. IACR Trans. Cryptogr. Hardw. Embed. Syst. **3**, 2021 (2021)
18. Boneh, D., Dagdelen, Ö., Fischlin, M., Lehmann, A., Schaffner, C., Zhandry, M.: Random oracles in a quantum world. In: Lee, D.H., Wang, X. (eds.) ASIACRYPT 2011. LNCS, vol. 7073, pp. 41–69. Springer, Heidelberg (2011). https://doi.org/10.1007/978-3-642-25385-0_3
19. Boneh, D., Ishai, Y., Passelègue, A., Sahai, A., Wu, D.J.: Exploring crypto dark matter: - new simple PRF candidates and their applications. In: Beimel, A., Dziembowski, S. (eds.) TCC 2018. LNCS, vol. 11240, pp. 699–729. Springer, Cham (2018). https://doi.org/10.1007/978-3-030-03810-6_25
20. Bos, J., et al.: CRYSTALS - Kyber: A CCA-Secure Module-Lattice-Based KEM. In: IEEE EuroS&P (2018)
21. Bos, J.W., Gourjon, M., Renes, J., Schneider, T., van Vredendaal, C.: Masking KYBER: First- and higher-order implementations. IACR Trans. Cryptogr. Hardw. Embed. Syst. **4**, 2021 (2021)
22. Bronchain, O., Cassiers, G.: Bitslicing arithmetic/Boolean masking conversions for fun and profit with application to lattice-based kems (2022)
23. Bronchain, O., Schneider, T., Standaert, F.: Reducing risks through simplicity: high side-channel security for lazy engineers. J. Cryptogr. Eng. **11**(1), 39–55 (2021)
24. Bronchain, O., Standaert, F.: Breaking masked implementations with many shares on 32-bit software platforms or when the security order does not matter. IACR Trans. Cryptogr. Hardw. Embed. Syst. **2021**(3), 202–234 (2021)
25. Cassiers, G., Grégoire, B., Levi, I., Standaert, F.: Hardware private circuits: from trivial composition to full verification. IEEE Trans. Comput. **70**(10), 1677–1690 (2021)
26. Cassiers, G., Standaert, F.: Provably secure hardware masking in the transition- and glitch-robust probing model: better safe than sorry. IACR Trans. Cryptogr. Hardw. Embed. Syst. **2021**(2), 136–158 (2021)
27. Chen, C., et al.: NTRU algorithm specifications and supporting documentation. NIST PQC Round **3**, 41 (2020)

28. Coron, J., Giraud, C., Prouff, E., Renner, S., Rivain, M., Vadnala, P.K.: Conversion of security proofs from one leakage model to another: a new issue. In: COSADE (2012)
29. Coron, J., Prouff, E., Rivain, M., Roche, T.: Higher-order side channel security and mask refreshing. In: FSE (2013)
30. D'Anvers, J.-P., Guo, Q., Johansson, T., Nilsson, A., Vercauteren, F., Verbauwhede, I.: Decryption failure attacks on IND-CCA secure lattice-based schemes. In: PKC (2019)
31. D'Anvers, J.-P., Karmakar, A., Sinha Roy, S., Vercauteren, F.: Saber: module-LWR based key exchange, CPA-secure encryption and CCA-secure KEM. In: Joux, A., Nitaj, A., Rachidi, T. (eds.) AFRICACRYPT 2018. LNCS, vol. 10831, pp. 282–305. Springer, Cham (2018). https://doi.org/10.1007/978-3-319-89339-6_16
32. D'Anvers, J.-P., Orsini, E., Vercauteren, F.: Error term checking: Towards chosen ciphertext security without re-encryption. In: AsiaPKC (2021)
33. D'Anvers, J.-P., Rossi, M., Virdia, F.: *(One) Failure Is Not an Option*: bootstrapping the search for failures in lattice-based encryption schemes. In: Canteaut, A., Ishai, Y. (eds.) EUROCRYPT 2020. LNCS, vol. 12107, pp. 3–33. Springer, Cham (2020). https://doi.org/10.1007/978-3-030-45727-3_1
34. Dobraunig, C., et al.: Isap v2.0. IACR Trans. Symmetric Cryptol. **2020**(S1) (2020)
35. Dobraunig, C., Eichlseder, M., Mendel, F., Schläffer, M.: Ascon v1.2: Lightweight authenticated encryption and hashing. J. Cryptol. **34**(3), 33 (2021)
36. Dobraunig, C., Koeune, F., Mangard, S., Mendel, F., Standaert, F.-X.: Towards fresh and hybrid re-keying schemes with beyond birthday security. In: Homma, N., Medwed, M. (eds.) CARDIS 2015. LNCS, vol. 9514, pp. 225–241. Springer, Cham (2016). https://doi.org/10.1007/978-3-319-31271-2_14
37. Duc, A., Faust, S., Standaert, F.-X.: Making Masking Security Proofs Concrete. In: Oswald, E., Fischlin, M. (eds.) EUROCRYPT 2015. LNCS, vol. 9056, pp. 401–429. Springer, Heidelberg (2015). https://doi.org/10.1007/978-3-662-46800-5_16
38. Duman, J., Hövelmanns, K., Kiltz, E., Lyubashevsky, V., Seiler, G., Unruh, D.: A thorough treatment of highly-efficient NTRU instantiations. Cryptology ePrint Archive: Report 2021/1352 (2021)
39. Duval, S., Méaux, P., Momin, C., Standaert, F.: Exploring crypto-physical dark matter and learning with physical rounding towards secure and efficient fresh re-keying. IACR Trans. Cryptogr. Hardw. Embed. Syst. **1**, 2021 (2021)
40. Dziembowski, S., Faust, S., Herold, G., Journault, A., Masny, D., Standaert, F.-X.: Towards sound fresh re-keying with hard (physical) learning problems. In: Robshaw, M., Katz, J. (eds.) CRYPTO 2016. LNCS, vol. 9815, pp. 272–301. Springer, Heidelberg (2016). https://doi.org/10.1007/978-3-662-53008-5_10
41. Fritzmann, T., Beirendonck, M.V., Roy, D.B., Karl, P., Schamberger, T., Verbauwhede, I., Sigl, G.: Masked accelerators and instruction set extensions for post-quantum cryptography. IACR Trans. Cryptogr. Hardw. Embed. Syst. **1**, 2022 (2022)
42. Fujisaki, E., Okamoto, T.: Secure integration of asymmetric and symmetric encryption schemes. In: Wiener, M. (ed.) CRYPTO 1999. LNCS, vol. 1666, pp. 537–554. Springer, Heidelberg (1999). https://doi.org/10.1007/3-540-48405-1_34
43. Fujisaki, E., Okamoto, T.: Secure integration of asymmetric and symmetric encryption schemes. J. Cryptol. **26**(21), 80–101 (2013)
44. Gilbert, H., Robshaw, M.J.B., Seurin, Y.: HB$^{\#}$: increasing the security and efficiency of HB$^+$. In: Smart, N. (ed.) EUROCRYPT 2008. LNCS, vol. 4965, pp. 361–378. Springer, Heidelberg (2008). https://doi.org/10.1007/978-3-540-78967-3_21

45. Guo, C., Pereira, O., Peters, T., Standaert, F.-X.: Authenticated encryption with nonce misuse and physical leakage: definitions, separation results and first construction. In: Schwabe, P., Thériault, N. (eds.) LATINCRYPT 2019. LNCS, vol. 11774, pp. 150–172. Springer, Cham (2019). https://doi.org/10.1007/978-3-030-30530-7_8

46. Hoffmann, C., Libert, B., Momin, C., Peters, T., Standaert, F.: Towards leakage-resistant post-quantum cca-secure public key encryption. IACR Cryptol. ePrint Arch., 873 (2022)

47. Hofheinz, D., Hövelmanns, K., Kiltz, E.: A modular analysis of the Fujisaki-Okamoto transformation. In: Kalai, Y., Reyzin, L. (eds.) TCC 2017. LNCS, vol. 10677, pp. 341–371. Springer, Cham (2017). https://doi.org/10.1007/978-3-319-70500-2_12

48. Hofheinz, D., Kiltz, E.: Secure hybrid encryption from weakened key encapsulation. In: Menezes, A. (ed.) CRYPTO 2007. LNCS, vol. 4622, pp. 553–571. Springer, Heidelberg (2007). https://doi.org/10.1007/978-3-540-74143-5_31

49. Ishai, Y., Sahai, A., Wagner, D.: Private circuits: securing hardware against probing attacks. In: Boneh, D. (ed.) CRYPTO 2003. LNCS, vol. 2729, pp. 463–481. Springer, Heidelberg (2003). https://doi.org/10.1007/978-3-540-45146-4_27

50. Katsumata, S., Yamada, S.: Partitioning via non-linear polynomial functions: more compact Ibes from ideal lattices and bilinear maps. In: Cheon, J.H., Takagi, T. (eds.) ASIACRYPT 2016. LNCS, vol. 10032, pp. 682–712. Springer, Heidelberg (2016). https://doi.org/10.1007/978-3-662-53890-6_23

51. Kiltz, E., Pietrzak, K., Venturi, D., Cash, D., Jain, A.: Efficient authentication from hard learning problems. J. Cryptol. 30(4), 1238–1275 (2017)

52. Lyubashevsky, V., Peikert, C., Regev, O.: On ideal lattices and learning with errors over rings. In: Gilbert, H. (ed.) EUROCRYPT 2010. LNCS, vol. 6110, pp. 1–23. Springer, Heidelberg (2010). https://doi.org/10.1007/978-3-642-13190-5_1

53. Mangard, S., Oswald, E., Popp, T.: Power analysis attacks - revealing the secrets of smart cards. Springer, New York (2007). https://doi.org/10.1007/978-0-387-38162-6

54. Mangard, S., Popp, T., Gammel, B.M.: Side-channel leakage of masked CMOS gates. In: Menezes, A. (ed.) CT-RSA 2005. LNCS, vol. 3376, pp. 351–365. Springer, Heidelberg (2005). https://doi.org/10.1007/978-3-540-30574-3_24

55. Medwed, M., Standaert, F.-X., Großschädl, J., Regazzoni, F.: Fresh re-keying: security against side-channel and fault attacks for low-cost devices. In: Bernstein, D.J., Lange, T. (eds.) AFRICACRYPT 2010. LNCS, vol. 6055, pp. 279–296. Springer, Heidelberg (2010). https://doi.org/10.1007/978-3-642-12678-9_17

56. Micciancio, D., Regev, O.: Worst-case to average-case reductions based on Gaussian measures. SIAMJC 37(1), 267–302 (2007)

57. Ngo, K., Dubrova, E., Guo, Q., Johansson, T.: A side-channel attack on a masked IND-CCA secure SABER KEM implementation. IACR Trans. Cryptogr. Hardw. Embed. Syst. 2021(4) (2021)

58. Nikova, S., Rijmen, V., Schläffer, M.: Secure hardware implementation of nonlinear functions in the presence of glitches. J. Cryptol. 24(2), 292–321 (2011)

59. Persichetti, E.: Improving the efficiency of code-based cryptography. PhD thesis, Univ. of Auckland (2012)

60. Ravi, P., Roy, S.S., Chattopadhyay, A., Bhasin, S.: Generic side-channel attacks on CCA-secure lattice-based PKE and KEMs. IACR Trans. Cryptogr. Hardw. Embed. Syst. 2020 (3) (2020)

61. Regev, O.: On lattices, learning with errors, random linear codes, and cryptography. In: STOC (2005)

62. Saito, T., Xagawa, K., Yamakawa, T.: Tightly-secure key-encapsulation mechanism in the quantum random oracle model. In: Nielsen, J.B., Rijmen, V. (eds.) EURO-CRYPT 2018. LNCS, vol. 10822, pp. 520–551. Springer, Cham (2018). https://doi.org/10.1007/978-3-319-78372-7_17

63. Shoup, V.: A proposal for an ISO standard for public key encryption. Manuscript, December 2001

64. Ueno, R., Xagawa, K., Tanaka, Y., Ito, A., Takahashi, J., Homma, N.: Curse of re-encryption: A generic power/EM analysis on post-quantum KEMs. IACR Trans. Cryptogr. Hardw. Embed. Syst. **2022**(1) (2022)

65. Veyrat-Charvillon, N., Gérard, B., Standaert, F.-X.: Soft analytical side-channel attacks. In: Sarkar, P., Iwata, T. (eds.) ASIACRYPT 2014. LNCS, vol. 8873, pp. 282–296. Springer, Heidelberg (2014). https://doi.org/10.1007/978-3-662-45611-8_15

66. Veyrat-Charvillon, N., Medwed, M., Kerckhof, S., Standaert, F.-X.: Shuffling against side-channel attacks: a comprehensive study with cautionary note. In: Wang, X., Sako, K. (eds.) ASIACRYPT 2012. LNCS, vol. 7658, pp. 740–757. Springer, Heidelberg (2012). https://doi.org/10.1007/978-3-642-34961-4_44

Attacks

The Hidden Number Problem with Small Unknown Multipliers: Cryptanalyzing MEGA in Six Queries and Other Applications

Nadia Heninger[iD] and Keegan Ryan[(✉)][iD]

University of California, San Diego, USA
nadiah@cs.ucsd.edu, kryan@eng.ucsd.edu

Abstract. In recent work, Backendal, Haller, and Paterson identified several exploitable vulnerabilities in the cloud storage provider MEGA. They demonstrated an RSA key recovery attack in which a malicious server could recover a client's private RSA key after 512 client login attempts. We show how to exploit additional information revealed by MEGA's protocol vulnerabilities to give an attack that requires only six client logins to recover the secret key.

Our optimized attack combines several cryptanalytic techniques. In particular, we formulate and give a solution to a variant of the hidden number problem with small unknown multipliers, which may be of independent interest. We show that our lattice construction for this problem can be used to give improved results for the implicit factorization problem of May and Ritzenhofen.

1 Introduction

MEGA is an encrypted cloud storage provider whose protocols are designed to protect a client's data and secret key against a malicious server or malicious entity in the backend infrastructure. In a recent paper [2], Backendal, Haller, and Paterson detail multiple exploitable flaws in MEGA's protocols including a full key recovery attack [2, Section III].

In this attack, a malicious MEGA server uses a victim client as a decryption oracle to learn information about mauled encryptions of the user's private RSA key. In Backendal, Haller, and Paterson's original work, the attacker learns one bit of information about the key per query, and thus needs at least 512 client login attempts to recover enough information to efficiently recover the rest of the secret RSA key.

We observe that the attacker can learn up to 43 bytes of information per query, and give an algorithm to efficiently exploit this information for an improved attack that only requires six login attempts from a victim client. This brings the attack into a much more realistic range of failed login attempts that would be tolerated by a human user.

© International Association for Cryptologic Research 2023
A. Boldyreva and V. Kolesnikov (Eds.): PKC 2023, LNCS 13940, pp. 147–176, 2023.
https://doi.org/10.1007/978-3-031-31368-4_6

Our work does not exploit any new vulnerabilities in MEGA's protocol; instead, we show that the risk to unpatched clients was significantly underestimated in [2]. MEGA patched the original issue by adding additional payload validation and emphasized in their blog post about the vulnerabilities [24] that only clients who have logged in more than 512 times are vulnerable. Their patch is effective at preventing our attack as well.

1.1   Technical Overview

Our full attack exploits the interplay between the symmetric and asymmetric cryptographic operations in MEGA's design and has several stages.

We wish to draw the reader's attention to one new subproblem that our new attack needed to solve, which we had not seen articulated before in the literature. We call this problem the Hidden Number Problem with Small Unknown Multipliers (HNP-SUM).

Definition 1 (HNP with Small Unknown Multipliers). *Given integer inputs N, a_i, T, and E such that for $1 \leq i \leq n$ there exist integers x, t_i, e_i satisfying*

$$a_i \equiv t_i x + e_i \pmod{N}$$
$$|t_i| \leq T$$
$$|e_i| \leq E,$$

the goal of the adversary is to recover the vector of t_i values up to sign and common divisor.

The reason we only require recovery of the collection of $t_1, \ldots, t_n$ up to sign and common divisor g is because if $t_1, \ldots, t_n, x$ satisfy the HNP-SUM equations, then so do $-t_1, \ldots, -t_n, -x$ and $t_1/g, \ldots, t_n/g, gx$.

This problem can be viewed as a variant of the hidden number problem in which the multipliers t_i are unknown, but known to be small, or a variant of the approximate GCD problem [15] with an additional modular reduction step with an unrelated modulus N.

We develop an efficient lattice-based approach that solves HNP-SUM heuristically. We apply our approach to the cryptanalysis of MEGA, enabling the attack to succeed in as few as six login attempts with high probability. Our definition of HNP-SUM also leads to a new approach for solving the implicit factoring problem, first introduced by May and Ritzenhofen in PKC 2009 [21].

Theorem 1. *Let N, a_i, T, E, and n define an instance of HNP-SUM as in Definition 1 with t_i generated uniformly at random. There exists a heuristic polynomial time algorithm that solves HNP-SUM when*

$$T^{(n+1)/(n-1)} E \lesssim N.$$

Although the exponential approximation factor of polynomial time lattice reduction algorithms does influence these bounds, the effect is minimal for small to medium n. A bound with additional terms is explored in Lemma 4.

Our lattice construction has dimension $n+1$ and entries of bit length $\log_2 N$. It is based on the observation that $t_2 a_1 - t_1 a_2 \equiv t_2 e_1 - t_1 e_2 \pmod{N}$ is a small integer linear combination modulo N that can be found by lattice reduction. There is a natural way to extend the lattice construction for $n > 2$, but the analysis becomes substantially more involved. To successfully recover the t_i, we must first use lattice reduction to find a basis for a dense sublattice of rank $n - 1$, and we then use the Hermite Normal Form to calculate the t_i from the sublattice. We analyze the sublattice structure heuristically to derive the bound in Theorem 1.

We give our detailed analysis in Sect. 3. We first analyze the $n = 2$ case, and we then extend our approach for $n > 2$.

1.2 Applying HNP-SUM to MEGA Cryptanalysis

In the MEGA attack context of [2], the server possesses an encrypted copy of the user's RSA private key, which is encrypted using AES-ECB with a key derived from the user's password. Encrypting the RSA private key held by the server is meant to stop a malicious server from decrypting the user's files while allowing a user to log in on a new client and decrypt their own files using only a password.

During the login process, the server sends the user the symmetrically encrypted RSA private key and a challenge ciphertext encrypted to the user's RSA public key. The user decrypts the RSA private key using their password, decrypts the challenge RSA ciphertext with the RSA private key they just decrypted, and responds to the server with the most significant bytes of the RSA plaintext. If these bytes match the server's RSA plaintext, this is intended to confirm that the user knows the RSA private key and therefore knows the password.

In the attack of Backendal, Haller, and Paterson, a malicious server uses a victim client as a decryption oracle to recover the symmetrically wrapped private RSA key. During the login procedure, the malicious server can send the user a mauled version of the user's encrypted private key. Because the private key is encrypted with ECB mode, it is possible for the attacker to selectively modify specific fields in the private key, and the victim client uses this maliciously modified private key to decrypt the server's RSA ciphertext c. The encrypted private key is a custom data structure encoding the prime factors p and q of N, the decryption exponent d, and the RSA-CRT coefficient $u \equiv q^{-1} \pmod{p}$.

The value that the client sends back to the server is

$$\mathrm{MSB}((u(m_p - m_q)q + m_q) \bmod N)$$

where m_p and m_q are $(c^d \bmod p)$ and $(c^d \bmod q)$ respectively.

In our attack, the attacker swaps ciphertext blocks into the location encoding u, and observes the client's decrypted values to learn information about u. In a toy simplification of our attack, consider the case where block swaps result in u being a single 128-bit block of AES plaintext. This gives an instance of HNP-SUM; u is the small unknown multiplier, $(m_p - m_q)q$ is the hidden number, and the most significant bytes after shifting by m_q give the approximation.

Solving HNP-SUM reveals the value of the unknown multiplier u and thus the corresponding block of AES-encrypted plaintext, providing the attacker with an AES decryption oracle that can be used to decrypt arbitrary blocks of the symmetrically encrypted RSA private key, eventually revealing the entire key.

In the actual attack, the attacker is significantly more constrained, and we detail the multiple steps that make it possible to perform the block swapping attack and obtain HNP-SUM samples that are sufficiently bounded and recoverable. We detail a fast attack that recovers the victim's RSA private key with 16 login attempts in a few seconds with success rate 93.9% and a small attack that recovers the victim's key with 6 login attempts in 4.5 h with success rate 97.7%.

Disclosure. The details of the attack of Backendal, Haller, and Paterson and associated patches were made public June 21, 2022. We notified MEGA of the improved cryptanalysis on July 13, 2022, which they acknowledged immediately after in an update to their blog post. In response to our improved cryptanalysis, they have updated their guidance to acknowledge that the potential exposure applies to "the vast majority of users" and underscore the importance of installing the patch.

1.3   Applying HNP-SUM to Implicit Factoring

In the implicit factoring problem [21], the adversary is given k (unbalanced) RSA moduli of the form $N_i = p_i q_i$, where the p_i share some bits in common. The bit length of q_i is α, and t is the number of bits shared by the p_i. Depending on the variant of the implicit factoring problem, these t bits may be least significant bits, most significant bits, a mix of both, or a block of t contiguous bits in the middle of p_i [27].

All four cases can be reduced to instances of HNP-SUM. When the t middle bits at offset l are shared, we have $p_i = 2^{l+t}\tilde{p}_i' + 2^l p_{mid} + \tilde{p}_i$, giving

$$N_i \equiv q_i(2^l p_{mid}) + (q_i \tilde{p}_i) \pmod{2^{l+t}}.$$

This is an instance of HNP-SUM with small unknown multiplier q_i, hidden number $2^l p_{mid}$, and approximation $N_i \bmod 2^{l+t}$. Solving HNP-SUM reveals q_i, which reveals the factorization of the N_i.

Our reduction to HNP-SUM gives a new lattice-based approach to solving the implicit factoring problem. We find that the case of shared middle bits can be heuristically solved when $t \geq 2\frac{k}{k-1}\alpha$ and the other three cases can be solved when $t \geq \frac{k}{k-1}\alpha$. For the shared middle bit case, our construction is significantly more efficient than the existing literature, since it requires a lattice dimension of $k+1$, where prior work used a lattice of dimension $\Theta(k^2)$. Our bounds match the heuristic bounds of existing non-Coppersmith lattice-based solution methods [9, 21], but do not improve the bounds of the Coppersmith-based approaches [20, 25, 27–29]. In addition, our lattice approach is the first non-Coppersmith approach to our knowledge that solves the mixed least significant and most significant bits case.

2   Background

2.1   Lattices

Our algorithms make use of integer lattices in multiple ways. Given a collection of vectors $B \subset \mathbb{Z}^m$, the lattice $\mathcal{L}(B) = \{\sum_{\vec{b}_i \in B} c_i \vec{b}_i \mid c_i \in \mathbb{Z}\}$ is the set of integer linear combinations of vectors in B. The dimension of the lattice is m. The rank d of the lattice is the rank of the matrix B. In this work, we represent basis vectors as the rows of the matrix $B \in \mathbb{Z}^{d \times m}$. A lattice does not have a unique basis, but the lattice determinant, calculated as $\det(\mathcal{L}(B)) = \sqrt{\det(BB^T)}$ is an invariant of the lattice.

The Hermite Normal Form (HNF) of a lattice $\mathcal{L}$ is a unique representation for a basis for $\mathcal{L}$. The HNF is upper triangular, the elements along the diagonal, known as the pivots, are positive, and elements above pivots are positive and bounded above by the pivot. Given any basis B, it is possible to compute HNF($\mathcal{L}(B)$) in polynomial time [18].

The successive minima $\lambda_i(\mathcal{L}(B))$ of a lattice are defined as the lengths of the i shortest linearly independent vectors in $\mathcal{L}(B)$. The Gaussian Heuristic [10] predicts that, for a random lattice, the successive minima approximate

$$\lambda_i(\mathcal{L}(B)) \approx \sqrt{\frac{d}{2\pi e}}(\det(\mathcal{L}(B)))^{1/d}.$$

While it is trivial to construct lattices that do not follow the Gaussian Heuristic, it is frequently a useful tool for predicting the successive minima of lattices.

Lattice reduction algorithms input a basis B and output a basis B' for the same lattice with vectors satisfying some reducedness definition, typically ensuring that the output basis vectors are bounded and closer to orthogonal. The LLL algorithm [19] runs in polynomial time and returns [22, Theorem 9] a basis B' satisfying

$$\|\vec{b'}_1\|_2 \leq \alpha^{(d-1)/4} \det(\mathcal{L}(B))^{1/d}$$
$$\|\vec{b'}_i\|_2 \leq \alpha^{(d-1)/2} \lambda_i(\mathcal{L}(B))$$

for some $\alpha^{1/4} > 1.07$. That is, the lengths of the vectors are exponentially close to their optimal values. For random lattices, LLL lattice reduction achieves an even better approximation factor $\alpha^{1/4} \approx 1.02$ [23], so in typical cryptographic applications the approximation is very close or exact for small dimension lattices.

A surprisingly large number of cryptanalysis problems can be expressed in terms of finding short vectors in a lattice, and lattice reduction is a powerful tool for solving these problems. One example is an approach by Coppersmith [7] and later reinterpreted by Howgrave-Graham [14] to find small solutions to polynomials modulo integers. Coppersmith techniques are powerful, but Coppersmith lattices frequently have large dimension and large entries, so lattice reduction is expensive. In the case of multivariate polynomials, Coppersmith's method involves additional heuristic assumptions and a sometimes expensive Gröbner basis calculation [3,17].

2.2   The Hidden Number Problem

The Hidden Number Problem (HNP), introduced by Boneh and Venkatesan [6], poses the problem of recovering a hidden integer x from knowledge of a modulus N, multipliers t_i, and approximations $a_i = t_i x + e_i \pmod{N}$. In most presentations, these approximations a_i are given by an oracle that outputs the most significant bits of $t_i x \pmod{N}$, but we make the error term e_i more explicit in our generalization.

Boneh and Venkatesan gave an efficient lattice-based algorithm to solve this problem, and Bleichenbacher gave a Fourier analysis-based approach [8]. It is also possible to recover x from knowledge of the least significant bits of $t_i x \pmod{N}$ or some combination of the most and least significant bits [13].

A number of variants of HNP have been proposed in the literature. The Extended Hidden Number Problem (EHNP) considers the case when there are multiple contiguous blocks of unknown bits in $t_i x \pmod{N}$. This was defined by Hlaváč and Rosa [12] who also gave a lattice-based algorithm to solve it. EHNP is used as part of our cryptanalysis of MEGA and is discussed further in Sect. 4.4. The Hidden Number Problem with Chosen Multipliers (HNP-CM) considers t_i chosen adversarially instead of sampled at random [5], and can be solved without using lattice techniques via the ACGS algorithm [1]. In the Modular Inversion Hidden Number Problem (MIHNP), one wishes to recover a hidden number x from t_i and the most significant bits of $(x + t_i)^{-1} \pmod{N}$, and it can be solved via Coppersmith techniques [4]. The Hidden Number Problem with Hidden Multipliers (HNP-HM) recovers x from knowledge of the most significant bits of x, t_i, and $t_i x \pmod{N}$, and it can be solved using lattice techniques [16].

Our definition of HNP-SUM is similar to HNP-HM, but there are differences that prevent us from applying HNP-HM. First, HNP-HM requires uniformly distributed t_i, which our small unknown multipliers do not satisfy. HNP-HM also assumes the same number of bits of x and $t_i x \pmod{N}$ are known, whereas in our case the bounds T and E may not be equal. Finally, our goal in HNP-SUM is to recover the multipliers t_i and not the hidden number x. This is because for many parameters, the hidden number may not be unique: if x satisfies $a_i \approx t_i x \pmod{N}$, then it is likely $x + 1$ satisfies $a_i \approx t_i(x + 1) \pmod{N}$ as well.

3   Solving HNP-SUM

3.1   Solving HNP-SUM with $n = 2$

Before we solve HNP-SUM in the general case, we consider the case where $n = 2$. We are given N, a_1, a_2, T, and E satisfying

$$a_1 \equiv t_1 x + e_1 \pmod{N}$$
$$a_2 \equiv t_2 x + e_2 \pmod{N}$$
$$|t_1|, |t_2| \leq T$$
$$|e_1|, |e_2| \leq E.$$

First we observe that the following linear expression is small modulo N. This is analogous to an observation by Faugère et al. [9] with an additional modular reduction in our setting.

$$t_2 a_1 - t_1 a_2 \equiv t_2(t_1 x + e_1) - t_1(t_2 x + e_2) \qquad (\text{mod } N)$$
$$\equiv t_2 e_1 - t_1 e_2 \qquad (\text{mod } N)$$

Since both the t_i and e_i are bounded, this defines a linear system $y a_1 + z a_2$ (mod N) that has a small output $t_2 e_1 - t_1 e_2$ when evaluated at a small point $(t_2, -t_1)$. In order to find this small solution, we can look for a small vector in the lattice spanned by the rows of the following basis:

$$B = \begin{bmatrix} E & 0 & a_1 \\ 0 & E & a_2 \\ 0 & 0 & N \end{bmatrix}$$

The vector $\vec{v} = (Et_2, -Et_1, t_1 e_2 - t_2 e_1)$ is small and is contained in this lattice, so we might hope that lattice reduction will find it.

However, there might be a small obstruction if t_1 and t_2 are not relatively prime. Note that if t_1 and t_2 share a common factor g, then the vector $\vec{v}/g = (Et_2/g, -Et_1/g, t_1 e_2/g - t_2 e_1/g)$ is also in the lattice, and it is shorter than $\vec{v}$. We observe experimentally that lattice reduction typically outputs one of the vectors $\pm \vec{v}/g$. For our definition of HNP-SUM, we only require finding t_i up to sign and common factor, but we the issue of common factors also appears for $n > 2$ and requires more analysis to work around.

Theorem 2. *HNP-SUM defined as in Definition 1 with two samples is solvable in heuristic polynomial time when*

$$T^3 E \lesssim N.$$

Proof. The Gaussian Heuristic predicts that $\lambda_1(\mathcal{L}(B)) \approx (E^2 N)^{1/3}$, and we also have $\lambda_1(\mathcal{L}(B)) \leq \|\vec{v}/g\|_2 \approx ET$. If $T^3 E \lesssim N$, then $ET \lesssim (E^2 N)^{1/3}$ and the Gaussian Heuristic is invalid. Instead of behaving like a random lattice, $\mathcal{L}(B)$ contains an unexpectedly short vector, which is heuristically the shortest vector in the lattice. If $\vec{v}/g$ is the shortest vector by some small constant factor, then the LLL algorithm applied to B finds $\pm \vec{v}/g$, which reveals (t_1, t_2) up to sign and common factor.

3.2 Construction for $n > 2$

The approach for solving HNP-SUM with $n > 2$ is a natural extension of the previous section. Inspired by the construction for $n = 2$, we study the lattice spanned by the rows of the basis matrix

$$B = \begin{bmatrix} E & & & & a_1 \\ & E & & & a_2 \\ & & \ddots & & \vdots \\ & & & E & a_n \\ & & & & N \end{bmatrix}$$

where all unspecified entries are 0. The rank of the lattice is $n + 1$ and the determinant is $E^n N$. In the $n = 2$ case, lattice reduction can be used to find $t_2, -t_1$ such that $t_2 a_1 - t_1 a_2 \equiv t_2 e_1 - t_1 e_2 \pmod{N}$ is small. For $n > 2$, we have many such small linear combinations from each pair (a_i, a_j) and combinations of these pairs.

Unlike the $n = 2$ case, reducing this lattice does not result in a single short vector. Instead, we empirically observe that lattice reduction returns $n - 1$ linearly independent short vectors of the same length, corresponding to a dense sublattice of rank $n - 1$. This sublattice is related to the (t_i, t_j) pairs and must be postprocessed to recover the individual unknown multipliers t_i.

More concretely, we consider the sublattice $\mathcal{L}(B_{sub})$ containing the set of (linearly dependent) short vectors

$$\vec{v}_{i,j} = t_j \vec{b}_i / \gcd(t_i, t_j) + t_i \vec{b}_j / \gcd(t_i, t_j) - k_{i,j} \vec{b}_{n+1}$$

$$B_{sub} = \{\vec{v}_{i,j} \mid i, j \in \{1, \ldots, n\}, i \neq j\}$$

where $\vec{b}_i$ is the ith row vector of B. Vector $\vec{b}_{n+1}$ is included to achieve modular reduction by N, and $k_{i,j}$ is set so the last entry of $\vec{v}_{i,j}$ is $(t_j e_1 - t_i e_2)/\gcd(t_i, t_j)$. With this definition, B_{sub} contains the short vectors

$$\vec{v}_{i,j} = (0, \ldots, Et_j, \ldots, -Et_i, \ldots, 0, t_j e_i - t_i e_j)/\gcd(t_i, t_j).$$

Clearly $\mathcal{L}(B_{sub})$ is a sublattice of $\mathcal{L}(B)$, but it is not obvious what the rank or determinant of $\mathcal{L}(B_{sub})$ is or how to recover the t_i from knowledge of this particular sublattice.

Section 3.3 explores an alternative basis H for this sublattice that gives insight into its structure. Section 3.4 shows how to recover the unknown multipliers from a basis of the sublattice by computing the Hermite Normal Form of the basis. Section 3.5 bounds the determinant of this sublattice, and finally Sect. 3.6 gives heuristic bounds for when lattice reduction can be used to find a basis of this sublattice.

3.3   Alternative Basis for the Sublattice

We begin by constructing matrix $H \in \mathbb{Z}^{n-1 \times n+1}$, which we show is a basis for $\mathcal{L}(B_{sub})$. Although H is not the HNF of the lattice, it is closely related. We define the rows of H by

$$\vec{h}_i = \begin{cases} \sum_{j=i+1}^{n} u_{i,j} \vec{v}_{i,j} & \text{for } i < n - 1 \\ \vec{v}_{i,i+1} & \text{for } i = n - 1 \end{cases}$$

where $u_{i,j}$ are integer values found by the extended GCD algorithm such that $\sum_{j=i+1}^{n} u_{i,j} \frac{t_j}{\gcd(t_i,t_j)} = \gcd(\frac{t_{i+1}}{\gcd(t_i,t_{i+1})}, \ldots, \frac{t_n}{\gcd(t_i,t_n)}) = \frac{\gcd(t_{i+1},\ldots,t_n)}{\gcd(t_i,\ldots,t_n)} = \tilde{g}_i$. This gives H the structure

$$H = \begin{bmatrix} \tilde{g}_1 E & * & \cdots & * & * & * & * \\ & \tilde{g}_2 E & \cdots & * & * & * & * \\ & & \ddots & \vdots & \vdots & \vdots & \vdots \\ & & & \tilde{g}_{n-2} E & * & * & * \\ & & & & \frac{t_n E}{\gcd(t_{n-1},t_n)} & \frac{-t_{n-1}E}{\gcd(t_{n-1},t_n)} & \frac{t_n e_{n-1}-t_{n-1}e_n}{\gcd(t_{n-1},t_n)} \end{bmatrix}$$

where the entries below the diagonal are zero.

Lemma 1. H *is a basis for the sublattice* $\mathcal{L}(B_{sub})$. *That is,* $\mathcal{L}(B_{sub}) = \mathcal{L}(H)$.

The construction of H makes it clear that $\vec{h}_i \in \mathcal{L}(B_{sub})$, and it is straightforward but tedious to show inclusion in the other direction. We include a proof of Lemma 1 in the full version of this paper [26].

Like the HNF, H is upper triangular, and the elements along the diagonal of H reveal the pivots of the HNF. Although the entries above the diagonal may not be in the necessary range for the HNF, that is easily fixed by doing simple row operations that do not modify the values along the diagonal.

3.4 Recovering Unknown Multipliers

At this point, we assume that we have applied a lattice reduction algorithm to B and have obtained a basis B'_{sub} for $\mathcal{L}(B_{sub})$. We compute $H' = \mathrm{HNF}(B'_{sub}) = \mathrm{HNF}(H)$ in polynomial time and learn the pivots $\tilde{g}_1 E, \ldots, \tilde{g}_{n-2} E$ as well as the values $\frac{\pm t_n E}{\gcd(t_{n-1},t_n)}, \frac{\mp t_{n-1} E}{\gcd(t_{n-1},t_n)}$.

Setting $G = \gcd(t_1, \ldots, t_n)$, the definition of $\tilde{g}_i$ shows that the product of the these are $\prod_{i=1}^{n-2} \tilde{g}_i = \frac{\gcd(t_{n-1},t_n)}{G}$, so knowledge of the HNF allows us to compute $\left(\prod_{i=1}^{n-2} \tilde{g}_i\right) \frac{\pm t_n}{\gcd(t_{n-1},t_n)} = \pm t_n/G$. Similarly, we can compute $\mp t_{n-1}/G$, revealing the pair (t_{n-1}, t_n) up to sign and division by G.

Note that the ordering of the samples a_i is arbitrary, and by reordering and repeating the process, we can learn any pair (t_i, t_j) up to sign and division by G. Rather than performing multiple lattice reductions, we can just reorder the columns of B'_{sub} and recompute the HNF for each (t_i, t_j) pair we wish to recover. By recovering $(t_1, t_n), (t_2, t_n), \ldots, (t_{n-1}, t_n)$ up to sign and division by G, we learn $\vec{t}' = \pm(t_1, t_2, \ldots, t_n)/G$, which is $\vec{t}$ up to sign and division. This is a valid solution for HNP-SUM.

3.5 Sublattice Determinant

The previous sections show the existence of a sublattice $\mathcal{L}(B_{sub})$ of rank $n - 1$. Experimentally, we observe that lattice reduction finds this sublattice. Our goal is to heuristically understand the properties of the sublattice in order to characterize when we expect our lattice attack to succeed. We make the following heuristic observation by calculating the sublattice basis H for random instances of HNP-SUM and computing the determinant.

Heuristic 1. Let $N, a_i, T, E, t_i, e_i, x$ define an instance of HNP-SUM with x, t_i, e_i drawn uniformly at random from their respective ranges. Let $\mathcal{L}(B_{sub})$ be the sublattice defined in Sect. 3.3. Then experimentally

$$\det(\mathcal{L}(B_{sub})) \approx 0.35 n E^{n-1} T.$$

While the heuristic suffices to predict the behavior of our method on random instances of HNP-SUM, we can also prove a weaker version of our heuristic for a restricted class of HNP-SUM instances. Note that although this analytic bound is slightly worse, it has the same structure as our heuristic, providing further evidence for the claims of our heuristic approach.

Lemma 2. *Let the rows of $H \in \mathbb{Z}^{n-1 \times n+1}$ define a basis for the sublattice $\mathcal{L}(B_{sub})$ associated with an instance (N, a_i, T, E) of HNP-SUM where the two values of t_i with the largest magnitude are coprime.*
The determinant of the sublattice is bounded:

$$\det(\mathcal{L}(B_{sub})) < n(2E)^{n-1} T.$$

The proof for this lemma considers the special structure of H which arises from the coprimality of the two large t_i and is included in the full version [26].

3.6 Sublattice Recovery via Lattice Reduction

In the previous sections, we demonstrated the existence of a sublattice $\mathcal{L}(B_{sub})$ of rank $n - 1$ with heuristic determinant approximately $n E^{n-1} T$. It remains to establish the conditions under which lattice reduction finds this sublattice. LLL lattice reduction on B finds short vectors that approximate the successive minima λ_i of $\mathcal{L}(B)$. To show that lattice reduction finds the sublattice of rank $n - 1$, we first estimate the successive minima, and then we argue that the first $n - 1$ vectors found by lattice reduction must belong to the sublattice and therefore form a basis.

Since the determinant of $\mathcal{L}(B)$ depends on N and E and there exists a dense sublattice with determinant that depends on T and E, the Gaussian Heuristic does not hold in general for our lattice. However, we make the following heuristic assumption which leads to accurate bounds for our method.

Heuristic 2. Let B be the basis of rank $n + 1$ for an instance of HNP-SUM. Let $\mathcal{L}(B_{sub})$ be the sublattice specified in Sect. 3.2 and let $\mathcal{L}(B_\perp)$ be the rank-2 lattice formed by projecting $\mathcal{L}(B)$ orthogonally to the span of B_{sub}. We assume the successive minima of $\mathcal{L}(B_{sub})$ and the successive minima of $\mathcal{L}(B_\perp)$ each follow the Gaussian Heuristic.

We can use this heuristic to infer the successive minima of $\mathcal{L}(B)$. A proof of Lemma 3 is in the full version [26].

Lemma 3. *Let N, n, T, E be parameters for an instance of HNP-SUM where $n^{2n/(n-1)}ET^{(n+1)/(n-1)} \lesssim N$. Let B the constructed lattice basis, and assume Heuristic 1 and Heuristic 2 hold. Then the successive minima of $\mathcal{L}(B)$ follow*

$$\lambda_i(\mathcal{L}(B)) \approx \begin{cases} n^{(n+1)/(2n-2)}ET^{1/(n-1)} & 1 \leq i \leq n-1 \\ \sqrt{\frac{NE}{nT}} & n \leq i \leq n+1 \end{cases}$$

up to a small constant factor, and the vectors corresponding to the first $n-1$ minima are in $\mathcal{L}(B_{sub})$.

If the rank of the lattice is small enough that we can recover the shortest vectors exactly, then this reveals a basis for $\mathcal{L}(B_{sub})$, and Sect. 3.4 shows how to recover the unknown multipliers. If the rank of the lattice is too large, we can use LLL lattice reduction to find a basis for the sublattice. Proving this is straightforward given Lemma 3.

Lemma 4. *Let N, n, T, E be parameters for an instance of HNP-SUM where $\alpha^n n^{2n/(n-1)}ET^{(n+1)/(n-1)} \lesssim N$ for some fixed approximation factor $\alpha > 4/3$, and assume Heuristics 1 and 2 hold. Let $\mathcal{L}(B_{sub})$ be the sublattice as before. It is possible to recover a basis for $\mathcal{L}(B_{sub})$ in polynomial time.*

For small to medium values of n, the LLL approximation factor α and the term $n^{2n/(n-1)}$ change the exact bounds by only a few bits, so for most cases in practice, it suffices to use the heuristic $ET^{(n+1)/(n-1)} \lesssim N$. Combining Lemma 4 with the method in Sect. 3.4 leads to a proof of Theorem 1.

3.7   Experimental Evaluation

We implemented our algorithm for solving HNP-SUM using Python and Sage-Math. We use SageMath to compute the Hermite Normal Form and a custom C++ implementation to perform lattice reduction. We experimentally measured the success rate of our algorithm for various parameters. We randomly generated 2048-bit moduli and, depending on our choice of n, E, and T, we generated t_i and e_i uniformly at random to construct the HNP-SUM samples a_i. Our experiments reduced lattices of dimension up to 31 and entries of size 2048 bits, and lattice reduction took under a half second to complete on a single thread of an Intel Xeon E5-2699A processor running at 2.4 GHz. Our results in Fig. 1 show that our predicted bound $T^{(n+1)/(n-1)}E \lesssim N$ is accurate to within a few bits in practice.

4   Application: Cryptanalyzing MEGA

We present two novel and overlapping key recovery attacks on MEGA. The first (*fast*) attack requires as few as 16 login attempts (with 17 login attempts on average) and takes only a few seconds to complete. The second (*small*) attack requires only 6 login attempts to succeed with 98% probability, but it is more

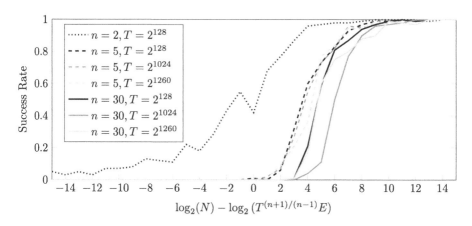

$$\log_2(N) - \log_2\left(T^{(n+1)/(n-1)}E\right)$$

Fig. 1. Success Rate of our HNP-SUM method. We generated random instances of HNP-SUM with $N \approx 2^{2048}$, $n \in \{2, 5, 30\}$, and $T \in \{2^{128}, 2^{1024}, 2^{1260}\}$. We set E to be close to the threshold value predicted by our bound $T^{(n+1)/(n-1)}E \lesssim N$, skipping the cases $n = 2, T \geq 2^{1024}$ for which no E satisfies the bound. Each data point is averaged from 100 sample instances. In all cases, the actual threshold is within a small factor of the predicted threshold, showing that our heuristic assumptions are valid. We see that the threshold is slightly higher for larger n, suggesting that the bounds likely have a secondary dependence on n as well.

computationally intensive. This latter attack can be performed in 4.5 h on an 88-core machine, but we include both because the former can be easily verified and includes some interesting additional analysis steps. Both of these attacks proceed in roughly the same series of stages with only minor variations in how the stage is completed in both the fast attack and the small attack. While solving HNP-SUM is a stage in both attacks, a number of additional stages are needed to preprocess and postprocess the leakage from the client to get it into the correct form. As a motivating application of HNP-SUM, we describe the relevant details of MEGA's protocol and the sequence of stages that allows for more efficient key recovery.

In MEGA's login protocol, the server sends the client an RSA private key that is encrypted using AES in ECB mode. The client decrypts the RSA private key, uses this RSA private key to decrypt a session ID that the server has encrypted to the RSA public key, and sends the result to the server.

The attack of Backendal, Haller, and Paterson modifies the ECB-encrypted ciphertext of the RSA private key and the encrypted session ID to obtain one bit of information about the secret key per login. However, the client is using the modified secret key to send 43 contiguous bytes of information from the result of the RSA decryption to the server. In our attack, the adversary swaps blocks in the ECB-encrypted wrapped RSA key before sending it to the client and then analyzes the resulting message from the client to obtain more information about the RSA secret key per victim client login attempt.

In the first stage of analysis, the attacker represents the 43-byte leakage from the client in terms of the unknown AES plaintext blocks. Second, these algebraic representations are manipulated so that the attacker learns information about the most significant bytes (MSBs) of an unknown value, not just about a contiguous subsequence of bytes. In the fast attack, this is done using an approach from solutions to the Extended Hidden Number Problem [12], and in the small attack, this is done by brute forcing unknown most significant bytes. Third, in the fast attack, these approximations of the MSBs are refined by combining approximations together so more MSBs are known. This is why the fast attack requires more samples than the small attack. Fourth, the (refined) approximations are used to solve for the value of unknown multipliers in the algebraic representation via HNP-SUM. These unknown multipliers correspond to differences between plaintext blocks in the encoded RSA private key. Fifth, we use the RSA equations to brute force a block of plaintext bytes of the RSA private exponent in the encoded key, and the plaintext differences reveal the values of other plaintext blocks. Finally, the plaintext blocks containing the MSBs of one of the RSA factors are analyzed in a Coppersmith attack [7] to recover the full factorization and private key.

Section 4.3 through 4.8 discuss each of the stages in turn. Section 4.9 analyzes the overall complexity of the attack.

4.1   Attack Context for MEGA

When a MEGA user attempts to log in for the first time on a new client, the client is only in possession of an AES secret key derived from the user's password. To function properly, the client requires a copy of the user's RSA private key. The server possesses the user's RSA public key and a copy of the user's RSA private key encrypted using the AES key in ECB mode, so in theory the private key is hidden from the server, but the client can obtain the private RSA key by decrypting the encrypted private key from the server with the password-derived AES secret key. It is the malicious server's goal is to recover the user's private RSA key.

During the login process, the server creates a 43-byte session identifier (SID), which it encrypts using the RSA public key and sends to the client alongside the wrapped private key. The client uses the AES key to unwrap the RSA private key, then uses the parameters in the unwrapped key to decrypt the RSA ciphertext and retrieve the SID. The client then sends the retrieved SID to the server. The malicious server wishes to use the SID value sent from the client to infer information about the parameters in the unwrapped private key.

Several of the exact implementation details are relevant for our improved attack, so we recount them here. The remaining details can be found in Backendal, Haller, and Paterson's paper [2, Section II]. We denote the RSA public key by (N, e), where the factors of modulus N are p and q. The public RSA exponent is e and the private exponent is d. The public RSA exponent is set by the client; the web client[1] uses $e = 257$, and the SDK[2] uses $e = 17$. MEGA clients use RSA-CRT for decryption, so let $u \leftarrow q^{-1} \bmod p$ be the coefficient used during CRT operations.

The private key is encoded as

$$sk_{share}^{encoded} \leftarrow \ell(q) \mid q \mid \ell(p) \mid p \mid \ell(d) \mid d \mid \ell(u) \mid u \mid P.$$

ℓ encodes the bit length of different values as a 2-byte integer, all integers are stored in big-endian format, and P is an 8-byte padding value unknown to the adversary. We wish to highlight that q is 1024 bits in length, so $\ell(q)$ is 0x0400, and since the secret values are of predictable size, they appear at predictable offsets within the plaintext. We also highlight that the private key encodes the full private exponent d and does not include the private exponents d_p, d_q that are frequently stored for use in RSA-CRT decryption. Finally, we note that due to the length fields, the 1024-bit u value spans 9 AES plaintext blocks, and the first and last of those contain the length and padding fields respectively. As in the original attack, we constrain our attacker to not alter this metadata so that the decrypted RSA key maintains correct length encodings and padding.

This encoding of the private key is 656 bytes, or 41 AES blocks. The encoded private key is encrypted using AES in ECB mode, which means that each 16-byte plaintext block is encrypted independently. That is,

$$ct_1 \mid ct_2 \mid \cdots \mid ct_{41} = \mathrm{E_{AES}}(pt_1) \mid \mathrm{E_{AES}}(pt_2) \mid \cdots \mid \mathrm{E_{AES}}(pt_{41}).$$

Decryption of the encrypted private key also processes 16-byte blocks independently, enabling malleability attacks where the malicious server alters individual blocks of ciphertext to alter the corresponding blocks of plaintext in the private key encoding.

When the honest server constructs the RSA plaintext with the 43-byte SID, it places the SID in bytes 3-45 of the 256-byte RSA plaintext m. Prior to patching, clients extract these bytes from the RSA decryption output without checking the validity of the remainder of the decryption output. However, there is special behavior in the client's extraction function that checks if byte 2 is nonzero, and if this is the case it extracts bytes 2-44. This detail has no consequence for the RSA key extraction attack in [2], but it is a necessary aspect of our small attack. If we assume the output bytes of the RSA decryption function are uniformly distributed, clients have probability $255/256$ of returning $SID \leftarrow m[2:44]$. We temporarily set this detail aside and assume that all SIDs returned by the client are composed of these bytes, and we revisit it in Sect. 4.9.

MEGA clients use Garner's formula [11] to perform RSA-CRT decryption, the process of decrypting an RSA ciphertext c to message m. These equations, as well as the SID extraction step, are detailed below.

---

[1] https://github.com/meganz/webclient/blob/9fca1d0b7d8a65b9d483a10e798f1 f67d1fb8f1e/js/crypto.js#L207.

[2] https://github.com/meganz/sdk/blob/849aea4d49e2bf24e06d1a3451823e02abd 76f39/src/crypto/cryptopp.cpp#L798.

$$m_p \leftarrow c^{d \bmod (p-1)} \bmod p$$
$$m_q \leftarrow c^{d \bmod (q-1)} \bmod q$$
$$m \leftarrow ((m_p - m_q)u \bmod p)q + m_q$$
$$SID \leftarrow m[2:44]$$

4.2   Original MEGA Attack of Backendal, Haller, and Paterson

In the original attack, the adversary alters ciphertext block ct_{40}, which is the last ciphertext block corresponding to only bytes of u, and no length fields or padding bytes. The attacker sends this altered wrapped key and RSA ciphertext $q_{guess}^e \bmod N$ to the client. The client decrypts and decodes the wrapped key to obtain private key (q, p, d, u', P) where $u' \neq u$ is not the correct value of $q^{-1} \bmod p$ to use during RSA-CRT decryption.

If $q_{guess} < q$, then $m_p \equiv m_q \pmod{p}$, so $(m_p - m_q)u = 0$ and $m = m_q < q$. Thus all SID bytes are 0. If $q_{guess} \geq q$, then $m_p \not\equiv m_q \pmod{p}$, so $h \neq 0$ and $m > q$. Thus the SID bytes are nonzero with high probability. The attack therefore uses whether SID is zero or nonzero as an oracle for whether the attacker-chosen q_{guess} is smaller or larger than the secret q. The adversary does a binary search on the value of q until sufficiently many most significant bits of q are known.

Once enough of the most significant bits of q are known, the attacker then uses a cryptanalytic technique by Coppersmith [7] to recover the least significant bits of q, and thus obtain the full factorization of N. Asymptotically, this attack recovers the factorization of N in polynomial time once the attacker knows the most significant half of bits of q. In the context of MEGA, that is 512 bits, which requires 512 login attempts to obtain. In practice, this attack can be prohibitively slow at the asymptotic limit, and implementations of Coppersmith's method often use additional most significant bits, which makes the implementation faster and more understandable. The proof-of-concept code associated with the original attack uses 683 most significant bits and therefore requires 683 login attempts.

We observe that although the client provides the adversary with 344 bits of SID per login attempt, this original attack only uses this data to refine the knowledge of the private key by a single bit. It is natural to wonder if the client's responses can be exploited in a more sample-efficient way, recovering the same private key with fewer login attempts. This is what our new attacks accomplish.

4.3   Expressing Leakage Algebraically

We begin our cryptanalysis by demonstrating how to algebraically express the information returned during a login attempt. As in the original attack, the adversary alters ciphertext blocks corresponding to the value of u, and therefore the client uses the altered u' value when performing decryption, but the remaining private key values are unaltered. In our attack, the adversary also picks an RSA ciphertext c at random, and reuses the same c for each login attempt. Both the (modified) wrapped key and RSA ciphertext are sent to the client during a login attempt.

By combining Garner's formula for RSA decryption with the extraction of the SID s' with altered value u', this gives the congruence

$$(m_p - m_q)u'q + m_q \equiv e_1'2^{b_1} + s'2^{b_2} + 2^{b_2-1} + e_2' \pmod{N}.$$

The left hand side expresses the output of the decryption function in terms of its input, and the right hand side expresses the output in terms of the known SID bytes $s' = m'[2 : 44]$ and the other unknown bytes $e_1' = m'[1]$ and $e_2' = m'[45 : 256] - 2^{b_2-1}$. The 2^{b_2-1} term is present so that unknown e_2' may be positive or negative and so $|e_2'|$ is minimized.

We can construct a similar equation using altered value u'' and SID s''.

$$(m_p - m_q)u''q + m_q \equiv e_1''2^{b_1} + s''2^{b_2} + 2^{b_2-1} + e_2'' \pmod{N}.$$

Subtracting these two congruences, we have

$$(u' - u'')(m_p - m_q)q \equiv (e_1' - e_1'')2^{b_1} + (s' - s'')2^{b_2} + (e_2' - e_2'') \pmod{N}.$$

The adversary can give extra structure to $(u' - u'')$ by carefully manipulating the AES-encrypted key. The value u used by the client during RSA decryption is decoded from the nine AES-decrypted blocks $D_{AES}(ct_{33} \mid ct_{34} \mid \cdots \mid ct_{41})$. Plaintext blocks pt_{33} and pt_{41} also include some bytes of d, the encoding of $\ell(u)$, and padding P. Now observe that if the attacker swaps out some of these ciphertext blocks encrypting u with ciphertext blocks ct_i, ct_j of their choosing, the decrypted and decoded value of u used by the client will contain bits from pt_i and pt_j. Consider what happens when the client decodes u' and u'' from the following two ciphertexts, which differ in the second-to-last block:

$$u' = \text{Decode}[D_{AES}(ct_{33}) \mid D_{AES}(ct_i) \mid \cdots \mid D_{AES}(ct_i) \mid D_{AES}(ct_i) \mid D_{AES}(ct_{41})]$$

$$u'' = \text{Decode}[D_{AES}(ct_{33}) \mid D_{AES}(ct_i) \mid \cdots \mid D_{AES}(ct_i) \mid D_{AES}(ct_j) \mid D_{AES}(ct_{41})],$$

After decryption, all of the plaintext blocks that contain only bits of u are replaced with pt_i, except for one in the second plaintext which is replaced with pt_j. The plaintext blocks that contain length encoding data or padding are not modified, so validation of the plaintext succeeds. With this construction, $(u' - u'')$ has special structure, because the only difference between the two is in block 40, which corresponds to bytes 105 through 120 of the encoded u. Therefore,

$$u' - u'' = (pt_i - pt_j)2^{64}.$$

For simplicity, in the future we will denote $\delta_{i,j} = pt_i - pt_j$, and observe that $|\delta_{i,j}| < 2^{128}$.

We will also consider $u' - u'''$ when u''' was decoded from the ciphertext

$$u''' = \text{Decode}[D_{AES}(ct_{33}) \mid D_{AES}(ct_i) \mid \cdots \mid D_{AES}(ct_j) \mid D_{AES}(ct_i) \mid D_{AES}(ct_{41})]$$

which differs only in block 39. By the same logic as before,

$$u' - u''' = (pt_i - pt_j)2^{196} = 2^{128}\delta_{i,j}2^{64}.$$

This generalizes so that the adversary can construct values of u with difference $\delta_{i,j}2^{128t+64}$ for $t \in \{0, 1, \ldots, 6\}$, corresponding to the 7 modifiable ciphertext blocks that contain only bytes of u and no padding bytes.

4.4   Obtaining Most Significant Bytes

For any AES ciphertext block indices i and j, Sect. 4.3 gives us the capability to construct an equation involving the differences of the corresponding plaintexts $\delta_{i,j} = pt_i - pt_j$. Specifically, we have

$$\delta_{i,j}2^{128t+64}(m_p - m_q)q \equiv (e'_1 - e''_1)2^{b_1} + (s' - s'')2^{b_2} + (e'_2 - e''_2) \pmod{N}.$$

In this equation, the adversary knows $(s' - s'')$ because it is the difference of two SIDs, and the adversary also knows t, b_1, b_2, and N. The adversary does not know $2^{64}(m_p - m_q)q \bmod N$, but this value is constant throughout the attack. The adversary does not know $(e'_1 - e''_1)$ or $(e'_2 - e''_2)$, but knows they are bounded by $|e'_1 - e''_1| \leq E_1 = 2^8$ and $|e'_2 - e''_2| \leq E_2 = 2^{b_2}$.

The goal of this phase is to learn the most significant bytes of some algebraic expression. This is a generally useful goal because it allows us to represent the error in the approximation as some bounded variable, and it is frequently possible to efficiently solve the problem of recovering bounded variables using lattice methods.

We now detail two approaches for obtaining the most significant bytes of this representation.

Brute Force. Because e'_1 and e''_1 are both single-byte values, $e'_1 - e''_1$ takes on one of 511 values. We can brute force these values and expect to eventually guess the correct value. Therefore, assuming we have guessed correctly, we can compute $a = (e'_1 - e''_1)2^{b_1} + (s' - s'')2^{b_2}$ and write

$$2^{128t}\delta_{i,j}x \equiv a - \varepsilon \pmod{N}$$

where $x = 2^{64}(m_p - m_q)q \bmod N$ is unknown but constant throughout the attack. This is beginning to resemble a sample for an instance of HNP-SUM with unknown multiplier $2^{128t}\delta_{i,j}$ and error ε which is unknown and bounded by $|\varepsilon| \leq 2^{b_2} = 2^{1696}$.

Extended Hidden Number Problem. We observe that the problem of converting a sample with a known block of contiguous bytes into a sample with known most significant bytes (MSBs) resembles the Extended Hidden Number Problem (EHNP) [12], specifically the Hidden Number Problem with two holes (HNP-2H). To obtain the MSBs, we search for a known multiplier C which simultaneously makes the unknown terms $(e'_1 - e''_1)C2^{b_1} \bmod N$ and $(e'_2 - e''_2)C \bmod N$ small. If we assume $|e'_1 - e''_1| < E_1$ and $|e'_2 - e''_2| < E_2$, such a value of C can be found by reducing the lattice defined by the rows of the basis matrix $B =$

$$\begin{bmatrix} E_1 N & 0 \\ E_1 2^{b_1} & E_2 \end{bmatrix}.$$

Lattice reduction finds the shortest vector $v = (E_1(C2_1^b \bmod N), E_2C)$ with $\|v\|_2 \leq \frac{2}{\sqrt{3}}\det B^{1/2} = \frac{2}{\sqrt{3}}\sqrt{E_1E_2N}$. Thus

$$|(e_1' - e_1'')C2^{b_1} + (e_2' - e_2'')C \bmod N|$$
$$\leq |e_1' - e_1''||C2^{b_1} \bmod N| + |e_2' - e_2''||C|$$
$$\leq E_1|C2^{b_1} \bmod N| + E_2|C|$$
$$\leq \|v\|_2 + \|v\|_2$$
$$\leq \frac{4}{\sqrt{3}}\sqrt{E_1E_2N}.$$

We set $C = v_2/E_2$ and note that C does not depend on information leaked from the client, and thus can be reused for every sample.

We therefore let $x = C(m_p - m_q)q \bmod N$, $a = C(s' - s'')2^{b_2}$, and $\varepsilon = -(e_1' - e_1'')C2^{b_1} - (e_2' - e_2'')C \bmod N$. This yields

$$2^{128t}\delta_{i,j}x \equiv a - \varepsilon \pmod{N}.$$

This also resembles a sample for an instance of HNP-SUM with unknown multiplier $2^{128t}\delta_{i,j}$, known approximation a that depends on the SIDs and C, and error ε which is unknown and bounded by $|\varepsilon| \leq \frac{4}{\sqrt{3}}\sqrt{E_1E_2N} \leq 2^{1878}$.

The approach using the EHNP technique therefore produces a similar equation to the brute-force approach, but the bound on the unknown ε is larger. In fact, this approach loses about half of the information exposed by the client; instead of knowing 43 MSBs, this transformation gives information about only 21.25 MSBs.

4.5   Refining Approximations

Our ability to solve HNP-SUM depends on the bounds for the multiplier and the error, and the error in the HNP-SUM samples we can obtain via the EHNP method is too large to be recovered. When using the EHNP method, it is therefore necessary to combine multiple HNP-SUM samples together to obtain a sample with smaller error. For the particular context of this attack, this sample refinement is possible.

Specifically, for any AES block indices i, j and choice of $t \in \{0, 1, \ldots, 6\}$, the adversary uses Sect. 4.4 to learn a_t satisfying

$$2^{128t}\delta_{i,j}x \equiv a_t - \varepsilon_t \pmod{N}.$$

$\delta_{i,j} = pt_i - pt_j$ is the difference of two plaintexts and is bounded $|\delta_{i,j}| \leq 2^{128}$. We also have bound $|\varepsilon_t| < E$. The goal of the adversary is to *refine* the approximation by computing $\tilde{a}$ satisfying

$$\delta_{i,j}x \equiv \tilde{a} - \tilde{\varepsilon} \pmod{N}$$

where $|\tilde{\varepsilon}| \leq \tilde{E} \leq E$.

Since the new bound on the error is smaller, this is equivalent to learning additional MSBs of $\delta_{i,j}x$.

We simplify the problem to a single refinement step using two approximations. Once we show that this is possible, it is clear that this can be repeated multiple times to refine the approximation further. We state the problem generically.

Approximation Refinement Problem. Assume the adversary is given $a_1, a_2, r \neq 0, N, E_1$ and E_2 satisfying

$$y \equiv a_1 - \varepsilon_1 \pmod{N}$$
$$ry \equiv a_2 - \varepsilon_2 \pmod{N}$$
$$|\varepsilon_1| \leq E_1$$
$$|\varepsilon_2| \leq E_2$$
$$2|r|E_1 + 1 \leq N - 2E_2.$$

If $\min((2E_2 + 1)/|r|, 2E_1 + 1) < 2\tilde{E}$, then the attacker's goal is to return $\tilde{a}$ such that there exists $\tilde{\varepsilon}$ satisfying $|\tilde{\varepsilon}| \leq \tilde{E}$ and

$$y \equiv \tilde{a} + \tilde{\varepsilon} \pmod{N}.$$

Intuitively, we consider the intersection of the set of y values satisfying the first congruence with the set of y values satisfying the second congruence. Because of the constraints on the parameters, the intersection is a single interval with easily computed bounds.

To solve this problem, observe that there exists y satisfying $y \in [a_1 - E_1, a_1 + E_1]$. Without loss of generality, assume $r > 0$. so therefore $ry \in S_1 = [r(a_1 - E_1), r(a_1 + E_1)]$. Also observe that

$$ry \in S_2 = \bigcup_{k=-\infty}^{\infty} [a_2 - E_2 + kN, a_2 + E_2 + kN],$$

so we wish to find the intersection of S_1 and S_2. Because S_2 consists of the union of intervals of size $2E_2 + 1$, repeated at multiples of N, the gaps between these intervals are $N - 2E_2 - 1$. Since the size of S_1 is $2rE_1 + 1 \leq N - 2E_2$, S_1 intersects with at most one interval, and we know there exists ry, the intersection of S_1 and S_2 is a single interval. Therefore we compute

$$k^* \leftarrow \left\lceil \frac{r(a_1 - E_1) - (a_2 + E_2)}{N} \right\rceil$$
$$low \leftarrow \max(r(a_1 - E_1), a_2 - E_2 + k^*N)$$
$$high \leftarrow \min(r(a_1 + E_1), a_2 + E_2 + k^*N)$$

and observe

$$ry \in S_1 \cap S_2 = [low, high] \Rightarrow y \in \left[\left\lceil \frac{low}{r} \right\rceil, \left\lfloor \frac{high}{r} \right\rfloor \right].$$

The size of this interval is at most $\min((2E_2 + 1)/r, 2E_1 + 1) < 2\tilde{E}$, so we let $\tilde{a}$ be its midpoint (or as close as possible if there are an even number of elements) and we have solved the problem.

To apply this to our specific problem, observe that this means that we can refine the EHNP sample $\delta_{i,j}x \equiv a_0 - \varepsilon_0 \pmod{N}$ with $2^{128}\delta_{i,j}x \equiv a_1 - \varepsilon_1 \pmod{N}$ to quality $\tilde{E} = 2^{1750}$ because $r = 2^{128}$, $E_1 = E_2 = 2^{1878}$, $N \approx 2^{2048}$. Similar logic shows that we can iterate this process, using the three samples $\{a_0, a_1, a_2\}$ to obtain a refined sample of the form

$$\delta_{i,j}x \equiv \tilde{a} - \tilde{\varepsilon} \pmod{N} \text{ with } |\tilde{\varepsilon}| \leq 2^{1622}.$$

This increases the number of known MSBs from about 21 to 53 and produces an HNP-SUM sample with small enough error to enable finding a solution.

4.6   Recovering Unknown Multipliers

We now turn to the goal of recovering unknown and small multipliers. For arbitrarily many (i, j) pairs, the attacker knows $a_{i,j}$ such that

$$a_{i,j} \equiv \delta_{i,j}x + e_{i,j} \pmod{N}$$

where $|\delta_{i,j}| \leq T = 2^{128}$ and $|e_{i,j}| < E$. The value of E depends on if the adversary initially used the brute-force strategy (giving $E = 2^{1696}$) in Sect. 4.4 or the EHNP strategy (4.4) plus refinement (4.5) (giving $E = 2^{1622}$).

This is an instance of HNP-SUM, because we have samples $a_{i,j}$, small unknown multipliers $\delta_{i,j}$, and small errors $e_{i,j}$. We use the lattice approach detailed in Sect. 3 to recover the values of $\delta_{i,j}$ up to sign and division by a common and small factor. Because the $\delta_{i,j}$ involve bytes of cryptographic material and are essentially random, the greatest common divisor of the unknown multipliers in our attack is likely to be 1 or some very small value. It is therefore possible to brute force the sign and possible common factors to recover the $\delta_{i,j}$ exactly.

By examining the heuristic condition $T^{(n+1)/(n-1)}E \lesssim N$, we observe that $n = 3$ samples are necessary for the brute-force strategy, and $n = 2$ samples are necessary for the strategy of EHNP plus refinement.

4.7   Recovering Plaintexts

By combining the capabilities of Sects. 4.3 through 4.6, the adversary can learn $\delta_{i,j} = pt_i - pt_j$ for any pair (i, j) of plaintext blocks (up to sign). Note that recovering any single plaintext pt_i therefore reveals any other plaintext $pt_j = pt_i - \delta_{i,j}$. To accomplish this, we make use of the fact that $\ell(q)$ is 2 bytes of known plaintext and a property of the RSA equations.

When the public modulus e is small, it is easy to compute the most significant bits of the private modulus d. The least significant bits of d are not easy to compute, so this does not impact the security of RSA. To see why this is the case, observe that the RSA equation implies

$$d \equiv e^{-1} \pmod{(p-1)(q-1)}$$
$$\Rightarrow ed - 1 \equiv 0 \pmod{(p-1)(q-1)}$$
$$\Rightarrow ed - 1 = k(p-1)(q-1)$$
$$\Rightarrow k = e\frac{d}{(p-1)(q-1)} - \frac{1}{(p-1)(q-1)}$$
$$\Rightarrow k \leq e.$$

Thus if e is small, all possible values of k can be brute forced. A typical choice of e is 65537, which leads to an easy brute-force attack. MEGA's web client uses $e = 257$, and the SDK uses $e = 17$, so brute forcing k is even easier in this scenario. If k is known, then

$$d = (k(p-1)(q-1) + 1)/e$$
$$= (k(pq - (p+q) + 1) + 1)/e$$
$$= \frac{kN + k + 1}{e} - \frac{p+q}{e}.$$

The second term is unknown, but it is about as small as p and q, which are about half the size of d. The first term is known and with high probability reveals the most significant bits of d.

To use this in the attack, we first recover $\delta_{18,1} = pt_{18} - pt_1$. pt_{18} contains 16 significant bytes of d and pt_1 contains the length encoding $\ell(q)$. We guess all possible values of k from 1 to e, and for each guess, we determine what the significant bytes of d would be if that guess of k were correct. This gives a candidate value for pt_{18}, which we can use to compute a candidate pt_1. If the candidate pt_1 has valid length padding, the candidate pt_{18} may be correct. The odds of a false positive are acceptably small, around $e/2^{16}$, so for small e this is likely to reveal the true value of pt_{18}. Once pt_{18} is known, this reveals pt_j for every known $\delta_{18,j}$.

4.8   Recovering the Factorization

Section 4.7 demonstrates how to recover arbitrary plaintext blocks in the encoded RSA private key. This could be used to recover every plaintext block in the encoded key, but as in the attack of Backendal, Haller, and Paterson there is a more efficient solution to learning the factorization. We can recover every plaintext block corresponding to the most significant bytes of prime factor q, then use Coppersmith's method [7] to recover the full factorization.

For the 2048-bit modulus N with 1024-bit prime factors p and q, this requires at least 512 of the most significant bits. However, there is a trade-off between how many of the most significant bits are known, how complex the implementation is, and how long it takes the implementation to run. The proof-of-concept code for the original attack requires 683 bits and involves a dimension-3 lattice constructed with Coppersmith degree 2 and multiplicity 1. We improve the implementation by increasing the Coppersmith degree to 4 and multiplicity to 2, resulting in a lattice of dimension 5. Our improved implementation recovers the factorization with only 624 most significant bits. This corresponds to the most significant bits of q encoded in the first 5 plaintext blocks $pt_1, pt_2, \ldots, pt_5$ of the encoded private key. With the improved implementation, recovering these 5 plaintext values suffices to recover the full factorization.

4.9 Complexity

In this section, we analyze the overall complexity of both the *fast* attack requiring an expected 17 login attempts and the *small* attack requiring an expected 6.1 login attempts. Because both of our attacks share many steps, we begin by describing the overlap.

Both approaches assume that the 43 bytes returned by the client are at a fixed location in the output of the RSA decryption function, but this is optimistic. As described in Sect. 4.1, the client returns bytes 2-44 when byte 2 is nonzero, and bytes 3-45 otherwise. This can be modeled as the attacker querying an oracle which has some small probability of returning an incorrect answer. For both of our approaches, we assume that all s responses from the oracle are correct. Empirically, the analysis steps succeed when this is true and fails otherwise. If the analysis fails, the RSA ciphertext is re-randomized and the entire attack is repeated, collecting s fresh oracle responses. Under the simplifying assumption that the probability the oracle returns a correct response for a particular input is independently distributed and equal to 255/256 (byte 2 is nonzero), the probability that all s responses are correct is $(255/256)^s$. Therefore the expected number of oracle queries before the full attack is successful is $s(256/255)^s$.

Both approaches also overlap in the final stages of the attack, so much of the complexity analysis is repeated. For the Coppersmith attack in Sect. 4.8 to succeed, we assume the attack has successfully recovered 5 plaintext blocks $pt_1, \ldots, pt_5$. To acquire these 5 plaintexts, Sect. 4.7 processes differences between these plaintexts and a plaintext pt_{18} involving MSBs of RSA private exponent d. That is, this part of the attack requires knowledge of $\delta_{18,1}, \ldots, \delta_{18,5}$. These 5 values are obtained using the technique of Sect. 4.6 from five high-quality approximations.

The two approaches differ in how they obtain these five approximations.

Fast Attack. In the fast attack, we obtain the five high-quality approximations using Sect. 4.5 to refine 15 lower-quality approximations. For each high-quality approximation involving $\delta_{18,j}$, we assume we have lower-quality approximations of $\delta_{18,j}x$, $2^{128}\delta_{18,j}x$, and $2^{256}\delta_{18,j}x$ for a fixed and unknown x.

We obtain these lower-quality approximations using the EHNP technique in Sect. 4.4. This approach requires minimal guesswork, and it would still work if the 43 contiguous bytes were present at a different fixed offset. The disadvantage is that the EHNP transformation increases the error bounds, so we need more samples. As input to the EHNP transformation, we require 15 algebraic relationships involving $2^{128t}\delta_{18,j}$ for $t \in \{0, 1, 2\}$ and $j \in \{1, 2, \ldots, 5\}$.

As described in Sect. 4.3, each algebraic relationship involves taking the difference between two client responses involving different manipulations of the wrapped RSA private key. This naively means that the attack could be performed with 30 client interactions, but because each $\delta_{18,j}$ involves the same plaintext block pt_{18}, one single client response can be reused in all 15 client response pairs. In particular, the shared ciphertext leads to the client decoding the u value as

$$\text{Decode}[\text{D}_{\text{AES}}(ct_{33}) \mid \text{D}_{\text{AES}}(ct_{18}) \mid \cdots \mid \text{D}_{\text{AES}}(ct_{18}) \mid \text{D}_{\text{AES}}(ct_{18}) \mid \text{D}_{\text{AES}}(ct_{41})].$$

This results in a total of $s = 16$ error-free oracle responses sufficing to recover the RSA private key, or $16(256/255)^{16} \approx 17.03$ login attempts on average. None of the steps in this approach are particularly expensive, so the overall private key recovery is fast.

Small Attack. In the small attack, the five high-quality approximations are obtained by using the brute-force technique described in Sect. 4.4. The inputs to the brute-force technique are five algebraic relationships from Sect. 4.3, and brute force attempts to recover the unknown term $e'_1 - e''_1$, which can take on one of 511 values. Instead of trying all of the $(511)^5 \approx 2^{45}$ possibilities, we improve the complexity by focusing on three algebraic relationships at a time. This gives a more tractable brute-force cost of around 2^{27}.

For every combination of prefixes for the three algebraic relationships, we apply the lattice methods in Sect. 3 for $n = 3$ to recover candidate unknown multipliers. If this attempt succeeds and yields valid multipliers, the guessed prefixes may be correct. If the attempt fails, the guessed prefixes are probably incorrect. In practice, this approach reliably returns the correct prefixes.

Table 1. Average number of logins and average wall time required for each attack. The reported ranges represent a 95% confidence interval for the measured value.

Approach	Sample Size	Exp. Logins	Avg. Logins	Avg. Time (s)
Original [2]	10000	683	683 ± 0	9.46 ± 0.02
Fast Attack	10000	17.03	17.06 ± 0.08	5.59 ± 0.66
Small Attack	100	6.14	6.18 ± 0.20	16214 ± 522

Next, we take two samples with recovered prefixes and one sample with an unknown prefix and repeat the brute-force process to recover the unknown prefix. This is faster than brute forcing prefixes for three samples simultaneously. We repeat this process to recover all unknown prefixes. This results in five high-quality approximations from give algebraic relations.

Using the same argument as in the fast attack, the 5 algebraic relationships can be obtained using 6 correct oracle responses, which happens with probability $(255/256)^6 \approx 98\%$. The expected number of oracle responses needed for a successful attack would be $6(256/255)^6 \approx 6.14$. The most expensive step is brute forcing the triple of unknown prefixes, but this step is easily parallelized.

4.10   Experimental Evaluation

We benchmarked both of our new attacks[3] against the abstract proof-of-concept code of the attack in [2]. Both attacks are implemented in Python and use the lattice reduction implementation in SageMath. We ran all our attacks on an 88-core Intel Xeon E5-2699A processor running at 2.4 GHz. The original attack and our fast attack are single-threaded, and our small attack implementation is multithreaded. Table 1 reports a 95% confidence interval for each measurement.

As expected, there is good agreement between the measurements and the expected complexity calculated in Sect. 4.9. The measured time includes the time to simulate the client-server interactions, explaining why the original attack, which includes more login attempts but fewer analysis steps, takes longer on average to perform. The small attack takes an average of 4 h 30 min of wall-clock time to complete the analysis parallelized across 88 cores. Although this computational effort is not small, it is eminently tractable. We therefore conclude that the risk of these vulnerabilities was not limited to users who attempted to log in over 500 times, and instead show that users who attempted to log in at least 6 times may potentially be at risk. This illustrates the importance of updating clients to the latest patched version.

Table 2. Comparison of non-Coppersmith methods solving the implicit factoring problem. Our approach achieves the same heuristic bounds as in prior work with smaller lattices. Neither our bounds nor the bounds reported in prior work include higher-order terms to account for the approximation factor of lattice reduction algorithms, but experimentally the bounds are accurate for small to medium values of k.

Bits Shared	Approach	Bound	Rank	Dimension	Our Bound	Rank	Dimension
LSBs	[21]	$t \geq \frac{k}{k-1}\alpha$	k	k	$t \geq \frac{k}{k-1}\alpha$	$k+1$	$k+1$
MSBs	[9]	$t \geq \frac{k}{k-1}\alpha$	k	$\frac{k(k+1)}{2}$	$t \geq \frac{k}{k-1}\alpha$	$k+1$	$k+1$
Middle	[9]	$t \geq 2\frac{k}{k-1}\alpha$	$\frac{k(k+1)}{2}$	$\frac{k(k+1)}{2}$	$t \geq 2\frac{k}{k-1}\alpha$	$k+1$	$k+1$
LSBs and MSBs	-	-	-	-	$t \geq \frac{k}{k-1}\alpha$	$k+1$	$k+1$

5   Application: Implicit Factoring

In the implicit factoring problem, introduced by May and Ritzenhofen in 2009 [21], one wishes to factor k RSA moduli of the form $N_i = p_i q_i$ where the factors p_i share t bits in common, but the value of these bits is not known.

---

[3] Our implementation is available at https://github.com/keeganryan/attacks-poc.

This problem is typically considered in the context of unbalanced b-bit RSA moduli where $p_i \gg q_i$; the size of q_i is α bits

The original presentation considered the case of p_i sharing least significant bits (LSBs), and Sarkar and Maitra [27] expanded the definition to consider shared most significant bits (MSBs), a mix of shared LSBs and MSBs, and shared bits in the middle. They also gave Coppersmith-like approaches to solve these cases. Faugère, Marinier, and Renault [9] gave a simpler lattice construction for shared MSBs and shared middle bits, but they observed that their approach cannot be applied to moduli that have factors sharing a mix of LSBs and MSBs.

Apart from [21] and [9], methods to solve the implicit factoring problem have relied on Coppersmith-like techniques [20, 25, 27–29]. While these methods often yield superior bounds, they often require lattices of higher dimension, more involved analyses, and Gröbner basis calculations to recover the solutions to multivariate polynomial systems.

We show that HNP-SUM can be used to solve the implicit factoring problem when LSBs, MSBs, a mix of LSBs and MSBs, or middle bits are shared. While our lattice construction does not improve on the bounds of the Coppersmith-like techniques, it is the first non-Coppersmith technique to solve the mixed LSBs/MSBs problem, and it is the most efficient method to our knowledge which solves the shared middle bits problem for $k > 2$. Compared to the lattices of dimension $O(k^2)$ in [9], our lattice has rank and dimension $k+1$. All of our attacks achieve the same heuristic bounds as their non-Coppersmith counterparts, and a comparison of these approaches is given in Table 2.

5.1   LSBs or MSBs Shared

We begin by considering the case where LSBs are shared, MSBs are shared, or some mix are shared. The input to the problem is k RSA moduli $N_i = p_i q_i$ where $N_i < 2^b$, $q_i < \alpha$, and the p_i share several bits. Let the $t_1 \geq 0$ least significant and $t_2 \geq 0$ most significant bits be shared. This setup includes the cases where only LSBs or only MSBs are shared by setting t_1 or t_2 to 0. We have $p_i = p_{shared} + 2^{t_1} \tilde{p}_i$ where $\tilde{p}_i < 2^{b-\alpha-t_1-t_2}$. We rewrite this as

$$2^{-t_1} N_i \equiv 2^{-t_1} p_i q_i$$
$$\equiv q_i(2^{-t_1} p_{shared}) + (\tilde{p}_i q_i) \qquad (\text{mod } M)$$

where $M = 2^{b+t_1+t_2-\alpha} + 1$. Observe that this is an instance of HNP-SUM with samples $a_i = 2^{-t_1} N_i \bmod M$, unknown multipliers q_i, hidden number $x = 2^{-t_1} p_{shared} \bmod M$, and error $e_i = \tilde{p}_i q_i$. This gives bounds $T = 2^\alpha$ and $E = 2^{b-\alpha-t_1-t_2+\alpha}$, so Theorem 1 heuristically recovers the factors q_i when

$$(2^\alpha)^{(k+1)/(k-1)} 2^{b-t_1-t_2} \lesssim 2^{b+t_1+t_2-\alpha} + 1,$$

or equivalently

$$t_1 + t_2 \gtrsim \frac{k}{k-1}\alpha.$$

This gives a unified heuristic bound for the cases where LSBs are shared, MSBs are shared, or a mix of LSBs and MSBs are shared.

Justifying the Bounds. Although the choice of modulus M seems arbitrary, there is good justification for it. Note that the congruence would hold for larger choices of M, and a larger modulus would suggest the ability to solve HNP-SUM for larger T and E, and this would therefore imply the ability to solve the implicit factoring problem when arbitrarily few bits are shared. Increasing the modulus does improve the bounds up to a certain point, but this argument fails because beyond that point, Heuristic 2 is no longer satisfied. In particular, the projected sublattice of rank 2 contains a short vector of length $\approx 2^{b-\alpha}$ in violation of the Gaussian Heuristic. Since the sublattice recovery depends on the shortest vector in the projected sublattice, the ability to recover the sublattice is unchanged.

We experimentally observe that the point at which Heuristic 2 begins to fail is usually $\approx 2^{b+t_1+t_2-\alpha}$, and using a significantly larger modulus does not improve upon the predicted bounds. In practice, we set M to be slightly larger because there is a small chance that Heuristic 2 holds for a slightly larger modulus, and making M larger by a handful of bits barely affects running time. We also make M odd to ensure 2^{-t_1} exists in the ring of integers modulo M.

5.2   Middle Bits Shared

We next consider the case where we are given k RSA moduli $N_i = p_i q_i$ with $N_i < 2^b$, $q_i < 2^\alpha$ and the $(l, l+t)$ middle bits of p_i are shared. That is, $p_i = \tilde{p}_i' 2^{l+t} + p_{mid} 2^l + \tilde{p}_i$ where $\tilde{p}_i' < 2^{b-\alpha-l-t}$ and $\tilde{p}_i < 2^l$. We rewrite this as

$$N_i \equiv 2^{l+t} \tilde{p}_i' q_i + 2^l p_{mid} q_i + \tilde{p}_i q_i \equiv q_i(2^l p_{mid}) + (\tilde{p}_i q_i) \pmod{2^{l+t}}$$

Table 3. Shared Least Significant Bits. We compared our lattice construction for solving implicit factoring against [21] for $b = 2048$, $\alpha = 512$, and various shared bits t. The row in bold represents the first value of t for which the condition $t \geq \frac{k}{k-1}\alpha$ is satisfied and we expect the lattice methods to succeed. We see that our approach is approximately as powerful as [21] or a bit stronger, and the success rate follows the predicted bound to within a couple of bits.

$k = 2$			$k = 5$			$k = 30$		
Leakage (t)	[21]	Ours	Leakage (t)	[21]	Ours	Leakage (t)	[21]	Ours
1022	0%	0%	638	0%	0%	528	0%	0%
1023	0%	0%	639	0%	0%	529	0%	0%
1024	**35%**	**44%**	**640**	**0%**	**0%**	**530**	**0%**	**0%**
1025	100%	100%	641	7%	34%	531	0%	78%
1026	100%	100%	642	89%	96%	532	53%	100%
1027	100%	100%	643	100%	100%	533	100%	100%
1028	100%	100%	644	100%	100%	534	100%	100%

Table 4. Shared Most Significant Bits. We compare our construction against [9] for $b = 2048$, $\alpha = 512$, and various t. The row in bold represents the first value of t for which $t \geq \frac{k}{k-1}\alpha$. As was the case for LSBs, our performance is close to [9] and the predicted bound, although this time it is slightly weaker.

$k = 2$			$k = 5$			$k = 30$		
Leakage (t)	[9]	Ours	Leakage (t)	[9]	Ours	Leakage (t)	[9]	Ours
1022	0%	0%	638	0%	0%	528	0%	0%
1023	0%	0%	639	0%	0%	529	0%	0%
1024	**9%**	**2%**	**640**	**0%**	**0%**	**530**	**0%**	**0%**
1025	71%	28%	641	5%	1%	531	50%	34%
1026	100%	98%	642	75%	43%	532	98%	97%
1027	100%	100%	643	99%	96%	533	100%	100%
1028	100%	100%	644	100%	100%	534	100%	100%

and observe that this gives an instance of HNP-SUM with $a_i = N_i$, $t_i = q_i$, $x = (2^l p_{mid})$, and $e_i = \tilde{p}_i q_i$. This gives bounds $T = 2^\alpha$ and $E = 2^{\alpha+l}$, so Theorem 1 heuristically recovers the t_i when

$$(2^\alpha)^{(k+1)/(k-1)} 2^{\alpha+l} \lesssim 2^{l+t} \Leftrightarrow t \gtrsim \frac{2k}{k-1}\alpha.$$

5.3   Experimental Evaluation

We implemented our reductions from implicit factoring to HNP-SUM and the lattice methods described in [21] and [9]. We performed experiments on 2048-bit moduli for $k \in \{2, 5, 30\}$ and several t around the boundary for which we predict the instance is solvable. In all cases, we find that our predicted bound is within a couple bits of what we observed. We attempted to solve 100 instances for each combination of parameters and report the results in Tables 3 through 6.

Our implementation was mostly written in Python and Sage. We also use a custom C++ lattice reduction implementation. We ran each attack instance on a single thread of an 88-core Intel Xeon E5-2699A processor running at 2.4 GHz. While our attack averaged under a second in all cases and the prior approaches were similarly fast in most cases, [9] was significantly slower for $k = 30$.

This was primarily due to the cost of lattice reduction. When solving the case of shared MSBs with $k = 30$, we reduce a lattice of rank 30, dimension 465, and entries of size 2048 bits. In the case of shared middle bits, both the rank and dimension are 465. Our custom lattice reduction implementation took around 10 s per instance in the first case and 4 min in the second.

Our experiments demonstrate that our heuristically derived bounds are accurate for a variety of parameters. Our methods are more efficient than prior work, and our reduction to HNP-SUM provides a straightforward lattice-based cryptanalysis to solve the implicit factoring problem in all shared-bit contexts.

Table 5. Shared MSBs and LSBs. We determine the success rate of our construction for $b = 2048$, $\alpha = 512$, and various t with the shared bits split evenly between the MSBs and LSBs. There is no non-Coppersmith method we are aware of to compare against, but the performance of our method closely approximates the predicted bound.

$k = 2$		$k = 5$		$k = 30$	
Leakage (t)	Ours	Leakage (t)	Ours	Leakage (t)	Ours
1022	0%	638	0%	528	0%
1023	0%	639	0%	529	0%
1024	**2%**	**640**	**0%**	**530**	**0%**
1025	36%	641	0%	531	36%
1026	91%	642	51%	532	95%
1027	100%	643	98%	533	100%
1028	100%	644	100%	534	100%

Table 6. Shared Middle Bits. We compare our construction against [9] for $b = 2048$, $\alpha = 380$, and various t around the boundary $t \geq 2\frac{k}{k-1}\alpha$. We find that our approach closely matches the predicted bound. However, the approach of [9] for $k = 30$ fails for all these values of t. This is because the lattice approximation factor is quite significant for lattices of rank $k(k+1)/2 = 465$, and lattice reduction failed to find the shortest vector for these parameters.

$k = 2$			$k = 5$			$k = 30$		
Leakage (t)	[9]	Ours	Leakage (t)	[9]	Ours	Leakage (t)	[9]	Ours
1518	0%	0%	948	0%	0%	785	0%	0%
1519	1%	1%	949	0%	0%	786	0%	0%
1520	**7%**	**10%**	**950**	**0%**	**0%**	**787**	**0%**	**0%**
1521	35%	38%	951	0%	0%	788	0%	0%
1522	69%	66%	952	9%	6%	789	0%	11%
1523	88%	90%	953	40%	38%	790	0%	44%
1524	91%	93%	954	68%	67%	791	0%	53%
1525	96%	96%	955	86%	84%	792	0%	67%
1526	100%	99%	956	93%	93%	793	0%	89%
1527	99%	99%	957	93%	93%	794	0%	93%

Acknowledgment. We thank Miro Haller and Kenny Paterson for their helpful comments on an earlier draft, insightful discussions, and providing further context. This material is based upon work supported by the National Science Foundation under grants no. 2048563 and 1913210.

References

1. Alexi, W., Chor, B., Goldreich, O., Schnorr, C.P.: RSA and Rabin functions: certain parts are as hard as the whole. SIAM J. Comput. **17**(2), 194–209 (1988). https://doi.org/10.1137/0217013
2. Backendal, M., Haller, M., Paterson, K.G.: MEGA: malleable encryption goes awry. In: 2023 IEEE Symposium on Security and Privacy (SP), pp. 450–467 (2023). https://doi.org/10.1109/SP46215.2023.00026
3. Bauer, A., Joux, A.: Toward a rigorous variation of coppersmith's algorithm on three variables. In: Naor, M. (ed.) EUROCRYPT 2007. LNCS, vol. 4515, pp. 361–378. Springer, Heidelberg (2007). https://doi.org/10.1007/978-3-540-72540-4_21
4. Boneh, D., Halevi, S., Howgrave-Graham, N.: The modular inversion hidden number problem. In: Boyd, C. (ed.) ASIACRYPT 2001. LNCS, vol. 2248, pp. 36–51. Springer, Heidelberg (2001). https://doi.org/10.1007/3-540-45682-1_3
5. Boneh, D., Shparlinski, I.E.: On the unpredictability of bits of the elliptic curve Diffie-Hellman scheme. In: Kilian, J. (ed.) CRYPTO 2001. LNCS, vol. 2139, pp. 201–212. Springer, Heidelberg (2001). https://doi.org/10.1007/3-540-44647-8_12
6. Boneh, D., Venkatesan, R.: Hardness of computing the most significant bits of secret keys in Diffie-Hellman and related schemes. In: Koblitz, N. (ed.) CRYPTO 1996. LNCS, vol. 1109, pp. 129–142. Springer, Heidelberg (1996). https://doi.org/10.1007/3-540-68697-5_11
7. Coppersmith, D.: Finding a small root of a bivariate integer equation; factoring with high bits known. In: Maurer, U. (ed.) EUROCRYPT 1996. LNCS, vol. 1070, pp. 178–189. Springer, Heidelberg (1996). https://doi.org/10.1007/3-540-68339-9_16
8. De Mulder, E., Hutter, M., Marson, M.E., Pearson, P.: Using Bleichenbacher's solution to the hidden number problem to attack nonce leaks in 384-bit ECDSA. In: Bertoni, G., Coron, J.-S. (eds.) CHES 2013. LNCS, vol. 8086, pp. 435–452. Springer, Heidelberg (2013). https://doi.org/10.1007/978-3-642-40349-1_25
9. Faugère, J.-C., Marinier, R., Renault, G.: Implicit factoring with shared most significant and middle bits. In: Nguyen, P.Q., Pointcheval, D. (eds.) PKC 2010. LNCS, vol. 6056, pp. 70–87. Springer, Heidelberg (2010). https://doi.org/10.1007/978-3-642-13013-7_5
10. Gama, N., Nguyen, P.Q.: Predicting lattice reduction. In: Smart, N. (ed.) EUROCRYPT 2008. LNCS, vol. 4965, pp. 31–51. Springer, Heidelberg (2008). https://doi.org/10.1007/978-3-540-78967-3_3
11. Garner, H.L.: The residue number system. In: Papers Presented at the the 3–5 March 1959, Western Joint Computer Conference, pp. 146–153. IRE-AIEE-ACM 1959 (Western), Association for Computing Machinery, New York, NY, USA (1959). https://doi.org/10.1145/1457838.1457864
12. Hlaváč, M., Rosa, T.: Extended hidden number problem and its cryptanalytic applications. In: Biham, E., Youssef, A.M. (eds.) SAC 2006. LNCS, vol. 4356, pp. 114–133. Springer, Heidelberg (2007). https://doi.org/10.1007/978-3-540-74462-7_9
13. Howgrave-Graham, N.A., Smart, N.P.: Lattice attacks on digital signature schemes. Des. Codes Crypt. **23**(3), 283–290 (2001). https://doi.org/10.1023/A:1011214926272
14. Howgrave-Graham, N.: Finding small roots of univariate modular equations revisited. In: Darnell, M. (ed.) Cryptography and Coding 1997. LNCS, vol. 1355, pp. 131–142. Springer, Heidelberg (1997). https://doi.org/10.1007/BFb0024458

15. Howgrave-Graham, N.: Approximate integer common divisors. In: Silverman, J.H. (ed.) CaLC 2001. LNCS, vol. 2146, pp. 51–66. Springer, Heidelberg (2001). https://doi.org/10.1007/3-540-44670-2_6

16. Howgrave-Graham, N.A., Nguyen, P.Q., Shparlinski, I.E.: Hidden number problem with hidden multipliers, timed-release crypto, and noisy exponentiation. Math. Comput. **72**(243), 1473–1485 (2003)

17. Jutla, C.S.: On finding small solutions of modular multivariate polynomial equations. In: Nyberg, K. (ed.) EUROCRYPT 1998. LNCS, vol. 1403, pp. 158–170. Springer, Heidelberg (1998). https://doi.org/10.1007/BFb0054124

18. Kannan, R., Bachem, A.: Polynomial algorithms for computing the Smith and Hermite normal forms of an integer matrix. SIAM J. Comput. **8**(4), 499–507 (1979). https://doi.org/10.1137/0208040

19. Lenstra, A.K., Lenstra, H.W., Lovász, L.: Factoring polynomials with rational coefficients. Math. Ann. **261**(4), 515–534 (1982). https://doi.org/10.1007/BF01457454

20. Lu, Y., Peng, L., Zhang, R., Hu, L., Lin, D.: Towards optimal bounds for implicit factorization problem. In: Dunkelman, O., Keliher, L. (eds.) SAC 2015. LNCS, vol. 9566, pp. 462–476. Springer, Cham (2016). https://doi.org/10.1007/978-3-319-31301-6_26

21. May, A., Ritzenhofen, M.: Implicit factoring: on polynomial time factoring given only an implicit hint. In: Jarecki, S., Tsudik, G. (eds.) PKC 2009. LNCS, vol. 5443, pp. 1–14. Springer, Heidelberg (2009). https://doi.org/10.1007/978-3-642-00468-1_1

22. Nguyen, P.Q.: Hermite's constant and lattice algorithms. In: Nguyen, P., (eds.) The LLL Algorithm. Information Security and Cryptography, pp. 19–69. Springer, Heidelberg (2010). https://doi.org/10.1007/978-3-642-02295-1

23. Nguyen, P.Q., Stehlé, D.: LLL On the average. In: Hess, F., Pauli, S., Pohst, M. (eds.) ANTS 2006. LNCS, vol. 4076, pp. 238–256. Springer, Heidelberg (2006). https://doi.org/10.1007/11792086_18

24. Ortmann, M.: MEGA security update (2022). https://blog.mega.io/mega-security-update/

25. Peng, L., Hu, L., Xu, J., Huang, Z., Xie, Y.: Further improvement of factoring RSA moduli with implicit hint. In: Pointcheval, D., Vergnaud, D. (eds.) AFRICACRYPT 2014. LNCS, vol. 8469, pp. 165–177. Springer, Cham (2014). https://doi.org/10.1007/978-3-319-06734-6_11

26. Ryan, K., Heninger, N.: The hidden number problem with small unknown multipliers: cryptanalyzing MEGA in six queries and other applications. Cryptology ePrint Archive, Report 2022/914 (2022). https://eprint.iacr.org/2022/914

27. Sarkar, S., Maitra, S.: Further results on implicit factoring in polynomial time. Adv. Math. Commun. **3**(2), 205–217 (2009). https://doi.org/10.3934/amc.2009.3.205

28. Sarkar, S., Maitra, S.: Approximate integer common divisor problem relates to implicit factorization. IEEE Trans. Inf. Theory **57**(6), 4002–4013 (2011). https://doi.org/10.1109/TIT.2011.2137270

29. Wang, S., Qu, L., Li, C., Fu, S.: A better bound for implicit factorization problem with shared middle bits. Sci. Chin. Inf. Sci. **61**(3), 1–10 (2017). https://doi.org/10.1007/s11432-017-9176-5

Hull Attacks on the Lattice Isomorphism Problem

Léo Ducas[1,2] and Shane Gibbons[1,2(✉)]

[1] Cryptology Group, CWI, Amsterdam, The Netherlands
{leo.ducas,shane.gibbons}@cwi.nl
[2] Mathematical Institute, Leiden University, Leiden, The Netherlands

Abstract. The lattice isomorphism problem (LIP) asks one to find an isometry between two lattices. It has recently been proposed as a foundation for cryptography in two independent works [Ducas & van Woerden, EUROCRYPT 2022, Bennett *et al.* preprint 2021]. This problem is the lattice variant of the code equivalence problem, on which the notion of the *hull* of a code can lead to devastating attacks.

In this work we study the cryptanalytic role of an adaptation of the hull to the lattice setting, namely, the s-hull. We first show that the s-hull is not helpful for creating an arithmetic distinguisher. More specifically, the genus of the s-hull can be efficiently predicted from s and the original genus and therefore carries no extra information.

However, we also show that the hull can be helpful for geometric attacks: for certain lattices the minimal distance of the hull is relatively smaller than that of the original lattice, and this can be exploited. The attack cost remains exponential, but the constant in the exponent is halved. This second result gives a counterexample to the general hardness conjecture of LIP proposed by Ducas & van Woerden.

Our results suggest that one should be very considerate about the geometry of hulls when instantiating LIP for cryptography. They also point to unimodular lattices as attractive options, as they are equal to their dual and their hulls, leaving only the original lattice to an attacker. Remarkably, this is already the case in proposed instantiations, namely the trivial lattice $\mathbb{Z}^n$ and the Barnes-Wall lattices.

Keywords: Lattice Isomorphism · Hull · Code Equivalence · Graph isomorphism · Cryptanalysis

1 Introduction

The lattice isomorphism problem (LIP) is the problem of finding an isometry between two lattices, given that such an isometry exists. It has long been a problem of interest in the geometry of numbers [17–19,23], in complexity theory [12], and has recently been proposed as a foundation for cryptography [4,10,11].

The problem can be viewed as the lattice analogue of the code equivalence problem; a problem that has received significant cryptanalytic attention [2,5,13, 20]. It should be noted that some of those attacks can be devastating for certain

© International Association for Cryptologic Research 2023
A. Boldyreva and V. Kolesnikov (Eds.): PKC 2023, LNCS 13940, pp. 177–204, 2023.
https://doi.org/10.1007/978-3-031-31368-4_7

choices of codes; in particular the code equivalence problem is easy for codes with small or trivial *hull* [2,20].

The hull of a code is defined as the intersection of the code with its dual. Critically, taking the hull is equivariant under isometries. The potential relevance of the hull for lattices was notified by Couvreur and Debris-Alazard, as briefly mentioned in [11]. Ducas and van Woerden [11] note that while the naïve hull of an integral lattice L is always itself since $L \subset L^*$, one can more generally define the s-hull $H_s(L) = L \cap sL^*$ for any non-zero rational scaling factor $s \in \mathbb{R}^\times$. They left any further cryptanalytic consideration to future work. This work explores precisely that cryptanalytic boulevard.

Prior Attacks on LIP. The algorithms to solve LIP, and its distinguishing version ΔLIP, are based on two kinds of invariants [11]. The first kind is an arithmetic invariant, namely the genus of a lattice or a quadratic form, and is efficiently computable (given the factorisation of the determinant)[7, Ch. 15], but only decide a coarser notion of equivalence. When instantiating ΔLIP, one must therefore take care to choose two lattices in the same genus; otherwise ΔLIP becomes easy to solve.

The second kind of invariants are geometric invariants: essentially the set of shortest vectors of that lattice. Once these shortest vectors are found in both lattices, finding the lattice isomorphism reduces to finding a graph isomorphism [23], a problem that has long been suspected to be easy, and was finally proven to be solvable in quasipolynomial time [1]. However, some lattices may have an exponential number of shortest vectors, which leads to an exponentially-sized graph resulting in superexponential complexity $\exp(n^{O(1)})$ in the dimension n in the worst-case. Alternatively, one can use the quasi-exponential algorithm of Haviv and Regev [12], which also resorts to enumeration of all short vectors up to a rather large radius in both L and its dual L^*.

Hence, the hardness of LIP essentially appears at least as hard as finding the shortest vectors in either the primal or the dual, and this hardness varies significantly depending on the geometry of the lattice and its dual. This is formulated as Conjecture 7.1 in [11] for comparing the cryptographic hardness of LIP over different lattices.

1.1 Contributions

This work is concerned with whether the hull can be helpful in mounting attacks against LIP (or its distinguishing variant ΔLIP). More specifically, can the hull be used to improve either of the two types of attacks above? Our answer is negative for the first attack, and positive for the second attack. More specifically:

- In Sect. 4, we prove that the genus of the s-hull of a lattice L is entirely determined by s and the genus of L. This means that taking the hull is not helpful to mount an attack based solely on arithmetic invariants.
- In Sect. 5, we show that for certain lattices, the s-hull can have a significantly different geometry than the original lattice, making finding an isometry

between hulls significantly easier than between the original lattices (yet still exponential time). We can then reconstruct an isometry between the original lattices in quasipolynomial time.

Significance. The second contribution (Sect. 5) directly contradicts the general hardness conjecture made by Ducas and van Woerden in [11]. Their definition of the gap, supposedly driving the hardness of LIP, only considers the geometry of the lattice L and its dual L^*. The conjecture should be adapted to include the s-hull of L for all relevant s. This is a rather clean redefinition, as L and L^* are themselves s-hulls or a scaling of s-hulls of L for certain s. This is detailed in our conclusion Sect. 6, where we prove in particular that, fortunately, there is only a finite number of relevant values $s \in \mathbb{R}^{\times}$ to consider.

We note that the lattices we consider, which act as a counter-example, are not necessarily a natural choice for instantiating LIP for cryptographic application, but instead they warn that the hull attack can be relevant. This is fortunately inconsequential when instantiating LIP with the trivial lattice $\mathbb{Z}^n$ as proposed in [4,10] since $L = L^*$, hence $H_s(L)$ is merely the scaling $\mathrm{lcm}(1, s) \cdot L$ for all $s \in \mathbb{Q}^{\times}$ and $H_s(L)$ is the zero lattice if $s \notin \mathbb{Q}^{\times}$.

More generally, choosing a unimodular lattice $(L = L^*)$ avoids having to consider hull attacks. This is in fact the case for (half of) an attractive family of lattices for LIP-based cryptography; namely the Barnes-Wall lattices with their associated efficient decoder [14].

1.2   Technical Overview

Genus of the Hull. The difficulty of analysing the genus of the hull comes from the lack of an explicit basis of it given a basis of the original lattice. However, we note that the dual of the hull can easily be described by a generating set. It is still possible to define a quadratic form out of such a generating set that is not a basis, but this quadratic form is only semi-definite. Most of our technical work lies in a careful extension of the genus theory to semi-definite forms.

A Lattice with a Better Attack via the Hull. Contrary to codes, the hull of an integer lattice is always full-dimensional, so the problem will not become easier directly via a reduction in the dimension. However, it might be possible to make its geometry weaker.

To do so, we consider construction A over a random code of length n and rate $1/2$ (*i.e.* a random p-ary lattice with $n/2$ equations). Because the hull of such a code is typically trivial (*i.e.* empty), the hull of the associated lattice is also "trivial", namely it is $p\mathbb{Z}^n$. Such a lattice has a minimal distance $\Theta(\sqrt{n})$ smaller than Minkowski's bound, and is therefore heuristically easier for LIP than a random lattice. On the contrary the lattice itself (and its dual), being random, are close to Minkowski's bound.

This gives a lattice for which LIP is significantly easier in the hull than the original lattice: according to heuristics and experiments [10], an SVP oracle with dimension $n/2 + o(n)$ suffices. Although this only solves LIP for the hull, which differs from the original lattice, this is still helpful. The automorphism group of $\mathbb{Z}^n$ is the group of signed permutations, that is, the orthonormal transformations corresponding to permuting basis vectors and swapping them with their negatives. All that remains to be recovered is an isomorphism that is a signed permutation with respect to the canonical basis of $\mathbb{Z}^n$. This leftover problem reduces to a signed permutation equivalence problem on the underlying code we started with. Finally, since the hull of that code was trivial to start with, this instance of the signed permutation equivalence problem is solvable in quasipolynomial time in n by an adaptation of the algorithm of Bardet *et al.* [2].

2   Preliminaries

2.1   Lattices and Codes

A lattice L is a discrete additive subgroup of $\mathbb{R}^n$, with inner product given by the usual dot product or Euclidean inner product $\langle \cdot, \cdot \rangle$, that is

$$\langle (x_1, \ldots, x_n), (y_1, \ldots, y_n) \rangle = (x_1, \ldots, x_n) \cdot (y_1, \ldots, y_n) = \sum_{1 \leq i \leq n} x_i y_i.$$

A set of linearly independent column vectors $B = (b_0, b_1, \ldots, b_{m-1})$ such that $L = B\mathbb{Z}^m$ is a basis of L. Such a lattice then has rank m. The determinant of the lattice with basis B is

$$\det(L) = \sqrt{\det(B^T B)}.$$

This value is independent of the choice of basis. The dual L^* of a lattice L is then defined as

$$L^* := \{x \in \operatorname{span}(L) : \langle x, L \rangle \subseteq \mathbb{Z}\}.$$

For a basis B of a lattice L, the dual of this basis can be defined as the pseudoinverse

$$B^* := B^T_{\text{left inverse}} = B(B^T B)^{-1}. \tag{1}$$

Importantly, the dual of B is a basis of the dual lattice.

Lemma 1. *Let $L \subseteq \mathbb{R}^n$ be a full rank lattice with basis B and dual L^*. The following are equivalent:*

1. the lattice satisfies $L \subseteq L^*$,
2. for all $x, y \in L$, $\langle x, y \rangle \in \mathbb{Z}$,
3. the matrix $B^T B$ has integer coefficients,.

Proof. 1. $\implies$ 2.: Let $x, y \in L$. Then by 1., $x, y \in L^*$, so $\langle x, y \rangle = \langle y, x \rangle \in \mathbb{Z}$.
2. $\implies$ 3.: Consider the i, j coefficient in $B^T B$. This is the inner product of basis vector i with basis vector j. By 2., this inner product is an integer.
3. $\implies$ 1.: Every lattice point can be written in the form Bz for some $z \in \mathbb{Z}^n$. Let $x = Bz \in L$. Then for any $y = Bw \in L$, $\langle x, y \rangle = z^T B^T Bw \in \mathbb{Z}$, since $B^T B$, z and w have integer coefficients. Thus $x \in L^*$. $\square$

Definition 1. *A lattice that meets the conditions of Lemma 1 is called an* integral lattice[1].

By Lemma 1, integrality is independent of the choice of basis, and so every basis B of the lattice has the condition that $B^T B$ has integer coefficients.

Lemma 2. *Let L be a full rank integral lattice with basis B. Then*

$$\det(B^T B)L^* \subseteq L$$

Proof. Let $B^* = (B^{-1})^T$ be a dual basis of L, and set $Q := B^T B$. By Lemma 1, Q has integer coefficients, and thus has adjugate $\mathrm{adj}(Q) = \det(Q)Q^{-1}$ with integer coefficients.

$$\mathrm{adj}(Q)B = \det(Q)Q^{-1}B = \det(Q)(B^{-1})^T B^{-1} B = \det(Q)(B^{-1})^T = \det(Q)B^*$$

This means $MB = \det(Q)B^*$ for an integer matrix $M \in \mathbb{Z}^{n \times n}$, and thus the lattice generated by B contains the lattice generated by $\det(Q)B^*$. □

Definition 2. *An integral lattice with unit determinant is called a* unimodular *lattice.*

A consequence of Lemmas 1 and 2 is that a lattice is unimodular if and only if it satisfies $L = L^*$.

A particular class of integral lattices of interest are q-ary lattices, namely lattices L such that

$$q\mathbb{Z}^n \subseteq L \subseteq \mathbb{Z}^n,$$

for some $q \in \mathbb{Z}$. Such a lattice can be written in many ways. Two useful formulations that we will require later on are the following.

Definition 3. *Let $0 < m \le n$ be integers, $q \in \mathbb{Z}$ and $A \in \mathbb{Z}^{n \times m}$ an integer matrix. Define the parity check lattice*

$$\Lambda_q^{\perp}(A) = \{x \in \mathbb{Z}^n : Ax = 0 \mod q\}.$$

Define also

$$\Lambda_q(A) = A\mathbb{Z}^m + q\mathbb{Z}^n.$$

When q is prime, such lattices correspond to the so-called *Construction A* over a code [8].

Definition 4. *Let q be a prime power. An $[n, k]_q$ linear code is a k-dimensional vector subspace $C \subseteq \mathbb{F}_q^n$. If $G \in \mathbb{F}_q^{n \times k}$ is full rank such that $C = G\mathbb{F}_q^k$, then G is a generator matrix for C. The dual $C^{\perp}$ of the code C is the $[n, n - k]_q$ linear subspace $C^{\perp} \subseteq \mathbb{F}_q^n$ given by:*

$$C^{\perp} := \{y \in \mathbb{F}_q^n : y \cdot x = 0 \quad \forall x \in C\}.$$

A generator matrix for the dual is called a parity check matrix *and is usually given the symbol H.*

---

[1] Not to be confused with an integer lattice. Every integer lattice is integral, but the converse is not true.

Note that the correspondence with lattices only works for p-ary codes for primes p, since we must include the elements of C in $\mathbb{Z}^n$. This is not possible with elements of $\mathbb{F}_q^n$.

Definition 5 (Construction A). *Let p be a prime, $n > 0$ an integer, and let C be a linear code in $\mathbb{F}_p^n$. If $\pi : \mathbb{Z}^n \to \mathbb{F}_p^n$ is the coordinate-wise projection modulo p, the* Construction A *lattice of C is*

$$L_p(C) = \pi^{-1}[C].$$

This can also be defined as

$$L_p(C) = \iota(C) + p\mathbb{Z}^n.$$

$\iota : \mathbb{F}_p^n \to \mathbb{Z}^n$ *is the obvious inclusion of elements in $\mathbb{F}_p$ into the integers.*

By abuse of notation, we will leave out the map ι, and simply write our lattices as $C + p\mathbb{Z}^n$. It can be easily shown that $L_p(C)$ and $L_p(C^\perp)$ are the dual of one another, up to a p-scaling. That is,

$$C^\perp + p\mathbb{Z}^n = p\left(C + p\mathbb{Z}\right)^*,$$

and as a consequence of duality,

$$C + p\mathbb{Z}^n = p\left(C^\perp + p\mathbb{Z}^n\right)^*.$$

This paper is concerned with deciding whether two lattices are isomorphic, and if so, finding the isomorphism.

Definition 6 (Lattice Isomorphism). *Two lattices L, $L' \subseteq \mathbb{R}^n$ are said to be isomorphic if there exists some* orthonormal *transformation $O \in \mathcal{O}_n(\mathbb{R})$ such that*

$$L' = O \cdot L.$$

Such an orthonormal $O \in \mathcal{O}_n(\mathbb{R})$ is sometimes called an isometry.

Computationally, we work in terms of bases of lattices, instead of L itself. A lattice of rank greater than 1 has infinitely many bases, which differ by unimodular basis transformations. That is, two bases B, $B' \in \mathbb{R}^{n \times m}$ generate isomorphic lattices if there exists some orthonormal transformation $O \in \mathcal{O}_n(\mathbb{R})$ and some *unimodular* $U \in \mathrm{GL}_m(\mathbb{Z})$ such that

$$B' = OBU.$$

Two computational problems arise from the idea of isomorphism. Informally, Definition 7 below is about deciding whether two given bases generate isomorphic lattices. Definition 8 is about finding the isomorphism, if it exists.

Definition 7 (Decision-LIP). *Given two bases B, $B' \in \mathbb{R}^{n \times m}$, decide whether there exists an isometry $O \in \mathcal{O}_n(\mathbb{R})$ and a change-of-basis $U \in \mathrm{GL}_m(\mathbb{Z})$ such that*

$$B' = OBU.$$

Definition 8 (Search-LIP). *Given two bases* B, $B' \in \mathbb{R}^{n \times m}$ *that generate isomorphic lattices, find* $O \in \mathcal{O}_n(\mathbb{R})$ *and* $U \in \mathrm{GL}_m(\mathbb{Z})$ *such that*

$$B' = OBU.$$

We usually call this second problem LIP instead of search-LIP. Finally, we will use the shorthand $\mathbb{Z}$LIP for instances of LIP on lattices isomorphic to the lattice $\mathbb{Z}^n$.

Similar notions exist for codes. Instead of isomorphism, in coding theory we consider whether two codes are "equivalent" or not, with finer and coarser forms of equivalence, each of which are isometries with respect to the Hamming metric.

Definition 9 (Linear Code Equivalence). *Two linear* $[n, k]_q$ *codes* C, $C' \subseteq \mathbb{F}_q^n$ *are said to be* linearly equivalent *(sometimes just "code equivalent") if there exists an* n-*permutation* $\sigma \in \mathcal{S}_n$ *and* $(a_1, a_2, \ldots, a_n) \in (\mathbb{F}_q^\times)^n$ *such that*

$$C' = \left\{ (a_1 x_{\sigma^{-1}(1)}, a_2 x_{\sigma^{-1}(2)}, \ldots, a_n x_{\sigma^{-1}(n)}) : (x_1, x_2, \ldots, x_n) \in C \right\}.$$

Equivalently, C *and* C' *are linearly equivalent if there exists a permutation matrix* P *and an* $n \times n$ *diagonal matrix* D *with non-zero diagonal entries such that*

$$C' = DPC.$$

A matrix of the form DP *is called a* monomial matrix, *and has one non-zero entry on each row and column.*

If we restrict $a_1, a_2, \ldots, a_n \in \mathbb{F}_q^\times$ *to be only* ± 1, *then the codes are said to be* signed permutation equivalent.

If we further restrict $a_1, a_2, \ldots, a_n \in \mathbb{F}_q^\times$ *to be all* 1, *then the codes are said to be* permutation equivalent.

Permutation equivalence is a finer type of equivalence than linear equivalence. Somewhere between these two types of equivalence is *signed permutation* equivalence. When $char(\mathbb{F}_q) \neq 2$, this is strictly coarser than permutation equivalence, and when $\mathbb{F}_q \neq \mathbb{F}_2, \mathbb{F}_3$ it is strictly finer than linear equivalence. For completeness, we gave the definitions for q a power of a prime, but for our purposes, we will only allow q to be a prime, p.

Definition 10 (CEP, SPEP, PEP). *The* Code Equivalence Problem (CEP)/ Signed Permutation Equivalence Problem (SPEP)/ Permutation Equivalence Problem (PEP) *is the problem of, given two linear codes* C, C' *that are linearly/signed permutation/permutation equivalent, finding the matrices* P *and* D *such that* $C' = DPC$.

Note that for SPEP, D *has coefficients equal to* ± 1, *while for PEP,* D *is forced to be the identity matrix.*

Many approaches to solving CEP, PEP or SPEP depend on the dimension of a certain subcode called the hull. We later provide a natural generalisation of this to lattices, and relate the hull of the Construction A lattice to the hull of the original code.

Definition 11. *Let C be an $[n, k]_q$ linear code with $[n, n - k]_q$-linear dual $C^{\perp}$. The* hull *of the code C is the linear subspace*

$$\mathcal{H}(C) = C \cap C^{\perp}.$$

If the code C has generator matrix G, and parity check matrix H, then the hull of C is the kernel of

$$[G|H].$$

Knowing that the hull of a code can be useful for code equivalence, it is natural to want to define the *hull* of a lattice in the same way, with the intention of using it for LIP. But immediately we find that if we define the hull exactly the same way we get no extra information. The dual L^* of an integral lattice L contains the original lattice L, so

$$L \cap L^* = L. \tag{2}$$

We therefore adjust the definition of the hull in a natural way. We scale the dual before taking the intersection, since scaling is a linear transformation that is equivariant under the action of $\mathcal{O}_n(\mathbb{R})$. This maintains the property of the hull that we want to exploit: that the geometry of the hull is equivariant under isometries.

Definition 12 (s-Hull). *For $s \in \mathbb{R}^{\times}$, the s-hull of a lattice L is defined as the sublattice*

$$H_s(L) = L \cap sL^*. \tag{3}$$

We will see later that when L is an integral lattice, the hull is $\{0\}$ when $s \notin \mathbb{Q}^{\times}$. The following lemma will later be helpful to decide which $s \in \mathbb{R}^{\times}$ give non-zero hulls

Lemma 3. *Let L be a full rank integral lattice with basis B and Gram matrix $Q = B^T B$. Then for any $s \in \mathbb{R}^{\times}$, the s-hull of L is given by:*

$$H_s(L) = \{h \in L : \langle h, L \rangle \subseteq s\mathbb{Z}\}. \tag{4}$$

Furthermore, if $s \in \mathbb{Z}$, then

$$H_s = B\Lambda_s^{\perp}(Q). \tag{5}$$

Proof. Let L be such a lattice, with basis B and let $s \in \mathbb{R}^{\times}$. Let $h \in H_s(L)$. By definition, $h \in L$ and $h = sx$ for some $x \in L^*$. Equivalently,

$$h/s \in L^* \iff \langle h/s, L \rangle \subseteq \mathbb{Z} \iff \langle h, L \rangle \subseteq s\mathbb{Z}.$$

And thus

$$H_s(L) = \{h \in L : \langle h, L \rangle \subseteq s\mathbb{Z}\}.$$

Any $h \in L$ can be written Bx for some $x \in \mathbb{Z}^n$. So we have

$$H_s(L) = \{Bx : x \in \mathbb{Z}^n, \langle Bx, L \rangle \subseteq s\mathbb{Z}\}$$
$$= \{Bx : x \in \mathbb{Z}^n, x^T B^T Bx \in s\mathbb{Z}^n\}.$$

If s is an integer then we can write the right hand side concisely as

$$= \left\{ Bx : x \in \Lambda_s^\perp (B^T B) \right\}$$
$$= B\Lambda_s^\perp (Q).$$

$\square$

In Sect. 2.5, after we have introduced the p-adic numbers, we will show that for integral lattices, only integer values of s that divide $\det(Q)$ are useful for our attack.

The p-hull of a Construction A lattice relates to the hull of an $\mathbb{F}_p$ code in a simple way. Note that the hull of a lattice does not have a smaller dimension than the original lattice, while the hull of a code often does. However, the hull of a lattice usually has a larger determinant.

Lemma 4. *Let C be an $[n,k]_p$ code in $\mathbb{F}_p^n$ for some prime p, and let $L = L_p(C) = C + p\mathbb{Z}^n$. Then*

$$H_p(L) = \mathcal{H}(C) + p\mathbb{Z}^n. \tag{6}$$

This is an immediate consequence of the definitions above. Thus, not only do we have a correspondence between p-ary lattices and $\mathbb{F}_p$ codes, but we also have a correspondence between their hulls.

The relative hardness of equivalence problems is well studied. For example, [2] show that when the hull of a code is trivial, PEP can be reduced to the graph isomorphism problem, which is solvable in quasipolynomial time [1].

The support splitting algorithm ($\mathcal{SSA}$) by Sendrier [20] can efficiently find the permutation between two codes C, C' when the hull has small dimension. It relies on the fact that the weight enumerator of a code (similar to the theta series of a lattice) is invariant up to permutation, and is easy to calculate when the dimension of the code is small.

Finally, note that the hull of a random code is trivial with high probability [20], and therefore via (6) the p-hull of a random p-ary lattice is equal to $p\mathbb{Z}^n$ with high probability. When this is the case, the above results about code equivalence allow us to exploit the code-lattice correspondence for LIP.

2.2 Quadratic Forms

Definition 13. *Let Q be an $n \times n$ symmetric matrix over a ring R. The quadratic form defined by the matrix Q is the map $q_Q : R^n \to R$ given by*

$$x \mapsto x^T Q x.$$

If $R \subseteq \mathbb{R}$, then such a form is called positive definite *if for all $x \in \mathbb{R}^n \setminus \{0\}$ we have $q_Q(x) > 0$. An integral* quadratic form *is a quadratic form over $\mathbb{Z}$.*

Definition 14 (Equivalence of Quadratic Forms). *Let q_1, q_2 be quadratic forms of dimension n over a ring R. Then q_1 is* equivalent *to q_2 over R, written $q_1 \sim_R q_2$ (or just $q_1 \sim q_2$ if the ring is clear from context), if there exists a matrix $H \in \mathrm{GL}_n(R)$ such that for all $x \in R^n$,*

$$q_1(x) = q_2(Hx).$$

Given two symmetric $n \times n$ matrices Q_1 and Q_2, the corresponding quadratic forms are equivalent over R, written $Q_1 \sim_R Q_2$ if and only if there exists a $H \in \mathrm{GL}_n(R)$ such that

$$Q_1 = H^T Q_2 H.$$

Definition 15 (Corresponding Quadratic Form). *A lattice with a basis $B \in \mathbb{R}^{n \times n}$ has a* corresponding quadratic form, *whose defining matrix is given by $B^T B$.*

Quadratic forms are more convenient to handle than lattices, because we can avoid computation with real valued elements of $\mathcal{O}_n(\mathbb{R})$. Note that two isomorphic lattices with bases B, B' with $B = OB'$ for some $O \in \mathcal{O}_n(\mathbb{R})$ give the same quadratic form:

$$B^T B = (OB')^T OB' = B'^T O^T OB' = B'^T B'.$$

If we consider equivalence over quadratic forms instead, we retain all geometric information and neglect any specific embedding of the lattice. Therefore, we often use 'lattice' and 'quadratic form' interchangeably, even though there is no bijection between the two. Definition 14 with $H \in \mathrm{GL}_n(\mathbb{Z})$ lead us to the following lemma.

Lemma 5. *Let L, L' be two lattices in $\mathbb{R}^n$. Then L, L' are isomorphic if and only if they have corresponding quadratic forms that are equivalent over $\mathbb{Z}$.*

2.3   The p-adic Numbers

The real numbers $\mathbb{R}$ are the *completion* of $\mathbb{Q}$ with respect to the usual absolute-value $|\cdot|_\infty : \mathbb{R} \to \mathbb{R}_{\geq 0}$. That is to say, every Cauchy sequence in $\mathbb{Q}$ converges to an element of $\mathbb{R}$. If we define another valuation on $\mathbb{Q}$, then we may get another inequivalent completion. For any prime $p \in \mathbb{Z}_{\geq 0}$, one can construct the p-adic valuation:

$$|\cdot|_p : \mathbb{Q} \to \mathbb{R}_{\geq 0}$$
$$x \mapsto p^{-c}$$

where $c \in \mathbb{Z}$ is such that $x = p^c \frac{a}{b}$, and a and b are coprime to p. By convention, $|0|_p = 0$ (but this also follows intuitively from the fact that $p^n \mid 0$ for all $n \in \mathbb{N}$).

Definition 16 (p-adic Numbers). *The completion of $\mathbb{Q}$ with respect to the p-adic absolute value is called the p-adic numbers (or p-adic rationals), denoted $\mathbb{Q}_p$.*

$$\mathbb{Q}_p \cong \left\{ \sum_{r=-\infty}^{\infty} a_r p^r : 0 \leq a_r < p, a_r \neq 0 \text{ for finitely many negative indices } r \right\}.$$

These sums always converge with respect to the p-adic absolute value. Addition and multiplication are defined in the natural way: for example, if $p = 2$, any element of $\mathbb{Q}_2$ can be expressed as an infinite binary expansion to the left, with the usual rules for adding and multiplying. The completion $\mathbb{Q}_p$ is a field, and has a ring of integers $\mathbb{Z}_p$.

$$\mathbb{Z}_p \cong \left\{ \sum_{r=0}^{\infty} a_r p^r : 0 \leq a_r < p \right\}$$
$$= \left\{ a_0 + a_1 p^1 + a_2 p^2 + \ldots : 0 \leq a_r < p \right\}.$$

The units of the ring of integers $\mathbb{Z}_p^\times$ are those with non-zero a_0. This type of construction is an example of a *local field*. Arithmetic in $\mathbb{Q}_p$ or $\mathbb{Z}_p$ is said to happen *locally* at the prime p. Note that there is a canonical inclusion $\mathbb{Z} \hookrightarrow \mathbb{Z}_p$, and $\mathbb{Q} \hookrightarrow \mathbb{Q}_p$, which maps an integer or rational number to its (finite) base-p expansion.

Definition 17 (p-Part, p-Prime-Part, Valuation). *Let p be a prime, and let $\alpha \in \mathbb{Q}_p$. Then α can be written in the form*

$$\alpha = p^s \beta$$

for some $s \in \mathbb{Z}$ and β coprime to p. The p-part of α is p^s, while the p-prime-part of α is β. The p-adic order or valuation of α is s.

Definition 18. *The* Legendre symbol *at an odd prime p, $\left(\frac{\cdot}{p}\right) : \mathbb{Z} \to \{0, \pm 1\}$ is given by*

$$\left(\frac{n}{p}\right) = \begin{cases} 0 & \text{if } p \mid n \\ 1 & \text{if } \exists\, a \in \mathbb{F}_p^* \text{ such that } a^2 = n \mod p \\ -1 & \text{if } \nexists\, a \in \mathbb{F}_p^* \text{ such that } a^2 = n \mod p. \end{cases}$$

The Legendre symbol is not defined at $p = 2$; instead there is an analogous symbol that we will use later.

Definition 19. *The* Kronecker symbol *$\left(\frac{\cdot}{2}\right) : \mathbb{Z} \to \{0, \pm 1\}$ is given by*

$$\left(\frac{n}{2}\right) := \begin{cases} 0 & \text{if } n \text{ is even,} \\ 1 & \text{if } n \equiv \pm 1 \mod 8, \\ -1 & \text{if } n \equiv \pm 3 \mod 8. \end{cases}$$

2.4   Genus Symbol

Definition 20 (Genus). *Two quadratic forms Q_1 and Q_2 lie in the same* genus *if they are equivalent over $\mathbb{R}$ and over the p-adic integers $\mathbb{Z}_p$ for all primes p.*

The genus is coarser than the integer equivalence class of a quadratic form (*i.e.* Definition 14 with $R = \mathbb{Z}$). Locally, we may consider the equivalence class of a quadratic form at a single prime p. The *Jordan decomposition* of a quadratic form f at a prime p is defined as follows. For any odd finite prime p, an integer quadratic form is equivalent over $\mathbb{Z}_p$ to a direct sum:

$$f = f_1 \oplus p f_p \oplus p^2 f_{p^2} \oplus \dots, \tag{7}$$

where each f_{p^i} is a quadratic form over the p-adic integers and whose determinant is not divisible by p. The Jordan decomposition at -1 is the decomposition

$$f = f_1 \oplus (-1) f_{-1},$$

where both f_1 and f_{-1} are positive definite.[2]

Quadratic forms corresponding to lattices are always postivie definite, and so they are always equivalent over $\mathbb{R}$. This is because for any basis B, and any non-zero $x \in \mathbb{R}^n$, the quadratic form $B^T B$ has the condition that $x^T B^T B x = \|Bx\|^2 > 0$.

The Jordan decomposition at $p = 2$ is a direct sum of blocks of the form

$$(qx), \text{ or } \begin{pmatrix} qa & qb \\ qb & qc \end{pmatrix}$$

with $x, b, ac - b^2$ coprime to 2, and a, c divisible by 2. If the elements in the main diagonal of a block are all divisible by 2, then it is called type II. If there is at least one element coprime to 2 in the main diagonal, then it is called type I, and the block has another invariant called the *oddity* relating to its trace. This diagonalisation is not unique, since different combinations of type I and type II submatrices can represent the same quadratic form. What is unique, however, is a canonical symbol representing the quadratic form, which we briefly discuss later.

For all p, the Jordan decomposition has an associated p-adic *symbol*, and any two forms with the same p-adic symbol are equivalent over $\mathbb{Z}_p$ [6,16].

Definition 21 (Genus Symbol). *For $p \neq 2$, the symbol at p of a quadratic form with Jordan decomposition*

$$f = f_1 \oplus p f_p \oplus p^2 f_{p^2} \oplus \dots \oplus p^r f_{p^r},$$

---

[2] Here, -1 is the preferred notation for the infinite prime or ∞. As Conway and Sloane say in [7], 'Unfortunately the pernicious habit has grown up of calling them "infinite primes" instead. [...] the unconventional name -1 made things so much more simple that its omission would be indefensible.'.

is the sequence

$$1^{\varepsilon_0 n_0}, \; p^{\varepsilon_1 n_1}, \; (p^2)^{\varepsilon_2 n_2}, \; \ldots, \; (p^r)^{\varepsilon_r n_r}$$

where $\varepsilon_q = \left(\frac{\det f_q}{p} \right)$ *and* $n_q = \dim f_q$ *for each* q *a power of* p

If any of these terms have dimension zero, they are not included in the symbol (*e.g.* if there is no f_1 component in the decomposition, then $n_0 = 0$ and we omit $1^{\varepsilon_0 n_0}$). Two quadratic forms are equivalent over $\mathbb{Z}_p$ for an odd p if and only if they have the same genus symbol at p [6,16].

The same is not fully true for $p = 2$. The symbol at $p = 2$ is more complicated to define, but we know sufficient and necessary conditions for two forms to be equivalent over $\mathbb{Z}_2$ [7,16] To any quadratic form f over $\mathbb{Z}_2$, one can associate an *oddity*, which is an integer modulo 8. We refer to [7, Chapter 15, 5.1] for the definition and the properties that we need. Suppose f has Jordan decomposition

$$f = f_1 \oplus 2f_2 \oplus 4f_4 \oplus \ldots \oplus 2^r f_{2^r}.$$

The *sign* ε_q of f_q is the Kronecker symbol $\left(\frac{\det(f_q)}{2} \right) \in \{\pm 1\}$. To such a Jordan decomposition one associates a genus symbol depending on the dimension, sign, type and oddity of each f_q. A form over $\mathbb{Z}_2$ may have multiple Jordan decompositions with different signs and oddities of the f_q. Still, one may attach a *canonical symbol* to each form in such a way that two forms are equivalent over $\mathbb{Z}_2$ if and only if their canonical symbols agree. For a complete description of the canonical symbol, see [7, Chapter 15, 7.3–7.6].

Finally, we note here that "computing the genus" of Q really amounts to computing the genus symbol at each prime dividing $2 \det(Q)$. For any prime, computing with $\mathbb{Z}_p$ can be seen as computing in $\mathbb{Z}/p^k\mathbb{Z}$, where $k = \mathrm{ord}_p(\det(Q)) + 1$ [9]. In particular, computing the genus symbol at p can be done in time polynomial in $n, \log(\det(Q))$, $\mathrm{ord}_p(\det(Q))$, and $\log(p)$. There still remains the matter of factorising $2 \det(Q)$.

2.5   Relevant Values of s for the s-Hull

In this section, we reduce the amount of values of $s \in \mathbb{R}^\times$ that can give a different s-hull attack. That is, we find a finite set of representatives $S \subset \mathbb{R}$ such that every s-hull is a scaling of $H_t(L)$ for some $t \in S$. Recall from Lemma 3 that the s-hull can be written as

$$H_s(L) = \{h \in L : \langle h, L \rangle \subseteq s\mathbb{Z}\}, \tag{8}$$

and when s is an integer, it can be written as

$$H_s(L) = B\Lambda_s^\perp (B^T B). \tag{9}$$

In particular, for an integral lattice this means that only rational values of s are relevant. Otherwise, $\frac{\langle h, \lambda \rangle}{s}$ would never be an integer for $\lambda \in \Lambda$, so the hull would be $\{0\}$. Furthermore, if $s = a/b \in \mathbb{Q}^\times$, then $H_s(L) = H_a(L)$. This can be seen by noting that for all $h = Bx \in H_s(L)$, $x^T B^T B x = v$ for some $v \in \mathbb{Z}^n$. Eq. (8) tells us that $v = (a/b)u$ for some $u \in \mathbb{Z}^n$, and a, b are coprime, we must have that $b \mid u_i$ for all $u_i \in u$. Therefore, $v \in a\mathbb{Z}^n$. So we need only consider integer values of s.

The set of integers is still a countably infinite set, but below we see that in general, an s-hull is a scaling of the s'-hull for some s' that divides $\det(Q)$. In geometric terms, there are only finitely many different hulls. The below lemma shows that we do not need to consider the factors of s that are coprime to $\det(Q)$.

Lemma 6 *Let L be a full rank integral lattice with basis $B \in \mathbb{R}^{n \times m}$ and corresponding quadratic form $Q = B^T B \in \mathbb{Z}^{m \times m}$. For any nonzero $s \in \mathbb{Z}$, let $s = s's''$, where $s', s'' \in \mathbb{Z}$ and s'' is coprime to $\det(Q)$. Then*

$$H_s(L) = s'' H_{s'}(L).$$

Proof Let $s = s's''$ be as above. Using Eq. (9), we know $H_s(L) = B\Lambda_s^\perp(Q)$. Now, $\Lambda_s^\perp(Q) = \{x \in \mathbb{Z}^n : Qx = 0 \mod s\}$. Since s', s'' are coprime, a solution x to equation $Qx = 0 \mod s$ must be a solution modulo s' and modulo s'' also. Since Q is full rank modulo s'', the only solution is $x = 0 \mod s''$. Via the Chinese remainder theorem,

$$\Lambda_s^\perp(Q) = \{x \in \mathbb{Z}^n : Qx = 0 \mod s\}$$
$$= \{s''x \in \mathbb{Z}^n : Qx = 0 \mod s'\}$$
$$= s''\Lambda_{s'}^\perp(Q),$$

and the result follows. □

The above result now means that if $\det(Q) = p_1^{e_1} \dots p_r^{e_r}$ for some primes p_i and exponents, then all s-hulls are either $\{0\}$ or a scaling of a t-hull where t is a product of the p_i's to any exponent. Finally, we can show that an s-hull for some $s \nmid \det(Q)$ is simply a scaling of one of the s'-hulls for some $s' \mid \det(Q)$.

Lemma 7 *Let L be a integral lattice with basis B and corresponding quadratic form $Q = B^T B$. For any nonzero $s \in \mathbb{Z}$, and any prime p, let $s = qp^{k+r}$ for some integer q, where k is the largest power of p dividing $\det(Q)$, and r an integer greater than or equal to 0. Then*

$$H_s(L) = p^r H_{qp^k}(L). \tag{10}$$

Proof Via the Chinese remainder theorem, we need only show that this is true for $s = p^{k+r}$. This is equivalent to showing $\Lambda_{p^{k+r}}^\perp(Q) = p^r \Lambda_{p^k}^\perp(Q)$, via Eq. (9). It can be shown that $\Lambda_{p^t}^\perp(Q) = p^t(\Lambda_{p^t}(Q)^*)$, for any t. Thus taking the dual of both lattices means that instead of Eq. (10) we equivalently want to show

$$\Lambda_{p^{k+r}}(Q) = \Lambda_{p^k}(Q). \tag{11}$$

The inclusion $\subseteq$ is immediate from the definition of the q-ary lattices. The reverse inclusion is proven by showing $p^k \mathbb{Z}^m \subseteq \Lambda_{p^{k+r}}(Q) = Q\mathbb{Z}^m + p^{k+r}\mathbb{Z}^m$. That is, for every $Y \in \mathbb{Z}^m$, there exists a solution $X \in \mathbb{Z}/p^{k+r}\mathbb{Z}$ to

$$QX = p^k Y \mod p^{k+r}. \tag{12}$$

Consider the equation in $\mathbb{Q}_p$, the p-adic numbers. Then

$$Q^{-1} \in \frac{1}{\det(Q)} \mathbb{Z}_p^{m \times m} = \frac{1}{p^k} \mathbb{Z}_p^{m \times m}.$$

The second equality is because the p-prime part of $\det(Q)$ is a unit in $\mathbb{Z}_p$. So set $Q^{-1} = p^{-k} Q'^{-1}$ for some $Q' \in \mathbb{Z}_p^{m \times m}$. Let $X := Q'Y \in \mathbb{Z}_p$. Reducing modulo p^{k+r} gives a solution to Eq. (12)   □

Corollary 1. *Let $m > 0$ and $A \in \mathbb{Z}^{m \times m}$ be a square matrix with non-zero determinant. Then for any prime p, there exists some $k \leq \mathrm{ord}_p(\det(A))$ such that*

$$\Lambda_{p^r}(A) = \Lambda_{p^k}(A)$$

for all $r \geq k$.

The above discussion, particularly Lemmas 6 and 7 say that any s-hull is either $\{0\}$ or a scaling of a t-hull for some integer $t \mid \det(Q)$. In summary, we have the following lemma.

Lemma 8. *Let L be a integral lattice with basis B and corresponding quadratic form $Q = B^T B$, and let $s \in \mathbb{R}^\times$. Denote the s-hull of L by $H_s(L)$.*

1. *If s is irrational, then $H_s(L) = \{0\}$.*
2. *If $s = a/b \in \mathbb{Q}$, then $H_s(L) = H_a(L)$.*
3. *If $s = rt \in \mathbb{Z}$, where $t \in \mathbb{Z}$ is the largest over all factorisations of s such that $t \mid \det(Q)$, then $H_s(L) = rH_t(L)$.*

3   Extensions of the Definition of the Genus

The genus is well-defined for integral lattices. We would like a more generalised version of this for rational quadratic forms and even for semidefinite forms. Semidefinite forms arise when we consider a generating set of a lattice rather than a basis. This will be useful when calculating the genus of the hull of a lattice. The concept of equivalence over $\mathbb{Z}_p$ is still valid when the entries are elements of $\mathbb{Q}_p$, similar to how $\mathbb{Z}$-equivalence is still relevant to quadratic forms with rational coefficients. We therefore provide a natural extension of the genus definition above, which applies to quadratic forms over $\mathbb{Q}$ (and $\mathbb{Q}_p$). Consider two rational quadratic forms Q, Q' that are equivalent over $\mathbb{Z}_p$. Then $\exists H \in \mathrm{GL}_n(\mathbb{Z}_p)$ such that

$$H^T Q H = Q'.$$

Any scaling $\lambda Q, \lambda Q'$, with non-zero $\lambda \in \mathbb{Q}$ are also equivalent via the same H. This motivates the following definition of the genus symbol of a rational quadratic form. The difference is that we only need to multiply by the p-part of a least common multiple (LCM) of the denominators, ensuring that λQ has coefficients in $\mathbb{Z}_p$.

Definition 22 (Genus Symbol for Rational Forms). *For $p \neq 2$, let f be a positive definite rational quadratic form and let $\lambda = p^s$ be the p-part of the LCM of the denominators of the coefficients in f. If λf has Jordan decomposition*

$$\lambda f = f_1 \oplus p f_p \oplus p^2 f_{p^2} \oplus \ldots \oplus p^r f_{p^r},$$

and genus symbol

$$1^{\varepsilon_0 n_0}, \ p^{\varepsilon_1 n_1}, \ (p^2)^{\varepsilon_2 n_2}, \ \ldots, \ (p^r)^{\varepsilon_r n_r},$$

then the symbol at p of f is

$$(p^{-s})^{\varepsilon_0 n_0}, \ (p^{1-s})^{\varepsilon_1 n_1}, \ (p^{2-s})^{\varepsilon_2 n_2}, \ \ldots, \ (p^{r-s})^{\varepsilon_r n_r}.$$

This is consistent with the original definition of the genus symbol at p when f has coefficients in $\mathbb{Z}$. In that case, $\lambda = 1$.

The effect on the symbol at 2 is the same for the sign, dimension, and powers of p, however the oddity and type of each f_i would remain the same. This is because these last two values are independent of the powers of 2 in the decomposition. We do not include an explicit definition of the symbol here, because for our purposes, we only need the fact that the quadratic forms are equivalent over $\mathbb{Z}_2$, not necessarily their genus symbols.

Next we define an equivalence relation that allows us to augment the genus symbol further to include semi-definite forms.

Definition 23. *Define the equivalence relation $\equiv$ of quadratic forms as follows. Let Q be a semidefinite symmetric matrix. Then*

$$Q \equiv \begin{pmatrix} Q & 0 \\ 0 & 0 \end{pmatrix} \quad and \quad \begin{pmatrix} Q & 0 \\ 0 & 0 \end{pmatrix} \equiv Q \tag{13}$$

where the larger matrix is the square block matrix consisting of Q and a zero row and zero column.

In particular, this means that a quadratic form Q is equivalent via $\equiv$ to the same quadratic form with any number of zero rows and zero columns added on (so long as the matrix remains square). This is not too drastic, since integral quadratic forms can also be written in terms of polynomials. If $(Q_{ij})_{1 \leq i,j \leq n}$ is a quadratic form, the corresponding polynomial in n variables is

$$\sum_{1 \leq i,j \leq n} Q_{ij} X_i X_j.$$

Including zero-rows and zero-columns to the matrix Q amounts to adding extra variables to this sum whose coefficients are always zero. This does not change the polynomial itself, only the number of variables in the polynomial. The above equivalence essentially says that quadratic forms whose polynomials are equal but with different numbers of variables are equivalent.

The following definition combines $\equiv$ and $\sim$ into one type of equivalence.

Definition 24. *Let R be an integral domain with field of fractions F. Let Q_1 and Q_2 be two symmetric semidefinite $n \times n$ matrices with coefficients in F such that*

$$Q_1 \sim \begin{pmatrix} Q_1' & 0 \\ 0 & 0 \end{pmatrix}$$

and

$$Q_2 \sim \begin{pmatrix} Q_2' & 0 \\ 0 & 0 \end{pmatrix},$$

where Q_1', Q_2' are positive definite of rank m and the 0 blocks are size $(n-m) \times m$, $(n-m) \times (n-m)$ and $m \times (n-m)$ as required. The corresponding quadratic forms are equivalent over R, written $Q_1 \cong Q_2$, when there exists $H \in \mathrm{GL}_m(R)$ such that

$$Q_1' = H^T Q_2' H.$$

Proposition 1. *Let Q, Q', S, S', be quadratic forms such that $Q \equiv S$ and $Q' \equiv S'$ where Q, Q' have the same dimension and S, S' have the same dimension. Then $Q \sim Q'$ if and only if $S \sim S'$.*

Informally, in the following diagram we want to show that when Q, Q' have the same dimension, $S \sim S'$ if and only if $Q \sim Q'$, where S, S' are the result of adding the same number of zero-rows and zero-columns to Q, Q', respectively.

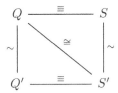

Proof. Let Q, Q' be $n \times n$ positive definite symmetric matrices. The positive definiteness assumption is without loss of generality since for any symmetric semidefinite matrices, A, B, C, equivalence means $A \equiv B$ and $B \equiv C$ implies $A \equiv C$. Graphically, the equivalence looks like this:

$$Q \overset{\equiv}{\text{------}} \begin{pmatrix} Q & 0_{n \times 1} \\ 0_{1 \times n} & 0_{1 \times 1} \end{pmatrix}$$

$$\begin{pmatrix} Q & 0_{n \times k} \\ 0_{k \times n} & 0_{k \times k} \end{pmatrix}$$

We also know by assumption that $S \sim T := \begin{pmatrix} Q & 0 \\ 0 & 0 \end{pmatrix}$ and $S' \sim T' := \begin{pmatrix} Q' & 0 \\ 0 & 0 \end{pmatrix}$, where the 0's are zero matrices of size $n \times k, k \times n$, and $k \times k$, ensuring S and S'

are square. This is by definition of the equivalence $\sim$. If Q and Q' are equivalent via some U, then T, T' are equivalent via $\begin{pmatrix} U & 0 \\ 0 & \mathbb{I}_k \end{pmatrix}$, and therefore $S \sim S'$.

For the other direction, assume that $S \sim S'$. Then $T \sim T'$, and there exists some unimodular matrix U such that $U^T T U = T'$. Let

$$U := \left(\begin{array}{c|c} U_1 & U_2 \\ \hline U_3 & U_4 \end{array} \right),$$

where the U_1 is size $n \times n$, U_2 is size $n \times k$, U_3 is size $k \times n$, and U_4 is size $k \times k$. Then we have

$$\left(\begin{array}{c|c} U_1^T Q U_1 & U_1^T Q U_2 \\ \hline U_2^T Q U_1 & U_2^T Q U_2 \end{array} \right) = \begin{pmatrix} Q' & 0 \\ 0 & 0 \end{pmatrix}.$$

Because Q is positive definite, U_2 is the zero matrix. Since $\det(U) = \det(U_1)\det(U_4)$ is a unit, then $\det(U_1)$ is a unit, and U_1 is unimodular.   □

Finally, a fact that we use in Sect. 4 is that if $Q \sim Q'$ via the action of some $H \in \mathrm{GL}_n(R)$, then $Q^{-1} \sim Q'^{-1}$ via the action of $H^{-T} \in \mathrm{GL}_n(R)$. Thus the genus of the dual of a lattice is decided by the genus of the primal lattice, and vice versa.

4   The Genus of the Hull

The below proposition can be summed up by saying that knowing the genus of the s-hull of a lattice L does not provide any more information than knowing s and the genus of L. Equivalently, the s-hull of two lattices are equivalent over $\mathbb{Z}_p$ if the original lattices are equivalent over $\mathbb{Z}_p$.

Proposition 2. *Let L and L' be two integral lattices admitting respective quadratic forms Q, $Q' \in \mathbb{Z}^{m \times m}$ that are equivalent over $\mathbb{Z}_p$, via some transformation*

$$U^T Q U = Q'.$$

Then any quadratic forms corresponding to the s-hulls of these lattices, Q_H and $Q_{H'}$, are also equivalent over $\mathbb{Z}_p$.

Proof. Let $s = \alpha p^v$ for some α coprime to p. Then, when considered as a lattice over $\mathbb{Z}_p$, $sL^* = p^v(\alpha L^*) = p^v L^*$. So without loss of generality[3], let $s = p^v$ for some non-negative v. Let H_s be the s-hull of L. A convenient path when dealing with intersections is to note that for two lattices, the sum of their duals is the dual of their intersection. Applying this principle to Eq. (3), we get that the dual of the s-hull can be written as

$$H_s^* = L^* + (sL^*)^*$$

$$= L^* + \frac{1}{s}L.$$

---

[3] In general, if $L = B \cdot R^m$ is a lattice, then $\alpha L = L$ when α is a unit in R.

Thus H_s^* has a column-wise generating set

$$\frac{1}{s}\left(B \mid sB^*\right),$$

which has corresponding quadratic form

$$Q_{H^*} = \frac{1}{s^2}\begin{pmatrix} B^T B & s\mathbb{I} \\ s\mathbb{I} & s^2(B^{*T}B^*) \end{pmatrix}. \tag{14}$$

For ease of notation, let $Q = B^T B$, $Q^{-1} = B^{*T}B^* = (B^T B)^{-1}$. Thus

$$Q_{H^*} = \frac{1}{s^2}\begin{pmatrix} Q & s\mathbb{I} \\ s\mathbb{I} & s^2 Q^{-1} \end{pmatrix}.$$

The same is true for L', the dual of whose s-hull has quadratic form given by

$$Q'_{H^*} = \frac{1}{s^2}\begin{pmatrix} Q' & s\mathbb{I} \\ s\mathbb{I} & s^2 Q'^{-1} \end{pmatrix}.$$

Now, let U be the unimodular transform in $\mathbb{Z}_p$ such that

$$U^T Q U = Q'.$$

Let $\hat{U} := \begin{pmatrix} U^T & 0 \\ 0 & U^{-1} \end{pmatrix}$, which is unimodular in $\mathbb{Z}_p$. One can verify that

$$\hat{U} Q_{H^*} \hat{U}^T = Q'_{H^*},$$

which is the required result.   □

The matrix $U_p \in \mathbb{Z}_p^{m \times m}$ which sends a basis of the hull of L to the same for L' can be found in the following manner. The generating set of H_s^* we saw above differs by a unimodular transformation to a basis $(BM)^*$ of H_s^*, where M is a basis of $\Lambda_s^{\perp}(Q)$. The same is true for $(H'_s)^*$. The quadratic forms of the generating sets of the duals differ by the matrix $\hat{U}$ from the proof. Combining these three transformations in the correct order gives us the matrix U that satisfies

$$U^T \begin{pmatrix} (BM)^* & 0 \\ 0 & 0 \end{pmatrix} U = \begin{pmatrix} (B'M')^* & 0 \\ 0 & 0 \end{pmatrix}.$$

Since BM and $B'M'$ are full rank, $n \times n$ matrices, this forces the top-left $n \times n$ submatrix of U, which we may call U_1, to satisfy

$$U_1^T (BM)^* U_1 = (B'M')^*.$$

Thus $U_p = U_1^{-T}$.

5   A Lattice with a Better Attack via the Hull

This section demonstrates how the hull attack can be useful on certain types of lattice. This is ultimately acts as a counterexample to [11, Conjecture 7.1] (Conjecture 1 below). They compare the length of the shortest vectors in the lattice to the expected length of a shortest vector in a *random* lattice of the same volume, *i.e.* the Gaussian heuristic.

$$\mathrm{gh}(L) := \det(L)^{1/n} \cdot \frac{1}{\sqrt{\pi}} \cdot \Gamma(1 + n/2)^{1/n} \approx \det(L)^{1/n} \cdot \sqrt{\frac{n}{2\pi e}}.$$

The first minimum of L and its dual L^* are both expected to be near the expected length of a shortest vector in a random lattice of the same dimension n.

Since LIP attacks can also be launched in the dual, they define the quantity

$$\mathrm{gap}(L) = \max\left\{\frac{\mathrm{gh}(L)}{\lambda_1(L)}, \frac{\mathrm{gh}(L^*)}{\lambda_1(L^*)}\right\}$$

as driving the hardness of attacks. A gap of 1 means that LIP is essentially as hard as solving SVP in a random lattice with the same dimension as n; larger gaps allow one to resort to the BKZ algorithm, and only solve SVP in dimension $\beta < n$. Using our notation, the conjecture is as follows.

Conjecture 1. For any two lattices L_0, L_1 admitting quadratic forms Q_0, Q_1 in the same genus, and $1 \leq \mathrm{gap}(L_i) \leq f$, the best attack against an instance of ΔLIP with L and L' requires solving f-approx-SVP for both L_0 and L_1.

In this statement, f is not quantified, but an existence quantification would be vacuously satisfied by any sufficiently large f. Indeed, this conjecture is motivated by attacks that solve f-SVP with $f = \min\{\mathrm{gap}(L_i)\}$. We therefore take

$$f = \min\{\mathrm{gap}(L_0), \mathrm{gap}(L_1)\}$$

as their original estimate for hardness.

Choose parameters p, n, k. Let C be a random, rate $1/2$, p-ary code of length n. Then let $L = C + p\mathbb{Z}^n$ be the Construction A lattice associated to this code. Direct LIP attacks based on SVP on lattices such as these (or their duals) cost $2^{0.292n+o(n)}$ [3]. But with high probability, the p-hull of such a lattice is $p\mathbb{Z}^n$. An instance of $\mathbb{Z}$LIP can be solved using the Blockwise Korkine Zolotarev (BKZ) algorithm with block size $\beta = n/2 + o(n)$ [10,11], in time $2^{0.292\beta+o(\beta)} = 2^{0.292n/2+o(n)}$ [3]. Section 5.1 tells us that for lattices with trivial hull, if an isomorphism from these hulls to $\mathbb{Z}^n$ can be found, then LIP can be reduced to an instance of SPEP on codes of length n, via a Karp reduction. Meanwhile, Sect. 5.2 shows that these instances of SPEP are equivalent to solving PEP on codes of length $2n$ with trivial hull. We also show that the PEP instances relevant to LIP are exactly those cases that reduce via [2] to an instance of graph isomorphism, GI, of size $2n$, and in particular are solvable in quasipolynomial time [1], or $2^{O((\log n)^c)}$ for some c.

5.1   When the Hull Is Trivial

In Sect. 2.1, Lemma 4, we saw that the hull of a p-lattice corresponds to the hull of a code over $\mathbb{F}_p$. From [20], we know that the hull of a random code is trivial with high probability, which implies that the hull of a Construction A lattice is $p\mathbb{Z}^n$ with high probability. We consider LIP for lattices that are isomorphic to $C + p\mathbb{Z}^n$, where C has trivial hull.

Lemma 9. *Let $C \subseteq \mathbb{F}_p^n$ be an $[n,k]_p$ code whose hull is $\{0\}$. For $i = 1, 2$, let $O_i \in \mathcal{O}_n(\mathbb{R})$ be two orthonormal transformations, and $L_i = O_i(C + p\mathbb{Z}^n)$ be two lattices which are isomorphic. An instance of LIP on L_1, L_2 can be solved using two oracle calls to $\mathbb{Z}$LIP and one oracle call to SPEP on C.*

Proof. A lattice $L = O(C + p\mathbb{Z}^n)$ has determinant p^{n-k}. Therefore if p is not known, it can be found by taking i-th roots of $\det(L)$ (which is efficiently calculable) for $i \in \{n - k, n - k - 1, \ldots, 1\}$, and checking if the answer is an integer. Since L is a lattice isomorphic to a Construction A lattice, Lemma 4 gives that:

$$\mathcal{H}_p(L) = pO\mathbb{Z}^n,$$

that is, the p-hull is isomorphic to $p\mathbb{Z}^n$ via the same rotation O. If we then solved $\mathbb{Z}$LIP to find an isomorphism from $p\mathbb{Z}^n$ to $\mathcal{H}_p(L)$, then we would get *some* isomorphism $\hat{O} := O\sigma$, where $O \in \mathcal{O}_n(\mathbb{R})$ and σ is a signed permutation. This is because every such isomorphism is in the coset $O\mathrm{Aut}(p\mathbb{Z}^n) \subseteq \mathcal{O}_n(\mathbb{R})$, where $\mathrm{Aut}(p\mathbb{Z}^n) = \{O \in \mathcal{O}_n(\mathbb{R}) : pO\mathbb{Z}^n = p\mathbb{Z}^n\}$. To see this, consider two isomorphisms

$$\varphi : \mathcal{H}_p(L) \to p\mathbb{Z}^n$$

and

$$\psi : \mathcal{H}_p(L) \to p\mathbb{Z}^n.$$

Then $\psi\varphi^{-1} \in \mathrm{Aut}(p\mathbb{Z}^n)$, and therefore it must be a signed permutation. Therefore, any φ and ψ as above differ only by a signed permutation.

Now, if we apply the inverse of isomorphism $\hat{O}$ to L, we get some lattice $L' := \hat{O}^{-1}L = \sigma^{-1}C + p\mathbb{Z}^n$. If we reduce this modulo p, we then get a basis for the code $\sigma^{-1}C$ over $\mathbb{F}_p$.

If instead we are given two lattices of the form $O_i(C + p\mathbb{Z}^n)$ for $i = 1, 2$, then we can apply the above argument to get two codes over $\mathbb{F}_p$ that differ by a signed permutation, *i.e.*

$$\sigma_1^{-1}C_1 = C = \sigma_2^{-1}C_2,$$

or equivalently

$$C_1 = \sigma_1\sigma_2^{-1}C_2.$$

We therefore have reduced the problem of finding the isomorphism between these two lattices to the problem of finding the signed permutation sending one code to another.   □

It still remains to analyse the hardness of these instances of SPEP.

5.2   Signed Permutation Equivalence and Graph Isomorphism

Below, we adapt a method by Sendrier and Simos in [21], involving the *closure* of a code, to show how SPEP on an instance of two length n codes reduces to PEP on an instance of two length $2n$ codes. Crucially, we show that if a code has trivial hull, and char$(\mathbb{F}_q) \neq 2$, then the length $2n$ closure in Definition 25 also has a trivial hull, unlike the closure in [21]. Using Bardet, Otmani and Saeed-Taha's reduction [2] from PEP to Graph Isomorphism when the hull is trivial, we can conclude that SPEP on linear codes with trivial hulls is solvable in quasipolynomial time [1].

The closure $\tilde{C}$ in [22] is with respect to $\mathcal{I}_n \times \mathbb{F}_q^*$ (where $\mathcal{I}_n = \{1, \ldots, n\}$), and allows a reduction from linear code equivalence of C and C' to permutation code equivalence of $\tilde{C}$ and $\tilde{C'}$. This new code has length $(q-1)n$, and is self-dual when $q \geq 5$. The weak self-duality of the closure means that the hull has maximal possible dimension. But the expected run time of the $\mathcal{SSA}$ [20] algorithm is exponential in the dimension of the hull, as is the reduction to graph isomorphism [2].

Instead, we use the closure with respect to $\mathcal{I}_n \times \{\pm 1\}$ (Definition 25). The critical difference this makes is that the hull of the signed closure of the code is equal to the signed closure of the hull. In this case, signed permutation on a code of length n with trivial hull reduces to permutation equivalence on a code of length $2n$ with trivial hull. One can use this closure to reduce signed permutation equivalence to graph isomorphism.

Definition 25. *Let $C \subseteq \mathbb{F}_q^n$ be a linear code of dimension k. The* signed closure *$C^{\pm}$ of the code C is the linear code of length $2n$ and dimension k over $\mathbb{F}_q$ given by:*

$$C^{\pm} := \{(x_1, -x_1, x_2, -x_2, \ldots, x_n, -x_n) : (x_i)_{i \in \mathcal{I}_n} \in C\}.$$

When $q \neq 2, 3$ the following lemma is not an immediate corollary of Theorem 1 in [22], since we are using a different concept of closure. However, the proof follows the exact same strategy as Lemma 4 from [21], using the set of indices $\mathcal{I}_n \times \{\pm 1\}$ instead of $\mathcal{I}_n \times \mathbb{F}_q^*$.

Lemma 10. *Let C, $C' \subseteq \mathbb{F}_q^n$ be linear codes. Then C and C' are signed permutation equivalent if and only if $C^{\pm}$ and $C'^{\pm}$ are permutation equivalent.*

Constructive Proof. Let C and C' be signed permutation equivalent, via $\sigma \in \mathcal{S}_n$ and $(v_1, v_2, \ldots, v_n) \in \{\pm 1\}^n$. Thus

$$C' = \left\{\left(v_1 x_{\sigma^{-1}(1)}, v_2 x_{\sigma^{-1}(2)}, \ldots, v_n x_{\sigma^{-1}(n)}\right) : (x_1, x_2, \ldots, x_n) \in C\right\}.$$

Let $C^{\pm}$ and $C'^{\pm}$ be their respective signed closures. Throughout the proof, for a code C'', we denote $\mathrm{Aut}_P(C'')$ for the group of permutations on the coordinates of C'' that leave C'' unchanged. Similarly, we write $\mathrm{Aut}_{SP}(C'')$ to be the group of *signed* permutations on the coordinates of C'' that leave C'' unchanged.

The permutation π such that

$$C'^{\pm} = \left\{\left(x^{\pm}_{\pi^{-1}(1)}, x^{\pm}_{\pi^{-1}(2)}, \ldots, x^{\pm}_{\pi^{-1}(2n)}\right) : (x_1^{\pm}, x_2^{\pm}, \ldots, x_{2n}^{\pm}) \in C^{\pm}\right\}$$

is constructed as follows. For any $i \in \{1, \ldots, n\}$ with $a_i = -1$, permute rows $2i - 1$ and $2i$ in the code $C^{\pm}$. Then for all i, swap row $2i - 1$ with $2\sigma^{-1}(i) - 1$, and swap row $2i$ with row $2\sigma^{-1}(i)$. By construction, this permutation sends the closure of C to the closure of C'.

The other direction is the construction from Lemma 4 of [21], translated to the simpler case we are dealing with. Let C and C' have permutation-equivalent closures. That is,

$$C'^{\pm} = \left\{ \left(x^{\pm}_{\pi^{-1}(1)}, x^{\pm}_{\pi^{-1}(2)}, \ldots, x^{\pm}_{\pi^{-1}(n)} \right) : (x^{\pm}_1, x^{\pm}_2, \ldots, x^{\pm}_n) \in C^{\pm} \right\}$$

for some $\pi \in \mathcal{S}_{2n}$.

Let $G^{\pm}$ and $G'^{\pm}$ be generator matrices of $C^{\pm}$ and $C'^{\pm}$ respectively, with rows $(g^{\pm}_i)_{i \in \mathcal{I}_n}$ and $(g'^{\pm}_i)_{i \in \mathcal{I}_n}$. We call $\{g^{\pm}_{2i-1}, g^{\pm}_{2i}\}$ the ith pair of rows of $G^{\pm}$, and we say that a permutation $\pi \in \mathcal{S}_{2n}$ *preserves the pair* $\{g^{\pm}_{2i-1}, g^{\pm}_{2i}\}$ if

$$\{\pi(2i - 1), \pi(2i)\} = \{2k - 1, 2k\}$$

for some k. That is, the ith pair of $C^{\pm}$ becomes the kth pair of $C'^{\pm}$, even though π does not necessarily preserve the ordering of the pair.

From [21], if $\pi \in \mathcal{S}_{2n}$ preserves all pairs, then it can be lifted to some $(\sigma, v) \in \mathcal{S}_n \times \{\pm 1\}^n$. For all $i \in \{1, \ldots, n\}$, define

$$v_i = \begin{cases} 1 & \text{if } \pi(2i - 1) = 2k - 1 \text{ for some } k \ (\textit{i.e. the ordering is preserved}) \\ -1 & \text{if } \pi(2i - 1) = 2k \text{ for some } k \ (\textit{i.e. the ordering is not preserved}), \end{cases}$$

and $v = (v_1, \ldots, v_n)$. In both cases above, the ith pair of $C^{\pm}$ is sent to the kth pair of $C'^{\pm}$, and so define $\sigma(i) = k$. The details of why this is correct are left to the proof of [21, Lemma 4]. That proof does not make explicit what happens when the permutation π does not preserve all pairs $i = 1, \ldots n$. We make this explicit below for our definition of the closure.

The key point is that if $\pi : C^{\pm} \to C'^{\pm}$ does not preserve all pairs, then there exists an $\alpha \in \text{Aut}_{\text{P}}(C'^{\pm})$ such that $\alpha\pi : C^{\pm} \to C'^{\pm}$ does preserve all pairs, and can then be lifted back to some signed permutation $(\sigma, v) \in \mathcal{S}_n \times \{\pm 1\}^n$.

We construct the automorphism α as a product of permutations α_i that swap rows. Let $i \in \{1, \ldots, n\}$. If π preserves the ith pair, then set $\alpha_i = \text{id}$. If π does not preserve the ith pair, then either

(a) $\pi(2i - 1)$ is odd, or
(b) $\pi(2i - 1)$ is even

In case (a), $\{\pi(2i - 1), \pi(2i)\} = \{2k - 1, r\}$ for some arbitrary index r. The action of π on $C^{\pm}$ sends the closure of a codeword in C to the closure of a codeword in C'. So

$$g'^{\pm}_{2k-1} = -g'^{\pm}_r,$$

since rows in the same pair in $C'^{\pm}$ are the negative of one another. But also, because rows in $C^{\pm}$ in the same pair are the negative of one another we have

$$g'^{\pm}_{2k} = -g'^{\pm}_{2k-1} = g'^{\pm}_r.$$

Therefore, we can define $\alpha_i \in \mathrm{Aut_P}(C'^{\pm})$ to be the automorphism of $C'^{\pm}$ that swaps row $2k$ for row r (*i.e.* swapping the identical row vectors $g'^{\pm}_{2k}$ and $g'^{\pm}_r$).

In case (b), $\{\pi(2i-1), \pi(2i)\} = \{2k, r\}$ for some arbitrary index r. The action of π on $C^{\pm}$ sends the closure of a codeword in C to the closure of a codeword in C'. So again since rows in the same pair of $C^{\pm}$ are negatives of one another,

$$g'^{\pm}_{2k} = -g'^{\pm}_r.$$

But also, the same is true for $C'^{\pm}$, so

$$g'^{\pm}_{2k-1} = -g'^{\pm}_{2k} = g'^{\pm}_r.$$

So we can define $\alpha_i \in \mathrm{Aut_P}(C'^{\pm})$ to be the automorphism of $C'^{\pm}$ that swaps row $2k - 1$ for row r (*i.e.* swapping the identical row vectors $g'^{\pm}_{2k-1}$ and $g'^{\pm}_r$).

Now, we construct α by first finding α_1 using π, then finding α_2 using $\alpha_1\pi$ and so on, finding α_i using $\alpha_{i-1}\alpha_{i-2}\ldots\alpha_1\pi$. Each α_i only swaps rows that are not already preserved by $\alpha_{i-1}\alpha_{i-2}\ldots\alpha_1\pi$. Therefore, $\alpha_1\pi$ preserves the first pair, and by induction, $\alpha_i\alpha_{i-1}\ldots\alpha_1\pi$ preserves the first i pairs. Finally, $\alpha_n\ldots\alpha_1\pi$ preserves every pair. Thus we set

$$\alpha = \alpha_n\ldots\alpha_1 \in \mathrm{Aut_P}(C'^{\pm}).$$

The permutation $\alpha\pi : C^{\pm} \to C'^{\pm}$ preserves pairs and therefore lifts to some element in $(\sigma, v) \in \mathcal{S}_n \times \{\pm 1\}$. □

We have therefore reduced from SPEP on a code of length n to PEP on a code of length $2n$. One of the problems that [22] find with this approach is that the closure of a code is almost always a hard instance of PEP. That is, the closure is almost always weakly self-dual, with hull of maximal dimension. The following result shows that this is *not* the case for the signed closure when $\mathrm{char}(\mathbb{F}_q) \neq 2$. In fact, we have a stronger statement.

Lemma 11. *Let C be a linear code over finite field $\mathbb{F}_q$ whose characteristic is not 2. The signed closure of the hull of a code C is the hull of the signed closure $C^{\pm}$.*

Proof. C and $C^{\pm}$ have the same dimension. Let x, $y \in C$ have closures $\tilde{x}$ and $\tilde{y}$ respectively.

$$\tilde{x} \cdot \tilde{y} = x_1 y_1 + (-x_1)(-y_1) + \ldots x_n y_n + (-x_n)(-y_n) = 2(x \cdot y).$$

If $x \cdot y = 0$, then $\tilde{x} \cdot \tilde{y} = 0$. If $x \cdot y \neq 0$, then $\tilde{x} \cdot \tilde{y} \neq 0$, using $\mathrm{char}(\mathbb{F}_q) \neq 2$. So for any two codewords in $\tilde{x}$, $\tilde{y} \in C^{\pm}$, we have $\tilde{x} \cdot \tilde{y} \neq 0$ if and only if $x \cdot y \neq 0$. The result follows. □

6   Conclusion

6.1   Revising LIP Hardness Conjecture

We have demonstrated that there are some lattices for which the hull attack is relevant: finding shortest vectors in the hull is easier than in the original lattice, and once they are found the isomorphism between the original lattices can be recovered in quasipolynomial time. This constitutes a counter-example to the (Strong) hardness conjecture made by Ducas and van Woerden [11, Conjecture 7.1] (Conjecture 1 in the present paper).

Our attack mandates the following revision, replacing the gap by the hull-gap as follows:

$$\text{hullgap}(L) = \max_{s \in \mathbb{R}^\times} \text{gap}(H_s(L)).$$

Note that the set we are maximising over includes the one from the original definition so that $\text{hullgap}(L) \geq \text{gap}(L)$; indeed, for an integral lattice we have $H_1(L) = L$.

One may also be concerned that the above definition requires considering infinitely many different $s \in \mathbb{R}^\times$; this is in fact not the case. The gap of a lattice is the same as the gap of any non-zero scaling of that lattice. So, using Lemma 8, we need only check the gap of the s-Hull for those integers $s \mid \det(B^T B)$. For example, for q-ary lattices of determinant q^k, one need only consider integer divisors of q^k. If q is prime, only $s \in \{q^i : i \in 0, \ldots k\}$ are relevant.

The above two remarks are explained for integral lattices, but also apply to lattices whose Gram matrices are rational, simply by scaling the lattice up by the gcd of the denominators of the Gram matrix. Thus we replace the gap in [11, Conjecture 7.1] with the quantity below.

$$\text{hullgap}(L) = \max_{\substack{s \in \mathbb{Z} \\ s \mid \det(Q) \\ \gcd(Q) \mid s}} \text{gap}(H_s(L)).$$

6.2   Unimodular Lattices

We recall that an integral lattice is unimodular if it is equal to its dual; and this is equivalent to its associated quadratic form being unimodular. In particular, all the hulls of such lattices are merely scalings of the original lattice, and taking the hull is therefore not helpful. Such choices of lattice avoid the consideration discussed above. This is the case of the trivial lattice $\mathbb{Z}^n$, as used in [4,10].

Half the Barnes-Wall Lattices are Unimodular (up to Scaling). Another lattice of interest in cryptography to instantiate LIP with is the Barnes-Wall lattice, as suggested in [10]. A simple construction for the Barnes-Wall lattices is given in [15], which shows that they are a scaling of a unimodular lattice. This means that they are equal to their own hull, and not subject to any hull attack.

For convenience, we give the construction by Miccianccio and Nicolosi [14], showing that at least half of them are unimodular, and therefore are not subject to any hull attack. More specifically, the Barnes-Wall lattices have ranks $n = 2^k$ for integers k, and we will show that they are unimodular when k is odd.

Miccianccio and Nicolosi [14] propose a simple and explicit construction of the Barnes-Wall lattice over the Gaussian integers $\mathbb{Z}[i]$, via an explicit column basis:

$$B_k = \begin{bmatrix} 1 & 0 \\ 1 & 1+i \end{bmatrix}^{\otimes k}.$$

Note that this lattice has rank $n = 2^{k+1}$ over the rational integers $\mathbb{Z}$. The associated hermitian form over $\mathbb{Z}[i]$ is given by :

$$Q_k = (\overline{B_1}^T B_1)^{\otimes k} = \begin{bmatrix} 2 & 1-i \\ 1+i & 2 \end{bmatrix}^{\otimes k}.$$

Furthermore, $Q_{2k} = Q_2^{\otimes k}$, and one can check that:

$$\frac{1}{2} \cdot Q_2 = \begin{bmatrix} 2 & 1+i & 1+i & i \\ 1-i & 2 & 1 & 1+i \\ 1-i & 1 & 2 & 1+i \\ -i & 1-i & 1-i & 2 \end{bmatrix}$$

is indeed integral over $\mathbb{Z}[i]$, and has determinant 1 over $\mathbb{Z}[i]$. It is therefore also the case that $Q_{2k}/2^k$ has determinant 1 for any integer $k \geq 1$. That is, the Barnes-Wall lattices of ranks 2^{2k+1} are unimodular (up to scaling).

6.3   Open Question

The counter-example we have provided remains mild: it only increases the gap from 1 to $O(\sqrt{n})$, and therefore only halves the blocksize required for an attack. A natural question is whether one can find lattices for which the gap of the hull increases much more consequentially, and whether this indeed leads to an attack on LIP, in either its distinguishing or search version.

Acknowledgements. The authors would like to thank Peter Bruin, Eamonn Postlethwaite, Ludo Pulles, Wessel van Woerden and the anonymous reviewers for their helpful discussion and feedback. Authors Léo Ducas and Shane Gibbons are supported by ERC Starting Grant 947821 (ARTICULATE).

References

1. Babai, L.: Graph isomorphism in quasipolynomial time (2015). https://arxiv.org/abs/1512.03547
2. Bardet, M., Otmani, A., Saeed-Taha, M.: Permutation code equivalence is not harder than graph isomorphism when hulls are trivial. In: 2019 IEEE International Symposium on Information Theory (ISIT). IEEE (2019). https://doi.org/10.1109/isit.2019.8849855
3. Becker, A., Ducas, L., Gama, N., Laarhoven, T.: New directions in nearest neighbor searching with applications to lattice sieving. In: Proceedings of the Annual ACM-SIAM Symposium on Discrete Algorithms, vol. 1, pp. 10–24 (2016). https://doi.org/10.1137/1.9781611974331.ch2

4. Bennett, H., Ganju, A., Peetathawatchai, P., Stephens-Davidowitz, N.: Just how hard are rotations of $\mathbb{Z}^n$? Algorithms and cryptography with the simplest lattice. Cryptology eprint Archive, Paper 2021/1548 (2021). https://eprint.iacr.org/2021/1548

5. Beullens, W.: Not enough LESS: an improved algorithm for solving code equivalence problems over $\mathbb{F}_q$. In: Dunkelman, O., Jacobson, Jr., M.J., O'Flynn, C. (eds.) SAC 2020. LNCS, vol. 12804, pp. 387–403. Springer, Cham (2021). https://doi.org/10.1007/978-3-030-81652-0_15

6. Cassels, J.W.S.: Rational quadratic forms. Academic Press, New York (1978)

7. Conway, J.H., Sloane, N.J.A.: Sphere packings, lattices and groups, vol. 290. Springer Science & Business Media (2013). https://doi.org/10.1007/978-1-4757-6568-7

8. Costa, S.I.R., Oggier, F., Campello, A., Belfiore, J.-C., Viterbo, E.: Lattices from codes. In: Lattices Applied to Coding for Reliable and Secure Communications. SM, pp. 37–58. Springer, Cham (2017). https://doi.org/10.1007/978-3-319-67882-5_3

9. Dubey, C., Holenstein, T.: Computing the p-adic canonical quadratic form in polynomial time (2014). https://doi.org/10.48550/ARXIV.1409.6199. https://arxiv.org/abs/1409.6199

10. Ducas, L., Postlethwaite, E.W., Pulles, L.N., van Woerden, W.: Hawk: module LIP makes lattice signatures fast, compact and simple. In: Agrawal, S., Lin, D. (eds.) Advances in Cryptology - ASIACRYPT 2022. ASIACRYPT 2022. Lecture Notes in Computer Science, vol. 13794, pp. 65–94. Springer, Cham (2022). https://doi.org/10.1007/978-3-031-22972-5_3

11. Ducas, L., van Woerden, W.: On the lattice isomorphism problem, quadratic forms, remarkable lattices, and cryptography. In: Dunkelman, O., Dziembowski, S. (eds.) Advances in Cryptology - EUROCRYPT 2022. EUROCRYPT 2022. Lecture Notes in Computer Science, vol. 13277, pp. 643–673. Springer, Cham (2022). https://doi.org/10.1007/978-3-031-07082-2_23

12. Haviv, I., Regev, O.: On the lattice isomorphism problem. In: Proceedings of the Twenty-Fifth Annual ACM-SIAM Symposium on Discrete Algorithms, pp. 391–404. SIAM (2014)

13. Leon, J.: Computing automorphism groups of error-correcting codes. IEEE Trans. Inf. Theory **28**(3), 496–511 (1982)

14. Micciancio, D., Nicolosi, A.: Efficient bounded distance decoders for Barnes-wall lattices. In: 2008 IEEE International Symposium on Information Theory, pp. 2484–2488 (2008). https://doi.org/10.1109/ISIT.2008.4595438

15. Nebe, G., Rains, E.M., Sloane, N.J.A.: A simple construction for the Barnes-wall lattices (2000). http://neilsloane.com/doc/bw.pdf

16. O'Meara, O.T.: Introduction to quadratic forms. Springer, Heidelberg (1971). https://doi.org/10.1007/978-3-642-62031-7

17. Plesken, W., Pohst, M.: Constructing integral lattices with prescribed minimum. I. Math. Comput. **45**(171), 209–221 (1985)

18. Plesken, W., Souvignier, B.: Computing isometries of lattices. J. Symb. Comput. **24**(3–4), 327–334 (1997)

19. Schurmann, A.: Computational geometry of positive definite quadratic forms: Polyhedral reduction theories, algorithms, and applications, vol. 48. American Mathematical Society (2009)

20. Sendrier, N.: Finding the permutation between equivalent codes: the support splitting algorithm. IEEE Trans. Inf. Theory **46**(4), 1193–1203 (2000)

21. Sendrier, N., Simos, D.: How easy is code equivalence over $\mathbb{F}_q$. In: International Workshop on Coding and Cryptography - WCC 2013, Apr 2013, Bergen, Norway (2013). https://hal.inria.fr/hal-00790861v2
22. Sendrier, N., Simos, D.E.: The hardness of code equivalence over $\mathbb{F}_q$ and its application to code-based cryptography. In: Gaborit, P. (ed.) PQCrypto 2013. LNCS, vol. 7932, pp. 203–216. Springer, Heidelberg (2013). https://doi.org/10.1007/978-3-642-38616-9_14
23. Sikiric, M.D., Haensch, A., Voight, J., van Woerden, W.: A canonical form for positive definite matrices. In: ANTS, vol. 14, p. 179 (2020)

A Key-Recovery Attack Against Mitaka in the t-Probing Model

Thomas Prest[(✉)] [ID]

PQShield, Paris, France
thomas.prest@pqshield.com

Abstract. MITAKA is a lattice-based signature proposed at Eurocrypt 2022. A key advertised feature of MITAKA is that it can be masked at high orders efficiently, making it attractive in scenarios where side-channel attacks are a concern. MITAKA comes with a claimed security proof in the t-probing model.

We uncover a flaw in the security proof of MITAKA, and subsequently show that it is not secure in the t-probing model. For any number of shares $d \geq 4$, probing $t < d$ variables per execution allows an attacker to recover the private key efficiently with approximately 2^{21} executions. Our analysis shows that even a constant number of probes suffices ($t = 3$), as long as the attacker has access to a number of executions that is linear in d/t.

Keywords: MITAKA · t-probing model · cryptanalysis

1 Introduction

In the last decade, post-quantum cryptography has been an extremely dynamic research and engineering field. One of the main catalysts of this dynamism is the NIST post-quantum cryptography standardization project, which in July 2022 has announced its first standards for key establishment and stateless digital signatures [NIS22]. Two of the three selected standards for signatures are based on lattices: Dilithium [LDK+22] and Falcon [PFH+22]. Dilithium and Falcon are both based on structured lattices. They achieve good computational and bandwidth efficiency, and the underlying mathematical assumptions are well-understood.

When considering concrete security, it becomes important to consider side-channel attacks, in which adversaries may learn information about the behavior of the device executing the algorithm. Side-channel attacks based on power consumption [KJJ99], running time [Koc96], electromagnetic emissions [GMO01] and even acoustic emissions [AA04,GST14] have shown to be relevant.

The main countermeasure against side-channel attacks is masking [ISW03]. It consists of splitting sensitive information in d shares (concretely: $x = x_0 + \cdots + x_{d-1}$), and of performing secure computation using MPC-based techniques.

© International Association for Cryptologic Research 2023
A. Boldyreva and V. Kolesnikov (Eds.): PKC 2023, LNCS 13940, pp. 205–220, 2023.
https://doi.org/10.1007/978-3-031-31368-4_8

In practice, the cost of a side-channel attack is expected to grow exponentially in the number of shares d [DFS19].

In parallel, leakage models have been developed in order to reason and prove statements about side-channel countermeasures. The most standard model is the t-probing model [ISW03], in which an attacker is allowed to learn the value of t variables during each execution of the protected algorithm. While not being the most realistic leakage model, the t-probing model is arguably the easiest to work in, especially when considering masking. In addition, proving security in this model is usually a good indicator of security, especially when augmenting the t-probing model with proof frameworks such as the SNI, PINI or IOS models.

Unfortunately, Dilithium and Falcon are not straightforward to mask. In the case of Dilithium, sampling from specific distributions and rejection sampling are two examples of operations that require conversions between Boolean and arithmetic representations (called A2B and B2A conversions), which is expensive when operating on masked values. Falcon seems even more challenging to mask, due to its intricate use of floating-point operations.

MITAKA [EFG+22] is a variant of Falcon that was proposed in order to address these caveats. One of the main advertised features of MITAKA is that it is easy to mask. This was done by proposing new algorithms for performing masked operations. One such algorithm is GaussShareByShare (Algorithm 3), which performs Gaussian sampling over the integers efficiently and with no A2B or B2A conversion. MITAKA comes complete with a claimed security proof in the t-probing model [EFG+22, Theorems 4 and 5], for $t < d$.

1.1 Our Contribution

We show that MITAKA is insecure in the t-probing model. More precisely, by targeting one specific call to GaussShareByShare, and probing $t < d$ specific values inside that execution, a t-probing attacker can compute a vector that is correlated to the private key $\mathbf{b}_0$. By combining sufficiently many of these vectors, the attacker can compute an estimator $\widehat{\mathbf{b}_0}$ that is a noisy version of the $\mathbf{b}_0$, which can then be recovered by lattice reduction attacks, or simple rounding, depending on the number of probes t, masking order d and number of executions N.

Concretely, we are able to recover the private key with $N = 2^{21}$ executions of the signing algorithm and, for each execution, the values of the probed variables, which we call traces. The efficiency behavior of our attack is illustrated in Fig. 1.

More worryingly, our attack remains feasible even if d is polynomially large and t is constant, since we only need the number of traces N to be linear in d/t. A generic countermeasure against our attack is to replace GaussShareByShare by more classical conversion-based techniques, but we expect this to incur a significant overhead on the computational cost of MITAKA.

As part of our attack, we propose in Sect. 5.4 a simple trick which speeds up considerably the recovery of $\mathbf{b}_0$ from the estimator $\widehat{\mathbf{b}_0}$ in many relevant regimes. This trick also applies to a recently proposed power analysis on Falcon [GMRR22], and may have other applications as well.

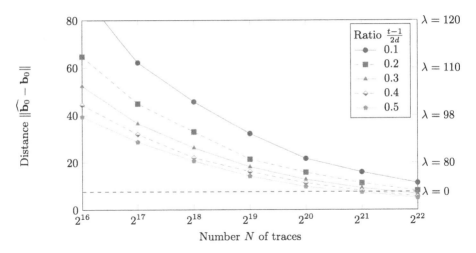

Fig. 1. Distance of the estimator $\widehat{\mathbf{b_0}}$ to the private key $\mathbf{b_0}$ as a function of the number of traces (x-axis) and the ratio $\frac{t-1}{2d}$. The marks $\{\lambda = x\}$ on the right side indicate the core-SVP hardness of the lattice problem we need to solve. Under the line $\{\text{- - -}\}$, $\mathbf{b_0}$ can be recovered in polynomial time (Sect. 5.4).

2 Preliminaries

Given $n \in \mathbb{N}, n > 0$, we may note $[n] = \{0, \ldots, n-1\}$.

2.1 Operators and Relations

As a mnemonic device, we note out $:= f(\mathsf{in})$ (resp. out $\leftarrow f(\mathsf{in})$ and $f(\mathsf{in}) \rightarrow$ out) to indicate that out is a deterministic (resp. randomized) function of in.

We assume familiarity with the asymptotic notation: $O(\cdot), o(\cdot), \Theta(\cdot)$, Knuth's $\Omega(\cdot)$ and so on. We use the notation $x \sim y$ as shorthand for $x - y = o(x)$.

We employ the notation $x \overset{s}{\sim} X$ to indicate that the distribution of x is statistically close to X. Finally, $F \simeq G$ indicates that F and G are isomorphic.

2.2 Cyclotomic Fields

For efficiency reasons, schemes such as Falcon and MITAKA work over cyclotomic number fields. Given $n \in \mathbb{N}$ a fixed power-of-two and $\zeta \in \mathbb{C}$ a primitive $2n$-root of unity, we define the cyclotomic field $\mathcal{K}$ and its corresponding ring of integers $\mathcal{R} \subset \mathcal{K}$:

$$\mathcal{K} = \mathbb{Q}(\zeta) \simeq \mathbb{Q}[x]/(x^n + 1)$$
$$\mathcal{R} = \mathbb{Z}[\zeta] \simeq \mathbb{Z}[x]/(x^n + 1)$$

It is often convenient to think of and represent elements of $\mathcal{K}$ and $\mathcal{R}$ as polynomials modulo $(x^n + 1)$. We can embed $\mathcal{K}$ (and thus $\mathcal{R}$) with an inner product:

$$\langle a, b \rangle_{\mathcal{K}} = a^* \cdot b,$$

where a^* is the adjoint of a, that is the unique $a^* \in \mathcal{K}$ such that $a^*(\zeta^k) := \overline{a(\zeta^k)}$ for all odd values of k, where $\bar{\cdot}$ denotes the complex conjugation in $\mathbb{C}$. We note $\mathbb{R}^{++} = \{x \in \mathbb{R} | x > 0\}$, and $a \in \mathcal{K}^{++}$ if $a^*(\zeta^k) \in \mathbb{R}^{++}$ for all odd values of k.

The polynomial representation of elements in $\mathcal{K}$ naturally entails a mapping $\mathcal{K} \to \mathbb{R}^n$, which allows to define, for $a, b \in \mathcal{K}$, the dot product $\langle a, b \rangle_{\mathbb{R}}$ as the usual dot product of their vectors of coefficients. We note that $\langle a, a \rangle_{\mathbb{R}} > 0$, so we can likewise define the norm $\|a\|_{\mathbb{R}} = \sqrt{\langle a, a \rangle_{\mathbb{Q}}}$.

2.3   Vectors and Matrices

We note vectors (resp. matrices) with entries in $\mathbb{Q}$ or $\mathcal{K}$ using lowercase (resp. uppercase) bold letters, for example $\mathbf{v}$ (resp. $\mathbf{M}$). We use the column convention for matrices.

We also note $\mathbf{x}^*$ the transposition of the coefficient-wise adjoint of $\mathbf{x}$. We extend the inner product $\langle \cdot, \cdot \rangle_{\mathcal{K}}$ to vectors $\mathbf{a} = (a_i), \mathbf{b} = (b_i) \in \mathcal{K}^m$:

$$\langle \mathbf{a}, \mathbf{b} \rangle_{\mathcal{K}} = \sum_i \langle a_i, b_i \rangle_{\mathcal{K}}$$

Likewise, we extend the notations $\langle \cdot, \cdot \rangle_{\mathbb{R}}$, $\| \cdot \|_{\mathbb{R}}$, and the notion of self-adjointness to vectors. We say that $\mathbf{a}$ and $\mathbf{b}$ are $\mathcal{K}$-orthogonal if $\langle \mathbf{a}, \mathbf{b} \rangle_{\mathcal{K}} = 0_{\mathcal{K}}$. Given a full-rank matrix $\mathbf{B} \in \mathcal{K}^{k \times \ell}$, the Gram-Schmidt orthogonalization of $\mathbf{B}$ is the unique pair $(\mathbf{U}, \tilde{\mathbf{B}})$ such that $\mathbf{U} \in \mathcal{K}^{\ell \times \ell}$ is upper triangular with 1's on the diagonal, the columns of $\tilde{\mathbf{B}} \in \mathcal{K}^{k \times \ell}$ are pairwise orthogonal and:

$$\mathbf{B} = \tilde{\mathbf{B}} \cdot \mathbf{U}. \tag{1}$$

We say that $\mathbf{M} \in \mathbb{K}^{m \times m}$ is self-adjoint if the matrix obtained by transposing $\mathbf{M}$, followed by entry-wise application of the adjoint operator, is $\mathbf{M}$. $\mathbf{M}$ is positive definite if (i) it is self-adjoint, and (ii) $\langle \mathbf{a}, \mathbf{M} \cdot \mathbf{a} \rangle_{\mathcal{K}} \in \mathcal{K}^{++}$ for any non-zero $\mathbf{a} \in \mathcal{K}^m$.

2.4   Lattices and Gaussians

A lattice $\mathcal{L}$ is a discrete subgroup of $\mathbb{R}^m$. Given a full-rank matrix $\mathbf{B} \in \mathbb{R}^{m \times n}$, the set $\mathcal{L}(\mathbf{B}) := \mathbf{B} \cdot \mathbb{Z}^n$ is a lattice. This representation is useful for algorithmic purposes. We can generalize this definition and define structured lattices by replacing $(\mathbb{R}, \mathbb{Z})$ in the definitions above with $(\mathcal{K}, \mathcal{R})$.

Structured lattices are convenient due to their compact representation, however they can also be interpreted as standard lattices since $\mathcal{R}$ is a $\mathbb{Z}$-module of rank n. More concretely, given $a \in \mathcal{K}$, we note $\mathcal{A}(a)$ the matrix $\mathcal{A}(a) = [\mathbf{a}_0, \ldots, \mathbf{a}_{n-1}]$ where each column $\mathbf{a}_i$ is the vector of coefficients of $x \cdot a$. Note that $\mathcal{A}(a)$ is the matrix representation of the endomorphism $f \mapsto a \cdot f$ in the canonical basis of $\mathcal{K}$. In addition, $\mathcal{A} : a \in \mathcal{K} \mapsto \mathcal{A}(a) \in \mathbb{Q}^{n \times n}$ is a ring morphism.

Given a positive definite $\Sigma \in \mathcal{K}^{m \times m}$, we note $\rho_{\sqrt{\Sigma}}$ the Gaussian function defined over $\mathcal{K}^m$ as

$$\rho_{\sqrt{\Sigma}}(\mathbf{x}) = \exp\left(-\frac{\|\mathbf{x}^* \cdot \Sigma^{-1} \cdot \mathbf{x}\|_{\mathbb{R}}^2}{2}\right). \tag{2}$$

We may note $\rho_{\sqrt{\Sigma},\mathbf{c}}(\mathbf{x}) = \rho_{\sqrt{\Sigma}}(\mathbf{x} - \mathbf{c})$. When Σ is of the form $\sigma \cdot \mathbf{I}_m$, where $\sigma \in \mathcal{K}^{++}$ and $\mathbf{I}_m$ is the identity matrix, we note $\rho_{\sigma,\mathbf{c}}$ as shorthand for $\rho_{\sqrt{\Sigma},\mathbf{c}}$. For any countable set $S \subset \mathcal{K}^m$, we note $\rho_{\sqrt{\Sigma},\mathbf{c}}(S) = \sum_{\mathbf{x} \in \mathcal{K}^m} \rho_{\sqrt{\Sigma},\mathbf{c}}(\mathbf{x})$ whenever this sum converges. Finally, when $\rho_{\sqrt{\Sigma},\mathbf{c}}(S)$ converges, the discrete Gaussian distribution $D_{S,\mathbf{c},\sqrt{\Sigma}}$ is defined over S by its probability distribution function:

$$D_{S,\sqrt{\Sigma},\mathbf{c}}(\mathbf{x}) = \frac{\rho_{\sqrt{\Sigma},\mathbf{c}}(\mathbf{x})}{\rho_{\sqrt{\Sigma},\mathbf{c}}(S)}. \tag{3}$$

We may also work with *continuous* Gaussians. Given $\sigma \in \mathcal{K}^{++}$, we note $\mathcal{N}_{\mathcal{K},\sigma}$ the unique distribution over $\mathcal{K}$ which probability distribution function is proportional to $\rho_\sigma(x)$. When $\sigma = 1$, we may omit it from the subscript. We note that $\sigma_2 \cdot \mathcal{N}_{\mathcal{K},\sigma_1} \sim \mathcal{N}_{\mathcal{K},\sigma_1 \cdot \sigma_2}$.

2.5   Masking

Given a finite field $\mathbb{F}$, masking a value $x \in \mathbb{F}$ consists of splitting it as:

$$x = \sum_{j \in [d]} x_j \tag{4}$$

We say that $(x_j)_{j \in [d]}$ is a valid d-sharing of x, and note it $[\![x]\!]$, if x and $(x_j)_{j \in [d]}$ satisfy (4). Note that for all $x \in \mathbb{F}$, there exist $|\mathbb{F}|^{d-1}$ valid d-sharings of x. We also note Decode the algorithm that maps a valid sharing $(x_j)_{j \in [d]} \in \mathbb{F}^d$ of x to the plain value $x = \sum_{j \in [d]} x_j$.

The t-probing model stipulates that for each execution of an algorithm Alg, the adversary can select t intermediate variables $(v_i)_{i \in [t]}$ inside Alg and is able to learn the values of $(v_i)_{i \in [t]}$ during this execution. Masked security proofs for MITAKA are realized in the t-probing model, using a modular proof framework which we informally refer to as the SNI (strong non-interference) model. For the purpose of this paper, it suffices to focus on one notion of the SNI framework called t-NIo, which we recall in Definition 1.

Definition 1 (t-NIo, [BBE+18]). *A masked algorithm (gadget) with public outputs X is t-NIo (Non-Interfering with public outputs) if and only if every set of at most t intermediate variables can be perfectly simulated with the public outputs and at most t shares of each input.*

3   Description of MITAKA

The GPV framework [GPV08] proposed a blueprint for obtaining lattice-based signatures in the hash-then-sign paradigm. MITAKA instantiates the GPV framework with NTRU lattices.

3.1   Private and Public Keys

In MITAKA, the private key is a structured matrix:

$$\mathbf{B} = \begin{bmatrix} \mathbf{b}_0 & \mathbf{b}_1 \end{bmatrix} = \begin{bmatrix} f & F \\ g & G \end{bmatrix} \tag{5}$$

where $f, g, F, G \in \mathcal{R}$ satisfy the NTRU equation in $\mathcal{R}$:

$$f \cdot G - g \cdot F = q \tag{6}$$

Concretely, this quadruple can be generated by first sampling $\mathbf{b}_0 = \begin{bmatrix} f \\ g \end{bmatrix}$, then resolving (6), which can be done efficiently [PP19]. For security, f, g, F, G are required to have small coefficients.

The public key is $h = g \cdot f^{-1} \bmod q$. If we note $\mathbf{A} = \begin{bmatrix} -h & 1 \end{bmatrix}$, we can see that $\mathbf{A} \cdot \mathbf{B} = 0 \bmod q$.

3.2   Signing Procedure

Algorithm 1 describes the signing procedure of MITAKA. In practice, only the first half s_1 of the short vector $\mathbf{s} = (s_1, s_2)$ is actually output by Algorithm 1. However, s_2 can be re-computed from a valid signature, so we can assume without loss of generality that $\mathbf{s}$ is output entirely.

Algorithm 1. Signing(sk, msg) → sig

Require: A message msg, a signing key sk, a bound γ
Ensure: A signature sig of msg under sk
1: **repeat**
2:     salt ← $\{0, 1\}^k$
3:     $\mathbf{c} := (0, H(\mathsf{salt} \| \mathsf{msg}))$
4:     $\mathbf{v} \leftarrow \mathsf{HybridSampler}(\mathsf{sk}, \mathbf{c})$ ▷ Algorithm 2
5:     $\mathbf{s} := \mathbf{c} - \mathbf{v}$ ▷ By construction, $\mathbf{s}$ is short
6: **until** $\|\mathbf{s}\| \leq \gamma$
7: **return** sig := (salt, $\mathbf{s}$)

Algorithm 2 (HybridSampler) is at the core of the signing procedure. Given a target vector $\mathbf{c}$ and a short basis $\mathbf{B}$ of a lattice $\mathcal{L}$, it outputs a lattice point $\mathbf{v} \in \mathcal{L}$ close to $\mathbf{c}$.

Algorithm 2 is designed so that $\mathbf{v}$ is distributed statistically close to $D_{\mathcal{L},\mathbf{c},\sigma}$. This ensures that $\mathbf{v}$ leaks no information about the short basis $\mathbf{B}$. In order to achieve this, continuous Gaussians (Line 3) and discrete Gaussians (Line 4) are employed in a careful manner. Our attack will learn some intermediate variables such that, conditioned on the values of these variables, the distribution of $\mathbf{v}$ is no longer independent of $\mathbf{B}$.

Algorithm 2. HybridSampler$(\mathbf{B}, r, \mathbf{c}) \to \mathbf{v}$

Require: A target center $\mathbf{c} \in \mathcal{K}^2$, a matrix $\mathbf{B} = [\mathbf{b}_0, \mathbf{b}_1]$
Precompute: The Gram-Schmidt orthogonalization $\tilde{\mathbf{B}} = [\tilde{\mathbf{b}}_0, \tilde{\mathbf{b}}_1]$ of $\mathbf{B}$. Standard
$\quad$ deviations $\sigma_i = \sqrt{\frac{\sigma^2}{\langle \tilde{\mathbf{b}}_i, \tilde{\mathbf{b}}_i \rangle_{\mathcal{K}}} - r^2} \in \mathcal{K}^{++}$ for $i \in \{0,1\}$ and a fixed parameter σ
Ensure: $\mathbf{v} \overset{s}{\sim} D_{\mathcal{L}(\mathbf{B}),\mathbf{c},\sigma}$
1: $(\mathbf{c}_2, \mathbf{v}_2) := (\mathbf{c}, \mathbf{0})$
2: **for** $i \in \{1, 0\}$ **do**
3: $\quad d_i \leftarrow \frac{\langle \tilde{\mathbf{b}}_i, \mathbf{c}_{i+1} \rangle_{\mathcal{K}}}{\langle \tilde{\mathbf{b}}_i, \tilde{\mathbf{b}}_i \rangle_{\mathcal{K}}} - \sigma_i \cdot \mathcal{N}_{\mathcal{K}}$
4: $\quad z_i \leftarrow D_{\mathbb{Z}, d_i, r}$ $\qquad\qquad\qquad\qquad\qquad$ ▷ When masked, use Algorithm 3
5: $\quad (\mathbf{c}_i, \mathbf{v}_i) := (\mathbf{c}_{i+1}, \mathbf{v}_{i+1}) + z_i \cdot (-\mathbf{b}_i, \mathbf{b}_i)$
6: **end for**
7: **return** $\mathbf{v}_0$

In a masked setting, the masked generation of $[\![z_i]\!]$ from $[\![d_i]\!]$ in Line 4 of Algorithm 2 is performed by Algorithm 3 (GaussShareByShare). Whereas a generic approach would perform this step by leveraging costly A2B and B2A conversions, Algorithm 3 foregoes this approach in favor of a more efficient one, by sampling each share of $[\![z_i]\!]$ independently and in parallel.

Algorithm 3. GaussShareByShare$([\![c]\!], r) \to [\![z]\!]$

Require: A standard deviation r, an arithmetic masking $[\![c]\!]$ for $c \in \frac{1}{C} \cdot \mathbb{Z}$, $B = \left\lceil \sqrt{2d} \right\rceil$.
Ensure: An arithmetic masking $[\![z]\!]$, where $z \overset{s}{\sim} D_{\mathbb{Z},c,r}$
1: **repeat**
2: $\quad$ **for** $j \in [d]$ **do**
3: $\quad\quad z_j \leftarrow D_{\frac{1}{B} \cdot \mathbb{Z}, c_j, \frac{r}{\sqrt{d}}}$
4: $\quad$ **end for**
5: $\quad$ acc $:= $ Decode $\left((z_j \bmod 1)_{j \in [d]} \right)$
6: **until** acc $= 0$
7: **return** $[\![z]\!] := (z_j)_{j \in [d]}$

3.3 The Proof Outline of MITAKA and Its Flaw

We refer to [EFG+22] for the full security proof of MITAKA, which is quite extensive due to the constraints of the t-probing model. The relevant part for us is [EFG+22, Lemma 3], which claims that Algorithm 3 is t-NIo (Definition 1). While no formal proof for [EFG+22, Lemma 3] is given, [EFG+22] informally argues that it follows from the fact that the input $[\![c]\!] = (c_i)_{i \in [d]}$ is uniform and each share is processed independently and in parallel. We illustrate this reasoning in Fig. 2; any subset $(c_i)_{i \in S}$ is perfectly uniform as long as $|S| < d$, and similarly for $(z_i)_{i \in S}$.

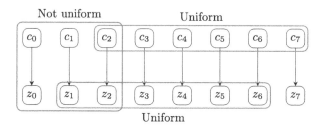

Fig. 2. Illustrating Algorithm 3 (Lines 2 to 4). Probing exclusively the input or output values yields a perfectly uniform subset (Green), but probing them conjointly does not (Red). (Color figure online)

Unfortunately, there is a flaw in this reasoning: while it is true that any set of $t < d$ shares of $[\![c]\!]$ or $[\![z]\!]$ would look uniform, the joint distribution of any subset of input values $(c_i)_{i \in S}$ and the corresponding output values $(z_i)_{i \in S}$ is not uniform. Indeed, for any $j \in [d]$, $c_j - z_j$ follows a Gaussian distribution. Moreover, we show in the next section that the observed value of this Gaussian is statistically correlated to the private key, and turn this observation into an attack.

4   Our Attack

At its heart, our attack is a simple statistical, averaging-based attack.

In Sect. 4.1, we show in that by probing the appropriate values in Algorithm 3, we are able, for each execution i of Algorithm 1, to compute a scalar $w_i \in \mathbb{R}$ such that $w_i \cdot \mathbf{b}_0$ correlates positively with the signature vector $\mathbf{s}_i$.

Once sufficiently many pairs $(\mathbf{s}_i, w_i)_i$ are collected, we show in Sect. 4.2 how we can compute a noisy estimator of $\mathbf{b}_0$, then recover $\mathbf{b}_0$ exactly via lattice-reduction (Sect. 5.3), pure rounding (Sect. 5.2), or guessing plus linear algebra (Sect. 5.4), depending on the regime.

4.1   Placing the Probes

Suppose Algorithm 2 is used to sample $\mathbf{v} \overset{s}{\sim} D_{\mathcal{L}(\mathbf{B}), \mathbf{c}, \sigma}$. Let us note $\mathbf{v} = \mathbf{B} \cdot \begin{bmatrix} \mathbf{z}_0 \\ \mathbf{z}_1 \end{bmatrix}$, and let $c \in \mathbb{R}$ the first coefficient of $\mathbf{z}_0$. We target the execution of Algorithm 3 when it is used in Algorithm 2 with $[\![c]\!]$ as input. We target c in particular because the signature $\mathbf{s}$ contains $c \cdot \mathbf{b}_0$ as an additive term, so learning $\mathbf{s}$ plus information about c provides information about $\mathbf{b}_0$. As illustrated in Fig. 2 (Red), during that specific execution of Algorithm 3, we probe:

1. the first t_1 coefficients $(c_j)_{j \in [t_1]}$ of $[\![c]\!]$;
2. the first t_1 coefficients $(z_j)_{j \in [t_1]}$ of $[\![z]\!]$;
3. the Boolean value acc.

As long as $t := 2 \cdot t_1 + 1 < d$, this is consistent with what is allowed within the t-probing model. Note that our choice of probes requires $d \geq 4$. Once acc $= 0$, we know that $[\![z]\!] = (z_j)_{j \in [d]}$ is output and incorporated in the signature. We compute:

$$w = \sum_{j \in [t_1]} (c_j - z_j) \qquad (7)$$

We say that the trace associated to a given execution is trace $= (\mathbf{s}, w)$, where $\mathbf{s}$ is the vector such that $\mathbf{A} \cdot \mathbf{s} = H(\mathsf{salt} \| \mathsf{msg})$, which is output as part of the signing procedure.

4.2 Recovering the Signing Key

We show how to exploit traces in order to recover the private key $\mathbf{b}_0$. Since the product $w \cdot \mathbf{b}_0$ is an additive component of the signature vector $\mathbf{s}$, there is a slight but exploitable correlation between $\mathbf{s}$ and $w \cdot \mathbf{b}_0$, more precisely the dot product $\langle \mathbf{s}, w \cdot \mathbf{b}_0 \rangle_{\mathbb{R}} = \langle w \cdot \mathbf{s}, \mathbf{b}_0 \rangle_{\mathbb{R}}$ will tend to be slightly larger than zero. We formalize this intuition by computing a real-valued estimator for $\mathbf{b}_0$ from a set of N traces $(\mathsf{trace}_i = (\mathbf{s}_i, w_i))_{i \in [N]}$:

$$\widehat{\mathbf{b}_0} = \frac{1}{\left(\sum_{i \in [N]} w_i^2 \right)} \cdot \left(\sum_{i \in [N]} w_i \cdot \mathbf{s}_i \right). \qquad (8)$$

We now study the distribution of signatures, conditioned on additional information. A valid signature $\mathbf{s}$ satisfies $\mathbf{s} \overset{s}{\sim} D_{\mathcal{L}-\mathbf{c}, \sigma}$. If we note $V = \mathrm{Span}_{\mathbb{R}}(\mathbf{b}_0)$, we can decompose $\mathbf{s}$ over $V \oplus V^\perp$:

$$\mathbf{s} = \bar{\mathbf{s}} + \overset{\perp}{\mathbf{s}}, \qquad \text{where} \qquad \begin{cases} \bar{\mathbf{s}} \overset{s}{\sim} D_{\mathrm{Proj}(\{\mathcal{L}-\mathbf{c}\}, V), \sigma} \\ \overset{\perp}{\mathbf{s}} \overset{s}{\sim} D_{\mathrm{Proj}(\{\mathcal{L}-\mathbf{c}\}, V^\perp), \sigma} \end{cases} \qquad (9)$$

Since $\overset{\perp}{\mathbf{s}} \perp \mathbf{b}_0$, the distribution of $\overset{\perp}{\mathbf{s}}$ is independent of w. On the other hand, we use the following heuristic for the conditional distribution of $\bar{\mathbf{s}}$:

$$\bar{\mathbf{s}} | w \overset{s}{\sim} w \cdot \mathbf{b}_0 + D_{\mathrm{Proj}(\{\mathcal{L}-\mathbf{c}-w \cdot \mathbf{b}_0\}, V), \sigma^*}, \qquad \text{where} \qquad \sigma^* = \sqrt{\sigma^2 - \frac{t_1}{d} \cdot r^2} \quad (10)$$

Let us note $\mathbf{w} = (w_i)_{i \in [N]}$. Summing the equation above for all traces, we obtain:

$$\sum_{i \in [N]} w_i \cdot \mathbf{s}_i \quad \overset{s}{\sim} \quad \sum_{i \in [N]} w_i \cdot \bar{\mathbf{s}}_i \quad + \quad \sum_{i \in [N]} w_i \cdot \overset{\perp}{\mathbf{s}}_i \tag{11}$$

$$\overset{s}{\sim} \|\mathbf{w}\|^2 \cdot \mathbf{b}_0 \tag{12}$$

$$+ D_{\mathrm{Proj}\left(\left\{\sum_i w_i (\mathcal{L} - \mathbf{c}_i - w_i \cdot \mathbf{b}_0)\right\}, V\right), \sigma^* \|\mathbf{w}\|} \tag{13}$$

$$+ D_{\mathrm{Proj}\left(\left\{\sum_i w_i (\mathcal{L} - \mathbf{c}_i)\right\}, V^\perp\right), \sigma \cdot \|\mathbf{w}\|} \tag{14}$$

Dividing everything by $\|\mathbf{w}\|^2$ gives the distribution of our estimator $\widehat{\mathbf{b}}_0$:

$$\widehat{\mathbf{b}}_0 \quad \overset{s}{\sim} \quad \mathbf{b}_0 + X, \tag{15}$$

where X is the random variable corresponding to summing (13) and (14), then dividing the result by $\|\mathbf{w}\|^2$. X is subgaussian for the Gaussian parameter $\sigma / \|\mathbf{w}\|$, so we model X in a way that is simpler, more conservative for an attacker, and essentially tight in our context:

$$X \overset{s}{\sim} D_{\frac{1}{\|\mathbf{w}\|^2}\left\{\sum_i w_i (\mathcal{L} - \mathbf{c}_i - w_i \cdot \mathbf{b}_0)\right\}, \sigma_X}, \tag{16}$$

where $\sigma_X = \sigma / \|\mathbf{w}\|$. Since we modeled each w_i as a Gaussian of standard deviation $r\sqrt{\frac{t_1}{d}}$, $\|\mathbf{w}\|^2$ is a χ^2 distribution with N degrees of freedom, scaled by a factor $\frac{r^2 \cdot t_1}{d}$. This implies that with probability $\Omega(1)$:

$$\sigma_X \leq \sigma \cdot \sqrt{\frac{d}{r^2 \cdot t_1 \cdot N}} \tag{17}$$

For a continuous $2n$-dimensional Gaussian Z of parameter σ_X, the probability that $\|Z\|_\infty \leq t$ is lower bounded as follows:

$$\mathbb{P}[\|Z\|_\infty \leq t] \geq \left(1 - 2e^{-t^2/2\sigma_X^2}\right)^{2n} \tag{18}$$

While X is discretized, we assume for the rest of our analysis that it behaves like a continuous Gaussian: $X \sim \mathcal{N}_{\mathbb{R}^{2n}, \sigma_X}$. In this case, (18) guarantees that $\|X\|_\infty \leq 1/2$ with probability $\geq 1/2$ if:

$$\sigma_X \leq \frac{1}{\sqrt{8 \cdot \log_2(4 \cdot n)}}. \tag{19}$$

Combining (17) with (19) gives the following success condition:

$$N \geq \frac{8 \cdot \log_2(4 \cdot n) \cdot d \cdot \sigma^2}{t_1 \cdot r^2} \tag{20}$$

If (20) is satisfied, then with good probability $\lfloor \widehat{\mathbf{b}}_0 \rceil = \mathbf{b}_0$ and we can recover $\mathbf{b}_0$. The second private basis vector $\mathbf{b}_1$ can be recovered by solving (6).

Note that (20) indicates that even if the masking order d is polynomially high and the number of probes per execution $t = 2 \cdot t_1 + 1$ is constant, a polynomial number of traces N suffices to ensure key recovery with $\Omega(1)$ probability.

5   Concrete Results

We tested the viability of our attack via experiments. To the best of our knowledge, there is no masked implementation of MITAKA, including private ones. We instead rely on an *unmasked* C implementation [Esp22] of MITAKA.

5.1   Simulating the Leakage

The implementation of [Esp22] does not use Algorithm 3 to sample $[\![z_i]\!]$. Instead, it directly samples $z_i \leftarrow D_{\mathbb{Z},d_i,r}$. We can nevertheless simulate the computation of the value w. Let X, Y be two independent Gaussians of center 0 and standard deviation σ_X, σ_Y. Given the sum $Z = X + Y$, it is well-known that the conditional distribution of X given the realization $Z = z$ is distributed as a Gaussian of mean $z \cdot \frac{\sigma_X^2}{\sigma_X^2 + \sigma_Y^2}$ and variance $\frac{\sigma_X^2 \cdot \sigma_Y^2}{\sigma_X^2 + \sigma_Y^2}$. This provides a simple way to simulate the computation of w in Algorithm 3:

1. Sample $z \leftarrow D_{\mathbb{Z},d,r}$ corresponding to the $[\![z]\!]$ output by Algorithm 3. This sample is easily obtained from the C implementation.
2. Compute $w = (c - z) \cdot \frac{t_1}{d} + r\sqrt{\frac{t_1(d-t_1)}{d^2}} \cdot \mathcal{N}_{\mathbb{R}}$.

One subtlety that this simulation does not capture is that each share of z belongs to $\frac{1}{B} \cdot \mathbb{Z}$, whereas our simulated w is not discretized in any way. This seems unimportant as the discretization (or lack thereof) of w does not seem to have an influence on the feasibility of our attack.

With this method of simulating the computation of w, we can now compute our estimator $\widehat{\mathbf{b}_0}$ using (8). Following (15), the difference $\widehat{\mathbf{b}_0} - \mathbf{b}_0$ follows an isotropic continuous Gaussian distribution X of standard deviation σ_X given by (17). We distinguish three regimes for X: low-, moderate- and high-noise, see Fig. 3. We cover each regime in a distinct section (Sects. 5.2 to 5.4), since we employ (slightly) different strategies for each setting.

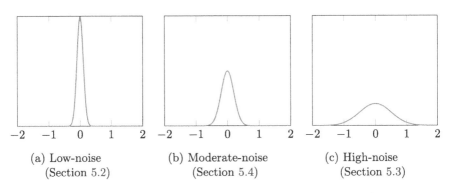

(a) Low-noise
(Section 5.2)

(b) Moderate-noise
(Section 5.4)

(c) High-noise
(Section 5.3)

Fig. 3. Three regimes for the coefficient-wise distribution of $(\widehat{\mathbf{b}_0} - \mathbf{b}_0)$

5.2   Low-noise Regime: $\|\widehat{\mathbf{b}_0} - \mathbf{b}_0\|_\infty < 1/2$

Following our analysis in Sect. 4.2, satisfying (20) guarantees with probability $\Omega(1)$ that we fall into this regime. In this case, $\lfloor\widehat{\mathbf{b}_0}\rceil = \mathbf{b}_0$.

Although the required number of samples N is polynomial, this number may be moderately large in practice. In our experiments, we found that for MITAKA-512 and for $\frac{t_1}{d} \approx \frac{1}{2}$, setting $N \approx 2^{22}$ provides a good chance of success.

5.3   High-noise Regime: $\|\widehat{\mathbf{b}_0} - \mathbf{b}_0\| < \sqrt{q}$

If N is large but does not satisfy (20), we can still recover $\mathbf{b}_0$ from the estimator $\widehat{\mathbf{b}_0}$ via lattice reduction methods. We first recall the Gaussian Heuristic.

Definition 2. *Let $gh(\mathcal{L})$ be the expected first minimum of a lattice $\mathcal{L}$ according to the Gaussian Heuristic. For a lattice $\mathcal{L} \subset \mathbb{R}^m$ generated by a full-rank matrix full-rank $\mathbf{M} \in \mathbb{R}^{m \times m}$, it is given by:*

$$gh(\mathcal{L}) = \sqrt{\frac{m}{2\pi e}} \cdot \det(\mathbf{M})^{1/m}. \tag{21}$$

Consider the rounded estimator: $\breve{\mathbf{b}}_0 = \lfloor\widehat{\mathbf{b}_0}\rceil \in \mathcal{R}^2$. If we note $\mathbf{e} = \breve{\mathbf{b}}_0 - \mathbf{b}_0$, it holds that $\|\mathbf{e}\|^2 \leq \|\widehat{\mathbf{b}_0} - \mathbf{b}_0\|^2 + n^2/2$. On the other hand, in the parameter regime of MITAKA, $\mathbf{b}_0$ is the shortest vector in the NTRU lattice: $\|\mathbf{b}_0\| \approx 2\sqrt{q}$.[1] Since $\|\widehat{\mathbf{b}_0} - \mathbf{b}_0\| < \sqrt{q}$, we can expect $\mathbf{e}$ to be much shorter than the shortest vector in the NTRU lattice. This allows us to use Kannan's embedding; a good reference for this technique is [AGVW17], which methodology we follow here. We first generate the matrix $\mathbf{M}$:

$$\mathbf{M} = \left[\begin{array}{cc|c} \mathbf{I}_n & & \breve{\mathbf{b}}_0 \\ \mathbf{H} & q\mathbf{I}_n & \\ \hline & & 1 \end{array}\right] \in \mathbb{Z}^{d \times d} \tag{22}$$

where $d = 2n + 1$ and $\mathbf{H} = \mathcal{A}(h)$. By construction, we expect $\begin{bmatrix} \mathbf{e} \\ 1 \end{bmatrix}$ to be the shortest vector of $\mathbf{M}$. Therefore, we apply the BKZ lattice reduction algorithm to $\mathbf{M}$ with blocksize β in order to recover $\mathbf{e}$. Under the geometric series assumption, $\mathbf{e}$ can be found if:

$$\sqrt{\frac{\beta}{d}} \cdot \sqrt{\|\mathbf{e}\|^2 + 1} \leq \delta_\beta^{2\cdot\beta - d} \cdot \det(\mathbf{M})^{1/d}, \tag{23}$$

where $\delta_\beta = \left(\frac{(\pi\beta)^{1/\beta}\cdot\beta}{2\pi e}\right)^{1/(2(\beta-1))}$ [Che13, Eq. (4.2)]. The corresponding core-SVP hardness λ for our key-recovery attack can be determined by computing $\lambda = \lfloor 0.292 \cdot \beta \rfloor$ for the minimal value of β such that (23) is satisfied. Alternatively, one may also use the nearest-colattice algorithm of [EK20].

---

[1] In [EFG+22], it is shown that $\|\mathbf{b}_0\| \leq \alpha\sqrt{q}$, with $\alpha \approx 2.04$ for MITAKA-512 and $\alpha \approx 2.33$ for MITAKA-1024.

5.4   Moderate-noise Regime: $\|\widehat{\mathbf{b}_0} - \mathbf{b}_0\|_\infty < 1$

If it is the case that:

$$\frac{1}{2} < \|\widehat{\mathbf{b}_0} - \mathbf{b}_0\|_\infty < 1,$$

then we are in an paradoxical situation: $\widehat{\mathbf{b}_0}$ is very close to $\mathbf{b}_0$, but rounding its coefficients will return a different vector from $\mathbf{b}_0$. Worse, several dozens of coefficients may be erroneous, and an exhaustive search of these coefficients may be expensive in practice. Similarly, lattice reduction as in Sect. 5.3 may be expensive. We now describe a simple trick that allows to recover $\mathbf{b}_0$ with high probability and little to no computation effort.

Observation 1. By construction, when interpreted as a vector in $\mathbb{Z}^{2n}$, $\mathbf{b}_0$ satisfies:

$$\mathbf{A} \cdot \mathbf{b}_0 = \mathbf{0} \bmod q, \tag{24}$$

Recall that $\widehat{\mathbf{b}_0}$ is equal to $\mathbf{b}_0$ plus Gaussian noise of standard deviation σ_X. The fact $\|\widehat{\mathbf{b}_0} - \mathbf{b}_0\|_\infty < 1$ implies that σ_X is small (concretely, $\sigma_X \le 0.25$ if $n = 512$). This in turn implies that errors close to 1 in absolute value are likely to be rare, which leads to our first key observation:

If a coefficient of $\widehat{\mathbf{b}_0}$ is close to an integer, then the corresponding coefficient of $\mathbf{b}_0$ is highly likely to be equal to this integer.

Observation 2. We now observe that recovering half of the coefficients of $\mathbf{b}_0$ is sufficient to recover it entirely. Suppose we have guessed n of the $2 \cdot n$ entries of $\mathbf{b}_0$. We can rearrange the entries of $\mathbf{b}_0$ as $\begin{bmatrix} \mathbf{x} \\ \mathbf{y} \end{bmatrix}$, where $\mathbf{y}$ corresponds to coefficients of $\mathbf{b}_0$ that were successfully guessed, and $\mathbf{x}$ are the remaining ones. By rearranging the columns of $\mathbf{A}$ in the same way, (24) becomes v:

$$[\mathbf{A}_1 \ \mathbf{A}_2] \cdot \begin{bmatrix} \mathbf{x} \\ \mathbf{y} \end{bmatrix} = \mathbf{0} \bmod q, \tag{25}$$

If $\mathbf{A}_1$ is invertible, then we can recover $\mathbf{x}$ by computing $\mathbf{x} = -\mathbf{A}_1^{-1} \cdot \mathbf{A}_2 \cdot \mathbf{y}$. In practice, we observe that $\mathbf{A}_1$ is invertible more often than not.

Example 1. We illustrate this strategy with a toy example over $\mathbb{Z}_q$, $q = 19$. Let:

$$\mathbf{A} = \begin{bmatrix} 12 & 9 & 10 & 5 \\ 9 & 7 & 5 & 15 \end{bmatrix} \in \mathbb{Z}_q^{2 \times 4} \qquad \text{and} \qquad \mathbf{b} = \begin{bmatrix} 7 & 6 & 1 & 18 \end{bmatrix}^t.$$

One can check that $\mathbf{A} \cdot \mathbf{b} = \mathbf{0} \bmod q$. Our estimator will be a noisy version of $\mathbf{b}$, for example $\widehat{\mathbf{b}} = \begin{bmatrix} 7.1 & 6.4 & 1.6 & 18.1 \end{bmatrix}^t$. Naively rounding $\widehat{\mathbf{b}}$ gives $\lfloor \widehat{\mathbf{b}} \rceil = \begin{bmatrix} 7 & 6 & 2 & 18 \end{bmatrix}^t \ne \mathbf{b}$. In contrast, guessing half of the coefficients (precisely, the half which are closer to an integer) gives $\mathbf{b} = \begin{bmatrix} 7 & * & * & 18 \end{bmatrix}^t$, and which point the remaining half of $\mathbf{b}$ can be computed by solving the linear system $\mathbf{A} \cdot \mathbf{b} = \mathbf{0} \bmod q$.

Success probability. Recall that $X = \widehat{\mathbf{b}_0} - \mathbf{b}_0$. This attack succeeds if there exists $\epsilon > 0$ such that, with probability $\Omega(1)$:

1. No coefficient of X is larger in absolute norm than $1 - \epsilon$.
2. At least half of the coefficients of X are in $[-\epsilon, \epsilon]$;

Item 1 ensures that "guessing to the nearest integer" all coefficient of $\widehat{\mathbf{b}_0}$ that are ϵ-close to an integer will indeed return the correct coefficient of $\mathbf{b}_0$, and is true if $\mathbb{P}[\|X\|_\infty < 1 - \epsilon] \leq 1/2$. Item 2 ensures there are n such coefficients. Following our modelization of X as a $(2 \cdot n)$-dimensional Gaussian of standard deviation σ_X, the conditions above can be expressed, using Gaussian tail bounds, as:

$$\left(1 - 2 \cdot e^{-\frac{(1-\epsilon)^2}{2 \cdot \sigma_X^2}}\right)^{2n} < \frac{1}{2}, \tag{26}$$

$$\text{where} \quad \epsilon = \min\left\{\epsilon^* \mid \mathcal{N}_{\mathbb{R},\sigma_X}([-\epsilon^*, \epsilon^*]) \geq \frac{1}{2}\right\}. \tag{27}$$

For $n = 512$, our attack is effective when $\sigma_X \lesssim 0.214$. In contrast, for this value of σ_X, pure rounding (Sect. 5.2) succeeds[2] with probability at most 2^{-29}. Similarly, on average 21 coefficients of $\widehat{\mathbf{b}_0}$ will round incorrectly, so that a pure lattice reduction approach (Sect. 5.3) would require a blocksize $\beta = 196$ and be costly to carry out. In comparison, our guessing-based approach is inexpensive and succeeds with high probability. Concretely, it allows us to decrease N to 2^{21}.

Refinement. This "smart guessing" technique can be refined to remain effective even if we guess less than half of the coefficients of $\mathbf{b}_0$. Suppose that with probability $1/2$, we can guess k of the $2n$ coefficients of $\mathbf{b}_0$. This is the case if (26) is satisfied, and by replacing (27) by this relaxed condition:

$$\epsilon = \min\left\{\epsilon^* \mid \mathcal{N}_{\mathbb{R},\sigma_X}([-\epsilon^*, \epsilon^*]) \geq \frac{k}{2n}\right\}. \tag{28}$$

We then rewrite (24) as (25), except that now $\mathbf{A}_1 \in \mathbb{Z}_q^{n \times (2n-k)}$ and $\mathbf{A}_2 \in \mathbb{Z}_q^{n \times k}$. We put $\mathbf{A}_1$ in systematic form ($\mathbf{M} \times \mathbf{A}_1 = [\mathbf{I}_n \; \bar{\mathbf{A}}_1]$) so that (25) becomes:

$$\bar{\mathbf{A}}_1 \cdot \mathbf{x}_2 + \mathbf{x}_1 = \mathbf{z}, \quad \text{where} \quad \begin{cases} \mathbf{z} = -\mathbf{M} \cdot \mathbf{A}_2 \cdot \mathbf{y} \in \mathbb{Z}_q^n \\ (\mathbf{x}_2, \mathbf{x}_1) \in \mathbb{Z}^{n-k} \times \mathbb{Z}^n \end{cases} \tag{29}$$

(29) can be interpreted as an LWE problem with a secret of dimension $n - k$, which indeed becomes vacuous when $k = n$. Unfortunately, due to Gaussian cut-off effects, this optimization does not seem to significantly increase the range of σ_X covered by our technique. We still provide it here for reference.

---

[2] Alternatively, (19) implies that pure rounding requires $\sigma_X \gtrsim 0.1066$ to be practical. Hence it is applicable on a more narrow range than our guessing-based approach.

Remark 1. We expect the guessing trick to also apply to a recent power analysis attack on FALCON by Guerreau et al. [GMRR22]. Similarly to our attack, their attack recovers a noisy estimator of b_0, where the noise decreases with the number of traces. It then recovers b_0 either by rounding (as in Sect. 5.2) or via lattice reduction (as in Sect. 5.3). Our guessing-based approach is applicable in regimes that are out of reach for pure rounding, but for which the cost of lattice reduction remains prohibitive.

Remark 2. After the initial completion of this work, we realized that a similar guessing trick was described in [DDGR20, §6.1], although with a different perspective (the *"LWE with side information"* framework). We invite the interested reader to read [DDGR20, §6.1] for a complementary point of view.

6   Conclusion

We have proposed a key-recovery attack against MITAKA in the t-probing model. Given a masked implementation of MITAKA with $d \geq 4$ shares, an attacker with the capability of probing $t < d$ variables per execution can recover the private key efficiently with $N = 2^{21}$ executions of the signing algorithm. More generally, our attack can be carried as long as $N = \Omega(d/t)$.

As part of our attack, we proposed a guessing-based trick which significantly reduces the computational cost of our attack for many relevant regimes.

Acknowledgements. I would like to thank Mélissa Rossi, Thomas Espitau, Alexandre Wallet, Morgane Guerreau and Eamonn Postlethwaite for useful discussions about [EFG+22], [GMRR22], and the attack presented in this paper. I am particularly grateful to my PQShield colleagues Rafaël del Pino and Fabrice Mouhartem for discussing the subtleties of lattice attacks with me. Finally, I would like to thank the anonymous reviewers of PKC 2023 for their insightful comments.

References

[AA04]   Asonov, D., Agrawal, R.: Keyboard acoustic emanations. In: 2004 IEEE Symposium on Security and Privacy, pp. 3–11. IEEE Computer Society Press, May 2004

[AGVW17]   Albrecht, M.R., Göpfert, F., Virdia, F., Wunderer, T.: Revisiting the expected cost of solving uSVP and applications to LWE. In: Takagi, T., Peyrin, T. (eds.) ASIACRYPT 2017. LNCS, vol. 10624, pp. 297–322. Springer, Cham (2017). https://doi.org/10.1007/978-3-319-70694-8_11

[BBE+18]   Barthe, G., et al.: Masking the GLP lattice-based signature scheme at any order. In: Nielsen, J.B., Rijmen, V. (eds.) EUROCRYPT 2018. LNCS, vol. 10821, pp. 354–384. Springer, Cham (2018). https://doi.org/10.1007/978-3-319-78375-8_12

[Che13]   Chen, Y.: Réduction de réseau et sécurité concrète du chiffrement complètement homomorphe. Ph.D. thesis (2013). https://archive.org/details/PhDChen13

[DDGR20]   Dachman-Soled, D., Ducas, L., Gong, H., Rossi, M.: LWE with side information: Attacks and concrete security estimation. Cryptology ePrint Archive, Report 2020/292 (2020). https://eprint.iacr.org/2020/292

[DFS19] Duc, A., Faust, S., Standaert, F.-X.: Making masking security proofs concrete (or how to evaluate the security of any leaking device), extended version. J. Cryptol. **32**(4), 1263–1297 (2019)

[EFG+22] Espitau, T., et al.: A simpler, parallelizable, maskable variant of falcon. In: Dunkelman, O., Dziembowski, S. (eds.), EUROCRYPT 2022, Part III, LNCS, vol. 13277, pp. 222–253. Springer, Heidelberg (2022). https://doi. org/10.1007/978-3-031-07082-2_9

[EK20] Espitau, T., Kirchner, P.: The nearest-colattice algorithm. Cryptology ePrint Archive, Report 2020/694 (2020). https://eprint.iacr.org/2020/694

[Esp22] Espitau, T.: Supporting code for MITAKA signature (EUROCRYPT 2022). GitHub (2022). https://github.com/espitau/Mitaka-EC22

[GMO01] Gandolfi, K., Mourtel, C., Olivier, F.: Electromagnetic analysis: concrete results. In: Koç, Ç.K., Naccache, D., Paar, C. (eds.) CHES 2001. LNCS, vol. 2162, pp. 251–261. Springer, Heidelberg (2001). https://doi.org/10. 1007/3-540-44709-1_21

[GMRR22] Guerreau, M., Martinelli, A., Ricosset, T., Rossi, M.: The hidden parallelepiped is back again: power analysis attacks on falcon. IACR Trans. Cryptographic Hardware Embedded Syst. **2022**(3), 141–164 (2022)

[GPV08] Gentry, C., Peikert, C., Vaikuntanathan, V.: Trapdoors for hard lattices and new cryptographic constructions. In: Ladner, R.E., Dwork, C. (eds.) 40th ACM STOC, pp. 197–206. ACM Press, May 2008

[GST14] Genkin, D., Shamir, A., Tromer, E.: RSA key extraction via low-bandwidth acoustic cryptanalysis. In: Garay, J.A., Gennaro, R. (eds.) CRYPTO 2014. LNCS, vol. 8616, pp. 444–461. Springer, Heidelberg (2014). https://doi. org/10.1007/978-3-662-44371-2_25

[ISW03] Ishai, Y., Sahai, A., Wagner, D.: Private circuits: securing hardware against probing attacks. In: Boneh, D. (ed.) CRYPTO 2003. LNCS, vol. 2729, pp. 463–481. Springer, Heidelberg (2003). https://doi.org/10.1007/978-3-540-45146-4_27

[KJJ99] Kocher, P., Jaffe, J., Jun, B.: Differential power analysis. In: Wiener, M. (ed.) CRYPTO 1999. LNCS, vol. 1666, pp. 388–397. Springer, Heidelberg (1999). https://doi.org/10.1007/3-540-48405-1_25

[Koc96] Kocher, P.C.: Timing attacks on implementations of Diffie-Hellman, RSA, DSS, and other systems. In: Koblitz, N. (ed.) CRYPTO 1996. LNCS, vol. 1109, pp. 104–113. Springer, Heidelberg (1996). https://doi.org/10.1007/ 3-540-68697-5_9

[LDK+22] Lyubashevsky, V., et al.: CRYSTALS-DILITHIUM. Technical report, National Institute of Standards and Technology (2022). https://csrc.nist. gov/Projects/post-quantum-cryptography/selected-algorithms-2022

[NIS22] NIST. Nistir 8413 - status report on the third round of the NIST postquantum cryptography standardization process (2022). https://doi.org/ 10.6028/NIST.IR.8413

[PFH+22] Prest, T., et al.: FALCON. Technical report, National Institute of Standards and Technology (2022). https://csrc.nist.gov/Projects/postquantum-cryptography/selected-algorithms-2022

[PP19] Pornin, T., Prest, T.: More efficient algorithms for the NTRU key generation using the field norm. In: Lin, D., Sako, K. (eds.) PKC 2019. LNCS, vol. 11443, pp. 504–533. Springer, Cham (2019). https://doi.org/10.1007/ 978-3-030-17259-6_17

Signatures

Hardening Signature Schemes via Derive-then-Derandomize: Stronger Security Proofs for EdDSA

Mihir Bellare[1]([⊠]), Hannah Davis[1], and Zijing Di[2]

[1] University of California San Diego, La Jolla, USA
{mihir,h3davis}@eng.ucsd.edu
[2] Stanford University, Stanford, USA
zidi@stanford.edu

Abstract. We consider a transform, called Derive-then-Derandomize, that hardens a given signature scheme against randomness failure and implementation error. We prove that it works. We then give a general lemma showing indifferentiability of a class of constructions that apply a shrinking output transform to an MD-style hash function. Armed with these tools, we give new proofs for the widely standardized and used EdDSA signature scheme, improving prior work in two ways: (1) we give proofs for the case that the hash function is an MD-style one, reflecting the use of SHA512 in the NIST standard, and (2) we improve the tightness of the reduction so that one has guarantees for group sizes in actual use.

1 Introduction

In designing schemes, and proving them secure, theoreticians implicitly assume certain things, such as on-demand fresh randomness and correct implementation. In practice, these assumptions can fail. Weaknesses in system random-number generators are common and have catastrophic consequences. (An example relevant to this paper is the well-known key-recovery attack on Schnorr signatures when signing reuses randomness. Another striking example are Ps and Qs attacks [25,29].) Meanwhile, implementation errors can be exploited, as shown by Bleichenbacher's attack on RSA signatures [15].

In light of this, practitioners may try to "harden" theoretical schemes before standardization and usage. A prominent and highly successful instance is EdDSA, a hardening of the Schnorr signature scheme proposed by Bernstein, Duif, Lange, Schwabe, and Yang (BDLSY) [14]. It incorporates explicit, simple key-derivation, makes signing deterministic, adds protection against sidechannel attacks via "clamping," and for simplicity confines itself to a single hash function, namely SHA512. The scheme is widely standardized [27,34] and used [26].

There is however a subtle danger here, namely that the hardening attempt introduces new vulnerabilities. In other words, hardening needs to be done right; if not, it may even "soften" the scheme! Thus it is crucial that the hardened scheme be vetted via a proof of security. This is of particular importance for

© International Association for Cryptologic Research 2023
A. Boldyreva and V. Kolesnikov (Eds.): PKC 2023, LNCS 13940, pp. 223–250, 2023.
https://doi.org/10.1007/978-3-031-31368-4_9

EdDSA given its widespread deployment. In that regard, Brendel, Cremers, Jackson and Zhao (BCJZ) [16] showed that EdDSA is secure if the Discrete-Log (DL) problem is hard and the hash function is modeled as a random oracle. This is significant as a first step but has at least two important limitations: (1) Due to the extension attack, a random oracle is not an appropriate model for the SHA512 hash function EdDSA actually uses, and (2) the reduction is so loose that there is no security guarantee for group sizes in use today.

Extrapolating EdDSA, the first part of this paper defines a general hardening transform on signature schemes called Derive-then-Derandomize (**DtD**), and proves its soundness. Next we prove the indifferentiability of a general class of constructions, that we call shrink-MD; it includes the well-studied chop-MD construction [19] and also the modulo-a-prime construction arising in EdDSA. Armed with these results, the second part of the paper returns to give new proofs for EdDSA that in particular fill the above gaps. We begin with some background.

RESPECTING HASH STRUCTURE IN PROOFS. Recall that the MD-transform [20, 31] defines a hash function $H = \mathbf{MD}[h] : \{0,1\}^* \to \{0,1\}^{2k}$ by iterating an underlying compression function $h : \{0,1\}^{b+2k} \to \{0,1\}^{2k}$. (See Sect. 2 for details.) SHA256 and SHA512 are obtained in this way, with (b,k) being $(512, 128)$ and $(1024, 256)$, respectively. This structure gives rise to attacks, of which the most well known is the extension attack. The latter allows an attacker given $t \leftarrow \mathbf{MD}[h](e_2\|M)$, where e_2 is a secret unknown to the attacker and $M \in \{0,1\}^*$ is public, to compute $t' = \mathbf{MD}[h](e_2\|M')$, for some $M' \in \{0,1\}^*$ of its choice. This has been exploited to violate the UF-security of the so-called prefix message authentication code $\mathsf{pfMAC}_{e_2}(M) = H(e_2\|M)$ when H is an MD-hash function; HMAC [4] was designed to overcome this.

A proof of security of a scheme (such as EdDSA) that uses a hash function H will often model H as a random oracle [10], in what we'll call the (H, H)-model: scheme algorithms, and the adversary, both have oracle access to the same random H. However the presence of the above-discussed structure in "real" hash functions led Dodis, Ristenpart and Shrimpton (DRS) [21] to argue that the "right" model in which to prove security of a scheme that uses $H = \mathbf{MD}[h]$ is to model the compression function h —rather than the hash function $H = \mathbf{MD}[h]$— as a random oracle. We'll call this the $(\mathbf{MD}[h], h)$-model: the adversary has oracle access to a random h, with scheme algorithms having access to $\mathbf{MD}[h]$. There is now widespread agreement with the DRS thesis that proofs of security of MD-hash-using schemes should use the $(\mathbf{MD}[h], h)$ model.

Giving from-scratch proofs in the $(\mathbf{MD}[h], h)$ model is, however, difficult. Maurer, Renner and Holenstein (MRH) [30] show that if a construction $\mathbf{F}$ is indifferentiable (abbreviated indiff) and a scheme is secure in the (H, H) model, then it remains secure in the $(\mathbf{F}[h], h)$ model. (This requires the game defining security of the scheme to be single-stage [38], which is true for the relevant ones here.) Unfortunately, $\mathbf{F} = \mathbf{MD}$ is provably *not* indiff [19], due exactly to the extension attack. So the MRH result does not help with $\mathbf{MD}$. This led to a search for indiff variants. DRS [21] and YMO [42] (independently) offer public-indiff and show that it suffices to prove security, in the $(\mathbf{MD}[h], h)$ model, of schemes that use $\mathbf{MD}$ in some restricted way. However, EdDSA does not obey these restrictions. Thus, other means are needed.

THE EdDSA SCHEME. The Edwards curve Digital Signature Algorithm (EdDSA) is a Schnorr-based signature scheme introduced by Bernstein, Duif, Lange, Schwabe and Yang [14]. Ed25519, which uses the Curve25519 Edwards curve and SHA512 as the hash function, is its most popular instance. The scheme is standardized by NIST [34] and the IETF [27]. It is used in TLS 1.3, OpenSSH, OpenSSL, Tor, GnuPGP, Signal and WhatsApp. It is also the preferred signature scheme of the Corda, Tezos, Stellar and Libra blockchain systems. Overall, IANIX [26] reports over 200 uses of Ed25519. Proving security of this scheme is accordingly of high importance.

Figure 4 shows EdDSA on the right, and, on the left, the classic Schnorr scheme [40] on which EdDSA is based. The schemes are over a cyclic, additively-written group $\mathbb{G}$ of prime order p with generator B. The public verification key is A. The Schnorr hash function has range $\mathbb{Z}_p = \{0, \ldots, p-1\}$, while, for EdDSA, function H_1 has range $\{0,1\}^{2k}$ where k, the bit-length of p, is 256 for Ed25519. Functions H_2, H_3 have range $\mathbb{Z}_p$.

EdDSA differs from Schnorr in significant ways. While the Schnorr secret key s is in $\mathbb{Z}_p$, the EdDSA secret key sk is a k-bit string. This is hashed and the $2k$-bit result is split into k-bit halves $e_1 \| e_2$. A Schnorr secret-key s is derived by applying to e_1 a clamping function CF that zeroes out the three least significant bits of e_1. (Note: This means s is *not* uniformly distributed over $\mathbb{Z}_p$.) Clamping increases resistance to side-channel attacks [14]. Signing is made deterministic by a standard de-randomization technique [9,12,23,33], namely obtaining the Schnorr randomness r by hashing the message M with a secret-key dependent string e_2. We note that all of H_1, H_2, H_3 are instantiated via the same hash function, namely SHA512.

PRIOR WORK AND OUR QUESTIONS. Recall that the security goal for a signature scheme is UF (UnForgeability under Chosen-Message Attack) [24]. Schnorr is well studied, and proven UF under DL (Discrete Log in $\mathbb{G}$) when H is a random oracle [1,37]. The provable security of EdDSA, however, received surprisingly little attention until the work of Brendel, Cremers, Jackson and Zhao (BCJZ) [16]. They take the path also used for Schnorr and other identification-based signature schemes [1,37], seeing EdDSA as the result of the Fiat-Shamir transform on an underlying identification scheme EdID that they define, proving security of the latter under DL, and concluding UF of EdDSA under DL when H is a random oracle. This is an important step forward, but the BCJZ proof [16] remains in the (H, H) model. We ask and address the following two questions.

1. Can We Prove Security in the $(\mathbf{MD}[h], h)$ model? The NIST standard [34] mandates that Ed25519 uses SHA512, which is an MD-hash function. Accordingly, as explained above, the BCJZ proof [16], being in the (H, H) model, does not guarantee security; to do the latter, we need a proof in the $(\mathbf{MD}[h], h)$ model.

The gap is more than cosmetic. As we saw above with the example of the prefix MAC, a scheme could be secure in the (H, H) model, yet totally insecure in the more realistic $(\mathbf{MD}[h], h)$ model, and thus also in practice. And EdDSA skirts close to the edge: line 14 is using the prefix-MAC that the extension attack breaks, and overlaps in inputs across the three uses of H could lead to failures. Intuitively what prevents attacks is that the MAC outputs are taken modulo p, and inputs to H in two of the three uses involve secrets. Thus, we'd expect that the scheme is indeed secure in the $(\mathbf{MD}[h], h)$ model.

Proving this, however, is another matter. We already know that $\mathbf{MD}$ is not indiff. It is public indiff [21,42], but this will not suffice for EdDSA because H_1, H_2 are being called on secrets. We ask, first, can EdDSA be proved secure in the $(\mathbf{MD}[h], h)$ model, and second, can this be done in some modular way, rather than from scratch?

2. Can We Improve Reduction Tightness? The reduction of BCJZ [16] is so loose that, in the 256-bit curve over which Ed25519 is implemented, it guarantees little security. Let's elaborate. Given an adversary A_{UF} violating the UF-security of EdDSA with probability ϵ_{UF}, the reduction builds an adversary A_{DL} breaking DL with probability $\epsilon_{DL} = \epsilon_{UF}^2 / q_h$ where q_h is the number of H-queries of A_{UF} and the two adversaries have about the same running time t. (The square arises from the use of rewinding, analyzed via the Reset Lemma of [8].) In an order p elliptic curve group, $\epsilon_{DL} \approx t^2/p$ so we get $\epsilon_{UF} = t \cdot \sqrt{q_h/p}$. Ed25519 has $p \approx 2^{256}$. Say $t = q_h = 2^{70}$, which (as shown by BitCoin mining capability) is not far from attacker reach. Then $\epsilon_{DL} = 2^{-116}$ is small but $\epsilon_{UF} = 2^{70} \cdot 2^{-(256-70)/2} = 2^{-23}$ is in comparison quite high.

Now, one might say that one would not expect better because the same reduction loss is present for Schnorr. The classical reductions for Schnorr [1,37] did indeed display the above loss, but that has changed: recent advances for Schnorr include a tighter reduction from DL [39], an almost-tight reduction from the MBDL problem [5] and a tight reduction from DL in the Algebraic Group Model [22]. We'd like to put EdDSA on par with the state of the art for Schnorr. We ask, first, is this possible, and second, is there a modular way to do it that leverages, rather than repeats, the (many, complex) just-cited proofs for Schnorr?

CONTRIBUTIONS FOR EdDSA. We simultaneously simplify and strengthen the security proofs for EdDSA as follows.

1. Reduction from Schnorr. Rather than, as in prior work, give a reduction from DL or some other algebraic problem, we give a simple, direct reduction from Schnorr itself. That is, we show that if the Schnorr signature scheme is UF-secure, then so is EdDSA. Furthermore, the reduction is *tight* up to a constant factor. This allows us to leverage prior work [5,22,39] to obtain tight proofs for EdDSA under various algebraic assumptions and justify security for group sizes in actual use. But there are two further dividends. First, Schnorr [40] is over 30 years old and has withstood the tests of time and cryptanalysis, so our proof that EdDSA is just as secure as Schnorr allows the former to inherit, and benefit from, this confidence. Second, our result formalizes and proves what was the intuition and belief in the first place [14], namely that, despite the algorithmic differences, EdDSA is a sound hardening of Schnorr.

2. Accurate Modeling of the Hash Function. As noted above, BCJZ [16] assume the hash function H is a random oracle, but this, due to the extension attack, is not an accurate model for the MD-hash function SHA512 used by EdDSA. We fill this gap by instead proving security in the $(MD[h], h)$ model, where $H = MD[h]$ is derived via the MD-transform [20,31] and the compression function h is a random oracle.

APPROACH AND BROADER CONTRIBUTIONS. The above-mentioned results on EdDSA are obtained as a consequence of more general ones.

3. The DtD Transform and Its Soundness. We extend the hardening technique used in EdDSA to define a general transform that we call Derive-then-Derandomize (**DtD**). It takes an *arbitrary* signature scheme DS, and with the aid of a PRG H_1 and a PRF H_2, constructs a hardened signature scheme $\overline{DS}$. We provide (Theorem 1) a strong and general validation of **DtD**, showing that $\overline{DS}$ is UF-secure assuming DS is UF-secure. Moreover *the reduction is tight* and the proof is simple. This shows that the EdDSA hardening method is generically sound.

4. Indifferentiability of Shrink-MD. It is well-known that **MD** is not indifferentiable [30] from a random oracle, but that the **Chop-MD** [19], which truncates the output of an **MD** hash by some number of bits, is indifferentiable. Unfortunately, we identified gaps in two prominent proofs of indifferentiability of **Chop-MD** [19,32]. EdDSA uses a similar construction that reduces the **MD** hash output modulo a prime p sufficiently smaller than the size of the range of **MD**, due to which we refer to this construction as **Mod-MD**. The **Mod-MD** construction has not been proven indifferentiable. We simultaneously give new proofs of indifferentiability for **Chop-MD** and **Mod-MD** as part of a more general class of constructions that we call **Shrink-MD** functors. These are constructions of the form $Out(MD)$ where Out is some output-processing function, and we prove indifferentiability under certain "shrinking" conditions on Out.

5. Application to EdDSA. EdDSA is obtained as the result $\overline{DS}$ of the **DtD** transform applied to the DS = Schnorr signature scheme, and with the PRG and PRF defined via **MD**, specifically $H_1(sk) = MD[h](sk)$ and $H_2(e_2, M) = MD[h](e_2 \| M)$ mod p where p is the prime order of the underlying group. Additionally, the hash function used in Schnorr is also $H_3(X) = MD[h](X)$ mod p. Due to Theorem 1 validating **DtD**, we are left to show the PRG security of H_1, the PRF security of H_2 and the UF-security of Schnorr, all with h modeled as a random oracle. We do the first directly. We obtain the second as a consequence of the indifferentiability of **Mod-MD**. (In principle it follows from the PRF security of AMAC [3], but we found it difficult to extract precise bounds via this route.) For the third, we again exploit indifferentiability of **Mod-MD**, together with a technique from BCJZ [16] to handle clamping, to reduce to the UF security of regular Schnorr, where the hash function is modeled as a random oracle. Putting all this carefully together yields our above-mentioned results for EdDSA. We note that one delicate and important point is that the idealized compression function h is *the same* across H_1, H_2 and H_3, meaning these are not independent. This is handled through the building blocks in Theorem 1 being functors [7] rather than functions.

DISCUSSION AND RELATED WORK. Both BCJZ [16] and CGN [17] note that there are a few versions of EdDSA out there, the differences being in their verification algorithms. What Fig. 4 shows is the most basic version of the scheme, but we will be able to cover the variants too, in a modular way, by reducing from Schnorr with the same verification algorithm.

BBT [3] define the function AMAC[h] to take a key e_2 and message M, and return $\mathbf{MD}[h](e_2\|M)$ mod p. This is the H_2 in EdDSA. We could exploit their results to conclude PRF security of H_2, but it requires putting together many different pieces from their work, and it is easier and more direct to establish PRF security of H_2 by using our lemma on the indifferentiability of **Mod-MD**.

In the Generic Group Model (GGM) [41], it is possible to prove UF-security of Schnorr under standard (rather than random oracle) model assumptions on the hash functions [18,35]. But use of the GGM means the result applies to a limited class of adversaries. Our results, following the classical proofs for identification-based signatures [1,28,36,37], instead use the standard model for the group, while modeling the hash function (in our case, the compression function) as a random oracle.

In an earlier version of this paper, our proofs had relied on a variant of indifferentiability that we had introduced. At the suggestion of a Crypto 2022 reviewer, this has been dropped in favor of a direct proof based on PRG and PRF assumptions on H_1, H_2. We thank the (anonymous) reviewer for this suggestion.

Theorem 1 is in the standard model if the PRG, PRF and starting signature scheme DS are standard-model, hence can be viewed as a standard-model justification of the hardening template underlying EdDSA. However, when we want to justify EdDSA itself, we need to consider the specific, **MD**-based instantiations of the PRG, PRF and Schnorr hash function, and for these we use the model where the compression function is ideal.

Several works study de-randomization of signing by deriving the coins via a PRF applied to the message, considering different ways to key the PRF [9,12, 23,33]. We use their techniques in the proof of Theorem 1.

One might ask how to view the UF-security of Schnorr signatures as an assumption. What is relevant is not its form (it is interactive) but that (1) it can be seen as a hub from where one can bridge to other assumptions that imply it, such as DL (non-tightly) [1,37] or MBDL (tightly) [5], and (2) it is validated by decades of cryptanalysis.

Our results have been stated for UF but extend to SUF (Strong unforgeability), meaning our proofs also show SUF-security of EdDSA in the ($\mathbf{MD}[h], h$) model assuming SUF security of Schnorr, with a tight (up to the usual constant factor) reduction.

EdDSA could be used with other hash functions such as SHAKE. The extension attack does not apply to the latter, so the proof of BCJZ [16] applies, but gives a loose reduction from DL; our results still add something, namely a tight reduction from Schnorr and thus improved tightness in several ways as discussed above.

2   Preliminaries

NOTATION. If n is a positive integer, then $\mathbb{Z}_n$ denotes the set $\{0, \ldots, n-1\}$ and $[n]$ or $[1..n]$ denote the set $\{1, \ldots, n\}$. If $\boldsymbol{x}$ is a vector then $|\boldsymbol{x}|$ is its length (the number of its coordinates), $\boldsymbol{x}[i]$ is its i-th coordinate and $[\boldsymbol{x}] = \{\; \boldsymbol{x}[i] \;:\; 1 \le i \le |\boldsymbol{x}| \;\}$ is the set of all its coordinates. A string is identified with a vector over $\{0,1\}$, so that if x is a string then $x[i]$ is its i-th bit and $|x|$ is its length. We denote $x[i..j]$ the i-th bit to the j-th bit of string x. By ε we denote the empty vector or string. The size of a set S is denoted $|S|$. For sets D, R let $\mathsf{AF}(D,R)$ denote the set of all functions $f : D \to R$. If $f : D \to R$ is a function then $\mathsf{Img}(f) = \{\; f(x) \;:\; x \in D \;\} \subseteq R$ is its image. We say that f is *regular* if every $y \in \mathsf{Img}(f)$ has the same number of pre-images under f. By $\{0,1\}^{\le L}$ we denote the set of all strings of length at most L. For any variables a and b, the expression $[[a = b]]$ denotes the Boolean value true when a and b contain the same value and false otherwise.

Let S be a finite set. We let $x \leftarrow_\$ S$ denote sampling an element uniformly at random from S and assigning it to x. We let $y \leftarrow A[\mathsf{O}_1, \ldots](x_1, \ldots; r)$ denote executing algorithm A on inputs $x_1, \ldots$ and coins r with access to oracles $\mathsf{O}_1, \ldots$ and letting y be the result. We let $y \leftarrow_\$ A[\mathsf{O}_1, \ldots](x_1, \ldots)$ be the resulting of picking r at random and letting $y \leftarrow A[\mathsf{O}_1, \ldots](x_1, \ldots; r)$ be the equivalent. We let $\mathrm{OUT}(A[\mathsf{O}_1, \ldots](x_1, \ldots)])$ denote the set of all possible outputs of A when invoked with inputs $x_1, \ldots$ and oracles $\mathsf{O}_1, \ldots$. Algorithms are randomized unless otherwise indicated. Running time is worst case.

GAMES. We use the code-based game playing framework of [11]. (See Fig. 1 for an example.) Games have procedures, also called oracles. Among the oracles are INIT and a FIN. In executing an adversary $\mathcal{A}$ with a game G, the adversary may query the oracles at will. We require that the adversary's first oracle query be to INIT and its last to FIN and it query these oracles at most once. The value return by the FIN procedure is taken as the game output. By $G(\mathcal{A}) \Rightarrow y$ we denote the event that the execution of game G with adversary $\mathcal{A}$ results in output y. We write $\Pr[G(\mathcal{A})]$ as shorthand for $\Pr[G(\mathcal{A}) \Rightarrow \mathsf{true}]$, the probability that the game returns true.

In writing game or adversary pseudocode, it is assumed that Boolean variables are initialized to false, integer variables are initialized to 0 and set-valued variables are initialized to the empty set $\emptyset$.

We adopt the convention that the running time of an adversary is the time for the execution of the game with the adversary, so that the time for oracles to respond to queries is included, and similarly for the number of queries to an oracle. In particular, the number of queries to a random oracle FO includes those made by scheme algorithms executed by game procedures. By $Q_{\mathcal{A}}^{\mathsf{O}}$ we denote the number of queries made by $\mathcal{A}$ and the game to oracle O in the execution. With $q_{\mathcal{A}}^{\mathsf{O}}$ we count only queries made directly by $\mathcal{A}$ to O, not by other game oracles or scheme algorithms. These counts are all worst case.

GROUPS. Throughout the paper, we fix integers k and b, an odd prime p, and a positive integer f such that $2^f < p$. We then fix two groups: $\mathbb{G}$, a group of order $p \cdot 2^f$ whose elements are k-bit strings, and its cyclic subgroup $\mathbb{G}_p$ of order p. We prove in our full version [6] that this subgroup is unique, and that it has an efficient membership test. We also assume an efficient membership test for $\mathbb{G}$. We will use additive notation for the group operation, and we let $0_{\mathbb{G}}$ denote the identity element of $\mathbb{G}$. We let $\mathbb{G}_p^* = \mathbb{G} \setminus \{0_{\mathbb{G}}\}$ denote the set of non-identity elements of $\mathbb{G}_p$, which is its set of generators. We fix a distinguished generator $B \in \mathbb{G}_p^*$. Then for any $X \in \mathbb{G}^*$, the discrete logarithm base B of X is denoted $\mathsf{DL}_{\mathbb{G},B}(X)$, and it is in the set $\mathbb{Z}_{|\mathbb{G}|}$. The instantiation of $\mathbb{G}$ used in Ed25519 is described in our full version [6].

3   Functor Framework

Our treatment relies on the notion of functors [7], which are functions that access an idealized primitive. We give relevant definitions, starting with signature schemes whose security is measured relative to a functor. Then we extend the notions of PRGs and PRFs to functors.

FUNCTION SPACES. In using the random oracle model [10], works in the literature sometimes omit to say what exactly are the domain and range of the underlying functions, and, when multiple functions are present, whether or not they are independent. (Yet, implicitly their proofs rely on certain choices.) For greater precision, we use the language of function spaces of [7], which we now recall.

A *function space* O is a set of tuples $\mathsf{H} = (\mathsf{H}_1, \ldots, \mathsf{H}_n)$ of functions. The integer n is called the arity of the function space, and can be recovered as O.arity. We view H as taking an input X that it parses as (i, x) to return $\mathsf{H}_i(x)$.

FUNCTORS. Following [7], we use the term functor for a transform that constructs one function from another. A functor $\mathbf{F} : \mathsf{SS} \to \mathsf{ES}$ takes as oracle a function h from a starting function space SS and returns a function $\mathbf{F}[\mathsf{h}]$ in the ending function space ES. (The term is inspired by category theory, where a functor maps from one category into another. In our case, the categories are function spaces.) If ES has arity n, then we also refer to n as the arity of $\mathbf{F}$, and write $\mathbf{F}_i$ for the functor which returns the i-th component of $\mathbf{F}$. That is, $\mathbf{F}_i[\mathsf{h}]$ lets $\mathsf{H} \leftarrow \mathbf{F}[\mathsf{h}]$ and returns H_i.

MD FUNCTOR. We are interested in the Merkle-Damgård [20,31] transform. This transform constructs a hash function with domain $\{0,1\}^*$ from a compression function $\mathsf{h} : \{0,1\}^{b+2k} \to \{0,1\}^{2k}$ for some integers b and k. The compression function takes a $2k$-bit chaining variable y and a b-bit block B to return a $2k$ bit output $\mathsf{h}(y\|B)$. In the case of SHA512, the hash function used in EdDSA, the compression function sha512 has $b = 1024$ and $k = 256$ (so the chaining variable is 512 bits and a block is 1024 bits), while $b = 512$ and $k = 128$ for SHA256. In our language, the Merkle-Damgård transform is a functor $\mathbf{MD} : \mathsf{AF}(\{0,1\}^{b+2k}, \{0,1\}^{2k}) \to \mathsf{AF}(\{0,1\}^*, \{0,1\}^{2k})$. It is parameterized by a padding function pad that takes the length ℓ of an input to the hash function and returns a padding string such that $\ell + |\mathsf{pad}(\ell)|$ is a multiple of b. Specifically, $\mathsf{pad}(\ell)$ returns $10^* \langle \ell \rangle$ where $\langle \ell \rangle$ is a 64-bit, resp. 128-bit encoding of ℓ for SHA256 resp. SHA512, and 0^* indicates the minimum number p of 0s needed to make $\ell + 1 + p + 64$, resp. $\ell + 1 + p + 128$ a multiple of b. We also fix an "initialization vector" $IV \in \{0,1\}^{2k}$. Given oracle h, the functor defines hash function $\mathsf{H} = \mathbf{MD}[\mathsf{h}] : \{0,1\}^* \to \{0,1\}^{2k}$ as follows:

Functor $\mathbf{MD}[\mathsf{h}](X)$
___
$y[0] \leftarrow IV$
$P \leftarrow \mathsf{pad}(|X|)$; $X'[1] \dots X'[m] \leftarrow X \| P$ // Split $X \| P$ into b-bit blocks
For $i = 1, \dots, m$ do $y[i] \leftarrow \mathsf{h}(y[i-1] \| X'[i])$
Return $y[m]$

Strictly speaking, the domain is only strings of length less than 2^{64} resp. 2^{128}, but since this is huge in practice, we view the domain as $\{0,1\}^*$.

SIGNATURE SCHEME SYNTAX. We give an enhanced, flexible syntax for a signature scheme DS. We want to cover ROM schemes, which means scheme algorithms have oracle access to a function H, but of what range and domain? Since these can vary from scheme to scheme, we have the scheme begin by naming the function space DS.FS from which H is drawn. We see the key-generation algorithm DS.Kg as first picking a signing key $sk \leftarrow_{\$} \mathsf{DS.SK}$ via a signing-key generation algorithm DS.SK, then obtaining the public verification key $vk \leftarrow \mathsf{DS.PK}[\mathsf{H}](sk)$ by applying a deterministic verification-key generation algorithm DS.PK, and finally returning (vk, sk). (For simplicity, DS.SK, unlike other scheme algorithms, does not have access to H.) We break it up like this because we may need to explicitly refer to the sub-algorithms in constructions. Continuing, via $\sigma \leftarrow \mathsf{DS.Sign}[\mathsf{H}](sk, vk, M; r)$ the signing algorithm takes sk, vk, a message $M \in \{0,1\}^*$, and randomness r from the randomness space DS.SR of the algorithm, to return a signature σ. As usual, $\sigma \leftarrow_{\$} \mathsf{DS.Sign}[\mathsf{H}](sk, vk, M)$ is shorthand for picking $r \leftarrow_{\$} \mathsf{DS.SR}$ and returning $\sigma \leftarrow \mathsf{DS.Sign}[\mathsf{H}](sk, vk, M; r)$. Via $b \leftarrow \mathsf{DS.Vf}[\mathsf{H}](vk, M, \sigma)$, the verification algorithm obtains a boolean decision $b \in \{\mathsf{true}, \mathsf{false}\}$ about the validity of the signature. The correctness requirement is that for all $\mathsf{H} \in \mathsf{DS.FS}$, all $(vk, sk) \in \mathsf{OUT}(\mathsf{DS.Kg}[\mathsf{H}])$, all $M \in \{0,1\}^*$ and all $\sigma \in \mathsf{OUT}(\mathsf{DS.Sign}[\mathsf{H}](sk, vk, M))$ we have $\mathsf{DS.Vf}[\mathsf{H}](vk, M, \sigma) = \mathsf{true}$.

UF SECURITY. We want to discuss security of a signature scheme DS under different ways in which the functions in DS.FS are chosen or built. Game $\mathbf{G}^{\mathrm{uf}}_{\mathsf{DS},\mathbf{FF}}$ in Fig. 1 is thus parameterized by a functor $\mathbf{FF} : \mathsf{SS} \to \mathsf{DS.FS}$. At line 1, a starting function h is chosen from the starting space of the functor, and then the function $\mathsf{H} \in \mathsf{DS.FS}$ that the scheme algorithms (key-generation, signing and verification) get as oracle is determined as $\mathsf{H} \leftarrow \mathbf{FF}[\mathsf{h}]$. The adversary, however, via oracle FO, gets access to h, which here is the random oracle. The rest is as

Game $\mathbf{G}_{\mathsf{DS},\mathbf{FF}}^{\mathrm{uf}}$ INIT:

1 h ←$ SS ; H ← $\mathbf{FF}$[FO] ; (vk, sk) ←$ DS.Kg[H] ; Return vk

SIGN(M):
2 σ ←$ DS.Sign[H](sk, vk, M) ; $S \leftarrow S \cup \{M\}$; Return σ

FO(X):
3 Return h(X)

FIN(M_*, σ_*):
4 If $(M_* \in S)$ then return false
5 Return DS.Vf[H](vk, M_*, σ_*)

Game $\mathbf{G}_{\mathbf{P}}^{\mathrm{prg}}$ INIT:

1 h ←$ SS ; c ←$ $\{0,1\}$
2 s ←$ $\{0,1\}^k$; $y_1 \leftarrow \mathbf{P}$[FO]$(s)$
3 y_0 ←$ $\{0,1\}^\ell$
4 Return y_c

FO(X):
5 Return h(X)

FIN(c'):
6 Return $(c = c')$

Game $\mathbf{G}_{\mathbf{F}}^{\mathrm{prf}}$ INIT:

1 h ←$ SS ; c ←$ $\{0,1\}$; K ←$ $\{0,1\}^k$

FN(X):
2 If YT$[X] \neq \bot$ then
3   If $(c = 1)$ then YT$[X] \leftarrow \mathbf{F}$[FO]$(K, X)$
4   Else YT$[X]$ ←$ R
5 Return YT$[X]$

FO(X):
6 Return h(X)

FIN(c'):
7 Return $(c = c')$

Fig. 1. Top: Game defining UF security of signature scheme DS relative to functor $\mathbf{FF} : \mathsf{SS} \to \mathsf{DS.FS}$. Bottom Left: Game defining PRG security of functor $\mathbf{P} : \mathsf{SS} \to \mathsf{AF}(\{0,1\}^k, \{0,1\}^\ell)$. Bottom Right: Game defining PRF security of functor $\mathbf{F} : \mathsf{SS} \to \mathsf{AF}(\{0,1\}^k \times \{0,1\}^*, R)$.

---

per the usual unforgeability definition. (Given in the standard model in [24] and extended to the ROM in [10].) We define the UF advantage of adversary $\mathcal{A}$ as $\mathbf{Adv}_{\mathsf{DS},\mathbf{FF}}^{\mathrm{uf}}(\mathcal{A}) = \Pr[\mathbf{G}_{\mathsf{DS},\mathbf{FF}}^{\mathrm{uf}}(\mathcal{A})].$

PRGs AND PRFs. The usual definition of a PRGs is for a function; we define it instead for a functor $\mathbf{P}$. The game $\mathbf{G}_{\mathbf{P}}^{\mathrm{prg}}$ is in Fig. 1. It picks a function h from the starting space SS of the functor. The functor now determines a function $\mathbf{P}[\mathsf{h}] : \{0,1\}^k \to \{0,1\}^\ell$. The game then follows the usual PRG one for this function, additionally giving the adversary oracle access to h via oracle FO. We let $\mathbf{Adv}_{\mathbf{P}}^{\mathrm{prg}}(\mathcal{A}) = 2\Pr[\mathbf{G}_{\mathbf{P}}^{\mathrm{prg}}(\mathcal{A})] - 1.$

$\overline{\mathsf{DS}}.\mathsf{SK}$:

1 $\overline{sk} \leftarrow\!\!\$ \, \{0,1\}^k$; Return $\overline{sk}$

$\overline{\mathsf{DS}}.\mathsf{PK}[\mathsf{H}](\overline{sk})$:

2 $e_1\|e_2 \leftarrow \mathsf{H}_1(\overline{sk})$; $sk \leftarrow \mathsf{CF}(e_1)$
3 $vk \leftarrow \mathsf{DS}.\mathsf{PK}[\mathsf{H}_3](sk)$
4 Return vk

$\overline{\mathsf{DS}}.\mathsf{Sign}[\mathsf{H}](\overline{sk}, vk, M)$:

5 $e_1\|e_2 \leftarrow \mathsf{H}_1(\overline{sk})$; $sk \leftarrow \mathsf{CF}(e_1)$
6 $r \leftarrow \mathsf{H}_2(e_2, M)$
7 $\sigma \leftarrow \mathsf{DS}.\mathsf{Sign}[\mathsf{H}_3](sk, vk, M; r)$
8 Return σ

$\overline{\mathsf{DS}}.\mathsf{Vf}[\mathsf{H}](vk, M, \sigma)$:

9 Return $\mathsf{DS}.\mathsf{Vf}[\mathsf{H}_3](vk, M, \sigma)$

$\mathsf{DS}^*.\mathsf{SK}$:

1 $\overline{sk} \leftarrow\!\!\$ \, \{0,1\}^k$; Return $\overline{sk}$

$\mathsf{DS}^*.\mathsf{PK}[\mathsf{G}](\overline{sk})$:

2 $sk \leftarrow \mathsf{CF}(\overline{sk})$
3 $vk \leftarrow \mathsf{DS}.\mathsf{PK}[\mathsf{G}](sk)$
4 Return vk

$\mathsf{DS}^*.\mathsf{Sign}[\mathsf{G}](\overline{sk}, vk, M)$:

5 $sk \leftarrow \mathsf{CF}(\overline{sk})$
6 $\sigma \leftarrow\!\!\$ \, \mathsf{DS}.\mathsf{Sign}[\mathsf{G}](sk, vk, M)$
7 Return σ

$\mathsf{DS}^*.\mathsf{Vf}[\mathsf{G}](vk, M, \sigma)$:

8 Return $\mathsf{DS}.\mathsf{Vf}[\mathsf{G}](vk, M, \sigma)$

Fig. 2. Left: The signature scheme $\overline{\mathsf{DS}} = \mathbf{DtD}[\mathsf{DS}, \mathsf{CF}]$ constructed by the $\mathbf{DtD}$ transform applied to signature scheme DS and clamping function $\mathsf{CF}: \{0,1\}^k \rightarrow$ $\mathsf{OUT}(\mathsf{DS}.\mathsf{SK})$. **Right:** The signature scheme $\overline{\mathsf{DS}} = \mathbf{JCl}[\mathsf{DS}, \mathsf{CF}]$ constructed by the $\mathbf{JCl}$ transform.

Similarly we extend the usual definition of PRG security to a functor $\mathbf{F}$, via game $\mathbf{G}_{\mathbf{F}}^{\mathrm{prf}}$ of Fig. 1. Here, for h in the starting space SS of the functor, the defined function maps as $\mathbf{F}[\mathsf{h}] : \{0,1\}^k \times \{0,1\}^* \rightarrow R$ for some k and range set R. We let $\mathbf{Adv}_{\mathbf{F}}^{\mathrm{prf}}(\mathcal{A}) = 2\Pr[\mathbf{G}_{\mathbf{F}}^{\mathrm{prf}}(\mathcal{A})] - 1$.

4 The Soundness of Derive-then-Derandomize

We specify a general signature-hardening transform that we call Derive-then-Derandomize ($\mathbf{DtD}$) and prove that it preserves the security of the starting signature scheme.

THE $\mathbf{DtD}$ TRANSFORM. Let DS be a given signature scheme that we call the base signature scheme. It will be the (general) Schnorr scheme in our application. Assume for simplicity that its function space $\mathsf{DS}.\mathsf{FS}$ has arity 1.

The $\mathbf{DtD}$ (derive then de-randomize) transform constructs a signature scheme $\overline{\mathsf{DS}} = \mathbf{DtD}[\mathsf{DS}, \mathsf{CF}]$ based on DS and a function $\mathsf{CF}: \{0,1\}^k \rightarrow$ $\mathsf{OUT}(\mathsf{DS}.\mathsf{SK})$, called the clamping function, that turns a k-bit string into a signing key for DS. The algorithms of $\overline{\mathsf{DS}}$ are shown in Fig. 2. They have access to oracle H that specifies sub-functions $\mathsf{H}_1, \mathsf{H}_2, \mathsf{H}_3$. Function $\mathsf{H}_1 : \{0,1\}^k \rightarrow \{0,1\}^{2k}$ expands the signing key $\overline{sk}$ of $\overline{\mathsf{DS}}$ into sub-keys e_1 and e_2. The clamping function is applied to e_1 to get a signing key for the base scheme, and its associated verification key is returned as the one for the new scheme at line 4. At line 6, function $H_2 : \{0,1\}^k \times \{0,1\}^* \to \mathsf{DS.SR}$ is applied to the second sub-key e_2 and the message M to determine signing randomness r for the line 5 invocation of the base signing algorithm. Finally, $H_3 \in \mathsf{DS.FS}$ is an oracle for the algorithms of DS. Formally the oracle space $\overline{\mathsf{DS}}.\mathsf{FS}$ of $\overline{\mathsf{DS}}$ is the arity 3 space consisting of all $H = (H_1, H_2, H_3)$ that map as above.

Viewing the PRG H_1, PRF H_2 and oracle H_3 for the base scheme as specified in the function space is convenient for our application to EdDSA, where they are all based on **MD** with the *same* underlying idealized compression function.

JUST CLAMP. Given a signature scheme DS and a clamping function $\mathsf{CF} : \{0,1\}^k \to \mathsf{OUT}(\mathsf{DS.SK})$, it is useful to also consider the signature scheme $\mathsf{DS}^* = \mathbf{JCl}[\mathsf{DS}, \mathsf{CF}]$ that does just the clamping. The scheme is shown in Fig. 2. Its oracle space is the same as that of DS and is assumed to have arity 1. On the right of Fig. 2 the function drawn from it is denoted G; it will be the same as H_3 on the left.

SECURITY OF **DtD**.b We study the security of the scheme $\overline{\mathsf{DS}} = \mathbf{DtD}[\mathsf{DS}, \mathsf{CF}]$ obtained via the **DtD** transform.

When we prove security of $\overline{\mathsf{DS}}$, it will be with respect to a functor **FF** that constructs all of H_1, H_2, H_3. This means that these three functions could all depend on the same starting function that **FF** uses, and in particular not be independent of each other. An important element of the following theorem is that it holds even in this case, managing to reduce security to conditions on the individual functors despite their using related (in fact, the same) underlying starting function.

Theorem 1. *Let* DS *be a signature scheme. Let* $\mathsf{CF} : \{0,1\}^k \to \mathsf{OUT}(\mathsf{DS.SK})$ *be a clamping function. Let* $\overline{\mathsf{DS}} = \mathbf{DtD}[\mathsf{DS}, \mathsf{CF}]$ *and* $\mathsf{DS}^* = \mathbf{JCl}[\mathsf{DS}, \mathsf{CF}]$ *be the signature schemes obtained by the above transforms. Let* $\mathbf{FF} : \mathsf{SS} \to \overline{\mathsf{DS}}.\mathsf{FS}$ *be a functor that constructs the function* H *that algorithms of* $\overline{\mathsf{DS}}$ *use as an oracle. Let* $\mathcal{A}$ *be an adversary attacking the* $\mathbf{G}^{\mathrm{uf}}$ *security of* $\overline{\mathsf{DS}}$. *Then there are adversaries* $\mathcal{A}_1, \mathcal{A}_2, \mathcal{A}_3$ *such that*

$$\mathbf{Adv}_{\overline{\mathsf{DS}},\mathbf{FF}}^{\mathrm{uf}}(\mathcal{A}) \le \mathbf{Adv}_{\mathbf{FF}_1}^{\mathrm{prg}}(\mathcal{A}_1) + \mathbf{Adv}_{\mathbf{FF}_2}^{\mathrm{prf}}(\mathcal{A}_2) + \mathbf{Adv}_{\mathsf{DS}^*,\mathbf{FF}_3}^{\mathrm{uf}}(\mathcal{A}_3) .$$

The constructed adversaries preserve the number of FO *queries of* $\mathcal{A}$ *and approximately preserve its running time. Adversary* $\mathcal{A}_2$ *makes* $Q_{\mathrm{SIGN}}^{\mathcal{A}}$ *queries to* FN. *Adversary* $\mathcal{A}_3$ *makes* $Q_{\mathrm{SIGN}}^{\mathcal{A}}$ *queries to* SIGN.

Proof (Theorem 1). The proof uses code-based game playing [11]. Consider the games of Fig. 3. Let $\epsilon_i = \Pr[\mathsf{G}_i(\mathcal{A})]$ for $i = 0, 1, 2$.

Game G_0 is the $\mathbf{G}^{\mathrm{uf}}$ game for $\overline{\mathsf{DS}}$ except that the signature of M is stored in table ST at line 8 and, at line 5, if a signature for M already exists, it is returned directly. Since signing in $\overline{\mathsf{DS}}$ is deterministic, meaning the signature is always the same for a given message and signing key, this does not change what SIGN returns, and thus

$$\mathbf{Adv}_{\overline{\mathsf{DS}},\mathbf{FF}}^{\mathrm{uf}}(\mathcal{A}) = \epsilon_0$$

$$= (\epsilon_0 - \epsilon_1) + (\epsilon_1 - \epsilon_2) + \epsilon_2 .$$

We bound each of the three terms above in turn.

Games G_0, G_1, G_2 INIT:

1 $h \leftarrow_\$ SS$
2 $\overline{sk} \leftarrow_\$ \{0,1\}^k$; $e_1\|e_2 \leftarrow \mathbf{FF}_1[\text{FO}](\overline{sk})$ // Game G_0
3 $e_1\|e_2 \leftarrow_\$ \{0,1\}^{2k}$ // Games G_1, G_2
4 $sk \leftarrow \text{CF}(e_1)$; $vk \leftarrow \text{DS.PK}[\mathbf{FF}_3[\text{FO}]](sk)$; Return vk

SIGN(M):

5 If $\text{ST}[M] \neq \bot$ then return $\text{ST}[M]$
6 $r \leftarrow \mathbf{FF}_2[\text{FO}](e_2, M)$ // Games G_0, G_1
7 $r \leftarrow_\$ \text{DS.SR}$ // Game G_2
8 $\text{ST}[M] \leftarrow \text{DS.Sign}[\mathbf{FF}_3[\text{FO}]](sk, vk, M; r)$; Return $\text{ST}[M]$

FO(X):

9 Return $h(X)$

FIN(M_*, σ_*):

10 If $(\text{ST}[M_*] \neq \bot)$ then return false
11 Return $\text{DS.Vf}[\mathbf{FF}_3[\text{FO}]](vk, M_*, \sigma_*)$

Fig. 3. Games for proof of Theorem 1. A line annotated with names of games is included only in those games.

The change in moving to game G_1 is at line 3, where we sample $e_1\|e_2$ uniformly from the set $\{0,1\}^{2k}$ rather than obtaining it via $\mathbf{FF}_1[\text{FO}]$ as in game G_0. We build PRG adversary $\mathcal{A}_1$ such that

$$\epsilon_0 - \epsilon_1 \leq \mathbf{Adv}^{\text{prg}}_{\mathbf{FF}_1}(\mathcal{A}_1) . \tag{1}$$

Adversary $\mathcal{A}_1$ is playing game $\mathbf{G}^{\text{prg}}_{\mathbf{FF}_1}$. It gets its challenge via $e_1\|e_2 \leftarrow \mathbf{G}^{\text{prg}}_{\mathbf{FF}_1}.\text{INIT}$. It lets $sk \leftarrow \text{CF}(e_1)$ and $vk \leftarrow \text{DS.PK}[\mathbf{FF}_3[\mathbf{G}^{\text{prg}}_{\mathbf{FF}_1}.\text{FO}]](sk)$ where $\mathbf{G}^{\text{prg}}_{\mathbf{FF}_1}.\text{FO}$ is the oracle provided in its own game. It runs $\mathcal{A}$, returning vk in response to $\mathcal{A}$'s INIT query. It answers SIGN queries as do G_0, G_1 except that it uses $\mathbf{G}^{\text{prg}}_{\mathbf{FF}_1}.\text{FO}$ in place of FO at lines 6,8. As part of this simulation, it maintains table ST. It answers FO queries via $\mathbf{G}^{\text{prg}}_{\mathbf{FF}_1}.\text{FO}$. When $\mathcal{A}$ calls FIN(M_*, σ_*), adversary $\mathcal{A}_1$ lets $c' \leftarrow 1$ if $\text{DS.Vf}[\mathbf{FF}_3[\mathbf{G}^{\text{prg}}_{\mathbf{FF}_1}.\text{FO}]](vk, M_*, \sigma_*)$ is true and $\text{ST}[M_*] = \bot$, and otherwise lets $c' \leftarrow 0$. It then calls $\mathbf{G}^{\text{prg}}_{\mathbf{FF}_1}.\text{FIN}(c')$. When the challenge bit c in game $\mathbf{G}^{\text{prg}}_{\mathbf{FF}_1}$ is $c = 1$, the view of $\mathcal{A}$ is as in G_0, and when $c = 0$ it is as in G_1, which explains Eq. (1).

Moving to G_2, the change is that line 6 is replaced by line 7, meaning signing coins are now chosen at random from the randomness space DS.SR of DS. We build PRF adversary $\mathcal{A}_2$ such that

$$\epsilon_1 - \epsilon_2 \leq \mathbf{Adv}^{\text{prf}}_{\mathbf{FF}_2}(\mathcal{A}_2) . \tag{2}$$

Adversary $\mathcal{A}_2$ is playing game $\mathbf{G}^{\text{prf}}_{\mathbf{FF}_2}$. It picks $e_1\|e_2 \leftarrow_\$ \{0,1\}^{2k}$. It lets $sk \leftarrow \text{CF}(e_1)$ and $vk \leftarrow \text{DS.PK}[\mathbf{FF}_3[\mathbf{G}^{\text{prf}}_{\mathbf{FF}_2}.\text{FO}]](sk)$ where $\mathbf{G}^{\text{prf}}_{\mathbf{FF}_2}.\text{FO}$ is the oracle provided in its own game. It runs $\mathcal{A}$, returning vk in response to $\mathcal{A}$'s INIT query. It answers SIGN queries as does G_1 except that it uses $\mathbf{G}_{\mathbf{FF}_2}^{\mathrm{prf}}.\mathrm{FN}$ in place of $\mathbf{FF}_2[\mathrm{FO}]$ at line 6 and $\mathbf{G}_{\mathbf{FF}_2}^{\mathrm{prf}}.\mathrm{FO}$ in place of FO in line 8. As part of this simulation, it maintains table ST. It answers FO queries via $\mathbf{G}_{\mathbf{FF}_2}^{\mathrm{prf}}.\mathrm{FO}$. When $\mathcal{A}$ calls $\mathrm{FIN}(M_*, \sigma_*)$, adversary $\mathcal{A}_2$ lets $c' \leftarrow 1$ if $\mathsf{DS.Vf}[\mathbf{FF}_3[\mathbf{G}_{\mathbf{FF}_2}^{\mathrm{prf}}.\mathrm{FO}]](vk, M_*, \sigma_*)$ is true and $\mathrm{ST}[M_*] = \bot$, and otherwise lets $c' \leftarrow 0$. It then calls $\mathbf{G}_{\mathbf{FF}_2}^{\mathrm{prf}}.\mathrm{FIN}(c')$. When the challenge bit c in game $\mathbf{G}_{\mathbf{FF}_2}^{\mathrm{prf}}$ is $c = 1$, the view of $\mathcal{A}$ is as in G_1, and when $c = 0$ it is as in G_2, which explains Eq. (2).

Finally we build adversary $\mathcal{A}_3$ such that

$$\epsilon_2 \leq \mathbf{Adv}_{\mathsf{DS}^*, \mathbf{FF}_3}^{\mathrm{uf}}(\mathcal{A}_3) . \tag{3}$$

Adversary $\mathcal{A}_3$ is playing game $\mathbf{G}_{\mathsf{DS}^*, \mathbf{FF}_3}^{\mathrm{uf}}$. It lets $vk \leftarrow \mathbf{G}_{\mathsf{DS}^*, \mathbf{FF}_3}^{\mathrm{uf}}.\mathrm{INIT}$. It runs $\mathcal{A}$, returning vk in response to $\mathcal{A}$'s INIT query. When $\mathcal{A}$ makes query M to SIGN, it answers as per the following:

If $\mathrm{ST}[M] \neq \bot$ then return $\mathrm{ST}[M]$
$\mathrm{ST}[M] \leftarrow_{\$} \mathbf{G}_{\mathsf{DS}^*, \mathbf{FF}_3}^{\mathrm{uf}}.\mathrm{SIGN}(M)$; Return $\mathrm{ST}[M]$

Note that memoizing signatures in ST is important here to ensure that the SIGN queries of $\mathcal{A}$ are correctly simulated. It answers FO queries via $\mathbf{G}_{\mathsf{DS}^*, \mathbf{FF}_3}^{\mathrm{uf}}.\mathrm{FO}$. When $\mathcal{A}$ calls $\mathrm{FIN}(M_*, \sigma_*)$, adversary $\mathcal{A}_2$ calls $\mathbf{G}_{\mathsf{DS}^*, \mathbf{FF}_3}^{\mathrm{uf}}.\mathrm{FIN}(M_*, \sigma_*)$. The distribution of signatures that $\mathcal{A}$ is given, and of the keys underlying them, is as in G_2, which explains Eq. (3).

Note that the constructed adversaries having access to oracle FO in their games is important to their ability to simulate $\mathcal{A}$ faithfully.

With regard to the costs (number of queries, running time) of the constructed adversaries, recall that we have defined these as the costs in the execution of the adversary with the game that the adversary is playing, so for example the number of queries to FO includes the ones made by algorithms executed in the game. When this is taken into account, queries to FO are preserved, and the other claims are direct. □

SECURITY OF JCl. We have now reduced the security of $\overline{\mathsf{DS}}$ to that of DS^*. To further reduce the security of DS^* to that of DS, we give a general result on clamping. Let $\mathcal{K} = \mathrm{OUT}(\mathsf{DS.SK})$ and let $\mathsf{CF} : \{0,1\}^k \to \mathcal{K}$ be a clamping function. As per terminology in Sect. 2, recall that $\mathrm{Img}(\mathsf{CF}) = \{\mathsf{CF}(\overline{sk}) : |\overline{sk}| = k\} \subseteq \mathcal{K}$ is the image of the clamping function, and CF is regular if every $y \in \mathrm{Img}(\mathsf{CF})$ has the same number of pre-images under CF.

Theorem 2. *Let* DS *be a signature scheme such that* $\mathsf{DS.SK}$ *draws its signing key* $sk \leftarrow_{\$} \mathcal{K}$ *at random from a set* $\mathcal{K}$. *Let* $\mathsf{CF} : \{0,1\}^k \to \mathcal{K}$ *be a regular clamping function. Let* $\delta = |\mathrm{Img}(\mathsf{CF})|/|\mathcal{K}| > 0$. *Let* $\mathsf{DS}^* = \mathbf{JCl}[\mathsf{DS}, \mathsf{CF}]$ *be the signature scheme obtained by the just-clamp transform. Let* $\mathbf{FF} : \mathsf{SS} \to \mathsf{DS.FS}$ *be any functor. Let* $\mathcal{B}$ *be an adversary attacking the* $\mathbf{G}^{\mathrm{uf}}$ *security of* DS^*. *Then*

$$\mathbf{Adv}_{\mathsf{DS}^*, \mathbf{FF}}^{\mathrm{uf}}(\mathcal{B}) \leq (1/\delta) \cdot \mathbf{Adv}_{\mathsf{DS}, \mathbf{FF}}^{\mathrm{uf}}(\mathcal{B}) .$$

DS.SK:	$\overline{\text{DS}}$.SK:
1 $s \leftarrow_\$ \mathbb{Z}_p$	1 $sk \leftarrow_\$ \{0,1\}^k$; Return sk
2 Return s	$\overline{\text{DS}}$.PK(sk):
DS.PK(s):	2 $e_1\|e_2 \leftarrow H_1(sk)$; $s \leftarrow CF(e_1)$
3 $A \leftarrow s \cdot B$; Return A	3 $A \leftarrow s \cdot B$; Return A
DS.Sign[H](s, A, M):	$\overline{\text{DS}}$.Sign[H](sk, A, M):
4 $r \leftarrow_\$ \mathbb{Z}_p$; $R \leftarrow r \cdot B$	4 $e_1\|e_2 \leftarrow H_1(sk)$; $s \leftarrow CF(e_1)$
5 $c \leftarrow H(R\|A\|M)$	5 $r \leftarrow H_2(e_2, M)$; $R \leftarrow r \cdot B$
6 $z \leftarrow (sc + r) \mod p$	6 $c \leftarrow H_3(R\|A\|M)$
7 Return (R, z)	7 $z \leftarrow (sc + r) \mod p$
DS.Vf[H](A, M, σ):	8 Return (R, z)
8 $(R, z) \leftarrow \sigma$	$\overline{\text{DS}}$.Vf[H](A, M, σ):
9 $c \leftarrow H(R\|A\|M)$	9 $(R, z) \leftarrow \sigma$
10 Return VF(A, R, c, z)	10 $c \leftarrow H_3(R\|A\|M) \mod p$
	11 Return VF(A, R, c, z)

CF(e) // $e \in \{0,1\}^k$:	sVF(A, R, c, z):
12 $t \leftarrow 2^{k-2}$	1 Return $(z \cdot B = c \cdot A + R)$
13 for $i \in [4..k-2]$	
14 $\quad t \leftarrow t + 2^{i-1} \cdot e[i]$	pVF(A, R, c, z):
15 $s \leftarrow t \mod p$	1 Return $2^f(z \cdot B) = 2^f(c \cdot A + R)$
16 return s	

Fig. 4. Top Left: the Schnorr scheme. **Top Right:** The EdDSA scheme. **Bottom Left:** EDDSA clamping function (generalized for any k; in the original definition, $k = 256$). **Bottom Right:** Strict and Permissive verification algorithms as choices for VF.

Proof (Theorem 2). We consider running $\mathcal{B}$ in game $\mathbf{G}^{uf}_{DS,FF}$, where the signing key is $sk \leftarrow_\$ \mathcal{K}$. With probability δ we have $sk \in \text{Img}(CF)$. Due to the regularity of CF, key sk now has the same distribution as a key $CF(\overline{sk})$ for $\overline{sk} \leftarrow_\$ \{0,1\}^k$ drawn in game $\mathbf{G}^{uf}_{DS^*,FF}$. Thus $\mathbf{Adv}^{uf}_{DS,FF}(\mathcal{B}) \geq \delta \cdot \mathbf{Adv}^{uf}_{DS^*,FF}(\mathcal{B})$. $\qquad\square$

5 Security of EdDSA

THE SCHNORR SCHEME. Let the prime-order group $\mathbb{G}_p$ of k-bit strings with generator B be as described in Sect. 2. The algorithms of the Schnorr signature scheme DS = Sch are shown on the left in Fig. 4. The function space DS.FS is $AF(\{0,1\}^*, \mathbb{Z}_p)$. (Implementations may use a hash function that outputs a string and embed the result in $\mathbb{Z}_p$ but following prior proofs [1] we view the hash function as directly mapping into $\mathbb{Z}_p$.) Verification is parameterized by an algorithm VF to allow us to consider strict and permissive verification in a modular way. The corresponding choices of verification algorithms are at the bottom of Fig. 4. The signing randomness space is $\mathsf{DS.SR} = \mathbb{Z}_\mathsf{p}$.

Schnorr signatures have a few variants that differ in details. In Schnorr's paper [40], the challenge is $c = \mathsf{H}(\mathsf{R}\|M) \bmod \mathsf{p}$. Our inclusion of the public key in the input to H follows Bernstein [13] and helps here because it is what EdDSA does. It doesn't affect security. (The security of the scheme that includes the public key in the hash input is implied by the security of the one that doesn't via a reduction that includes the public key in the message.) Also in [40], the signature is (c, z). The version we use, where it is (R, z), is from [1]. However, BBSS [2] shows that these versions have equivalent security.

THE EDDSA SCHEME. Let the prime-order group $\mathbb{G}_\mathsf{p}$ of k-bit strings with generator B be as before and assume $2^{k-5} < \mathsf{p} < 2^k$. Let $\mathsf{CF} : \{0,1\}^k \to \mathbb{Z}_\mathsf{p}$ be the clamping function shown at the bottom of Fig. 4. The algorithms of the scheme $\overline{\mathsf{DS}}$ are shown on the right side of Fig. 4. The key length is k. As before, the verification algorithm VF is a parameter. The H available to the algorithms defines three sub-functions. The first, $\mathsf{H}_1 : \{0,1\}^k \to \{0,1\}^{2k}$, is used at lines 2,4, where its output is parsed into k-bit halves. The second, $\mathsf{H}_2 : \{0,1\}^k \times \{0,1\}^* \to \mathbb{Z}_\mathsf{p}$, is used at line 5 for de-randomization. The third, $\mathsf{H}_3 : \{0,1\}^* \to \mathbb{Z}_\mathsf{p}$, plays the role of the function H for the Schnorr schemes. Formally, $\overline{\mathsf{DS}}.\mathsf{FS}$ is the arity-3 function space consisting of all H mapping as just indicated.

In [14,16], the output of the clamping is an integer that (in our notation) is in the range $2^{k-2}, \ldots, 2^{k-1} - 8$. When used in the scheme, however, it is (implicitly) modulo p. It is convenient for our analysis, accordingly, to define CF to be the result modulo p of the actual clamping. Note that in EdDSA the prime p has magnitude a little more than 2^{k-4} and less than 2^{k-3}.

There are several versions of EdDSA depending on the choice for verification algorithms: strict, permissive or batch VF. We specify the first two choices in Fig. 4. Our results hold for all choices of VF, meaning EdDSA is secure with respect to VF assuming Schnorr is secure with respect to VF. It is in order to make this general claim that we abstract out VF.

SECURITY OF EdDSA WITH INDEPENDENT ROs. As a warm-up, we show security of EdDSA when the three functions it uses are independent random oracles, the setting assumed by BCJZ [16]. However, while they assume hardness of DL, our result is more general, assuming only security of Schnorr with a monolithic random oracle. We can then use known results on Schnorr [1,37] to recover the result of BCJZ [16], but the proof is simpler and more modular. Also, other known results on Schnorr [5,22,39] can be applied to get better bounds. Following this, we will turn to the "real" case, where the three functions are all MD with a random compression function.

The Theorem below is for a general prime $\mathsf{p} > 2^{k-5}$ but in EdDSA the prime is $2^{k-4} < \mathsf{p} < 2^{k-3}$ so the value of δ below is $\delta = 2^{k-5}/\mathsf{p} > 2^{k-5}/2^{k-3} = 1/4$, so the factor $1/\delta$ is ≤ 4. We capture the three functions of EdDSA being independent random oracles by setting functor $\mathbf{P}$ below to the identity functor, and similarly capture Schnorr being with a monolithic random oracle by setting $\mathbf{R}$ to be the identity functor.

Functor $\mathbf{S}_1[\mathsf{h}](sk)$: $/\!\!/$ $|sk| = k$

2 $e \leftarrow \mathbf{MD}[\mathsf{h}](sk)$; Return e $/\!\!/$ $|e| = 2k$

Functor $\mathbf{S}_2[\mathsf{h}](e_2, M)$: $/\!\!/$ $|e_2| = k$

3 Return $\mathbf{MD}[\mathsf{h}](e_2\|M) \bmod \mathsf{p}$

Functor $\mathbf{S}_3[\mathsf{h}](X)$: $/\!\!/$ also called **Mod-MD**

4 Return $\mathbf{MD}[\mathsf{h}](X) \bmod \mathsf{p}$

Fig. 5. The arity-3 functor $\mathbf{S}$ for EdDSA. Here $\mathsf{h} : \{0,1\}^{b+2k} \to \{0,1\}^{2k}$ is a compression function.

Theorem 3. *Let* DS *be the* Schnorr *signature scheme of Fig. 4. Let* CF: $\{0,1\}^k \to \mathbb{Z}_\mathsf{p}$ *be the clamping function of Fig. 4. Assume* $\mathsf{p} > 2^{k-5}$ *and let* $\delta = 2^{k-5}/\mathsf{p}$. *Let* $\overline{\mathsf{DS}} = \mathbf{DtD}[\mathsf{DS}, \mathsf{CF}]$ *be the* EdDSA *signature scheme. Let* $\mathbf{R} : \mathsf{AF}(\{0,1\}^*, \mathbb{Z}_\mathsf{p}) \to \mathsf{AF}(\{0,1\}^*, \mathbb{Z}_\mathsf{p})$ *be the identity functor. Let* $\mathbf{P} : \overline{\mathsf{DS}}.\mathsf{FS} \to \overline{\mathsf{DS}}.\mathsf{FS}$ *be the identity functor. Let* $\mathcal{A}$ *be an adversary attacking the* $\mathbf{G}^{\mathrm{uf}}$ *security of* $\overline{\mathsf{DS}}$. *Then there is an adversary* $\mathcal{B}$ *such that*

$$\mathbf{Adv}^{\mathrm{uf}}_{\overline{\mathsf{DS}},\mathbf{P}}(\mathcal{A}) \leq (1/\delta) \cdot \mathbf{Adv}^{\mathrm{uf}}_{\mathsf{DS},\mathbf{R}}(\mathcal{B}) + \frac{2 \cdot Q^{\mathcal{A}}_{\mathrm{FO}}}{2^k} .$$

Adversary $\mathcal{B}$ *preserves the queries and running time of* $\mathcal{A}$.

Proof (Theorem 3). Let $\mathsf{DS}^* = \mathbf{JCl}[\mathsf{Sch}, \mathsf{CF}]$. By Theorem 1, we have

$$\mathbf{Adv}^{\mathrm{uf}}_{\overline{\mathsf{DS}},\mathbf{P}}(\mathcal{A}) \leq \mathbf{Adv}^{\mathrm{prg}}_{\mathbf{P}_1}(\mathcal{A}_1) + \mathbf{Adv}^{\mathrm{prf}}_{\mathbf{P}_2}(\mathcal{A}_2) + \mathbf{Adv}^{\mathrm{uf}}_{\mathsf{DS}^*,\mathbf{P}_3}(\mathcal{A}_3) .$$

It is easy to see that

$$\mathbf{Adv}^{\mathrm{prg}}_{\mathbf{P}_1}(\mathcal{A}_1) \leq \frac{Q^{\mathcal{A}_1}_{\mathrm{FO}}}{2^k} = \frac{Q^{\mathcal{A}}_{\mathrm{FO}}}{2^k}$$

$$\mathbf{Adv}^{\mathrm{prf}}_{\mathbf{P}_2}(\mathcal{A}_2) \leq \frac{Q^{\mathcal{A}_2}_{\mathrm{FO}}}{2^k} = \frac{Q^{\mathcal{A}}_{\mathrm{FO}}}{2^k} .$$

Under the assumption $\mathsf{p} > 2^{k-5}$ made in the theorem, BCJZ [16] established that $|\mathrm{Img}(\mathsf{CF})| = 2^{k-5}$. So $|\mathrm{Img}(\mathsf{CF})|/|\mathbb{Z}_\mathsf{p}| = 2^{k-5}/\mathsf{p} = \delta$. Let $\mathcal{B} = \mathcal{A}_3$ and note that $\mathbf{P}_3 = \mathbf{R}$. So by Theorem 2 we have

$$\mathbf{Adv}^{\mathrm{uf}}_{\mathsf{DS}^*,\mathbf{P}_3}(\mathcal{A}_3) \leq (1/\delta) \cdot \mathbf{Adv}^{\mathrm{uf}}_{\mathsf{DS},\mathbf{R}}(\mathcal{B}) . \qquad (4)$$

Collecting terms, we obtain the claimed bound stated in Theorem 3. $\qquad \square$

ANALYSIS OF THE $\mathbf{S}$ FUNCTOR. Let $\overline{\mathsf{DS}}$ be the result of the $\mathbf{DtD}$ transform applied to Sch and a clamping function $\mathsf{CF}: \{0,1\}^k \to \mathbb{Z}_\mathsf{p}$. Security of EdDSA is captured as security in game $\mathbf{G}^{\mathrm{uf}}_{\overline{\mathsf{DS}},\mathbf{S}}$ when $\mathbf{S}$ is the functor that builds the component hash functions in the way that EdDSA does, namely from a MD-hash function. To evaluate this security, we start by defining the functor $\mathbf{S}$ in

Games G_0, $\boxed{G_1}$ INIT:

  1 $sk \leftarrow\!\!\$\ \{0,1\}^k$; $e \leftarrow\!\!\$\ \{0,1\}^{2k}$
  2 Return e

FO(X):

  3 If $\mathrm{FT}[X] \neq \bot$ then return $\mathrm{FT}[X]$
  4 $Y \leftarrow\!\!\$\ \{0,1\}^{2k}$
  5 If $X = IV\|sk\|P$ then bad $\leftarrow$ true ; $\boxed{Y \leftarrow e}$
  6 $\mathrm{FT}[X] \leftarrow Y$; Return $\mathrm{FT}[X]$

FIN(c'):

  7 Return ($c' = 1$)

Fig. 6. Games G_0 and G_1 in the proof of Lemma 4. Boxed code is only in G_1.

Fig. 5. It is an arity-3 functor, and we separately specify $\mathbf{S}_1, \mathbf{S}_2, \mathbf{S}_3$. (Functor $\mathbf{S}_3$ will be called **Mod-MD** in later analyses.) The starting space, from which h is drawn, is $\mathsf{AF}(\{0,1\}^{b+2k}, \{0,1\}^{2k})$, the set of compression functions. The prime p is as before, and is public.

We want to establish the three assumptions of Theorem 1. Namely: (1) $\mathbf{S}_1$ is PRG-secure (2) $\mathbf{S}_2$ is PRF secure and (3) security holds in game $\mathbf{G}^{\mathrm{uf}}_{\mathsf{Sch}^*, \mathbf{S}_3}$ where $\mathsf{Sch}^* = \mathbf{JCl}[\mathsf{Sch}, \mathsf{CF}]$. Bridging from Sch^* to Sch itself will use Theorem 2.

Lemma 4. *Let functor* $\mathbf{S}_1 : \mathsf{AF}(\{0,1\}^{b+2k}, \{0,1\}^{2k}) \to \mathsf{AF}(\{0,1\}^k, \{0,1\}^{2k})$ *be defined as in Fig. 5. Let* $\mathcal{A}_1$ *be an adversary. Then*

$$\mathbf{Adv}^{\mathrm{prg}}_{\mathbf{S}_1}(\mathcal{A}_1) \leq \frac{\mathrm{Q}^{\mathcal{A}_1}_{\mathrm{FO}}}{2^k} \qquad (5)$$

Proof (Lemma 4). Since the input sk to $\mathbf{S}_1[\mathsf{h}]$ is k-bits long, the **MD** transform defined in Sect. 3 only iterates once and the output is $e = \mathsf{h}(IV\|sk\|P)$, for padding $P \in \{0,1\}^{3k}$ and initialization vector $IV \in \{0,1\}^{2k}$ that are fixed and known. Now consider the games in Fig. 6, where the boxed code is only in G_1. Then we have

$$\mathbf{Adv}^{\mathrm{prg}}_{\mathbf{S}_1}(\mathcal{A}_1) = \Pr[G_1(\mathcal{A}_1)] - \Pr[G_0(\mathcal{A}_1)]$$
$$\leq \Pr[G_0(\mathcal{A}_1) \text{ sets bad}]$$
$$\leq \frac{\mathrm{Q}^{\mathcal{A}_1}_{\mathrm{FO}}}{2^k} .$$

The second line above is by the Fundamental Lemma of Game Playing, which applies since G_0, G_1 are identical-until-bad. $\qquad \square$

Lemma 5. *Let functor* $\mathbf{S}_2 : \mathsf{AF}(\{0,1\}^{b+2k}, \{0,1\}^{2k}) \to \mathsf{AF}(\{0,1\}^k \times \{0,1\}^*, \mathbb{Z}_p)$ *be defined as in Fig. 5. Let ℓ be an integer such that all messages queried to* FO *are no more than $b \cdot (\ell - 1) - k$ bits long. Let $\mathcal{A}_2$ be an adversary. Then*

$$\mathbf{Adv}_{\mathbf{S}_2}^{\mathrm{prf}}(\mathcal{A}_2) \leq \frac{Q_{\mathrm{FO}}^{\mathcal{A}_2}}{2^k} + \frac{2p(q_{\mathrm{FO}}^{\mathcal{A}_2} + \ell Q_{\mathrm{FN}}^{\mathcal{A}_2})}{2^{2k}} + \frac{(q_{\mathrm{FO}}^{\mathcal{A}_2} + \ell Q_{\mathrm{FN}}^{\mathcal{A}_2})^2}{2^{2k}} + \frac{p q_{\mathrm{FO}}^{\mathcal{A}_2} \cdot \ell Q_{\mathrm{FN}}^{\mathcal{A}_2}}{2^{2k}}.$$

Proof (Lemma 5). In Sect. 6, we prove the indifferentiability of functor $\mathbf{S}_3$ (c.f. Figure 5), which we also call **Mod-MD**. Define $\mathbf{R} : \mathsf{AF}(\{0,1\}^*, \mathbb{Z}_p) \to \mathsf{AF}(\{0,1\}^k \times \{0,1\}^*, \mathbb{Z}_p)$ to be the identity functor such that $\mathbf{R}[\mathsf{H}](x, y) = \mathsf{H}(x \,\|\, y)$ for all x, y, H in the appropriate domains. Notice that when $\mathbf{R}$ is given access to the **Mod-MD** functor as its oracle, the resulting functor is exactly $\mathbf{S}_2$. Using this property, we will reduce the PRF security of functor $\mathbf{S}_2$ to the indifferentiability of **Mod-MD**.

For any simulator algorithm $\mathcal{S}$, the indifferentiability composition theorem [30] grants the existence of distinguisher $\mathcal{D}$ and adversary $\mathcal{A}_5$ such that

$$\mathbf{Adv}_{\mathbf{S}_2}^{\mathrm{prf}}(\mathcal{A}_2) \leq \mathbf{Adv}_{\mathbf{R}}^{\mathrm{prf}}(\mathcal{A}_5) + \mathbf{Adv}_{\mathbf{Mod\text{-}MD}, \mathcal{S}}^{\mathrm{indiff}}(\mathcal{D}).$$

We let $\mathcal{S}$ be the simulator guaranteed by Theorem 8 and separately bound each of these terms. Adversary $\mathcal{A}_5$ simulates the PRF game for its challenger $\mathcal{A}_2$ by forwarding all FN queries to its own FN oracle and answering FO queries using the simulator, which has access to the FO oracle of $\mathcal{A}_5$. Since the simulator is efficient and makes at most one query to its oracle each time it is run, we can say the runtime of $\mathcal{A}_5$ is approximately the same as that of $\mathcal{A}_2$. $\mathcal{A}_5$ makes the same number of FN and FO queries as $\mathcal{A}_2$.

Next, we want to compute $\mathbf{Adv}_{\mathbf{R}}^{\mathrm{prf}}(\mathcal{A}_5)$. When $\mathbf{R}$ is evaluated with access to a random function h, its outputs are random unless the adversary makes a relevant query involving the secret key. The adversary can only distinguish if the output of FN is randomly sampled or from $\mathbf{R}[\mathsf{h}]$ if it queries FO on the k-bit secret key (e_2), which has probability $\frac{1}{2^k}$ for a single query. Taking a union bound over all FO queries, we have

$$\mathbf{Adv}_{\mathbf{R}}^{\mathrm{prf}}(\mathcal{A}_5) \leq \frac{Q_{\mathrm{FO}}^{\mathcal{A}_2}}{2^k}.$$

Distinguisher $\mathcal{D}$ simulates the PRF game for $\mathcal{A}_2$, by replacing functor **Mod-MD** with its own PRIV oracle within the FN oracle and forwarding $\mathcal{A}_2$'s direct FO queries to PUB. $\mathcal{D}$ hence makes $Q_{\mathcal{A}_2}^{\mathrm{FN}}$ queries to PRIV of maximum length $b \cdot (\ell - 1)$ and $q_{\mathcal{A}_2}^{\mathrm{FO}}$ to PUB. To bound the second term, we apply Theorem 8 on the indifferentiability of shrink-MD transforms. This theorem is parameterized by two numbers γ and ϵ; in Sect. 6, we show that **Mod-MD** belongs to the shrink-MD class for $\gamma = \lfloor \frac{2^{2k}}{p} \rfloor$ and $\epsilon = \frac{p}{2^{2k}}$. Then the theorem gives

$$\mathbf{Adv}_{\mathbf{Mod\text{-}MD}, \mathcal{S}}^{\mathrm{indiff}}(\mathcal{D}) \leq 2(Q_{\mathrm{PUB}}^{\mathcal{D}} + \ell Q_{\mathrm{PRIV}}^{\mathcal{D}})\epsilon + \frac{(Q_{\mathrm{PUB}}^{\mathcal{D}} + \ell Q_{\mathrm{PRIV}}^{\mathcal{D}})^2}{2^{2k}} + \frac{Q_{\mathrm{PUB}}^{\mathcal{D}} \cdot \ell Q_{\mathrm{PRIV}}^{\mathcal{D}}}{\gamma}.$$

By substituting $Q_{\mathrm{PUB}}^{\mathcal{D}} = q_{\mathrm{FO}}^{\mathcal{A}_2}$ and $Q_{\mathrm{PRIV}}^{\mathcal{D}} = Q_{\mathrm{FN}}^{\mathcal{A}_2}$, we obtain the bound stated in the theorem. $\square$

The following considers the UF security of $\mathsf{DS}^* = \mathbf{JCl}[\mathsf{Sch}, \mathsf{CF}]$ with the hash function being an MD one, and reduces this to the UF security of the same scheme with the hash function being a monolithic random oracle. Formally, the latter is captured by game $\mathbf{G}^{\mathrm{uf}}_{\mathsf{DS}^*, \mathbf{R}}$ where $\mathbf{R}$ is the identity functor.

Lemma 6. *Let functor* $\mathbf{S}_3 : \mathsf{AF}(\{0,1\}^{b+2k}, \{0,1\}^{2k}) \rightarrow \mathsf{AF}(\{0,1\}^*, \mathbb{Z}_\mathsf{p})$ *be defined as in Fig. 5. Assume* $2^k > \mathsf{p}$. *Let* $\mathsf{DS}^* = \mathbf{JCl}[\mathsf{Sch}, \mathsf{CF}]$ *where* $\mathsf{CF} : \{0,1\}^k \rightarrow \mathbb{Z}_p$ *is a clamping function. Let* $\mathbf{R} : \mathsf{AF}(\{0,1\}^*, \mathbb{Z}_\mathsf{p}) \rightarrow \mathsf{AF}(\{0,1\}^*, \mathbb{Z}_\mathsf{p})$ *be the identity functor, meaning* $\mathbf{R}[\mathsf{H}] = \mathsf{H}$. *Let* $\mathcal{A}_3$ *be a* $\mathbf{G}^{\mathrm{uf}}$ *adversary making* $\mathrm{Q}^{\mathcal{A}_3}_{\mathrm{FO}}, \mathrm{Q}^{\mathcal{A}_3}_{\mathrm{SIGN}}$ *queries to its respective oracles, and let* ℓ *be an integer such that the maximum message length* $\mathcal{A}_3$ *queries to* SIGN *is at most* $b \cdot (\ell - 1) - 2k$ *bits. Then we can construct adversary* $\mathcal{A}_4$ *such that*

$$\mathbf{Adv}^{\mathrm{uf}}_{\mathsf{DS}^*, \mathbf{S}_3}(\mathcal{A}_3) \leq \mathbf{Adv}^{\mathrm{uf}}_{\mathsf{DS}^*, \mathbf{R}}(\mathcal{A}_4) + \frac{2\mathsf{p}(q^{\mathcal{A}_3}_{\mathrm{FO}} + \ell \mathrm{Q}^{\mathcal{A}_3}_{\mathrm{SIGN}})}{2^{2k}} \tag{6}$$

$$+ \frac{(q^{\mathcal{A}_3}_{\mathrm{FO}} + \ell \mathrm{Q}^{\mathcal{A}_3}_{\mathrm{SIGN}})^2}{2^{2k}} + \frac{\mathsf{p}q^{\mathcal{A}_3}_{\mathrm{FO}} \cdot \ell \mathrm{Q}^{\mathcal{A}_3}_{\mathrm{SIGN}}}{2^{2k}}. \tag{7}$$

Adversary $\mathcal{A}_4$ *has approximately equal runtime and query complexity to* $\mathcal{A}_3$.

Proof (Theorem 6). Again, we rely on the indifferentiability of functor $\mathbf{S}_3 = $ **Mod-MD**, as shown in Sect. 6. The general indifferentiability composition theorem [30] states that for any simulator $\mathcal{S}$ and adversary $\mathcal{A}_3$, there exist distinguisher $\mathcal{D}$ and adversary $\mathcal{A}_4$ such that

$$\mathbf{Adv}^{\mathrm{uf}}_{\mathsf{DS}^*, \mathbf{S}_3}(\mathcal{A}_3) \leq \mathbf{Adv}^{\mathrm{uf}}_{\mathsf{DS}^*, \mathbf{R}}(\mathcal{A}_4) + \mathbf{Adv}^{\mathrm{indiff}}_{\mathbf{S}_3, \mathcal{S}}(\mathcal{D}).$$

Let $\mathcal{S}$ be the simulator whose existence is implied by Theorem 8. The distinguisher runs the unforgeability game for its adversary, replacing $\mathbf{S}_3[\mathrm{FO}]$ in scheme algorithms and adversarial FO queries with its PRIV and PUB oracles respectively. It makes $q^{\mathcal{A}_3}_{\mathrm{FO}}$ queries to PUB and $\mathrm{Q}^{\mathcal{A}_3}_{\mathrm{SIGN}}$ queries to PRIV, and the maximum length of any query to PRIV is $b \cdot (\ell - 1)$ bits because each element of group $\mathbb{G}_\mathsf{p}$ is a k-bit string (c.f. Section 2). We apply Theorem 8 to obtain the bound

$$\mathbf{Adv}^{\mathrm{indiff}}_{\mathbf{S}_3, \mathcal{S}}(\mathcal{D}) \leq 2(q^{\mathcal{A}_3}_{\mathrm{FO}} + \ell \mathrm{Q}^{\mathcal{A}_3}_{\mathrm{SIGN}})\epsilon + \frac{(q^{\mathcal{A}_3}_{\mathrm{FO}} + \ell \mathrm{Q}^{\mathcal{A}_3}_{\mathrm{SIGN}})^2}{2^{2k}} + \frac{q^{\mathcal{A}_3}_{\mathrm{FO}} \cdot \ell \mathrm{Q}^{\mathcal{A}_3}_{\mathrm{SIGN}}}{\gamma}.$$

Adversary $\mathcal{A}_4$ is a wrapper for $\mathcal{A}_3$, which answers all of its queries to FO by running $\mathcal{S}$ with access to its own FO oracle; since the simulator runs in constant time and makes only one query to its oracle, the runtime and query complexity approximately equal those of $\mathcal{A}_3$.

Substituting $\frac{1}{\gamma} \geq \frac{\mathsf{p}}{2^{2k}}$ and $\epsilon = \frac{\mathsf{p}}{2^{2k}}$ gives the bound. □

SECURITY OF EdDSA WITH MD. We now want to conclude security of EdDSA, with an MD-hash function, assuming security of Schnorr with a monolithic random oracle. The Theorem is for a general prime p in the range $2^k > \mathsf{p} > 2^{k-5}$ but in EdDSA the prime is $2^{k-4} < \mathsf{p} < 2^{k-3}$ so the value of δ below is

$\delta = 2^{k-5}/p > 2^{k-5}/2^{k-3} = 1/4$, so the factor $1/\delta$ is ≤ 4. Again recall our convention that query counts of an adversary include those made by oracles in its game, implying for example that $Q_{FO}^{\mathcal{A}} \geq Q_{SIGN}^{\mathcal{A}}$.

Theorem 7. *Let* DS *be the* Schnorr *signature scheme of Fig. 4. Let* CF $: \{0,1\}^k$ $\rightarrow \mathbb{Z}_p$ *be the clamping function of Fig. 4. Assume* $2^k > p > 2^{k-5}$ *and let* $\delta = 2^{k-5}/p$. *Let* $\overline{DS} = DtD[DS, CF]$ *be the* EdDSA *signature scheme. Let* $\mathbf{R} : AF(\{0,1\}^*, \mathbb{Z}_p) \rightarrow AF(\{0,1\}^*, \mathbb{Z}_p)$ *be the identity functor. Let* $\mathbf{S}$ *be the functor of Fig. 5. Let* $\mathcal{A}$ *be an adversary attacking the* $\mathbf{G}^{uf}$ *security of* $\overline{DS}$. *Again let* $b \cdot (\ell - 1) - 2k$ *be the maximum length in bits of a message input to* SIGN. *Then there is an adversary* $\mathcal{B}$ *such that*

$$\mathbf{Adv}_{\overline{DS},\mathbf{S}}^{uf}(\mathcal{A}) \leq (1/\delta) \cdot \mathbf{Adv}_{DS,\mathbf{R}}^{uf}(\mathcal{B}) + \frac{Q_{FO}^{\mathcal{A}}}{2^{k-1}} + \frac{p(q_{FO}^{\mathcal{A}} + \ell Q_{SIGN}^{\mathcal{A}})}{2^{2k-2}}$$
$$+ \frac{(q_{FO}^{\mathcal{A}} + \ell Q_{SIGN}^{\mathcal{A}_2})^2}{2^{2k-1}} + \frac{p q_{FO}^{\mathcal{A}} \cdot \ell Q_{SIGN}^{\mathcal{A}}}{2^{2k-1}} .$$

Adversary $\mathcal{B}$ *preserves the queries and running time of* $\mathcal{A}$.

Proof (Theorem 7). Let $DS^* = JCl[Sch, CF]$. By Theorem 1, we have

$$\mathbf{Adv}_{\overline{DS},\mathbf{S}}^{uf}(\mathcal{A}) \leq \mathbf{Adv}_{\mathbf{S}_1}^{prg}(\mathcal{A}_1) + \mathbf{Adv}_{\mathbf{S}_2}^{prf}(\mathcal{A}_2) + \mathbf{Adv}_{DS^*,\mathbf{S}_3}^{uf}(\mathcal{A}_3).$$

Now applying Lemma 4, we have

$$\mathbf{Adv}_{\mathbf{S}_1}^{prg}(\mathcal{A}_1) \leq \frac{Q_{FO}^{\mathcal{A}}}{2^k} .$$

Applying Lemma 5, we have

$$\mathbf{Adv}_{\mathbf{S}_2}^{prf}(\mathcal{A}_2) \leq \frac{Q_{FO}^{\mathcal{A}_2}}{2^k} + \frac{2p(q_{FO}^{\mathcal{A}_2} + \ell Q_{FN}^{\mathcal{A}_2})}{2^{2k}} + \frac{(q_{FO}^{\mathcal{A}_2} + \ell Q_{FN}^{\mathcal{A}_2})^2}{2^{2k}} + \frac{p q_{FO}^{\mathcal{A}_2} \cdot \ell Q_{FN}^{\mathcal{A}_2}}{2^{2k}}.$$

We substitute $Q_{FO}^{\mathcal{A}_2} = Q_{FO}^{\mathcal{A}}$, $q_{FO}^{\mathcal{A}_2} = q_{FO}^{\mathcal{A}}$ and $Q_{FN}^{\mathcal{A}_2} = Q_{SIGN}^{\mathcal{A}}$. By Lemma 6 we obtain

$$\mathbf{Adv}_{DS^*,\mathbf{S}_3}^{uf}(\mathcal{A}_3) \leq \mathbf{Adv}_{DS^*,\mathbf{R}}^{uf}(\mathcal{B}) + \frac{2p(Q_{FO}^{\mathcal{A}_3} + \ell Q_{SIGN}^{\mathcal{A}_3})}{2^{2k}}$$
$$+ \frac{(Q_{FO}^{\mathcal{A}_3} + \ell Q_{SIGN}^{\mathcal{A}_3})^2}{2^{2k}} + \frac{p Q_{FO}^{\mathcal{A}_3} \cdot \ell Q_{SIGN}^{\mathcal{A}_3}}{2^{2k}} .$$

Recall that adversary $\mathcal{A}_3$ has the same query complexity as $\mathcal{A}$.

Under the assumption $p > 2^{k-5}$ made in the theorem, BCJZ [16] established that $|Img(CF)| = 2^{k-5}$. So $|Img(CF)|/|\mathbb{Z}_p| = 2^{k-5}/p = \delta$. So by Theorem 2 we have

$$\mathbf{Adv}_{DS^*,\mathbf{R}}^{uf}(\mathcal{B}) \leq (1/\delta) \cdot \mathbf{Adv}_{DS,\mathbf{R}}^{uf}(\mathcal{B}) . \tag{8}$$

By substituting with the number of queries made by $\mathcal{A}$ as in Theorem 1 and collecting terms, we obtain the claimed bound stated in Theorem 7. $\square$

We can now obtain security of EdDSA under number-theoretic assumptions via known results on the security of Schnorr. Namely, we use the known results to bound $\mathbf{Adv}_{\mathsf{DS},\mathbf{R}}^{\mathrm{uf}}(\mathcal{B})$ above. From [1,37] we can get a bound and proof based on the DL problems, and from [39] with a better bound. We can also get an almost tight bound under the MBDL assumption via [5] and a tight bound in the AGM via [22].

6   Indifferentiability of Shrink-MD Class of Functors

INDIFFERENTIABILITY. We want the tuple of functions returned by a functor $\mathbf{F} : \mathsf{SS} \to \mathsf{ES}$ to be able to "replace" a tuple drawn directly from ES. Indifferentiability is a way of defining what this means. We adapt the original MRH definition of indifferentiability [30] to our game-based model in Fig. 7. In this game, $\mathcal{S}$ is a simulator algorithm. The advantage of an adversary $\mathcal{A}$ against the indifferentiability of functor $\mathbf{F}$ with respect to simulator $\mathcal{S}$ is defined to be

$$\mathbf{Adv}_{\mathbf{F},\mathcal{S}}^{\mathrm{indiff}}(\mathcal{A}) := 2\Pr[\mathbf{G}_{\mathbf{F},\mathcal{S}}^{\mathrm{indiff}}(\mathcal{A}) \Rightarrow 1] - 1.$$

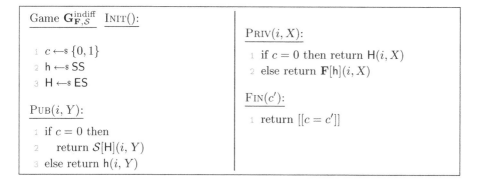

Fig. 7. The game $\mathbf{G}_{\mathbf{F},\mathcal{S}}^{\mathrm{indiff}}$ measuring indifferentiability of a functor $\mathbf{F}$ with respect to simulator $\mathcal{S}$.

MODIFYING THE MERKLE-DAMGÅRD TRANSFORM. Coron et al. showed that the Merkle-Damgård transform is not indifferentiable with respect to any efficient simulator due to its susceptibility to length-extension attacks [19]. In the same work, they analysed the indifferentiability of several closely related indifferentiable constructions, including the "chop-MD" construction. Chop-MD is a functor with the same domain as the MD transform; it simply truncates a specified number of bits from the output of MD. The $\mathbf{S}_3$ functor of Fig. 5 operates similarly to the chop-MD functor, except that $\mathbf{S}_3$ reduces the output modulo a prime p instead of truncating. This small change introduces some bias into the resulting construction that affects its indifferentiability due to the fact that the outputs of the MD transform, which are $2k$-bit strings, are not distributed uniformly over $\mathbb{Z}_p$.

In this section, we establish indifferentiability for a general class of functors that includes both chop-MD and $\mathbf{S}_3$. We rely on the indifferentiability of $\mathbf{S}_3$ in Sect. 5 as a stepping-stone to the unforgeability of EdDSA; however, we think our proof for chop-MD is of independent interest and improves upon prior work.

The original analysis of the chop-MD construction [19] was set in the ideal cipher model and accounted for some of the structure of the underlying compression function. A later proof by Fischlin and Mittelbach [32] adapts the proof strategy to the simpler construction we address here and works in the random oracle model as we do. Both proofs, however, contain a subtle gap in the way they use their simulators.

At a high level, both proofs define stateful simulators S which simulate a random compression function by sampling uniform answers to some queries and programming others with the help of their random oracles. These simulators are not perfect, and fail with some probability that the proofs bound. In the ideal indifferentiability game, the PUB oracle answers queries using the simulator and the PRIV oracle answers queries using a random oracle. Both proofs at some point replace the random oracle H in PRIV with **Chop-MD**[S] and claim that because **Chop-MD**[S[H]](X) will always return H(X) if the simulator does not fail, the adversary cannot detect the change. This argument is not quite true, because the additional queries to S made by the PRIV oracle can affect its internal state and prevent the simulator from failing when it would have in the previous game. In our proof, we avoid this issue with a novel simulator with *two internal states* to enforce separation between PRIV and PUB queries that both run the simulator.

Our result establishes indifferentiability for all members of the **Shrink-MD** class of functors, which includes any functor built by composing of the MD transform with a function $\mathsf{Out} : \{0,1\}^{2k} \to S$ that satisfies three conditions, namely that for some $\gamma, \epsilon \geq 0$,

1. For all $y \in S$, we can efficiently sample from the uniform distribution on the preimage set $\{\mathsf{Out}^{-1}(y)\}$. We permit the sampling algorithm to fail with probability at most ϵ, but require that upon failure the algorithm outputs a (not necessarily random) element of $\{\mathsf{Out}^{-1}(y)\}$.
2. For all $y \in S$, it holds that $\gamma \leq |\{\mathsf{Out}^{-1}(y)\}|$.
3. The statistical distance $\delta(D)$ between the distribution

$$D := z \leftarrow_\$ \mathsf{Out}^{-1}(y) : y \leftarrow_\$ S$$

and the uniform distribution on $\{0,1\}^{2k}$ is bounded above by ϵ.

In principle, we wish γ to be large and ϵ to be small; if this is so, then the set S will be substantially smaller than $\{0,1\}^{2k}$ and the function Out "shrinks" its domain by mapping it onto a smaller set.

Both chop-MD and mod-MD are members of the **Shrink-MD** class of functors; we briefly show the functions that perform bit truncation and modular reduction by a prime satisfy our three conditions. Truncation by any number of bits trivially satisfies condition (1) with $\epsilon = 0$.

Reduction modulo p also satisfies condition (1) because the following algorithm samples from the equivalence class of x modulo p with failure probability at most $\frac{p}{2^{2k}}$. Let ℓ be the smallest integer such that $\ell > \frac{2^{2k}}{p}$. Sample $w \leftarrow_\$ [0 \ldots \ell-1]$ and output $w \cdot p + x$, or x if $w \cdot p + x > 2^{2k}$. We say this algorithm "fails" in the latter case, which occurs with probability at most $\frac{1}{\ell} < \frac{p}{2^{2k}}$. In the event the algorithm does not fail, it outputs a uniform element of the equivalence class of x.

Bellare et al. showed that the truncation of n trailing bits satisfies condition (2) for $\gamma = 2^{2k-n}$ and reduction modulo prime p satisfies (2) for $\gamma = \lfloor 2^{2k}/p \rfloor$. It is clear that sampling from the preimages of a random $2k - n$-bit string under n-bit truncation produces a uniform $2k$-bit string, so truncation satisfies condition (3) with $\epsilon = 0$. Also from Bellare et al. [3], we have that the statistical distance between a uniform element of $\mathbb{Z}_p$ and the modular reduction of a uniform $2k$-bit string is $\epsilon = \frac{p}{2^{2k}}$. The statistical distance of our distribution $z \leftarrow_\$ \mathsf{Out}^{-1}(Y)$ for uniform Y over S from the uniform distribution over $\{0,1\}^{2k}$ is bounded above by the same ϵ; hence condition (3) holds.

Given a set S and a function $\mathsf{Out} : \{0,1\}^{2k} \to S$, we define the functor $\mathbf{F}_{S,\mathsf{Out}}$ as the composition of Out with $\mathbf{MD}$. In other words, for any $x \in \{0,1\}^*$ and $h \in \mathsf{AF}(\{0,1\}^{b+2k}, \{0,1\}^{2k})$, let $\mathbf{F}_{S,\mathsf{Out}}[h](x) := \mathsf{Out}(\mathbf{MD}[h](x))$.

Theorem 8. *Let k be an integer and S a set of bitstrings. Let $\mathsf{Out} : \{0,1\}^{2k} \to S$ be a function satisfying conditions (1), (2), and (3) above with respect to $\gamma, \epsilon > 0$. Let $\mathbf{MD}$ be the Merkle-Damgård functor(c.f. Section 2) $\mathbf{F}_{S,\mathsf{Out}} := \mathsf{Out} \circ \mathbf{MD}$ be the functor described in the prior paragraph. Let pad be the padding function used by $\mathbf{MD}$, and let unpad be the function that removes padding from its input (i.e., for all $X \in \{0,1\}^*$, it holds that $\mathsf{unpad}(X \parallel \mathsf{pad}(|X|)) = X$). Assume that unpad returns $\perp$ if its input is incorrectly padded and that unpad is injective on its support. Then there exists a simulator $\mathcal{S}$ such that for any adversary $\mathcal{A}$ making PRIV queries of maximum length $b \cdot (\ell - 1)$ bits then*

$$\mathbf{Adv}_{\mathbf{F},\mathcal{S}}^{\mathrm{indiff}}(\mathcal{A}) \leq 2(Q_{\mathrm{PUB}}^{\mathcal{A}} + \ell Q_{\mathrm{PRIV}}^{\mathcal{A}})\epsilon + \frac{(Q_{\mathrm{PUB}}^{\mathcal{A}} + \ell Q_{\mathrm{PRIV}}^{\mathcal{A}})^2}{2^{2k}} + \frac{Q_{\mathrm{PUB}}^{\mathcal{A}} \cdot \ell Q_{\mathrm{PRIV}}^{\mathcal{A}}}{\gamma}.$$

We prove the theorem in the game-based framework in our full version [6]. Here, we give a brief overview of our proof strategy and its differences from previous indifferentiability proofs for the chop-MD construction [19,32].

Our simulator, $\mathcal{S}$, is defined in Fig. 8. It is inspired by, but distinct from, that of Mittelbach and Fischlin's simulator for the chop-MD construction ([32] Fig. 17.4.), which in turn adapts the simulator of Coron et al. [19] from the ideal cipher model to the random oracle model. These simulators all present the interface of a random compression function h and internally maintain a graph in which each edge represents an input-output pair under the simulated compression function. The intention is that each path through this graph will represent a possible evaluation of $\mathbf{F}_{S,\mathsf{Out}}[h]$. The fundamental difference between our simulator and previous ones is that we maintain two internal graphs instead of one: one graph for all queries, and one graph for public interface queries only.

This novel method of using two graphs avoids the gap in prior proofs described above by tracking precisely which parts of the simulator's state are influenced by private and public interface queries respectively.

In our proof, we transform the ideal indifferentiability game by evaluating our functor $\mathbf{F}$ in each query to the PRIV oracle. Initially, we discard the output of this evaluation and use a separate graph in our simulator so that these additional queries do not influence the PUB oracle. In later games, we bound the probability that the private queries influence the public graph in a way that is detectable by the adversary (such as creating collisions, cycles, or duplicate edges in the public simulator's graph), and begin using the same graph for both types of query. We also claim that if the graph is free of collisions, cycles, and duplicate edges, then we can respond to PRIV queries with the evaluation of $\mathbf{F}$ without detection. We then use the statistical closeness of sampling a random preimage of a random element (property (3) of Out) to argue that our simulator is honestly behaving as a random oracle except with some small probability. The resulting game is then equivalent to the real indifferentiability game, and the theorem follows by collecting the bounded differences between each pair of adjacent games.

Simulator $\mathcal{S}[\mathsf{H}](Y, \mathcal{G})$:

1 $(y, m) \leftarrow Y$
2 if $\exists z$ such that $(y, z, m) \in \mathcal{G}.\mathsf{edges}$
3   return z
4 $M \leftarrow \mathcal{G}.\mathrm{FindPath}(IV, y)$
5 if $M \neq \bot$ and $\mathsf{unpad}(M \parallel m) \neq \bot$ then
6   if $\mathrm{T_h}[Y, M] \neq \bot$ then $z \leftarrow \mathrm{T_h}[Y, M]$
7   else $z \leftarrow_\$ \mathsf{Out}^{-1}(\mathsf{H}(\mathsf{unpad}(M \parallel m)))$
8      $\mathrm{T_h}[Y, M] \leftarrow z$
9 else if $\mathrm{T_h}[Y] \neq \bot$ then $z \leftarrow \mathrm{T_h}[Y]$
10 else $z \leftarrow_\$ \{0, 1\}^{2k}$; $\mathrm{T_h}[Y] \leftarrow z$
11 add (y, z, m) to $\mathcal{G}.\mathsf{edges}$
12 add (y, z, m) to $\mathcal{G}_{\mathtt{all}}.\mathsf{edges}$
13 return z

Fig. 8. Indifferentiability simulator for the proof of Theorem 8.

Acknowledgments. Bellare and Davis are supported in part by NSF grant CNS-2154272. We thank the (anonymous) reviewers of Crypto 2022, Asiacrypt 2022 and CT-RSA 2023 for their valuable comments. We thank Joseph Jaeger for his helpful comments and discussions about the correctness of chop-MD proofs in the literature.

References

1. Abdalla, M., An, J.H., Bellare, M., Namprempre, C.: From identification to signatures via the fiat-shamir transform: minimizing assumptions for security and forward-security. In: Knudsen, L.R. (ed.) EUROCRYPT 2002. LNCS, vol. 2332, pp. 418–433. Springer, Heidelberg (2002). https://doi.org/10.1007/3-540-46035-7_28

2. Backendal, M., Bellare, M., Sorrell, J., Sun, J.: The Fiat-Shamir zoo: relating the security of different signature variants. In: Gruschka, N. (ed.) NordSec 2018. LNCS, vol. 11252, pp. 154–170. Springer, Cham (2018). https://doi.org/10.1007/978-3-030-03638-6_10

3. Bellare, M., Bernstein, D.J., Tessaro, S.: Hash-function based PRFs: AMAC and its multi-user security. In: Fischlin, M., Coron, J.-S. (eds.) EUROCRYPT 2016. Part I, volume 9665 of LNCS, pp. 566–595. Springer, Heidelberg (2016)

4. Bellare, M., Canetti, R., Krawczyk, H.: Keying hash functions for message authentication. In: Koblitz, N. (ed.) CRYPTO'96. LNCS, vol. 1109, pp. 1–15. Springer, Heidelberg (1996)

5. Bellare, M., Dai, W.: The multi-base discrete logarithm problem: tight reductions and non-rewinding proofs for schnorr identification and signatures. In: Bhargavan, K., Oswald, E., Prabhakaran, M. (eds.) INDOCRYPT 2020. LNCS, vol. 12578, pp. 529–552. Springer, Cham (2020). https://doi.org/10.1007/978-3-030-65277-7_24

6. Bellare, M., Davis, H., Di, Z.: Hardening Signature Schemes via Derive-then-Derandomize: Stronger Security Proofs for EdDSA. Cryptology ePrint Archive, February 2023. http://eprint.iacr.org

7. Bellare, M., Davis, H., Günther, F.: Separate your domains: NIST PQC KEMs, oracle cloning and read-only Indifferentiability. In: Canteaut, A., Ishai, Y. (eds.) EUROCRYPT 2020. LNCS, vol. 12106, pp. 3–32. Springer, Cham (2020). https://doi.org/10.1007/978-3-030-45724-2_1

8. Bellare, M., Palacio, A.: GQ and Schnorr identification schemes: proofs of security against impersonation under active and concurrent attacks. In: Yung, M. (ed.) CRYPTO 2002. LNCS, vol. 2442, pp. 162–177. Springer, Heidelberg (2002). https://doi.org/10.1007/3-540-45708-9_11

9. Bellare, M., Poettering, B., Stebila, D.: From identification to signatures, tightly: a framework and generic transforms. In: Cheon, J.H., Takagi, T. (eds.) ASIACRYPT 2016. LNCS, vol. 10032, pp. 435–464. Springer, Heidelberg (2016). https://doi.org/10.1007/978-3-662-53890-6_15

10. Bellare, M., Rogaway, P.: Random oracles are practical: a paradigm for designing efficient protocols. In: Denning, D.E., Pyle, R., Ganesan, R., Sandhu, R.S., Ashby, V. (eds.) ACM CCS 93, pp. 62–73. ACM Press, November 1993

11. Bellare, M., Rogaway, P.: The security of triple encryption and a framework for code-based Game-Playing Proofs. In: Vaudenay, S. (ed.) EUROCRYPT 2006. LNCS, vol. 4004, pp. 409–426. Springer, Heidelberg (2006). https://doi.org/10.1007/11761679_25

12. Bellare, M., Tackmann, B.: Nonce-based cryptography: retaining security when randomness fails. In: Fischlin, M., Coron, J.-S. (eds.) EUROCRYPT 2016. LNCS, vol. 9665, pp. 729–757. Springer, Heidelberg (2016). https://doi.org/10.1007/978-3-662-49890-3_28

13. Bernstein, D.J.: Multi-user Schnorr security, revisited. Cryptology ePrint Archive, Report 2015/996 (2015). https://eprint.iacr.org/2015/996

14. Bernstein, D.J., Duif, N., Lange, T., Schwabe, P., Yang, B.-Y.: High-speed high-security signatures. J. Cryptographic Eng. **2**(2), 77–89 (2012)
15. Bleichenbacher, D.: A forgery attack on RSA signatures based on implementation errors in the verification. Rump Session Presentation, Crypto 2006, August 2006
16. Brendel, J., Cremers, C., Jackson, D., Zhao, M.: The provable security of Ed25519: theory and practice. In: 2021 IEEE Symposium on Security and Privacy, pages 1659–1676. IEEE Computer Society Press, May 2021
17. Chalkias, K., Garillot, F., Nikolaenko, V.: Taming the many EdDSAs. In: van der Merwe, T., Mitchell, C., Mehrnezhad, M. (eds.) SSR 2020. LNCS, vol. 12529, pp. 67–90. Springer, Cham (2020). https://doi.org/10.1007/978-3-030-64357-7_4
18. Chen, Y., Lombardi, A., Ma, F., Quach, W.: Does Fiat-Shamir require a cryptographic hash function? In: Malkin, T., Peikert, C. (eds.) CRYPTO 2021. LNCS, vol. 12828, pp. 334–363. Springer, Cham (2021). https://doi.org/10.1007/978-3-030-84259-8_12
19. Coron, J.-S., Dodis, Y., Malinaud, C., Puniya, P.: Merkle-Damgård revisited: how to construct a hash function. In: Shoup, V. (ed.) CRYPTO 2005. LNCS, vol. 3621, pp. 430–448. Springer, Heidelberg (2005)
20. Damgård, I.B.: A design principle for hash functions. In: Brassard, G. (ed.) CRYPTO 1989. LNCS, vol. 435, pp. 416–427. Springer, New York (1990). https://doi.org/10.1007/0-387-34805-0_39
21. Dodis, Y., Ristenpart, T., Shrimpton, T.: Salvaging Merkle-Damgård for practical applications. In: Joux, A. (ed.) EUROCRYPT 2009. LNCS, vol. 5479, pp. 371–388. Springer, Heidelberg (2009)
22. Fuchsbauer, G., Plouviez, A., Seurin, Y.: Blind schnorr signatures and signed ElGamal encryption in the algebraic group model. In: Canteaut, A., Ishai, Y. (eds.) EUROCRYPT 2020. Part II, volume 12106 of LNCS, pp. 63–95. Springer, Heidelberg (2020)
23. Goldreich, O.: Two remarks concerning the Goldwasser-Micali-Rivest signature scheme. In: Odlyzko, A.M. (ed.) CRYPTO 1986. LNCS, vol. 263, pp. 104–110. Springer, Heidelberg (1987). https://doi.org/10.1007/3-540-47721-7_8
24. Goldwasser, S., Micali, S., Rivest, R.L.: A digital signature scheme secure against adaptive chosen-message attacks. SIAM J. Computi. **17**(2), 281–308 (1988)
25. Heninger, N., Durumeric, Z., Wustrow, E., Halderman, J.A.: Mining your PS and QS: detection of widespread weak keys in network devices. In: Kohno, T. (ed.) USENIX Security 2012, pp. 205–220. USENIX Association, August 2012
26. IANIX. Things that use Ed25519. https://ianix.com/pub/ed25519-deployment.html
27. S. Josefsson and I. Liusvaara. Edwards-curve digital signature algorithm (EdDSA). RFC 8032, January 2017. https://datatracker.ietf.org/doc/html/rfc8032
28. Kiltz, E., Masny, D., Pan, J.: Optimal security proofs for signatures from identification schemes. In: Robshaw, M., Katz, J. (eds.) CRYPTO 2016. LNCS, vol. 9815, pp. 33–61. Springer, Heidelberg (2016). https://doi.org/10.1007/978-3-662-53008-5_2
29. Lenstra, A.K., Hughes, J.P., Augier, M., Bos, J.W., Kleinjung, T., Wachter, C.: Ron was wrong, whit is right. Cryptology ePrint Archive, Report 2012/064 (2012). https://eprint.iacr.org/2012/064
30. Maurer, U.M., Renner, R., Holenstein, C.: Indifferentiability, impossibility results on reductions, and applications to the random oracle methodology. In: Naor, M. (ed.) TCC 2004. LNCS, vol. 2951, pp. 21–39. Springer, Heidelberg (2004)

31. Merkle, R.C.: A certified digital signature. In: Brassard, G. (ed.) CRYPTO 1989. LNCS, vol. 435, pp. 218–238. Springer, New York (1990). https://doi.org/10.1007/0-387-34805-0_21

32. Mittelbach, A., Fischlin, M.: The Theory of Hash Functions and Random Oracles. Springer, Cham(2021). https://doi.org/10.1007/978-3-030-63287-8

33. M'Raïhi, D., Naccache, D., Pointcheval, D., Vaudenay, S.: Computational alternatives to random number generators. In: Tavares, S., Meijer, H. (eds.) SAC 1998. LNCS, vol. 1556, pp. 72–80. Springer, Heidelberg (1999). https://doi.org/10.1007/3-540-48892-8_6

34. National Institute of Standards and Technology. Digital Signature Standard (DSS). FIPS PUB 186–5, October 2019. https://nvlpubs.nist.gov/nistpubs/FIPS/NIST.FIPS.186-5-draft.pdf

35. Neven, G., Smart, N.P., Warinschi, B.: Hash function requirements for Schnorr signatures. J. Math. Cryptol. 3(1), 69–87 (2009)

36. Ohta, K., Okamoto, T.: On concrete security treatment of signatures derived from identification. In: Krawczyk, H. (ed.) CRYPTO'98. LNCS, vol. 1462, pp. 354–369. Springer, Heidelberg (1998). https://doi.org/10.1007/BFb0055741

37. Pointcheval, D., Stern, J.: Security arguments for digital signatures and blind signatures. J. Cryptol. 13(3), 361–396 (2000)

38. Ristenpart, T., Shacham, H., Shrimpton, T.: Careful with composition: limitations of the indifferentiability framework. In: Paterson, K.G. (ed.) EUROCRYPT 2011. LNCS, vol. 6632, pp. 487–506. Springer, Heidelberg (2011). https://doi.org/10.1007/978-3-642-20465-4_27

39. Rotem, L., Segev, G.: Tighter security for Schnorr identification and signatures: a high-moment forking lemma for Σ-protocols. In: Malkin, T., Peikert, C. (eds.) CRYPTO 2021. LNCS, vol. 12825, pp. 222–250. Springer, Cham (2021). https://doi.org/10.1007/978-3-030-84242-0_9

40. Schnorr, C.-P.: Efficient signature generation by smart cards. J. Cryptol. 4(3), 161–174 (1991)

41. Shoup, V.: Lower bounds for discrete logarithms and related problems. In: Fumy, W. (ed.) EUROCRYPT'97. LNCS, vol. 1233, pp. 256–266. Springer, Heidelberg (1997)

42. Yoneyama, K., Miyagawa, S., Ohta, K.: Leaky random oracle. IEICE Trans. Fundam. Electron. Commun. Comput. Sci. 92(8), 1795–1807 (2009)

Security Analysis of RSA-BSSA

Anna Lysyanskaya$^{(\boxtimes)}$ [ID]

Brown University Providence, Providence, RI 02912, USA
anna_lysyanskaya@brown.edu

Abstract. In a blind signature scheme, a user can obtain a digital signature on a message of her choice without revealing anything about
the message or the resulting signature to the signer. Blind signature
schemes have recently found applications for privacy-preserving web
browsing and ad ecosystems, and as such, are ripe for standardization.
In this paper, we show that the recent proposed standard of Denis,
Jacobs and Wood [16,17] constitutes a strongly one-more-unforgeable
blind signature scheme in the random-oracle model under the one-more-
RSA assumption. Further, we show that the blind version of RSA-
FDH proposed and analyzed by Bellare, Namprempre, Pointcheval and
Semanko [6] does not satisfy blindness when the public key is chosen
maliciously, but satisfies a weaker notion of a blind token.

1 Introduction

A blind signature scheme is a digital signature scheme that allows the signature
recipient to obtain a digital signature on a message of the recipient's choice without revealing this message to the signer. The key feature of a blind signature
protocol is that the resulting signature cannot be linked to a particular protocol
run. If the recipient ran the protocol n times and, as a result, produced n signatures and provided them to the signer in a randomly permuted order, the signer
would not be able to identify which signature corresponded to which protocol
run any better than by guessing at random. Just as in a regular digital signature
scheme, in order to verify a signature, a verifier (a third party, distinct from the
signer or the signature recipient) runs a non-interactive verification algorithm.

Applications. Blind signatures were first introduced by David Chaum [13,14].
The motivating application was untraceable electronic cash (ecash) [13,15]: a
bank can issue electronic coins by issuing blind signatures. A message represents
a coin's serial number, while the bank's signature on it attests that it is indeed a
valid coin. The fact that it was issued via a blind signing protocol means that one
cannot trace which coin was issued to which user, and therefore cannot surmise
how a particular user Alice spent her money.

Blind signatures protect a user's privacy even while ensuring they are qualified for a particular transaction. For example, suppose that a user has convinced
a server that he is a human (rather than a bot) by solving a CAPTCHA. Then
the server may issue such a user a blind signature (or several blind signatures)

© International Association for Cryptologic Research 2023
A. Boldyreva and V. Kolesnikov (Eds.): PKC 2023, LNCS 13940, pp. 251–280, 2023.
https://doi.org/10.1007/978-3-031-31368-4_10

that allow this user to convince other servers that he is a human and not a bot without needing to perform additional CAPTCHAs; however, even if all these servers compare transaction logs, they cannot tell which user it was. This simple scenario is of a growing importance in practice; for example, in is used in VPN by Google One[1], Apple's iCloud Private Relay[2] and Apple's Safari browser proposal for privacy-preserving click measurements[3].

Definitions. A blind signature scheme must satisfy correctness, blindness, and strong one-more unforgeability [1,25,28,33]. Correctness means that an honest verifier will always accept a signature issued by an honest signer to an honest recipient; here, by "honest" we mean one that follows the prescribed algorithms. Blindness, as we explained above, means that the malicious signer learns nothing about a message during the signing protocol, and a signature cannot be linked to the specific protocol execution in which it was computed. This must hold even if the signer's public key is chosen maliciously. Finally, strong one-more unforgeability means that, if an adversary acts as the recipient n times, then it cannot produce $n+1$ distinct message-signature pairs better than with negligible probability. It is important that unforgeability hold even when the adversary engages in several sessions with the signer at the same time; i.e. it is important that unforgeability should hold in the *concurrent* setting.

Standardization. Blind signatures have been studied for almost forty years. They have well-understood definitions of security [1,25,28,33]. Numerous constructions have also been proposed [2,3,5,6,11,13,19,23,24,27,28]. Finally, as we argued above, they are highly desirable in practice. Of course, even a well-understood cryptographic primitive should not get adopted for widespread use without undergoing a thorough standardization process through software standardization bodies such as the IETF.

The first proposed IETF standard for a blind signature scheme is the RSA-BSSA proposal by Denis, Jacobs and Wood [16,17]. The scheme they proposed for standardization is, in a nutshell, the blind version of RSA-PSS [8,9,29,30] along the lines proposed by Chaum [13,14]. However, as the analysis in this paper makes clear, care must be taken to ensure that the message being signed comes from a high-entropy distribution; in the event that it doesn't, a random salt value must be appended to it.

The key generation and verification algorithms are (essentially) the same as in RSA-PSS, except that, in case the message msg does not come from a high-entropy distribution, a salt value rand must be concatenated to the message msg. More precisely, if msg does not come from a high-entropy distribution, this paper's analysis recommends that the blind signing algorithm consist of three steps: first, on input a message msg and the RSA public key (N, e), the user chooses a random salt value rand and computes an RSA-PSS encoding m of

---

[1] https://one.google.com/about/vpn/howitworks.

[2] https://www.apple.com/privacy/docs/iCloud_Private_Relay_Overview_Dec2021. PDF.

[3] https://webkit.org/blog/11940/pcm-click-fraud-prevention-and-attribution-sent-to-advertiser/.

$\mathtt{msg} \circ \mathtt{rand}$ (where '$\circ$' denotes concatenation), picks a blinding value r and sends the value $z = mr^e \bmod N$ to the signer. Using his secret key d, the signer computes $s = z^d \bmod N$ and sends it to the user, who derives the signature $\sigma = s/r \bmod N$; it is easy to see that $\sigma^e = s^e/r^e = z/r^e = m \bmod N$, and thus, constitutes a valid RSA-PSS signature on the user's message $\mathtt{msg} \circ \mathtt{rand}$. In case $\mathtt{msg}$ comes from a high-entropy distribution, $\mathtt{rand}$ is not needed, and m is computed as a PSS encoding of $\mathtt{msg}$; the rest of the signing algorithm is the same. As we will see in Sect. 4, either the high entropy of $\mathtt{msg}$, or the additional salt value $\mathtt{rand}$ are necessary to ensure that the scheme is provably blind in the event that the signer's key was chosen maliciously. This has resulted in IETF discussions on amending the draft[4].

As pointed out by Denis, Jacobs and Wood [16,17], the message-response (i.e., two-move) structure of this protocol makes it desirable. The security game for strong one-more unforgeability for a two-move protocol is the same whether in the sequential or the concurrent setting. In contrast, a recent result [10] gave an attack on popular three-move blind signature protocols (such as the blind version of the Schnorr signature [28,31,32] or anonymous credentials light [4]) in the concurrent setting, making them poor candidates for standardization. Moreover, a three-message (or more) protocol would require the signer to keep state, which is a significant complication when it comes to system design, making the concurrently secure blind signature schemes of Abe [2] and Tessaro and Zhu [35] less suitable in practice.

The choice of blind RSA-PSS over blind RSA-FDH [6] is motivated by the popularity of (non-blind) RSA-PSS, ensuring that, at least as far as verifying the signatures is concerned, no new software need be developed. That way, even unsophisticated participants have easy access to the digital tools they need to take advantage of the privacy-preserving features offered by blind signatures.

Why standardize and adopt an RSA-based scheme now, instead of a post-quantum one? Indeed it is possible that, with the advent of quantum computing, decades from now another scheme will have to replace this RSA-based one. Yet, this will have no consequences on today's clients and servers if the users' privacy is protected even from quantum computers (for example, if it holds unconditionally). The consequences to the servers are minimized because a blind signature ceases to be relevant after a relatively brief amount of time, so the lifetime of a signing key would be measured in weeks rather than years.

This paper's contributions and organization. We show that the proposed RSA-BSSA standard [16] constitutes a one-more unforgeable blind signature scheme. One-more unforgeability holds in the random-oracle model under the one-more-RSA assumption introduced by Bellare, Namprempre, Pointcheval and Semanko (BNPS) [6]. Blindness of the RSA-BSSA holds in the random-oracle model.

We also show that Chaum-BNPS's blind RSA-FDH [6,14] is not blind in the malicious-signer model, i.e., it can only be shown to be blind if the signer's key pair is generated honestly (see Sect. 4.4). However, we show in Sect. 4.4 that even in the case of a malicious signer, it satisfies the weaker notion of a blind token which we introduce in Sect. 2.3.

---

[4] https://github.com/cfrg/draft-irtf-cfrg-blind-signatures/pull/105.

The rest of this paper is organized as follows: In Sect. 2 we recall the definition of security for blind signature schemes. Our definitions are tailor-made for two-move blind signature schemes, because in the case of two-move signatures the issues of composition with other protocols go away (as discussed above). Other than that, our definitions are standard [1,25,28,33]. We include bibliographic notes explaining that at the end of Sects. 2.1 and 2.2 that provide definitions of one-more unforgeability and blindness, respectively.

In Sect. 3 we give an overview of RSA-BSSA. We begin by giving a basic version of the scheme, in which the blind signature that a user obtains is a standard RSA-PSS signature on the user's message msg (i.e. there is no rand). We also give two modifications of the basic scheme: a variant in which the signer's RSA public key (N, e) is enhanced in a way that ensures that the exponent e is relatively prime to $\varphi(N)$ using a technique of Goldberg, Reyzin, Sagga and Baldimtsi [21]. Finally, in Sect. 3.3 we give the variant that corresponds to the RSA-BSSA proposal from February 2022 [16]; in this variant, the public key is a standard RSA public key (N, e) and the signature on a message msg consists of a salt rand and the PSS signature on (msg ∘ rand).

In Sect. 4 we justify the salt rand: we show why it is difficult to prove that the basic scheme is blind without introducing additional assumptions, and show that, in the random-oracle model, both modifications give rise to blind signature schemes. We also show that the basic scheme is a blind token. Finally, in Sect. 5 we show that the basic scheme and both variants are one-more-unforgeable under the one-more-RSA assumption in the random-oracle model.

2 Definition of a Two-Move Blind Signature Scheme

The definition of a blind signature scheme we provide here applies only to two-move blind signatures; see prior work for more general definitions [8,9,29,30]. First, in Definition 1 let us give the input-output specification for the five algorithms that constitute a two-move blind signature scheme. The key generation algorithm KeyGen and the signature verification algorithm Verify have the same input-output behavior as in a regular digital signature scheme.

The signing algorithm is broken down into three steps: (1) The signature recipient runs the Blind algorithm to transforms a message msg into its blinded form blinded_msg; blinded_msg is sent to the signer. (2) The signer runs the algorithm BSig(SK, blinded_msg) to compute its response blinded_sig, and then sends it to the signature recipient. (3) The signature recipient uses the algorithm Finalize to transform blinded_sig into a valid signature σ on its message msg. More precisely:

Definition 1 (Input-output specification for a two-move blind signature scheme). *Let $\mathcal{S} = $ (KeyGen, Blind, BSig, Finalize, Verify) be a set of polynomial-time algorithms with the following input-output specifications:*

KeyGen(1^k) → (PK, SK) *is a probabilistic algorithm that takes as input 1^k (the security parameter represented in unary) and outputs the public signature verification key PK and a secret signing key SK.*

Blind(PK, msg) → (blinded_msg, inv) *is a probabilistic algorithm that takes as input the public key PK and a string* msg *and outputs a blinded message* blinded_msg *(which will be sent to the signer) and an auxiliary string* inv *(which will be used by* Finalize *to derive the final signature* σ*).*

BSig(SK, blinded_msg) → blinded_sig *is an algorithm (possibly a probabilistic one) that takes as input the secret signing key SK and a string* blinded_msg *and outputs a blinded signature* blinded_sig*.*

Finalize(PK, inv, blinded_sig) → σ *is an algorithm that takes as input the public signature verification key PK, an auxiliary string* inv *and a blinded signature and outputs a signature* σ*.*

Verify(PK, msg, σ) *is an algorithm that either accepts or rejects.*

Next, let us define what it means for $\mathcal{S}$ to constitute a *correct* blind signature scheme. On a high level, correctness means that if a signature σ was produced after both the signature recipient and the signer followed their corresponding algorithms, then this signature will be accepted by Verify. More formally:

Definition 2 (Correct two-move blind signature). *Let* $\mathcal{S}$ = (KeyGen, Blind, BSig, Finalize, Verify) *be a set of polynomial-time algorithms that satisfy the input-output specification for a two-move blind signature scheme (Definition 1).* $\mathcal{S}$ *constitutes a correct two-move blind signature scheme if for all k,* (PK, SK) *output by* KeyGen(1^k)*, strings* msg*,* (blinded_msg, inv) *output by* Blind(PK, msg)*,* blinded_sig *output by* BSig(SK, blinded_msg)*, and* σ *output by* Finalize(PK, inv, blinded_sig)*,* Verify(PK, msg, σ) *accepts.*

2.1   Strong One-More Unforgeability

As discussed above, a blind signature scheme must satisfy one-more unforgeability: an adversarial user who obtained ℓ signatures from the signer cannot produce $\ell + 1$ distinct message-signature pairs. Since we are limiting our attention to two-move blind signatures, the security experiment that captures it can allow the adversary oracle access to the algorithm BSig(SK, ·). More formally:

Definition 3 (Strong one-more-unforgeability). *Let* $\mathcal{S}$ = (KeyGen, Blind, BSig, Finalize, Verify) *be a set of polynomial-time algorithms that satisfy the input-output specification for a two-move blind signature scheme (Definition 1). For an oracle Turing machine* $\mathcal{A}$*, the success probability* $p_{\mathcal{A}}^{\mathcal{S}}(k)$ *of* $\mathcal{A}$ *in breaking the strong one-more unforgeability of* $\mathcal{S}$ *is the probability that* $\mathcal{A}$ *is successful in the following experiment parameterized by* k*:*

Experiment set-up *The key pair is generated:* $(PK, SK) \leftarrow$ KeyGen(1^k)*.*

Adversary's execution *The adversary* $\mathcal{A}$ *is given oracle access to* BSig(SK, ·) *and is run on input PK;* $\mathcal{A}^{\text{BSig}(SK, \cdot)}(PK)$ *terminates with a set of message-signature pairs on its output tape:* $((\text{msg}_1, \sigma_1), \dots, (\text{msg}_n, \sigma_n))$*, and a set of query-response pairs on its query tape:*

$$((\text{blinded\_msg}_1, \text{blinded\_sig}_1), \dots, (\text{blinded\_msg}_\ell, \text{blinded\_sig}_\ell)).$$

The success criterion *The number of distinct message-signature pairs* (msg_i, σ_i) *such that* $\mathsf{Verify}(PK, \mathsf{msg}_i, \sigma_i) = 1$ *is at least* $\ell + 1$, *i.e.* $\mathcal{A}$ *outputs more distinct signatures than the number of queries it made to* BSig.

$\mathcal{S}$ *satisfies the strong one-more-unforgeability property if for any polynomial-time adversary* $\mathcal{A}$, *the value* $p_{\mathcal{A}}^{\mathcal{S}}(k)$ *is negligible.*

The history of this definition. Chaum's original blind signatures papers [13,14] did not contain a formal definition; in fact, they preceded the formal definition of security for a digital signature scheme.

The regular definition of unforgeability for digital signature schemes [22] does not apply to blind signatures. In the regular definition, the adversary wins the unforgeability game if it produces a signature on a message that the challenger never signed. However, the challenger in the blind signature game has no way of knowing which messages it has signed — that's the whole point of blindness, and ideally, we want it to hold unconditionally.

Thus, Pointcheval and Stern [27,28] came up with the notion of *one-more unforgeability* in which the adversary is considered successful if it outputs more distinct signed messages than the number of blind signing sessions it participated in. Pointcheval and Stern considered a more general structure of a blind signing protocol, not just the message-response exchange a-la our Blind, BSig, Finalize structure, and thus the issue of self-composition (i.e. what happened if the messages from the signer were adversarially interleaved with those of the adversarial users) needed to be carefully defined in their work. But, as Bellare et al. observed [6], for a protocol that has this simple two-move (i.e. message-response) structure, self-composition is for free, and so the one-more-unforgeability game can be formalized in relatively simple terms.

A stronger definition of unforgeability for blind signatures was given by Schröder and Unruh [33]. They consider the case when the adversary observes the inputs and outputs of *honest* users who engage in ℓ blind signing protocols to obtain signatures on fewer than ℓ distinct messages (i.e. some message is getting signed more than once). The adversary should not be able to get a signature on an additional message by directing honest users to get more than one signature on the same message. Schröder and Unruh showed that Pointcheval and Stern's one-more-unforgeability definition is not sufficient to prevent the adversary from taking advantage of honest users this way; but strong one-more unforgeability is. Following their work, strong one-more unforgeability is the standard notion of unforgeability for blind signature schemes.

Our formulation of strong one-more unforgeability in Definition 3 uses Definition 6.1 of Bellare et al. [6], which is their definition of one-more unforgeability, as a starting point. Their formulation is tailored specifically to one-more unforgeability of the blind RSA-FDH, while ours generally applies to any two-move protocol consisting of Blind, BSig, and Finalize. We also modified the success criterion to correspond to strong one-more unforgeability.

One might wonder why the security game is for only one signer. Indeed, we could extend the game to require that the adversary specify a number of signers and interact with each signer before outputting a set of message-signature pairs. The adversary would be deemed successful if, for one of the signers, the number of valid message-signature pairs from this signer produced by the adversary was greater than the number of the adversary's queries to this signer. It is easy to see that extending the security game to such a multi-signer scenario would not make the definition stronger: a scheme that satisfies one-more unforgeability with one signer will also satisfy it with multiple (say, n) signers. The reduction would randomly pick one of the signers and would set up the game so that it knows the secret key of all but the selected signer; the selected signer is the one from the one-more-unforgeability challenger with one signer. If the adversary succeeds and the reduction guessed the signer correctly, then the reduction will succeed as well; since the guess is correct with probability $1/n$, this shows that the two definitions are equivalent up to a security loss of $1/n$. Although not addressed explicitly in the literature cited above, this is well-understood in the context of regular digital signatures [20] and thus it is the single-signer definitions that are standard in the blind signatures literature.

2.2   Blindness

Finally, a blind signature scheme must satisfy *blindness*, that is, it should be impossible to determine which query to the (adversarial) signer resulted in the (honest) signature recipient deriving a particular message-signature pair. For this security game, the adversary picks the public key adversarially; it also picks two messages whose signatures the challenger will try to obtain. The challenger will try to obtain signatures on these messages in random order selected by picking a random bit b; the adversary's goal is to tell in what order. The adversary gets to see the resulting signatures before producing an output.

A trivial strategy for the adversary would be to issue a valid signature in response to one of the queries but not the other. In order to rule out this strategy, the challenger allows the adversary to see the resulting signatures only if both of them verify. If one (or both) of the signatures does not verify, the adversary will have to guess the bit b based on its view of the interaction with the user in the blind signing protocol.

The formal definition below applies only to two-move blind signature schemes, but it can be generalized to any protocol structure.

Definition 4 (Blindness). *Let $\mathcal{S} = (\mathsf{KeyGen}, \mathsf{Blind}, \mathsf{BSig}, \mathsf{Finalize}, \mathsf{Verify})$ be a set of polynomial-time algorithms that satisfy the input-output specification for a two-move blind signature scheme (Definition 1). For an interactive algorithm $\mathcal{A}$, let $q_{\mathcal{A}}^{\mathcal{S}}(k, b)$ be the probability that $\mathcal{A}$ outputs 0 in the following experiment parameterized by k and the bit b:*

$\mathcal{A}$ **is invoked** *$\mathcal{A}(1^k)$ selects a public key PK (whose length is appropriate for the security parameter k) and two messages msg_0 and msg_1.*

$\mathcal{A}$ **acts as the blind signer** *For $i \in \{0, 1\}$, the challenger computes the values $(\mathtt{blinded\_msg}_i, \mathtt{inv}_i) \leftarrow \mathsf{Blind}(PK, \mathsf{msg}_i)$ and sends $(\mathtt{blinded\_msg}_b,$*

$\texttt{blinded\_msg}_{1-b}$) *to* $\mathcal{A}$, *receiving* ($\texttt{blinded\_sig}_b$, $\texttt{blinded\_sig}_{1-b}$) *in response.*

$\mathcal{A}$ receives the signatures *For $i \in \{0,1\}$, the challenger computes*

$$\sigma_i = \mathsf{Finalize}(PK, \texttt{inv}_i, \texttt{blinded\_sig}_i)$$

If $\mathsf{Verify}(PK, \texttt{msg}_0, \sigma_0) = \mathsf{Verify}(PK, \texttt{msg}_1, \sigma_1) = 1$, *it sends* (σ_0, σ_1) *to* $\mathcal{A}$; *else it sends* $\perp$ *to* $\mathcal{A}$.

$\mathcal{A}$'s output $\mathcal{A}$ *outputs some value* $\texttt{output}$.

$\mathcal{A}$'s advantage $\mathbf{Adv}^{\mathcal{S}}_{\mathcal{A}}(k)$ *in breaking the blindness of* $\mathcal{S}$ *is defined as* $\mathbf{Adv}^{\mathcal{S}}_{\mathcal{A}}(k) := |q^{\mathcal{S}}_{\mathcal{A}}(k,0) - q^{\mathcal{S}}_{\mathcal{A}}(k,1)|$. $\mathcal{S}$ *satisfies blindness if for any probabilistic polynomial-time* $\mathcal{A}$, $\mathbf{Adv}^{\mathcal{S}}_{\mathcal{A}}(k)$ *is negligible.*

The history of this definition. The first formalization of the blindness property of a digital signature scheme was given by Juels, Luby and Ostrovsky [25]; in this initial formulation, the public key for the scheme was generated honestly. Abdalla, Namprepre and Neven [1] improved the definition by considering a signer who is already adversarial at key generation time; they also gave a more careful treatment of the compositional issues. The definition given above corresponds to the Abdalla et al. version of the blindness definition as it applies to the case of a two-move signing protocol. It is considered standard in the literature.

Again, one might wonder why the number of messages in the security game is limited to just two, $\texttt{msg}_0$ and $\texttt{msg}_1$; and why the user just interacts with the signer $\mathcal{A}$ once. It is relatively straightforward to show that extending the definition to allow more than two messages or to give the signer more chances to interact with the challenger will not strengthen the definition: a reduction playing middleman between the multi-message or multi-interaction adversary and the two-message single interaction challenger will inherit a non-negligible fraction of the adversary's advantage.

2.3   A New Definition: Blind Tokens

In certain applications, the messages being signed are chosen at random from some message space $\mathcal{M}$. If all goes well during the signing protocol, the user gets a unique authenticated token, i.e. a signature on this random message. This token should be *blind*, i.e. unlinkable to the specific interaction with the signer in which it was obtained. If for some reason the signing protocol fails to return a valid signature on this message, the message may be discarded.

Let us formalize the blindness requirement of such applications by introducing a new cryptographic primitive: a *blind token* scheme. A blind token scheme will have the same input-output specification as a blind signature scheme, and must also be strongly one-more unforgeable; however, the notion of blindness it needs to satisfy is somewhat weaker. Unlike the blind signature blindness experiment, here the two messages $\texttt{msg}_0$ and $\texttt{msg}_1$ are picked from the same distribution $\mathcal{M}$. The adversary has some influence on how they are picked: $\mathcal{M}$ takes as input the adversary's public key PK as well as some auxiliary input *aux*. In the full version of this paper [26], we also give a version of this definition that corresponds to the one-more unforgeability, rather than strong one-more unforgeability.

Definition 5 (Strongly unforgeable blind token scheme). *Let* $S =$ KeyGen, Blind, BSig, Finalize, Verify *be a set of polynomial-time algorithms that satisfy the input-output specification for a two-move blind signature scheme (Definition 1) and the strong one-more unforgeability property (Definition 3). Let* $\mathcal{M}$ *be a message sampling algorithm that, on input the security parameter* 1^k, *a public key* PK, *and auxiliary input* aux, *outputs a string* msg.

For an interactive algorithm $\mathcal{A}$ *and an efficient message sampling algorithm* $\mathcal{M}$, *let* $q_{\mathcal{A}}^{S,\mathcal{M}}(k,b)$ *be the probability that* $\mathcal{A}$ *outputs 0 in the following experiment parameterized by the security parameter* k *and the bit* b:

$\mathcal{A}$ **is invoked** $\mathcal{A}(1^k)$ *selects a public key* PK *(whose length is appropriate for the security parameter* k*), and auxiliary input* aux *for the message sampling algorithm.*

$\mathcal{A}$ **acts as the blind signer** *For* $i \in \{0,1\}$, *let* $\mathrm{msg}_i \leftarrow \mathcal{M}(1^k, PK, aux)$ *be messages randomly selected by the challenger, who then proceeds to compute the values* $(\mathrm{blinded\_msg}_i, \mathrm{inv}_i) \leftarrow \mathrm{Blind}(PK, \mathrm{msg}_i)$ *and send* $(\mathrm{blinded\_msg}_b,$ $\mathrm{blinded\_msg}_{1-b})$ *to* $\mathcal{A}$, *receiving* $(\mathrm{blinded\_sig}_b,\ \mathrm{blinded\_sig}_{1-b})$ *in response.*

$\mathcal{A}$ **receives the signatures** *For* $i \in \{0,1\}$, *the challenger computes*

$$\sigma_i = \mathrm{Finalize}(PK, \mathrm{inv}_i, \mathrm{blinded\_sig}_i)$$

If $\mathrm{Verify}(PK, \mathrm{msg}_0, \sigma_0)$ $=$ $\mathrm{Verify}(PK, \mathrm{msg}_1, \sigma_1)$ $=$ 1, *it sends* $(\mathrm{msg}_0, \sigma_0, \mathrm{msg}_1, \sigma_1)$ *to* $\mathcal{A}$; *else it sends* $\perp$ *to* $\mathcal{A}$.
$\mathcal{A}$**'s output** $\mathcal{A}$ *outputs some value* output.

$\mathcal{A}$*'s advantage* $\mathbf{Adv}_{\mathcal{A}}^{S,\mathcal{M}}(k)$ *is defined as* $\mathbf{Adv}_{\mathcal{A}}^{S,\mathcal{M}}(k) := |q_{\mathcal{A}}^{S,\mathcal{M}}(k,0) - q_{\mathcal{A}}^{S,\mathcal{M}}(k,1)|$. S *is a strongly unforgeable blind token scheme for message space* $\mathcal{M}$ *if for any probabilistic polynomial-time* $\mathcal{A}$, $\mathbf{Adv}_{\mathcal{A}}^{S,\mathcal{M}}(k)$ *is negligible.*

The motivation for this definition. This definition is new; generally, when analyzing proposed standards, introducing new notions of security is a bad idea. An algorithm adapted for practical use should satisfy a notion of security that is well-understood and established. Unfortunately, as we will see in Sect. 4.4, at least one scheme that is already used in practice does not satisfy the established definition of a blind signature scheme; however, we show that it satisfies Definition 5, and therefore can still be used securely in some limited applications.

In the ecash application as originally envisioned by Chaum, the message msg is simply a string that is sampled uniformly at random; it should be long enough that it is unlikely that the same string can be sampled twice. Once the user obtains the signature σ on msg, the pair (msg, σ) can be viewed as an e-coin. msg is the coin's serial number, while σ can be thought of as its proof of validity. However, if the user fails to obtain σ for this msg, then msg has no value and can be discarded. The reason that blind tokens give users of this system the desired privacy is that each user draws the serial numbers for her coins from exactly the same distribution as all the other users.

3   The RSA-BSSA Scheme

Let us review the blind signature scheme from the RSA blind signature scheme with appendix (RSA-BSSA) proposal by Denis, Jacobs and Wood [16,17].

High-level description of the basic scheme. In the RSA-PSS signature scheme [8, 9,29,30], the signature on a message M is the RSA inverse of a special encoding (called the *PSS encoding*) m of M. At a high level, the basic version of RSA-BSSA is reminiscent of Chaum's original blind signature scheme: it is the blind version of the RSA-PSS signature scheme. Following RSA-PSS, the key generation algorithm generates an RSA key pair $PK = (N, e)$, $SK = d$, where $ed \equiv 1 \bmod \varphi(N)$. Following Chaum, in order to obtain a blind signature on a message M, the user first generates a PSS encoding m of M, then blinds it using a random $r \leftarrow \mathbb{Z}_N^*$ obtaining $z = mr^e \bmod N$, which is (hopefully) an element of $\mathbb{Z}_N^*$ that is distributed independently of M. Then he gets from the signer the blinded signature $y = z^d \bmod N$, and unblinds it to obtain and output $s = yr^{-1} \bmod N$. To verify a signature s on a message M, follow the same algorithm as RSA-PSS verification: check that the PSS decoding of $m = s^e \bmod N$ is the message M. Let us fill in the missing details.

Hash functions. For the PSS encoding, the scheme will use two cryptographic hash functions Hash and MGF the same way that PSS does. Both Hash and MGF take as input a string of bytes S and an integer ℓ, and output a string of ℓ bytes. In the security analysis, both will be treated as random oracles. Even though their input-output specifications and security requirements match, it may be helpful to have functions with different implementations because, as their names suggest, the function Hash will potentially take a long string S and output a shorter string; while MGF (which stands for "mask generation function") will take as input a short "seed" string and output a longer one.

Other subroutines. Since we are analyzing not just an algorithm but a proposed standard, it is important to note that any software program implementing this standard will have to recognize two distinct types: integers (on which integer operations are performed) and strings of bytes (that lend themselves to string operations, such as concatenation and exclusive-or). I2OSP is a procedure that converts an integer into an octet string (an octet is just the IETF terminology for the eight-bit byte). On input an integer and the desired length ℓ, it outputs the binary representation of the integer using ℓ octets if ℓ is sufficiently large, or fails otherwise. OS2IP reverses this process: given a string, it interprets it as the binary representation of an integer and outputs that integer.

Parameters. The scheme is parameterized by k, which is the bit length of the RSA modulus (strictly speaking, there are two parameters: *kLen* and *kBits*, representing its length in bytes and in bits, respectively; but for the purposes of the analysis the bit length is sufficient). The value $emLen = \lceil (k-1)/8 \rceil$ denotes the number of octets needed to represent a PSS encoding; i.e., a PSS encoding will always take up exactly $k-1$ bits.

As in PSS, the choice of the functions Hash and MGF and the parameters $hLen$ and $sLen$ are additional design choices (parameters, if you will) that define an instantiation of the scheme. The value $hLen$ denotes the length in octets of the output of the hash function Hash that's used in the scheme. It is important that $hLen$ be set up in such a way that, in the random oracle model, the probability that two distinct inputs to Hash($\cdot, hLen$) yield the same output (i.e. collide) be minuscule; an adversary whose running time is t can generate at most t such inputs; thus 2^{4hLen} needs to be a generous upper bound on t. The value $sLen$ denotes the length (in octets) of the salt of the PSS encoding.

Our security analysis requires that $emLen \geq \max(2hLen, hLen + sLen) + 2$.

PSS encoding and decoding procedures. Recall that, in RSA-PSS, the signing algorithm is broken down into two steps. The first step does not involve the secret key: it simply encodes the input message in a special way. The second step uses the secret key in order to compute the signature corresponding to the encoding obtained in step one. Analogously, signature verification consists of two steps as well: the first step uses the public key in order to compute what may turn out to be an encoding of the message; the second step verifies that the string obtained in step one is indeed a valid encoding of the message.

When describing RSA-BSSA below, we invoke the encoding and decoding procedures from the IETF standard [30]: PSSEncode(msg, ℓ) is the function that, on input a message msg and an integer ℓ, produces a string EM (encoded message) of $\lceil \ell/8 \rceil$ octets whose ℓ rightmost bits constitute a PSS encoding of msg. PSSVerify(msg, EM, ℓ) verifies that EM is consistent with the output of PSSEncode(msg, ℓ). For an RSA modulus of bit length k, the PSS scheme will use $\ell = k - 1$, so EM will be of length $emLen = \lceil (k-1)/8 \rceil$.

Specifically (but briefly), PSSEncode(msg, ℓ) works as follows: first, hash msg to obtain mHash = Hash(msg, $hLen$), and pick a random string salt of length $sLen$ bytes (octets). Compute $H = $ Hash($0^{64} \circ$ mHash $\circ$ salt), and use it to compute a mask dbMask = MGF($H, emLen - hLen - 1$) and use it to mask the salt: maskedDB = DB $\oplus$ dbMask, where DB is salt padded (to make sure that the resulting string is of the correct length) with a pre-defined string. Then output the encoded message EM = maskedDB $\circ H \circ 0xBC$.

In turn, PSSVerify(msg, EM, ℓ) begins by parsing EM = maskedDB $\circ H \circ 0xBC$. Then it computes dbMask as above to unmask salt from maskedDB (it rejects if the padding was incorrect) and verifies that $H = $ Hash($0^{64} \circ$ mHash $\circ$ salt) for mHash = Hash(msg, $hLen$). See the full version of this paper for details about the history of PSS. In Appendix B we provide a more detailed description of the verification algorithm for PSS.

3.1 The Basic Scheme

We begin by describing the basic scheme in which the user obtains from the signer an RSA-PSS signature on the message msg. As usual, the scheme consists of a key generation algorithm, a protocol for obtaining signatures, and a signature verification algorithm.

Key generation The key generation algorithm is the standard RSA key generation: The public key is $PK = (N, e)$, where N is an RSA modulus of length k (k is given as input to the key generation algorithm, in unary, i.e. 1^k), and e is relatively prime to $\varphi(N)$. The secret key is $SK = (N, d)$ such that $ed \equiv 1 \bmod \varphi(N)$. The exact specification is as described in the PKCS#1 standard.

Blind signing protocol The protocol consists of three algorithms: Blind, BSig, and Finalize. On input a message msg that the client wishes to get a signature for, the client runs Blind(PK, msg) and obtains (blinded_msg, inv). The server runs the algorithm BSig(SK, blinded_msg) and outputs a blinded signature blinded_sig. The user runs Finalize(PK, msg, blinded_sig, inv) to derive the signature σ. The three algorithms are as follows:

Blind(PK, msg) Compute a PSS encoding of msg: EM = PSSEncode(msg, $k -$ 1), and let $m = $ OS2IP(EM) be the corresponding integer. Next, sample $r \leftarrow \mathbb{Z}_N^*$, compute $z = mr^e \bmod N$, and make sure that $z \in \mathbb{Z}_N^*$. Compute $r_{inv} = r^{-1} \bmod N$, and output (z, r_{inv}) as octet strings, i.e., output blinded_msg = I2OSP(z, $kLen$), inv = I2OSP(r_{inv}, $kLen$).

BSig(SK, blinded_msg) First, check that the string blinded_msg is of bit length k, and reject if it is not. Next, convert into a k-bit integer $m = $ OS2IP(blinded_msg). Output the binary representation of $s = m^d \bmod N$, i.e. blinded_sig = I2OSP(s, $kLen$).

Finalize(PK, msg, blinded_sig, inv) Convert blinded_sig and inv into integers using the OS2IP procedure: $z = $ OS2IP(blinded_sig), $r_{inv} = $ OS2IP(inv); compute $s = zr_{inv} \bmod N$. The signature is the binary representation of s, i.e. $\sigma = $ I2OSP(s, $kLen$). Finally, if PSSVerify(PK, msg, σ), then output σ, else fail.

Verification The verification algorithm calls PSSVerify(PK, msg, σ). (Described in more detail in Appendix B.)

The following theorem follows easily by inspection:

Theorem 1. *The RSA-BSSA scheme is correct.*

As we will show in Sect. 5, it also satisfies one-more unforgeability under the one-more-RSA assumption [6]. However, as we will explain in more detail in Sect. 4, it is not clear whether or not this construction satisfies blindness.

3.2   RSA-BSSA, Version A

The basic construction described above (Sect. 3.1) results in a perfectly blind signing protocol whenever $PK = (N, e)$ where the public exponent e is relatively prime to $\varphi(N)$: in that case, for any $m \in \mathbb{Z}_N^*$, selecting $r \leftarrow \mathbb{Z}_N^*$ uniformly at random and outputting $z = mr^e$ ensures that z is a uniformly random element of $\mathbb{Z}_N^*$. This is because, of course, if there exists d such that $ed \equiv 1 \bmod \varphi(N)$, then for each $z \in \mathbb{Z}_N^*$, there exists a unique $r = (z/m)^d$ such that $z = mr^e$.

Thus, in order to ensure blindness, it is sufficient to ensure that e is relatively prime to $\varphi(N)$. Consider the following variant of RSA-BSSA, in which a public key contains a proof that e is relatively prime to $\varphi(N)$ as described by Goldberg, Reyzin, Sagga and Baldimtsi [21].

It will require the additional parameter κ, which is a statistical security parameter. Further, it will require a function R_k that, on input three integers, outputs a random integer $0 \le a < 2^{k-1}$; such R_k can be constructed, for example, from MGF. Let e' be a prime that is small enough that checking that $(N, e) \in L_{e'}$ can be done efficiently, where $L_{e'} = \{(N, e) \mid N, e > 0 \text{ and no prime less than } e' \text{ divides } e\}$. In practice, e is often prime and small enough that setting $e' = e$ works. We let e' be a system-wide parameter, so each procedure below receives it as input. Finally, let $\ell = \lceil \kappa / \log_2(e') \rceil$.

Key generation On input the desired modulus length k and a statistical security parameter κ, run the RSA key generation algorithm as in the basic protocol (Sect. 3.1) to obtain (N, e) and d. Next, compute a proof π that e is relatively prime to $\varphi(N)$, as follows: for $1 \le i \le \ell$, let $a_i = R_k(N, e, i)$, compute $b_i = a_i{}^d \bmod N$, and let $\pi = b_1, \dots, b_\ell$.
The public key is $PK = (N, e, \pi)$, the secret key is $SK = (N, d)$.

Blind signing protocol Before running the signing protocol, the user verifies that the public key $PK = (N, e, \pi)$ is well-formed: let $\pi = b_1, \dots, b_\ell$; for $1 \le i \le \ell$, check that $b_i^e = R_k(N, e, i) \bmod N$. If one of the checks fails, fail. Else, run the Blind, BSig, and Finalize algorithms as described in Sect. 3.1.

Verification As in Sect. 3.1, return PSSVerify(PK, msg, σ).

3.3   RSA-BSSA, Version B

As we will see in Sect. 4.2, another way to ensure blindness is to modify the construction in such a way that the value mHash incorporated into the PSS encoding of the message to be signed reveals nothing about this message. This calls for a simple modification of the basic protocol that requires that, instead of invoking the signing protocol directly on the message msg, the user invokes it on the message msg' = msg ∘ rand, where rand is a random value of κ bits, where κ is a security parameter. More precisely:

Key generation Run the RSA key generation algorithm as in the basic protocol (Sect. 3.1) to obtain $PK = (N, e)$ and $SK = d$.

Blind signing protocol The user generates a random string rand of κ bits, and runs the signing protocol in Sect. 3.1 on input msg' = msg ∘ rand, and obtains from it the signature σ' on the message msg'. Output the signature $\sigma = (\sigma', \text{rand})$.

Verification Following Sect. 3.1, on input msg and $\sigma = (\sigma', \text{rand})$, the verification algorithm makes sure that rand consists of κ bits, rejects if it does not, and then returns the output of PSSVerify(PK, msg', σ'), where msg' = msg ∘ rand.

4 Blindness of RSA-BSSA

In the blindness experiment, the adversary picks the modulus N; thus we cannot assume that it is a proper RSA modulus. Therefore, in order to understand how much information such an adversary can learn in the blindness experiment, we must consider the structure of the group $\mathbb{Z}_N^*$ for arbitrary N.

Lemma 1. *Let $N > 1$ be any odd integer, let $N = \prod_{i=1}^{\ell} p_i^{\alpha_i}$ be is its prime factorization. Then $\mathbb{Z}_N^*$ is of size $\varphi(N) = \prod_{i=1}^{\ell} \varphi(p_i^{\alpha_i}) = \prod_{i=1}^{\ell} p_i^{\alpha_i - 1}(p_i - 1)$ is isomorphic to $\mathbb{Z}_{\varphi(p_1^{\alpha_1})} \times \mathbb{Z}_{\varphi(p_2^{\alpha_2})} \times \ldots \times \mathbb{Z}_{\varphi(p_\ell^{\alpha_\ell})}$.*

For the proof, we refer to Sect. 7.5 of Shoup [34]. The lemma implies that every element $x \in \mathbb{Z}_N^*$ can be viewed as a vector $(x_1, \ldots, x_\ell) \in \mathbb{Z}_{p_1^{\alpha_1 - 1}(p_1 - 1)} \times \mathbb{Z}_{p_2^{\alpha_2 - 1}(p_2 - 1)} \times \ldots \times \mathbb{Z}_{p_\ell^{\alpha_\ell - 1}(p_\ell - 1)}$, and vice versa.

Let Ψ_N denote this isomorphism; when N is clear from the context, we will write it as Ψ. Moreover, there is a (not necessarily efficient) algorithm that computes Ψ_N, as follows: on input $x \in \mathbb{Z}_N^*$, compute $x_i = x \bmod p_i^{\alpha_i}$, and then find $\chi_i \in \mathbb{Z}_{p_i^{\alpha_i - 1}(p_i - 1)}$ such that $x = g_i^{\chi_i}$, where g_i is a generator of $\mathbb{Z}_{p_i^{\alpha_i}}^*$ (it exists by Theorem 7.28 in Shoup [34]).

We also refer the reader to Shoup [34] for the Chinese Remainder Theorem; below, by $CRT(x_1, \ldots, x_\ell)$ we denote the element $x \in \mathbb{Z}_N$ such that $x = x_i \bmod p_i^{\alpha_i}$, where $N = \prod_{i=1}^{\ell} p_i^{\alpha_i}$ is the prime factorization of N.

Definition 6 (Roots and residues). *Let N and e be any positive integers, and let $m \in \mathbb{Z}_N^*$. Let the set $Roots_{N,e}(m) = \{s \in \mathbb{Z}_N^* \mid s^e = m\}$. Let the set $Residues_{N,e} = \{m \in \mathbb{Z}_N^* \mid Roots_{N,e}(m) \neq \emptyset\}$.*

Lemmas 2, 3 and 4, and Corollaries 1 and 2 are well-known; for completeness, their proofs are included in the full version of this paper [26].

Lemma 2. *Let $N > 1$ be any odd integer. If an integer e is relatively prime to $\varphi(N)$, then the distribution $D_0(N, e) = \{r \leftarrow \mathbb{Z}_N^* : r\}$ is identical to the distribution $D_1(N, e) = \{r \leftarrow \mathbb{Z}_N^* : r^e\}$.*

Lemma 3. *Let $p > 2$ be a prime number, and let $e \geq 2$ and $\alpha \geq 1$ be integers. Let $g = \gcd(e, p^{\alpha-1}(p-1))$. Then for any $m \in Residues_{p^\alpha, e}$, $|Roots_{p^\alpha, e}(m)| = g$. I.e. either $m \notin Residues_{p^\alpha, e}$), or it has exactly g e^{th} roots.*

Corollary 1. *Let $p > 2$ be a prime number, and let $e > 1$ and $\alpha \geq 1$ be integers. Let $g = \gcd(e, p^{\alpha-1}(p-1))$, and let $q = p^{\alpha-1}(p-1)/g$. Let $m \in Residues_{p^\alpha, e}$, and let $s \in Roots_{p^\alpha, e}(m)$. Then $Roots_{p^\alpha, e}(m) = \{s_k \mid 0 \leq k \leq g - 1, s_k = \Psi^{-1}(\sigma + kq)\}$, where $\sigma = \Psi(s)$.*

Lemma 4. *Let $N > 1$ be an odd integer, and let $\prod_{i=1}^{\ell} p_i^{\alpha_i}$ be its prime factorization. Let $e > 1$ be an integer. Let $g_i = \gcd(e, p_i^{\alpha_i - 1}(p_i - 1))$. Then for any $m \in Residues_{N,e}$, $|Roots_{N,e}(m)| = \prod_{i=1}^{\ell} g_i$.*

Corollary 2. Let $N > 1$ be an odd integer, and let $\prod_{i=1}^{\ell} p_i^{\alpha_i}$ be its prime factorization. Let $e > 1$ be an integer. Let $g_i = \gcd(e, p_i^{\alpha_i-1}(p_i - 1))$, and let $q_i = p_i^{\alpha_i-1}(p_i - 1)/g_i$. Let $m \in Residues_{N,e}$, let s be its eth root, and let $\Psi(s) = (\sigma_1, \ldots, \sigma_\ell)$. Then $Roots_{N,e}(m) = \{ CRT(s_{1,k_1}, \ldots, s_{\ell,l_\ell}) \mid \forall 1 \leq i \leq \ell, 0 \leq k_i \leq g_i - 1, s_{i,k_i} = \Psi_{p_i^{\alpha_i}}^{-1}(\sigma_i + k_i q_i)\}$.

Lemma 5. Let $N > 1$ be an odd integer, and $e > 1$ be an integer. Then r selected as follows is a uniformly random element of $\mathbb{Z}_N^*$: first, select y uniformly at random from $Residues_{N,e}$. Then, select r uniformly at random from $Roots_{N,e}(y)$.

Proof. By Lemma 4, every element of $Residues_{N,e}$ has the same number of roots, and so selecting a random element of $Residues_{N,e}$ and then picking one of its roots at random is equivalent to picking a random element of $\mathbb{Z}_N^*$. □

Lemma 6. Let $N > 1$ be an odd integer, and $e > 1$ be an integer. Let $m \in Residues_{N,e}$. Let z be selected uniformly at random from $Residues_{N,e}$; let $y = z/m$. Then y is a uniformly random element of $Residues_{N,e}$.

Proof. Let $y \in Residues_{N,e}$. y is selected whenever the experiment chooses $z = my$; this happens with probability $1/|Residues_{N,e}|$. □

In our analysis below, it will be important that even if the adversary picks an eth root u of the value $z = mr^e$ (recall that z is what the signature recipient sends to the signer in order to get the message signed), it still cannot alter the distribution of the resulting signature. We will see that the signature $s = u/r$ is a member of $Roots_{N,e}(m)$ that is independent of u as long as r had been picked uniformly at random. In other words, as long as r is picked uniformly at random, s is random as well, no matter what the adversary does. This is captured in the following lemma:

Lemma 7. Let $N > 1$ be an odd integer, and $e > 1$ be an integer. Then for all $m, z \in Residues_{N,e}$, $u \in Roots_{N,e}(z)$, the following outputs a uniformly random element of $Roots_{N,e}(m)$: pick $r \leftarrow Roots_{N,e}(z/m)$, output u/r.

Proof. Consider $N = p^\alpha$ for some prime p; the general case follows via the Chinese Remainder Theorem. Let s_0 be the smallest (in absolute value) element of $Roots_{p^\alpha,e}(m)$, and let r_0 be the smallest element of $Roots_{p^\alpha,e}(z/m)$. Let $\Psi(s_0) = \sigma$, $\Psi(r_0) = \rho$, $\Psi(u) = \upsilon$, $g = \gcd(e, p^{\alpha-1}(p-1))$, and $q = p^{\alpha-1}(p-1)/g$.

By Corollary 1, $Roots_{p^\alpha,e}(m) = \{s_k \mid 0 \leq k \leq g-1, s_k = \Psi^{-1}(\sigma + kq)\}$. Since u/r_0 is an eth root of m, $u/r_0 = \Psi^{-1}(\sigma + nq)$ for some $0 \leq n < g$. Also by Corollary 1, $Roots_{p^\alpha,e}(m/z) = \{r_k \mid 0 \leq k \leq g-1, r_k = \Psi^{-1}(\rho+kq)\}$. Selecting r_k uniformly at random corresponds to picking $k \leftarrow \{0, \ldots, g-1\}$, and results in outputting $u/r_k = \Psi^{-1}(\upsilon - (\rho+kq)) = \Psi^{-1}((\upsilon-\rho) - kq) = \Psi^{-1}((\sigma+nq) - kq) = \Psi^{-1}(\sigma + (n - k)q)$. Since k is random, $n - k \bmod g$ is also a random element of $\{0, \ldots, g-1\}$, and therefore the output $r_k u = s_{(n-k) \bmod g}$ is uniformly random element of $Roots_{p^\alpha,e}(m)$. □

4.1   Blindness of the Signing Protocol

Let us consider $\mathcal{A}$'s interaction with the blindness challenger, and then analyze what information $\mathcal{A}$ learns as a result of this interaction. For simplicity, below we omit the integer-to-string conversions and, when clear from context that integers in question are elements of $\mathbb{Z}_N^*$, we omit "$\bmod N$."

$\mathcal{A}$ **is invoked** $\mathcal{A}(1^k)$ selects a public key $PK = (N, e)$ and two messages $\mathtt{msg}_0$ and $\mathtt{msg}_1$.

$\mathcal{A}$ **acts as the blind signer** For $j \in \{0, 1\}$, the challenger computes $\mathtt{EM}_j = \mathsf{PSSEncode}(\mathtt{msg}_j, k - 1)$; let $m_j = \mathsf{OS2IP}(\mathtt{EM}_j)$ be the corresponding integer. Next, sample $r_j \leftarrow \mathbb{Z}_N$, compute $z_j = m_j r_j^e$. Compute $\mathtt{inv}_j = r_j^{-1}$. The challenger sends to $\mathcal{A}$ the values z_b and z_{1-b}.

$\mathcal{A}$ **receives the signatures** Upon receipt of u_b and u_{1-b} from the signer, the challenger computes $s_0 = u_0/r_0$ and $s_1 = u_1/r_1$. If both signatures verify, i.e. $s_0^e = m_0$ and $s_1^e = m_1$, it sends (s_0, s_1) to $\mathcal{A}$; else it sends $\bot$ to $\mathcal{A}$.

$\mathcal{A}$'**s output** $\mathcal{A}$ outputs some value $\mathtt{output}$.

Claim 1. *If e is relatively prime to $\varphi(N)$, then z_0 and z_1 (sent to $\mathcal{A}$ while it is acting as the blind signer) are both random elements of $\mathbb{Z}_N^*$ and are distributed independently of b, m_0 and m_1.*

Proof. Follows immediately from Lemma 2.   □

Claim 2. *If e is relatively prime to $\varphi(N)$, then $\mathcal{A}$'s view after receiving the signatures is independent of the bit b.*

Proof. $\mathcal{A}$ already knows, based on the values u_b and u_{1-b} it sent to the challenger in the previous step, whether it will receive the signatures or $\bot$. If it receives the signatures, then there are unique values $r_{0,b}, r_{1,b}$ consistent with either $b \in \{0, 1\}$, and they were equally likely to have been chosen; see Lemma 2. If $\mathcal{A}$ does not receive the signatures, then $\mathcal{A}$ learns nothing.   □

If e is not relatively prime to $\varphi(N)$, then there are two cases, based on whether the signatures output by $\mathsf{Finalize}$ pass verification. The easy case is when the signatures output by $\mathsf{Finalize}$ do not both pass verification; then, the challenger sends $\bot$ to the adversary and thus no additional information is revealed in this step. Let us show that:

Claim 3. *If both signatures verify, $s_0^e = m_0$ and $s_1^e = m_1$, then $\mathcal{A}$'s view in the blindness experiment is independent of b.*

Proof. Let us condition on the event that the signatures pass verification. In this case, the values m_0, m_1 computed by the challenger, as well as the value z_b and z_{1-b} the challenger sent to the signer must all be in the set $Residues_{N,e}$. Let us consider a series of experiments.

Our first experiment is the case of running the blindness challenger with $b = 0$: The challenger begins by sampling m_0 and m_1 as PSS encodings of

$\mathtt{msg}_0$ and $\mathtt{msg}_1$. Then, it samples $r_0 \leftarrow \mathbb{Z}_N^*$, $r_1 \leftarrow \mathbb{Z}_N^*$, computes $z_0 = m_0 r_0^e$ and $z_1 = m_1 r_1^e$, and sends $(z, z') = (z_0, z_1)$ to the adversary. The adversary responds with (u_0, u_1), and the challenger computes the signatures $s_0 = u_0/r_0$ and $s_1 = u_1/r_1$.

By Lemma 5, instead of choosing r_0 and r_1 uniformly at random from $\mathbb{Z}_N^*$ and then setting $z_0 = r_0^e m_0$ and $z_1 = r_1^e m_1$, one could equivalently choose y_0, y_1 uniformly at random from $Residues_{N,e}$, and then let $z_0 = y_0 m_0$, $z_1 = y_1 m_1$, $r_0 \leftarrow Roots_{N,e}(y_0)$, $r_1 \leftarrow Roots_{N,e}(y_1)$; let us call the resulting experiment A_0. By Lemma 6, this is equivalent to choosing z_0 and z_1 uniformly at random from $Residues_{N,e}$, and letting $r_0 \leftarrow Roots_{N,e}(z_0/m_0)$, $r_1 \leftarrow Roots_{N,e}(z_1/m_1)$; let us call the resulting experiment B_0. By Lemma 7, this is equivalent to picking z_0 and z_1 uniformly at random from $Residues_{N,e}$ and sending the adversary the pair $(z, z') = (z_0, z_1)$, and upon receipt of u_0 and u_1 such that $u_0^e = z_0$ and $u_1^e = z_1$, outputting $s_0 \leftarrow Roots_{N,e}(m_0)$, $s_1 \leftarrow Roots_{N,e}(m_1)$; let us call the resulting experiment C_0.

Let us obtain a new experiment, C_1, by modifying C_0: let $(z, z') = (z_1, z_0)$, while everything else stays the same. C_1 gives the adversary identical view to C_0. Let B_1 be the same as B_0 except for $(z, z') = (z_1, z_0)$; by Lemma 7, the adversary's view here is identical to C_1. Let A_1 be identical to A_0 except $(z, z') = (z_1, z_0)$; by Lemma 6, it is identical to B_1. Finally, by Lemma 5, A_1 gives the adversary the same view as the challenger when $b = 1$.   □

Rephrasing Claims 1, 2 and 3, we get the following two lemmas:

Lemma 8. *Let $E_{relprime}^{\mathcal{A}}$ be the event that $\mathcal{A}$ playing the blindness game with the challenger for the basic version of RSA-BSSA sets $PK = (N, e)$ such that e is relatively prime to $\varphi(N)$. Conditioned on $E_{relprime}^{\mathcal{A}}$, $\mathcal{A}$ receives the same view in the blindness experiment for $b = 0$ as for $b = 1$.*

Lemma 9. *Let $E_{goodsigs}^{\mathcal{A}}$ be the event that in the blindness game with adversary $\mathcal{A}$, the challenger for the basic version of RSA-BSSA obtains two signatures that pass verification. Conditioned on $E_{goodsigs}^{\mathcal{A}}$, $\mathcal{A}$ receives the same view in the blindness experiment for $b = 0$ as for $b = 1$.*

When blindness might not hold. Based on the above analysis, the only situation in which $\mathcal{A}$'s view may depend on b is when e is not relatively prime to $\varphi(N)$ and the challenger fails to output two valid signatures. In this situation, z_b may leak enough information about m_b that it might be possible to infer whether $m_b = \mathsf{PSSEncode}(\mathtt{msg}_0)$ or $m_b = \mathsf{PSSEncode}(\mathtt{msg}_1)$, revealing b.

For example, for a prime p such that $e \mid p - 1$, x and y are in the same e^{th} residue class modulo p if there exists $r \in \mathbb{Z}_p^*$ such that $x = yr^e \bmod p$. There are e distinct e^{th} residue classes modulo p when $e \mid p - 1$; they correspond to the e values of $\Psi_p(x) \bmod e$. Thus, determining e^{th} residue class modulo p of an unknown x provides $\log e$ bits of information about x.

Suppose $N = \prod_{i=1}^{\ell} p_i$ such that $e \mid p_i - 1$ for $1 \leq i \leq \ell$, where each p_i is a distinct prime number. Then $z_b = m_b r^e \bmod p_i$ is the same e^{th} residue class as $m_b \bmod p_i$. Thus, z_b reveals $\ell \log e$ bits of information about m_b. If each p_i

is only slightly larger than e, then z reveals (in the information-theoretic sense) more than half the bits of m_b. It is unclear how these information-theoretic bits correspond to physical bits; therefore, we must consider the worst case, in which they reveal a significant number of bits of the encoded message EM. Especially devastating would be the case when the revealed bits correspond to H and the bits of maskedDB just to the left of H; by XORing those bits with $MGF(H, lenDB)$, $\mathcal{A}$ can recover salt, and check whether $H = \mathsf{Hash}(M')$ where M' encodes mHash $= \mathsf{Hash}(\mathsf{msg}_0, hLen)$ with salt (which corresponds to $b = 0$) or mHash $= \mathsf{Hash}(\mathsf{msg}_1, hLen)$ with salt (which corresponds to $b = 1$).

As we will see below, variants A and B of RSA-BSSA prevent this situation in two distinct ways. Variant A makes it extremely unlikely that e is not relatively prime to $\varphi(N)$. Variant B ensures that recovering mHash does not help in checking whether it corresponds to msg_0 or msg_1: any value mHash is equally likely to correspond to either, depending on the choice of the randomizer rand.

4.2   Blindness of Variants a and B

Theorem 2. *RSA-BSSA, Version A, satisfies blindness (Definition 4).*

Proof. This follows by the soundness of the proof due to Goldberg et al. [21]. □

Theorem 3. *RSA-BSSA, Version B, satisfies blindness in the random-oracle model (Definition 4).*

Proof. For $j \in \{0, 1\}$, let m_j be the integer that corresponds to PSSEncode($\mathsf{msg}_j \circ \mathsf{rand}_j$) for a random string rand_j of κ bits, and $z_j = m_j r_j^e$. Let $(z, z') = (z_b, z_{1-b})$ be the values that the challenger sends to the adversary $\mathcal{A}$ in the blindness experiment with the bit b. In order to see that (z, z') are distributed independently of the bit b it is sufficient to show that $\mathsf{mHash}_b = \mathsf{Hash}(\mathsf{msg}_b \circ \mathsf{rand}_b, hLen)$ is distributed independently of b for a randomly chosen rand_b, since PSSEncode just feeds its input string to Hash.

Let us model Hash as a random oracle. Consider a modified blindness experiment in which the challenger also controls the random oracle Hash:

$\mathcal{A}$ **is invoked** $\mathcal{A}(1^k)$ selects a public key $PK = (N, e)$ and msg_0 and msg_1.

$\mathcal{A}$ **acts as the blind signer** For $j \in \{0, 1\}$, compute $\mathsf{EM}_j = \mathsf{PSSEncode}(\mathsf{msg}_j, k - 1)$ differently from the blindness challenger, as follows: instead of picking rand_j first, and then setting mHash_j, leave rand_j undefined for now and let mHash_j be a random string of length $8hLen$. Next, follow the protocol and let $m_j = \mathsf{OS2IP}(\mathsf{EM}_j)$ be the corresponding integer. Next, sample $r_j \leftarrow \mathbb{Z}_N^*$, compute $z_j = m_j r_j^e \bmod N$ and make sure $z_j \in \mathbb{Z}_N^*$. Compute $\mathsf{inv}_j = r_j^{-1} \bmod N$. The challenger sends to $\mathcal{A}$ the values z_b and z_{1-b}.

$\mathcal{A}$ **receives the signatures** Upon receipt of u_b and u_{1-b} from the signer, the challenger checks that $z_j = u_j^e$ for each $j \in \{0, 1\}$; if these fail, send $\perp$ to $\mathcal{A}$. If these checks pass, then choose random κ-bit strings rand_0 and rand_1 and set the random oracle so that $\mathsf{mHash}_j = \mathsf{Hash}(\mathsf{msg}_j \circ \mathsf{rand}_j, hLen)$; if setting the random oracle this way fails (i.e., the value $\mathsf{Hash}(\mathsf{msg}_j \circ \mathsf{rand}_j, hLen)$ is already defined), then this experiment fails.

Else, for each $j \in \{0, 1\}$, compute $s_j = u_j/r_j$ and send (s_0, s_1) to $\mathcal{A}$.

$\mathcal{A}$ **queries** Hash Since in this modified blindness experiment, the challenger controls the random oracle, we must also describe how it handles the adversary's queries to Hash. As usual, when $\mathcal{A}$ queries a value (v, ℓ) such that $\mathsf{Hash}(v, \ell)$ has not yet been defined, respond with a random string of length 8ℓ; when querying for a string whose value has already been defined, return that value.

$\mathcal{A}$'s **output** At the end of its execution, $\mathcal{A}$ produces some output. At that point, if rand_0 and rand_1 are still undefined, choose random κ-bit strings rand_0 and rand_1 and set the random oracle so that $\mathsf{mHash}_j = \mathsf{Hash}(\mathsf{msg}_j \circ \mathsf{rand}_j, hLen)$; if setting the random oracle this way fails (i.e., the value $\mathsf{Hash}(\mathsf{msg}_j \circ \mathsf{rand}_j, hLen)$ is already defined), then this experiment fails.

Our theorem will follow by putting together the following three claims:

Claim 4. *Conditioned on the event that the modified blindness experiment does not fail, the view $\mathcal{A}$ receives in the modified blindness experiment above is independent of the bit b.*

Claim 5. *Conditioned on the event that the modified blindness experiment does not fail, the view $\mathcal{A}$ receives in the modified blindness experiment above is identical to the view it receives in the actual blindness experiment.*

Claim 6. *Let $\mathcal{A}$'s running time be t. Then the modified blindness experiment fails with probability $O(t2^{-\kappa})$.*

To see that the theorem follows from the claims, consider a sequence of experiments: (1) blindness game with $b = 0$; (2) modified blindness game with $b = 0$; (3) modified blindness game with $b = 1$; (4) blindness game with $b = 1$. (1) and (2) are indistinguishable by combining Claims 5 and 6; similarly (3) and (4). (2) and (3) are indistinguishable by combining Claims 4 and 6.

We conclude our proof of the theorem by proving these claims.

Proof of Claim 4. This claim follows by construction. Note that in the step when $\mathcal{A}$ acts as the blind signer, the challenger does not even need to have b already defined: it can set mHash_b and mHash_{1-b} without knowing b and compute m_b and m_{1-b} from them; similarly it can sample r_b and compute z_b. If it needs to know b in the step where $\mathcal{A}$ receives the signatures, the challenger is already assured that m_0 and m_1 are both in $Residues_{N,e}$, and so by Lemma 9, $\mathcal{A}$'s view is independent of b.

Proof of Claim 5. In the random-oracle model, the only difference between the modified experiment above and the real blindness experiment is the point in time in which the values rand_0 and rand_1 are defined: whether they are already defined when $\mathcal{A}$ acts as the blind signer, or whether this does not happen until the step where $\mathcal{A}$ receives the signatures or (in the event it does not) the output step. If we condition on the event that the modified experiment does not fail, then we know that $\mathcal{A}$ has never over the course of its execution queried Hash on the values $(\mathtt{msg}_0 \circ \mathtt{rand}_0, hLen)$ and $(\mathtt{msg}_1 \circ \mathtt{rand}_1, hLen)$. In that case, whether $\mathtt{rand}_0$ and $\mathtt{rand}_1$ were already defined or not, is independent of $\mathcal{A}$'s view, and therefore the modified blindness experiment is identical to the original one.

Proof of Claim 6. The modified experiment fails if the adversary ever queries Hash on input $(\mathtt{msg}_j \circ \mathtt{rand}_j, hLen)$ for $j \in \{0,1\}$. In t steps, $\mathcal{A}$ may query at most t such strings. $\mathtt{rand}_j$ is a random κ-bit string, so the probability it's among the t that $\mathcal{A}$ has queried, is $t2^{-\kappa}$. □

4.3   The Basic Version Is a Blind Token Scheme

Theorem 4. *The basic version of RSA-BSSA is a strongly unforgeable blind token scheme (Definition 5) under the one-more-RSA assumption.*

Proof. First, note that the basic version of RSA-BSSA satisfies the input-output specification for a two-move blind signature scheme (Definition 1) and the strong one-more unforgeability property (Definition 3). The first follows by inspection; the second, by Theorem 6. Thus, it is sufficient to show that for any $\mathcal{A}$, the view in the experiment described in Definition 5 is independent of the bit b.

Note that in the blind token security game, unless the challenger obtains two valid signatures, the adversary's view is independent of b based on how the game unfolds. Thus, an adversary $\mathcal{A}$ guessing b correctly in that game more often than half the time must be one for whom the challenger obtains two valid signatures. Then consider the following reduction $\mathcal{B}$ that plays the (usual) blindness game with a blind signature challenger for RSA-BSSA and uses $\mathcal{A}$ to contradict Lemma 9: it obtains from $\mathcal{A}$ the values (N, e) and the auxiliary data needed to sample the messages $\mathtt{msg}_0$ and $\mathtt{msg}_1$ and proceeds to sample them. Then it sends (N, e) and $\mathtt{msg}_0$ and $\mathtt{msg}_1$ to its challenger, and from then on, it passes messages back and forth from its challenger to $\mathcal{A}$, and outputs whatever $\mathcal{A}$ outputs. If $\mathcal{A}$ is successful, then $\mathcal{B}$ is successful. But $\mathcal{A}$ can only be successful (as we observed above) when the challenger outputs two valid signatures, and by Lemma 9, under these circumstances $\mathcal{B}$ cannot be successful, which is a contradiction. □

4.4   Blindness of Chaum-RSA-FDH

Consider Bellare et al. [6]'s version of Chaum blind signature; we will call it *Chaum-RSA-FDH* from now on. Chaum-RSA-FDH works as follows: Following RSA-FDH, the key generation algorithm generates an RSA key pair $PK = (N, e)$, $SK = d$, where $ed \equiv 1 \bmod \varphi(N)$. Following Chaum, in order to obtain a blind signature on a message M, the user first blinds it using a random $r \leftarrow \mathbb{Z}_N^*$ obtaining $z = \mathsf{Hash}(M)r^e \bmod N$. Then he sends z to the signer and gets back the blinded signature $y = z^d \bmod N$, and unblinds it to obtain and output $s = yr^{-1} \bmod N$. The resulting value passes RSA-FDH verification: $s^e = y^e r^{-e} = zr^{-e} = \mathsf{Hash}(M)r^e r^{-e} = \mathsf{Hash}(M)$.

Let (N, e) be such that e is not relatively prime to $\varphi(N)$. Let $U = \{u \mid u^e \equiv 1 \bmod N\}$; by Lemma 4, when e divides some prime factors of N, $|U| \geq e$. Let $\equiv_e$ be the following equivalence relation: $a \equiv_e b$ if there exist α, β and $u \in U$ such that $a = \alpha^e u \bmod N$ and $b = \beta^e u \bmod N$. It is easy to see that $\equiv_e$ partitions $\mathbb{Z}_N^*$ into $|U|$ equivalence classes. There is an efficient algorithm that, on input the factorization of N, a and b, determines whether $a \equiv_e b$. Moreover, for any $a, r \in \mathbb{Z}_N^*$, $a \equiv_e ar^e$.

In order to break blindness of Chaum-RSA-FDH, the adversary picks (N, e) such that it knows the factorization of N, and such that $e \mid \varphi(N)$. Next, it picks two messages M_0 and M_1 to send to the challenger, such that $1 \not\equiv_e$ Hash$(M_0) \not\equiv_e$ Hash$(M_1) \not\equiv_e 1$. The challenger computes $z_0 = $ Hash$(M_0)r_0^e$ and $z_1 = $ Hash$(M_1)r_1^e$, and sends them to the adversary in random order: (z_b, z_{1-b}). In order to determine the bit b, the adversary checks whether $z_b \equiv_e$ Hash(M_0); if so, it returns 0, else it returns 1.

Bibliographic note. Before the community settled on what is now considered to be the right definition of blindness [1], the definition due to Juels, Ostrovsky and Luby [25] was the standard one. That definition's security experiment for blindness did not envision that the adversarial signer may generate the signing key in a malicious way, rather than following the key generation algorithm. Bellare, Namprempre, Pointcheval and Semanko showed that the Chaum-RSA-FDH scheme was a secure blind signature under the old definition [25]. As we saw, their result does not hold under the more modern definition of blindness that came several years after their paper came out. Fortunately, Chaum-RSA-FDH is a strongly one-more-unforgeable blind token scheme, i.e., it satisfies Definition 5.

Theorem 5. *The Chaum-RSA-FDH scheme described in Sect. 4.4 is a strongly one-more-unforgeable blind token scheme for any efficiently samplable message space $\mathcal{M}$.*

Proof. (Sketch) It is easy to see that the scheme satisfies the input-output structure and the correctness requirements. As for strong one-more unforgeability: Bellare, Namprempre, Pointcheval and Semanko [6] showed that it was one-more-unforgeable under the one-more-RSA assumption. Strong one-more unforgeability follows because RSA-FDH is deterministic, i.e., there is a unique signature corresponding to each message. Thus we just need to show that for any $\mathcal{A}$, $\mathcal{A}$'s advantage in the blind token experiment described in Definition 5 is negligible; in fact we will see that it is 0.

Let $\mathcal{A}$ be an adversary playing the blind token game; let us consider the view $\mathcal{A}$ receives given a fixed $b \in \{0, 1\}$. When it is first invoked (step 1), it produces $PK = (N, e)$ and some string aux. Next (step 2), $\mathtt{msg}_0$ and $\mathtt{msg}_1$ are selected by the challenger by running $\mathcal{M}(1^k, PK, aux)$; let $x_0 = $ Hash$(\mathtt{msg}_0)$ and $x_1 = $ Hash$(\mathtt{msg}_1)$. Let r_0 and r_1 be sampled at random from $\mathbb{Z}_N^*$, and let $z_0 = x_0 r_0^e$ and $z_1 = x_1 r_1^e$ be the blinded messages the challenger sends to $\mathcal{A}$ (step 3), and let s_0 and s_1 be the values $\mathcal{A}$ sends in return — the order in which they are sent depends on b (step 4). Next (step 5) if $s_0^e = z_0$ and $s_1^e = z_1$, the challenger computes $\sigma_0 = s_0/r_0$ and σ_1/r_1 and sends to the adversary the values $(\mathtt{msg}_0, \sigma_0)$ and $(\mathtt{msg}_1, \sigma_1)$, else it sends it $\perp$.

Consider an alternative pair of experiments for $b \in \{0, 1\}$; here the challenger is computationally unbounded. The challenger begins by selecting $\mathtt{msg}_0$ and $\mathtt{msg}_1$

from $\mathcal{M}(1^k, PK, aux)$. We have two cases: Case A, in which there exist (σ_0, σ_1) such that $\sigma_0^e = \mathsf{Hash}(\mathsf{msg}_0)$ and $(\sigma_1)^e = \mathsf{Hash}(\mathsf{msg}_1)$; and Case B, in which the pair exist (σ_0, σ_1) does not exist. Since this challenger is unbounded, it identifies which case it is in, and acts as follows:

In Case A, in Step 2, the challenger picks z and z^* uniformly at random from $\mathbb{Z}_N^*$ and sends (z, z^*) to $\mathcal{A}$. It receives (s, s^*). In step 5, if $s^e \neq z$ or $(s^*)^e \neq (z^*)^e$, then it sends $\perp$ to $\mathcal{A}$. Else, it samples valid signatures σ_0 and σ_1 for msg_0 and msg_1, respectively, and sends to the adversary $\mathcal{A}$ the values $(\mathsf{msg}_0, \sigma_0)$ and $(\mathsf{msg}_1, \sigma_1)$.

In Case B, the challenger follows the protocol.

It is easy to see that, in the alternative experiment, the adversary's view is independent of b. To see that the alternative experiment gives $\mathcal{A}$ a view that's identical to the blind token game in Case A, note that the challenger choosing $r_0 = s/\sigma_0$ and $r_1 = s^*/\sigma_1$ in step 3 corresponds to having $b = 0$ in the blind token game, while choosing $r_0 = s^*/\sigma_0$ and $r_1 = s/\sigma_1$ corresponds to $b = 1$. Since r_0 and r_1 are chosen uniformly at random, the two options are equally likely. In Case B, since one or both signatures don't exist, the adversary's view is independent of b as well, since the pair of messages $(\mathsf{msg}_0, \mathsf{msg}_1)$ is just as likely as $(\mathsf{msg}_1, \mathsf{msg}_2)$. $\qquad\qquad\square$

5   Unforgeability of RSA-BSSA

Recall that an algorithm $\mathcal{A}$ is said to break the security of a cryptographic scheme *in the random-oracle model* [7] if its success probability is non-negligible when a specific component of the scheme, typically a hash function, is replaced by a random oracle. Security in the random-oracle model means that no polynomial-time algorithm can break the scheme in the random-oracle model.

A proof of security in the random-oracle model does not, in fact, imply a proof of security in the plain model (i.e. where no component of the scheme is modeled as a random oracle) [12]. However, it is considered evidence of security that's good enough in practice.

In a random-oracle-based reduction, the reduction is typically privy to all the hash function queries the adversary issues. Another privilege that such a reduction has (in the standard, so-called "programmable" random-oracle model — these different flavors are explored by Fischlin et al. [18]) is that it can answer such a query with any value it desires. Since the adversary expects the answers to its queries to be truly random, as long as the reduction's responses are distributed at random (or are indistinguishable from random), the adversary's success probability will be as high when interacting with the reduction as when attacking the scheme.

We will prove strong one-more unforgeability of RSA-BSSA in the random-oracle model under the one-more-RSA assumption introduced by Bellare, Namprempre, Pointcheval and Semanko [6]. They also showed that the one-more-RSA assumption (stated formally in Appendix A) holds if an only if the following problem, called the alternative chosen-target RSA inversion (RSA-ACTI) problem, is hard:

Definition 7 (RSA-ACTI [6]). *Let $\mathcal{A}$ be an oracle Turing machine. For the security parameter k, let the experiment $\mathbf{Exp}_{\mathcal{A}}^{rsa-acti}(k)$ be defined as follows:*

RSA key pair generation *The challenger generates an RSA public key (N, e) and secret key d corresponding to the security parameter k. Let us define the following oracles:*
1. *The RSA inversion oracle $\mathcal{O}_I(\cdot, N, d)$ that, on input $y \in \mathbb{Z}_N^*$, returns x such that $x^e = y \bmod N$; i.e., it returns $y^d \bmod N$ where $ed \equiv 1 \bmod \varphi(N)$.*
2. *An oracle $\mathcal{O}_R(\cdot, N)$ that, when queried, issues a random RSA inversion challenge point, i.e. a random element of $\mathbb{Z}_N^*$. By y_i, let us denote the outcome of the ith such query.*

$\mathcal{A}$ is invoked The challenger invokes $\mathcal{A}^{\mathcal{O}_I(\cdot,N,d),\mathcal{O}_R(\cdot,N)}(N, e)$ and responds to its oracle queries. Eventually, $\mathcal{A}$ terminates.

$\mathcal{A}$'s success criterion Let ℓ be the number of queries $\mathcal{A}$ issued to $\mathcal{O}_I(\cdot, N, d)$. Let $(y_1, \ldots, y_n)$ be the values $\mathcal{A}$ received from $\mathcal{O}_R(\cdot, N)$. Let $(z_1, \ldots, z_n)$ be $\mathcal{A}$'s output. For $1 \le i \le n$, z_i is correct if $z_i^e = y_i \bmod N$. $\mathcal{A}$ is successful if $|\{i : z_i \text{ is correct}\}| \ge \ell + 1$.

By $\mathbf{Adv}_{\mathcal{A}}^{rsa-acti}(k)$ we denote the probability that $\mathcal{A}$ is successful in $\mathbf{Exp}_{\mathcal{A}}^{rsa-acti}(k)$. The RSA-ACTI problem is hard if for any probabilistic polynomial-time $\mathcal{A}$, $\mathbf{Adv}_{\mathcal{A}}^{rsa-acti}(k)$ is negligible.

Theorem 6. *Let $\mathcal{A}$ be an algorithm that breaks strong one-more unforgeability of the basic RSA-BSSA scheme (Definition 3) where both $\mathsf{Hash}(\cdot, \ell)$ and $\mathsf{MGF}(\cdot, \ell)$ are random oracles for every integer ℓ. Let $t_{\mathcal{A}}(k)$ be an upper bound on its running time; let $p_{\mathcal{A}}(k)$ be its success probability.*

Then there exists an algorithm $\mathcal{B}$ that solves the RSA-ACTI problem (Definition 7) in $t^{\mathcal{B}}(k) = O(poly(k) + t^{\mathcal{A}}(k))$ time with probability $p_{\mathcal{B}}(k) = p_{\mathcal{A}}(k) - \Theta(t_{\mathcal{A}}^2(k)2^{-8hLen})$.

This theorem, i.e. the unforgeability of the *basic* RSA-BSSA scheme, implies unforgeability of variants A and B. For variant A, the additional proof that's part of the public key can be simulated in the random-oracle model as shown by Goldberg et al. [21]. For variant B, unforgeability follows from that of the basic scheme, since a signature in variant B on message `msg` with randomness `rand` is also a signature in the basic scheme on message `msg ∘ rand`.

Corollary 3. *Let $\mathcal{A}$ be an algorithm that breaks strong one-more unforgeability of RSA-BSSA variants A or B (Definition 3) where both $\mathsf{Hash}(\cdot, \ell)$ and $\mathsf{MGF}(\cdot, \ell)$ are random oracles for every integer ℓ. Let $t_{\mathcal{A}}(k)$ be an upper bound on its running time; let $p_{\mathcal{A}}(k)$ be its success probability.*

Then there exists an algorithm $\mathcal{B}$ that solves the RSA-ACTI problem (Definition 7) in $t^{\mathcal{B}}(k) = O(poly(k) + t^{\mathcal{A}}(k))$ time with probability $p_{\mathcal{B}}(k) = p_{\mathcal{A}}(k) - \Theta(t_{\mathcal{A}}^2(k)2^{-8hLen})$.

Proof. (of Theorem 6) Let $q_{\mathsf{Hash}}^{\mathcal{A}}(PK; R)$, $q_{\mathsf{MGF}}^{\mathcal{A}}(PK; R)$ and $q_{\mathsf{BSig}}^{\mathcal{A}}(PK; R)$ be the number of queries $\mathcal{A}$ makes to Hash, MGF and BSig respectively when interacting with it challenger on input a specific public key PK; R denotes the randomness of the experiment (i.e., both the random tape of $\mathcal{A}$ and that of the challenger). When PK and R are clear from context, we will write $q^{\mathcal{A}}_{\mathsf{Hash}}$, $q^{\mathcal{A}}_{\mathsf{MGF}}$ and $q^{\mathcal{A}}_{\mathsf{BSig}}$.

Without loss of generality, let us assume that $\mathcal{A}$'s output is either empty (i.e., $\mathcal{A}$ fails to win the game) or consists solely of $q^{\mathcal{A}}_{\mathsf{BSig}} + 1$ message-signature pairs that pass verification. Let us call such an $\mathcal{A}$ a "high-achieving adversary" in the sequel. The reason we can assume that $\mathcal{A}$ is high-achieving is that, if it's not, we could modify $\mathcal{A}$ into an algorithm $\mathcal{A}'$ that verifies $\mathcal{A}$'s output and, if $\mathcal{A}$ succeeded, outputs the first $q^{\mathcal{A}}_{\mathsf{BSig}} + 1$ pairs that pass verification. By definition of one-more unforgeability, $\mathcal{A}'$ succeeds with the same probability as $\mathcal{A}$, and has a comparable running time.

We will construct the reduction $\mathcal{B}$ that will use a high-achieving $\mathcal{A}$ as a subroutine.

Input to the reduction. The reduction plays the role of the attacker in experiment $\mathsf{Exp}^{rsa-acti}_{\mathcal{B}}(k)$. Thus, it takes as input the RSA public key (N, e) that had been generated by RSA's key generation on input the security parameter k.

The oracle the reduction may use. As described in Definition 7, $\mathcal{B}$ has access to two oracles:

1. The RSA inversion oracle $\mathcal{O}_I(\cdot, N, d)$ that, on input $y \in \mathbb{Z}^*_N$, returns x such that $x^e = y \bmod N$; i.e., it returns $y^d \bmod N$ where $ed \equiv 1 \bmod \varphi(N)$.
2. An oracle $\mathcal{O}_R(\cdot, N)$ that, when queried, issues a random RSA inversion challenge point, i.e. a random element of $\mathbb{Z}^*_N$. By y_i, let us denote the outcome of the ith such query.

How the reduction interacts with $\mathcal{A}$. The adversary $\mathcal{A}$ is attacking the strong one-more unforgeability property of the RSA-BSSA scheme as described in Definition 3. Thus, $\mathcal{A}$ will need to receive PK as input; the reduction sets $PK = (N, e)$, where (N, e) is its own input. Since the reduction is in the random-oracle model, $\mathcal{A}$ will expect oracle access to Hash and MGF, which $\mathcal{B}$ will respond to as described below. $\mathcal{A}$ will also engage with the signer in the blind signing protocol; in the case of RSA-BSSA, this will involve oracle access to $\mathsf{BSig}(SK, \cdot)$; below, we describe how $\mathcal{B}$ will handle this as well. Finally, $\mathcal{A}$ terminates and produces some output; below, we describe how $\mathcal{B}$ uses $\mathcal{A}$'s output to compute a solution to the RSA-ACTI problem.

How the reduction will handle $\mathcal{A}$'s queries to $\mathsf{Hash}(\cdot, \cdot)$. A relevant query to $\mathsf{Hash}(\cdot, \cdot)$ is (v, ℓ) such that $\ell = hLen$ and the first eight bytes of v are all 0.

Let (v, ℓ) be a query that is *not* relevant. A value v that is derived as part of signature verification must begin with 64 0s; if v is not of that form, we know that we will never encounter the need to calculate $\mathsf{Hash}(v, hLen)$ as part of verifying a signature. (A detailed description of the signature verification algorithm provided in Appendix B clarifies this point; see Step 6.) We also know that for any length $\ell \neq hLen$, $\mathsf{Hash}(v, \ell)$ is not computed as part of signature verification. Thus, there is no need to prepare a response to this query in any special way. In response to (v, ℓ), the reduction returns a randomly sampled string h of ℓ bytes and stores $((v, \ell), h)$ for future reference.

In contrast, the response to the ith relevant query is set up in such a way that, should that query be part of the successful verification of one of the signatures returned by the adversary, it should allow the reduction to invert RSA at a challenge point y_i.

More precisely: Let the ith relevant query to Hash be the pair $(v_i, hLen)$. Parse v_i as follows: $v_i = 0^{64} \circ \mathtt{mHash}_i \circ \mathtt{salt}_i$. Implicitly, $\mathtt{mHash}_i$ is computed from some unknown M_i, and $\mathtt{salt}_i$ are the last $lenSalt$ bits of v_i.

Our goal is to ensure that, if the adversary ever returns (M, σ) that passes the verification algorithm such that $\mathtt{mHash} = \mathtt{mHash}_i$, and $\mathtt{salt} = \mathtt{salt}_i$, then $\sigma^e = y_i r_i^e \mod N$ for some challenge point y_i and a value r_i known to the reduction. Then the reduction can invert RSA at y_i by outputting σ / r_i.

First, the reduction obtains the challenge y_i by querying $\mathcal{O}_R(\cdot, N)$. Next, it samples from $\mathbb{Z}_N^*$ until it finds a value r_i such that, for $w_i = y_i r_i^e$, $w_i < 2^{k-1}$ (i.e. $k - 1$ bits are sufficient to encode it) and the binary representation of w_i ends in the byte $0xBC$. In expectation, it will take between 256 and 512 attempts to find such r_i, depending on how close N is to 2^k: at least half the time, $w_i < 2^{k-1}$, and conditioned on that, it starts with $0xBC$ one in every 256 tries.

Next, execute the following steps that determine how to fix MGF in one point, and what value to return in response to this query. The goal is to ensure that, if (M, σ) is a message-signature pair accepted by the verification algorithm, and $v_i = 0^{64} \circ \mathtt{mHash} \circ \mathtt{salt}$ is the input to Hash computed as part of verification (i.e. it is the value M' computed in Step 6 and queried in Step 7 of the detailed verification algorithm in Appendix B), then $\sigma^e \mod N = w_i$.

1. Set $\mathtt{EM}_i = \mathsf{I2OSP}(w_i, emLen)$ (recall that $emLen = \lceil (k - 1)/8 \rceil$).
2. Parse $\mathtt{EM}_i = \mathtt{maskedDB}_i \circ H_i \circ 0xBC$ (as described in Step 2 of the verification procedure in Appendix B). Since the reduction used the sampling procedure above to obtain w_i, $\mathtt{EM}_i$ ends in the byte $0xBC$.
3. In order to ensure that $\mathtt{DB}_i$ that will be computed in Step 4 (of the detailed verification procedure) contains the same salt value as v_i, carry out the following steps:
   - Let $\mathtt{mHash}_i$ and $\mathtt{salt}_i$ be the strings of $hLen$ and $sLen$ bytes, respectively, such that $v_i = 0^{64} \circ \mathtt{mHash}_i \circ \mathtt{salt}_i$.
   - Let $\mathtt{DB}_i = 0^a \circ 0 \times 01 \circ \mathtt{salt}_i$, where $a = 8(lenDB - 1 - sLen)$.
   - Let $\mathtt{dbMask}'_i = \mathtt{DB}_i \oplus \mathtt{maskedDB}_i$. Note that $\mathtt{dbMask}'_i$ must start with 0^p, since $\mathtt{DB}_i$ starts with 0s, and the fact that $\mathtt{maskedDB}$ is the beginning of the string output by I2OSP ensures that it begin with p 0s. Let $\mathtt{dbMask}_i$ be the result of replacing the first p bits of $\mathtt{dbMask}'_i$ with random bits.
   - If $\mathsf{MGF}(H_i, lenDB)$ is already defined, fail. Else, set it to the value $\mathtt{dbMask}_i$.
4. Set $\mathsf{Hash}(v_i, hLen) = H_i$, save (i, v_i, w_i, r_i, H_i) for future reference.

Return H_i.

How the reduction will handle $\mathcal{A}$'s queries to $\mathsf{MGF}(\cdot, \cdot)$. Let u be a query to MGF. Case 1: $\mathsf{MGF}(u, \ell)$ is already fixed as a result of a previous query to Hash or MGF;

then return the value $\mathsf{MGF}(u, \ell)$. Case 2: $\mathsf{MGF}(u, \ell)$ is not yet fixed; then return a random string of ℓ octets.

How the reduction will handle $\mathcal{A}$'s queries to $\mathsf{BSig}(SK, \cdot)$. Once `blinded_msg` from the adversary $\mathcal{A}$ is received, compute $m = \mathsf{OS2IP}(\texttt{blinded\_msg})$. If $m \geq N$, then it fails. Otherwise, it sends m to its RSA inversion oracle $\mathcal{O}_I(\cdot, N, d)$. In turn, $\mathcal{O}_I(m, N, d)$ returns s such that $s^e = m \bmod N$. $\mathcal{B}$ computes `blinded_sig` = $\mathsf{I2OSP}(s, kLen)$ and returns it to $\mathcal{A}$.

How the reduction will process $\mathcal{A}$'s output. At the end of its execution, the adversary $\mathcal{A}$ outputs a set of message-signature pairs $\{(M_j, \sigma_j)\}$. First, $\mathcal{B}$ verifies these message-signature pairs, as follows: it runs the verification algorithm as described in Appendix B. When the verification algorithm queries Hash and MGF for a value previously queried by $\mathcal{A}$, Hash and MGF return the same string as was returned to $\mathcal{A}$. When the verification algorithm queries Hash and MGF for a value not previously queried by $\mathcal{A}$, Hash and MGF return random strings.

Next, $\mathcal{B}$ fails if some message-signature pair (M_j, σ_j) is accepted by the verification algorithm, and yet $\mathcal{A}$ had not made the queries to Hash and MGF that the verification algorithm just made when verifying (σ_j, M_j).

Else, $\mathcal{B}$ proceeds as follows. Recall that n is the number of queries that $\mathcal{B}$ has made to its challenge oracle, i.e. the number of challenge points y_j that $\mathcal{B}$ has received. For $1 \leq i \leq n$, initialize $z_i = \perp$. Next, for each j such that (M_j, σ_j) is accepted by the verification algorithm, find i such that $\sigma_j^e \bmod N \equiv w_i$. (If no such i exists, fail.) Then $\sigma_j^e = y_i r_i^e \bmod N$, so $y_i = (\sigma_j/r_i)^e$ and so $\mathcal{B}$ has inverted RSA at y_i; set $z_i = \sigma_j/r_i$.

$\mathcal{B}$ outputs $z_1, \dots, z_n$.

Analysis of the reduction. To conclude our proof of security, we need to prove the following three claims. First, we show that an adversary that wins the strong one-more-forgery game against RSA-BSSA must (other than with very small probability) query MGF and Hash for all the values that will be queried over the course of the verification of its signatures. This will allow us to assume that we are dealing with the adversary that always makes these queries prior to outputting its signatures and makes sure that verification accepts; we will call such an adversary a "make-sure" adversary. More formally:

Claim 7. *Let $\mathcal{A}$ be a high-achieving adversary that wins the strong one-more-forgery game against RSA-BSSA in the random-oracle model with probability $p_{\mathcal{A}}(k)$. Let E be the event that $\mathcal{A}$ wins the game and for each of the message-signature pairs it produced, it issued the queries to both $\mathsf{MGF}(\cdot, lenDB)$ and $\mathsf{Hash}(\cdot, hLen)$ needed for verifying the message-signature pair some time during the course of its execution. Then $\Pr[E] \geq p_{\mathcal{A}}(k) - \Theta(t_{\mathcal{A}}^2(k) 2^{-8hLen})$.*

Next, we show that for a "make-sure" $\mathcal{A}$, our reduction succeeds. This is done in two steps: (1) showing that the view that the reduction provides for $\mathcal{A}$ is identical to its view in the one-more-forgery game in the random-oracle model; (2) showing that whenever a "make-sure" $\mathcal{A}$ is successful, the reduction succeeds in the RSA-ACTI game. More formally:

Claim 8. *Let $\mathcal{A}$ be any adversary. In the random-oracle model, the view that $\mathcal{A}$ receives when interacting with the strong one-more unforgeability game challenger for RSA-BSSA is identical to the one $\mathcal{A}$ obtains in an interaction with the reduction $\mathcal{B}$ whenever $\mathcal{B}$ does not fail while answering $\mathcal{A}$'s queries. Moreover, the probability that $\mathcal{B}$ fails while answering a query from $\mathcal{A}$ is $O(t^2(k)2^{-8hLen})$.*

Claim 9. *Let $\mathcal{A}$ be an adversary that wins the strong one-more unforgeability game against RSA-BSSA in the random-oracle model with probability $p_{\mathcal{A}}(k)$. Then $\mathcal{B}$ wins the RSA-ACTI game with probability $p_{\mathcal{A}}(k) - \Theta(t_{\mathcal{A}}^2(k)2^{-8hLen})$.*

The proofs of Claims 7, 8 and 9 are in the full version of this paper [26]. □

Acknowledgments. I thank Frederic Jacobs for numerous discussions about RSA-BSSA, and to Chris Wood and Steve Myers for helpful feedback. I am also grateful to the anonymous referees for constructive comments. This paper was supported by Apple Inc. I also acknowledge the support of NSF awards #2154170 and #2154941.

A   Statement of Computational Hardness Assumptions

Bellare, Namprempre, Pointcheval and Semanko [5,6] introduced the RSA known-target inversion problem (RSA-KTI) defined below; the definition we give here is identical to theirs:

Definition 8. (Known-Target Inversion Problem: RSA-KTI [6]). *Let $\mathcal{A}$ be an oracle Turing machine. For the security parameter k and any function $m : \mathbb{N} \mapsto \mathbb{N}$, let the experiment $\mathbf{Exp}_{\mathcal{A},m}^{rsa-kti}(k)$ be defined as follows:*

RSA key pair generation *The challenger generates an RSA public key (N, e) and secret key d corresponding to the security parameter k. Let $\mathcal{O}_I(\cdot, N, d)$ be the RSA inversion oracle; i.e., on input $y \in \mathbb{Z}_N^*$, it returns $x = y^d \bmod N$.*
Challenge values are selected *For $1 \leq i \leq m(k) + 1$, pick $y_i \leftarrow \mathbb{Z}_N^*$.*
$\mathcal{A}$ is invoked *The challenger invokes $\mathcal{A}^{\mathcal{O}_I(\cdot, N, d)}(N, e, k, y_1, \ldots, y_{m(k)+1})$ and responds to its oracle queries. Eventually, $\mathcal{A}$ terminates.*
$\mathcal{A}$'s success criterion *$\mathcal{A}$ is successful if (1) it issued no more than $m(k)$ queries to $\mathcal{O}_I(\cdot, N, d)$; and (2) $\mathcal{A}$ output is $(z_1, \ldots, z_{m(k)+1})$ such that, for all $1 \leq i \leq m(k) + 1$, $z_i^e = y_i \bmod N$.*

By $\mathbf{Adv}_{\mathcal{A},m}^{rsa-kti}(k)$ we denote the probability that $\mathcal{A}$ is successful in $\mathbf{Exp}_{\mathcal{A},m}^{rsa-kti}(k)$. The RSA-KTI[m] problem is hard if for any probabilistic polynomial-time $\mathcal{A}$, $\mathbf{Adv}_{\mathcal{A},m}^{rsa-kti}(k)$ is negligible; the RSA-KTI problem is hard if the RSA-KTI[m] problem is hard for any polynomially bounded m.

Assumption A1. (One-more-RSA Assumption [6]) *The known-target inversion problem RSA-KTI is intractable.*

Bellare et al. then reduced breaking the assumption (i.e., solving RSA-KTI) to solving the seemingly easier RSA-ACTI problem stated in Definition 7. (See Theorems 4.1 and 5.4 in Bellare et al. [6].) Thus, to prove security of the scheme, it is sufficient to give a polynomial-time reduction that breaks RSA-ACTI with access to an adversary $\mathcal{A}$ attacking the scheme.

B   The Verification Algorithm, Step by Step

For the security analysis, it is helpful to recall all the steps that the signature verification algorithm will take (rather than deferring to subroutines that are defined elsewhere). The notation $0xUV$, where U and V are hexadecimal digits, denote the value of an octet, or byte; e.g., $0 \times 3a$ corresponds to the binary string 00111100. The symbol $\circ$ denotes concatenation. Using the PSS encoding from the PKCS#1 standard [29,30], verifying a signature σ for a message M consists of the following steps (note: these steps are equivalent to those in the PKCS# standard, but not described in exactly the same way):

1. Compute the encoded message $\mathtt{EM} = \mathsf{I2OSP}(\sigma^e \bmod N, emLen)$. Specifically, I2OSP will reject if $\sigma^e \bmod N$ is greater than 2^{8emLen}; else, it outputs $emLen = \lceil(k-1)/8\rceil$ octets that, when viewed as a binary integer, equal $\sigma^e \bmod N$. Note that, whenever $k-1$ is not a multiple of 8, this will always result in having $\mathtt{EM}$ (viewed as a bit string) start with up to 7 zeroes. Let $0 \le p \le 7$ be such that for maximal positive integer m, $k-1 = 8m+(8-p)$. I.e. p is the number of extra bits we get when converting the bit representation of a $k-1$-but integer into the byte representation of the same integer.
2. If $\mathtt{EM}$ doesn't end in the byte $0xBC$, reject. Else, parse $\mathtt{EM}$ as follows: the first $lenDB = emLen - hLen - 1$ bytes are the string $\mathtt{maskedDB}$; the next $hLen$ bytes are the string H, and the last byte, as we already know, is $0xBC$. To summarize, $\mathtt{EM} = \mathtt{maskedDB} \circ H \circ 0xBC$.
3. Let $\mathtt{dbMask} = \mathsf{MGF}(H, lenDB)$.
4. Let $\mathtt{DB'} = \mathtt{maskedDB} \oplus \mathtt{dbMask}$; let $\mathtt{DB}$ be the same string as $\mathtt{DB'}$ except that the first p bits are set to 0. (This is because, since we set p to be $0 \le p \le 7$ be such that for some integer m, $k-1 = 8m+(8-p)$, the first p bits of the byte encoding of a $k-1$-bit integer are always 0, so the value we "unmask" starts at bit $p+1$.)
5. If $\mathtt{DB}$ does not start with $lenDB - 1 - sLen$ 0×00 octets followed by 0×01, then reject. Else, let $\mathtt{salt}$ be the last $sLen$ octets of $\mathtt{DB}$. To summarize, $\mathtt{DB} = 0 \times 00 \ldots 0 \times 00 \circ 0 \times 01 \circ \mathtt{salt}$.
6. Let $M' = 0^{64} \circ \mathtt{mHash} \circ \mathtt{salt}$, where $\mathtt{mHash} = \mathsf{CRHF}(M)$. (As usual, by 0^{64} we denote a binary string of 64 zeroes; we can also think of it as a string of eight bytes, each set to 0×00.)
7. If $H = \mathsf{Hash}(M', hLen)$, accept, else, reject.

References

1. Abdalla, M., Namprempre, C., Neven, G.: On the (Im)possibility of blind message authentication codes. In: Pointcheval, D. (ed.) CT-RSA 2006. LNCS, vol. 3860, pp. 262–279. Springer, Heidelberg (2006). https://doi.org/10.1007/11605805_17
2. Abe, M.: A secure three-move blind signature scheme for polynomially many signatures. In: Pfitzmann, B. (ed.) EUROCRYPT 2001. LNCS, vol. 2045, pp. 136–151. Springer, Heidelberg (2001). https://doi.org/10.1007/3-540-44987-6_9

3. Abe, M., Okamoto, T.: Provably secure partially blind signatures. In: Bellare, M. (ed.) CRYPTO 2000. LNCS, vol. 1880, pp. 271–286. Springer, Heidelberg (2000). https://doi.org/10.1007/3-540-44598-6_17

4. Baldimtsi, F., Lysyanskaya, A.: Anonymous credentials light. In: ACM CCS 2013, pp. 1087–1098. ACM Press, November (2013)

5. Bellare, M., Namprempre, C., Pointcheval, D., Semanko, M.: The power of RSA inversion oracles and the security of Chaum's RSA-based blind signature scheme. In: Syverson, P. (ed.) FC 2001. LNCS, vol. 2339, pp. 319–338. Springer, Heidelberg (2002). https://doi.org/10.1007/3-540-46088-8_25

6. Bellare, M., Namprempre, C., Pointcheval, D., Semanko, M.: The One-More-RSA-inversion problems and the security of Chaum's blind signature scheme. J. Cryptol. 16(3), 185–215 (2003). https://doi.org/10.1007/s00145-002-0120-1

7. Bellare, M., Rogaway, P.: Random oracles are practical: a paradigm for designing efficient protocols. In: ACM CCS 93, pp. 62–73. ACM Press, November (1993)

8. Bellare, M., Rogaway, P.: The exact security of digital signatures-how to sign with RSA and Rabin. In: Maurer, U. (ed.) EUROCRYPT 1996. LNCS, vol. 1070, pp. 399–416. Springer, Heidelberg (1996). https://doi.org/10.1007/3-540-68339-9_34

9. Bellare, M., Rogaway, P.: PSS: provably secure encoding method for digital signatures. Submission to IEEE P1363 (1998)

10. Benhamouda, F., Lepoint, T., Loss, J., Orrù, M., Raykova, M.: On the (in)security of ROS. In: Canteaut, A., Standaert, F.-X. (eds.) EUROCRYPT 2021. LNCS, vol. 12696, pp. 33–53. Springer, Cham (2021). https://doi.org/10.1007/978-3-030-77870-5_2

11. Boldyreva, A.: Threshold signatures, multi signatures and blind signatures based on the gap-diffie-hellman-group signature scheme. In: Desmedt, Y.G. (ed.) PKC 2003. LNCS, vol. 2567, pp. 31–46. Springer, Heidelberg (2003). https://doi.org/10.1007/3-540-36288-6_3

12. Canetti, R., Goldreich, O., Halevi, S.: The random oracle methodology, revisited (preliminary version). In: 30th ACM STOC, pp. 209–218. ACM Press, May (1998)

13. Chaum, D.: Blind signatures for untraceable payments. In: CRYPTO'82, pp. 199–203. Plenum Press, New York, USA (1982)

14. Chaum, D.: Blind signature systems. In: CRYPTO '83, pp. 153–156. Plenum (1983)

15. Chaum, D., Fiat, A., Naor, M.: Untraceable electronic cash. In: Goldwasser, S. (ed.) CRYPTO 1988. LNCS, vol. 403, pp. 319–327. Springer, New York (1990). https://doi.org/10.1007/0-387-34799-2_25

16. IETF Draft. Denis, F., Jacobs, F., Wood, C.A.: RSA blind signatures, Feb (2022). https://datatracker.ietf.org/doc/draft-irtf-cfrg-rsa-blind-signatures/

17. IETF Draft. Denis, F., Jacobs, F., Wood, C.A.: RSA blind signatures, March 2021. https://datatracker.ietf.org/doc/html/draft-wood-cfrg-rsa-blind-signatures-00

18. Fischlin, M., Lehmann, A., Ristenpart, T., Shrimpton, T., Stam, M., Tessaro, S.: Random Oracles with(out) programmability. In: Abe, M. (ed.) ASIACRYPT 2010. LNCS, vol. 6477, pp. 303–320. Springer, Heidelberg (2010). https://doi.org/10.1007/978-3-642-17373-8_18

19. Fuchsbauer, G., Plouviez, A., Seurin, Y.: Blind schnorr signatures and signed elgamal encryption in the algebraic group model. In: Canteaut, A., Ishai, Y. (eds.) EUROCRYPT 2020. LNCS, vol. 12106, pp. 63–95. Springer, Cham (2020). https://doi.org/10.1007/978-3-030-45724-2_3

20. Galbraith, S.D., Malone-Lee, J., Smart, N.P.: Public key signatures in the multiuser setting. Inf. Process. Lett. 83(5), 263–266 (2002)

21. Goldberg, S., Reyzin, L., Sagga, O., Baldimtsi, F.: Efficient noninteractive certification of RSA moduli and beyond. In: Galbraith, S.D., Moriai, S. (eds.) ASIACRYPT 2019. LNCS, vol. 11923, pp. 700–727. Springer, Cham (2019). https://doi.org/10.1007/978-3-030-34618-8_24

22. Goldwasser, S., Micali, S., Rivest, R.: A digital signature scheme secure against adaptive chosen-message attacks. SIAM J. Comput. **17**(2), 281–308 (1988)

23. Hauck, E., Kiltz, E., Loss, J.: A modular treatment of blind signatures from identification schemes. In: EUROCRYPT 2019, Part III, volume 11478 of LNCS, pp. 345–375. Springer, Heidelberg, May (2019). https://doi.org/10.1007/978-3-030-17659-4_12

24. Hauck, E., Kiltz, E., Loss, J., Nguyen, N.K.: Lattice-based blind signatures, revisited. In: Micciancio, D., Ristenpart, T. (eds.) CRYPTO 2020. LNCS, vol. 12171, pp. 500–529. Springer, Cham (2020). https://doi.org/10.1007/978-3-030-56880-1_18

25. Juels, A., Luby, M., Ostrovsky, R.: Security of blind digital signatures (extended abstract). In: CRYPTO'97, volume 1294 of LNCS, pp. 150–164. Springer, Heidelberg, August (1997). https://doi.org/10.1007/BFb0052233

26. Lysyanskaya, A.: Security analysis of RSA-BSSA. IACR Cryptol. ePrint Arch., p. 895 (2022)

27. Pointcheval, D., Stern, J.: Provably secure blind signature schemes. In: ASIACRYPT'96, volume 1163 of LNCS, pp. 252–265. Springer, Heidelberg, November 1996. https://doi.org/10.1007/BFb0034852

28. Pointcheval, D., Stern, J.: Security arguments for digital signatures and blind signatures. J. Crypt. **13**(3), 361–396 (2000)

29. IETF RFC3447. Jonsson, J., Kaliski, B.: Public-Key Cryptography Standards (PKCS) #1: RSA Cryptography Specifications Version 2.1, February (2003). https://datatracker.ietf.org/doc/html/rfc3447

30. IETF RFC8017. Moriarty, K., Ed., Kaliski, B., Jonsson, J., Rusch, A.: PKCS #1: RSA Cryptography Specifications Version 2.2, November (2016). https://datatracker.ietf.org/doc/html/rfc8017

31. Schnorr, C.-P.: Efficient signature generation by smart cards. J. Crypt. **4**(3), 161–174 (1991)

32. Schnorr, C.P.: Security of blind discrete log signatures against interactive attacks. In: Qing, S., Okamoto, T., Zhou, J. (eds.) ICICS 2001. LNCS, vol. 2229, pp. 1–12. Springer, Heidelberg (2001). https://doi.org/10.1007/3-540-45600-7_1

33. Schröder, D., Unruh, D.: Security of blind signatures revisited. In: PKC 2012, vol. 7293 of LNCS, pp. 662–679. Springer, Heidelberg, May (2012)

34. Shoup, V.: A Computational Introduction to Number Theory and Algebra, 2nd edn. Cambridge University Press, Cambridge (2009)

35. Tessaro, S., Zhu, C.: Short pairing-free blind signatures with exponential security. In: EUROCRYPT 2022, Part II, vol. 13276 of LNCS, pp. 782–811. Springer, Heidelberg, May/June (2022). https://doi.org/10.1007/978-3-031-07085-3_27

Extendable Threshold Ring Signatures
with Enhanced Anonymity

Gennaro Avitabile[1(✉)], Vincenzo Botta[2], and Dario Fiore[1]

[1] IMDEA Software Institute, Madrid, Spain
avitabilegenn@gmail.com, {gennaro.avitabile,dario.fiore}@imdea.org
[2] University of Warsaw, Warsaw, Poland
v.botta@uw.edu.pl

Abstract. Threshold ring signatures are digital signatures that allow t parties to sign a message while hiding their identity in a larger set of n users called "ring". Recently, Aranha et al. [PKC 2022] introduced the notion of *extendable* threshold ring signatures (ETRS). ETRS allow one to update, in a non-interactive manner, a threshold ring signature on a certain message so that the updated signature has a greater threshold, and/or an augmented set of potential signers. An application of this primitive is anonymous count me in. A first signer creates a ring signature with a sufficiently large ring announcing a proposition in the signed message. After such cause becomes *public*, other parties can anonymously decide to support that proposal by producing an updated signature. Crucially, such applications rely on partial signatures being posted on a *publicly accessible* bulletin board since users may not know/trust each other.

In this paper, we first point out that even if anonymous count me in was suggested as an application of ETRS, the anonymity notion proposed in the previous work is insufficient in many application scenarios. Indeed, the existing notion guarantees anonymity only against adversaries who just see the last signature, and are not allowed to access the "full evolution" of an ETRS. This is in stark contrast with applications where partial signatures are posted in a public bulletin board. We therefore propose stronger anonymity definitions and construct a new ETRS that satisfies such definitions. Interestingly, while satisfying stronger anonymity properties, our ETRS asymptotically improves on the two ETRS presented in prior work [PKC 2022] in terms of both time complexity and signature size. Our ETRS relies on extendable non-interactive witness-indistinguishable proof of knowledge (ENIWI PoK), a novel technical tool that we formalize and construct, and that may be of independent interest. We build our constructions from pairing groups under the SXDH assumption.

Keywords: Threshold Ring Signatures · Anonymity · Malleable Proof Systems

G. Avitabile and V. Botta—Work done mainly while working at University of Salerno, Italy.

A. Boldyreva and V. Kolesnikov (Eds.): PKC 2023, LNCS 13940, pp. 281–311, 2023.
https://doi.org/10.1007/978-3-031-31368-4_11

1 Introduction

Anonymity is a central requirement in several privacy-preserving technologies. Notable examples are e-voting protocols [34], anonymous authentication [30], and privacy-protecting cryptocurrencies [35]. A central cryptographic primitive that can be used to provide anonymity in applications is ring signatures [33]. Ring signatures [33] are digital signatures which allow one user to sign a message while hiding her identity in a larger group called ring $\mathcal{R}$. In practice, the signing algorithm, aside the message, takes as input a set of public keys (i.e., the ring) and one of the corresponding secret keys. The produced signature guarantees that one of the public keys in the ring signed the message, while hiding which one of the secret keys was used to create the signature. Clearly, the larger is $\mathcal{R}$ the greater is the anonymity provided to the signer. Constructions for ring signatures are known from a variety of cryptographic tools such as RSA [17], pairing groups [10,16,37], non-interactive zero-knowledge proofs [3,11,22], and lattices [9,19,27,28]. A practical application of ring signature is whistleblowing. By signing a message, a member of a company can report a wrong practice of the company itself while hiding his identity among all the other employees.

Threshold ring signatures [12] enrich ring signatures by allowing t signers to hide their identity within the ring. The signature guarantees that t members of $\mathcal{R}$ signed the message without revealing which ones. Ring signatures can be seen as threshold ring signatures with $t = 1$. Some threshold ring signatures also enjoy a property called flexibility [29,31]. They allow new signers to join already produced signatures: a signature on a message m that was already created with threshold t for a ring $\mathcal{R}$ can be transformed into a new signature on message m with threshold $t + 1$ w.r.t. the same ring $\mathcal{R}$. The interesting aspect of flexible threshold ring signatures is that the update does not require the participation of any previous signer. Nevertheless, until recently, all known threshold ring signatures did not offer an analogous property that would allow extending the ring. In other words, all previous constructions required to fix the ring from the beginning and did not allow to modify it further.

This problem has been addressed for the first time in the recent work of Aranha et al. [2] which has put forth the notion of *extendable* threshold ring signatures (ETRS). ETRS, aside the join operation, also provide an *extend* operation: any signature with ring $\mathcal{R}$ can be transformed by anybody into a signature with ring $\mathcal{R}'$ s.t. $\mathcal{R} \subset \mathcal{R}'$. After the extend operation, all signers in $\mathcal{R}'$ can join the signature.

On Count-me-in Applications. Aranha et al. [2] observe how the richer flexibility of ETRS can enable more advanced forms of whistleblowing or anonymous petitions. The first signer could create a ring signature with a sufficiently large ring announcing a proposition in the signed message. After such cause becomes *public*, other parties could support the cause via extend and/or join operations. As also reported in [2], an observer who has seen signatures on an old ring $\mathcal{R}$ and on a new ring $\mathcal{R}'$ can always compute $\mathcal{R}' \setminus \mathcal{R}$, and this can help narrowing down the identity of the signers. This problem is inherent in the functionality provided by ETRS, and it worsens as t approaches the size of the ring. A clear example is the one of a signature w.r.t. ring $\mathcal{R}$ with threshold $t = n - 1$, where $n = |\mathcal{R}|$, which is transformed into a signature with threshold $t = n' - 1$ w.r.t. $\mathcal{R}', |\mathcal{R}'| = n' = n + 1$ (i.e., the threshold is increased by one and the final ring contains an additional public key of a user A). By looking at the two signatures, one can infer that one signer of the last signature either comes from $|\mathcal{R}|$ or it is A with probability $\frac{1}{2}$.

In [2], the authors address this issue by proposing an anonymity definition in which the adversary is restricted to see only the signature obtained eventually, after all the extend and join operations have been applied. However, this restriction hinders the use of ETRS in real-world count-me-in applications since it bears an implicit requirement: the signers should privately interact to incrementally produce the ETRS and then only the final signature can be made public to the outside world. This means that *all* the possible advocates of a proposal should be given access to a private bulletin board where partial signatures are posted (it can be implemented using a blockchain). Additionally, the abstract of [2] informally mentions the importance of *fellow signer anonymity* (FSA), a property stating that "it is often crucial for signers to remain anonymous even from their fellow signers". Such requirement was previously formally modeled in [29], but it is not captured by the anonymity definitions of [2]. Indeed, it is unclear how such property could be guaranteed when anonymity is only formulated w.r.t. an adversary who cannot see intermediate signatures (as real signers would) and does not have the secret key of any of the signers (as in the definition of [2]).

1.1   Our Contributions

In this work, we address the aforementioned shortcomings of ETRS. First, we propose a stronger security definition that guarantees anonymity even against adversaries that see the full "evolution" of a signature. Second, we propose a new ETRS construction that achieves our strong anonymity definition, and also improves in efficiency over previous work (cfr., Table 1). Our construction relies on extendable non-interactive witness indistinguishable proof of knowledge (ENIWI PoK), a novel technical tool that we formalize and construct, and that may be of independent interest. In what follows, we present our contributions in more detail.

Stronger Anonymity for ETRS. Even though certain leaks are inherent when the adversary gets to see several ETRS, one should aim at building a scheme which leaks nothing more than that. To this regard, we start from the anonymity definition proposed in [2] and we make it stronger as follows. We allow the adversary $\mathcal{A}$ to see all the ETRS that led to the final signature. In a nutshell, $\mathcal{A}$ outputs two sequences of operations which at every step lead to an ETRS on the same message, with the same ring, and the same threshold in both sequences. The challenger $\mathcal{C}$ picks one of such sequences at random, executes it, and gives to $\mathcal{A}$ the corresponding outputs of each step. We then require that $\mathcal{A}$ only has a negligible advantage in guessing which sequence was applied. We also propose a security game that models fellow signer anonymity for ETRS.

Constructing ETRS. In [2], two constructions of ETRS are proposed: the first one is obtained from extendable same-message linkable ring signatures (SMLERS)[1], while the second one is constructed from signatures of knowledge (SoK) for the discrete log relation, public key encryption (PKE), and the discrete log assumption. The first scheme achieves our stronger anonymity notion but suffers quite high complexity; for instance, the signature size is $\mathcal{O}(tn)$. The second scheme in [2] is more compact but does not fulfill our stronger anonymity notion. Indeed, anyone who sees an ETRS before and after a join operation can easily pinpoint the exact signer who joined the signature (see Appendix A.1 of [5] for more details). It follows that such scheme is also not fellow-signer anonymous, since no secret key is required to carry out the above attack.

We construct an ETRS which fulfills our stronger anonymity definition and is also fellow-signer anonymous. As shown in Table 1, our ETRS also generally improves the constructions given in [2] in terms of both time complexity and signature size. In Appendix A.1 of [5], we give a high-level overview of both ETRS presented in [2]. To build our ETRS, we introduce the notion of ENIWI PoK, which may be of independent interest. We then show how to build an ETRS from an ENIWI PoK for a hard relation, and an IND-CPA homomorphic public key encryption scheme.

Table 1. Comparison of signature size, time complexities, and anonymity guarantees of our ETRS and the ones presented in [2]. Let $|\mathcal{R}| = n$ and t be the threshold. In the DL + SoK + PKE construction of [2] signature size and time complexities both depend on a fixed upper bound on the ring size N. We say that a scheme achieves weak anonymity if it achieves the anonymity property of [2], and strong anonymity if our stronger anonymity definition is satisfied. FSA stands for fellow-signer anonymity.

Scheme	Size	Sign	Join	Extend	Verify	Anonymity	FSA
SMLERS [2]	$\mathcal{O}(tn)$	$\mathcal{O}(tn)$	$\mathcal{O}(n)$	$\mathcal{O}(tn)$	$\mathcal{O}(tn)$	Strong	Yes
DL + SoK + PKE [2]	$\mathcal{O}(N)$	$\mathcal{O}(N^2)$	$\mathcal{O}(N^2)$	$\mathcal{O}(N^2)$	$\mathcal{O}(N^2)$	Weak	No
Ours	$\mathcal{O}(n)$	$\mathcal{O}(n)$	$\mathcal{O}(n)$	$\mathcal{O}(n)$	$\mathcal{O}(n)$	Strong	Yes

ENIWI *PoKs.* In [14], Chase et al. examined notions of malleability for non-interactive proof systems. They defined the notion of allowable transformation $T = (T_x, T_w)$ w.r.t. a relation $R_{\mathcal{L}}$. A transformation is allowable w.r.t. $R_{\mathcal{L}}$ if on input $(x, w) \in R_{\mathcal{L}}$ it gives as output $(T_x(x) = x', T_w(w) = w') \in R_{\mathcal{L}}$.

---

[1] SMLERS were introduced in [2] as well. A SMLERS is a ring signature which is also extendable. In addition, it allows to link two signatures produced by the same signer on the same message, even on different rings. The SMLERS of [2] is obtained from signatures of knowledge for the discrete log relation, collision-resistant hash functions, and the discrete log assumption.

Then, a proof system is said to be malleable w.r.t. an allowable transformation $T = (T_x, T_w)$, if there exists a poly-time algorithm that on input the initial statement x, the transformation T, and an accepting proof Π, gives an accepting proof Π' for the transformed statement x'. They also considered more complex transformations including n statements and proofs. They showed that Groth-Sahai (GS) proofs [24] are malleable w.r.t. the language of sets of pairing product equations and they define a set of elementary allowable transformations which can be used to build more complex ones, including conjunctions and disjunctions. They also observed that since GS is re-randomizable, a transformation of a proof followed by its re-randomization is indistinguishable from a proof computed from scratch for statement x' using witness w'. They called this property derivation privacy.

In this paper, we further explore the notion of malleability for non-interactive witness indistinguishable (NIWI) proofs of knowledge (PoKs) in the context of threshold relations. A threshold relation $R_{\mathcal{L}^{tr}}$ is defined w.r.t. a relation $R_{\mathcal{L}}$ as $R_{\mathcal{L}^{tr}} = \{(x = (k, x_1, \ldots, x_n), w = ((w_1, \alpha_1), \ldots, (w_k, \alpha_k)))|1 \leq \alpha_1 < \ldots < \alpha_k \leq n \wedge \forall\, j \in [k] : (x_{\alpha_j}, w_j) \in R_{\mathcal{L}}\}$. Let $\mathcal{L}^{tr}$ be the corresponding NP language. In words, the prover wants to prove it has k witnesses for k *different* statements out of n statements. The transformations we explore are extend and add operations:

– **Extend**: transform a proof for $(k, x_1, \ldots, x_n) \in \mathcal{L}^{tr}$ into a proof for $(k, x_1, \ldots, x_n, x_{n+1}) \in \mathcal{L}^{tr}$.
– **Add**: transform a proof for $(k, x_1, \ldots, x_n) \in \mathcal{L}^{tr}$ into a proof for $(k+1, x_1, \ldots, x_n) \in \mathcal{L}^{tr}$.

While the extend operation can be realized without using any private input of the "previous" prover, as modelled in [14], the same does not hold for the add operation. Indeed, thanks to extractability, an accepting proof for $(k + 1, x_1, \ldots, x_n) \in \mathcal{L}^{tr}$ can only be generated by the prover, except with negligible probability, using $k + 1$ witnesses for $k + 1$ different statements out of all the n statements. It follows that the add transformation must require a witness for statement x_i, with index $i \in [n]$ that was not previously used, and it cannot produce an accepting proof for the updated statement on input a witness for a previously used index. It is straightforward to notice that this fact could be used to check whether or not a given witness was used in the proof, thus violating witness indistinguishability.

Therefore, we put forth the new notion of ENIWI PoK. In an ENIWI PoK, when the prover computes a proof Π for a statement $x = (k, x_1, \ldots, x_n)$, it also outputs a list of auxiliary values $\mathsf{AUX} = (\mathsf{aux}_1, \ldots, \mathsf{aux}_n)$. The auxiliary value aux_i will be later used to perform the add operation via an additional algorithm called PrAdd. PrAdd, on input an accepting proof Π for $(k, x_1, \ldots, x_n) \in \mathcal{L}^{tr}$, a witness w_i for a not previously used index i s.t. $(x_i, w_i) \in R_{\mathcal{L}}$, and the corresponding auxiliary value aux_i, outputs a proof Π' for $(k + 1, x_1, \ldots, x_n) \in \mathcal{L}^{tr}$. Analogously, there is an additional algorithm $\mathsf{PrExtend}$ that is used to perform the extend operation. $\mathsf{PrExtend}$ does not require any auxiliary value. $\mathsf{PrExtend}$, on input an accepting proof for $(k, x_1, \ldots, x_n) \in \mathcal{L}^{tr}$, and a statement x_{n+1}, outputs a proof Π' for $(k, x_1, \ldots, x_{n+1}) \in \mathcal{L}^{tr}$ and the auxiliary value aux_{n+1} related to statement x_{n+1}. The auxiliary value aux_{n+1} can later be used to perform an add operation using witness w_{n+1} s.t. $(x_{n+1}, w_{n+1}) \in R_{\mathcal{L}}$. The verification algorithm is left unaltered and does not take any auxiliary value in input.

Similarly to derivation privacy, we require that the outputs of both the extend and add operations followed by a re-randomization are indistinguishable from proofs created using the regular prover algorithm. Regarding witness indistinguishability, we have to treat the auxiliary values in a special manner. Indeed, giving out all the auxiliary values would at least reveal the indices of the used witnesses. Therefore, we propose a new notion called extended witness indistinguishability. In this notion, the adversary $\mathcal{A}$ samples a $x = (k, x_1, \ldots, x_n)$ and two witnesses w^i as $((w_1^i, \alpha_1^i) \ldots, (w_k^i, \alpha_k^i))$, s.t. $(x, w^i) \in R_{\mathcal{L}^{tr}}$ for $i \in \{0, 1\}$. Recall that $\alpha_j \in [n]$, with $j \in [k]$, indicates that w_j is a witness s.t. $(x_{\alpha_j}, w_j) \in R_{\mathcal{L}}$. Then, the challenger $\mathcal{C}$ outputs a proof computed using one of the two witnesses, but it only gives to $\mathcal{A}$ a *subset* of all the auxiliary values. Such subset includes the auxiliary values only related to certain indices, namely $(\{1, \ldots, n\} \setminus (\{\alpha_1^0, \ldots, \alpha_n^0\} \cup \{\alpha_1^1, \ldots, \alpha_n^1\})) \cup (\{\alpha_1^0, \ldots, \alpha_n^0\} \cap \{\alpha_1^1, \ldots, \alpha_n^1\})$. In words, those are the auxiliary values related to the indices for which one of the following conditions holds: (i) the index was not used in either w^0 or w^1; (ii) the index was used in both w^0 and w^1. We require that $\mathcal{A}$ has negligible advantage in guessing whether w^0 or w^1 was used to create the proof. The idea is that if we build upon a NIWI and if the auxiliary values are only tied to the *indices* of the used witness and not to their concrete values, then giving the auxiliary values for the "irrelevant" positions to $\mathcal{A}$ does not give $\mathcal{A}$ any advantage. Although it could seem a cumbersome notion, ENIWI is enough to obtain strongly anonymous ETRS, and could possibly have other applications.

High-level Overview of our ENIWI. We propose an ENIWI for the base relation $R_{\mathcal{L}}$ of pairing product equations (PPEs) in which all the variables are elements of group two, public constants are either paired with secret values or with the public generator, and the target element is the neutral element.

We build our ENIWI from GS proofs. GS is a commit-and-prove system where secret variables are first committed and the prover algorithm takes as input the committed values as well as the commitments randomnesses to create some proof elements. The proof can be verified on input the statement, the commitments, and proof elements. We first modify known techniques to get disjunctions of PPEs [13,23] into a technique to get proofs of partial satisfiability of k out of n PPEs. Such transformation modifies the starting PPEs via some additional variables $\hat{M}_i$ with $i \in [n]$ s.t. k of the PPEs are left unaltered while $n - k$ of them now admit the trivial solution, thus allowing for simulation. The value of $\hat{M}_i$ is constrained to two values, depending on whether or not the proof for the i-th equation should be simulated. We then observe that such proofs can be turned into an ENIWI provided with the extend and the add operations. The auxiliary values can be seen as the commitment openings related to such variables which enable to replace an $\hat{M}_i$ allowing for simulation (i.e., an $\hat{M}_i$ that makes the corresponding PPE admit the trivial solution) with a new one preventing simulation (i.e., an $\hat{M}_i$ that leaves the corresponding PPE unaltered). The idea is that to perform the add operation, the old commitment to a variable

$\hat{M}_i$ would be replaced with a fresh one. Then, aux_i would allow to erase from the proof element the contribution related to the old committed variable and to subsequently put in the contribution of the freshly committed variable. The extend operation is more straightforward since it does not need to erase any contribution, but only to add the contribution of a new variable. At a high level, extended witness indistinguishability is achieved since the $\hat{M}_i$ variables are only tied to the particular equation being simulated or not, but not to the actual value of any of the variables. Proofs can also be re-randomized leveraging the re-randomizability of GS and by appropriately updating the auxiliary values after the re-randomization.

High-level Overview of our ETRS. To get an ETRS, we just need a way to turn an ENIWI in a signature scheme preserving its extendability properties. In [20], it is shown how to create a signature of knowledge (SoK) from a NIWI PoK in the random oracle model (ROM). In a nutshell, the message is hashed to produce the CRS which is then used to prove the statement of the SoK. The resulting proof constitutes the signature. We leverage their technique to create an ETRS starting from an ENIWI PoK. The idea is that since the transformation given in [20] just modifies how the CRS is generated, we are able to replace the NIWI PoK with an ENIWI PoK to get an ETRS instead of a regular signature. In our ETRS, the i-th signer has as public key a statement x_i for a hard relation $R_{\mathcal{L}}$ for which it exists an ENIWI, along with the public key pk_e^i of an IND-CPA public key encryption scheme (PKE) which is homomorphic w.r.t. the update operation of the auxiliary values. The corresponding secret key is w_i s.t. $(x_i, w_i) \in R_{\mathcal{L}}$, along with the secret key of the encryption scheme sk_e^i. The first signer S hashes the message m to get the CRS, then S uses her own witness to create a proof for $(1, x_1, \ldots, x_n) \in R_{\mathcal{L}^{tr}}$. By creating such proof, the signer will also get auxiliary values $(\mathsf{aux}_1, \ldots, \mathsf{aux}_n)$. Since publishing the auxiliary values in the clear would reveal the identity of the signer, each individual aux_i is encrypted using the public key of the i-th signer[2]. A new signer willing to join will decrypt aux_i and run PrAdd to update the proof. To extend the ring, it suffices to run PrExtend to update the proof. Finally, to ensure anonymity we exploit the fact that ENIWI PoKs are re-randomizable. We re-randomize all the proofs after running either PrAdd or PrExtend. We additionally exploit the homomorphic property of the encryption scheme to update the auxiliary values after each re-randomization. We prove the security of our ETRS in the ROM.

Both the constructions presented in [2] use SoKs for the discrete log relation as a building block without specifying a concrete instantiation. Whether they require the ROM or not depends on whether there exists a practical[3] SoK

---

[2] Notice that for anonymity to hold, it is crucial that the witness indistinguishability property holds even if the auxiliary values related to unused positions are accessible by the adversary. Indeed, in our anonymity notion the adversary is allowed to corrupt all non-signers, thus getting their decryption keys and the related auxiliary values.

[3] Chase and Lysyanskaya [15] proposed a generic construction under standard complexity assumptions in the common random string model, but it is not practical since it uses general non-interactive zero-knowledge (NIZK) proofs.

without random oracles for that relation. The authors also provide an implementation in which they use the Schnorr identification scheme with the Fiat-Shamir transform as a SoK. Such SoK requires the ROM. In our ETRS, all operations require linear time in n as the number of equations to be proved linearly depends on n. Additionally, GS proofs have constant size for each type of equation, therefore the size of the ETRS is $\mathcal{O}(n)$. Note that both time complexity and signature size do not depend on t.

2   Related Work

Threshold ring signatures were introduced by Bresson et al. [12]. They provided a construction based on RSA. The size of the signature is $\mathcal{O}(n \log n)$, where n is the size of the ring. Subsequent works proposed new constructions from a variety of assumptions focused on either relaxing the setup assumptions, reducing the signature size, or getting rid of the ROM.

Several works have signatures of size linear in n [1,26,32], while some others proposed constructions with signature size that can be sub-linear in n [4,6,36][4], or even $\mathcal{O}(t)$ [25,29]. Some works have also focused on providing post-quantum security [1,8,26].

In [31], the concept of flexibility was introduced. A flexible threshold ring signature scheme allows one to modify an already created signature on a message m with threshold t and ring $\mathcal{R}$ into a new signature on message m with threshold $t + 1$ w.r.t. $\mathcal{R}$, without the intervention of the previous signers.

Usually, threshold ring signatures are formulated as an interactive protocol run among the signers. Some schemes have a weaker requirement [4,6], where the signers just have to interact with one party called the aggregator. After having interacted with all the signers, the aggregator just compiles all the received contributions into one threshold ring signatures which can then be publicly posted. Munch-Hansen et al. [29] presented a threshold ring signature based on RSA accumulators with size $\mathcal{O}(t)$. Their scheme also achieves flexibility. Moreover, they introduce a stronger anonymity property that demands that a signer cannot be deanonymized even by their fellow signers. In this scenario, having non-interactive signing is crucial since the deanonymization could be done by exploiting communication meta-data such as the IP address. The same applies to signatures using an aggregator, unless the aggregator is trusted. Recently, Aranha et al. [2] have further enhanced the functionality of threshold ring signature by proposing extendable threshold ring signatures ETRS. ETRS are flexible and they also allow to extend the ring of a given signature without the need of any secret.

3   Preliminaries

In this section, we introduce the assumptions and the cryptographic tools our constructions rely on. We defer to the full version [5] for more widely known defi-

---

[4] In particular, [36] has size $\mathcal{O}(t\sqrt{n})$, [6] is $\mathcal{O}(t \log n)$, and [4] is $\mathcal{O}(\log n)$.

nitions and assumptions. When referring to an NP language $\mathcal{L}$ we call $R_{\mathcal{L}}$ the corresponding NP relation. We work over bilinear groups $\mathsf{gk} = (p, \hat{\mathbb{G}}, \check{\mathbb{H}}, \mathbb{T}, e, \hat{g}, \check{h}) \leftarrow \mathcal{G}(1^\lambda)$. $\mathcal{G}(1^\lambda)$ is a generator algorithm that on input the security parameter, outputs the description of a bilinear group. We call such description group key gk. $\hat{\mathbb{G}}, \check{\mathbb{H}}, \mathbb{T}$ are prime p order groups, $\hat{g}, \check{h}$ are generators of $\hat{\mathbb{G}}, \check{\mathbb{H}}$ respectively, and $e : \hat{\mathbb{G}} \times \check{\mathbb{H}} \rightarrow \mathbb{T}$ is a non-degenerate bilinear map. In this paper, we will use additive notation for the group operations and multiplicative notation for the bilinear map e.

Assumption 1 (Double Pairing Fixed Term Assumption) *We say the double pairing fixed term assumption holds relative to $\hat{\mathbb{G}}$ if for* $\mathsf{gk} = (p, \hat{\mathbb{G}}, \check{\mathbb{H}}, \mathbb{T}, e, \hat{g}, \check{h}) \leftarrow \mathcal{G}(1^\lambda)$, *and for all PPT adversaries $\mathcal{A}$ we have*

$$\Pr\left[\hat{a}, \hat{b} \leftarrow_{\$} \hat{\mathbb{G}} \setminus (\hat{0}, \hat{0}); \check{b}' \leftarrow \mathcal{A}(\mathsf{gk}, \hat{a}, \hat{b}) : \check{b}' \in \check{\mathbb{H}}, \hat{a} \cdot \check{h} + \hat{b} \cdot \check{b}' = 0_{\mathbb{T}}\right] \leq \mathsf{negl}(\lambda).$$

Lemma 1. *If the double pairing fixed term assumption holds for gk, then the Decisional Diffie-Hellman assumption holds for $\hat{\mathbb{G}}$.*

See [5] for the proof.

3.1 Groth-Sahai Proofs

The Groth-Sahai proof system [24] is a proof system for the language of satisfiable equations (of types listed below) over a bilinear group $\mathsf{gk} = (p, \hat{\mathbb{G}}, \check{\mathbb{H}}, \mathbb{T}, e, \hat{g}, \check{h}) \leftarrow \mathcal{G}(1^\lambda)$. The prover wants to show that there is an assignment of all the variables that satisfies the equation. Such equations can be of four types:

Pairing-Product Equations (PPE): For public constants $\hat{a}_j \in \hat{\mathbb{G}}$, $\check{b}_i \in \check{\mathbb{H}}$, $\gamma_{ij} \in \mathbb{Z}_p$, $t_{\mathbb{T}} \in \mathbb{T}$: $\sum_i \hat{x}_i \cdot \check{b}_i + \sum_j \hat{a}_j \cdot \check{y}_j + \sum_i \sum_j \gamma_{ij} \hat{x}_i \cdot \check{y}_j = t_{\mathbb{T}}$.

Multi-Scalar Multiplication Equation in $\hat{\mathbb{G}}$ ($\mathsf{ME}_{\hat{\mathbb{G}}}$): For public constants $\hat{a}_j \in \hat{\mathbb{G}}$, $b_i \in \mathbb{Z}_p$, $\gamma_{ij} \in \mathbb{Z}_p$, $\hat{t} \in \hat{\mathbb{G}}$: $\sum_i \hat{x}_i b_i + \sum_j \hat{a}_j y_j + \sum_i \sum_j \gamma_{ij} \hat{x}_i y_j = \hat{t}$.

Multi-Scalar Multiplication Equation in $\check{\mathbb{H}}$ ($\mathsf{ME}_{\check{\mathbb{H}}}$): For public constants $a_j \in \mathbb{Z}_p$, $\check{b}_i \in \check{\mathbb{H}}$, $\gamma_{ij} \in \mathbb{Z}_p$, $\check{t} \in \check{\mathbb{H}}$: $\sum_i x_i \check{b}_i + \sum_j a_j \check{y}_j + \sum_i \sum_j \gamma_{ij} x_i \check{y}_j = \check{t}$.

Quadratic Equation in $\mathbb{Z}_p$ (QE): For public constants $a_j \in \mathbb{Z}_p$, $b_i \in \mathbb{Z}_p$, $\gamma_{ij} \in \mathbb{Z}_p$, $t \in \mathbb{Z}_p$: $\sum_i x_i b_i + \sum_j a_j y_j + \sum_i \sum_j \gamma_{ij} x_i y_j = t$.

Here, we formalize the GS proof system as in [18]. The GS proof system is a commit-and-prove system. Each committed variable is also provided with a public label that specifies the type of input (i.e., scalar or group element). Accordingly, the prover algorithm takes as input a label L which indicates the type of equation to be proved (i.e., $L \in \{\mathsf{PPE}, \mathsf{ME}_{\hat{\mathbb{G}}}, \mathsf{ME}_{\check{\mathbb{H}}}, \mathsf{QE}\}$). GS features the following PPT algorithms, the common reference string crs and the group key gk are considered as implicit input of all the algorithms.

- crs $\leftarrow$$ CRSSetup(gk): on input the group key, output the common reference string.
- $(l, c) \leftarrow$ Com$(l, w; r)$: return a commitment (l, c) to message w according to the label l and randomness r.
- $\pi \leftarrow$ Prove$(L, x, (l_1, w_1, r_1), \ldots, (l_n, w_n, r_n))$: consider statement x as an equation of type specified by L, and on input a list of commitment openings produce a proof π.
- $0/1 \leftarrow$ PrVerify$(x, (l_1, c_1), \ldots, (l_n, c_n), \pi)$: given committed variables, statement x, and proof π, output 1 to accept and 0 to reject.
- $((l_1, c_1'), \ldots, (l_n, c_n'), \pi') \leftarrow$ RandPr$(L, (l_1, c_1), \ldots, (l_n, c_n), \pi; r)$: on input equation type specified by L, a list of commitments, a proof π, and a randomness r, output a re-randomized proof along with the corresponding list of re-randomized commitments.

GS can be also used to prove that a set of equations S, with possibly shared variables across the equations, has a satisfying assignment. To do so, the prover has to reuse the same commitments for the shared variables while executing the Prove algorithm for each individual equation. The above description can also fit the interface of NIWI PoK (see Appendix A.2 of [5]). Indeed, the Prove algorithm can just launch the Com and the Prove algorithm above with the appropriate labels, and return as a proof both the commitments and the proof elements. Similarly, the PrVerify and RandPr algorithms of the NIWI PoK interface have just to appropriately parse their inputs and call the PrVerify and RandPr algorithms described above.

The GS proof system is proved to be a NIWI for all types of the above equations under the SXDH assumption. In addition, it is a NIWI PoK for all equations involving solely group elements. To be more specific, Escala and Groth formulated the notion of F-knowledge [18] (i.e., a variation of adaptive extractable soundness, see Definition 14 of [5]) for a commit-and-prove system. In a nutshell, it requires the existence of an Ext_2 algorithm that, on input a valid commitment and the extraction key produced by Ext_1, outputs a function F of the committed value. They prove that GS enjoys F-knowledge. For commitments to group elements, F is identity function. Regarding commitments to scalars, F is a one-way function that uniquely determines the committed value.

Internals of GS Proofs. In [18], the authors provide a very fine-grained description of GS proofs. In this description, we report only the aspects that are relevant to our constructions. It is possible to write the equations of Sect. 3.1 in a more compact way. Consider $\hat{\boldsymbol{x}} = (\hat{x}_1, \ldots, \hat{x}_m)$ and $\check{\boldsymbol{y}} = (\check{y}_1, \ldots, \check{y}_n)$, which may be both public constants (i.e., written before as $\hat{a}_j, \check{b}_i$) or secret values. Let $\Gamma = \{\gamma_{ij}\}_{i=1,j=1}^{m,n} \in \mathbb{Z}_p^{m \times n}$. We can now write a PPE as $\hat{\boldsymbol{x}} \Gamma \check{\boldsymbol{y}} = t_{\mathbb{T}}$. Similarly, a $\mathsf{ME}_{\hat{\mathbb{G}}}$, a $\mathsf{ME}_{\hat{\mathbb{H}}}$, and a QE can be written as $\hat{\boldsymbol{x}} \Gamma \boldsymbol{y} = \hat{t}$, $\boldsymbol{x} \Gamma \check{\boldsymbol{y}} = \check{t}$, and $\boldsymbol{x} \Gamma \boldsymbol{y} = t$. This holds for $\hat{\boldsymbol{x}} \in \hat{\mathbb{G}}^{1 \times m}$, $\check{\boldsymbol{y}} \in \check{\mathbb{H}}^{n \times 1}$, $\boldsymbol{x} \in \mathbb{Z}_p^{1 \times m}$, $\boldsymbol{y} \in \mathbb{Z}_p^{n \times 1}$. Additionally, for equations of type $\mathsf{ME}_{\hat{\mathbb{G}}}$, $\mathsf{ME}_{\hat{\mathbb{H}}}$, and QE, we can, without loss of generality, assume the target element to be the neutral element. For PPE we will restrict ourselves to the case in which $t_{\mathbb{T}} = 0_{\mathbb{T}}$, and no public constants are paired with each other, unless one of the two is a generator specified in the public parameters. The structure of the crs is clear from Fig. 1, where the Ext_1 algorithm is shown.

$(\mathsf{crs}, xk) \leftarrow \mathsf{Ext}_1(\mathsf{gk})$

Parse $\mathsf{gk} = (p, \hat{\mathbb{G}}, \check{\mathbb{H}}, \mathbb{T}, e, \hat{g}, \check{h})$

$\rho \leftarrow_\$ \mathbb{Z}_p, \xi \leftarrow_\$ \mathbb{Z}_p^*$ and $\sigma \leftarrow_\$ \mathbb{Z}_p, \psi \leftarrow_\$ \mathbb{Z}_p^*$

$\hat{v} = (\xi\hat{g}, \hat{g})^\top$ and $\check{v} = (\psi\check{h}, \check{h})$

$\hat{w} = \rho\hat{v}$ and $\check{w} = \sigma\check{v}$

$\hat{u} = \hat{w} + (\hat{0}, \hat{g})^\top$ and $\check{u} = \check{w} + (\check{0}, \hat{g})$

$\boldsymbol{\xi} = (-\xi^{-1} \mod p, 1)$ and

$\boldsymbol{\psi} = (-\psi^{-1} \mod p, 1)^\top$

$\mathsf{crs} = (\hat{u}, \hat{v}, \hat{w}, \check{u}, \check{v}, \check{w})$

$xk = (\boldsymbol{\xi}, \boldsymbol{\psi})$

return (crs, xk)

Fig. 1. Generation of the CRS along with the extraction key in the GS proof system.

In Fig. 2, we report the commitment labels and corresponding commit algorithm that are of interest for this work.

Input	Randomness	Output	Input	Randomness	Output
$\mathsf{pub}_{\hat{\mathbb{G}}}, \hat{x}$	$r = 0, s = 0$	$\hat{c} = e^\top \hat{x}$	$\mathsf{pub}_{\check{\mathbb{H}}}, \check{y}$	$r = 0, s = 0$	$\check{d} = \check{y}e$
$\mathsf{com}_{\hat{\mathbb{G}}}, \hat{x}$	$r, s \leftarrow_\$ \mathbb{Z}_p$	$\hat{c} = e^\top \hat{x} + \hat{v}r + \hat{w}s$	$\mathsf{com}_{\check{\mathbb{H}}}, \check{x}$	$r, s \leftarrow_\$ \mathbb{Z}_p$	$\check{d} = \check{y}e + r\check{v} + s\check{w}$
$\mathsf{base}_{\hat{\mathbb{G}}}, \hat{g}$	$r = 0, s = 0$	$\hat{c} = e^\top \hat{g}$	$\mathsf{base}_{\check{\mathbb{H}}}, \check{h}$	$r = 0, s = 0$	$\check{d} = \check{h}e$
$\mathsf{sca}_{\hat{\mathbb{G}}}, x$	$r \leftarrow_\$ \mathbb{Z}_p, s = 0$	$\hat{c} = \hat{u}x + \hat{v}r$	$\mathsf{sca}_{\check{\mathbb{H}}}, y$	$r \leftarrow_\$ \mathbb{Z}_p, s = 0$	$\check{d} = y\check{u} + r\check{v}$

Fig. 2. GS commit labels and corresponding commit algorithm, $e = (0, 1)$.

In Fig. 3 and in Fig. 4, we report the prover and verifier algorithm respectively. We defer to Appendix A.4 of [5] for more details on GS internals.

4 Extendable Threshold Ring Signature

A non-interactive extendable threshold ring signature scheme ETRS is defined as a tuple of six PPT algorithms ETRS = (Setup, KeyGen, Sign, Verify, Join, Extend), where the public parameters pp produced by Setup are implicitly available to all the other algorithms:

- pp ← Setup(1^λ): on input the security parameter, outputs public parameters pp.

$\mathsf{Prove}(L, \Gamma, \{(l_{x_i}, x_i, (r_{x_i}, s_{x_i}))\}_{i=1}^m, \{(l_{y_j}, y_j, (r_{y_j}, s_{y_j}))\}_{j=1}^n)$

---

if $x \in \hat{\mathbb{G}}^m$ define $\hat{C} = e^\top x + \hat{v} r_x + \hat{w} s_x$ else if $x \in \mathbb{Z}_p^m$ define $\hat{C} = \hat{u} x + \hat{v} r_x$

if $y \in \check{\mathbb{H}}^n$ define $\check{D} = e^\top y + r_y \check{v} + s_y \check{w}$ else if $y \in \mathbb{Z}_p^n$ define $\check{D} = \check{u} y + r_y \check{v}$

Set $\alpha = \beta = \gamma = \delta = 0$

if $L = \mathrm{PPE}$ $\alpha, \beta, \gamma, \delta \leftarrow\!\!\$\ \mathbb{Z}_p$

if $L = \mathrm{ME}_{\hat{\mathbb{G}}}$ $\alpha, \beta \leftarrow\!\!\$\ \mathbb{Z}_p$

if $L = \mathrm{ME}_{\check{\mathbb{H}}}$ $\alpha, \gamma \leftarrow\!\!\$\ \mathbb{Z}_p$

if $L = \mathrm{QE}$ $\alpha \leftarrow\!\!\$\ \mathbb{Z}_p$

$\check{\pi}_{\hat{v}} = r_x \Gamma \check{D} + \alpha \check{v} + \beta \check{w}$ $\hat{\pi}_{\check{v}} = (\hat{C} - \hat{v} r_x - \hat{w} s_x) \Gamma r_y - \hat{v} \alpha - \hat{w} \gamma$

$\check{\pi}_{\hat{w}} = s_x \Gamma \check{D} + \gamma \check{v} + \delta \check{w}$ $\hat{\pi}_{\check{w}} = (\hat{C} - \hat{v} r_x - \hat{w} s_x) \Gamma s_y - \hat{v} \beta - \hat{w} \delta$

return $\boldsymbol{\pi} = (\check{\pi}_{\hat{v}}, \hat{\pi}_{\check{v}}, \check{\pi}_{\hat{w}}, \hat{\pi}_{\check{w}})$

Fig. 3. Prover algorithm of the GS proof system.

$\mathsf{PrVerify}(L, \Gamma, \{(l_{x_i}, \hat{c}_i)\}_{i=1}^m, \{(l_{y_j}, \check{d}_j)\}_{j=1}^n), \boldsymbol{\pi})$

Check that the equation has a valid format.

Check $\hat{C} = (\hat{c}_1 \ldots \hat{c}_m) \in \hat{\mathbb{G}}^{2 \times m}$ and $\check{D} = (\check{d}_1 \ldots \check{d}_n)^\top \in \check{\mathbb{H}}^{n \times 2}$

Check $\boldsymbol{\pi} = (\check{\pi}_{\hat{v}}, \check{\pi}_{\hat{w}}, \hat{\pi}_{\check{v}}, \hat{\pi}_{\check{w}}) \in \check{\mathbb{H}}^{2 \times 1} \times \check{\mathbb{H}}^{2 \times 1} \times \hat{\mathbb{G}}^{1 \times 2} \times \hat{\mathbb{G}}^{1 \times 2}$

Check $\hat{C} \Gamma \check{D} = \hat{v} \check{\pi}_{\hat{v}} + \hat{w} \check{\pi}_{\hat{w}} + \hat{\pi}_{\check{v}} \check{v} + \hat{\pi}_{\check{w}} \check{w}$

return 1 if and only if all checks pass and 0 otherwise.

Fig. 4. Verifier algorithm of the GS proof system.

- $(\mathsf{pk}, \mathsf{sk}) \leftarrow \mathsf{KeyGen}()$: generates a new public and secret key pair.
- $\sigma \leftarrow \mathsf{Sign}(m, \{\mathsf{pk}_i\}_{i \in \mathcal{R}}, \mathsf{sk})$: returns a signature with threshold $t = 1$ using the secret key sk corresponding to a public key pk_i with $i \in \mathcal{R}$.
- $0/1 \leftarrow \mathsf{Verify}(t, m, \{\mathsf{pk}_i\}_{i \in \mathcal{R}}, \sigma)$: verifies a signature σ for the message m against the public keys $\{\mathsf{pk}_i\}_{i \in \mathcal{R}}$ with threshold t. Outputs 1 to accept, and 0 to reject.
- $\sigma' \leftarrow \mathsf{Join}(m, \{\mathsf{pk}_i\}_{i \in \mathcal{R}}, \mathsf{sk}, \sigma)$: it takes as input a signature σ for message m produced w.r.t. ring $\mathcal{R}$ with threshold t, and the new signer secret key sk (whose corresponding pk is included in $\mathcal{R}$). It outputs a new signature σ' with threshold $t + 1$.
- $\sigma' \leftarrow \mathsf{Extend}(m, \sigma, \{\mathsf{pk}_i\}_{i \in \mathcal{R}}, \{\mathsf{pk}_i\}_{i \in \mathcal{R}'})$: extends the signature σ with threshold t for the ring $\mathcal{R}$ into a new signature σ' with threshold t for the larger ring $\mathcal{R} \cup \mathcal{R}'$.

To formalize the properties of ETRS, we use the notion of ladder as in [2]. A ladder lad is a sequence of tuples (action, input), where action takes a value in the set $\{\mathsf{Sign}, \mathsf{Join}, \mathsf{Extend}\}$ and the value of input depends on the value of action. If action $= \mathsf{Sign}$, then input is a pair $(\mathcal{R}, i)$, where $\mathcal{R}$ is the ring for the signature and i is the signer's identity. If action $= \mathsf{Join}$, then input is an identifier i that identifies the signer that joins the signature. If action = Extend, then input is a ring $\mathcal{R}$ that is the ring to use to extend the previous ring. We notice that a ladder unequivocally determines a sequence of ETRS, each one with a specific ring and threshold value. In Fig. 7, the algorithm Proc is described. Proc takes as input a message, a ladder, and a corresponding list of keys, and outputs the sequence of all the signatures that correspond to each step of the ladder. It outputs $\perp$ whenever the ladder has an inconsistent sequence of actions or is incompatible with the list of keys provided in the input.

Definition 1 (Correctness for ETRS). *For all $\lambda \in \mathbb{N}$, for any message $m \in \{0,1\}^*$, for any ladder* lad *of polynomial size identifying a ring $\mathcal{R}$, it holds that:*

$$\Pr\left[\begin{array}{c} \left(\bigwedge_{j=1}^{\ell} \mathsf{Verify}(t, m, \{\mathsf{pk}_i\}_{i\in\mathcal{R}}, \sigma_j) = 1\right) \\ \vee (\Sigma, t, \mathcal{R}) = \perp \end{array} \middle| \begin{array}{c} \mathsf{pp} \leftarrow \mathsf{Setup}(1^\lambda); \\ \mathsf{L}_{\mathsf{keys}} \leftarrow \{\mathsf{KeyGen}()\}_{i\in\mathcal{R}}; \\ (\Sigma, t, \mathcal{R}) \leftarrow \mathsf{Proc}(m, \mathsf{L}_{\mathsf{keys}}, \mathsf{lad}); \\ \{\sigma_1, \ldots, \sigma_\ell\} = \Sigma \end{array}\right] = 1.$$

Definition 2 (Unforgeability for ETRS). *An extendable threshold ring signature scheme* ETRS *is said to be unforgeable if for all PPT adversaries $\mathcal{A}$, the success probability in the experiment of Fig. 5 is*

$$\Pr\left[\mathsf{Exp}_{\mathcal{A},\mathsf{ETRS}}^{cmEUF}(\lambda) = win\right] \leq \mathsf{negl}(\lambda).$$

Definition 3 (Anonymity for ETRS). *An extendable threshold ring signature scheme* ETRS *is said to provide anonymity if for all PPT adversaries $\mathcal{A}$, the success probability in the anonymous extendability experiment of Fig. 6 is* $\Pr\left[\mathsf{Exp}_{\mathcal{A},\mathsf{ETRS}}^{ANEXT}(\lambda) = win\right] \leq \frac{1}{2} + \mathsf{negl}(\lambda).$ *In this experiment, the ladders submitted by $\mathcal{A}$ are said to be well-formed if all the actions in the ladders are pairwise of the same type, and they have the same ring as input.*

Remarks on Anonymity and Unforgeability for ETRS. We modify the definition of anonymity for ETRS in [2] making it stronger. The difference is that the adversary now gets to see all the intermediate ETRS instead of just the final one (see lines 11 and 12 of Chal in Fig. 6). This modification enables count-me-in applications where partial signatures get publicly posted. In addition, in the experiment, we add the checks of lines 15 and 17 to rule out a trivial attack inherent to any ETRS. Indeed, since the Join operation cannot increase the threshold of an ETRS when using a secret key that was already used before, $\mathcal{A}$ could use this fact to distinguish between the ladders.

The Combine algorithm is introduced in [2] as a procedure to combine together two signatures on the same message with two different (not necessarily disjoint) rings. The output is a signature having as ring the union of the two rings and as threshold the cardinality of the union of the signers sets of the starting signatures. The Combine algorithm can be run without knowing any secret key. In [2], the authors showed that the Join operation can be obtained

$\mathsf{Exp}^{\mathsf{cmEUF}}_{\mathcal{A},\mathsf{ETRS}}(\lambda)$	$\mathsf{OKey}(i,\mathsf{pk})$
1 : $L_{\mathsf{keys}}, L_{\mathsf{corr}}, L_{\mathsf{sign}}, L_{\mathsf{join}} \leftarrow \emptyset$	1 : **if** $\mathsf{pk} = \bot$
2 : $pp \leftarrow \mathsf{ETRS.Setup}(1^\lambda)$	2 : $(\mathsf{pk}_i, \mathsf{sk}_i) \leftarrow \mathsf{ETRS.KeyGen}()$
3 : $\mathsf{O} \leftarrow \{\mathsf{OSign}, \mathsf{OKey}, \mathsf{OCorr}, \mathsf{OJoin}\}$	3 : $L_{\mathsf{keys}} \leftarrow L_{\mathsf{keys}} \cup \{(i, \mathsf{pk}_i, \mathsf{sk}_i)\}$
4 : $(t^*, m^*, \mathcal{R}^*, \sigma^*) \leftarrow \mathcal{A}^{\mathsf{O}}(pp)$	4 : **else**
5 : $q_1 \leftarrow |\{(m^*, \mathcal{R}, \cdot) \in L_{\mathsf{sign}} : \mathcal{R} \subseteq \mathcal{R}^*\}|$	5 : $L_{\mathsf{corr}} \leftarrow L_{\mathsf{corr}} \cup \{i\}$
6 : $q_2 \leftarrow |\{(m^*, i, \cdot) \in L_{\mathsf{join}} : i \in \mathcal{R}^*\}|$	6 : $\mathsf{pk}_i \leftarrow \mathsf{pk}$
7 : $q \leftarrow q_1 + q_2$	7 : $L_{\mathsf{keys}} \leftarrow L_{\mathsf{keys}} \cup \{(i, \mathsf{pk}_i, \bot)\}$
8 : **if** $|\mathcal{R}^* \cap L_{\mathsf{corr}}| + q \geq t^*$	8 : **return** pk_i
9 : **return** *lose*	
10 : **if** $\mathsf{Verify}(t^*, m^*, \{\mathsf{pk}_j\}_{j \in \mathcal{R}^*}, \sigma^*) = 0$	$\mathsf{OCorr}(i)$
11 : **return** *lose*	1 : **if** $(i, \mathsf{pk}_i, \mathsf{sk}_i) \in L_{\mathsf{keys}} \wedge \mathsf{sk}_i \neq \bot$
12 : **return** *win*	2 : $L_{\mathsf{corr}} \cup \{i\}$
	3 : **return** $(\mathsf{pk}_i, \mathsf{sk}_i)$
$\mathsf{OSign}(m, \mathcal{R}, i)$	4 : **return** $\bot$
1 : **if** $(i \in L_{\mathsf{corr}} \vee i \notin \mathcal{R})$ **return** $\bot$	$\mathsf{OJoin}(m, \mathcal{R}, i, \sigma)$
2 : **for** $j \in \mathcal{R}$	
3 : **if** $(j, \mathsf{pk}_j, \cdot) \notin L_{\mathsf{keys}}$	1 : **if** $i \in L_{\mathsf{corr}}$ **return** $\bot$
4 : **return** $\bot$	2 : **for** $j \in \mathcal{R}$
5 : $\sigma \leftarrow \mathsf{ETRS.Sign}(m, \{\mathsf{pk}_j\}_{j \in \mathcal{R}}, \mathsf{sk}_i)$	3 : **if** $((j, \mathsf{pk}_j, \cdot) \notin L_{\mathsf{keys}})$
6 : $L_{\mathsf{sign}} \leftarrow L_{\mathsf{sign}} \cup \{(m, \mathcal{R}, i)\}$	4 : **return** $\bot$
7 : **return** σ	5 : $\sigma' \leftarrow \mathsf{Join}(m, \{\mathsf{pk}_j\}_{j \in \mathcal{R}}, \mathsf{sk}_i, \sigma)$
	6 : $L_{\mathsf{join}} \leftarrow L_{\mathsf{join}} \cup \{(m, i, \sigma)\}$
	7 : **return** σ'

Fig. 5. Unforgeability game for ETRS (security experiment and oracles). This notion is reported from [2].

as the concatenation of the Sign operation and the Combine operation. In order to avoid the same attack described before, the checks in lines 11 and 13 of the experiment of Fig. 6 are needed. We notice that our ETRS only provides a weaker form of Combine in which the starting rings are disjoint (cfr., Sect. 6). A similar discussion holds for lines $5 - 8$ of the unforgeability experiment in Fig. 5. In particular, they rule out trivial attacks due to $\mathcal{A}$ asking too many sign, join, or corruption queries.

Fellow-signer Anonymity. We also define a stronger version of anonymity called fellow-signer anonymity. This game models the requirement that even a signer cannot determine any of the other signers by just looking at all the signatures that were produced. It is straightforward to notice that fellow-signer anonymity implies anonymity for ETRS.

Definition 4 (Fellow Signer Anonymity for ETRS). *An extendable threshold ring signature scheme* ETRS *is said to provide fellow signer anonymity if for all PPT adversaries* $\mathcal{A}$, *the success probability in the experiment of Fig. 8 is*
$$\Pr\left[\mathsf{Exp}^{ANFS}_{\mathcal{A},\mathsf{ETRS}}(\lambda) = win\right] \leq \tfrac{1}{2} + \mathsf{negl}(\lambda).$$

5 Extendable Non-interactive Witness Indistinguishable Proof of Knowledge

Given an NP language $\mathcal{L}$ with associated poly-time relation $R_{\mathcal{L}}$, we define the related threshold relation $R_{\mathcal{L}^{tr}}$ as follows. We name the corresponding language $\mathcal{L}^{tr}$.

$\mathsf{Exp}^{ANEXT}_{\mathcal{A},\mathsf{ETRS}}(\lambda)$	$\mathsf{Chal}_b(m^*, \mathsf{lad}_0^*, \mathsf{lad}_1^*)$
1 : $b \leftarrow\$ \{0,1\}, \mathsf{L}_{\mathsf{keys}}, \mathsf{L}_{\mathsf{corr}}, \mathsf{L}_{\mathsf{sign}}, \mathsf{L}_{\mathsf{join}} \leftarrow \emptyset$	1 : if $(\mathsf{lad}_0^*, \mathsf{lad}_1^*)$ is not well-formed
2 : $pp \leftarrow \mathsf{ETRS.Setup}(1^\lambda)$	2 : return $\bot$
3 : $O \leftarrow \{\mathsf{OSign}, \mathsf{OKey}, \mathsf{OCorr}, \mathsf{OJoin}\}$	3 : if $\exists i \in \mathsf{lad}_0^*.\mathcal{S}$ s.t. $i \in \mathsf{L}_{\mathsf{corr}}$
4 : $(m^*, \mathsf{lad}_0^*, \mathsf{lad}_1^*) \leftarrow \mathcal{A}^O(pp)$	4 : return $\bot$
5 : $\Sigma \leftarrow \mathsf{Chal}_b(m^*, \mathsf{lad}_0^*, \mathsf{lad}_1^*)$	5 : if $\exists i \in \mathsf{lad}_1^*.\mathcal{S}$ s.t. $i \in \mathsf{L}_{\mathsf{corr}}$
6 : $b^* \leftarrow \mathcal{A}^O(\Sigma)$	6 : return $\bot$
7 : if $\exists i \in \mathsf{lad}_0^*.\mathcal{S}$ s.t. $i \in \mathsf{L}_{\mathsf{corr}}$	7 : $val_0 \leftarrow \mathsf{Proc}(m^*, \mathsf{L}_{\mathsf{keys}}, \mathsf{lad}_0^*)$
8 : return *lose*	8 : $val_1 \leftarrow \mathsf{Proc}(m^*, \mathsf{L}_{\mathsf{keys}}, \mathsf{lad}_1^*)$
9 : if $\exists i \in \mathsf{lad}_1^*.\mathcal{S}$ s.t. $i \in \mathsf{L}_{\mathsf{corr}}$	9 : if $val_0 = \bot \vee val_1 = \bot$
10 : return *lose*	10 : return $\bot$
11 : if $\exists (m^*, \cdot, i) \in \mathsf{L}_{\mathsf{sign}}$ for $i \in \mathsf{lad}_0^*.\mathcal{S}$	11 : Parse val_0 as $(\Sigma_0, t_0, \mathcal{R}_0)$
12 : return *lose*	12 : Parse val_1 as $(\Sigma_1, t_1, \mathcal{R}_1)$
13 : if $\exists (m^*, \cdot, i) \in \mathsf{L}_{\mathsf{sign}}$ for $i \in \mathsf{lad}_1^*.\mathcal{S}$	13 : $\Sigma \leftarrow \Sigma_b$
14 : return *lose*	14 : return Σ
15 : if $\exists (m^*, i, \cdot) \in \mathsf{L}_{\mathsf{join}}$ for $i \in \mathsf{lad}_0^*.\mathcal{S}$	
16 : return *lose*	
17 : if $\exists (m^*, i, \cdot) \in \mathsf{L}_{\mathsf{join}}$ for $i \in \mathsf{lad}_1^*.\mathcal{S}$	
18 : return *lose*	
19 : if $b^* \neq b$ **return** *lose*	
20 : **return** *win*	

Fig. 6. Anonymous extendability game. We use lad.$\mathcal{S}$ to indicate the set of signers of a ladder lad. We propose a stronger notion compared to [2]. Indeed, in our definition, the adversary gets to see all the intermediate signatures instead of only the final ETRS.

Proc(m, $\mathsf{L_{keys}}$, lad)

1 : $\Sigma \leftarrow \emptyset, t = 0$

2 : Parse lad as $((\mathsf{action}^1, \mathsf{input}^1), \ldots, (\mathsf{action}^l, \mathsf{input}^l))$

3 : **if** $\mathsf{action}^1 \neq \mathsf{Sign}$ **return** $\bot$

4 : **else**

5 :   Parse input^1 as $(\mathcal{R}^1, i^1)$

6 :   **for** $j \in \mathcal{R}^1$ **if** $(j, \mathsf{pk}_j, \cdot) \notin \mathsf{L_{keys}}$ **return** $\bot$

7 :   **if** $sk_{i^1} = \bot \vee i^1 \notin \mathcal{R}^1$ **return** $\bot$

8 : $\mathcal{R} \leftarrow \mathcal{R}^1, \mathcal{S} \leftarrow \{i^1\}$

9 : $\sigma \leftarrow \mathsf{Sign}(m, \{\mathsf{pk}_j\}_{j \in \mathcal{R}}, sk_{i^1}), \Sigma \leftarrow \Sigma \cup \{\sigma\}$

10 : **for** $l' \in [2, \ldots, l]$

11 :   **if** $\mathsf{action}^{l'} = \mathsf{Sign}$ **return** $\bot$

12 :   **else**

13 :   **if** $\mathsf{action}^{l'} = \mathsf{Join}$ parse $\mathsf{input}^{l'}$ as $(i^{l'})$

14 :   **if** $i^{l'} \notin \mathcal{R} \vee i^{l'} \in \mathcal{S}$ **return** $\bot$

15 : $\sigma \leftarrow \mathsf{Join}(m, \{\mathsf{pk}_j\}_{j \in \mathcal{R}}, sk_{i}^{l'}, \sigma)$

16 : $\Sigma \leftarrow \Sigma \cup \{\sigma\}, \mathcal{S} \leftarrow \mathcal{S} \cup \{i^{l'}\}, t = t + 1$

17 :   **if** $\mathsf{action}^{l'} = \mathsf{Extend}$ parse $\mathsf{input}^{l'}$ as $(\mathcal{R}^{l'})$

18 :   **for** $j \in \mathcal{R}^{l'}$ **if** $(j, \mathsf{pk}_j, \cdot) \notin \mathsf{L_{keys}}$ **return** $\bot$

19 : $\sigma \leftarrow \mathsf{Extend}(m, \sigma, \{\mathsf{pk}_j\}_{j \in \mathcal{R}}, \{\mathsf{pk}_j\}_{j \in \mathcal{R}^{l'}})$

20 : $\mathcal{R} \leftarrow \mathcal{R} \cup \mathcal{R}^{l'}, \Sigma \leftarrow \Sigma \cup \{\sigma\}$

21 :   **else return** $\bot$

22 : **return** $(\Sigma, t, \mathcal{R})$

Fig. 7. Process algorithm for ETRS.

$$R_{\mathcal{L}^{tr}} = \{(x = (k, x_1, \ldots, x_n), w = ((w_1, \alpha_1), \ldots, (w_k, \alpha_k)))|$$
$$1 \leq \alpha_1 < \ldots < \alpha_k \leq n \wedge \forall\, j \in [k] : (x_{\alpha_j}, w_j) \in R_{\mathcal{L}}\}.$$

An extendable non-interactive proof system for a threshold relation $R_{\mathcal{L}^{tr}}$ consists of the following PPT algorithms. The group key $\mathsf{gk} \leftarrow \mathcal{G}(1^\lambda)$ is considered as an implicit input to all algorithms:

– $\mathsf{crs} \leftarrow_\$ \mathsf{CRSSetup}(\mathsf{gk})$: on input the group key gk, output a uniformly random[5] common reference string $\mathsf{crs} \in \{0, 1\}^\lambda$.

---

[5] Here we are also assuming that the crs is uniformly random since it is needed by our ETRS construction.

$\mathsf{Exp}_{\mathcal{A},\mathsf{ETRS}}^{\mathsf{ANFS}}(\lambda)$	$\mathsf{Chal}_b(m^*,\mathsf{lad}^*,i^*,j^*)$
1: $b \leftarrow\!\!\$\ \{0,1\}$	1: **if** $i^* \in \mathsf{L}_{\mathsf{corr}} \vee j^* \in \mathsf{L}_{\mathsf{corr}}$
2: $\mathsf{L}_{\mathsf{keys}}, \mathsf{L}_{\mathsf{corr}}, \mathsf{L}_{\mathsf{sign}}, \mathsf{L}_{\mathsf{join}} \leftarrow \emptyset$	2: $\quad$ **return** $\bot$
3: $pp \leftarrow \mathsf{ETRS.Setup}(1^\lambda)$	3: $\mathsf{lad}^*.add((\mathsf{Extend}, \{i^*\}))$
4: $\mathsf{O} \leftarrow \{\mathsf{OSign}, \mathsf{OKey}, \mathsf{OCorr}, \mathsf{OJoin}\}$	4: $\mathsf{lad}^*.add((\mathsf{Extend}, \{j^*\}))$
5: $(m^*, \mathsf{lad}^*, i^*, j^*) \leftarrow \mathcal{A}^{\mathsf{O}}(pp)$	5: **if** $b = 0$
6: $\Sigma \leftarrow \mathsf{Chal}_b(m^*, \mathsf{lad}^*, i^*, j^*)$	6: $\quad \mathsf{lad}^*.add((\mathsf{Join}, i^*))$
7: $b^* \leftarrow \mathcal{A}^{\mathsf{O}}(\Sigma)$	7: **if** $b = 1$
8: **if** $i^* \in \mathsf{L}_{\mathsf{corr}} \vee j^* \in \mathsf{L}_{\mathsf{corr}}$	8: $\quad \mathsf{lad}^*.add((\mathsf{Join}, j^*))$
9: $\quad$ **return** *lose*	9: $val \leftarrow \mathsf{Proc}(m^*, \mathsf{L}_{\mathsf{keys}}, \mathsf{lad}^*)$
10: **if** $\exists\, (m^*, \cdot, i^*) \in \mathsf{L}_{\mathsf{sign}} \vee (m^*, \cdot, j^*) \in \mathsf{L}_{\mathsf{sign}}$	10: **if** $val = \bot$
11: $\quad$ **return** *lose*	11: $\quad$ **return** $\bot$
12: **if** $\exists\, (m^*, i^*, \cdot) \in \mathsf{L}_{\mathsf{join}} \vee (m^*, j^*, \cdot) \in \mathsf{L}_{\mathsf{join}}$	12: **else**
13: $\quad$ **return** *lose*	13: $\quad$ Parse val as $(\Sigma, t, \mathcal{R})$
14: **if** $b^* \neq b$	14: **return** Σ
15: $\quad$ **return** *lose*	
16: **return** *win*	

Fig. 8. Fellow signer anonymity game. We use $\mathsf{lad}.\mathcal{S}$ to indicate the set of signers of a ladder lad and $\mathsf{lad}.add$ to indicate that we are adding the pair $(\mathsf{action}, \mathsf{input})$ as the last element of the ladder.

- $(\Pi, (\mathsf{aux}_1, \ldots, \mathsf{aux}_n)) \leftarrow \mathsf{Prove}(\mathsf{crs}, (k, x_1, \ldots, x_n), ((w_1, \alpha_1) \ldots, (w_k, \alpha_k)))$: on input $((k, x_1, \ldots, x_n), ((w_1, \alpha_1) \ldots, (w_k, \alpha_k))) \in R_{\mathcal{L}^{tr}}$, output a proof Π and auxiliary values $(\mathsf{aux}_1, \ldots, \mathsf{aux}_n)$. The auxiliary value aux_i is used later on to perform an add operation using a witness for a not previously used statement x_i.

- $0/1 \leftarrow \mathsf{PrVerify}(\mathsf{crs}, (k, x_1, \ldots, x_n), \Pi)$: on input statement $(k, x_1, \ldots, x_n)$, and a proof Π, output 1 to accept and 0 to reject.

- $(\Pi', \mathsf{aux}_{n+1}) \leftarrow \mathsf{PrExtend}(\mathsf{crs}, (k, x_1, \ldots, x_n), x_{n+1}, \Pi)$: on input statements $(k, x_1, \ldots, x_n)$, x_{n+1}, and a proof Π for $(k, x_1, \ldots, x_n) \in \mathcal{L}^{tr}$, output an updated proof Π' for $(k, x_1, \ldots, x_n, x_{n+1}) \in \mathcal{L}^{tr}$, and additional auxiliary value aux_{n+1}. The auxiliary value aux_{n+1} is used later on to perform an add operation using a witness for x_{n+1}.

- $(\Pi', \mathsf{aux}'_\alpha) \leftarrow \mathsf{PrAdd}(\mathsf{crs}, (k, x_1, \ldots, x_n), (w, \alpha), \mathsf{aux}, \Pi)$: on input statement $(k, x_1, \ldots, x_n)$, witness (w, α), auxiliary value aux, and proof Π for $(k, x_1, \ldots, x_n) \in \mathcal{L}^{tr}$, output an updated proof Π' for $(k+1, x_1, \ldots, x_n) \in \mathcal{L}^{tr}$, and updated auxiliary value aux'_α.

- $(\Pi', r = (r_1, \ldots, r_n)) \leftarrow \mathsf{RandPr}(\mathsf{crs}, (k, x_1, \ldots, x_n), \Pi)$: on input statement x and proof Π for $x \in \mathcal{L}^{tr}$, output a re-randomized proof Π' and update randomness r_i (related to auxiliary value aux_i) with $i \in [n]$.

– $\text{aux}'_i \leftarrow \text{AuxUpdate}(\text{crs}, \text{aux}_i, r_i)$: on input auxiliary value aux_i, and update randomness r_i, output updated auxiliary value aux'_i. AuxUpdate is used to update the auxiliary values after a proof has been re-randomized. The used input randomness is the one given in output by RandPr. To simplify the notation, we write $\text{AUX}' \leftarrow \text{AuxUpdate}(\text{crs}, \text{AUX}, r)$ to indicate that a list of auxiliary values is updated by appropriately parsing AUX and r and running the update operation on each element of the list.

– $0/1 \leftarrow \text{AuxVerify}(\text{crs}, (k, x_1, \ldots, x_n), ((w_1, \alpha_1) \ldots, (w_k, \alpha_k)), (\text{aux}_1, \ldots, \text{aux}_n), \Pi)$: on input statement $(k, x_1, \ldots, x_n)$, witness $((w_1, \alpha_1) \ldots, (w_k, \alpha_k))$, auxiliary values $(\text{aux}_1, \ldots, \text{aux}_n)$, and proof Π, output 1 if the auxiliary values are consistent with the statement, the proof, and the witness. Return 0 otherwise. If AuxUpdate returns 1, we are guaranteed that the subsequent extend/add operations can be correctly executed[6].

An extendable non-interactive proof system is said to be an extendable non-interactive witness indistinguishable (ENIWI) proof of knowledge if it satisfies adaptive extractable soundness (Definition 14 of [5]) and the following properties.

Definition 5 (Completeness). *An extendable non-interactive proof system for $R_{\mathcal{L}^{tr}}$ is complete if $\forall \lambda \in \mathbb{N}$, $\text{gk} \leftarrow \mathcal{G}(1^\lambda)$, $\text{crs} \leftarrow_\$ \text{CRSSetup}(\text{gk})$, $(x, w) \in R_{\mathcal{L}^{tr}}$, and $(\Pi, \text{AUX}) \leftarrow \text{Prove}(\text{crs}, x, w)$ it holds that*

$$\Pr[\text{PrVerify}(\text{crs}, x, \Pi) = 1 \wedge \text{AuxVerify}(\text{crs}, x, w, \text{AUX}, \Pi) = 1] = 1$$

Definition 6 (Transformation Completeness). *An extendable non-interactive proof system for $R_{\mathcal{L}^{tr}}$ is transformation complete if $\forall \lambda \in \mathbb{N}$, $\text{gk} \leftarrow \mathcal{G}(1^\lambda)$, $\text{crs} \leftarrow_\$ \text{CRSSetup}(\text{gk})$, $(x, w) \in R_{\mathcal{L}^{tr}}$, and (Π, AUX) such that $\text{PrVerify}(\text{crs}, x, \Pi) = 1$ and $\text{AuxVerify}(\text{crs}, x, w, \text{AUX}, \Pi) = 1$ the following holds with probability 1:*

– *$\text{AuxVerify}(\text{crs}, x, w, \text{AUX}', \Pi') = 1$, where $(\Pi', r) \leftarrow \text{RandPr}(\text{crs}, x, \Pi)$ and $\text{AUX}' \leftarrow \text{AuxUpdate}(\text{crs}, \text{AUX}, r)$.*
– *Parse x as $(k, x_1, \ldots, x_n)$ and w as $((w_1, \alpha_1) \ldots, (w_k, \alpha_k))$. $(\Pi', \text{aux}') \leftarrow \text{PrAdd}(\text{crs}, x, (w', \alpha'), \text{aux}, \Pi)$, modify AUX replacing $\text{aux}_{\alpha'}$ with aux'. If $\alpha' \notin \{\alpha_1, \ldots \alpha_k\}$ and $(x_{\alpha'}, w') \in R_{\mathcal{L}}$, then $\text{PrVerify}(\text{crs}, (k + 1, x_1, \ldots, x_n), \Pi') = 1$, and $\text{AuxVerify}(\text{crs}, (k+1, x_1, \ldots, x_n), ((w_1, \alpha_1) \ldots, (w_k, \alpha_k), (w', \alpha')), \text{AUX}, \Pi') = 1$.*
– *$(\Pi', \text{aux}_{n+1}) \leftarrow \text{PrExtend}(\text{crs}, x, x_{n+1}, \Pi)$, modify AUX adding auxiliary value aux_{n+1}. Then, $\text{PrVerify}(\text{crs}, (k, x_1, \ldots, x_{n+1}), \Pi') = 1$, and $\text{AuxVerify}(\text{crs}, (k, x_1, \ldots, x_{n+1}), w, \text{AUX}, \Pi') = 1$.*

Definition 7 (Re-Randomizable Addition). *Consider the following experiment:*

– $\text{gk} \leftarrow \mathcal{G}(1^\lambda)$

---

[6] We introduce AuxVerify merely as an internal utility to simplify the description of our definitions.

- crs $\leftarrow$\$ CRSSetup(gk)
- $(x, w, \Pi^*, \mathsf{AUX}^*) \leftarrow \mathcal{A}(\mathsf{crs})$
- *Parse* x *as* $(k, x_1, \ldots, x_n)$ *and* w *as* $((w_1, \alpha_1) \ldots (w_k, \alpha_k))$
- *If* $(x, w) \notin R_{\mathcal{L}^{tr}}$ *or* PrVerify(crs, $(k - 1, x_1, \ldots, x_n), \Pi^*) = 0$ *or* AuxVerify(crs, $(k - 1, x_1, \ldots, x_n), ((w_1, \alpha_1) \ldots, (w_{k-1}, \alpha_{k-1})), \mathsf{AUX}^*, \Pi^*) = 0$ *output* $\perp$ *and abort. Otherwise, sample* $b \leftarrow$\$ $\{0, 1\}$ *and do the following:*
  - *If* $b = 0$, $(\Pi_0, \mathsf{AUX}_0) \leftarrow$ Prove(crs, x, w); $(\Pi, r) \leftarrow$ RandPr(crs, x, Π_0), $\mathsf{AUX} \leftarrow$ AuxUpdate(crs, AUX_0, r)
  - *If* $b = 1$, $(\Pi_1, \mathsf{aux}^*) \leftarrow$ PrAdd(crs, $x, (w_k, \alpha_k), \mathsf{AUX}^*, \Pi^*$). *Replace in* AUX^* *the value* aux_{α_k} *with* aux^*. $(\Pi, r) \leftarrow$ RandPr(crs, x, Π_1), $\mathsf{AUX} \leftarrow$ AuxUpdate(crs, AUX^*, r)
- $b' \leftarrow \mathcal{A}(\Pi, \mathsf{AUX})$

We say that the proof system has re-randomizable addition if for every PPT $\mathcal{A}$, *there exists a negligible function* $\nu(\cdot)$, *such that* $\Pr[b = b'] \leq 1/2 + \nu(\lambda)$.

Definition 8 (Re-Randomizable Extension). *Consider the following experiment:*

- gk $\leftarrow \mathcal{G}(1^\lambda)$
- crs $\leftarrow$\$ CRSSetup(gk)
- $(x, w, x_n, \Pi^*, \mathsf{AUX}^*) \leftarrow \mathcal{A}(\mathsf{crs})$
- *Parse* x *as* $(k, x_1, \ldots, x_{n-1})$
- *If* $(x, w) \notin R_{\mathcal{L}^{tr}}$ *or* PrVerify(crs, $x, \Pi^*) = 0$ *or* AuxVerify(crs, $x, w, \mathsf{AUX}^*, \Pi^*) = 0$ *output* $\perp$ *and abort. Otherwise, sample* $b \leftarrow$\$ $\{0, 1\}$ *and do the following:*
  - *If* $b = 0$ $(\Pi_0, \mathsf{AUX}_0) \leftarrow$ Prove(crs, $(k, x_1, \ldots, x_n), w$); $(\Pi, r) \leftarrow$ RandPr(crs, $(k, x_1, \ldots, x_n), \Pi_0$), $\mathsf{AUX} \leftarrow$ AuxUpdate(crs, AUX_0, r)
  - *If* $b = 1$ $(\Pi_1, \mathsf{aux}^*) \leftarrow$ PrExtend(crs, x, x_n, Π^*). *Append the value* aux^* *to* AUX^*. $(\Pi, r) \leftarrow$ RandPr(crs, $(k, x_1, \ldots, x_n), \Pi_1$), $\mathsf{AUX} \leftarrow$ AuxUpdate(crs, AUX^*, r)
- $b' \leftarrow \mathcal{A}(\Pi, \mathsf{AUX})$

We say that the proof system has re-randomizable extension if, for every PPT $\mathcal{A}$, *there exists a negligible function* $\nu(\cdot)$, *such that* $\Pr[b = b'] \leq 1/2 + \nu(\lambda)$.

Definition 9 (Extended Witness Indistinguishability). *Consider the following experiment.*

- gk $\leftarrow \mathcal{G}(1^\lambda)$
- crs $\leftarrow$\$ CRSSetup(gk)
- $(x, w^0, w^1) \leftarrow \mathcal{A}(\mathsf{crs})$
- *Parse* x *as* $(k, x_1, \ldots, x_n)$, w^i *as* $((w_1^i, \alpha_1^i) \ldots (w_k^i, \alpha_k^i))$, *for* $i \in \{0, 1\}$
- *If* $(x, w^0) \notin R_{\mathcal{L}^{tr}}$ *or* $(x, w^1) \notin R_{\mathcal{L}^{tr}}$ *output* $\perp$ *and abort. Otherwise, sample* $b \leftarrow$\$ $\{0, 1\}$ *and do the following:*
  - $(\Pi, (\mathsf{aux}_1, \ldots, \mathsf{aux}_n)) \leftarrow$ Prove(crs, x, w_b).
  - *Set* $I_0 = \{\alpha_1^0, \ldots, \alpha_k^0\}$, $I_1 = \{\alpha_1^1, \ldots, \alpha_k^1\}$, $I = I_0 \cap I_1$, $S = ([n] \setminus (I_0 \cup I_1)) \cup I$, *and* $\mathsf{AUX} = \{\mathsf{aux}_i\}_{i \in S}$.
- $b' \leftarrow \mathcal{A}(\Pi, \mathsf{AUX})$

The proof system has extended witness indistinguishability (EWI) if for every PPT $\mathcal{A}$, *there exists a negligible function* $\nu(\cdot)$, *such that* $\Pr[b = b'] \leq 1/2 + \nu(\lambda)$.

6   Our Extendable Threshold Ring Signature

In Fig. 9, we show our ETRS from an ENIWI PoK ENIWI for a *hard* relation $R_{\mathcal{L}}$, and an IND-CPA public key encryption scheme PKE which is homomorphic w.r.t. ENIWI.AuxUpdate. By *hard* relation we mean that a PPT $\mathcal{A}$ who is given $x \in \mathcal{L}$, has negligible probability of providing a witness w such $(x, w) \in R_{\mathcal{L}}$. We also require that $R_{\mathcal{L}}$ is public coin samplable, meaning that it is possible to efficiently sample random $x \in \mathcal{L}$. We omit the Setup algorithm from the description since it simply runs the setup algorithm of PKE and samples a hash function mapping arbitrary strings into elements in the correct space[7].

Instantiating our ETRS. We work over a bilinear group $\mathsf{gk} = (p, \hat{\mathbb{G}}, \check{\mathbb{H}}, \mathbb{T}, e, \hat{g}, \check{h})$ for which the SXDH assumption is believed to hold. In Sect. 7.3, we show an ENIWI PoK having as base relation pairing product equations in which all the variables are elements of $\check{\mathbb{H}}$, public constants are either paired with secret values or with $\check{h}$, and the target element is $0_{\mathbb{T}}$. In particular, we can use as base relation the following: $R_{\mathcal{L}} = \{(x = (\hat{a}, \hat{b}, \check{h}), w = \check{b}' | \hat{a} \cdot \check{h} + \hat{b} \cdot \check{b}' = 0_{\mathbb{T}}\}$. In Lemmma 1, we prove that this is a hard relation under the DDH assumption in $\hat{\mathbb{G}}$. Additionally, since in our ENIWI AuxUpdate simply consists of applying the group operation between two elements of $\check{\mathbb{H}}$, we can use ElGamal instantiated in $\check{\mathbb{H}}$ as public key encryption scheme.

Remark on Malicious Extenders. As in [2], we do not consider security definitions accounting for malicious signers that try to prevent future signers from joining the signature. For example, in our construction a malicious extender could just encrypt a wrong auxiliary value. An approach that could be investigated to tackle this issue is adding a NIZK proving that the content of the encrypted auxiliary values is s.t. AuxVerify = 1. Such NIZK would need to be malleable so that it could be updated after every re-randomization step, as well as whenever the signature is extended.

On Combining Signatures. One might wonder if concrete instantiations of our ETRS could also support the Combine operation as described in [2]. Whenever there is a shared public key (i.e., statement) in two ETRS, such signatures cannot be combined. Indeed, consider the case of two proofs over the same ring where there is a common base statement for which a corresponding witness was used in both proofs. Then, the combined proof should not have a resulting threshold that counts it twice. This means that the output of Combine would be different depending on whether two NIWI proofs on the same statement used the same witness or not. This is in clear contradiction with the witness indistinguishability property. On the other hand, the above observation does not exclude the possibility of having a weaker form of Combine where the starting signatures are constrained to have disjoint rings. Indeed, our instantiation of Sect. 7.3 could be

---

[7] We need a cryptographic hash function that allows to hash directly to both the source groups of the pairing group. See [21] for more details.

easily modified to support the corresponding Combine operation. Such operation exploits basically the same technique of the extend operation, and thus we omit its description.

6.1   Security of Our Extendable Threshold Ring Signature

Theorem 1. *Let* ENIWI *be an extendable non-interactive witness indistinguishable proof of knowledge for a hard relation* $R_{\mathcal{L}}$, *and* PKE *be an* IND-CPA *public key encryption scheme which is homomorphic w.r.t.* ENIWI.AuxUpdate, *then the scheme of Fig. 9 is an extendable threshold ring signature scheme.*

We prove Theorem 1 using Lemma 2 and Lemma 3.

Lemma 2. *The signature scheme described in Fig. 9 is unforgeable according to Definition 2.*

Proof Sketch. The basic idea of the proof is to turn an adversary $\mathcal{A}$ breaking the unforgeability with non-negligible probability into another adversary $\mathcal{B}$ that extracts a witness for an instance $x \in \mathcal{L}$ of the hard relation, which is sampled by a challenger $\mathcal{C}$. In order to build this reduction, we need to show how to simulate all the oracle queries of $\mathcal{A}$ during the game. We do this by showing a series of hybrid games, starting from the game described in Fig. 5.

The first change consists into replying to Join queries by computing every time a new proof from scratch using ENIWI.Prove, instead of updating the current proof using PrAdd. This change is not detected by $\mathcal{A}$ thanks to the re-randomizable addition of the ENIWI.

The second change is that $\mathcal{B}$ can guess j^*, that is the index of the random oracle query in which $\mathcal{A}$ will query the message used in the forgery, and i^*, that is the index of a "new" signer used to create the forgery for m_{j^*}. We notice that, by the rules of the unforgeability game (see checks of lines $5 - 8$ of the unforgeability experiment in Fig. 5), this index i^* must exist, $\mathcal{A}$ never makes a corruption query for i^*, and it does not ask for any Sign/Join query involving i^* on message m_{j^*}. Whenever $\mathcal{B}$ discovers that it did not guess such indices correctly, $\mathcal{B}$ aborts. Nevertheless, since these indices can be kept perfectly hidden in $\mathcal{A}$'s view, $\mathcal{B}$ guesses these two indices with noticeable probability.

The next change consists into programming the random oracle to switch to an extraction-mode crs for the query on message m_{j^*}. Additionally, for each $j \neq j^*$, we can program the random oracle to output a $\mathsf{pk}_{\mathsf{O}_j}$ for which $\mathcal{B}$ knows the witness w_{1_j} s.t. $(x_{1_j}, w_{1_j}) \in R_{\mathcal{L}}$. Every Join/Sign query involving the signer i^* and a message m_j, with $j \neq j^*$, is answered using w_{1_j} instead of w_{i^*}. This change is not detectable by $\mathcal{A}$ thanks to the extended WI and the adaptive extractable soundness of ENIWI. Indeed, extended WI guarantees that $\mathcal{A}$ cannot notice the change of the used witness, and the adaptive extractable soundness guarantees that the probability of extracting a witness for statement x_{i^*} from the forgery does not change, except up to a negligible factor. Importantly, in order to reduce the indistinguishability of these changes to these two properties

---

$\mathsf{Sign}(m, \{\mathsf{pk}_i\}_{i \in \mathcal{R}}, \mathsf{sk})$

1 : $A \leftarrow \emptyset$

2 : $(\mathsf{crs}, \mathsf{pk}_O = (x_1, \mathsf{pk}_e^1)) \leftarrow H(m)$

3 : Parse $\{\mathsf{pk}_i\}_{i \in \mathcal{R}} = (\mathsf{pk}_2, \ldots, \mathsf{pk}_{n+1})$

4 : Parse $\mathsf{pk}_i = (x_i, \mathsf{pk}_e^i)$ for $i \in [n+1]$

5 : Parse $\mathsf{sk} = (w, \mathsf{sk}_e)$

6 : if $\not\exists x_j, j \in [n+1]$ s.t. $(x_j, w) \in R_{\mathcal{L}}$

7 :   return $\perp$

8 : Let $x = (1, x_1, \ldots, x_n, x_{n+1})$

9 : $(\Pi, \mathsf{AUX}) \leftarrow \mathsf{Prove}(x, (w, j))$

10 : for $i \in [n+1]$

11 :   if $i = j \lor i = 1$

12 : $a \leftarrow \mathsf{Enc}(\perp, \mathsf{pk}_e^j)$

13 :   else

14 : $a \leftarrow \mathsf{Enc}(\mathsf{AUX}[i], \mathsf{pk}_e^i)$

15 : $A \leftarrow A \cup a$

16 : return $\sigma = (1, \Pi, A)$

$\mathsf{Extend}(m, \sigma, \{\mathsf{pk}_i\}_{i \in \mathcal{R}}, \mathsf{pk}^*)$

1 : if $\mathsf{pk}^* \in \{\mathsf{pk}_i\}_{i \in \mathcal{R}}$ return $\perp$

2 : $(\mathsf{pk}_O = (x_1, \mathsf{pk}_e^1)) \leftarrow H(m)$

3 : Parse $\{\mathsf{pk}_i\}_{i \in \mathcal{R}} = (\mathsf{pk}_2, \ldots, \mathsf{pk}_{n+1})$

4 : Parse $\mathsf{pk}_i = (x_i, \mathsf{pk}_e^i)$ for $i \in [n+1]$

5 : Parse $\mathsf{pk}^* = (x_{n+2}, \mathsf{pk}_e^{n+2})$

6 : Parse $\sigma = (k, \Pi, A)$

7 : Let $x = (k, x_1, \ldots, x_{n+1})$

8 : $(\Pi, \mathsf{aux}) \leftarrow \mathsf{PrExtend}(x, x_{n+2}, \Pi)$

9 : $a \leftarrow \mathsf{Enc}(\mathsf{aux}, \mathsf{pk}_e^{n+2})$

10 : $A \leftarrow A \cup a$

11 : Let $\bar{x} = (k, x_1, \ldots, x_{n+2})$

12 : $(\Pi, r_1, \ldots, r_{n+2}) \leftarrow \mathsf{RandPr}(\bar{x}, \Pi)$

13 : for $a_i \in A$

14 : $a_i \leftarrow \mathsf{Eval}(a_i, r_i, \mathsf{pk}_e^i)$

15 : return $\sigma = (k, \Pi, A)$

$\mathsf{KeyGen}()$

1 : $(\mathsf{pk}_e, \mathsf{sk}_e) \leftarrow \mathsf{KeyGen}()$

2 : Sample $(x, w) \in R_{\mathcal{L}}$

3 : $(\mathsf{pk} = (x, \mathsf{pk}_e), \mathsf{sk} = (w, \mathsf{sk}_e))$

4 : return $(\mathsf{pk}, \mathsf{sk})$

$\mathsf{Join}(m, \{\mathsf{pk}_i\}_{i \in \mathcal{R}}, \mathsf{sk}, \sigma)$

1 : $(\mathsf{pk}_O = (x_1, \mathsf{pk}_e^1)) \leftarrow H(m)$

2 : Parse $\{\mathsf{pk}_i\}_{i \in \mathcal{R}} = (\mathsf{pk}_2, \ldots, \mathsf{pk}_{n+1})$

3 : Parse $\mathsf{pk}_i = (x_i, \mathsf{pk}_e^i)$ for $i \in [n+1]$

4 : Parse $\mathsf{sk} = (w, \mathsf{sk}_e)$

5 : if $\not\exists x_j, j \in [n+1]$ s.t $(x_j, w) \in R_{\mathcal{L}}$

6 :   return $\perp$

7 : Parse $\sigma = (k, \Pi, A), A = (a_1, \ldots, a_{n+1})$

8 : Parse $\mathsf{sk} = (w, \mathsf{sk}_e)$

9 : $\mathsf{aux} \leftarrow \mathsf{Dec}(a_j, \mathsf{sk}_e)$

10 : Let $x = (k, x_1, \ldots, x_{n+1})$

11 : $(\Pi, \mathsf{aux}_j') \leftarrow \mathsf{PrAdd}(x, (w, j), \mathsf{aux}, \Pi)$

12 : Set $a_j \in A$ as $a_j \leftarrow \mathsf{Enc}(\perp, \mathsf{pk}_e^j)$

13 : $k \leftarrow k + 1$

14 : $(\Pi, r_1, \ldots, r_{n+1}) \leftarrow \mathsf{RandPr}(x, \Pi)$

15 : for $a_i \in A$

16 : $a_i \leftarrow \mathsf{Eval}(a_i, r_i, \mathsf{pk}_e^i)$

17 : return $\sigma = (k, \Pi, A)$

$\mathsf{Verify}(t, m, \{\mathsf{pk}_i\}_{i \in \mathcal{R}}, \sigma)$

1 : $(\mathsf{crs}, \mathsf{pk}_O = (x_1, \mathsf{pk}_e^1)) \leftarrow H(m)$

2 : Parse $\{\mathsf{pk}_i\}_{i \in \mathcal{R}} = (\mathsf{pk}_2, \ldots, \mathsf{pk}_{n+1})$

3 : Parse $\mathsf{pk}_i = (x_i, \mathsf{pk}_e^i)$ for $i \in [n+1]$

4 : Parse $\sigma = (k, \Pi, A)$

5 : Let $x = (k, x_1, \ldots, x_{n+1})$

6 : if $k < t$

7 :   return 0

8 : else

9 :   return $\mathsf{PrVerify}(x, \Pi)$

Fig. 9. ETRS from ENIWI PoK and IND-CPA homomorphic PKE. For space reasons, we directly write the internal algorithms of the schemes (e.g., Prove instead of ENIWI.Prove), and we omit crs from ENIWI algorithms input considering it as implicit. We use $\mathsf{AUX}[i]$ to indicate the i-th element of list AUX.

of the ENIWI we take advantage of the fact that we have a *different* CRS for every message. Finally, after applying all these changes, $\mathcal{B}$ can set x_{i^*} as the x received from $\mathcal{C}$. Given the forgery generated by $\mathcal{A}$, $\mathcal{B}$ can extract a witness for statement x, breaking the hardness of $R_\mathcal{L}$.

Let $\Pr\left[\mathsf{Exp}^{\mathrm{cmEUF}}_{\mathcal{A},\mathsf{ETRS}}(\lambda) = win\right]$ be the probability that the adversary wins the unforgeability game, we have that: $\Pr\left[\mathsf{Exp}^{\mathrm{cmEUF}}_{\mathcal{A},\mathsf{ETRS}}(\lambda) = win\right] \leq \epsilon_{rr} + q_m(\epsilon_{crs} + (q_{KG} + 1)(\epsilon_{HR} + \epsilon_{EWI}))$, where q_{KG} and q_m are polynomial bounds on the number of key generation queries and random oracle queries that $\mathcal{A}$ can do. While ϵ_{rr}, ϵ_{crs}, ϵ_{HR}, ϵ_{EWI} are the advantages in the re-randomizable addition game of ENIWI, in distinguishing a regular CRS from an extraction-mode CRS, in the hard relation game, and in the extended witness indistinguishability game respectively. We defer to [5] for the complete proof.

Lemma 3. *The signature scheme described in Fig. 9 satisfies the anonymity property of Definition 3.*

Proof Sketch. Through a sequence of indistinguishable hybrids, we switch from a challenger $\mathcal{B}$ using lad_0 to a $\mathcal{B}$ using lad_1. We show that at every hybrid, $\mathcal{B}$ can exploit $\mathcal{A}$ distinguishing between the two hybrids to break some properties of the underlying primitives. First, $\mathcal{B}$ changes the way it processes the ladders and replies to Join queries. In particular, $\mathcal{B}$ computes every time a new proof from scratch using ENIWI.Prove, instead of running the Join/Extend algorithms, analogously to the proof of unforgeability. After that, when processing the ladders, $\mathcal{B}$ will encrypt $\perp$ in all signers' ciphertexts. This change is not detected by $\mathcal{A}$ thanks to the IND-CPA property of the encryption scheme. At the end, $\mathcal{B}$ fixes the ladder used in the anonymity game to be lad_1. This change is unnoticeable thanks to the extended WI of ENIWI. We defer to [5] for the complete proof.

Lemma 4. *The signature scheme described in Fig. 9 enjoys fellow-signer anonymity (cfr., Definition 4).*

The proof follows essentially the same path of the one of Lemma 3.

7 Our Extendable Non-Interactive Witness Indistinguishable Proof of Knowledge

In this section, we first show how to extend the GS proof system to define a proof system for a threshold relation. After that, we show how to further modify such scheme to get our ENIWI PoK.

7.1 GS Proofs of Partial Satisfiability

In [13,23], it is shown how to transform n sets of certain types of equations $S_1, \ldots, S_n$ to a set of equations S' s.t. S' is satisfied whenever one of $S_1, \ldots, S_n$ is satisfied. A witness for S_i, with $i \in [n]$, is easily mapped to a witness for S'. Indeed, this transformation realizes a disjunction. The transformation works by assuming that $S_1, \ldots, S_n$ have independent variables, adding variables $b_1, \ldots b_{n-1} \in \{0,1\}$, and defining $b_n = 1 - b_1 - \ldots - b_{n-1}$. Then, for $i \in [n]$, b_i is used to modify all the equations in S_i so that they remain the same if $b_i = 1$, but they admit the trivial solution for $b_i = 0$. Slightly increasing the overhead of these compilers, it is also possible to implement partial satisfiability proofs for an arbitrary threshold k, meaning that S' is satisfied iff k of $S_1, \ldots, S_n$ are satisfied. To do so, the main idea is to define $b_n \in \{0,1\}$, and to prove that $b_1 + \ldots + b_n = k$.

A case which is relevant to this paper is when $S_1, \ldots, S_n$ contain only PPEs with $t_{\mathbb{T}} = 0_{\mathbb{T}}$, all the variables of the PPEs are elements of $\hat{\mathbb{H}}$, and public constants are either paired with secret values or with $\hat{h}$. In this case, the prover would:

1. Add variables $b_1, \ldots, b_n$ and prove that $b_i \in \{0,1\} \; \forall i \in [n]$. This can be done with quadratic equations, by adding the equations $b_i(1 - b_i) = 0$. Let us define such equations to be of type $\mathcal{B}$, we will refer to a specific equation using $\mathcal{B}_i$.
2. Add variables $\hat{M}_1, \ldots, \hat{M}_n$ and prove $b_i \hat{g} - \hat{M}_i = 0$, with $i \in [n]$. This can be done via multi-scalar multiplication equations in $\hat{\mathbb{G}}$. Since $b_i \in \{0,1\}$, it follows that $\hat{M}_i \in \{\hat{0}, \hat{g}\}$. Let us define such equations to be of type $\mathcal{M}$.
3. Add equation $\sum_{i=1}^{n} \hat{M}_i \cdot \hat{h} - k\hat{g} \cdot \hat{h} = 0_{\mathbb{T}}$. Since $\hat{M}_i \in \{\hat{0}, \hat{g}\}$, this equation implies that exactly k of the $\hat{M}_i$, with $i \in [n]$, are equal to $\hat{g}$. Let us call such equation as $\mathcal{K}$.
4. For each S_i, with $i \in [n]$, let Q_i be the number of equations in S_i, let $J_{i,q}$ be the number of variables in the equation $q \in [Q_i]$ of S_i. For each variable $\breve{y}_{i,q,j}$ with $q \in [Q_i], j \in [J_{i,q}]$, define variable $\breve{x}_{i,q,j}$ and add equation $\hat{M}_i \cdot \breve{y}_{i,q,j} - \hat{M}_i \cdot \breve{x}_{i,q,j} = 0_{\mathbb{T}}$. Since k of the $\hat{M}_i$ are equal to $\hat{g}$, this implies that for k equations sets it must hold that all $\breve{y}_{i,q,j} = \breve{x}_{i,q,j}$. Let us define such equations to be of type $\mathcal{Y}$.
5. For each equation in each S_i, replace all the original $\breve{y}_{i,q,j}$ with the corresponding $\breve{x}_{i,q,j}$. This allows to set all $\breve{x}_{i,q,j} = \breve{y}_{i,q,j} = \breve{0}$ for each set S_i for which the prover does not have a satisfying assignment. For the k sets for which the prover does have a satisfying assignment, the prover sets $\breve{y}_{i,q,j} = \breve{x}_{i,q,j}$. Let us define such equations to be of type $\mathcal{X}$.

7.2   High-level Overview of Our ENIWI

We construct our ENIWI by observing that GS proofs of partial satisfiability can be updated in two ways:

– **Extend**: consider a proof Π for a set of equations S which is satisfied if k out of n of the original equations sets $S_1, \ldots, S_n$ are satisfied. On input a new equations set S_{n+1} and the proof Π, compute a new equations set S' which is satisfied if k out of the $n + 1$ equations sets $S_1, \ldots, S_n, S_{n+1}$ are satisfied. Output S' and the corresponding updated proof Π'.

- **Add**: consider a proof Π for a set of equations S which is satisfied if k out n of the original equations sets $S_1, \ldots, S_n$ are satisfied. On input the proof Π for S, a witness for an equations set S_i with $i \in [n]$ which was not previously used to create Π, and some corresponding auxiliary information aux_i, compute a new equations set S' which is satisfied if $k + 1$ out of the n equations sets $S_1, \ldots, S_n$ are satisfied. Output S' and the corresponding updated proof Π'.

In particular, one can notice that each step of the partial satisfiability proof described in Sect. 7.1 only adds equations featuring independent variables, except for step 3. In step 3, one equation is added combining all variables $\hat{M}_i$ with $i \in [n]$. The equation is $\sum_{i=1}^{n} \hat{M}_i \cdot \check{h} - k\hat{g} \cdot \check{h} = 0_{\mathbb{T}}$. Let us compute the GS proof for such equation. Let crs be $(\hat{u}, \hat{v}, \hat{w}, \check{u}, \check{v}, \check{w})$.

- Variables $\hat{M}_i$ are committed as group elements (i.e., with label $\mathsf{com}_{\hat{\mathbb{G}}}$), thus $\hat{c}_{\hat{M}_i} = e^{\top} \hat{M}_i + \hat{v} r_i + \hat{w} s_i$, with $r_i, s_i \xleftarrow{\$} \mathbb{Z}_p$.
- $\hat{g}$ is the base element of $\hat{\mathbb{G}}$, thus it is publicly committed with label $\mathsf{base}_{\hat{\mathbb{G}}}$ as $\hat{c}_{\hat{g}} = (0, \hat{g})^{\top}$.
- $\check{h}$ is the base element of $\check{\mathbb{H}}$, and thus it is publicly committed with label $\mathsf{base}_{\check{\mathbb{H}}}$ as $(0, \check{h})$.

This results in $\hat{C} = (\hat{c}_{\hat{M}_1}, \ldots, \hat{c}_{\hat{M}_n}, \hat{c}_{\hat{g}})$, $\check{D} = (0, \check{h})$, $\boldsymbol{r}_x = (r_1, \ldots, r_n, 0)^{\top}$, $\boldsymbol{s}_x = (s_1, \ldots, s_n, 0)^{\top}$, $\boldsymbol{r}_y = 0$, $\boldsymbol{s}_y = 0$.

This means that $\hat{\boldsymbol{\pi}}_{\check{v}} = -\hat{\boldsymbol{v}}\alpha - \hat{\boldsymbol{w}}\gamma$ and $\hat{\boldsymbol{\pi}}_{\check{w}} = -\hat{\boldsymbol{v}}\beta - \hat{\boldsymbol{w}}\delta$, with $\alpha, \gamma, \beta, \delta$ being random elements in $\mathbb{Z}_p$.

Let us compute $\boldsymbol{r}_x \Gamma \check{D} = (r_1, \ldots, r_n, 0)^{\top} (1, \ldots, 1, -k)(0, \check{h}) = (0, \sum_{i=1}^{n} r_i \check{h})$. Similarly, we have that $\boldsymbol{s}_x \Gamma \check{D} = (0, \sum_{i=1}^{n} s_i \check{h})$. Let us define $\mathsf{aux}_i = (\mathsf{aux}_i^1, \mathsf{aux}_i^2) = (r_i \check{h}, s_i \check{h})$. This means that $\check{\boldsymbol{\pi}}_{\hat{v}} = \boldsymbol{r}_x \Gamma \check{D} + \alpha \check{\boldsymbol{v}} + \beta \check{\boldsymbol{w}} = (0, \sum_{i=1}^{n} \mathsf{aux}_i^1) + \alpha \check{\boldsymbol{v}} + \beta \check{\boldsymbol{w}}$ and $\check{\boldsymbol{\pi}}_{\hat{w}} = \boldsymbol{s}_x \Gamma \check{D} + \delta \check{\boldsymbol{v}} + \gamma \check{\boldsymbol{w}} = (0, \sum_{i=1}^{n} \mathsf{aux}_i^2) + \delta \check{\boldsymbol{v}} + \gamma \check{\boldsymbol{w}}$. We notice that the proof elements for equation $\mathcal{K}$ are essentially a sum of n independent contributions (i.e., the aux_i values) for each of the involved n variables (i.e., $\hat{M}_i$ with $i \in [n]$). We can exploit this fact to perform the extend and add operations in the following way. Let us consider the steps of Sect. 7.1.

- **Extend**: Add new equations of types $\mathcal{B}, \mathcal{M}, \mathcal{Y}, \mathcal{X}$ by defining the corresponding new independent variables, and compute the related GS proofs. Modify equation $\mathcal{K}$ to be $\sum_{i=1}^{n+1} \hat{M}_i \cdot \check{h} - k\hat{g} \cdot \check{h} = 0_{\mathbb{T}}$ and update $\check{\boldsymbol{\pi}}_{\hat{v}}$ and $\check{\boldsymbol{\pi}}_{\hat{w}}$ as $\check{\boldsymbol{\pi}}_{\hat{v}} = \check{\boldsymbol{\pi}}_{\hat{v}} + (0, r_{n+1} \check{h})$, $\check{\boldsymbol{\pi}}_{\hat{w}} = \check{\boldsymbol{\pi}}_{\hat{w}} + (0, s_{n+1} \check{h})$, where r_{n+1} and s_{n+1} are the randomnesses used to commit to the new variable $\hat{M}_{n+1} = \hat{0}$.
- **Add**: Replace the committed variables for the equations $\mathcal{B}_i, \mathcal{M}_i, \mathcal{Y}_i, \mathcal{X}_i$ with new committed variables $b_i = 1$, $\hat{M}_i = \hat{g}$, and $\check{y}_{i,q,j} = \check{x}_{i,q,j}$. Replace the old corresponding GS proofs with freshly computed ones. Modify equation $\mathcal{K}$ to be $\sum_{i=1}^{n} \hat{M}_i \cdot \check{h} - (k+1)\hat{g} \cdot \check{h} = 0_{\mathbb{T}}$, and update $\check{\boldsymbol{\pi}}_{\hat{v}}$ and $\check{\boldsymbol{\pi}}_{\hat{w}}$ as $\check{\boldsymbol{\pi}}_{\hat{v}} = \check{\boldsymbol{\pi}}_{\hat{v}} - (0, \mathsf{aux}_i^1) + (0, r_i' \check{h})$, $\check{\boldsymbol{\pi}}_{\hat{w}} = \check{\boldsymbol{\pi}}_{\hat{w}} - (0, \mathsf{aux}_i^2) + (0, s_i' \check{h})$, where r_i' and s_i' are the randomnesses used for the fresh commitment to $\hat{M}_i = \hat{g}$.

After any of the two above modifications, the resulting proof is an accepting proof for the updated threshold relation. Indeed, both the extend and add operation symbolically compute the proofs in the same way a prover for the updated threshold relation would do from scratch.

7.3   Our ENIWI

Our ENIWI is an ENIWI PoK over the language of sets of pairing product equations where all the variables are elements of $\check{\mathbb{H}}$, public constants are either paired with secret values or with $\check{h}$, and the target element is $0_\mathbb{T}$. For simplicity, we consider each statement x_i as containing only one equation.

- crs $\leftarrow$ CRSSetup(gk): run GS.Setup(gk). This results in crs $= (\hat{u}, \hat{v}, \hat{w}, \check{u}, \check{v}, \check{w})$.
- $(\Pi, (\mathsf{aux}_1, \ldots, \mathsf{aux}_n)) \leftarrow$ Prove(crs, $(k, x_1, \ldots, x_n), ((w_1, \alpha_1) \ldots (w_k, \alpha_k)))$: on input $((k, x_1, \ldots, x_n), ((w_1, \alpha_1) \ldots (w_k, \alpha_k))) \in$ rl, define $A = \{\alpha_1, \ldots, \alpha_k\}^8$ and do the following.
  1. For each equation x_i, $i \in [n]$, define new variables and equations:
     - Define variable $b_i = 1$ if $i \in A$, and $b_i = 0$ otherwise.
     - Define quadratic equation $\mathcal{B}_i$ as $b_i(1 - b_i) = 0$.
     - Define variables $\hat{M}_i = \hat{g}$ if $i \in A$, and $\hat{M}_i = \hat{0}$ otherwise.
     - Define multi-scalar multiplication equation $\mathcal{M}_i$ as $b_i\hat{g} - \hat{M}_i = 0$.
     - Let J_i be the number of variables in equation x_i. For each variable $\check{y}_{i,j}$, with $j \in [J_i]$, define a variable $\check{x}_{i,j}$. Set $\check{x}_{i,j} = \check{y}_{i,j}$, if $i \in A$, and $\check{x}_{i,j} = \check{0}$ otherwise.
     - For each variable $\check{y}_{i,j}$, with $j \in [J_i]$, define pairing product equation $\mathcal{Y}_{i,j}$ as $\hat{M}_i \cdot \check{y}_{i,j} - \hat{M}_i \cdot \check{x}_{i,j} = 0_\mathbb{T}$.
     - Modify pairing product equation x_i by replacing each variable $\check{y}_{i,j}$, with $j \in [J_i]$, with variable $\check{x}_{i,j}$. Let us call such modified equation $\mathcal{X}_i$.

     Moreover, define pairing product equation $\mathcal{K}$ as $\sum_{i=1}^n \hat{M}_i \cdot \check{h} - k\hat{g} \cdot \check{h} = 0_\mathbb{T}$. At the end of this step, there will be n equations of types $\mathcal{B}, \mathcal{M}, \mathcal{X}$, $n \sum_{i=1}^n J_i$ equations of type $\mathcal{Y}$, and one equation of type $\mathcal{K}$.
  2. For each equation of types $\mathcal{B}, \mathcal{M}, \mathcal{Y}, \mathcal{X}$ generate appropriate commitments (using GS.Com) to all variables, resulting in lists of commitments $C_\mathcal{B}, C_\mathcal{M}, C_\mathcal{Y}, C_\mathcal{X}$ respectively[9]. Then, for each equation of types $\mathcal{B}, \mathcal{M}, \mathcal{Y}, \mathcal{X}$, run GS.Prove with the obvious inputs obtaining proof elements lists $\pi_\mathcal{B}, \pi_\mathcal{M}, \pi_\mathcal{Y}, \pi_\mathcal{X}$. For example, $\pi_\mathcal{B}$ contains proof elements $\pi_{\mathcal{B}i}$, with $i \in [n]$, each of them obtained running GS.Prove for equation $\mathcal{B}_i$ using commitments $C_{\mathcal{B}i}$ (and related randomnesses) from $C_\mathcal{B}$.

---

[8] A indicates what are the k equations the prover has a satisfying assignment for.
[9] Whenever different equations share the same variables, we can think of the commitments lists as containing copies of the exact same commitments. Clearly, in practice data does not need to be replicated.

Moreover, for equation $\mathcal{K}$ do the following[10]:

- Commit to $\hat{M}_i$, with $i \in [n]$, with label $\mathsf{com}_{\hat{\mathbb{G}}}$ and randomness (r_i, s_i), i.e., $(\mathsf{com}_{\hat{\mathbb{G}}}, \hat{c}_{\hat{M}_i}) \leftarrow \mathsf{GS.Com}(\mathsf{com}_{\hat{\mathbb{G}}}, \hat{M}_i; (r_i, s_i))$, resulting in $\hat{c}_{\hat{M}_i} = e^{\top}\hat{M}_i + \hat{v}r_i + \hat{w}s_i$.
- Commit to $\hat{g}$ with label $\mathsf{base}_{\hat{\mathbb{G}}}$ and randomness $(0, 0)$, i.e., $(\mathsf{base}_{\hat{\mathbb{G}}}, \hat{c}_{\hat{g}}) \leftarrow \mathsf{GS.Com}(\mathsf{base}_{\hat{\mathbb{G}}}, \hat{g}; (0, 0))$, resulting in $\hat{c}_{\hat{g}} = (0, \hat{g})^{\top}$.
- Commit to $\check{h}$ with label $\mathsf{base}_{\check{\mathbb{H}}}$ and randomness $(0, 0)$, i.e., $(\mathsf{base}_{\check{\mathbb{H}}}, \check{d}_{\check{h}}) \leftarrow \mathsf{GS.Com}(\mathsf{base}_{\check{\mathbb{H}}}, \check{h}; (0, 0))$, resulting in $\check{d}_{\check{h}} = (0, \check{h})$.

Do the following steps:

- Define $\hat{C} = (\hat{c}_{\hat{M}_1}, \ldots, \hat{c}_{\hat{M}_n}, \hat{c}_{\hat{g}})$, $\check{D} = (0, \check{h})$, $\boldsymbol{r}_x = (r_1, \ldots, r_n, 0)^{\top}$, $\boldsymbol{s}_x = (s_1, \ldots, s_n, 0)^{\top}$, $\boldsymbol{r}_y = 0$, $\boldsymbol{s}_y = 0$. This means that $\hat{\boldsymbol{\pi}}_{\check{v}} = -\hat{v}\alpha - \hat{w}\gamma$ and $\hat{\boldsymbol{\pi}}_{\check{w}} = -\hat{v}\beta - \hat{w}\delta$.
- Compute $\boldsymbol{r}_x \Gamma \check{D} = (r_1, \ldots, r_n, 0)^{\top}(1, \ldots, 1, -k)(0, \check{h}) = (0, \sum_{i=1}^n r_i \check{h})$. Similarly, we have that $\boldsymbol{s}_x \Gamma \check{D} = (0, \sum_{i=1}^n s_i \check{h})$. Define $\mathsf{aux}_i = (\mathsf{aux}_i^1, \mathsf{aux}_i^2) = (r_i \check{h}, s_i \check{h})$, with $i \in [n]$.
- Compute $\check{\boldsymbol{\pi}}_{\hat{v}} = \boldsymbol{r}_x \Gamma \check{D} + \alpha \check{v} + \beta \check{w} = (0, \sum_{i=1}^n \mathsf{aux}_i^1) + \alpha \check{v} + \beta \check{w}$ and $\check{\boldsymbol{\pi}}_{\hat{w}} = \boldsymbol{s}_x \Gamma \check{D} + \delta \check{v} + \gamma \check{w} = (0, \sum_{i=1}^n \mathsf{aux}_i^2) + \delta \check{v} + \gamma \check{w}$.

Let $\pi_{\mathcal{K}} = (\hat{\boldsymbol{\pi}}_{\check{v}}, \hat{\boldsymbol{\pi}}_{\check{w}}, \check{\boldsymbol{\pi}}_{\hat{v}}, \check{\boldsymbol{\pi}}_{\hat{w}})$ and $C_{\mathcal{K}} = (\hat{C}, \check{D})$. Output $(\Pi = (\boldsymbol{C}_{\mathcal{B}}, \boldsymbol{C}_{\mathcal{M}}, \boldsymbol{C}_{\mathcal{Y}}, \boldsymbol{C}_{\mathcal{X}}, C_{\mathcal{K}}, \boldsymbol{\pi}_{\mathcal{B}}, \boldsymbol{\pi}_{\mathcal{M}}, \boldsymbol{\pi}_{\mathcal{Y}}, \boldsymbol{\pi}_{\mathcal{X}}, \pi_{\mathcal{K}}), \mathsf{AUX} = (\mathsf{aux}_1, \ldots, \mathsf{aux}_n))$.

- $0/1 \leftarrow \mathsf{PrVerify}(\mathsf{crs}, (k, x_1, \ldots, x_n), \Pi)$ reconstruct equations of type $\mathcal{B}, \mathcal{M}, \mathcal{Y}, \mathcal{X}, \mathcal{K}$, appropriately parse Π, and for every equation run $\mathsf{GS.PrVerify}$ with the obvious inputs. For example, the proof for equation $\mathcal{B}_i$ is verified giving, after appropriate parsing, commitments $\boldsymbol{C}_{\mathcal{B}_i}$ and proof element $\boldsymbol{\pi}_{\mathcal{B}_i}$ in input to $\mathsf{GS.PrVerify}$. Return 1 iff all the calls to $\mathsf{GS.PrVerify}$ return 1.
- $(\Pi', \mathsf{aux}_{n+1}) \leftarrow \mathsf{PrExtend}(\mathsf{crs}, (k, x_1, \ldots, x_n), x_{n+1}, \Pi)$ do the following:
  1. Parse Π as $(\boldsymbol{C}_{\mathcal{B}}, \boldsymbol{C}_{\mathcal{M}}, \boldsymbol{C}_{\mathcal{Y}}, \boldsymbol{C}_{\mathcal{X}}, C_{\mathcal{K}}, \boldsymbol{\pi}_{\mathcal{B}}, \boldsymbol{\pi}_{\mathcal{M}}, \boldsymbol{\pi}_{\mathcal{Y}}, \boldsymbol{\pi}_{\mathcal{X}}, \pi_{\mathcal{K}})$, $\mathsf{AUX} = (\mathsf{aux}_1, \ldots, \mathsf{aux}_n)$.
  2. For each of the 4 equation types $\mathcal{B}, \mathcal{M}, \mathcal{Y}, \mathcal{X}$, add a new equation related to x_{n+1} by defining the corresponding new independent variables, $b_{n+1} = 0, \hat{M}_{n+1} = \hat{0}$ and all the $\check{y}_{n+1,j} = \check{0}$, with $j \in [J_{n+1}]$.
  3. Compute commitments to new variables and appropriately add them to $\boldsymbol{C}_{\mathcal{B}}, \boldsymbol{C}_{\mathcal{M}}, \boldsymbol{C}_{\mathcal{Y}}, \boldsymbol{C}_{\mathcal{X}}$.
  4. Compute the related new GS proofs and add them to $\boldsymbol{\pi}_{\mathcal{B}}, \boldsymbol{\pi}_{\mathcal{M}}, \boldsymbol{\pi}_{\mathcal{Y}}, \boldsymbol{\pi}_{\mathcal{X}}$ accordingly.
  5. Parse $\pi_{\mathcal{K}}$ as $(\hat{\boldsymbol{\pi}}_{\check{v}}, \hat{\boldsymbol{\pi}}_{\check{w}}, \check{\boldsymbol{\pi}}_{\hat{v}}, \check{\boldsymbol{\pi}}_{\hat{w}})$ and update $\check{\boldsymbol{\pi}}_{\hat{v}}$ and $\check{\boldsymbol{\pi}}_{\hat{w}}$ as $\check{\boldsymbol{\pi}}_{\hat{v}} = \check{\boldsymbol{\pi}}_{\hat{v}} + (0, r_{n+1}\check{h}), \check{\boldsymbol{\pi}}_{\hat{w}} = \check{\boldsymbol{\pi}}_{\hat{w}} + (0, s_{n+1}\check{h})$, where r_{n+1} and s_{n+1} are the randomnesses used to commit to the new variable $\hat{M}_{n+1} = \hat{0}$.
  6. Set $\mathsf{aux}_{n+1} = (\mathsf{aux}_{n+1}^1, \mathsf{aux}_{n+1}^2) = (r_{n+1}\check{h}, s_{n+1}\check{h})$.
  7. Output $(\Pi, \mathsf{aux}_{n+1})$.
- $(\Pi', \mathsf{aux}'_{\alpha}) \leftarrow \mathsf{PrAdd}(\mathsf{crs}, (k, x_1, \ldots, x_n), (w, \alpha), \mathsf{aux}, \Pi)$ do the following:
  1. Parse Π as $(\boldsymbol{C}_{\mathcal{B}}, \boldsymbol{C}_{\mathcal{M}}, \boldsymbol{C}_{\mathcal{Y}}, \boldsymbol{C}_{\mathcal{X}}, C_{\mathcal{K}}, \boldsymbol{\pi}_{\mathcal{B}}, \boldsymbol{\pi}_{\mathcal{M}}, \boldsymbol{\pi}_{\mathcal{Y}}, \boldsymbol{\pi}_{\mathcal{X}}, \pi_{\mathcal{K}})$.

---

[10] We report the whitebox computation of the GS prover to show how to compute the auxiliary values. Furthermore, for sake of clarity, we report again commitments to variables $\hat{M}_i$ with $i \in [n]$, which were already created to prove other equations.

2. For each of the 4 equation types $\mathcal{B}, \mathcal{M}, \mathcal{Y}, \mathcal{X}$, replace the variables in equations related to x_α (i.e., $\mathcal{B}_\alpha, \mathcal{M}_\alpha, \mathcal{X}_\alpha$, and all $\mathcal{Y}_{\alpha,j}$ with $j \in J_\alpha$) as follows: $b_\alpha = 1$, $\hat{M}_\alpha = \hat{g}$ and all the $\check{y}_{\alpha,j} = \check{x}_{\alpha,j}$, with $j \in [J_\alpha]$.

3. Replace the commitments related to equations $\mathcal{B}_\alpha, \mathcal{M}_\alpha, \mathcal{X}_\alpha$, and all $\mathcal{Y}_{\alpha,j}$, with $j \in J_\alpha$ with freshly generated ones updating $C_\mathcal{B}, C_\mathcal{M}, C_\mathcal{Y}, C_\mathcal{X}$ accordingly.

4. Replace the GS proofs related to equations $\mathcal{B}_\alpha, \mathcal{M}_\alpha, \mathcal{X}_\alpha$, and all $\mathcal{Y}_{\alpha,j}$ with $j \in J_\alpha$, with freshly generated ones replacing proof elements of $\boldsymbol{\pi}_\mathcal{B}, \boldsymbol{\pi}_\mathcal{M}, \boldsymbol{\pi}_\mathcal{Y}, \boldsymbol{\pi}_\mathcal{X}$ accordingly.

5. Parse $\pi_\mathcal{K}$ as $(\hat{\boldsymbol{\pi}}_{\check{v}}, \hat{\boldsymbol{\pi}}_{\check{w}}, \check{\boldsymbol{\pi}}_{\hat{v}}, \check{\boldsymbol{\pi}}_{\hat{w}})$ and update $\check{\boldsymbol{\pi}}_{\hat{v}}$ and $\check{\boldsymbol{\pi}}_{\hat{w}}$ as $\check{\boldsymbol{\pi}}_{\hat{v}} = \check{\boldsymbol{\pi}}_{\hat{v}} - (0, \mathsf{aux}_\alpha^1) + (0, r'_\alpha \check{h})$, $\check{\boldsymbol{\pi}}_{\hat{w}} = \check{\boldsymbol{\pi}}_{\hat{w}} - (0, \mathsf{aux}_\alpha^2) + (0, s'_\alpha \check{h})$, where r'_α and s'_α are the randomnesses used for the fresh commitment to $\hat{M}_\alpha = \hat{g}$.

6. Set $\mathsf{aux}'_\alpha = (\mathsf{aux}_\alpha^1, \mathsf{aux}_\alpha^2) = (r'_\alpha \check{h}, s'_\alpha \check{h})$.

7. Output $(\Pi, \mathsf{aux}'_\alpha)$.

- $(\Pi', r_1, \ldots, r_n) \leftarrow \mathsf{RandPr}(\mathsf{crs}, (k, x_1, \ldots, x_n), \Pi)$:

1. Run GS.RandPr on each of the proofs, appropriately fixing the random coins when randomizing proofs related to equations involving shared variables (i.e., s.t. we end up again with shared variables having the exact same commitments). Let r'_i, s'_i, with $i \in [n]$ be the randomnesses used to update commitments to all $\hat{M}_i$, with $i \in [n]$. Define $r_i = (r'_i, s'_i)$. Let randomized proof elements and commitments be contained in Π'.

2. Output $(\Pi', r_1, \ldots, r_n)$

- $\mathsf{aux}' \leftarrow \mathsf{AuxUpdate}(\mathsf{crs}, \mathsf{aux}, r)$:

1. Parse r as (r', s'), and aux as $(\mathsf{aux}^1, \mathsf{aux}^2)$.

2. Output $\mathsf{aux}' = (\mathsf{aux}^1 + r'\check{h}, \mathsf{aux}^2 + s'\check{h})$.

- $0/1 \leftarrow \mathsf{AuxVerify}(\mathsf{crs}, (k, x_1, \ldots, x_n), ((w_1, \alpha_1) \ldots, (w_k, \alpha_k)), (\mathsf{aux}_1, \ldots, \mathsf{aux}_n), \Pi)$:

1. Parse Π as $(C_\mathcal{B}, C_\mathcal{M}, C_\mathcal{Y}, C_\mathcal{X}, C_\mathcal{K}, \boldsymbol{\pi}_\mathcal{B}, \boldsymbol{\pi}_\mathcal{M}, \boldsymbol{\pi}_\mathcal{Y}, \boldsymbol{\pi}_\mathcal{X}, \pi_\mathcal{K})$. Parse $C_\mathcal{K}$ as $\hat{C} = (\hat{c}_{\hat{M}_1}, \ldots, \hat{c}_{\hat{M}_n}, \hat{c}_{\hat{g}})$ and $\check{D} = (0, \check{h})$.

2. Check that $(\mathsf{aux}_{\alpha_1}, \ldots, \mathsf{aux}_{\alpha_k})$ all open $(\hat{c}_{\hat{M}_{\alpha_1}}, \ldots, \hat{c}_{\hat{M}_{\alpha_k}})$ to $\hat{g}$. Namely, check that $\hat{c}_{\hat{M}_i} \cdot (\check{h}, \check{h}) + \hat{\boldsymbol{v}} \cdot (-\mathsf{aux}_i^1, -\mathsf{aux}_i^1) + \hat{\boldsymbol{w}} \cdot (-\mathsf{aux}_i^2, -\mathsf{aux}_i^2) = (\hat{0}, \hat{g})^\top \cdot (\check{h}, \check{h})$, for all $i \in A$.

3. Check that remaining auxiliary values open commitments $\hat{c}_{\hat{M}_i}$ with $i \in [n] \setminus A$ to $\hat{0}$. Namely, check that $\hat{c}_{\hat{M}_i} \cdot (\check{h}, \check{h}) + \hat{\boldsymbol{v}} \cdot (-\mathsf{aux}_i^1, -\mathsf{aux}_i^1) + \hat{\boldsymbol{w}} \cdot (-\mathsf{aux}_i^2, -\mathsf{aux}_i^2) = (\hat{0}, \hat{0})^\top \cdot (\check{h}, \check{h})$, for all $i \in [n] \setminus A$.

Theorem 2. *If* GS *(cfr., Sect. 3.1) is a NIWI for all equation types and a NIWI PoK for pairing product equations, then the construction above is an* ENIWI *PoK. The base relation $R_\mathcal{L}$ consists of pairing product equations in which all the variables are elements of $\check{\mathbb{H}}$, public constants are either paired with secret values or with $\check{h}$, and the target element is $0_\mathbb{T}$.*

See [5] for the proof.

Acknowledgements. This result is part of projects that have received funding from the European Research Council (ERC) under the European Union's Horizon 2020 research and innovation program under projects PICOCRYPT (grant agreement No. 101001283) and PROCONTRA (grant agreement No. 885666), from the Spanish Government under project PRODIGY (TED2021-132464B-I00), and from the Madrid Regional Government under project BLOQUES (S2018/TCS-4339). The last two projects are co-funded by European Union EIE, and NextGenerationEU/PRTR funds.

References

1. Aguilar Melchor, C., Cayrel, P.-L., Gaborit, P.: A new efficient threshold ring signature scheme based on coding theory. In: Buchmann, J., Ding, J. (eds.) PQCrypto 2008. LNCS, vol. 5299, pp. 1–16. Springer, Heidelberg (2008). https://doi.org/10.1007/978-3-540-88403-3_1

2. Aranha, D.F., Hall-Andersen, M., Nitulescu, A., Pagnin, E., Yakoubov, S.: Count me in! extendability for threshold ring signatures. In: Hanaoka, G., Shikata, J., Watanabe, Y. (eds.) Public-Key Cryptography – PKC 2022. PKC 2022. Lecture Notes in Computer Science, vol. 13178, pp. 379–406. Springer, Cham (2022). https://doi.org/10.1007/978-3-030-97131-1_13

3. Attema, T., Cramer, R., Fehr, S.: Compressing proofs of k-out-Of-n partial knowledge. In: Malkin, T., Peikert, C. (eds.) CRYPTO 2021. LNCS, vol. 12828, pp. 65–91. Springer, Cham (2021). https://doi.org/10.1007/978-3-030-84259-8_3

4. Attema, T., Cramer, R., Rambaud, M.: Compressed Σ-protocols for bilinear group arithmetic circuits and application to logarithmic transparent threshold signatures. In: Tibouchi, M., Wang, H. (eds.) ASIACRYPT 2021. LNCS, vol. 13093, pp. 526–556. Springer, Cham (2021). https://doi.org/10.1007/978-3-030-92068-5_18

5. Avitabile, G., Botta, V., Fiore, D.: Extendable threshold ring signatures with enhanced anonymity. ePrint, Report 2022/1568

6. Avitabile, G., Botta, V., Friolo, D., Visconti, I.: Efficient proofs of knowledge for threshold relations. In: Atluri, V., Di Pietro, R., Jensen, C.D., Meng, W. (eds.) Computer Security – ESORICS 2022. ESORICS 2022. Lecture Notes in Computer Science, vol. 13556, pp. 42–62. Springer, Cham (2022). https://doi.org/10.1007/978-3-031-17143-7_3

7. Belenkiy, M., Camenisch, J., Chase, M., Kohlweiss, M., Lysyanskaya, A., Shacham, H.: Randomizable proofs and delegatable anonymous credentials. In: Halevi, S. (ed.) CRYPTO 2009. LNCS, vol. 5677, pp. 108–125. Springer, Heidelberg (2009). https://doi.org/10.1007/978-3-642-03356-8_7

8. Bettaieb, S., Schrek, J.: Improved lattice-based threshold ring signature scheme. In: Gaborit, P. (ed.) PQCrypto 2013. LNCS, vol. 7932, pp. 34–51. Springer, Heidelberg (2013). https://doi.org/10.1007/978-3-642-38616-9_3

9. Beullens, W., Katsumata, S., Pintore, F.: Calamari and Falafl: logarithmic (linkable) ring signatures from isogenies and lattices. In: Moriai, S., Wang, H. (eds.) ASIACRYPT 2020. LNCS, vol. 12492, pp. 464–492. Springer, Cham (2020). https://doi.org/10.1007/978-3-030-64834-3_16

10. Boneh, D., Gentry, C., Lynn, B., Shacham, H.: Aggregate and verifiably encrypted signatures from bilinear maps. In: Biham, E. (ed.) EUROCRYPT 2003. LNCS, vol. 2656, pp. 416–432. Springer, Heidelberg (2003). https://doi.org/10.1007/3-540-39200-9_26

11. Bootle, J., Cerulli, A., Chaidos, P., Ghadafi, E., Groth, J., Petit, C.: Short accountable ring signatures based on DDH. In: Pernul, G., Ryan, P.Y.A., Weippl, E. (eds.) ESORICS 2015. LNCS, vol. 9326, pp. 243–265. Springer, Cham (2015). https://doi.org/10.1007/978-3-319-24174-6_13

12. Bresson, E., Stern, J., Szydlo, M.: Threshold ring signatures and applications to Ad-hoc groups. In: Yung, M. (ed.) CRYPTO 2002. LNCS, vol. 2442, pp. 465–480. Springer, Heidelberg (2002). https://doi.org/10.1007/3-540-45708-9_30

13. Camenisch, J., Chandran, N., Shoup, V.: A public key encryption scheme secure against key dependent chosen plaintext and adaptive chosen ciphertext attacks. In: Joux, A. (ed.) EUROCRYPT 2009. LNCS, vol. 5479, pp. 351–368. Springer, Heidelberg (2009). https://doi.org/10.1007/978-3-642-01001-9_20

14. Chase, M., Kohlweiss, M., Lysyanskaya, A., Meiklejohn, S.: Malleable proof systems and applications. In: Pointcheval, D., Johansson, T. (eds.) EUROCRYPT 2012. LNCS, vol. 7237, pp. 281–300. Springer, Heidelberg (2012). https://doi.org/10.1007/978-3-642-29011-4_18

15. Chase, M., Lysyanskaya, A.: On signatures of knowledge. In: Dwork, C. (ed.) CRYPTO 2006. LNCS, vol. 4117, pp. 78–96. Springer, Heidelberg (2006). https://doi.org/10.1007/11818175_5

16. Chow, S.S.M., Wei, V.K.W., Liu, J.K., Yuen, T.H.: Ring signatures without random oracles. In: ASIACCS 06, pp. 297–302. ACM Press (2006)

17. Dodis, Y., Kiayias, A., Nicolosi, A., Shoup, V.: Anonymous identification in *Ad Hoc* groups. In: Cachin, C., Camenisch, J.L. (eds.) EUROCRYPT 2004. LNCS, vol. 3027, pp. 609–626. Springer, Heidelberg (2004). https://doi.org/10.1007/978-3-540-24676-3_36

18. Escala, A., Groth, J.: Fine-tuning Groth-Sahai proofs. In: Krawczyk, H. (ed.) PKC 2014. LNCS, vol. 8383, pp. 630–649. Springer, Heidelberg (2014). https://doi.org/10.1007/978-3-642-54631-0_36

19. Esgin, M.F., Steinfeld, R., Sakzad, A., Liu, J.K., Liu, D.: Short lattice-based one-out-of-many proofs and applications to ring signatures. In: Deng, R.H., Gauthier-Umaña, V., Ochoa, M., Yung, M. (eds.) ACNS 2019. LNCS, vol. 11464, pp. 67–88. Springer, Cham (2019). https://doi.org/10.1007/978-3-030-21568-2_4

20. Faonio, A., Fiore, D., Nizzardo, L., Soriente, C.: Subversion-resilient enhanced privacy ID. In: Galbraith, S.D. (ed.) CT-RSA 2022. LNCS, vol. 13161, pp. 562–588. Springer, Cham (2022). https://doi.org/10.1007/978-3-030-95312-6_23

21. Galbraith, S.D., Paterson, K.G., Smart, N.P.: Pairings for cryptographers. Discrete Appl. Math. **156**(16), 3113–3121 (2008)

22. Goel, A., Green, M., Hall-Andersen, M., Kaptchuk, G.: Stacking sigmas: A framework to compose Σ-protocols for disjunctions. In: Dunkelman, O., Dziembowski, S. (eds.) Advances in Cryptology – EUROCRYPT 2022. EUROCRYPT 2022. Lecture Notes in Computer Science, vol. 13276, pp. 458–487. Springer, Cham (2022). https://doi.org/10.1007/978-3-031-07085-3_16

23. Groth, J.: Simulation-sound NIZK proofs for a practical language and constant size group signatures. In: Lai, X., Chen, K. (eds.) ASIACRYPT 2006. LNCS, vol. 4284, pp. 444–459. Springer, Heidelberg (2006). https://doi.org/10.1007/11935230_29

24. Groth, J., Sahai, A.: Efficient non-interactive proof systems for bilinear groups. In: Smart, N. (ed.) EUROCRYPT 2008. LNCS, vol. 4965, pp. 415–432. Springer, Heidelberg (2008). https://doi.org/10.1007/978-3-540-78967-3_24

25. Haque, A., Krenn, S., Slamanig, D., Striecks, C.: Logarithmic-size (linkable) threshold ring signatures in the plain model. In: Hanaoka, G., Shikata, J., Watanabe, Y. (eds) Public-Key Cryptography – PKC 2022. PKC 2022. Lecture Notes in Computer Science, vol. 13178, pp. 437–467. Springer, Cham (2022). https://doi.org/10.1007/978-3-030-97131-1_15

26. Haque, A., Scafuro, A.: Threshold ring signatures: new definitions and post-quantum security. In: Kiayias, A., Kohlweiss, M., Wallden, P., Zikas, V. (eds.) PKC 2020. LNCS, vol. 12111, pp. 423–452. Springer, Cham (2020). https://doi.org/10.1007/978-3-030-45388-6_15

27. Liu, Z., Nguyen, K., Yang, G., Wang, H., Wong, D.S.: A lattice-based linkable ring signature supporting stealth addresses. In: Sako, K., Schneider, S., Ryan, P.Y.A. (eds.) ESORICS 2019. LNCS, vol. 11735, pp. 726–746. Springer, Cham (2019). https://doi.org/10.1007/978-3-030-29959-0_35

28. Lu, X., Au, M.H., Zhang, Z.: Raptor: a practical lattice-based (linkable) ring signature. In: Deng, R.H., Gauthier-Umaña, V., Ochoa, M., Yung, M. (eds.) ACNS 2019. LNCS, vol. 11464, pp. 110–130. Springer, Cham (2019). https://doi.org/10.1007/978-3-030-21568-2_6

29. Munch-Hansen, A., Orlandi, C., Yakoubov, S.: Stronger notions and a more efficient construction of threshold ring signatures. In: Longa, P., Ràfols, C. (eds.) LATIN-CRYPT 2021. LNCS, vol. 12912, pp. 363–381. Springer, Cham (2021). https://doi.org/10.1007/978-3-030-88238-9_18

30. Naor, M.: Deniable ring authentication. In: Yung, M. (ed.) CRYPTO 2002. LNCS, vol. 2442, pp. 481–498. Springer, Heidelberg (2002). https://doi.org/10.1007/3-540-45708-9_31

31. Okamoto, T., Tso, R., Yamaguchi, M., Okamoto, E.: A k-out-of-n ring signature with flexible participation for signers. ePrint, Report 2018/728 (2018)

32. Petzoldt, A., Bulygin, S., Buchmann, J.: A multivariate based threshold ring signature scheme. Appl. Algebra Eng. Commun. Comput. **24**(3–4), 255–275 (2013)

33. Rivest, R.L., Shamir, A., Tauman, Y.: How to leak a secret. In: Boyd, C. (ed.) ASIACRYPT 2001. LNCS, vol. 2248, pp. 552–565. Springer, Heidelberg (2001). https://doi.org/10.1007/3-540-45682-1_32

34. Russo, A., Anta, A.F., Vasco, M.I.G., Romano, S.P.: Chirotonia: a Scalable and Secure e-Voting Framework based on Blockchains and Linkable Ring Signatures. In: 2021 IEEE International Conference on Blockchain (Blockchain), pp. 417–424 (2021)

35. Thyagarajan, S.A.K., Malavolta, G., Schmid, F., Schröder, D.: Verifiable timed linkable ring signatures for scalable payments for monero. In: Atluri, V., Di Pietro, R., Jensen, C.D., Meng, W. (eds.) Computer Security – ESORICS 2022. ESORICS 2022. Lecture Notes in Computer Science, vol. 13555, pp. 467–486. Springer, Cham (2022). https://doi.org/10.1007/978-3-031-17146-8_23

36. Yuen, T.H., Liu, J.K., Au, M.H., Susilo, W., Zhou, J.: Efficient linkable and/or threshold ring signature without random oracles. Comput. J. **56**(4), 407–421 (2013)

37. Zhang, F., Kim, K.: ID-Based blind signature and ring signature from pairings. In: Zheng, Y. (ed.) ASIACRYPT 2002. LNCS, vol. 2501, pp. 533–547. Springer, Heidelberg (2002). https://doi.org/10.1007/3-540-36178-2_33

Tracing a Linear Subspace: Application to Linearly-Homomorphic Group Signatures

Chloé Hébant[1], David Pointcheval[2], and Robert Schädlich[2(✉)]

[1] Cosmian, Paris, France
[2] DIENS, École normale supérieure, PSL University, CNRS, Inria, Paris, France
robert.schaedlich@ens.fr

Abstract. When multiple users have power or rights, there is always the risk of corruption or abuse. Whereas there is no solution to avoid those malicious behaviors, from the users themselves or from external adversaries, one can strongly deter them with tracing capabilities that will later help to revoke the rights or negatively impact the reputation. On the other hand, privacy is an important issue in many applications, which seems in contradiction with traceability.

In this paper, we first extend usual tracing techniques based on codes so that not just one contributor can be traced but the full collusion. In a second step, we embed suitable codes into a set $\mathcal{V}$ of vectors in such a way that, given a vector $\mathbf{U} \in \mathsf{span}(\mathcal{V})$, the underlying code can be used to efficiently find a minimal subset $\mathcal{X} \subseteq \mathcal{V}$ such that $\mathbf{U} \in \mathsf{span}(\mathcal{X})$.

To meet privacy requirements, we then make the vectors of $\mathsf{span}(\mathcal{V})$ anonymous while keeping the efficient tracing mechanism. As an interesting application, we formally define the notion of linearly-homomorphic group signatures and propose a construction from our codes: multiple signatures can be combined to sign any linear subspace in an anonymous way, but a tracing authority is able to trace back all the contributors involved in the signatures of that subspace.

1 Introduction

In any multi-user setting, a user can always share its secret key with a non-legitimate one or get corrupted, which delegates all its rights. One way to escape from such a situation is to make it useless: in threshold cryptography, such keys are useless unless enough keys are obtained. Another approach consists in deterring traitors to share their keys by activity tracing. This idea has been introduced by Chor *et al.* in [7], initially to recover the origin of a pirate decoder box decrypting broadcast messages, such as for PayTV. In this use-case, tracing one traitor at a time makes sense, as the broadcast can continue after having revoked the first traitor. If the pirate decoder is still effective, other traitors can sequentially be traced and revoked. However, things are different if the setting is rather "static", such as when signatures are created jointly by several users. Here, tracing one traitor at a time is meaningless, as the signature cannot be

© International Association for Cryptologic Research 2023
A. Boldyreva and V. Kolesnikov (Eds.): PKC 2023, LNCS 13940, pp. 312–341, 2023.
https://doi.org/10.1007/978-3-031-31368-4_12

replayed to retrieve all the traitors one after one. We therefore develop techniques that allow to retrieve not only one but all the actual contributors.

1.1   Contributions

Linearly-Homomorphic Group Signatures. In this work, we build multi-user signatures that include tracing capabilities. More specifically, we combine functionality and security guarantees of group signatures [2,6] and linearly-homomorphic signatures [4]. The former roughly guarantees that, given signatures for vector messages $\mathbf{M}_1, \ldots, \mathbf{M}_n$, anyone can sign elements in the span of these messages. The latter is a multi-user signature scheme which allows members of a (fixed) *group* to sign anonymously on behalf of this group, except towards an authority called the *group manager* that is able to revoke anonymity. Our new primitive puts linearly-homomorphic signatures into a multi-user setting with broad functionality by allowing the aggregation of arbitrary signatures, whether freshly created by different group members or previously aggregated. In addition, this comes along with the strong security guarantees of a group signature. From a privacy point of view, signatures can only be associated with a group, but not with individual members. Group members act thus anonymously, even towards other members of the group. However, to avoid malicious behavior, the group manager is able to recover the actual creators of a signature. We emphasize that, in contrast to classic group signatures, a linearly-homomorphic group signature can have multiple contributors after aggregation, which generally requires the group manager to identify a set of signers rather than a single one. As a corrupted group member can always mix their own signatures with that of honest signers, it is crucial for the group manager to recover *all* contributors to a signature. Any strict subset of the contributors is vacuous, as there is no guarantee that it contains the malicious ones.

Linear-Subspace Tracing. Our main technical contribution is the construction of an object that we call a *linear-subspace tracing* (LST) scheme. Let $\mathbb{U}$ be a vector space and c a positive integer, as a bound on the size of the collusion. Informally, a LST scheme solves the problem of finding sets $\mathcal{V} \subset \mathbb{U}$ such that the following task can be solved *efficiently* and *uniquely*:

> *On input a vector* $\mathbf{U} \in \bigcup_{\mathcal{X} \subseteq \mathcal{V}, |\mathcal{X}| \leq c} \mathsf{span}(\mathcal{X})$, *recover a minimal (a.k.a. the smallest) subset* $\mathcal{X}_0 \subseteq \mathcal{V}$ *such that* $\mathbf{U} \in \mathsf{span}(\mathcal{X}_0)$.

As each subset of $\mathcal{V}$ spans a linear subspace, solving this task can be viewed as "tracing" the smallest subspace that contains the given vector $\mathbf{U}$. Of course, there exist trivial constructions. For example, given $\mathbb{U} = \mathbb{Z}_p^\ell$ for a prime p and a positive integer ℓ, one can choose $\mathcal{V} = \{\mathbf{e}_i : i \in [\ell]\}$ where $\mathbf{e}_i$ denotes the i-th standard unit vector. It even allows large collusions, as one can take $c = \ell$, where ℓ is the cardinality of the set $\mathcal{V}$ and also the maximal size c of the collusion. However, the situation gets more intricate when we try to make the construction more efficient (i.e., for a dimension ℓ smaller than the cardinality n of the set) but for possibly bounded collusions (of maximal size $c \leq n$). Note that in the example above the required dimension of $\mathbb{U}$ grows linearly with the cardinality $\mathcal{V}$, as $n = \ell$. In this work, we consider vector spaces where the discrete logarithm problem in the additive group is assumed to be hard. We present LST schemes for vector spaces of dimension $\ell = \Omega(c^2 \cdot \log(n/\varepsilon))$, where ε denotes the maximum acceptable probability that the tracing will fail.

To meet privacy requirements, we also construct an *anonymous* LST scheme, which informally means that recovering the set $\mathcal{X}_0$ is computationally hard except one holds a special tracing key. We are able to prove anonymity without increasing the lower bound on ℓ. However, we need the stronger assumption that the Decisional Diffie-Hellman problem (instead of only the discrete logarithm) is hard in the additive group of the vector space.

Fully IPP Codes. A formal model to address the traitor tracing problem are codes with the *Identifiable Parent Property (IPP)* introduced by Hollmann *et al.* [10]. A word $\mathbf{u} = (u_k)$ is a *descendant* of a coalition $\mathcal{X}$ of codewords if every letter u_k is present in at least one codeword of $\mathcal{X}$ at the same position k. Conversely, the elements of $\mathcal{X}$ are called parents. Intuitively, a code $\mathcal{C}$ satisfies the Identifiable Parent Property if for any descendant of $\mathcal{C}$, *at least one* parent codeword can be identified with certainty. In contrast, this work pursues the stronger goal of identifying *all* parent codewords of a word $\mathbf{u}$. We formalize this aspect by defining a variant of IPP codes that we call *fully* IPP (FIPP), as it allows to identify a full coalition instead of just a single parent codeword. For consistency, we then must require that there exists a unique minimal (w.r.t. $\subseteq$) set $\mathcal{X}_0$ among all sets $\mathcal{X} \subseteq \mathcal{C}$ with the property that $\mathbf{u}$ is a descendant of $\mathcal{X}$. Otherwise, it would be impossible to determine which of several minimal subsets was used to derive $\mathbf{u}$.

In the literature, IPP codes are only considered with respect to the above-mentioned notion of descendants. However, the general concept of IPP (or FIPP) can also be studied using other descendancy relations. We primarily use FIPP codes as a building block for our LST scheme. Since this use case differs significantly from the original purpose of tracing traitors in broadcast encryption, a modified definition of descendants proves to be more suitable. We therefore note that our construction of FIPP codes is not a contribution to the theory of classical IPP codes. We use the terminology merely to give the reader a better intuition. For readers familiar with fingerprinting codes [5,13], we further remark that—like the standard definition of descendants—our new version can be seen as a strengthening of the Marking assumption. As the concepts of IPP and fingerprinting codes are very similar, our construction could also be interpreted as a fingerprinting code with a modified Marking assumption.

1.2   Technical Overview

Constructing FIPP Codes. We start with the definition of descendants used throughout this work. Let $\mathcal{Q} = \{a_1, \ldots, a_n, \perp, \top\}$ be an alphabet with two distinguished letters: the *neutral* letter $\top$ and the letter $\perp$ which represents a *collision*. Roughly, a word $\mathbf{u} = (u_k)$ is defined to be a *descendant* of a coalition $\mathcal{X}$

of codewords if there exists a subset $\mathcal{X}_0 \subseteq \mathcal{X}$ such that the following condition is satisfied for all positions k: if all letters that occur at the k-th position of a codeword in $\mathcal{X}_0$ equal either $\top$ or some $a \in \mathcal{Q}$, then $u_k = a$ too. Otherwise, $u_k = \bot$. Intuitively, descendants preserve information at those positions where all parents coincide or equal the neutral letter $\top$, but lose all information elsewhere (since there is a collision of different letters). The condition that there exists a subset $\mathcal{X}_0$ of $\mathcal{X}$ is necessary to cover the case that not all codewords of $\mathbf{X}$ are actively used to derive the descendant $\mathbf{u}$. However, for ease of exposition, we implicitly assume that $\mathcal{X}_0 = \mathcal{X}$ here.

We next describe the construction of our FIPP codes $\mathcal{C} = \{\mathbf{w}_1, \ldots, \mathbf{w}_n\}$ with respect to this definition of descendants. Recall that $\mathcal{Q}$ is of the form $\{a_1, \ldots, a_n, \bot, \top\}$. In our construction, we impose the restriction that the i-th codeword $\mathbf{w}_i$ includes only the letters a_i and $\top$. In this case, the descendancy definition implies that any word containing the letter a_i must have $\mathbf{w}_i$ as a parent codeword since there is no other way to derive a word which contains this letter. Thus, the choice of $\mathbf{w}_1, \ldots, \mathbf{w}_n$ boils down to a balls-into-bins problem, where we must arrange the letters of the codewords in such a way that the number of collisions is small. Our approach is very simple: we divide all codewords into multiple blocks of equal size. Then for each $i \in [n]$, $\mathbf{w}_i$ is chosen such that each of its blocks contains the letter a_i at exactly one position, and $\top$ elsewhere.

Let $\mathbf{u}$ be a descendant of a coalition $\mathcal{X} \subseteq \mathcal{C}$. The tracing algorithm simply outputs the set $\{\mathbf{w}_i \in \mathcal{C} : \mathbf{u} \text{ contains } a_i\}$. As argued above, this method never "accuses" a wrong codeword. Conversely, we need to bound the probability that a parent codeword $\mathbf{w}_i$ is not detected. This happens if there are collisions in *all* positions of $\mathbf{u}$ where $\mathbf{w}_i$ contains the latter a_i. Inside a fixed block, this probability is constant. Since the blocks of $\mathbf{w}_i$ are chosen independently, the probability that there is such a collision in all blocks of $\mathbf{u}$ decreases exponentially in the number of blocks. Thus, each parent codeword of $\mathbf{u}$ is detected with high probability.

Embedding Codewords into Vectors. We next describe our construction of a LST scheme. We start with the generation of the set $\mathcal{V}$ of vectors. At a high level, we embed a FIPP code $\mathcal{C} = \{\mathbf{w}_1, \ldots, \mathbf{w}_n\}$ into the set $\mathcal{V} = \{\mathbf{V}_1, \ldots, \mathbf{V}_n\}$ such that vectors in the span of an arbitrary subset $\mathcal{X} = \{\mathbf{V}_{i_1}, \ldots, \mathbf{V}_{i_d}\} \subseteq \mathcal{V}$ represent descendants of the corresponding set $\mathcal{Y} = \{\mathbf{w}_{i_1}, \ldots, \mathbf{w}_{i_d}\}$ of codewords. Thus, given a vector $\mathbf{U} \in \bigcup_{\mathcal{X} \subseteq \mathcal{V}, |\mathcal{X}| \leq c} \mathsf{span}(\mathcal{X})$, we can compute the smallest subset $\mathcal{X}_0 \subseteq \mathcal{V}$ such that $\mathbf{U} \in \mathsf{span}(\mathcal{X}_0)$ by recovering the word $\mathbf{u}$ embedded in the vector $\mathbf{U}$, followed by an execution of the code's tracing algorithm which reveals all parents of $\mathbf{u}$.

More specifically, we embed codewords of length ℓ into vectors of $\mathbb{G}^{2\ell}$ where $\mathbb{G}$ is a cyclic group of prime order p with a generator G. For each $i \in [n]$, we sample a random scalar $s_i \xleftarrow{\$} \mathbb{Z}_p$. We then construct $\mathbf{V}_i$ by replacing each occurrence of the letter a_i in the codeword $\mathbf{w}_i$ with the tuple $(G, s_i \cdot G)$ and each occurrence of $\top$ with (G, G). Let k be a position where all codewords in $\mathcal{Y}$ agree with either $\top$ or the letter a_{i_j} for some $j \in [d]$. Note that the construction of our FIPP code ensures that such positions exist for all choices of j with high probability. A simple computation shows that the coordinates $(2k - 1, 2k)$ of any vector $\mathbf{U}$ in the span of $\mathcal{X}$ are of the form $(H, s_i \cdot H)$, for some $H \in \mathbb{G}$. If we identify each element of $\{(H, s_i \cdot H) : H \in \mathbb{G}^*\}$ with the letter a_i for $i \in [n]$, then vectors in the span of $\mathcal{X}$ correspond to descendants of $\mathcal{Y}$ as desired. Note that it is easy to recover the descendant $\mathbf{u}$ of $\mathcal{Y}$ corresponding to $\mathbf{U}$ even if the discrete logarithm problem in $\mathbb{G}$ is hard. Indeed, this can be done by testing for each tuple (H, H') of $\mathbf{U}$ if $H' = s \cdot H$ for some $s \in \{s_1, \ldots, s_n\}$. Once $\mathbf{u}$ is recovered, one runs the code's tracing algorithm to obtain its parents.

Anonymization. The basic idea to obtain anonymous versions $\mathbf{V}'_1, \ldots, \mathbf{V}'_n$ of $\mathbf{V}_1, \ldots, \mathbf{V}_n$ is to encrypt them component-wise using the ElGamal encryption scheme [8]. It is well-known that this encryption scheme is partially homomorphic. In our context, this means that for all coefficients $\omega_1, \ldots, \omega_n$, $\sum_{i=1}^{n} \omega_i \cdot \mathbf{V}'_i$ is a component-wise encryption of $\sum_{i=1}^{n} \omega_i \cdot \mathbf{V}_i$. Thus, the tracing of an encrypted vector can be done by first decrypting it and passing the resulting vector to the original tracing algorithm. Since the security of ElGamal is based on the DDH assumption, it is straightforward to exploit the random self-reducibility of the DDH problem. If we reuse the same randomness in the encryption of all components of a vector $\mathbf{V}_i$, then one component of all ciphertexts is equal and, thus, must be included only once in the anonymous version of $\mathbf{V}_i$. This leads us to a more efficient transformation where anonymous vectors have only one additional coordinate.

Linearly-Homomorphic Group Signatures. We finally explain how our LST scheme can be used to build linearly-homomorphic group signatures. A well-known blueprint for the construction of group signatures works as follows (see [2]): each group member has a secret signing key that includes a key pair of a classical signature scheme certified by the group manager. To sign a message m in the name of the group, a group member signs m using its private key and encrypts this signature together with certificate and identity information under a public encryption key held by the group manager. The final group signature consists of this ciphertext accompanied by a non-interactive zero-knowledge proof that it contains what it is supposed to contain.

To make this framework linearly-homomorphic, one needs to define a suitable aggregation operation for signatures. In particular, it raises the question of how to aggregate the ciphertexts which encrypt the identities. Naively, one could simply append all the ciphertexts when aggregating a signature. One disadvantage of this method is that the size of signatures grows linearly with the number of involved signers. But even worse, this construction leaks the information of how many signers participated in the creation of the signature, thus breaking anonymity. Therefore, one needs a mechanism which allows to aggregate the ciphertexts in such a way that

1. the aggregated ciphertext does not leak the number of signers (nor any other information about the identities of the signers), and
2. the originally encrypted identities can be recovered after decryption of the aggregated ciphertext.

To solve the first issue, it is straightforward to use a (partially) homomorphic encryption scheme like ElGamal, and to aggregate signatures by applying the homomorphic operation of the encryption scheme. The second requirement, however, is much more challenging.

Tracing Contributors to a Signature. As a starting point, one could assign a codeword of a classical traceable code (e.g. IPP codes or fingerprinting codes) to each group member. One then forces group members to sign messages together with an encryption of a vector which embeds the signer's codeword in the exponents. This must be done in such a way that the homomorphic operation of the encryption scheme respects the descendancy relation (resp. the Marking assumption in the context of fingerprinting codes). Then, to trace a signature, one decrypts the vector, recovers the challenge word from the exponents and runs the code's tracing algorithm.

This idea, however, runs into a major problem. For the unforgeability of the underlying linearly-homomorphic signature scheme, the discrete logarithm problem must be hard in the additive group of the vector space. Therefore, we cannot hope to recover the challenge word from the exponents to run the tracing algorithm. Also, running the tracing algorithm directly in the exponent seems difficult.

As a solution we use our above-described code construction which comes with the property that embeddings of codewords into vectors can still be traced, even if the discrete logarithm is hard. (Recall that we call this object a LST scheme.) Roughly, we assign to each group member a vector of a set $\mathcal{V} = \{\mathbf{V}_1, \ldots, \mathbf{V}_n\}$ generated using a LST scheme. We force group members to sign each message together with their respective vector. When multiple signatures are aggregated, one obtains a new vector $\mathbf{U}$ which lies in the span of those vectors $\mathbf{V}_i$ whose associated group members contributed to the derived signature. Using the tracing algorithm of the LST scheme, it is possible to recover exactly the subset of $\mathcal{V}$ which corresponds to the contributors of the signature. To achieve privacy for the group members, we use an anonymous LST scheme where the tracing key is only known to the group manager.

1.3   Organization

The rest of the article is organized as follows. The next section recalls assumptions and definitions that we will use in the paper. Section 3 formally introduces FIPP codes and presents a construction with respect to our new definition of descendant. Section 4 defines and provides a construction of a LST scheme which is made anonymous in Sect. 5. Finally, our work can be used to create a linearly-homomorphic group signature scheme for which a formal model is provided in Sect. 6 and the construction in Sect. 7.

2   Preliminaries

For integers i and j, we write $[i; j]$ to denote the integer interval $\{k \in \mathbb{Z} : i \leq k \leq j\}$. By default, we set $[j] = [1, j]$. For any $q \geq 2$, we let $\mathbb{Z}_q$ denote the ring of integers with addition and multiplication modulo q. Furthermore, for an integer n and a group $(\mathbb{G}, +)$ of prime order p, we interpret $\mathbb{G}^n$ as a vector space over $\mathbb{Z}_p$ in the usual way. We denote the zero element of this vector space by $\mathbf{0}^{(n)}$. Given a vector $\boldsymbol{\omega} = (\omega_i)_{i=1}^n \in \mathbb{Z}_p^n$ and a group element $G \in \mathbb{G}$, we write $\boldsymbol{\omega} \cdot G$ to denote the vector $(\omega_i \cdot G)_{i=1}^n$. Also, we refer to the set of generators of a cyclic group $\mathbb{G}$ by $\mathbb{G}^*$. Given a set $\mathcal{X}$ and an integer $0 \leq c \leq |\mathcal{X}|$, we denote by $\mathcal{P}_c(\mathcal{X})$ the set of all subsets of size at most c, i.e. $\mathcal{P}_c(\mathcal{X}) = \{\mathcal{X}' \subseteq \mathcal{X} : |\mathcal{X}'| \leq c\}$.

2.1   Hardness Assumptions

We recall the assumptions needed for our constructions.

Definition 1 (Discrete Logarithm (DL) Assumption). *The* DL *assumption in a group* $(\mathbb{G}, +)$, *of prime order p with generator G, states that given $H = x \cdot G$, no algorithm can efficiently recover x.*

Definition 2 (Decisional Diffie-Hellman (DDH) Assumption). *The* DDH *assumption in a group* $(\mathbb{G}, +)$, *of prime orders p with generator G, states that no algorithm can efficiently distinguish the two distributions*

$$D_0 = \left\{ (x \cdot G, y \cdot G, xy \cdot G) : x, y \xleftarrow{\$} \mathbb{Z}_p \right\}$$

$$D_1 = \left\{ (x \cdot G, y \cdot G, z \cdot G) : x, y, z \xleftarrow{\$} \mathbb{Z}_p \right\}$$

We prove some of our results in the *algebraic group model* (AGM) – a computational model in which all adversaries are modeled as algebraic. Let $\mathbb{G}$ be a group of prime order p. Roughly, an algorithm A is called *algebraic* if for all group elements $G \in \mathbb{G}$ output by A, it additionally provides the representation of G relative to all previously received group elements. For a clean definition of the AGM see [9].

Real-world implementations of bilinear structures sometimes allow the construction of group elements without knowing their discrete logarithm. Therefore, it seems important to prove results in a model that takes this property of concrete instantiations into account, e.g. a variant of the generic group model (GGM) where the adversary has access to an oracle that generates random group elements. We remark that besides the classical GGM, this (and similar) modifications are also covered by the AGM. Intuitively, an adversary in the "GGM-R" (GGM with additional oracle for random group elements) can be used to construct an algebraic adversary since all generated random elements and all group operations computed by the GGM-R adversary are known and, thus, the GGM-R simulator is able to extract itself the representations of all elements submitted by the adversary.

2.2   Linearly-Homomorphic Signatures

Linearly-homomorphic signatures were originally introduced by Boneh *et al.* in [4]. Our definition is similar to that in [12].

Definition 3 (Linearly-Homomorphic Signature Scheme (LH-Sig)). *A LH-Sig scheme with tag space $\mathcal{T}$ and message space $\mathbb{G}^n$, for a cyclic group $(\mathbb{G}, +)$ of prime order p and a positive integer n, is a collection of five polynomial-time algorithms defined as follows.*

Setup(1^λ): *On input the security parameter λ, this algorithm returns the public parameters* pp.

KeyGen(pp): *On input the public parameters* pp, *this algorithm returns a key pair* (sk, pk). *We will assume that* pk *implicitly contains* pp *and* sk *implicitly contains* pk.

Sign(sk, τ, **M**): *On input a secret key* sk, *a tag $\tau \in \mathcal{T}$ and a message $\mathbf{M} \in \mathbb{G}^n$, this algorithm returns a signature Σ of $\mathbf{M}$ under the tag τ.*

DeriveSign(pk, τ, $(\omega_j, \Sigma_j)_{j=1}^d$): *On input a public key* pk, *a tag $\tau \in \mathcal{T}$ and d tuples of weights $\omega_j \in \mathbb{Z}_p$ and signatures Σ_j, this algorithm returns a signature Σ on the vector $\mathbf{M} = \sum_{j=1}^d \omega_j \cdot \mathbf{M}_j$ under the tag τ, where Σ_j is a signature on the message $\mathbf{M}_j \in \mathbb{G}^n$ under τ.*

Verify(pk, τ, **M**, Σ): *On input a public key* pk, *a tag $\tau \in \mathcal{T}$, a message $\mathbf{M} \in \mathbb{G}^n$ and a signature Σ, this algorithm returns 1 if $\tau \in \mathcal{T}$ and Σ is valid relative to* pk *and τ, and 0 otherwise.*

Correctness. The basic consistency requirement of every signature scheme is that honestly generated signatures must be accepted as valid. In the case of a LH-Sig scheme we distinguish between (a) "initial" and (b) "derived" signatures. Let (sk, pk) ← KeyGen(Setup(1^λ)) be any key pair and τ be any tag in $\mathcal{T}$. Then,

(a) for every message $\mathbf{M} \in \mathbb{G}^n$ and $\Sigma \leftarrow$ Sign(sk, τ, **M**), the scheme satisfies Verify(pk, τ, **M**, Σ) = 1, and

(b) for any list $(\omega_j, \mathbf{M}_j, \Sigma_j)_{j=1}^d$ such that Verify(pk, τ, $\mathbf{M}_j$, Σ_j) = 1 for each $j \in [d]$, if $\Sigma \leftarrow$ DeriveSign(pk, τ, $(\omega_j, \Sigma_j)_{j=1}^d$), then Verify(pk, τ, $\sum_{j=1}^d \omega_j \cdot \mathbf{M}_j$, Σ) = 1.

Security. We recall the unforgeability notion of [12], using our notations.

Definition 4 (Unforgeability of LH-Sig). *For a PPT adversary A and a LH-Sig scheme $\Sigma = $ (Setup, KeyGen, Sign, DeriveSign, Verify) with message space $\mathbb{G}^n$ and tag space $\mathcal{T}$, we define the experiment $\mathbf{Exp}_{\Sigma,A}^{\mathrm{unf}}(1^\lambda)$ as shown in Fig. 1.*

The oracles $\mathcal{O}$Sign, $\mathcal{O}$DeriveSign and $\mathcal{O}$Reveal can be called in any order and any number of times. For a tag $\tau \in \mathcal{T}$, $\mathcal{S}_\tau$ denotes the set of messages $\mathbf{M} \in \mathbb{G}^n$ such that the tuple $(\tau, \mathbf{M})$ is in the set $\mathcal{S}$ maintained by the challenger. The challenger also maintains a table $\mathcal{H}$ that contains tuples of the form $(h, (\tau, \mathbf{M}, \Sigma))$, where h is a handle, $\tau \in \mathcal{T}$, $\mathbf{M} \in \mathbb{G}^n$ and Σ is a signature on $\mathbf{M}$ under τ. We define a lookup operation $\mathsf{Lookup}_\mathcal{H}$ that, on input a set *of handles* $\{h_1, \ldots, h_d\}$, *retrieves the tuples* $\{(h_j, (\tau_j, \mathbf{M}_j, \Sigma_j))\}_{j=1}^d$ *from* $\mathcal{H}$ *and returns* $\{(\tau_j, \mathbf{M}_j, \Sigma_j)\}_{j=1}^d$. *If there exists a* $j \in [d]$ *such that there does not exist a tuple of the form* $(h_j, (\cdot, \cdot, \cdot))$ *in* $\mathcal{H}$, *then the* Lookup$_{\mathcal{H}}$ *algorithm returns an error message that causes the oracle to abort immediately with return value* $\perp$.

We say that a *LH-Sig* scheme is unforgeable if for any PPT adversary A, there exists a negligible function negl such that

$$\mathbf{Adv}_{\Sigma,A}^{\mathrm{unf}}(\lambda) = \Pr\left[\mathbf{Exp}_{\Sigma,A}^{\mathrm{unf}}(1^\lambda) = 1\right] \leq \mathsf{negl}(\lambda).$$

Since $\mathbb{G}^n$ forms a vector space over $\mathbb{Z}_p$, it is consistent to write span($\mathcal{A}$) for the subspace spanned by a subset $\mathcal{A}$ of $\mathbb{G}^n$. As usual, we set span($\emptyset$) = $\{\mathbf{0}^{(n)}\}$.

Initialize(1^λ):
(pk, sk) ← KeyGen(Setup(1^λ))
$\mathcal{H} \leftarrow \emptyset; \mathcal{S} \leftarrow \emptyset$
Return pk

$\mathcal{O}$Sign(τ, $\mathbf{M}$):
$\Sigma \leftarrow$ Sign(sk, τ, $\mathbf{M}$)
Pick new handle h
$\mathcal{H} \leftarrow \mathcal{H} \cup \{(h, (\tau, \mathbf{M}, \Sigma))\}$
Return h

$\mathcal{O}$Reveal(h):
$(\tau, \mathbf{M}, \Sigma) \leftarrow$ Lookup$_{\mathcal{H}}(h)$
$\mathcal{S} \leftarrow \mathcal{S} \cup \{(\tau, \mathbf{M})\}$
Return Σ

$\mathcal{O}$DeriveSign($(h_j, \omega_j)_{j=1}^d$):
$\{(\tau_j, \mathbf{M}_j, \Sigma_j)\}_{j=1}^d \leftarrow$ Lookup$_{\mathcal{H}}(\{h_j\}_{j=1}^d)$
If $\exists j \in [2; d]$ s.t. $\tau_j \neq \tau_1$, return $\perp$
$\mathbf{M} \leftarrow \sum_{j=1}^d \omega_j \cdot \mathbf{M}_j$
$\Sigma \leftarrow$ DeriveSign(pk, τ_1, $(\omega_j, \Sigma_j)_{j=1}^d$)
Pick new handle h
$\mathcal{H} \leftarrow \mathcal{H} \cup \{(h, (\tau_1, \mathbf{M}, \Sigma))\}$
Return h

Finalize(τ, $\mathbf{M}$, Σ):
If Verify(pk, τ, $\mathbf{M}$, Σ) = 0, return 0
If $\mathbf{M} \in$ span($\mathcal{S}_\tau$), return 0
Return 1

Fig. 1. Security game $\mathbf{Exp}_{\Sigma,A}^{\mathrm{unf}}(1^\lambda)$ for unforgeability

As in [12], we will also consider a weaker notion of unforgeability. A *one-time* linearly-homomorphic signature (OT-LH-Sig) is a LH-Sig scheme, where the tag space is a singleton $\mathcal{T} = \{\varepsilon\}$. Consequently, we can drop the tags τ given as argument to the algorithms Sign, DeriveSign and Verify.

Privacy. Given signatures on messages $\mathbf{M}_1, \ldots, \mathbf{M}_d \in \mathbb{G}^n$, it may be desirable that derived signatures on a message $\mathbf{M} \in$ span($\{\mathbf{M}_1, \ldots, \mathbf{M}_d\}$) do not leak information about $\mathbf{M}_1, \ldots, \mathbf{M}_d$ beyond what is revealed by $\mathbf{M}$. A strong definition that formalizes this property is given by Ahn *et al.* [1] under the name *context hiding*. We state a slightly different version here. The details are explained in the full version [11].

Definition 5 (Context Hiding). *A LH-Sig scheme* Σ = (Setup, KeyGen, Sign, DeriveSign, Verify) *with message space* $\mathbb{G}^n$ *and tag space* $\mathcal{T}$ *is called perfectly (resp. statistically, computationally) context-hiding if*

– *for any key pair* $(\mathsf{pk}, \mathsf{sk}) \leftarrow \mathsf{KeyGen}(\mathsf{Setup}(1^\lambda))$ *and any tag* $\tau \in \mathcal{T}$,
– *for any tuple of messages* $\mathcal{M} = (\mathbf{M}_j)_{j=1}^d \in (\mathbb{G}^n)^d$ *and any tuple of coefficients* $\boldsymbol{\omega} = (\omega_j)_{j=1}^d \in \mathbb{Z}_p^d$, *and*
– *for any tuple of signatures* $\mathcal{S} = (\Sigma_j)_{j=1}^d$, *where* Σ_j *is a signature returned by* Sign *on input* $(\mathsf{sk}, \tau, \mathbf{M}_j)$ *with a nonzero probability,*

the following distribution ensembles are perfectly (resp. statistically, computationally) indistinguishable:

$$\mathcal{D}_0 = \left\{ \left(\mathsf{sk}, (\Sigma_j)_{j=1}^d, \mathsf{Sign}(\mathsf{sk}, \tau, \textstyle\sum_{j=1}^d \omega_j \cdot \mathbf{M}_j)\right) \right\}_{\mathsf{sk}, \tau, \mathcal{M}, \omega, \mathcal{S}}$$

$$\mathcal{D}_1 = \left\{ \left(\mathsf{sk}, (\Sigma_j)_{j=1}^d, \mathsf{DeriveSign}\left(\mathsf{pk}, \tau, (\omega_j, \Sigma_j)_{j=1}^d\right)\right) \right\}_{\mathsf{sk}, \tau, \mathcal{M}, \omega, \mathcal{S}}$$

The definition states that a signature on a message $\mathbf{M}$ derived from a collection of signatures $(\Sigma_j)_{j=1}^d$ on messages $(\mathbf{M}_j)_{j=1}^d$ is indistinguishable from a fresh signature on $\mathbf{M}$, even if the original signatures are known. Consequently, the derived signature is independent of $(\Sigma_j)_{j=1}^d$ and cannot reveal any information about $(\mathbf{M}_j)_{j=1}^d$ beyond what is revealed by $\mathbf{M}$.

Remark 6. As observed by Ahn *et al.*, the context hiding property can be used to simplify the security experiment for unforgeability. For a LH-Sig scheme Σ and a PPT adversary A, we define the experiment $\mathbf{Exp}_{\Sigma,A}^{\mathrm{unf'}}(1^\lambda)$ as shown in Fig. 2. If a LH-Sig scheme is context hiding and unforgeable with respect to $\mathbf{Exp}_{\Sigma,A}^{\mathrm{unf'}}(1^\lambda)$, then it is also unforgeable with respect to $\mathbf{Exp}_{\Sigma,A}^{\mathrm{unf}}(1^\lambda)$. For a proof, see Lemma A.4 of [1]. We exploit this observation in Sect. 6 to simplify the definition of traceability within our model of a linearly-homomorphic group signature (LH-GSig) scheme.

Initialize(1^λ):	Finalize$(\tau, \mathbf{M}, \Sigma)$:
$(\mathsf{pk}, \mathsf{sk}) \leftarrow \mathsf{KeyGen}(\mathsf{Setup}(1^\lambda)); \ \mathcal{S} \leftarrow \emptyset$	If $\mathsf{Verify}(\mathsf{pk}, \tau, \mathbf{M}, \Sigma) = 0$, return 0
Return pk	If $\mathbf{M} \in \mathsf{span}(\mathcal{S}_\tau)$, return 0
	Return 1
$\mathcal{O}\mathsf{Sign}(\tau, \mathbf{M})$:	
$\mathcal{S} \leftarrow \mathcal{S} \cup \{(\tau, \mathbf{M})\}$	
Return $\Sigma \leftarrow \mathsf{Sign}(\mathsf{sk}, \tau, \mathbf{M})$	

Fig. 2. Simplified security game $\mathbf{Exp}_{\Sigma,A}^{\mathrm{unf'}}(1^\lambda)$ for unforgeability

3 Codes with the Fully Identifiable Parent Property

Let $\mathcal{Q}$ be an alphabet. A set $\mathcal{C} = \{\mathbf{w}^{(1)}, \ldots, \mathbf{w}^{(n)}\} \subseteq \mathcal{Q}^\ell$ is called a *code* of size n and *length* ℓ. Each $\mathbf{w}^{(i)} \in \mathcal{C}$ is called a *codeword*. Furthermore, we say a subset $\mathcal{X} \subseteq \mathcal{C}$ is a *coalition*. For $k \in [\ell]$, let $\mathcal{Q}_k(\mathcal{X})$ denote the set of letters $a \in \mathcal{Q}$ for which there exists a codeword $\mathbf{w}^{(i)} = (w_1^{(i)}, \ldots, w_\ell^{(i)}) \in \mathcal{X}$ such that $w_k^{(i)} = a$.

We recall some standard terminology that goes back to Chor *et al.* [7]. A word $\mathbf{u} = (u_k)_{k=1}^\ell \in \mathcal{Q}^\ell$ is called a *descendant* of a coalition $\mathcal{X}$ if for any $k \in [\ell]$, $u_k \in \mathcal{Q}_k(\mathcal{X})$. In this case, the elements of $\mathcal{X}$ are called *parent codewords* of $\mathbf{u}$. We denote by $\mathsf{Desc}(\mathcal{X})$ the set of all descendants of $\mathcal{X}$. Furthermore, for a positive integer c, we write $\mathsf{Desc}_c(\mathcal{C})$ for the set of all descendants of coalitions that contain at most c codewords, i.e.

$$\mathsf{Desc}_c(\mathcal{C}) = \bigcup_{\mathcal{X} \in \mathcal{P}_c(\mathcal{C})} \mathsf{Desc}(\mathcal{X}).$$

For a positive integer c and a word $\mathbf{u} \in \mathsf{Desc}_c(\mathcal{C})$, we write $\mathsf{Par}_c(\mathbf{u})$ for the set of all coalitions $\mathcal{X}$ of size at most c such that $\mathbf{u} \in \mathsf{Desc}(\mathcal{X})$, i.e. $\mathsf{Par}_c(\mathbf{u}) = \{\mathcal{X} \in \mathcal{P}_c(\mathcal{C}) : \mathbf{u} \in \mathsf{Desc}(\mathcal{X})\}$. Then one defines codes with the *identifiable parent property (IPP)* as follows.

Definition 7 (IPP Code). *A code $\mathcal{C}$ is called c-IPP if for any $\mathbf{u} \in \mathsf{Desc}_c(\mathcal{C})$, the intersection of all $\mathcal{X} \in \mathsf{Par}_c(\mathbf{u})$ is nonempty.*

Intuitively, a code $\mathcal{C}$ is IPP if for every descendant $\mathbf{u} \in \mathsf{Desc}_c(\mathcal{C})$ at least one parent codeword can be identified with certainty. In this paper, we pursue the stronger goal to identify not only one parent but a full coalition $\mathcal{X} \subseteq \mathcal{C}$ such that $\mathbf{u} \in \mathsf{Desc}(\mathcal{X})$. In order not to falsely include codewords into $\mathcal{X}$, we must require that there is a smallest coalition with this property. Then we define the notion of a *fully IPP (FIPP)* code as follows.

Definition 8 (FIPP Code). *A code $\mathcal{C}$ is called c-FIPP if for any $\mathbf{u} \in \mathsf{Desc}_c(\mathcal{C})$, there exists a smallest element $\mathcal{X}_0$ in $\mathsf{Par}_c(\mathbf{u})$ with respect to the usual inclusion.*

While IPP codes for the standard definition of descendants have been the subject of intensive studies, little is known about other derivation models. Here, we introduce a novel definition of descendancy.

Definition 9 (Descendant). *Let $\mathcal{Q} = \{a_1, \ldots, a_n, \bot, \top\}$, where $\bot$ and $\top$ are two distinguished letters. We say that a word $\mathbf{u} = (u_k)_{k=1}^\ell \in \mathcal{Q}^\ell$ is a descendant of a set $\mathcal{X}$ if there exists a nonempty subset $\mathcal{X}_0 \subseteq \mathcal{X}$ that satisfies the following condition for each $k \in [\ell]$.*

1. *If $\mathcal{Q}_k(\mathcal{X}_0) = \{a\}$ for some $a \in \mathcal{Q}$, then $u_k = a$.*
2. *Else, if $\mathcal{Q}_k(\mathcal{X}_0) = \{\top, a\}$ for some $a \in \mathcal{Q} \setminus \{\top\}$, then $u_k = a$.*
3. *Else, $u_k = \bot$.*

In the remainder of this article, we consider IPP and FIPP codes always with respect to Definition 9. We postpone the motivation of this new derivation model to Sect. 4 where we present a natural application.

Construction. We present an extremely simple construction of a c-FIPP code $\mathcal{C}$ of size n and length ℓ over the alphabet $\mathcal{Q} = \{a_1, \ldots, a_n, \top, \bot\}$.

In the construction, ℓ appears as the product of two positive integers J and K. For convenience, we use tuples $(k,j) \in [K] \times [J]$ to index the letters of codewords. However, they can simply be thought of as a single vector of length ℓ, consisting of K blocks with J coordinates each. For $i \in [n]$, let $\mathcal{S}_i^{(J)} \subseteq \mathcal{Q}^J$ be the set that contains all sequences $(s_1, \ldots, s_J)$ with the property that there exists a $j \in [J]$ such that $s_j = a_i$ and $s_{j'} = \top$ for all $j' \in [J] \setminus \{j\}$. Furthermore, we define $\mathcal{S}_i^{(K,J)} = \times_{k=1}^K \mathcal{S}_i^{(J)}$.

Theorem 10. *Let n, c and $J > c$ be positive integers. If $\mathbf{w}^{(i)} \xleftarrow{\$} \mathcal{S}_i^{(K,J)}$ for each $i \in [n]$, then the code $\mathcal{C} = \{\mathbf{w}^{(1)}, \ldots, \mathbf{w}^{(n)}\}$ is c-FIPP with probability at least $1 - \mathsf{negl}(K)$ for some negligible function negl.*

Proof. Let $\mathcal{Q}' = \mathcal{Q} \setminus \{\top, \bot\}$. For $\mathbf{u} = (u_{k,j})_{k \in [K], j \in [J]} \in \mathsf{Desc}_c(\mathcal{C})$, we set $\mathcal{U} = \{u_{k,j} : k \in [K], j \in [J]\} \cap \mathcal{Q}'$ and $\mathcal{X}_0 = \{\mathbf{w}^{(i)} : a_i \in \mathcal{U}\}$. First, observe that $\mathcal{X}_0$ is smaller than or equal to every element of $\mathsf{Par}_c(\mathbf{u})$. This can be seen as follows. Every letter in $\mathcal{U}$ occurs only in one codeword, and $\mathcal{X}_0$ contains exactly this collection of codewords. Furthermore, descendants can only contain letters of $\mathcal{Q}'$ if they already appeared in at least one parent codeword. Hence, $\mathcal{X}_0$ is a subset of each $\mathcal{X} \in \mathsf{Par}_c(\mathbf{u})$. This property implies in particular that $|\mathcal{X}_0| \leq c$.

It remains to show that $\mathbf{u} \in \mathsf{Desc}(\mathcal{X}_0)$. Since $\mathbf{u} \in \mathsf{Desc}_c(\mathcal{C})$, there exists a set $\mathcal{X}' \subseteq \mathcal{C}$ in $\mathsf{Par}_c(\mathbf{u})$. Let $\mathcal{X}_0'$ denote a possible choice for the specific subset of $\mathcal{X}'$ whose existence is required in our definition of descendants (Definition 9). Note that the elements in $\mathcal{X}' \setminus \mathcal{X}_0'$ are irrelevant for the descendancy of $\mathbf{u}$ which implies that $\mathbf{u} \in \mathsf{Desc}(\mathcal{X}_0')$. Then it suffices to show that $\mathcal{X}_0 = \mathcal{X}_0'$ with high probability. (In this case it follows in particular that the above choice of $\mathcal{X}_0'$ is unique.) First, since $\mathbf{u} \in \mathsf{Desc}(\mathcal{X}_0')$, we have that $\mathcal{X}_0' \in \mathsf{Par}_c(\mathbf{u})$ and, thus, $\mathcal{X}_0 \subseteq \mathcal{X}_0'$. For the other inclusion, we define $\mathcal{I} = \{i \in [n] : \mathbf{w}^{(i)} \in \mathcal{X}_0'\}$. Furthermore, for $i \in [n]$, we parse $\mathbf{w}^{(i)} = (w_{k,j}^{(i)})_{k \in [K], j \in [J]}$ and let $\mathbf{d}^{(i)} = (d_1^{(i)}, \ldots, d_K^{(i)}) \in [J]^K$ such that

$$\left(w_{1,d_1^{(i)}}^{(i)}, \ldots, w_{K,d_K^{(i)}}^{(i)}\right) = (a_i, \ldots, a_i),$$

i.e. $\mathbf{d}^{(i)}$ contains the positions of the letter a_i in each of the K blocks of $\mathbf{w}^{(i)}$. Let E denote the event that there exists an $i_0 \in \mathcal{I}$ with the property that for all $k \in [K]$, there exists an $i_k \in \mathcal{I} \setminus \{i_0\}$ such that $d_k^{(i_k)} = d_k^{(i_0)}$. Note that E corresponds exactly to the event that $\mathcal{X}_0 \subsetneq \mathcal{X}_0'$. For a fixed choice of $i_0 \in \mathcal{I}$, the probability that for all $k \in [K]$, there exists such an $i_k \in \mathcal{I} \setminus \{i_0\}$ with the property that $d_k^{(i_k)} = d_k^{(i_0)}$, is bounded by $(c/J)^K$. Thus, $\Pr[E] \leq c \cdot (c/J)^K$.

Finally, applying the union bound over all possible coalitions $\mathcal{X}_0' \subseteq \mathcal{C}$ of size at most c implies the result for all $\mathbf{u} \in \mathsf{Desc}_c(\mathcal{C})$. Hence, we conclude that $\mathcal{C}$ is c-FIPP with probability at least $1 - c \cdot n^c \cdot (c/J)^K = 1 - \mathsf{negl}(K)$. $\square$

Remark 11 (Efficiency). For a practical usability of a FIPP code, one needs efficient generation and tracing algorithms. The code generation in our construction is trivial as one only samples $\mathbf{w}^{(i)} \xleftarrow{\$} \mathcal{S}_i^{(K,J)}$ for each $i \in [n]$. Furthermore, we observe that the proof of Theorem 10 does not only show the existence of a smallest set $\mathcal{X}_0$ but also shows how to construct this set efficiently. Indeed, on input a descendant $\mathbf{u} = (u_{k,j})_{k \in [K], j \in [J]} \in \mathsf{Desc}_c(\mathcal{C})$, the tracing algorithm simply returns the set $\{u_{k,j} : k \in [K], j \in [J]\} \setminus \{\top, \bot\}$.

Another aspect of efficiency considers the length of the code. Let ε denote the acceptable error probability. If one chooses, say, $J = 2c$, then the proof of Theorem 10 yields that $K = \mathcal{O}(c \cdot \log(n/\varepsilon))$, which in turn implies that $\ell = \mathcal{O}(c^2 \cdot \log(n/\varepsilon))$. Furthermore, our alphabet has size $\mathcal{O}(n)$. Thus, our codewords have representations on $\mathcal{O}(c^2 \cdot \log(n/\varepsilon) \cdot \log n)$ bits. It is interesting to compare this bound with the "naive" FIPP code $\mathcal{C} = \{\mathbf{w}^{(i)} = (\delta_{i,j})_{j=1}^n\}_{i=1}^n$, where $\delta_{i,j} = \bot$ if $i = j$, and $\delta_{i,j} = \top$ otherwise. This code uses the binary alphabet $\mathcal{Q} = \{\top, \bot\}$. Codewords in the naive solution thus require $\mathcal{O}(n)$ bits which grows asymptotically faster (in n) than our bound $\mathcal{O}(c^2 \cdot \log(n/\varepsilon) \cdot \log n)$, with reasonable trade-off on c and ε.

4   An Efficient Tracing Algorithm for Linear Subspaces

Let $\mathbb{U}$ be a vector space over a field $\mathbb{K}$ and let $\mathcal{V} = \{\mathbf{V}_1, \ldots, \mathbf{V}_n\} \subset \mathbb{U}$. Given a vector $\boldsymbol{\omega} = (\omega_i)_{i=1}^n \in \mathbb{K}^n$, we write $N_{\boldsymbol{\omega}} = |\{i \in [n] : \omega_i \neq 0\}|$. Then for a positive integer c, we denote $\mathsf{span}_c(\mathcal{V}) = \bigcup_{\mathcal{X} \in \mathcal{P}_c(\mathcal{V})} \mathsf{span}(\mathcal{X})$. Also, we call $\mathcal{V}$ c-linearly independent if the following implication is satisfied for every $\boldsymbol{\omega} = (\omega_i)_{i=1}^n \in \mathbb{K}^n$:

$$\sum_{i=1}^n \omega_i \cdot \mathbf{V}_i = 0 \implies N_{\boldsymbol{\omega}} = 0 \vee N_{\boldsymbol{\omega}} > c$$

Intuitively, c-linear independence states that for each vector $\mathbf{U}$ in $\mathsf{span}_c(\mathcal{V})$, there exists a unique choice of coefficients $\omega_1, \ldots, \omega_n$ such that $\sum_{i=1}^n \omega_i \cdot \mathbf{V}_i = \mathbf{U}$ and there are at most c nonzero coefficients. However, the definition does not exclude that there may exist coefficients $\omega_1', \ldots, \omega_n'$ that also satisfy $\sum_{i=1}^n \omega_i' \cdot \mathbf{V}_i = \mathbf{U}$, but with more than c coefficients being nonzero.

Definition 12. (Linear-Subspace Tracing (LST) Scheme). *Let $\mathbb{U}$ be a vector space and c a positive integer. A LST scheme (for linear subspaces of $\mathbb{U}$) is a tuple of two polynomial-time algorithms defined as follows.*

$\mathsf{Gen}(1^\lambda, 1^n)$: *On input the security parameter λ and a positive integer n, this algorithm returns a tracing key tk and a c-linearly independent set $\mathcal{V} \subseteq \mathbb{U}$ of size n.*

$\mathsf{Trace}(\mathsf{tk}, \mathbf{U})$: *On input a tracing key tk and a vector $\mathbf{U} \in \mathsf{span}_c(\mathcal{V})$, this algorithm returns a set $\mathcal{I} \subseteq [n]$.*

For a PPT adversary A and a LST scheme $\mathsf{T} = (\mathsf{Gen}, \mathsf{Trace})$, the experiment $\mathbf{Exp}_{\mathsf{T},A}^{\text{c-cor}}(1^\lambda, 1^n)$ is defined as shown in Fig. 3. We say that a LST scheme T is c-correct if for any PPT adversary A and any polynomial $n = n(\lambda)$, there exists a negligible function negl such that

$$\mathbf{Adv}_{\mathsf{T},A}^{\text{c-cor}}(\lambda, n) = \Pr\left[\mathbf{Exp}_{\mathsf{T},A}^{\text{c-cor}}(1^\lambda, 1^n) = 1\right] \leq \mathsf{negl}(\lambda).$$

$$\begin{aligned}
&(\mathsf{tk}, \mathcal{V} = \{\mathbf{V}_1, \ldots, \mathbf{V}_n\}) \leftarrow \mathsf{Gen}(1^\lambda, 1^n)\\
&\mathcal{X} \stackrel{\$}{\leftarrow} \mathcal{P}_c(\mathcal{V}); \ \mathbf{U} \leftarrow A(\mathsf{tk}, \mathcal{X}); \ \mathcal{I} \leftarrow \mathsf{Trace}(\mathsf{tk}, \mathbf{U})\\
&\text{If } \mathbf{U} \notin \mathsf{span}(\mathcal{X}), \text{ return } 0\\
&\text{If } \{\mathbf{V}_i : i \in \mathcal{I}\} \neq \bigcap_{\mathcal{X}' \subseteq \mathcal{X}, \mathbf{U} \in \mathsf{span}(\mathcal{X}')} \mathcal{X}', \text{ return } 1\\
&\text{Return } 0
\end{aligned}$$

Fig. 3. Security game $\mathbf{Exp}_{\mathsf{T},A}^{c\text{-}\mathrm{cor}}(1^\lambda, 1^n)$ for c-correctness

As mentioned above, c-linear independence of the set $\mathcal{V}$ ensures that vectors in $\mathsf{span}_c(\mathcal{V})$ have a unique representation as a linear combination with at most c coefficients being nonzero. The correctness condition states that the tracing algorithm returns (the indices of) these nonzero coefficients with overwhelming probability.

Construction. Let $\mathbb{G}$ be a group of prime order p in which the DL problem is hard. In the following, we construct a LST scheme $\mathsf{T} = (\mathsf{Gen}, \mathsf{Trace})$ for subspaces of $\mathbb{G}^\ell$, where $\ell = \Theta(c^2 \cdot \log(n/\varepsilon))$ and ε is the maximum acceptable probability that the tracing will fail. We view the construction as an implementation of the FIPP code presented in Sect. 3.

Intuitively, the Gen algorithm first chooses a random alphabet $\mathcal{Q}$, along with a tracing key tk that serves as a description of $\mathcal{Q}$. Then it generates a FIPP code $\mathcal{C} = \{\mathbf{w}^{(i)} : i \in [n]\}$ of length ℓ' and chooses a (random) representative $\mathbf{V}^{(i)} \in \mathbb{G}^\ell$ for each codeword $\mathbf{w}^{(i)}$ and $\ell = 2 \cdot \ell'$. (We will detail below what "represent" means exactly in our context.) Finally, the Gen algorithm returns tk and $\mathcal{V} = \{\mathbf{V}^{(i)} : i \in [n]\}$. We then show that if a vector $\mathbf{U}$ is in the span of some set $\{\mathbf{V}^{(i_1)}, \ldots, \mathbf{V}^{(i_{c'})}\} \in \mathcal{P}_c(\mathcal{V})$, then the word $\mathbf{u} \in \mathcal{Q}^{\ell'}$ which is represented by $\mathbf{U}$ is in $\mathsf{Desc}(\{\mathbf{w}^{(i_1)}, \ldots, \mathbf{w}^{(i_{c'})}\})$ with overwhelming probability. Thus, it is enough to recover $\mathbf{u}$ from $\mathbf{U}$ and to utilize the tracing mechanism of the FIPP code explained in Remark 11.

An overview of the implementation of our LST scheme $\mathsf{T} = (\mathsf{Gen}, \mathsf{Trace})$ is depicted in Fig. 4. We explain the details of the construction below. We place special emphasis on the connections to the FIPP code from Sect. 3.

Generation. At first, the Gen algorithm samples a vector $\mathbf{s} = (s_i)_{i=1}^n \stackrel{\$}{\leftarrow} (\mathbb{Z}_p^*)^n$. This vector specifies the alphabet $\mathcal{Q} = \mathcal{Q}_\mathbf{s}$ and serves as the tracing key tk. Formally, $\mathcal{Q}$ is a partition of $\mathbb{G} \times \mathbb{G}$ and the letters are the disjoint subsets of $\mathcal{Q}$, which can be seen as classes of equivalence, defined as follows: for $i \in [n]$, we set $a_i = \{(G, s_i \cdot G) : G \in \mathbb{G}^*\}$, $\top = \{(0, 0)\}$, and $\bot = (\mathbb{G} \times \mathbb{G}) \setminus (\top \cup \bigcup_{i=1}^n a_i)$.

In the second step, the generation algorithm generates the codewords. According to Remark 11, one samples $\mathbf{w}^{(i)} \stackrel{\$}{\leftarrow} \mathcal{S}_i^{(K,J)}$ for each $i \in [n]$, where $\mathbf{w}^{(i)} \in \mathcal{Q}^{\ell'}$ and $\ell' = K \cdot J$ for suitable polynomials $K(\lambda)$ and $J(\lambda)$. Strictly speaking, these codewords are a sequence of classes of $\mathcal{Q}$. However, since the size of these classes can be exponential, we choose a representative $(G_i, s_i \cdot G_i) \stackrel{\$}{\leftarrow} a_i$

Gen($1^\lambda, 1^n$):	Trace(tk = $(s_i)_{i=1}^n, \mathbf{U}$):
$\mathbf{s} = (s_i)_{i=1}^n \xleftarrow{\$} (\mathbb{Z}_p^*)^n$	Parse $\mathbf{U} = (U_{k,j})_{k\in[K], j\in[J]}$
For $i \in [n]$:	$\mathcal{I} \leftarrow \emptyset$
$\mathbf{d}_i = (d_{i,k})_{k=1}^K \xleftarrow{\$} [J]^K$; $G_i \xleftarrow{\$} \mathbb{G}^*$	For $k \in [K]$, $j \in [J]$ and $i \in [n]$:
$\mathbf{V}^{(i)} \leftarrow (V_{k,j}^{(i)})_{k\in[K], j\in[J]}$ where	Parse $U_{k,j} = (G, H)$
$V_{k,j}^{(i)} = \begin{cases} (G_i, s_i \cdot G_i) & \text{if } j = d_{i,k} \\ (0,0) & \text{otherwise} \end{cases}$	If $s_i \cdot G = H$, then $\mathcal{I} \leftarrow \mathcal{I} \cup \{i\}$
	Return $\mathcal{I}$
Return (tk $\leftarrow \mathbf{s}, \mathcal{V} \leftarrow \{\mathbf{V}^{(i)}\}_{i=1}^n$)	

Fig. 4. Our LST scheme

for each letter $a_i \in \mathcal{Q}$. Furthermore, since $\top$ is a singleton, there is only one possible choice for a representative. Then we construct $\mathbf{V}^{(i)}$ by replacing each occurrence of the letter a_i in $\mathbf{w}^{(i)}$ with the selected representative $(G_i, s_i \cdot G_i)$ and each letter $\top$ with the tuple $(0,0)$.

More straightforward, the construction of the vectors $\mathbf{V}^{(i)}$ can be described as follows. For each $i \in [n]$, one samples a random tuple $\mathbf{d}_i = (d_{i,1}, \ldots, d_{i,K}) \xleftarrow{\$} [J]^K$ and a group generator $G_i \xleftarrow{\$} \mathbb{G}^*$, and sets

$$\mathbf{V}^{(i)} = \left(V_{k,j}^{(i)} = \begin{cases} (G_i, s_i \cdot G_i) & \text{if } j = d_{i,k} \\ (0,0) & \text{otherwise} \end{cases} \right)_{k\in[K], j\in[J]}$$

We emphasize that the random choice of both the vector $\mathbf{s}$ and the representatives of the letters is crucial to achieve correctness against arbitrary PPT adversaries.

Tracing. Let $\mathbf{U} = (U_{k,j})_{k\in[K], j\in[J]} \in \mathcal{P}_c(\mathcal{V})$. The crucial part is to recover the word $\mathbf{u} \in \mathcal{Q}^\ell$ which is represented by $\mathbf{U}$. That is, for each coordinate $(k,j) \in [K] \times [J]$, we need to identify the letter $a \in \mathcal{Q}$ such that $U_{k,j} \in a$.

Since the DL problem is assumed to be hard in $\mathbb{G}$, the scalar s cannot be recovered from a tuple $(G, s \cdot G) \in \mathbb{G} \times \mathbb{G}$. However, since we deal only with a polynomial number n, and thus with a polynomial-size alphabet $\mathcal{Q}_\mathbf{s}$, we can test for each $k \in [K]$, $j \in [J]$ and $i \in [n]$ if $U_{k,j} \in a_i$. Once we have recovered $\mathbf{u}$, we simply use the tracing mechanism explained in Remark 11.

Correctness. To prove correctness of the LST scheme T, one needs to show that each vector $\mathbf{U}$ in the span of some set $\mathcal{X} \in \mathcal{P}_c(\mathcal{V})$ represents a descendant of the set containing all codewords that are represented by an element of $\mathcal{X}$.

To state this result more formally, we introduce the following notations. First, recall that a vector $\mathbf{s} \in (\mathbb{Z}_p^*)^n$ defines an equivalence relation $\mathcal{Q}_\mathbf{s}$ on $\mathbb{G} \times \mathbb{G}$. So it is consistent to write $[(G, H)]_\mathbf{s}$ (or simply $[(G, H)]$ if $\mathbf{s}$ is fixed) for the letter $a \in \mathcal{Q}$ which contains $(G, H) \in \mathbb{G} \times \mathbb{G}$. Similarly, for a vector $\mathbf{V} = (V_i)_{i=1}^\ell \in (\mathbb{G} \times \mathbb{G})^\ell$,

$[V_1] \cdots [V_n]$ denotes the word $\mathbf{w} \in \mathcal{Q}^\ell$ which is represented by $\mathbf{V}$. For convenience, we also refer to $\mathbf{w}$ by $[\mathbf{V}]$ and, for a set $\mathcal{V} = \{\mathbf{V}_1, \ldots, \mathbf{V}_n\} \subseteq (\mathbb{G} \times \mathbb{G})^\ell$, we denote the set $\{[\mathbf{V}_1], \ldots, [\mathbf{V}_n]\}$ by $[\mathcal{V}]$.

Theorem 13. *Let* $(\mathsf{tk}, \mathcal{V}) \leftarrow \mathsf{Gen}(1^\lambda, 1^n)$ *and let* A *be any algebraic PPT algorithm that on input* tk *and a set* $\mathcal{X} \in \mathcal{P}_c(\mathcal{V})$ *returns a nonzero vector* $\mathbf{U} \in \mathrm{span}(\mathcal{X})$. *Then it holds* $[\mathbf{U}] \in \mathsf{Desc}([\mathcal{X}])$ *with overwhelming probability under the* DL *assumption.*

For the proof, we need the following lemma.

Lemma 14. *Let* $(\mathbb{G}, +)$ *be a group of prime order* p, $s \in \mathbb{Z}_p^*$ *and* $n > 2$. *Given* n *tuples* (G_i, s_i), *for* $G_i \xleftarrow{\$} \mathbb{G}^*$ *and* $s_i \xleftarrow{\$} \mathbb{Z}_p^*$, *it is computationally hard under the* DL *assumption to output* $(\omega_1, \ldots, \omega_n) \in \mathbb{Z}_p^n$ *such that* $\omega_i \neq 0$ *for at least two* $i \in [n]$ *and*

$$s \cdot \sum_{i=1}^n \omega_i \cdot G_i = \sum_{i=1}^n \omega_i s_i \cdot G_i.$$

A proof of Lemma 14 is provided in the full version [11].

Proof (of Theorem 13). Let $\mathsf{tk} = \mathbf{s} = (s_i)_{i=1}^n$ and $\mathcal{V} = \{\mathbf{V}^{(1)}, \ldots, \mathbf{V}^{(n)}\}$. We assume that the entries of $\mathbf{s}$ are pairwise distinct, which is correct with overwhelming probability. Also, without loss of generality, we assume that $\mathcal{X} = \{\mathbf{V}^{(1)}, \ldots, \mathbf{V}^{(c)}\}$. Note that if $[\mathcal{V}]$ is c-FIPP, then $\mathcal{X}$ is c-linearly independent. (This can be seen in the proof of Theorem 10.) Since $\mathcal{X}$ contains c elements and is c-linearly independent, it follows that there exist unique coefficients $\omega_1, \ldots, \omega_c$ in $\mathbb{Z}_p$ such that $\mathbf{U} = \sum_{j=1}^c \omega_j \cdot \mathbf{V}^{(i)}$. These coefficients are provided by the (algebraic) adversary A. We set $\mathcal{X}_0 = \{\mathbf{V}^{(i)} \in \mathcal{X} : \omega_i \neq 0\}$.

Fix any $(k, j) \in [K] \times [J]$. We consider several cases that correspond to those in Definition 9.

1. $\mathcal{Q}_{k,j}([\mathcal{X}_0]) = \{a\}$ *for some* $a \in \mathcal{Q}$. We split this case into two subcases.
   (a) $\mathcal{Q}_{k,j}([\mathcal{X}_0]) = \{\top\}$. In this case, we have $V_{k,j}^{(i)} = (0, 0)$ for all $i \in [c]$ satisfying $\omega_i \neq 0$, which implies that also $U_{k,j} = \sum_{i=1}^c \omega_i \cdot V_{k,j}^{(i)} = (0, 0)$. Thus, $[U_{k,j}] = \top$.
   (b) $\mathcal{Q}_{k,j}([\mathcal{X}_0]) = \{a_i\}$ *for some* $i \in [c]$. Since we assume that $s_1, \ldots, s_n$ are pairwise distinct, it follows that $\mathcal{X}_0 = \{\mathbf{V}^{(i)}\}$ and $V_{k,j}^{(i)} = (G_i, s_i \cdot G_i)$ for some $G_i \in \mathbb{G}^*$. Due to the DL assumption, the probability that $\omega_i \cdot G_i = 0$ is negligible. Thus, $[U_{k,j}] = [\omega_i \cdot (G_i, s_i \cdot G_i)] = a_i$ with overwhelming probability.
   The case $\mathcal{Q}_{k,j}([\mathcal{X}_0]) = \bot$ cannot occur since elements of $\bot$ do not appear as components in the vectors in $\mathcal{V}$.
2. $\mathcal{Q}_{k,j}([\mathcal{X}_0]) = \{\top, a_i\}$ *for some* $i \in [c]$. This case can be seen as the combination of the cases 1. (a) and 1. (b). That is, we have $\omega_{i'} = 0$ or $V_{k,j}^{(i')} = (0, 0)$

for all $i' \in [c] \setminus \{i\}$, and $V_{k,j}^{(i)} = (G_i, s_i \cdot G_i)$ for some $G_i \in \mathbb{G}^*$. Again by the DL assumption, it follows that

$$U_{k,j} = \sum_{i'=1}^{c} \omega_{i'} \cdot V_{k,j}^{(i')} = (\omega_i \cdot G_i, \omega_i s_i \cdot G_i) \in a_i.$$

3. *None of the previous cases applies.* Let $\mathcal{J} = \{i \in [c] : V_{k,j}^{(i)} \neq (0,0)\}$. If there exists at most one $i \in \mathcal{J}$ such that $\omega_i \neq 0$, then we can argue as in one of the previous cases. Otherwise, the argumentation is as follows. There exist generators $(G_i)_{i \in \mathcal{J}}$ such that $V_{k,j}^{(i)} = (G_i, s_i \cdot G_i)$ for each $i \in \mathcal{J}$. Fix some $s \in \mathbb{Z}_p$. By Lemma 14, it follows that a vector $\boldsymbol{\omega} = (\omega_i)_{i \in \mathcal{J}}$ that has at least two nonzero entries and satisfies

$$U_{k,j} = \sum_{i \in \mathcal{J}} \omega_i \cdot V_{k,j}^{(i)} = \left(\sum_{i \in \mathcal{J}} \omega_i \cdot G_i, s \cdot \sum_{i \in \mathcal{J}} \omega_i \cdot G_i \right)$$

can be used to solve discrete logarithms in $\mathbb{G}$. Applying a union bound over all values of $s \in \{0, s_1, \ldots, s_n\}$ implies that $U_{k,j} \in \top \cup \bigcup_{i=1}^{n} a_i$ with negligible probability, i.e. $[U_{k,j}] = \bot$ with overwhelming probability.

Finally, the statement of the theorem follows by a union bound over all $(k,j) \in [K] \times [J]$. $\qquad \square$

Remark 15 (Efficiency Improvement and Dynamic Generation). Let $i \in [n]$. Note that the vector $\mathbf{V}^{(i)} \in \mathbb{G}^{J \cdot K}$ in Fig. 4 is computed from $\mathbf{d}_i \in [J]^K$, $G_i \in \mathbb{G}$ and $s_i \in \mathbb{Z}_p$. Since these three values require far less memory than $\mathbf{V}^{(i)}$, it would be desirable to use these three values as an efficient representation of $\mathbf{V}^{(i)}$. Clearly, $\mathbf{d}_i$ and G_i can be recovered from $\mathbf{V}^{(i)}$ and, thus, must not be hidden. Furthermore, Theorem 13 explicitly covers the case that the vector $\mathsf{tk} = (s_i)_{i=1}^{n}$ is known to the adversary. Thus, knowledge of the scalar s_i does not affect the correctness of the LST scheme. So $(\mathbf{d}_i, G_i, s_i)$ can indeed be used as an efficient representation of $\mathbf{V}^{(i)}$.

Moreover, we observe that the vectors $\mathbf{V}^{(1)}, \ldots, \mathbf{V}^{(n)}$ are generated independently, and the length of the code depends only on the security parameter but not on n (as long as it is polynomially in the security parameter). Therefore, the total number of vectors must not be fixed in advance, but new ones can be added dynamically.

5   Linear-Subspace Tracing and Anonymity

Equivalent vectors $\mathbf{V}_1, \mathbf{V}_2 \in \mathbb{G}^\ell$ (i.e. $[\mathbf{V}_1] = [\mathbf{V}_2]$) are publicly linkable, as the nonzero positions are publicly available. However, in some situations it may be desirable that users act anonymously, with unlinkable actions, except with respect to the authority holding the tracing key. We thus now explain how to make vectors anonymous.

Definition 16 (Anonymity). *For a LST scheme* T = (Gen, Trace) *and a PPT adversary A, we define the experiment* $\mathbf{Exp}^{ano}_{T,A}(1^\lambda, 1^n)$ *as shown in Fig. 5. The "Subspace or Full space" oracle* $\mathcal{O}SoF$ *can be called any number of times.*

We say that a LST scheme is anonymous if for any PPT adversary A and any polynomial $n = n(\lambda)$, there exists a negligible function negl such that

$$\mathbf{Adv}^{ano}_{T,A}(\lambda, n) = \left| \Pr\left[\mathbf{Exp}^{ano}_{T,A}(1^\lambda, 1^n) = 1\right] - \frac{1}{2} \right| \leq negl(\lambda).$$

Initialize$(1^\lambda, 1^n)$:
$b \xleftarrow{\$} \{0,1\}$; (tk, $\mathcal{V}$) $\leftarrow$ Gen$(1^\lambda, 1^n)$
Return $\mathcal{V}$

Finalize(b'): Return $(b = b')$

$\mathcal{O}SoF(\mathcal{X})$:
If $\mathcal{X} \nsubseteq \mathcal{V}$, return $\bot$
$\mathbf{V}_0 \xleftarrow{\$} \text{span}(\mathcal{X})$; $\mathbf{V}_1 \xleftarrow{\$} \text{span}(\mathcal{V})$
Return $\mathbf{V}_b$

Fig. 5. Security game $\mathbf{Exp}^{ano}_{T,A}(1^\lambda, 1^n)$ for anonymity

Let T′ = (Gen′, Trace′) be the LST scheme for linear subspaces of $\mathbb{G}^{\ell'}$ defined in Fig. 4. Recall that $\ell' = 2KJ$ where K and J are specified by the underlying FIPP code. Let (tk′, $\mathcal{V}' = \{\mathbf{V}'_i\}_{i=1}^n$) $\leftarrow$ Gen′$(1^\lambda, 1^n)$. Note that even if the tracing algorithm cannot be run directly without the tracing key tk′, the scheme is still not anonymous because the vectors in $\mathcal{V}'$ do not hide the embedded vectors $\mathbf{d}_1, \ldots, \mathbf{d}_n$. Hence, to break anonymity it is enough to compare the positions of the nonzero entries of the challenge vector with those of $\mathbf{V}_1, \ldots, \mathbf{V}_n$. Nevertheless, the scheme can easily be made anonymous.

Construction. As above, let (tk′, $\mathcal{V}' = \{\mathbf{V}'_i\}_{i=1}^n$) $\leftarrow$ Gen′$(1^\lambda, 1^n)$. The basic idea to obtain anonymous versions of $\mathbf{V}'_1, \ldots, \mathbf{V}'_n$ is to encrypt them component-wise using the ElGamal encryption scheme [8]. That is, we sample a vector $\mathbf{x} = (x_k)_{k=1}^{\ell'} \xleftarrow{\$} \mathbb{Z}_p^{\ell'}$ where, for each $k \in [\ell']$, x_k serves as the secret key for the k-th component. The corresponding vector of public keys is $\mathbf{X} = \mathbf{x} \cdot G$ for some fixed generator $G \in \mathbb{G}^*$. Since each ElGamal ciphertext consists of two group elements, component-wise encryption of $\mathbf{V}'_i$ with $\mathbf{X}$ yields a vector $\mathbf{V}_i$ of length $2\ell'$. It is well-known that the ElGamal encryption scheme is partially homomorphic. In our context, this means that, for all coefficients $\omega_1, \ldots, \omega_n$, $\sum_{i=1}^n \omega_i \cdot \mathbf{V}_i$ is a component-wise encryption of $\sum_{i=1}^n \omega_i \cdot \mathbf{V}'_i$. Thus, the tracing of a vector $\mathbf{U}$ can be done by first decrypting it and passing the resulting vector $\mathbf{U}'$ to the algorithm Trace′. The output $\mathcal{I}'$ of the tracing of $\mathbf{U}'$ is exactly the wanted output $\mathcal{I}$ for the tracing of $\mathbf{U}$.

Since the security of ElGamal is based on the DDH assumption, it is straightforward to exploit the random self-reducibility of the DDH problem here. If we reuse the same randomness in the encryption of all components of a vector $\mathbf{V}'_i$, $i \in [n]$, then one component of all ciphertexts is equal and, thus, must be included only once in the anonymous version $\mathbf{V}_i$ of $\mathbf{V}'_i$. This leads us to a more efficient anonymous transformation of T' where the vectors have only length $\ell = \ell' + 1$ instead of $2\ell'$.

The full scheme is depicted in Fig. 6. The correctness of the construction is a direct consequence of the correctness of T' and the fact that the ElGamal encryption scheme is partially homomorphic.

$\mathsf{Gen}(1^\lambda, 1^n)$:
$(\mathsf{tk}', \mathcal{V}' = \{\mathbf{V}'_i\}_{i=1}^n) \leftarrow \mathsf{Gen}'(1^\lambda, 1^n)$
Choose any $G \in \mathbb{G}^*$
$\mathbf{x} \xleftarrow{\$} \mathbb{Z}_p^{\ell'}$; $\mathbf{X} \leftarrow \mathbf{x} \cdot G$
For $i \in [n]$:
$\quad r_i \xleftarrow{\$} \mathbb{Z}_p$; $\mathbf{V}_i \leftarrow r_i \cdot G \parallel r_i \cdot \mathbf{X} + \mathbf{V}'_i$
Return $(\mathsf{tk} \leftarrow (\mathsf{tk}', \mathbf{x}), \mathcal{V} \leftarrow \{\mathbf{V}_i\}_{i=1}^n)$

$\mathsf{Trace}(\mathsf{tk}, \mathbf{U} = (U_k)_{k=0}^{\ell'})$:
$\mathbf{U}' \leftarrow (U_1, \ldots, U_{\ell'})$
Return $\mathcal{I} \leftarrow \mathsf{Trace}'(\mathsf{tk}', \mathbf{U}' - \mathbf{x} \cdot U_0)$

Fig. 6. Our anonymous LST scheme T

Theorem 17. *The LST scheme T is anonymous under the DDH assumption in $\mathbb{G}$. More precisely, it holds that $\mathbf{Adv}_{\mathsf{T},A}^{\mathrm{ano}}(\lambda, n) \leq \mathbf{Adv}_{\mathbb{G}}^{\mathrm{ddh}}(\lambda)$ for any PPT adversary A, where $\mathbf{Adv}_{\mathbb{G}}^{\mathrm{ddh}}(\lambda)$ denotes the best advantage a PPT algorithm can get in solving the DDH problem in $\mathbb{G}$.*

Proof. The proof is done via a sequence of hybrid games. The advantage of an adversary A in game $\mathcal{G}_i$ is denoted by

$$\mathbf{Adv}(\mathcal{G}_i) = \left| \Pr[\mathcal{G}_i = 1] - \frac{1}{2} \right|.$$

Hybrid Game $\mathcal{G}_0$. This corresponds to the real security game $\mathbf{Exp}_{\mathsf{T},A}^{\mathrm{ano}}(1^\lambda, 1^n)$. We recall the construction of the set $\mathcal{V}$. First, the Gen algorithm samples random vectors $\mathbf{s} = (s_i)_{i=1}^n \xleftarrow{\$} (\mathbb{Z}_p^*)^n$ and $\mathbf{x} \xleftarrow{\$} \mathbb{Z}_p^{\ell'}$ and computes $\mathbf{X} = \mathbf{x} \cdot G$ for some fixed generator $G \in \mathbb{G}^*$. Then, for each $i \in [n]$, the algorithm samples $\mathbf{d}_i = (d_{i,1}, \ldots, d_{i,K}) \xleftarrow{\$} [J]^K$, $G_i \xleftarrow{\$} \mathbb{G}^*$ and $r_i \xleftarrow{\$} \mathbb{Z}_p$, and computes $\mathbf{V}_i = (r_i \cdot G \parallel r_i \cdot \mathbf{X} + \mathbf{V}'_i)$ where

$$\mathbf{V}'_i = \left(V'_{i,k,j} = \begin{cases} (G_i, s_i \cdot G_i) & \text{if } j = d_{i,k} \\ (0, 0) & \text{otherwise} \end{cases} \right)_{k \in [K], j \in [J]}.$$

Hybrid Game $\mathcal{G}_1$. We slightly modify the Gen algorithm. Instead of sampling $\mathbf{x} \xleftarrow{\$} \mathbb{Z}_p^n$ and computing $\mathbf{X} = \mathbf{x} \cdot G$, it directly samples $\mathbf{X} \xleftarrow{\$} \mathbb{G}^{\ell'}$ now. Furthermore, the algorithm samples a vector $\mathbf{t} = (t_i)_{i=1}^n \xleftarrow{\$} (\mathbb{Z}_p^*)^n$ and sets $\mathbf{V}_i = (r_i \cdot G \parallel r_i \cdot \mathbf{X} + \mathbf{v}_i' \cdot G)$ where the vector $\mathbf{v}_i' \in \mathbb{Z}_p^{\ell'}$ is defined as follows

$$\mathbf{v}_i' = \left(v_{i,k,j}' = \begin{cases} (t_i, s_i t_i) & \text{if } j = d_{i,k} \\ (0,0) & \text{otherwise} \end{cases} \right)_{k \in [K], j \in [J]}.$$

Since the distribution of $\mathcal{V}$ does not change, it follows $\mathbf{Adv}(\mathcal{G}_1) = \mathbf{Adv}(\mathcal{G}_0)$.

Hybrid Game $\mathcal{G}_2$. We embed a Diffie-Hellman tuple (X, Y, Z) in basis G. The challenger samples $\boldsymbol{\mu}, \boldsymbol{\nu} \xleftarrow{\$} \mathbb{Z}_p^{\ell'}$ and sets $\mathbf{X} = \boldsymbol{\mu} \cdot X + \boldsymbol{\nu} \cdot G$. Clearly, this does not change the distribution of $\mathbf{X}$. Furthermore, we modify the implementation of $\mathcal{OS}$oF. First, if $b = 1$, we simply replace $\mathcal{X}$ with $\mathcal{V}$ and continue as in the case $b = 0$. On input a set $\mathcal{X} = \{\mathbf{V}_{i_1}, \ldots, \mathbf{V}_{i_d}\} \subseteq \mathcal{V}$, the oracle samples random scalars $\omega_1, \ldots, \omega_d \xleftarrow{\$} \mathbb{Z}_p$ and computes $\mathbf{U}_1 = (\omega_1 r_{i_1} \cdot Y \parallel r_{i_1} \cdot \mathbf{Z} + \mathbf{v}_{i_1}' \cdot Y)$ where $\mathbf{Z} = \omega_1 \boldsymbol{\mu} \cdot Z + \omega_1 \boldsymbol{\nu} \cdot Y$. Subsequently, it returns $\mathbf{U} = \mathbf{U}_1 + \sum_{j=2}^d \omega_j \cdot \mathbf{V}_{i_j}$. Note that if $Y = y \cdot G$ for some (unknown) $y \in \mathbb{Z}_p$, then $\mathbf{U}_1 = \omega_1 y \cdot \mathbf{V}_{i_1}$, i.e. $\mathbf{U}_1$ is a random multiple of $\mathbf{V}_{i_1}$. Thus, the oracle still returns a uniformly random element of $\mathsf{span}(\mathcal{X})$ which implies that the games $\mathcal{G}_3$ and $\mathcal{G}_2$ are again perfectly indistinguishable and $\mathbf{Adv}(\mathcal{G}_2) = \mathbf{Adv}(\mathcal{G}_1)$.

Hybrid Game $\mathcal{G}_3$. We replace the above Diffie-Hellman tuple with a random tuple $(X, Y, Z) \xleftarrow{\$} \mathbb{G}^3$. Thus, we have $\mathbf{Adv}(\mathcal{G}_3) \geq \mathbf{Adv}(\mathcal{G}_2) - \mathbf{Adv}_{\mathbb{G}}^{\mathrm{ddh}}(\lambda)$. Moreover, we observe that $\mathbf{Z}$ (and thus $\mathbf{U}$) are uniformly random vectors in $\mathbb{G}^\ell$ now. Therefore, it follows that $\mathbf{Adv}(\mathcal{G}_3) = 0$.

Using a hybrid argument, we conclude that $\mathbf{Adv}_{\mathsf{T},A}^{\mathrm{ano}}(\lambda, n) \leq \mathbf{Adv}_{\mathbb{G}}^{\mathrm{ddh}}(\lambda)$. $\quad\square$

Remark 18 (Randomizability). Let $\mathsf{T} = (\mathsf{Gen}, \mathsf{Trace})$ be a LST scheme and let $(\mathsf{tk}, \mathcal{V} = \{\mathbf{V}_i\}_{i=1}^n) \leftarrow \mathsf{Gen}(1^\lambda, 1^n)$. Given a vector $\mathbf{U} \in \mathsf{span}(\mathcal{X})$ for some subset $\mathcal{X} \subseteq \mathcal{V}$, it is easy to find another vector $\mathbf{U}'$ in $\mathsf{span}(\mathcal{X})$ unlinkable to $\mathbf{U}$. Indeed, one can simply sample a scalar $\omega \xleftarrow{\$} \mathbb{Z}_p$ and set $\mathbf{U}' = \omega \cdot \mathbf{U}$. Then the unlinkability follows from the DL assumption in $\mathbb{G}$. This randomization is even possible without knowledge of the vectors in $\mathcal{X}$.

However, this method creates several unlinkable representations of the same subspace $\mathsf{span}(\mathcal{X})$ rather than of the same vector $\mathbf{U}$. To achieve the latter, one can add a dummy vector $\mathbf{V}_0$ by running $(\mathsf{tk}, \mathcal{V} = \{\mathbf{V}_i\}_{i=0}^n) \leftarrow \mathsf{Gen}(1^\lambda, 1^{n+1})$ instead of $\mathsf{Gen}(1^\lambda, 1^n)$. Then one sets $\mathcal{V}' = \{\mathbf{V}_i\}_{i=1}^n$ and defines an equivalence relation on $\mathsf{span}(\mathcal{V}) \times \mathsf{span}(\mathcal{V})$ where vectors are equivalent if and only if their orthogonal projection onto the subspace $\mathsf{span}(\mathcal{V}')$ is equal. The randomization of a vector $\mathbf{U}$ inside its equivalence class can be done by sampling a scalar $\omega \xleftarrow{\$} \mathbb{Z}_p$ and computing $\mathbf{U}' = \mathbf{U} + \omega \cdot \mathbf{V}_0$. If the vector $\mathbf{V}_0$ is public, then the randomization can be done by everyone. Furthermore, if T is anonymous, then, for any $\mathbf{U}_1, \mathbf{U}_2 \in \mathsf{span}(\mathcal{V})$, the distributions $\{(\mathbf{U}_1, \mathbf{U}_2, \mathbf{U}_1', \mathbf{U}_2')\}$ and $\{(\mathbf{U}_1, \mathbf{U}_2, \mathbf{U}_2', \mathbf{U}_1')\}$ are computationally indistinguishable, where $\mathbf{U}_1' = \mathbf{U}_1 + \omega_1 \cdot \mathbf{V}_0$ and $\mathbf{U}_2' = \mathbf{U}_2 + \omega_2 \cdot \mathbf{V}_0$ for $\omega_1, \omega_2 \xleftarrow{\$} \mathbb{Z}_p$. If T is $(c+1)$-correct, then the "randomizable" variant (where $\mathbf{V}_0$ is public) is still c-correct. Indeed, one can simply run Trace and remove the index 0 from its output set.

Note that in our concrete construction (Fig. 6), a randomizable, c-correct LST scheme can even be obtained from a c-correct LST scheme (instead of a $(c+1)$-correct scheme). Using the notation of Fig 6, if one chooses $\mathbf{V}_0 = (r_0 \cdot G \parallel r_0 \cdot \mathbf{X} + \mathbf{V}_0')$ for $\mathbf{V}_0' = \mathbf{0}^{(\ell')}$, then the ElGamal encryption preserves all security guarantees, but one avoids interferences of $\mathbf{V}_0'$ with $\mathbf{V}_1', \ldots, \mathbf{V}_n'$ inside the underlying scheme T'. Thus, c-correctness suffices.

Remark 19 (Strong Correctness). It is worth mentioning that the encrypted LST scheme in Fig. 6 also satisfies a stronger correctness notion. The security experiment in Fig. 3 states that the adversary sees only c out of the n vectors in $\mathcal{V} = \{\mathbf{V}_1, \ldots, \mathbf{V}_n\}$. As mentioned above, for the non-encrypted LST scheme described in Fig. 4, this is a necessary restriction since a vector $\mathbf{V}_i \in \mathcal{V}$ does not hide the embedded vector $\mathbf{d}_i$ chosen during its creation. If an adversary A knew more than c vectors, then it could specifically create "collisions", i.e. it could combine vectors $\mathbf{V}_{i_0}$ and $\mathbf{V}_{i_1}$ for which the corresponding vectors $\mathbf{d}_{i_1}$ and $\mathbf{d}_{i_1}$ coincide in some positions.

However, in the encrypted scheme it follows from the semantic security of the ElGamal encryption scheme that the vectors $\mathbf{d}_1, \ldots, \mathbf{d}_n$ cannot be efficiently recovered from $\mathbf{V}_1, \ldots, \mathbf{V}_n$. Thus, even if the adversary knows the entire set $\mathcal{V}$, it is not able to determine which of the vectors must be combined to create many collisions. (Intuitively, the tracing fails if for one vector, the adversary can create a collision in each of its K blocks.) Therefore, we do not need to bound the number of vectors an adversary is allowed to see, but only the number of vectors it is allowed to combine in the challenge vector $\mathbf{U}$. This stronger security game is shown in Fig. 7.

$$
\begin{array}{|l|}
\hline
(\mathsf{tk}, \mathcal{V} = \{\mathbf{V}_1, \ldots, \mathbf{V}_n\}) \leftarrow \mathsf{Gen}(1^\lambda, 1^n) \\
\mathbf{U} \leftarrow A(\mathsf{tk}, \mathcal{V}); \; \mathcal{I} \leftarrow \mathsf{Trace}(\mathsf{tk}, \mathbf{U}) \\
\text{If } \mathbf{U} \notin \mathsf{span}_c(\mathcal{V}), \text{ return } 0 \\
\text{If } \{\mathbf{V}_i : i \in \mathcal{I}\} \neq \bigcap_{\mathcal{X} \subseteq \mathcal{V}, \mathbf{U} \in \mathsf{span}(\mathcal{X})} \mathcal{X}, \text{ return } 1 \\
\text{Return } 0 \\
\hline
\end{array}
$$

Fig. 7. Security game $\mathsf{Exp}_{T,A}^{\text{c-scor}}(1^\lambda, 1^n)$ for strong c-correctness

6   A Model for Linearly-Homomorphic Group Signatures

Group signatures were originally proposed by [6], with a formal security model in [2]. We build on their definition by combining it with linearly-homomorphic signatures. More precisely, we define a linearly-homomorphic group signature scheme as follows.

Definition 20 (Linearly-Homomorphic Group Signature (LH-GSig)). *A LH-GSig scheme with tag space $\mathcal{T}$ and message space $\mathbb{Z}_p^n$, for a positive integer n and a prime number p, consists of the following polynomial-time algorithms.*

$\mathsf{GKg}(1^\lambda, 1^\kappa)$: *This algorithm takes as input a tuple $(1^\lambda, 1^\kappa)$, where λ is the security parameter and κ is the group size, and returns a tuple $(\mathsf{gpk}, \mathsf{gmsk}, \mathbf{gsk})$, where gpk is the group public key, gmsk is the group manager's secret key and $\mathbf{gsk}$ is a κ-vector of keys with $\mathsf{gsk}[i]$ being the secret signing key of group member $i \in [\kappa]$. We will assume that gmsk and all $\mathsf{gsk}[i]$ implicitly contain gpk.*

$\mathsf{GSig}(\mathsf{gsk}[i], \tau, \mathbf{m})$: *On input a secret signing key $\mathsf{gsk}[i]$ for some $i \in [\kappa]$, a tag $\tau \in \mathcal{T}$ and a message $\mathbf{m} \in \mathbb{Z}_p^n$, this algorithm returns a signature Σ of $\mathbf{m}$ under the tag τ.*

$\mathsf{GDrv}(\mathsf{gpk}, \tau, (\omega_j, \Sigma_j)_{j=1}^d)$: *On input the group public key gpk, a tag $\tau \in \mathcal{T}$ and d tuples of weights $\omega_j \in \mathbb{Z}_p$ and signatures Σ_j, this algorithm returns a signature Σ on the vector $\mathbf{m} = \sum_{j=1}^d \omega_j \cdot \mathbf{m}_j$ under the tag τ, where Σ_j is a signature on the message $\mathbf{m}_j \in \mathbb{Z}_p^n$ under τ.*

$\mathsf{GVf}(\mathsf{gpk}, \tau, \mathbf{m}, \Sigma)$: *On input the group public key gpk, a tag $\tau \in \mathcal{T}$, a message $\mathbf{m} \in \mathbb{Z}_p^n$ and a signature Σ, this algorithm returns 1 if $\tau \in \mathcal{T}$ and Σ is valid relative to gpk and τ, and 0 otherwise.*

$\mathsf{Open}(\mathsf{gmsk}, \tau, \mathbf{m}, \Sigma)$: *On input the group manager's secret key gmsk, a tag $\tau \in \mathcal{T}$, a vector $\mathbf{m} \in \mathbb{Z}_p^n$ and a signature Σ, this algorithm returns a subset $\mathcal{A} \subseteq [\kappa]$ containing the signers of Σ if $\mathsf{GVf}(\mathsf{gpk}, \tau, \mathbf{m}, \Sigma) = 1$, and $\perp$ otherwise.*

Correctness. LH-GSig schemes must meet two correctness requirements concerning the verification and the opening of signatures. The former is very similar to the case of LH-Sig schemes (Definition 3). Let $(\mathsf{gpk}, \mathsf{gmsk}, \mathbf{gsk}) \leftarrow \mathsf{GKg}(1^\lambda, 1^\kappa)$ be any keys and τ be any tag in $\mathcal{T}$. Then,

(a) for each $\mathbf{m} \in \mathbb{Z}_p^n$, $i \in [\kappa]$ and $\Sigma \leftarrow \mathsf{GSig}(\mathsf{gsk}[i], \tau, \mathbf{m})$, the scheme satisfies $\mathsf{GVf}(\mathsf{gpk}, \tau, \mathbf{m}, \Sigma) = 1$, and

(b) for any list $(\omega_j, \mathbf{m}_j, \Sigma_j)_{j=1}^d$ such that $\mathsf{GVf}(\mathsf{gpk}, \tau, \mathbf{m}_j, \Sigma_j) = 1$ for each $j \in [d]$, if $\Sigma \leftarrow \mathsf{GDrv}(\mathsf{gpk}, \tau, (\omega_j, \Sigma_j)_{j=1}^d)$, then $\mathsf{GVf}(\mathsf{gpk}, \tau, \sum_{j=1}^d \omega_j \cdot \mathbf{m}_j, \Sigma) = 1$.

The second aspect asks that the opening algorithm correctly recovers the identity of the signers from an honestly generated signature. Note that, since LH-GSig schemes allow the combination of signatures issued by different group members, the opening algorithm returns a subset of $[\kappa]$ rather than a single element. For a LH-GSig scheme Σ, a positive integer c and a PPT adversary A, we define the experiment $\mathbf{Exp}_{\Sigma, A}^{c\text{-cor}}(1^\lambda, 1^\kappa)$ as shown in Fig. 8. We say that openings of Σ are c-correct if for any PPT adversary A and any integer κ, there exists a negligible function negl such that

$$\mathbf{Adv}_{\Sigma,A}^{c\text{-cor}}(\lambda, \kappa) = \Pr\left[\mathbf{Exp}_{\Sigma,A}^{c\text{-cor}}(1^\lambda, 1^\kappa) = 1\right] \leq \mathsf{negl}(\lambda).$$

Initialize($1^\lambda, 1^\kappa$):	$\mathcal{O}\mathsf{GSig}(i, \tau, \mathbf{m})$:
$\mathcal{H} \leftarrow \emptyset$	$\Sigma \leftarrow \mathsf{GSig}(\mathsf{gsk}[i], \tau, \mathbf{m})$
$(\mathsf{gpk}, \mathsf{gmsk}, \mathbf{gsk}) \leftarrow \mathsf{KeyGen}(1^\lambda, 1^\kappa)$	Pick new handle h
Return gpk	If $\mathbf{m} = \mathbf{0}^{(n)}$, then $\mathcal{I} \leftarrow \emptyset$; else $\mathcal{I} \leftarrow \{i\}$
	$\mathcal{H} \leftarrow \mathcal{H} \cup \{(h, (\tau, \mathcal{I}, \mathbf{m}, \Sigma))\}$
$\mathcal{O}\mathsf{GDrv}((h_j, \omega_j)_{j=1}^d)$:	Return (h, Σ)
$\{(\tau_j, \mathcal{I}_j, \mathbf{m}_j, \Sigma_j)\}_j \leftarrow \mathsf{Lookup}_{\mathcal{H}}(\{h_j\}_{j=1}^d)$	
If $\exists j \in [2; d]$ s.t. $\tau_j \neq \tau_1$, return $\bot$	Finalize(h):
$\mathbf{m} \leftarrow \sum_{j=1}^d \omega_j \cdot \mathbf{m}_j$	$(\tau, \mathcal{I}, \mathbf{m}, \Sigma) \leftarrow \mathsf{Lookup}_{\mathcal{H}}(h)$
$\Sigma \leftarrow \mathsf{GDrv}(\mathsf{pk}, \tau_1, (\omega_j, \Sigma_j)_{j=1}^d)$	If $|\mathcal{I}| \leq c$ and $\mathsf{Open}(\mathsf{gmsk}, \mathbf{m}, \Sigma) \neq \mathcal{I}$,
Pick new handle h	return 1
$\mathcal{H} \leftarrow \mathcal{H} \cup \{(h, (\tau_1, \mathcal{I} = \bigcup_{j=1}^d \mathcal{I}_j, \mathbf{m}, \Sigma))\}$	Return 0
Return (h, Σ)	

Fig. 8. Security game $\mathbf{Exp}_{\Sigma,A}^{c\text{-cor}}(1^\lambda, 1^\kappa)$ for c-correctness of openings

Since the unforgeability of LH-Sig schemes does not exclude that signatures of the zero vector can be created without knowledge of the secret key, we prefer not to trace signers of this vector in general. However, if desired, our construction could easily be modified to allow the creation of deliberately traceable signatures on the zero vector.

Security – Anonymity. Intuitively, anonymity requires that an adversary not in possession of the group manager's secret key gmsk cannot efficiently recover the identities of the signers from a signature. As usual, to win the security game an adversary does not need to recover the identity of a signer from a signature, but it only needs to distinguish which of two (collections of) signers of its choice signed a target message of its choice.

Definition 21 (Anonymity). *For a LH-GSig scheme Σ and a PPT adversary A, we define the experiment $\mathbf{Exp}_{\Sigma,A}^{\mathrm{ano}}(1^\lambda, 1^\kappa)$ as shown in Fig. 9. The "Fresh or Derived" oracle $\mathcal{O}\mathsf{FoD}$ can be called any number of times.*

We say that a LH-GSig scheme Σ is anonymous if for any PPT adversary A and any polynomial $\kappa = \kappa(\lambda)$, there exists a negligible function negl such that

$$\mathbf{Adv}_{\Sigma,A}^{\mathrm{ano}}(\lambda, \kappa) = \left| \Pr\left[\mathbf{Exp}_{\Sigma,A}^{\mathrm{ano}}(1^\lambda, 1^\kappa) = 1\right] - \frac{1}{2} \right| \leq \mathsf{negl}(\lambda).$$

Initialize$(1^\lambda, 1^\kappa)$:	$\mathcal{O}\mathsf{FoD}(i, \tau, (\omega_j, \mathbf{m}_j, i_j)_{j=1}^d)$:
$b \xleftarrow{\$} \{0,1\}$	$\Sigma_0^* \leftarrow \mathsf{GSig}(\mathbf{gsk}[i], \tau, \sum_{j=1}^d \omega_j \cdot \mathbf{m}_j)$
$(\mathsf{gpk}, \mathsf{gmsk}, \mathbf{gsk}) \leftarrow \mathsf{KeyGen}(1^\lambda, 1^\kappa)$	$(\Sigma_j \leftarrow \mathsf{GSig}(\mathbf{gsk}[i_j], \tau, \mathbf{m}_j))_{j=1}^d$
Return $\mathbf{gsk}$	$\Sigma_1^* \leftarrow \mathsf{GDrv}(\tau, (\omega_j, \Sigma_j)_{j=1}^d)$
	Return $(\Sigma_b^*, (\Sigma_j)_{j=1}^d)$
Finalize(b'): Return $(b = b')$	

Fig. 9. Security game $\mathbf{Exp}_{\Sigma,A}^{\mathrm{ano}}(1^\lambda, 1^\kappa)$ for anonymity

Our definition captures various cases. This means the adversary can win the security game if it is able to distinguish the given signatures in either of the following scenarios:

- The adversary is given two fresh signatures created by running the Sign algorithm on input the signing keys of two different group members.
- The adversary is given a fresh signature created by running Sign and a derived signature created using the DeriveSign algorithm and a set of "parent" signatures
- The adversary is given two signatures derived from different sets of parent signatures.

Also, our security game ensures that signatures created by the same group members are unlinkable. This is a consequence of the fact that the adversary is given **gsk** (i.e. all signing keys). Therefore, it can simulate a signing oracle itself.

On the other hand, note that the adversary in $\mathbf{Exp}_{\Sigma,A}^{\mathrm{ano}}(1^\lambda, 1^\kappa)$ does not have access to an opening oracle. As observed by Bellare *et al.* [2], this would require to use an IND-CCA secure encryption scheme. However, such encryption schemes are not malleable which is crucial for our signature scheme to be linearly homomorphic. We therefore adapt the IND-CPA version of anonymity proposed by Boneh *et al.* with the suggested relaxations. For more details see Sect. 5.1 of [3].

Security – Traceability. In case of misuse, signer anonymity can be revoked by the group manager. For this to be an effective mechanism, we require that no colluding subset of group members (of size at most c) can create signatures that are opened incorrectly or cannot be opened at all. This is even true if the coalition is in possession of the group manager's secret key gmsk.

Definition 22 (Traceability). *For a LH-GSig scheme Σ with tag space $\mathcal{T}$ and message space $\mathbb{Z}_p^n$, a positive integer c and a PPT adversary A we define the experiment $\mathbf{Exp}_{\Sigma,A}^{c\text{-tr}}(1^\lambda, 1^\kappa)$ as shown in Fig. 10.*

The oracles $\mathcal{O}\mathsf{GSig}$ and $\mathcal{O}\mathsf{Corrupt}$ can be called in any order and any number of times. For a tag $\tau \in \mathcal{T}$, $\mathcal{S}_\tau$ denotes the set of all $i \in [\kappa]$ such that there exists a tuple $(\tau, i, \cdot) \in \mathcal{S}$. Similarly, for a tag τ and an $i \in [\kappa]$, we define $\mathcal{S}_{\tau,i}$ to be the set that contains all $\mathbf{m} \in \mathbb{Z}_p^n$ such that $(\tau, i, \mathbf{m}) \in \mathcal{S}$.

We say that a LH-GSig scheme Σ is c-traceable if for any PPT adversary A and any polynomial $\kappa = \kappa(\lambda)$, there exists a negligible function negl such that

$$\mathbf{Adv}_{\Sigma,A}^{c\text{-tr}}(\lambda, \kappa) = \Pr\left[\mathbf{Exp}_{\Sigma,A}^{c\text{-tr}}(1^\lambda, 1^\kappa) = 1\right] \leq \mathsf{negl}(\lambda).$$

Initialize($1^\lambda, 1^\kappa$):

(gpk, gmsk, **gsk**) $\leftarrow$ GKg($1^\lambda, 1^\kappa$)
$\mathcal{C} \leftarrow \emptyset; \mathcal{S} \leftarrow \emptyset$
Return gmsk

$\mathcal{O}$GSig($\tau, i, \mathbf{m}$):
$\overline{\mathcal{S} \leftarrow \mathcal{S} \cup \{(\tau, i, \mathbf{m})\}}$
Return $\Sigma \leftarrow$ GSig(gsk$[i], \tau, \mathbf{m}$)

$\mathcal{O}$Corrupt(i):
$\overline{\mathcal{C} \leftarrow \mathcal{C} \cup \{i\}}$; return gsk$[i]$

Finalize($\tau, \mathbf{m}, \Sigma$):
Return 0 if
  − Verify(gpk, $\tau, \mathbf{m}, \Sigma$) = 0, or
  − $\mathbf{m} = \mathbf{0}^{(n)}$, or
  − $|\mathcal{C} \cup \mathcal{S}_\tau| > c$
Return 1 if
  − Open(gmsk, $\mathbf{m}, \Sigma$) = $\emptyset$, or
  − Open(gmsk, $\mathbf{m}, \Sigma$) $\not\subseteq \mathcal{C} \cup \mathcal{S}_\tau$, or
  − Open(gmsk, $\mathbf{m}, \Sigma$) = $\mathcal{A}$, $\mathcal{A} \cap \mathcal{C} = \emptyset$
    and $\mathbf{m} \notin \mathrm{span}(\bigcup_{i \in \mathcal{A}} \mathcal{S}_{\tau,i})$
Return 0

Fig. 10. Security game $\mathbf{Exp}_{\Sigma,A}^{c\text{-tr}}(1^\lambda, 1^\kappa)$ for c-traceability

---

A reasonable notion of traceability should in particular imply unforgeability. If one removes the adversary's access to $\mathcal{O}$Corrupt and provides only the group public key gpk instead of the group manager's secret key gmsk, then $\mathbf{Exp}_{\Sigma,A}^{c\text{-tr}}(1^\lambda, 1^\kappa)$ roughly equals $\mathbf{Exp}_{\Sigma,A}^{\mathsf{unf}'}(1^\lambda)$ as defined in Fig. 2. However, according to Remark 6, to obtain equivalence to the more general security experiment $\mathbf{Exp}_{\Sigma,A}^{\mathsf{unf}}(1^\lambda)$ as defined in Fig. 1, the signatures must in addition be context hiding. But this property is always implied by the anonymity of a LH-GSig scheme. Thus, by a proof similar to that of Lemma A.4 in [1], one can replace the oracles $\mathcal{O}$Sign, $\mathcal{O}$DeriveSign and $\mathcal{O}$Reveal in $\mathbf{Exp}_{\Sigma,A}^{\mathsf{unf}}(1^\lambda)$ with the single oracle $\mathcal{O}$GSig as in $\mathbf{Exp}_{\Sigma,A}^{c\text{-tr}}(1^\lambda, 1^\kappa)$. So our traceability notion implies indeed a general variant of unforgeability.

Remark 23. One-time linearly-homomorphic signatures (without tags) have the general problem that everyone can create a signature for any message in the span of previously signed messages. Therefore, the more signatures are available, the less meaningful individual signatures become. To overcome this problem, one introduces tags and allows aggregation only if signatures were created with respect to the same tag. In this way, the number of signatures that can be combined is decreased, and individual signatures gain more significance.

The tracing mechanism in our LH-GSig model faces a very similar issue. Indeed, the fact of being traced becomes less significant the more signatures are available, which is due to basic attacks of the following shape: suppose two honest signers B and C have published signatures Σ_B and Σ_C of respective messages $\mathbf{m}_B$ and $\mathbf{m}_C$. Whenever a malicious signer A wants to sign an evil message $\mathbf{m}_A$, it may instead sign $\mathbf{m}_A - (\mathbf{m}_B + \mathbf{m}_C)$ and combine that signature with Σ_B and Σ_C to obtain a signature for $\mathbf{m}_A$. Every signature produced in this way traces back to A, B and C, and the tracing authority has no chance to identify the malicious signer among these three.

We think that this weakness in the traceability should be seen in the same spirit as the previously mentioned lack of significance in the context of general linearly-homomorphic signatures. Therefore, it seems natural to defeat attacks like the one described above by applying the same countermeasures, i.e. to introduce tags (such as a time stamp). This lowers the number of signatures available during a certain time period and, in particular, it prevents the malicious signer A from reusing the signatures Σ_B and Σ_C forever. In many practical scenarios it seems unlikely that a malicious signer knows signatures of the same (honest) signers in every time interval. However, if the malicious signer mixes its signature in each time interval with signatures from different signers (or it does not mix its signatures at all), then A will soon be identified as the unique common point. A second countermeasure is discussed in the full version [11].

7   Generic Construction of a LH-GSig Scheme

7.1   Properties of LH-Sig Schemes

We introduce two properties of LH-Sig schemes that we exploit in our LH-GSig construction.

Zero-Signability. Note that signatures of the zero vector are never considered a valid forgery in the security game $\mathbf{Exp}^{\mathrm{unf}}_{\Sigma, A}(1^\lambda)$ (Fig. 1). Thus, the definition of LH-Sig schemes does not preclude signatures of the zero vector to be efficiently computable without knowledge of the signing key, but it does not require it either. If signatures of the zero vector can be computed under any tag, then we call a LH-Sig scheme zero-signable.

Definition 24 (Zero-Signability). *A LH-Sig scheme* Σ = (Setup, KeyGen, Sign, DeriveSign, Verify) *with message space* $\mathbb{G}^n$ *and tag space* $\mathcal{T}$ *is called zero-signable if there exists a polynomial-time algorithm* ZSign *of the following shape:*

ZSign(pk, τ): *On input a public key* pk *and a tag* $\tau \in \mathcal{T}$, *this algorithm returns a signature* Σ *on* $\mathbf{0}^{(n)}$ *under* τ *that is valid with respect to* pk.

Universality. We consider a LH-Sig scheme Σ = (Setup, KeyGen, Sign, DeriveSign, Verify). Let (sk, pk) $\leftarrow$ KeyGen(Setup(1^λ)). Abusing notation, Sign(sk, τ, $\mathbf{M}$) denotes the set of all signatures output by the Sign algorithm on input (sk, τ, $\mathbf{M}$) with a nonzero probability. A signature Σ on a message $\mathbf{M}$ is called *universal* with respect to sk if $\Sigma \in \bigcap_{\tau \in \mathcal{T}}$ Sign(sk, τ, $\mathbf{M}$).

The unforgeability implies that the Sign algorithm outputs universal signatures only with negligible probability. Nevertheless, knowledge of the secret key sk may enable an efficient computation of such signatures. In this case, we call the LH-Sig scheme universal.

Definition 25 (Universality). *A LH-Sig scheme* $\Sigma = $ (Setup, KeyGen, Sign, DeriveSign, Verify) *with message space* $\mathbb{G}^n$ *and tag space* τ *is called universal if there exists a polynomial-time algorithm* USign *of the following shape:*

USign(sk, **M**): *On input a signing key* sk *and a message* $\mathbf{M} \in \mathbb{G}^n$, *this algorithm returns a signature* Σ *on* $\mathbf{M}$ *that is universal with respect to* sk.

Note that each OT-LH-Sig scheme is trivially universal. We present a generic conversion of a OT-LH-Sig scheme into a universal, zero-signable LH-Sig scheme with tag space $\mathbb{Z}_p^*$ in the full version [11].

Remark 26. Let $\Sigma' = $ (Setup', KeyGen', Sign', DeriveSign', Verify') be a LH-Sig scheme with message space $\mathcal{M}' = \mathbb{G}^n$ and tag space $\mathcal{T}'$. Then Σ' can easily be turned into a LH-Sig scheme $\Sigma = $ (Setup', KeyGen', Sign, DeriveSign', Verify) with message space $\mathcal{M} = \mathbb{Z}_p^n$ (and tag space $\mathcal{T} = \mathcal{T}'$) by fixing a generator $G \in \mathbb{G}^*$ and replacing scalar messages $\mathbf{m} \in \mathbb{Z}_p^n$ with $\mathbf{m} \cdot G$, i.e. Sign(sk, τ, $\mathbf{m}$) runs Sign'(sk, τ, $\mathbf{m} \cdot G$) and Verify(pk, τ, $\mathbf{m}$, Σ) runs Verify'(pk, τ, $\mathbf{m} \cdot G$, Σ).

For $k \in [n]$, let $\mathbf{e}_k$ denote the k-th standard unit vector in $\mathbb{Z}_p^n$ and let $\mathbf{E}_k = \mathbf{e}_k \cdot G$. If Σ' is zero-signable, then universal signatures $\Sigma_1, \ldots, \Sigma_n$ of $\mathbf{E}_1, \ldots, \mathbf{E}_n$ suffice to sign any message $\mathbf{m} = (m_i)_{i=1}^n \in \mathbb{Z}_p^n$ under an arbitrary tag $\tau \in \mathcal{T}$. Indeed, a signature Σ of $\mathbf{m}$ can be obtained by setting $m_0 = 1$ and computing $\Sigma_0 \leftarrow $ ZSign'(pk, τ) and $\Sigma \leftarrow $ DeriveSign'(pk, τ, $(m_k, \Sigma_k)_{k=0}^n$).

7.2   High-level Description

Our c-traceable LH-GSig scheme with message space $\mathbb{Z}_p^n$ and tag space $\mathcal{T}$ is based on the following building blocks:

- an anonymous, $(c+1)$-correct LST scheme T = (Gen, Trace) for linear subspaces of $\mathbb{G}^\ell$, and
- a universal, zero-signable and context-hiding LH-Sig scheme $\Sigma' = $ (Setup', KeyGen', Sign', DeriveSign', Verify') with message space $\mathbb{G}^{n+\ell}$ and tag space $\mathcal{T}' = \mathcal{T}$, and the additional algorithms ZSign' and USign'.

Let $(\text{tk}, \mathcal{V} = \{\mathbf{V}_i\}_{i=1}^\kappa) \leftarrow \text{Gen}(1^\lambda, 1^\kappa)$ and $(\text{sk}', \text{pk}') \leftarrow \text{KeyGen}'(\text{Setup}'(1^\lambda))$. At a high level, we use the idea of Remark 26 that universal signatures of the unit vectors suffice to sign any message in $\mathbb{Z}_p^n$ under any tag $\tau \in \mathcal{T}$. However, to enable tracing, we provide the i-th group member, for $i \in [\kappa]$, with universal signatures $(\sigma_{i,k})_{k=1}^n$ on $(\mathbf{E}_k \parallel \mathbf{V}_i)_{k=1}^n$ instead of just $(\mathbf{E}_k)_{k=1}^n$. To sign a message $\mathbf{m} = (m_k)_{k=1}^n \in \mathbb{Z}_p^n$, the i-th group member proceeds exactly as in Remark 26. That is, it computes $\sigma_\tau \leftarrow $ ZSign'(pk', τ) and $\sigma \leftarrow $ DeriveSign'(pk, τ, $(m_k, \sigma_{i,k})_{k \in [n] \cup \{\tau\}}$) for $m_\tau = 1$. Then it outputs the signature $\Sigma = (\sigma, \mathbf{C} = \sum_{k=1}^n m_k \cdot \mathbf{V}_i)$, i.e. Σ-signatures are tuples that consists of a Σ'-signature and a vector in $\mathbb{G}^\ell$. For the verification one simply checks that Verify'(pk', τ, $(\mathbf{m} \parallel \mathbf{C})$, σ) = 1.

This method obviously generalizes to signature derivations. Given a tag τ and d tuples $(\omega_j, \Sigma_j = (\sigma_j, \mathbf{C}_j))_{j=1}^d$ where Σ_j is a signature on a message $\mathbf{m}_j$ under τ, one obtains a message on $\mathbf{m} = \sum_{j=1}^d \mathbf{m}_j$ by deriving a Σ'-signature

$\sigma \leftarrow$ DeriveSign$'($pk$', \tau, (\omega_j, \sigma_j)_{j=0}^d)$ and outputting $\Sigma = (\sigma, \mathbf{C} = \sum_{j=1}^d \omega_j \cdot \mathbf{C}_j)$. Note that $\mathbf{C}$ is in the span of $\{\mathbf{C}_j\}_{j=1}^d$. Hence, the LST scheme T can be used to recover all group members who participated in the creation of Σ.

However, this construction is not anonymous. While the first component of a Σ-signature is a signature of the *context-hiding* signature scheme Σ', the second component can be used to link signatures created by the same group members. Therefore, we add a randomization mechanism as described in Remark 18. More precisely, we run $($tk$, \mathcal{V} = \{\mathbf{V}_0, \ldots, \mathbf{V}_\kappa\}) \leftarrow$ Gen$(1^\lambda, 1^{\kappa+1})$ and $\sigma_0 \leftarrow$ USign$'($sk$', (\mathbf{0}^{(n)} \parallel \mathbf{V}_0))$, and include $(\mathbf{V}_0, \sigma_0)$ in the group public key. Given a Σ signature $\Sigma = (\sigma, \mathbf{C})$ on a message $\mathbf{m}$ under a tag τ, one can randomize it by sampling a random scalar $\omega_0 \xleftarrow{\$} \mathbb{Z}_p$ and setting $\tilde{\Sigma} = (\tilde{\sigma}, \tilde{\mathbf{C}})$ for $\tilde{\sigma} \leftarrow$ DeriveSign$'($pk$', \tau, ((1, \sigma), (\omega_0, \sigma_0)))$ and $\tilde{\mathbf{C}} \leftarrow \mathbf{C} + \omega_0 \cdot \mathbf{V}_0$. By the anonymity of the LST scheme T, it follows that $\mathbf{C}$ and $\tilde{\mathbf{C}}$ cannot be linked. Furthermore, since σ_0 is a signature on the vector $(\mathbf{0}^{(n)} \parallel \mathbf{V}_0)$, $\tilde{\sigma}$ is a Σ'-signature on $\mathbf{m} \parallel \tilde{\mathbf{C}}$. This in turn implies that $\tilde{\Sigma} = (\tilde{\sigma}, \tilde{\mathbf{C}})$ is still a Σ-signature on the original message $\mathbf{m}$.

7.3   Our Scheme

Figure 11 depicts our LH-GSig scheme. The LST scheme $\mathsf{T} = ($Gen, Trace$)$ can be instantiated from the construction presented in Fig. 6. For the LH-Sig scheme $\Sigma' = ($Setup$'$, KeyGen$'$, Sign$'$, DeriveSign$'$, Verify$')$, we provide a construction in the full version [11]. While both components are proven secure in the AGM, the security analysis of our (generic) LH-GSig scheme is done in the standard model.

The correctness of verifications follows from the correctness of the underlying LH-Sig scheme Σ'. The c-correctness of openings is a consequence of the $(c+1)$-correctness of the LST scheme T. Security is stated in the following theorems.

Theorem 27. *Let c be a positive integer. If Σ' is unforgeable and T is $(c+1)$-correct, then Σ is c-traceable.*

Theorem 28. *If Σ' is (computationally) context hiding and T is anonymous, then Σ is anonymous. More precisely, it holds that*

$$\mathbf{Adv}_{\Sigma, A}^{\mathrm{ano}}(\lambda, \kappa) \leq \mathbf{Adv}_{\mathsf{T}}^{\mathrm{ano}}(\lambda, \kappa + 1) + Q \cdot \mathbf{Adv}_{\Sigma'}^{\mathrm{ch}}(\lambda)$$

for any PPT adversary A, where Q is the number of queries to $\mathcal{O}$FoD and $\mathbf{Adv}_{\Sigma, A}^{\mathrm{ch}}(\lambda)$ the best advantage a PPT algorithm can get in distinguishing the distributions $\mathcal{D}_0$ and $\mathcal{D}_1$ in the definition of context hiding (Definition 5).

The theorems are proven in the full version [11].

Note that we could slightly relax the condition on Σ' to be universal. For the scheme to work, it is not important that the signatures σ_0 and $(\sigma_{i,k})_{i \in [\kappa], k \in [n]}$ are valid with respect to each tag $\tau \in \mathcal{T}$. In fact, they do not even have to be valid with respect to any tag, as their validity is never checked. In the scheme,

$$
\begin{aligned}
&\underline{\mathsf{GKg}(1^\lambda, 1^\kappa):} \\
&(\mathsf{sk}', \mathsf{pk}') \leftarrow \mathsf{KeyGen}'(\mathsf{Setup}'(1^\lambda)) \\
&\text{Choose any } G \in \mathbb{G}^* \\
&(\mathsf{tk}, \{\mathbf{V}_i\}_{i=0}^\kappa) \leftarrow \mathsf{Gen}(1^\lambda, 1^{\kappa+1}) \\
&\sigma_0 \leftarrow \mathsf{USign}'(\mathsf{sk}', (\mathbf{0}^{(n)} \parallel \mathbf{V}_0)) \\
&\text{For } i \in [\kappa]: \\
&\quad (\sigma_{i,k} \leftarrow \mathsf{USign}'(\mathsf{sk}', \mathbf{e}_k \cdot G \parallel \mathbf{V}_i))_{k=1}^n \\
&\quad \mathsf{gsk}[i] \leftarrow ((\sigma_{i,k})_{k=1}^n, \mathbf{V}_i) \\
&\mathsf{gpk} \leftarrow (\mathsf{pk}', G, \mathbf{V}_0, \sigma_0); \ \mathsf{gmsk} \leftarrow \mathsf{tk} \\
&\text{Return } (\mathsf{gpk}, \mathsf{gmsk}, \mathbf{gsk})
\end{aligned}
$$

$$
\begin{aligned}
&\underline{\mathsf{GDrv}(\mathsf{gpk}, \tau, (\omega_j, \Sigma_j = (\sigma_j, \mathbf{C}_j))_{j=1}^d):} \\
&\omega_0 \xleftarrow{\$} \mathbb{Z}_p; \ \mathbf{C}_0 \leftarrow \mathbf{V}_0; \ \mathbf{C} \leftarrow \sum_{j=0}^d \omega_j \cdot \mathbf{C}_j \\
&\sigma \leftarrow \mathsf{DeriveSign}'(\mathsf{pk}', \tau, (\omega_j, \sigma_j)_{j=0}^d) \\
&\text{Return } \Sigma \leftarrow (\sigma, \mathbf{C})
\end{aligned}
$$

$$
\begin{aligned}
&\underline{\mathsf{GSig}(\mathsf{gsk}[i] = ((\sigma_k)_{k=1}^n, \mathbf{V}), \tau, \mathbf{m}):} \\
&(\Sigma_k \leftarrow (\sigma_k, \mathbf{V}))_{k=1}^n \\
&\sigma_\tau \leftarrow \mathsf{ZSign}'(\mathsf{pk}', \tau); \ \Sigma_\tau \leftarrow (\sigma_\tau, \mathbf{0}^{(\ell)}) \\
&\text{Parse } \mathbf{m} = (m_k)_{k=1}^n; \ m_\tau \leftarrow 1 \\
&\Sigma \leftarrow \mathsf{GDrv}(\mathsf{gpk}, \tau, (m_k, \Sigma_k)_{k \in [n] \cup \{\tau\}}) \\
&\text{Return } \Sigma
\end{aligned}
$$

$$
\begin{aligned}
&\underline{\mathsf{GVf}(\mathsf{gpk}, \tau, \mathbf{m}, \Sigma = (\sigma, \mathbf{C})):} \\
&\text{Return } b \leftarrow \mathsf{Verify}'(\mathsf{pk}', \tau, \mathbf{m} \cdot G \parallel \mathbf{C}, \sigma)
\end{aligned}
$$

$$
\begin{aligned}
&\underline{\mathsf{Open}(\mathsf{gmsk}, \tau, \mathbf{m}, \Sigma = (\sigma, \mathbf{C})):} \\
&\text{If } \mathsf{GVf}(\mathsf{gpk}, \tau, \mathbf{m}, \Sigma) = 0, \text{ return } \bot \\
&\mathcal{A} \leftarrow \mathsf{Trace}(\mathsf{gmsk}, \mathbf{C}) \\
&\text{Return } \mathcal{A} \setminus \{0\}
\end{aligned}
$$

Fig. 11. Our LH-GSig scheme

they are only passed to the DeriveSign′ algorithm together with another signature σ_τ which is valid with respect to a tag $\tau \in \mathcal{T}$. Therefore, it is sufficient to require that this derivation works correctly and returns a signature also valid with respect to τ.

Also, note that OT-LH-Sig schemes are in particular universal. Hence, each zero-signable and context-hiding OT-LH-Sig can be used to construct a one-time LH-GSig scheme.

Some efficiency improvements are discussed in the full version [11].

7.4 Efficiency

The size of signatures in the c-traceable LH-GSig scheme Σ presented in Fig. 11 depends mainly on the instantiation of the underlying LH-Sig and LST schemes denoted Σ' and T respectively. More precisely, a Σ-signature consists of a Σ'-signature and a vector $\mathbf{C}$ with entries in $\mathbb{G}_1$ whose dimension depends on T. In the full version [11], we present an instantiation for Σ' where signatures consist of a small constant number of elements of $\mathbb{G}_1$. For T, if one uses our LST scheme presented in Sects. 4 and 5, then signatures consist of $\Theta(c^2 \cdot \log(\kappa/\varepsilon))$ group elements where κ denotes the size of the group and ε is the maximum acceptable probability that the tracing will fail. On the other hand, a naive solution which uses a LST scheme based on the "naive FIPP code" described in Remark 11 (i.e. each group member puts its identity in a separate coordinate) would yield signatures of size $\mathcal{O}(\kappa)$ group elements. Thus, Σ-signatures in the naive solution grow asymptotically faster (in the size of the group) than in our construction.

Acknowledgments. This work was supported by the France 2030 ANR Project ANR-22-PECY-003 SecureCompute.

References

1. Ahn, J.H., Boneh, D., Camenisch, J., Hohenberger, S., shelat, a., Waters, B.: Computing on authenticated data. Cryptology ePrint Archive, Report 2011/096 (2011). https://eprint.iacr.org/2011/096
2. Bellare, M., Micciancio, D., Warinschi, B.: Foundations of group signatures: formal definitions, simplified requirements, and a construction based on general assumptions. In: Biham, E. (ed.) EUROCRYPT 2003. LNCS, vol. 2656, pp. 614–629. Springer, Heidelberg (2003). https://doi.org/10.1007/3-540-39200-9_38
3. Boneh, D., Boyen, X., Shacham, H.: Short group signatures. In: Franklin, M. (ed.) CRYPTO 2004. LNCS, vol. 3152, pp. 41–55. Springer, Heidelberg (2004). https://doi.org/10.1007/978-3-540-28628-8_3
4. Boneh, D., Freeman, D., Katz, J., Waters, B.: Signing a linear subspace: signature schemes for network coding. In: Jarecki, S., Tsudik, G. (eds.) PKC 2009. LNCS, vol. 5443, pp. 68–87. Springer, Heidelberg (2009). https://doi.org/10.1007/978-3-642-00468-1_5
5. Boneh, D., Shaw, J.: Collusion-secure fingerprinting for digital data. In: Coppersmith, D. (ed.) CRYPTO 1995. LNCS, vol. 963, pp. 452–465. Springer, Heidelberg (1995). https://doi.org/10.1007/3-540-44750-4_36
6. Chaum, D., van Heyst, E.: Group signatures. In: Davies, D.W. (ed.) EUROCRYPT 1991. LNCS, vol. 547, pp. 257–265. Springer, Heidelberg (1991). https://doi.org/10.1007/3-540-46416-6_22
7. Chor, B., Fiat, A., Naor, M.: Tracing traitors. In: Desmedt, Y.G. (ed.) CRYPTO 1994. LNCS, vol. 839, pp. 257–270. Springer, Heidelberg (1994). https://doi.org/10.1007/3-540-48658-5_25
8. ElGamal, T.: A public key cryptosystem and a signature scheme based on discrete logarithms. In: Blakley, G.R., Chaum, D. (eds.) CRYPTO 1984. LNCS, vol. 196, pp. 10–18. Springer, Heidelberg (1985). https://doi.org/10.1007/3-540-39568-7_2
9. Fuchsbauer, G., Kiltz, E., Loss, J.: The algebraic group model and its applications. In: Shacham, H., Boldyreva, A. (eds.) CRYPTO 2018. LNCS, vol. 10992, pp. 33–62. Springer, Cham (2018). https://doi.org/10.1007/978-3-319-96881-0_2
10. Hollmann, H.D., van Lint, J.H., Linnartz, J.P., Tolhuizen, L.M.: On codes with the identifiable parent property. J. Comb. Theory Ser. A **82**(2), 121–133 (1998)
11. Hébant, C., Pointcheval, D., Schädlich, R.: Tracing a linear subspace: Application to linearly-homomorphic group signatures. Cryptology ePrint Archive, Report 2023/138 (2023). https://eprint.iacr.org/2023/138
12. Libert, B., Peters, T., Joye, M., Yung, M.: Linearly homomorphic structure-preserving signatures and their applications. In: Canetti, R., Garay, J.A. (eds.) CRYPTO 2013. LNCS, vol. 8043, pp. 289–307. Springer, Heidelberg (2013). https://doi.org/10.1007/978-3-642-40084-1_17
13. Tardos, G.: Optimal probabilistic fingerprint codes. In: 35th ACM STOC, pp. 116–125. ACM Press (2003). https://doi.org/10.1145/780542.780561

Isogenies

SCALLOP: Scaling the CSI-FiSh

Luca De Feo[1] , Tako Boris Fouotsa[2] , Péter Kutas[3,4],
Antonin Leroux[5,11,12,13](✉), Simon-Philipp Merz[6], Lorenz Panny[7],
and Benjamin Wesolowski[8,9,10]

[1] IBM Research Europe, Zürich, Switzerland
scallop@defeo.lu
[2] EPFL, Lausanne, Switzerland
tako.fouotsa@epfl.ch
[3] Eötvös Loránd University, Budapest, Hungary
[4] University of Birmingham, Birmingham, UK
p.kutas@bham.ac.uk
[5] DGA-MI, Bruz, France
[6] Royal Holloway, University of London, Egham, UK
research@simon-philipp.com
[7] Academia Sinica, Taipei, Taiwan
lorenz@yx7.cc
[8] Univ. Bordeaux, CNRS, Bordeaux INP, IMB, UMR 5251,
33400 Talence, France
[9] INRIA, IMB, UMR 5251, 33400 Talence, France
[10] ENS de Lyon, CNRS, UMPA, UMR 5669, Lyon, France
[11] IRMAR, Université de Rennes, Rennes, France
[12] LIX, CNRS, Ecole Polytechnique, Institut Polytechnique de Paris,
Palaiseau, France
antonin.leroux@polytechnique.org
[13] INRIA, Saclay, France

Abstract. We present SCALLOP: SCALable isogeny action based on
Oriented supersingular curves with Prime conductor, a new group action
based on isogenies of supersingular curves. Similarly to CSIDH and
OSIDH, we use the group action of an imaginary quadratic order's class
group on the set of oriented supersingular curves. Compared to CSIDH,
the main benefit of our construction is that it is easy to compute the
class-group structure; this data is required to uniquely represent — and
efficiently act by — arbitrary group elements, which is a requirement in,
e.g., the CSI-FiSh signature scheme by Beullens, Kleinjung and Vercauteren. The index-calculus algorithm used in CSI-FiSh to compute

Author list in alphabetical order; see https://ams.org/profession/leaders/CultureStat
ement04.pdf. This research was funded in part by the EPSRC under grants
EP/S01361X/1 and EP/P009301/1, the National Research, Development and Innovation Office within the Quantum Information National Laboratory of Hungary, the
János Bolyai Research Scholarship of the Hungarian Academy of Sciences and by the
ÚNKP-22-5 New National Excellence Program, the Agence Nationale de la Recherche
under grant ANR MELODIA (ANR-20-CE40-0013), and the France 2030 program
under grant agreement No. ANR-22-PETQ-0008 PQ-TLS. Date of this document:
2023-04-05.

A. Boldyreva and V. Kolesnikov (Eds.): PKC 2023, LNCS 13940, pp. 345–375, 2023.
https://doi.org/10.1007/978-3-031-31368-4_13

the class-group structure has complexity $L(1/2)$, ruling out class groups much larger than CSIDH-512, a limitation that is particularly problematic in light of the ongoing debate regarding the quantum security of cryptographic group actions.

Hoping to solve this issue, we consider the class group of a quadratic order of large prime conductor inside an imaginary quadratic field of small discriminant. This family of quadratic orders lets us easily determine the size of the class group, and, by carefully choosing the conductor, even exercise significant control on it — in particular supporting highly smooth choices. Although evaluating the resulting group action still has subexponential asymptotic complexity, a careful choice of parameters leads to a practical speedup that we demonstrate in practice for a security level equivalent to CSIDH-1024, a parameter currently firmly out of reach of index-calculus-based methods. However, our implementation takes 35 s (resp. 12.5 min) for a single group-action evaluation at a CSIDH-512-equivalent (resp. CSIDH-1024-equivalent) security level, showing that, while feasible, the SCALLOP group action does not achieve realistically usable performance yet.

1   Introduction

Isogeny-based cryptography was first proposed by Couveignes [21] in 1996, but not published at the time. The same idea was independently rediscovered by Rostovtsev and Stolbunov later [50]. Couveignes and Rostovtsev–Stolbunov (CRS) suggested a post-quantum key exchange based on the group action of an ideal class group on a class of ordinary elliptic curves. However, this scheme is very slow.

A major breakthrough for isogeny-based group actions was the invention of CSIDH [13]. The construction follows a similar blueprint as the CRS key exchange but the class group of an imaginary quadratic order acts on the set of supersingular elliptic curves defined over a prime field, rather, and this makes the scheme a lot faster for various reasons. CSIDH was the first efficient post-quantum action and its efficient public-key validation gives rise to non-interactive key exchange. While it is well known that CSIDH, like CRS, is susceptible to a quantum subexponential attack, the concrete size of parameters to achieve a certain security level has been a matter of debate [10,16,48].

Colò and Kohel generalized CSIDH-like schemes to obtain the "Oriented Supersingular Isogeny Diffie–Hellman" (OSIDH) key exchange [19], introducing the notion of orientations to handle the action of a generic class group on a set of supersingular curves. Since then, the OSIDH key exchange has been broken for the suggested parameters [23], but its generalisation of CSIDH remains a useful framework.

The first attempt to build isogeny-based signatures was outlined in Stolbunov's PhD thesis, where the Fiat–Shamir transform is applied to a Σ-protocol [52]. However, to instantiate the scheme it would be necessary to sample uniformly from the acting class group and, crucially, to compute a canonical representative for each class group element efficiently. The first requirement could be approximated sufficiently well, but the second one remained elusive. Instead of using canonical representatives, De Feo and Galbraith proposed the signature scheme SeaSign [26] which uses an abundantly redundant representation together with rejection sampling to make the distribution of class group elements independent from the secret key. Though it provides short signatures, signing time is still impractical for the fastest parameter set (2 min), even after further optimisations by Decru, Panny and Vercauteren [30].

Computing the class group structure of the acting group solves both challenges left to instantiate Stolbunov's signature scheme. By providing a simple canonical representation for class group elements, it also gives an easy way to sample uniformly, instead of resorting to expensive statistical methods. In 2019, Beullens, Kleinjung and Vercauteren [9] conducted a record breaking class group computation to find the class group structure and relation lattice of the class group of the imaginary quadratic field corresponding to the smallest CSIDH parameter set, CSIDH-512. This let them efficiently instantiate Stolbunov's signature, leading to CSI-FiSh [9]. CSI-FiSh is very efficient and is a building block for many other schemes such as threshold signatures [11,22,29], ring signatures [8,40]) and group signatures [7,18]. Furthermore, it is a basis for other primitives such as updatable encryption [42].

Unfortunately, the best known algorithms to compute the class group structure have complexity $L_\Delta(1/2)$, using the classic L-notation

$$L_x(\alpha) = \exp\left(O\left((\log x)^\alpha (\log\log x)^{1-\alpha}\right)\right),$$

where Δ denotes the discriminant of the number field. Instantiating CSI-FiSh for larger security levels of CSIDH would require class group computations that are currently out of reach. Yet, especially in light of recent debate about CSIDH's concrete quantum security, it is desirable to have an efficient isogeny-based signature scheme (and all the aforementioned primitives) at higher security levels.

This motivates the search for other isogeny actions that have better control on the class group, it is thus natural to look at orientations different from the one in CSIDH. However, choosing an orientation poses several challenges. First, it is usually hard to compute an orientation even if one knows that the curve is oriented by a particular order as discussed in [25]. Secondly, disclosing the orientation in the public key requires an efficient representation of the orientation. Then, the resulting group action should be efficiently computable. Finally, for a general orientation it is unclear how the structure of the class group can be computed, whereas special orientations may not lead to cryptographically secure group actions (see [19,23] and [2, Theorem 11.4]).

1.1   Contribution

We present SCALLOP, a new isogeny-based group action on supersingular curves. Following a standard approach [13,19], we use the group action of the class group of an imaginary quadratic order on a set of oriented supersingular curves. In an attempt to solve the scaling issue of CSI-FiSh, we explore the situation where the quadratic order $\mathfrak{O}$ of discriminant Δ has a large prime conductor f inside an imaginary quadratic field of very small discriminant d_0, i.e.

$\Delta = f^2 d_0$. There are exact formulas and results to compute the structure of the class group in this case.

To make the computation of the resulting group action efficient, we study how to obtain effective and (hopefully) secure $\mathfrak{O}$-orientations for a generic quadratic order $\mathfrak{O}$, something known only in the special case of CSIDH, where $\mathfrak{O} = \mathbb{Z}[\sqrt{-p}]$, prior to our work. In particular, we introduce a generic framework to evaluate the group action when $\mathfrak{O}$ contains a generator α such that the principal ideal $\mathfrak{O}\alpha$ can be factored as $\mathfrak{L}_1^2\mathfrak{L}_2$ for two ideals $\mathfrak{L}_1, \mathfrak{L}_2$ of smooth coprime norm. We then show how to instantiate this framework when $\mathfrak{O}$ is an order of large prime conductor and we provide an algorithm to perform the computation as efficiently as possible in this context. In particular, we provide a way to choose the conductor such that $\mathfrak{O}$ has a generator α of the correct form with essentially optimal size. As is customary in isogeny-based cryptography, this setup also requires to carefully select the characteristic of the finite field $\mathbb{F}_p$ for an efficient evaluation of the group action.

To generate concrete parameters, we also provide an efficient algorithm to generate an initial effective $\mathfrak{O}$-orientation, something that can always be done in polynomial time (using the maximal-order-to-supersingular-elliptic-curve algorithm from [32]) but might be very costly in practice.

Our new group action still requires a precomputation of complexity $L_\Delta(1/2)$: Here the main algorithmic task is to compute a *lattice of relations* for the class group, which can be used later to obtain a "short representative" of any given class in $\mathrm{Cl}(\mathfrak{O})$. Computing relations in the class group amounts to solving discrete logarithms in a subgroup of some finite field (unrelated to $\mathbb{F}_p$), whose order we can somewhat control by choosing the conductor.

Despite the fact that our choice of conductor is very constrained by the requirements on the generator α (see Sect. 5.1), we show that we have a search space large enough to obtain a fairly smooth class number. Thus, we were able to instantiate the SCALLOP group action for security levels that remain entirely out of reach for the CSI-FiSh approach, using only modest computational resources. Concretely, we give parameters for our group action with security comparable to CSIDH-512 and CSIDH-1024. This leads to an isogeny-based Fiat–Shamir signature analogous to CSI-FiSh for parameters twice as large as CSI-FiSh.

1.2   Technical Overview

We give below a list of tasks and constraints required to create a setup analogous to CSI-FiSh. Then, we briefly explain how our new group action is evaluated and how it compares to CSI-FiSh.

We distinguish two phases in setting-up an isogeny-based group action: an offline and an online one. The offline phase is the main novelty introduced in CSI-FiSh compared to CSIDH [13]. It is performed just once at parameter generation. We do not need it to be efficient, but we want it to be feasible. This precomputation is crucial to the efficiency of the online phase, which is executed at every group action evaluation (hence dozens of times for each signature) and needs to be as fast as possible.

In the following, let $\mathfrak{O}$ be an imaginary quadratic order.

Evaluating Isogeny Group Actions. Abstractly, a group action is defined by a group G, a set X, and a map $\star : G \times X \to X$ satisfying some set of axioms. Algorithmically, we ask that elements of G and X have a representation, and that for any $g \in G$ and $x \in X$ it is feasible to compute $g \star x$. These, and other requirements, have been formalized under the names of Hard Homogenous Space (HHS) [21] or Effective Group Action (EGA) [1].

In the specific case of isogeny actions, the set X is a set of elliptic curves, which can be represented by an appropriate invariant, e.g. the j-invariant. The group $G = \mathrm{Cl}(\mathfrak{O})$ tends to be cyclic, or nearly cyclic, thus its elements could be uniquely represented as powers $\mathfrak{a}^e$ of some generator $\mathfrak{a}$. However it is not true in general that $\mathfrak{a}^e \star E$ can be efficiently evaluated for every exponent e and every curve E. Instead, there exist a list of ideals $\mathfrak{l}_1, \dots, \mathfrak{l}_n$ of small norm, spanning $\mathrm{Cl}(\mathfrak{O})$ and such that the actions $\mathfrak{l}_i \star E$ can be efficiently evaluated for every $\mathfrak{l}_i$ and every E. Then, the action of any ideal of the form $\mathfrak{b} = \prod_{i=1}^n \mathfrak{l}_i^{e_i}$ can be efficiently evaluated as soon as the *exponent vector* $(e_1, \dots, e_n) \in \mathbb{Z}^n$ has small norm. This setup is called a Restricted EGA (REGA) in [1].

To go from a REGA to an EGA, we need a way to rewrite any ideal class $\mathfrak{a}^e$ as a product $\mathfrak{a}^e = \prod_{i=1}^n \mathfrak{l}_i^{e_i}$ with small exponents. The main advance in CSI-FiSh was the computation of the *lattice of relations* of the ideals $\mathfrak{l}_1, \dots, \mathfrak{l}_n$ in CSIDH-512, i.e. the lattice $\mathcal{L}$ spanned by the vectors $(e_1, \dots, e_n)$ such that $\prod \mathfrak{l}_i^{e_i}$ is principal. If the $\mathfrak{l}_i$ span $\mathrm{Cl}(\mathfrak{O})$, then $\mathbb{Z}^n / \mathcal{L}$ is isomorphic to $\mathrm{Cl}(\mathfrak{O})$. Then, assuming $\mathfrak{a} = \mathfrak{l}_1$, finding a decomposition of $\mathfrak{a}^e$ with short exponents amounts to solving a Closest Vector Problem (CVP) in the lattice of relations for the vector $(e, 0, \dots, 0)$.

Our aim is to replicate this strategy for the relation lattices associated to the class groups we are interested in.

The Offline Phase. The goal of this phase is to precompute the relation lattice of the class group $\mathrm{Cl}(\mathfrak{O})$, and produce a reduced basis of it. The main steps are:

1. Compute the class number and the structure of the class group.
2. Generate the lattice of relations $\mathcal{L}$.
3. Compute a reduced basis of $\mathcal{L}$ suitable for solving approximate-CVP.

In CSI-FiSh, the first item is obtained as a byproduct of the second, which is performed using index calculus, for an asymptotic cost of $L_\Delta(1/2)$. The last step is a standard lattice-basis reduction (typically done using BKZ); although, depending on the approximation factor, this step may even have exponential complexity, it is the fastest one in practice.

In this work we change the way the first two steps are performed. First, we choose $\mathfrak{O}$ so that the class group structure comes for free: We select a quadratic order $\mathfrak{O} = \mathbb{Z} + f\mathfrak{O}_0$ of large conductor f inside a maximal quadratic order $\mathfrak{O}_0$ of small discriminant d_0. Computing the class group structure, then, amounts to factoring f, which we choose to be a prime.

Secondly, by choosing $\mathfrak{O}_0$ and f carefully, not only can we compute the group structure, but we can even control it to some extent. In particular, we search for the prime f such that the class number of $\mathfrak{O}$, given by $f - \left(\frac{d_0}{f}\right)$, is some-what smooth, so that computing discrete logarithms in $\mathrm{Cl}(\mathfrak{O})$ becomes feasible. Then, instead of using index calculus, we directly obtain the lattice of relations by computing the discrete logarithm relationships between the generators $\mathfrak{l}_1, \ldots, \mathfrak{l}_n$. Asymptotically, an $L_f(1/2)$-long search for f is expected to yield an $L_f(1/2)$-smooth class number: At this level of detail in the analysis, no obvious improvement over index calculus stands out, however the constants hidden in the exponents turn out to be much more favorable to our setup, as our experiments confirm.

The final step, BKZ reduction, is unchanged.

In the Online Phase. we evaluate the group action. The inputs are an oriented curve E and an integer e, the output is the oriented curve $\mathfrak{a}^e \star E$, where $\mathfrak{a}$ is some fixed generator (e.g. $\mathfrak{a} = \mathfrak{l}_1$). This phase consists of two steps:

1. Solving approximate-CVP to find a decomposition $\mathfrak{a}^e = \prod_i \mathfrak{l}_i^{e_i}$ with small exponents.
2. Using isogeny computations to evaluate $\left(\prod_i \mathfrak{l}_i^{e_i}\right) \star E$.

In SCALLOP the first step is identical to CSI-FiSh: We use Babai's nearest plane algorithm [4] to find a vector close to $(e, 0, \ldots, 0)$. The cost of this step is negligible, however the quality of the output depends on the quality of the basis computed in the offline phase, and has a big impact on the cost of the next step. In practice, the dimension of the lattices we consider is small enough that we can compute a nearly optimal basis, thus the approximation factor for CVP will be rather small. However, from an asymptotic point of view, there is a trade-off between the time spent reducing the lattice in the offline phase, and the approximation factor achieved in the online phase. The break-even point happens at $L(1/2)$, exactly like in CSI-FiSh.

The isogeny computation step is where we deviate most from CSI-FiSh. Indeed in CSI-FiSh there is an implicit orientation by the order $\mathfrak{O} = \mathbb{Z}[\sqrt{-p}]$, which is easily computed via Frobenius endomorphisms. In contrast, in SCAL-LOP we need an explicit representation of the orientation, that we transport along the group action. It is thus not surprising that, for the same parameter sizes, our algorithms are significantly slower than CSI-FiSh. Nonetheless we show there are choices of orientations for which it is at least feasible to run them.

Concretely, we choose a quadratic order $\mathfrak{O}$ that contains a generator α of smooth norm of size roughly equal to $\mathrm{disc}(\mathfrak{O})$ (essentially, the smallest size we could hope for). The orientation is then represented by an endomorphism ω corresponding to the principal ideal $\mathfrak{O}\alpha$, encoded as the composition of two isogenies of degree roughly equal to $\sqrt{\mathrm{disc}(\mathfrak{O})}$. The endomorphism ω plays here the same role as the Frobenius endomorphism in CSI-FiSh: An ideal $\mathfrak{l}_i$ acts through an isogeny of degree ℓ_i whose kernel is stabilized by ω, to compute $\mathfrak{l}_i \star E$ it is thus sufficient to evaluate ω on $E[\ell_i]$ and determine its eigenspaces.

In Sect. 5.1, we justify the concrete choices for $\mathfrak{O}$ in more detail and we present all required precomputations. The full description of the algorithm for the online phase is given in Sect. 5.2.

Organisation of the Paper. The rest of this paper is organized as follows. Section 2 introduces the necessary mathematical background. In Sect. 3, we introduce our generic framework for effective orientation and group action computation. Then, we introduce the security notions related to group actions in Sect. 4. In Sect. 5, we explain in detail how the SCALLOP group action works. In Sect. 6, we discuss the concrete instantiation of the scheme. Finally, we analyze one particular angle of attack against the scheme in Sect. 7.

2 Preliminaries

2.1 Elliptic Curves and Isogenies

Elliptic Curves. In this work we consider elliptic curves defined over a finite field $\mathbb{F}_{p^2}$, which can be represented, for example, by a Weierstrass equation

$$E \; : \; y^2 = x^3 + ax + b, \;\; a, b \in \mathbb{F}_{p^2}.$$

For a field extension k of $\mathbb{F}_{p^2}$, we write $E(k)$ for the group of k-rational points of E. We denote by $[n]P$ the nth scalar multiple of a point P, and by $E[n]$ the n-torsion subgroup of $E(\overline{\mathbb{F}}_{p^2})$, so $E[n] \simeq (\mathbb{Z}/n\mathbb{Z})^2$ as soon as $p \nmid n$.

Isogenies. An *isogeny* $\varphi : E_1 \to E_2$ is a non-constant morphism sending the identity of E_1 to that of E_2. The degree of an isogeny is its degree as a rational map (see [51]). An isogeny of degree d, or d-isogeny, is necessarily *separable* when $p \nmid d$, which implies $d = \# \ker \varphi$. An isogeny is said to be *cyclic* when its kernel is a cyclic group. For any $\varphi : E_1 \to E_2$, there exists a unique dual isogeny $\hat{\varphi} : E_2 \to E_1$, satisfying $\varphi \circ \hat{\varphi} = [\deg(\varphi)]$.

Endomorphism Ring. An isogeny from a curve E to itself, or the constant zero map, is an *endomorphism*. The set $\mathrm{End}(E)$ of all endomorphisms of E forms a ring under addition and composition. For elliptic curves defined over a finite field, $\mathrm{End}(E)$ is isomorphic either to an order of a quadratic imaginary field or a maximal order in a quaternion algebra. In the first case, the curve is said to be *ordinary* and otherwise *supersingular*. We focus on the supersingular case, here, and we write $\mathcal{S}(p)$ for the set of isomorphism classes of supersingular curves defined over a field of characteristic p. It is a finite set containing roughly $p/12$ classes, and each class admits a representative over $\mathbb{F}_{p^2}$. The Frobenius isogeny $\pi : (x, y) \to (x^p, y^p)$ is the only inseparable isogeny between supersingular curves and it has degree p. We write $\pi : E \to E^p$. For any supersingular curve E we have $\mathrm{End}(E) \cong \mathrm{End}(E^p)$, but $E \cong E^p$ if and only if E has an isomorphic model over $\mathbb{F}_p$.

A concrete example: $j = 1728$. Let $p \equiv 3 \pmod 4$, and let $\mathcal{E}_0/\mathbb{F}_{p^2}$ be the curve $y^2 = x^3 + x$ of j-invariant 1728. Its endomorphism ring is isomorphic to the maximal order $\mathcal{O}_0 = \langle 1, i, \frac{i+j}{2}, \frac{1+k}{2} \rangle$ with $i^2 = -1$, $j^2 = -p$ and $k = ij$. Moreover, we have explicit endomorphisms π and ι such that $\mathrm{End}(E_0) = \langle 1, \iota, \frac{\iota+\pi}{2}, \frac{1+\iota\pi}{2} \rangle$, where π is the Frobenius isogeny and ι is the map $(x, y) \mapsto (-x, \sqrt{-1}y)$.

2.2 Representing and Evaluating Isogenies

Vélu's formulas [53] let us compute any separable isogeny φ of degree D, given $\ker \varphi$. They take $\widetilde{O}(\sqrt{D})$ operations over the field of definition of $\ker \varphi$ [6]. An isogeny of degree D can be decomposed into a sequence of isogenies of degrees the prime factors of D, thus the efficiency of any isogeny computation mainly depends on the largest prime factor $\ell | D$, and the size of the field extension containing $E[\ell] \cap \ker \varphi$. Hence, we will focus on isogenies of smooth degree where the related torsion groups $E[\ell]$ are defined over $\mathbb{F}_{p^2}$.

In practice, we encode cyclic D-isogenies as tuples (E, P), where P is a generator of $\ker \phi$. We call this a *kernel representation*. It can be compressed to only $O(\log(p) + \log(D))$ bits using techniques similar to SIDH key compression [3, 20, 46, 56] (even when P is defined over a large field extension of $\mathbb{F}_{p^2}$). Such compression becomes relevant when large degree isogenies are exchanged as part of a key agreement message or cryptographic signature.

Pullback and Push-forward. Let us take two coprime integers A, B. Any isogeny of degree AB can be factored in two ways as $\varphi_A \circ \varphi_B$ or $\psi_B \circ \psi_A$, where φ_A, ψ_A (resp. φ_B, ψ_B) have degree A (resp. B). This creates a commutative diagram, where $\ker \varphi_A = \varphi_B(\ker \psi_A)$ and $\ker \psi_B = \psi_A(\ker \varphi_B)$. Given ψ_A and φ_B we define φ_A (resp. ψ_B) as the *pushforward* of ψ_A through φ_B (resp. φ_B through ψ_A), which we denote by $\varphi_A = [\varphi_B]_*\psi_A$ (resp. $\psi_B = [\psi_A]_*\varphi_B$). There is also a dual notion of *pullback*, denoted by $[\cdot]^*\cdot$, so that $\psi_A = [\varphi_B]^*\varphi_A$ and $\varphi_B = [\psi_A]^*\psi_B$.

2.3 Orientation of Supersingular Curves and Ideal Group Action

For the rest of this article, we fix a quadratic imaginary field K and a quadratic order $\mathfrak{O}$ of discriminant $D < 0$ in K. We will consider primitive $\mathfrak{O}$-orientations of supersingular curves. The notion of orientation in Definition 1 below corresponds to that of *primitive orientation with a p-orientation* in [19], and it is equivalent under the Deuring correspondence to *optimal embeddings* of quadratic orders inside maximal orders of $B_{p,\infty}$. The same notion is referred to as normalized optimal embeddings in [5].

Definition 1. *For any elliptic curve E, a K-orientation is a ring homomorphism $\iota : K \hookrightarrow \mathrm{End}(E) \otimes \mathbb{Q}$. A K-orientation induces an $\mathfrak{O}$-orientation if $\iota(\mathfrak{O}) = \mathrm{End}(E) \cap \iota(K)$. In that case, the pair (E, ι) is called a $\mathfrak{O}$-oriented curve and E is an $\mathfrak{O}$-orientable curve.*

In what follows, we consider the elements of $\mathcal{S}(p)/\pi$ rather than $\mathcal{S}(p)$ because the Frobenius π creates two orientations (one in E and one in $E^{(p)}$) from each optimal embedding of $\mathfrak{O}$ in a maximal quaternion order of $B_{p,\infty}$. Note that this is not the convention taken in [47, 55], where orientations are not considered up to Galois conjugacy.

Definition 2. *$\mathcal{S}_{\mathfrak{O}}(p)$ is the set of $\mathfrak{O}$-oriented curves (E, ι) up to isomorphisms and Galois conjugacy.*

The following proposition follows from the results proven by Onuki [47, Proposition 3.2, Proposition 3.3, Theorem 3.4] and gives a way to compute $\#\mathcal{S}_{\mathfrak{O}}(p)$.

Proposition 3. *The set $\mathcal{S}_{\mathfrak{O}}(p)$ is not empty if and only if p does not split in K and does not divide the conductor of $\mathfrak{O}$. When these conditions are satisfied, and p is not ramified in K, we have $\#\mathcal{S}_{\mathfrak{O}}(p) = h(\mathfrak{O})$.*

When p is ramified in K, the situation is a bit more complicated but it can be shown [2] that

$$\#\mathcal{S}_{\mathfrak{O}}(p) \in \left\{ \frac{1}{2}h(\mathfrak{O}), h(\mathfrak{O}) \right\}.$$

When $\mathcal{S}_{\mathfrak{O}}(p)$ is not empty, the set of invertible $\mathfrak{O}$-ideals acts on $\mathfrak{O}$-orientations via an operation that we write $\mathfrak{a} \star (E, \iota) = (E_{\mathfrak{a}}, \iota_{\mathfrak{a}})$. Principal ideals act trivially, thus the operation $\star$ defines a group action of $\mathrm{Cl}(\mathfrak{O})$ on $\mathcal{S}_{\mathfrak{O}}(p)$, which we also denote by $\star$. Onuki proved that this group action is free and transitive.

Concretely, this action is computed using isogenies. For an ideal $\mathfrak{a}$ in $\mathfrak{O}$ and an $\mathfrak{O}$-orientation (E, ι_E), we define $E[\mathfrak{a}] = \bigcap_{\alpha \in \mathfrak{a}} \ker \iota_E(\alpha)$ and write $\varphi_{\mathfrak{a}}^E$ for the isogeny of kernel $E[\mathfrak{a}]$. We have

$$\varphi_{\mathfrak{a}}^E : E \to E_{\mathfrak{a}} = E/E[\mathfrak{a}] \quad \text{and} \quad \iota_{\mathfrak{a}}^E(x) = \frac{1}{n(\mathfrak{a})} \varphi_{\mathfrak{a}}^E \circ \iota(x) \circ \hat{\varphi}_{\mathfrak{a}}^E. \tag{1}$$

When $\mathfrak{a}$ does not factor as $n\mathfrak{b}$ for some integer $n > 1$, we say that $\mathfrak{a}$ is *primitive*. In that case, the corresponding isogeny $\varphi_{\mathfrak{a}}^E$ is cyclic.

It will be useful for us to consider a generator α of $\mathfrak{O}$ (an element such that $\mathfrak{O} = \mathbb{Z}[\alpha]$). In that case, every ideal $\mathfrak{a}$ can be written as $\langle x + \alpha y, n(\mathfrak{a}) \rangle$ for some $x, y \in \mathbb{Z}$. Note that this choice of generator is not unique: if α is a generator, any $\alpha + k$ will also be generators with $k \in \mathbb{Z}$.

Although an orientation may exist it is not always clear how to represent it and compute with it. Informally, an *effective orientation* is one that comes with efficient representations and algorithms. We will give a more formal, and slightly more specific definition in Sect. 3.2.

3   The Generic Group Action

This section introduces our general framework for evaluating group actions of oriented curves. The algorithm we outline below is not designed to be particularly efficient. Later, in Sect. 5.2, we will describe in detail a version and parameter choices that make it somewhat practical.

The key to our technique is having a generator of smooth norm for the quadratic order. To simplify the exposition, we restrict to quadratic orders $\mathfrak{O}$ with a generator α of norm $L_1^2 L_2$, where L_1 and L_2 are two smooth coprime integers and the principal ideal $\mathfrak{O}\alpha$ is equal to $\mathfrak{L}_1^2 \mathfrak{L}_2$ for some primitive ideals $\mathfrak{L}_1, \mathfrak{L}_2$. We will further refine these constraints in Sect. 5.1 for an efficient instantiation.

We now present a few generic properties, then, in Sect. 3.2, we describe how the orientation by such an order can be made effective.

3.1 Factorization of Ideals and Decomposition of Isogenies

We recall from Eq. (1) that if (E, ι_E) is an oriented curve and $\mathfrak{a}$ is an ideal, the action $\mathfrak{a} \star (E, \iota_E)$ is computed via an isogeny denoted by $\varphi_{\mathfrak{a}}^E$.

Proposition 4. *If $\mathfrak{a}$ can be factored as $\mathfrak{a}_1\mathfrak{a}_2$, then the isogeny $\varphi_{\mathfrak{a}}^E$ can be decomposed as $\varphi_{\mathfrak{a}_2}^{E_{\mathfrak{a}_1}} \circ \varphi_{\mathfrak{a}_1}^E$. Moreover, if $\mathfrak{a}_1$ and $\mathfrak{a}_2$ have coprime norms, then $\varphi_{\mathfrak{a}_2}^{E_{\mathfrak{a}_1}} = [\varphi_{\mathfrak{a}_1}^E]_* \varphi_{\mathfrak{a}_2}^E$.*

Proof. The fact that we can factor $\varphi_{\mathfrak{a}}^E$ is standard and the formula to compute $\varphi_{\mathfrak{a}_2}^{E_{\mathfrak{a}_1}}$ follows from Lemma 5 below.   □

Lemma 5. *Let $\mathfrak{a}, \mathfrak{b}$ be two ideals such that $E[\mathfrak{a}] \cap E[\mathfrak{b}] = \{0\}$. Let $\varphi_{\mathfrak{a}}^E : E \to E_{\mathfrak{a}} := E/E[\mathfrak{a}]$ be the isogeny corresponding to the action of $\mathfrak{a}$ on (E, ι_E). Then $E_{\mathfrak{a}}[\mathfrak{b}] = \varphi_{\mathfrak{a}}^E(E[\mathfrak{b}])$.*

Proof. Firstly, let us suppose that $a = n(\mathfrak{a})$ and $b = n(\mathfrak{b})$ are coprime. Then the lemma follows from the usual commutative diagram obtained by decomposing the isogeny $\varphi_{\mathfrak{ab}}^E$ as $\varphi_{\mathfrak{b}}^{E_{\mathfrak{a}}} \circ \varphi_{\mathfrak{a}}^E$ with $E_{\mathfrak{a}}[\mathfrak{b}] = \ker \varphi_{\mathfrak{b}}^{E_{\mathfrak{a}}} = \varphi_{\mathfrak{a}}^E(E[\mathfrak{b}])$.

Secondly, let us suppose that $a = b$. Then since $E[\mathfrak{a}] \cap E[\mathfrak{b}] = \{0\}$, we have $\mathfrak{b} = \bar{\mathfrak{a}}$ and $\mathfrak{b} \star \mathfrak{a} \star (E, \iota_E) = (E, \iota_E)$. It follows that $E_{\mathfrak{a}}[\mathfrak{b}] = E_{\mathfrak{a}}[\bar{\mathfrak{a}}] = \ker \hat{\varphi}_{\mathfrak{a}}^E = \varphi_{\mathfrak{a}}^E(E[\mathfrak{a}]) = \varphi_{\mathfrak{a}}^E(E[\mathfrak{a}] \oplus E[\mathfrak{b}]) = \varphi_{\mathfrak{a}}^E(E[\mathfrak{b}])$.

Lastly, suppose generally that $\gcd(a, b) = c$, writing $a = ca'$, $b = cb'$, $\mathfrak{a} = \mathfrak{c}\mathfrak{a}'$ and $\mathfrak{b} = \bar{\mathfrak{c}}\mathfrak{b}'$. Then $E_{\mathfrak{a}}[\mathfrak{b}] = E_{\mathfrak{a}}[\bar{\mathfrak{c}}] \oplus E_{\mathfrak{a}}[\mathfrak{b}']$. Combining the first case and the second one, we have $E_{\mathfrak{a}}[\bar{\mathfrak{c}}] = \varphi_{\mathfrak{c}}^{E_{\mathfrak{a}'}}(E_{\mathfrak{a}'}[\bar{\mathfrak{c}}]) = \varphi_{\mathfrak{c}}^{E_{\mathfrak{a}'}} \circ \varphi_{\mathfrak{a}'}^E(E[\bar{\mathfrak{c}}]) = \varphi_{\mathfrak{a}}^E(E[\bar{\mathfrak{c}}])$ and $E_{\mathfrak{a}}[\mathfrak{b}'] = \varphi_{\mathfrak{c}}^{E_{\mathfrak{a}'}}(E_{\mathfrak{a}'}[\mathfrak{b}']) = \varphi_{\mathfrak{c}}^{E_{\mathfrak{a}'}} \circ \varphi_{\mathfrak{a}'}^E(E[\mathfrak{b}']) = \varphi_{\mathfrak{a}}^E(E[\mathfrak{b}'])$. Hence $E_{\mathfrak{a}}[\mathfrak{b}] = \varphi_{\mathfrak{a}}^E(E[\mathfrak{b}])$.   □

When using Lemma 5, we will in general specify the tuple $(E, \mathfrak{a}, \mathfrak{b})$ at hand.

3.2 Effective Orientation

Let us take an $\mathfrak{O}$-orientation (E, ι_E). Through ι_E, we obtain an endomorphism $\omega_E \in \mathrm{End}(E)$ as $\iota_E(\alpha)$. This endomorphism ω_E has degree $L_1^2 L_2$ and it can be decomposed as $\omega_E = \hat{\varphi}_{\mathfrak{L}_1^{-1}}^E \circ \varphi_{\mathfrak{L}_1 \mathfrak{L}_2}^E$, as Proposition 4 shows. Thus, we obtain a representation of ω_E from the kernel representations of the two isogenies $\hat{\varphi}_{\mathfrak{L}_1^{-1}}^E$ and $\varphi_{\mathfrak{L}_1 \mathfrak{L}_2}^E$. This idea of decomposing an endomorphism into a cycle of two isogenies is now quite standard in isogeny-based cryptography (see for instance [28,49]).

Formally, we have the following definition.

Definition 6. *Let $(E, \iota_E) \in \mathcal{S}_{\mathfrak{O}}(p)$ where $\mathfrak{O} = \mathbb{Z}[\alpha]$ with $\alpha = \mathfrak{L}_1^2 \mathfrak{L}_2$. An effective orientation for (E, ι_E) is a tuple $s_E = (E, P_E, Q_E)$ where (E, P_E) and (E, Q_E) are the respective kernel representations of the isogenies $\varphi_{\mathfrak{L}_1 \mathfrak{L}_2}^E$ and $\varphi_{\mathfrak{L}_1}^E$ (of respective degree $L_1 L_2$ and L_1).*

Remark 7. When it comes to using an effective orientation as public key, it is important to represent it in a canonical way. For example, when performing a key exchange with SCALLOP, the shared key (which is an oriented curve), must be canonically represented so that both parties can get the same shared key. Given $s_E = (E, P_E, Q_E)$, one computes canonical generators P'_E and Q'_E of the groups $\langle P_E \rangle$ and $\langle Q_E \rangle$ respectively. The effective representation $s'_E = (E, P'_E, Q'_E)$ is then refered to as the canonical effective representation for (E, ι_E).

Since L_1 and L_2 are coprime, $P_E = R_E + S_E$ where R_E and S_E are points of order L_1 and L_2 respectively. Given P_E, one recovers $R_E = [\lambda_2 L_2]P_E$ and $S_E = [\lambda_1 L_1]P_E$, where λ_1 is the inverse of $L_1 \bmod L_2$ and λ_2 is the inverse of $L_2 \bmod L_1$. Conversely, given R_E and S_E, one recovers $P_E = R_E + S_E$. In some cases, such as the statement and proof of Proposition 9, we may directly assume ω_E is represented as (R_E, S_E, Q_E), for simplicity.

3.3   The Group Action Computation from the Effective Orientation

Let $\mathfrak{a}$ be an ideal of $\mathfrak{O}$, our goal now is to understand how to compute an effective orientation $\omega_{E_\mathfrak{a}}$ for $\mathfrak{a} \star (E, \iota_E)$ from the effective orientation ω_E.

By Proposition 4, we know that we can focus on the case where $\mathfrak{a} = \mathfrak{l}$ is a prime ideal. If we know how to compute $\varphi_{\mathfrak{l}}^E$ and the effective orientation $\omega_{E_\mathfrak{l}}$ for $(E_\mathfrak{l}, \iota_{E_\mathfrak{l}}) = \mathfrak{l} \star (E, \iota_E)$, from $\mathfrak{l}$ and ω_E, then we can recursively compute the action of any ideal $\mathfrak{a}$ from its factorization as a product of prime ideals. So we need to focus on two operations: computing $\varphi_{\mathfrak{l}}^E$ and computing $\omega_{E_\mathfrak{l}}$.

Computation of the Group Action Isogeny. The computation of $\varphi_{\mathfrak{l}}^E$ can be done from $\ker \varphi_{\mathfrak{l}}^E = E[\mathfrak{l}]$ using Vélu's formulas [53]. Thus, the main operation is the computation of $E[\mathfrak{l}]$ from ω_E. Proposition 8 provides this operation.

Proposition 8. *When ℓ is split in $\mathfrak{O} = \mathbb{Z}[\alpha]$, and $\mathfrak{l}$ is a prime ideal above ℓ, there exists $\lambda \in \mathbb{Z}$ such that $\mathfrak{l} = \langle \alpha - \lambda, \ell \rangle$. Then, $\ker \varphi_{\mathfrak{l}}^E = E[\mathfrak{l}] = E[\ell] \cap \ker \rho_E$ where $\rho_E = \omega_E - [\lambda]_E$.*

Proof. It suffices to see that $n(\alpha - \lambda) = \lambda^2 - \lambda \operatorname{tr}(\alpha) + n(\alpha)$ has two solutions modulo ℓ if and only if $\operatorname{disc} \mathfrak{O} = \operatorname{tr}(\alpha)^2 - 4n(\alpha)$ is a non-zero square modulo ℓ which is exactly the case where ℓ splits in $\mathfrak{O}$. The ideal $\langle \alpha - \lambda, \ell \rangle$ has norm ℓ because $\alpha - \lambda \notin \ell\mathfrak{O}$ (because ℓ is split in $\mathfrak{O}$). Then the result follows from the definition of $\varphi_{\mathfrak{l}}^E$. □

The computation of a generator of $\ker \varphi_{\mathfrak{l}}^E$ from Proposition 8 is quite standard in the literature on isogeny-based cryptography. It suffices, for instance, to evaluate $\omega_E - [n(\alpha)/\lambda]$ (or $\omega_E - \operatorname{tr}(\alpha)$ if $\lambda = 0$) on a basis P, Q of $E[\ell]$, then at least one of the two images will generate $E[\mathfrak{l}]$. From this, we derive the kernel representation of $\varphi_{\mathfrak{l}}^E$.

Computation of the New Effective Orientation. Computing $\omega_{E_{\mathfrak{l}}}$ is less straightforward. There are basically two cases depending on whether ℓ is coprime with $n(\alpha) = \deg \omega_E$ or not. The first case is by far the simplest: When ℓ and $n(\alpha)$ are coprime, applying Proposition 4 to $\omega_E = \hat{\varphi}^E_{\mathfrak{L}_1^{-1}} \circ \varphi^E_{\mathfrak{L}_1 \mathfrak{L}_2}$ shows that $\omega_{E_{\mathfrak{l}}} = [\varphi^E_{\mathfrak{l}}]_* \omega_E$. Thus, it suffices to push the generators of $\hat{\varphi}^E_{\mathfrak{L}_1^{-1}}$ and $\varphi^E_{\mathfrak{L}_1 \mathfrak{L}_2}$ through $\varphi^E_{\mathfrak{l}}$ to get a kernel representation for $\omega_{E_{\mathfrak{l}}}$.

The story is more complicated when ℓ and $n(\alpha)$ are not coprime because the pushforward of ω_E is not well-defined in this case. Let us treat the simplified case where $L_1 = \ell$ (and so $n(\alpha) = \ell^2 L_2$ for some L_2 coprime with ℓ), as the generic case can be handled with similar ideas. The full algorithm to handle the generic case is given in Sect. 5.2.

When $n(\alpha) = \ell^2 L_2$, there are two possibilities: either $\mathfrak{L}_1 = \mathfrak{l}$ or $\mathfrak{L}_1 = \mathfrak{l}^{-1}$ as there are no further primitive ideals of norm dividing ℓ. If we have a method to solve the former, we can derive a method to solve the latter by considering the dual of the endomorphism ω_E. Thus, we focus on $\mathfrak{L}_1 = \mathfrak{l}$.

Proposition 9. *Let α be a generator of $\mathfrak{O}$ of norm $\ell^2 L_2$ with $\mathfrak{O}\alpha = \mathfrak{l}^2 \mathfrak{L}_2$ as above. Then $\omega_E = \iota(\alpha)$ can be decomposed as $\hat{\varphi}^E_{\bar{\mathfrak{l}}} \circ \varphi^{E_{\mathfrak{l}}}_{\mathfrak{L}_2} \circ \varphi^E_{\mathfrak{l}}$. Suppose that ω_E is represented as (R_E, S_E, Q_E) where $E[\mathfrak{l}] = \langle R_E \rangle$, $E[\mathfrak{L}_2] = \langle S_E \rangle$ and $E[\bar{\mathfrak{l}}] = \langle Q_E \rangle$. The effective orientation of the curve $E_{\mathfrak{l}}$ is $(R_{E_{\mathfrak{l}}}, S_{E_{\mathfrak{l}}}, Q_{E_{\mathfrak{l}}})$ where:*

$$Q_{E_{\mathfrak{l}}} = \varphi^E_{\mathfrak{l}}(Q_E)$$
$$R_{E_{\mathfrak{l}}} = \widehat{\varphi^{E_{\mathfrak{l}}}_{\mathfrak{L}_2}} \circ \varphi^E_{\bar{\mathfrak{l}}}(R_E)$$
$$S_{E_{\mathfrak{l}}} = \varphi^E_{\mathfrak{l}}(S_E).$$

Proof. By the definitions of the group action and of the effective orientation, $\omega_E = \iota(\alpha)$ implies $\omega_{E_{\mathfrak{l}}} = \iota_{\mathfrak{l}}(\alpha)$. This is why we obtain the two decompositions $\hat{\varphi}^E_{\bar{\mathfrak{l}}} \circ \varphi^{E_{\mathfrak{l}}}_{\mathfrak{L}_2} \circ \varphi^E_{\mathfrak{l}}$ for ω_E and $\hat{\varphi}^E_{\bar{\mathfrak{l}}} \circ \varphi^{E_{\mathfrak{l}^2}}_{\mathfrak{L}_2} \circ \varphi^{E_{\mathfrak{l}}}_{\mathfrak{l}}$ for $\omega_{E_{\mathfrak{l}}}$ from the factorization $\mathfrak{O}\alpha = \mathfrak{l}^2 \mathfrak{L}_2$. The rest of the proposition follows by applying Lemma 5 to $(E, \mathfrak{l}, \bar{\mathfrak{l}})$, $(E, \overline{\mathfrak{L}_2 \mathfrak{l}}, \mathfrak{l})$, and $(E, \mathfrak{l}, \mathfrak{L}_2)$ respectively. □

Note that Proposition 9 remains valid when we replace the ideal $\mathfrak{l}$ by any ideal of smooth norm dividing $\alpha\mathfrak{O}$. This will be the case in Sect. 5 where we evaluate the action of a product of prime ideals $\mathfrak{l}_i$ where some $\mathfrak{l}_i^2$ divide $\alpha\mathfrak{O}$ and others do not.

In Sect. 5, we introduce a concrete instantiation of the general principle described above. There, we provide a detailed and efficient version of the algorithms outlined in this section.

Comparison with CSIDH. In CSIDH [13], the effective orientation is obtained through the Frobenius endomorphism, which has norm p and is thus coprime to the norm of all ideals we need to evaluate. Thus, we are in the easy case. Moreover, the situation of CSIDH is particularly simple because the kernel of $\varphi^E_{\mathfrak{l}}$ can be directly obtained as one of the two subgroups of order ℓ stable under Frobenius.

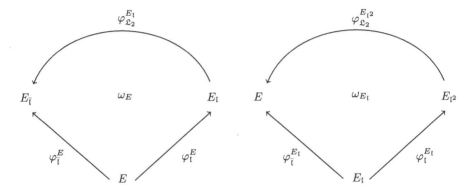

Fig. 1. A picture of the effective orientation computation from Proposition 9.

4   Security of a Group Action

In this section, we define the security notions associated to a cryptographic group action — a (very) hard homogenous space — and we review the best known attacks. A (free and transitive) group action $\star$ of a group G on a set X is a *hard homogenous space* if it can be computed efficiently and the following problems are hard.

Problem 10 *(Vectorisation). Given $x, y \in X$, find $g \in G$ such that $y = g \star x$.*

Problem 11 *(Parallelisation). Given $x, g \star x, h \star x \in X$ (for undisclosed $g, h \in G$), find $(gh) \star x$.*

It is a *very hard homogenous space* if the following problem is hard.

Problem 12 *(Decisional Parallelisation). Given $x, y, u, v \in X$, decide whether there exists $g \in G$ such that $y = g \star x$ and $v = g \star u$.*

The vectorisation and parallelisation problems, when instantiated with our group action of the class group of $\mathfrak{O}$ on $\mathcal{S}_{\mathfrak{O}}(p)$, are also known as the problems $\mathfrak{O}$-VECTORISATION and $\mathfrak{O}$-DIFFIEHELLMAN, studied in [55]. For simplicity, assume that the factorization of $\mathrm{disc}(\mathfrak{O})$ is known, and that it has $O(\log\log|\mathrm{disc}(\mathfrak{O})|)$ distinct prime factors[1], as will be the case of our construction.

The two problems $\mathfrak{O}$-VECTORISATION and $\mathfrak{O}$-DIFFIEHELLMAN are equivalent under quantum reductions (see [35,45] for reductions that are polynomial in the cost of evaluating the group action, or [55] for reductions that are polynomial in the instance lengths).

Furthermore, these problems are closely related to the endomorphism ring problem, a foundational problem of isogeny-based cryptography: given a supersingular curve E, compute a basis of the endomorphism ring $\mathrm{End}(E)$ (i.e., four

---

[1] Note that the average number of distinct prime factors of integers up to n is indeed $O(\log\log n)$.

endomorphisms of E that generate $\mathrm{End}(E)$ as a lattice). More precisely, the problem $\mathfrak{O}$-VECTORISATION is equivalent to the following oriented version of the endomorphism ring problem (see [55, Figure 1]).

Problem 13 *($\mathfrak{O}$-ENDRING)*. *Given an effectively oriented curve $(E, \iota_E) \in S_{\mathfrak{O}}(p)$, compute a basis of the endomorphism ring $\mathrm{End}(E)$.*

Clearly, $\mathfrak{O}$-ENDRING reduces to the standard endomorphism ring problem, but the converse is not known to be true. In fact, $\mathfrak{O}$-ENDRING currently seems simpler than the endomorphism ring problem as long as $|\mathrm{disc}(\mathfrak{O})| < p^2$. Precisely,

- The endomorphism ring problem can be solved in time $(\log p)^{O(1)} p^{1/2}$ (see [31, 33]), and
- The problem $\mathfrak{O}$-ENDRING can be solved in time $l^{O(1)} |\mathrm{disc}(\mathfrak{O})|^{1/4}$ with l the length of the input (see [55, Proposition 3]).

Write $\mathfrak{O} = \mathbb{Z} + f \mathfrak{O}_0$ where f is the conductor of $\mathfrak{O}$ and $\mathfrak{O}_0$ is the maximal order. Better algorithms than the above are known when $\mathfrak{O}_0$ has small class group and f is powersmooth (see [55, Theorem 5]), or even smooth in certain situations (as discussed in [19], or more generally [55, Corollary 6]). We will protect against such attacks by choosing f a large prime. This is in fact one key difference between OSIDH [19] and our construction. In OSIDH [19], the setting is similar, but f is smooth (a power of two), and the f-torsion is defined over $\mathbb{F}_{p^2}$. For this not to be a vulnerability, OSIDH is forced to only reveal partial information on the orientations, which must be done carefully, lest the attacks of [23] apply. An unfortunate side effect is that, without the full orientation, OSIDH does not actually provide an effective group action.

In summary, the fastest known generic *classical* method to solve the vectorisation problem associated to the group action has complexity

$$\min\left((\log p)^{O(1)} p^{1/2}, \log(p + d)^{O(1)} d^{1/4} \right)$$
$$= \log(p + d)^{O(1)} \min\left(p^{1/2}, f^{1/2} \right),$$

where $d = |\mathrm{disc}(\mathfrak{O})|$. A precise estimate of the $O(1)$ appearing in the complexity of [55, Proposition 3] would provide a more precise estimation of the cost of an attack.

Regarding quantum security, there is an asymptotically faster heuristic algorithm, which runs in subexponential time (see [55, Proposition 4]). It relies on Kuperberg's algorithm [39] for the Abelian hidden shift problem, and runs in time

$$\log(p)^{O(1)} L_{\mathrm{disc}(\mathfrak{O})}(1/2).$$

Note that in special cases the hidden shift problem can be solved in polynomial time as discussed in [14, 17, 37]. These include groups isomorphic to $(\mathbb{Z}/\ell\mathbb{Z})^k$ where ℓ is a small prime and groups of the form $(\mathbb{Z}/2\mathbb{Z})^k \times (\mathbb{Z}/q\mathbb{Z})^r$ where q is a small prime. In general class groups rarely have this structure and for the parameter sets proposed, we can easily see that these attacks do not apply.

Finally, let us discuss the hardness of the Decisional Parallelisation problem. Clearly, it is not harder than vectorisation, hence the algorithms discussed above apply. The only known method that may outperform them is an algorithm to distinguish the action of ideal classes *up to squares*. More precisely, to each odd prime divisor $m \mid \operatorname{disc}(\mathfrak{O})$ is associated a quadratic character, i.e., a group homomorphism

$$\chi_m : \operatorname{Cl}(\mathfrak{O}) \longrightarrow \{\pm 1\},$$

Given oriented curves (E, ι) and $(E^{\mathfrak{a}}, \iota^{\mathfrak{a}})$, the algorithm of [12] (a generalisation of [15]) allows one to evaluate $\chi_m([\mathfrak{a}])$ in time polynomial in m. In fact, the algorithm requires finding random points in $E[m]$, and solving a discrete logarithm in a group of order m. Hence the quantum complexity may be as low as polynomial in $\log(m)$ and k if the points of $E[m]$ are defined over $\mathbb{F}_{p^k}$. There may also be two additional computable characters if $\operatorname{disc}(\mathfrak{O})$ is even. Clearly, if $[\mathfrak{a}] \in \operatorname{Cl}(\mathfrak{O})^2$ is a square, then $\chi_m([\mathfrak{a}]) = 1$, so one can prevent this attack by using $\operatorname{Cl}(\mathfrak{O})^2$ instead of $\operatorname{Cl}(\mathfrak{O})$. Another way to prevent this attack is to ensure that all prime factors of $\operatorname{disc}(\mathfrak{O})$ are large, and $E[m]$ lives in a large field extension, so no character can be computed efficiently.

5   SCALLOP: a Secure and Efficient Group Action

We finally propose an efficient instantiation of the effective group action outlined in Sect. 3. Our main algorithm is given in Sect. 5.2, but we need to motivate our parameter choices first. This is what we do in Sect. 5.1, where we also explain all the required precomputations.

5.1   Parameter Choice and Precomputation

The content of this section covers all the choices of parameters and precomputations required to make the SCALLOP group action computation secure and efficient. All the algorithms described here have to be run only once, at the moment of generating public parameters. We refer the reader to Sect. 1.2 for a list of all the requirements of that precomputation to obtain a construction similar to CSI-FiSh.

Choice of Quadratic Order. Our main motivation is to obtain a quadratic order $\mathfrak{O}$ of large discriminant, but with an easy to compute structure of the class group. In general, this is a very hard problem for classical computers, the best algorithm being index calculus, with a complexity of $L_{\operatorname{disc}(\mathfrak{O})}(1/2)$. But there are some special cases where the structure is easily determined, e.g. when

$$\mathfrak{O} = \mathbb{Z} + f\mathfrak{O}_0, \tag{2}$$

where $\mathfrak{O}_0$ is a quadratic maximal order of small discriminant and f is in $\mathbb{Z}$. In that case, we deduce directly the structure of $\operatorname{Cl}(\mathfrak{O})$ from that of $\operatorname{Cl}(\mathfrak{O}_0)$ and the factorization of f. In practice, we propose to take $\mathfrak{O}_0$ of class number one (e.g. the Gauss integers) and f a prime number (also for security, as discussed in Sect. 4).

We give below a formula for the class number of such an order. The group structure, which turns out to be cyclic when $\mathfrak{O}_0$ has class number one, is described in the full version of this paper [24, Appx. A].

Proposition 14. *Let f be a prime integer and let $\mathfrak{O}_0$ be a quadratic order of class number h_0, discriminant d_0 and let u_0 denote $|\mathfrak{O}_0^\times|/2$. The class number of $\mathbb{Z} + f\mathfrak{O}_0$ is equal to $\left(f - \left(\frac{d_0}{f}\right)\right)\frac{h_0}{u_0}$.*

Note that u_0 is one for all orders corresponding to curves with j-invariant different from 0 or 1728. From now on, we write d_0 for disc($\mathfrak{O}_0$), and we assume the class number is one. It is not too difficult to generalize the algorithms below to larger class numbers, as long as d_0 is small.

Choice of Conductor. We argued that we need a prime f for security, and to avoid factoring. Prime numbers also have the advantage of being abundant and easy to generate. Apart from this, our choice of f will be determined by efficiency constraints. In particular, to use the algorithm outlined in Sect. 3, we require that there exists a generator α with norm equal to $L_1^2 L_2$ to obtain effective $\mathfrak{O}$-orientations. Since the manipulation of this effective orientation requires computing L_1- and L_2-isogenies, we need L_1 and L_2 to be smooth. Moreover, we need L_2 to be small for the algorithm SetUpCurve described below.

Finally, there is a third requirement that we will motivate a bit later: that $f - (\frac{d_0}{f})$ is as smooth as possible. This last constraint impacts the efficiency of the offline phase of our scheme. As such, it is less important than the smoothness of $L_1 L_2$, which impacts the cost of the online phase. This is why our approach consists in finding a set of candidates for f that closely match the first two constraints, before sieving through the set to find the best candidate for the last requirement. In Sect. 6.1, we provide more details on how we select the parameters and we give some concrete examples of cryptographic size.

For a given $\mathfrak{O}$, finding a generator α of smooth norm is quite hard. Indeed, for a generic $\mathfrak{O}$, the size of the α of smallest smooth norm will be very large compared to f. This is why we choose the conductor f (and thus the order $\mathfrak{O}$) at the same time as the generator α. Our method allows us to find a conductor f and an α of smooth norm of optimal size (i.e., $n(\alpha) \approx f^2$). To do that, we first target a smooth norm $L_1^2 L_2$, and then we find a suitable conductor f.

Concretely, we fix a collection of principal ideals of small prime norm in $\mathfrak{O}_0$. Let us write α_0 for a generator of $\mathfrak{O}_0$ and $\mathfrak{l}_1, \ldots, \mathfrak{l}_m$ for the collection of principal ideals and $\ell_1, \ldots, \ell_m$ for the associated split primes. Because the ℓ_i are split, there are two principal ideals of norm ℓ_i in $\mathfrak{O}_0$: $\mathfrak{l}_i$ and its conjugate $\overline{\mathfrak{l}}_i$, which, by a slight abuse of notation, we write $\mathfrak{l}_i^{-1}$. We denote by L the product $\prod_{i=1}^m \ell_i$. For some $n_1 < n_2 \leq m$, we consider the products $\prod_{i=1}^{n_1} \mathfrak{l}_i^{b_i} \prod_{i=n_1+1}^{n_2} \mathfrak{l}_i^{c_i}$ where all $b_i \in \{-2, 2\}$ and $c_i \in \{-1, 1\}$, then we get 2^{n_2} principal ideals of norm $L_1^2 L_2$ with $L_1 = \prod_{i=1}^{n_1} \ell_i$ and $L_2 = \prod_{i=n_1+1}^{n_2} \ell_i$. It suffices to obtain one such ideal of the form $\langle L_1^2 L_2, \alpha \rangle$ where $\alpha = x + f\alpha_0$ for some prime number f to get that $\mathbb{Z} + f\mathfrak{O}_0 = \mathbb{Z}[\alpha]$

where α has norm $L_1^2 L_2$ as we desire. Each product has probability roughly $1/\log(L_1^2 L_2)$ to satisfy the desired property. This gives a set of size $2^m/\log(L)$ to sieve through in order to find the best candidate with respect to our third requirement (we have the estimate $m = O(\log(L_1^2 L_2)/\log\log(L_1^2 L_2))$, see for instance [36, Chapter 22]). Up to exchanging $\mathfrak{l}_i$ and $\mathfrak{l}_i^{-1}$, we can assume that all the b_i and c_i are positive and so we have $\mathfrak{O}_0 \alpha = \prod_{i=1}^{n_1} \mathfrak{l}_i^2 \prod_{i=n_1+1}^{n_2} \mathfrak{l}_i$.

Remark 15. Note that for a fixed $\mathfrak{O}_0$ of discriminant d_0, the choice of class group determines $\left(\frac{d_0}{p}\right)$ to be 1 or -1. This is the only condition imposed on the prime characteristic p by the choice of class group. Thus, we will be able to choose p in a way that enables efficient computations after a suitable $\mathfrak{O}$ has been found.

Computing the Relation Lattice. Knowing the order of $\mathrm{Cl}(\mathfrak{O})$ is not enough for our application. Indeed, we want to be able to efficiently evaluate the action of any ideal class, which, by virtue of Proposition 4, calls for a way to compute for any class a representative that factors as a short product of ideals of small norm. For that, we follow the method introduced in [9].

The first step is to choose a set $\{\mathfrak{l}_1, \ldots, \mathfrak{l}_m, \ldots, \mathfrak{l}_n\}$ of $n = O(\log(f))$ ideals of small prime norm,[2] and to generate its *lattice of relations* $\mathcal{L}$, i.e. the lattice spanned by the vectors $(e_1, \ldots, e_n) \in \mathbb{Z}^n$ such that the ideal $\prod_{i=1}^n \mathfrak{l}_i^{e_i}$ is principal in $\mathfrak{O}$. [9] uses an index calculus method, with complexity $L_f(1/2)$, to compute a basis of $\mathcal{L}$. But another basis is simply given by the relations $\mathfrak{a}^{h(\mathfrak{O})} = 1$ and $\mathfrak{a}^{x_i} = \mathfrak{l}_i$, where $\mathfrak{a}$ is any generator of $\mathrm{Cl}(\mathfrak{O})$ and the x_i are the discrete logarithms to base $\mathfrak{a}$. If we force $\mathrm{Cl}(\mathfrak{O})$ to have smooth order, we can efficiently compute these discrete logarithms using the Pohlig–Hellman method.

This explains why we search for f such that $f - \left(\frac{d_0}{f}\right)$ is as smooth as possible (recall Proposition 14). Unfortunately, we could not find a method to significantly bias $f - \left(\frac{d_0}{f}\right)$ towards being smooth, thus our method still has subexponential complexity: Heuristically, if we sieve through $L_f(1/2)$ candidates we expect to find one that is $L_f(1/2)$-smooth, then solving discrete logarithms also takes $L_f(1/2)$ operations.

Although it looks like we haven't improved over index calculus, the constant hidden in (the exponent of) $L_f(1/2)$ is better for our method—which indeed performs much better in practice—and is the only reason we were able to instantiate parameters twice as large as those of CSI-FiSh (see Sect. 6).

After having computed a basis for $\mathcal{L}$, the second step, which we do identically to [9], is to apply a lattice reduction algorithm to obtain a shorter basis. Here we need to strike a balance between the time spent reducing and the quality of the output: For example, using BKZ with block size in $O(\sqrt{n})$, running in time $L_{\exp(n)}(1/2)$, we achieve an approximation factor of $L_{\exp(n)}(1/2)$ (see [43, Theorem 3]). In practice, however, the lattice rank n tends to be relatively small, letting us compute a nearly optimal basis in negligible time, as already observed in [9].

---

[2] This set contains the ideals $\mathfrak{l}_1, \ldots, \mathfrak{l}_m$ that divide $\mathfrak{O}_0 \alpha$, but can be larger in general.

Finally, any time we are given an ideal class, say $\mathfrak{l}_1^e$, we use Babai's nearest plane algorithm [4] to find a vector $\boldsymbol{v}$ close to $\boldsymbol{e} = (e, 0, \ldots, 0)$, whence we deduce a representative $\mathfrak{l}_1^{e-v_1} \prod_{i=2}^n \mathfrak{l}_i^{-v_i} \equiv \mathfrak{l}_1^e$. The cost of evaluating the group action by this representative, using the algorithms of Sect. 3, will be proportional to the norm of $\boldsymbol{e} - \boldsymbol{v}$. Hence the better the basis of $\mathcal{L}$ has been reduced, the faster the evaluation will be.

Choice of Prime Characteristic. When it comes to the choice of p, we want to find a prime that maximizes the efficiency of evaluating the group action. We have two requirements: that the effective orientations (E, P_E, Q_E) (see Definition 6) can be manipulated efficiently, and that the isogenies associated to the ideals $\mathfrak{l}_i$ can be evaluated efficiently.

For the first requirement, we will force the points P_E and Q_E representing the kernel of $\omega_E = \iota_E(\alpha)$ to be defined over $\mathbb{F}_{p^2}$. Recall that P_E has order $L_1 L_2$ and Q_E has order L_1, hence it is sufficient to choose $L_1 L_2 \mid (p^2 - 1)$.

Similarly, for the second requirement, we want each of the $E[\mathfrak{l}_i]$ to be defined over $\mathbb{F}_{p^2}$ in order to apply the most efficient versions of Vélu's formulas, i.e. we want $n(\mathfrak{l}_i) = \ell_i \mid (p^2 - 1)$. Point in case, $\ell_1, \ldots, \ell_m$ must already divide $p^2 - 1$. Write $L = L_1 L_2 L_3 = \prod_{i=1}^n \ell_i$, then it suffices to select $p = cL \pm 1$ for some small cofactor c.

Finally we want that $\mathcal{S}_{\mathfrak{O}_0}(p)$ is not empty, implying that p must not split in $\mathfrak{O}_0$. For instance, if $\mathfrak{O}_0 = \mathbb{Z}[i]$, we need $p \equiv 3 \pmod 4$. In any case, finding such a prime p can be done after a logarithmic number of tries for a cofactor c. Alternatively, one might take $c = 1$ and play with the split prime factors dividing $L_1 L_2 L_3$ until $L \pm 1$ is prime and split in $\mathfrak{O}_0$.

In fact, we also need p to be large enough to prevent generic attacks (see Sect. 4). Luckily, with the choices outlined above, we will obtain a prime p that is a lot larger than the minimal security requirement.

Generation of a Starting Curve. After we have chosen parameters $\mathfrak{O}_0, L, \alpha, f, p$, generated and reduced the lattice of relations $\mathcal{L}$, the last step of precomputation is the generation of a first orientation (E, ι_E) in $\mathcal{S}_{\mathfrak{O}}(p)$. After this last part is done, we will be able to do everything with the group action algorithm. This algorithm will be described later in full detail as Algorithm 3, but for now, we focus on the computation of one (E, ι_E) with the corresponding embedding $\omega_E = \iota_E(\alpha)$. The goal of this paragraph is to explain how the algorithm SetUp-Curve works (see Algorithm 1).

First, let us take $(E_0, \iota_0) \in \mathcal{S}_{\mathfrak{O}_0}(p)$, and $\mathcal{O}_0 \cong \text{End}(E_0)$ a maximal order in $B_{p,\infty}$. When d_0 is small enough, $\mathcal{O}_0$ is a special extremal order as defined in [38]. This means that we can efficiently find elements $\gamma \in \mathcal{O}_0$ of norm M as soon as $M > p$. For instance, when $p \equiv 3 \pmod 4$, we can do this in the endomorphism ring of the curve of j-invariant 1728 with the FullRepresentInteger algorithm from [28, Algorithm 1]. Moreover, we can evaluate any endomorphism of $\text{End}(E_0)$ efficiently, because we have the nice representation explicited at the end of Sect. 2.1. By a result from [44], the orientations in $\mathcal{S}_{\mathfrak{O}}(p)$ are obtained from the orientations of $\mathcal{S}_{\mathfrak{O}_0}(p)$ through f-isogenies, this is what we explain in Proposition 16.

Proposition 16. *Let $\mathfrak{O}_0$ be a quadratic order, and $(E_0, \iota_0) \in \mathcal{S}_{\mathfrak{O}_0}(p)$, let f be a prime integer and $\mathfrak{O} = \mathbb{Z} + f\mathfrak{O}_0$. If $\varphi : E_0 \to E$ is not one of the $1 + \left(\frac{d_0}{f}\right)$ isogenies corresponding to prime ideals above f, then there exists $\iota_E : \mathfrak{O} \hookrightarrow \mathrm{End}(E)$ and $(E, \iota_E) \in \mathcal{S}_{\mathfrak{O}}(p)$. Moreover $\iota_E(\alpha) = [\varphi]_* \iota_0(\alpha)$ for any $\alpha \in \mathfrak{O}$.*

Now the idea is to compute the kernel of $\iota_0(\alpha)$ (in fact the kernel of the two isogenies of degree L in the decomposition of $\iota_0(\alpha)$) and push that kernel through the isogeny φ. Let us write this kernel as G. The only problem is that in our case f is a large prime, ruling out Vélu's formulas for evaluating φ. Since we know $\mathrm{End}(E_0)$, our idea is to use the method described in [41, Algorithm 2] (or [34]) to evaluate isogenies of large prime degree: represent φ as an ideal I_φ of norm f and compute $J \sim I_\varphi$ where $S = n(J)$, is smooth. Then, evaluate φ, using ψ the isogeny corresponding to J. This is also similar to the key generation of the SQISign signature protocol [27]. Here, we can even use the alternative key generation method described in [27, Appendix D] for better efficiency. Indeed, we can choose almost any isogeny of degree f (by Proposition 16, there are at most two isogenies of degree f that do not create a $\mathfrak{O}$-orientation). Thus, we need to find an endomorphism of norm fS for some smooth integer S. Of course, the simplest situation would be to take $S = 1$, but this is not possible because $f \approx L_1 \sqrt{L_2}$ is strictly smaller than p, and we can only find endomorphisms of norm larger than p in $\mathrm{End}(E_0)$. Another natural choice would be to take S dividing L but we need S to be coprime with $L_1 L_2$ because our goal is to evaluate the isogeny of degree S on the $L_1 L_2$-torsion to compute the kernel representation of ω_E. Thus, we can use only the L_3-torsion which is not enough in itself because $fL_3 < p$. We are not going to assume anything specific about the cofactor c (defined along with the prime p as $p = cL \pm 1$), in particular c might not be coprime to L so we may not be able to use it in S. However, c quantifies the size of the additional torsion we need, since we have $c\sqrt{L_2} \approx p/(fL_3)$. What we know for sure is that c is small. Thus, if L_2 is small as well, we can select a small prime ℓ_0 coprime with $L_1 L_2$ and take $S = L_3 \ell_0^h$ for some h such that $\ell_0^h > p/(fL_3)$. Since h and ℓ_0 are small, we can simply brute-force through all ℓ_0^h-isogenies until one works, i.e., until we obtain an endomorphism of the right norm and trace after pushing the kernel representation through the considered isogeny of degree ℓ_0^h.

This yields the SetUpCurve algorithm that we describe below as Algorithm 1. The orientation $(E_0, \iota_0) \in \mathcal{S}_{\mathfrak{O}_0}(p)$, and an explicit isomorphism $\rho_0 : \mathcal{O}_0 \hookrightarrow \mathrm{End}(E_0)$ are considered as implicit parameters of this algorithm. The output is a kernel representation of $\iota_E \omega_E$ as in Definition 6.

For a kernel representation s and any morphism ψ, we write $\psi(s)$ for the kernel representation of the group obtained by pushing through ψ the kernel corresponding to s.

Proposition 17. SetUpCurve *is correct and terminates in $O(c\sqrt{L_2}\mathsf{poly}(\log (pcL_2))$ where c is one of $(p \pm 1)/L$.*

Proof. To prove correctness, we need to verify that the output s_E is an effective orientation in $\mathcal{S}_{\mathfrak{O}}(p)$. Let us assume that the verification made in the loop passed.

Algorithm 1. SetUpCurve(p, f)

Input: A prime p of the form $p = cL_1L_2L_3 \pm 1$ and a prime f such that there exists $\mathfrak{O}_0$ of discriminant d_0 where p is not split and $\mathfrak{O} = \mathbb{Z} + f\mathfrak{O}_0$ contains an element of norm $L_1^2L_2$.

Output: An effective orientation s_E for $(E, \iota_E) \in \mathcal{S}_{\mathfrak{O}}(p)$.

1: Let ℓ_0 be the smallest prime coprime with L_1L_2.
2: Compute s_0 the kernel representation of $\omega_0 = \iota_0(\alpha)$.
3: Set h such that $\ell_0^h > p/(fL_3)$ and compute $\gamma \in \mathcal{O}_0$ of norm $fL_3\ell_0^h$ with Full-RepresentInteger.
4: Compute the kernel representation $s = \rho_0(\gamma)(s_0)$.
5: Use ρ_0 to compute the isogeny $\psi : E_0 \rightarrow E'$ of norm L_3 corresponding to the ideal $\langle \overline{\gamma}, L_3 \rangle$.
6: Make the list $(\varphi_i : E' \rightarrow E_i)_{1 \leq i \leq m}$ of all isogenies of degree ℓ_0^h from E'.
7: **for** $i \in [1, m]$: **do**
8:    Compute $s_i = \varphi_i \circ \psi(s)$ and verify that it is a kernel representation for an endomorphism ω_i of norm $n(\alpha)$ and that it is not s_0.
9:    If yes, verify that $\mathrm{tr}(\omega_i)$ is the same as $\mathrm{tr}(\alpha)$. If yes, break from the loop.
10: **end for**
11: Set $E = E_i$, and $s_E = s_i$.
12: **return** Output s_E.

We will start by proving correctness under that assumption, then we will justify why the verification always passes. When the verification passes, it means that s_E is the kernel representation for an endomorphism ω_E of the same norm and trace as α. This implies that $\mathbb{Z}[\omega_E] \cong \mathbb{Z}[\alpha]$ and so by definition we get that s_E is a correct effective orientation.

Now, let us justify that there always is an i that passes the verification. The element $\gamma \in \mathcal{O}_0$ provides us with a principal ideal $\mathcal{O}_0\gamma$, whose corresponding isogeny $\rho_0(\varphi_\gamma)$ is an endomorphism of E_0. Moreover, we have that (up to composing with some isomorphisms if necessary) $\varphi_\gamma = \psi' \circ \varphi \circ \varphi_f$ where $\varphi_f : E_0 \rightarrow E$ has degree f, $\varphi : E \rightarrow E'$ has degree ℓ_0^h and $\psi' : E' \rightarrow E_0$ has degree L_3. By Proposition 16, E is an $\mathfrak{O}$-orientable curve unless φ_f corresponds to one of the $1 + \left(\frac{d_0}{f} \right)$ horizontal f-isogenies of domain E_0. Let us assume for now that it is not. By Proposition 16, we know that the endomorphism $\omega_E = \iota_E(\alpha)$ can be obtained by pushing forward ω_0 through φ_f. Thus, we need to show that $s = \varphi_f(s_0)$. By design, the ideal $\langle \overline{\gamma}, L_3 \rangle$ corresponds to the isogeny $\hat{\psi}'$. Thus, we have that the isogeny ψ computed in Step 5, is the isogeny $\hat{\psi}'$. Then, if we take the index i_0 such that $\varphi_{i_0} = \hat{\varphi}$, we get that E_{i_0} is the curve E that we are looking for. Then, $s_{i_0} = \varphi_{i_0} \circ \psi \circ \psi' \circ \varphi \circ \phi_f(s) = \varphi_f(s)$ and this proves the result. To finish the proof of correctness, we simply need to address the case where φ_f might be one of the bad isogenies. What happens in that case, is that $[\varphi_f]_*\iota_0(\alpha) = \iota_0(\alpha)$ (so we obtain an embedding that is not primitive, since it is the corresponding to ι_0). Thus, the additional verification that s_i is not s_0 prevents the bad case from happening and so we know that s_E is an effective orientation of $\mathcal{S}_{\mathfrak{O}}(p)$.

Regarding complexity, we have $\ell_0^h < \ell_0 p/(fL_3)$ and since we have $f = O(L_1\sqrt{L_2})$, the loop is repeated at most $O(c\sqrt{L_2})$ times. The computations over the quaternions are in $O(\mathsf{poly}(\log(p)))$. Then, since we have the explicit isomorphism ρ_0, we can compute ψ and evaluate $\rho_0(\gamma)$ over the L-torsion in $O(\mathsf{poly}(\log(p)))$ (remember that the L-torsion is defined over $\mathbb{F}_{p^2}$ and $L < p$). Then, the computation of each φ_i is in $O(\mathsf{poly}(\log(pL_2c)))$ and computing s_i and checking the trace has $O(\mathsf{poly}(\log(p)))$ complexity with the CheckTrace algorithm introduced in [41]. This proves the result.   □

5.2   The Group Action Computation

Now that we have our starting curve E and an effective orientation ω_E, it remains to see how we can compute $E_{\mathfrak{a}}$ and the kernel representation of $\omega_{E_{\mathfrak{a}}}$ for any ideal $\mathfrak{a}$. For efficiency reasons, we restrict ourselves to the case where $\mathfrak{a}$ has a smooth norm. Also, we target the case where $n(\mathfrak{a}) = \prod_{i=1}^{n} \ell_i^{e_i}$ because this is the one where we will be able to compute the corresponding isogeny efficiently.

Since we only have the L-torsion available, we can factor $\mathfrak{a}$ as the product of $e = \max_{1 \le i \le n} e_i$ ideals whose norm is dividing L and treat each of them independently.

Thus, our main algorithm is GroupActionSmall (Algorithm 2) that performs the group action computation for one ideal of degree dividing L. The final algorithm GroupAction (described as Algorithm 3) is simply the consecutive execution of this sub-algorithm on all factors.

When the ideal has degree dividing L. Let us fix some notation. We write $\mathfrak{L}_1 = \prod_{i=1}^{n_1} \mathfrak{l}_i$, $\mathfrak{L}_2 = \prod_{i=n_1+1}^{n_2} \mathfrak{l}_i$ and $\mathfrak{L}_3 = \prod_{i=n_2+1}^{n} \mathfrak{l}_i$. With these definitions we have $\mathfrak{O}\alpha = \mathfrak{L}_1^2\mathfrak{L}_2$. Equivalently, this means that we can write ω_E as $\hat{\varphi}_{\mathfrak{L}_1^{-1}}^{E} \circ \varphi_{\mathfrak{L}_1\mathfrak{L}_2}^{E}$. The kernel of ω_E is made of two subgroups that we write $\langle P_E \rangle, \langle Q_E \rangle$ with $\langle P_E \rangle = \ker \varphi_{\mathfrak{L}_1\mathfrak{L}_2}^{E}$ and $\langle Q_E \rangle = \ker \varphi_{\mathfrak{L}_1^{-1}}^{E}$. Let us take the input ideal $\mathfrak{a}$, it can be factored as $\mathfrak{a}_1, \mathfrak{a}_2, \mathfrak{a}_3$ where $n(\mathfrak{a}_i)|L_i$. And for $i = 1, 2$ we also factor $\mathfrak{a}_i$ as $\mathfrak{b}_i\mathfrak{c}_i$ where $\mathfrak{b}_i|\mathfrak{L}_i$ and $\mathfrak{c}_i|\mathfrak{L}_i^{-1}$ and $\gcd(n(\mathfrak{b}_i), n(\mathfrak{c}_i)) = 1$. We write $\mathfrak{K}_i = \mathfrak{L}_i/\mathfrak{b}_i$ and $\mathfrak{J}_1 = \mathfrak{L}_1^{-1}/\mathfrak{c}_1$. Given an ideal $\mathfrak{a}$ whose norm divides L, we use Algorithm 2 (GroupActionSmall) to compute the action of $\mathfrak{a}$ on (E, s_E).

Figure 2 provides a visualization of the different isogenies involved in Algorithm 2.

Proposition 18. GroupActionSmall *is correct and runs in time* $\tilde{O}(B)$ *where B is the largest factor of L.*

Proof. To prove correctness, we need to verify that $s_{E_{\mathfrak{a}}} = (P_{E_{\mathfrak{a}}}, Q_{E_{\mathfrak{a}}})$ represents the two correct subgroups, that is $E_{\mathfrak{a}}[\mathfrak{L}_1\mathfrak{L}_2] = \langle P_{E_{\mathfrak{a}}} \rangle$ and $E_{\mathfrak{a}}[\mathfrak{L}_1^{-1}] = \langle Q_{E_{\mathfrak{a}}} \rangle$. By definition of the effective orientation, we have $E[\mathfrak{L}_1\mathfrak{L}_2] = \langle P_E \rangle$ and $E[\mathfrak{L}_1^{-1}] = \langle Q_E \rangle$.

Algorithm 2. GroupActionSmall$(((E, \iota_E), \mathfrak{a}))$

Input: An effective $\mathfrak{D}$-orientation s_E for (E, ι_E) and an ideal $\mathfrak{a} = \mathfrak{b}_1 \mathfrak{b}_2 \mathfrak{c}_1 \mathfrak{c}_2 \mathfrak{a}_3$ such that
    $\mathfrak{b}_i | \mathfrak{L}_i$ and $\mathfrak{c}_i | \mathfrak{L}_i^{-1}$ for $i = 1, 2$ and $n(\mathfrak{a}_3) | L_3$.
Output: An effective $\mathfrak{D}$-orientation $s_{E_\mathfrak{a}}$ for $(E_\mathfrak{a}, \iota_{E_\mathfrak{a}})$.
1: Parse s_E as E, P_E, Q_E.
2: Compute $\varphi^E_{\mathfrak{b}_1 \mathfrak{b}_2}$ from its kernel $\langle \left[\frac{L_1 L_2}{n(\mathfrak{b}_1 \mathfrak{b}_2)} \right] P_E \rangle$
3: Compute $P^*_{E_{\mathfrak{b}_1 \mathfrak{b}_2}} = \varphi^E_{\mathfrak{b}_1 \mathfrak{b}_2}(P_E)$, $Q_{E_{\mathfrak{b}_1 \mathfrak{b}_2}} = \varphi^E_{\mathfrak{b}_1 \mathfrak{b}_2}(Q_E)$ and $\varphi^E_{\mathfrak{b}_1 \mathfrak{b}_2}(E[n(\mathfrak{c}_2)L_3])$.
4: Compute $\varphi^{E_{\mathfrak{b}_1 \mathfrak{b}_2}}_{\hat{\mathfrak{R}}_1 \hat{\mathfrak{R}}_2}$ from its kernel $\langle P^*_{E_{\mathfrak{b}_1 \mathfrak{b}_2}} \rangle$.
5: Compute $Q_{E_{\mathfrak{L}_1 \mathfrak{L}_2}} = \varphi^{E_{\mathfrak{b}_1 \mathfrak{b}_2}}_{\hat{\mathfrak{R}}_1 \hat{\mathfrak{R}}_2}(Q_{E_{\mathfrak{b}_1 \mathfrak{b}_2}})$ and $\varphi^{E_{\mathfrak{b}_1 \mathfrak{b}_2}}_{\hat{\mathfrak{R}}_1 \hat{\mathfrak{R}}_2}(E_{\mathfrak{b}_1 \mathfrak{b}_2}[n(\mathfrak{b}_1 \mathfrak{b}_2 \mathfrak{c}_2)L_3])$.
6: Compute $\varphi^E_{\mathfrak{c}_1}$ from its kernel $\langle [\frac{L_1}{n(\mathfrak{c}_1)}] Q_E \rangle$
7: Compute $P_{E_{\mathfrak{c}_1}} = \varphi^E_{\mathfrak{c}_1}(P_E)$, $Q^*_{E_{\mathfrak{c}_1}} = \varphi^E_{\mathfrak{c}_1}(Q_E)$ and $\varphi^E_{\mathfrak{c}_1}(E[n(\mathfrak{c}_2)L_3])$.
8: Compute $\varphi^{E_{\mathfrak{c}_1}}_{\mathfrak{J}_1}$ from its kernel $\langle Q^*_{E_{\mathfrak{c}_1}} \rangle$
9: Compute $P_{E_{\mathfrak{L}_1 \mathfrak{L}_2}} = \varphi^{E_{\mathfrak{c}_1}}_{\mathfrak{J}_1}(P_{E_{\mathfrak{c}_1}})$ and $\varphi^{E_{\mathfrak{c}_1}}_{\mathfrak{J}_1}(E[n(\mathfrak{c}_1 \mathfrak{c}_2)L_3])$.
10: From the action of $\varphi^{E_{\mathfrak{b}_1 \mathfrak{b}_2}}_{\hat{\mathfrak{R}}_1 \hat{\mathfrak{R}}_2}$ on $E_{\mathfrak{b}_1 \mathfrak{b}_2}[n(\mathfrak{b}_1 \mathfrak{b}_2)]$, compute $\hat{\varphi}^{E_{\mathfrak{b}_1 \mathfrak{b}_2}}_{\hat{\mathfrak{R}}_1 \hat{\mathfrak{R}}_2}([\frac{L_1 L_2}{n(\mathfrak{b}_1 \mathfrak{b}_2)}] P_{E_{\mathfrak{L}_1 \mathfrak{L}_2}})$
    and add it up to $P^*_{E_{\mathfrak{b}_1 \mathfrak{b}_2}}$ to recover $P_{E_{\mathfrak{b}_1 \mathfrak{b}_2}}$.
11: From the action of $\varphi^{E_{\mathfrak{c}_1}}_{\mathfrak{J}_1}$ on $E_{\mathfrak{c}_1}[n(\mathfrak{c}_1)]$, compute $\hat{\varphi}^{E_{\mathfrak{c}_1}}_{\mathfrak{J}_1}([\frac{L_1}{n(\mathfrak{c}_1)}] Q_{E_{\mathfrak{L}_1 \mathfrak{L}_2}})$ and add it
    up to $Q^*_{E_{\mathfrak{c}_1}}$ to recover $Q_{E_{\mathfrak{c}_1}}$.
12: From the action of $\varphi^E_{\mathfrak{b}_1 \mathfrak{b}_2}$, $\varphi^{E_{\mathfrak{b}_1 \mathfrak{b}_2}}_{\hat{\mathfrak{R}}_1 \hat{\mathfrak{R}}_2}$, $\varphi^E_{\mathfrak{c}_1}$ and $\varphi^{E_{\mathfrak{c}_1}}_{\mathfrak{J}_1}$ on the respective $n(\mathfrak{c}_2)L_3$-torsion
    groups, compute $\omega_{E_{\mathfrak{b}_1 \mathfrak{b}_2}}(E_{\mathfrak{b}_1 \mathfrak{b}_2}[n(\mathfrak{c}_2)L_3])$ and deduce $E_{\mathfrak{b}_1 \mathfrak{b}_2}[\mathfrak{c}_2 \mathfrak{a}_3]$.
13: Compute $\varphi^{E_{\mathfrak{b}_1 \mathfrak{b}_2}}_{\mathfrak{c}_1}$ from its kernel $\langle \left[\frac{L_1}{n(\mathfrak{c}_1)} \right] Q_{E_{\mathfrak{b}_1 \mathfrak{b}_2}} \rangle$
14: Compute $P_{E_{\mathfrak{a}_1 \mathfrak{b}_2}} = \varphi^{E_{\mathfrak{b}_1 \mathfrak{b}_2}}_{\mathfrak{a}_1 \mathfrak{b}_2}(P_{E_{\mathfrak{b}_1 \mathfrak{b}_2}})$ and $E_{\mathfrak{a}_1 \mathfrak{b}_2}[\mathfrak{c}_2 \mathfrak{a}_3] = \varphi^{E_{\mathfrak{b}_1 \mathfrak{b}_2}}_{\mathfrak{c}_1}(E_{\mathfrak{b}_1 \mathfrak{b}_2}[\mathfrak{c}_2 \mathfrak{a}_3])$.
15: Compute $\varphi^{E_{\mathfrak{c}_1}}_{\mathfrak{b}_1 \mathfrak{b}_2}$ from its kernel $\langle \left[\frac{L_1 L_2}{n(\mathfrak{b}_1 \mathfrak{b}_2)} \right] P_{E_{\mathfrak{c}_1}} \rangle$
16: Compute $Q_{E_{\mathfrak{a}_1 \mathfrak{b}_2}} = \varphi^{E_{\mathfrak{c}_1}}_{\mathfrak{b}_1 \mathfrak{b}_2}(Q_{E_{\mathfrak{c}_1}})$.
17: Compute $\varphi^{E_{\mathfrak{a}_1 \mathfrak{b}_2}}_{\mathfrak{c}_2 \mathfrak{a}_3} = \varphi^{E_{\mathfrak{a}_1 \mathfrak{a}_2}}_{\mathfrak{a}_3} \circ \varphi^{E_{\mathfrak{a}_1 \mathfrak{b}_2}}_{\mathfrak{c}_2}$ from its kernel $E_{\mathfrak{a}_1 \mathfrak{b}_2}[\mathfrak{c}_2 \mathfrak{a}_3]$.
18: Compute $P_{E_\mathfrak{a}} = \varphi^{E_{\mathfrak{a}_1 \mathfrak{b}_2}}_{\mathfrak{c}_2 \mathfrak{a}_3}(P_{E_{\mathfrak{a}_1 \mathfrak{b}_2}})$ and $Q_{E_\mathfrak{a}} = \varphi^{E_{\mathfrak{a}_1 \mathfrak{b}_2}}_{\mathfrak{c}_2 \mathfrak{a}_3}(Q_{E_{\mathfrak{a}_1 \mathfrak{b}_2}})$.
19: Compute the canonical effective orientation $s_{E_\mathfrak{a}}$ for $(E_\mathfrak{a}, \iota_{E_\mathfrak{a}})$ from $E_\mathfrak{a}, P_{E_\mathfrak{a}}$ and
    $Q_{E_\mathfrak{a}}$ (see Remark 7).
20: **return** $s_{E_\mathfrak{a}}$.

From the computation of the isogenies $\varphi^E_{\mathfrak{b}_1 \mathfrak{b}_2}$, $\varphi^{E_{\mathfrak{b}_1 \mathfrak{b}_2}}_{\hat{\mathfrak{R}}_1 \hat{\mathfrak{R}}_2}$, $\varphi^E_{\mathfrak{c}_1}$ and $\varphi^{E_{\mathfrak{c}_1}}_{\mathfrak{J}_1}$ in step 2,
4, 6 and 8 respectively, and their evaluation on the respective $n(\mathfrak{c}_2 \mathfrak{a}_3)$ torsion
groups in step 3, 5, 7 and 9, we successfully recover the action of

$$\omega_{E_{\mathfrak{b}_1 \mathfrak{b}_2}} = \varphi^E_{\mathfrak{b}_1 \mathfrak{b}_2} \circ \hat{\varphi}^E_{\mathfrak{c}_1} \circ \hat{\varphi}^{E_{\mathfrak{c}_1}}_{\mathfrak{J}_1} \circ \varphi^{E_{\mathfrak{b}_1 \mathfrak{b}_2}}_{\hat{\mathfrak{R}}_1 \hat{\mathfrak{R}}_2}$$

on $E_{\mathfrak{b}_1 \mathfrak{b}_2}[n(\mathfrak{c}_2)L_3]$ in step 12. Since $n(\mathfrak{c}_2)L_3$ is smooth, we efficiently solve some
two-dimensional discrete logarithms in the group $E_{\mathfrak{b}_1 \mathfrak{b}_2}[n(\mathfrak{c}_2)L_3]$ to successfully
recover $E_{\mathfrak{b}_1 \mathfrak{b}_2}[\mathfrak{c}_2 \mathfrak{a}_3]$ in step 12.

Applying Lemma 5 to $(E, \mathfrak{b}_1 \mathfrak{b}_2, \mathfrak{L}^{-1})$, we get that $\langle Q_{E_{\mathfrak{b}_1 \mathfrak{b}_2}} \rangle = E_{\mathfrak{b}_1 \mathfrak{b}_2}[\mathfrak{L}_1^{-1}]$ in step 3. Meanwhile, in step 3 $\langle P^*_{E_{\mathfrak{b}_1 \mathfrak{b}_2}} \rangle = \langle \varphi^E_{\mathfrak{b}_1 \mathfrak{b}_2}(P_E) \rangle$ generates the proper
subgroup of $E_{\mathfrak{b}_1 \mathfrak{b}_2}[\mathfrak{L}_1 \mathfrak{L}_2]$ of order $L_1 L_2 / n(\mathfrak{b}_1 \mathfrak{b}_2)$.

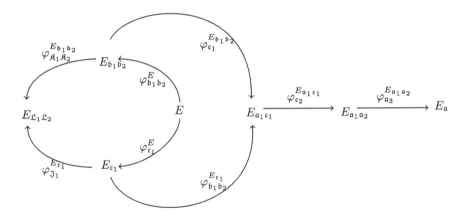

Fig. 2. A picture of the isogenies and curves involved in GroupActionSmall.

To recover the remaining part of the group $E_{\mathfrak{b}_1\mathfrak{b}_2}[\mathfrak{L}_1\mathfrak{L}_2]$, one applies the formulas given in Proposition 9: that is, one recovers the part of $E_{\mathfrak{b}_1\mathfrak{b}_2}[\mathfrak{L}_1\mathfrak{L}_2]$ lost when evaluating $\varphi^E_{\mathfrak{b}_1\mathfrak{b}_2}$ on P_E by evaluating

$$\varphi^E_{(\mathfrak{L}_1 K_1 K_2)^{-1}} = \hat{\varphi}^{E_{\mathfrak{b}_1\mathfrak{b}_2}}_{\hat{\mathfrak{K}}_1 \hat{\mathfrak{K}}_2} \circ \varphi^{E_{\mathfrak{c}_1}}_{\mathfrak{J}_1} \circ \varphi^E_{\mathfrak{c}_1}$$

on $[\frac{L_1 L_2}{n(\mathfrak{b}_1\mathfrak{b}_2)}] P_E$. This is done in step 10 where $E_{\mathfrak{b}_1\mathfrak{b}_2}[\mathfrak{L}_1\mathfrak{L}_2] = \langle P_{E_{\mathfrak{b}_1\mathfrak{b}_2}} \rangle$.

Reasoning similarly for $\mathfrak{c}_1$ and $\mathfrak{L}_1\mathfrak{L}_2$, we get that in step 7, we have the equality $\langle P_{E_{\mathfrak{c}_1}} \rangle = E_{\mathfrak{c}_1}[\mathfrak{L}_1\mathfrak{L}_2]$ and that step 11 successfully recovers $Q_{E_{\mathfrak{c}_1}}$ such that $E_{\mathfrak{c}_1}[\mathfrak{L}_1^{-1}] = \langle Q_{E_{\mathfrak{c}_1}} \rangle$.

Applying Lemma 5 to $(E_{\mathfrak{c}_1}, \mathfrak{b}_1\mathfrak{b}_2, \mathfrak{L}^{-1})$, $(E_{\mathfrak{b}_1\mathfrak{b}_2}, \mathfrak{c}_1, \mathfrak{L}_1\mathfrak{L}_2)$ and $(E_{\mathfrak{b}_1\mathfrak{b}_2}, \mathfrak{c}_1, \mathfrak{c}_2\mathfrak{a}_3)$ respectively, we get that

$$E_{\mathfrak{a}_1\mathfrak{b}_2}[\mathfrak{L}_1^{-1}] = \varphi^{E_{\mathfrak{c}_1}}_{\mathfrak{b}_1\mathfrak{b}_2}\left(E_{\mathfrak{c}_1}[\mathfrak{L}_1^{-1}]\right) = \varphi^{E_{\mathfrak{c}_1}}_{\mathfrak{b}_1\mathfrak{b}_2}(\langle Q_{E_{\mathfrak{c}_1}} \rangle) = \langle Q_{E_{\mathfrak{a}_1\mathfrak{b}_2}} \rangle$$

as computed in step 16,

$$E_{\mathfrak{a}_1\mathfrak{b}_2}[\mathfrak{L}_1\mathfrak{L}_2] = \varphi^{E_{\mathfrak{b}_1\mathfrak{b}_2}}_{\mathfrak{c}_1}\left(E_{\mathfrak{b}_1\mathfrak{b}_2}[\mathfrak{L}_1\mathfrak{L}_2]\right) = \varphi^{E_{\mathfrak{b}_1\mathfrak{b}_2}}_{\mathfrak{c}_1}(\langle P_{E_{\mathfrak{b}_1\mathfrak{b}_2}} \rangle) = \langle P_{E_{\mathfrak{a}_1\mathfrak{b}_2}} \rangle$$

as computed in step 14 and

$$E_{\mathfrak{a}_1\mathfrak{b}_2}[\mathfrak{c}_2\mathfrak{a}_3] = \varphi^{E_{\mathfrak{b}_1\mathfrak{b}_2}}_{\mathfrak{c}_1}\left(E_{\mathfrak{b}_1\mathfrak{b}_2}[\mathfrak{c}_2\mathfrak{a}_3]\right)$$

as computed in step 14.

In step 17 and 18, we compute $\varphi^{E_{\mathfrak{a}_1\mathfrak{b}_2}}_{\mathfrak{c}_2\mathfrak{a}_3}$ and applying Lemma 5 to $(E_{\mathfrak{a}_1\mathfrak{b}_2}, \mathfrak{c}_2\mathfrak{a}_3, \mathfrak{L}^{-1})$ and $(E_{\mathfrak{a}_1\mathfrak{b}_2}, \mathfrak{c}_2\mathfrak{a}_3, \mathfrak{L}_1\mathfrak{L}_2)$ respectively, we get

$$E_{\mathfrak{a}}[\mathfrak{L}_1^{-1}] = \varphi^{E_{\mathfrak{a}_1\mathfrak{b}_2}}_{\mathfrak{c}_2\mathfrak{a}_3}\left(E_{\mathfrak{a}_1\mathfrak{b}_1}[\mathfrak{L}_1^{-1}]\right) = \varphi^{E_{\mathfrak{a}_1\mathfrak{b}_2}}_{\mathfrak{c}_2\mathfrak{a}_3}(\langle Q_{\mathfrak{a}_1\mathfrak{b}_1} \rangle) = \langle Q_{E_{\mathfrak{a}}} \rangle$$

Algorithm 3. GroupAction($(E, \iota_E), \mathfrak{d}$)

Input: An effective $\mathfrak{O}$-orientation s_E for (E, ι_E) and $\mathfrak{d} = \mathfrak{l}_1^{e_1} \cdots \mathfrak{l}_n^{e_n}$.
Output: An effective $\mathfrak{O}$-orientation $s_{E_\mathfrak{d}}$ for $(E_\mathfrak{d}, \iota_{E_\mathfrak{d}})$
1: **while** some $e_i \neq 0$ **do**
2:     $\mathfrak{a} = 1$
3:     **for** $i \in \{1, \cdots, n\}$ **do**
4:         **if** $e_i < 0$ **then**
5:             $\mathfrak{a} = \mathfrak{a} * \mathfrak{l}_i^{-1}, e_i = e_i + 1$
6:         **else if** $e_i > 0$ **then**
7:             $\mathfrak{a} = \mathfrak{a} * \mathfrak{l}_i, e_i = e_i - 1$
8:         **end if**
9:     **end for**
10:     $s_E = \mathsf{GroupActionSmall}(s_E, \mathfrak{a})$
11: **end while**
12: **return** s_E.

---

and

$$E_\mathfrak{a}[\mathfrak{L}_1 \mathfrak{L}_2] = \varphi_{\mathfrak{c}_2 \mathfrak{a}_3}^{E_{\mathfrak{a}_1 \mathfrak{b}_2}} (E_{\mathfrak{a}_1 \mathfrak{b}_1}[\mathfrak{L}_1 \mathfrak{L}_2]) = \varphi_{\mathfrak{c}_2 \mathfrak{a}_3}^{E_{\mathfrak{a}_1 \mathfrak{b}_2}} (\langle P_{\mathfrak{a}_1 \mathfrak{b}_1} \rangle) = \langle P_{E_\mathfrak{a}} \rangle.$$

Algorithm 2 mostly consists of scalar multiplications, isogenies and discrete logarithm computations. The running time of scalar multiplications is polynomial in $\log(p)$ and $\log(L)$. Since the degrees of the isogenies computed, and the orders of the groups in which the discrete logarithms are computed divide L, then these operations can be performed in time $\tilde{O}(B)$ where B is the largest factor of L. Hence the overall complexity of Algorithm 2, ignoring logarithmic factors, is $\tilde{O}(B)$.   □

The Full Algorithm. Now, Algorithm 3 describes the group action evaluation. It is simply made of consecutive executions of $\mathsf{GroupActionSmall}$ preceded with a little initialization.

6   Concrete Instantiation

In this section, we report on the concrete choices we made to instantiate a signature scheme analogous to CSI-FiSh on top of our SCALLOP group action. For the construction of the signature scheme it suffices to replace the CSIDH group action by the SCALLOP group action. Since this does not provide any new insights, we refer the reader to [9] for the detailed description of the scheme instead. The security of the new signature scheme based on the SCALLOP group action relies on the problems introduced in Sect. 4. For the concrete instantiation we target two levels of security: matching the security of CSIDH-512 and of CSIDH-1024. To obtain class groups of the same size, we take prime conductors of size 256 and 512 bits respectively.

6.1   Parameter Selection

As outlined in Sect. 5, we start by choosing the conductor f. To this end, we fix $\mathfrak{O}_0 = \mathbb{Z}[i]$ to be the Gaussian integers. Then, we consider the smallest $n_1 + n_2$ split primes ℓ_i. As before, let $\mathfrak{l}_i$ denote split ideals associated to the primes ℓ_i. We partition the primes into two sets P_1 and P_2 of respective size n_1 and n_2 such that $L_1 = \prod_{\ell_i \in P_1} \ell_i$ and $L_2 = \prod_{\ell_i \in P_2} \ell_i$. For such a fixed partition, we iterate through choices for $b_i \in \{-2, 2\}$ and $c_i \in \{-1, 1\}$ to generate candidates for the orientation $\alpha \in \mathbb{Z}[i]$ as

$$\prod_{\ell_i \in P_1} \mathfrak{l}_i^{b_i} \prod_{\ell_i \in P_2} \mathfrak{l}_i^{c_i}.$$

By construction, each candidate is of smooth norm $L_1^2 L_2$.

For each candidate, we test whether the coefficient f of the imaginary part is prime. If this is the case, we try to factor $f + 1$, if $f \equiv 3 \pmod 4$, or $f - 1$ otherwise. Factoring is done using the ECM method with early abort in case a factor larger than a given smoothness bound is found or no further factor is discovered within a given time frame.

We ran this method and the algorithm SetUpCurve to find a conductor and a starting oriented curve for parameters with the same security level as CSIDH-512 and CSIDH-1024 respectively. The result are reported in the full version [24, Appx. B]. In both cases, the computation ran in minutes on a laptop.

6.2   Performance

Size of Public Keys. Public keys are represented as effective orientations (E, P_E, Q_E) (see Definition 6), with all constants defined over $\mathbb{F}_{p^2}$, so they are approximately six times larger than CSIDH keys. However, using standard compression techniques, we can represent them using only two $\mathbb{F}_p$-elements and two integers modulo $L_1 L_2$, which would give keys of approximately 1600 bits for SCALLOP-512 and 2300 bits for SCALLOP-1024.

Implementation. We implemented our group action in C++, making use of assembly-language field arithmetic. In our proof-of-concept implementation, applying the action of one arbitrary class-group element takes about 35 s for the smaller parameter set and 12.5 min for the larger parameter set on a single core of an Intel i5-6440HQ processor running at 3.5 GHz. Note that our implementation is not side-channel resistant.

While the current implementation is not fully optimized, for instance it does not yet use the $\sqrt{\text{élu}}$ algorithm [6], we do not expect to gain an order of magnitude by implementing all the possible optimizations. Thus, even if our implementation demonstrates feasibility, it seems that the SCALLOP group action is not yet ready for cryptographic applications.

Our code is available at https://github.com/isogeny-scallop/scallop.

7   Security Discussion: Evaluating the Descending Isogeny

We discuss a conceivable strategy to break the hardness assumptions of our proposed group action in the following. Recall that $\mathfrak{O}$-VECTORISATION is essentially equivalent to $\mathfrak{O}$-ENDRING, hence it would be sufficient to devise an algorithm that computes the endomorphism ring of any $\mathfrak{O}$-oriented curve, say (E_1, ι_1). Given an $\mathfrak{O}_0$-oriented curve (E_0, ι_0) with known endomorphism ring and $\mathfrak{O}_0$ of class number one, there exists a unique descending isogeny

$$\varphi : (E_0, \iota_0) \longrightarrow (E_1, \iota_1),$$

which has degree f. To compute $\mathrm{End}(E_1)$, one could try the following:

1. Find an algorithm to evaluate φ on input points efficiently.
2. Using Step 1, try to convert φ into its corresponding left $\mathrm{End}(E_0)$-ideal I_φ.
3. Deduce $\mathrm{End}(E_1)$ as the right-order of I_φ.

Note that this problem is related to the SubOrder to Ideal Problem (SOIP) introduced by Leroux [41]. It is quite obvious that the problem we study here is harder than the SOIP since the SOIP provides to the attacker several effective orientations of different quadratic orders (instead of one in our case). We refer to [41, section 4] for a study of the SOIP. Below, we will try to explain why applying efficiently the attack outlined above appears complicated.

In particular, the first two steps seem challenging. Since we chose $\deg(\varphi) = f$ to be a large prime, there is no hope to evaluate φ, Step 1, using standard algorithms such as Vélu's formulas, which have polynomial complexity in $\deg(\varphi)$. However, even if one managed to solve Step 1, it is not clear how to solve Step 2 (which is somewhat equivalent to the SOIP, see [41, Proposition 14]). Known algorithms to convert an isogeny into an ideal require working within the torsion subgroup $E[\deg(\varphi)]$. Our parameter choice ensures this torsion to be defined over an extension field of exponentially large degree.

Despite these obstacles, let us investigate a possible solution to Step 1, which does not necessarily need to rely on Vélu's formulas, or knowing $\ker(\varphi)$.

Let us introduce a vector notation for arithmetic on the curves. Given a pair of points $B = (P, Q)$, and a vector of two integers $v = (x, y)$, we write $v \cdot B = xP + yQ$. Fix a positive integer n coprime with p and the norm of $\mathfrak{a}$. Let $B_0 = (P_0, Q_0)$ and $B_1 = (P_1, Q_1)$ be bases of $E_0[n]$ and $E_1[n]$ respectively. Let $\psi : E_0 \to E_1$ be an isogeny. The restriction of ψ on the n-torsion is characterised by the matrix $M_\psi \in M_{2\times 2}(\mathbb{Z}/n\mathbb{Z})$ such that for any $v \in (\mathbb{Z}/n\mathbb{Z})^2$, we have $\psi(v \cdot B_0) = (M_\psi v) \cdot B_1$. We call M_ψ the matrix form of ψ with respect to B_0 and B_1.

In the following, we show that even for φ of large prime degree, it is possible to learn information about M_φ, effectively identifying a 1-dimensional subvariety of $M_{2\times 2}(\mathbb{Z}/n\mathbb{Z})$ containing it. Yet, this is not enough to solve Step 1.

Let $e_n(-, -)$ denote the Weil pairing on points of order dividing n. The following lemma fixes the determinant of M_φ.

Lemma 19. *If $e_n(P_0, Q_0) = e_n(P_1, Q_1)$, then $\det(M_\varphi) \equiv \deg(\varphi) \bmod n$.*

Proof. Write $M_\varphi = \left(\begin{smallmatrix} a & b \\ c & d \end{smallmatrix}\right)$. We have

$$e_n(P_0, Q_0)^{\deg(\varphi)} = e_n(\varphi(P_0), \varphi(Q_0)) = e_n(aP_1 + cQ_1, bP_1 + dQ_1)$$
$$= e_n(P_1, Q_1)^{ad-bc} = e_n(P_0, Q_0)^{\det(M_\varphi)}.$$

The result follows from the non-degeneracy of the Weil pairing. $\qquad\square$

For random bases B_0 and B_1, $e_n(P_0, Q_0) = e_n(P_1, Q_1)$ is unlikely. However, at the cost of solving one discrete logarithm in a group of order n, this condition on the bases can be enforced. This can be done in classical exponential time in the size of the largest prime factor of n, or in quantum polynomial time in $\log(n)$.

Due to φ being a descending isogeny, we observe that M_φ satisfies further certain linear relations: Writing $\mathfrak{O}_0 = \mathbb{Z}[\omega]$ and $\mathfrak{O} = \mathbb{Z}[f\omega]$, we have $\iota_1(f\omega) = \varphi \circ \iota_0(\omega) \circ \hat{\varphi}$, hence

$$AM_\varphi = M_\varphi B$$

where A is the matrix of $\iota_1(f\omega)$ (with respect to B_1), and B is the matrix of $f\iota_0(\omega)$ (with respect to B_0). Note that the matrices A and B can be computed in quantum polynomial time (or in classical exponential time in the size of the largest prime factor). This is because the endomorphisms can be evaluated in polynomial time on the points of the basis, and the matrix coefficients follow from a discrete logarithm computation as above.

For simplicity, assume that n is prime. Then, $M_{2\times2}(\mathbb{Z}/n\mathbb{Z})$ is an $\mathbb{F}_n$-vector space. The space $\mathcal{M}$ of solutions M of $AM_\varphi = M_\varphi B$ has dimension 2. Indeed, if M is one solution with non-zero determinant, then XM is a solution if and only if X commutes with A. Note that a solution exists, since M_φ itself has non-zero determinant by Lemma 19. The space of matrices that commute with A is the span of A and the identity matrix I_2, which has rank 1 if A is a scalar matrix, and 2 otherwise. Since n is coprime with the norm of $\mathfrak{a}$, the endomorphism $\iota_1(f\omega)$ does not act like a scalar on the n-torsion, so A is not a scalar matrix, and the space of solutions $\mathcal{M}$ has dimension 2.

Together with Lemma 19, we have reduced our search space for M_φ to the one-dimensional $\mathbb{F}_n$-variety

$$\mathcal{M}_f = \{M \in \mathcal{M} \mid \det(M) = f\}.$$

It is unclear how to reduce this space further, narrowing down M_φ. One may be tempted to use pairing equations as in Lemma 19 with the Tate pairing instead of the Weil pairing. However, the curves having trace $\pm 2p$, the Tate pairing is alternating (see [54, Theorem 3.17]), and thereby provides the same condition as the Weil pairing. In conclusion, it appears that all the available information is insufficient to evaluate the descending isogeny φ on any input efficiently.

References

1. Alamati, N., De Feo, L., Montgomery, H., Patranabis, S.: Cryptographic group actions and applications. In: Moriai, S., Wang, H. (eds.) ASIACRYPT 2020. LNCS, vol. 12492, pp. 411–439. Springer, Cham (2020). https://doi.org/10.1007/978-3-030-64834-3_14

2. Arpin, S., Chen, M., Lauter, K.E., Scheidler, R., Stange, K.E., Tran, H.T.N.: Orienteering with one endomorphism. arXiv preprint arXiv:2201.11079 (2022)

3. Azarderakhsh, R., Jao, D., Kalach, K., Koziel, B., Leonardi, C.: Key compression for isogeny-based cryptosystems. In: Proceedings of the 3rd ACM International Workshop on ASIA Public-Key Cryptography, pp. 1–10. ACM (2016)

4. Babai, L.: On Lovász' lattice reduction and the nearest lattice point problem. Combinatorica **6**(1), 1–13 (1986)

5. Belding, J.V.: Number theoretic algorithms for elliptic curves. University of Maryland, College Park (2008)

6. Bernstein, D.J., De Feo, L., Leroux, A., Smith, B.: Faster computation of isogenies of large prime degree. ANTS (2020)

7. Beullens, W., Dobson, S., Katsumata, S., Lai, Y.F., Pintore, F.: Group signatures and more from isogenies and lattices: Generic, simple, and efficient. In: Dunkelman, O., Dziembowski, S. (eds.) Advances in Cryptology – EUROCRYPT 2022. EUROCRYPT 2022. Lecture Notes in Computer Science, vol. 13276, pp. 95–126. Springer, Cham (2022). https://doi.org/10.1007/978-3-031-07085-3_4

8. Beullens, W., Katsumata, S., Pintore, F.: Calamari and Falafl: logarithmic (linkable) ring signatures from isogenies and lattices. In: Moriai, S., Wang, H. (eds.) ASIACRYPT 2020. LNCS, vol. 12492, pp. 464–492. Springer, Cham (2020). https://doi.org/10.1007/978-3-030-64834-3_16

9. Beullens, W., Kleinjung, T., Vercauteren, F.: CSI-FiSh: efficient isogeny based signatures through class group computations. In: Galbraith, S.D., Moriai, S. (eds.) ASIACRYPT 2019. LNCS, vol. 11921, pp. 227–247. Springer, Cham (2019). https://doi.org/10.1007/978-3-030-34578-5_9

10. Bonnetain, X., Schrottenloher, A.: Quantum security analysis of CSIDH. In: Canteaut, A., Ishai, Y. (eds.) EUROCRYPT 2020. LNCS, vol. 12106, pp. 493–522. Springer, Cham (2020). https://doi.org/10.1007/978-3-030-45724-2_17

11. Campos, F., Muth, P.: On actively secure fine-grained access structures from isogeny assumptions. In: Cheon, J.H., Johansson, T. (eds) Post-Quantum Cryptography. PQCrypto 2022. Lecture Notes in Computer Science, vol. 13512, pp. 375–398. Springer, Cham (2022). https://doi.org/10.1007/978-3-031-17234-2_18

12. Castryck, W., Houben, M., Vercauteren, F., Wesolowski, B.: On the decisional Diffie-Hellman problem for class group actions on oriented elliptic curves. Research in Number Theory 8 (2022). https://doi.org/10.1007/s40993-022-00399-6

13. Castryck, W., Lange, T., Martindale, C., Panny, L., Renes, J.: CSIDH: an efficient post-quantum commutative group action. In: Peyrin, T., Galbraith, S. (eds.) ASIACRYPT 2018. LNCS, vol. 11274, pp. 395–427. Springer, Cham (2018). https://doi.org/10.1007/978-3-030-03332-3_15

14. Castryck, W., van der Meeren, N.: Two remarks on the vectorization problem. Cryptology ePrint Archive (2022)

15. Castryck, W., Sotáková, J., Vercauteren, F.: Breaking the decisional Diffie-Hellman problem for class group actions using genus theory. In: Micciancio, D., Ristenpart, T. (eds.) Advances in Cryptology - CRYPTO 2020. Lecture Notes in Computer Science, vol. 12171, pp. 92–120. Springer (2020). https://doi.org/10.1007/978-3-030-56880-1_4

16. Chávez-Saab, J., Chi-Domínguez, J.J., Jaques, S., Rodríguez-Henríquez, F.: The SQALE of CSIDH: sublinear Vélu quantum-resistant isogeny action with low exponents. J. Cryptogr. Eng. **12**(3), 349–368 (2022)
17. Childs, A.M., van Dam, W.: Quantum algorithms for algebraic problems. Rev. Mod. Phys. **82**(1), 1 (2010)
18. Chung, K.M., Hsieh, Y.C., Huang, M.Y., Huang, Y.H., Lange, T., Yang, B.Y.: Group signatures and accountable ring signatures from isogeny-based assumptions. arXiv preprint arXiv:2110.04795 (2021)
19. Colò, L., Kohel, D.: Orienting supersingular isogeny graphs. Number-Theoretic Methods in Cryptology 2019 (2019)
20. Costello, C., Jao, D., Longa, P., Naehrig, M., Renes, J., Urbanik, D.: Efficient compression of SIDH public keys. In: Coron, J.-S., Nielsen, J.B. (eds.) EUROCRYPT 2017. LNCS, vol. 10210, pp. 679–706. Springer, Cham (2017). https://doi.org/10.1007/978-3-319-56620-7_24
21. Couveignes, J.M.: Hard homogeneous spaces. Cryptology ePrint Archive, Report 2006/291 (2006)
22. Cozzo, D., Smart, N.P.: Sashimi: Cutting up CSI-FiSh secret keys to produce an actively secure distributed signing protocol. In: Ding, J., Tillich, J.-P. (eds.) PQCrypto 2020. LNCS, vol. 12100, pp. 169–186. Springer, Cham (2020). https://doi.org/10.1007/978-3-030-44223-1_10
23. Dartois, P., De Feo, L.: On the security of OSIDH. In: Hanaoka, G., Shikata, J., Watanabe, Y. (eds.) Public-Key Cryptography – PKC 2022. PKC 2022. Lecture Notes in Computer Science, vol. 13177, pp. 52–81. Springer, Cham (2022). https://doi.org/10.1007/978-3-030-97121-2_3
24. De Feo, L., et al.: SCALLOP: scaling the CSI-FiSh. Cryptology ePrint Archive, Report 2023/058 (2023). https://eprint.iacr.org/2023/058
25. De Feo, L., et al.: SÉTA: Supersingular encryption from torsion attacks. In: ASIACRYPT (2021)
26. De Feo, L., Galbraith, S.D.: SeaSign: compact isogeny signatures from class group actions. In: Ishai, Y., Rijmen, V. (eds.) EUROCRYPT 2019. LNCS, vol. 11478, pp. 759–789. Springer, Cham (2019). https://doi.org/10.1007/978-3-030-17659-4_26
27. De Feo, L., Kohel, D., Leroux, A., Petit, C., Wesolowski, B.: SQISign: compact post-quantum signatures from quaternions and isogenies. In: Moriai, S., Wang, H. (eds.) ASIACRYPT 2020. LNCS, vol. 12491, pp. 64–93. Springer, Cham (2020). https://doi.org/10.1007/978-3-030-64837-4_3
28. De Feo, L., Leroux, A., Longa, P., Wesolowski, B.: New algorithms for the Deuring correspondence: towards practical and secure SQISign signatures. Eurocrypt 2023 (2023)
29. De Feo, L., Meyer, M.: Threshold schemes from isogeny assumptions. In: Kiayias, A., Kohlweiss, M., Wallden, P., Zikas, V. (eds.) PKC 2020. LNCS, vol. 12111, pp. 187–212. Springer, Cham (2020). https://doi.org/10.1007/978-3-030-45388-6_7
30. Decru, T., Panny, L., Vercauteren, F.: Faster SeaSign signatures through improved rejection sampling. In: Ding, J., Steinwandt, R. (eds.) PQCrypto 2019. LNCS, vol. 11505, pp. 271–285. Springer, Cham (2019). https://doi.org/10.1007/978-3-030-25510-7_15
31. Delfs, C., Galbraith, S.D.: Computing isogenies between supersingular elliptic curves over $\mathbb{F}_p$. Des. Codes Crypt. **78**(2), 425–440 (2016)
32. Eisenträger, K., Hallgren, S., Lauter, K., Morrison, T., Petit, C.: Supersingular isogeny graphs and endomorphism rings: reductions and solutions. In: Nielsen, J.B., Rijmen, V. (eds.) EUROCRYPT 2018. LNCS, vol. 10822, pp. 329–368. Springer, Cham (2018). https://doi.org/10.1007/978-3-319-78372-7_11

33. Eisenträger, K., Hallgren, S., Leonardi, C., Morrison, T., Park, J.: Computing endomorphism rings of supersingular elliptic curves and connections to path-finding in isogeny graphs. Open Book Series **4**(1), 215–232 (2020)

34. Fouotsa, T.B., Kutas, P., Merz, S.P., Ti, Y.B.: On the isogeny problem with torsion point information. In: Hanaoka, G., Shikata, J., Watanabe, Y. (eds) Public-Key Cryptography – PKC 2022. PKC 2022. Lecture Notes in Computer Science(), vol 13177, pp. 142–161. Springer, Cham (2022). https://doi.org/10.1007/978-3-030-97121-2_6

35. Galbraith, S., Panny, L., Smith, B., Vercauteren, F.: Quantum equivalence of the DLP and CDHP for group actions. Math. Cryptol. **1**(1), 40–44 (2021)

36. Hardy, G.H., Wright, E.M., et al.: An introduction to the theory of numbers. Oxford University Press (1979)

37. Ivanyos, G.: On solving systems of random linear disequations. arXiv preprint arXiv:0704.2988 (2007)

38. Kohel, D.R., Lauter, K., Petit, C., Tignol, J.P.: On the quaternion ℓ-isogeny path problem. LMS J. Comput. Math. **17**(A), 418–432 (2014)

39. Kuperberg, G.: A subexponential-time quantum algorithm for the dihedral hidden subgroup problem. SIAM J. Comput. **35**(1), 170–188 (2005)

40. Lai, Y.F., Dobson, S.: Collusion resistant revocable ring signatures and group signatures from hard homogeneous spaces. Cryptology ePrint Archive (2021)

41. Leroux, A.: A new isogeny representation and applications to cryptography. In: Agrawal, S., Lin, D. (eds.) Advances in Cryptology - ASIACRYPT 2022, pp. 3–35. Springer, Cham (2022). https://doi.org/10.1007/978-3-031-22966-4_1

42. Leroux, A., Roméas, M.: Updatable encryption from group actions. Cryptology ePrint Archive (2022)

43. Li, J., Nguyen, P.Q.: A complete analysis of the BKZ lattice reduction algorithm. Cryptology ePrint Archive, Paper 2020/1237 (2020). https://eprint.iacr.org/2020/1237

44. Love, J., Boneh, D.: Supersingular curves with small noninteger endomorphisms. Open Book Ser. **4**(1), 7–22 (2020)

45. Montgomery, H., Zhandry, M.: Full quantum equivalence of group action DLog and CDH, and more. In: Agrawal, S., Lin, D. (eds.) Advances in Cryptology - ASIACRYPT 2022, pp. 3–32. Springer, Cham (2022). https://doi.org/10.1007/978-3-031-22963-3_1

46. Naehrig, M., Renes, J.: Dual isogenies and their application to public-key compression for isogeny-based cryptography. In: Galbraith, S.D., Moriai, S. (eds.) ASIACRYPT 2019. LNCS, vol. 11922, pp. 243–272. Springer, Cham (2019). https://doi.org/10.1007/978-3-030-34621-8_9

47. Onuki, H.: On oriented supersingular elliptic curves. Finite Fields Appl. **69**, 101777 (2021)

48. Peikert, C.: He gives C-sieves on the CSIDH. In: Canteaut, A., Ishai, Y. (eds.) EUROCRYPT 2020. LNCS, vol. 12106, pp. 463–492. Springer, Cham (2020). https://doi.org/10.1007/978-3-030-45724-2_16

49. de Quehen, V., et al.: Improved torsion-point attacks on SIDH variants. In: Malkin, T., Peikert, C. (eds) Advances in Cryptology – CRYPTO 2021. CRYPTO 2021. Lecture Notes in Computer Science, vol. 12827, pp. 432–470. Springer, Cham (2021). https://doi.org/10.1007/978-3-030-84252-9_15

50. Rostovtsev, A., Stolbunov, A.: Public-key cryptosystem based on isogenies. Cryptology ePrint Archive, Report 2006/145 (2006)

51. Silverman, J.H.: The arithmetic of elliptic curves, vol. 106 (2009)

52. Stolbunov, A.: Cryptographic schemes based on isogenies (2012)
53. Vélu, J.: Isogénies entre courbes elliptiques. Comptes-Rendus de l'Académie des Sciences, Série I **273**, 238–241 (1971)
54. Washington, L.C.: Elliptic curves: number theory and cryptography. Chapman and Hall/CRC, second edn. (2008). https://doi.org/10.1201/9781420071474
55. Wesolowski, B.: Orientations and the supersingular endomorphism ring problem. In: Dunkelman, O., Dziembowski, S. (eds.) Advances in Cryptology - EUROCRYPT 2022. Lecture Notes in Computer Science, vol. 13277, pp. 345–371. Springer (2022). https://doi.org/10.1007/978-3-031-07082-2_13
56. Zanon, G.H.M., Simplicio, M.A., Pereira, G.C.C.F., Doliskani, J., Barreto, P.S.L.M.: Faster isogeny-based compressed key agreement. In: Lange, T., Steinwandt, R. (eds.) PQCrypto 2018. LNCS, vol. 10786, pp. 248–268. Springer, Cham (2018). https://doi.org/10.1007/978-3-319-79063-3_12

Round-Optimal Oblivious Transfer and MPC from Computational CSIDH

Saikrishna Badrinarayanan[1], Daniel Masny[2], Pratyay Mukherjee[3],
Sikhar Patranabis[4(✉)], Srinivasan Raghuraman[5], and Pratik Sarkar[6]

[1] LinkedIn, Seattle, USA
[2] Meta, Menlo Park, USA
[3] Supra, Kolkata, India
[4] IBM Research India, Bengaluru, India
sikharpatranabis@gmail.com, sikhar.patranabis@ibm.com
[5] VISA Research, Palo Alto, USA
[6] Boston University, Boston, USA

Abstract. We present the first round-optimal and plausibly quantum-safe oblivious transfer (OT) and multi-party computation (MPC) protocols from the computational CSIDH assumption – the weakest and most widely studied assumption in the CSIDH family of isogeny-based assumptions. We obtain the following results:

- The *first* round-optimal maliciously secure OT and MPC protocols in the *plain model* that achieve (black-box) simulation-based security while relying on the computational CSIDH assumption.
- The *first* round-optimal maliciously secure OT and MPC protocols that achieves Universal Composability (UC) security in the presence of a trusted setup (common reference string plus random oracle) while relying on the computational CSIDH assumption.

Prior plausibly quantum-safe isogeny-based OT protocols (with/without setup assumptions) are either not round-optimal, or rely on potentially stronger assumptions.

We also build a 3-round maliciously-secure OT extension protocol where each base OT protocol requires only 4 isogeny computations. In comparison, the most efficient isogeny-based OT extension protocol till date due to Lai et al. [Eurocrypt 2021] requires 12 isogeny computations and 4 rounds of communication, while relying on the same assumption as our construction, namely the reciprocal CSIDH assumption.

1 Introduction

Oblivious transfer (OT) [Rab05, EGL82] is an interactive protocol between two parties: a sender and a receiver. Informally speaking, an OT protocol

S. Patranabis—Part of the work was done while the author was at VISA Research USA.

P. Sarkar—Supported by NSF Awards 1931714, 1414119, and the DARPA SIEVE program.

A. Boldyreva and V. Kolesnikov (Eds.): PKC 2023, LNCS 13940, pp. 376–405, 2023.
https://doi.org/10.1007/978-3-031-31368-4_14

involves a *sender* holding two messages m_0 and m_1, and a receiver holding a bit $b \in \{0,1\}$. At the end of the protocol, the receiver should only learn the message m_b and nothing about the other message m_{1-b}, while the sender should learn nothing about the bit b. OT serves as a fundamental building block in cryptography [Kil88], particularly in secure multi-party computation (MPC) [Yao86, IKO+11, BL18, GS18]. Round optimal OT protocols imply round-optimal MPC protocols [BL18, GS18, CCG+20] and hence are always desirable.

Quantum-Safe OT. With steady progress in quantum computing, the study of post-quantum cryptography has gained significant momentum in recent years, especially in light of Shor's algorithm [Sho94], which breaks traditional cryptographic assumptions such as factoring and discrete-log. OT protocols are known from various plausibly quantum-safe assumptions such as lattices [PVW08, BD18, MR19], codes [DvMN08, DNM12, MR19], and isogenies of elliptic curves [BOB18, Vit18, LGdSG21]. Unfortunately, many isogeny-based OT constructions [BOB18, dSGOPS20, Vit18] are now (classically) broken in light of the recent attacks on the Supersingular Isogeny Diffie-Hellman (SIDH) assumption [CD22, MM22, Rob22]. Hence, the only plausibly quantum-safe isogeny-based OT constructions are the ones based on the Commutative SIDH (CSIDH) [CLM+18] family of isogeny-based assumptions, which are not affected by the recent attacks on SIDH.

The CSIDH Family of Assumptions. The CSIDH family of (plausibly quantum-safe) isogeny-based assumptions includes the computational CSIDH assumption [CLM+18] (the CSIDH-equivalent of the traditional CDH assumption), the decisional CSIDH assumption [CSV20, ADMP20, BKW20] (the CSIDH-equivalent of the traditional DDH assumption), the reciprocal CSIDH assumption [LGdSG21], and certain variants of these assumptions [AEK+22]. Of these, the computational CSIDH assumption is the weakest assumption (equivalently, the hardest problem to solve). The decisional CSIDH assumption implies the computational CSIDH assumption, and has been shown to be broken for certain families of elliptic curves [CSV20]. Finally, the reciprocal CSIDH assumption is only *quantum-equivalent* to the computational CSIDH assumption; the corresponding classical equivalence is not known (see discussion in [LGdSG21]).

OT from CSIDH-Based Assumptions. Many recent works have constructed OT protocols from the CSIDH family of isogeny-based assumptions. We broadly categorize these OT constructions as: (i) OT protocols in the *plain model*, i.e., without any (trusted) setup assumptions, or (ii) OT protocols in the *setup model*, i.e., assuming the existence of some (trusted) setup and/or random oracles.

In the plain model, there exist round-optimal OT protocols achieving various security notions from the decisional CSIDH assumption [ADMP20, KM20] and the reciprocal CSIDH assumption [BPS22]. We present a summary of these protocols in Table 1. In the setup model, round-optimal OT protocols are known from the decisional CSIDH assumption [ADMP20, BKW20, AMPS21]. A recent work by Lai et al. [LGdSG21] proposed an elegant OT protocol from the reciprocal CSIDH assumption; however, their construction is *not* round-optimal. We summarize these protocols in Table 2.

Table 1. Comparison of plausibly quantum-safe maliciously secure OT protocols in the plain model from the CSIDH family of isogeny-based assumptions

Protocol	Computational Assumption	Rounds	Security Model
[ADMP20]-1	decisional CSIDH	2	semantic
[BPS22]-1	reciprocal CSIDH	3	semantic
[KM20]	decisional CSIDH	4	simulation-secure
[BPS22]-2	reciprocal CSIDH	4	simulation-secure
Our Protocol-1	**computational CSIDH**	**4**	**simulation-secure**

Table 2. Comparison of plausibly quantum-safe maliciously secure OT protocols in the setup model from the CSIDH family of isogeny-based assumptions. The protocols of [ADMP20, AMPS21] are in the CRS model. All other protocols are in the CRS+random oracle model.

Protocols	Computational Assumption	Rounds	Security Model
[ADMP20]-2	decisional CSIDH	2	UC-secure
[BKW20]	decisional CSIDH	2	UC-secure
[AMPS21]	decisional CSIDH	2	UC-secure
[LGdSG21]-1	reciprocal CSIDH	3	simulation-secure
[LGdSG21]-2	reciprocal CSIDH	4	UC-secure
Our Protocol-2	**computational CSIDH**	**2**	**UC-secure**

Notably, there exist no (round-optimal) OT protocols in the plain/setup model from the computational CSIDH assumption, which is the weakest (and most widely studied) assumption in the CSIDH family of isogeny-based assumptions. This motivates us to ask the following question:

Can we design round-optimal OT protocols from computational CSIDH?

1.1 Our Contributions

In this paper, we answer the above question in the affirmative by presenting the first round-optimal, maliciously secure, and plausibly quantum safe OT protocols in various settings from the computational CSIDH assumption. In particular, we propose two new round-optimal maliciously secure OT protocols in the plain and common reference string[1] (CRS) models, while relying on the computational CSIDH assumption. These also yield the first round-optimal MPC protocols in the respective settings from the computational CSIDH assumption. Our main contributions can be summarized as follows.

Round Optimal OT and MPC in the Plain Model. We propose the *first* round-optimal (4-round) OT protocol in the plain model while relying on the computational CSIDH assumption. Our construction satisfies perfect correctness and simulation-based security against malicious corruption of parties, which is the strongest notion of OT security that is achievable in the plain model. Our result is captured by the following (informal) theorem.

---

[1] The setup string is structured and it is sampled from a given distribution.

Theorem 1. (Informal) *Assuming computational CSIDH, there exists a 4-round OT protocol in the plain model that achieves perfect correctness and (black-box) simulation-security against malicious corruption of parties.*

In Table 1, we present a comparison of our proposed OT construction with known constructions of round-optimal OT in the plain model from the CSIDH family of assumptions. Additionally, by invoking known relationships between round-optimal OT and MPC in the plain model from [CCG+20], we achieve the following (informal) corollary.

Corollary 1. (Informal) *Assuming computational CSIDH, there exists a 4-round MPC protocol in the plain model with (black-box) simulation-security against malicious corruption of parties.*

This is the first round optimal MPC protocol achieving (black-box) simulation security in the plain model from the computational CSIDH assumption.

Round-Optimal OT and MPC assuming Trusted Setup. We propose the *first* round-optimal (2-round) OT protocol in the CRS plus random oracle model[2] while relying on the computational CSIDH assumption. Our construction satisfies perfect correctness and universal composability (UC)-security against malicious corruption of parties, which is the strongest notion of OT security that is achievable in the trusted setup model. Informally, we prove the following theorem.

Theorem 2. (Informal) *Assuming that the computational CSIDH assumption holds, there exists a 2-round OT protocol in the CRS plus random oracle model that is UC-secure against malicious corruption of parties.*

In Table 2, we present a comparison of our proposed OT construction with known constructions of round-optimal OT in the trusted setup model from the CSIDH family of assumptions. Finally, by invoking known relationships between round-optimal OT and MPC from [GS18], we achieve the following (informal) corollary (to

Corollary 2. (Informal) *Assuming that the computational CSIDH assumption holds, there exists a 2-round MPC protocol in the CRS plus random oracle model that is UC-secure against malicious corruption of parties.*

This yields the *first* construction of round-optimal MPC in the CRS plus random oracle model from the computational CSIDH assumption.

Efficient OT Extension. As an additional contribution, we propose the first UC-secure OT extension protocol that relies on the computational CSIDH assumption. Concretely, we show that an optimized variant of the recent 4-round OT protocol due to Lai et al. [LGdSG21] can be plugged into the OT extension compiler due to Canetti et al. [CSW20a] to build a UC-secure 3-round *OT extension protocol* in the random oracle model. This yields the most efficient (to

---

[2] The random oracles in our protocol are local to each session.

our knowledge) UC-secure OT extension protocol currently known from isogeny-based assumptions.[3]

Our construction of OT extension builds upon a maliciously secure base OT protocol that requires a total of 4 isogeny computations. On the other hand, the state-of-the-art 4-round maliciously secure protocol of [LGdSG21] incurs 12 isogeny computations, while relying on the same hardness assumption as our construction (the reciprocal CSIDH assumption).

1.2 Related Work

Lattice-Based OT. To the best of our knowledge, the first lattice-based oblivious transfer protocol was designed by Peikert, Vaikuntanathan and Waters [PVW08], that relies on LWE [Reg05]. Their OT protocol follows a more generic framework on dual encryption and achieves round-optimality as well as UC security in the CRS model. A recent result of Quach [Qua20] improves the [PVW08] construction so that the CRS can be reused by multiple OT executions. Another recent work by Büscher et al. [BDK+20] provided an instantiation of a lattice-based OT from additive homomorphic encryption. The OT construction of Brakerski and Döttling [BD18] provided the first two-round SSP OT (without a CRS).

An alternative to constructing an OT is to construct an oblivious pseudorandom function which implies [JL09] an OT. Albrecht, Davidson, Deo and Smart [ADDS21] showed how to construct an oblivious pseudorandom function from ideal lattices using non-interactive zero-knowledge arguments [CSW22, PS19, CCH+19].

Code-Based OT. There are two OT constructions based on the code-based assumptions [DvMN08, DNM12]. Both of these constructions use the specific assumption underlying the McEliece cryptosystems [McE78]. Among these, only the latter achieves UC security. Recently, Bitansky and Freizeit [BF22] showed how to realize a statistically sender-private (SSP) OT protocol with semantic security against a computationally bounded sender and an unbounded receiver while relying on the learning with parity (LPN) assumption plus Nissan Wigderson style derandomization.

Generic OT Constructions. Generic approaches to realize OT [BGJ+18, MR19, FMV19, DGH+20] rely on public-key encryption schemes with specific properties. Unfortunately, known public-key encryption schemes from isogeny-based assumptions (including the CSIDH family of assumptions) do not satisfy any of these properties. For example, to use any isogeny-based PKE in the framework of [MR19], one inherently needs the ability to hash into a curve in the family of supersingular elliptic curves, which is not known so far (see [Pet17, DMPS19, CPV20, BBD+22, MMP22] for more details). For the constructions of Badrinarayanan et al. [BGJ+18] and Friolo et al. [FMV19] in

---

[3] We note that while prior works on OT from isogenies do not explicitly construct OT extension protocols, they do yield base OT protocols that can be converted in a generic manner into full-fledged OT extension protocols.

the plain model, one needs a PKE with dense public-key space – this is again not known to exist from isogeny-based assumptions. Döttling et al. [DGH+20] provided a generic approach to obtain 2-round UC-secure OT in the CRS model from protocols satisfying very mild form of security, known as elementary OT – this gives 2-round OT from LPN [ACPS09]. The work of [AMPS21] also follows a similar route to build adaptively secure OT from a mild strengthening of elementary OT.

Prior Isogeny-Based OT. Prior works [BOB18, dSGOPS20, Vit18, BKW20] have realized isogeny-based OT constructions from the well-known SIDH assumption and its variants. Unfortunately, these constructions are now (classically) broken in light of the recent attacks on the SIDH assumption [CD22, MM22]. The construction of [BKW20] was, in fact, broken in its original form by an earlier attack proposed in [BKM+21].

Prior works have realized OT protocols in the plain model achieving various security notions from the decisional CSIDH assumption [ADMP20, KM20] and the reciprocal CSIDH assumption [BPS22]. The authors of [ADMP20] showed how to construct a 2-round SSP OT protocol with semantic security against a computationally bounded sender and an unbounded receiver from the decisional CSIDH assumption. The authors of [KM20] showed how to construct a 4-round OT protocol with full-fledged simulation security from any 2-round SSP OT protocol. The authors of [BPS22] showed how to construct a 3-round statistically receiver-private (SRP) OT protocol with semantic security against a computationally bounded receiver and an unbounded sender from the reciprocal CSIDH assumption. They also showed a construction of 4-round OT protocol with full-fledged simulation security from any 3-round SRP OT protocol. See Table 1 for a comparison of our proposed OT protocol in the plain model with these prior OT protocols.

In the setup model, round-optimal OT protocols are known from the decisional CSIDH assumption [ADMP20, BKW20, AMPS21]. The OT construction of [BKW20] was not explicitly described, but follows implicitly from the construction of oblivious PRF from decisional CSIDH (plus random oracles) in the same paper. The work of [AMPS21] presents the first adaptively secure OT protocol from isogenies. Their protocol is round optimal and relies on decisional CSIDH assumption. The recent work by Lai et al. [LGdSG21] proposed an elegant OT protocol from the reciprocal CSIDH assumption (plus random oracles); however, the simulation-secure and UC-secure versions of their construction require 3 rounds and 4 rounds, respectively, and are hence not round-optimal.

2 Preliminaries

Notation. For $a \in \mathbb{N}$ such that $a \geq 1$, we denote by $[a]$ the set of integers lying between 1 and a (both inclusive). We use κ to denote the security parameter, and denote by $\mathsf{poly}(\kappa)$ and $\mathsf{negl}(\kappa)$ any generic (unspecified) polynomial function and negligible function in κ, respectively. For a finite set S, we use $s \leftarrow_R S$ to sample uniformly from the set S. For a probability distribution $\mathcal{D}$ on a finite set S, we use $s \leftarrow_R \mathcal{D}$ to sample from $\mathcal{D}$. We use the notations $\overset{s}{\approx}$ and $\overset{c}{\approx}$ to denote statistical and computational indistinguishability of distributions, respectively.

2.1   Basic Cryptographic Primitives

Weak Unpredictable Function (wUF) [ADMP20]. Let K, X, and Y be sets indexed by κ. A weak unpredictable function (wUF) family is a family of efficiently computable functions $\{F(k, \cdot) : X \to Y\}_{k \in K}$ such that for all PPT adversaries $\mathcal{A}$ we have the following:

$$\Pr[\mathcal{A}^{F_k^\$}(1^\kappa, x^*) = F(k, x^*)] \leq \mathsf{negl}(\kappa),$$

where $k \leftarrow_R K$, $x^* \leftarrow_R X$, and $F_k^\$$ is a *randomized* oracle that when queried samples $x \leftarrow_R X$ and outputs $(x, F(k, x))$.

Weak Pseudorandom Function (wPRF). Let K, X, and Y be sets indexed by κ. A weak pseudorandom function (wPRF) is a family of efficiently computable functions $\{F(k, \cdot) : X \to Y\}_{k \in K}$ such that for all PPT adversaries $\mathcal{A}$ we have the following:

$$\left| \Pr[\mathcal{A}^{F_k^\$}(1^\kappa) = 1] - \Pr[\mathcal{A}^{\pi^\$}(1^\kappa) = 1] \right| \leq \mathsf{negl}(\kappa),$$

where $k \leftarrow_R k$, $F_k^\$$ is a randomized oracle that when queried samples $x \leftarrow_R X$ and outputs $(x, F(k, x))$, and $\pi^\$$ is a randomized oracle that when queried samples $x \leftarrow_R X$ and $y \leftarrow_R Y$, and outputs (x, y).

2.2   Cryptographic Group Actions

In this section we recall the definitions of cryptographic group actions from [ADMP20]. We note here that the authors of [ADMP20] use the definitions of Brassard and Yung [BY91] and Couveignes [Cou06] as starting points to provide definitions that allow for easy use of isogenies (in particular, isogeny families such as CSIDH [CLM+18] and CSI-FiSh [BKV19]) in cryptographic protocols. We begin by recalling the definition of a group action.

Definition 1. (Group Action [BY91, Cou06, ADMP20]). *A group G is said to act on a set X if there is a map $\star : G \times X \to X$ that satisfies:*

1. *Identity: If e is the identity element of G, then for any $x \in X$, we have $e \star x = x$.*
2. *Compatibility: For any $g, h \in G$ and any $x \in X$, we have $(gh) \star x = g \star (h \star x)$.*

Throughout this paper, we use the abbreviated notation $(G, X, \star)$ to denote a group action.

Remark 1. If $(G, X, \star)$ is a group action, for any $g \in G$ the map $\pi_g : x \mapsto g \star x$ defines a permutation of X.

Properties of Group Actions. We consider group actions $(G, X, \star)$ that satisfy one or more of the following properties:

1. *Abelian:* The group G is abelian.
2. *Transitive:* For every $x_1, x_2 \in X$, there exists a group element $g \in G$ such that $x_2 = g \star x_1$. For such a transitive group action, the set X is called a *homogeneous space* for G.
3. *Faithful:* For each group element $g \in G$, either g is the identity element or there exists a set element $x \in X$ such that $x \neq g \star x$.
4. *Free:* For each group element $g \in G$, g is the identity element if and only if there exists some set element $x \in X$ such that $x = g \star x$.
5. *Regular: Both* free *and* transitive.

Remark 2. If a group action is regular, then for any $x \in X$, the map $f_x : g \mapsto g \star x$ defines a bijection between G and X; in particular, if G (or X) is finite, then we must have $|G| = |X|$.

Effective Group Action (EGA). We now recall the definition of an *effective* group action (abbreviated throughout as an EGA) from [ADMP20]. At a high level, an EGA is an abelian and regular group action with certain special computational properties that allow it to be useful for cryptographic applications. Formally, an abelian and regular group action $(G, X, \star)$ is *effective* if the following properties are satisfied:

1. The group G is finite and there exist efficient (PPT) algorithms for:
   (a) Membership testing, i.e., to decide if a given bit string represents a valid group element in G.
   (b) Equality testing, i.e., to decide if two bit strings represent the same group element in G.
   (c) Sampling, i.e., to sample an element g from a distribution G on G. In this paper, We consider distributions that are statistically close to uniform.
   (d) Operation, i.e., to compute gh for any $g, h \in G$.
   (e) Inversion, i.e., to compute g^{-1} for any $g \in G$.
2. The set X is finite and there exist efficient algorithms for:
   (a) Membership testing, i.e., to decide if a bit string represents a valid set element.
   (b) Unique representation, i.e., given any arbitrary set element $x \in X$, compute a string $\hat{x}$ that canonically represents x.
3. There exists a distinguished element $x_0 \in X$, called the *origin*, such that its bit-string representation is known.
4. There exists an efficient algorithm that given (some bit-string representations of) any $g \in G$ and any $x \in X$, outputs $g \star x$.

Restricted Effective Group Action (REGA). From the point of view of cryptographic applications, one can view EGA as an abstraction that captures the CSI-FiSh [BKV19] family of isogenies, where we can compute the group action operation $\star$ efficiently for any element g in the group G. However, this is not the case for the CSIDH family of isogenies [CLM+18], where we can only compute the group action operation $\star$ efficiently for "certain" elements in the group G (more specifically, a generating set of small cardinality). To model such families of isogenies, the authors of [ADMP20] introduced a weaker or *restricted* variant of EGA (abbreviated throughput as REGA). We refer the reader to the full version [BMM+22] for more details on REGA.

Hardness Assumptions over EGA. The definitions of Effective Group Action (EGA) and Restricted Effective Group Action (REGA) can be recalled from [ADMP20]. We now define certain hardness assumptions pertaining to an EGA following conventions introduced in [ADMP20].

Definition 2. (Weak Unpredictable EGA [ADMP20]). *An EGA $(G, X, \star)$ is weakly unpredictable if the family of functions (more specifically, permutations) $\{\pi_g : X \to X\}_{g \in G}$ is weakly unpredictable, where π_g is defined as $\pi_g : x \mapsto g \star x$.*

Definition 3. (Weak Pseudorandom EGA [ADMP20]). *An EGA $(G, X, \star)$ is weakly pseudorandom if the family of functions (more specifically, permutations) $\{\pi_g : X \to X\}_{g \in G}$ is weakly pseudorandom, where π_g is defined as $\pi_g : x \mapsto g \star x$.*

Throughout this paper, we will use the abbreviations wU-EGA and wPR-EGA to refer to a weak unpredictable and weak pseudorandom (abelian and regular) EGA, respectively. We can similarly define wU-REGA and wPR-REGA, where in the corresponding definitions, all group elements are sampled from a distribution that is statistically close to uniform. Finally, we state the following theorem (imported from [ADMP20]).

Theorem 3. [ADMP20]. *Assuming that the computational (resp., decisional) CSIDH assumption holds, there exists a wU-REGA (resp., wPR-REGA).*

All of the protocols proposed in this paper can be instantiated using both EGA and REGA (and hence from both CSI-FiSh [BKV19] and CSIDH [CLM+18]). For simplicity of representation, we describe our constructions from an EGA; the corresponding REGA-based constructions follow analogously.

2.3 Oblivious Transfer (OT)

In this section, we present preliminary background material on oblivious transfer (OT) protocols.

The Ideal Functionality for OT. The ideal functionality $\mathcal{F}_{\mathsf{OT}}$ for any OT protocol is described in Fig. 1. We adopt this description essentially verbatim from prior works [CLOS02, PVW08, DGH+20].

$$\mathcal{F}_{\mathsf{OT}}$$

$\mathcal{F}_{\mathsf{OT}}$ interacts with an ideal sender S and an ideal receiver R as follows:

- On input $(\mathsf{Choose}, \mathsf{rec}, \mathsf{sid}, b)$ from R where $b \in \{0,1\}$; if no message of the form $(\mathsf{rec}, \mathsf{sid}, b)$ has been recorded in the memory, store $(\mathsf{rec}, \mathsf{sid}, b)$ and send $(\mathsf{rec}, \mathsf{sid})$ to S.

- On input $(\mathsf{Transfer}, \mathsf{sen}, \mathsf{sid}, (\mathsf{m}_0, \mathsf{m}_1))$ from S with $\mathsf{m}_0, \mathsf{m}_1 \in \{0,1\}^n$, if no message of the form $(\mathsf{sen}, \mathsf{sid}, (\mathsf{m}_0, \mathsf{m}_1))$ is recorded and a message of the form $(\mathsf{rec}, \mathsf{sid}, b)$ is stored, send $(\mathsf{sent}, \mathsf{sid}, \mathsf{m}_b)$ to R and $(\mathsf{sent}, \mathsf{sid})$ to S. Ignore future messages with the same sid.

Fig. 1. The ideal functionality $\mathcal{F}_{\mathsf{OT}}$ for Oblivious Transfer

Two-Round Oblivious Transfer in the CRS Model. We first formally define a two-round oblivious transfer (OT) protocol in the CRS model. A two-round OT protocol in the CRS model is a tuple of four algorithms of the form $\mathsf{OT} = (\mathsf{Setup}, \mathsf{OTR}, \mathsf{OTS}, \mathsf{OTD})$ described below:

- $\mathsf{Setup}(1^\kappa)$: Takes as input the security parameter κ and outputs a CRS string crs and a trapdoor td.[4]

- $\mathsf{OTR}(\mathsf{crs}, b \in \{0,1\})$: Takes as input the crs and a bit $b \in \{0,1\}$, and outputs the receiver's message ot_1 and the receiver's (secret) internal state st.

- $\mathsf{OTS}(\mathsf{crs}, \mathsf{ot}_1, \mathsf{m}_0, \mathsf{m}_1)$: Takes as input the crs, the receiver's message ot_1, a pair of input strings $(\mathsf{m}_0, \mathsf{m}_1)$, and outputs the sender's message ot_2.

- $\mathsf{OTD}(\mathsf{crs}, \mathsf{st}, \mathsf{ot}_2)$: Takes as input the crs, the sender's message ot_2, and the receiver's internal state st, and outputs a message string m'.

Correctness. A two-round OT protocol in the CRS model is said to be correct if for any $b \in \{0,1\}$ and any $(\mathsf{m}_0, \mathsf{m}_1)$, letting $(\mathsf{crs}, \mathsf{td}) \leftarrow_R \mathsf{Setup}(1^\kappa)$ and $(\mathsf{ot}_1, \mathsf{st}) \leftarrow_R \mathsf{OTR}(\mathsf{crs}, b)$, we have $\mathsf{OTD}(\mathsf{crs}, \mathsf{st}, \mathsf{OTS}(\mathsf{crs}, \mathsf{ot}_1, \mathsf{m}_0, \mathsf{m}_1)) = \mathsf{m}_b$.

Four-Round Oblivious Transfer in the Plain Model. We also formally define a four-round oblivious transfer (OT) protocol in the plain model. A four-round OT protocol in the plain model is a tuple of five algorithms of the form $\mathsf{OT} = (\mathsf{OTR}_1, \mathsf{OTS}_1, \mathsf{OTR}_2, \mathsf{OTS}_2, \mathsf{OTD})$ described below:

- $\mathsf{OTR}_1(1^\kappa, b)$: Given κ and a bit $b \in \{0,1\}$, output message ot_1 and (secret) receiver state st_R.
- $\mathsf{OTS}_1(1^\kappa, (\mathsf{m}_0, \mathsf{m}_1), \mathsf{ot}_1)$: Given κ, a pair of strings $(\mathsf{m}_0, \mathsf{m}_1)$, and a message ot_1, output message ot_2 and (secret) sender state st_S.
- $\mathsf{OTR}_2(\mathsf{st}_\mathsf{R}, \mathsf{ot}_2)$: Given receiver state st_R and a message ot_2, output message ot_3 and an updated receiver state st_R.

---

[4] For standard two-round OT protocols, the setup algorithm need not output a trapdoor td, but we include it for certain security properties described subsequently.

- $\mathsf{OTS}_2(\mathsf{st}_S, \mathsf{ot}_3)$: Given sender state st_S and message ot_3, output message ot_4.
- $\mathsf{OTD}(\mathsf{st}_R, \mathsf{ot}_4)$: Given receiver state st_R and message ot_4, output string m'.

Correctness. A four-round OT protocol in the plain model is said to be correct if for any bit $b \in \{0, 1\}$ and any pair of strings $\mathsf{m}_0, \mathsf{m}_1$, letting

$$(\mathsf{ot}_1, \mathsf{st}_R) = \mathsf{OTR}_1(1^\kappa, b), \quad (\mathsf{ot}_2, \mathsf{st}_S) = \mathsf{OTS}_1(1^\kappa, (\mathsf{m}_0, \mathsf{m}_1), \mathsf{ot}_1),$$
$$(\mathsf{ot}_3, \mathsf{st}_R) = \mathsf{OTR}_2(\mathsf{st}_R, \mathsf{ot}_2), \quad \mathsf{ot}_4 = \mathsf{OTS}_2(\mathsf{st}_S, \mathsf{ot}_3),$$

and finally
$$\mathsf{m}' = \mathsf{OTD}(\mathsf{st}_R, \mathsf{ot}_4),$$

we have $\mathsf{m}' = \mathsf{m}_b$ with overwhelming probability.

Simulation Security in the Plain Model. We say that any 4-round OT protocol in the plain model is simulation-secure against maliciously corrupt parties if it implements the $\mathcal{F}_{\mathsf{OT}}$ functionality in the plain model. For our construction of 4-round OT protocol in the plain model, we prove security in the standalone setting.

UC Security and Simulation Security. We refer the reader to the full version [BMM+22, CSW20b] for the formal definitions of UC security and simulation security of OT protocols in the aforementioned settings, namely two-round protocols in the CRS model and four-round protocols in the plain model.

3 Round-Optimal UC-Secure OT from wU-EGA

In this section, we demonstrate how to construct a two-round UC-secure OT protocol in the CRS model based on any weak unpredictable effective group action (EGA) (Definition 2). For background material on EGA, see Sect. 2.2. For simplicity, we begin with a construction of two-round (round optimal) OT in the CRS model that is UC-secure against a *malicious* sender but only a *semi-honest* receiver. Subsequently, we show how to augment the construction in order to also achieve UC-security against a malicious receiver.

3.1 Warm-Up: 2-Round UC-OT Against Semi-honest Receiver

We provide a brief overview of our protocol. The initial protocol is described as follows. The crs consists of two set elements $(x_0, x_1) = (g_0 \star x, g_1 \star x)$. The receiver has its input choice bit b. It constructs the OT receiver message z by sampling a random group element $r \leftarrow_R G$ as follows:

$$z = r \star x_b$$

The sender has input messages $(m_0, m_1) \in \{0, 1\}^\kappa$. The sender uses z and the crs $= (x_0, x_1)$ to compute the second OT message by sampling random group elements $k_0, k_1 \leftarrow_R G$ as follows:

$$y_0 = k_0 \star x_0, \quad \gamma_0 = H(k_0 \star z) \oplus m_0,$$

$$y_1 = k_1 \star x_1, \quad \gamma_1 = H(k_1 \star z) \oplus m_1.$$

The receiver uses the randomness r to decrypt m_b as follows:

$$m_b = \gamma_b \oplus H(r \star y_b).$$

Let td denote the trapdoor of the CRS as follows:

$$\mathsf{crs} = (g_0 \star x, g_1 \star x), \quad \mathsf{td} = g_1(g_0)^{-1},$$

The protocol is secure against a malicious sender since z perfectly hides b. If $b = 0$, then the honest receiver constructs $z = r \star x_0$. The same z can be opened to choice bit $b = 1$ with randomness r' (by using the trapdoor td) as follows:

$$z = r \star x_0 = r \cdot (g_1(g_0)^{-1}) \star x_1 \text{ where } r' = rg_1(g_0)^{-1}.$$

Using the above observation, the simulator constructs $z = r \star x_0$ and extracts m_0 and m_1 using randomness r and r' respectively. Next, we argue security against a semi-honest receiver. We show that if the receiver computes m_{1-b} by querying $H(k_1 \star z)$ to the random oracle then one can build an adversary for breaking the weak unpredictability property. The details of our reduction can be found in Sect. 3.1. Our reduction requires the knowledge of the receiver's randomness r to plug in the challenge instance of the weak unpredictability game into the sender's OT messages. Also, z perfectly hides b and as a result the simulator cannot extract the corrupt receiver's choice bit b during simulation. These are the reasons due to which the current construction only attains malicious security against a corrupt sender. Our construction and proof sketch follows.

The Construction. Let $(G, X, \star)$ be a wU-EGA with x being a publicly available element in the set X. Also let $H : X \to \{0, 1\}^\ell$ be a hash function (modeled in the proof as a random oracle). Our construction is a tuple of four PPT algorithms (Setup, OTR, OTS, OTD) as follows:

- Setup(1^λ): Sample $g_0, g_1 \leftarrow_R G$ and output $\mathsf{crs} = (x_0, x_1)$ where

$$x_0 = g_0 \star x, \quad x_1 = g_1 \star x.$$

- OTR(crs, b): Sample uniformly at random $r \leftarrow_R G$ and compute $z = r \star x_b$. Output the receiver message $\mathsf{ot}_1 = z$ and the receiver state $\mathsf{st} = (b, r)$.
- OTS($\mathsf{crs}, (m_0, m_1), \mathsf{ot}_1$): Parse $\mathsf{crs} = (x_0, x_1)$ and $\mathsf{ot}_1 = z$. Sample uniformly at random $k_0, k_1 \leftarrow_R G$ and output the sender message $\mathsf{ot}_2 = (y_0, y_1, \gamma_0, \gamma_1)$, where

$$y_0 = k_0 \star x_0, \quad \gamma_0 = H(k_0 \star z) \oplus m_0,$$

$$y_1 = k_1 \star x_1, \quad \gamma_1 = H(k_1 \star z) \oplus m_1.$$

- OTD(st, ot$_2$): Parse st $= (b, r)$ and ot$_2 = (y_0, y_1, \gamma_0, \gamma_1)$, and output the recovered message as

$$m' = \gamma_b \oplus H(r \star y_b).$$

Correctness. Correctness of the scheme follows by inspection.

Security. We state and prove the following theorem.

Theorem 4. *Assuming that $(G, X, \star)$ be a wU-EGA and H is a random oracle, the above construction implements the $\mathcal{F}_{OT}$ functionality in the common reference string + random oracle model against a malicious sender and a semi-honest receiver.*

Security Against Malicious Sender (Informal). Note that the receiver's choice bit b is hidden statistically. Also, note that z is in fact an equivocal commitment to b given the "discrete log" of x_1 w.r.t. x_0, i.e. the group element $g_1(g_0)^{-1}$. Hence, the simulator can generate a CRS-trapdoor pair (crs, td) as

$$\mathsf{crs} = (g_0 \star x, g_1 \star x), \quad \mathsf{td} = g_1(g_0)^{-1},$$

and recover both the sender messages m$_0$ and m$_1$.

Security Against Semi-honest Receiver (Informal). We will prove the following lemma:

Lemma 1. *Assuming that $(G, X, \star)$ be a wU-EGA and H is a random oracle, the above construction is UC-secure in the common reference string + random oracle model against a semi-honest receiver.*

Proof. Given an wU-EGA challenge of the form $(x, x^*, y = k \star x)$, the goal is to predict $y^* = k \star x^*$. Suppose $\mathcal{A}$ is an adversary that breaks OT security. We show that there exists an adversary $\mathcal{A}'$ for wu-EGA given $\mathcal{A}$. The reduction proceeds as follows (the reduction already knows the corrupt receiver's choice bit b and output m$_b$, and simulates hash function H as a random oracle):

- Simulate the CRS as $\mathsf{crs} = (x_0, x_1)$ where :

$$x_b = x^*, \quad x_{1-b} = x.$$

- On behalf of the receiver, sample $r \leftarrow_R G$ and compute $z = r \star x_b$. Output the receiver message ot$_1 = z$.
- On behalf of the sender, sample $k' \leftarrow_R G$ and output simulated sender OT message as ot$_2' = (y_0, y_1, \gamma_0, \gamma_1)$ where

$$y_b = k' \star x_b, \quad \gamma_b = H(k' \star z) \oplus \mathsf{m}_b, y_{1-b} = y, \quad \gamma_{1-b} \leftarrow_R \{0, 1\}^\ell.$$

Let E be the event that $\mathcal{A}$ queries the random oracle with input $k \star z$. Let us denote the real world (resp. simulated) OT sender message as ot_2 (resp. ot_2'). Then, we denote the advantage of a corrupt receiver breaking sender privacy as follows.

$$
\begin{aligned}
& \big| \Pr[\mathcal{A}(\mathsf{ot}_2) \to 1] - \Pr[\mathcal{A}(\mathsf{ot}_2') \to 1] \big| \\
&= \big| (\Pr[\mathcal{A}(\mathsf{ot}_2) \to 1 | E] \cdot \Pr[E] + \Pr[\mathcal{A}(\mathsf{ot}_2) \to 1 | \overline{E}] \cdot \Pr[\overline{E}]) \\
&\qquad - (\Pr[\mathcal{A}(\mathsf{ot}_2') \to 1 | E] \cdot \Pr[E] - \Pr[\mathcal{A}(\mathsf{ot}_2') \to 1 | \overline{E}] \cdot \Pr[\overline{E}]) \big| \\
&= \big| (\Pr[\mathcal{A}(\mathsf{ot}_2) \to 1 | E] \cdot \Pr[E] - \Pr[\mathcal{A}(\mathsf{ot}_2') \to 1 | E] \cdot \Pr[E]) \\
&\qquad + (\Pr[\mathcal{A}(\mathsf{ot}_2) \to 1 | \overline{E}] \cdot \Pr[\overline{E}] - \Pr[\mathcal{A}(\mathsf{ot}_2') \to 1 | \overline{E}] \cdot \Pr[\overline{E}]) \big| \\
&= \big| \Pr[E] \cdot (\Pr[\mathcal{A}(\mathsf{ot}_2) \to 1 | E] - \Pr[\mathcal{A}(\mathsf{ot}_2') \to 1 | E]) \\
&\qquad - \Pr[\overline{E}] \cdot (\Pr[\mathcal{A}(\mathsf{ot}_2) \to 1 | \overline{E}] - \Pr[\mathcal{A}(\mathsf{ot}_2') \to 1 | \overline{E}]) \big| \\
&\leq \Pr[E] \cdot \big| \Pr[\mathcal{A}(\mathsf{ot}_2) \to 1 | E] - \Pr[\mathcal{A}(\mathsf{ot}_2') \to 1 | E] \big| \\
&\qquad + \Pr[\overline{E}] \cdot \big| \Pr[\mathcal{A}(\mathsf{ot}_2) \to 1 | \overline{E}] - \Pr[\mathcal{A}(\mathsf{ot}_2') \to 1 | \overline{E}] \big| \\
&\leq \Pr[E] + \big| \Pr[\mathcal{A}(\mathsf{ot}_2) \to 1 | \overline{E}] - \Pr[\mathcal{A}(\mathsf{ot}_2') \to 1 | \overline{E}] \big|.
\end{aligned}
$$

where ot_2 is computed honestly following the honest sender algorithm and (m_0, m_1), and ot_2' is computed as described above. The second last inequality follows due to triangle inequality. Rearranging the terms yields the following inequality:

$$
\big| \Pr[\mathcal{A}(\mathsf{ot}_2) \to 1] - \Pr[\mathcal{A}(\mathsf{ot}_2') \to 1] \big| - \big| \Pr[\mathcal{A}(\mathsf{ot}_2) \to 1 | \overline{E}] - \Pr[\mathcal{A}(\mathsf{ot}_2') \to 1 | \overline{E}] \big| \leq \Pr[E]
$$

Note that the simulation is perfect assuming event E does not occur, since H is a random oracle and since

$$
y_{1-b} = y = k \star x = k \star x_{1-b}.
$$

In such a case, an honestly computed γ_{1-b} is indistinguishable from a random γ_{1-b} if the adversary $\mathcal{A}$ does not query H on $k \star z$. This follows from the random oracle assumption. Thus the following occurs with negligible probability:

$$
\big| \Pr[\mathcal{A}(\mathsf{ot}_2) \to 1 | \overline{E}] - \Pr[\mathcal{A}(\mathsf{ot}_2') \to 1 | \overline{E}] \big| \leq \mathsf{neg}(\kappa).
$$

This reduces the above equation to the following:

$$
\big| \Pr[\mathcal{A}(\mathsf{ot}_2) \to 1] - \Pr[\mathcal{A}(\mathsf{ot}_2') \to 1] \big| - \mathsf{neg}(\kappa) \leq \Pr[E]
$$

Next, we construct our adversary $\mathcal{A}'$ for wU-EGA provided event E occurs, i.e. $\mathcal{A}$ queries H on $k \star z$. The adversary $\mathcal{A}$ distinguishes ot_2 and ot_2' if it obtains information about m_{1-b}. Given the simulated ensemble,

$$
(\mathsf{crs}, b, \mathsf{m}_b, \mathsf{ot}_1 = z, \mathsf{ot}_2' = (y_0, y_1, \gamma_0, \gamma_1)),
$$

if $\mathcal{A}$ manages to recover message m_{1-b} by querying (conditioned on occurrence of event E) the random oracle on $z^* = k \star z$, then the following holds true:

$$z^* = k \star z = k \star (r \star x_b) = r \star (k \star x_b) = r \star (k \star x^*) = r \star y^*.$$

Hence, the adversary $\mathcal{A}'$ recovers (with non-negligible probability)

$$y^* = r^{-1} \star z^*,$$

thereby violating the weak unpredictability of the EGA. Thus, the advantage of an adversary $\mathcal{A}'$ in the weak unpredictability game will be as follows:

$$\big| \Pr[\mathcal{A}(\mathsf{ot}_2) \to 1] - \Pr[\mathcal{A}(\mathsf{ot}_2') \to 1] \big| \leq \Pr[E] \leq \Pr[\mathcal{A}' \text{ wins wU-EGA game}]$$

$$\leq \mathsf{neg}(\kappa).$$

This completes the proof of Lemma 1 and, hence, the proof of Theorem 4.   □

3.2   2-Round Maliciously Secure UC-OT

We now show how to augment the construction in order to also achieve UC-security against a malicious receiver. We add security against a malicious receiver by forcing the receiver to send a non-interactive witness indistinguishable (NIWI) proof of knowledge π proving correct construction of its OT message corresponding to the following statement:

$$\exists b \in \{0, 1\}, r \in G : z = r \star x_b$$

The sender verifies the proof as part of the OT protocol. The proof allows a simulator to extract the choice bit b and randomness r to complete reduction. The knowledge of r is required for the security reductions among the hybrids. The NIWI can be performed by applying Fiat-Shamir Transform on the Sigma protocols of [DG19].[5] We refer to the full version [BMM+22] for the complete protocol. This yields the first round optimal OT from weak unpredictability property and it can be instantiated based on computational CSIDH assumption.

Additional Requirement. Let $(G, X, \star)$ be a wU-EGA with x being a publicly available element in the set X. We denote the NIWI proof of knowledge (NIWI-POK) system as follows:

$$\mathsf{NIWI} = (\mathsf{NIWI.Prove}, \mathsf{NIWI.Verify}),$$

that is capable of generating proofs for OR relations of the following form with respect to a tuple $(x_0, x_1, z) \in X \times X \times X$:

$$\exists r \in G : (z = r \star x_0) \vee (z = r \star x_1),$$

where the tuple (x_0, x_1, z) is the proof statement and the witness is a tuple of the form $(r, b) \in G \times \{0, 1\}$.

---

[5] The recent work of [BDK+22] constructs a similar NIZK. But it is based on the decisional CSIDH assumption, and is hence insufficient for our purpose.

Our Protocol-1. Let $(G, X, \star)$ be a wU-EGA with x being a publicly available element in the set X. Also let $H : X \to \{0,1\}^\ell$ be a hash function (modeled in the proof as a random oracle). Our construction is a collection of four PPT algorithms $(\mathsf{Setup}, \mathsf{OTR}, \mathsf{OTS}, \mathsf{OTD})$ as follows:

- $\mathsf{Setup}(1^\lambda)$: Sample $g_0, g_1 \leftarrow_R G$, and output $\mathsf{crs} = (x_0, x_1)$, where

$$x_0 = g_0 \star x, \quad x_1 = g_1 \star x.$$

- $\mathsf{OTR}(\mathsf{crs}, b)$: Sample uniformly at random $r \leftarrow_R G$ and compute $z = r \star x_b$. Output the receiver message $\mathsf{ot}_1 = (z, \pi)$ and the receiver state $\mathsf{st} = (b, r)$, where

$$\pi \leftarrow_R \mathsf{NIWI.Prove}((x_0, x_1, z), (r, b)).$$

- $\mathsf{OTS}(\mathsf{crs}, (\mathsf{m}_0, \mathsf{m}_1), \mathsf{ot}_1)$: Parse $\mathsf{ot}_1 = (z, \pi)$ and proceed as follows:
  - If $\mathsf{NIWI.Verify}((x_0, x_1, z), \pi) = 0$, output $\bot$.
  - Otherwise, sample uniformly at random $k_0, k_1 \leftarrow_R G$ and output the sender message $\mathsf{ot}_2 = (y_0, y_1, \gamma_0, \gamma_1)$, where

$$y_0 = k_0 \star x_0, \quad \gamma_0 = H(k_0 \star z) \oplus \mathsf{m}_0,$$

$$y_1 = k_1 \star x_1, \quad \gamma_1 = H(k_1 \star z) \oplus \mathsf{m}_1.$$

- $\mathsf{OTD}(\mathsf{st}, \mathsf{ot}_2)$: Parse $\mathsf{st} = (b, r)$ and $\mathsf{ot}_2 = (y_0, y_1, \gamma_0, \gamma_1)$, and output the recovered message as

$$\mathsf{m}' = \gamma_b \oplus H(r \star y_b).$$

Correctness. Correctness of the scheme follows by inspection.

Security Proof. The security of our protocol is summarized below.

Theorem 5. *Assuming that $(G, X, \star)$ is a wU-EGA, NIWI is a NIWI proof of knowledge, and H is a random oracle, then Protocol-1 (i.e. the above construction) implements the $\mathcal{F}_{\mathsf{OT}}$ functionality in the common reference string + random oracle model and it is UC-secure against malicious adversaries.*

Proof. At a high level, the proof is very similar to the proof for our semi-honest construction, with the additional guarantees provided by the (NIWI-POK) system allowing us to prove security against a malicious receiver. The detailed proof is deferred to the full version [BMM+22]. ∎

Instantiation from wU-REGA. We finally note that our constructions and proofs work in essentially the same way from a restricted EGA provided that we can sample group elements from a distribution that is *statistically* close to uniform over the group G while retaining the ability to efficiently compute the action. We note that this is plausibly the case with respect to the instantiation of restricted EGA from CSIDH and other similar isogeny-based assumptions. We refer the reader to [DG19, ADMP20] for more details.

Leveraging this observation and Theorem 3 together with Theorem 5, we get the following corollary.

Corollary 3. *If the computational CSIDH assumption holds and if H is a random oracle, there exists a 2-round OT protocol that implements the $\mathcal{F}_{OT}$ functionality in the common reference string + random oracle model and achieves UC-security against malicious adversaries.*

4   Round-Optimal OT in Plain Model from wU-EGA

In this section we construct our round optimal OT with simulation-based security in the plain model from wU-EGA assumption.

4.1   Overview

We build upon the two round semi-honest OT protocol from Sec. 3.1. It can be observed that the receiver's choice bit b is perfectly hidden in the receiver OT message $\mathsf{ot}_1 = z$ (computed using randomness $g \in G$), even if the OT parameters (x_0, x_1) are generated by a malicious sender. We need to extract the receiver's choice bit and randomness to enable simulation security against a corrupt receiver. We rely on a three round WI proof of knowledge (denoted as WI) for this purpose, where the receiver proves that for statement (x_0, x_1, z) and witness (g, b) the following holds true:

$$\mathcal{C}_1((x_0, x_1, z), (g, b)) = 1, \quad \text{iff } z = g \star x_b.$$

We require the WI proof system to be input-delayed where only the last message of the WI proof system depends on the statement being proven. We refer to [BPS22, BMM+22] for formal definitions. In our protocol the receiver sends the first message π_1^{WI} of the proof in the first round, the sender sends the OT parameters (x_0, x_1) and the second round message π_2^{WI} of the proof in the second round, the receiver computes z and the final round message π_3^{WI} of the proof as the third OT message and the sender verifies the proof and sends $(y_0, y_1, \gamma_0, \gamma_1)$ as the final OT message. The receiver uses (g, b) to decrypt m_b. The simulator against a corrupt receiver invokes the witness extractor of WI to extract (g, b). The knowledge of g also allows us to break wU-EGA assumption when a malicious receiver computes both (m_0, m_1). Meanwhile, receiver privacy follows the witness indistinguishability of the proof system. For every z, there always exists g_0 and g_1 such that $z = g_0 \star x_0 = g_1 \star x_1$.

Next, we need to extract a corrupt sender's input messages (m_0, m_1) from $(y_0, y_1, \gamma_0, \gamma_1)$ to enable simulation security against a corrupt sender. We rely on a four round ZK proof of knowledge (denoted as ZK) for this purpose, where the sender proves that for statement (x, x_0, x_1) and witness (g_0, g_1) the following holds true:

$$\mathcal{C}_2((x_0, x_1), (g_0, g_1)) = 1, \quad \text{iff } x_0 = g_0 \star x, x_1 = g_1 \star x.$$

We require the ZK proof system to be input-delayed where only the last message of the WI proof system depends on the statement being proven. We refer to

[BPS22,BMM+22] for formal definitions. In our protocol the receiver sends the first message π_1^{ZK} of the proof along with π_1^{WI} in the first round, the sender sends the OT parameters (x_0, x_1), the second round message π_2^{ZK} of the proof and $\pi_2 WI$ in the second round, the receiver computes z and π_3^{WI} and the third round message π_3^{ZK} of the proof as the third OT message and the sender verifies the WI proof, computes the final round message of ZK proof as π_4^{ZK} and sends $(y_0, y_1, \gamma_0, \gamma_1, \pi_4^{ZK})$ as the final OT message. The receiver verifies the ZK proof and then computes the output. The simulator against a corrupt sender invokes the witness extractor of ZK to extract (g_0, g_1) and compute (m_0, m_1). Meanwhile, the simulator against a corrupt receiver uses the ZK simulator to simulate the ZK proof.

The three round input-delayed WI proof system can be obtained [PRS02, KM20,BPS22] from non-interactive commitment schemes using the protocol of [FLS99]. The commitment scheme can be obtained from wU-EGA assumption via injective trapdoor one way function. The four round input-delayed ZK proof system can be constructed [PRS02,KM20,BPS22] from two-round statistically hiding commitment scheme which in turn can be constructed[6] from wU-EGA. As a result, we obtain the *first* round-optimal OT in plain model from wU-EGA which satisfies simulation security. Formal details of the protocol follows. We denote our plain model OT protocol as Protocol-2.

4.2   Our Protocol-2

Let $WI = (WI_1, WI_2, WI_3, WI_4)$ be a three round delayed input WI proof of knowledge for the following language $\mathcal{L}_1$ consisting of statement (x_0, x_1, z), witness (g, b) and NP verification circuit $\mathcal{C}_1$ described as follows, where $x_0, x_1, z \in X, g \in G, b \in \{0, 1\}$.

$$\mathcal{C}_1((x_0, x_1, z), (g, b)) = 1, \quad \text{if } z = g \star x_b$$
$$= 0, \quad \text{otherwise}$$

Let $ZK = (ZK_1, ZK_2, ZK_3, ZK_4, ZK_5)$ be a four round delayed input ZK proof of knowledge for the following language $\mathcal{L}_2$ consisting of statement (x, x_0, x_1), witness (g_0, g_1) and NP verification circuit $\mathcal{C}_2$ described as follows, where $x, x_0, x_1 \in X, g_0, g_1 \in G$.

$$\mathcal{C}_2((x, x_0, x_1), (g_0, g_1)) = 1, \quad \text{if } x_0 = g_0 \star x, x_1 = g_1 \star x$$
$$= 0, \quad \text{otherwise}$$

Receiver has choice bit $b \in \{0, 1\}$. Sender has input bit-messages $(m_0, m_1) \in \{0, 1\}$. x is a public set element. $H : X \rightarrow \{0, 1\}$ is the Goldreich-Levin hash function. We describe our OT protocol as follows:

---

[6] The verifier sends (x_0, x_1) as the first round message by sampling $g_0, g_1 \leftarrow_R G$ and computing $x_0 = g_0 \star x, x_1 = g_1 \star x$. The committer commits to bit b by sampling g and computing the commitment as $z = g \star x_b$. The decommitment is (g, b). Bit b remains perfectly hidden. Binding follows from wU-EGA assumption since openings $(s_0, 0)$ and $(s_1, 1)$ for bits 0 and 1 help to find $r = s_0 \cdot s_1^{-1}$ such that $x_1 = r \star x_0$.

- $\mathsf{OTR}_1(1^\kappa, b)$: The receiver performs the following:
  - Runs the first round of WI on the security parameter to obtain $(\pi_1^{\mathsf{WI}}, \mathsf{st}_\mathsf{R}^{\mathsf{WI}}) \leftarrow \mathsf{WI}_1(1^\kappa, \mathcal{C}_1)$ for $\mathcal{L}_1$ with NP-verification circuit $\mathcal{C}_1$.
  - Runs the first round of ZK on the security parameter to obtain $(\pi_1^{\mathsf{ZK}}, \mathsf{st}_\mathsf{R}^{\mathsf{ZK}}) \leftarrow \mathsf{ZK}_1(1^\kappa, \mathcal{C}_2)$ for $\mathcal{L}_2$ with NP-verification circuit $\mathcal{C}_2$.
  - Sends $\mathsf{ot}_1 = (\pi_1^{\mathsf{WI}}, \pi_1^{\mathsf{ZK}})$ as the first OT message and saves $\mathsf{st}_\mathsf{R} = (b, \mathsf{st}_\mathsf{R}^{\mathsf{WI}}, \mathsf{st}_\mathsf{R}^{\mathsf{ZK}})$ as the internal receiver state.

- $\mathsf{OTS}_1(1^\kappa, (\mathsf{m}_0, \mathsf{m}_1), \mathsf{ot}_1)$: The sender computes the following:
  - Samples $g_0, g_1 \leftarrow_R G$ and computes the OT parameters as $x_0 = g_0 \star x$ and $x_1 = g_1 \star x$.
  - Computes second message of WI as $(\pi_2^{\mathsf{WI}}, \mathsf{st}_\mathsf{S}^{\mathsf{WI}}) \leftarrow \mathsf{WI}_2(1^\kappa, \mathcal{C}_1, \pi_1^{\mathsf{WI}})$.
  - Computes second message of ZK as $(\pi_2^{\mathsf{ZK}}, \mathsf{st}_\mathsf{S}^{\mathsf{ZK}}) \leftarrow \mathsf{ZK}_2(1^\kappa, \mathcal{C}_2, \pi_1^{\mathsf{ZK}})$.
  - Sends $\mathsf{ot}_2 = (x_0, x_1, \pi_2^{\mathsf{WI}}, \pi_2^{\mathsf{ZK}})$ as the second OT message and it stores $\mathsf{st}_\mathsf{S} = (\mathsf{m}_0, \mathsf{m}_1, x_0, x_1, \mathsf{ot}_1, \mathsf{st}_\mathsf{S}^{\mathsf{WI}}, \mathsf{st}_\mathsf{S}^{\mathsf{ZK}})$ as the internal sender state.

- $\mathsf{OTR}_2(\mathsf{st}_\mathsf{R}, \mathsf{ot}_2)$: The receiver does the following:
  - Samples $g \leftarrow_R G$ and computes $z = g \star x_b$.
  - Compute third message of WI as $\pi_3^{\mathsf{WI}} \leftarrow \mathsf{WI}_3((x_0, x_1, z), (g, b), \mathsf{st}_\mathsf{R}^{\mathsf{WI}}, \pi_2^{\mathsf{WI}})$ corresponding to statement (x_0, x_1, z) and witness (g, b).
  - Compute third message of ZK as $(\pi_3^{\mathsf{ZK}}, \mathsf{st}_\mathsf{R}^{\mathsf{ZK}}) \leftarrow \mathsf{ZK}_3(\mathsf{st}_\mathsf{R}^{\mathsf{ZK}}, \pi_2^{\mathsf{ZK}})$.
  - Sends the third OT message $\mathsf{ot}_3 = (z, \pi_3^{\mathsf{WI}}, \pi_3^{\mathsf{ZK}})$ and updates its internal state as $\mathsf{st}_\mathsf{R} = (b, g, \mathsf{st}_\mathsf{R}^{\mathsf{ZK}})$.

- $\mathsf{OTS}_2(\mathsf{st}_\mathsf{S}, \mathsf{ot}_3)$: The sender computes the following:
  - The sender aborts if the WI proof fails to verify on statement (x_0, x_1, z), i.e. $\mathsf{WI}_4((x_0, x_1, z), \mathsf{st}_\mathsf{S}^{\mathsf{WI}}, \pi_3^{\mathsf{WI}}) = 0$.
  - The sender computes the fourth message of ZK as $\pi_4^{\mathsf{ZK}} \leftarrow \mathsf{ZK}_3((x, x_0, x_1), (g_0, g_1), \mathsf{st}_\mathsf{S}^{\mathsf{ZK}}, \pi_3^{\mathsf{ZK}})$ corresponding to statement (x, x_0, x_1) and witness (g_0, g_1).
  - Sample uniformly at random $k_0, k_1 \leftarrow_R G$ and compute $(y_0, y_1, \gamma_0, \gamma_1)$, where
  $$y_0 = k_0 \star x_0, \quad \gamma_0 = H(k_0 \star z) \oplus \mathsf{m}_0,$$
  $$y_1 = k_1 \star x_1, \quad \gamma_1 = H(k_1 \star z) \oplus \mathsf{m}_1.$$
  - The sender sends fourth OT message $\mathsf{ot}_4 = (y_0, y_1, \gamma_0, \gamma_1, \pi_4^{\mathsf{ZK}})$ to the receiver.

- $\mathsf{OTD}(\mathsf{st}_\mathsf{R}, \mathsf{ot}_2)$: The receiver computes the following:
  - The receiver aborts if the ZK proof fails to verify on statement (x, x_0, x_1), i.e. $\mathsf{ZK}_5((x, x_0, x_1), \mathsf{st}_\mathsf{R}^{\mathsf{ZK}}, \pi_4^{\mathsf{ZK}}) = 0$.
  - The receiver parses $\mathsf{st}_\mathsf{R} = (b, g)$ and $\mathsf{ot}_4 = (y_0, y_1, \gamma_0, \gamma_1, \pi_4^{\mathsf{ZK}})$, and outputs the recovered message as m' where
  $$\mathsf{m}' = \gamma_b \oplus H(r \star y_b).$$

We show that the above protocol provides indistinguishability based security against a malicious sender and simulation based security against a corrupt receiver by proving the following theorem.

Theorem 6. *Let* $WI = (WI_1, WI_2, WI_3, WI_4)$ *be a three round delayed input WI proof of knowledge for the following language* $\mathcal{L}_1$, $ZK = (ZK_1, ZK_2, ZK_3, ZK_4, ZK_5)$ *be a four round delayed input ZK proof of knowledge for the following language* $\mathcal{L}_2$, *and* $(G, X, \star)$ *be a wU-EGA, then Protocol-2 (i.e. the above construction) provides receiver privacy against a malicious sender and provides simulation-based security against a malicious receiver.*

Proof. We first argue that our protocol satisfies simulation-based security against a corrupt sender and then we argue the same against a corrupt receiver. The formal proof details can be found in the full version [BMM+22].

Simulation Against Corrupt Sender. Assume $x_1 = r \star x_0$. It can be observed that z perfectly hides b since for every $g_0 \in G$ there exists $g_1 = g_0 \cdot r^{-1}$ such that $z = g_0 \star x_0 = g_1 \star x_1$. When $b == 0$, the WI proof is constructed with the group element g_0 such that $z = g_0 \star x_0$. Meanwhile, when $b == 1$ the WI proof is constructed using g_1 as $z = g_1 \star x_1$ where g_0 and g_1 satisfies the above relation. A malicious sender distinguishing between a run of the OT protocol with receiver input choice bit $b = 0$ from a run of the OT protocol with receiver input choice bit $b = 1$ breaks the WI property of the proof system. Moreover, the simulator can extract both m_0 and m_1 given the trapdoors g_0 and g_1. The simulator obtains these trapdoors by invoking the ZK witness extractor algorithm $\mathsf{Ext}^{\mathsf{ZK}}$ on π^{ZK}.

Simulation Against Corrupt Receiver. The simulator invokes the WI witness extractor algorithm, denoted as $\mathsf{Ext}^{\mathsf{WI}}$, to extract the witness (g, b) from the proof. The simulator invokes the $\mathcal{F}_{\mathsf{OT}}$ functionality with the extracted choice bit b to obtain m_b. The simulator constructs ot_4 with inputs (m_0, m_1), where $m_{1-b} = 0$. The ZK proof is constructed by invoking the ZK simulator, denoted as $\mathcal{S}^{\mathsf{ZK}}$. An adversary breaks the security of the protocol if the WI proof is accepting and yet the witness extractor failed to extract a witness, or the corrupt receiver distinguishes the simulated ZK proof from a real one. In the later case, it breaks ZK property. In the former case, the corrupt receiver breaks the proof of knowledge property of the WI protocol. The other case, where the extractor extracts multiple valid witnesses also leads to an abort by the simulator. That event occurs when the receiver breaks the wU-EGA property. $\square$

The three round input-delayed WI proof system can be obtained [PRS02, KM20, BPS22] from non-interactive commitment schemes using the protocol of [FLS99]. The commitment scheme can be obtained from wU-EGA assumption via injective trapdoor one way function. The four round input-delayed ZK proof system can be constructed [PRS02, KM20, BPS22] from two-round statistically hiding commitment scheme which in turn can be constructed from wU-EGA. As a result, we obtain the *first* round-optimal OT in plain model from wU-EGA which satisfies simulation security. Our result is summarized in Thm. 7.

Theorem 7. *Assuming $(G, X, \star)$ is a wU-EGA, there exists a four-round oblivious transfer protocol in the plain model that provides simulation based security against malicious corruptions of the parties.*

5   OT Extension from Reciprocal EGA

In this section, we discuss our three round OT extension protocol following a roadmap of observations. The maliciously secure OT protocol in [LGdSG21] fails to achieve UC security in three rounds, and would require four rounds.[7] However, their construction relies on an efficient two round semi-honest OT protocol. We observe that this semi-honest protocol can be used to implement a batch of $\ell = \mathcal{O}(\kappa)$ OTs, satisfying malicious security notions which are weaker than UC-security. This semi-honest to malicious security transformation requires a few additional checks, incurring $\mathcal{O}(1)$ cheap symmetric operations per OT. Finally, we show that this weaker notion of malicious security suffices for [KOS15] OT extension by applying the result of [CSW20a]. We begin by introducing some additional definitions and notations surrounding EGA and REGA.

5.1   Reciprocal EGA and Reciprocal CSIDH

The OT protocol of Lai et al. [LGdSG21] is based on the reciprocal CSIDH assumption, and relies on crucially on the *quadratic twist* of an elliptic curve, which can be computed efficiently in the CSIDH setting (see [LGdSG21] for details). In this section, we adopt an abstraction of the quadratic twist and the reciprocal CSIDH assumption in the framework of (R)EGA from [BPS22].

The Twist Map. Let $(G, X, \star)$ be an EGA (equivalently an REGA) as described above. We define a "twist" as a map $\mathcal{T} : X \to X$ that satisfies the following properties:

- For any $g \in G$ and any $x \in X$ we have $\mathcal{T}(g \star x) = g^{-1} \star \mathcal{T}(x)$.
- For any $x \in X$ and any *uniform* $g \leftarrow_R G$, we have: $g \star x \approx_s \mathcal{T}(g \star x)$.
- There exists a "twist-invariant" element $x_0 \in X$ such that $\mathcal{T}(x_0) = x_0$.

The Reciprocal EGA Assumption. Given an EGA $(G, X, \star)$, we say that the reciprocal assumption holds if for any security parameter $\kappa \in \mathbb{N}$ and for any PPT adversary $\mathcal{A}$, the following holds with overwhelmingly large probability:

$$\Pr[\mathsf{Expt}^{\mathsf{recEGA}}(\kappa, \mathcal{A}) = 1] < \mathsf{negl}(\kappa),$$

where the experiment $\mathsf{Expt}^{\mathsf{recEGA}}(\kappa, \mathcal{A})$ is as defined in Fig. 2.

Remark 3. We can similarly define a reciprocal REGA assumption where, in the corresponding experiment, all group elements (more concretely, the group elements g and s) are sampled from a distribution that is statistically close to uniform over the group G.

---

[7] This was pointed out by the authors of [LGdSG21] in their Eurocrypt 2021 presentation.

Experiment $\mathsf{Expt}^{\mathsf{recEGA}}(\kappa, \mathcal{A})$:

1. The challenger generates the description of an EGA $(G, X, \star)$ along with the "twist" map $\mathcal{T} : X \to X$ and a special "twist-invariant" element $x_{\mathcal{T}} \in X$.

2. The challenger then samples $g \leftarrow_R G$, sets $x = g \star x_{\mathcal{T}}$, and provides to the adversary $\mathcal{A}$ the tuple $(G, X, \star, \mathcal{T}, x_{\mathcal{T}}, x)$.

3. The adversary $\mathcal{A}$ outputs an element $z \in X$.

4. The challenger samples $s \leftarrow_R G$ and provides to the adversary $\mathcal{A}$ the set element $y = s \star x$.

5. The adversary $\mathcal{A}$ eventually outputs a pair of set elements $(z_0, z_1) \in X \times X$.

6. Output 1 if $(z_0, z_1) = (s \star z, s^{-1} \star z)$. Output 0 otherwise.

Fig. 2. The Reciprocal EGA Experiment

Finally, we import the following theorem from [LGdSG21].

Theorem 8. [LGdSG21]. *Assuming that the reciprocal CSIDH assumption holds, there exists an REGA satisfying the reciprocal REGA assumption.*

5.2   OT Construction of [LGdSG21]

We briefly recall the semi-honest OT construction of [LGdSG21]. Let $(G, X, \star)$ be an EGA with x_0 being a publicly available element in the set X where reciprocal EGA assumption holds. Let $H : X \to \{0, 1\}^\kappa$ be a hash function (modeled in the proof as a random oracle). Let $\mathcal{T} : X \to X$ denote the twist operation. Receiver R has input choice bit $b \in \{0, 1\}$ and sender has inputs messages $(m_0, m_1) \in \{0, 1\}^\kappa$. It is a tuple of five PPT algorithms $(\mathsf{Setup}, \mathsf{OTR}, \mathsf{OTS}_1, \mathsf{OTD})$ as follows:

- $\mathsf{Setup}(1^\lambda)$: Sample a trusted set element x_0 such that $\mathcal{T}(x_0) = x_0$. Sample $g \leftarrow_R G$ and output $\mathsf{crs} = x = g \star x_0$.

- $\mathsf{OTR}(\mathsf{crs}, \mathbf{b})$: Sample $r \leftarrow_R G$ and compute $z \in X$ as follows:

$$z = r \star x \text{ if } b = 0, \quad z = \mathcal{T}(r \star x) \text{ if } b = 1,$$

Output the receiver message $\mathsf{ot}_1 = z$ and the receiver state $\mathsf{st} = (b, r)$.

- $\mathsf{OTS}(\mathsf{crs}, \mathsf{ot}_1)$: Sample uniformly at random $s \leftarrow_R G$ and compute sender's OT message $y \in X$ and sender's random pads - $(a_0, a_1) \in \{0, 1\}^\kappa$ as follows:

$$y = s \star x, \quad c_0 = H(s \star z) \oplus \mathsf{m}_0 \quad c_1 = H(s \star \mathcal{T}(z)) \oplus \mathsf{m}_1.$$

Send the sender OT message as $\mathsf{ot}_2 = (y, c_0, c_1)$.

- $\mathsf{OTD}(\mathsf{st}, \mathsf{ot}_2)$: Parse $\mathsf{st} = (b, r)$ and $\mathsf{ot}_2 = (y, c_0, c_1)$, and recover the output message $m_b = c_b \oplus H(r \star y)$.

Security Against Malicious Sender. At a high level, z perfectly hides the choice bit b as $(r \star x)$ and $\mathcal{T}(r \star x)$ are statistically indistinguishable. A corrupt sender's inputs can even be extracted by a simulator (see [LGdSG21] for details).

Security Against Malicious Receiver. A corrupt receiver cannot compute both m_0 and m_1 since it requires to query H on $(q_0, q_1) = (s \star z, s \star \mathcal{T}(z))$. Given q_1, one can compute $s^{-1} \star z = \mathcal{T}(z)$. This breaks the reciprocal EGA assumption since the adversary computes $(s \star z, s^{-1} \star z)$ where $y = s \star x$ is generated by the challenger after it receives adversarially generated set element $z \in X$. However, the simulator is unable to extract a corrupt receiver's input choice bit since it is statistically hidden.

To achieve security against a malicious receiver, the work of [LGdSG21] adds an interactive challenge-proof-verify mechanism. The sender computes a challenge that challenges the receiver to prove that it knows randomness r such that $z = r \star x$ or $z = \mathcal{T}(r \star x)$. Upon receiving the challenge, the receiver decrypts m_b and computes the proof using randomness r. It sends the proof to the sender, who verifies it and completes the protocol. The proof is sent in the third round of the protocol, thus blowing up the round complexity to three rounds. This approach successfully extracts a corrupt receiver's input if it computes a correct proof to the sender's challenger. However, their challenge-proof-verify mechanism incurs an additional overhead of 7 isogeny computation. We note that this 3 round maliciously secure OT construction suffices for simulation-based security but they would need an additional round for UC security. We refer to their Eurocrypt presentation for details.

5.3   Constructing OT Extension Protocols from Reciprocal (R)EGA

We build an inexpensive challenge-proof-verify mechanism on top of the above semi-honest by relying only on symmetric key operations to obtain custom OT protocols. These custom OT protocols are used to instantiate the maliciously secure base OT protocols in the [KOS15] (KOS) OT extension paradigm using ideas from [CSW20a].

Observations from [CSW20a]**.** The work of [CSW20a] (abbreviated henceforth as CSW) made crucial observations that suffices for the base-OT protocols in KOS: 1) The base OT protocols are run in a batch of $\ell = \mathcal{O}(\kappa) > 3\mu$ OTs together, where μ is the statistical security parameter. Simulation based security should hold for non-aborting parties for the batch together. 2) A corrupt sender is allowed to launch selective failure attack on the base-OTs since the receiver possesses random choice bits. 3) The base-OT protocols needs to satisfy simulation-based security only for non-aborting parties, in case of an abort semantic security suffices. The OT functionality $\mathcal{F}_{\mathsf{SF\text{-}ROT}}$ with selective failure attack, which is weaker than UC-OT functionality, suffices for the base OT in KOS. We show a technique that builds upon the semi-honest OT protocol of [LGdSG21] to implement $\mathcal{F}_{\mathsf{SF\text{-}ROT}}$ against malicious adversaries. Our transformation only relies on cheap symmetric key operations. This reduces our isogeny computations for each base OT to 5 and it also yields the first OT extension protocol based on isogenies.

Overview. We build upon the semi-honest protocol of [LGdSG21]. Recall that their two round protocol (described in Sect. 5.2) is secure against a malicious sender and a semi-honest receiver since the simulator fails to extract the corrupt receiver's input. They add a challenge-proof-verify mechanism to tackle a malicious receiver but that doubles their isogeny computations. Instead, we take a different route and construct the same challenge-proof-verify mechanism by solely relying on symmetric key operations. Our mechanism is inspired from the work of CSW and we describe it as follows.

Let us denote the two messages of the OT sender for the ith OT as $p_{0,i}$ and $p_{1,i}$ respectively. Let $H_1 : X \rightarrow \{0,1\}^\kappa, H_2 : \{0,1\}^\kappa \rightarrow \{0,1\}^\kappa, H_3 : \{0,1\}^{\ell\kappa} \rightarrow \{0,1\}^\kappa, H_4 : \{0,1\}^{2\kappa} \rightarrow \{0,1\}^\kappa$ be different hash functions (modeled in the proof as a random oracle). Let us denote the choice bit of the receiver for the ith OT as b_i. The sender constructs a challenge chall_i using the two messages as follows:

$$\mathsf{chall}_i = u_{0,i} \oplus u_{1,i}, \quad \text{where } u_{0,i} = H_2(i, p_{0,i}), \quad u_{1,i} = H_2(i, p_{1,i}).$$

The receiver is required to compute the response as $u_{0,i}$ and send it back to the sender as the proof. The receiver decrypts $p_{b_i,i}$ and computes $u_{0,i}$ as follows:

$$u_{0,i} = \mathsf{chall}_i \cdot b_i \oplus H_2(p_{b_i,i}).$$

Note that the receiver needs to query the random oracle H_2 in order to compute $u_{0,i}$ correctly and hence the simulator successfully extracts b_i if the receiver computes the correct response $u_{0,i}$. However, a corrupt sender can extract b_i by constructing chall_i maliciously. It samples a random chall'_i and sends it to the receiver. If the receiver responds with the correct $u_{0,i}$ then the sender sets $b_i = 0$ else it sets $b_i = 1$.

We tackle this problem by relying on the observation that the OT protocol can allow selective failure attack and it can allow the sender to guess $\mathcal{O}(\kappa)$ choice bits of the receiver. This suffices for the KOS base OT protocols. Using this observation we make the sender prove that the batch of ℓ challenges were correctly computed. The sender computes the response ans of receiver proof using a random oracle H_3 as follows:

$$\mathsf{ans} = H_3(u_{0,1}, u_{0,2}, \ldots u_{0,\ell}).$$

The sender sends proof of correct computation by sending the proof $\mathsf{pf} = H_2(\mathsf{ans})$ to the receiver along with the challenger. The sender sets the output of ℓ random OTs as $(\mathbf{a}_0, \mathbf{a}_1)$ where $\mathbf{a}_0 = \{a_{0,i}\}_{i\in[\ell]}$ and $\mathbf{a}_1 = \{a_{1,i}\}_{i\in[\ell]}$ is defined as follows for $i \in [\ell]$:

$$a_{0,i} = H_4(\mathsf{ans}, p_{0,i}), \quad a_{1,i} = H_4(\mathsf{ans}, p_{1,i}).$$

Upon receiving the sender's OT message, the receiver computes $p_{b_i,i}$ corresponding to its choice bit b_i. It computes $\{u_{0,i}\}_{i\in[\ell]}$ and recomputes ans to verify pf. If the verification succeeds then the receiver sends ans to the sender as the response and computes the OT output as $a_{b_i,i} = H_4(\text{ans}, p_{b_i,i})$. If a corrupt receiver computes the correct ans then a simulator extracts every $\{b_i\}_{i\in[\ell]}$ by observing the queries made to H_2 and H_3. Without computing the correct ans the corrupt receiver cannot compute the OT output $a_{b_i,i}$. Hence, the simulator successfully extracts all the choice bits of the receiver if the receiver needs to compute the output of any single OT. Meanwhile, a corrupt sender can launch a selective failure attack only if it correctly guesses the value of receiver computed ans to verify pf. This is performed by guessing the $u_{0,i}$ values computed by the receiver and for that the sender needs to guess the receiver's choice bit in the OT protocols. The base OT protocols in KOS are random OTs. The sender guesses κ choice bits of the receiver with only $2^{-\kappa}$ probability. Thus, our OT protocol allows selective failure attack and it implements the $\mathcal{F}_{\text{SF-ROT}}$ functionality. Formal details of our protocol follows and the security proof is deferred to the full version [BMM+22].

Our Protocol-3. Let $(G, X, \star)$ be an EGA with x_0 being a publicly available element in the set X where reciprocal EGA assumption holds. Also let $H_1 : X \to \{0,1\}^\kappa, H_2 : \{0,1\}^\kappa \to \{0,1\}^\kappa, H_3 : \{0,1\}^{\ell\kappa} \to \{0,1\}^\kappa, H_4 : \{0,1\}^{2\kappa} \to \{0,1\}^\kappa$ be different hash functions (modeled in the proof as a random oracle). Our construction is a tuple of five PPT algorithms $(\text{Setup}, \text{OTR}_1, \text{OTS}_1, \text{OTR}_2, \text{OTS}_2)$:

- $\text{Setup}(1^\lambda)$: Sample a trusted set element x_0 such that $\mathcal{T}(x_0) = x_0$. Sample $g \leftarrow_R G$ and output $\text{crs} = x = g \star x_0$.
- $\text{OTR}_1(\text{crs}, \mathbf{b})$: Sample $\mathbf{r} \leftarrow_R G^\ell$ and compute $\mathbf{z} \in X^\ell$ as follows for $i \in [\ell]$:

$$z_i = r_i \star x \text{ if } b_i = 0, \quad z_i = \mathcal{T}(r_i \star x) \text{ if } b_i = 1,$$

  Output the receiver message $\text{ot}_1 = \mathbf{z}$ and the receiver state $\text{st} = (\mathbf{b}, \mathbf{r})$.
- $\text{OTS}_1(\text{crs}, \text{ot}_1)$: Sample uniformly at random $\mathbf{s} \leftarrow_R G^\ell$ and compute sender's OT message $\mathbf{y} \in X^\ell$ and sender's random inputs messages as $(\mathbf{p}_0, \mathbf{p}_1) \in \{0,1\}^{\kappa \times \ell}$ as follows for $i \in [\ell]$:

$$y_i = s_i \star x, \quad p_{0,i} = H_1(i, s_i \star z_i) \quad p_{1,i} = H_1(i, s_i \star \mathcal{T}(z_i)).$$

  Compute the challenge **chall** for receiver proof as follows for $i \in [\ell]$:

$$\text{chall}_i = u_{0,i} \oplus u_{1,i}, \quad \text{where } u_{0,i} = H_2(i, p_{0,i}), \quad u_{1,i} = H_2(i, p_{1,i}).$$

  Compute the response $\text{ans} = H_3(u_{0,1}, u_{0,2}, \ldots u_{0,\ell})$ of receiver proof. Compute the sender's proof $\text{pf} = H_2(\text{ans})$. Send the sender OT message as $\text{ot}_2 = (\mathbf{y}, \textbf{chall}, \text{pf})$. Store $(\text{ans}, \mathbf{p}_0, \mathbf{p}_1)$ as the internal state.
- $\text{OTR}_2(\text{st}, \text{ot}_2)$: Parse $\text{st} = (\mathbf{b}, \mathbf{r})$ and $\text{ot}_2 = (\mathbf{y}, \textbf{chall}, \text{pf})$, and recover the output pads $\mathbf{p} = \{p_i\}_{i\in[\ell]}$ as follows for $i \in [\ell]$ as $p_i = H_1(r_i \star y_i)$. Compute the intermediate proof response as follows for $i \in [\ell]$: $u_i' = \text{chall}_i \cdot b_i \oplus H_2(i, p_i)$, and compute the receiver's proof response ans' as $\text{ans}' = H_3(u_1', u_2', \ldots u_\ell')$. The receiver aborts if $H_2(\text{ans}') \neq \text{pf}$. Else, the receiver responds to the sender's challenge by sending $\text{ot}_3 = \text{ans}'$ to the sender. The receiver computes the OT output as $\mathbf{m} = \{m_i\}_{i\in[\ell]} = \{H_4(\text{ans}', p_i)\}_{i\in[\ell]}$ for $i \in [\ell]$. Output $(\mathbf{b}, \mathbf{m})$ as the random OT receiver output.

– $\mathsf{OTS}_2(\mathsf{ans}, \mathsf{ot}_3)$: Parse $\mathsf{ot}_3 = \mathsf{ans}'$. The sender aborts if $\mathsf{ans}' \neq \mathsf{ans}$. Else, the sender sets the output as $(\mathbf{a}_0, \mathbf{a}_1)$ where $\mathbf{a}_0 = \{a_{0,i}\}_{i \in [\ell]}$ and $\mathbf{a}_1 = \{a_{1,i}\}_{i \in [\ell]}$ is defined as follows for $i \in [\ell]$:

$$a_{0,i} = H_4(\mathsf{ans}, p_{0,i}), \quad a_{1,i} = H_4(\mathsf{ans}, p_{1,i}).$$

Further Optimizations. It can be observed that the sender can reuse the randomness s for multiple OT protocols by using reusing the same y for all the OT protocols. This translates into a $\mathsf{poly}(\kappa)$ loss in the security parameter since the reduction to reciprocal EGA assumption needs to guess the session where a corrupt receiver breaks the assumption. The security loss can be compensated by increasing the security parameter accordingly. This optimization reduces the number of isogeny computations to 4 for each OT. Meanwhile, the semi-honest OT protocol of [LGdSG21] requires 5 isogeny computations.

Acknowledgments. We thank the anonymous reviewers of IACR PKC 2023 for their helpful comments and suggestions. Pratik Sarkar is supported by NSF Awards 1931714, 1414119, and the DARPA SIEVE program.

References

[ACPS09] Applebaum, B., Cash, D., Peikert, C., Sahai, A.: Fast cryptographic primitives and circular-secure encryption based on hard learning problems. In: Halevi, S. (ed.) CRYPTO 2009. LNCS, vol. 5677, pp. 595–618. Springer, Heidelberg (2009). https://doi.org/10.1007/978-3-642-03356-8_35

[ADDS21] Albrecht, M.R., Davidson, A., Deo, A., Smart, N.P.: Round-optimal verifiable oblivious pseudorandom functions from ideal lattices. In: Garay, J.A. (ed.) PKC 2021. LNCS, vol. 12711, pp. 261–289. Springer, Cham (2021). https://doi.org/10.1007/978-3-030-75248-4_10

[ADMP20] Alamati, N., De Feo, L., Montgomery, H., Patranabis, S.: Cryptographic group actions and applications. In: Moriai, S., Wang, H. (eds.) ASIACRYPT 2020, Part II. LNCS, vol. 12492, pp. 411–439. Springer, Cham (2020). https://doi.org/10.1007/978-3-030-64834-3_14

[AEK+22] Abdalla, M., Eisenhofer, T., Kiltz, E., Kunzweiler, S., Riepel, D.: Password-authenticated key exchange from group actions. In: Dodis, Y., Shrimpton, T. (eds.) CRYPTO 2022. LNCS, vol. 13508, pp. 699–728. Springer, Cham (2022). https://doi.org/10.1007/978-3-031-15979-4_24

[AMPS21] Alamati, N., Montgomery, H., Patranabis, S., Sarkar, P.: Two-round adaptively secure MPC from isogenies, LPN, or CDH. In: Tibouchi, M., Wang, H. (eds.) ASIACRYPT 2021. LNCS, vol. 13091, pp. 305–334. Springer, Cham (2021). https://doi.org/10.1007/978-3-030-92075-3_11

[BBD+22] Booher, J., et al.: Failing to hash into supersingular isogeny graphs. Cryptology ePrint Archive, Paper 2022/518 (2022). https://eprint.iacr.org/2022/518

[BD18] Brakerski, Z., Döttling, N.: Two-message statistically sender-private OT from LWE. In: Beimel, A., Dziembowski, S. (eds.) TCC 2018, Part II. LNCS, vol. 11240, pp. 370–390. Springer, Cham (2018). https://doi.org/10.1007/978-3-030-03810-6_14

[BDK+20] Büscher, N., et al.: Secure two-party computation in a quantum world. In: Conti, M., Zhou, J., Casalicchio, E., Spognardi, A. (eds.) ACNS 2020. LNCS, vol. 12146, pp. 461–480. Springer, Cham (2020). https://doi.org/10.1007/978-3-030-57808-4_23

[BDK+22] Beullens, W., Dobson, S., Katsumata, S., Lai, Y.-F., Pintore, F.: Group signatures and more from isogenies and lattices: generic, simple, and efficient. **13276**, 95–126 (2022)

[BF22] Bitansky, N., Freizeit, S.: Statistically sender-private OT from LPN and derandomization. In: Dodis, Y., Shrimpton, T. (eds.) CRYPTO 2022. LNCS, vol. 13508, pp. 699–728. Springer, Cham (2022). https://doi.org/10.1007/978-3-031-15982-4_21

[BGJ+18] Badrinarayanan, S., Goyal, V., Jain, A., Kalai, Y.T., Khurana, D., Sahai, A.: Promise zero knowledge and its applications to round optimal MPC. In: Shacham, H., Boldyreva, A. (eds.) CRYPTO 2018, Part II. LNCS, vol. 10992, pp. 459–487. Springer, Cham (2018). https://doi.org/10.1007/978-3-319-96881-0_16

[BKM+21] Basso, A., Kutas, P., Merz, S.-P., Petit, C., Sanso, A.: Cryptanalysis of an oblivious PRF from supersingular isogenies. In: Tibouchi, M., Wang, H. (eds.) ASIACRYPT 2021, Part I. LNCS, vol. 13090, pp. 160–184. Springer, Cham (2021). https://doi.org/10.1007/978-3-030-92062-3_6

[BKV19] Beullens, W., Kleinjung, T., Vercauteren, F.: CSI-FiSh: efficient isogeny based signatures through class group computations. In: Galbraith, S.D., Moriai, S. (eds.) ASIACRYPT 2019. LNCS, vol. 11921, pp. 227–247. Springer, Cham (2019). https://doi.org/10.1007/978-3-030-34578-5_9

[BKW20] Boneh, D., Kogan, D., Woo, K.: Oblivious Pseudorandom Functions from Isogenies. In: Moriai, S., Wang, H. (eds.) ASIACRYPT 2020, Part II. LNCS, vol. 12492, pp. 520–550. Springer, Cham (2020). https://doi.org/10.1007/978-3-030-64834-3_18

[BL18] Benhamouda, F., Lin, H.: k-Round multiparty computation from k-Round oblivious transfer via garbled interactive circuits. In: Nielsen, J.B., Rijmen, V. (eds.) EUROCRYPT 2018, Part II. LNCS, vol. 10821, pp. 500–532. Springer, Cham (2018). https://doi.org/10.1007/978-3-319-78375-8_17

[BMM+22] Badrinarayanan, S., Masny, D., Mukherjee, P., Patranabis, S., Raghuraman, S., Sarkar, P.: Round-optimal oblivious transfer and MPC from computational CSIDH. IACR Cryptology ePrint Archive, p. 1511 (2022). https://eprint.iacr.org/2022/1511

[BOB18] Barreto, P., Oliveira, G., Benits, W.: Supersingular isogeny oblivious transfer. Cryptology ePrint Archive, Report 2018/459 (2018). https://eprint.iacr.org/2018/459

[BPS22] Badrinarayanan, S., Patranabis, S., Sarkar, P.: Statistical security in two-party computation revisited. In: Kiltz, E., Vaikuntanathan, V. (eds.) TCC 2022, Part II. LNCS, vol. 13748, pp. 181–210. Springer, Cham (2022). https://doi.org/10.1007/978-3-031-22365-5_7

[BY91] Brassard, G., Yung, M.: One-way group actions. In: Menezes, A.J., Vanstone, S.A. (eds.) CRYPTO 1990. LNCS, vol. 537, pp. 94–107. Springer, Heidelberg (1991). https://doi.org/10.1007/3-540-38424-3_7

[CCG+20] Rai Choudhuri, A., Ciampi, M., Goyal, V., Jain, A., Ostrovsky, R.: Round
optimal secure multiparty computation from minimal assumptions. In:
Pass, R., Pietrzak, K. (eds.) TCC 2020, Part II. LNCS, vol. 12551,
pp. 291–319. Springer, Cham (2020). https://doi.org/10.1007/978-3-030-
64378-2_11

[CCH+19] Canetti, R., et al.: Fiat-Shamir: from practice to theory. In: Charikar,
M., Cohen, E. (eds.) 51st ACM STOC, pp. 1082–1090. ACM Press, June
2019

[CD22] Castryck, W., Decru, T.: An efficient key recovery attack on SIDH
(preliminary version). IACR Cryptology ePrint Archive, p. 975 (2022).
https://eprint.iacr.org/2022/975

[CLM+18] Castryck, W., Lange, T., Martindale, C., Panny, L., Renes, J.: CSIDH:
an efficient post-quantum commutative group action. In: Peyrin, T., Galbraith, S. (eds.) ASIACRYPT 2018, Part III. LNCS, vol. 11274, pp. 395–
427. Springer, Cham (2018). https://doi.org/10.1007/978-3-030-03332-
3_15

[CLOS02] Canetti, R., Lindell, Y., Ostrovsky, R., Sahai, A.: Universally composable
two-party and multi-party secure computation. In: 34th ACM STOC, pp.
494–503. ACM Press, May 2002

[Cou06] Couveignes, J.-M.: Hard homogeneous spaces. Cryptology ePrint
Archive, Report 2006/291 (2006). https://eprint.iacr.org/2006/291

[CPV20] Castryck, W., Panny, L., Vercauteren, F.: Rational isogenies from irrational endomorphisms. In: Canteaut, A., Ishai, Y. (eds.) EUROCRYPT
2020, Part II. LNCS, vol. 12106, pp. 523–548. Springer, Cham (2020).
https://doi.org/10.1007/978-3-030-45724-2_18

[CSV20] Castryck, W., Sotáková, J., Vercauteren, F.: Breaking the decisional
Diffie-Hellman problem for class group actions using genus theory. In:
Micciancio, D., Ristenpart, T. (eds.) CRYPTO 2020, Part II. LNCS, vol.
12171, pp. 92–120. Springer, Cham (2020). https://doi.org/10.1007/978-
3-030-56880-1_4

[CSW20a] Canetti, R., Sarkar, P., Wang, X.: Blazing fast OT for three-round UC
OT extension. In: Kiayias, A., Kohlweiss, M., Wallden, P., Zikas, V.
(eds.) PKC 2020, Part II. LNCS, vol. 12111, pp. 299–327. Springer, Cham
(2020). https://doi.org/10.1007/978-3-030-45388-6_11

[CSW20b] Canetti, R., Sarkar, P., Wang, X.: Efficient and round-optimal oblivious
transfer and commitment with adaptive security. In: Moriai, S., Wang,
H. (eds.) ASIACRYPT 2020. LNCS, vol. 12493, pp. 277–308. Springer,
Cham (2020). https://doi.org/10.1007/978-3-030-64840-4_10

[CSW22] Canetti, R., Sarkar, P., Wang, X.: Triply adaptive UC NIZK. In: Agrawal,
S., Lin, D. (eds.) ASIACRYPT 2022. LNCS, vol. 13792, pp. 466–495.
Springer, Cham (2022). https://doi.org/10.1007/978-3-031-22966-4_16

[DG19] De Feo, L., Galbraith, S.D.: SeaSign: compact isogeny signatures from
class group actions. In: Ishai, Y., Rijmen, V. (eds.) EUROCRYPT 2019,
Part III. LNCS, vol. 11478, pp. 759–789. Springer, Cham (2019). https://
doi.org/10.1007/978-3-030-17659-4_26

[DGH+20] Döttling, N., Garg, S., Hajiabadi, M., Masny, D., Wichs, D.: Two-round
oblivious transfer from CDH or LPN. In: Canteaut, A., Ishai, Y. (eds.)
EUROCRYPT 2020, Part II. LNCS, vol. 12106, pp. 768–797. Springer,
Cham (2020). https://doi.org/10.1007/978-3-030-45724-2_26

[DMPS19] De Feo, L., Masson, S., Petit, C., Sanso, A.: Verifiable delay functions from supersingular isogenies and pairings. In: Galbraith, S.D., Moriai, S. (eds.) ASIACRYPT 2019, Part I. LNCS, vol. 11921, pp. 248–277. Springer, Cham (2019). https://doi.org/10.1007/978-3-030-34578-5_10

[DNM12] David, B.M., Nascimento, A.C.A., Müller-Quade, J.: Universally composable oblivious transfer from lossy encryption and the McEliece assumptions. In: Smith, A. (ed.) ICITS 2012. LNCS, vol. 7412, pp. 80–99. Springer, Heidelberg (2012). https://doi.org/10.1007/978-3-642-32284-6_5

[dSGOPS20] de Saint Guilhem, C.D., Orsini, E., Petit, C., Smart, N.P.: Semicommutative masking: a framework for isogeny-based protocols, with an application to fully secure two-round isogeny-based OT. In: Krenn, S., Shulman, H., Vaudenay, S. (eds.) CANS 2020. LNCS, vol. 12579, pp. 235–258. Springer, Cham (2020). https://doi.org/10.1007/978-3-030-65411-5_12

[DvMN08] Dowsley, R., van de Graaf, J., Müller-Quade, J., Nascimento, A.C.A.: Oblivious transfer based on the McEliece assumptions. In: Safavi-Naini, R. (ed.) ICITS 2008. LNCS, vol. 5155, pp. 107–117. Springer, Heidelberg (2008). https://doi.org/10.1007/978-3-540-85093-9_11

[EGL82] Even, S., Goldreich, O., Lempel, A.: A randomized protocol for signing contracts. In: Chaum, D., Rivest, R.L., Sherman, A.T. (eds.) CRYPTO'82, pp. 205–210. Plenum Press, New York (1982)

[FLS99] Feige, U., Lapidot, D., Shamir, A.: Multiple noninteractive zero knowledge proofs under general assumptions. SIAM J. Comput. 29(1), 1–28 (1999)

[FMV19] Friolo, D., Masny, D., Venturi, D.: A black-box construction of fully-simulatable, round-optimal oblivious transfer from strongly uniform key agreement. In: Hofheinz, D., Rosen, A. (eds.) TCC 2019, Part I. LNCS, vol. 11891, pp. 111–130. Springer, Cham (2019). https://doi.org/10.1007/978-3-030-36030-6_5

[GS18] Garg, S., Srinivasan, A.: Two-round multiparty secure computation from minimal assumptions. In: Nielsen, J.B., Rijmen, V. (eds.) EUROCRYPT 2018, Part II. LNCS, vol. 10821, pp. 468–499. Springer, Cham (2018). https://doi.org/10.1007/978-3-319-78375-8_16

[IKO+11] Ishai, Y., Kushilevitz, E., Ostrovsky, R., Prabhakaran, M., Sahai, A.: Efficient non-interactive secure computation. In: Paterson, K.G. (ed.) EUROCRYPT 2011. LNCS, vol. 6632, pp. 406–425. Springer, Heidelberg (2011). https://doi.org/10.1007/978-3-642-20465-4_23

[JL09] Jarecki, S., Liu, X.: Efficient oblivious pseudorandom function with applications to adaptive OT and secure computation of set intersection. In: Reingold, O. (ed.) TCC 2009. LNCS, vol. 5444, pp. 577–594. Springer, Heidelberg (2009). https://doi.org/10.1007/978-3-642-00457-5_34

[Kil88] Kilian, J.: Founding cryptography on oblivious transfer. In: 20th ACM STOC, pp. 20–31. ACM Press, May 1988

[KM20] Khurana, D., Mughees, M.H.: On statistical security in two-party computation. In: Pass, R., Pietrzak, K. (eds.) TCC 2020, Part II. LNCS, vol. 12551, pp. 532–561. Springer, Cham (2020). https://doi.org/10.1007/978-3-030-64378-2_19

[KOS15] Keller, M., Orsini, E., Scholl, P.: Actively secure OT extension with optimal overhead. In: Gennaro, R., Robshaw, M. (eds.) CRYPTO 2015, Part I. LNCS, vol. 9215, pp. 724–741. Springer, Heidelberg (2015). https://doi.org/10.1007/978-3-662-47989-6_35

[LGdSG21] Lai, Y.-F., Galbraith, S.D., Delpech de Saint Guilhem, C.: Compact, efficient and UC-secure isogeny-based oblivious transfer. In: Canteaut, A., Standaert, F.-X. (eds.) EUROCRYPT 2021. LNCS, vol. 12696, pp. 213–241. Springer, Cham (2021). https://doi.org/10.1007/978-3-030-77870-5_8

[McE78] McEliece, R.J.: A public-key cryptosystem based on algebraic coding theory. Coding Thv **4244**, 114–116 (1978)

[MM22] Maino, L., Martindale, C.: An attack on SIDH with arbitrary starting curve. IACR Cryptology ePrint Archive, p. 1026 (2022). https://eprint.iacr.org/2022/1026

[MMP22] Mula, M., Murru, N., Pintore, F.: On random sampling of supersingular elliptic curves. Cryptology ePrint Archive, Paper 2022/528 (2022). https://eprint.iacr.org/2022/528

[MR19] Masny, D., Rindal, P.: Endemic oblivious transfer. In: ACM CCS 2019, pp. 309–326. ACM Press (2019)

[Pet17] Petit, C.: Faster algorithms for isogeny problems using torsion point images. In: Takagi, T., Peyrin, T. (eds.) ASIACRYPT 2017, Part II. LNCS, vol. 10625, pp. 330–353. Springer, Cham (2017). https://doi.org/10.1007/978-3-319-70697-9_12

[PRS02] Prabhakaran, M., Rosen, A., Sahai, A.: Concurrent zero knowledge with logarithmic round-complexity. In: 43rd FOCS, pp. 366–375. IEEE Computer Society Press, November 2002

[PS19] Peikert, C., Shiehian, S.: Noninteractive zero knowledge for NP from (plain) learning with errors. In: Boldyreva, A., Micciancio, D. (eds.) CRYPTO 2019, Part I. LNCS, vol. 11692, pp. 89–114. Springer, Cham (2019). https://doi.org/10.1007/978-3-030-26948-7_4

[PVW08] Peikert, C., Vaikuntanathan, V., Waters, B.: A framework for efficient and composable oblivious transfer. In: Wagner, D. (ed.) CRYPTO 2008. LNCS, vol. 5157, pp. 554–571. Springer, Heidelberg (2008). https://doi.org/10.1007/978-3-540-85174-5_31

[Qua20] Quach, W.: UC-secure OT from LWE, revisited. In: Galdi, C., Kolesnikov, V. (eds.) SCN 2020. LNCS, vol. 12238, pp. 192–211. Springer, Cham (2020). https://doi.org/10.1007/978-3-030-57990-6_10

[Rab05] Rabin, M.O.: How to exchange secrets with oblivious transfer. Cryptology ePrint Archive, Report 2005/187 (2005). https://eprint.iacr.org/2005/187

[Reg05] Regev, O.: On lattices, learning with errors, random linear codes, and cryptography. In: Gabow, H.N., Fagin, R. (eds.) 37th ACM STOC, pp. 84–93. ACM Press, May 2005

[Rob22] Robert, D.: Breaking SIDH in polynomial time. Cryptology ePrint Archive, Paper 2022/1038 (2022). https://eprint.iacr.org/2022/1038

[Sho94] Peter W. Shor. Algorithms for quantum computation: Discrete logarithms and factoring. In 35th FOCS, pages 124–134. IEEE Computer Society Press, November 1994

[Vit18] Vitse, V.: Simple oblivious transfer protocols compatible with kummer and supersingular isogenies. Cryptology ePrint Archive, Report 2018/709 (2018). https://eprint.iacr.org/2018/709

[Yao86] Yao, A.C.-C.: How to generate and exchange secrets (extended abstract). In: 27th FOCS, pp. 162–167. IEEE Computer Society Press, October 1986

Generic Models for Group Actions

Julien Duman[ID], Dominik Hartmann[(✉)][ID], Eike Kiltz[ID],
Sabrina Kunzweiler[ID], Jonas Lehmann[ID], and Doreen Riepel[ID]

Ruhr-Universität Bochum, Bochum, Germany
{julien.duman,dominik.hartmann,eike.kiltz,sabrina.kunzweiler,
jonas.lehmann-c6j,doreen.riepel}@rub.de

Abstract. We define the Generic Group Action Model (GGAM), an adaptation of the Generic Group Model to the setting of group actions (such as CSIDH). Compared to a previously proposed definition by Montgomery and Zhandry (ASIACRYPT '22), our GGAM more accurately abstracts the security properties of group actions.

We are able to prove information-theoretic lower bounds in the GGAM for the discrete logarithm assumption, as well as for non-standard assumptions recently introduced in the setting of threshold and identification schemes on group actions. Unfortunately, in a natural quantum version of the GGAM, the discrete logarithm assumption does not hold.

To this end we also introduce the weaker Quantum Algebraic Group Action Model (QAGAM), where every set element (in superposition) output by an adversary is required to have an explicit representation relative to known elements. In contrast to the Quantum Generic Group Action Model, in the QAGAM we are able to analyze the hardness of group action assumptions: We prove (among other things) the equivalence between the discrete logarithm assumption and non-standard assumptions recently introduced in the setting of QROM security for Password-Authenticated Key Exchange, Non-Interactive Key Exchange, and Public-Key Encryption.

Keywords: Group Actions · CSIDH · Algebraic Group Action Model · Generic Group Action Model

1 Introduction

GROUP ACTIONS. Group actions are considered a promising candidate for building post-quantum secure cryptography. While similar to the well-known prime-order groups, group actions are more limited and provide less structure. For a group $(\mathcal{G}, \circ)$ with neutral element $e \in \mathcal{G}$ and a set $\mathcal{X}$, a group action is a map

$$\star : \mathcal{G} \times \mathcal{X} \to \mathcal{X}$$

that is compatible with the group operation in $\mathcal{G}$. That is, $e \star x = x$ for all $x \in \mathcal{X}$ and $(g \circ h) \star x = g \star (h \star x)$ for all $g, h \in \mathcal{G}$ and $x \in \mathcal{X}$. It can be thought of as an

© International Association for Cryptologic Research 2023
A. Boldyreva and V. Kolesnikov (Eds.): PKC 2023, LNCS 13940, pp. 406–435, 2023.
https://doi.org/10.1007/978-3-031-31368-4_15

analogue to the exponentiation in a multiplicative prime-order group, which leads to natural analogues of problems such as the discrete logarithm problem in group actions (GA-DLOG). The similarity to prime-order groups allows the adaptation of several basic schemes to group actions [14,17,19,28,37,41]. Crucially, there is no group law on $\mathcal{X}$. This makes group actions resilient against well-known quantum attacks on groups such as Shor's algorithm [39]. To date, the best known quantum attacks on group actions are based on Kuperberg's algorithm [29] which has subexponential runtime.

The most prominent example for a cryptographic group action to date is the CSIDH group action [14], which is based on isogenies between supersingular elliptic curves. While promising, isogeny-based cryptography is still fairly new and has not been as thoroughly studied as traditional cryptography based on the discrete logarithm problem in prime order groups or the RSA problem. This lack of analysis was exemplified by the recent attacks on the SIDH assumption [13, 30,36], which completely break SIDH and related schemes, but have no impact on the security of CSIDH.

GENERIC MODELS. A useful tool for analyzing cryptographic problems are generic models. One popular model in the setting of prime-order groups is Shoup's Generic Group Model (GGM) [40]. The GGM replaces group elements with random labels (without any algebraic meaning) and only allows computation of the group law via an oracle. In the GGM one can provide information-theoretic lower bounds on the number of calls to the group oracle for certain cryptographic problems. For example, in the GGM the discrete logarithm problem over groups of prime order p can only be solved with at least $\sqrt{p}$ calls to the group oracle.

Another useful model in the setting of prime-order groups is the Algebraic Group Model (AGM) [22]. In the AGM all algorithms know the group structure and can compute group operations. However, adversaries are restricted to only producing new group elements by combining previously known group elements via the group law, i.e. they have to behave "algebraically". This is enforced by requiring algebraic adversaries to provide a representation of their output group elements relative to their inputs. While this model cannot be used to prove lower bounds for cryptographic assumptions, it has proven useful for relating the hardness of different assumptions and cryptographic protocols [7,22,32].

GENERIC MODELS FOR GROUP ACTIONS. The GGM has recently been adapted to the group action setting by Montgomery and Zhandry [33] in order to prove the generic quantum equivalence of GA-DLOG and GA-CDH in the setting of restricted effective group actions (REGA).[1] We refer to this as the MZ-Generic Group Action Model (MZ-GGAM). The MZ-GGAM encodes elements from the group $\mathcal{G}$ and the set $\mathcal{X}$ with random labels and provides oracles for both the

---

[1] In a REGA (not considered in this work) the group action evaluation cannot be performed efficiently for arbitrary group elements, but it is necessary to find a suitable representation of the element first. In particular, this is the case when the group structure is unknown.

group law in $\mathcal{G}$ and the group action $\star$ on $\mathcal{X}$. Additionally, they define the MZ-Quantum Generic Group Action Model (MZ-QGGAM), a quantum analogue of the MZ-GGAM providing quantum access to the two oracles.

While the definition of the MZ-GGAM seems reasonable when considering REGAs, we believe that it does not accurately capture the security properties of general effective group actions (EGA). Why? One could simply use group $\mathcal{G}$ and ignore set $\mathcal{X}$ and mapping $\star$. In the MZ-GGAM one can prove the hardness of standard assumption like the discrete logarithm in group $\mathcal{G}$, even though group actions are "not supposed" to source their hardness from problems over $\mathcal{G}$. This simple observation allows to provably port all standard group-based cryptography to the MZ-GGAM. That is, in the MZ-GGAM group actions actually have more structure than prime-order groups (though they should not). Furthermore, in the MZ-Quantum Generic Group Action Model one can efficiently compute discrete logarithms over $\mathcal{G}$ by applying Shor's algorithm [39], hence learn the entire group structure of $\mathcal{G}$. This shows that hiding the structure of group $\mathcal{G}$ with random labels is useless in a quantum setting.

1.1   Contributions

We propose an alternative definition of the generic group model for group actions (GGAM) and analyze several standard and non-standard assumptions in it. We also consider a quantum version, QGGAM, and show that the group action discrete logarithm problem (GA-DLOG) does *not* hold in it. Furthermore, we define a (quantum) algebraic group model for group actions, AGAM and QAGAM, and use it to relate the hardness of several useful group-action assumptions.

We will now go over our results in a bit more detail.

Generic Group Action Model. We propose a new definition of the Generic Group Action Model (GGAM), which differs from the previous definition MZ-GGAM of [33] in that we only encode elements from the set $\mathcal{X}$ and not from group $\mathcal{G}$. Our definition assumes $\mathcal{G}$ to be cyclic of order N (see the full version for a generalization to non-cyclic abelian group actions). In a quantum setting the isomorphism between $\mathcal{G}$ and $\mathbb{Z}_N$ is efficiently computable with Shor's algorithm, so we can assume it to be known with some quantum precomputation. Hence in our GGAM we set $\mathcal{G} := \mathbb{Z}_N$, which also models the fact that a group action should not source its hardness from group $\mathcal{G}$, an important security feature of group actions.

RELATION TO THE GENERIC GROUP MODEL. While it seems intuitive that hardness results in the GGM (over prime-order groups) should carry over to the more restricted GGAM (over group actions), there are some subtleties in formalizing this. We prove a "lifting lemma" which states that all hardness results in the GGM for a group of prime order p carry over to the GGAM if the order N of the group action satisfies $N = p - 1$. Looking ahead, this restriction is a consequence of how the GGAM can be embedded in the GGM.

GENERIC GROUP ACTION MODEL WITH TWISTS. We extend the definition of the GGAM to the GGAM with Twists ($\text{GGAM}^\top$), which models group actions like CSIDH more closely. More specifically, we include a twisting algorithm that allows to compute $-\mathfrak{a} \star x$ from $\mathfrak{a} \star x$ efficiently for any $\mathfrak{a} \in \mathbb{Z}_N$ and $x \in \mathcal{X}$. This allows us to capture a wider variety of practical group action instantiations. Unfortunately, there is no analogue to twisting in the prime order group setting, therefore we can not prove a lifting lemma from the GGM to the $\text{GGAM}^\top$.

GENERIC LOWER BOUNDS. Next, we prove explicit lower bounds on the success probability of generic adversaries on GA-DLOG, as well as two non-standard assumptions in the $\text{GGAM}^\top$ that were recently introduced in the context of threshold schemes [18], identification schemes [5] and password-authenticated key exchange [1]. Our proofs are rather straightforward and adapt well-known proof techniques from the GGM. The resulting bounds are almost the same bounds as in the GGM except for constant factors due to the (potentially) composite order of the group action. This actually highlights that there are cases where group action based assumptions become potentially easier. Our analysis makes it simple to detect and to subsequently exclude those cases in the assumption.

Generic Models in the Quantum Setting. We define the Quantum Generic Group Action Model (QGGAM), an extension of the GGAM to the quantum setting where the adversary has quantum access to the group action oracle. Similar to the classical setting, the group $\mathcal{G}$ is simply modeled as $\mathbb{Z}_N$. We first show that our QGGAM is in fact equivalent to the MZ-GGAM, while it is conceptually much simpler. Unfortunately, we observe that even GA-DLOG is information-theoretically *easy* in the QGGAM. This is due to a generic algorithm by Ettinger and Høyer [21], which breaks GA-DLOG with polynomially many quantum group-action queries plus (classical) exponential time to solve the Trigonometric Approximation Problem (TAP). TAP is a purely combinatorial problem which is independent of the group action. Since the QGGAM is an information-theoretic model which only counts the number of oracle queries, this constitutes an efficient quantum attack against GA-DLOG in the QGGAM. One interpretation of this result is that the quantum hardness of GA-DLOG is a combinatorial property rather than an algebraic one.

ALGEBRAIC GROUP ACTION MODEL. We define the group action analogue of the AGM [22] in the quantum setting, which we call the Quantum Algebraic Group Action Model with twists ($\text{QAGAM}^\top$) and without twists (QAGAM). While there cannot exist any meaningful bounds in the QGGAM, we are still able to quantum-relate the following assumptions in the $\text{QAGAM}/\text{QAGAM}^\top$.

- **Assumptions for KEM/NIKE.** The Group Action Quantum Strong Computational Diffie-Hellman assumption (GA-QSt-CDH) is the CDH assumption for group actions, where the adversary is furthermore given *quantum access* to (fixed-base) DDH oracles. GA-QSt-CDH assumptions are required to prove active security of group-action Hashed ElGamal encryption and

Diffie-Hellman NIKE protocols in the QROM (used, for example, in Post-Quantum WireGuard and OPTLS) [19]. There is no known security analysis of GA-QSt-CDH. We prove that GA-QSt-CDH is equivalent to the GA-DLOG assumption in the $\mathrm{QAGAM}^\top$, therefore giving the first indication towards its quantum security. Our proof relies on the semi-classical one-way to hiding lemma.

- **Assumptions for PAKE.** We consider the Group Action Quantum Strong Square-Inverse Diffie-Hellman(GA-QSt-SqInvDH) assumption [1] in the $\mathrm{QAGAM}^\top$. This non-standard assumption is a combination of the Square-DH and Inversion-DH assumption relative to a flexible base, where an adversary is furthermore given quantum access to DDH oracles as in the GA-QSt-CDH assumption. The GA-QSt-SqInvDH assumption is required to prove security of a recently proposed PAKE protocol in the QROM [1]. We again prove that GA-QSt-SqInvDH is equivalent to the GA-DLOG assumption in the $\mathrm{QAGAM}^\top$, therefore giving the first indication towards its quantum security.

- **Assumptions for ElGamal.** We study the Quantum CCA1 (QCCA1) security of the Group Action plain (unhashed) ElGamal KEM. QCCA1 security means that the adversary is allowed to ask the decryption oracle with ciphertexts in superposition, but only before seeing the challenge ciphertext. We prove its QCCA1 security to be equivalent to the Group Action q-Decisional Diffie-Hellman Problem (GA-q-DDH) in the $\mathrm{QAGAM}^\top$.

2 Preliminaries

In this section, we fix some notation that will be used throughout the paper and recall standard definitions.

2.1 Notation

For integers m, n where $m < n$, $[m, n]$ denotes the set $\{m, m + 1, ..., n\}$. For $m = 1$, we simply write $[n]$. By $\log(x)$ we denote the logarithm over the reals with base 2. For a (finite) set S, $s \leftarrow_\$ S$ denotes that s is sampled uniformly and independently at random from S. $y \leftarrow \mathcal{A}(x_1, x_2, ...)$ denotes that on input $x_1, x_2, ...$ the probabilistic algorithm $\mathcal{A}$ returns y. $\mathcal{A}^\mathrm{O}$ denotes that algorithm $\mathcal{A}$ has access to oracle O. An adversary is a probabilistic algorithm. The notation $[\![B]\!]$, where B is a boolean statement, refers to a bit that is 1 if the statement is true and 0 otherwise.

2.2 Security Games

We define code based security games similar to [8]. A game G is defined as an algorithm (which we call the challenger) that provides a main procedure and (possibly zero) oracle procedures. An algorithm $\mathcal{A}$ playing game G gets an initial input from the challenger and can subsequently interact with (possibly zero) oracles. In the case of quantum algorithms, the oracles can be queried in superposition. At the end of its execution, $\mathcal{A}$ has to provide some output to the challenger. We say that $\mathcal{A}$ *wins* (or *solves*) the game G if the challenger accepts the output, which we write as $\text{G}^{\mathcal{A}} \Rightarrow 1$. We define the *success probability* of $\mathcal{A}$ as $\Pr[\text{G}^{\mathcal{A}} \Rightarrow 1]$. Note that we will use the words "game" and "problem" interchangeably.

2.3 Quantum Notation

We recall some quantum computation preliminaries and notation as stated in [20]. Additional quantum preliminaries can be found in the full version.

QUBIT. A qubit $|x\rangle = \alpha|0\rangle + \beta|1\rangle$ is a 2-dimensional unit vector with coefficients in $\mathbb{C}$, i.e. $x = (\alpha, \beta) \in \mathbb{C}^2$ fulfilling the normalization constraint $|\alpha|^2 + |\beta|^2 = 1$. When neither $\alpha = 1$ nor $\beta = 1$, we say that $|x\rangle$ is in *superposition*.

n-QUBIT STATE. An n-bit quantum register $|x\rangle = \sum_{i=1}^{2^n-1} \alpha_i|i\rangle$ is a unit vector of $\mathbb{C}^{2^n} = (\mathbb{C}^2)^{\otimes n}$, that is $\alpha_i \in \mathbb{C}$ and $\sum_{i=0}^{2^n-1} |\alpha_i|^2 = 1$. We call the set $\{|0\rangle, |1\rangle, \ldots, |2^n - 1\rangle\}$ the *computational basis*. When $|x\rangle$ can not be written as the tensor product of single qubits, we say that $|x\rangle$ is *entangled*.

MEASUREMENT. Unless otherwise stated, measurements are done in the computational basis. After measuring a quantum register $|x\rangle = \sum_{i=0}^{2^n-1} \alpha_i|i\rangle$ in the computational basis, the state *collapses* and $|x\rangle = \pm|i\rangle$ with probability $|\alpha_i|^2$.

QUANTUM ALGORITHMS. A quantum algorithm $\mathcal{A}$ is a series of unitary operations U_i, where unitary operations are defined as to map unit vectors to unit vectors, preserving the normalization constraint of quantum registers. A quantum oracle algorithm $\mathcal{A}^{\text{O}}$ is defined similarly, except it can query the oracle O after (or before) executing a unitary U_i. Since quantum computation needs to be reversible, we model an oracle $\text{O} : X \to Y$ by a unitary U_{O} that maps $|x\rangle|y\rangle \mapsto |x\rangle|y \oplus \text{O}(x)\rangle$. We only consider sequential quantum algorithms (see the full version).

QUANTUM-ACCESS OF ORACLES. For an oracle O, we are going to write $|\text{O}\rangle$ to denote that it can be queried on quantum inputs and O if it can not (which means that its inputs are implicitly measured). For an oracle which allows partial quantum-access, we write $|\cdot\rangle$ to denote the inputs which are quantum (i.e., not measured), for example $\text{O}(\cdot, |\cdot\rangle)$ means that the first input is classical (i.e., implicitly measured on query) and the second is quantum. Alternatively to $|\text{O}\rangle$ we might also write $\text{O}(|\cdot\rangle, |\cdot\rangle)$, if O takes two inputs. While such a (partially) quantum oracle formally needs an additional ancillary input to write its result, we omit this to keep the interfaces between classical and quantum oracles aligned.

3 Group Actions

In this section, we introduce cyclic effective group actions (with twists). We explain that this abstract framework models the group action underlying the isogeny-based protocol CSIDH [14]. Further we define the two standard group action assumptions in our setting: Group Action Discrete Logarithm Problem and the Group Action Computational Diffie-Hellman Problem.

3.1   Definitions

We first recall the definition of (effective) group actions from [3] and then introduce cyclic effective group actions (with twists).

Definition 1 (Group Action). *Let $(\mathcal{G}, \circ)$ be a group with identity element $e \in \mathcal{G}$, and $\mathcal{X}$ a set. A map*

$$\star : \mathcal{G} \times \mathcal{X} \to \mathcal{X}$$

is a group action if it satisfies the following properties:

1. *Identity: $e \star x = x$ for all $x \in \mathcal{X}$.*
2. *Compatibility: $(g \circ h) \star x = g \star (h \star x)$ for all $g, h \in \mathcal{G}$ and $x \in \mathcal{X}$.*

We use the shorthand notation $(\mathcal{G}, \mathcal{X}, \star)$ to denote the group action. A group action is called regular, *if for all $x, y \in \mathcal{X}$, there exists precisely one $g \in \mathcal{G}$ s.t. $y = g \star x$.*

Example 1. Let $(\mathbb{G}, \circ)$ be a group of prime order p. Then the group $(\mathbb{Z}_p^*, \cdot)$ acts on $\mathbb{G}$ in a natural way:

$$\star : \mathbb{Z}_p^* \times \mathbb{G} \to \mathbb{G},$$
$$(a, g) \mapsto g^a = \underbrace{(g \circ \cdots \circ g)}_{a \text{ times}}.$$

The identity property is trivially satisfied: $1 \star g = g^1 = g$. Compatibility is verified as follows:

$$(a \cdot b) \star g = g^{a \cdot b} = (g^a)^b = a \star (b \star g).$$

Note that the group action is not regular since $g^a \neq e \in \mathbb{G}$ for all $a \in \mathbb{Z}_p^*$. However it can be easily made regular by restricting the action to the set $\mathcal{X} = \mathbb{G} \setminus \{e\}$.

We would like to stress that exponentiation does *not* define a group action of $(\mathbb{Z}_p, +)$ on $\mathbb{G}$, since consecutive exponentiation behaves multiplicatively.

Definition 2 (Effective Group Action). *Let $(\mathcal{G}, \mathcal{X}, \star)$ be a group action satisfying the following properties:*

1. *$\mathcal{G}$ is finite and there exist efficient algorithms for membership testing, equality testing, (random) sampling, group operation and inversion.*
2. *The set $\mathcal{X}$ is finite and there exist efficient algorithms for membership testing and to compute a unique representation.*
3. *There exists a distinguished element $\tilde{x} \in \mathcal{X}$ with known representation.*
4. *There exists an efficient algorithm to evaluate the group action, i.e. to compute $g \star x$ given g and x.*

Then we call $\tilde{x} \in \mathcal{X}$ the origin *and $(\mathcal{G}, \mathcal{X}, \star, \tilde{x})$ an* effective group action *(EGA).*

For an EGA it is a priori not assumed that the structure of the group $\mathcal{G}$ is known. Indeed this reflects the reality for some group actions used in cryptography. However, the security of these protocols should not be based on the difficulty of computing the group structure. Consequently, in this work we focus on known-order groups (see also [3, Definition 3.9]). Moreover, we restrict our attention to cyclic groups of known order. This is not a serious restriction. For example in isogeny-based group actions, the group $\mathcal{G}$ is guaranteed to be "almost" cyclic, hence the security is dominated by its largest cyclic component (cf. Section 3.2). For completeness, we provide an alternative set of definitions for non-cyclic abelian groups in the full version.

Definition 3 (Cyclic Effective Group Action). *Let $(\mathcal{G}, \mathcal{X}, \star, \tilde{x})$ be an effective group action satisfying the following properties:*

1. *The group $\mathcal{G}$ is cyclic of order N for some known $N \in \mathbb{N}$.*
2. *There exists a generator $g \in \mathcal{G}$ with known representation (that is $\mathcal{G} = \langle g \rangle$).*
3. *For any element $h \in \mathcal{G}$, the element $\mathfrak{a} \in \mathbb{Z}_N$ satisfying $h = g^{\mathfrak{a}}$ is efficiently computable.*
4. *The group action is regular.*

Then we say that $(\mathcal{G}, \mathcal{X}, \star, \tilde{x})$ is a cyclic (known-order) effective group action (CEGA). *In other words, a* CEGA *is an* EGA *for which there exists an isomorphism $\phi : (\mathbb{Z}_N, +) \to (\mathcal{G}, \circ)$ efficiently computable in both directions. We therefore denote any* CEGA *equivalently by $(\mathbb{Z}_N, \mathcal{X}, \diamond, \tilde{x})$ where*

$$\diamond : \mathbb{Z}_N \times \mathcal{X} \to \mathcal{X},$$
$$(\mathfrak{a}, x) \mapsto \underbrace{(g \circ \cdots \circ g)}_{\mathfrak{a} \ times} \star x.$$

Remark 1. We stress that for a CEGA the compatibility property of a group action turns into $\mathfrak{a} \diamond (\mathfrak{b} \diamond x) = (\mathfrak{a} + \mathfrak{b}) \diamond x$.

Similar to the framework suggested in [1], we also introduce CEGA with twists which reflects a property inherent to CSIDH-based group actions.

Definition 4 (Cyclic Effective Group Action with Twists). *Let $(\mathbb{Z}_N, \mathcal{X}, \diamond, \tilde{x})$ be a* CEGA. *We call it a Cyclic Effective Group Action with Twists* (CEGAT) *if there is an efficient algorithm that, given $x = \mathfrak{a} \diamond \tilde{x}$, computes $x^t = -\mathfrak{a} \diamond \tilde{x}$.*

Remark 2. In practice, the requirements from the definition of EGA are often too strong. Therefore the weaker notion of *restricted effective group actions* (REGA) is introduced in [3]. In the design of protocols it is important to have this limitation in mind. For instance, the CSIDH protocol [14] is modeled as a REGA. For certain CSIDH parameter sets, the group structure has already been computed in [9] which converts it into a known-order REGA. Moreover the authors show that in this case it can even be modeled as a known-order EGA.[2]

---

[2] As is pointed out in [3], knowing the group structure of a REGA does not automatically covert it to an EGA, but there are some subtleties to consider. In particular, the evaluation of the group action might require to solve a lattice problem. However, in all known instantiations this problem is easy to solve [9].

In any case, in this work we are only concerned with analyzing the security of protocols. It is clear that the security should not be based on the difficulty of computing the group structure. Even more, knowing the group structure only makes a potential adversary stronger. Consequently, it makes sense to only consider *known-order effective group actions*.

3.2   The CSIDH Group Action

An important example of group actions used in cryptography are provided by isogeny-based group actions, in particular by CSIDH [14].

Let p be a large prime of the form $p = 4 \cdot \ell_1 \cdots \ell_n - 1$, where the ℓ_i are small distinct odd primes. Fix the elliptic curve $E_0 : y^2 = x^3 + x$ over $\mathbb{F}_p$. This is a supersingular curve and its $\mathbb{F}_p$-rational endomorphism ring is $\mathcal{O} = \mathbb{Z}[\pi]$, where π is the Frobenius endomorphism. Let $\mathcal{E}\ell\ell_p(\mathcal{O})$ be the set of elliptic curves defined over $\mathbb{F}_p$, with endomorphism ring $\mathcal{O}$. The ideal class group $cl(\mathcal{O})$ acts on the set $\mathcal{E}\ell\ell_p(\mathcal{O})$, i.e. there is a map

$$\star : cl(\mathcal{O}) \times \mathcal{E}\ell\ell_p(\mathcal{O}) \to \mathcal{E}\ell\ell_p(\mathcal{O})$$

satisfying the properties from Definition 1 [14, Theorem 7].

CSIDH-512 is a CEGAT. The structure of the group $cl(\mathcal{O})$ is unknown for large parameter sets. Assuming the Generalized Riemann Hypothesis, it can be computed in classical subexponential time using the Hafner–McCurley algorithm [23]. Moreover there exist quantum algorithms by Biasse and Song [10] to compute the class group $cl(\mathcal{O})$ in polynomial time. The class group computation has been successfully performed for the parameters of CSIDH-512 [9]. In particular, the authors showed that $cl(\mathcal{O})$ is a cyclic group of order

$$\begin{aligned} N = {} & 3 \cdot 37 \cdot 1407181 \cdot 51593604295295867744293584889 \\ & \cdot 31599414504681995853008278745587832204909 \\ \approx {} & 2^{257} \end{aligned} \tag{1}$$

generated by the element $g = (3, \pi - 1) \in cl(\mathcal{O})$. Moreover it is shown that $cl(\mathcal{O})$ can be identified with $\mathbb{Z}_N$ via an efficiently computable isomorphism

$$\phi : \mathbb{Z}_N \to cl(\mathcal{O}), \quad \mathfrak{a} \mapsto g^{\mathfrak{a}}.$$

Consequently, the CSIDH-512 group action can be viewed as a CEGA. Moreover as any CSIDH-based group action, it is possible to compute twists of elements efficiently, hence it may also be viewed as a CEGAT.

Remark 3. While not all class groups appearing in isogeny-based cryptography are cyclic, it makes sense to model these groups as CEGATs when analyzing their security. This is justified by the fact that heuristically the class groups are close to being cyclic, see also [14, §7.1]. More precisely, the odd part of a randomly chosen class group of an imaginary quadratic field is very likely to be cyclic. In case it is not cyclic, the group is with overwhelming probability of the form $\mathbb{Z}_{N_1} \times \mathbb{Z}_{N_2}$ with $N_2 \ll N_1$, hence its complexity is dominated by the cyclic component $\mathbb{Z}_{N_1}$. More details on these heuristics can be found in [16, §9.1]. Further, we note that genus theory implies that the even part of $cl(\mathcal{O})$ is trivial for all CSIDH parameters.

3.3   Group Action Assumptions

For cryptographic applications, we are interested in CEGA(T)s that come equipped with the following two properties:

- Given $x \in \mathcal{X}$, it is hard to find $\mathfrak{a} \in \mathbb{Z}_N$ with $\mathfrak{a} \diamond \tilde{x} = x$.
- Given $x = \mathfrak{a} \diamond \tilde{x}$, $y = \mathfrak{b} \diamond \tilde{x}$, it is hard to find $z \in \mathcal{X}$ with $z = (\mathfrak{a} + \mathfrak{b}) \diamond \tilde{x}$.

In [3] such group actions are called *cryptographic group actions*, and in [17] they are called *hard homogeneous spaces*. The two hardness assumptions are the natural generalizations of the discrete logarithm assumption and the Diffie-Hellman assumption in the traditional group based setting. In analogy to this setting, we make the following definitions.

Definition 5 (Group Action Discrete Logarithm Problem). *Let* CEGA(T) $= (\mathbb{Z}_N, \mathcal{X}, \diamond, \tilde{x})$ *be a cyclic effective group action (with twists). We say that an adversary $\mathcal{A}$ solves the group action discrete logarithm problem* (GA-DLOG) *if $\mathcal{A}(\tilde{x}, \mathfrak{a} \diamond \tilde{x}) = \mathfrak{a}$ for $\mathfrak{a} \leftarrow_\$ \mathbb{Z}_N$.*

Definition 6 (Group Action Computational Diffie-Hellman Problem). *Let* CEGA(T) $= (\mathbb{Z}_N, \mathcal{X}, \diamond, \tilde{x})$ *be a cyclic effective group action (with twists). We say that an adversary $\mathcal{A}$ solves the group action computational Diffie-Hellman problem* (GA-CDH) *if $\mathcal{A}(\tilde{x}, \mathfrak{a} \diamond \tilde{x}, \mathfrak{b} \diamond \tilde{x}) = (\mathfrak{a} + \mathfrak{b}) \diamond \tilde{x}$ for $\mathfrak{a}, \mathfrak{b} \leftarrow_\$ \mathbb{Z}_N$.*

4   Generic Group Action Model

In this section we adapt the well-known Generic Group Model (GGM) of Shoup [40] to the group action setting. In Sect. 4.1 we introduce the Generic Group Action Model and relate it to the GGM. We extend the definition to also include twists in Sect. 4.2 and quantum queries in Sect. 4.3. There, we also show that GA-DLOG does not hold when allowing quantum queries. Finally, we compare our model to the model of [33] in Sect. 4.4.

As explained in the preceding section, we focus on CEGAs for the underlying group action of our generic models. For completeness a natural extension to known-order effective group actions is explained in the full version.

4.1   Definitions and Relations

Generic Group Model. Recall that in the GGM we associate to a group $(\mathbb{G}, \odot, e)$ of prime order p and neutral element e a set of labels $\mathcal{T} \subset \{0, 1\}^*$ and an injective labeling function $\sigma_{\mathbb{G}} : \mathbb{G} \to \mathcal{T}$. We require $|\mathcal{T}| = |\mathbb{G}|$, but we

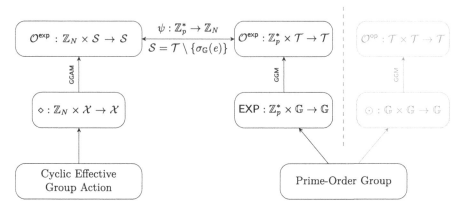

Fig. 1. Schematic overview of the relation between GGAM and GGM where $N = p - 1$.

assume that labels are sufficiently long to ensure that finding a label that has a corresponding preimage in $\mathbb{G}$ is hard. A generic algorithm is subsequently given abstract access to $\mathbb{G}$ via two oracles $\mathcal{O}^{\mathsf{op}} : \mathcal{T} \times \mathcal{T} \to \mathcal{T}$ and $\mathcal{O}^{\mathsf{exp}} : \mathbb{Z}_p^* \times \mathcal{T} \to \mathcal{T}$.[3] The first oracle takes as input two labels $\sigma_{\mathbb{G}}(g)$ and $\sigma_{\mathbb{G}}(h)$ and returns $\sigma_{\mathbb{G}}(g \odot h)$. Similarly, the second oracle takes as input a label $\sigma_{\mathbb{G}}(g)$ and an exponent $k \in \mathbb{Z}_p^*$ and returns $\sigma_{\mathbb{G}}(g^k)$. Here we restrict the exponent k to be in $\mathbb{Z}_p^*$ instead of $\mathbb{Z}_p$. This restriction is without loss of generality, as $\mathcal{O}^{\mathsf{exp}}(0, \sigma_{\mathbb{G}}(g)) = \sigma_{\mathbb{G}}(e)$ for all $g \in \mathbb{G}$, which is trivial to compute even without the oracle. However, it allows us to view $\mathcal{O}^{\mathsf{exp}}$ as the *regular* group action shown in Example 1. Lastly, we call p the *order* of the GGM.

Let $\mathcal{A}$ be a generic algorithm playing a game G. We say $\mathcal{A}$ is a (ϵ, t, q)-algorithm if its has success probability $\Pr[\mathrm{G}^{\mathcal{A}} \Rightarrow 1] = \epsilon$, time complexity t and query complexity q. Here, the query complexity refers to the amount of queries to $\mathcal{O}^{\mathsf{exp}}$ and $\mathcal{O}^{\mathsf{op}}$. We call a generic (ϵ, t, q)-algorithm *pseudoefficient* if $q \in \mathcal{O}(poly(\log p))$ and simply *efficient* if both $t, q \in \mathcal{O}(poly(\log p))$.

Generic Group Action Model (GGAM). The Generic Group Action Model is now defined similarly to the GGM. We associate to a cyclic effective group action $\mathsf{CEGA} = (\mathbb{Z}_N, \mathcal{X}, \diamond, \tilde{x})$ a set of labels $\mathcal{S} \subset \{0, 1\}^*$ and an injective labeling function $\sigma_{\mathcal{X}} : \mathcal{X} \to \mathcal{S}$. We again assume that $\mathcal{X}$ and $\mathcal{S}$ have the same cardinality. Subsequently, a generic group action algorithm has access to an oracle $\mathcal{O}^{\mathsf{exp}} : \mathbb{Z}_N \times \mathcal{S} \to \mathcal{S}$ which abstractly computes the group action. In particular, on input $\mathfrak{a} \in \mathbb{Z}_N$ and a label $\sigma_{\mathcal{X}}(x)$ for $x \in \mathcal{X}$, the oracle returns $\sigma_{\mathcal{X}}(\mathfrak{a} \diamond x)$. While this is slightly ambiguous with the $\mathcal{O}^{\mathsf{exp}}$ in the GGM, it is easy to see that the $\mathcal{O}^{\mathsf{exp}}$ in the GGM and the $\mathcal{O}^{\mathsf{exp}}$ in the GGAM are virtually identical and, as we will argue next, can be translated into one another. We call N the *order* of the GGAM.

---

[3] We include $\mathcal{O}^{\mathsf{exp}}$ as a distinct oracle for convenience even though it can be simulated efficiently via $\mathcal{O}^{\mathsf{op}}$ and a square-and-multiply approach.

Lastly, a generic (ϵ, t, q)-algorithm playing a game G is called pseudoefficient if $q \in \mathcal{O}(poly(\log N))$ and overall efficient if $t, q \in \mathcal{O}(poly(\log N))$.

One can now observe that the definition of the GGAM almost matches the definition of the GGM except for the $\mathcal{O}^{op}$ oracle. In fact, the only other difference between both models is the fact that in the GGM, $\mathcal{O}^{exp}$ takes as input an exponent in $\mathbb{Z}_p^*$ whereas in the GGAM, the exponents are in $\mathbb{Z}_N$. Assuming $N = p - 1$, this change is w.l.o.g. as there exists an isomorphism $\psi : \mathbb{Z}_p^* \to \mathbb{Z}_N$ which a (pseudoefficient) generic algorithm can easily compute. Also note that $\mathcal{S}$ and $\mathcal{T}$ can be identified except for the label $\sigma_{\mathbb{G}}(e) = \sigma_{\mathbb{G}}(g^0)$ since $0 \notin \mathbb{Z}_p^*$, but this label can simply be ignored. The relation between the GGM and the GGAM is visualized in Fig. 1.

From the construction of the GGAM we easily see that it is a stronger (i.e. more restricted) version of the GGM if we assume $N + 1$ being prime. We therefore get the following observation.

Lemma 1 (Lifting Lemma). *Let p be a prime and define $N = p - 1$. Let G be a game in the GGAM of order N and let $\mathcal{A}$ be a generic (ϵ, t, q)-algorithm winning G in the GGAM. Then there exists a generic (ϵ, t', q)-algorithm $\mathcal{B}$ that wins G in the GGM of order p with runtime $t' \leq q + t$.*

Proof. From the observations above, it is straight forward to translate the algorithm $\mathcal{A}$ in the GGAM to an algorithm $\mathcal{B}$ in the GGM: Because the label sets $\mathcal{S}$ and $\mathcal{T}$ can be identified except for $\sigma_{\mathbb{G}}(e)$, we just have to worry about translating oracle queries between the GGAM and GGM. As Fig. 1 shows, this boils down to computing the isomorphism ψ in the backwards direction, i.e. computing $\psi^{-1} : \mathbb{Z}_N \to \mathbb{Z}_p^*$. This can be done efficiently via $\mathfrak{a} \mapsto g^{\mathfrak{a}}$ for some generator $g \in \mathbb{Z}_p^*$. Therefore the runtime of $\mathcal{B}$ increases by the number of evaluations of ψ^{-1}, which itself is exactly the amount q of oracle queries that $\mathcal{A}$ issues. □

Remark 4. Note that when viewing G in the GGM we might lose some (trivial) instances. More specifically, the game G in Lemma 1 is defined in the GGAM first, which means that the label $\sigma_{\mathbb{G}}(e)$ cannot occur in an instance of G as it is not defined in the GGAM. For example, in the case of DLOG this means that the instance $(g, g^0) = (g, e)$ cannot occur in the GGM as $\psi(0)$ is undefined and therefore this does not have a corresponding instance in GA-DLOG. Yet this is only a formal restriction that does not affect the hardness of G in the GGM.

Intuitively, Lemma 1 states that hardness result in the GGM can be lifted to the GGAM as long as $N = p - 1$. Most importantly the lemma also applies to the hardness of solving GA-DLOG and GA-CDH [40].

Corollary 1. *Assume $N + 1$ being prime. For a generic (ϵ, t, q)-algorithm solving either GA-DLOG or GA-CDH in the GGAM of order N we have $\epsilon \leq q^2/N$.*

Note that the *Baby-Step Giant-Step Algorithm* [38] can be easily adapted to the group action setting. This adaption yields a generic algorithm for solving GA-DLOG which matches the bound from Corollary 1.

We remark again that Lemma 1 and Corollary 1 only apply if $N + 1$ is a prime number. Therefore hardness results in the GGM only carry over to the GGAM under this restriction. For specific assumptions we can prove their hardness irrespective of $N + 1$ being prime as we show in the next section, however a universal lifting theorem might not be achievable. We leave this as an interesting topic for future work.

4.2 Generic Group Action Model with Twists

We introduce the Generic Group Action Model with Twists $(\mathsf{GGAM}^\top)$ which extends the above GGAM for CEGATs. Recall that current instantiations of group actions like CSIDH are indeed modeled more accurately by a CEGAT as they come with an additional twisting functionality which allows to efficiently compute $-\mathfrak{a} \diamond \tilde{x}$ from $\mathfrak{a} \diamond \tilde{x}$. Since this functionality is not present in the current definition of the GGAM, some attacks may not be captured for a large class of widely used group actions. This makes an important difference when analyzing the generic hardness of non-standard assumptions. It is therefore desirable to adapt the GGAM to this setting. In particular, we extend the definition of the GGAM by an additional oracle $\mathcal{O}^{\mathsf{tw}} : \mathcal{S} \to \mathcal{S}$ that computes $\sigma_\mathcal{X}(-\mathfrak{a} \diamond \tilde{x})$ for a given input $\sigma_\mathcal{X}(\mathfrak{a} \diamond \tilde{x})$.

Note that twists do not have an analogue in the standard prime order group setting. This means that Lemma 1 does not apply to the $\mathsf{GGAM}^\top$ even if $N + 1$ is prime. Below we provide two separating examples.

Example 2. The security of the password-autheticated key exchange scheme TBPEKE [35] relies on the so-called *Simultaneous Diffie-Hellman assumption.* Translated to the group action notation, an adversary is given three elements $x = \mathfrak{g} \diamond \tilde{x}$, $y_1 = \mathfrak{a}_1 \diamond x$, $y_2 = \mathfrak{a}_2 \diamond x \in \mathcal{X}$ and is supposed to output three elements z, r_1, $r_2 \in \mathcal{X}$ satisfying $r_1 = -\mathfrak{a}_1 \diamond z$ and $r_2 = -\mathfrak{a}_2 \diamond z$. The authors show that a generic (ϵ, t, q)-algorithm solving this problem in the GGM of order p, has success probability $\epsilon \leq q^2 + 20/2p$. In contrast to that, an adversary in the $\mathsf{GGAM}^\top$ only needs three calls to the $\mathcal{O}^{\mathsf{tw}}$ oracle in order to find a valid solution: $z = \mathcal{O}^{\mathsf{tw}}(x)$, $r_1 = \mathcal{O}^{\mathsf{tw}}(y_1)$, $r_2 = \mathcal{O}^{\mathsf{tw}}(y_2)$.

Example 3. Another simple separating example is the *Inverse Diffie-Hellman Problem (IDHP).* Adapted to our group action notation, an adversary is given $\mathfrak{a} \diamond \tilde{x}$ for $\mathfrak{a} \leftarrow_\$ \mathbb{Z}_N$ and is asked to compute $-\mathfrak{a} \diamond \tilde{x}$. From the definition of $\mathcal{O}^{\mathsf{tw}}$ it is obvious that IDHP is easy in $\mathsf{GGAM}^\top$. In the GGAM, however, IDHP must be as hard as CDH (assuming $N + 1$ being prime). The reason is that IDHP and CDH are equivalent in the GGM [6], implying that both have the same lower bound in the GGM. Due to Lemma 1, the lower bound for IDHP must therefore hold in the GGAM. We thus have that IDHP is easy in the $\mathsf{GGAM}^\top$ but provably hard in the GGAM if $N + 1$ is prime.

The two examples show that results in the $\mathsf{GGAM}^\top$ and the GGAM are incomparable. However, we can still analyze specific problems directly in the $\mathsf{GGAM}^\top$ by adapting the information theoretic arguments used in the GGM.

With this we get a similar bound for the discrete logarithm assumption, as well as bounds for the non-standard Group Action k-power Decisional Diffie-Hellman Problem (Definition 7) and the Group Action Discrete Logarithm Problem with Auxilary Input (Definition 8). Our analysis further shows that some assumptions possess instances which are potentially easier to solve. We are further able to argue that information-theoretically there are only a hand full of these cases which are all linked to the composite nature of N. Before we proceed to study these problems, we recall a useful lemma needed for our analysis.

Lemma 2. *Let $a, b \in \mathbb{Z}$, $N \in \mathbb{N}$ and denote $d = \gcd(a, N)$. Then the equation $a \cdot x \equiv b \pmod{N}$ has precisely d solutions if d divides b and no solutions otherwise.*

Theorem 1. *For every generic (ϵ, t, q)-algorithm $\mathcal{A}$ winning the GA-DLOG game in the $GGAM^\top$ of order N, we have $\epsilon \leq 2q^2/N$.*

Note that the bound differs from the GGM bound by a factor of 2. This is due to the fact that N is potentially composite, leading to polynomials of degree 1 with two roots in the reduction. This factor can be removed by requiring that $\gcd(2, N) = 1$. The latter is always true when instantiating the group action with CSIDH.

Proof. The proof idea is very similar to classical proofs of DLOG in the GGM. The discrete logarithm challenge is replaced by an indeterminate $\mathbf{X}$ and the labeling function is extended to polynomials $f_i(X)$. If the value of $\mathbf{X}$ (and therefore the DLOG solution) is only chosen after the adversary finished, the probability of success is exactly $1/N$. However, we have to ensure that this change is undetected. The only problem that can occur is that the adversary makes two queries (which are now on polynomials $f_i(\mathbf{X}), f_j(\mathbf{X})$) that result in different labels since $f_i(\mathbf{X}) \neq f_j(\mathbf{X})$, but both polynomials evaluate to the same value on the chosen challenge. However, we can bound the probability of this event by predicting the number of roots of $f_i(\mathbf{X}) - f_j(\mathbf{X})$, yielding the well-known bounds.

While our proof follows the same idea, there are some intricacies we have to consider. First, the order N of the group action is potentially composite, so by Lemma 2, for a polynomial of the form $\mathfrak{a}\mathbf{X} + \mathfrak{b} \equiv 0 \pmod{N}$, there are $d = \gcd(\mathfrak{a}, N)$ many roots if d divides $\mathfrak{b}$ and none otherwise. On the other hand, an adversary is limited to the $\mathcal{O}^{\mathsf{exp}}$ and the $\mathcal{O}^{\mathsf{tw}}$, so all equations that it can compute are of the form $\mathfrak{g} \pm \mathbf{X}$ or $\mathfrak{g} \pm 2\mathbf{X}$, thus every equation has at most two roots.

Overall with exactly the same argument as in the GGM the theorem follows with the additional factor 2.   □

In [18] the authors define the so called k-*power Decisional Diffie-Hellman Group Action Problem* in order to build threshold schemes. We give an equivalent definition that is written in additive notation and analyze its hardness in the $GGAM^\top$.

Definition 7 (Group Action k-power Decisional Diffie-Hellman Problem). *Let* CEGAT $= (\mathbb{Z}_N, \mathcal{X}, \diamond, \tilde{x})$ *and* $1 < k < N - 1$. *For* $\mathfrak{a}, \mathfrak{c} \leftarrow_\$ \mathbb{Z}_N$ *define* $w_0 = k \cdot \mathfrak{a} \diamond \tilde{x}$ *and* $w_1 = \mathfrak{c} \diamond \tilde{x}$. *We say that an adversary $\mathcal{A}$ solves the Group Action k-power Decisional Diffie-Hellman Problem* (GA-k-PDDH) *if*

$$\mathcal{A}(k, \mathfrak{a} \diamond \tilde{x}, w_b, w_{1-b}) = b$$

for $b \leftarrow_\$ \{0, 1\}$.

Theorem 2. *For every generic (ϵ, t, q)-algorithm $\mathcal{A}$ winning* GA-k-PDDH *in the* $GGAM^\top$ *of order N, we have*

$$\epsilon \leq \frac{1}{2} + \frac{2 \cdot d_{max} \cdot q^2}{N} \ ,$$

where $d_{max} = \max\{\gcd(2k, N), \gcd(k \pm 1, N)\}$.

Proof. The proof uses an argument similar to the original proof of DDH in the GGM by Shoup [40], however there are again some subtleties. Fix some $1 < k < N - 1$. We define indeterminates $\mathbf{X}, \mathbf{Y}, \mathbf{Z}$ that represent the values $\mathfrak{a} \diamond \tilde{x}$, w_b and w_{1-b}, respectively. An algorithm can implicitly build polynomials $f_i(\mathbf{X}, \mathbf{Y}, \mathbf{Z})$ of the following forms:

$$\mathfrak{g}, \qquad \mathfrak{g} \pm \mathbf{X}, \qquad \mathfrak{g} \pm \mathbf{Y}, \qquad \text{and} \qquad \mathfrak{g} \pm \mathbf{Z} \qquad (\text{mod } N) \ .$$

As in the proof of Theorem 1 we are now interested in the number of roots of $f_i(\mathbf{X}, \mathbf{Y}, \mathbf{Z}) - f_j(\mathbf{Y}, \mathbf{Y}, \mathbf{Z})$. More specifically, we have to keep in mind that either $\mathbf{Y}$ or $\mathbf{Z}$ is set to $k \cdot \mathbf{X}$ at the end of the game, meaning that we have to bound the probability that either

$$f_i(\mathbf{X}, \mathbf{Y}, k \cdot \mathbf{Y}) - f_j(\mathbf{Y}, \mathbf{Y}, k \cdot \mathbf{X}) \equiv 0 \mod N \tag{2}$$

or

$$f_i(\mathbf{X}, k \cdot \mathbf{X}, \mathbf{Z}) - f_j(\mathbf{X}, k \cdot \mathbf{x}, \mathbf{Z}) \equiv 0 \mod N \tag{3}$$

for a random assignment of $\mathbf{X}$, $\mathbf{Y}$ and $\mathbf{Z}$. Listing all possibilities for these differences is tedious, therefore we restrict our attention to the polynomial in $\mathbf{X}$ and leave the remaining polynomials (in either $\mathbf{Y}$ or $\mathbf{Z}$) unspecified. In the case of Eq. (2) we get

$$\pm k \cdot \mathbf{X} + f(\mathbf{Y}), \quad \pm(k+1)\mathbf{X} + f(\mathbf{Y}), \quad \pm(k-1)\mathbf{X} + f(\mathbf{Y}),$$

$$\pm \mathbf{X} + f(\mathbf{Y}), \quad \pm 2\mathbf{X} + f(\mathbf{Y}), \quad \pm 2k \cdot \mathbf{X} + f(\mathbf{Y}) \ .$$

and analogously for Eq. (3). The likelihood of an assignment being a root now mainly depends on the choice of $\mathbf{X}$. Recall from Lemma 2 that an equation of the form $\mathfrak{a}\mathbf{X} + \mathfrak{b} \equiv 0 \pmod{N}$ has at most $\gcd(\mathfrak{a}, N)$ solutions. In our setting, $\mathfrak{a} \in \{\pm 1, \pm 2, \pm k, \pm(k-1), \pm(k+1), \pm 2k\}$, hence

$$\gcd(\mathfrak{a}, N) \leq d_{\max} = \max\{\gcd(2k, N), \gcd(k \pm 1, N)\} \ .$$

In conclusion, the probability that an assignment for $\mathbf{X}$ is a root of one polynomial in Eq. (2) is bounded by $d_{\max}/N$ and the same holds for polynomials in eq. (3). Therefore, choosing the bit b after the adversary has finished fails with probability $2 \cdot d_{\max}/N$. Of course, an adversary can still guess the (now information theoretically hidden) bit b with constant probability $1/2$, which immediately yields the overall bound. $\qquad\square$

Remark 5. The authors in [18] already noted that in the presence of twists GA-k-PDDH is easy for $k = N - 1$. Generically, the problem can be solved by sending one query to the twist oracle. Therefore we excluded this case in our definition of the problem. Moreover our analysis in the $\mathsf{GGAM}^\top$ indicates that there are more choices for $1 < k < N-1$ for which GA-k-PDDH becomes potentially easier. In light of Theorem 2, we advise to only use a stronger version of GA-k-PDDH, where it is additionally assumed that $d_{\max} = \max\{\gcd(2k, N), \gcd(k\pm 1, N)\} = 1$.

Remark 6. It is also possible to consider a version of GA-k-PDDH where all elements are given relative to some $x = \mathfrak{h} \diamond \tilde{x}$. A correct GA-$k$-PDDH tuple would thus contain the element $z = (k \cdot \mathfrak{a} + \mathfrak{h}) \diamond \tilde{x}$. This makes the analysis more intricate but does not change the overall bound.

Baghery, Cozzo and Pederson [5] introduce the vectorization problem with auxiliary inputs to construct a new identification scheme and thus a signature scheme based on CSIDH. The problem has already been analyzed by [26] in the standard model. It is similar to q-DLOG [11] or DLOG with auxiliary inputs [15] in the prime-order group setting. In the following we first recall the problem and then analyze its hardness in the $\mathsf{GGAM}^\top$.

Definition 8 Group Action Discrete Logarithm Problem with Auxilary Input [5]). *Let* $\mathsf{CEGAT} = (\mathbb{Z}_N, \mathcal{X}, \diamond, \tilde{x})$. *We say that an adversary* $\mathcal{A}$ *solves the Group Action Discrete Logarithm Problem with Auxilary Input* (GA-DLAI) *if*

$$\mathcal{A}(k_0, \ldots, k_{m-1}, x_0, \ldots, x_{m-1}) = \mathfrak{a}$$

where the k_i *are given by*

$$k_0 = 0, k_1 = 1 \text{ and } 1 < k_i < N \text{ for } i > 1$$

under the restriction

$$\forall i \neq j : \gcd(k_i - k_j, N) = 1 \qquad and \qquad \forall i, j : \gcd(k_i + k_j, N) = 1$$

and the x_i *are given by* $x_i = k_i \cdot \mathfrak{a} \diamond \tilde{x}$ *for* $\mathfrak{a} \leftarrow_\$ \mathbb{Z}_N$.

Theorem 3. *For any generic* (ϵ, q, t)*-adversary* $\mathcal{A}$ *winning* GA-DLAI *in the* $GGAM^\top$ *of order* N*, we have* $\epsilon \leq q^2/N$.

Proof. The proof is almost identical to the proofs of Theorem 1 and Theorem 2. Here, the cases where an equation has more than one root are excluded by the requirement that $\gcd(k_i - k_j, N) = 1$ for $i \neq j$ and $\gcd(k_i + k_j, N) = 1$ for all i, j. ☐

4.3   Quantum Generic Group Action Model

Isogeny-based group actions are a strong candidate for post-quantum secure cryptography. Therefore, group action based assumptions should also be analyzed in the presence of quantum adversaries. One might hope that the GGAM can be adapted to the quantum setting where a quantum algorithm can query $\mathcal{O}^{\mathsf{exp}}$ in superposition. Formally this change is simple, that is, we define the quantum oracle $\mathcal{O}^{\mathsf{exp}}(\sum_{x,y,z} \alpha_{x,y,z} |x, y, z\rangle) = \sum_{x,y,z} \alpha_{x,y,z} |x, y, z \oplus \mathcal{O}^{\mathsf{exp}}(x, y)\rangle$.[4] In the following, we will denote this model by QGGAM and naturally extend the notion of a (ϵ, t, q)-algorithm to the quantum setting. In practice, however, making the oracle quantum accessible creates a lot of problems, especially regarding one of the main purposes of the GGAM: information-theoretic lower bounds.

The most glaring issue is an algorithm by Ettinger and Høyer [21] that can be used to solve GA-DLOG pseudoefficiently in the QGGAM.

Theorem 4. *There exists a generic quantum (ϵ, t, q)-algorithm that solves* GA-DLOG *in the QGGAM of order N with $\epsilon = 1 - \frac{1}{2N}$, $t \in \mathcal{O}(\sqrt{N})$ and $q = \lceil 64 \ln N \rceil$.*

In its purest form the Ettinger-Høyer algorithm solves the well-known *Dihedral Hidden Subgroup Problem (DHSP)* with polynomially many quantum oracle queries (see [27] for a survey on the DHSP). Because GA-DLOG and many other group action based assumptions reduce to some form of the DHSP, its hardness plays a central role in group action based cryptography [34]. Although there have been improvements towards solving the DHSP more efficiently, the currently fastest (generic) algorithm still has an overall subexponential complexity.

Theorem 5 (Kuperberg's algorithm, [29]). *There exists a generic quantum (ϵ, t, q)-algorithm that solves* GA-DLOG *in the QGGAM of order N with $\epsilon \approx 1$ and $t, q \in \mathcal{O}(2^{\sqrt{\log N}})$.*

In the standard model, Kuberberg's algorithm has the more favorable trade off between the time complexity t and query complexity q, therefore making it the best currently known algorithm against DHSP. Because of its overall subexponential complexity, the DHSP (and by extension GA-DLOG) remain hard in the standard model, which starkly contrasts the situation in the QGGAM.

We conclude that in the QGGAM we cannot give lower bounds on computational problems because even GA-DLOG can be solved with polynomial oracle complexity. Since the exponential time of the Ettinger-Høyer algorithm stems

---

[4] This was already observed in [33]. A more thorough comparison can be found in Sect. 4.4.

from solving a combinatorial problem, one can assume that the hardness of GA-DLOG is thus not an algebraic one but a combinatorial one. We discuss this more in the full version.

4.4 Comparison with the Generic Model by Montgomery and Zhandry

In [33] the authors define a different variant of the GGAM, which we call the MZ-GGAM, where the group $\mathcal{G}$ of a group action $(\mathcal{G}, \mathcal{X}, \star, \tilde{x})$ is also modeled as a generic group. Consequently, the authors define *two* labeling functions, one for $\mathcal{G}$ and one for $\mathcal{X}$, as well as corresponding oracles for the operation in $\mathcal{G}$ and for the group action. In particular, DLOG is assumed to be hard in the group $\mathcal{G}$. In the following, we want to argue that this model and especially its quantum counterpart does not capture the widely used class of *(cyclic) effective* group actions very well. To simplify the exposition, we assume that in line with our setup the group $\mathcal{G}$ is cyclic. Clearly, the discussion translates to the setting of a general abelian group as well. For more details on the functionality of our GGAM in this setting, the reader is referred to the full version.

For the discussion we introduce the (somewhat informal) notation $[\mathcal{X}]$ resp. $[\mathcal{G}]$ to denote that a set (resp. group) is idealized in the sense of the generic group model. That is, its elements are represented by labels and algorithms are provided with oracles to compute the group action (resp. group operation). With this notation our GGAM would be written as $(\mathbb{Z}_N, [\mathcal{X}], \diamond, \tilde{x})$, while the MZ-GGAM of [33] can be seen as $([\mathcal{G}], [\mathcal{X}], \star, \tilde{x})$.

Our discussion mainly focuses on the generic group $[\mathcal{G}]$, which is the main difference between the two models. We first cover the classical setting where we observe that the MZ-GGAM can be used to simulate a classical GGM. The reason for this is straightforward: Per definition, the MZ-GGAM provides an algorithm with a generic group $[\mathcal{G}]$. In fact, any game or algorithm in the GGM can be compiled in the MZ-GGAM by just ignoring $[\mathcal{X}]$ and solely using $[\mathcal{G}]$ for computations. We thus have that, intuitively, the GGM is fully contained in the MZ-GGAM. A more formal statement would be that the GGM is *indifferentiable* from the MZ-GGAM (see [31] for a definition of indifferentiability). We leave out this rigorous discussion in the interest of space. This connection is not desirable as the computational hardness of group actions should not stem from the hardness of the group itself but instead should stem from the hardness of inverting the group action. Phrased differently: even if DLOG were easy in $\mathcal{G}$, we still require that GA-DLOG is hard in $(\mathcal{G}, [\mathcal{X}], \star, \tilde{x})$.

The last fact is emphasized when looking at the *quantum* setting. Here, we can easily compute an isomorphism $\psi : [\mathcal{G}] \rightarrow \mathbb{Z}_N$ via Shor's algorithm [39] for a suitable $N \in \mathbb{N}$, making the generic group $[\mathcal{G}]$ obsolete for algebraic purposes. Additionally, even constructions like the random oracle from a generic group in [42] are likely to be adaptable to the QGGAM as they only require access to a random labeling function.

Of course, the issues discussed in Sect. 4.3 regarding the quantum hardness of GA-DLOG also apply to the MZ-QGGAM. Hence there is no reason to insist on a generic group $[\mathcal{G}]$ as any hardness assumption imposed on $\mathcal{G}$ can be circumvented by quantum preprocessing. We therefore believe that even in the classical setting, our weaker definition models the computational complexity of (cyclic) effective group actions in a more realistic way.

5   Algebraic Group Action Model

In this section we introduce the Algebraic Group Action Model and use it to prove several results. In Sect. 5.1 we formally define the Algebraic Group Action Model in several variants (classic/quantum and with/without twists). In Sect. 5.2 we use the quantum version to reduce different non-standard assumptions to GA-DLOG.

5.1   Definition and Relations

We define the Algebraic Group Action Model (AGAM) similar to the AGM of [22] with the difference that the underlying algebraic structure is now an effective group action instead of a prime-order group. Like in the GGAM, we assume that DLOG is easy in $\mathcal{G}$ and therefore make exclusive use of cyclic effective group actions.[5]

Definition 9 ((Quantum) Algebraic Group Action Algorithms). *Let* CEGA $= (\mathbb{Z}_N, \mathcal{X}, \diamond, \tilde{x})$ *be a fixed cyclic effective group action. An algorithm* $\mathcal{A}$ *is called* algebraic *if for each output element* $y \in \mathcal{X}$ *it additionally provides a representation relative to a previously received set element. Concretely, if* $(x_1, \ldots, x_\ell) \in \mathcal{X}^\ell$ *is the list of received set elements so far,* $\mathcal{A}$ *additionally provides a group element* $\mathfrak{a} \in \mathbb{Z}_N$ *and an index* $i \in \{1, \ldots, \ell\}$ *such that* $y = \mathfrak{a} \diamond x_i$. *We denote*

$$y_{(i,\mathfrak{a})} = \mathfrak{a} \diamond x_i.$$

If an oracle is queried on some set elements, then $\mathcal{A}$ *also has to provide a representation for each set element contained in that query.*

Analogously, a quantum *adversary is algebraic if for every output state* $|y\rangle$ *it additionally outputs a* quantum representation, *i.e. a quantum state* $|i, \mathfrak{a}\rangle$ *s.t.* $|y\rangle = |\mathfrak{a} \diamond x_i\rangle$. *Similarly to the classical case, we write* $|y_{(i,\mathfrak{a})}\rangle$. *Note that the representation is entangled with the group element.*

Additionally, if the group action supports twists (i.e. it is a CEGAT*), we extend the representation by a bit* b, *indicating whether the base element was twisted before applying the group action. Formally, we then have*

$$y_{(i,\mathfrak{a},b)} = \begin{cases} \mathfrak{a} \diamond x_i & \text{if } b = 0, \\ \mathfrak{a} \diamond x_i{}^t & \text{if } b = 1. \end{cases}$$

As in the AGM we require that all auxiliary input provided to the adversary which is not in $\mathcal{X}$ *does not depend on elements from* $\mathcal{X}$.

---

[5] To capture general abelian groups, a similar approach as described for the GGAM in the full version applies.

Remark 7. As noted in [25,43], it is somewhat imprecise to require auxiliary inputs to be independent of set element inputs, as there might be arbitrary, information theoretically hidden set elements encoded in them. However, generally it is clear in practice whether such dependencies exist, so we do not specify this further. Additionally, all adversaries that we consider only receive set elements as inputs, so it is clear either way that there are no "hidden" set elements.

Remark 8. We assume that all representations provided by an adversary in the QAGAM are correct. While it is not as straight forward as in the classical setting to actually check this correctness, this is without loss of generality. Instead of providing the representation *and* the group element itself, we could instead require the adversary to only provide the representation and have the reduction/oracle compute the group element itself. This makes everything consistent and correct. Alternatively, an approach similar to the semi-classical O2H is possible, where the reduction measures whether the representation is correct, however this introduces a small error probability.

Let G_1, G_2 be two security games in the (Q)AGAM and assume that there exists an algebraic (ϵ, t)-algorithm $\mathcal{A}$ winning game G_2. We say that G_1 *reduces to* G_2 if there exists an *efficient* (quantum) algorithm $\mathcal{R}$ (called the *reduction*) such that $\mathcal{R}^{\mathcal{A}}$ is an (ϵ', t')-algorithm that wins G_1 with time complexity $t' \in \mathcal{O}(poly(t))$ and success probability $\epsilon' \in \Omega(poly(\epsilon))$. If $\mathcal{R}$ is algebraic, then we have that $\mathcal{R}^{\mathcal{A}}$ is an algebraic algorithm as well.

While the GGAM can not be lifted (in a useful way) to the quantum setting (see Sect. 4.3), the QAGAM is indeed useful for studying the relation between assumptions in the presence of a quantum adversary. Firstly, this is due to the fact that the AGAM is not used to prove lower bounds but instead upper bounds via reductions as described above. This means that all reductions from the AGAM can be immediately lifted to the QAGAM, as a quantum algorithm can perform all classical operations. Secondly, some assumptions are inherently quantum. They can for example include oracles which can be queried on quantum superpositions. For such queries, a classical representation is implausible, as it potentially has exponential size and would require an adversary to always know all amplitudes of the states it queries to oracles, which is unreasonable even for algebraic adversaries. Therefore, the QAGAM is necessary when considering such assumptions. We analyze two inherently quantum assumptions in Sect. 5.2.

Relation Between AGAM and AGM. Similarly to the GGM and GGAM, it is possible relate the AGM to the AGAM. While the intuition behind this relation is similar to the generic case, it is a lot more complicated to formalize. The main complication stems from the fact that we do not have the useful formal limitations of the generic group model. Specifically, while it is easy to simply omit an oracle in an idealized model, formalizing the set of allowed operations of an arbitrary algorithm on some group or group action requires more rigor in order to make no arbitrary limitations. While this is possible via the abstraction of group schemes [2, 4, 24] (which can also be adapted to group actions), it is not very insightful.

Additionally, relating the AGAM to the AGM is not very useful. While we can adapt lower bounds from the GGM to the GGAM, we could only hope to adapt *upper bounds* from the AGAM to the AGM. However, it is very likely that there are actually better upper bounds that can be proven in the AGM as we have more freedom there. So we only get "upper bounds on upper bounds", which are of limited use.

Relation between AGAM and AGAM$^\top$. As in the GGAM, one generally can not directly translate results from the AGAM to the AGAM$^\top$ or vice versa. For the direction from AGAM to AGAM$^\top$, the examples from Sect. 4.2 apply as well. In the other direction, the situation is a bit more nuanced. Since the reduction can depend on the representations provided by the adversary, there are situations where the reduction only uses the twisting functionality of the group action, if the adversary does so as well. In this case the reduction can be moved from the AGAM$^\top$ to the AGAM. In all other cases, directly transfering reductions seems impossible and both models have to be considered.

5.2 Results in the Quantum Algebraic Group Action Model with Twists

As a warm-up, we show the equivalence of GA-DLOG and GA-CDH in the (Q)AGAM$^\top$. As the implication from GA-CDH to GA-DLOG is obvious, we only show the non-trivial implication.

Theorem 6 (GA-DLOG $\Rightarrow$ GA-CDH in the (Q)AGAM$^\top$). *Let $\mathcal{A}$ be an algebraic (quantum) $(\epsilon_\mathcal{A}, t_\mathcal{A})$-adversary against the GA-CDH problem, then there exists an $(\epsilon_\mathcal{B}, t_\mathcal{B})$-adversary $\mathcal{B}$ against the GA-DLOG problem with*

$$\epsilon_\mathcal{A} \le \epsilon_\mathcal{B} \quad and \quad t_\mathcal{A} \approx t_\mathcal{B} .$$

Formally, we prove the theorem in the AGAM$^\top$. However, there are no quantum oracles and the proof adapts to the quantum setting without change.

Proof. We construct a reduction $\mathcal{B}$ against GA-DLOG as follows. $\mathcal{B}$ gets as input $x_1 := \mathfrak{a} \diamond \tilde{x}$ and chooses $\mathfrak{r} \leftarrow_\$ \mathbb{Z}_N$. It computes $x_2 := \mathfrak{r} \diamond x_1$ and then runs the algebraic adversary $\mathcal{A}$ against GA-CDH on (x_1, x_2). At some point $\mathcal{A}$ will output a solution z as well as a representation $(i, \mathfrak{s}, b)$. Note that if $\mathcal{A}$ wins, then $z = (2\mathfrak{a} + \mathfrak{r}) \diamond \tilde{x}$. For each $i \in \{0, 1, 2\}$ and $b \in \{0, 1\}$, we show how we can solve the GA-DLOG challenge from $\mathfrak{s}$.

- Case 1 ($i = 0$): Since the twist maps the origin $\tilde{x}$ to itself, we get $\mathfrak{s} \diamond \tilde{x} = (2\mathfrak{a} + \mathfrak{r}) \diamond \tilde{x}$ for both $b \in \{0, 1\}$. Thus, we have to solve $2\mathfrak{a} = \mathfrak{s} - \mathfrak{r} \bmod N$. If $\gcd(2, N) = 2$ and 2 divides $\mathfrak{s} - \mathfrak{r}$, then we get two solutions and we test which is the correct one. Otherwise, there exists exactly one solution.
- Case 2 ($i = 1$): For $b = 0$, we get $\mathfrak{s} \diamond (\mathfrak{a} \diamond \tilde{x}) = (2\mathfrak{a} + \mathfrak{r}) \diamond \tilde{x}$. Thus, we get $\mathfrak{a} = \mathfrak{s} - \mathfrak{r} \bmod N$. For $b = 1$, we get $\mathfrak{s} \diamond (-\mathfrak{a} \diamond \tilde{x}) = (2\mathfrak{a} + \mathfrak{r}) \diamond \tilde{x}$ and we have

to solve $3\mathfrak{a} = \mathfrak{s} - \mathfrak{r}$. If $\gcd(3, N) = 3$ and 3 divides $\mathfrak{s} - \mathfrak{r}$, then we get three solutions and we test which is the correct one. Otherwise, there exists exactly one solution.

- Case 3 ($i = 2$): For $b = 0$, we get $\mathfrak{s} \diamond ((\mathfrak{a} + \mathfrak{r}) \diamond \tilde{x}) = (2\mathfrak{a} + \mathfrak{r}) \diamond \tilde{x}$. Thus, $\mathfrak{a} = \mathfrak{s}$ is exactly the GA-DLOG solution. For $b = 1$, we get $\mathfrak{s} \diamond ((-\mathfrak{a} - \mathfrak{r}) \diamond \tilde{x}) = (2\mathfrak{a} + \mathfrak{r}) \diamond \tilde{x}$ and we have to solve $3\mathfrak{a} = \mathfrak{s} - 2\mathfrak{r}$, which we can do similar to case 2.

This concludes the proof of Theorem 6. □

An interesting new problem and its necessity to prove IND-CCA security of (plain) hashed ElGamal was put forward by [19]. They define different variants of the strong CDH problem, some of them allowing quantum queries to the decision oracle. We first recall the definition of the strongest version of their problem.

Definition 10 (Group Action Quantum Strong Computational Diffie-Hellman). *Let* $\mathsf{CEGA}(T) = (\mathbb{Z}_N, \mathcal{X}, \diamond, \tilde{x})$ *be a cyclic effective group action (with twists). We say that an adversary* $\mathcal{A}$ *solves the group action quantum strong computational Diffie-Hellman problem* (GA-QSt-CDH) *if* $\mathcal{A}^O(\tilde{x}, \mathfrak{a} \diamond \tilde{x}, \mathfrak{b} \diamond \tilde{x}) = (\mathfrak{a} + \mathfrak{b}) \diamond \tilde{x}$ *for* $\mathfrak{a}, \mathfrak{b} \leftarrow_\mathfrak{s} \mathbb{Z}_N$, *where* $\mathcal{A}$ *has access to decision oracles* $O := \{\mathsf{GA\text{-}DDH}_\mathfrak{a}(|\cdot, \cdot\rangle), \mathsf{GA\text{-}DDH}_\mathfrak{b}(|\cdot, \cdot\rangle)\}$.

On basis-state inputs (y, z), GA-DDH$_\mathfrak{a}$ *returns 1 if* $\mathfrak{a} \diamond y = z$ *and 0 otherwise.* GA-DDH$_\mathfrak{b}$ *is defined equivalently. Note that superposition queries are then implicitly defined by linearity (i.e.,* $O(\sum_x \alpha_x x) = \sum_x \alpha_x O(x)$).

Remark 9. The GA-QSt-CDH assumption is called Double-Sided Fully Quantum Group Action Strong Computational Diffie-Hellman Problemin [19]. They define additional variants where the adversary can only access one of the two decision oracles or has only partial quantum access (i.e. one of the inputs is implicitly measured). The GA-QSt-CDH assumption is the strongest of these assumptions, so the result we show in Theorem 7 applies to the weaker assumptions as well.

Now we show that in the $\mathsf{QAGAM}^\top$, this problem can actually be reduced to GA-DLOG using the semi-classical oneway-to-hiding lemma (see the full version).

Theorem 7 (GA-DLOG $\Rightarrow$ GA-QSt-CDH in the $\mathsf{QAGAM}^\top$). *Let* $\mathcal{A}$ *be an algebraic quantum* $(\epsilon_\mathcal{A}, t_\mathcal{A})$*-adversary against the* GA-QSt-CDH *problem making at most* q *decision oracle queries, then there exist* $(\epsilon_\mathcal{B}, t_\mathcal{B})$*-adversary* $\mathcal{B}$ *and* $(\epsilon_\mathcal{C}, t_\mathcal{C})$*-adversary* $\mathcal{C}$ *against* GA-DLOG *with*

$$\epsilon_\mathcal{A} \leq \sqrt{(q+1) \cdot \epsilon_\mathcal{B}} + \epsilon_\mathcal{C} \quad and \quad t_\mathcal{A} \approx t_\mathcal{B} \approx t_\mathcal{C} .$$

Proof. The main difficulty of the proof is to show that the reduction can simulate the quantum GA-DDH oracles. The main observation then is that if the algebraic adversary queries GA-DDH on points where it might learn something interesting, it already had to solve GA-DLOG. Therefore, we can assume that the adversary does not query those points (with noticeable probability amplitude) and we can remove them from the oracle using the semi-classical O2H lemma. This is done in the gamehop G_0 to G_1. On the remaining points where the adversary does

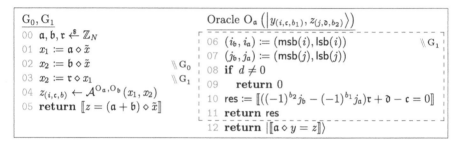

Fig. 2. Games G_0-G_1 for the proof of Theorem 7. The oracle O_b is simulated in the same way as O_a except for an additional $\mathfrak{r}$ in the boolean test in line 10. The variable d is defined as in Eq. (6). Lines 06 and 07 interpret i and j as a two digit binary number. Note that $i, j \leq 2$.

not learn anything of interest, the reduction knows how to simulate GA-DDH perfectly and we can solve GA-DLOG from the algebraic GA-CDH solution, which bounds the probability of winning in G_1. We proceed with the formal proof.

Let $\mathcal{A}$ be a quantum algebraic adversary against the GA-QSt-CDH game. Consider the games given in Fig. 2.

Game G_0. This is the definition of the GA-QSt-CDH game where we write O_a for GA-DDH$_a$ and likewise for O_b. We have

$$\Pr[G_0 \Rightarrow 1] = \epsilon_\mathcal{A}.$$

Game G_1. Here, we make two changes. The first change is a simple conceptual change. We use the random self-reducibility of GA-DLOG to set x_2 to $\mathfrak{r} \diamond x_1$ instead of $\mathfrak{b} \diamond \tilde{x}$ for $\mathfrak{r} \leftarrow_\$ \mathbb{Z}_N$. The second change is in the simulation of the decision oracles. We reprogram certain points of the decision oracle O_a and O_b to always output 0. More specifically, we reprogram those points to 0 which would allow us to solve GA-DLOG if the adversary gave us elements where GA-DDH returns 1. By the semi-classical oneway-to-hiding lemma (see full version) we can bound the difference between the games G_0 and G_1 by the probability of the adversary finding an element from the reprogrammed set of points $\mathcal{S}$. That is

$$|\Pr[G_0 \Rightarrow 1] - \Pr[G_1 \Rightarrow 1]| \leq \sqrt{(q+1)\Pr\left[\textsc{Find} \mid \mathcal{A}^{G \setminus \mathcal{S}}\right]},$$

where we define $\mathcal{S}$ as the set where the function SetTest defined in Fig. 3 returns 1.

We bound the right-hand-side, showing that

$$\Pr\left[\textsc{Find} \mid \mathcal{A}^{G \setminus \mathcal{S}}\right] \leq \epsilon_\mathcal{B}, \tag{4}$$

in the reduction $\mathcal{B}$ described in Fig. 3. The reduction simulates the oracles as in G_1 and simulates the semi-classical O2H oracle by considering the cases described below.

Reduction $\mathcal{B}(x_1 := \mathfrak{a} \diamond \tilde{x})$	Oracle $O_\mathfrak{a} \setminus \mathcal{S}(|\psi_{in}, \psi_{out}\rangle)$
00 $\mathfrak{r} \xleftarrow{\$} \mathbb{Z}_N$	12 $|\psi'_{in}, b\rangle \leftarrow O_\mathcal{S}^{SC}(|\psi_{in}, 0\rangle)$
01 $x_2 := \mathfrak{r} \diamond x_1$	13 if $b = 1$
02 $\mathcal{T} \leftarrow$ Run $\mathcal{A}^{O \setminus \mathcal{S}}(x_1, x_2)$ until FIND	14 FIND $:= 1$
and measure query register inputs	15 return $U_O(|\psi'_{in}, \psi_{out}\rangle)$
03 return FindSolution$(\mathcal{T}, x_1, x_2)$	

Oracle $O_\mathcal{S}^{SC}(|\psi_{in}, 0\rangle)$	FindSolution$(\mathcal{T}, x_1, x_2)$
04 Parse ψ_{in} as $\left|y_{(i,\mathfrak{c},b_1)}, z_{(j,\mathfrak{d},b_2)}\right\rangle$	16 Parse $\mathcal{T}$ as $(y_{(i,\mathfrak{c},b_1)}, z_{(j,\mathfrak{d},b_2)})$
05 $b := 0$	17 Run SetTest$(y_{(i,\mathfrak{c},b_1)}, z_{(j,\mathfrak{d},b_2)})$
06 $b \leftarrow$ Measure $\left[\text{SetTest}\left(\left|y_{(i,\mathfrak{c},b_1)}, z_{(j,\mathfrak{d},b_2)}\right\rangle\right)\right]$	returning $\mathfrak{a}'$ s.t. $\mathfrak{a}' \diamond \tilde{x} = x_1$
07 return $(|\psi'_{in}\rangle, b)$	18 return $\mathfrak{a}'$

SetTest $\left(\left|y_{(i,\mathfrak{c},b_1)}, z_{(j,\mathfrak{d},b_2)}\right\rangle\right)$

08 if $d \neq 0$

09    $\mathcal{T} := \text{Solve}(\mathfrak{a} + \mathfrak{c} + (-1)^{b_1}(i_\mathfrak{a}\mathfrak{a} + i_\mathfrak{b}(\mathfrak{r} + \mathfrak{a})) =$
      $\mathfrak{d} + (-1)^{b_2}(j_\mathfrak{a}\mathfrak{a} + j_\mathfrak{b}(\mathfrak{r} + \mathfrak{a})))$

10   return $\exists \mathfrak{a}' \in \mathcal{T} : [\![\mathfrak{a}' \diamond \tilde{x} = x_1]\!]$

11 return 0

Fig. 3. Reduction $\mathcal{B}$ for bounding the difference between G_0 and G_1 for the proof of Theorem 7. The function Solve solves for $\mathfrak{a}$ and outputs a set of (possibly multiple) solutions. The oracle $O_\mathfrak{a}$ is simulated as in G_1. The simulation of $O_\mathfrak{b}$ is similar and explained in the proof. Line 17 is abuse of notation and queries a search version of SetTest instead of the decisional version. The variables $i_\mathfrak{a}$, $i_\mathfrak{b}$, $j_\mathfrak{a}$ and $j_\mathfrak{b}$ are defined as in Fig. 2. The variable d is defined as in Eq. (6).

Essentially, there are three cases when the algebraic adversary queries the decision oracle $O_\mathfrak{a}$. The first possibility is that the explanation of the adversary leads to an equation which we could solve for $\mathfrak{a}$ if GA-DDH returns 1 on that input. In that case the reduction solves GA-DLOG. If $\mathfrak{a}$ vanishes in the expression, we can simply simulate the GA-DDH oracle, since all variables necessary are known to the reduction. In the third case, $\mathfrak{a}$ does not vanish from the expression, but there is no solution, in which case 0 would have been returned anyway. To give a simple example of the first case, assume that $y = \mathfrak{c} \diamond x_1$ and $z = \mathfrak{d} \diamond \tilde{x}$, then $\mathfrak{a} = \mathfrak{d} - \mathfrak{c}$. To cover all cases we use variables $i_\mathfrak{a}$, $i_\mathfrak{b}$, $j_\mathfrak{a}$ and $j_\mathfrak{b}$ as defined in Fig. 2 and can then derive the DDH expression

$$\mathfrak{a} + \underbrace{\mathfrak{c} + (-1)^{b_1}(i_\mathfrak{a}\mathfrak{a} + i_\mathfrak{b}(\mathfrak{r} + \mathfrak{a}))}_{\diamond \tilde{x} = y} \equiv \underbrace{\mathfrak{d} + (-1)^{b_2}(j_\mathfrak{a}\mathfrak{a} + j_\mathfrak{b}(\mathfrak{r} + \mathfrak{a}))}_{\diamond \tilde{x} = z} \mod N. \quad (5)$$

This equation can be rearranged to

$$\underbrace{(1 + (-1)^{b_1}(i_\mathfrak{a} + i_\mathfrak{b}) - (-1)^{b_2}(j_\mathfrak{a} + j_\mathfrak{b}))}_{=:d \in [-1,3]} \mathfrak{a} \equiv ((-1)^{b_2}j_\mathfrak{b} - (-1)^{b_1}j_\mathfrak{a})\mathfrak{r}$$

$$+ \mathfrak{d} - \mathfrak{c} \mod N \quad (6)$$

which we can use to either solve GA-DLOG when $\mathfrak{a}$ does not vanish and otherwise simulate $O_\mathfrak{a}$. Clearly, the variable $\mathfrak{a}$ vanishes in the expression if $d = 0$, enabling us to extract a solution if $d \neq 0$. This is tested in G_1 before using the expression to simulate O_a. However, in the case $d \neq 0$ we still have to consider the fact that $d \mid N$ but d does not divide the right hand side of Eq. (6). Referring back to Lemma 2 we therefore have no solutions for a. This is a non-issue as we can just return 0 in that case as well. If $d = 0$ we test whether the right hand side evaluates to 0 as well. For simulating $O_b(y, z) = O_{r+a}(y, z) = O_a(r \diamond y, z)$ we proceed in the same way except that r is added to the left side of Eq. (5).

We have just shown Eq. 4. It remains to reduce G_1 to GA-DLOG. That is,

$$\Pr[G_1 \Rightarrow 1] \leq \epsilon_{\mathcal{C}} .$$

This is straightforward, the reduction $\mathcal{C}$ gets the GA-DLOG challenge $x_1 = a \diamond \tilde{x}$, samples $r \leftarrow_\$ \mathbb{Z}_N$ and sets $x_2 = r \diamond x_1$. Then $\mathcal{C}$ simulates G_1 and receives the GA-CDH solution and solves GA-DLOG as in Theorem 6. Adding up the terms yields the claimed bound and concludes the proof.   □

Now we want to analyze the strong square inverse Diffie-Hellman assumption introduced in [1] to prove security of their password-authenticated key exchange protocol. As pointed out in [19], a security proof in the quantum random oracle model will rely on a stronger version of the assumption, where decision oracles are queried in quantum superposition. This is similar to the case of hashed ElGamal and the GA-QSt-CDH assumption.

Definition 11 (Group Action Quantum Strong Square-Inverse Diffie-Hellman). *Let* CEGA$(T) = (\mathbb{Z}_N, \mathcal{X}, \diamond, \tilde{x})$ *be a cyclic effective group action (with twists). We say that an adversary $\mathcal{A}$ solves the group action quantum strong square-inverse Diffie-Hellman problem* (GA-QSt-SqInvDH) *if* $\mathcal{A}^O(\tilde{x}, a \diamond \tilde{x}) = (y, 2a \diamond y, -a \diamond y)$ *for* $a \leftarrow_\$ \mathbb{Z}_N$ *and some* $y \in \mathcal{X}$. *Here $\mathcal{A}$ has access to decision oracles* $O := \{$GA-DDH$_a(|\cdot\rangle, |\cdot\rangle),$ GA-DDH$_{2a}(|\cdot\rangle, |\cdot\rangle)\}$ *which are defined similarly to those in Definition 10.*

Theorem 8. *Let $\mathcal{A}$ be an $(\epsilon_{\mathcal{A}}, t_{\mathcal{A}})$-algebraic quantum adversary against the* GA-QSt-SqInvDH *problem that issues at most q decision oracle queries, then there exist an $(\epsilon_{\mathcal{B}}, t_{\mathcal{B}})$-adversary $\mathcal{B}$ and an $(\epsilon_{\mathcal{C}}, t_{\mathcal{C}})$-adversary $\mathcal{C}$ against the* GA-DLOG *problem with*

$$\epsilon_{\mathcal{A}} \leq \sqrt{(q+1) \cdot \epsilon_{\mathcal{B}}} + \epsilon_{\mathcal{C}} \quad and \quad t_{\mathcal{A}} \approx t_{\mathcal{B}} \approx t_{\mathcal{C}} .$$

Here the square-root term comes from the fact that we allow quantum queries to the decision oracles. When allowing for classical queries only, the bound would be tight. The proof is very similar to that of Theorem 7 and we defer it to the full version.

5.3   Security Analysis of ElGamal in the Quantum Algebraic Group Action Model with Twists

Similar to the analysis in the AGM of [22], we can prove IND-CCA1 security of group action ElGamal. Going even one step further, we are also able to analyze IND-QCCA1 security in the QAGAM$^\top$. This security notion, where the

Game IND-CCA1($\mathcal{A}$)	**Oracle** ENC	\\ only once
00 (pk, sk) $\leftarrow$ Gen	03 $b \xleftarrow{\$} \{0,1\}$	
01 $b' \leftarrow \mathcal{A}^{\text{ENC},\text{DECAPS}}$(pk)	04 (ct*, K_0) $\leftarrow$ Encaps(pk)	
02 **return** $[\![b = b']\!]$	05 $K_1 \xleftarrow{\$} \mathcal{K}$	
	06 **return** (ct*, K_b)	
	Oracle DECAPS(ct)	\\ only before ENC
	07 **return** Dec(sk, ct)	

Fig. 4. The IND-CCA1 game for a key encapsulation mechanism KEM.

adversary is allowed to ask for decapsulation queries in quantum superposition, was first proposed by Boneh and Zhandry in [12]. We recall the definition of a key encapsulation mechanism and the group action q-decisional Diffie-Hellman assumption below. This assumption is similar to those in Definitions 7 and 8. Lastly, we define the ElGamal KEM in Fig. 5.

KEY ENCAPSULATION MECHANISM. Let $\mathcal{PK}$, $\mathcal{SK}$, $\mathcal{C}$, $\mathcal{K}$ be sets. A *key encapsulation mechanism* KEM = (Gen, Encaps, Decaps) consists of the following three algorithms:

- Gen: The key generation algorithm outputs a public key pk $\in \mathcal{PK}$ and a secret key sk $\in \mathcal{SK}$.
- Encaps(pk): On input a public key pk, the encapsulation algorithm returns a ciphertext ct $\in \mathcal{C}$ and a key $K \in \mathcal{K}$, where ct is an encapsulation of K.
- Decaps(sk, ct): On input a secret key sk and a ciphertext ct, the decapsulation algorithm returns a key $K \in \mathcal{K}$ or a special failure symbol $\bot$.

We require perfect correctness, i.e. for all (pk, sk) $\leftarrow$ Gen, (ct, K) $\leftarrow$ Encaps(pk), we have Decaps(sk, ct) = K.

IND-CCA1 SECURITY. We define the IND-CCA1 security game (aka. lunchtime security) in Fig. 4. We say that an adversary $\mathcal{A}$ solves the IND-CCA1 game if the game outputs 1. Analogously, we define the IND-QCCA1 security game, where the only difference from the regular IND-CCA1 game is that an adversary has *quantum* access to the decapsulation oracle.

Definition 12 (Group Action q-Decisional Diffie-Hellman). *Let* CEGA(T) = $(\mathbb{Z}_N, \mathcal{X}, \diamond, \tilde{x})$. *We say that an adversary $\mathcal{A}$ solves the group action q-decisional Diffie-Hellman* (GA-q-DDH) *if*

$$\mathcal{A}(\tilde{x}, \mathfrak{a} \diamond \tilde{x}, 2\mathfrak{a} \diamond \tilde{x}, \ldots, q\mathfrak{a} \diamond \tilde{x}, \mathfrak{b} \diamond \tilde{x}, z_r) = r \ ,$$

where $\mathfrak{a}, \mathfrak{b} \leftarrow_{\$} \mathbb{Z}_N$, $z_0 := (\mathfrak{a} + \mathfrak{b}) \diamond \tilde{x}$, $z_1 \leftarrow_{\$} \mathcal{X}$ *and* $r \leftarrow_{\$} \{0, 1\}$.

Theorem 9 (GA-q-DDH $\implies$ IND-QCCA1 of ElGamal). *Let $\mathcal{A}$ be an algebraic quantum $(\epsilon_{\mathcal{A}}, t_{\mathcal{A}})$-adversary against the* IND-QCCA1 *security of ElGamal KEM making at most $q - 1$ quantum decapsulation queries, then there exists a quantum $(\epsilon_{\mathcal{B}}, t_{\mathcal{B}})$-adversary $\mathcal{B}$ against* GA-q-DDH *with*

$$\epsilon_{\mathcal{A}} \leq \epsilon_{\mathcal{B}} \quad \text{and} \quad t_{\mathcal{A}} \approx t_{\mathcal{B}} \ .$$

Gen	Encaps(pk)	Decaps(sk, ct)
00 $sk := \mathfrak{a} \xleftarrow{\$} \mathbb{Z}_N$	03 $\mathfrak{b} \xleftarrow{\$} \mathbb{Z}_N$	07 $K := sk \diamond ct$
01 $pk := \mathfrak{a} \diamond \tilde{x}$	04 $ct := \mathfrak{b} \diamond \tilde{x}$	08 **return** K
02 **return** (pk, sk)	05 $K := \mathfrak{b} \diamond pk$	
	06 **return** (ct, K)	

Fig. 5. The ElGamal KEM for $\mathsf{CEGA}(\mathsf{T}) = (\mathbb{Z}_N, \mathcal{X}, \diamond, \tilde{x})$.

Proof. We describe how the reduction works classically. Simulation of the quantum decapsulation oracle follows from linearity of quantum states and from the fact that all computations are deterministic from their inputs.

Let $(x_1, x_2, \ldots, x_q, y, z) := (\mathfrak{a} \diamond \tilde{x}, 2\mathfrak{a} \diamond \tilde{x}, \ldots, q\mathfrak{a} \diamond \tilde{x}, \mathfrak{b} \diamond \tilde{x}, z)$ be the GA-q-DDH challenge. The main idea of the proof is to use the x_i to simulate the decapsulation oracle together with the algebraic explanation provided by the algebraic adversary. If the adversary $\mathcal{A}$ uses twists, the reduction $\mathcal{B}$ can still simulate decapsulation queries by twisting the appropriate x_i. We will therefore define $x_{-i} := x_i^t$. The main observation is that an adversary can learn higher "powers" of $\mathfrak{a} \diamond \tilde{x}$, i.e. $k\mathfrak{a} \diamond \tilde{x}$ for $k \in [q]$, by querying $\mathfrak{a} \diamond \tilde{x}$ to the decapsulation oracle. $\mathcal{A}$ can then query the decapsulation oracle on ciphertexts which depend on answers to previous decapsulations and so on. Then the i-th answer to the decapsulation oracle can be written as

$$K_i = \mathfrak{d}_i \diamond x_{j_i} = (j_i \mathfrak{a} + \mathfrak{d}_i) \diamond \tilde{x}$$

where $|j_i| \leq i$. For the $i + 1$-th decapsulation query, we then have

$$\mathsf{Decaps}_{\mathfrak{a}}(c_{(k, \mathfrak{d}, r)}) = \mathfrak{a} \diamond c = (a + \mathfrak{d}) \diamond K_k^r$$
$$= (\mathfrak{a} + (-1)^t i_k \mathfrak{a} + \mathfrak{d}_k + \mathfrak{d}) \diamond \tilde{x} = (\mathfrak{d} + \mathfrak{d}_k) \diamond x_{(-1)^t i_k + 1},$$

where $K_k^r = K_k$ if $b = 0$ and K_k^t otherwise. With $i_{j+1} := (-1)^t i_k + 1$ and $\mathfrak{d}_i := \mathfrak{d} + \mathfrak{d}_k$, we get a representation for K_{j+1} as above, which can in turn be used to simulate the next decapsulation. Since $\mathcal{A}$ makes at most $q - 1$ decapsulation queries, we always have $|i_k| \leq q$, so the simulation always works.

Being able to simulate decapsulation queries, the adversary sets the ElGamal randomness carrier to be $\mathfrak{b} \diamond \tilde{x}$ and sets the KEM key to be z and uses the distinguishing bit to decide if it is in the real or random case of the GA-q-DDH problem. $\square$

Acknowledgments. The work of Julien Duman was supported by the German Federal Ministry of Education and Research (BMBF) in the course of the 6GEM Research Hub under Grant 16KISK037. Dominik Hartmann was supported by the European Union (ERC AdG REWORC - 101054911). Eike Kiltz was supported by the Deutsche Forschungsgemeinschaft (DFG, German research Foundation) as part of the Excellence Strategy of the German Federal and State Governments - EXC 2092 CASA - 390781972, and by the European Union (ERC AdG REWORC - 101054911). Sabrina Kunzweiler,

Jonas Lehmann and Doreen Riepel were funded by the Deutsche Forschungsgemeinschaft (DFG, German Research Foundation) under Germany's Excellence Strategy - EXC 2092 CASA - 390781972.

References

1. Abdalla, M., Eisenhofer, T., Kiltz, E., Kunzweiler, S., Riepel, D.: Password-authenticated key exchange from group actions. In: Dodis, Y., Shrimpton, T. (eds.) Advances in Cryptology - CRYPTO 2022. LNCSD, vol. 13508, pp. 699–728. Springer, Cham (2022). https://doi.org/10.1007/978-3-031-15979-4_24
2. Agrikola, T., Hofheinz, D.: Interactively secure groups from obfuscation. In: Abdalla, M., Dahab, R. (eds.) PKC 2018. LNCS, vol. 10770, pp. 341–370. Springer, Cham (2018). https://doi.org/10.1007/978-3-319-76581-5_12
3. Alamati, N., De Feo, L., Montgomery, H., Patranabis, S.: Cryptographic group actions and applications. In: Moriai, S., Wang, H. (eds.) ASIACRYPT 2020. LNCS, vol. 12492, pp. 411–439. Springer, Cham (2020). https://doi.org/10.1007/978-3-030-64834-3_14
4. Albrecht, M.R., Farshim, P., Hofheinz, D., Larraia, E., Paterson, K.G.: Multilinear maps from obfuscation. In: Kushilevitz, E., Malkin, T. (eds.) TCC 2016. LNCS, vol. 9562, pp. 446–473. Springer, Heidelberg (2016). https://doi.org/10.1007/978-3-662-49096-9_19
5. Baghery, K., Cozzo, D., Pedersen, R.: An isogeny-based ID protocol using structured public keys. In: Paterson, M.B. (ed.) IMACC 2021. LNCS, vol. 13129, pp. 179–197. Springer, Cham (2021). https://doi.org/10.1007/978-3-030-92641-0_9
6. Bao, F., Deng, R.H., Zhu, H.F.: Variations of Diffie-Hellman problem. In: Qing, S., Gollmann, D., Zhou, J. (eds.) ICICS 2003. LNCS, vol. 2836, pp. 301–312. Springer, Heidelberg (2003). https://doi.org/10.1007/978-3-540-39927-8_28
7. Bauer, B., Fuchsbauer, G., Loss, J.: A classification of computational assumptions in the algebraic group model. In: Micciancio, D., Ristenpart, T. (eds.) CRYPTO 2020. LNCS, vol. 12171, pp. 121–151. Springer, Cham (2020). https://doi.org/10.1007/978-3-030-56880-1_5
8. Bellare, M., Rogaway, P.: Code-based game-playing proofs and the security of triple encryption. Cryptology ePrint Archive, Report 2004/331 (2004), https://eprint.iacr.org/2004/331
9. Beullens, W., Kleinjung, T., Vercauteren, F.: CSI-FiSh: efficient isogeny based signatures through class group computations. In: Galbraith, S.D., Moriai, S. (eds.) ASIACRYPT 2019. LNCS, vol. 11921, pp. 227–247. Springer, Cham (2019). https://doi.org/10.1007/978-3-030-34578-5_9
10. Biasse, J.F., Song, F.: Efficient quantum algorithms for computing class groups and solving the principal ideal problem in arbitrary degree number fields. In: Proceedings of the Twenty-Seventh Annual ACM-SIAM Symposium on Discrete Algorithms, pp. 893–902. SIAM (2016)
11. Boneh, D., Boyen, X.: Short signatures without random oracles and the SDH assumption in bilinear groups. J. Cryptol. **21**(2), 149–177 (2007). https://doi.org/10.1007/s00145-007-9005-7
12. Boneh, D., Zhandry, M.: Secure signatures and chosen ciphertext security in a quantum computing world. In: Canetti, R., Garay, J.A. (eds.) CRYPTO 2013. LNCS, vol. 8043, pp. 361–379. Springer, Heidelberg (2013). https://doi.org/10.1007/978-3-642-40084-1_21

13. Castryck, W., Decru, T.: An efficient key recovery attack on SIDH (preliminary version). Cryptology ePrint Archive, Report 2022/975 (2022). https://eprint.iacr.org/2022/975

14. Castryck, W., Lange, T., Martindale, C., Panny, L., Renes, J.: CSIDH: an efficient post-quantum commutative group action. In: Peyrin, T., Galbraith, S. (eds.) ASIACRYPT 2018. LNCS, vol. 11274, pp. 395–427. Springer, Cham (2018). https://doi.org/10.1007/978-3-030-03332-3_15

15. Cheon, J.H.: Discrete logarithm problems with auxiliary inputs. J. Cryptol. **23**(3), 457–476 (2009). https://doi.org/10.1007/s00145-009-9047-0

16. Cohen, H., Lenstra, H.: Heuristics on class groups. In: Number theory, pp. 26–36. Springer (1984)

17. Couveignes, J.M.: Hard homogeneous spaces. Cryptology ePrint Archive, Report 2006/291 (2006). https://eprint.iacr.org/2006/291

18. De Feo, L., Meyer, M.: Threshold schemes from isogeny assumptions. In: Kiayias, A., Kohlweiss, M., Wallden, P., Zikas, V. (eds.) PKC 2020. LNCS, vol. 12111, pp. 187–212. Springer, Cham (2020). https://doi.org/10.1007/978-3-030-45388-6_7

19. Duman, J., Hartmann, D., Kiltz, E., Kunzweiler, S., Lehmann, J., Riepel, D.: Group action key encapsulation and non-interactive key exchange in the qrom. In: ASIACRYPT 2022 (2022)

20. Duman, J., Hövelmanns, K., Kiltz, E., Lyubashevsky, V., Seiler, G., Unruh, D.: A thorough treatment of highly-efficient NTRU instantiations. Cryptology ePrint Archive, Report 2021/1352 (2021). https://eprint.iacr.org/2021/1352

21. Ettinger, M., Høyer, P.: On quantum algorithms for noncommutative hidden subgroups. Adv. Appl. Math. **25**(3), 239–251 (2000). https://doi.org/10.1006/aama.2000.0699,https://www.sciencedirect.com/science/article/pii/S0196885800906997

22. Fuchsbauer, G., Kiltz, E., Loss, J.: The algebraic group model and its applications. In: Shacham, H., Boldyreva, A. (eds.) CRYPTO 2018. LNCS, vol. 10992, pp. 33–62. Springer, Cham (2018). https://doi.org/10.1007/978-3-319-96881-0_2

23. Hafner, J.L., McCurley, K.S.: A rigorous subexponential algorithm for computation of class groups. J. Am. Math. Soc. **2**(4), 837–850 (1989)

24. Kastner, J., Pan, J.: Towards instantiating the algebraic group model. Cryptology ePrint Archive, Report 2019/1018 (2019). https://eprint.iacr.org/2019/1018

25. Katz, J., Zhang, C., Zhou, H.S.: An analysis of the algebraic group model. Cryptology ePrint Archive, Report 2022/210 (2022). https://eprint.iacr.org/2022/210

26. Kim, T.: Security analysis of group action inverse problem with auxiliary inputs with application to CSIDH Parameters. In: Seo, J.H. (ed.) ICISC 2019. LNCS, vol. 11975, pp. 165–174. Springer, Cham (2020). https://doi.org/10.1007/978-3-030-40921-0_10

27. Kobayashi, H., Gall, F.: Dihedral hidden subgroup problem: A survey. Information and Media Technologies **1**, 178–185 (2006). https://doi.org/10.11185/imt.1.178

28. de Kock, B., Gjøsteen, K., Veroni, M.: Practical isogeny-based key-exchange with optimal tightness. In: Dunkelman, O., Jacobson, Jr., M.J., O'Flynn, C. (eds.) SAC 2020. LNCS, vol. 12804, pp. 451–479. Springer, Cham (2021). https://doi.org/10.1007/978-3-030-81652-0_18

29. Kuperberg, G.: A subexponential-time quantum algorithm for the dihedral hidden subgroup problem. SIAM J. Comput. **35**(1), 170–188 (2005)

30. Maino, L., Martindale, C.: An attack on SIDH with arbitrary starting curve. Cryptology ePrint Archive, Report 2022/1026 (2022). https://eprint.iacr.org/2022/1026

31. Maurer, U., Renner, R., Holenstein, C.: Indifferentiability, impossibility results on reductions, and applications to the random oracle methodology. In: Naor, M. (ed.) TCC 2004. LNCS, vol. 2951, pp. 21–39. Springer, Heidelberg (2004). https://doi.org/10.1007/978-3-540-24638-1_2

32. Mizuide, T., Takayasu, A., Takagi, T.: Tight reductions for Diffie-Hellman variants in the algebraic group model. In: Matsui, M. (ed.) CT-RSA 2019. LNCS, vol. 11405, pp. 169–188. Springer, Cham (2019). https://doi.org/10.1007/978-3-030-12612-4_9

33. Montgomery, H., Zhandry, M.: Full quantum equivalence of group action DLog and CDH, and more. In: ASIACRYPT 2022 (2022)

34. Peikert, C.: He gives C-sieves on the CSIDH. In: Canteaut, A., Ishai, Y. (eds.) EUROCRYPT 2020. LNCS, vol. 12106, pp. 463–492. Springer, Cham (2020). https://doi.org/10.1007/978-3-030-45724-2_16

35. Pointcheval, D., Wang, G.: VTBPEKE: verifier-based two-basis password exponential key exchange. In: Karri, R., Sinanoglu, O., Sadeghi, A.R., Yi, X. (eds.) ASIACCS 17, pp. 301–312. ACM Press (Apr 2017)

36. Robert, D.: Breaking SIDH in polynomial time. Cryptology ePrint Archive, Report 2022/1038 (2022). https://eprint.iacr.org/2022/1038

37. Rostovtsev, A., Stolbunov, A.: Public-Key Cryptosystem Based On Isogenies. Cryptology ePrint Archive, Report 2006/145 (2006). https://eprint.iacr.org/2006/145

38. Shanks, D.: Class number, a theory of factorization, and genera. In: Proc. of Symp. Math. Soc., 1971, vol. 20, pp. 41–440 (1971)

39. Shor, P.W.: Algorithms for quantum computation: Discrete logarithms and factoring. In: 35th FOCS, pp. 124–134. IEEE Computer Society Press (Nov 1994). https://doi.org/10.1109/SFCS.1994.365700

40. Shoup, V.: Lower bounds for discrete logarithms and related problems. In: Fumy, W. (ed.) EUROCRYPT 1997. LNCS, vol. 1233, pp. 256–266. Springer, Heidelberg (1997). https://doi.org/10.1007/3-540-69053-0_18

41. Yoneyama, K.: Post-quantum variants of ISO/IEC standards: compact chosen ciphertext secure key encapsulation mechanism from isogeny. In: Proceedings of the 5th ACM Workshop on Security Standardisation Research Workshop, SSR 2019, pp. 13–21. Association for Computing Machinery, New York (2019). https://doi.org/10.1145/3338500.3360336

42. Zhandry, M.: Redeeming reset indifferentiability and applications to post-quantum security. In: Tibouchi, M., Wang, H. (eds.) ASIACRYPT 2021, Part I. LNCS, vol. 13090, pp. 518–548. Springer, Heidelberg (2021). https://doi.org/10.1007/978-3-030-92062-3_18

43. Zhandry, M.: To label, or not to label (in generic groups). In: Dodis, Y., Shrimpton, T. (eds.) Advances in Cryptology - CRYPTO 2022. LNCS, vol. 13509, pp. 66–96. Springer, Cham (2022). https://doi.org/10.1007/978-3-031-15982-4_3

Crypto for Crypto

CRAFT: Composable Randomness Beacons and Output-Independent Abort MPC From Time

Carsten Baum[1,2], Bernardo David[3(✉)], Rafael Dowsley[4], Ravi Kishore[3], Jesper Buus Nielsen[2], and Sabine Oechsner[5]

[1] Technical University of Denmark, Lyngby, Denmark
cabau@dtu.dk
[2] Aarhus University, Aarhus, Denmark
{cbaum,jbn}@cs.au.dk
[3] IT University of Copenhagen, Copenhagen, Denmark
{beda,rava}@itu.dk
[4] Monash University, Melbourne, Australia
rafael@dowsley.net
[5] University of Edinburgh, Edinburgh, UK
s.oechsner@ed.ac.uk

Abstract. Recently, time-based primitives such as time-lock puzzles (TLPs) and verifiable delay functions (VDFs) have received a lot of attention due to their power as building blocks for cryptographic protocols. However, even though exciting improvements on their efficiency and security (*e.g.* achieving non-malleability) have been made, most of the existing constructions do not offer general composability guarantees and thus have limited applicability. Baum *et al.* (EUROCRYPT 2021) presented in TARDIS the first (im)possibility results on constructing TLPs with Universally Composable (UC) security and an application to secure two-party computation with output-independent abort (OIA-2PC), where an adversary has to decide to abort *before* learning the output. While these

C. Baum–Funded by the European Research Council (ERC) under the European Unions' Horizon 2020 program under grant agreement No 669255 (MPCPRO).
B. David–Supported by the Concordium Foundation and the Independent Research Fund Denmark grants number 9040-00399B (TrA^{2}C), 9131-00075B (PUMA) and 0165-00079B (P2DP).
R. Dowsley–Partially done while Rafael Dowsley was with Bar-Ilan University and supported by the BIU Center for Research in Applied Cryptography and Cyber Security in conjunction with the Israel National Cyber Bureau in the Prime Minister's Office.
R. Kishore–Supported by the Independent Research Fund Denmark grant number 9131-00075B (PUMA).
J.B. Nielsen–Partially funded by The Concordium Foundation; The Danish Independent Research Council under Grant-ID DFF-8021-00366B (BETHE); The Carlsberg Foundation under the Semper Ardens Research Project CF18-112 (BCM).
S. Oechsner–Supported by Input Output (iohk.io) through their funding of the Edinburgh Blockchain Technology Lab. Partially done while Sabine Oechsner was with Aarhus University and supported by the Danish Independent Research Council under Grant-ID DFF-8021-00366B (BETHE) and Concordium Foundation.

© International Association for Cryptologic Research 2023
A. Boldyreva and V. Kolesnikov (Eds.): PKC 2023, LNCS 13940, pp. 439–470, 2023.
https://doi.org/10.1007/978-3-031-31368-4_16

results establish the feasibility of UC-secure TLPs and applications, they are limited to the two-party scenario and suffer from complexity overheads. In this paper, we introduce the first UC constructions of VDFs and of the related notion of publicly verifiable TLPs (PV-TLPs). We use our new UC VDF to prove a folklore result on VDF-based randomness beacons used in industry and build an improved randomness beacon from our new UC PV-TLPs. We moreover construct the first multiparty computation protocol with punishable output-independent aborts (POIA-MPC), *i.e.* MPC with OIA and financial punishment for cheating. Our novel POIA-MPC both establishes the feasibility of (non-punishable) OIA-MPC and significantly improves on the efficiency of state-of-the-art OIA-2PC and (non-OIA) MPC with punishable aborts.

1   Introduction

Time has always been an important, although sometimes overlooked, resource in cryptography. Recently, there has been a renewed interest in time-based primitives such as Time-Lock Puzzles (TLPs) [39] and Verifiable Delay Functions (VDFs) [12]. TLPs allow a sender to commit to a message in such a way that it can be obtained by a receiver only after a certain amount of time, during which the receiver must perform a sequence of computation steps. On the other hand, a VDF works as a pseudorandom function that is evaluated by performing a certain number of computation steps (which take time), after which it generates both an output and a proof that this number of steps has been performed to obtain the output. A VDF guarantees that evaluating a certain number of steps takes at least a certain amount of time and that the proof obtained with the output can be verified in time essentially independent of the number of steps.

Both TLPs and VDFs have been investigated extensively in recent work which focusses on improving their efficiency [11,38,41], obtaining new properties [25] and achieving stronger security guarantees [22,26,31]. These works are motivated by the many applications of TLPs and VDFs, such as randomness beacons [12,13], partially fair secure computation [20] and auctions [13]. In particular, all these applications use TLPs and VDFs concurrently composed with other cryptographic primitives and sub-protocols. However, most of current constructions of TLPs [11,13,26,31,39] and all known constructions of VDFs [12,22,25,38,41] do not offer general composability guarantees, meaning it is not possible to easily and securely use those in more complex protocols.

The current default tool for proving security of cryptographic constructions under general composability is the Universal Composability (UC) framework [14]. However, the UC framework is inherently asynchronous and does not capture time, meaning that a notion of passing time has to be added in order to analyze time-based constructions in UC. Recently, TARDIS [6] introduced a suitable time model and the first UC construction of TLPs, proven secure under the iterated squaring assumption of [39] using a programmable random oracle. [6] also shows that a programmable random oracle is *necessary* for realizing such time-based primitives in the UC framework.

Besides analyzing the (im)possibility of constructing UC TLPs, TARDIS [6] showed that UC TLPs can be used to construct UC-secure Two-Party Computation with Output-Independent Abort (OIA-2PC), where the adversary must decide whether to cause an abort *before* learning the output of the computation. OIA-2PC itself implies fair coin tossing, an important task used in randomness beacons. However, while these results showcase the power of UC TLPs, they are restricted to the two-party setting and incur a high concrete complexity. Moreover, their results do not extend to VDFs. This leaves an important gap, since many TLP applications (*e.g.* auctions [13]) are intrinsically multiparty and VDFs are used in practice for building randomness beacons [12,40]. The TARDIS TLP formalization and its applications also give adversaries exactly as much power in breaking the time-based assumption as the honest parties, which appears very restrictive and unrealistic.

1.1   Our Contributions

In this work, we present the first UC-secure constructions of VDFs and introduce the related notion of Publicly Verifiable TLPs, which we also construct. Using these primitives as building blocks, we construct a new more efficient randomness beacon and Multiparty Computation with Output-Independent Abort (OIA-MPC) and Punishable Abort. Our constructions are both practical and proven secure under general composition, and support adversaries who can break the timing assumptions faster than honest parties.

UC Verifiable Delay Functions. We introduce the *first* UC definition of VDFs [12], which is a delicate task and a contribution on its own. We also present a matching construction that consists in compiling a trapdoor VDF [41] into a UC-secure VDF in the random oracle model while only increasing the proof size by a small constant. Even though we manage to construct a very simple and efficient compiler, the security proof for this construction is highly detailed and complex. Based on our UC VDF, we give the *first* security proof of a folklore randomness beacon construction [12].

UC Publicly Verifiable Time-Lock Puzzles (PV-TLP). We introduce publicly verifiable TLPs (PV-TLP), presenting an ideal functionality and a UC-secure construction for this primitive. A party who solves a PV-TLP (or its creator) can prove to any third party that a certain message was contained in the PV-TLP (or that it was invalid) in way that verifying the proof takes constant time. We show that the TLP of [6] allows for proving that a message was contained in a valid TLP. Next, we introduce a new UC-secure PV-TLP scheme based on trapdoor VDFs that allows for a solver to prove that a puzzle is invalid, similarly to the construction of [26], which does not achieve UC security.

Efficient UC Randomness Beacon from PV-TLP. Building on our new notion (and construction) of PV-TLPs, we introduce a new provably secure randomness beacon protocol. Our construction achieves far better best case scenario efficiency than the folklore VDF-based construction [12]. Our novel PV-TLP-based construction *requires only $O(n)$ broadcasts (as does [12]) to generate a* *uniformly random output*, where n is the number of parties. Differently from the VDF-based construction [12], whose execution time is *at least* the worst case communication channel delay, our protocol outputs a random value as soon as all messages are delivered, achieving in the optimistic case an *execution as fast as 2 round trip times in the communication channel*. This construction and its proof require not only a simple application of UC PV-TLPs but also a careful analysis of the relative delays between PV-TLPs broadcast channels/public ledgers and PV-TLPs. We not only present this new protocol but also provide a full security proof in the partially synchronous model (where the communication delay is unknown), characterizing the protocol's worst case execution time in terms of the communication delay upper bound. In comparison, no security proof for the construction of [12] is presented in their work.

UC Multiparty Computation (MPC) with Output Independent Abort (OIA-MPC). We construct the first UC-secure protocol for Multiparty Computation with Output Independent Abort (OIA-MPC), which is a stronger notion of MPC where aborts by cheaters must be made before they know the output. This notion is a generalization of the limited OIA-2PC result from [6]. As our central challenge, we identify the necessity of synchronizing honest parties so that their views allow them to agree on the same set of cheaters. We design a protocol that only requires that honest parties are not too much out of sync when the protocol starts and carefully analyze its security.

UC MPC with Punishable Output Independent Abort (POIA-MPC) from PV-TLP. We construct the first protocol for Multiparty Computation with Punishable Output Independent Abort (POIA-MPC), generalizing OIA-MPC to a setting where i) outputs can be publicly verified; and ii) cheaters in the output stage can be identified and financially punished. Our construction employs our new publicly verifiable TLPs to construct a commitment scheme with delayed opening. To use this simple commitment scheme, we improve the currently best [4] techniques for publicly verifiable MPC with cheater identification in the output stage. We achieve this by eliminating the need for homomorphic commitments, which makes our construction highly efficient. We do not punish cheating that occurs before the output phase (i.e. before the output can be known), as this requires expensive MPC with publicly verifiable identifiable abort [8,30,34]. Our approach is also taken in other previous works [1,4,10,35].

1.2 Related Work

The recent work of Baum et al. [6] introduced the first construction of a composable TLP, while previous constructions such as [11,13,39] were only proven to be stand-alone secure. As an intermediate step towards composable TLPs, non-malleable TLPs were constructed in [26,31]. The related notion of VDFs has been investigated in [12,22,25,38,41]. Also for these constructions, composability guarantees have so far not been shown. Hence, issues arise when using these primitives as building blocks in more complex protocols, since their security is not guaranteed when they are composed with other primitives.

Randomness beacons that resist adversarial bias have been constructed based on publicly verifiable secret sharing (PVSS) [16,33] and on VDFs [12], although neither of these constructions is composable. The best UC-secure randomness beacons based on PVSS [17] still require $O(n^2)$ communication where n is the number of parties even if only one single value is needed. UC-secure randomness beacons based on verifiable random functions [2,21] can be biased by adversaries.

Fair secure computation (where honest parties always obtain the output if the adversary learns it) is known to be impossible in the standard communication model and with dishonest majority [18], which includes the 2-party setting. Couteau et al. [20] presented a secure two-party fair exchange protocol for the "best possible" alternative, meaning where an adversary can decide to withhold the output from an honest party but must make this decision independently of the protocol output. Baum et al. [6] showed how to construct a secure 2-party computation protocol with output-independent abort and composition guarantees. Neither of these works considers the important multiparty setting.

Another work which considers fairness is that of Garay *et al.* [27], which introduced the notion of resource-fairness for protocols in UC. Their work is able to construct fair MPC in a modified UC framework, while we obtain OIA-MPC which can be used to obtain partially fair secure computation (as defined in [28]). The key difference is that their resource-fairness framework needs to modify the UC framework in such a way that environments, adversaries and simulators must have an a priori bounded running time. Being based on the TARDIS model of [6], our work uses the standard UC framework without such stringent (and arguably unrealistic) modifications/restrictions.

An alternative, recently popularized idea is to circumvent the impossibility result of [18] by imposing financial penalties. In this model, cheating behavior is punished using cryptocurrencies and smart contracts, which incentivizes rational adversaries to act honestly. Works that achieve fair output delivery with penalties such as [1,4,10,35] allow the adversary to make the abort decision *after* he sees the output. Therefore financial incentives must be chosen according to the adversary's worst-case gain. Our POIA-MPC construction forces the adversary to decide before seeing the output and incentives can be based on the expected gain of cheating in the computation instead. All these mentioned works as well as ours focus on penalizing cheating during the output phase only, as current MPC protocols with publicly verifiable cheater identification are costly [7,8,34].

2   Preliminaries

We use the (Global) Universal Composability or (G)UC model [14,15] for analyzing security and refer interested readers to the original works for more details.

In UC protocols are run by interactive Turing Machines (iTMs) called *parties*. A protocol π will have n parties which we denote as $\mathcal{P} = \{\mathcal{P}_1, \ldots, \mathcal{P}_n\}$. The *adversary* $\mathcal{A}$, which is also an iTM, can corrupt a subset $I \subset \mathcal{P}$ as defined by the security model and gains control over these parties. The parties can exchange messages via resources, called *ideal functionalities* (which themselves are iTMs) and which are denoted by $\mathcal{F}$.

As usual, we define security with respect to an iTM $\mathcal{Z}$ called *environment*. The environment provides inputs to and receives outputs from the parties $\mathcal{P}$. To define security, let $\pi^{\mathcal{F}_1,\cdots} \circ \mathcal{A}$ be the distribution of the output of an arbitrary $\mathcal{Z}$ when interacting with $\mathcal{A}$ in a real protocol instance π using resources $\mathcal{F}_1, \ldots$. Furthermore, let $\mathcal{S}$ denote an *ideal world adversary* and $\mathcal{F} \circ \mathcal{S}$ be the distribution of the output of $\mathcal{Z}$ when interacting with parties which run with $\mathcal{F}$ instead of π and where $\mathcal{S}$ takes care of adversarial behavior.

Definition 1. *We say that $\mathcal{F}$ UC-securely implements π if for every iTM $\mathcal{A}$ there exists an iTM $\mathcal{S}$ (with black-box access to $\mathcal{A}$) such that no environment $\mathcal{Z}$ can distinguish $\pi^{\mathcal{F}_1,\cdots} \circ \mathcal{A}$ from $\mathcal{F} \circ \mathcal{S}$ with non-negligible probability.*

In the security experiment $\mathcal{Z}$ may arbitrarily activate parties or $\mathcal{A}$, though *only one iTM (including $\mathcal{Z}$) is active at each point of time*. We denote with λ the statistical and τ the computational security parameter.

Public Verifiability in UC. We model the public verification of protocol outputs, for simplicity, by having a static set of verifiers $\mathcal{V}$. These parties exist during the protocol execution (observing the public protocol transcript) but only act when they receive an input to be publicly verified. Converting our approach to dynamic sets of verifiers (as in e.g. [3]) is possible using standard techniques.

2.1 The TARDIS [6] Composable Time Model

The TARDIS [6] model expresses time within the GUC framework in such a way that protocols can be made oblivious to clock ticks. To achieve this, TARDIS provides a global ticker functionality $\mathcal{G}_{\text{ticker}}$ as depicted in Fig. 1. This global ticker provides "ticks" to ideal functionalities in the name of the environment. A tick represents a discrete unit of time which can only be advanced, and moreover only by one unit at a time. Parties observe events triggered by elapsed time, but not the time as it elapses in $\mathcal{G}_{\text{ticker}}$. Ticked functionalities can freely interpret ticks and perform arbitrary internal state changes. To ensure that all honest parties can observe all relevant timing-related events, $\mathcal{G}_{\text{ticker}}$ only progresses if all honest parties have signaled to it that they have been activated (in arbitrary order). An honest party may contact an arbitrary number of functionalities before asking $\mathcal{G}_{\text{ticker}}$ to proceed. We refer to [6] for more details.

How We Use the TARDIS [6] Model. To control the observable side effects of ticks, the protocols and ideal functionalities presented in this work are restricted to interact in the[1] "pull model". This precludes functionalities from implicitly providing communication channels between parties. Parties have to actively query functionalities in order to obtain new messages, and they obtain the activation token back upon completion. Ticks to ideal functionalities are modeled as follows: upon each activation, a functionality first checks with $\mathcal{G}_{\text{ticker}}$ if a tick

---

[1] The pull model, a standard approach in networking, has been used in previous works before such as [32].

Functionality $\mathcal{G}_{\mathsf{ticker}}$

Initialize a set of registered parties $\mathtt{Pa} = \emptyset$, a set of registered functionalities $\mathtt{Fu} = \emptyset$, a set of activated parties $L_{\mathsf{Pa}} = \emptyset$, and a set of functionalities $L_{\mathsf{Fu}} = \emptyset$ that have been informed about the current tick.

Party registration: Upon receiving $(\mathtt{register}, \mathsf{pid})$ from honest party $\mathcal{P}$ with pid pid, add pid to $\mathtt{Pa}$ and send $(\mathtt{registered})$ to $\mathcal{P}$.

Functionality registration: Upon receiving $(\mathtt{register})$ from functionality $\mathcal{F}$, add $\mathcal{F}$ to $\mathtt{Fu}$ and send $(\mathtt{registered})$ to $\mathcal{F}$.

Tick: Upon receiving $(\mathtt{tick})$ from the environment, do the following:
1. If $\mathtt{Pa} = L_{\mathsf{Pa}}$, reset $L_{\mathsf{Pa}} = \emptyset$ and $L_{\mathsf{Fu}} = \emptyset$, and send $(\mathtt{ticked})$ to the adversary $\mathcal{S}$.
2. Else, send $(\mathtt{notticked})$ to the environment.

Ticked request: Upon receiving $(\mathtt{ticked?})$ from functionality $\mathcal{F} \in \mathtt{Fu}$: If $\mathcal{F} \notin L_{\mathsf{Fu}}$, add $\mathcal{F}$ to L_{Fu} and send $(\mathtt{ticked})$ to $\mathcal{F}$. Otherwise send $(\mathtt{notticked})$ to $\mathcal{F}$.

Record party activation: Upon receiving $(\mathtt{activated})$ from party $\mathcal{P}$ with pid $\mathsf{pid} \in \mathtt{Pa}$, add pid to L_{Pa} and send $(\mathtt{recorded})$ to $\mathcal{P}$.

Fig. 1. Global ticker functionality $\mathcal{G}_{\mathsf{ticker}}$ (from [6]).

has happened and if so, may act accordingly. For this, it will execute code in a special **Tick** interface.

In comparison to [6], after every tick, each ticked functionality $\mathcal{F}$ that we define (unless mentioned otherwise) allows $\mathcal{A}$ to provide an optional $(\mathsf{Schedule}, \mathsf{sid}, \mathcal{D})$ message parameterized by a queue $\mathcal{D}$. This queue contains commands to $\mathcal{F}$ which specify if the adversary wants to abort $\mathcal{F}$ or how it will schedule message delivery to individual parties in $\mathcal{P}$. The reason for this approach is that it simplifies the specification of a correct $\mathcal{F}$. This is because it makes it easier to avoid edge cases where an adversary could influence the output message buffer of $\mathcal{F}$ such that certain conditions supposedly guaranteed by $\mathcal{F}$ break. As mentioned above, an adversary *does not have* to send $(\mathsf{Schedule}, \mathsf{sid}, \mathcal{D})$ - each $\mathcal{F}$ can take care of guaranteed delivery itself. On the other hand, $\mathcal{D}$ can depend on information that the adversary learns when being activated after a tick event.

Modeling Start (De)synchronization. In the 2-party setting considered in TARDIS [6] there is no need to capture the fact that parties receive inputs and start executing protocols at different points in time, since parties can adopt the default behavior of waiting for a message from the other before progressing. However, in the multiparty setting (and specially in applications sensitive to time), start synchronization is an important issue that has been observed before in the literature (*e.g.* [32, 36]) although it is often overlooked. In the spirit of the original TARDIS model, we flesh out this issue by ensuring that time progresses regardless of honest parties having received their inputs (meaning that protocols may be insecure if a fraction of the parties receive inputs "too late"). Formally, we require that every (honest) party sends (activated) to $\mathcal{G}_{\text{ticker}}$ during every activation regardless of having received its input. We explicitly address the start synchronization conditions required for our protocols to be secure.

Ticked Functionalities. We explicitly mention when a functionality $\mathcal{F}$ is "ticked". Each such $\mathcal{F}$ internally has two lists $\mathcal{M}, \mathcal{Q}$ which are initially empty. The functionality will use these to store messages that the parties ought to obtain. $\mathcal{Q}$ contains messages to parties that are currently buffered. Actions by honest parties can add new messages to $\mathcal{Q}$, while actions of the adversary can change the content of $\mathcal{Q}$ in certain restricted ways or move messages from $\mathcal{Q}$ to $\mathcal{M}$. $\mathcal{M}$ contains all the "output-ready" messages that can be read by the parties directly. The content of $\mathcal{M}$ cannot be changed by $\mathcal{A}$ and he cannot prevent parties from reading it. "Messages" from $\mathcal{F}$ may e.g. be messages that have been sent between parties or delayed responses from $\mathcal{F}$ to a request from a party.

We assume that each ticked functionality $\mathcal{F}$ has two special interfaces. One, as mentioned above, is called **Tick** and is activated internally, as outlined before, upon activation of $\mathcal{F}$ if a tick event just happened on $\mathcal{G}_{\text{ticker}}$. The second is called **Fetch Messages**. This latter interface allows parties to obtain entries of $\mathcal{M}$. The interface works identically for all ticked functionalities as follows:

Fetch Message: Upon receiving (Fetch, sid) by $\mathcal{P}_i \in \mathcal{P}$ retrieve the set L of all entries $(\mathcal{P}_i, \text{sid}, \cdot)$ in $\mathcal{M}$, remove L from $\mathcal{M}$ and send (Fetch, sid, L) to $\mathcal{P}_i$.

Macros. A recurring pattern in ticked functionalities in [6] is that the functionality $\mathcal{F}$, upon receiving a request (Request, sid, m) by party $\mathcal{P}_i$ must first internally generate unique message IDs mid to balance message delivery with the adversarial option to delay messages. $\mathcal{F}$ then internally stores the message to be delivered together with the mid in $\mathcal{Q}$ and finally hands out i, mid to the ideal adversary $\mathcal{S}$ as well as potentially also m. This allows $\mathcal{S}$ to influence delivery of m by $\mathcal{F}$ at will by referring to each unique mid. We now define macros that simplify the aforementioned process. When using the macros we will sometimes leave out certain options if their choice is clear from the context.

Macro "*Notify the parties $T \subseteq \mathcal{P}$ about a message with prefix* Request *from* $\mathcal{P}_i$ *via* $\mathcal{Q}$ *with delay* Δ" expands to

1. Let $T = \{\mathcal{P}_{i_1}, \ldots, \mathcal{P}_{i_k}\}$. Sample unused message IDs $\text{mid}_{i_1}, \ldots, \text{mid}_{i_k}$.
2. Add $(\Delta, \text{mid}_{i_j}, \text{sid}, \mathcal{P}_{i_j}, (\text{Request}, i))$ to $\mathcal{Q}$ for each $\mathcal{P}_{i_j} \in T$.

Macro "*Send message m with prefix* Request *received from party* $\mathcal{P}_i$ *to the parties* $T \subseteq \mathcal{P}$ *via* $\mathcal{Q}$ *with delay* Δ" expands to

1. Let $T = \{\mathcal{P}_{i_1}, \ldots, \mathcal{P}_{i_k}\}$. Sample unused message IDs $\text{mid}_{i_1}, \ldots, \text{mid}_{i_k}$.
2. Add $(\Delta, \text{mid}_{i_j}, \text{sid}, \mathcal{P}_{i_j}, (\text{Request}, i, m))$ to $\mathcal{Q}$ for each $\mathcal{P}_{i_j} \in T$.

Macro. *"Notify $\mathcal{S}$ about a message with prefix* Request" expands to "Send (Request, sid, i, $\mathsf{mid}_{i_1}, \ldots, \mathsf{mid}_{i_k}$) to $\mathcal{S}$." Finally, the **Macro** *"Send m with prefix* Request *and the IDs to* $\mathcal{S}$" expands to "Send (Request, sid, i, m, $\mathsf{mid}_{i_1}, \ldots, \mathsf{mid}_{i_k}$) to $\mathcal{S}$."

If honest parties send messages via simultaneous broadcast (ensuring simultaneous arrival), then we will only choose *one* mid for all messages. As the adversary can influence delivery on mid-basis, this ensures simultaneous delivery. We indicate this by using the prefix "simultaneously" in the first two macros.

2.2 Trapdoor Verifiable Sequential Computation

Functionality $\mathcal{F}_{\mathsf{psc}}$ is presented in Fig. 2 and captures the notion of a generic stand alone trapdoor verifiable sequential computation scheme (a generalization of a trapdoor VDF) in a similar way as the iterated squaring assumption from [39] is captured in [6]. More concretely, $\mathcal{F}_{\mathsf{psc}}$ allows the evaluation of Γ computational steps taking as input an initial state el and outputting a final state $\mathtt{el}_\Gamma$ along with a proof π. A verifier can use π to check that a state $\mathtt{el}'_\Gamma$ was indeed obtained after Γ computational steps starting from el. Each computational step takes a tick to happen, and parties who are currently performing a computation must activate $\mathcal{F}_{\mathsf{psc}}$ in order for their computation to advance when the next tick happens. The proof π' can be verified with respect to $\mathtt{el}, \mathtt{el}_\Gamma, \Gamma$ in time essentially independent of Γ. Since current techniques (*e.g.* [25,38,41]) for verifying such a proof require non-constant computational time, we model the number of ticks necessary for each by function $g(\Gamma)$. The implementation of $\mathcal{F}_{\mathsf{psc}}$ is presented in the full version [5] due to space limitations.

$\mathcal{F}_{\mathsf{psc}}$ must be used to capture a stand alone verifiable sequential computation because, as observed in [6], exposing the actual states from a concrete computational problem would allow the environment to perform several computational steps without activating other parties (and essentially breaking the hardness assumption). However, notice that $\mathcal{F}_{\mathsf{psc}}$ does not guarantee that the states it outputs are uniformly random or non-malleable, as it allows the adversary to choose the representation of each state, which is crucial in our proof. What $\mathcal{F}_{\mathsf{psc}}$ does guarantee is that proofs are only generated and successfully verified if the claimed number of computational steps is indeed correct, also guaranteeing that the transition between states el and nxt is injective.

2.3 Multi-party Message Delivery

Ticked Authenticated Broadcast. In Fig. 3 we describe a ticked functionality $\mathcal{F}_{\mathsf{BC},\mathsf{delay}}^{\Gamma,\Delta}$ for delayed authenticated simultaneous broadcast. $\mathcal{F}_{\mathsf{BC},\mathsf{delay}}^{\Gamma,\Delta}$ allows each party $\mathcal{P}_i \in \mathcal{P}$ to broadcast one message m_i in such a way that each m_i is delivered to all parties at the same tick (although different messages m_i, m_j may be delivered at different ticks). This functionality guarantees messages to be delivered at most Δ ticks after they were input. Moreover, it requires that all

---

Functionality $\mathcal{F}_{\mathsf{psc}}$

$\mathcal{F}_{\mathsf{psc}}$ interacts with a set of parties $\mathcal{P} = \{\mathcal{P}_i, \dots, \mathcal{P}_n\}$, an owner $\mathcal{P}_o \in \mathcal{P}$ (if $\mathcal{P}_o = \perp$, no $\mathcal{P}_i \in \mathcal{P}$ can access **Trapdoor Solve**) and an adversary $\mathcal{S}$. It is parameterized by an adversarial slack parameter $0 \leq \epsilon \leq 1$, state space $\mathcal{ST}$, a proof space $\mathcal{PROOF}$ and a function $g : \{0,1\}^* \mapsto \mathbb{N}$ determining the number of ticks for verifying proofs. $\mathcal{F}_{\mathsf{psc}}$ has initially empty lists prf, L and $\mathcal{Q}_v$ (proofs being verified); and flags f_i for $i = 1, \dots, n$ that are initially set to zero.

Trapdoor Solve: Upon receiving $(\mathsf{TdSolve}, \mathsf{sid}, \mathsf{el}_0, \Gamma)$ from $\mathcal{P}_o$ where $\Gamma \in \mathbb{N}^+$ and $\mathsf{el}_0 \in \mathcal{ST}$, sample Γ random distinct states $\mathsf{el}_j \xleftarrow{\$} \mathcal{ST}$ for $j \in \{1, \dots, \Gamma\}$ and add $(\mathsf{el}_{j-1}, \mathsf{el}_j)$ to steps. Also sample proof $\pi \xleftarrow{\$} \mathcal{PROOF}$. Add $(\mathsf{el}_0, \Gamma, \mathsf{el}_\Gamma, \pi)$ to prf and output $(\mathsf{sid}, \mathsf{el}_0, \Gamma, \mathsf{el}_\Gamma, \pi)$ to $\mathcal{P}_o$.

Solve: Upon receiving $(\mathsf{Solve}, \mathsf{sid}, \mathsf{el}_0, \Gamma)$ from $\mathcal{P}_i \in \mathcal{P}$ where $\mathsf{el}_0 \in \mathcal{ST}$, append $(\mathcal{P}_i, \mathsf{sid}, \mathsf{el}_0, \Gamma, \mathsf{el}_0, 0)$ to L and send $(\mathsf{Solve}, \mathsf{sid}, \mathsf{el}_0, \Gamma)$ to $\mathcal{S}$.

Advance State: Upon receiving $(\mathsf{AdvanceState}, \mathsf{sid})$ from $\mathcal{P}_i \in \mathcal{P}$, set $f_i = 1$.

Tick:
  - For each $(\mathcal{P}_i, \mathsf{sid}, \mathsf{el}_0, \Gamma, \mathsf{el}_c, c) \in L$, if $f_i = 1$ proceed as follows:
    1. If there is no el_{c+1} such that $(\mathsf{el}_c, \mathsf{el}_{c+1}) \in$ steps then sample $\mathsf{el}_{c+1} \xleftarrow{\$} \mathcal{ST}$, and append $(\mathsf{el}_c, \mathsf{el}_{c+1})$ to steps.
    2. Output $(\mathsf{el}_c, \mathsf{el}_{c+1})$ to $\mathcal{S}$ and update $(\mathcal{P}_i, \mathsf{sid}, \mathsf{el}_0, \Gamma, \mathsf{el}_c, c)$ by setting $c = c + 1$.
    3. If $c \geq \epsilon\Gamma$ and $(\mathsf{el}_0, \Gamma, \mathsf{el}_\Gamma, \pi) \in$ prf, output $(\mathsf{GetEsPf}, \mathsf{el}_0, \Gamma, \mathsf{el}_c, \mathsf{el}_{c+1}, \dots, \mathsf{el}_\Gamma, \pi)$ to $\mathcal{S}$.
    4. Else If $c \geq \epsilon\Gamma$ but $(\mathsf{el}_0, \Gamma, \mathsf{el}_\Gamma, \pi) \notin$ prf, then for $j \in \{c+1, \dots, \Gamma\}$ sample state $\mathsf{el}_j \xleftarrow{\$} \mathcal{ST}$ and add $(\mathsf{el}_{j-1}, \mathsf{el}_j)$ to steps. Also sample proof $\pi \xleftarrow{\$} \mathcal{PROOF}$, and add $(\mathsf{el}_0, \Gamma, \mathsf{el}_\Gamma, \pi)$ to prf. Finally, output $(\mathsf{GetEsPf}, \mathsf{el}_0, \Gamma, \mathsf{el}_c, \mathsf{el}_{c+1}, \dots, \mathsf{el}_\Gamma, \pi)$ to $\mathcal{S}$.
    5. If $c = \Gamma$, output $(\mathsf{GetPf}, \mathsf{sid}, \mathsf{el}_0, \Gamma, \mathsf{el}_\Gamma, \pi)$ to $\mathcal{P}_i$, and remove $(\mathcal{P}_i, \mathsf{sid}, \mathsf{el}_0, \Gamma, \mathsf{el}_\Gamma, \Gamma)$ from L.
  - For each $(\mathcal{P}_i, \mathsf{sid}, c, \mathsf{el}_I, \Gamma, \mathsf{el}_O, \pi) \in \mathcal{Q}_v$, if $f_i = 1$ proceed as follows:
    1. If $c = 0$: remove $(\mathcal{P}_i, \mathsf{sid}, 0, \mathsf{el}_I, \Gamma, \mathsf{el}_O, \pi)$ from $\mathcal{Q}_v$ and set $b = 1$ if $(\mathsf{el}_I, \Gamma, \mathsf{el}_O, \pi) \in$ prf, otherwise set $b = 0$, and output $(\mathsf{Verified}, \mathsf{sid}, \mathsf{el}_I, \Gamma, \mathsf{el}_O, \pi, b)$ to $\mathcal{P}_i$.
    2. Else, if $c > 0$: update $(\mathcal{P}_i, \mathsf{sid}, c, \mathsf{el}_I, \Gamma, \mathsf{el}_O, \pi)$ by setting $c = c - 1$.

Set flag $f_i = 0$ for $i = 1, \dots, n$.

Verify: Upon receiving $(\mathsf{Verify}, \mathsf{sid}, \mathsf{el}_I, \Gamma, \mathsf{el}_O, \pi)$ from $\mathcal{P}_i \in \mathcal{P}$ where $\pi \in \mathcal{PROOF}$, add $(\mathcal{P}_i, \mathsf{sid}, g(\Gamma), \mathsf{el}_I, \Gamma, \mathsf{el}_O, \pi)$ to $\mathcal{Q}_v$.

Fig. 2. Ticked Functionality $\mathcal{F}_{\mathsf{psc}}$ for trapdoor provable sequential computations.

parties $\mathcal{P}_i \in \mathcal{P}$ must provide inputs m_i within a period of Γ ticks, modeling a start synchronization requirement. If this loose start synchronization condition is not fulfilled, the functionality no longer provides any guarantees, allowing

Functionality $\mathcal{F}_{\mathsf{BC},\mathsf{delay}}^{\Gamma,\Delta}$

The ticked functionality $\mathcal{F}_{\mathsf{BC},\mathsf{delay}}^{\Gamma,\Delta}$ is parameterized by maximal input desynchronization Γ, parties $\mathcal{P} = \{\mathcal{P}_1, \ldots, \mathcal{P}_n\}$ and adversary $\mathcal{S}$. $\mathcal{S}$ may corrupt a strict subset $I \subset \mathcal{P}$. The functionality uses the identifier ssid to distinguish different instances per sid. $\mathcal{F}_{\mathsf{BC},\mathsf{delay}}^{\Gamma,\Delta}$ for each ssid has internal states $\mathsf{st}_{\mathsf{ssid}}, \mathsf{done}_{\mathsf{ssid}}$ that are initially $\perp$.

Init: In the beginning of the execution, $\mathcal{F}_{\mathsf{BC},\mathsf{delay}}^{\Gamma,\Delta}$ waits for input (Delay, Δ) from $\mathcal{S}$. Upon receiving (Delay, Δ) from $\mathcal{S}$ where $\Delta \in \mathbb{N}$ and $\Delta \geq \Gamma$, $\mathcal{F}_{\mathsf{BC},\mathsf{delay}}^{\Gamma,\Delta}$ proceeds to the next steps using Δ as its internal (unknown to honest parties) delay parameter.

Send: Upon receiving an input $(\mathsf{Send}, \mathsf{sid}, \mathsf{ssid}, m_i)$ from an honest party $\mathcal{P}_i$:

1. If $\mathsf{st}_{\mathsf{ssid}} = \perp$ then set $\mathsf{st}_{\mathsf{ssid}} = \Gamma$. If either $\mathsf{st}_{\mathsf{ssid}} = \top$ or $\mathcal{P}_i$ sent $(\mathsf{Send}, \mathsf{sid}, \mathsf{ssid}, \cdot)$ before then go to **Total Breakdown**.

2. For all $\mathcal{P}_j \in \mathcal{P}$, add $(\Delta, \mathsf{sid}, \mathcal{P}_j, (\mathcal{P}_i, m_i, \mathsf{ssid}))$ to $\mathcal{Q}$.

3. If all honest parties sent $(\mathsf{Send}, \mathsf{sid}, \mathsf{ssid}, \cdot)$ then set $\mathsf{done}_{\mathsf{ssid}} = \top$.

4. Send $(\mathsf{Send}, \mathsf{sid}, \mathsf{ssid}, \mathcal{P}_i, m_i)$ to $\mathcal{S}$.

Total Breakdown: Doing a total breakdown means the ideal functionality from now on relays all inputs to $\mathcal{S}$, otherwise ignores the input and lets $\mathcal{S}$ determine all outputs from then on. The ideal functionality becomes a proxy for $\mathcal{S}$.

Tick:

1. If $\mathsf{st}_{\mathsf{ssid}} = a$ for $a \geq 0$:

   (a) If $a > 0$ then set $\mathsf{st}_{\mathsf{ssid}} = a - 1$.

   (b) If $a = 0$ and if there is $\mathcal{P}_i \in \mathcal{P} \setminus I$ that did not send $(\mathsf{Send}, \mathsf{sid}, \mathsf{ssid}, \cdot)$ then go to **Total Breakdown**, otherwise set $\mathsf{st}_{\mathsf{ssid}} = \top$.

   (c) If $\mathsf{done}_{\mathsf{ssid}} = \top$ then wait for m_i from $\mathcal{S}$ for each $\mathcal{P}_i \in I$ and, if $\mathcal{S}$ sends it, then add $(a, \mathsf{sid}, \mathcal{P}_j, (\mathcal{P}_i, m_i, \mathsf{ssid}))$ to $\mathcal{Q}$ for all $\mathcal{P}_j \in \mathcal{P}$, and set $\mathsf{st}_{\mathsf{ssid}} = \top$.

2. Remove each $(0, \mathsf{sid}, \mathcal{P}_i, M)$ from $\mathcal{Q}$ and add $(\mathsf{sid}, \mathcal{P}_i, M)$ to $\mathcal{M}$.

3. Replace each $(\mathsf{cnt}, \mathsf{sid}, \mathcal{P}_i, M)$ in $\mathcal{Q}$ with $(\mathsf{cnt} - 1, \mathsf{sid}, \mathcal{P}_i, M)$.

Upon receiving $(\mathsf{Schedule}, \mathsf{sid}, \mathsf{ssid}, \mathcal{D})$ from $\mathcal{S}$:

   – If $(\mathsf{Deliver}, \mathsf{sid}, \mathsf{ssid}) \in \mathcal{D}$ and $\mathsf{done}_{\mathsf{ssid}} = \top$ then, for all $\mathcal{P}_i \in \mathcal{P}$, remove $(\mathsf{cnt}, \mathsf{sid}, \mathcal{P}_j, (\mathcal{P}_i, m_i, \mathsf{ssid}))$ from $\mathcal{Q}$ and add $(\mathsf{sid}, \mathcal{P}_j, (\mathcal{P}_i, m_i, \mathsf{ssid}))$ to $\mathcal{M}$.

Fig. 3. Ticked ideal functionality $\mathcal{F}_{\mathsf{BC},\mathsf{delay}}^{\Gamma,\Delta}$ for synchronized authenticated broadcast with maximal message delay Δ.

the adversary to freely manipulate message delivery (specified in **Total Breakdown**).

In comparison to the two-party secure channel functionality $\mathcal{F}_{\mathsf{smt},\mathsf{delay}}^{\Delta}$ of [6], our broadcast functionality $\mathcal{F}_{\mathsf{BC},\mathsf{delay}}^{\Gamma,\Delta}$ uses a scheduling-based approach and explicitly captures start synchronization requirements. Using scheduling makes formalizing the multiparty case much easier while requiring start synchronization allows us to realize the functionality as discussed below. This also means that $\mathcal{F}_{\mathsf{BC},\mathsf{delay}}^{\Gamma,\Delta}$ is not a simple generalization of the ticked channels of [6].

We briefly discuss how to implement $\mathcal{F}_{\mathsf{BC},\mathsf{delay}}^{\Gamma,\Gamma,\Delta}$. We could start from a synchronous broadcast protocol like [24] or the one in [23] with early stopping. These protocols require all parties to start in the same round and that they terminate within some known upper bound. For $t < n/3$ corruptions we could use [19] to first synchronize the parties before running such a broadcast. If $t \geq n/3$ we can get rid of the requirement that they start in the same round using the round stretching techniques of [37]. This will maintain that the parties terminate within some known upper bound. Then use n instances of such a broadcast channel to let each party broadcast a value. When starting the protocols at time t a party $\mathcal{P}_i$ knows that all protocol instances terminate before time $t + \Delta$ so it can wait until time $t + \Delta$ and collect the set of outputs. Notice that by doing so the original desynchronization Γ is maintained. When using protocols with early stopping [23], the parties might terminate down to one round apart in time. But this will be one of the stretched rounds, so it will increase the original desynchronization by a constant factor.

We stress that other broadcast channels than the one in $\mathcal{F}_{\mathsf{BC},\mathsf{delay}}^{\Gamma,\Delta}$ may also be modeled using [6], although these may not be applicable to instantiate OIA-MPC as we do in Sect. 6.

Ticked Public Ledger. In order to define a ledger functionality $\mathcal{F}_{\mathsf{Ledger}}$, we adapt ideas from Badertscher et al. [3]. The ledger functionality $\mathcal{F}_{\mathsf{Ledger}}$ is, due to space limitations, presented in the full version [5]. There, we also describe it in more detail. The original ledger functionality of Badertscher et al. [3] keeps track of many relevant times and interacts with a global clock in order to take actions at the appropriate time. Our ledger functionality $\mathcal{F}_{\mathsf{Ledger}}$, on the other hand, only keeps track of a few counters. The counters are updated during the ticks, and the appropriate actions are done if some of them reach zero. We also enforce liveness and chain quality properties, and our ledger functionality can be realized by the same protocols as [3].

3   Publicly Verifiable Time-Lock Puzzles

In this section, we describe an ideal functionality $\mathcal{F}_{\mathsf{TLP}}$ for publicly verifiable TLPs. Intuitively, a publicly verifiable TLP allows a prover who performs all computational steps needed for solving a PV- TLP to later convince a verifier that the PV-TLP contained a certain message or that it was invalid. The verifier only needs constant time to verify this claim. The ideal functionality $\mathcal{F}_{\mathsf{TLP}}$ as presented in Figs. 4 and 5 models exactly that behavior: $\mathcal{F}_{\mathsf{TLP}}$ has an extra interface for any verifier to check whether a certain solution to a given PV-TLP is correct. Moreover, $\mathcal{F}_{\mathsf{TLP}}$ allows the adversary to obtain the message from a PV-TLP with Γ steps in just $\epsilon\Gamma$ steps for $0 < \epsilon \leq 1$, modeling the slack between concrete computational complexities for honest parties and for the adversary is sequential computation assumptions.

Functionality $\mathcal{F}_{\mathsf{TLP}}$ allows the owner to create a new TLP containing message m to be solved in Γ steps by activating it with $(\mathsf{CreatePuzzle}, \mathsf{sid}, \Gamma, m)$. Other parties can request the solution of a TLP puz generated by the owner of $\mathcal{F}_{\mathsf{TLP}}$ by activating it with message (Solve, sid, puz). After every tick when a party activates $\mathcal{F}_{\mathsf{TLP}}$ with message (AdvanceState, sid), one step of this party's previosly requested puzzle solutions is evaluated. When $\epsilon \Gamma$ steps have been computed, $\mathcal{F}_{\mathsf{TLP}}$ leaks message m contained in the puzzle puz to the adversary $\mathcal{S}$. When all Γ steps of a puzzle solution requested by a party are evaluated, $\mathcal{F}_{\mathsf{TLP}}$ outputs m and a proof π that m was indeed contained in puz to that party. Finally, a party who has a proof π that a message m was contained in puz can verify this proof by activating $\mathcal{F}_{\mathsf{TLP}}$ with message (Verify, sid, puz, m, π).

Functionality $\mathcal{F}_{\mathsf{TLP}}$ (Part 1)

$\mathcal{F}_{\mathsf{TLP}}$ is parameterized by a computational security parameter τ, a message space $\{0,1\}^\tau$, a state space $\mathcal{ST}$, a tag space $\mathcal{TAG}$, a proof space $\mathcal{PROOF}$, a slack parameter $0 < \epsilon \leq 1$ and a function $g : \{0,1\}^\star \mapsto \mathbb{N}$ (determining how many ticks it takes to verify a proof). $\mathcal{F}_{\mathsf{TLP}}$ interacts with a set of parties $\mathcal{P} = \{\mathcal{P}_1, \ldots, \mathcal{P}_n\}$, an owner $\mathcal{P}_o \in \mathcal{P}$ and an adversary $\mathcal{S}$. $\mathcal{F}_{\mathsf{TLP}}$ maintains flags f_i for $i = 1, \ldots, n$ that are initially set to 0 and initially empty lists steps (honest state transitions), omsg (output messages and proofs), $\mathcal{Q}_\mathsf{v}$ (proofs being verified), L (puzzles being solved).

Create puzzle: Upon receiving the first message (CreatePuzzle, sid, Γ, m) from $\mathcal{P}_o$ where $\Gamma \in \mathbb{N}^+$ and $m \in \{0,1\}^\tau$, proceed as follows:
1. If $\mathcal{P}_o$ is honest, sample tag $\xleftarrow{\$} \mathcal{TAG}$, st$_0$ $\xleftarrow{\$} \mathcal{ST}$, and proof $\pi \xleftarrow{\$} \mathcal{PROOF}$. If $\mathcal{P}_o$ is corrupted, let $\mathcal{S}$ provide values tag, st$_0$, and the proof π.
2. If (tag, st$_0, \pi) \notin \mathcal{TAG} \times \mathcal{ST} \times \mathcal{PROOF}$ or there exists (st$'_0, \Gamma', tag', m', \pi) \in$ omsg then $\mathcal{F}_{\mathsf{TLP}}$ halts. Otherwise, append (puz $=$ (st$_0, \Gamma, $tag), m, π) to omsg, and output (CreatedPuzzle, sid, puz, π) to $\mathcal{P}_o$ and (CreatedPuzzle, sid, puz) to $\mathcal{S}$.

Solve: Upon receiving (Solve, sid, puz $=$ (st$_0, \Gamma, $tag)) from $\mathcal{P}_i \in \mathcal{P}$, add ($\mathcal{P}_i$, sid, puz, st$_0$, 0) to L and send (Solve, sid, puz) to $\mathcal{S}$.

Advance State: Upon receiving (AdvanceState, sid) from $\mathcal{P}_i \in \mathcal{P}$, set $f_i = 1$.

Public Verification: Upon receiving (Verify, sid, puz $=$ (st, $\Gamma, $tag), m, π) from a party $\mathcal{P}_i \in \mathcal{P}$, add ($\mathcal{P}_i$, sid, $g(\Gamma)$, st, $\Gamma, $tag, m, π) to $\mathcal{Q}_\mathsf{v}$.

Fig. 4. Ticked Functionality $\mathcal{F}_{\mathsf{TLP}}$ for publicly verifiable time-lock puzzles (Part 1).

In the full version [5], we show that the TLP from [6] realizes a slightly weaker version of $\mathcal{F}_{\mathsf{TLP}}$ and present a new Protocol π_{tlp} that realizes $\mathcal{F}_{\mathsf{TLP}}$ (*i.e.* proving Theorem 1). Protocol π_{tlp} is constructed from a standalone trapdoor VDF modeled by $\mathcal{F}_{\mathsf{psc}}$. A puzzle owner $\mathcal{P}_o$ uses the trapdoor to compute the VDF on a random input st$_0$ for the number of steps Γ required by the PV-TLP, obtaining the corresponding output st$_\Gamma$ and proof π. The owner then computes tag$_1$ $= H_1($st$_0, \Gamma, st_\Gamma, \pi) \oplus m$, tag$_2$ $= H_2($st$_0, \Gamma, st_\Gamma, \pi, tag_1, m)$ and tag $=$ (tag$_1$, tag$_2$), where m is the message in the puzzle, using random oracles H_1 and H_2. The final puzzle is puz $=$ (st$_0, \Gamma, $tag). A solver computes

Γ steps of the trapdoor VDF with input st_0 to get a proof of PV-TLP solution $\pi' = (\mathsf{st}_\Gamma, \pi)$, which can be used to check the consistency of tag and retrieve m. If tag is not consistent, π' can also be used to verify this fact.

Theorem 1. *Protocol π_{tlp} (G)UC-realizes $\mathcal{F}_{\mathsf{TLP}}$ in the $\mathcal{G}_{\mathsf{ticker}}, \mathcal{G}_{\mathsf{rpoRO}}, \mathcal{F}_{\mathsf{psc}}$-hybrid model with computational security against a static adversary. For every static adversary $\mathcal{A}$ and environment $\mathcal{Z}$, there exists a simulator $\mathcal{S}$ s.t. $\mathcal{Z}$ cannot distinguish π_{tlp} composed with $\mathcal{G}_{\mathsf{ticker}}, \mathcal{G}_{\mathsf{rpoRO}}, \mathcal{F}_{\mathsf{psc}}$ and $\mathcal{A}$ from $\mathcal{S}$ composed with $\mathcal{F}_{\mathsf{TLP}}$.*

Functionality $\mathcal{F}_{\mathsf{TLP}}$ (Part 2)

Tick: – For all $(\mathcal{P}_i, \mathsf{sid}, \mathsf{puz} = (\mathsf{st}_0, \Gamma, \mathsf{tag}), \mathsf{st}_c, c) \in L$, if $f_i = 1$ proceed as follows:

1. If there is no st_{c+1} such that $(\mathsf{st}_c, \mathsf{st}_{c+1}) \in \mathsf{steps}$:

   (a) If $\mathcal{P}_o$ is honest, sample $\mathsf{st}_{c+1} \overset{\$}{\leftarrow} \mathcal{ST}$, and append $(\mathsf{st}_c, \mathsf{st}_{c+1})$ to steps.

   (b) If $\mathcal{P}_o$ is corrupted, send $(\mathsf{sid}, \mathsf{adv}, \mathsf{st}_c)$ to $\mathcal{S}$ and wait for $(\mathsf{sid}, \mathsf{adv}, \mathsf{st}_c, \mathsf{st}_{c+1})$. If $\mathsf{st}_{c+1} \notin \mathcal{ST}$ then halt. Otherwise, append $(\mathsf{st}_c, \mathsf{st}_{c+1})$ to steps.

2. Output $(\mathsf{st}_c, \mathsf{st}_{c+1})$ to $\mathcal{S}$ and update $(\mathcal{P}_i, \mathsf{sid}, \mathsf{puz}, \mathsf{st}_c, c) \in L$ by setting $c = c+1$.

3. If $c \geq \epsilon\Gamma$ and there is no $(\mathsf{st}_c, \mathsf{st}_{c+1}), (\mathsf{st}_{c+1}, \mathsf{st}_{c+2}), \dots, (\mathsf{st}_{\Gamma-1}, \mathsf{st}_\Gamma) \in \mathsf{steps}$:

   (a) If $\mathcal{P}_o$ is honest, sample $\mathsf{st}_j \overset{\$}{\leftarrow} \mathcal{ST}$ for $j = c+1, c+2, \dots, \Gamma$, and output $(\mathsf{st}_{j-1}, \mathsf{st}_j)$ to $\mathcal{S}$ and append $(\mathsf{st}_{j-1}, \mathsf{st}_j)$ to steps. If $(\mathsf{st}_0, \Gamma, \mathsf{tag}, m, \pi) \notin \mathsf{omsg}$, set $m = \perp$, sample $\pi \overset{\$}{\leftarrow} \mathcal{PROOF}$ and append $(\mathsf{st}_0, \Gamma, \mathsf{tag}, \perp, \pi) \in \mathsf{omsg}$. Finally, output $(\mathsf{Solved}, \mathsf{sid}, \mathsf{puz}, m, \pi)$ to $\mathcal{S}$.

   (b) Else (if $\mathcal{P}_o$ is corrupted), send $(\mathsf{GetSts}, \mathsf{sid}, \mathsf{puz})$ to $\mathcal{S}$, wait for $\mathcal{S}$ to answer with $(\mathsf{GetSts}, \mathsf{sid}, \mathsf{puz}, \mathsf{st}_c, \mathsf{st}_{c+1}, \dots, \mathsf{st}_\Gamma)$. For $j = c+1, \dots, \Gamma$, if $\mathsf{st}_j \notin \mathcal{ST}$ or $(\mathsf{st}_{j-1}, \mathsf{st}'_j) \in \mathsf{steps}$, then $\mathcal{F}_{\mathsf{TLP}}$ halts, else, append $(\mathsf{st}_{j-1}, \mathsf{st}_j)$ to steps.

4. Else If $c \geq \epsilon\Gamma$ and there exist $(\mathsf{st}_c, \mathsf{st}_{c+1}), \dots, (\mathsf{st}_{\Gamma-1}, \mathsf{st}_\Gamma) \in \mathsf{steps}$, or if $(\mathsf{puz}' = (\mathsf{st}_0, \Gamma, \mathsf{tag}'), m', \pi') \in \mathsf{omsg}$ s.t. $\mathsf{tag}' \neq \mathsf{tag}$ (*i.e.* a puzzle with same st_0, Γ has been solved) or $\mathcal{P}_o$ is corrupted and $(\mathsf{puz}, m, \pi) \notin \mathsf{omsg}$, send $(\mathsf{GetMsg}, \mathsf{sid}, \mathsf{puz})$ to $\mathcal{S}$, wait for $\mathcal{S}$ to answer with $(\mathsf{GetMsg}, \mathsf{sid}, \mathsf{puz}, m, \pi)$. If $\pi \notin \mathcal{PROOF}$ or $(\mathsf{st}'_0, \Gamma', \mathsf{tag}', m', \pi) \in \mathsf{omsg}$, $\mathcal{F}_{\mathsf{TLP}}$ halts, else, append $(\mathsf{st}_0, \Gamma, \mathsf{tag}, m, \pi)$ to omsg.

5. If $c = \Gamma$, remove $(\mathcal{P}_i, \mathsf{sid}, \mathsf{puz}, \mathsf{st}_c, c) \in L$ and send $(\mathsf{Solved}, \mathsf{sid}, \mathsf{puz}, m, \pi)$ to $\mathcal{P}_i$.

– For each $(\mathcal{P}_i, \mathsf{sid}, c, \mathsf{st}, \Gamma, \mathsf{tag}, m, \pi) \in \mathcal{Q}_{\mathsf{v}}$, if $f_i = 1$ proceed as follows: 1. If $c = 0$, remove $(\mathcal{P}_i, \mathsf{sid}, 0, \mathsf{st}, \Gamma, \mathsf{tag}, m, \pi)$ from $\mathcal{Q}_{\mathsf{v}}$, set $b = 1$ if $(\mathsf{st}, \Gamma, \mathsf{tag}, m, \pi) \in \mathsf{omsg}$, otherwise set $b = 0$ and output $(\mathsf{Verified}, \mathsf{sid}, \mathsf{puz} = (\mathsf{st}, \Gamma, \mathsf{tag}), m, \pi, b)$ to $\mathcal{P}_i$; 2. Else, if $c > 0$: update $(\mathcal{P}_i, \mathsf{sid}, c, \mathsf{st}, \Gamma, \mathsf{tag}, m, \pi) \in \mathcal{Q}_{\mathsf{v}}$ by setting $c = c - 1$. Set $f_i = 0$ for $i = 1, \dots, n$.

Fig. 5. Ticked Functionality $\mathcal{F}_{\mathsf{TLP}}$ for publicly verifiable time-lock puzzles (Part 2).

4   Universally Composable Verifiable Delay Functions

We present a generic UC construction of VDFs as modeled in functionality $\mathcal{F}_{\mathsf{VDF}}$ (Fig. 6) from a generic verifiable sequential computation scheme modeled in functionality $\mathcal{F}_{\mathsf{psc}}$ (Fig. 2) and a global random oracle $\mathcal{G}_{\mathsf{rpoRO}}$. Our construction is presented in protocol π_{VDF} (Fig. 7).

Functionality $\mathcal{F}_{\mathsf{VDF}}$

$\mathcal{F}_{\mathsf{VDF}}$ is parameterized by a computational security parameter τ, a state space $\mathcal{ST}$, a proof space $\mathcal{PROOF}$, a slack parameter $0 < \epsilon \leq 1$ and a function $g : \{0,1\}^* \mapsto \mathbb{N}$ (determining how many ticks it takes to verify a proof). $\mathcal{F}_{\mathsf{VDF}}$ interacts with a set of parties $\mathcal{P} = \{\mathcal{P}_1, \ldots, \mathcal{P}_n\}$, and an adversary $\mathcal{S}$. $\mathcal{F}_{\mathsf{VDF}}$ maintains flags f_i for $i = 1, \ldots, n$ that are initially set to 0 and initially empty lists **steps** (state transitions), $\mathcal{Q}_{\mathsf{v}}$ (proofs being verified), L (proofs being computed), and OUT (outputs).

Solve: Upon receiving (Solve, sid, in, Γ) from $\mathcal{P}_i \in \mathcal{P}$ where $in \in \mathcal{ST}$ and $\Gamma \in \mathbb{N}$, add $(\mathcal{P}_i, \mathsf{sid}, in, \Gamma, in, 0)$ to L and send (Solve, sid, in, Γ) to $\mathcal{S}$.

Advance State: Upon receiving (AdvanceState, sid) from $\mathcal{P}_i \in \mathcal{P}$, set $f_i = 1$.

Tick: – For each $(\mathcal{P}_i, \mathsf{sid}, in, \Gamma, \mathbf{st}_c, c) \in L$, if $f_i = 1$ proceed as follows:

1. If there is no $\mathbf{st}_{c+1}$ such that $(\mathbf{st}_c, \mathbf{st}_{c+1}) \in \mathsf{steps}$, send (sid, adv, $\mathbf{st}_c$) to $\mathcal{S}$ and wait for (sid, adv, $\mathbf{st}_c, \mathbf{st}_{c+1}$). If $\mathbf{st}_{c+1} \notin \mathcal{ST}$ or $(\mathbf{st}_c, \mathbf{st}'_{c+1}) \in \mathsf{steps}$ for some $\mathbf{st}'_{c+1} \in \mathcal{ST}$ then halt. Otherwise, append $(\mathbf{st}_c, \mathbf{st}_{c+1})$ to **steps**. Finally update $(\mathcal{P}_i, \mathsf{sid}, in, \Gamma, \mathbf{st}_c, c) \in L$ by setting $c = c + 1$.

2. If $c \geq \epsilon\Gamma$ and there is no $(\mathbf{st}_c, \mathbf{st}_{c+1}), (\mathbf{st}_{c+1}, \mathbf{st}_{c+2}), \ldots, (\mathbf{st}_{\Gamma-1}, out) \in \mathsf{steps}$, sample $out \xleftarrow{\$} \mathcal{ST}$, send (GetStsPf, sid, $in, \Gamma, \mathbf{st}_c, out$) to $\mathcal{S}$, wait for $\mathcal{S}$ to answer with (GetStsPf, sid, $\mathbf{st}_{c+1}, \ldots, \mathbf{st}_{\Gamma-1}, \Pi$). If $\mathbf{st}_j \notin \mathcal{ST}$ or $(\mathbf{st}_{j-1}, \mathbf{st}'_j) \in \mathsf{steps}$, for $j \in \{c+1, \ldots, \Gamma-1\}$, or $\Pi \notin \mathcal{PROOF}$, or there exists $(in', \Gamma', out', \Pi) \in \mathsf{OUT}$, $\mathcal{F}_{\mathsf{VDF}}$ halts. Otherwise, append $(\mathbf{st}_{j-1}, \mathbf{st}_j)$ to **steps**, for $j \in \{c+1, \ldots, \Gamma-1\}$, append $(\mathbf{st}_{\Gamma-1}, out)$ to **steps** and (in, Γ, out, Π) to OUT.

3. If $c = \Gamma$, remove $(\mathcal{P}_i, \mathsf{sid}, in, \Gamma, out, \Gamma) \in L$, send (Proof, sid, in, Γ, out, Π) to $\mathcal{P}_i$.

– For each $(\mathcal{P}_i, \mathsf{sid}, c, in, \Gamma, out, \Pi) \in \mathcal{Q}_{\mathsf{v}}$, if $f_i = 1$ proceed as follows: 1. If $c = 0$, remove $(\mathcal{P}_i, \mathsf{sid}, 0, in, \Gamma, out, \Pi)$ from $\mathcal{Q}_{\mathsf{v}}$, set $b = 1$ if $(in, \Gamma, out, \Pi) \in \mathsf{OUT}$, otherwise set $b = 0$ and output (Verified, sid, in, Γ, out, Π, b) to $\mathcal{P}_i$; 2. If $c > 0$, update $(\mathcal{P}_i, \mathsf{sid}, c, in, \Gamma, out, \Pi) \in \mathcal{Q}_{\mathsf{v}}$ by setting $c = c - 1$. Set $f_i = 0$ for $i = 1, \ldots, n$.

Verification: Upon receiving (Verify, sid, in, Γ, out, Π) from a party $\mathcal{P}_i \in \mathcal{P}$, add $(\mathcal{P}_i, \mathsf{sid}, g(\Gamma), in, \Gamma, out, \Pi)$ to $\mathcal{Q}_{\mathsf{v}}$.

Fig. 6. Ticked Functionality $\mathcal{F}_{\mathsf{VDF}}$ for Verifiable Delay Functions.

Verifiable Delay Functions. We model the UC VDF in Functionality $\mathcal{F}_{\mathsf{VDF}}$. It ensures that each computational step of the VDF evaluation takes at least a fixed amount of time (one tick) and guarantees that the output obtained after a number of steps is uniformly random and unpredictable even to the adversary. However, it allows that the adversary obtains the output of evaluating a VDF for Γ steps in only $\epsilon\Gamma$ steps for $0 < \epsilon \leq 1$, modeling the slack between concrete computational complexities for honest parties and for the adversary in sequential computation assumptions. Naturally, $\mathcal{F}_{\mathsf{VDF}}$ also provides a proof that each output has been correctly obtained by computing a certain number of steps on a given input. As it is the case with $\mathcal{F}_{\mathsf{psc}}$, the time required to verify such proofs is variable and modeled as a function $g(\Gamma)$. Moreover, $\mathcal{F}_{\mathsf{VDF}}$ allows the ideal adversary to choose the representation of intermediate computational steps involved in evaluating the VDF, even though the output is guaranteed to be random. Another particularity of $\mathcal{F}_{\mathsf{VDF}}$ used in the proof is a leakage of each evaluation performed by an honest party at the tick when the result is returned to the original caller. This leakage neither affects the soundness of the VDF nor the randomness of its output, but is necessary for simulation.

Functionality $\mathcal{F}_{\mathsf{VDF}}$ allows for a party to start evaluating the VDF for Γ steps on an input in by activating it with message $(\mathsf{Solve}, \mathsf{sid}, in, \Gamma)$. After this initial request, the party needs to activate $\mathcal{F}_{\mathsf{VDF}}$ with message $(\mathsf{AdvanceState}, \mathsf{sid})$ on Γ different ticks in order to receive the result of the VDF evaluation. This is taken care of by the Tick interface of $\mathcal{F}_{\mathsf{VDF}}$, whose instructions are executed after every new tick, causing $\mathcal{F}_{\mathsf{VDF}}$ to iterate over every pending VDF evaluation request from parties who have activated $\mathcal{F}_{\mathsf{VDF}}$ in the previous tick. Each evaluation is performed by asking the adversary for a representation of the next intermediate state st_{c+1}. When $\epsilon\Gamma$ steps have been evaluated, $\mathcal{F}_{\mathsf{VDF}}$ leaks the output out to the adversary $\mathcal{S}$. When all Γ steps have been evaluated by $\mathcal{F}_{\mathsf{VDF}}$, it outputs out and a proof Π that this output was obtained from in after Γ steps. Moreover, parties who have an input in and a potential proof Π that out was obtained as output after evaluating the VDF for Γ steps on this input can activate $\mathcal{F}_{\mathsf{VDF}}$ with message $(\mathsf{Verify}, \mathsf{sid}, in, \Gamma, out, \Pi)$ to verify the proof. Once a proof verification request has been made, the party needs to activate $\mathcal{F}_{\mathsf{VDF}}$ with message $(\mathsf{AdvanceState}, \mathsf{sid})$ on $g(\Gamma)$ different ticks to receive the result of the verification.

Construction. Our protocol π_{VDF} realizing $\mathcal{F}_{\mathsf{VDF}}$ in the $\mathcal{F}_{\mathsf{psc}}, \mathcal{G}_{\mathsf{rpoRO}}$-hybrid model is described in Fig. 7. We use an instance of $\mathcal{F}_{\mathsf{psc}}$ where $\mathcal{P}_o = \perp$, meaning that no party in $\mathcal{P}$ has access to the trapdoor evaluation interface. Departing from $\mathcal{F}_{\mathsf{psc}}, \mathcal{G}_{\mathsf{rpoRO}}$ this protocol works by letting the state el_1 be the VDF input in. Once all the Γ solution steps are computed and the final state and proof el_Γ, π are obtained, the output is defined as $out = H(\mathsf{sid}|\Gamma|\mathsf{el}_\Gamma|\pi)$ where H is an instance of $\mathcal{G}_{\mathsf{rpoRO}}$ and the VDF proof is defined as $\Pi = (\mathsf{el}_\Gamma, \pi)$. Verification of an output out obtained from input in with proof Π consists of again setting the initial state $\mathsf{el}_1' = in$ and the output $out' = H(sid|\Gamma|\mathsf{el}_\Gamma|\pi)$, then checking that $out = out'$ and verifying with $\mathcal{F}_{\mathsf{psc}}$ that π is valid with respect to $\Gamma, \mathsf{el}_1', \mathsf{el}_\Gamma$. The security of Protocol π_{VDF} is formally stated in Theorem 2, and the proof is presented in the full version [5] due to space limitations.

Theorem 2. *Protocol π_{VDF} (G)UC-realizes $\mathcal{F}_{\mathsf{VDF}}$ in the $\mathcal{G}_{\mathsf{ticker}}, \mathcal{G}_{\mathsf{rpoRO}}, \mathcal{F}_{\mathsf{psc}}$-hybrid model with computational security against a static adversary: there exists a simulator $\mathcal{S}$ such that for every static adversary $\mathcal{A}$ no environment $\mathcal{Z}$ can distinguish π_{VDF} composed with $\mathcal{G}_{\mathsf{rpoRO}}, \mathcal{F}_{\mathsf{psc}}$ and $\mathcal{A}$ from $\mathcal{S}$ composed with $\mathcal{F}_{\mathsf{VDF}}$.*

5   UC-Secure Semi-synchronous Randomness Beacons

We model a randomness beacon as a publicly verifiable coin tossing functionality $\mathcal{F}_{\mathsf{RB}}{}^{\Delta_{\mathsf{TLP-RB}}}$ presented in Fig. 8. Even though this functionality does not periodi-

---

Protocol π_{VDF}

Protocol π_{VDF} is parameterized by a security parameter τ and is executed by a set of parties $\mathcal{P} = \{\mathcal{P}_1, \ldots, \mathcal{P}_n\}$ interacting with functionalities $\mathcal{G}_{\mathsf{ticker}}, \mathcal{G}_{\mathsf{rpoRO}}, \mathcal{F}_{\mathsf{psc}}$ (whose state space is $\mathcal{ST}$, proof space is $\mathcal{PROOF}$ and $\mathcal{P}_o = \perp$, i.e. no $\mathcal{P}_i \in \mathcal{P}$ can access the trapdoor solve interface). All parties locally keep initially empty lists L and $\mathcal{Q}_v$.

Solve: Upon receiving input (Solve, sid, in, Γ) where $in \in \mathcal{ST}$ and $\Gamma \in \mathbb{N}$, $\mathcal{P}_i$ sends (Solve, sid, in, Γ) to $\mathcal{F}_{\mathsf{psc}}$, and adds (sid, in, Γ) to L.

Advance State: Upon receiving input (AdvanceState, sid), $\mathcal{P}_i$ sends (AdvanceState, sid) to $\mathcal{F}_{\mathsf{psc}}$.

Tick: $\mathcal{P}_i$ processes proofs being computed or verified as follows:

1. Upon receiving (GetPf, sid, $in, \Gamma, \mathsf{el}_\Gamma, \pi$) from $\mathcal{F}_{\mathsf{psc}}$ s.t. there is (sid, in, Γ) $\in L$:
   (a) Send (Hash-Query, $(in|\Gamma|\mathsf{el}_\Gamma|\pi)$) to $\mathcal{G}_{\mathsf{rpoRO}}$, getting (Hash-Confirm, h).
   (b) Set $out = h$ and $\Pi = (\mathsf{el}_\Gamma, \pi)$; output (Proof, sid, in, Γ, out, Π) and remove (sid, in, Γ) from L.

2. Upon receiving (Verified, sid, $in, \Gamma, \mathsf{el}_\Gamma, \pi, b$) from $\mathcal{F}_{\mathsf{psc}}$ s.t. there is $(\mathcal{P}_i, \mathsf{sid}, in, \Gamma, out, \Pi = (\mathsf{el}_\Gamma, \pi)) \in \mathcal{Q}_v$:
   (a) Send (Hash-Query, $(in|\Gamma|\mathsf{el}_\Gamma|\pi)$) to $\mathcal{G}_{\mathsf{rpoRO}}$, getting (Hash-Confirm, h).
   (b) Set $b' = 0$ if $b = 0$ or $h \neq out$, otherwise set $b' = 1$. Output (Verified, sid, in, Γ, out, Π, b') and remove $(\mathcal{P}_i, \mathsf{sid}, in, \Gamma, out, \Pi)$ from $\mathcal{Q}_v$.

Verification: Upon receiving input (Verify, sid, in, Γ, out, Π), $\mathcal{P}_i$ parses $\Pi = (\mathsf{el}_\Gamma, \pi)$, and sends (Verify, sid, $in, \Gamma, \mathsf{el}_\Gamma, \pi$) to $\mathcal{F}_{\mathsf{psc}}$, and adds $(\mathcal{P}_i, \mathsf{sid}, in, \Gamma, out, \Pi)$ to $\mathcal{Q}_v$.

Fig. 7. Protocol π_{VDF} realizing Verifiable Delay Functions functionality $\mathcal{F}_{\mathsf{VDF}}$ in the $\mathcal{F}_{\mathsf{psc}}, \mathcal{G}_{\mathsf{rpoRO}}$-hybrid model.

cally produce new random values as in some notions of randomness beacons, it can be periodically queried by the parties when they need new randomness.

5.1 Randomness Beacons from TLPs

In order to construct a UC-secure randomness beacon from TLPs and a semi-synchronous broadcast channel $\mathcal{F}_{\mathsf{BC},\mathsf{delay}}^{\Gamma,\Delta}$ (with finite but unknown delay Δ), we depart from a simple commit-then-open protocol for n parties with honest majority where commitments are substituted by publicly verifiable TLPs as captured in $\mathcal{F}_{\mathsf{TLP}}$. Such a protocol involves each party $\mathcal{P}_i$ posting a TLP containing a random value r_i, waiting for a set of at least $1 + n/2$ TLPs to be received and then opening their TLPs, which can be publicly verified. The output is defined as $r = r_{j_1} \oplus \cdots \oplus r_{j_{1+n/2}}$, where values r_j are valid TLP openings. If an adversary tries to bias the output by refusing to reveal the opening of its TLP, the honest parties can recover by solving the TLP themselves.

To ensure the adversary cannot bias/abort this protocol, we must ensure two conditions: 1. At least $1 + n/2$ TLPs are broadcast and at least 1 is generated

---

Functionality $\mathcal{F}_{\mathsf{RB}}{}^{\Delta_{\mathsf{TLP-RB}}}$

$\mathcal{F}_{\mathsf{RB}}{}^{\Delta_{\mathsf{TLP-RB}}}$ is parameterized by delay $\Delta_{\mathsf{TLP-RB}}$ and interacts with parties $\mathcal{P} = \{\mathcal{P}_1, \ldots, \mathcal{P}_n\}$, verifiers $\mathcal{V}$ and an adversary $\mathcal{S}$ through the following interfaces:

Toss: Upon receiving $(\text{Toss}, \mathsf{sid})$ from all honest parties in $\mathcal{P}$, sample $x \xleftarrow{\$} \{0,1\}^\tau$ and send $(\text{Tossed}, \mathsf{sid}, x)$ to all parties in $\mathcal{P}$ via $\mathcal{Q}$ with delay $\Delta_{\mathsf{TLP-RB}}$.

Verify: Upon receiving $(\text{Verify}, \mathsf{sid}, x)$ from $\mathcal{V}_j \in \mathcal{V}$, if $(\text{Tossed}, \mathsf{sid}, x)$ has been sent to all parties in $\mathcal{P}$ set $f = 1$, else set $f = 0$. Send $(\text{Verify}, \mathsf{sid}, x, f)$ to $\mathcal{V}_j$.

Tick:
1. Remove each $(0, \mathsf{mid}, \mathsf{sid}, \mathcal{P}_i, m)$ from $\mathcal{Q}$ and instead add $(\mathcal{P}_i, \mathsf{sid}, m)$ to $\mathcal{M}$.
2. Replace each $(\mathsf{cnt}, \mathsf{mid}, \mathsf{sid}, \mathcal{P}_i, m)$ in $\mathcal{Q}$ with $(\mathsf{cnt} - 1, \mathsf{mid}, \mathsf{sid}, \mathcal{P}_i, m)$.

Fig. 8. Ticked Functionality $\mathcal{F}_{\mathsf{RB}}{}^{\Delta_{\mathsf{TLP-RB}}}$ for Randomness Beacons.

by an honest party (*i.e.* it contains an uniformly random r_i); 2. The adversary must broadcast its TLPs before the honest TLPs open, so it does not learn any of the honest parties' r_i and cannot choose its own r_is in any way that biases the output. While condition 1 is trivially guaranteed by honest majority, we ensure condition 2 by dynamically adjusting the number of steps δ needed to solve the TLPs *without prior knowledge of the maximum broadcast delay* Δ. Every honest party checks that at least $1 + n/2$ TLPs have been received from distinct parties *before* a timeout of $\epsilon\delta$ ticks (*i.e.* the amount of ticks needed for the adversary to solve honest party TLPs) counted from the moment they broadcast their own TLPs. If this is not the case, the honest parties increase δ and repeat the protocol from the beginning until they receive at least $1+n/2$ TLPs from distinct parties before the timeout. In the optimistic scenario where all parties follow the protocol (*i.e.* revealing TLP openings) and where the protocol is not repeated, this protocol terminates as fast as all publicly verifiable openings to the TLPs are revealed with computational and broadcast complexities of $O(n)$. Otherwise, the honest parties only have to solve the TLPs provided by corrupted parties (who do not post a valid opening after the commitment phase).

We design and prove security of our protocol with an honest majority in the semi-synchronous model where $\mathcal{F}_{\mathsf{BC},\mathsf{delay}}^{\Gamma,\Delta}$ has a finite but unknown maximum delay Δ. However, *if we were in a synchronous setting with a known broadcast delay* Δ, *we could achieve security with a dishonest majority* by proceeding to the **Opening Phase** after a delay of $\delta > \Delta$, since there would be a guarantee that all honest party TLPs have been received.

We describe protocol $\pi_{\mathsf{TLP-RB}}$ in Fig. 9 and state its security in Theorem 3. The proof is presented in the full version [5] due to space limitations.

Theorem 3. *If Δ is finite (though unknown) and all $\mathcal{P}_i \in \mathcal{P}$ receive inputs within a delay of δ ticks of each other, Protocol $\pi_{\mathsf{TLP-RB}}$ UC-realizes $\mathcal{F}_{\mathsf{RB}}{}^{\Delta_{\mathsf{TLP-RB}}}$ in the $\mathcal{F}_{\mathsf{TLP}}, \mathcal{F}_{\mathsf{BC},\mathsf{delay}}^{\Gamma,\Delta}$-hybrid model with computational security against static*

Protocol $\pi_{\text{TLP-RB}}$

The protocol is executed by parties $\mathcal{P} = \{\mathcal{P}_1, \ldots, \mathcal{P}_n\}$ out of which $t < n/2$ are corrupted and verifiers $\mathcal{V}$, who interact with $\mathcal{F}_{\text{BC,delay}}^{\Gamma, \Delta}$ and instances $\mathcal{F}_{\text{TLP}}^i$ of $\mathcal{F}_{\text{TLP}}$ with slack parameter ϵ for which $\mathcal{P}_i$ acts as $\mathcal{P}_o$. The initial delay parameter is δ.

Toss: On input $(\text{Toss}, \text{sid})$, all parties in $\mathcal{P}$ proceed as follows:

1. **Commitment Phase:** For $i \in \{1, \ldots, n\}$, party $\mathcal{P}_i$ proceeds as follows:
   (a) Sample $r_i \xleftarrow{\$} \{0,1\}^\tau$ and send $(\text{CreatePuzzle}, \text{sid}, \delta, r_i)$ to $\mathcal{F}_{\text{TLP}}^i$, receiving $(\text{CreatedPuzzle}, \text{sid}, \text{puz}_i, \pi_i)$ in response.
   (b) Send $(\text{Send}, \text{sid}, \text{ssid}, \text{puz}_i)$ to $\mathcal{F}_{\text{BC,delay}}^{\Gamma, \Delta}$ and send (activated) to $\mathcal{G}_{\text{ticker}}$.
   (c) Wait for $\mathcal{P}_j \in \mathcal{P}$ to broadcast their TLPs within $\epsilon\delta$ ticks (*i.e.* before the adversary solves puz_i) by sending $(\text{Solve}, \text{sid}, \text{puz}' = (\text{st}', \epsilon\delta, \text{tag}'))$ to $\mathcal{F}_{\text{TLP}}$ (*i.e.* solving a dummy TLP with $\epsilon\delta$ steps to count the ticks) and proceeding as follows when activated: i. Send $(\text{Fetch}, \text{sid})$ to $\mathcal{F}_{\text{BC,delay}}^{\Gamma, \Delta}$, receiving $(\text{Fetch}, \text{sid}, L)$; ii. Check that there exist $1 + n/2$ messages $(\mathcal{P}_i, \text{sid}, (\mathcal{P}_j, \text{puz}_j, \text{ssid}))$ in L from different $\mathcal{P}_j$ and, if yes, let $\mathcal{C} = \{\mathcal{P}_j\}_{1 \leq j \leq 1+n/2}$ and proceed to the **Opening Phase**, else, send (activated) to $\mathcal{G}_{\text{ticker}}$; iii. If $(\text{Solved}, \text{sid}, \text{puz}', \perp, \pi')$ is received from $\mathcal{F}_{\text{TLP}}$, $\epsilon\delta$ ticks have passed, so increment δ and go to Step 1(a).

2. **Opening Phase:** All parties $\mathcal{P}_i \in \mathcal{C}$ proceed as follows:
   (a) Send $(\text{Send}, \text{sid}, \text{ssid}', r_i, \pi_i)$ to $\mathcal{F}_{\text{BC,delay}}^{\Gamma, \Delta}$.
   (b) Wait δ ticks for all $\mathcal{P}_j \in \mathcal{C}$ to broadcast their TLP solutions by sending $(\text{Solve}, \text{sid}, \text{puz}_i)$ to $\mathcal{F}_{\text{TLP}}$ and only proceeding to Step 2(c) when $(\text{Solved}, \text{sid}, \text{puz}_i, r_i, \pi_i)$ is received from $\mathcal{F}_{\text{TLP}}$, sending (activated) to $\mathcal{G}_{\text{ticker}}$ otherwise;
   (c) Send $(\text{Fetch}, \text{sid})$ to $\mathcal{F}_{\text{BC,delay}}^{\Gamma, \Delta}$, receiving $(\text{Fetch}, \text{sid}, L)$. Check that every message of the form $(\mathcal{P}_i, \text{sid}, (\mathcal{P}_j, r_j, \pi_j, \text{ssid}'))$ from $\mathcal{P}_j \in \mathcal{C}$ is a valid solution to puz_j by sending $(\text{Verify}, \text{sid}, \text{puz}_j, r_j, \pi_j)$ to $\mathcal{F}_{\text{TLP}}^j$ and checking that the answer received later is $(\text{Verified}, \text{sid}, \text{puz}_j, r_j, \pi_j, 1)$. Send (activated) to $\mathcal{G}_{\text{ticker}}$. If this check passes for all puz_j from $\mathcal{P}_j \in \mathcal{C}$, compute $r = \bigoplus_{r_i \in \mathcal{V}} r_i$, output $(\text{Tossed}, \text{sid}, r)$ and skip **Recovery Phase**. Otherwise, proceed.

3. **Recovery Phase:** For $i \in \{1, \ldots, n\}$, party $\mathcal{P}_i$ proceeds as follows:
   (a) For each j such that $\mathcal{P}_j \in \mathcal{C}$ did not send a valid solution of puz_j, send $(\text{Solve}, \text{sid}, \text{puz}_j)$ to $\mathcal{F}_{\text{TLP}}$. When activated, if $(\text{Solved}, \text{sid}, \text{puz}_j, r_j, \pi_j)$ is received from $\mathcal{F}_{\text{TLP}}$, send $(\text{Send}, \text{sid}, \text{ssid}'', (r_j, \pi_j))$ to $\mathcal{F}_{\text{BC,delay}}^{\Gamma, \Delta}$ and (activated) to $\mathcal{G}_{\text{ticker}}$.
   (b) Let $\mathcal{G}$ be the set of all solutions $r_j \neq \perp$ of puz_j such that $\mathcal{P}_j \in \mathcal{C}$ (*i.e.* $\mathcal{G}$ is the set of solutions r_j from valid TLPs posted in the commitment phase). Compute $r = \bigoplus_{r_j \in \mathcal{G}} r_j$, output $(\text{Tossed}, \text{sid}, r)$ and send (activated) to $\mathcal{G}_{\text{ticker}}$.

4. **Verify:** On input $(\text{Verify}, \text{sid}, x)$, $\mathcal{V}_j \in \mathcal{V}$ proceeds as follows:
   (a) Send $(\text{Fetch}, \text{sid})$ to $\mathcal{F}_{\text{BC,delay}}^{\Gamma, \Delta}$, receiving $(\text{Fetch}, \text{sid}, L)$ and determining $\mathcal{C}$ by looking for the first $1 + n/2$ messages of the form $(\mathcal{P}_i, \text{sid}, (\mathcal{P}_j, \text{puz}_j, \text{ssid}))$;
   (b) Check that each message of the form $(\mathcal{P}_i, \text{sid}, (\mathcal{P}_h, r_j, \pi_j, \text{ssid}'))$ in L for $\mathcal{P}_j \in \mathcal{C}$ and $\mathcal{P}_h \in \mathcal{P}$ (*i.e.* solutions to a puzzle puz_j from a party $\mathcal{P}_j \in \mathcal{C}$ sent by $\mathcal{P}_j$ or by any party $\mathcal{P}_h \in \mathcal{P}$ who solved an unopened puz_j in the recovery phase) contains a valid solution to puz_j by sending $(\text{Verify}, \text{sid}, \text{puz}_j, r_j, \pi_j)$ to $\mathcal{F}_{\text{TLP}}^j$ and checking that the answer is $(\text{Verified}, \text{sid}, \text{puz}_j, r_j, \pi_j, 1)$;
   (c) Let $\mathcal{G}$ be the set of all r_j such that $\mathcal{P}_j \in \mathcal{C}$, r_j is a valid solution of puz_j and $r_j \neq \perp$. If $x = \bigoplus_{r_j \in \mathcal{G}} r_j$, set $f = 1$, else set $f = 0$, output $(\text{Verify}, \text{sid}, x, f)$.

Fig. 9. Protocol $\pi_{\text{TLP-RB}}$ for a randomness beacon based on PV-TLPs.

adversaries corrupting $t < \frac{n}{2}$ parties in $\mathcal{P}$ for $\Delta_{\mathsf{TLP-RB}} = 3(\epsilon^{-1}\Delta + 1) + \sum_{i=1}^{\epsilon^{-1}\Delta} i$, where ϵ is $\mathcal{F}_{\mathsf{TLP}}$'s slack parameter. There exists a simulator $\mathcal{S}$ such that for every static adversary $\mathcal{A}$, and any environment $\mathcal{Z}$, the environment cannot distinguish an execution of $\pi_{\mathsf{TLP-RB}}$ by $\mathcal{A}$ composed with $\mathcal{F}_{\mathsf{TLP}}, \mathcal{F}_{\mathsf{BC,delay}}^{\Gamma,\Delta}$ from an ideal execution with $\mathcal{S}$ and $\mathcal{F}_{\mathsf{RB}}{}^{\Delta_{\mathsf{TLP-RB}}}$.

5.2   Using a Public Ledger $\mathcal{F}_{\mathsf{Ledger}}$ with $\pi_{\mathsf{TLP-RB}}$

Instead of using a delayed broadcast $\mathcal{F}_{\mathsf{BC,delay}}^{\Gamma,\Delta}$, we can instantiate Protocol $\pi_{\mathsf{TLP-RB}}$ using a public ledger $\mathcal{F}_{\mathsf{Ledger}}$ for communication. In this case, we must parameterize the TLPs with a delay δ that is large enough to guarantee that all honest parties (including desynchronized ones) agree on the set of the first $t + 1$ TLPs that are posted on the ledger before proceeding to the **Opening Phase**. We describe an alternative Protocol $\pi_{\mathsf{TLP-RB-LEDGER}}$ that behaves exactly as Protocol $\pi_{\mathsf{TLP-RB}}$ but leverages $\mathcal{F}_{\mathsf{Ledger}}$ for communication.

Protocol. $\pi_{\mathsf{TLP-RB-LEDGER}}$: This protocol is exactly the same as $\pi_{\mathsf{TLP-RB}}$ except for using $\mathcal{F}_{\mathsf{Ledger}}$ for communication instead of $\mathcal{F}_{\mathsf{BC,delay}}^{\Gamma,\Delta}$ in the following way:

- At every point of $\pi_{\mathsf{TLP-RB}}$ where parties send $(\mathsf{Send}, \mathsf{sid}, \mathsf{ssid}, m)$ to $\mathcal{F}_{\mathsf{BC,delay}}^{\Gamma,\Delta}$, instead they send $(\mathsf{Submit}, \mathsf{sid}, m)$ to $\mathcal{F}_{\mathsf{Ledger}}$.
- At every point of $\pi_{\mathsf{TLP-RB}}$ where parties send $(\mathsf{Fetch}, \mathsf{sid})$ to $\mathcal{F}_{\mathsf{BC,delay}}^{\Gamma,\Delta}$ and check for messages in $(\mathsf{Fetch}, \mathsf{sid}, L)$, instead they send $(\mathsf{Read}, \mathsf{sid})$ to $\mathcal{F}_{\mathsf{Ledger}}$ and check for messages in $(\mathsf{Read}, \mathsf{sid}, \mathsf{state}_i)$.

Theorem 4. *If $\Delta = \mathsf{maxTXDelay} + \mathsf{emptyBlocks} \cdot \mathsf{slackWindow}$ (computed from $\mathcal{F}_{\mathsf{Ledger}}$'s parameters) is finite (though unknown), Protocol $\pi_{\mathsf{TLP-RB-LEDGER}}$ UC-realizes $\mathcal{F}_{\mathsf{RB}}{}^{\Delta_{\mathsf{TLP-RB}}}$ in the $\mathcal{F}_{\mathsf{TLP}}, \mathcal{F}_{\mathsf{Ledger}}$-hybrid model with computational security against a static adversary corrupting $t < \frac{n}{2}$ parties in $\mathcal{P}$ for $\Delta_{\mathsf{TLP-RB}} = 3(\epsilon^{-1}\Delta + 1) + \sum_{i=1}^{\epsilon^{-1}\Delta} i$, where ϵ is $\mathcal{F}_{\mathsf{TLP}}$'s slack parameter. Formally, there exists a simulator $\mathcal{S}$ such that for every static adversary $\mathcal{A}$, and any environment $\mathcal{Z}$, the environment cannot distinguish an execution of $\pi_{\mathsf{TLP-RB-LEDGER}}$ by $\mathcal{A}$ composed with $\mathcal{F}_{\mathsf{TLP}}, \mathcal{F}_{\mathsf{Ledger}}$ from an ideal execution with $\mathcal{S}$ and $\mathcal{F}_{\mathsf{RB}}{}^{\Delta_{\mathsf{TLP-RB}}}$.*

Proof. The proof is presented in the full version [5] due to space limitations.

5.3   Randomness Beacons from VDFs

It has been suggested that VDFs can be used to obtain a randomness beacon [12] via a simple protocol where parties post plaintext values $r_1, \ldots, r_n$ on a public ledger and then evaluate a VDF on input $H(r_1|\ldots|r_n)$, where $H()$ is a cryptographic hash function, in order to obtain a random output r. However, despite being used in industry [40], the security of this protocol was never formally proven due to the lack of composability guarantees for VDFs. Our work settles this question by formalizing Protocol $\pi_{\mathsf{VDF-RB}}$ and proving Theorem 5 (in the full version [5]), which characterizes the worst case execution time.

Theorem 5. *If $\Delta = \mathsf{maxTXDelay} + \mathsf{emptyBlocks} \cdot \mathsf{slackWindow}$ (computed from $\mathcal{F}_{\mathsf{Ledger}}$'s parameters) is finite (but unknown), Protocol $\pi_{\mathsf{VDF-RB}}$ UC-realizes $\mathcal{F}_{\mathsf{RB}}{}^{\Delta_{\mathsf{TLP-RB}}}$ in the $\mathcal{F}_{\mathsf{VDF}}, \mathcal{F}_{\mathsf{Ledger}}$-hybrid model with computational security against static adversaries corrupting $t < n/2$ parties for $\Delta_{\mathsf{TLP-RB}} = 2(\epsilon^{-1}\Delta + 1) + \sum_{i=1}^{\epsilon^{-1}\Delta} i$, where ϵ is $\mathcal{F}_{\mathsf{VDF}}$'s slack parameter. There is a simulator $\mathcal{S}$ s.t. for every static adversary $\mathcal{A}$, and any environment $\mathcal{Z}$, $\mathcal{Z}$ cannot distinguish an execution of $\pi_{\mathsf{VDF-RB}}$ by $\mathcal{A}$ composed with $\mathcal{F}_{\mathsf{VDF}}, \mathcal{F}_{\mathsf{Ledger}}$ from an ideal execution with $\mathcal{S}$ and $\mathcal{F}_{\mathsf{RB}}{}^{\Delta_{\mathsf{TLP-RB}}}$.*

6   MPC with (Punishable) Output-Independent Abort

In this section we will describe how to construct a protocol that achieves MPC with output-independent abort. The starting point of this construction will be MPC with secret-shared output[2], which is a strictly weaker primitive, as well as the broadcast as modeled in $\mathcal{F}_{\mathsf{BC,delay}}^{\Gamma,\Delta}$ and Commitments with Delayed Openings $\mathcal{F}_{\mathsf{com}}^{\Delta,\delta,\zeta}$. In the full version [5], we subsequently show how to financially penalize cheating behavior in the protocol (POIA-MPC).

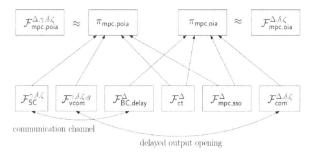

Fig. 10. How MPC with (Punishable) Output-Independent Abort is constructed.

6.1   Functionalities for Output-Independent Abort

We begin by mentioning the functionalities that are used in our construction and which have not appeared in previous work (when modeled with respect to time). These functionalities are:

---

[2] For the sake of efficiency we focus on an output phase that uses additive secret sharing. However, the core MPC computation could use any secret sharing scheme, while only the output phase is restricted to additive secret sharing. This approach can be generalized by using a generic MPC protocol that computes an additive secret sharing of the output as part of the evaluated circuit, although at an efficiency cost. We remark that efficient MPC protocols matching our requirements do exist, e.g. [29].

1. $\mathcal{F}_{\mathsf{mpc,sso}}^{\Delta}$ (Fig. 11 and Fig. 12) for secure MPC with secret-shared output.
2. $\mathcal{F}_{\mathsf{mpc,oia}}^{\Delta,\delta,\zeta}$ (Fig. 13 and Fig. 14) for OIA-MPC.

In the full version [5], we also introduce the following functionalities:

1. $\mathcal{F}_{\mathsf{ct}}^{\Delta}$ for coin-flipping with abort.
2. $\mathcal{F}_{\mathsf{com}}^{\Delta,\delta,\zeta}$ for commitments with delayed non-interactive openings.
3. $\mathcal{F}_{\mathsf{vcom}}^{\gamma,\delta,\zeta,g}$ for commitments with verifiable delayed non-interactive openings.
4. $\mathcal{F}_{\mathsf{SC}}^{\gamma,\delta,\zeta}$ which is an abstraction of a smart contract.
5. $\mathcal{F}_{\mathsf{mpc,poia}}^{\Delta,\gamma,\delta,\zeta}$ for POIA-MPC.

Before formally introducing all functionalities and explaining them in more detail, we show how they are related in our construction in Fig. 10. As can be seen there our approach is twofold. First, we will realize $\mathcal{F}_{\mathsf{mpc,oia}}^{\Delta,\delta,\zeta}$ via the protocol $\pi_{\mathsf{mpc,oia}}$ relying on $\mathcal{F}_{\mathsf{BC,delay}}^{\Gamma,\Delta}, \mathcal{F}_{\mathsf{ct}}^{\Delta}, \mathcal{F}_{\mathsf{mpc,sso}}^{\Delta}$ and $\mathcal{F}_{\mathsf{com}}^{\Delta,\delta,\zeta}$. Then, we will show how to implement $\mathcal{F}_{\mathsf{mpc,poia}}^{\Delta,\gamma,\delta,\zeta}$ via the protocol $\pi_{\mathsf{mpc,poia}}$ (a generalization of $\pi_{\mathsf{mpc,oia}}$) which uses $\mathcal{F}_{\mathsf{SC}}^{\gamma,\delta,\zeta}, \mathcal{F}_{\mathsf{ct}}^{\Delta}, \mathcal{F}_{\mathsf{mpc,sso}}^{\Delta}$ as well as $\mathcal{F}_{\mathsf{vcom}}^{\gamma,\delta,\zeta,g}$. As mentioned in Fig. 10, $\mathcal{F}_{\mathsf{vcom}}^{\gamma,\delta,\zeta,g}$ and $\mathcal{F}_{\mathsf{SC}}^{\gamma,\delta,\zeta}$ are modifications of $\mathcal{F}_{\mathsf{com}}^{\Delta,\delta,\zeta}$ and $\mathcal{F}_{\mathsf{BC,delay}}^{\Gamma,\Delta}$. We now describe the functionalities required to build $\pi_{\mathsf{mpc,oia}}$ in more detail.

MPC with Secret-Shared Output. The functionality $\mathcal{F}_{\mathsf{mpc,sso}}^{\Delta}$ is formally introduced in Fig. 11 and Fig. 12. It directly translates an MPC protocol with secret-shared output into the TARDIS model, but does not make use of any tick-related properties beyond scheduling of message transmission. The functionality supports computations on secret input where the output of the computation is additively secret-shared among the participants. Additionally, it allows parties to sample random values, compute linear combinations of outputs and those random values and allows to reliably but unfairly open secret-shared values. $\mathcal{F}_{\mathsf{mpc,sso}}^{\Delta}$ can be instantiated from many different MPC protocols, such as those based on secret-sharing [9] or multiparty BMR [29].

Commitments with Delayed Openings. We describe the functionality $\mathcal{F}_{\mathsf{com}}^{\Delta,\delta,\zeta}$ for commitments with delayed non-interactive openings in the full version [5]. The functionality distinguishes between a sender $\mathcal{P}_{\mathsf{Send}}$, which can make commitments, and a set of receivers, which obtain the openings. Compared to regular commitments with a normal **Open** that immediately reveals the output to all parties, $\mathcal{P}_{\mathsf{Send}}$ is also allowed to perform a **Delayed Open**, where there is a delay between the choice of a sender to open a commitment (or not) and the actual opening towards receivers and the adversary.

While both **Commit** and **Open** directly resemble their counterparts in a normal commitment functionality, the **Delayed Open** logic is not as straightforward. What happens during such a delayed open is that first all honest parties will simultaneously learn that indeed an opening will happen in the future - for which they obtain a message DOpen. Additionally, $\mathcal{F}_{\mathsf{com}}^{\Delta,\delta,\zeta}$ stores the openings

---

Functionality $\mathcal{F}_{\mathsf{mpc,sso}}^{\Delta}$ (Computation, Message Handling)

The ticked functionality interacts with n parties $\mathcal{P} = \{\mathcal{P}_1, \ldots, \mathcal{P}_n\}$ and an adversary $\mathcal{S}$ which may corrupt a strict subset $I \subset \mathcal{P}$.

Init: On first input $(\mathsf{Init}, \mathsf{sid}, C)$ by $\mathcal{P}_i \in \mathcal{P}$:
1. Send message C to the parties $\mathcal{P} \setminus \{\mathcal{P}_i\}$ via $\mathcal{Q}$ with delay Δ.
2. If each party sent $(\mathsf{Init}, \mathsf{sid}, C)$ then store C. Send C and the IDs to $\mathcal{S}$.

Input: On first input $(\mathsf{Input}, \mathsf{sid}, i, x_i)$ by $\mathcal{P}_i \in \mathcal{P}$:
1. Notify parties $\mathcal{P} \setminus \{\mathcal{P}_i\}$ via $\mathcal{Q}$ with delay Δ. Then accept x_i as input for $\mathcal{P}_i$.
2. Send m and the IDs to $\mathcal{S}$ if $\mathcal{P}_i \in I$, otherwise notify $\mathcal{S}$ about a message with prefix Input.

Computation: On first input $(\mathsf{Compute}, \mathsf{sid})$ by $\mathcal{P}_i \in \mathcal{P}$ and if $x_1, \ldots, x_n$ were accepted:
1. Notify parties $\mathcal{P} \setminus \{\mathcal{P}_i\}$ via $\mathcal{Q}$ with delay Δ. If all parties sent $(\mathsf{Compute}, \mathsf{sid})$ compute and store $(y_1, \ldots, y_m) \leftarrow C(x_1, \ldots, x_n)$.
2. Notify $\mathcal{S}$ about a message with prefix $\mathsf{Compute}$.

Tick:
1. Remove each $(0, \mathsf{mid}, \mathsf{sid}, \mathcal{P}_i, m)$ from $\mathcal{Q}$ and instead add $(\mathcal{P}_i, \mathsf{sid}, m)$ to $\mathcal{M}$.
2. Replace each $(\mathtt{cnt}, \mathsf{mid}, \mathsf{sid}, \mathcal{P}_i, m)$ in $\mathcal{Q}$ with $(\mathtt{cnt} - 1, \mathsf{mid}, \mathsf{sid}, \mathcal{P}_i, m)$.
Upon receiving $(\mathsf{Schedule}, \mathsf{sid}, \mathcal{D})$ from $\mathcal{S}$:
- If $(\mathsf{Deliver}, \mathsf{sid}, \mathsf{mid}) \in \mathcal{D}$ then remove each $(\mathtt{cnt}, \mathsf{mid}, \mathsf{sid}, \mathcal{P}_i, m)$ from $\mathcal{Q}$ and add $(\mathcal{P}_i, \mathsf{sid}, m)$ to $\mathcal{M}$.
- If $(\mathsf{Abort}, \mathsf{sid}) \in \mathcal{D}$ then add $(\mathcal{P}_i, \mathsf{sid}, \mathsf{Abort})$ to $\mathcal{M}$ for each $i \in [n]$ and ignore all further messages with this sid except to **Fetch Message**.

Fig. 11. Ticked Functionality $\mathcal{F}_{\mathsf{mpc,sso}}^{\Delta}$ for MPC with Secret-Shared Output and Linear Secret Share Operations.

in an internal queue $\mathcal{O}$. These openings *can not be rescheduled by the adversary*, and therefore it will take δ ticks before honest parties learn the opening of the commitment. This means that for honest parties, it may take up to $\Delta + \delta$ ticks depending on when DOpen is obtained. The simulator will already learn the opening after $\zeta \leq \delta$ ticks, similar to how it might solve $\mathcal{F}_{\mathsf{TLP}}$ faster. $\mathcal{F}_{\mathsf{com}}^{\Delta,\delta,\zeta}$ ensures that *all honest parties will learn the delayed opening simultaneously*.

In the full version [5], we provide a secure instantiation of a publicly verifiable version of $\mathcal{F}_{\mathsf{com}}^{\Delta,\delta,\zeta}$. Since we do not require homomorphic operations, this means that it can be realized with a much simpler protocol than the respective two-party functionality in [6].

In Fig. 13 and Fig. 14 we describe the functionality $\mathcal{F}_{\mathsf{mpc,oia}}^{\Delta,\delta,\zeta}$ for MPC with output-independent abort.

In terms of the actual secure computation, our functionality is identical with $\mathcal{F}_{\mathsf{mpc,sso}}^{\Delta}$, although it does not reveal the concrete shares to the parties and the

---

Functionality $\mathcal{F}_{\mathsf{mpc,sso}}^{\Delta}$ (Computation on Outputs)

Share Output: Upon first input (ShareOutput, sid, $\mathcal{T}$) by $\mathcal{P}_i \in \mathcal{P}$ for fresh identifiers $\mathcal{T} = \{\mathsf{cid}_1, \ldots, \mathsf{cid}_m\}$ and if **Computation** was finished:

1. Notify parties $\mathcal{P} \setminus \{\mathcal{P}_i\}$ via $\mathcal{Q}$ with delay Δ.

2. If all parties sent ShareOutput:
   (a) Send (RequestShares, sid, $\mathcal{T}$) to $\mathcal{S}$, which replies with (OutputShares, sid, $\{s_{j,\mathsf{cid}}\}_{\mathsf{cid} \in \mathcal{T}, \mathcal{P}_j \in I}$). Then for each $\mathcal{P}_j \in \mathcal{P} \setminus I, h \in [m]$ sample $s_{j,\mathsf{cid}_h} \leftarrow \mathbb{F}$ uniformly random conditioned on $y_h = \bigoplus_{k \in [n]} s_{k,\mathsf{cid}_h}$.
   (b) For $\mathsf{cid} \in \mathcal{T}$ store $(\mathsf{cid}, s_{1,\mathsf{cid}}, \ldots, s_{n,\mathsf{cid}})$ and for each $\mathcal{P}_j \in \mathcal{P} \setminus I$ send $s_{j,\mathsf{cid}}$ with prefix OutputShares to party $\mathcal{P}_j$ via $\mathcal{Q}$ with delay Δ. Finally notify $\mathcal{S}$ about the message with prefix OutputShares.

3. Notify $\mathcal{S}$ about a message with the prefix ShareOutput.

Share Random Value: Upon input (ShareRandom, sid, $\mathcal{T}$) by all parties with fresh identifiers $\mathcal{T}$:

1. Notify parties $\mathcal{P} \setminus \{\mathcal{P}_i\}$ via $\mathcal{Q}$ with delay Δ.

2. If all parties sent ShareRandom:
   (a) Send (RequestShares, sid, $\mathcal{T}$) to $\mathcal{S}$, which replies with (RandomShares, sid, $\{s_{j,\mathsf{cid}}\}_{\mathsf{cid} \in \mathcal{T}, \mathcal{P}_j \in I}$). Then for each $\mathcal{P}_j \in \mathcal{P} \setminus I, \mathsf{cid} \in \mathcal{T}$ sample $s_{j,\mathsf{cid}} \leftarrow \mathbb{F}$ uniformly at random.
   (b) For $\mathsf{cid} \in \mathcal{T}$ store $(\mathsf{cid}, s_{1,\mathsf{cid}}, \ldots, s_{n,\mathsf{cid}})$ and for each $\mathcal{P}_j \in \mathcal{P} \setminus I$ send $s_{j,\mathsf{cid}}$ with prefix RandomShares to party $\mathcal{P}_j$ via $\mathcal{Q}$ with delay Δ. Finally notify $\mathcal{S}$ about the message with prefix RandomShares.

3. Notify $\mathcal{S}$ about a message with the prefix ShareRandom.

Linear Combination: Upon input (Linear, sid, $\{(\mathsf{cid}, \alpha_{\mathsf{cid}})\}_{\mathsf{cid} \in \mathcal{T}}, \mathsf{cid}'$) from all parties: If all $\alpha_{\mathsf{cid}} \in \mathbb{F}$, all $(\mathsf{cid}, s_{1,\mathsf{cid}}, \ldots, s_{n,\mathsf{cid}})$ have been stored and cid' is unused, set $s_i' \leftarrow \sum_{\mathsf{cid} \in \mathcal{T}} \alpha_{\mathsf{cid}} \cdot s_{i,\mathsf{cid}}$ and record $(\mathsf{cid}', s_1', \ldots, s_n')$.

Reveal: Upon input (Reveal, sid, $\mathcal{T}$) by $\mathcal{P}_i \in \mathcal{P}$ for identifiers $\mathcal{T}$ and if $(\mathsf{cid}, s_1, \ldots, s_n)$ is stored for each $\mathsf{cid} \in \mathcal{T}$:

1. Notify the parties $\mathcal{P} \setminus \{\mathcal{P}_i\}$ via $\mathcal{Q}$ with delay Δ. Then notify $\mathcal{S}$ about a message with prefix Reveal.

2. If all parties sent (Reveal, sid, $\mathcal{T}$) then send (Reveal, sid, $\{(\mathsf{cid}, s_{1,\mathsf{cid}}, \ldots, s_{n,\mathsf{cid}})\}_{\mathsf{cid} \in \mathcal{T}}$) to $\mathcal{S}$.

3. If $\mathcal{S}$ sends (DeliverReveal, sid, $\mathcal{T}$) then send message $\{(\mathsf{cid}, s_{1,\mathsf{cid}}, \ldots, s_{n,\mathsf{cid}})\}_{\mathsf{cid} \in \mathcal{T}}$ with prefix DeliverReveal to parties $\mathcal{P}$ via $\mathcal{Q}$ with delay Δ and notify $\mathcal{S}$ about a message with prefix DeliverReveal.

Fig. 12. Ticked Functionality $\mathcal{F}_{\mathsf{mpc,sso}}^{\Delta}$ for MPC with Secret-Shared Output and Linear Secret Share Operations, Part 2.

adversary during the sharing. The output-independent abort property of our functionality is then achieved as follows: in order to reveal the output of the computation, each party will have to send Reveal to $\mathcal{F}_{\mathsf{mpc,oia}}^{\Delta,\delta,\zeta}$. Once all honest parties and the verifiers thus learn that the parties indeed are synchronized by

---

Functionality $\mathcal{F}_{\mathsf{mpc,oia}}^{\Delta,\delta,\zeta}$ (Computation, Sharing)

The ticked functionality runs with n parties $\mathcal{P} = \{\mathcal{P}_1,\ldots,\mathcal{P}_n\}$ and an adversary $\mathcal{S}$ who may corrupt a strict subset $I \subset \mathcal{P}$. $\mathcal{F}_{\mathsf{mpc,oia}}^{\Delta,\delta,\zeta}$ is parameterized by $\Delta, \delta, \zeta \in \mathbb{N}^+, \zeta \leq \delta$, has an initially empty list $\mathcal{O}$ and set J as well as a state $\mathtt{st}$ initially $\bot$.

Init: On first input $(\mathsf{Init}, \mathsf{sid}, C)$ by $\mathcal{P}_i \in \mathcal{P}$:
1. Send message C to the parties $\mathcal{P} \setminus \{\mathcal{P}_i\}$ via $\mathcal{Q}$ with delay Δ.
2. If each party sent $(\mathsf{Init}, \mathsf{sid}, C)$ then store C locally. Send C and the IDs to $\mathcal{S}$.

Input: On first input $(\mathsf{Input}, \mathsf{sid}, i, x_i)$ by $\mathcal{P}_i \in \mathcal{P}$:
1. Notify parties $\mathcal{P} \setminus \{\mathcal{P}_i\}$ via $\mathcal{Q}$ with delay Δ. Then accept x_i as input for $\mathcal{P}_i$.
2. Send x_i and the IDs to $\mathcal{S}$ if $\mathcal{P}_i \in I$, otherwise notify $\mathcal{S}$ about a message with prefix Input.

Computation: On first input $(\mathsf{Compute}, \mathsf{sid})$ by $\mathcal{P}_i \in \mathcal{P}$ and if all $\{x_i\}_{i \in [n]}$ were accepted:
1. Notify parties $\mathcal{P} \setminus \{\mathcal{P}_i\}$ via $\mathcal{Q}$ with delay Δ.
2. If each party sent $(\mathsf{Compute}, \mathsf{sid})$ compute $y = C(x_1,\ldots,x_n)$ and store y.
3. Notify $\mathcal{S}$ about a message with prefix $\mathsf{Compute}$.

Share: On first input $(\mathsf{Share}, \mathsf{sid})$ by party $\mathcal{P}_i$, if y has been stored and if $\mathtt{st} = \bot$:
1. Notify parties $\mathcal{P} \setminus \{\mathcal{P}_i\}$ via $\mathcal{Q}$ with delay Δ.
2. If all parties sent Share then:
   (a) Send $(\mathsf{Shares?}, \mathsf{sid})$ to $\mathcal{S}$.
   (b) Upon $(\mathsf{DeliverShares}, \mathsf{sid})$ from $\mathcal{S}$ send a message with prefix $\mathsf{DeliverShares}$ to each $\mathcal{P}_j \in \mathcal{P} \setminus I$ via $\mathcal{Q}$ with delay Δ. Then notify $\mathcal{S}$ about messages with prefix $\mathsf{DeliverShares}$ and the IDs.
   (c) Otherwise, if $\mathcal{S}$ sends $(\mathsf{Abort}, \mathsf{sid})$ then send Abort to all parties
3. Notify $\mathcal{S}$ about a message with prefix Share.

Reveal: Upon first message $(\mathsf{Reveal}, \mathsf{sid}, i)$ by each party $\mathcal{P}_i \in \mathcal{P}$, if **Share** has finished, if no $\mathsf{DeliverShare}$ message is in $\mathcal{Q}$ and if $\mathtt{st} = \bot$ or $\mathtt{st} = \mathtt{sync}$:
1. Simultaneously send a message i with prefix Reveal to parties $\mathcal{P} \setminus \{\mathcal{P}_i\}$ via $\mathcal{Q}$ with delay Δ.
2. Set $\mathtt{st} = \mathtt{sync}$ and notify $\mathcal{S}$ about a message with prefix Reveal.

Fig. 13. Ticked $\mathcal{F}_{\mathsf{mpc,oia}}^{\Delta,\delta,\zeta}$ Functionality for MPC with Output-Independent Abort.

seeing that *the first synchronization message arrives at all parties* ($\mathtt{st} = \mathtt{sync}$ and $\mathtt{f} = \top$), the internal state of the functionality changes. From this point on, the adversary can, within an additional time-frame of ζ ticks, decide whether to reveal its shares or not. Then, once these ζ ticks passed, $\mathcal{S}$ will obtain the output y of the computation *after* having provided the set of aborting parties J. If $J = \emptyset$ then $\mathcal{F}_{\mathsf{mpc,oia}}^{\Delta,\delta,\zeta}$ will, within δ additional ticks, simultaneously output y to all honest parties, while it otherwise outputs the set J.

Functionality $\mathcal{F}_{\mathsf{mpc,oia}}^{\Delta,\delta,\zeta}$ **(Timing)**

Tick:

1. Set $\mathbf{f} \leftarrow \bot$, remove each $(0, \mathsf{mid}, \mathsf{sid}, \mathcal{P}_i, m)$ from $\mathcal{Q}$ and instead add $(\mathcal{P}_i, \mathsf{sid}, m)$ to $\mathcal{M}$. If $m = (\mathsf{Reveal}, i)$ then set $\mathbf{f} \leftarrow \top$.

2. Replace each $(\mathtt{cnt}, \mathsf{mid}, \mathsf{sid}, \mathcal{P}_i, m)$ in $\mathcal{Q}$ with $(\mathtt{cnt} - 1, \mathsf{mid}, \mathsf{sid}, \mathcal{P}_i, m)$.

3. If $\mathtt{st} = \mathtt{wait}(x)$ & $x \geq 0$:
   If $x \geq 0$: Set $\mathtt{st} = \mathtt{wait}(x - 1)$.

   If $x = 0$:
   (a) Send $(\mathsf{Abort?}, \mathsf{sid})$ to $\mathcal{S}$ and wait for response $(\mathsf{Abort}, \mathsf{sid}, J)$ with $J \subseteq I$.

   (b) If $J = \emptyset$ then send message y with prefix Output to each party $\mathcal{P} \setminus I$ via $\mathcal{Q}$ with delay δ. If $J \neq \emptyset$ then send message J with prefix Abort to each party $\mathcal{P} \setminus I$ via $\mathcal{Q}$ with delay δ.

   (c) Send $(\mathsf{Output}, \mathsf{sid}, y)$ and the IDs to $\mathcal{S}$.

4. If $\mathtt{st} = \mathtt{sync}$ and $f = \top$ then set $\mathtt{st} = \mathtt{wait}(\zeta)$ and send $(\mathsf{RevealStart}, \mathsf{sid})$ to $\mathcal{S}$.
   Upon receiving $(\mathsf{Schedule}, \mathsf{sid}, \mathcal{D})$ from $\mathcal{S}$:
   - If $(\mathsf{Deliver}, \mathsf{sid}, \mathsf{mid}) \in \mathcal{D}$ then remove each $(\mathtt{cnt}, \mathsf{mid}, \mathsf{sid}, \mathcal{P}_i, m)$ from $\mathcal{Q}$ and add $(\mathcal{P}_i, \mathsf{sid}, m)$ to $\mathcal{M}$.
   - If $(\mathsf{Abort}, \mathsf{sid}) \in \mathcal{D}$ and $\mathtt{st} = \bot$ then add $(\mathcal{P}_i, \mathsf{sid}, \mathsf{Abort})$ to $\mathcal{M}$ for each $\mathcal{P}_i \in \mathcal{P}$ and ignore all further messages with this sid except to **Fetch Message**.

Fig. 14. Ticked $\mathcal{F}_{\mathsf{mpc,oia}}^{\Delta,\delta,\zeta}$ Functionality for MPC with Output-Independent Abort.

The additional up to δ ticks between the adversary learning y and the honest parties learning y or J is due to our protocol and will be more clear later.

Coin Tossing. $\pi_{\mathsf{mpc,oia}}$ additionally requires a functionality for coin tossing $\mathcal{F}_{\mathsf{ct}}^{\Delta}$, which we present in the full version [5]. Note that $\mathcal{F}_{\mathsf{ct}}^{\Delta}$ can easily be realized in the $\mathcal{F}_{\mathsf{BC,delay}}^{\Gamma,\Delta}, \mathcal{F}_{\mathsf{com}}^{\Delta,\delta,\zeta}$-hybrid model.

6.2   Building MPC with Output-Independent Abort

We will now describe how to construct an MPC protocol that guarantees output-independent abort. Although this might appear like a natural generalization of [6], constructing the protocol is far from trivial as we must take care that all honest parties agree on the same set of cheaters. Our protocol works as follows:

1. The parties begin by sending a message $beat$ (i.e. a heartbeat) to the functionality $\mathcal{F}_{\mathsf{BC,delay}}^{\Gamma,\Delta}$. Throughout the protocol, they do the following in parallel to running the MPC protocol, unless mentioned otherwise:
   - All parties wait for a broadcast message $beat$ from all parties on $\mathcal{F}_{\mathsf{BC,delay}}^{\Gamma,\Delta}$. If some parties did not send their message to $\mathcal{F}_{\mathsf{BC,delay}}^{\Gamma,\Delta}$ in one iteration then all parties abort. Otherwise, they send $beat$ in another iteration to $\mathcal{F}_{\mathsf{BC,delay}}^{\Gamma,\Delta}$.

Protocol $\pi_{\mathsf{mpc,oia}}$ (Computation, Share)

All parties $\mathcal{P}$ have access to one instance of the functionalities $\mathcal{F}^{\Delta}_{\mathsf{mpc,sso}}$, $\mathcal{F}^{\Delta}_{\mathsf{ct}}$ and $\mathcal{F}^{\Gamma,\Delta}_{\mathsf{BC,delay}}$. Furthermore, each $\mathcal{P}_i \in \mathcal{P}$ has it's own $\mathcal{F}^{\Delta,\delta,\varsigma,i}_{\mathsf{com}}$ where it acts as the dedicated sender and all other parties of $\mathcal{P}$ are receivers. Throughout the protocol, we say "$\mathcal{P}_i$ ticks" when we mean that it sends (activated) to $\mathcal{G}_{\mathsf{ticker}}$. We say that "$\mathcal{P}_i$ waits" when we mean that it, upon each activation, first checks if the event happened and if not, sends (activated) to $\mathcal{G}_{\mathsf{ticker}}$.

Upon every activation: Let c be a counter that is initially 0. $\mathcal{P}_i$ sends (Send, sid, c, $beat$) to the functionality $\mathcal{F}^{\Gamma,\Delta}_{\mathsf{BC,delay}}$ (with c as ssid). Throughout $\pi_{\mathsf{mpc,oia}}$, each $\mathcal{P}_i$ waits for $\mathcal{F}^{\Gamma,\Delta}_{\mathsf{BC,delay}}$ to return $(\mathcal{P}_j, c, beat)$ for all other $\mathcal{P}_j \in \mathcal{P}$. If it does, then each $\mathcal{P}_i$ increases c by 1 and sends (Send, sid, c, $beat$) to $\mathcal{F}^{\Gamma,\Delta}_{\mathsf{BC,delay}}$. Otherwise the parties abort.

Init: Each $\mathcal{P}_i \in \mathcal{P}$ sends (Init, sid, C) to $\mathcal{F}^{\Delta}_{\mathsf{mpc,sso}}$ and ticks. It waits until it obtains messages C with prefix Init from $\mathcal{F}^{\Delta}_{\mathsf{mpc,sso}}$ for every other party $\mathcal{P} \setminus \{\mathcal{P}_i\}$.

Input: Each $\mathcal{P}_i \in \mathcal{P}$ sends (Input, sid, i, x_i) to $\mathcal{F}^{\Delta}_{\mathsf{mpc,sso}}$ and ticks. It waits until it obtains messages j with prefix Input from $\mathcal{F}^{\Delta}_{\mathsf{mpc,sso}}$ for every $\mathcal{P}_j \in \mathcal{P} \setminus \{\mathcal{P}_i\}$.

Computation: Each $\mathcal{P}_i \in \mathcal{P}$ sends (Computation, sid) to $\mathcal{F}^{\Delta}_{\mathsf{mpc,sso}}$ and ticks. It waits until it obtains messages with prefix Computation from $\mathcal{F}^{\Delta}_{\mathsf{mpc,sso}}$ for every $\mathcal{P} \setminus \{\mathcal{P}_i\}$.

Share:

1. Set $\mathcal{T}_y = \{\mathsf{cid}_{y,j}\}_{j\in[m]}$, $\mathcal{T}_r = \{\mathsf{cid}_{r,k}\}_{k\in[\lambda]}$ and $\mathcal{T}_t = \{\mathsf{cid}_{t,k}\}_{k\in[\lambda]}$.

2. Each $\mathcal{P}_i \in \mathcal{P}$ sends (ShareOutput, sid, $\mathcal{T}_y$) to $\mathcal{F}^{\Delta}_{\mathsf{mpc,sso}}$ and ticks. Then it waits until it obtains a message $\{y_{i,\mathsf{cid}}\}_{\mathsf{cid}\in\mathcal{T}_y}$ with prefix OutputShares from $\mathcal{F}^{\Delta}_{\mathsf{mpc,sso}}$.

3. Each $\mathcal{P}_i \in \mathcal{P}$ sends (ShareRandom, sid, $\mathcal{T}_r$) to $\mathcal{F}^{\Delta}_{\mathsf{mpc,sso}}$ and ticks. It then waits until it obtains a message $\{r_{i,\mathsf{cid}}\}_{\mathsf{cid}\in\mathcal{T}_r}$ with prefix RandomShares from $\mathcal{F}^{\Delta}_{\mathsf{mpc,sso}}$. Set $\boldsymbol{y}_i = (y_{i,\mathsf{cid}_{y,1}}, \ldots, y_{i,\mathsf{cid}_{y,m}})$ and equivalently define $\boldsymbol{r}_i$.

4. Each $\mathcal{P}_i \in \mathcal{P}$ sends (Commit, sid, cid_i, $(\boldsymbol{y}_i, \boldsymbol{r}_i)$) to $\mathcal{F}^{\Delta,\delta,\varsigma,i}_{\mathsf{com}}$ and ticks. It then waits for messages (Commit, sid, cid_j) from $\mathcal{F}^{\Delta,\delta,\varsigma,j}_{\mathsf{com}}$ of all other $\mathcal{P}_j \in \mathcal{P} \setminus \{\mathcal{P}_i\}$.

5. Each $\mathcal{P}_i \in \mathcal{P}$ sends (Toss, sid, $m \cdot \lambda$) to $\mathcal{F}^{\Delta}_{\mathsf{ct}}$ and ticks. It then waits for the message (Coins, sid, $\mathbf{A}$) where $\mathbf{A} \in \mathbb{F}^{\lambda \times m}$.

6. Each $\mathcal{P}_i \in \mathcal{P}$ for $k \in [\lambda]$ sends (Linear, sid, $\{(\mathsf{cid}_{v,j}, \mathbf{A}[k,j])\}_{j\in[m]} \cup \{(\mathsf{cid}_{r,k}, 1)\}$, $\mathsf{cid}_{t,k}$) to $\mathcal{F}^{\Delta}_{\mathsf{mpc,sso}}$.

7. Each $\mathcal{P}_i \in \mathcal{P}$ sends (Reveal, sid, $\mathcal{T}_t$) to $\mathcal{F}^{\Delta}_{\mathsf{mpc,sso}}$ and ticks. It then waits for the message $\{(\mathsf{cid}, t_{1,\mathsf{cid}}, \ldots, t_{n,\mathsf{cid}})\}_{\mathsf{cid}\in\mathcal{T}_t}$ with prefix DeliverReveal from $\mathcal{F}^{\Delta}_{\mathsf{mpc,sso}}$. Set $\boldsymbol{t}_j = (t_{j,\mathsf{cid}_{t,1}}, \ldots, t_{j,\mathsf{cid}_{t,\lambda}})$ for each $j \in [n]$.

Fig. 15. Protocol $\pi_{\mathsf{mpc,oia}}$ for MPC with Output-Independent Abort.

The purpose of the heartbeat is to ensure that honest parties are synchronized throughout the protocol, allowing them to later achieve agreement on the corrupt parties.

Protocol $\pi_{\mathsf{mpc,oia}}$ (Reveal)

Reveal: If **Share** completed successfully:

1. Each party changes the messages to $\mathcal{F}_{\mathsf{BC,delay}}^{\Gamma,\Delta}$ to $(\mathsf{Send}, \mathsf{sid}, c, \mathit{ready})$. Upon receiving the first $(\mathcal{P}_j, \mathit{ready}, c)$ for all $\mathcal{P}_j \in \mathcal{P}$ from $\mathcal{F}_{\mathsf{BC,delay}}^{\Gamma,\Delta}$, each $\mathcal{P}_i$ sends $(\mathsf{DOpen}, \mathsf{sid}, \mathsf{cid}_j)$ to $\mathcal{F}_{\mathsf{com}}^{\Delta,\delta,\varsigma,j}$ for each $\mathcal{P}_j \in \mathcal{P}$ and ticks. It also stops sending beat to $\mathcal{F}_{\mathsf{BC,delay}}^{\Gamma,\Delta}$.

2. Each $\mathcal{P}_i \in \mathcal{P}$ waits until $\mathcal{F}_{\mathsf{com}}^{\Delta,\delta,\varsigma,i}$ returns $(\mathsf{DAdvOpened}, \mathsf{sid}, \mathsf{cid}_i)$. Then $\mathcal{P}_i$ checks if it obtained a message with prefix DOpen from all other $\mathcal{F}_{\mathsf{com}}^{\Delta,\delta,\varsigma,j}$. Let $J_1 \subset \mathcal{P}$ be the set of parties such that $\mathcal{P}_i$ did not obtain DOpen before it received $\mathsf{DAdvOpened}$.

3. Each $\mathcal{P}_i \in \mathcal{P}$ waits until it obtains $(\mathsf{DOpened}, \mathsf{sid}, (\mathsf{cid}_j, (\boldsymbol{y}_j, \boldsymbol{r}_j)))$ for each $\mathcal{P}_j \in \mathcal{P} \setminus (J_1 \cup \{\mathcal{P}_i\})$ from the respective instance of $\mathcal{F}_{\mathsf{com}}^{\Delta,\delta,\varsigma,j}$. It then defines J_2 as the set of all parties $\mathcal{P}_j$ such that $\boldsymbol{t}_j \neq \boldsymbol{r}_j + \mathbf{A}\boldsymbol{y}_j$.

4. If $J_1 \cup J_2 = \emptyset$ then each $\mathcal{P}_i \in \mathcal{P}$ outputs $(\mathsf{Output}, \mathsf{sid}, \boldsymbol{y} = \bigoplus_{j \in [n]} \boldsymbol{y}_j)$ and terminates. Otherwise it outputs $(\mathsf{Abort}, \mathsf{sid}, J_1 \cup J_2)$.

Fig. 16. Protocol $\pi_{\mathsf{mpc,oia}}$ for MPC with Output-Independent Abort.

2. The parties provide inputs x_i to $\mathcal{F}_{\mathsf{mpc,sso}}^{\Delta}$, perform the computation using $\mathcal{F}_{\mathsf{mpc,sso}}^{\Delta}$ and obtain secret shares $\boldsymbol{y}_1, \ldots, \boldsymbol{y}_n$ of the output $\boldsymbol{y}$. They also sample a blinding value $\boldsymbol{r}_i \in \mathbb{F}^\lambda$ for each $\mathcal{P}_i$ inside $\mathcal{F}_{\mathsf{mpc,sso}}^{\Delta}$. $\boldsymbol{y}_i, \boldsymbol{r}_i$ is opened to $\mathcal{P}_i$.

3. Next, the parties commit to both $\boldsymbol{y}_i, \boldsymbol{r}_i$ using $\mathcal{F}_{\mathsf{com}}^{\Delta,\delta,\varsigma}$ towards all parties. Dishonest parties may commit to a different value than the one they obtained from $\mathcal{F}_{\mathsf{mpc,sso}}^{\Delta}$ and consistency must therefore be checked.

4. All parties use the coin-flipping functionality to sample a uniformly random matrix $\mathbf{A} \in \mathbb{F}^{\lambda \times m}$. This matrix is used to perform the consistency check.

5. For each $i \in [n]$ the parties compute and open $\boldsymbol{t}_i = \boldsymbol{r}_i + \mathbf{A}\boldsymbol{y}_i$ using $\mathcal{F}_{\mathsf{mpc,sso}}^{\Delta}$. Due to the blinding value $\boldsymbol{r}_i$ opening $\boldsymbol{t}_i$ will not leak any information about $\boldsymbol{y}_i$ of $\mathcal{P}_i \in \mathcal{P} \setminus I$ to the adversary.

6. Each party that obtained $\boldsymbol{t}_i$ changes the next beat message to ready. Once parties receive ready from all other parties and are thus synchronized, they simultaneously perform a delayed open of $\boldsymbol{y}_i, \boldsymbol{r}_i$ using their commitments (and ignore $\mathcal{F}_{\mathsf{BC,delay}}^{\Gamma,\Delta}$ from now on). Parties which don't open commitments in time or whose opened values do not yield $\boldsymbol{t}_i$ are considered as cheaters.

Intuitively, our construction has output-independent abort because of the timing of the opening: Until Step 6., the adversary may abort at any time but no such abort will provide it with information about the output. Once the opening phase begins, parties can easily verify if an opening by an adversary is valid or not - because he committed to its shares before $\mathbf{A}$ was chosen and the probability of a collision with $\boldsymbol{t}_i$ for different choices of $\boldsymbol{y}_i', \boldsymbol{r}_i'$ can be shown to be negligible in λ as this is exactly the same as finding a collision to a universal hash function. The decision to initiate its opening, on the other hand, will arrive at each honest party before the honest party's delayed opening result is available to the adversary - which will be ensured by the appropriate choice of $\zeta > \Delta$. In turn, an adversary must thus send its opening message before learning the shares of an honest party, which is exactly the property of output-independent abort. At the same time, honest parties have their DOpen message delivered after Δ steps already and will never be identified as cheaters.

Concerning agreement on the output of the honest parties, we see that if all honest parties initially start almost synchronized (i.e. at most Γ ticks apart) then if they do not abort during the protocol they will simultaneously open their commitments. Therefore, using $\mathcal{F}_{\mathsf{BC},\mathsf{delay}}^{\Gamma,\Delta}$ guarantees that they all have the same view of all adversarial messages during the **Reveal** phase.

Interestingly, our construction does not need homomorphic commitments as was necessary in [4,6] to achieve their verifiable or output-independent abort in UC. Clearly, our solution can also be used to improve these protocols and to simplify their constructions. The full protocol can be found in Fig. 15 and Fig. 16. We now prove the following Theorem:

Theorem 6. *Let λ be the statistical security parameter and $\zeta > \Delta$. Assume that all honest parties obtain their inputs at most Γ ticks apart. Then the protocol $\pi_{\mathsf{mpc},\mathsf{oia}}$ GUC-securely implements the ticked functionality $\mathcal{F}_{\mathsf{mpc},\mathsf{oia}}^{\Delta,\delta,\zeta}$ in the $\mathcal{F}_{\mathsf{mpc},\mathsf{sso}}^{\Delta}, \mathcal{F}_{\mathsf{com}}^{\Delta,\delta,\zeta}, \mathcal{F}_{\mathsf{ct}}^{\Delta}, \mathcal{F}_{\mathsf{BC},\mathsf{delay}}^{\Gamma,\Delta}$-hybrid model against any static adversary corrupting up to $n-1$ parties in $\mathcal{P}$. The transcripts are statistically indistinguishable.*

To prove security, we will construct a PPT simulator $\mathcal{S}$ and then argue indistinguishability of the transcripts of $\pi_{\mathsf{mpc},\mathsf{oia}} \circ \mathcal{A}$ and $\mathcal{F}_{\mathsf{mpc},\mathsf{oia}}^{\Delta,\delta,\zeta} \circ \mathcal{S}$. The proof is presented in the full version [5] due to space limitations.

References

1. Andrychowicz, M., Dziembowski, S., Malinowski, D., Mazurek, Ł: Fair two-party computations via bitcoin deposits. In: Böhme, R., Brenner, M., Moore, T., Smith, M. (eds.) FC 2014. LNCS, vol. 8438, pp. 105–121. Springer, Heidelberg (2014). https://doi.org/10.1007/978-3-662-44774-1_8
2. Badertscher, C., Gazi, P., Kiayias, A., Russell, A., Zikas, V.: Ouroboros genesis: composable proof-of-stake blockchains with dynamic availability. In: ACM CCS 2018, Oct. (2018)
3. Badertscher, C., Maurer, U., Tschudi, D., Zikas, V.: Bitcoin as a transaction ledger: a composable treatment. In: Katz, J., Shacham, H. (eds.) CRYPTO 2017. LNCS, vol. 10401, pp. 324–356. Springer, Cham (2017). https://doi.org/10.1007/978-3-319-63688-7_11
4. Baum, C., David, B., Dowsley, R.: Insured MPC: efficient secure computation with financial penalties. In: FC 2020, Feb. (2020)
5. Baum, C., David, B., Dowsley, R., Kishore, R., Nielsen, J.B., Oechsner, S.: Craft: composable randomness beacons and output-independent abort MPC from time. Cryptology ePrint Archive, Paper 2020/784 (2020). https://eprint.iacr.org/2020/784

6. Baum, C., David, B., Dowsley, R., Nielsen, J.B., Oechsner, S.: TARDIS: a foundation of time-lock puzzles in UC. In: Canteaut, A., Standaert, F.-X. (eds.) EUROCRYPT 2021. LNCS, vol. 12698, pp. 429–459. Springer, Cham (2021). https://doi.org/10.1007/978-3-030-77883-5_15
7. Baum, C., Orsini, E., Scholl, P.: Efficient secure multiparty computation with identifiable abort. In: Hirt, M., Smith, A. (eds.) TCC 2016. LNCS, vol. 9985, pp. 461–490. Springer, Heidelberg (2016). https://doi.org/10.1007/978-3-662-53641-4_18
8. Baum, C., Orsini, E., Scholl, P., Soria-Vazquez, E.: Efficient constant-round MPC with identifiable abort and public verifiability. In: Micciancio, D., Ristenpart, T. (eds.) CRYPTO 2020. LNCS, vol. 12171, pp. 562–592. Springer, Cham (2020). https://doi.org/10.1007/978-3-030-56880-1_20
9. Bendlin, R., Damgård, I., Orlandi, C., Zakarias, S.: Semi-homomorphic encryption and multiparty computation. In: Paterson, K.G. (ed.) EUROCRYPT 2011. LNCS, vol. 6632, pp. 169–188. Springer, Heidelberg (2011). https://doi.org/10.1007/978-3-642-20465-4_11
10. Bentov, I., Kumaresan, R.: How to use bitcoin to design fair protocols. In: Garay, J.A., Gennaro, R. (eds.) CRYPTO 2014. LNCS, vol. 8617, pp. 421–439. Springer, Heidelberg (2014). https://doi.org/10.1007/978-3-662-44381-1_24
11. Bitansky, N., Goldwasser, S., Jain, A., Paneth, O., Vaikuntanathan, V., Waters, B.: Time-lock puzzles from randomized encodings. In: ITCS 2016, Jan. (2016)
12. Boneh, D., Bonneau, J., Bünz, B., Fisch, B.: Verifiable delay functions. In: Shacham, H., Boldyreva, A. (eds.) CRYPTO 2018. LNCS, vol. 10991, pp. 757–788. Springer, Cham (2018). https://doi.org/10.1007/978-3-319-96884-1_25
13. Boneh, D., Naor, M.: Timed commitments. In: Bellare, M. (ed.) CRYPTO 2000. LNCS, vol. 1880, pp. 236–254. Springer, Heidelberg (2000). https://doi.org/10.1007/3-540-44598-6_15
14. Canetti, R.: Universally composable security: a new paradigm for cryptographic protocols. In: 42nd FOCS, Oct. (2001)
15. Canetti, R., Dodis, Y., Pass, R., Walfish, S.: Universally composable security with global setup. In: Vadhan, S.P. (ed.) TCC 2007. LNCS, vol. 4392, pp. 61–85. Springer, Heidelberg (2007). https://doi.org/10.1007/978-3-540-70936-7_4
16. Cascudo, I., David, B.: SCRAPE: scalable randomness attested by public entities. In: ACNS 17, July (2017)
17. Cascudo, I., David, B.: ALBATROSS: publicly attestable batched randomness based on secret sharing. In: Moriai, S., Wang, H. (eds.) ASIACRYPT 2020. LNCS, vol. 12493, pp. 311–341. Springer, Cham (2020). https://doi.org/10.1007/978-3-030-64840-4_11
18. Cleve, R.: Limits on the security of coin flips when half the processors are faulty (extended abstract). In: 18th ACM STOC, May (1986)
19. Coan, B.A., Dolev, D., Dwork, C., Stockmeyer, L.J.: The distributed firing squad problem. SIAM J. Comput. 18(5), 990–1012 (1989)
20. Couteau, G., Roscoe, A.W., Ryan, P.Y.A.: Partially-fair computation from timed-release encryption and oblivious transfer. In: ACISP 21, Dec. (2021)
21. David, B., Gaži, P., Kiayias, A., Russell, A.: Ouroboros Praos: an adaptively-secure, semi-synchronous proof-of-stake blockchain. In: Nielsen, J.B., Rijmen, V. (eds.) EUROCRYPT 2018. LNCS, vol. 10821, pp. 66–98. Springer, Cham (2018). https://doi.org/10.1007/978-3-319-78375-8_3

22. De Feo, L., Masson, S., Petit, C., Sanso, A.: Verifiable delay functions from supersingular isogenies and pairings. In: Galbraith, S.D., Moriai, S. (eds.) ASIACRYPT 2019. LNCS, vol. 11921, pp. 248–277. Springer, Cham (2019). https://doi.org/10.1007/978-3-030-34578-5_10

23. Dolev, D., Reischuk, R., Strong, H.R.: Early stopping in byzantine agreement. J. ACM **37**(4), 720–741 (1990)

24. Dolev, D., Strong, H.R.: Polynomial algorithms for multiple processor agreement. In: Proceedings of the 14th Annual ACM Symposium on Theory of Computing, pp. 401–407. ACM (1982)

25. Ephraim, N., Freitag, C., Komargodski, I., Pass, R.: Continuous verifiable delay functions. In: Canteaut, A., Ishai, Y. (eds.) EUROCRYPT 2020. LNCS, vol. 12107, pp. 125–154. Springer, Cham (2020). https://doi.org/10.1007/978-3-030-45727-3_5

26. Freitag, C., Komargodski, I., Pass, R., Sirkin, N.: Non-malleable time-lock puzzles and applications. In: Nissim, K., Waters, B. (eds.) TCC 2021. LNCS, vol. 13044, pp. 447–479. Springer, Cham (2021). https://doi.org/10.1007/978-3-030-90456-2_15

27. Garay, J., MacKenzie, P., Prabhakaran, M., Yang, K.: Resource fairness and composability of cryptographic protocols. In: Halevi, S., Rabin, T. (eds.) TCC 2006. LNCS, vol. 3876, pp. 404–428. Springer, Heidelberg (2006). https://doi.org/10.1007/11681878_21

28. Gordon, S.D., Katz, J.: Partial fairness in secure two-party computation. J. Crypt. (1), Jan. (2012)

29. Hazay, C., Scholl, P., Soria-Vazquez, E.: Low cost constant round MPC combining BMR and oblivious transfer. In: Takagi, T., Peyrin, T. (eds.) ASIACRYPT 2017. LNCS, vol. 10624, pp. 598–628. Springer, Cham (2017). https://doi.org/10.1007/978-3-319-70694-8_21

30. Ishai, Y., Ostrovsky, R., Zikas, V.: Secure multi-party computation with identifiable abort. In: Garay, J.A., Gennaro, R. (eds.) CRYPTO 2014. LNCS, vol. 8617, pp. 369–386. Springer, Heidelberg (2014). https://doi.org/10.1007/978-3-662-44381-1_21

31. Katz, J., Loss, J., Xu, J.: On the security of time-lock puzzles and timed commitments. In: Pass, R., Pietrzak, K. (eds.) TCC 2020. LNCS, vol. 12552, pp. 390–413. Springer, Cham (2020). https://doi.org/10.1007/978-3-030-64381-2_14

32. Katz, J., Maurer, U., Tackmann, B., Zikas, V.: Universally composable synchronous computation. In: Sahai, A. (ed.) TCC 2013. LNCS, vol. 7785, pp. 477–498. Springer, Heidelberg (2013). https://doi.org/10.1007/978-3-642-36594-2_27

33. Kiayias, A., Russell, A., David, B., Oliynykov, R.: Ouroboros: a provably secure proof-of-stake blockchain protocol. In: Katz, J., Shacham, H. (eds.) CRYPTO 2017. LNCS, vol. 10401, pp. 357–388. Springer, Cham (2017). https://doi.org/10.1007/978-3-319-63688-7_12

34. Kiayias, A., Zhou, H.-S., Zikas, V.: Fair and robust multi-party computation using a global transaction ledger. In: Fischlin, M., Coron, J.-S. (eds.) EUROCRYPT 2016. LNCS, vol. 9666, pp. 705–734. Springer, Heidelberg (2016). https://doi.org/10.1007/978-3-662-49896-5_25

35. Kumaresan, R., Bentov, I.: How to use bitcoin to incentivize correct computations. In: ACM CCS 2014, Nov. (2014)

36. Kushilevitz, E., Lindell, Y., Rabin, T.: Information-theoretically secure protocols and security under composition. In: 38th ACM STOC, May (2006)

37. Lindell, Y., Lysyanskaya, A., Rabin, T.: Sequential composition of protocols without simultaneous termination. In: Ricciardi, A., editor, PODC 2002 (2002)

38. Pietrzak, K.: Simple verifiable delay functions. In: ITCS 2019, Jan. (2019)
39. Rivest, R.L., Shamir, A., Wagner, D.A.: Time-lock puzzles and timed-release crypto (1996)
40. VDF Alliance Team. Vdf alliance (2020). https://www.vdfalliance.org/what-we-do
41. Wesolowski, B.: Efficient verifiable delay functions. In: Ishai, Y., Rijmen, V. (eds.) EUROCRYPT 2019. LNCS, vol. 11478, pp. 379–407. Springer, Cham (2019). https://doi.org/10.1007/978-3-030-17659-4_13

Efficient and Universally Composable Single Secret Leader Election from Pairings

Dario Catalano[1], Dario Fiore[2], and Emanuele Giunta[2,3,4(✉)]

[1] Università di Catania, Catania, Italy
catalano@dmi.unict.it
[2] IMDEA Software Institute, Madrid, Spain
{dario.fiore,emanuele.giunta}@imdea.org
[3] Universidad Politecnica de Madrid, Madrid, Spain
[4] Scuola Superiore di Catania, Catania, Italy

Abstract. Single Secret Leader Election (SSLE) protocols allow a set of users to elect a leader among them so that the identity of the winner remains secret until she decides to reveal herself. This notion was formalized and implemented in a recent result by Boneh, *et al.* (ACM Advances on Financial Technology 2020) and finds important applications in the area of Proof of Stake blockchains.

In this paper we put forward new SSLE solutions that advance the state of the art both from a theoretical and a practical front. On the theoretical side we propose a new definition of SSLE in the universal composability framework. We believe this to be the right way to model security in highly concurrent contexts such as those of many blockchain related applications. Next, we propose a UC-realization of SSLE from public key encryption with keyword search (PEKS) and based on the ability of distributing the PEKS key generation and encryption algorithms. Finally, we give a concrete PEKS scheme with efficient distributed algorithms for key generation and encryption and that allows us to efficiently instantiate our abstract SSLE construction.

Our resulting SSLE protocol is very efficient, does not require participants to store any state information besides their secret keys and guarantees so called *on-chain efficiency*: the information to verify an election in the new block should be of size at most logarithmic in the number of participants. To the best of our knowledge, this is the first efficient SSLE scheme achieving this property.

1 Introduction

Leader Election protocols are of fundamental importance to realize consensus in distributed systems. The rise of blockchain and its numerous applications brought renewed interest on this topic and motivated the need to consider consensus protocols that also provide some secrecy guarantees. This is the case, for example, of leader elections in the context of Proof of Stake blockchains (e.g., [AMM18, GHM+17, KKKZ19, GOT19]) where one may wish to randomly select

© International Association for Cryptologic Research 2023
A. Boldyreva and V. Kolesnikov (Eds.): PKC 2023, LNCS 13940, pp. 471–499, 2023.
https://doi.org/10.1007/978-3-031-31368-4_17

a *secret* leader, i.e., a leader that remains hidden until she reveals herself. In these contexts, leader-secrecy allows to protect against several attacks that would otherwise compromise the liveness of the blockchain. Indeed, if a malicious party could know the identity of a future leader, he could try to deny the leader's access to the network (using a denial of service attack, for instance) before the latter publishes her block, and this would affect, at least temporarily, the liveness and finality of the system. Bribery attacks could also be carried out with ease in order to influence the set of transactions that are going to be published.

Many existing solutions address this issue by secretly selecting a few potential leaders in *expectation* (e.g. [BGM16,BPS16]). This means that, for every given round, on expectation a single block leader is elected. Unfortunately, however, this also means that even many (or zero) leaders may be elected in any round.

This state of affairs led to the quest for an election protocol that secretly produces a *single* leader [Lab19], i.e., where *exactly* one single candidate is able to prove that she won the election. In principle this problem could be solved using general multiparty computation. What make such an approach problematic are however the efficiency requirements desired in a blockchain context. In particular, beyond being computationally efficient, the protocol should guarantee low communication complexity (i.e. the total number of exchanged messages should scale with $O(N)$ or better, where N is the number of miners/users), and more importantly it should be *on-chain efficient*: the amount of bits to store on chain, per new block, should be small (ideally logarithmic in N).

The question of finding such an election protocol was formally addressed in a recent work of Boneh *et al.* [BEHG20] who put forward the notion of *Single Secret Leader Election* (SSLE, from now on). Informally, an SSLE scheme is a distributed protocol that secretly elects a leader and satisfies *uniqueness* (at most one leader is elected), *fairness* (all participants have the same probability of becoming the leader) and *unpredictability* (if the adversary does not win the election, she should not be able to guess the leader better than at random). Boneh *et al.* [BEHG20] also proposed three constructions meeting this notion that are based on different approaches and that achieve different efficiency (and security) tradeoffs (cf. Table 1 for a summary).

Their first SSLE scheme relies on indistinguishability obfuscation (iO) [GGH+13] and its main advantage is to achieve the lowest communication complexity and on-chain efficiency; indeed every election involves a single constant-size message from the winner. At the same time, given the status of iO realizations, this SSLE protocol is of very limited (if any) practical interest.

The second construction in [BEHG20] builds on Threshold Fully homomorphic Encryption (TFHE) [BGG+18] and is asymptotically less efficient than the iO-based one: every election needs $O(t)$ communication (where t is a bound on the number of malicious users tolerated by the system) to partially decrypt a publicly computable ciphertext; after this round of communication, the winner can prove her victory. A nice aspect of the TFHE-based solution is that it actually requires only a *leveled* scheme for circuits that for, say, $N = 2^{16}$ participants, can be of depth as little as 10. However, other aspects of this solution make it far from practical. First, it is not on-chain efficient: to make the election verifiable, $O(t)$ bits of information must be stored in the new block (unless one applies a transformation through a general-purpose SNARK proof that t valid partial decryptions exist). Second, it requires large $O(N \log N)$ secret key shares, and no concrete distributed setup (for the TFHE scheme) is explicitly provided in [BGG+18]. So to the best of our knowledge one would have to rely on general multiparty computation techniques to achieve it.

The third SSLE construction in [BEHG20] is based on shuffling and the decisional Diffie-Hellman assumption. Asymptotically, it performs worse than the other two solutions: every new election requires to communicate and store in the new block a freshly shuffled list of N Diffie-Hellman pairs[1] (along with a NIZK of shuffle). Notice that this makes the solution inherently not on-chain efficient. The authors also describe a lightweight variant whose communication costs are $O(\sqrt{N})$, but the tradeoff here is a scheme with significantly lower security guarantees, as the secret leader is selected in a public subset of only $\sqrt{N}$ users.

We note also that both the iO and TFHE-based SSLE protocols need a trusted setup. The latter must be realized with a distributed protocol and should be in principle refreshed when new users join the system. On the other hand, the shuffle-based solution is essentially setup-free and thus can handle more easily users that join and leave the system dynamically.

Beyond efficiency considerations, another fundamental limitation of the constructions above is that they are proved secure with respect to a (stand-alone) game-based definition which makes their actual security in concurrent settings unclear. This is problematic in practice as it is hardly the case that distributed consensus protocols are executed stand-alone.

Given this state of affairs, the main question that motivates our work is:
is it possible to build an SSLE protocol that is on-chain efficient and achieves good practical performances while also realizing strong composability guarantees?

1.1 Our Contribution

In this paper we propose a new SSLE solution that answers the above question in the affirmative. Our first contribution is the proposal of a new definition of SSLE in the universal composability model [Can01] (see Sect. 3). We believe this to be the right notion to model security in the highly distributed, often concurrent, blockchain-like applications where electing a leader is required. Our new definition implies the game-based definition of Boneh *et al.* [BEHG20], but the converse is not true.

As a second contribution, we propose a UC-secure construction of SSLE. In particular, we give a generic protocol based on public key encryption with keyword search (PEKS) [BDOP04], and then propose an efficient instantiation of it based on pairings under the SXDH assumption. The latter is our main technical

---

[1] Precisely, when the winner no longer wants to participate in future elections, there is no need to shuffle for the next election; we ignore this special case in our analysis.

Table 1. Comparison between the SSLE solutions from [BEHG20] and the SSLE of this work. 'On-chain' refers to the amount of information to be stored on chain in the new block after every election. Shuffle-$\sqrt{N}$ achieves a weak unpredictability notion. Everywhere, in $O(\cdot)$ we include the fixed security parameter λ. κ is a statistical security parameter that gives meaningful security for $\kappa = \log N$.

SSLE	Security model	Election efficiency		
		Rounds	Comm.	On-chain
iO	Game-based	0	$O(1)$	$O(1)$
TFHE	Game-based	1	$O(t)$	$O(t)$
Shuffle-N	Game-based	1	$O(N)$	$O(N)$
Shuffle-$\sqrt{N}$	Game-based	1	$O(\sqrt{N})$	$O(\sqrt{N})$
Ours	UC	$1+1$	$O(t)$	$O(\kappa \log N)$

contribution: it is a protocol that achieves the same (asymptotic) communication complexity as the TFHE-based solution from [BEHG20] while achieving, in addition, on-chain efficiency and much better practical performance. We refer to Table 1 for a comparison between ours and the previous solutions and to the next section for an overview of our protocol. We note that, although our protocol requires a total of 2 rounds of communication to prepare an election, the first round can actually be executed in a preprocessing phase and shared to prepare many elections, thus making the online rounds effectively 1, as in the other solutions. Moreover, the protocol *does not* require parties to keep any state across rounds of communication, besides their secret keys.

An Overview of Our SSLE Protocol. Let us describe our protocol and its efficiency in slightly more detail. PEKS is a notion of functional encryption [BSW11, O'N10] in which given a ciphertext c encrypting a keyword w and secret key sk associated to another keyword w', the decryption allows one to learn if $w = w'$ and nothing more. Our SSLE protocol is based on the following simple idea. For every election a small subset of users generates a ciphertext c that encrypts a random keyword $j \in \{0, \dots, N-1\}$. At registration time, each user is given a secret key sk_i associated to an integer i, and can claim victory by giving a NIZK proof that she can decrypt the election's ciphertext.

More specifically, our protocol consists of two phases: (1) a setup (done rarely) in which the users run an MPC protocol to generate the public key of the PEKS and distribute its secret keys, (2) an election's procedure in which a randomly sampled committee of κ players generates a commitment to the election's ciphertext in a distributed way. The commitment is then opened in a distributed way. Whoever knows a secret key that decrypts the ciphertext is the leader.

We formalize this approach in a generic SSLE protocol that we prove UC-secure assuming ideal functionalities for the setup and encryption algorithms of any PEKS (see Sect. 4). Our main technical contribution, however is to design an efficient instantiation of this blueprint, by showing an "MPC-friendly" PEKS and by proposing very efficient (distributed) protocols for the setup and election phases. To devise such a PEKS we build on (a modified variant of) the functional encryption for orthogonality (OFE) scheme recently proposed by Wee [Wee17]. Furthermore we extend this functionality to test keywords equality mod N albeit the message space is over a large field $\mathbb{F}_q$. We refer to this new primitive as *modular PEKS*.

Informally, the committed ciphertexts created in the election procedure are (plain) El Gamal encryptions of Wee's ciphertexts. An immediate advantage of this approach is that it allows for a very efficient setup procedure: it merely consists in a threshold key generation for El Gamal followed by the key generation for the functional encryption scheme. When relying on a publicly available random beacon, we show that the latter can be realized efficiently in two rounds of communication, one of which only used to perform complaints.

More interestingly, however, our proposed scheme allows to complete step (2) efficiently both in terms of computation and communication. Indeed, our protocol manages to distributively create valid (committed) ciphertexts c (encrypting messages uniformly distributed in a given range) in one single round of communication! Moreover, this round of communication can be used to generate, in parallel, as many committed ciphertexts as one wishes, one for every future election. This way, the communication needed to perform an election effectively consists of only one round of communication in which $O(t)$ parties send their partial opening of the election's ciphertext.

We note that the naïve approach of posting all these $O(t)$ partial openings in the blockchain would destroy our claimed on-chain efficiency guarantees. Interestingly, we can do better than this. Parties can exchange the $O(t)$ partial openings off-chain and store on-chain only much shorter aggregate values that still enable anyone to verify the correctness of the election. Recall that opening our committed ciphertexts consists in, distributively, decrypting corresponding El Gamal ciphertexts. Simplifying things a bit, in our case this is achieved by letting players exchange partial decryption shares $(K_{1,i}, K_{2,i})$ together with corresponding NIZKs. These shares are then (locally) multiplied together to get values (K_1, K_2) that can be used to retrieve the encrypted ciphertext c. Whoever is able to decrypt c correctly can then claim victory. Concretely, in our protocol, a user can claim victory by posting on the blockchain only (K_1, K_2), together with a proof that she can correctly decrypt c. Surprisingly, we show that a potentially expensive aggregated NIZK proving correctness of (K_1, K_2) is not needed for our protocol to be secure, as we prove that coming up with different (K_1', K_2') which open the ElGamal commitment to another $c' \neq c$ that an adversary is able to decrypt, implies being able to break the underlying functional encryption scheme.

Concrete Efficiency and Comparison to Previous Solutions. To confirm the concrete performances of our protocol we measure them for $N = 2^{14}$ users, as suggested in [Lab19]. Our results show that the communication costs of an election are 34.0 KB to generate the committed election's ciphertext, 1.57 MB for the partial decryptions, and 256 B to claim victory. Importantly, out of all this information, only 34.3 KB per election have to be stored on-chain for verifiability.

The major cost in our protocol is that of setup, which for 2^{14} users would amount to 252 MB. This setup, however, is supposed to be performed rarely[2]. Indeed, in our protocol we can add new users to the system without running a full setup: they engage in a registration procedure that allows them to receive their secret keys, without altering the key material of other users. This can be done with only 73 KB of communication per registration. If we compare to the shuffle-N solution of Boneh et al. [BEHG20], our protocol can easily amortize the expensive setup and results in less communication. In the shuffle-N solution, the issue is that every time a new user is added (which always includes the winner of the previous election if he still wants to run) a new shuffle has to be communicated and posted on-chain: this is about 1 MB per shuffle for 2^{14} users. Concretely, if we assume 50 new users join before every election,[3] after 100 elections the shuffle-N scheme generates 6.2 GB to be communicated and stored on-chain, whereas our protocol involves 1.8 GB of off-chain communication and only 5.9 MB of on-chain storage.

Our Election Protocol More in Detail. At the heart of our protocol there is a very efficient method to generate committed ciphertexts of the form discussed above. Here we informally highlight the main ideas underlying this construction. Recall that we build our PEKS from a tailored variant of the functional encryption for orthogonality (OFE) scheme recently proposed by Wee [Wee17]. In OFE a ciphertext is associated to a vector $\mathbf{x}$, a secret key corresponds to a vector $\mathbf{y}$ and decryption allows one to learn if $\mathbf{y}^\top \mathbf{x} = 0$. The basic idea of our (modular) PEKS from OFE is inspired to a transformation from [KSW08] with a novel tweak.

In what follows, to keep the presentation intuitive, we present a simplified version of our methods that, in particular, supports vectors of dimension 2 (rather than 3 as in our actual scheme) and only allows to test equality of keywords (rather than equality mod N).

During setup, each party P_i receives a public and secret key $\mathsf{mpk}, \mathsf{sk}_i$ of the OFE scheme, where sk_i is associated to the vector $(1, i)$. If there were a magic way to directly produce an encryption c of $(m, -1)$ such that m is uniform over $[N]$ (and no user gains any extra information on m), then, using $\mathsf{FE.Dec}$, each party could test if $m = i$ by simply checking whether $(m, -1)^\top (1, i) = 0$. Clearly the only user able to do this could then claim victory. Unfortunately, since no such wizardry is currently known, we go for the next best option: we develop a very fast, one round protocol to jointly produce a *commitment* of such a c[4]. The commitment is just a (standard) El Gamal encryption of c that can be (distributively) opened in one round of communication.

---

[2] As in the TFHE solution, our protocol in practice requires periodic setup to refresh the secrets shared when many new users join (see Sect. 6 for a discussion on this).

[3] This number is justified by [Lab19], where $O(\log^2 N)$ new users are expected.

[4] We stress here that no efficient single round solution to directly produce c seems possible because of rushing attacks.

In this informal presentation, we explain how to generate the (committed) ciphertext, in the simpler case where m is allowed to lie in the slightly larger interval $[\kappa N]$. Our underlying ciphertexts have the following shape[5]

$$\mathbf{c}_0 = [s\mathbf{a}]_1 , \quad c_1 = [m\sigma + s\mathbf{a}^\top \mathbf{w}_1]_1 , \quad c_2 = [-\sigma + s\mathbf{a}^\top \mathbf{w}_2]_1 .$$

where $[\mathbf{a}]_1 , [\mathbf{a}^\top \mathbf{w}_1]_1 , [\mathbf{a}^\top \mathbf{w}_2]_1$ are public key elements and s, σ are random values.[6] Using the random beacon, we begin by generating a (small) election committee $Q \subseteq [N]$ of size κ and two (random) group elements G, H that can be interpreted as an ElGamal encryption of $[\sigma]_1$ in the following way

$$G = g^\theta, \qquad H = h^\theta [\sigma]_1$$

where (g, h) is the El Gamal public key and θ, σ are random and unknown to participants. Using this public information, each player $P_i \in Q$ can create (committed) encryptions of m_i by simply choosing random $r_i, \rho_i, s_i,$ and $m_i \in [N]$ and broadcasting $[s_i\mathbf{a}]_1$ together with

$$G^{m_i} \cdot g^{r_i} = g^{\theta m_i + r_i} \quad H^{m_i} \cdot h^{r_i} \cdot [s_i\mathbf{a}^\top \mathbf{w}_1]_1 = h^{\theta m_i + r_i} [m_i\sigma + s_i\mathbf{a}^\top \mathbf{w}_1]_1$$

$$G^{-1} \cdot g^{\rho_i} = g^{\rho_i - \theta} \quad H^{-1} \cdot h^{\rho_i} \cdot [s_i\mathbf{a}^\top \mathbf{w}_2]_1 = h^{\rho_i - \theta} [-\sigma + s_i\mathbf{a}^\top \mathbf{w}_2]_1$$

All these (committed) ciphertexts share the same randomness σ and can thus be multiplied together to produce the final (committed) ciphertext of the vector $(m = \sum_{i \in Q} m_i, -1)$. Note that the message m lies in the larger interval $[\kappa N]$ but $m \bmod N$ is uniform over $[N]$ as long as so is at least one of the m_i's. Finally, as mentioned earlier, our actual realization (cf. Section 2.5) works around this issue by managing to test equalities modulo N.

1.2 Other Related Work

Recently, the importance of SSLE solutions was confirmed by a study by Azouvi and Cappelletti [AC21]. Their analysis shows substantial security gains (when compared to probabilistic election schemes) both when considering the private attack (the worst attack on longest-chain protocols [DKT+20]) and grinding attacks. The problem of extending proof of stake systems to consider privacy was considered, among others, in [GOT19] and in [KKKZ19]. Leader election protocols were also considered by Algorand [GHM+17] and Fantomette [AMM18]. There the idea is to first identify few potential leaders (via a VRF) that then reveal themselves in order and choose the winner via some simple tie break method (e.g. lowest VRF output wins). The approach is efficient but has the drawback that the elected leader does not know she was elected until everybody else published their value. Moreover, implicitly requires all nodes to be able to see the winner's output: users not getting this information might incorrectly think that another leader was elected (causing the chain to fork). We stress that this cannot happen in our setting.

---

[5] For clarity note that group operations are denoted multiplicatively, and that we make use of the bracket notation, cf. Section 2.1.

[6] In Wee's scheme $\sigma = s\mathbf{a}^\top \mathbf{u}$, with $[\mathbf{a}^\top \mathbf{u}]_1$ being an extra element of the public key.

1.3 Organization

In the next section we start by introducing notation, computational assumptions and cryptographic primitives used by our schemes. There we also recall the game-based definition of SSLE from [BEHG20]. Next, in Sect. 3 we give our definition of SSLE in the universal composability framework. Section 5 includes our main contribution, that is our efficient SSLE protocol from the SXDH assumption (the generic SSLE construction from PEKS is given in Sect. 4). Finally, in Sect. 6 we discuss the efficiency of our protocol in a realistic scenario and compare it with the SSLE based on shuffles by Boneh et al. [BEHG20].

2 Preliminaries

2.1 Notation

$\lambda \in \mathbb{N}$ denotes the security parameter. A function $\varepsilon(\lambda)$ is said *negligible in* λ if it vanishes faster than the inverse of any polynomial in λ. $[n] = \{0, \ldots, n-1\}$. Bold font $(\mathbf{a}, \mathbf{u}, \mathbf{w}, \ldots)$ denotes vectors with entries in a given field or a group. $x \xleftarrow{\$} S$ means that x is sampled uniformly and with fresh randomness from S. N is the number of players and t the threshold parameter.

We denote with $\mathcal{G}(\lambda)$ a *bilinear group generator*, that is an algorithm which returns the description of a bilinear group $\mathsf{bg} = (q, \mathbb{G}_1, \mathbb{G}_2, \mathbb{G}_T, e, g_1, g_2)$, where $\mathbb{G}_1$, $\mathbb{G}_2$ and $\mathbb{G}_T$ are groups of the same prime order $q > 2^\lambda$, $g_1 \in \mathbb{G}_1$ and $g_2 \in \mathbb{G}_2$ are two generators, and $e : \mathbb{G}_1 \times \mathbb{G}_2 \to \mathbb{G}_T$ is an efficiently computable, non-degenerate, bilinear map. We use $g_T = e(g_1, g_2)$ as a canonical generator of $\mathbb{G}_T$. When $\mathbb{G}_1 = \mathbb{G}_2$, the groups are called *symmetric*; otherwise they are called *asymmetric*. In our work we use Type-III *asymmetric* bilinear groups [GPS08] where no efficiently computable isomorphism between $\mathbb{G}_1$ and $\mathbb{G}_2$ is known.

$\mathbb{F}_q$ is the finite field of prime cardinality q. Given a vector $\mathbf{a} = (a_i)_{i=1}^n \in \mathbb{F}_q^n$ and a group element g we denote $[\mathbf{a}]_g = (g^{a_1}, \ldots, g^{a_n})$. When the base is g_1, g_2 or g_T we replace the above notation with $[\mathbf{a}]_1$, $[\mathbf{a}]_2$ and $[\mathbf{a}]_T$ respectively. Operations with vectors in $\mathbb{G}^n$ are entry-wise, i.e., for $\mathbf{g}, \mathbf{h} \in \mathbb{G}^n$, $\mathbf{g} \cdot \mathbf{h} = (g_i \cdot h_i)_{i=1}^n$, $\mathbf{g}^a = (g_i^a)_{i=1}^n$. Pairings are the only exception where $e(\mathbf{g}, \mathbf{h}) = e(g_1, h_1) \cdot \ldots \cdot e(g_n, h_n)$ for $\mathbf{g} \in \mathbb{G}_1^n$ and $\mathbf{h} \in \mathbb{G}_2^n$. Similarly $\mathbf{g}^{\mathbf{a}} = g_1^{a_1} \cdot \ldots \cdot g_n^{a_n}$.

2.2 SXDH Assumption

Our efficient construction relies on the SXDH assumption in bilinear groups, which informally states that the classical DDH assumption holds in both $\mathbb{G}_1$ and $\mathbb{G}_2$. More formally,

Definition 1 (SXDH assumption). *Let $\mathcal{G}$ be a bilinear group generator. We say that the SXDH assumption holds for $\mathcal{G}$ if for every PPT adversary $\mathcal{A}$, and every $s \in \{1, 2\}$ there exists a negligible function ε such that:*

$$\left| \Pr\left[\mathcal{A}(\mathsf{bg}, [a]_s, [b]_s, [c]_s) = 1 \right] - \Pr\left[\mathcal{A}(\mathsf{bg}, [a]_s, [b]_s, [ab]_s) = 1 \right] \right| \leq \varepsilon(\lambda)$$

where the probabilities are over the random choice of $a, b, c \xleftarrow{\$} \mathbb{F}_q$ and $\mathsf{bg} = (q, \mathbb{G}_1, \mathbb{G}_2, \mathbb{G}_T, g_1, g_2) \xleftarrow{\$} \mathcal{G}(1^\lambda)$.

When the above assumption is considered in only one group $\mathbb{G}_s$, for either $s = 1$ or $s = 2$, we refer to it as DDH in $\mathbb{G}_s$. We call DDH^0 a game in which $\mathcal{A}$ received the first distribution and DDH^1 a game in which he receives the second one.

In the paper we also use an extension of DDH for vectors of n elements, called DDH_n, which says it is hard to distinguish $([a_1]_s, \ldots, [a_n]_s, [b]_s, [c_1]_s, \ldots, [c_n]_s)$, denoted as DDH_n^0, from $([a_1]_s, \ldots, [a_n]_s, [b]_s, [a_1 b]_s, \ldots, [a_n b]_s)$ denoted as DDH_n^1, for random $a_i, b, c_i \in \mathbb{F}_q$. We note that DDH_n can be reduced to DDH in the same group [NR97].

2.3   Functional Encryption

We recall the definition of Functional Encryption [BSW11,O'N10].

Definition 2. *A* functionality F *is a family of functions* $\mathsf{F} = \{f : \mathcal{X} \to \mathcal{Y}\}$, *where* $\mathcal{X}$ *is the plaintext space and* $\mathcal{Y}$ *is the output space.*

Definition 3. *A **functional encryption scheme** for a functionality* F *is a tuple* (FE.Setup, FE.Enc, FE.KeyGen, FE.Dec) *of* PPT *algorithms such that*

- FE.Setup$(1^\lambda) \xrightarrow{\$} (\mathsf{mpk}, \mathsf{msk})$ *generates the secret and public master keys.*
- FE.Enc$(m, \mathsf{mpk}; r) \to c$ *returns a ciphertext. Randomness* r *may be omitted.*
- FE.KeyGen$(f, \mathsf{msk}) \xrightarrow{\$} \mathsf{sk}_f$ *returns a key associated to the function* $f \in \mathsf{F}$.
- FE.Dec$(c, f, \mathsf{mpk}, \mathsf{sk}_f) \to x$ *a bit string.*

*The scheme is **correct** if for any* $m \in \mathcal{X}$ *and* $f \in \mathsf{F}$, *sampled* $\mathsf{mpk}, \mathsf{msk} \xleftarrow{\$}$ FE.Setup(1^λ), $c \xleftarrow{\$}$ FE.Enc(m, mpk), $\mathsf{sk}_f \xleftarrow{\$}$ FE.KeyGen(f, msk), *then up to negligible probability* FE.Dec$(c, f, \mathsf{mpk}, \mathsf{sk}_f) = f(m)$.

We recall the notion of selectively secure FE, which suffices for our goals.

Definition 4. *A functional encryption scheme achieves **selective security** if for any* PPT *algorithm* $\mathcal{A}$ *there exists a negligible function* ε *such that*

$$\mathsf{Adv}_{\mathsf{SSFE}}^{\mathcal{A}}(1^\lambda) = \left| \Pr\left[\mathsf{Exp}_{\mathsf{SSFE}}^{\mathcal{A}}(1^\lambda) = 1 \right] - \frac{1}{2} \right| \leq \varepsilon(\lambda).$$

2.4   Functional Encryption for Modular Keyword Search

Recall that the keyword search functionality [BDOP04,ABC+05] is defined as $\mathsf{F}_{\mathsf{ks}} = \{f_y : \mathcal{X} \to \{0,1\}\}$, where each function $f_y \in \mathsf{F}_{\mathsf{ks}}$ labelled by $y \in \mathcal{X}$ is such that $f_y(x)$ returns 1 if $x = y$ and 0 otherwise. Our realization works with a generalisation of the above where equality are checked modulo a given integer. Formally we consider the modular keyword search functionality $\mathsf{F}_{\mathsf{mks}}^{\kappa} = \{f_y : \mathbb{F}_q \times \mathbb{F}_q \to \{0,1\}\}$ parametrized by a positive integer κ of polynomial size, where each function f_y labelled by $y \in \mathbb{F}_q$ are such that $f_y(x, n)$ returns 1 if $x = y + \delta n$ for some $\delta \in [\kappa]$, and 0 otherwise. Observe that when $y \in [n]$ and $x \in [\kappa n]$, then $f_y(x, n) = 1$ if and only if $x = y \mod n$.

Selective Security Game $\mathsf{Exp}^{\mathcal{A}}_{\mathsf{SSFE}}(1^\lambda)$:

1 : $m_0, m_1 \leftarrow^{\$} \mathcal{A}$
2 : Sample $b \leftarrow^{\$} \{0,1\}$, $\mathsf{mpk}, \mathsf{msk} \leftarrow^{\$} \mathsf{FE.Setup}(1^\lambda)$, $c \leftarrow^{\$} \mathsf{FE.Enc}(m_b, \mathsf{mpk})$
3 : Send $\mathcal{A} \leftarrow \mathsf{mpk}, c$
4 : **When** $\mathcal{A}$ queries $f \in \mathsf{F}$, if $f(m_0) \neq f(m_1)$ then $\mathcal{A} \leftarrow \perp$. Otherwise:
5 : Compute $\mathsf{sk}_f \leftarrow^{\$} \mathsf{FE.KeyGen}(f, \mathsf{msk})$ and send $\mathcal{A} \leftarrow \mathsf{sk}_f$
6 : **When** $\mathcal{A} \rightarrow b'$: Return $b == b'$

Fig. 1. Selective security game for a FE scheme with functionality F

2.5 Our Realization of FE for Modular Keyword Search

We realize our FE scheme for the keyword search functionality $\mathsf{F}^{\kappa}_{\mathsf{mks}}$ through a more powerful scheme for the so-called *orthogonality* functionality [KSW08]. In the latter we have the message space $\mathcal{X} = \mathbb{F}_q^n$ and each function $f_{\mathbf{y}}$, defined by a vector $\mathbf{y} \in \mathbb{F}_q^n$, is such that $f_{\mathbf{y}}(\mathbf{x})$ returns 1 when $\mathbf{y}^\top \mathbf{x} = 0$ and 0 otherwise.

A general construction of FE for F_{ks} from an OFE scheme already appears in previous work [KSW08]. In this paper, we tweak that template in order to support the $\mathsf{F}^{\kappa}_{\mathsf{mks}}$ described earlier (see Fig. 2). The idea is that $m = \gamma + \delta n$ if and only if $(m, -1, -n)^\top (1, \gamma, \delta)$ for some $\delta \in [\kappa]$. Therefore, using an OFE scheme with dimension 3, a ciphertext for m and n is an encryption of the vector $\mathbf{x}_{m,n} = (m, -1, -n)$, while a key for γ is a collection of keys for the vectors $\mathbf{y}_{\gamma,\delta} = (1, \gamma, \delta)$, with $\delta \in [\kappa]$. This way, decryption can be realized by testing if one of the keys successfully decrypts.

$\mathsf{MKS.Setup}(1^\lambda)$:

$(\mathsf{mpk}', \mathsf{msk}') \leftarrow^{\$} \mathsf{FE.Setup}(1^\lambda, 3)$
Return $\mathsf{mpk}', \mathsf{msk}'$

$\mathsf{MKS.Enc}(m, n, \mathsf{mpk})$:

$\mathbf{x}_{m,n} \leftarrow (m, -1, -n)$
Return $c \leftarrow^{\$} \mathsf{FE.Enc}(\mathbf{x}_{m,n}, \mathsf{mpk})$

$\mathsf{MKS.KeyGen}(\gamma, \mathsf{msk})$:

For $\delta \in [\kappa]$:
$\mathsf{sk}_{\gamma,\delta} \leftarrow^{\$} \mathsf{FE.KeyGen}((1, y, \delta), \mathsf{msk})$
Return $\mathsf{sk}_\gamma \leftarrow (\mathsf{sk}_{\gamma,0}, \ldots, \mathsf{sk}_{,\gamma,\kappa-1})$

$\mathsf{MKS.Dec}(c, y, \mathsf{mpk}, \mathsf{sk}_y)$:

Set $\mathbf{y}_{\gamma,\delta} \leftarrow (1, \gamma, \delta)$ for all $\delta \in [\kappa]$
If $\exists \delta \in [\kappa]$: $\mathsf{FE.Dec}(c, \mathbf{y}_{\gamma,\delta}, \mathsf{mpk}, \mathsf{sk}_{\gamma,\delta}) = 1$
Return 1. **Else Return** 0

Fig. 2. Our FE for $\mathsf{F}^{\kappa}_{\mathsf{mks}}$ from and orthogonality functional encryption scheme

Note however that the resulting construction is secure under the weaker notion in which the adversary, who initially queries an encryption of (m_0, n_0) and (m_1, n_1), can only ask secret keys for keywords γ such that $\gamma \neq m_0 + \delta n_0$ and $\gamma \neq m_1 + \delta n_1$ for all $\delta \in [\kappa]$. This restriction (often referred to as weak

FE.Setup$(1^\lambda, n)$:	FE.KeyGen$(\mathbf{y}, \mathsf{msk})$:
Sample $\mathbf{a}, \mathbf{w}_1, \ldots, \mathbf{w}_n \xleftarrow{\$} \mathbb{F}_q^2$	$r \xleftarrow{\$} \mathbb{F}_q \setminus \{0\}$
$\mathsf{mpk} \leftarrow \left([\mathbf{a}]_1, [\mathbf{a}^\top \mathbf{w}_1]_1, \ldots, [\mathbf{a}^\top \mathbf{w}_n]_1\right)$	$\textbf{Return } \mathsf{sk}_\mathbf{y} \leftarrow \left[\sum_{i=1}^n r y_i \mathbf{w}_i\right]_2, [r]_2$
$\mathsf{msk} \leftarrow (\mathbf{w}_i)_{i=1}^n$ and $\textbf{return }$ $(\mathsf{mpk}, \mathsf{msk})$	
FE.Dec$(c, \mathbf{y}, \mathsf{mpk}, \mathsf{sk}_\mathbf{y})$:	FE.Enc$(\mathbf{x}, \mathsf{mpk})$:
Parse $c = (\mathbf{c}_0, c_i)_{i=1}^n$ with $\mathbf{c}_0 \in \mathbb{G}_1^2$	$\sigma, s \xleftarrow{\$} \mathbb{F}_q \setminus \{0\}$
Parse $\mathsf{sk}_\mathbf{y} = (\mathbf{d}_0, d_1)$ with $\mathbf{d}_0 \in \mathbb{G}_2^2$	$c_i \leftarrow [\sigma x_i + s \mathbf{a}^\top \mathbf{w}_i]_1$
$\textbf{Return } e(\mathbf{c}_0, \mathbf{d}_0) \overset{?}{=} e(c_1^{y_1} \cdots c_n^{y_n}, d_1) \neq 1$	$\textbf{Return } c \leftarrow \left([s\mathbf{a}]_1, c_1, \ldots, c_n\right).$

Fig. 3. Our simplified version of [Wee17] FE scheme for orthogonality

attribute-hiding) is sufficient in our application as we want to hide the winner's index $m \mod n$ only from those users that haven't won i.e. from those holding keys for $\gamma \neq m \mod n$.

Concretely, we instantiate the construction in Fig. 2, with a modified variant of the pairing-based FE for orthogonality proposed by Wee in [Wee17]. Our modified scheme is detailed in Fig. 3. In the full version we prove the following theorem.

Proposition 1. *The scheme in Fig. 3 is selective secure under the* SXDH *assumption*

2.6 Non Interactive Zero-Knowledge

A non-interactive zero-knowledge (NIZK) proof system for a relation $\mathcal{R}$ is a tuple of PPT algorithms $(\mathsf{NIZK.G}, \mathsf{NIZK.P}, \mathsf{NIZK.V})$ where: $\mathsf{NIZK.G}$ generates a common reference string crs; $\mathsf{NIZK.P}(\mathsf{crs}, x, w)$, given $(x, w) \in \mathcal{R}$, outputs a proof π; $\mathsf{NIZK.V}(\mathsf{crs}, x, \pi)$, given statement x and proof π outputs 0 (reject) or 1 (accept). We say that a NIZK for $\mathcal{R}$ is *correct* if for every $\mathsf{crs} \xleftarrow{\$} \mathsf{NIZK.G}(1^\lambda)$ and all $(x, w) \in \mathcal{R}$, $\mathsf{NIZK.V}(\mathsf{crs}, x, \mathsf{NIZK.P}(\mathsf{crs}, x, w)) = 1$ holds with probability 1. In our protocols we require the NIZKs to satisfy the notions of weak simulation extractability [Sah99] and zero-knowledge [FLS90].

About the first property, it only guarantees the extractability of proofs produced by the adversary that are not equal to proofs previously observed. For this reason we make them "unique" by adding implicitly a session ID to the statement. Concretely this means that in the Fiat Shamir transform, the hash function evaluations need to be salted with a unique session ID. Note that we won't detail how to handle these *sid* (and neither we do this for ideal functionalities invocations).

We now define three relations about group elements. The first one checks whether two vectors $\mathbf{g}, \mathbf{h} \in \mathbb{G}_1^n$ are proportional, i.e., there exists $x \in \mathbb{F}_q$ s.t.

$\mathbf{g}^x = \mathbf{h}$. The second one generalizes the previous to linear maps. The third one asks for solutions to the linear system $A\mathbf{x} = \mathbf{b}$ where $A, \mathbf{b}$ are given in the exponent and the last component x_n lies in a prescribed range. Formally

$$\mathcal{R}_{\mathsf{DDH}} = \{((\mathbf{g}, \mathbf{h}), x) \; : \; \mathbf{g}, \mathbf{h} \in \mathbb{G}^n, \; \mathbf{g}^x = \mathbf{h}\}$$
$$\mathcal{R}_{\mathsf{Lin}} = \{(([A]_1, [B]_1), X) \; : \; A \in \mathbb{F}_q^{k,m}, \; B \in \mathbb{F}_q^{k,n}, \; X \in \mathbb{F}_q^{m,n}, \; AX = B\}$$
$$\mathcal{R}_{\mathsf{LR}} = \{(([A]_1, [\mathbf{b}]_1, R), \mathbf{x}) \; : \; A \in \mathbb{F}_q^{m,n}, \; \mathbf{b} \in \mathbb{F}_q^m, \; \mathbf{x} \in \mathbb{F}_q^n, \; A\mathbf{x} = \mathbf{b}, \; x_n \in [R]\}$$

We also use $\mathcal{R}_{\mathsf{Enc}}$ and $\mathcal{R}_{\mathsf{Dec}}$ which relates to a given functional encryption scheme. The first one, given a ciphertext, requires knowledge of the message and randomness used to generate it. The second one instead, given a tuple (mpk, c, f, x) asks for a *correct secret key* sk_f that decrypts c to x. Below we also introduce a language $\mathcal{L}_{\mathsf{key}}$ to formally capture the notion of correct secret key.

$$\mathcal{L}_{\mathsf{key}} = \{(\mathsf{mpk}, f, \mathsf{sk}) : \forall m, r; \; c = \mathsf{FE.Enc}(m, \mathsf{mpk}; r) \Rightarrow \mathsf{FE.Dec}(c, f, \mathsf{mpk}, \mathsf{sk}) = f(m)\}$$
$$\mathcal{R}_{\mathsf{Dec}} = \{((\mathsf{mpk}, c, f, x), \mathsf{sk}) : (\mathsf{mpk}, f, \mathsf{sk}) \in \mathcal{L}_{\mathsf{key}}, \; \mathsf{FE.Dec}(c, f, \mathsf{mpk}, \mathsf{sk}) = x\}$$
$$\mathcal{R}_{\mathsf{Enc}} = \{((c, \mathsf{mpk}), (m, r)) : c = \mathsf{FE.Enc}(m, \mathsf{mpk}; r)\}.$$

Notice that, by abusing notation, standard asymmetric encryption, being a special case of FE, is also captured by this definition.

To construct our protocols, we assume the existence of a NIZK argument for each of these relations. We note that all of them can be proved through a sigma protocol, and that Fiat-Shamir based NIZKs from sigma protocols are weakly-simulation-extractable [FKMV12] based on a special property called quasi-unique responses. For the relations $\mathcal{R}_{\mathsf{DDH}}$ and $\mathcal{R}_{\mathsf{Lin}}$, we can use generalised Schnorr protocols provided in [Mau15]. For $\mathcal{R}_{\mathsf{LR}}$ we propose a variant of the folklore solution based on binary decomposition[7], in the full version. Still in the full version a sigma protocol for $\mathcal{R}_{\mathsf{Dec}}$ appears in the appendix.

2.7 UC Model and Ideal Functionalities

The celebrated UC model, introduced in the seminal work of Ran Canetti [Can01], is a framework that allows to prove security properties of a protocol that are preserved under composition. This is done by comparing the protocol to an ideal functionality $\mathcal{F}$ defined to capture the intended properties. A protocol securely realises $\mathcal{F}$ if it is indistinguishable from $\mathcal{F} \circ \mathcal{S}$ for a given PPT simulator $\mathcal{S}$. The distinguisher $\mathcal{Z}$, also called the *environment*, is granted the power to choose all parties' input, learn their output and corrupt any number of parties learning their internal state and influencing their behavior. The challenge for $\mathcal{S}$ is therefore to reproduce all the messages sent by uncorrupted parties in a consistent way with their input/output, even though $\mathcal{S}$ cannot access it. To make

---

[7] In this case the most efficient choice to date may be an adaptation of Bulletproofs [BBB+18]; however, to the best of our knowledge, this is only known to be simulation-extractable in the AGM [GOP+21]. We leave the exploration of this optimization for future work.

this possible in non trivial cases, functionalities are often designed to leak some information to $\mathcal{S}$ and allow the simulator to influence the result in some way.

In Fig. 4 we define two functionalities required in our construction: $\mathcal{F}_{zk}$ and $\mathcal{F}_{CT}^{\mathcal{D}}$ which respectively models a zero-knowledge proof of knowledge and a random beacon. The first one was introduced in [CF01], with the minor difference that in our case all the parties receive the output messages, deviation justified under the assumption of an authenticated broadcast channel. $\mathcal{F}_{CT}$ instead was introduced in [CD20] and realised assuming honest majority under standard assumptions. We remark that our use of the random oracle for the NIZK proofs is justified assuming a global random oracle in the GUC model [CJS14,CDG+18]. Finally, about our communication model, we assume an authenticated broadcast channel with known bounded delay [KMTZ13], which implies that messages sent in broadcast are eventually delivered with potentially different order. Although this introduce some degree of synchronicity, this is in line with previous work [BEHG20].

The ZK Functionality $\mathcal{F}_{zk}^{\mathcal{R}}$:
Upon receiving (prove, sid, x, w) from P_i, with sid being used by P_i for the first time: if $(x, w) \in \mathcal{R}$, broadcast (proof, sid, i, x).

The Coin Tossing Functionality $\mathcal{F}_{CT}^{\mathcal{D}}$:
Parametrized by a distribution $\mathcal{D}$. Upon receiving (toss, sid) from all the honest parties, sample $x \leftarrow^\$ \mathcal{D}$ and broadcast (tossed, sid, x)

Fig. 4. Description of the functionalities $\mathcal{F}_{zk}$ and $\mathcal{F}_{CT}$

3   Universally Composable SSLE

The notion of single secret leader election was introduced in [BEHG20] as a tuple of protocols (SSLE.Setup, SSLE.Reg, SSLE.Elect, SSLE.Claim, SSLE.Vrf) aimed at electing a unique leader among a set of participants who can stay hidden until she decide to reveal herself. Security of this primitive was captured through three game-based properties, namely *uniqueness*, *fairness* and *unpredictability*. However, the underlying security experiments fail to capture scenarios where multiple executions of the given procedures may occur concurrently. Moreover, as in most game-based notions, security is not guaranteed to hold when the primitive is used in a more complex protocol.

For this reason, we propose a definition of SSLE in the universal composability model. To this end, we define a functionality $\mathcal{F}_{SSLE}$ that performs elections and reveals the winners in an ideal way. A UC-secure SSLE scheme is then any protocol that securely realizes $\mathcal{F}_{SSLE}$.

At a high-level, $\mathcal{F}_{SSLE}$ consists of the following commands. By using (register) a user can register to an election. When all the honest users call (elect, eid), a new election with identifier eid is performed, that is, the ideal functionality samples a winner index j uniformly at random from the set of registered users. By using the (elect, eid) command, every honest user is informed by the ideal functionality on whether she is the winner of the election eid. Using (reveal, eid), an honest winning user instructs the ideal functionality to announce the election's outcome to everyone. Finally, the (fake_rejected, eid, j) command is reserved to the adversary and makes $\mathcal{F}_{\mathsf{SSLE}}$ announce to everyone that P_j is *not* the winner. This models a scenario in which an adversary who won an election deviates from the protocol to claim victory in spite of being the winning leader. The formal definition $\mathcal{F}_{\mathsf{SSLE}}$ is detailed in Fig. 5.

The SSLE functionality $\mathcal{F}_{\mathsf{SSLE}}$:
Initialise $E, R \leftarrow \varnothing$, $n \leftarrow 0$ and let $M \subseteq [N]$ be the set of corrupted parties. Upon receiving:

- (register) from P_i: add $R \leftarrow R \cup \{(i, n)\}$, broadcast (registered, i) and set $n \leftarrow n + 1$.

- (elect, eid) from all honest parties: if $R \neq \varnothing$ and eid was not requested before, sample $(j, \gamma) \leftarrow^{\$} R$ and send (outcome, eid, 1) to P_j and (outcome, eid, 0) to P_i for $(i, \cdot) \in R$, $i \neq j$. Store $E \leftarrow E \cup \{(eid, j)\}$.

- (reveal, eid) from P_i: if $(eid, i) \in E$ broadcast (result, eid, i). Otherwise broadcast (rejected, eid, i).

- (fake_rejected, eid, j) from $\mathcal{Z}$: if P_j is corrupted broadcast (rejected, eid, j).

Fig. 5. SSLE functionality executed among $P_1, \ldots, P_N$ and environment $\mathcal{Z}$

In order to capture constructions that are secure against adversaries capable of corrupting only a fraction of the participants, we distinguish two thresholds parameters: $t \in [N]$, which bounds corruptions among *all* users $P_1, \ldots, P_N$ (even those who are not registered), and $\vartheta : \mathbb{N} \rightarrow \mathbb{N}$, which upper bounds corruptions among the set of *currently registered* users depending on their number. Even though this notation is non-standard, it allows us to formalise standard assumptions such as the existence of an honest majority among *currently active* users, which is employed in several blockchain protocols. More formally, we give the following definitions.

Definition 5. *Let* $t \in [N]$ *and* $\vartheta : \mathbb{N} \rightarrow \mathbb{N}$. *A protocol* Π *is said to statically* (t, ϑ)-*threshold realise* $\mathcal{F}_{\mathsf{SSLE}}$ *if there exists a simulator* $\mathcal{S}$ *such that* Π *is indistinguishable from* $\mathcal{F}_{\mathsf{SSLE}} \circ \mathcal{S}$ *for all* PPT *environments* $\mathcal{Z}$ *that statically corrupt a set* M *of parties with* $|M| < t$ *and such that at each step, calling* R *the set of registered users,* $|R \cap M| < \vartheta(|R|)$.

Definition 6. *A* (t, ϑ)-*threshold statically secure UC-SSLE is a protocol* Π *that* (t, ϑ)-*securely realise* $\mathcal{F}_{\mathsf{SSLE}}$. *If* $t = N$ *and* $\vartheta = 1_{\mathbb{N}}$ *then* Π *is called a* *statically secure UC-SSLE.*

To further motivate our UC-secure notion of SSLE we compare it to the game-based one. First, with the following proposition, we show that the UC notion implies the game-based one. For the sake of generality we informally say that a property is (t, ϑ)-*threshold satisfied* if it holds against an adversary that corrupts at most t users and up to $\vartheta(|R|)$ of them belong to the set R of those currently registered at each step. For a more formal treatment see the full version of this paper, where also a proof of the following appears.

Proposition 2. *If Π is a (t, ϑ)-threshold statically secure UC-SSLE protocol, then its derived SSLE scheme described in Fig. 6 satisfies (t, ϑ)-threshold uniqueness, (t, ϑ)-threshold fairness and (t, ϑ)-threshold unpredictability.*

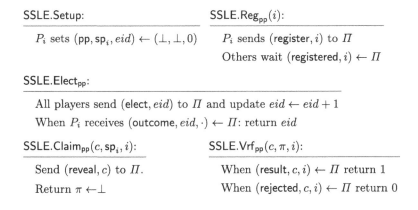

Fig. 6. The derived SSLE scheme from a UC-SSLE protocol Π

Second, we argue that our UC notion is strictly stronger than the game-based one. For this, we simply observe that taking one of the protocols from [BEHG20] (e.g., the one based on TFHE or the one based on Shuffling) they cannot be UC-secure if the zero-knowledge proofs they employ are not UC-secure.[8] In [BEHG20], these protocols are proven secure without making any UC assumption on these zero-knowledge proofs; so they constitute a counterexample of protocols that are secure in the game-based sense but would not be secure according to our UC notion.

3.1 A Parametrised Definition

Definition 6 provides a higher level of security with respect to the game-based definition in [BEHG20], but at the same time requires more structure from the

---

[8] Here, as the candidate protocol we are assuming the one where each sub protocol is used to implement the corresponding command, i.e., SSLE.Reg for register, SSLE.Elect for elect, etc.

underlying protocol and therefore may imply higher costs. In order to leverage security and efficiency we present here a "tunable" functionality $\mathcal{F}_{\mathsf{SSLE}}^{\kappa,\eta}$ which allows the adversary to control, with probability smaller than $2^{-\kappa}$, a given election and which may not elect any user with probability smaller than $2^{-\eta}$.

The Parametrised SSLE functionality $\mathcal{F}_{\mathsf{SSLE}}^{\kappa,\eta}$:

Initialise $E, R \leftarrow \varnothing, n \leftarrow 0$ and let $M \subseteq [N]$ be the set of corrupted parties. Upon receiving:

- (register) from P_i: add $R \leftarrow R \cup \{(i,n)\}$, broadcast (registered, i) and set $n \leftarrow n+1$.

- (elect, eid) from honest parties: if eid was not requested before leak to $\mathcal{Z}$ (electing, eid). Upon receiving (prob, eid, p_1, p_2) with $p_1 \leq 2^{-\kappa}, p_2 \leq 2^{-\eta}$:

  With probability p_1 leak (corrupted, eid) and wait for the adversary to reply with (infl, eid, j). Else, with probability p_2 set $j \leftarrow \perp$. If the previous actions are not performed, sample $(j, \cdot) \leftarrow^{\$} R$.

  Send (outcome, $eid, 1$) to P_j and (outcome, $eid, 0$) to P_i for $(i, \cdot) \in R$, $i \neq j$. Add $E \leftarrow E \cup \{(eid, j)\}$.

- (reveal, eid) from P_i: if $(eid, i) \in E$ broadcast (result, eid, i). Otherwise broadcast (rejected, eid, i).

- (fake_rejected, eid, j) from $\mathcal{Z}$: if P_j is corrupted broadcast (rejected, eid, j).

Fig. 7. Parametrised SSLE executed among $P_1, \ldots, P_N$ and environment $\mathcal{Z}$

Setting $\kappa = \eta = \Theta(\lambda)$ we get back a functionality equivalent to $\mathcal{F}_{\mathsf{SSLE}}$. However for smaller κ, η, we can now capture schemes achieving weaker (but still meaningful!) fairness and unpredictability notions. These might be acceptable/sufficient in practical scenarios, especially if they lead to significant efficiency gains. In the full version we show that applying the construction in Fig. 6 to a protocol realizing $\mathcal{F}_{\mathsf{SSLE}}^{\kappa,\eta}$ yields an SSLE scheme with $(2^{-\kappa} + 2^{-\eta})$-fairness and $\xi(\kappa)$-unpredictability with

$$\xi(\kappa) = \sup_{n \in \mathbb{N}} \left(\frac{n}{n - \vartheta(n)} \right) \cdot \frac{1}{2^{\kappa}} \cdot \frac{2^{\eta}}{2^{\eta} - 1}.$$

For fairness, the $2^{-\kappa} + 2^{-\eta}$ bound simply means that for $\kappa, \eta = \log N$ an adversary controlling T parties, wins the election with probability $(T+2)/N$. This is the same winning probability of an adversary that runs a perfectly fair election but corrupts two single extra players.

4   UC-secure SSLE from FE for Modular Keyword Search

We now present a generic construction of a UC-SSLE protocol based on modular keyword search FE. This, besides being of interest on its own, serves as a warm-up for our efficient construction of Sect. 5. More specifically, assuming for the sake of abstraction the existence of a protocol Π which securely distributes keys and, on request, produces ciphertexts encrypting random messages in a given set, we UC-realise $\mathcal{F}_{\mathsf{SSLE}}^{\kappa,\eta}$.

Our construction roughly works as follows: Initially the public key mpk is distributed among the N users. To perform the n-th registration for P_i, parties run Π to give sk_n to P_i. When an election is requested, users generate with Π a challenge ciphertext c that encrypts a message m, n, with $m \in [\kappa n]$ such that $m \bmod n \sim U([n])$, and check whether they won or lost by decrypting. Whoever can decrypt c to 1 is the leader and can claim victory by broadcasting a NIZK argument of this.

Unfortunately, even if this solution can already be proven secure in the game-based definition, it is not UC-secure yet. The reason is technical: if at a given round a ciphertext c encrypting (m, n) with $m = \gamma + \delta n$ is returned, γ being associated to an honest user[9], the adversary could re-register malicious users until he gets sk_m and then test that $\mathsf{MKS.Dec}(c, m, \mathsf{mpk}, \mathsf{sk}_m) = 1$. This makes the protocol hard to simulate as the ciphertext produced needs to always contain the winner's index – which the simulator may not know in advance[10].

To prevent this issue we introduce a set S of forbidden keys: each time a user wins with key sk_γ, the indices $\gamma + \delta n$ for $\delta \in [\kappa]$ are added to S and, each time a new user joins, n is set to be the next integer not lying in S. However this introduce a probability $|[n] \cap S| \cdot n^{-1}$ to produce a ciphertext no one can decrypt, meaning that nobody is elected. A way to keep it smaller than $2^{-\eta}$ is to perform a new setup every time the above probability exceeds this bound.

To proceed we formally define a functionality $\mathcal{F}_{\mathsf{SnC}}$, Fig. 5, which shapes the behaviour and security of Π, and a protocol $\{P_{\mathsf{MKS-SSLE}}^{(i)} : i \in [N]\}$ in the $\mathcal{F}_{\mathsf{SnC}}$-hybrid model realising $\mathcal{F}_{\mathsf{SSLE}}^{\kappa,\eta}$. A proof of security appears in the full version.

Theorem 1. *The protocol* $\{P_{\mathsf{MKS-SSLE}}^{(i)} : i \in [N]\}$ *in Fig. 9 securely realises* $\mathcal{F}_{\mathsf{SSLE}}^{\kappa,\eta}$ *in the* $\mathcal{F}_{\mathsf{SnC}}$*-hybrid model for the class of* PPT *environments* $\mathcal{Z}$ *that statically corrupts up to N players for any positive* κ, η.

5   An Efficient UC-secure SSLE from SXDH

In this section we present our main contribution, an SSLE protocol that works over bilinear groups which we prove UC-secure under the SXDH assumption.

5.1   Intuition

At a high level we instantiate the generic protocol provided in the previous section with the modular KS scheme obtained applying the transformation in Fig. 2 to our OFE in Fig. 3. The main challenge here is to efficiently generate

---

[9] i.e. such that an honest user P_i posses the key sk_γ.

[10] When $\mathcal{F}_{\mathsf{SSLE}}^{\kappa,\eta}$ elects an honest user, the simulator learn its identity only after this party is instructed by the environment to claim victory through a reveal command.

The Setup and Challenge Functionality $\mathcal{F}_{\mathsf{SnC}}$:

Generate $\mathsf{crs} \leftarrow^\$ \mathsf{NIZK.G}_{\mathsf{Dec}}(1^\lambda)$, $\mathsf{mpk}, \mathsf{msk} \leftarrow^\$ \mathsf{KS.Setup}(1^\lambda)$. Set $S \leftarrow \varnothing$ and $n \leftarrow 0$. Upon receiving:

- (setup) from P_i: send $(\mathsf{input}, \mathsf{crs}, \mathsf{mpk})$ to P_i.

- (ch_request, eid) from all honest parties: If eid was not requested before, sample $m \leftarrow^\$ [\kappa n]$ and compute $c \leftarrow^\$ \mathsf{KS.Enc}((m, n), \mathsf{mpk})$. Broadcast (challenge, eid, c). If $m \notin S$, divide $m = \gamma + \delta n$ with $\gamma \in [n]$ and add $S \leftarrow S \cup \{\gamma + \delta' n : \delta' \in [\kappa]\}$.

- (keygen) from P_i: When honest users agree, $n \leftarrow n + 1$ until $n \notin S$, set $\mathsf{sk}_n \leftarrow \mathsf{MKS.KeyGen}(n, \mathsf{msk})$ send $(\mathsf{key}, \mathsf{sk}_n)$ to P_i and broadcast (key_request, i, n).

Fig. 8. Setup and Challenge functionality executed among $P_1, \ldots, P_N$

ciphertexts in a distributed way. To address this, the basic idea is to select a random committee $Q \subseteq [N]$, have each member P_j secretly sample a value $m_j \in [n]$, where n is the number of users currently registered, and jointly generate an encryption of $m = \sum_{j \in Q} m_j$.

A downside is that now $m \in [|Q| \cdot n]$. For this reason we set $\kappa \geq |Q|$, where κ parametrises the set of functions $\mathsf{F}^\kappa_{\mathsf{mks}}$ supported by our modular KS scheme. In this way, as in the generic construction, decryption allows the holder of a secret key sk_γ to learn only whether $m = \gamma \bmod n$ or not. Also, if at least one m_j is uniform over $[n]$, so is $m \bmod n$, implying that the election is fair. Finally, since $|Q| = \kappa$ is a small parameter, the decryption procedure in our scheme (Fig. 2) remains efficient.

The next step is to show in more detail how the committee can accomplish its task. The ciphertext we want to produce is the encryption of $(m, -1, -n)$ under our OFE scheme in Fig. 3 and has the following form

$$\mathbf{c}_0 = [s\mathbf{a}]_1, \; c_1 = \left[\sigma m + s\mathbf{a}^\top \mathbf{w}_1\right]_1, \; c_2 = \left[-\sigma + s\mathbf{a}^\top \mathbf{w}_2\right]_1, \; c_3 = \left[-n\sigma + s\mathbf{a}^\top \mathbf{w}_3\right]_1$$

with $s, \sigma \sim U(\mathbb{F}_q)$ and $[\mathbf{a}]_1$, $[\mathbf{a}^\top \mathbf{w}_\ell]_1$ being the public key. While $\mathbf{c}_0, c_2, c_3$ would be easy to generate in a distributed way, as they linearly depend on s, σ, in c_1 we need to compute a product $\sigma \cdot m$. Standard MPC techniques could solve this issue within a few rounds, however we opt for a solution that requires each user to only speak once.

First, we sample two group elements G, H through the random beacon and interpret them as the ElGamal encryption, with respect to a previously generated public key g, h, of $[\sigma]_1$. Next each player P_i for $i \in Q$ samples $m_i \in [n]$, $s_i \in [n]$, and, using the linearity of ElGamal, computes and randomise an encryption of

$$c_{1,i} = \left[\sigma m_i + s_i \mathbf{a}^\top \mathbf{w}_1\right]_1, \quad c_{2,i} = \left[-\sigma + s_i \mathbf{a}^\top \mathbf{w}_2\right]_1, \quad c_{3,i} = \left[-n\sigma + s_i \mathbf{a}^\top \mathbf{w}_3\right]_1$$

Finally he publish these encrypted values together with $\mathbf{c}_{0,i} = [s_i \mathbf{a}]_1$ in plain and a NIZK. At this point everyone can locally set $\mathbf{c}_0$ as the product of the $\mathbf{c}_{0,i}$'s and

---

Party $P_{\mathsf{MSK-SSLE}}^{(i)}$ **realising** $\mathcal{F}_{\mathsf{SSLE}}^{\kappa,\eta}$:

Set $C, R, \mathcal{K} \leftarrow \varnothing$, send setup to $\mathcal{F}_{\mathsf{SnC}}$ and wait for (input, crs, mpk). Upon receiving:

- register: send keygen to $\mathcal{F}_{\mathsf{SnC}}$ and wait for its reply (key, sk_γ). Store $\mathcal{K} \leftarrow \mathcal{K} \cup \{\mathsf{sk}_\gamma\}$.

- A request to generate a new secret key from $\mathcal{F}_{\mathsf{SnC}}$: accepts if there is no election currently in progress.

- (key_request, j, n) from $\mathcal{F}_{\mathsf{SnC}}$: return (registered, j) and set $R \leftarrow R \cup \{(j, n)\}$.

- (elect, eid): send (ch_request) to $\mathcal{F}_{\mathsf{SnC}}$. When it replies with (challenge, eid, c), if there exists $\mathsf{sk}_\gamma \in \mathcal{K}$ such that $1 \leftarrow \mathsf{MKS.Dec}(c, \gamma, \mathsf{mpk}, \mathsf{sk}_\gamma)$, return (outcome, $eid, 1$). Otherwise return (outcome, $eid, 0$). Add $C \leftarrow C \cup \{(c, eid)\}$.

- (reveal, eid): if $(eid, c) \in C$ and $1 \leftarrow \mathsf{KS.Dec}(c, i, \mathsf{mpk}, \mathsf{sk}_\gamma)$ for some $\mathsf{sk}_\gamma \in \mathcal{K}$, prove $\pi \leftarrow^{\$} \mathsf{NIZK.P_{Dec}}(\mathsf{mpk}, c, \gamma, \mathsf{sk}_\gamma)$ and broadcast (claim, eid, π, γ). Otherwise broadcast (claim, $eid, \bot$).

- (claim, eid, π, γ) from P_j: if $(j, \gamma) \in R$ and $1 \leftarrow \mathsf{NIZK.V_{Dec}}(\mathsf{crs}, \mathsf{mpk}, c, \gamma, \pi)$ return (result, eid, j), otherwise (rejected, eid, j)

Fig. 9. Reduction of $\mathcal{F}_{\mathsf{SSLE}}^{\kappa,\eta}$ to the Setup and Challenge functionality $\mathcal{F}_{\mathsf{SnC}}$

compute ElGamal encryptions of c_1, c_2, c_3 that are respectively the products of $c_{1,i}$, $c_{2,i}$ and $c_{3,i}$. The last step would then be to decrypt these three remaining components. To this aim we assume that the secret key x of the ElGamal public key $h = g^x$ was previously t-shared among all users, which allows us to perform a threshold decryption.

To complete the protocol we have to show how to distribute the setup and key generation of our FE scheme. For ease of exposition, we first present a protocol assuming an ideal setup functionality in Sect. 5.2, and then in Sect. 5.3 we show how this functionality can be UC-realized. In conclusion we point out that, as in the general construction in Sect. 4, we have to maintain a set S of keys that cannot be generated in order to keep the protocol simulatable, resulting occasionally in elections without leaders.

5.2 SSLE Protocol with Ideal Setup Functionality

In Fig. 11 we show a protocol that securely realizes the $\mathcal{F}_{\mathsf{SSLE}}^{\kappa,\eta}$ ideal functionality. To this end we use the following building blocks:

- The FE scheme for orthogonality in Fig. 3, denoted FE which we use to instantiate a modular KS scheme.
- NIZKs for $\mathcal{R}_{\mathsf{DDH}}, \mathcal{R}_{\mathsf{LR}}$ and $\mathcal{R}_{\mathsf{Dec}}$. For readability, we suppress the crs from the inputs of the prover and verifier algorithm.
- A functionality $\mathcal{F}_{\mathsf{SK}}$ that distributes public and private keys of our OFE scheme, and t-share a threshold ElGamal secret key – sending privately the share $f(j)$ to P_j and publicly $k_j = g^{f(j)}$.

– A random beacon $\mathcal{F}_{\mathsf{CT}}^{\mathsf{ch}}$ returning G, H, Q with $G, H \sim U(\mathbb{G}_1^2)$ and $Q \subseteq [N]$, $|Q| = \ell$ such that the probability that Q is contained in the set of corrupted parties is smaller than $2^{-\kappa}$. Note that $t < N/2$ implies $\ell \le \kappa$.

Each user maintains (or recovers from the public state) four sets $C, R, S, \mathcal{K}$ respectively containing previous challenges, currently registered users, forbidden keys and owned secret keys.

Elections begin by invoking $\mathcal{F}_{\mathsf{CT}}^{\mathsf{ch}}$ which returns (G, H, Q). In steps 6-8 users in Q interpret $(G, H) = (g^\theta, h^\theta \cdot [\sigma]_1)$ as an ElGamal encryption with $\sigma \sim U(\mathbb{F}_q)$, sample $m_i \in [n]$, $s_i \in \mathbb{F}_q$ and produce encrypted shares of the challenge components. Then they sample r_i and ρ_i to re-randomize these ciphertexts. Interestingly we observe that using the same randomness for the last two components does not affect security.

Next, in steps 11-15 we let $Q_0 \subseteq Q$ be the set of users who replied with a correct NIZK. Observe that, calling s, r, ρ, m the sum of the respective shares s_i, r_i, ρ_i and m_i over Q_0, then $G_1 = g^{r+\theta m}$ and $G_2 = g^{\rho+\theta}$. In order to decrypt each user produces $K_{1,i}, K_{2,i}$ that will open, through a Shamir reconstruction in the exponent, to $h^{r+\theta m}$ and $h^{\rho+\theta}$.

In steps 16-20, users locally multiply the elements sent by the committee and reconstruct, interpolating at the exponent, $K_1 = h^{r+\theta m}$ and $K_2 = h^{\rho+\theta}$. Since

$$\prod_{\mu \in Q_0} c_{1,\mu} = h^{r+\theta m}\left[m\sigma + s\mathbf{a}^\top \mathbf{w}_1\right]_1 \qquad H^{-1}\prod_{\mu \in Q_0} c_{2,\mu} = h^{-\rho-\theta}\left[-\sigma + s\mathbf{a}^\top \mathbf{w}_2\right]_1$$

$$H^{-n}\prod_{\mu \in Q_0} c_{3,\mu} = h^{-n(\rho+\theta)}\left[-n\sigma + s\mathbf{a}^\top \mathbf{w}_3\right]_1$$

applying K_1, K_2 they finally obtain all the components of the challenge c. At the end of an election (lines 20-22) each user verify whether or not he won by attempting to decrypt the produced challenge with the keys he stored in $\mathcal{K}$.

When a user wins and is instructed through a reveal command to claim victory, he sends both the elements K_1, K_2 previously computed and a proof of knowledge of a secret key $\mathsf{sk}_{\gamma,j}$ which decrypts the challenge to 1. The first part is required as we don't want to store on chain the threshold decryption. This may sound insecure at first, as another user could come up with different K_1', K_2' that let him win. Interestingly, in the proof of security we show that being able to do so implies breaking the selective security of our OFE.

Theorem 2. *The protocol in Fig. 11 (t, ϑ)-threshold securely realizes $\mathcal{F}_{\mathsf{SSLE}}^{\kappa,\eta}$ in the $(\mathcal{F}_{\mathsf{CT}}, \mathcal{F}_{\mathsf{SK}})$-hybrid model under the* SXDH *assumption, for $t = \lfloor N/2 \rfloor$ and $\vartheta(n) = \lfloor n/2 \rfloor$*

5.3   Realising the Setup

Here we describe how to realize the functionality $\mathcal{F}_{\mathsf{SK}}$ deployed in Protocol 11.

First of all, in order to emulate private communication channels, not available in our model but necessary to distribute secret parameters, we use an IND-CPA encryption scheme (AE.Setup, AE.Enc, AE.Dec). Second, as our NIZKs are

---

The Setup and Key Generation Functionality $\mathcal{F}_{SK}$

$n \leftarrow 0$, $S \leftarrow \varnothing$, $g \leftarrow^{\$} \mathbb{G}_1$, $f \leftarrow^{\$} \mathbb{F}_q[x]_{<t}$, mpk, msk $\leftarrow^{\$}$ FE.Setup($1^\lambda, 3$). Fix $h \leftarrow g^{f(-1)}$, $k_j \leftarrow g^{f(j)}$, pp $\leftarrow$ (mpk, $g, h, (k_j)_{j=0}^{N-1}$), leak (setup_leak, pp, $f(j))_{j \in M}$ and wait for (setup_infl, $\mathbf{w}_\alpha^*, f^*)_{\alpha=1}^3$ from the adversary $\mathcal{Z}$. Calling mpk $=$ $(\mathbf{z}_0, z_\alpha)_{\alpha=1}^3$, msk $= (\mathbf{w}_\alpha)_{\alpha=1}^3$, set

$$\text{mpk} \leftarrow (\mathbf{z}_0, z_\alpha \cdot \mathbf{z}_0^{\mathbf{w}_\alpha^*})_{\alpha=1}^3, \qquad \text{msk} \leftarrow (\mathbf{w}_\alpha + \mathbf{w}_\alpha^*)_{\alpha=1}^3, \qquad f \leftarrow f + f^*$$

and update pp. Upon receiving:

- (setup) from P_j: Send (input, pp, $f(j)$) to P_j.

- (update, γ, n) from honest players: $S \leftarrow S \cup \{\gamma + \delta n : \delta \in [\kappa]\}$.

- (keygen) from P_j: Broadcast (key_request). while $n \in S$, increase n by 1. Set $\text{sk}_{n,\delta} \leftarrow$ FE.KeyGen($\mathbf{y}_{n,\delta}$, msk) and send (key, $(\text{sk}_{n,\delta})_{\delta=0}^{\kappa-1}$) to P_j.

- (infl, $(\mathbf{w}_i^*)_{i=1}^3$) from the adversary $\mathcal{Z}$: For each key sk $= (\mathbf{d}, d)$ sent to P_j associated to a vector $\mathbf{y}$, compute sk$' = (\mathbf{d} \cdot [y_1 \mathbf{w}_1^* + y_2 \mathbf{w}_2^* + y_3 \mathbf{w}_3^*]_d, d)$ and send (key_update, sk$'$) to P_j. Update msk setting $\mathbf{w}_\alpha \leftarrow \mathbf{w}_\alpha + \mathbf{w}_\alpha^*$.

Fig. 10. Functionality $\mathcal{F}_{SK}$ among users $P_1, \ldots, P_N$ and environment $\mathcal{Z}$ which in Protocol 11 performs the setup and distributes keys on request

randomised sigma protocols compiled with Fiat-Shamir, they only need access to a random oracle and in particular there is no need to instantiate a crs. Next, we need to distribute the secret key of the Threshold ElGamal scheme. This is addressed by deploying standard techniques from verifiable secret sharing.

Finally we have to generate the public and secret keys of the FE scheme in Fig. 3. To this aim, recall that

$$\text{mpk} = [\mathbf{a}]_1, ([\mathbf{a}^\top \mathbf{w}_\alpha]_1)_{\alpha=1}^3, \qquad \text{sk}_{\mathbf{y}_{\gamma,\delta}} = [r(\mathbf{w}_1 + \gamma \mathbf{w}_2 + \delta \mathbf{w}_3)]_2, [r]_2.$$

Fixing $[\mathbf{a}]_1$ and $[r]_2$, which can be generated through a random beacon, the remaining components of these keys depends linearly on $\mathbf{w}_\alpha$. Therefore we can again select a random committee and let each member P_i sample $\mathbf{w}_{\alpha,i} \leftarrow^{\$} \mathbb{F}_q^2$. At a high level to produce either mpk or a secret key, users provide shares of it, which are then locally multiplied. When reconstructing a secret key moreover the receiver checks the shares and complain if they are malformed.

More in detail in our construction we will use

- NIZKs for $\mathcal{R}_{Enc}, \mathcal{R}_{Dec}$ and the ideal functionality $\mathcal{F}_{zk}^{Lin}$.
- Two random beacons $\mathcal{F}_{CT}^{stp}$ and $\mathcal{F}_{CT}^{sk}$ returning respectively $(Q, \mathbf{z}_0, g)$ and $(d_\delta)_{\delta=0}^{\kappa-1}$ with $\mathbf{z}_0 \sim U(\mathbb{F}_q^2)$, $g \sim U(\mathbb{G}_1)$, $d_\delta \sim U(\mathbb{G}_2)$ and $Q \subseteq [N]$, $|Q| = \ell$ such that the probability of Q containing only corrupted users is smaller than $2^{-\lambda}$. Notice that $t < N/2$ implies $\ell \leq \lambda$.

In steps 1-6 members of the committee sample a polynomial f_i used for the VSS, and shares $\mathbf{w}_{i,\alpha}$. The proof in line 4 guarantees that the adversary is aware of the plaintext $f_i(j)$ encrypted, preventing decryption-oracle attacks.

Party $P_{\mathsf{SSLE},\kappa}^{(i)}$ realising $\mathcal{F}_{\mathsf{SSLE}}^{\kappa,\eta}$:

Call $C, R, S, \mathcal{K} \leftarrow \varnothing$, $n \leftarrow 0$. Send setup to $\mathcal{F}_{\mathsf{SK}}$, wait for the reply $(\mathsf{input}, \mathsf{pp}, f(i))$ and parse $\mathsf{pp} = \mathsf{mpk}$, g, h, $k_0, \ldots, k_{N-1}$, with $\mathsf{mpk} = [\mathbf{a}]_1$, $[\mathbf{a}^\top \mathbf{w}_1]_1$, $[\mathbf{a}^\top \mathbf{w}_2]_1$, $[\mathbf{a}^\top \mathbf{w}_3]_1$ together with bilinear groups description. Upon receiving:

1 : (register): Send keygen to $\mathcal{F}_{\mathsf{SK}}$ and wait for $(\mathsf{key}, \mathsf{sk}_n)$; Add $\mathcal{K} \leftarrow \mathcal{K} \cup \mathsf{sk}_n$

2 : (key_requested, j) from $\mathcal{F}_{\mathsf{SK}}$: Wait for all elected leader to reveal themselves.

3 :   While $n \in S$, $n \leftarrow n+1$; $R \leftarrow R \cup \{(j,n)\}$, $n \leftarrow n+1$;   Return (registered, j)

4 : (elect, eid): Send (toss, eid) to $\mathcal{F}_{\mathsf{CT}}^{\mathsf{ch}}$

5 : (tossed, eid, G, H, Q) from $\mathcal{F}_{\mathsf{CT}}^{\mathsf{ch}}$, if $i \in Q$:

6 :   Sample $s_i, r_i, \rho_i \leftarrow^\$ \mathbb{F}_q$ and $m_i \leftarrow^\$ [n]$ and compute:

7 : $G_{1,i} \leftarrow g^{r_i} G^{m_i}$, $G_{2,i} \leftarrow g^{\rho_i}$, $\mathbf{c}_{0,i} \leftarrow [s_i \mathbf{a}]_1$, $c_{1,i} \leftarrow h^{r_i} H^{m_i} \cdot [s_i \mathbf{a}^\top \mathbf{w}_1]_1$

8 : $c_{2,i} \leftarrow h^{-\rho_i} \cdot [s_i \mathbf{a}^\top \mathbf{w}_2]_1$, $c_{3,i} \leftarrow h^{-n\rho_i} \cdot [s_i \mathbf{a}^\top \mathbf{w}_3]_1$

9 : $\pi_{\mathsf{LR},i} \leftarrow \mathsf{NIZK.P_{LR}}(\mathbf{S}, (\mathbf{c}_{0,i}, c_{1,i}, c_{2,i}, c_{3,i}, G_{1,i}, G_{2,i}), [n], (s_i, r_i, \rho_i, m_i))$

10 :   Broadcast (msg, $eid, \mathbf{c}_{0,i}, c_{1,i}, c_{2,i}, c_{3,i}, G_{1,i}, G_{2,i}, \pi_{\mathsf{LR},i}$)

11 : (msg, $eid, \mathbf{c}_{0,\nu}, c_{1,\nu}, c_{2,\nu}, c_{3,\nu}, G_{1,\nu}, G_{2,\nu}, \pi_{\mathsf{LR},\nu}$) from P_ν:

12 :   Let $Q_0 \subseteq Q$ be the set of ν such that $\pi_{\mathsf{LR},\nu}$ is accepted

13 : $G_1 \leftarrow \prod_{\nu \in Q_0} G_{1,\nu}$, $G_2 \leftarrow G \cdot \prod_{\nu \in Q_0} G_{2,\nu}$, $K_{1,i} \leftarrow G_1^{f(i)}$, $K_{2,i} \leftarrow G_2^{f(i)}$

14 : $\pi_{\mathsf{DDH},i} \leftarrow \mathsf{NIZK.P_{DDH}}((g, G_1, G_2), (k_i, K_{1,i}, K_{2,i}), f(i))$

15 :   Broadcast (open, $eid, K_{1,i}, K_{2,i}, \pi_{\mathsf{DDH},i}$)

16 : (open, $eid, K_{1,\nu}, K_{2,\nu}, \pi_{\mathsf{DDH},\nu}$) with valid proof, from a set $Z \subseteq [N]$ of t parties:

17 :   Reconstruct $K_j \leftarrow \prod_{\nu \in Z} K_{j,\nu}^{\lambda_\nu}$ with λ_ν the Lagrange coefficient for Z

18 : $\mathbf{c}_0 \leftarrow \prod_{\mu \in Q_0} \mathbf{c}_{0,\mu}$, $c_1 \leftarrow K_1^{-1} \cdot \prod_{\mu \in Q_0} c_{1,\mu}$, $c_2 \leftarrow H^{-1} K_2 \cdot \prod_{\mu \in Q_0} c_{2,\mu}$

19 : $c_3 \leftarrow H^{-n} K_2^n \cdot \prod_{\mu \in Q_0} c_{3,\mu}$, $c \leftarrow (\mathbf{c}_0, c_1, c_2, c_3)$

20 :   **If** there exists $\mathsf{sk}_{\gamma,\delta} \in \mathcal{K}$ which decrypts c to 1:

21 :   Return (outcome, $eid, 1$) and store $C \leftarrow C \cup \{(eid, K_1, K_2)\}$

22 :   **Else** return (outcome, $eid, 0$).

23 : (reveal, eid): **If** there exists $(eid, K_1, K_2) \in C$: compute c as in steps 18, 19

24 :   Find $\mathsf{sk}_{\gamma,\delta} \in \mathcal{K}$ which decrypts the challenge c to 1

25 :   Get $\pi \leftarrow \mathsf{NIZK.P_{Dec}}(\mathsf{mpk}, c, (\gamma, \delta), \mathsf{sk}_{\gamma,\delta})$ and send (claim, $eid, \pi, K_1, K_2, \gamma, \delta$)

26 :   **Else** broadcast an error message (claim, $eid, \perp$)

27 : (claim, $eid, \pi, K_1, K_2, \gamma, \delta$) from P_ν: compute c as in steps 18, 19

28 :   **If** $(\nu, \gamma) \in R$ and π is accepted: Send (update, γ, n) to $\mathcal{F}_{\mathsf{SK}}$

29 :   Update $S \leftarrow S \cup \{\gamma + \delta' n : \delta' \in [\kappa]\}$ and return (result, eid, ν)

30 :   **Else**: return (rejected, eid, ν)

Fig. 11. Protocol $P_{\mathsf{SSLE},\kappa}^{(i)}$. $\mathbf{S} \in \mathbb{G}_1^{7,4}$ represents the linear operations in lines 6-8.

In lines 7-15 users test the VSS by checking if the exponents of $h_\mu, (k_{i,\mu})_{i=0}^{N-1}$ lies in the right Reed-Solomon code. A standard test is to check orthogonality with a codeword in the dual space $\mathsf{RS}_{\mathbb{F},N+1,t}^{\perp}$. Next, consistency with $s_{i,\mu} = f_\mu(i)$ and $k_{i,\mu}$ is checked. If it fails the player will complain (lines 10-13) and remove P_μ from the committee.

Next, the generation of a new secret key begins by querying $\mathcal{F}_{\mathsf{CT}}^{\mathsf{sk}}$, line 20, which returns $(d_\delta)_{\delta=0}^{k-1}$, interpreted as the randomness of requested OFE keys. In lines 21-25 members of the committee generate the secret key share $\mathbf{d}_{n,\delta}^{(i)}$ and privately send it to the receiver. Again a NIZK is added to prevent any decryption-oracle attack.

Observe now that, for every $\mu \in Q$

$$(\mathbf{z}_0, z_{1,\mu}, z_{2,\mu}, z_{2,\mu}) = [\mathbf{a}]_1, [\mathbf{a}^\top \mathbf{w}_{1,\mu}]_1, [\mathbf{a}^\top \mathbf{w}_{2,\mu}]_1, [\mathbf{a}^\top \mathbf{w}_{3,\mu}]_1$$

is a master public key for our OFE scheme, and $(\mathbf{d}_{n,\delta}^{(\mu)}, d_\delta)$ is a secret key for $(1, n, \delta)$ in the same scheme. Hence the recipient, lines 26-31, verifies this key share by checking if it is able to decrypt an encryption of $\mathbf{0}$. Somewhat surprisingly in the proof of security we show that this is enough to ensure correctness of the key.

Finally, if the above check fails, the recipient broadcasts a complaint message exposing the malformed key. Every user then checks the complaint and, if legitimate, remove P_μ from the committee.

Theorem 3. *Protocol* $\{P_{\mathsf{SK}}^{(i)} : i \in [N]\}$ *securely realises* $\mathcal{F}_{\mathsf{SK}}$ *in the* $(\mathcal{F}_{\mathsf{CT}}, \mathcal{F}_{\mathsf{zk}})$ *hybrid model under the* SXDH *assumption for the class of* PPT *environments* $\mathcal{Z}$ *that statically corrupt up to* $\lfloor N/2 \rfloor$ *players.*

6 Efficiency Considerations

Overall communication costs of our protocol are summarised in Table 2. As mentioned in the previous section, however most of these messages are not required for verification and, in particular, they do not need to be stored on chain.

More in detail, for the VSS to generate the ElGamal public and secret keys, only aggregated elements $h, k_0, \ldots, k_{N-1}$ have to be placed on-chain, as those are the only ones required to verify the secret sharing. Next, during elections, we have to store the partial ciphertexts and related NIZKs sent by the committee, as these components are necessary to reconstruct the election's ciphertext. However, our specific OFE and protocol allow the winner to aggregate the expensive threshold decryption, without the need to also post a proof of correctness. Note that the same property does not hold for the first round, since together with the partial ciphertexts one would have to aggregate the corresponding NIZKs with more sophisticated tools. Finally we remark that it is also possible to avoid storing encrypted secret keys for our OFE on chain, using the chain only for disputes.

As shown in the Table, while election requires low communications, the setup is more expensive, requiring 252 MB for 2^{14} users. However, this is supposed to

Party $P_{\mathsf{SK}}^{(i)}$ realising $\mathcal{F}_{\mathsf{SK}}$:

Initially set $n \leftarrow 0$, $S \leftarrow \varnothing$. Create $(\mathsf{pk}_i, \mathsf{sk}_i) \leftarrow^{\$} \mathsf{AE.Setup}(1^\lambda)$, broadcast (user_key, pk_i), send (toss) $\rightarrow \mathcal{F}_{\mathsf{CT}}^{\mathsf{stp}}$ and wait for its reply (tossed, $Q, \mathbf{z}_0, g$)

1 : **If** $i \in Q$: Sample $f_i \leftarrow^{\$} \mathbb{F}_q[x]_{<t}$, $\mathbf{w}_{1,i}, \mathbf{w}_{2,i}, \mathbf{w}_{3,i} \leftarrow^{\$} \mathbb{F}_q^2$

2 :   Compute $h_i \leftarrow g^{f_i(-1)}$, $k_{j,i} \leftarrow g^{f_i(j)}$ and $z_{\alpha,i} \leftarrow \mathbf{z}_0^{\mathbf{w}_{\alpha,i}}$ for $j \in [N]$, $\alpha \in [3]$

3 : $c_{j,i} \leftarrow^{\$} \mathsf{AE.Enc}(f_i(j), \mathsf{pk}_j)$ with randomness $r_{j,i}$

4 : $\pi_{j,i} \leftarrow^{\$} \mathsf{NIZK.P}_{\mathsf{Enc}}(c_j, \mathsf{pk}_j, f_i(j), r_{j,i})$

5 :   Broadcast (msg, $h_i, (k_{j,i}, c_{j,i}, \pi_{j,i})_{j=0}^{N-1}$)

6 :   Send (prove, $(z_{\alpha,i})_{\alpha=1}^3, (\mathbf{w}_{\alpha,i})_{\alpha=1}^3$) to $\mathcal{F}_{\mathsf{zk}}^{\mathcal{R}_{\mathsf{Lin}}}$

7 : When $P_\mu \rightarrow$ (msg, $h_\mu, k_{j,\mu}, c_{j,\mu}, \pi_{j,\mu})_{j=0}^{N-1}$, $\mathcal{F}_{\mathsf{zk}}^{\mathcal{R}_{\mathsf{Lin}}} \rightarrow$ (proof, $\mu, z_{\alpha,\mu})_{\alpha=1}^3$ for $\mu \in Q_0$:

8 :   Set $\mathbf{k}_\mu = (h_\mu, k_{0,\mu}, \ldots, k_{N-1,\mu})$ and sample $\mathbf{v} \leftarrow^{\$} \mathsf{RS}_{\mathbb{F}, N+1, t}^{\perp}$.

9 :   If $\mathbf{k}_\mu^{\mathbf{v}} \neq 1$ or some $\pi_{j,\mu}$ is rejected: remove μ from Q_0.

10 :   Decrypt $s_{i,\mu} \leftarrow \mathsf{AE.Dec}(c_{i,\mu}, \mathsf{pk}_i, \mathsf{sk}_i)$. If $g^{s_{i,\mu}} \neq k_{i,\mu}$:

11 : $\pi \leftarrow \mathsf{NIZK.P}_{\mathsf{Dec}}(\mathsf{pk}_i, c_{i,\mu}, s_{i,\mu}, \mathsf{sk}_i)$, and broadcast (complain, $s_{i,\mu}, \mu, \pi$)

12 :   Upon receiving (complain, $\mu, s_{i,\mu}, \pi$) from P_j:

13 :   If π is accepting and $g^{s_{i,\mu}} \neq k_{i,\mu}$, remove μ from Q_0.

14 :   Compute and store $z_\alpha \leftarrow \prod_{\mu \in Q_0} z_{\alpha,\mu}$, $h \leftarrow \prod_{\mu \in Q_0} h_\mu$, $k_j \leftarrow \prod_{\mu \in Q_0} k_{j,\mu}$

15 :   mpk $\leftarrow (\mathbf{z}, z_1, z_2, z_3)$, pp $\leftarrow$ (mpk, $h, k_0, \ldots, k_{N-1}$), $s_i \leftarrow \prod_{\mu \in Q_0} s_{i,\mu}$

Fig. 12. Realisation $\mathcal{F}_{\mathsf{SK}}$, Initial setup phase

be performed rarely. Once this is done, our protocol allows new users to join providing them a new secret key, without updating the key material of other users. This registration takes only 73 KB of communication. Letting users leave the system on the other hand introduces some inefficiencies. The problem is that users who go away may still be elected, causing some elections to end without a winner. An obvious, but expensive, way to completely remove this problem is to perform a new setup every time that one or more users leave. However, one can also make a trade-off leaving the possibility that some elections finish without a winner, and redo the setup only when this probability (which for L inactive users out of N registered users is L/N) becomes too high.

Comparison with [BEHG20]. We now compare our UC-secure construction with the shuffle-based solution in [BEHG20], which we briefly recall here. Essentially the public state contains a list of Diffie-Hellman pairs $(K_{i,1}, K_{i,2})$, one for every user, and P_i's secret key is a discrete log k_i such that $K_{i,2} = K_{i,1}^{k_i}$. An election is performed by choosing one of those tuples through the random beacon and the leader claims victory by revealing its secret key. To achieve unpredictability, each time a pair is added by a user, he sends a shuffled and re-randomized list along with a NIZK. Note that every election involves at least the registration of the previous winner, who has "burnt" her secret key, if she desires to stay.

Party $P_{\mathsf{SK}}^{(i)}$ realising $\mathcal{F}_{\mathsf{SK}}$ upon receiving:

17 : (setup): Return $(\mathsf{input}, \mathsf{pp}, s_i)$

18 : (update, n, γ): set $S \leftarrow \{\gamma + \delta n \ : \ \delta \in [\kappa]\}$

19 : (keygen): Broadcast (key_request)

20 : (key_request) from P_j: Send $(\mathsf{toss}, rid|j)$ to $\mathcal{F}_{\mathsf{CT}}^{\mathsf{sk}}$ and return (key_requested, j)

21 : $(\mathsf{tossed}, rid|j, (d_\delta)_{\delta=0}^{\kappa-1})$ from $\mathcal{F}_{\mathsf{CT}}^{\mathsf{sk}}$, if $i \in Q$:

22 :   While $n \in S$, increase $n \leftarrow n + 1$

23 : $\mathbf{d}_{n,\delta}^{(i)} \leftarrow [\mathbf{w}_{1,i} + n\mathbf{w}_{2,i} + \delta\mathbf{w}_{3,i}]_{d_\delta}$, $\quad \mathbf{d}_n^{(i)} \leftarrow (\mathbf{d}_{n,\delta}^{(i)})_{\delta=0}^{\kappa-1}$

24 : $c_i \leftarrow^{\$} \mathsf{AE.Enc}(\mathbf{d}_n^{(i)}, \mathsf{pk}_j)$ with randomness r_i

25 : $\pi_i \leftarrow^{\$} \mathsf{NIZK.P}_{\mathsf{Enc}}(c_i, \mathsf{pk}_j, \mathbf{d}_n^{(i)}, r_i)$; Broadcast (key_partial, c_i, π_i, j, n)

26 : (key_partial, c_μ, π_μ, i, n) with accepting π_μ from P_μ for $\mu \in Q_n$:

27 :   for all $\mu \in Q_n$ get $(\mathbf{d}_{n,\delta}^{(\mu)})_{\delta=0}^{\kappa-1} \leftarrow \mathsf{AE.Dec}(c_i, \mathsf{sk}_i)$

28 :   If $e(\mathbf{z}_0, \mathbf{d}_{n,\delta}^{(\mu)}) \neq e(z_{1,\mu} \cdot z_{2,\mu}^n \cdot z_{3,\mu}^\delta, d_\delta)$:

29 :   Remove μ from Q and compute π a proof that c_μ encrypts $(\mathbf{d}_{n,\delta}^{(\mu)})_{\delta=0}^{\kappa-1}$

30 :   Broadcast (key_complain, $\mu, n, \delta, (\mathbf{d}_{n,\delta}^{(\mu)})_{\delta=0}^{\kappa-1}, \pi$)

31 :   Set $\mathsf{sk}_{n,\delta} \leftarrow \left(\prod_{\mu \in Q_n} \mathbf{d}_{n,\delta}^{(\mu)}, d_\delta \right)$ and return (key, $(\mathsf{sk}_{n,\delta})_{\delta=0}^{\kappa-1}$)

32 : (key_complain, $\mu, n, \delta, (\mathsf{sk}_{n,\delta}^{(\mu)})_{\delta=0}^{\kappa-1}, \pi$) from P_j with accepting π:

33 :   Perform the test on line 28. If the two terms differ:

34 :   Remove μ from Q_n, and P_μ's share from mpk

35 :   For each key received sk let $\mathbf{d}_\mu$ be P_μ's share

36 :   Parse $\mathsf{sk} = (\mathbf{d}, d)$, return (key_update, $(\mathbf{d} \cdot \mathbf{d}_\mu^{-1}, d)$)

Fig. 13. Realisation $\mathcal{F}_{\mathsf{SK}}$, Key Distribution phase

Moreover, this implies that the protocol requires at each round as many shuffles as the number of new users. Notably, all the lists and NIZKs have to be posted on chain in order to ensure verifiability.

In the high communication solution, denoted N-shuffle, each shuffles costs $2n$ group elements, while the more efficient and less secure one, denoted $\sqrt{N}$-shuffle, costs $2\sqrt{n}$ elements.

In light of the requirement in [Lab19] to support $O(\log^2 N)$ new users per round, we compare these solutions evaluating the cumulative cost of several elections, interleaving between every two a fixed amount of registrations. In Fig. 6 we provide the communication costs for such a scenario where we assume to start with 2^{14} users and then perform: 10 registrations for each election in the first column, 20 in the second column, and 30 in the third one. Furthermore

Table 2. Communication costs of our scheme, using ElGamal in place of the generic IND-CPA encryption. Size is computed assuming $\log |\mathbb{F}_q| = 256$, $\log |\mathbb{G}_1| = 512$, $\log |\mathbb{G}_2| = 256$, $\log |\mathbb{G}_T| = 3072$, $\lambda = 80$, $\kappa = \log N$, $t = \lfloor N/2 \rfloor$ and $N = 2^{14}$.

Procedure	Number of elements sent			Size	
	$\mathbb{F}_q$	$\mathbb{G}_1$	$\mathbb{G}_2$	off-chain	on-chain
VSS for ElGamal	$2\lambda N$	$2\lambda N + 2\lambda$	–	252 MB	1.05 MB
Distribute mpk	3λ	2λ	–	20.5 KB	20.5 KB
Election, 1st Round	$\kappa(6 + 2\log n)$	$\kappa(7 + \log n)$	–	34.0 KB	34.0 KB
Election, 2nd Round	$2(t + 1)$	$2(t + 1)$	–	1.57 MB	–
Election, Claim	1	2	3	256 B	256 B
Registration	λ	–	$2\kappa\lambda + 2\lambda$	73.3 KB	–

we let the same number of new users who joined the system leave it after each election. Note that, as mentioned earlier, this means some elections may have to be repeated in our case as users who leave may still be elected.

We remark that in those plots, the costs of the shuffle-based solutions do not even include the costs of setup[11], as it can be done only once in contrast to ours where we need to occasionally refresh the secret key material. In spite of that, the cost of our setup is quickly compensated by our lighter registration and election procedure, which makes our solution more suited to dynamic scenarios.

More Efficient SSLE with Game Based Security. We now remark that communication complexity can be further reduced in our construction at the cost of giving up UC security yet achieving the game-based security notion.

As we would not need any more to simulate each election, every secret key can now be produced without artificially skipping some of them. For the same reason, the NIZKs need not to be simulation-extractable, which allow us to use Bulletproofs for the range proofs. This reduces on-chain costs to $O(\kappa \log \log N)$.

Finally, when giving up UC security users who voluntarily leave the system can be handled by asking such users to reveal their own secret keys upon leaving, as done in [BEHG20]. This way, if a revoked user happens to be elected, everyone can detect it and immediately proceed to generate a new election's ciphertext. To keep round complexity low, one can also prepare several challenges per election, order them, remove those that can be decrypted with keys of users who left, and set the current challenge as the first of the remaining ones. This solution only works for non-UC security though, as the simulator should now generate on request honest user's secret key that are consistent with previous elections.

---

[11] I.e. the cost to generate a shuffled list containing the pairs of the initial users. This has cost $O(n^2)$ if everyone performs a shuffle, or $O(\kappa n)$ using an approach similar to ours where a random committee of κ users shuffle the initial list.

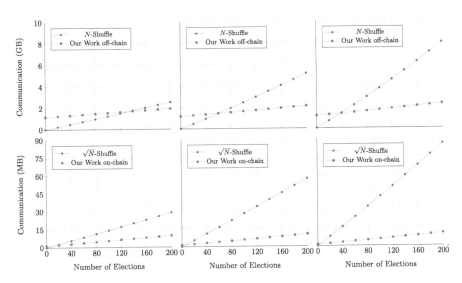

Fig. 14. Cumulative communication costs in this work and [BEHG20]. Initially the number of users is $N = 2^{14}$ and between every two elections 10 (left column), 20 (middle column) or 30 (right column) registrations occur, while the same amount of already registered users leave.

Acknowledgements. This work has received funding in part from the European Research Council (ERC) under the European Union's Horizon 2020 research and innovation program under project PICOCRYPT (grant agreement No. 101001283), by a research grant from Nomadic Labs and the Tezos Foundation, by the Programma ricerca di ateneo UNICT 2020-22 linea 2, by SECURING Project (PID2019-110873RJ-I00/MCIN/AEI/10.13039/501100011033), by the Spanish Government under projects SCUM (ref. RTI2018-102043-B-I00), CRYPTOEPIC (ref. UR2019-103816), RED2018-102321-T, and PRODIGY (TED2021-132464B-I00), and by the Madrid Regional Government under project BLOQUES (ref. S2018/TCS-4339). The last five projects are co-funded by European Union EIE, and NextGenerationEU/PRTR funds.

References

[ABC+05] Abdalla, M., et al.: Searchable encryption revisited: consistency properties, relation to anonymous IBE, and extensions. In: Shoup, V. (ed.) CRYPTO 2005. LNCS, vol. 3621, pp. 205–222. Springer, Heidelberg (2005). https://doi.org/10.1007/11535218_13

[AC21] Azouvi, S., Cappelletti, D.: Private attacks in longest chain proof-of-stake protocols with single secret leader elections. In: Proceedings of the 3rd ACM Conference on Advances in Financial Technologies, pp. 170–182 (2021)

[AMM18] Azouvi, S., McCorry, P., Meiklejohn, S.: Betting on blockchain consensus with fantomette. CoRR, abs/1805.06786 (2018)

[BBB+18] Bünz, B., Bootle, J., Boneh, D., Poelstra, A., Wuille, P., Maxwell, G.: Bulletproofs: short proofs for confidential transactions and more. In: 2018 IEEE Symposium on Security and Privacy, pp. 315–334. IEEE Computer Society Press, May (2018)

[BDOP04] Boneh, D., Di Crescenzo, G., Ostrovsky, R., Persiano, G.: Public key encryption with keyword search. In: Cachin, C., Camenisch, J. (eds.) EUROCRYPT 2004. LNCS, vol. 3027, pp. 506–522. Springer, Heidelberg (2004). https://doi.org/10.1007/978-3-540-24676-3_30

[BEHG20] Boneh, D., Eskandarian, S., Hanzlik, L., Greco, N.: Single secret leader election. In: Proceedings of the 2nd ACM Conference on Advances in Financial Technologies, pp. 12–24 (2020)

[BGG+18] Boneh, D., Gennaro, R., Goldfeder, S., Jain, A., Kim, S., Rasmussen, P.M.R., Sahai, A.: Threshold cryptosystems from threshold fully homomorphic encryption. In: Shacham, H., Boldyreva, A. (eds.) CRYPTO 2018. Part I, volume 10991 of LNCS, pp. 565–596. Springer, Heidelberg (2018). https://doi.org/10.1007/978-3-319-96884-1_19

[BGM16] Bentov, I., Gabizon, A., Mizrahi, A.: Cryptocurrencies without proof of work. In: Clark, J., Meiklejohn, S., Ryan, P.Y.A., Wallach, D.S., Brenner, M., Rohloff, K. (eds.) FC 2016 Workshops. LNCS, vol. 9604, pp. 142–157. Springer, Heidelberg (2016). https://doi.org/10.1007/978-3-662-53357-4_10

[BPS16] Bentov, I., Pass, R., Shi, E.: Snow white: provably secure proofs of stake. Cryptology ePrint Archive, Report 2016/919 (2016). http://eprint.iacr.org/2016/919

[BSW11] Boneh, D., Sahai, A., Waters, B.: Functional encryption: definitions and challenges. In: Ishai, Y. (ed.) TCC 2011. LNCS, vol. 6597, pp. 253–273. Springer, Heidelberg (2011). https://doi.org/10.1007/978-3-642-19571-6_16

[Can01] Canetti, R.: Universally composable security: a new paradigm for cryptographic protocols. In: 42nd FOCS, pp. 136–145. IEEE Computer Society Press, October (2001)

[CD20] Cascudo, I., David, B.: ALBATROSS: publicly attestable batched randomness based on secret sharing. In: Moriai, S., Wang, H. (eds.) ASIACRYPT 2020. Part III, volume 12493 of LNCS, pp. 311–341. Springer, Heidelberg (2020). https://doi.org/10.1007/978-3-030-64840-4_11

[CDG+18] Camenisch, J., Drijvers, M., Gagliardoni, T., Lehmann, A., Neven, G.: The wonderful world of global random oracles. In: Nielsen, J.B., Rijmen, V. (eds.) EUROCRYPT 2018. LNCS, vol. 10820, pp. 280–312. Springer, Cham (2018). https://doi.org/10.1007/978-3-319-78381-9_11

[CF01] Canetti, R., Fischlin, M.: Universally composable commitments. In: Kilian, J. (ed.) CRYPTO 2001. LNCS, vol. 2139, pp. 19–40. Springer, Heidelberg (2001). https://doi.org/10.1007/3-540-44647-8_2

[CJS14] Canetti, R., Jain, A., Scafuro, A.: Practical UC security with a global random oracle. In: Ahn, G.-J., Yung, M., Li, N., editors, ACM CCS 2014, pp. 597–608. ACM Press, November (2014)

[DKT+20] Dembo, A., et al.: Everything is a race and Nakamoto always wins. In: Ligatti, J., Ou, X., Katz, J., Vigna, G., editors, ACM CCS 20, pp. 859–878. ACM Press, November (2020)

[FKMV12] Faust, S., Kohlweiss, M., Marson, G.A., Venturi, D.: On the non-malleability of the fiat-shamir transform. In: Galbraith, S.D., Nandi, M. (eds.) INDOCRYPT 2012. LNCS, vol. 7668, pp. 60–79. Springer, Heidelberg (2012). https://doi.org/10.1007/978-3-642-34931-7_5

[FLS90] Feige, U., Lapidot, D., Shamir, A.: Multiple non-interactive zero knowledge proofs based on a single random string (Extended Abstract). In: 31st FOCS, pp. 308–317. IEEE Computer Society Press, October (1990)

[GGH+13] Garg, S., Gentry, C., Halevi, S., Raykova, M., Sahai, A., Waters, B.: Candidate indistinguishability obfuscation and functional encryption for all circuits. In: 54th FOCS, pp. 40–49. IEEE Computer Society Press, October (2013)

[GHM+17] Gilad, Y., Hemo, R., Micali, S., Vlachos, G., Zeldovich, N.: Algorand: scaling byzantine agreements for cryptocurrencies. In: Proceedings of the 26th Symposium on Operating Systems Principles, SOSP '17, pp. 51–68, New York, NY, USA (2017). Association for Computing Machinery

[GOP+21] Ganesh, C., Orlandi, C., Pancholi, M., Takahashi, A., Tschudi, D.: Fiat–shamir bulletproofs are non-malleable (in the Algebraic Group Model). Cryptology ePrint Archive, Paper 2021/1393 (2021). https://eprint.iacr.org/2021/1393

[GOT19] Ganesh, C., Orlandi, C., Tschudi, D.: Proof-of-stake protocols for privacy-aware blockchains. In: Ishai, Y., Rijmen, V. (eds.) EUROCRYPT 2019. Part I, volume 11476 of LNCS, pp. 690–719. Springer, Heidelberg (2019). https://doi.org/10.1007/978-3-030-17653-2_23

[GPS08] Galbraith, S.D., Paterson, K.G., Smart, N.P.: Pairings for cryptographers. Discrete Appl. Math. **156**(16), 3113–3121 (2008)

[KKKZ19] Kerber, T., Kiayias, A., Kohlweiss, M., Zikas, V.: Ouroboros crypsinous: privacy-preserving proof-of-stake. In: 2019 IEEE Symposium on Security and Privacy, pp. 157–174. IEEE Computer Society Press, May (2019)

[KMTZ13] Katz, J., Maurer, U., Tackmann, B., Zikas, V.: Universally composable synchronous computation. In: Sahai, A. (ed.) TCC 2013. LNCS, vol. 7785, pp. 477–498. Springer, Heidelberg (2013). https://doi.org/10.1007/978-3-642-36594-2_27

[KSW08] Katz, J., Sahai, A., Waters, B.: Predicate encryption supporting disjunctions, polynomial equations, and inner products. In: Smart, N.P. (ed.) EUROCRYPT 2008. LNCS, vol. 4965, pp. 146–162. Springer, Heidelberg (2008)

[Lab19] Labs, P.: Secret single-leader election (SSLE) (2019) . https://web.archive.org/web/20191228170149/https://github.com/protocol/research-RFPs/blob/master/RFPs/rfp-6-SSLE.md

[Mau15] Maurer, U.: Zero-knowledge proofs of knowledge for group homomorphisms. Designs Codes Crypt. **77**(2), 663–676 (2015)

[NR97] Naor, M., Reingold, O.: Number-theoretic constructions of efficient pseudorandom functions. In: 38th FOCS, pp. 458–467. IEEE Computer Society Press, October (1997)

[O'N10] O'Neill, A.: Definitional issues in functional encryption. Cryptology ePrint Archive, Report 2010/556 (2010). http://eprint.iacr.org/2010/556

[Sah99] Sahai, A.: Non-malleable non-interactive zero knowledge and adaptive chosen-ciphertext security. In: 40th FOCS, pp. 543–553. IEEE Computer Society Press, October (1999)

[Wee17] Wee, H.: Attribute-hiding predicate encryption in bilinear groups, revisited. In: Kalai, Y., Reyzin, L. (eds.) TCC 2017. Part I, volume 10677 of LNCS, pp. 206–233. Springer, Heidelberg (2017). https://doi.org/10.1007/978-3-319-70500-2_8

Simple, Fast, Efficient, and Tightly-Secure Non-malleable Non-interactive Timed Commitments

Peter Chvojka[1]([✉]) and Tibor Jager[2]

[1] IMDEA Software Institute, Madrid, Spain
chvojka.p@gmail.com
[2] University of Wuppertal, Wuppertal, Germany
jager@uni-wuppertal.de

Abstract. Timed commitment schemes, introduced by Boneh and Naor (CRYPTO 2000), can be used to achieve fairness in secure computation protocols in a simple and elegant way. The only known non-malleable construction in the standard model is due to Katz, Loss, and Xu (TCC 2020). This construction requires general-purpose zero knowledge proofs with specific properties, and it suffers from an inefficient commitment protocol, which requires the committing party to solve a computationally expensive puzzle.

We propose new constructions of non-malleable non-interactive timed commitments, which combine (an extension of) the Naor-Yung paradigm used to construct IND-CCA secure encryption with a non-interactive ZK proof for a simple algebraic language. This yields much simpler and more efficient non-malleable timed commitments in the standard model.

Furthermore, our constructions also compare favourably to known constructions of timed commitments in the random oracle model, as they achieve several further interesting properties that make the schemes very practical. This includes the possibility of using a homomorphism for the forced opening of multiple commitments in the sense of Malavolta and Thyagarajan (CRYPTO 2019), and they are the first constructions to achieve *public verifiability*, which seems particularly useful to apply the homomorphism in practical applications.

1 Introduction

Timed commitments make it possible to commit to a message with respect to some time parameter $T \in \mathbb{N}$, such that (1) the commitment is *binding* for the

Peter Chvojka has been partially funded by the European Research Council (ERC) under the European Union's Horizon 2020 research and innovation program under project PICOCRYPT (grant agreement No. 101001283), a research grant from Nomadic Labs and the Tezos Foundation, the Spanish Government under project PRODIGY (TED2021-132464B-I00), and the Madrid Regional Government under project BLO-QUES (S2018/TCS-4339), the last two projects are co-funded by European Union EIE, and NextGenerationEU/PRTR funds. Tibor Jager is supported by the European Research Council (ERC) under the European Union's Horizon 2020 research and innovation programme, grant agreement 802823.

© International Association for Cryptologic Research 2023
A. Boldyreva and V. Kolesnikov (Eds.): PKC 2023, LNCS 13940, pp. 500–529, 2023.
https://doi.org/10.1007/978-3-031-31368-4_18

committing party, (2) it is *hiding* the committed message for T units of time (*e.g.*, seconds, minutes, days), but (3) it can also forcibly be opened after time T in case the committing party refuses to open the commitment or becomes unavailable. This idea goes back to a seminal work by Rivest, Shamir, and Wagner [24] introducing the strongly related notion of *time-lock puzzles*, and Boneh and Naor [7] extended this idea to *timed commitments*, which have the additional feature that an opening to the commitment can be efficiently verified (and thus the commitment can be opened efficiently).

Achieving fairness via timed commitments. One prime application of timed commitments is to achieve *fairness* in secure two- or multi-party protocols. For instance, consider a simple sealed-bid auction protocol with n bidders $B_1, \ldots, B_n$, where every bidder B_i commits to its bid x_i and publishes the commitment $c_i = \mathsf{Com}(x_i, r_i)$ using randomness r_i. When all bidders have published their commitments, everyone reveals their bid x_i along with r_i, such that everyone can publicly verify that the claimed bid x_i is indeed consistent with the initial commitment c_i. The bidder with the maximal bid wins the auction. For this to be most practical, we want commitments to be *non-interactive*.

Now suppose that after the first $(n-1)$ bidders $B_1, \ldots, B_{n-1}$ have opened their commitments (x_i, r_i), the last bidder B_n claims that it has "lost" its randomness r_{i*}, *e.g.*, by accidentally deleting it. However, B_n also argues strongly and quite plausibly that it has made the highest bid x_{i*}. This is a difficult situation to resolve in practice:

- B_n *might indeed be honest.* In this case, it would be fair to accept its highest bid x_{i*}. One could argue that it is B_n's own fault and thus it should not win the auction, but at the same time a seller might strongly argue to accept the bid, as it is interested in maximising the price, and if B_n's claim is indeed true, then discarding the real highest bit could be considered unfair by the seller.
- *However,* B_n *might also be cheating.* Maybe it didn't commit to the highest bid, and now B_n tries to "win" the auction in an unfair way.

Timed commitments can resolve this situation very elegantly and without the need to resort to a third party that might collude with bidders, and thus needs to be trusted, or which might not even be available in certain settings, *e.g.*, in fully decentralized protocols, such as blockchain-based applications. In a timed commitment scheme, the parties create their commitments $c_i = \mathsf{Com}(x_i, r_i, T)$ with respect to a suitable time parameter T for the given application. In case one party is not able to or refuses to open its commitment, the other parties can force the commitment open in time T and thus resolve a potential dispute.

Requirements on Practical Timed Commitments. Several challenges arise when constructing timed commitments that can be used in practical applications.

Consistency of standard and forced opening. A first challenge to resolve when constructing a timed commitment scheme is to guarantee that the availability of an alternative way to open a commitment, by using the forced decommitment procedure, does not break the *binding* property. Standard and forced opening must be guaranteed to reveal the same message. Otherwise, a malicious party could create a commitment where standard and forced openings yields different values. Then it could decide in the opening phase whether it provide the "real" opening, or whether it refuses to open, such that the other parties will perform the forced opening.

Non-interactivity. Having non-interactive commitments is generally desirable to obtain protocols that do not require all parties to be online at the same time. Furthermore, certain applications inherently require the commitment scheme to be non-interactive. This includes, for example, protocols where the commitments are published in a public ledger (*e.g.*, a decentralized blockchain). Several examples of such applications are described in [20]. Non-interactivity also avoids concurrent executions of the commitment protocol, which simplifies the security model significantly.

Non-malleability. Non-malleability of a commitment guarantees that no party can turn a given commitment c that decommits to some value x into another commitment c' which decommits to a different value x', such that x and x' are related in some meaningful way. For instance, in the above example of an auction, a malicious party B_n could first wait for all other parties to publish their commitments. Then it would select the commitment c_i which most likely contains the highest bid x_i, and exploit the malleability of to create a new commitment c_n, which is derived from c_i and opens to $x_i + 1$. Hence, B_n would be able win the auction with a bid that is only slightly larger than the 2nd highest bit, which does not meet the intuitive security expectations on a secure auctioning protocol.

In order to achieve non-malleability for timed commitments, a recent line of works has explored the idea of *non-malleable time-locked commitments* and *puzzles* [1,12,17,25]. Existing constructions of timed commitments are either malleable, rely on the random oracle model, have highly non-tight security proof, which constructs a reduction that solves multiple instances of a puzzle, or require the sender of the commitment to invest as much effort to commit to a value as for the receiver to forcibly open the commitment. The only known standard model construction by Katz *et al.* [17] relies on non-interactive zero-knowledge proofs (NIZKs) for *general* NP relations with very specific properties.

Force opening many commitments at once via homomorphism. Yet another interesting property that can make timed commitments more practical is a possibility to aggregate multiple commitments into a *single* one, such that it is sufficient to force open only this commitment. The idea of homomorphic time-lock *puzzles* was introduced by Malavolta and Thyagarajan [20] and later adopted to the setting of non-interactive timed commitments in [25].

A homomorphic timed commitment scheme allows to efficiently evaluate a circuit C over a set of commitments $c_1, \ldots, c_n$, where c_i is a commitment to some value x_i for all i, to obtain a commitment c to $C(x_1, \ldots, x_n)$. If there are multiple parties $B_{i_1}, \ldots, B_{i_z}$ that refuse to open their commitments and it is not necessary to recover the full committed messages $x_{i_1}, \ldots, x_{i_z}$, but recovering $C(x_{i_1}, \ldots, x_{i_z})$ is sufficient, then one can use the homomorphism to compute a single commitment c that needs to be opened. Malavolta and Thyagarajan [20] describe several interesting applications, including e-voting and sealed-bid auctions over blockchains, multi-party coin flipping, and multi-party contract signing.

Public verifiability of commitments. Another property is *public verifiability* of a timed commitment, which requires that one can efficiently check whether a commitment is well-formed, such that a forced decommitment will yield a correct result.

Without public verifiability, timed commitments might not provide practical solutions for certain applications. For instance, a malicious party could output a malformed commitment that cannot be opened in time T, such that a protocol would fail again in case the malicious party refuses to open the commitment. This could pose a problem in time-sensitive applications, in particular if a large time parameter T is used, and also give rise do Denial-of-Service attacks. Note that public verifiability is particularly relevant for homomorphic commitments. When many commitments are aggregated into a single one, then it is essential that all these commitments are well-formed, as otherwise the forced opening may fail. Public verifiability allows to efficiently decide which subset of commitments is well-formed, and thus to include only these in the homomorphic aggregate.

Note that the requirement of public verifiability rules out several natural ways to achieve non-malleability, such as the Fujisaki-Okamoto transform [14,15] used by Ephraim *et al.* [12]. It seems that even in the random oracle model ZK proofs are required.

Public verifiability of forced opening. In scenarios when the forced opening is executed by untrusted party, it is desirable to be able efficiently check that forced opening has been executed properly without redoing an expensive sequential computation. This particularly useful when the forced opening computation is outsourced to untrusted server. This property was first suggested for time-lock puzzles by [12].

Our Contributions. We provide a simpler and more efficient approach to construct practical non-malleable timed commitments. We give the first constructions that simultaneously achieve non-interactivity, non-malleability, linear (*i.e.*, additive) or multiplicative homomorphism, public verifiability of commitments and public verifiability of forced opening. Moreover, all our reductions avoid the need to answer decommitment queries using the slow forced decommitment algorithm, which yields much tighter security. Instead of relying on expensive ZK proofs for general NP languages as prior work, we show how to use Fiat-Shamir [13] NIZKs derived from Sigma protocols for simple algebraic languages. Our constructions can be instantiated in the standard model by leveraging techniques from Libert *et al.* [18] and more efficiently in the random oracle model.

Table 1. Comparison of our constructions with related work. Column **Hom.** indicates whether the construction provides a linear/multiplicative homomorphism, **Std.** whether the construction has a standard-model proof, **Com?** whether it is publicly verifiable that commitments are well-formed, **FDec?** efficient public verifiability of forced decommitments, $|\mathsf{Com}|$ is the size of commitments, $|\pi_{\mathsf{Com}}|$ the size of proofs, t_{Com} the running time of the commitment algorithm, and **Tight** whether the proof avoids running the forced decommitment algorithm to respond to CCA queries.

Construction	Hom.	Std.	Setup	Com?	FDec?	$|\mathsf{Com}|$	$|\pi_{\mathsf{Com}}|$	t_{Com}	Tight
[12]	—	✗	—	✗	✓	$O(1)$	—	$O(\log T)$	✓
[17]	—	✓	priv.	✓	✗	$O(1)$	$O(1)$	$O(T)$	✓
[25]	linear	✗	pub.	✓	✗	$O(\lambda)$	$O(\lambda)$	$O(1)$	✗
Sect. 3.3	linear	✓	priv.	✓	✓	$O(1)$	$O(\log \lambda)$	$O(1)$	✓
Sect. 3.4	mult.	✓	priv.	✓	✓	$O(1)$	$O(\log \lambda)$	$O(1)$	✓
[9] - Sect. 4.3	linear	✗	priv.	✓	✓	$O(1)$	$O(1)$	$O(1)$	✓
[9] - Sect. 4.4	mult	✗	priv.	✓	✓	$O(1)$	$O(1)$	$O(1)$	✓

In more detail, we make the following contributions.

1. We begin by extending the formal definitions of prior work to cover *public verifiability* of forced opening in the setting of non-malleable non-interactive timed commitments.
2. We then give four constructions of non-interactive non-malleable timed commitments. All our constructions rely on a variation of the double encryption paradigm by Naor and Yung [21], which was also used by Katz *et al.* [17] and Thyagarajan *et al.* [25].

   However, in contrast to [17], we do not start from a timed public key encryption scheme, but build our timed commitment from scratch. This enables us avoid two out of the three NIZK proofs in their construction, and lets us replace the third by a proof for a variation of the DDH relation over groups of unknown order. We are able to instantiate the given NIZK both in the standard model and in the random oracle model [2]. Like the construction from [17] we support public verifiability of commitments. Another important advantage of our constructions over that of Katz *et al.* [17] is that it allows for fast commitment, whereas [17] requires to execute an expensive sequential computation in order to commit to a message. Additionally, we achieve public verifiability of forced opening and homomorphic properties.

In comparison, the non-interactive construction of David *et al.* [1] is in the programmable random oracle model, while ours can also be instantiated in the standard model. David *et al.* achieve fast commitments, however the construction does not provide public verifiability of commitments, public verifiability of forced opening nor homomorphic properties. The work of Ephraim et al. [12] does support fast commitments and public verifiability of forced opening, but is also in the (auxiliary non-programmable) random oracle model and does not support public verifiability of commitments and homomorphic properties. Thyagarajan *et al.* [25]

Table 2. Comparison of our construction [9](Section 4.3) with [25] for security level $\lambda = 128$ bits and taking into account the security loss for $Q = T = 2^{32}$.

Construction	|crs| (kB)	|Com| (kB)	|π_{Com}| (kB)	|m| (bits)
[25]	2.32	3321.41	8846.96	256
[9] - Sect. 4.3	1.92	1.54	1.55	3072

construct the first CCA-secure non-interactive timed commitment with transparent setup, meaning that randomness used in the setup can be made public. Their construction relies on class groups and CCA security is achieved using the Naor-Young paradigm. Additionally, the construction is linearly homomorphic. This is very similar to our work. The main disadvantage of this approach compared to our constructions is that the size of the resulting commitments is linear in security parameter and the security proof is extremely non-tight, since it relies on slow forced decommitment in several steps of the security proof. Moreover, it supports a significantly smaller message space and the construction is in the random oracle model. We provide a summary of the properties of our constructions in comparison to previous works in Table 1. Additionally, in Table 2 we provide a comparison of an instantiation of our construction of linearly homomorphic NITCs in the ROM with an instantiation of the construction from [25] which is also linearly homomorphic and in ROM. We compare the size of crs, commitments Com, proofs π_{Com}, and messages for security level $\lambda = 128$ bits and taking into account a security loss in the security proofs. Since in the majority of game hops of the security proof of [25] decommitment queries are answered using forced decommitment, the corresponding security loss is $Q \cdot T$ where Q is the number of decommitment queries and T is the time parameter of NITC. As an example, we assume that $Q = T = 2^{32}$, which results in the security loss of 2^{64}. Therefore to achieve 128 bits of security, one has to instantiate assumptions in [25] for security parameter $\lambda = 192$ bits.[1] According to [4] the fundamental discriminant Δ_K for this security parameter has size of 3598 bits, and similarly to [25] we define the message space $\mathbb{Z}_q$ for q which is 256 bits. Hence, Δ_q has size of $3588 + 2 \times 256 = 4110$ bits, size of $\tilde{q}$ is $\alpha = 3598/2 + 192 = 1991$ bits, and $\mathbb{Z}_p^*$ is instantiated for a prime p of size 3072 bits. To instantiate our construction it is sufficient to use recommended modulus size of 3072 bits, since our security proof is tight. We remark, that our constructions provide significantly smaller commitments and proofs and larger message space even if we don't take the security loss into account.

Technical Overview. The *binding* property of our commitment scheme will be relatively easy to argue, therefore let us focus on the *hiding* property and non-malleability. Like in [17], we prove this by considering an IND-CCA security experiment, where the adversary has access to a forced decommitment oracle. Even though the forced decommitment can be performed in polynomial time, this

---

[1] The choice of Q and T such that $QT = 2^{64}$ is convenient because it yields $\lambda = 192$ and [4] provides concrete parameters for this security parameter.

polynomial may be very large, if the time parameter T is large. Since the experiment needs to perform a forced decommitment for *every* decommitment query of the adversary, this would incur a very significant overhead and a highly lossy reduction. Hence, following Katz *et al.* [17], we aim to build commitment schemes where a reduction can perform a fast decommitment.

Recall that a classical approach to achieve IND-CCA security is to apply the Naor-Yung paradigm [21]. A natural approach to construct non-malleable timed commitments is therefore to apply this paradigm as follows. A commitment $c = (c_1, c_2, \pi)$ to a message m consists of a time-lock puzzle c_1 opening to m, a public key encryption of m, and a simulation-sound zero knowledge proof π that both contain the same message m, everything with respect to public parameters contained in a public common reference string. This scheme may potentially achieve all desired properties:

- Consistency of regular and forced opening can be achieved by using a suitable time-lock puzzle and public-key encryption scheme.
- The commitment is non-interactive.
- IND-CCA security follows from the standard Naor-Yung argument.
- The time-lock puzzle in the above construction can be instantiated based on repeated squaring [24], possibly using the variant of [20] that combines repeated squaring with Paillier encryption [22] to achieve a linear homomorphism.
- Public verifiability can be achieved by using a suitable proof system for π.

Furthermore, in the IND-CCA security proof, we can perform fast opening by decrypting c_2 with the secret key of the public key encryption scheme, which is indistinguishable from a forced opening using c_1 by the soundness of the proof. However, it turns out that concretely instantiating this scheme in a way that yields a practical construction is non-trivial and requires a very careful combination of different techniques.

Triple Naor-Yung. First of all, note that repeated squaring modulo a composite number $N = PQ$, where P and Q are different primes, is currently the only available choice to achieve a practical time-lock puzzle, hence we are bound to using this puzzle to instantiate c_1. Conveniently, this puzzle allows for a linear (*i.e.*, additive) homomorphism by following [20]. Then, in order to be able to instanatiate π efficiently, it would be convenient to use a standard Sigma protocol, which can then be made non-interactive via the Fiat-Shamir transform [13] in the random oracle model, or by leveraging techniques from Libert *et al.* [18] in the standard model. Since practically efficient Sigma protocols are only known for algebraic languages, such as that defined by the DDH relation, for example, we have to choose c_2 in a way which is "algebraically compatible" with c_1 and the available proofs π. If we instantiate c_1 with the homomorphic TLP from [20], then a natural candidate would be to instantiate c_2 also with Paillier encryption. Here we face the first technical difficulty:

- Efficient proof systems for π are only available, if both c_1 and c_2 use the same modulus N. Hence, we have to instantiate both with the same modulus N.

- When arguing that c_1 hides the committed message m in the Naor-Yung argument of the security proof, we will have to replace c_1 with a random puzzle, using the *strong sequential squaring* (SSS) assumption. At the same time, we have to be able to respond to decommitment queries using the decryption key of c_2. But this decryption key is the factorization P, Q of the common modulus N, and we cannot reduce to the hardness of SSS while knowing the factorization of N.

The first candidate approach to overcome this difficulty is to replace the Paillier encryption used in c_2 with an encryption scheme that does not require knowledge of the factorization of N, such as the "Paillier ElGamal" scheme from [20], which is defined over the subgroup $\mathbb{J}_N$ of elements of $\mathbb{Z}_N$ having Jacobi symbol 1, and which uses a discrete logarithm to decrypt but still requires the factorization of N to be hidden in order to be secure.

However, now we run into another difficulty. In the Naor-Yung argument, we will also have to replace c_2 with an encryption of a random message, in order to argue that our commitment scheme is hiding. In this part of the proof, we cannot know the secret key of c_2, that is, neither the aforementioned discrete logarithm, nor the factorization of N. However, we also cannot use c_1 to respond to decommitment queries, because then we would have to solve the time-lock puzzle, which cannot be done fast without knowledge of the factorization of N.

We resolve this problem by using "triple Naor-Yung". In our linearly homomorphic constructions, a commitment to m will have the form (c_1, c_2, c_3, π), where c_1 and c_2 are Paillier-ElGamal encryptions of m, and c_3 is the Paillier-style time-lock puzzle based on repeated squaring from [20]. All are with respect to the same modulus N, and thus allow for an efficient Sigma-protocol-based proof π that c_1, c_2, and c_3 all contain the same message. In the Naor-Yung-style IND-CCA security proof, we will first replace c_3 with a random puzzle, while using the discrete logarithm of the public key that corresponds to c_1 to perform fast decommitments. When we then replace c_2 with an encryption of a random message, we use the discrete logarithm of the public key that corresponds to c_1 to answer decommitment queries. Finally, we switch to using the discrete logarithm of the secret key corresponding to c_2 for decommitment queries, and replace c_1 with an encryption of a random message. Hence, throughout the argument we never require the factorization of N for fast decommitments.

Standard Naor-Yung works for multiplicative homomorphism. Next, we observe that the standard (*i.e.*, "two-ciphertext") Naor-Yung approach works, if a *multiplicative* homomorphism (or no homomorphism at all) is required. Concretely, a commitment will have the form (c_1, c_2, π), where c_1 is an ElGamal encryption and c_2 uses the "sequential-squaring-with-ElGamal-encryption" idea of [20]. By replacing the underlying group to the subgroup $\mathbb{QR}_N$ of quadratic residues modulo N, we can rely on the DDH assumption in $\mathbb{QR}_N$ and thus do not require the factorization of N to be hidden when replacing the ElGamal encryption c_1 with an encryption of a random message. While the construction idea and high-level arguments are very similar, the underlying groups and detailed arguments are some-what different, and thus we have to give a separate proof.

On separate proofs in the standard model and the ROM. The constructions sketched above can be instantiated relatively efficiently in the standard model, using the one-shot Fiat-Shamir arguments in the standard model by Libert *et al.* [18]. However, these proofs repeat the underlying Sigma protocol a logarithmic number of times, and thus it would be interesting to also consider constructions in the random oracle model. Since the syntactical definitions and properties of proof systems in the random oracle model are slightly different from that in [18], we give separate proofs for both random oracle constructions as well.

Shared randomness. To obtain commitments of smaller size we additionally apply the shared randomness technique from [3], where instead of producing two or three independent encryptions of the same message, we reuse the same randomness for encryption. This allows to save one group element in case of the standard Naor-Yung constructions and two group elements in the case of triple Naor-Yung.

Further Related Work. Time-lock puzzles based on randomized encodings were introduced in [8], but all known constructions of timed commitments rely on the repeated squaring puzzles of [24]. Timed commitments are also related to time-lock encryption scheme [19] and time-released encryption [10], albeit with different properties. The construction in [19] is based on an external "computational reference clock" (instantiated with a public block chain), whose output can be used to decrypt, such that decrypting parties do not have to perform expensive computations by solving a puzzle. The constructions of Chvojka *et al.* [10] are based on repeated squaring, however, the main difference is that the time needed for decryption starts to run from the point when *setup* is executed and not from the point when ciphertext is created.

2   Preliminaries

We denote our security parameter by λ. For $n \in \mathbb{N}$ we write 1^n to denote the n-bit string of all ones. For any element x in a set X, we use $x \xleftarrow{\$} X$ to indicate that we choose x uniformly at random from X. For simplicity we model all algorithms as Turing machines, however, all adversaries are modeled as non-uniform polynomial-size circuits to simplify concrete time bounds in the security definitions of non-interactive timed commitments and the strong sequential squaring assumption. All algorithms are randomized, unless explicitly defined as deterministic. For any PPT algorithm A, we define $x \leftarrow A(1^\lambda, a_1, \ldots, a_n)$ as the execution of A with inputs security parameter λ, $a_1, \ldots, a_n$ and fresh randomness and then assigning the output to x. We write $[n]$ to denote the set of integers $\{1, \ldots, n\}$ and $\lfloor x \rfloor$ to denote the greatest integer that is less than or equal to x.

Non-interactive timed commitments. The following definition of a non-interactive timed commitment scheme is from [17].

Definition 1. *A non-interactive timed commitments scheme* NITC *with message space* $\mathcal{M}$ *is a tuple of algorithms* NITC $=$ (PGen, Com, ComVrfy, DecVrfy, FDec) *with the following syntax.*

- crs $\leftarrow$ PGen($1^\lambda, T$) *is a probabilistic algorithm that takes as input the security parameter* 1^λ *and a hardness parameter* T *and outputs a common reference string* crs *and a secret key.*
- $(c, \pi_{\mathsf{Com}}, \pi_{\mathsf{Dec}}) \leftarrow$ Com(crs, m) *is a probabilistic algorithm that takes as input a common reference string* crs *and a message* m *and outputs a commitment* c *and proofs* $\pi_{\mathsf{Com}}, \pi_{\mathsf{Dec}}$.
- $0/1 \leftarrow$ ComVrfy(crs, c, π_{Com}) *is a deterministic algorithm that takes as input a common reference string* crs, *a commitment* c *and proof* π_{Com} *and outputs* 0 *(reject) or* 1 *(accept).*
- $0/1 \leftarrow$ DecVrfy(crs, c, m, π_{Dec}) *is a deterministic algorithm that takes as input a common reference string* crs, *a commitment* c, *a message* m *and proof* π_{Dec} *and outputs* 0 *(reject) or* 1 *(accept).*
- $m \leftarrow$ FDec(crs, c, π_{Com}) *is a deterministic forced decommit algorithm that takes as input a common reference string* crs *and a ciphertext* c *and outputs* $m \in \mathcal{M} \cup \{\perp\}$ *in time at most* $T \cdot \mathsf{poly}(\lambda)$.

We say NITC *is correct if for all* $\lambda, T \in \mathbb{N}$ *and all* $m \in \mathcal{M}$ *holds:*

$$\Pr\left[\begin{array}{l} \mathsf{FDec}(\mathsf{crs}, c) = m \\ \wedge\ \mathsf{ComVrfy}(\mathsf{crs}, c, \pi_{\mathsf{Com}}) = 1 : \\ \wedge\ \mathsf{DecVrfy}(\mathsf{crs}, c, m, \pi_{\mathsf{Dec}}) = 1 \end{array} \begin{array}{l} \mathsf{crs} \leftarrow \mathsf{PGen}(1^\lambda, T) \\ (c, \pi_{\mathsf{Com}}, \pi_{\mathsf{Dec}}) \leftarrow \mathsf{Com}(\mathsf{crs}, m) \end{array} \right] = 1.$$

The following definition is based on [17], however, adjusted to computational model considered by Bitansky *et al.* [5].

Definition 2. *A non-interactive timed commitment scheme* NITC *is* IND-CCA *secure with gap* $0 < \epsilon < 1$ *if there exists a polynomial* $\tilde{T}(\cdot)$ *such that for all polynomials* $T(\cdot) \geq \tilde{T}(\cdot)$ *and every non-uniform polynomial-size adversary* $\mathcal{A} = \{(\mathcal{A}_{1,\lambda}, \mathcal{A}_{2,\lambda})\}_{\lambda \in \mathbb{N}}$, *where the depth of* $\mathcal{A}_{2,\lambda}$ *is at most* $T^\epsilon(\lambda)$, *there exists a negligible function* $\mathsf{negl}(\cdot)$ *such that for all* $\lambda \in \mathbb{N}$ *it holds*

$$\mathbf{Adv}_{\mathcal{A}}^{\mathtt{NITC}} = \left| \Pr\left[b = b' : \begin{array}{r} \mathsf{crs} \leftarrow \mathsf{PGen}(1^\lambda, T(\lambda)) \\ (m_0, m_1, \mathsf{st}) \leftarrow \mathcal{A}_{1,\lambda}^{\mathsf{DEC}(\cdot, \cdot)}(\mathsf{crs}) \\ b \xleftarrow{\$} \{0,1\} \\ (c^*, \pi_{\mathsf{Com}}, \pi_{\mathsf{Dec}}) \leftarrow \mathsf{Com}(\mathsf{crs}, m_b) \\ b' \leftarrow \mathcal{A}_{2,\lambda}^{\mathsf{DEC}(\cdot)}(c^*, \pi^*_{\mathsf{Com}}, \mathsf{st}) \end{array} \right] - \frac{1}{2} \right| \leq \mathsf{negl}(\lambda),$$

where $|m_0| = |m_1|$ *and the oracle* DEC(c, π_{Com}) *returns the result of* FDec(crs, c) *if* ComVrfy(crs, c, π_{Com}) = 1, *otherwise it returns* $\perp$, *with the restriction that* $\mathcal{A}_{2,\lambda}$ *is not allowed to query the oracle* DEC($\cdot, \cdot$) *for a decommitment of the challenge commitment* $(c^*, \pi^*_{\mathsf{Com}})$.

As already observed in [17], a challenge for a security proof of a concrete timed commitment construction is that the reduction must be able to answer decommitment queries to $\mathsf{DEC}(\cdot, \cdot)$ in time which is independent of T, as otherwise one is not able to obtain a sound proof when reducing to a time-sensitive assumption, such as the strong sequential squaring assumption. This in particular means that decommitment queries in the security proof can not be simply answered by executing the forced decommitment algorithm FDec, as its runtime depends on T, but there must exist another way.

Remark 1. We note that our definition of the decommitment oracle DEC slightly differs from the original definition in [17], since we require that the oracle at first checks if the commitment is well formed and only then returns the result of FDec. All our constructions can achieve also the original definition, to this end we would simply include the proof π that the commitment is well-formed in the commitment and then directly perform the check if a commitment is well formed in algorithm FDec. However, in that case π_{Com} would be empty and the whole idea of the separation of a commitment from a proof of well-formedness would be meaningless.[2]

Definition 3. *We define the* $\mathsf{BND\text{-}CCA}_{\mathcal{A}}(\lambda)$ *experiment as follows:*

1. $\mathsf{crs} \leftarrow \mathsf{PGen}(1^\lambda, T(\lambda))$;
2. $(m, c, \pi_{\mathsf{Com}}, \pi_{\mathsf{Dec}}, m', \pi'_{\mathsf{Dec}}) \leftarrow \mathcal{A}_\lambda^{\mathsf{DEC}(\cdot, \cdot)}(\mathsf{crs})$, *where the oracle* $\mathsf{DEC}(c, \pi_{\mathsf{Com}})$ *returns* $\mathsf{FDec}(\mathsf{crs}, c)$ *if* $\mathsf{ComVrfy}(\mathsf{crs}, c, \pi_{\mathsf{Com}}) = 1$, *otherwise it returns* $\bot$;
3. *Output 1 iff* $\mathsf{ComVrfy}(\mathsf{crs}, c, \pi_{\mathsf{Com}}) = 1$ *and either:*
   - $m \neq m' \wedge \mathsf{DecVrfy}(\mathsf{crs}, c, m, \pi_{\mathsf{Dec}}) = \mathsf{DecVrfy}(\mathsf{crs}, c, m', \pi'_{\mathsf{Dec}}) = 1$;
   - $\mathsf{DecVrfy}(\mathsf{crs}, c, m, \pi_{\mathsf{Dec}}) = 1 \wedge \mathsf{FDec}(\mathsf{crs}, c) \neq m$.

A non-interactive timed commitment scheme NITC *is* BND-CCA *secure if for all non-uniform polynomial-size adversaries* $\mathcal{A} = \{\mathcal{A}_\lambda\}_{\lambda \in \mathbb{N}}$ *there is a negligible function* $\mathsf{negl}(\cdot)$ *such that for all* $\lambda \in \mathbb{N}$

$$\mathbf{Adv}_{\mathcal{A}}^{\mathtt{NITC}} = \Pr\left[\mathsf{BND\text{-}CCA}_{\mathcal{A}}(\lambda) = 1\right] \leq \mathsf{negl}(\lambda).$$

Next we define a new property of NITCs, which allows for efficient verification that a forced decommitment was executed correctly, without the need to execute expensive sequential computation. This property was first suggested for time-lock puzzles by [12] and denoted as public verifiability.

Definition 4. *A non-interactive timed commitments scheme* NITC *is publicly verifiable if* FDec *additionally outputs a proof* π_{FDec} *and has an additional algorithm* $\mathsf{FDecVrfy}$ *with the following syntax:*

- $0/1 \leftarrow \mathsf{FDecVrfy}(\mathsf{crs}, c, m, \pi_{\mathsf{FDec}})$ *is a deterministic algorithm that takes as input a common reference string* crs, *a commitment* c, *a message* m, *and a proof* π_{FDec} *and outputs 0 (reject) or 1 (accept) in time* $\mathsf{poly}(\log T, \lambda)$.

---

[2] Note that [17] FDec also implicitly checks well-formedness, as it runs a decryption algorithm, which verifies the NIZK proof.

Moreover, a publicly verifiable NITC must have the following properties:

– Completeness *for all* $\lambda, T \in \mathbb{N}$ *and all* $m \in \mathcal{M}$ *holds:*

$$\Pr \left[\mathsf{FDecVrfy}(\mathsf{crs}, c, m, \pi_{\mathsf{FDec}}) = 1 : \begin{array}{l} \mathsf{crs} \leftarrow \mathsf{PGen}(1^\lambda, T) \\ (c, \pi_{\mathsf{Com}}, \pi_{\mathsf{Dec}}) \leftarrow \mathsf{Com}(\mathsf{crs}, m) \\ (m, \pi_{\mathsf{FDec}}) \leftarrow \mathsf{FDec}(\mathsf{crs}, c) \end{array} \right] = 1.$$

– Soundness *for all non-uniform polynomial-size adversaries* $\mathcal{A} = \{\mathcal{A}_\lambda\}_{\lambda \in \mathbb{N}}$ *there is a negligible function* $\mathsf{negl}(\cdot)$ *such that for all* $\lambda \in \mathbb{N}$

$$\Pr \left[\begin{array}{c} \mathsf{FDecVrfy}(\mathsf{crs}, c, m', \pi'_{\mathsf{FDec}}) = 1 \\ \wedge\ \mathsf{ComVrfy}(\mathsf{crs}, c, \pi_{\mathsf{Com}}) = 1 : \\ \wedge\ m \neq m' \end{array} \begin{array}{l} \mathsf{crs} \leftarrow \mathsf{PGen}(1^\lambda, T) \\ (c, \pi_{\mathsf{Com}}, m', \pi'_{\mathsf{FDec}}) \leftarrow \mathcal{A}_\lambda(\mathsf{crs}) \\ (m, \pi_{\mathsf{FDec}}) \leftarrow \mathsf{FDec}(\mathsf{crs}, c) \end{array} \right] \leq \mathsf{negl}(\lambda).$$

The following definition is inspired by the definition of homomorphic time-lock puzzles of Malavolta *et al.* [20].

Definition 5. *A non-interactive timed commitments scheme* NITC *is homomorphic with respect to a class of circuits* $\mathcal{C} = \{\mathcal{C}_\lambda\}_{\lambda \in \mathbb{N}}$, *if there is an additional algorithm* Eval *with the following syntax:*

– $c \leftarrow \mathsf{Eval}(\mathsf{crs}, C, c_1, \ldots, c_n)$ *is a probabilistic algorithm that takes as input a common reference string* crs, *a circuit* $C \in \mathcal{C}_\lambda$, *and set of* n *commitments* $(c_1, \ldots, c_n)$. *It outputs a commitment* c.

Additionally, a homomorphic NITC fulfils the following properties:
Correctness: *for all* $\lambda, T \in \mathbb{N}$, $C \in \mathcal{C}_\lambda$, $(m_1, \ldots, m_n) \in \mathcal{M}^n$, *all* crs *in the support of* $\mathsf{PGen}(1^\lambda, T)$, *all* c_i *in the support of* $\mathsf{Com}(\mathsf{crs}, m_i)$ *we have:*

1. *There exists a negligible function* negl *such that*

$$\Pr[\mathsf{FDec}(\mathsf{crs}, \mathsf{Eval}(\mathsf{crs}, C, c_1, \ldots, c_n)) \neq C(m_1, \ldots, m_n)] \leq \mathsf{negl}(\lambda).$$

2. *The exists a fixed polynomial* poly *such that the runtime of* $\mathsf{FDec}(\mathsf{crs}, c)$ *is bounded by* $\mathsf{poly}(\lambda, T)$, *where* $c \leftarrow \mathsf{Eval}(\mathsf{crs}, C, c_1, \ldots, c_n)$.

Compactness: *for all* $\lambda, T \in \mathbb{N}$, $C \in \mathcal{C}_\lambda$, $(m_1, \ldots, m_n) \in \mathcal{M}^n$, *all* crs *in the support of* $\mathsf{PGen}(1^\lambda, T)$, *all* c_i *in the support of* $\mathsf{Com}(\mathsf{crs}, m_i)$, *the following two conditions are satisfied:*

1. *The exists a fixed polynomial* $\hat{\mathsf{poly}}$ *such that* $|c| = \hat{\mathsf{poly}}(\lambda, |C(m_1, \ldots, m_n)|)$, *where* $c \leftarrow \mathsf{Eval}(\mathsf{crs}, C, c_1, \ldots, c_n)$.
2. *The exists a fixed polynomial* $\tilde{\mathsf{poly}}$ *such that the runtime of* $\mathsf{Eval}(\mathsf{crs}, C, c_1, \ldots, c_n)$ *is bounded by* $\tilde{\mathsf{poly}}(\lambda, |C|)$.

$\mathsf{ExpSSS}_{\mathcal{A}}^b(\lambda):$

$(p, q, N, g) \leftarrow \mathsf{GenMod}(1^\lambda)$

$\mathsf{st} \leftarrow \mathcal{A}_{1,\lambda}(N, T(\lambda), g)$

$x \overset{\$}{\leftarrow} \mathbb{G}$

if $b = 0 : y := x^{2^{T(\lambda)}} \bmod N$

if $b = 1 : y \overset{\$}{\leftarrow} \mathbb{G}$

return $b' \leftarrow \mathcal{A}_{2,\lambda}(x, y, \mathsf{st})$

$\mathsf{ExpDCR}_{\mathcal{A}}^b(\lambda):$

$(p, q, N, g) \leftarrow \mathsf{GenMod}(1^\lambda)$

$y_1 \overset{\$}{\leftarrow} \mathbb{Z}_{N^2}^*$

$y_0 = y_1^N \bmod N^2$

return $b' \leftarrow \mathcal{A}_\lambda(N, y_b)$

Fig. 1. Security experiments for the strong sequential squaring assumption (left) and DCR (right).

Complexity assumptions. We base our constructions on the strong sequential squaring assumption. Let p, q be safe primes (i.e., such that $p = 2p' + 1, q = 2q' + 1$ for primes p', q'). We denote by $\varphi(\cdot)$ Euler's totient function, by $\mathbb{Z}_N^*$ the group $\{x \in \mathbb{Z}_N : \gcd(N, x) = 1\}$ and by $\mathbb{J}_N$ the cyclic subgroup of elements of $\mathbb{Z}_N^*$ with Jacobi symbol 1 which has order $|\mathbb{J}_N| = \frac{\varphi(N)}{2} = \frac{(p-1)(q-1)}{2}$. By $\mathbb{QR}_N$ we denote the cyclic group of quadratic residues modulo N which has order $|\mathbb{QR}_N| = \frac{\varphi(N)}{4} = \frac{(p-1)(q-1)}{4}$. To efficiently sample a random generator g from $\mathbb{J}_N$, it is sufficient to be able sample random element from $\mathbb{J}_N \setminus \mathbb{QR}_N$, since with all but negligible probability a random element of $\mathbb{J}_N \setminus \mathbb{QR}_N$ is a generator. Moreover, when the factors p, q are known, then it easy to check if the given element is a generator of $\mathbb{J}_N$ by testing possible orders.

To sample a random element of $\mathbb{J}_N \setminus \mathbb{QR}_N$, we can sample $r \overset{\$}{\leftarrow} \mathbb{Z}_N^*$ and let $g := -r^2 \bmod N$. Now notice that $r^2 \bmod N$ is a random element in the group of the quadratic residues and $-1 \bmod N \in \mathbb{J}_N \setminus \mathbb{QR}_N$. To see this, notice that for any safe prime p it holds that $p = 3 \bmod 4$. By Euler's criterion we have $\left(\frac{x}{p}\right) = x^{\frac{p-1}{2}} \bmod p$ for odd primes p and every x which is coprime to p. Therefore $\left(\frac{-1}{p}\right) = \left(\frac{-1}{q}\right) = -1$, meaning that $-1 \bmod N \in \mathbb{J}_N \setminus \mathbb{QR}_N$. By multiplying a fixed element of $\mathbb{J}_N \setminus \mathbb{QR}_N$ with a random element of $\mathbb{QR}_N$ we obtain a random element of $\mathbb{J}_N \setminus \mathbb{QR}_N$.

As mentioned above, to sample a random element from $\mathbb{QR}_N$, we can sample $r \overset{\$}{\leftarrow} \mathbb{Z}_N^*$ and let $g := r^2 \bmod N$. Again g is a generator of $\mathbb{QR}_N$ with all but negligible probability. When the factors p, q are known, then it easy to check if the given element is a generator of $\mathbb{QR}_N$ by checking if $g^{p'} \neq 1 \bmod N \land g^{q'} \neq 1 \bmod N$. Therefore we are able to efficiently sample a random generator of $\mathbb{QR}_N$.

Since our constructions relies on the strong sequential squaring assumption either in the group $\mathbb{J}_N$ [20] or in the group $\mathbb{QR}_N$ [17] for brevity we state the strong sequential squaring assumption in the group $\mathbb{G}$, where $\mathbb{G}$ is one of the mentioned groups. Let GenMod be a probabilistic polynomial-time algorithm which on input 1^λ outputs two λ-bit safe primes p and q, modulus $N = pq$ and a random generator g of the group $\mathbb{G}$.

Definition 6 (Strong Sequential Squaring Assumption (SSS)). *Consider the security experiment* $\mathsf{ExpSSS}_{\mathcal{A}}^{b}(\lambda)$ *in Fig. 1. The strong sequential squaring assumption with gap* $0 < \epsilon < 1$ *holds relative to* GenMod *if there exists a polynomial* $\tilde{T}(\cdot)$ *such that for all polynomials* $T(\cdot) \geq \tilde{T}(\cdot)$ *and for every non-uniform polynomial-size adversary* $\mathcal{A} = \{(\mathcal{A}_{1,\lambda}, \mathcal{A}_{2,\lambda})\}_{\lambda \in \mathbb{N}}$, *where the depth of* $\mathcal{A}_{2,\lambda}$ *is at most* $T^{\epsilon}(\lambda)$, *there exists a negligible function* $\mathsf{negl}(\cdot)$ *such that for all* $\lambda \in \mathbb{N}$

$$\mathbf{Adv}_{\mathcal{A}}^{\mathsf{SSS}} = \left| \Pr[\mathsf{ExpSSS}_{\mathcal{A}}^{0}(\lambda) = 1] - \Pr[\mathsf{ExpSSS}_{\mathcal{A}}^{1}(\lambda) = 1] \right| \leq \mathsf{negl}(\lambda).$$

Next we define the DDH experiment in the group $\mathbb{J}_N$, as originally stated by Castagnos *et al.* [11]. Castagnos *et al.* have shown that this problem is hard assuming that DDH is hard in the subgroups of $\mathbb{Z}_N^*$ of order p' and q' and that the quadratic residuosity problem is hard in $\mathbb{Z}_N^*$. We also define DDH experiment in the group of quadratic residues modulo N where the factors of N are given to an adversary. Castagnos *et al.* [11] have shown that DDH problem is hard in $\mathbb{QR}_N$ assuming that DDH is hard in the large prime-order subgroups of $\mathbb{Z}_N^*$. This is shown as part of the proof of their Theorem 9. We remark that even though in the mentioned proof the prime factors p, q are not given to DDH adversary in the group $\mathbb{QR}_N$, but the proof relies on the fact that the constructed reduction knows factors p, q. Therefore the proof is valid even if p, q are given to DDH adversary in $\mathbb{QR}_N$ as input.

$\mathsf{ExpJ_NDDH}_{\mathcal{A}}^{b}(\lambda)$:	$\mathsf{ExpQR_NDDH}_{\mathcal{A}}^{b}(\lambda)$:
$(p, q, N, g) \leftarrow \mathsf{GenMod}(1^\lambda)$	$(p, q, N, g) \leftarrow \mathsf{GenMod}(1^\lambda)$
$\alpha, \beta \xleftarrow{\$} [\varphi(N)/2]$	$\alpha, \beta \xleftarrow{\$} [\varphi(N)/4]$
if $b = 0 : \gamma = a \cdot b \bmod \varphi(N)/2$	if $b = 0 : \gamma = a \cdot b \bmod \varphi(N)$
if $b = 1 : \gamma \xleftarrow{\$} [\varphi(N)/2]$	if $b = 1 : \gamma \xleftarrow{\$} [\varphi(N)/4]$
return $b' \leftarrow \mathcal{A}_\lambda(N, g, g^\alpha, g^\beta, g^\gamma)$	return $b' \leftarrow \mathcal{A}_\lambda(N, p, q, g, g^\alpha, g^\beta, g^\gamma)$

Fig. 2. Security experiments for DDH in $\mathbb{J}_N$ and $\mathbb{QR}_N$.

Definition 7 (Decisional Diffie-Hellman in $\mathbb{J}_N$). *Consider the security experiment* $\mathsf{ExpJ_NDDH}_{\mathcal{A}}^{b}(\lambda)$ *in Fig. 2. The decisional Diffie-Hellman assumption holds relative to* GenMod *in* $\mathbb{J}_N$ *if for every non-uniform polynomial-size adversary* $\mathcal{A} = \{\mathcal{A}_\lambda\}_{\lambda \in \mathbb{N}}$ *there exists a negligible function* $\mathsf{negl}(\cdot)$ *such that for all* $\lambda \in \mathbb{N}$

$$\mathbf{Adv}_{\mathcal{A}}^{\mathsf{DDH}} = \left| \Pr[\mathsf{ExpJ_NDDH}_{\mathcal{A}}^{0}(\lambda) = 1] - \Pr[\mathsf{ExpJ_NDDH}_{\mathcal{A}}^{1}(\lambda) = 1] \right| \leq \mathsf{negl}(\lambda).$$

Definition 8 (Decisional Diffie-Hellman in $\mathbb{QR}_N$). *Consider the security experiment* $\mathsf{ExpQR_NDDH}_{\mathcal{A}}^{b}(\lambda)$ *in Fig. 2. The decisional Diffie-Hellman assumption holds relative to* GenMod *in* $\mathbb{QR}_N$ *if for every non-uniform polynomial-size adversary* $\mathcal{A} = \{\mathcal{A}_\lambda\}_{\lambda \in \mathbb{N}}$ *there exists a negligible function* $\mathsf{negl}(\cdot)$ *such that for all* $\lambda \in \mathbb{N}$

$$\mathbf{Adv}_{\mathcal{A}}^{\mathsf{DDH}} = \left| \Pr[\mathsf{ExpQR_NDDH}_{\mathcal{A}}^{0}(\lambda) = 1] - \Pr[\mathsf{ExpQR_NDDH}_{\mathcal{A}}^{1}(\lambda) = 1] \right| \leq \mathsf{negl}(\lambda).$$

Definition 9 (Decisional Composite Residuosity Assumption). *Consider the security experiment* $\mathsf{ExpDCR}_{\mathcal{A}}^b(\lambda)$ *in Fig. 1. The decisional composite residuosity assumption holds relative to* GenMod *if for every non-uniform polynomial-size adversary* $\mathcal{A} = \{\mathcal{A}_\lambda\}_{\lambda \in \mathbb{N}}$ *there exists a negligible function* $\mathsf{negl}(\cdot)$ *such that for all* $\lambda \in \mathbb{N}$

$$\mathbf{Adv}_{\mathcal{A}}^{\mathsf{DCR}} = \left| \Pr[\mathsf{ExpDCR}_{\mathcal{A}}^0(\lambda) = 1] - \Pr[\mathsf{ExpDCR}_{\mathcal{A}}^1(\lambda) = 1] \right| \leq \mathsf{negl}(\lambda).$$

When designing an efficient simulation sound NIZK for our scheme, we rely on factoring assumption.

Definition 10 (Factoring Assumption). *The* factoring assumption *holds relative to* GenMod *if for every non-uniform polynomial-size adversary* $\mathcal{A} = \{\mathcal{A}_\lambda\}_{\lambda \in \mathbb{N}}$ *there exists a negligible function* $\mathsf{negl}(\cdot)$ *such that for all* $\lambda \in \mathbb{N}$

$$\mathbf{Adv}_{\mathcal{A}}^{\mathtt{Factor}} = \Pr \left[N = p'q' : \begin{array}{r} (p, q, N, g) \leftarrow \mathsf{GenMod}(1^\lambda) \\ p', q' \leftarrow \mathcal{A}_\lambda(N), \\ \text{such that } p', q' \in \mathbb{N}; p', q' > 1 \end{array} \right] \leq \mathsf{negl}(\lambda).$$

To argue that our proof system fulfils required properties, we make of use the following lemma, which states that it is possible factorize N if a positive multiple of $\varphi(N)$ is known. The proof of this lemma is part of an analysis of [16, Theorem 8.50].

Lemma 1. *Let* $(p, q, N) \leftarrow \mathsf{GenMod}(1^\lambda)$ *and let* $M = \alpha\varphi(N)$ *for some positive integer* $\alpha \in \mathbb{Z}^+$. *There exists a PPT algorithm* $\mathsf{Factor}(N, M)$ *which, on input* (N, M), *outputs* $p', q' \in \mathbb{N}$, $p', q' > 1$ *such that* $N = p'q'$ *with probability at least* $1 - 2^{-\lambda}$.

On sampling random exponents for $\mathbb{J}_N$ *and* $\mathbb{QR}_N$. Since in our construction the order $\varphi(N)/2$ of the group $\mathbb{J}_N$ and the order $\varphi(N)/4$ of $\mathbb{QR}_N$ are unknown, we use the set $[\lfloor N/2 \rfloor]$, respectively $[\lfloor N/4 \rfloor]$, whenever we should sample from the sets $[\varphi(N)/2]$, respectively $[\varphi(N)/4]$ without knowing the factorization of N. Sampling from $[\lfloor N/2 \rfloor]$ is statistically indistinguishable from sampling from $[\varphi(N)/2]$ and similarly sampling from $[\lfloor N/4 \rfloor]$ is statistically indistinguishable from sampling from $[\varphi(N)/4]$.

Definition 11 (Statistical Distance). *Let* X *and* Y *be two random variables over a finite set* S. *The statistical distance between* X *and* Y *is defined as*

$$\mathbb{SD}(X, Y) = \frac{1}{2} \sum_{s \in S} |\Pr[X = s] - \Pr[Y = s]|.$$

Lemma 2. *Let* p, q *be primes,* $N = pq$, $\ell \in \mathbb{N}$ *such that* $\gcd(\ell, \varphi(N)) = \ell$ *and* X *and* Y *be random variables defined on domain* $[\lfloor N/\ell \rfloor]$ *as follows:*

$$\Pr[X = r] = 1/\lfloor N/\ell \rfloor \; \forall r \in [\lfloor N/\ell \rfloor] \text{ and } \Pr[Y = r] = \begin{cases} \ell/\varphi(N) & \forall r \in [\varphi(N)/\ell] \\ 0 & \textit{otherwise.} \end{cases}$$

Then

$$\mathbb{SD}(X,Y) \leq \frac{1}{p} + \frac{1}{q} - \frac{1}{N}.$$

The proof of this lemma can be found in the full version of this paper [9].

3   Standard Model Constructions

In this section we construct two non-malleable non-interactive timed commitment schemes whose security can be proven in standard model and which are either linearly (i.e., additively) or multiplicatively homomorphic. he constructions rely on non-interactive zero-knowledge proofs in the common reference string model.

3.1   Non-interactive Zero-Knowledge Proofs

We recall the definition of a simulation-sound non-interactive proof system (SS-NIZK) that we take from Libert *et al.* [18].

Definition 12. *A non-interactive zero-knowledge proof system Π for an NP language L associated with a relation $\mathcal{R}$ is a tuple of four PPT algorithms $(\mathsf{Gen_{par}}, \mathsf{Gen}_L, \mathsf{Prove}, \mathsf{Vrfy})$, which work as follows:*

- $\mathsf{crs} \leftarrow \mathsf{Setup}(1^\lambda, L)$ *takes a security parameter 1^λ and the description of a language L. It outputs a a common reference string crs.*
- $\pi \leftarrow \mathsf{Prove}(\mathsf{crs}, s, w)$ *is a PPT algorithm which takes as input the common reference string crs, a statement s, and a witness w such that $(s, w) \in \mathcal{R}$ and outputs a proof π.*
- $0/1 \leftarrow \mathsf{Vrfy}(\mathsf{crs}, s, \pi)$ *is a deterministic algorithm which takes as input the common reference string crs, a statement s and a proof π and outputs either 1 or 0, where 1 means that the proof is "accepted" and 0 means it is "rejected".*

Moreover, Π should satisfy the following properties.

- Completeness: *for all $(s, w) \in \mathcal{R}$ holds:*

$$\Pr[\mathsf{Vrfy}(\mathsf{crs}, s, \pi) = 1 : \mathsf{crs} \leftarrow \mathsf{Setup}(1^\lambda, L), \pi \leftarrow \mathsf{Prove}(\mathsf{crs}, s, w)] = 1.$$

- Soundness: *for all non-uniform polynomial-size adversaries $\mathcal{A} = \{\mathcal{A}_\lambda\}_{\lambda \in \mathbb{N}}$ there exists a negligible function $\mathsf{negl}(\cdot)$ such that for all $\lambda \in N$*

$$\mathbf{Snd}_\mathcal{A}^{\mathtt{NIZK}} = \Pr\left[\begin{array}{c} s \notin L\, \wedge \\ \mathsf{Vrfy}(\mathsf{crs}, s, \pi) = 1 \end{array} : \begin{array}{c} (\mathsf{crs} \leftarrow \mathsf{Setup}(1^\lambda, L) \\ (\pi, s) \leftarrow \mathcal{A}_\lambda(\mathsf{crs}, \tau_L) \end{array}\right] \leq \mathsf{negl}(\lambda),$$

where τ_L is membership testing trapdoor.

– Zero-Knowledge: *there is a PPT simulator* $(\mathsf{Sim}_1, \mathsf{Sim}_2)$, *such that for all non-uniform polynomial-size adversaries* $\mathcal{A} = \{\mathcal{A}_\lambda\}_{\lambda \in \mathbb{N}}$ *there exists a negligible function* $\mathsf{negl}(\cdot)$ *such that for all* $\lambda \in \mathbb{N}$:

$$\mathbf{ZK}_{\mathcal{A}}^{\mathtt{NIZK}} = \left| \Pr\left[\mathcal{A}_\lambda^{\mathsf{Prove}(\mathsf{crs},\cdot,\cdot),}(\mathsf{crs}, \tau_L) = 1 : \mathsf{crs} \leftarrow \mathsf{Setup}(1^\lambda, L)\right]\right.$$
$$\left. - \Pr\left[\mathcal{A}_\lambda^{\mathcal{O}(\mathsf{crs},\tau,\cdot,\cdot),}(\mathsf{crs}, \tau_L) = 1 : (\mathsf{crs}, \tau) \leftarrow \mathsf{Sim}_1(1^\lambda, L)\right]\right| \leq \mathsf{negl}(\lambda).$$

Here τ_L *is a membership testing trapdoor for language* L; $\mathsf{Prove}(\mathsf{crs}, \cdot, \cdot)$ *is an oracle that outputs* $\bot$ *on input* $(s, w) \notin \mathcal{R}$ *and outputs a valid proof* $\pi \leftarrow \mathsf{Prove}(\mathsf{crs}, s, w)$ *otherwise;* $\mathcal{O}(\mathsf{crs}, \tau, \cdot, \cdot)$ *is an oracle that outputs* $\bot$ *on input* $(s, w) \notin \mathcal{R}$ *and outputs a simulated proof* $\pi \leftarrow \mathsf{Sim}_2(\mathsf{crs}, \tau, s)$ *on input* $(s, w) \in \mathcal{R}$. *Note that the simulated proof is generated independently of the witness* w.

Remark 2. We have slightly modified the soundness and zero-knowledge definitions compared to [18]. Our soundness definition is adaptive and an adversary is given as input also a membership testing trapdoor τ_L. This notion is implied by the simulation-soundness as defined in Definition 13. Our zero-knowledge definition provides a membership testing trapdoor τ_L as an input for an adversary, whereas the definition of [18] lets an adversary generate the language L itself. The definition of [18] works in our constructions too, but we prefer to base our constructions on a slightly weaker definition.

Definition 13 (One-Time Simulation Soundness). *A NIZK for an NP language* L *with zero-knowledge simulator* $\mathsf{Sim} = (\mathsf{Sim}_0, \mathsf{Sim}_1)$ *is one-time simulation sound, if for all non-uniform polynomial-size adversaries* $\mathcal{A} = \{\mathcal{A}_\lambda\}_{\lambda \in \mathbb{N}}$ *there exists a negligible function* $\mathsf{negl}(\cdot)$ *such that for all* $\lambda \in \mathbb{N}$

$$\mathbf{SimSnd}_{\mathcal{A}}^{\mathtt{NIZK}} = \Pr\left[\begin{array}{c} s \notin L \wedge \\ (s, \pi) \neq (s', \pi') \wedge : \\ \mathsf{Vrfy}(\mathsf{crs}, s, \pi) = 1 \end{array} \begin{array}{c} (\mathsf{crs}, \tau) \leftarrow \mathsf{Sim}_1(1^\lambda, L) \\ (s, \pi) \leftarrow \mathcal{A}_\lambda^{\mathsf{Sim}_2(\mathsf{crs},\tau,\cdot)}(\mathsf{crs}, \tau_L) \end{array} \right] \leq \mathsf{negl}(\lambda),$$

where τ_L *is a membership testing trapdoor for language* L *and* $\mathsf{Sim}_2(\mathsf{crs}, \tau, \cdot)$ *is a single query oracle which on input* s' *returns* $\pi' \leftarrow \mathsf{Sim}(\mathsf{crs}, \tau, s')$.

Libert *et al.* [18] show that given an additively homomorphic encryption scheme, one can build a trapdoor Sigma protocol for the language defined below. Moreover, any trapdoor Sigma protocol can be turned into an unbounded simulation sound NIZK which directly implies existence of a one-time simulation sound NIZK. Since we use the term *trapdoor Sigma protocol* only as intermediate notion and never instantiate it, we do not state formal definition and only reference it for brevity. For more details about trapdoor Sigma protocols see e.g. [18].

Lemma 3 (Lemma D.1 [18]). *Let* $(\mathsf{Gen}, \mathsf{Enc}, \mathsf{Dec})$ *be an additively homomorphic encryption scheme where the message space* M, *randomness space* R *and the ciphertext space* C *form groups* $(M, +), (R, +)$ *and* $(C, \cdot)$. *Let the encryption* *scheme be such that for any public key* pk *generated using* $(\mathsf{pk}, \mathsf{sk}) \leftarrow \mathsf{Gen}(1^\lambda)$, *any messages* $m_1, m_2 \in M$ *and randomness* $r_1, r_2 \in R$ *holds*

$$\mathsf{Enc}(\mathsf{pk}, m_1; r_1) \cdot \mathsf{Enc}(\mathsf{pk}, m_2; r_2) = \mathsf{Enc}(\mathsf{pk}, m_1 + m_2; r_1 + r_2).$$

Let S *be a finite set of public cardinality such that uniform sampling from* S *is computationally indistinguishable from uniform sampling from* R. *Then there is an trapdoor Sigma protocol for the language* $L := \{c \in C | \exists r \in R : c = \mathsf{Enc}(\mathsf{pk}, 0; r)\}$ *of encryptions of zero, where* pk *is fixed by the language.*

Remark 3. We note that Libert *et al.* required that the order of the group $(R, +)$ is public and that this group is efficiently samplable, which is used in their proof of the zero-knowledge property. This is however, not necessary, since it is sufficient to be able to sample from a distribution which is computationally indistinguishable from the uniform distribution. This results in computational indistinguishability of real and simulated transcripts. In case of our constructions, we will sample randomness from a distribution which is statistically close and hence indistinguishable from the uniform distribution over R, which yields that the real and the simulated transcripts are statistically indistinguishable.

Additionally, Libert *et al.* construct a simulation sound non-interactive argument system from any trapdoor Sigma protocol relying on a strongly unforgeable one-time signature, a lossy public-key encryption scheme, an admissible hash function and a correlation intractable hash function.

Theorem 1 (Thm B.1, Thm. B.2 [18]). *Let* $(\mathsf{Gen}_{\mathsf{par}}, \mathsf{Gen}_L, \mathsf{Prove}, \mathsf{Vrfy})$ *be a trapdoor Sigma protocol for an NP language* L. *Then given a strongly unforgeable one-time signature scheme,* $\mathcal{R}$-*lossy public-key encryption scheme, a correlation intractable hash function and an admissible hash function, there is an unbounded simulation sound non-interactive zero-knowledge proof system for the language* L.

We note that in order to achieve negligible soundness error, it is needed to run the underlying trapdoor Sigma protocol $\mathcal{O}(\log \lambda)$ times in parallel. One run of the trapdoor Sigma protocol of Libert *et al.* for L, as defined above, corresponds to sending one ciphertext of the homomorphic encryption scheme and one random element $r \in R$.

3.2 Standard-Model Instantiation of SS-NIZKs

In this section we provide simulation sound NIZK proof systems for languages L_1 and L_2 that are used in our constructions. The languages are defined in the following way:

$$L_1 = \left\{ (c_0, c_1, c_2, c_3) | \exists (m, r) : \begin{array}{l} (\wedge_{i=1}^3 c_i = h_i^{rN}(1+N)^m \bmod N^2) \wedge \\ \qquad\qquad\qquad c_0 = g^r \bmod N \end{array} \right\} \text{ and}$$

$$L_2 = \left\{ (c_0, c_1, c_2) | \exists (m, r) : (\wedge_{i=1}^2 c_i = h_i^r m \bmod N) \wedge c_0 = g^r \bmod N \right\},$$

where g, h_1, h_2, h_3, N are parameters defining the languages.

Note that L_1 can be viewed as a set of all ciphertexts $(c_0, c_1 \cdot (c_2)^{-1}, c_3 \cdot (c_2)^{-1})$ that are encryptions of zero, where the corresponding public key is defined as $\mathsf{pk} := (g, (h_1 \cdot (h_2)^{-1}), (h_3 \cdot (h_2)^{-1}), N)$ and encryption is defined as $\mathsf{Enc}(\mathsf{pk} := (g, h, h'), m) : c := g^r \bmod N, c' := h^{rN}(1 + N)^m \bmod N^2, c' := h'^{rN}(1 + N)^m \bmod N^2$. L_2 can be viewed as a set of all ciphertexts $(c_0, c_1 \cdot (c_2)^{-1})$ that are encryptions of zero, where the corresponding public key is defined as $\mathsf{pk} := (g, (h_1 \cdot (h_2)^{-1})), N)$ and encryption is defined as $\mathsf{Enc}(\mathsf{pk} := (g, h), m) : c := g^r, c' := hg^m \bmod N$. Hence, both encryption schemes are additively homomorphic and by Lemma 3 we obtain a trapdoor Sigma protocol for the languages L_1, L_2. By Theorem 1 this yields unbounded simulation-sound NIZKs for these languages.

3.3   Construction of Linearly Homomorphic Non-malleable NITC

We start with a construction of linearly homomorphic non-malleable NITC. In our construction depicted in Fig. 3 we rely on a one-time simulation-sound NIZK for the following language:

$$L = \left\{ (c_0, c_1, c_2, c_3) | \exists (m, r) : \begin{array}{l} (\wedge_{i=1}^3 c_i = h_i^{rN}(1 + N)^m \bmod N^2) \wedge \\ c_0 = g^r \bmod N \end{array} \right\},$$

where g, h_1, h_2, h_3, N are parameters specifying the language.

Theorem 2. *If* $(\mathsf{NIZK.Setup}, \mathsf{NIZK.Prove}, \mathsf{NIZK.Vrfy})$ *is a one-time simulation-sound non-interactive zero-knowledge proof system for* L, *the strong sequential squaring assumption with gap* ϵ *holds relative to* GenMod *in* $\mathbb{J}_N$, *the Decisional Composite Residuosity assumption holds relative to* GenMod, *and the Decisional Diffie-Hellman assumption holds relative to* GenMod *in* $\mathbb{J}_N$, *then* $(\mathsf{PGen}, \mathsf{Com}, \mathsf{ComVrfy}, \mathsf{DecVrfy}, \mathsf{FDec})$ *defined in Fig. 3 is an IND-CCA-secure non-interactive timed commitment scheme with gap* $\underline{\epsilon}$, *for any* $\underline{\epsilon} < \epsilon$.

Proof. Completeness is implied by the completeness of the NIZK and can be verified by straightforward inspection.

To prove security we define a sequence of games $\mathsf{G}_0 - \mathsf{G}_{12}$. For $i \in \{0, 1, \ldots, 12\}$ we denote by $\mathsf{G}_i = 1$ the event that the adversary $\mathcal{A} = \{(\mathcal{A}_{1,\lambda}, \mathcal{A}_{2,\lambda})\}_{\lambda \in \mathbb{N}}$ outputs b' in the game G_i such that $b = b'$.

Game 0. Game G_0 corresponds to the original security experiment where decommitment queries are answered using FDec.

Game 1. In game G_1 decommitment queries are answered using the algorithm Dec defined in Fig. 4 with $i := 1$, meaning that secret key k_1 and ciphertext c_1 are used, to answer decommitment queries efficiently.

$\underline{\mathsf{PGen}(1^\lambda, T)}$

$(p, q, N, g) \leftarrow \mathsf{GenMod}(1^\lambda)$

$\varphi(N) := (p-1)(q-1)$

$k_1, k_2 \stackrel{\$}{\leftarrow} [\lfloor N/2 \rfloor]$

$t := 2^T \bmod \varphi(N)/2$

For $i \in [2] : h_i := g^{k_i} \bmod N$

$h_3 := g^t \bmod N$

$\mathsf{crs_{NIZK}} \leftarrow \mathsf{NIZK.Setup}(1^\lambda, L)$

return $\mathsf{crs} := (N, T, g, h_1, h_2, h_3, \mathsf{crs_{NIZK}})$

$\underline{\mathsf{Com}(\mathsf{crs}, m)}$

$r \stackrel{\$}{\leftarrow} [\lfloor N/2 \rfloor]$

$c_0 := g^r \bmod N$

For $i \in [3] : c_i := h_i^{rN}(1+N)^m \bmod N^2$

$c := (c_0, c_1, c_2, c_3), w := (m, r)$

$\pi_, \leftarrow \mathsf{NIZK.Prove}(\mathsf{crs_{NIZK}}, c, w)$

$\pi_{\mathsf{Dec}} := r$

return $(c, \pi_,, \pi_{\mathsf{Dec}})$

$\underline{\mathsf{ComVrfy}(\mathsf{crs}, c, \pi_,)}$

return $\mathsf{NIZK.Vrfy}(\mathsf{crs_{NIZK}}, c, \pi_,)$

$\underline{\mathsf{DecVrfy}(\mathsf{crs}, c, m, \pi_{\mathsf{Dec}})}$

Parse c as (c_0, c_1, c_2, c_3)

if $\wedge_{i=1}^3 c_i = h_i^{\pi_{\mathsf{Dec}}N}(1+N)^m \bmod N^2$

$\wedge c_0 = g^{\pi_{\mathsf{Dec}}} \bmod N$

return 1

return 0

$\underline{\mathsf{FDec}(\mathsf{crs}, c)}$

Parse c as (c_0, c_1, c_2, c_3)

Compute $\pi_{\mathsf{FDec}} := c_0^{2^T} \bmod N$

$m := \frac{c_3 \cdot \pi_{\mathsf{FDec}}^{-N}(\bmod N^2) - 1}{N}$

return (m, π_{FDec})

$\underline{\mathsf{FDecVrfy}(\mathsf{crs}, c, m, \pi_{\mathsf{FDec}})}$

Parse c as $(c_0, c_1, c_2, c_3$

if $c_3 = \pi_{\mathsf{FDec}}^N(1+N)^m \bmod N^2$

return 1

return 0

$\underline{\mathsf{Eval}(\mathsf{crs}, \oplus_N, c_1, \ldots, c_n)}$

Parse c_i as $(c_{i,0}, c_{i,1}, c_{i,2}, c_{i,3})$

Compute $c_0 := \prod_{i=1}^n c_{i,0} \bmod N, c_1 := \bot, c_2 := \bot, c_3 := \prod_{i=1}^n c_{i,3} \bmod N^2$

return $c := (c_0, c_1, c_2, c_3)$

Fig. 3. Construction of Linearly Homomorphic NITC in Standard Model. $\oplus_N$ refers to addition $\bmod N$

$\underline{\mathsf{Dec}(\mathsf{crs}, c, \pi_,, i)}$

Parse c as (c_0, c_1, c_2, c_3)

if $\mathsf{NIZK.Vrfy}(\mathsf{crs_{NIZK}}, (c_0, c_1, c_2, c_3), \pi_,) = 1$

Compute $y := c_0^{k_i} \bmod N$

return $\frac{c_i \cdot y^{-N}(\bmod N^2) - 1}{N}$

return $\bot$

Fig. 4. Decommitment oracle

Lemma 4. $|\Pr[\mathsf{G}_0 = 1] - \Pr[\mathsf{G}_1 = 1]| \leq \mathbf{Snd}_\mathcal{B}^{\mathsf{NIZK}}$.

Notice that if c_1 and c_3 contain the same message, both oracles answer decommitment queries consistently. Let E denote the event that the adversary $\mathcal{A}$ asks a decommitment query (c, π_{Com}) such that its decommitment using the key k_1 is different from its decommitment using FDec. Since G_0 and G_1 are identical until E happens, we bound the probability of E. Concretely, we have

$$|\Pr[G_0 = 1] - \Pr[G_1 = 1]| \leq \Pr[E].$$

We construct an adversary $\mathcal{B}$ that breaks soundness of the NIZK. It is given as input $\mathsf{crs}_{\mathtt{NIZK}}$ together with a membership testing trapdoor $\tau_L := (k_1, k_2, t)$ where $t := 2^T \bmod \varphi(N)/2$. The adversary $\mathcal{B}_\lambda(\mathsf{crs}_{\mathtt{NIZK}}, \tau_L)$ proceeds as follows:

1. It computes $h_1 := g^{k_1} \bmod N, h_2 := g^{k_2} \bmod N, h_3 := g^t \bmod N$ using the membership testing trapdoor $\tau_L := (k_1, k_2, t)$ and sets $\mathsf{crs} := (N, T, g, h_1, h_2, h_3, \mathsf{crs}_{\mathtt{NIZK}})$.
2. Then it runs $(m_0, m_1, \mathsf{st}) \leftarrow \mathcal{A}_{1,\lambda}(\mathsf{crs})$ and answers decommitment queries using k_1.
3. It samples $b \xleftarrow{\$} \{0, 1\}, r \xleftarrow{\$} [\lfloor N/2 \rfloor]$ and computes $c_0^* := g^r, c_1^* := h_1^{rN}(1 + N)^{m_b}, c_2^* := h_2^{rN}(1 + N)^{m_b}, c_3^* := h_3^{rN}(1 + N)^{m_b}$. It sets $(s := (c_0^*, c_1^*, c_2^*, c_3^*), w := (m, r))$ and runs $\pi^* \leftarrow \mathtt{NIZK.Prove}(s, w)$.
4. It runs $b' \leftarrow \mathcal{A}_{2,\lambda}(s, \pi^*, \mathsf{st})$ and answers decommitment queries using k_1.
5. Finally, it checks whether there exists a decommitment query (c, π_{Com}) such that $\mathsf{DEC}(\mathsf{crs}, c, \pi_{\mathsf{Com}}) \neq \mathsf{Dec}(\mathsf{crs}, c, \pi_{\mathsf{Com}}, 2)$. If E occurs, then this is the case, and it returns (c, π_{Com}). Notice that this check can be done efficiently with the knowledge of t, since instead of running FDec, $\mathcal{B}$ can verify the proof and compute $c_3 c_0^{-t} \bmod N$ which produces the same output as FDec.

$\mathcal{B}$ simulates G_1 perfectly and if the event E happens, then it outputs a valid proof for a statement which is not in the specified language L. Therefore we get

$$\Pr[E] \leq \mathbf{Snd}_{\mathcal{B}}^{\mathtt{NIZK}}.$$

Game 2. Game G_2 proceeds exactly as the previous game but we run the zero-knowledge simulator $(\mathsf{crs}, \tau) \leftarrow \mathsf{Sim}_1(1^\lambda, L)$ in PGen and produce a simulated proof for the challenge commitment as $\pi^* \leftarrow \mathsf{Sim}_2(\mathsf{crs}, \tau, (c_0^*, c_1^*, c_2^*, c_3^*))$. By zero-knowledge security of underlying NIZK we directly obtain

Lemma 5. $|\Pr[G_1 = 1] - \Pr[G_2 = 1]| \leq \mathbf{ZK}_{\mathcal{B}}^{\mathtt{NIZK}}.$

We construct an adversary $\mathcal{B} = \{\mathcal{B}_\lambda\}_{\lambda \in \mathbb{N}}$ against the zero-knowledge security of NIZK as follows: $\mathcal{B}_\lambda(\mathsf{crs}_{\mathtt{NIZK}}, \tau_L)$:

1. It sets $\mathsf{crs} := (N, T(\lambda), g, h_1, h_2, h_3, \mathsf{crs}_{\mathtt{NIZK}})$ and runs $(m_0, m_1, \mathsf{st}) \leftarrow \mathcal{A}_{1,\lambda}(\mathsf{crs})$ and answers decommitment queries using k_1, which is included in $\tau_L = (k_1, k_2, t)$.
2. It samples $b \xleftarrow{\$} \{0, 1\}, r \xleftarrow{\$} [\lfloor N/2 \rfloor]$ and computes $c_0^* := g^r, c_1^* := h_1^{rN}(1 + N)^{m_b}, c_2^* := h_2^{rN}(1 + N)^{m_b}, c_3^* := h_3^{rN}(1 + N)^{m_b}$. It submits $(s := (c_0^*, c_1^*, c_2^*, c_3^*), w := (m, r))$ to its oracle and obtains proof π^* as answer.
3. Then it runs $b' \leftarrow \mathcal{A}_{2,\lambda}((c_0^*, c_1^*, c_2^*, c_3^*), \pi^*, \mathsf{st})$ and answers decommitment queries using k_1.
4. Finally, it returns the truth value of $b = b'$.

If the proof π^* is generated using $\mathtt{NIZK.Prove}$, then $\mathcal{B}$ simulates G_1 perfectly. Otherwise π^* is generated using Sim_1 and $\mathcal{B}$ simulates G_2 perfectly. This proves the lemma.

Game 3. In G_3 we sample r uniformly at random from $[\varphi(N)/2]$.

Lemma 6. $|\Pr[G_2 = 1] - \Pr[G_3 = 1]| \leq \frac{1}{p} + \frac{1}{q} - \frac{1}{N}.$

Since the only difference between the two games is in the set from which we sample r, to upper bound the advantage of adversary we can use Lemma 2 with $\ell := 2$, which directly yields the required bound.

Game 4. In G_4 we sample $y_3 \xleftarrow{\$} \mathbb{J}_N$ and compute c_3^* as $y_3^N(1 + N)^{m_b}$.

Let $\tilde{T}_{\mathsf{SSS}}(\lambda)$ be the polynomial whose existence is guaranteed by the SSS assumption. Let $\mathsf{poly}_{\mathcal{B}}(\lambda)$ be the fixed polynomial which bounds the time required to execute Steps 1–2 and answer decommitment queries in Step 3 of the adversary $\mathcal{B}_{2,\lambda}$ defined below. Set $\underline{T} := (\mathsf{poly}_{\mathcal{B}}(\lambda))^{1/\varepsilon}$. Set $\tilde{T}_{\mathtt{NITC}} := \max(\tilde{T}_{\mathsf{SSS}}, \underline{T})$.

Lemma 7. *From any polynomial-size adversary* $\mathcal{A} = \{(\mathcal{A}_{1,\lambda}, \mathcal{A}_{2,\lambda})\}_{\lambda \in \mathbb{N}}$*, where depth of* $\mathcal{A}_{2,\lambda}$ *is at most* $T^\varepsilon(\lambda)$ *for some* $T(\cdot) \geq \underline{T}(\cdot)$ *we can construct a polynomial-size adversary* $\mathcal{B} = \{(\mathcal{B}_{1,\lambda}, \mathcal{B}_{2,\lambda})\}_{\lambda \in \mathbb{N}}$ *where the depth of* $\mathcal{B}_{2,\lambda}$ *is at most* $T^\varepsilon(\lambda)$ *with* $|\Pr[G_3 = 1] - \Pr[G_4 = 1]| \leq \mathbf{Adv}_{\mathcal{B}}^{\mathsf{SSS}}.$

The adversary $\mathcal{B}_{1,\lambda}(N, T(\lambda), g)$ proceeds as follows:

1. It samples $k_1, k_2 \xleftarrow{\$} [\lfloor N/2 \rfloor]$, computes $h_1 := g^{k_1} \bmod N, h_2 := g^{k_2} \bmod N, h_3 := g^{2^{T(\lambda)}} \bmod N$, runs $(\mathsf{crs}_{\mathtt{NIZK}}, \tau) \leftarrow \mathsf{NIZK.Sim}_1(1^\lambda, L)$ and sets $\mathsf{crs} := (N, T(\lambda), g, h_1, h_2, h_3, \mathsf{crs}_{\mathtt{NIZK}})$. Notice that value h_3 is computed by repeated squaring.
2. It runs $(m_0, m_1, \mathsf{st}) \leftarrow \mathcal{A}_{1,\lambda}(\mathsf{crs})$ and answers decommitment queries using k_1.
3. Finally, it outputs $(N, g, k_1, k_2, h_1, h_2, h_3, \mathsf{crs}_{\mathtt{NIZK}}, \tau, m_0, m_1, \mathsf{st})$

The adversary $\mathcal{B}_{2,\lambda}(x, y, (N, g, k_1, k_2, h_1, h_2, h_3, \mathsf{crs}_{\mathtt{NIZK}}, \tau, m_0, m_1, \mathsf{st}))$:

1. Samples $b \xleftarrow{\$} \{0, 1\}$, computes $c_0^* := x, c_1^* := x^{k_1 N}(1 + N)^{m_b}, c_2^* := x^{k_2 N}(1 + N)^{m_b}, c_3^* := y^N(1 + N)^{m_b}$.
2. Runs $\pi^* \leftarrow \mathsf{Sim}_2(\mathsf{crs}_{\mathtt{NIZK}}, \tau, (c_0^*, c_1^*, c_2^*, c_3^*))$.
3. Runs $b' \leftarrow \mathcal{A}_{2,\lambda}((c_0^*, c_1^*, c_2^*, c_3^*), \pi^*), \mathsf{st})$ and answers decommitment queries using k_1.
4. Returns the truth value of $b = b'$.

Since g is a generator of $\mathbb{J}_N$ and x is sampled uniformly at random from $\mathbb{J}_N$ there exists some $r \in [\varphi(N)/2]$ such that $x = g^r$. Therefore when $y = x^{2^T} = (g^{2^T})^r \bmod N$, then $\mathcal{B}$ simulates G_3 perfectly. Otherwise y is random value and $\mathcal{B}$ simulates G_4 perfectly.

Now we analyse the running time of the constructed adversary. Adversary $\mathcal{B}_1$ computes h_3 by $T(\lambda)$ consecutive squarings and because $T(\lambda)$ is polynomial in λ, $\mathcal{B}_1$ is efficient. Moreover, $\mathcal{B}_2$ fulfils the depth constraint:

$$\mathsf{depth}(\mathcal{B}_{2,\lambda}) = \mathsf{poly}_{\mathcal{B}}(\lambda) + \mathsf{depth}(\mathcal{A}_{2,\lambda}) \leq \underline{T}^\varepsilon(\lambda) + T^\varepsilon(\lambda) \leq 2\,T^\varepsilon(\lambda) = o(T^\varepsilon(\lambda)).$$

Also $T(\cdot) \geq \tilde{T}_{\mathtt{NITC}}(\cdot) \geq \tilde{T}_{\mathsf{SSS}}(\cdot)$ as required.

Game 5. In G_5 we sample $y_3 \xleftarrow{\$} \mathbb{Z}_{N^2}^*$ such that it has Jacobi symbol 1 and compute c_3^* as $y_3(1+N)^{m_b}$.

Lemma 8. $|\Pr[\mathsf{G}_4 = 1] - \Pr[\mathsf{G}_5 = 1]| \le \mathbf{Adv}_{\mathcal{B}}^{\mathrm{DCR}}.$

We construct an adversary $\mathcal{B} = \{\mathcal{B}_\lambda\}_{\lambda \in \mathbb{N}}$ against DCR. $\mathcal{B}_\lambda(N, y)$ works as follows:

1. It samples $g, y_3, x \xleftarrow{\$} \mathbb{J}_N, k_1, k_2 \xleftarrow{\$} [\lfloor N/2 \rfloor]$, computes $h_1 := g^{k_1} \bmod N, h_2 := g^{k_2} \bmod N, h_3 := g^{2^T} \bmod N$, runs $(\mathsf{crs}_{\mathsf{NIZK}}, \tau) \leftarrow \mathsf{NIZK.Sim}_1(1^\lambda, L)$ and sets $\mathsf{crs} := (N, T(\lambda), g, h_1, h_2, h_3, \mathsf{crs}_{\mathsf{NIZK}})$. Notice that value h_3 is computed by repeated squaring.
2. It runs $(m_0, m_1, \mathsf{st}) \leftarrow \mathcal{A}_{1,\lambda}(\mathsf{crs})$ and answers decommitment queries using k_1.
3. Then it samples $b \xleftarrow{\$} \{0,1\}, w \xleftarrow{\$} \mathbb{Z}_{N^2}^*$ such that $\left(\frac{y}{N}\right) = \left(\frac{w}{N}\right)$. We remark that computing Jacobi symbol can be done efficiently without knowing factorization of N.
4. It computes $c_0^* := x, c_1^* := x^{k_1 N}(1+N)^{m_b}, c_2^* := x^{k_2 N}(1+N)^{m_b}, c_3^* := y w^N(1+N)^{m_b}$. Runs $\pi^* \leftarrow \mathsf{Sim}_2(\mathsf{crs}_{\mathsf{NIZK}}, \tau, (c_0^*, c_1^*, c_2^*, c_3^*))$.
5. It runs $b' \leftarrow \mathcal{A}_{2,\lambda}((c_0^*, c_1^*, c_2^*, c_3^*), \pi^*, \mathsf{st})$ and answers decommitment queries using k_1.
6. Then it returns the truth value of $b = b'$.

If $y = v^N \bmod N^2$ then $y w^N = v^N w^N = (vw)^N$ and hence $y w^N$ is N-th residue. Moreover, the Jacobi symbol of yw is 1, since the Jacobi symbol is multiplicatively homomorphic. Therefore $\mathcal{B}$ simulates G_4 perfectly.

Otherwise, if y is uniform random element in $\mathbb{Z}_{N^2}^*$, then $y w^N$ is also uniform among all elements of $\mathbb{Z}_{N^2}^*$ that have Jacobi symbol 1 and $\mathcal{B}$ simulates G_5 perfectly. This proves the lemma.

We remark that at this point c_3^* does not reveal any information about b. Here we use that if $x = y \bmod N$ then $\left(\frac{x}{N}\right) = \left(\frac{y}{N}\right)$ and that there is an isomorphism $f : \mathbb{Z}_N^* \times \mathbb{Z}_N \to \mathbb{Z}_{N^2}^*$ given by $f(u, v) = u^N(1+N)^v = u^N(1+vN) \bmod N^2$ (see e.g. [16, Proposition 13.6]). Since $f(u, v) \bmod N = u^N + u^N vN \bmod N = u^N \bmod N$, that means that Jacobi symbol $\left(\frac{f(u,v)}{N}\right)$ depends only on u. Hence if $\left(\frac{f(u,v)}{N}\right) = 1$, then it must hold that $\left(\frac{f(u,r)}{N}\right) = 1$ for all $r \in \mathbb{Z}_N$. This implies that a random element $f(u, v)$ in $\mathbb{Z}_{N^2}^*$ with $\left(\frac{f(u,v)}{N}\right) = 1$ has a uniformly random distribution of v in $\mathbb{Z}_N$. Therefore if $y w^N = u^N(1+N)^v \bmod N^2$ then $y w^N(1+N)^{m_b} = u^N(1+N)^{m_b+v} \bmod N^2$. Since v is uniform in $\mathbb{Z}_N$, $(m_b + v)$ is also uniform in $\mathbb{Z}_N$, which means that ciphertext c_3^* does not reveal any information about b.

Game 6. In G_6 we sample k_2 uniformly at random from $[\varphi(N)/2]$.

Lemma 9. $|\Pr[\mathsf{G}_5 = 1] - \Pr[\mathsf{G}_6 = 1]| \le \frac{1}{p} + \frac{1}{q} - \frac{1}{N}.$

Again using a statistical argument this lemma directly follows from Lemma 2 with $\ell := 2$.

Game 7. In G_7 we sample $y_2 \xleftarrow{\$} \mathbb{J}_N$ and compute c_2^* as $y_2^N (1 + N)^{m_b}$.

Lemma 10. $|\Pr[\mathsf{G}_6 = 1] - \Pr[\mathsf{G}_7 = 1]| \le \mathbf{Adv}_{\mathcal{B}}^{\mathsf{DDH}}$.

We construct an adversary $\mathcal{B} = \{\mathcal{B}_\lambda\}_{\lambda \in \mathbb{N}}$ against DDH in the group $\mathbb{J}_N$.
$\mathcal{B}_\lambda(N, g, g^\alpha, g^\beta, g^\gamma)$ proceeds as follows:

1. It samples $k_1 \xleftarrow{\$} [\lfloor N/2 \rfloor]$, computes $h_1 := g^{k_1} \bmod N, h_3 := g^{2^T} \bmod N$, runs $(\mathsf{crs}_{\mathtt{NIZK}}, \tau) \leftarrow \mathtt{NIZK.Sim}_1(1^\lambda, L)$ and sets $\mathsf{crs} := (N, T, g, h_1, h_2 := g^\alpha, h_3, \mathsf{crs}_{\mathtt{NIZK}})$.
2. It runs $(m_0, m_1, \mathsf{st}) \leftarrow \mathcal{A}_{1,\lambda}(\mathsf{crs})$ and answers decommitment queries using k_1.
3. It samples $b \xleftarrow{\$} \{0, 1\}, y_3 \xleftarrow{\$} \mathbb{Z}_{N^2}^*$ such that it has Jacobi symbol 1 and computes $(c_0^*, c_1^*, c_2^*, c_3^*) := (g^\beta, (g^\beta)^{k_1 N}(1 + N)^{m_b}, (g^\gamma)^N(1 + N)^{m_b}, y_3(1 + N)^{m_b})$. Runs $\pi^* \leftarrow \mathsf{Sim}_2(\mathsf{crs}_{\mathtt{NIZK}}, \tau, (c_0^*, c_1^*, c_2^*, c_3^*))$.
4. It runs $b' \leftarrow \mathcal{A}_{2,\lambda}((c_0^*, c_1^*, c_2^*, c_3^*), \pi^*, \mathsf{st})$ and answers decommitment queries using k_1.
5. It returns the truth value of $b = b'$.

If $\gamma = \alpha\beta$, then $\mathcal{B}$ simulates G_6 perfectly. Otherwise g^γ is uniform random element in $\mathbb{J}_N$ and $\mathcal{B}$ simulates G_7 perfectly. This proves the lemma.

Game 8. In G_8 we sample k_2 uniformly at random from $[\lfloor N/2 \rfloor]$. Again by Lemma 2 with $\ell := 2$ we get

Lemma 11. $|\Pr[\mathsf{G}_7 = 1] - \Pr[\mathsf{G}_8 = 1]| \le \frac{1}{p} + \frac{1}{q} - \frac{1}{N}$.

Game 9. In G_9 we sample $y_2 \xleftarrow{\$} \mathbb{Z}_{N^2}^*$ such that it has Jacobi symbol 1 and compute c_2^* as $y_2(1 + N)^{m_b}$.

Lemma 12. $|\Pr[\mathsf{G}_8 = 1] - \Pr[\mathsf{G}_9 = 1]| \le \mathbf{Adv}_{\mathcal{B}}^{\mathsf{DCR}}$.

This can be proven in similar way as Lemma 8. We remark that at this point c_2^* does not reveal any information about b, with the same argument as in the transition from G_4 to G_5.

Game 10. In G_{10} we answer decommitment queries using Dec (Fig. 4) with $i := 2$ which means that secret key k_2 and ciphertext c_2 are used.

Lemma 13. $|\Pr[\mathsf{G}_9 = 1] - \Pr[\mathsf{G}_{10} = 1]| \le \mathbf{SimSnd}_{\mathcal{B}}^{\mathtt{NIZK}}$.

Let E denote the event that adversary $\mathcal{A}$ asks a decommitment query (c, π_{Com}) such that its decommitment using the key k_1 is different from its decommitment using the key k_2. Since G_9 and G_{10} are identical until E happens, it is sufficient to bound the probability of E. Concretely,
  $|\Pr[\mathsf{G}_9 = 1] - \Pr[\mathsf{G}_{10} = 1]| \le \Pr[\mathsf{E}]$.
  We construct an adversary $\mathcal{B}$ that breaks one-time simulation soundness of the NIZK. It is given as input $\mathsf{crs}_{\mathtt{NIZK}}$ together with a membership testing trapdoor $\tau_L := (k_1, k_2, t)$, where $t := 2^T \bmod \varphi(N)/2$. The adversary $\mathcal{B}_\lambda^{\mathsf{Sim}_2}(\mathsf{crs}_{\mathtt{NIZK}}, \tau_L)$ proceeds as follows:

1. It computes $h_1 := g^{k_1} \bmod N, h_2 := g^{k_2} \bmod N, h_3 := g^t \bmod N$ using the membership testing trapdoor τ_L and sets $\mathsf{crs} := (N, T, g, h_1, h_2, h_3, \mathsf{crs}_{\mathtt{NIZK}})$.
2. It runs $(m_0, m_1, \mathsf{st}) \leftarrow \mathcal{A}_{1,\lambda}(\mathsf{crs})$ and answers decommitment queries using k_2.
3. It samples $b \xleftarrow{\$} \{0,1\}, x \xleftarrow{\$} \mathbb{J}_N, y_2, y_3 \xleftarrow{\$} \mathbb{Z}_{N^2}^*$ and computes $(c_0^*, c_1^*, c_2^*, c_3^*) := (x, x^{k_1 N}(1+N)^{m_b}, y_2(1+N)^{m_b}, y_3(1+N)^{m_b})$. Forwards $(c_0^*, c_1^*, c_2^*, c_3^*)$ to simulation oracle Sim_2 and obtains a proof π^*.
4. It runs $b' \leftarrow \mathcal{A}_{2,\lambda}((c_0^*, c_1^*, c_2^*, c_3^*), \pi^*, \mathsf{st})$ and answers decommitment queries using k_2.
5. If there exists a decommitment query (c, π_{Com}) such that $\mathsf{Dec}(\mathsf{crs}, c, \pi_{\mathsf{Com}}, 1) \neq \mathsf{Dec}(\mathsf{crs}, c, \pi_{\mathsf{Com}}, 2)$, then it returns (c, π_{Com}). Note that such a query exists iff E happens.

$\mathcal{B}$ simulates G_{10} perfectly and if the event E happens, it outputs a valid proof for a statement which is not in the specified language L. Therefore we get $\Pr[\mathsf{E}] \leq \mathbf{SimSnd}_{\mathcal{B}}^{\mathtt{NIZK}}$.

Game 11. In G_{11} we sample k_1 uniformly at random from $[\varphi(N)/2]$. The following again follows directly from Lemma 2 with $\ell := 2$.

Lemma 14. $|\Pr[\mathsf{G}_{10} = 1] - \Pr[\mathsf{G}_{11} = 1]| \leq \frac{1}{p} + \frac{1}{q} - \frac{1}{N}$.

Game 12. In G_{12} we sample $y_1 \xleftarrow{\$} \mathbb{J}_N$ and compute c_1^* as $y_1^N(1+N)^{m_b}$.

Lemma 15. $|\Pr[\mathsf{G}_{11} = 1] - \Pr[\mathsf{G}_{12} = 1]| \leq \mathbf{Adv}_{\mathcal{B}}^{\mathsf{DDH}}$.

This can be proven in similar way as Lemma 10.

Game 13. In G_{13} we sample $y_1 \xleftarrow{\$} \mathbb{Z}_{N^2}^*$ such that it has Jacobi symbol 1 and compute c_1^* as $y_1(1+N)^{m_b}$.

Lemma 16. $|\Pr[\mathsf{G}_{12} = 1] - \Pr[\mathsf{G}_{13} = 1]| \leq \mathbf{Adv}_{\mathcal{B}}^{\mathsf{DCR}}$.

This can be proven in similar way as Lemma 8. We remark that at this point c_1^* does not reveal any information about b, with the same arguments as above.

Lemma 17. $\Pr[\mathsf{G}_{13} = 1] = \frac{1}{2}$.

Clearly, c_0^* is uniform random element in $\mathbb{J}_N$ and hence it does not contain any information about the challenge message. Since y_1, y_2, y_3 are sampled uniformly at random from $\mathbb{Z}_{N^2}^*$ the ciphertexts c_1^*, c_2^*, c_3^* are also uniform random elements in $\mathbb{Z}_{N^2}^*$ and hence do not contain any information about the challenge message m_b. Therefore, an adversary can not do better than guessing.

By combining Lemmas 4–17 we obtain the following:

$$\mathbf{Adv}_{\mathcal{A}}^{\mathtt{NITC}} = \left|\Pr[\mathsf{G}_0 = 1] - \frac{1}{2}\right| \leq \sum_{i=0}^{12} |\Pr[\mathsf{G}_i = 1] - \Pr[\mathsf{G}_{i+1} = 1]| + \left|\Pr[\mathsf{G}_{13} - \frac{1}{2}\right|$$

$$\leq \mathbf{Snd}_{\mathcal{B}}^{\mathtt{NIZK}} + \mathbf{ZK}_{\mathcal{B}}^{\mathtt{NIZK}} + \mathbf{Adv}_{\mathcal{B}}^{\mathsf{SSS}} + \mathbf{SimSnd}_{\mathcal{B}}^{\mathtt{NIZK}} + 2\mathbf{Adv}_{\mathcal{B}}^{\mathsf{DDH}} + 3\mathbf{Adv}_{\mathcal{B}}^{\mathsf{DCR}}$$

$$+ 4\left(\frac{1}{p} + \frac{1}{q} - \frac{1}{N}\right).$$

Theorem 3. $(\mathsf{PGen}, \mathsf{Com}, \mathsf{ComVrfy}, \mathsf{DecVrfy}, \mathsf{FDec})$ *defined in Fig. 3 is a BND-CCA-secure non-interactive timed commitment scheme.*

Proof. We show that the construction is actually perfectly binding. This is straightforward to show since Paillier encryption is perfectly binding. Therefore there is exactly one message/randomness pair (m, r) which can pass the check in $\mathsf{DecVrfy}$. Therefore the first winning condition of the BND-CCA experiment happens with probability 0. Moreover, since PGen is executed by the challenger, the value h_3 is computed correctly and therefore FDec reconstructs always the correct message m. Therefore the second winning condition of BND-CCA experiment happens with probability 0 as well.

Theorem 4. *If* $\mathsf{NIZK} = (\mathsf{NIZK.Setup}, \mathsf{NIZK.Prove}, \mathsf{NIZK.Vrfy})$ *is a non-interactive zero-knowledge proof system for L, then* $(\mathsf{PGen}, \mathsf{Com}, \mathsf{ComVrfy}, \mathsf{DecVrfy}, \mathsf{FDec},$ $\mathsf{FDecVrfy})$ *defined in Fig. 3 is a publicly verifiable non-interactive timed commitment scheme.*

Proof. Completeness is straightforward to verify. To prove soundness, notice that if the commitment verifies, then we know that $c_0 = g^r$ and $c_3 = h_3^r(1 + N)^m$ for honestly generated g and h_3 and some r and m. Otherwise, an adversary would be able to break soundness of the proof system. Since there is an isomorphism $f : \mathbb{Z}_N^* \times \mathbb{Z}_N \to \mathbb{Z}_{N^2}^*$ given by $f(a, b) = a^N(1+N)^b \bmod N^2$ (see e.g. [16, Proposition 13.6]) there exist unique values π_{FDec} and m such that $c_3 = \pi_{\mathsf{FDec}}^N(1 + N)^m \bmod N^2$. Therefore adversary is not able to provide a different message m' fulfilling the required equation. Finally, note that $\mathsf{FDecVrfy}$ is efficient, with a running time which is independent of T.

It is straightforward to verify that considering the Eval algorithm, our construction yields a *linearly homomorphic* NITC, which follows from the linear homorphism of Paillier, as also used in [20].

Theorem 5. *The NITC* $(\mathsf{PGen}, \mathsf{Com}, \mathsf{ComVrfy}, \mathsf{DecVrfy}, \mathsf{FDec}, \mathsf{FDecVrfy}, \mathsf{Eval})$ *defined in Fig. 3 is a linearly homomorphic non-interactive timed commitment scheme.*

3.4 Construction of Multiplicatively Homomorphic Non-malleable NITC

The construction described in this section is similar to that from Sect. 3.3, except that we replace Paillier encryption with ElGamal to obtain a multiplicative homomorphism and the construction is based on standard Naor-Yung paradigm. Our construction is given in Fig. 5 and we rely on a one-time simulation sound NIZK for the following language:

$$L = \left\{ (c_0, c_1, c_2) | \exists (m, r) : (\wedge_{i=1}^2 c_i = h_i^r m \bmod N) \wedge c_0 = g^r \bmod N \right\},$$

where g, h_1, h_2, N are parameters specifying the language.

$\mathsf{PGen}(1^\lambda, T)$	$\mathsf{Com}(\mathsf{crs}, m)$
$(p, q, N, g) \leftarrow \mathsf{GenMod}(1^\lambda)$	$r \xleftarrow{\$} [\lfloor N/4 \rfloor]$
$\varphi(N) := (p-1)(q-1)$	$c_0 := g^r \bmod N$
$k_1 \xleftarrow{\$} [\lfloor N/4 \rfloor]$	For $i \in [2] : c_i := h_i^r m \bmod N$
$t := 2^T \bmod \varphi(N)/4$	$c := (c_0, c_1, c_2), w := (m, r)$
$h_1 := g^{k_1} \bmod N$	$\pi, \leftarrow \mathsf{NIZK.Prove}(\mathsf{crs}_{\mathtt{NIZK}}, c, w)$
$h_2 := g^t \bmod N$	$\pi_{\mathsf{Dec}} := r$
$\mathsf{crs}_{\mathtt{NIZK}} \leftarrow \mathsf{NIZK.Setup}(1^\lambda, L)$	return $(c, \pi,, \pi_{\mathsf{Dec}})$
return $\mathsf{crs} := (N, T, g, h_1, h_2, \mathsf{crs}_{\mathtt{NIZK}})$	
$\mathsf{ComVrfy}(\mathsf{crs}, c, \pi,)$	$\mathsf{DecVrfy}(\mathsf{crs}, c, m, \pi_{\mathsf{Dec}})$
return $\mathsf{NIZK.Vrfy}(\mathsf{crs}_{\mathtt{NIZK}}, c, \pi)$	Parse c as (c_0, c_1, c_2)
	if $\wedge_{i=1}^2 c_i = h_i^{\pi_{\mathsf{Dec}}} m \bmod N \wedge c_0 = g^{\pi_{\mathsf{Dec}}} \bmod N$
	$\quad$ return 1
	return 0
$\mathsf{FDec}(\mathsf{crs}, c)$	$\mathsf{Eval}(\mathsf{crs}, \otimes_N, c_1, \ldots, c_n)$
Parse c as (c_0, c_1, c_2)	Parse c_i as $(c_{i,0}, c_{i,1}, c_{i,2})$
Compute $y := c_0^{2^T} \bmod N$	Compute $c_0 := \prod_{i=1}^n c_{i,0} \bmod N, c_1 := \perp$
$m := c_2 \cdot y^{-1} \bmod N$	Compute $c_2 := \prod_{i=1}^n c_{i,2} \bmod N$
return m	return $c := (c_0, c_1, c_2)$

Fig. 5. Construction of Multiplicatively Homomorphic NITC in Standard Model. $\otimes_N$ refers to multiplication $\bmod N$

Theorem 6. *If* $(\mathsf{NIZK.Setup}, \mathsf{NIZK.Prove}, \mathsf{NIZK.Vrfy})$ *is a one-time simulation-sound non-interactive zero-knowledge proof system for* L, *the strong sequential squaring assumption with gap* ϵ *holds relative to* GenMod *in* $\mathbb{QR}_N$, *and the Decisional Diffie-Hellman assumption holds relative to* GenMod *in* $\mathbb{QR}_N$, *then* $(\mathsf{PGen}, \mathsf{Com}, \mathsf{ComVrfy}, \mathsf{DecVrfy}, \mathsf{FDec})$ *defined in Fig. 5 is an IND-CCA-secure non-interactive timed commitment scheme with* $\underline{\epsilon}$, *for any* $\underline{\epsilon} < \epsilon$.

The proof can be found in the full version of this paper [9].

Theorem 7. $(\mathsf{PGen}, \mathsf{Com}, \mathsf{ComVrfy}, \mathsf{DecVrfy}, \mathsf{FDec})$ *defined in Fig. 5 is a BND-CCA-secure non-interactive timed commitment scheme.*

Proof. We show that the construction is perfectly binding. This is straightforward to show since ElGamal encryption is perfectly binding. Therefore there is exactly one message/randomness pair (m, r) which can pass the check in $\mathsf{DecVrfy}$. Therefore the first winning condition of BND-CCA experiment happens with probability 0. Moreover, since PGen is executed by the challenger, the value h_3 is computed correctly and therefore FDec reconstructs always the correct message m. Therefore the second winning condition of BND-CCA experiment happens with probability 0 as well.

It is straightforward to verify that considering Eval algorithm, our construction yields multiplicatively homomorphic NITC.

$\mathsf{FDec}(\mathsf{crs}, c)$	$\mathsf{FDecVrfy}(\mathsf{crs}, c, m, \pi_{\mathsf{FDec}})$
Parse c as (c_0, c_1, c_2)	Parse c as (c_0, c_1, c_2)
$y := c_0^{2^T} \bmod N, \pi_{\mathsf{PoE}} = \mathsf{PoE.Prove}(c_0, y)$	if $c_2 = m \cdot y \bmod N \wedge \mathsf{PoE.Vrfy}((c_0, y), \pi_{\mathsf{PoE}})$
$\pi_{\mathsf{FDec}} := (y, \pi_{\mathsf{PoE}}), m := c_2 \cdot y{-}1 \bmod N$	return 1
return (m, π_{FDec})	return 0

Fig. 6. FDec and FDecVrfy of Publicly Verifiable NITC

Theorem 8. *The NITC* $(\mathsf{PGen}, \mathsf{Com}, \mathsf{ComVrfy}, \mathsf{DecVrfy}, \mathsf{FDec}, \mathsf{FDecVrfy}, \mathsf{Eval})$ *defined in Fig. 5 is a multiplicatively homomorphic non-interactive timed commitment scheme.*

Remark 4 (Public Verifiability). It is natural to ask if it is possible to make the construction in Fig. 5 publicly verifiable. Since the output m of FDec is perfectly determined by value $y := c_0^{2^T} \bmod N$, it is possible to achieve public verifiability if one can efficiently check that indeed y equals to $c_0^{2^T} \bmod N$ without executing T squarings. However, this is exactly what proofs of exponentiation of Pietrzak [23] and Wesolowski [26] do. Concretely, [23,26] propose efficient proofs systems for the language $L' := \{(G, a, b, T) | a, b \in G \wedge b = a^{2^T}\}$ where G is some group where low order assumption [23] or adaptive root assumption [26] hold. We remark, that for both suggested proof systems G can be instantiated for example as $\mathbb{Z}_N^* / \{-1, 1\}$ [6,26] or as it is proposed by Pietrzak G can be instantiated as a group of signed quadratic residues $\mathbb{QR}_N^+ := \{|x| : x \in \mathbb{QR}_N\}$. One can argue that the strong sequential squaring assumption holds in $\mathbb{QR}_N^+$ (see e.g. [12,23]). Therefore by adjusting the construction in Fig. 5 to work in the group $\mathbb{QR}_N^+$, one can obtain publicly verifiable NITC by outputing in FDec the value y together with a proof of exponentiation that $y = c_0^{2^T} \bmod N$ and FDecVrfy just checks that the proof of exponentiation is valid and at the same time $c_2 = y \cdot m \bmod N$. For completeness we provide a description of these algorithms in Fig. 6, where we use $(\mathsf{PoE.Prover}, \mathsf{PoE.Vrfy})$ to denote a proof system for language L'. Both Pietrzak's and Wesolowski's proof system are interactive protocols which might be made non-interactive using Fiat-Shamir transformation. Thus we obtain a publicly verifiable NITC in ROM.

We defer the constructions of non-malleable non-interactive timed commitments in the random oracle model to the full version of this paper [9].

References

1. Baum, C., David, B., Dowsley, R., Nielsen, J.B., Oechsner, S.: TARDIS: a foundation of time-lock puzzles in UC. In: Canteaut, A., Standaert, F.-X. (eds.) EUROCRYPT 2021. LNCS, vol. 12698, pp. 429–459. Springer, Cham (2021). https://doi.org/10.1007/978-3-030-77883-5_15
2. Bellare, M., Rogaway, P.: Random oracles are practical: a paradigm for designing efficient protocols. In: Denning, D.E., Pyle, R., Ganesan, R., Sandhu, R.S., Ashby, V., (Eds.), ACM CCS 93, pp. 62–73. ACM Press, November (1993)

3. Biagioni, S., Masny, D., Venturi, D.: Naor-Yung paradigm with shared randomness and applications. In: Zikas, V., De Prisco, R. (eds.) SCN 2016. LNCS, vol. 9841, pp. 62–80. Springer, Cham (2016). https://doi.org/10.1007/978-3-319-44618-9_4

4. Biasse, J.-F., Jacobson, M.J., Silvester, A.K.: Security estimates for quadratic field based cryptosystems. In: Steinfeld, R., Hawkes, P. (eds.) ACISP 10. LNCS, vol. 6168, pp. 233–247. Springer, Heidelberg (2010)

5. Bitansky, N., Goldwasser, S., Jain, A., Paneth, O., Waters, V.V.: Time-lock puzzles from randomized encodings. In: Sudan, M., ed., ITCS 2016, pp. 345–356. ACM, January (2016)

6. Boneh, D., Bünz, B., Fisch, B.: A survey of two verifiable delay functions. Cryptology ePrint Archive, Report 2018/712 (2018). https://eprint.iacr.org/2018/712

7. Boneh, D., Naor, M.: Timed commitments. In: Bellare, M. (ed.) CRYPTO 2000. LNCS, vol. 1880, pp. 236–254. Springer, Heidelberg (2000). https://doi.org/10.1007/3-540-44598-6_15

8. Brakerski, Z., Döttling, N., Garg, S., Malavolta, G.: Leveraging linear decryption: rate-1 fully-homomorphic encryption and time-lock puzzles. In: Hofheinz, D., Rosen, A. (eds.) TCC 2019. Part II, volume 11892 of LNCS, pp. 407–437. Springer, Heidelberg (2019). https://doi.org/10.1007/978-3-030-36033-7_16

9. Chvojka, P., Jager, T.: Simple, fast, efficient, and tightly-secure non-malleable non-interactive timed commitments. Cryptology ePrint Archive, Paper 2022/1498 (2022). https://eprint.iacr.org/2022/1498

10. Chvojka, P., Jager, T., Slamanig, D., Striecks, C.: Versatile and sustainable timed-release encryption and sequential time-lock puzzles. ESORICS 2021, (2021). https://eprint.iacr.org/2020/739

11. Couteau, G., Peters, T., Pointcheval, D.: Encryption switching protocols. In: Robshaw, M., Katz, J. (eds.) CRYPTO 2016. Part I, volume 9814 of LNCS, pp. 308–338. Springer, Heidelberg (2016). https://doi.org/10.1007/978-3-662-53018-4_12

12. Ephraim, N., Freitag, C., Komargodski, I., Pass, R.: Non-malleable time-lock puzzles and applications. Cryptology ePrint Archive, Report 2020/779 (2020). https://eprint.iacr.org/2020/779

13. Fiat, A., Shamir, A.: How to prove yourself: practical solutions to identification and signature problems. In: Odlyzko, A.M. (ed.) CRYPTO'86. LNCS, vol. 263, pp. 186–194. Springer, Heidelberg (1987)

14. Fujisaki, E., Okamoto, T.: Secure integration of asymmetric and symmetric encryption schemes. In: Wiener, M.J. (ed.) CRYPTO'99. LNCS, vol. 1666, pp. 537–554. Springer, Heidelberg (1999). https://doi.org/10.1007/3-540-48405-1_34

15. Fujisaki, E., Okamoto, T.: Secure integration of asymmetric and symmetric encryption schemes. J. Crypt. **26**(1), 80–101 (2013)

16. Katz, J., Lindell, Y.: Introduction to Modern Cryptography, 2nd edn. Chapman and Hall/CRC Press, Boca Raton (2014)

17. Katz, J., Loss, J., Jiayu, X.: On the security of time-lock puzzles and timed commitments. In: Pass, R., Pietrzak, K. (eds.) TCC 2020. Part III, volume 12552 of LNCS, pp. 390–413. Springer, Heidelberg (2020). https://doi.org/10.1007/978-3-030-64381-2_14

18. Libert, B., Nguyen, K., Peters, T., Yung, M.: One-shot Fiat-Shamir-based NIZK arguments of composite residuosity in the standard model (2021)

19. Liu, J., Jager, T., Kakvi, S.A., Warinschi, B.: How to build time-lock encryption. Designs, Codes Crypt. **86**(11), 2549–2586 (2018). https://doi.org/10.1007/s10623-018-0461-x

20. Malavolta, G., Thyagarajan, S.A.K.: Homomorphic time-lock puzzles and applications. In: Boldyreva, A., Micciancio, D. (eds.) CRYPTO 2019. Part I, volume 11692 of LNCS, pp. 620–649. Springer, Heidelberg (2019). https://doi.org/10.1007/978-3-030-26948-7_22

21. Naor, M., Yung, M.: Public-key cryptosystems provably secure against chosen ciphertext attacks. In: 22nd ACM STOC, pp. 427–437. ACM Press, May (1990)

22. Paillier, P.: Public-key cryptosystems based on composite degree residuosity classes. In: Stern, J. (ed.) EUROCRYPT'99. LNCS, vol. 1592, pp. 223–238. Springer, Heidelberg (1999). https://doi.org/10.1007/3-540-48910-X_16

23. Krzyszt of Pietrzak. Simple verifiable delay functions. In: Blum, A., ed., ITCS 2019, vol. 124, pp. 60:1–60:15. LIPIcs, January (2019)

24. Ronald, L., Adi Shamir, R., Wagner, D.A.: Time-lock puzzles and timed-release crypto, Technical report (1996)

25. Thyagarajan, A.K., Castagnos, G., Laguillaumie, F., Malavolta, G.: Efficient CCA timed commitments in class groups. In: Vigna, G., Shi, E., eds., ACM CCS 2021, pp. 2663–2684. ACM Press, November (2021)

26. Wesolowski, B.: Efficient verifiable delay functions. In: Ishai, Y., Rijmen, V. (eds.) EUROCRYPT 2019. Part III, volume 11478 of LNCS, pp. 379–407. Springer, Heidelberg (2019). https://doi.org/10.1007/s00145-020-09364-x

Certifying Giant Nonprimes

Charlotte Hoffmann[1]([⊠]), Pavel Hubáček[2], Chethan Kamath[3],
and Krzysztof Pietrzak[1]

[1] Institute of Science and Technology Austria, Klosterneuburg, Austria
{charlotte.hoffmann,krzysztof.pietrzak}@ist.ac.at
[2] Institute of Mathematics, Czech Academy of Sciences, Prague, Czech Republic
hubacek@iuuk.mff.cuni.cz
[3] Tel Aviv University, Tel Aviv, Israel
ckamath@protonmail.com

Abstract. GIMPS and PrimeGrid are large-scale distributed projects dedicated to searching giant prime numbers, usually of special forms like Mersenne and Proth primes. The numbers in the current search-space are millions of digits large and the participating volunteers need to run resource-consuming primality tests. Once a candidate prime N has been found, the only way for another party to independently verify the primality of N used to be by repeating the expensive primality test. To avoid the need for second recomputation of each primality test, these projects have recently adopted certifying mechanisms that enable efficient verification of performed tests. However, the mechanisms presently in place only detect benign errors and there is no guarantee against adversarial behavior: a malicious volunteer can mislead the project to reject a giant prime as being non-prime.

In this paper, we propose a practical, cryptographically-sound mechanism for certifying the non-primality of Proth numbers. That is, a volunteer can – parallel to running the primality test for N – generate an efficiently verifiable proof at a little extra cost certifying that N is not prime. The interactive protocol has statistical soundness and can be made non-interactive using the Fiat-Shamir heuristic.

Our approach is based on a cryptographic primitive called Proof of Exponentiation (PoE) which, for a group $\mathbb{G}$, certifies that a tuple $(x, y, T) \in \mathbb{G}^2 \times \mathbb{N}$ satisfies $x^{2^T} = y$ (Pietrzak, ITCS 2019 and Wesolowski, J. Cryptol. 2020). In particular, we show how to adapt Pietrzak's PoE at a moderate additional cost to make it a cryptographically-sound certificate of non-primality.

1 Introduction

The search for giant primes has long focussed on primes of special forms due to the availability of faster, custom primality tests. Two of the most well-known examples are

A. Boldyreva and V. Kolesnikov (Eds.): PKC 2023, LNCS 13940, pp. 530–553, 2023.
https://doi.org/10.1007/978-3-031-31368-4_19

Mersenne numbers of the form $M_n = 2^n - 1$, for some $n \in \mathbb{N}$, which can be tested using the Lucas-Lehmer or the Lucas-Lehmer-Reisel test [23,25,35]; and

Proth numbers of the form $P_{k,n} = k2^n + 1$, for some $n \in \mathbb{N}$ and odd $k \in \mathbb{N}$, which can be tested using Proth's theorem [33].

To harness the computational resources required for finding giant primes, there are massive distributed projects like GIMPS (Great Internet Mersenne Prime Search) and PrimeGrid dedicated to the search for giant primes of special forms, including the ones above. A volunteer in such a distributed project can download an open-source software that locally carries out primality tests on candidate numbers, at the end of which, a candidate is either rejected as a composite number or confirmed as a new prime. The largest-known prime as of now is a Mersenne prime $(2^{82,589,933} - 1)$ with 24,862,048 decimal digits found by GIMPS [16].

Testing primality of giant numbers. The search for large primes is a time-consuming process: the GIMPS website warns that a single primality test could take up to a month. The reason for this is that these tests – whenever the prime candidate has no small prime factors[1] – require the computation of a very long sequence modulo an extremely large number. For example, Proth's theorem [33] states that $P_{k,n} = k2^n + 1$ is prime if and only if, for a quadratic non-residue x modulo $P_{k,n}$, it holds that

$$x^{k2^{n-1}} \equiv -1 \bmod P_{k,n}. \tag{1}$$

To date, the largest-known Proth prime is $10223 \cdot 2^{31,172,165} + 1$ [31]. Since n is of the order of magnitude 10^7 and the square-and-multiply algorithm is the fastest way currently known to carry out exponentiation, the test roughly requires 10^7 squarings modulo a 10^7-digit modulus. Unfortunately, performing this test does not yield an immediate witness that certifies the correctness of the result – in particular, if $P_{k,n}$ is composite, the test does not find a divisor of $P_{k,n}$.[2] Until very recently, the standard way for another party to independently validate the test result was by recomputing the result of Equation (1). In 2020, Pavel Atnashev demonstrated that a cryptographic primitive called *Proof of Exponentiation* (PoE) might be applicable in the context of these specialized primality tests to avoid the costly second recomputation.[3]

---

[1] GIMPS first tests by trial division whether a candidate number has any prime divisors of size up to a bound between 2^{66} and 2^{81}. Only when this is not the case is that they run a more expensive specialized primality test: details can be found on this page.

[2] Note that some primality tests, like, e.g., Miller-Rabin [27,34], can be modified to (sometimes) yield factors in case the number being tested is not a prime.

[3] More details can be found in this thread of mersenneforum.org. An implementation due to Atnashev is available on GitHub. The idea of using PoEs for certifying giant primes has been discussed also by Mihai Preda in another thread in the same forum already in August 2019.

PoEs and efficient verification of primality tests. For a group $\mathbb{G}$, a PoE [28,39] is an interactive protocol for the language

$$L_{\mathbb{G}} := \left\{ (x, y, T) \in \mathbb{G} \times \mathbb{G} \times \mathbb{N} : x^{2^T} = y \text{ over } \mathbb{G} \right\}. \tag{2}$$

In case the PoE is public-coin, it can be transformed into a non-interactive PoE using the Fiat-Shamir heuristic [14]. A PoE enables efficient verification of costly iterated exponentiation even without the knowledge of the order of the underlying group. Since the primality test using Proth's theorem amounts to iterated exponentiation, it seems immediate that one would attempt to exploit PoEs also towards efficient verifiability in the context of primality tests for giant numbers. The idea is for the volunteer to use the (non-interactive) PoE to compute – alongside the result of the test – a proof that helps any other party verify the result. For this approach to be feasible,

1. computing the proof should not require much more additional resource (relative to the iterated exponentiation induced by the specialized primality test), and
2. the cost of verifying a proof should be significantly lower than that of recomputing the exponentiation.

Recently, this approach has been deployed in both GIMPS [17] and PrimeGrid [32], where (non-interactive) Pietrzak's PoE [28] is used to certify (both primality and non-primality) of Mersenne and Proth numbers when used along with Lucas-Lehmer-Riesel test and Proth's theorem, respectively. In fact, one of the recently-found Proth primes, $68633 \cdot 2^{2715609} + 1$, has been certified so.

However, PoEs were constructed for groups whose order is hard to compute like, e.g., RSA group [36] or class group [11]. In such groups, the only known way to compute x^{2^T} is via T sequential squaring. On the other hand, if one party knows the group order, they can not only speed up this exponentiation[4] but also (in many groups) construct *false* Pietrzak PoEs that lead a verifier to accept proofs for false statements. In the context of primality testing the underlying group is $\mathbb{Z}_{P_{k,n}}$, so the group order is known whenever $P_{k,n}$ is prime. While this does not speed up the computation of the primality test (since the modulus is larger than the exponent), it removes the soundness guarantee of the protocol. As we discuss next, a malicious prover can falsely convince a verifier that *any* Proth prime is composite using Pietrzak's protocol in those groups.

1.1 Our Contribution

The statistical security guarantee of Pietrzak's PoE applies only to groups *without* low-order elements.[5] In groups with low-order elements, one additionally

---

[4] If the order of the group is known, then x^{2^T} can be computed efficiently using the shortcut: $y = x^e$ (over $\mathbb{G}$) for $e = 2^T \bmod \operatorname{ord}(\mathbb{G})$.

[5] Recall that the order of an element $g \in \mathbb{G}$, denoted $\operatorname{ord}(g)$, is the least integer such that $g^{\operatorname{ord}(g)} = 1$. An example of a group without low-order elements is *signed quadratic residues* QR_N^+, where N is sampled as the product of safe primes [15,21]. This is also the algebraic setting used in Pietrzak's VDF [28].

requires the *low-order assumption* [8] to hold, i.e., it must be computationally hard to find a group element of low order. Boneh, Bünz, and Fisch [8] described an attack on the soundness of Pietrzak's PoE when implemented in groups where low-order elements are easy to find (see Sect. 1.2). This presents an issue with its usage in the GIMPS and PrimeGrid projects since there are no guarantees on the structure of the group in these applications. In fact, if $P_{k,n}$ is prime, the order of the group is $P_{k,n} - 1 = k2^n$ so low-order elements (e.g., of order 2) do exist and can be found without much effort. We show in Appendix A how a malicious volunteer can exploit the attack from [8] to generate a proof that "certifies" an arbitrary Proth *prime* as composite with constant probability. Indeed, people at GIMPS and PrimeGrid were aware of this [3] and Pietrzak's PoE is currently employed in these projects more-or-less as a checksum to catch benign errors (e.g., hardware errors). When a volunteer is malicious and deliberately tries to mislead the project, there are no guarantees. This could force the volunteer network to waste additional computation and possibly postpone the discovery of another giant prime by years.

Are Cryptographically-Sound Certificates Possible? In our work, we explore whether any cryptographic guarantee for *practical* proofs is possible in the above scenarios. Whilst it is theoretically possible to use existing results to certify non-primality, these measures, as we discuss in Sect. 1.1, turn out to be too expensive. As a first step towards practical proofs, we show how to achieve soundness for proving *non-primality* of Proth numbers. That is, we construct an interactive protocol for the language

$$L := \{(k, n) \in \mathbb{N}^2 : k \text{ is odd and } P_{k,n} = k2^n + 1 \text{ is not a prime}\}. \quad (3)$$

While ideally, one would want to certify both primality and non-primality, the latter is much more important for projects like GIMPS and PrimeGrid: they worry about missing out on primes rather than false claims stating that a composite is a prime. Primes are very sparse[6], so double checking claims of primality is not a problem, but performing *each* primality check twice to catch benign errors or a malicious volunteer is almost twice as expensive as using a sound non-primality test as suggested in this work.

Our interactive protocol has statistical soundness: if the candidate number to be tested is indeed a Proth prime, then even a computationally unbounded malicious prover (a malicious volunteer) will not be able to convince the verifier (say a server run by the project) that it is composite.

Theorem 1 (Informal). *There is a practical public-coin statistically-sound interactive proof for the non-primality of Proth numbers.*

---

[6] For $N \in \mathbb{N}$, let $\pi(N)$ denote the number of primes less than N. By prime number theorem, asymptotically $\pi(N)$ approaches $N/\log(N)$. For the case of Proth numbers, however, even the question of whether there are infinitely many of them is open [9].

We provide an overview of our interactive protocol in the next section. Since it is public-coin, our interactive protocol can be made non-interactive via the Fiat-Shamir transform [14]. In general, the Fiat-Shamir transform only works for constant round protocols, which is not the case for our protocol, so showing that Fiat-Shamir works in our case needs a proof.

Corollary 1 (Informal). *In the random-oracle model, there is a practical statistically-sound non-interactive proof for the non-primality of Proth numbers.*

Concrete Efficiency. We defer exact details about the complexity of our protocol to Sect. 4.3. Here, we provide concrete (worst-case) numbers for our non-interactive proof using the largest Proth prime known to date as the candidate: $10223 \cdot 2^{31172165} + 1$ [31]. For $k = 10223$, $n = 31172165$ and security parameter $\lambda = 80$:

- the prover (additionally) stores 5584 group elements (which is around 20GB) and performs 13188 multiplications;
- the verifier performs 10046 multiplications; and
- the proof size is 26 elements of size 31172179, i.e., around 102 MB.

Note that recomputing the result of the primality test would take $n = 31172165$ multiplications, so our protocol reduces the number of multiplications by a factor of $\lfloor 31172165/(13188 + 10046) \rfloor = 1341$. Note that this takes the order of hours rather than days. In Sect. 4.4, we show that the additional cost of our protocol compared to the one that is being used now (which is not cryptographically sound) is moderate: In the above example, the prover performs 2021 and the verifier 4046 multiplications more than in the current implementation.

Applicability of Existing Statistically-Sound PoEs. The issue with low-order elements when using Pietrzak's PoE out-of-the-box can be resolved using alternative PoEs that are statistically sound in *arbitrary* groups.[7] Indeed, such PoEs were recently proposed [6,20]. [6] can be regarded as a parallel-repeated variant of Pietrzak's protocol but, to achieve statistical soundness, the number of repetitions is as large as the security parameter. This leads to significant overhead in terms of both proof-size and computation. For example, to compute the PoE of [6] for the Proth prime from Sect. 1.1, the prover needs to perform 893312 multiplications and it takes the verifier 318800 multiplications to verify the proof consisting of 2080 group elements (i.e., 8160 MB). This means that our protocol reduces the number of multiplications of [6] by a factor of 52 and the proof size by a factor of 80. The overall approach in [20] is similar to that in [6], but it improves on the complexity of [6] whenever it is possible to choose the

---

[7] One could also use SNARGs [22,26] for this purpose but, being a general-purpose primitive, the resulting schemes would not be practically efficient.

exponent to be a large q of a special form. In the primality testing application, we do not have the freedom to choose the exponent and, for the case of $q = 2$, the complexity of [20] is comparable to that of [6].

1.2 Technical Overview

Our starting point is Pietrzak's PoE (PPoE, Fig. 2), which is a statistically-sound $\log(T)$-round interactive protocol for the language $L_{\mathbb{G}}$ from Equation (2). We start with its overview (which is adapted from [20]). The protocol in [28] is recursive in the parameter T and involves $\log(T)$ rounds of interaction. To prove a (true) statement (x, y, T), the (honest) prover $\mathcal{P}$, in the first round, sends the "midpoint" $z := x^{2^{T/2}}$ to the verifier $\mathcal{V}$. This results in two *intermediate* statements $(x, z, T/2)$ and $(z, y, T/2)$. Next, $\mathcal{V}$ sends a random challenge r to $\mathcal{P}$, and they merge these two intermediate statements into a *new* statement $(x^r \cdot z, z^r \cdot y, T/2)$. The above steps constitute the "halving" sub-protocol, which is repeated $\log(T)$ times, halving the parameter T each time, until $\mathcal{P}$ and $\mathcal{V}$ arrive at a (base) statement for $T = 1$. At this point, $\mathcal{V}$ can efficiently check the correctness on its own by performing a single squaring.

Problem with low-order elements. The soundness argument in groups without low-order elements proceeds in a round-by-round manner as follows: when starting with a false statement, it is guaranteed that at least one of the two intermediate statements is false and one can argue that the new statement is false with high probability (over the choice of r). In groups that have easy-to-compute low-order elements, the above argument fails and we recall the attack described in [8]. In the following discussion, by a "μ-false" statement, we refer to a statement that is off a true statement by a factor of $\mu \in \mathbb{G}$. Suppose that $\mu \in \mathbb{G}$ has order 2 and let (x, y, T) be a true statement. For the μ-false statement $(x, y\mu, T)$, the cheating prover simply sends μz as its first message and the claim is that the new statement at the end of the first halving sub-protocol is true with probability $1/2$. To see this, note that the new statement is $(x^r \cdot \mu z, (\mu z)^r \cdot y, T/2)$ and whenever r is odd, it reduces to the true statement $(\mu \cdot x^r \cdot z, \mu \cdot z^r \cdot y, T/2)$ (since μ vanishes when exponentiated to an even power $T/2$). Thus, the verifier eventually accepts. Therefore, applying PPoE out-of-the-box as a certificate of non-primality for a Proth number $P_{k,n}$ is not sound since the group $\mathbb{Z}^*_{P_{k,n}}$ might have easy-to-find elements of low order. We show in Appendix A that this is indeed the case and it is not hard to generate PPoE proofs that "certify" a prime $P_{k,n}$ as composite.

Working around low-order elements. The way low-order elements are dealt with in [6,20] is via parallel repetition and/or by working with exponents q of a particular form. As explained in Sect. 1.1, we cannot exploit either of these techniques because of efficiency reasons and the restriction on the exponent placed by the primality test. Nevertheless, our interactive protocol, described in Figs. 1 and 3,

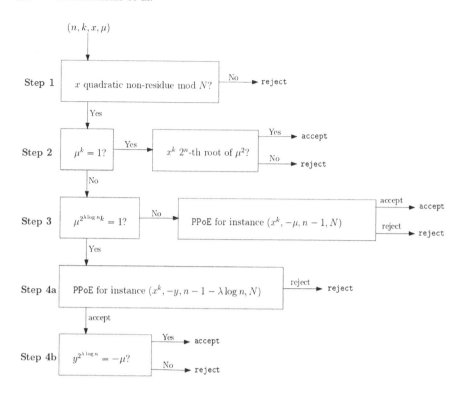

Fig. 1. Overview of the protocol in Fig. 3. All computations are done in the group $\mathbb{Z}_N^*$, where $N = k2^n + 1$.

builds on some of the ideas in [20, 28] to get around the issue of low-order elements for the specific exponentiation considered in Proth's test (Equation (1)). Below, we give an overview of how this is accomplished – we refer the readers to Sect. 4 for a more detailed overview.

For a prime $N := P_{k,n}$, suppose that $x \in \mathbb{Z}_N^*$ is a quadratic non-residue.[8] Suppose that a malicious prover $\mathcal{P}^*$ tries to convince the verifier $\mathcal{V}$ that

$$x^{k2^{n-1}} \equiv -\mu \bmod N, \quad 1 \neq \mu \in \mathbb{Z}_N^*. \tag{4}$$

Since N is a prime and the result must be -1 by Proth's theorem, the statement $(x, -\mu, k2^{n-1})$ corresponding to Equation (4) is μ-false. Our protocol exploits the fact that $\mathcal{V}$ does not care about the exact value of $x^{k2^{n-1}}$ and it rejects as long as the correct result is not equal to -1. This observation greatly simplifies the task for $\mathcal{V}$. As we show, it is sufficient to perform a few efficient checks on the order of μ, depending on which $\mathcal{V}$ can choose a sound method for verification. For ease of exposition, we restrict this overview to the case where k itself is prime.

---

[8] In the actual protocol, we explain how the verifier can check if the Jacobi symbol of x is -1 (Step 1 in Fig. 3).

- Our starting point is the case where $\text{ord}(\mu)$ is "large", by which we mean $\text{ord}(\mu) \nmid k2^{\lambda \log(n)}$ (Step 3). We show in this case that it is possible to use PPoE out of the box to prove the statement $(x^k, -\mu, n-1)$, which is equivalent to the statement in Equation (4). Key to proving this is the following observation on the fine-grained nature of soundness of PPoE: the "falseness" of a statement in each round of the sub-protocol cannot decrease by too much. More precisely, if the cheating prover starts with an α-false statement then the new statement is β-false for some β whose order cannot be much smaller than α's. Therefore, if the cheating prover starts off with a statement that is sufficiently false, which turns out to be when $\text{ord}(\alpha) = k2^{\lambda \log(n)}$, then the statement in the final round remains false with overwhelming probability and is rejected by the PPoE verifier. We formalise this observation in Lemma 1 and point out that, while a similar lemma was proved in [20], there are some crucial differences: see Remark 3.
- Next is the case where $\text{ord}(\mu)$ is "small and odd" (Step 2), i.e., in this overview $\text{ord}(\mu) = k$. In this case, $\mathcal{V}$ can verify the statement in Equation (4) *without* any help from $\mathcal{P}^*$ as follows: find the inverse of 2^n modulo k and raise μ^2 to that element.[9] By Equation (4), this yields the same element as x^k if the prover is honest. If N is prime, this will yield a different element than x^k as we show in Sect. 4.2. This quick verification is only possible since k and 2^n are coprime, so it can only be used in this case.
- Finally, consider the case where the order is "small and even", by which we mean $\text{ord}(\mu) \mid 2^{\lambda \log(n)}$ (Step 4). Here, we are in a situation where PPoE does not guarantee soundness (since the statement is not "false enough"). However, as in [20], it is possible to reduce the task of checking Equation (4) to that of verifying, using PPoE, the "smaller" statement obtained by taking the $2^{\lambda \log(n)}$-th root of Equation (4). To be precise, $\mathcal{P}$ and $\mathcal{V}$ verify the statement $(x^k, y, n - 1 - \lambda \log(n))$ using PPoE and, if convinced, $\mathcal{V}$ then checks whether $y^{2^{\lambda \log(n)}} = -\mu$, by itself, using a final exponentiation. This final exponentiation forces a malicious prover $\mathcal{P}^*$ to cheat with an element of high enough order during the PPoE. To see this, assume for example that $\mathcal{P}^*$ sends the honest result $y = x^{2^{n-1-\lambda \log(n)}}$. Then, $\mathcal{V}$'s final exponentiation leads to outright rejection since

$$y^{2^{\lambda \log(n)}} = \left(x^{k2^{n-1-\lambda \log(n)}}\right)^{2^{\lambda \log(n)}} = x^{k2^{n-1}} \neq -\mu.$$

On the other hand, $\mathcal{P}^*$ cheating with an element of such high order during the PPoE makes the verifier reject this PPoE with overwhelming probability (as in the first case).

We refer the reader to Sects. 3 and 4 for the formal analysis.

---

[9] Note that if μ has order k, then $-\mu$ has order $2k$ (which is not coprime to 2^{n-1}), which is the reason we have to square the statement in Equation (4) before computing the inverse of the exponent.

1.3   Related Work

General-purpose primality testing. Pratt showed that primality testing (of arbitrary integers) lies in the class **NP**, via the eponymous Pratt certificates [30] (an alternative certificate of primality is the Atkin-Goldwasser-Kilian-Morain certificate [2,18]). Coupled with the fact that non-primality has succinct certificates in the form of factorization (which can be efficiently checked by integer multiplication) placed primality testing in **NP** ∩ **co−NP**. Probabilistic tests like Solovay-Strassen [38], Miller-Rabin [27,34] and Baillie-PSW [4,29] soon followed, which placed primality testing in classes like **BPP**, **RP** or **ZPP**.[10] Finally, Agrawal, Kayal, and Saxena [1] settled the question by showing that primality testing is in **P**. We refer the readers to [1] for a more detailed exposition on (general-purpose) primality testing.

Giant prime numbers and custom primality tests. In addition to Mersenne numbers M_n and Proth numbers $P_{k,n}$, numbers of special form that have been targetted in the search for giant primes include Fermat numbers $F_n := 2^{2^n} + 1$ (which are a special case of Proth numbers), generalised Fermat numbers $F_{a,b,n} := a^{2^n} + b^{2^n}$ and Woodall numbers $W_n := n \cdot 2^n - 1$. We refer the readers to PrimePages for a more comprehensive list. These numbers of special forms are amenable to custom primality tests that run faster than general-purpose primality tests. For example, the Lucas-Lehmer (LL) test [23,25] is a deterministic primality test for M_n that runs in time $O(n \cdot \mu(n))$, where $\mu(n)$ denotes the complexity of multiplying two n-bit integers.[11] In comparison, for M_n, the complexity of deterministic AKS primality test is $\tilde{O}(n^6)$ and the complexity of probabilistic Miller-Rabin test is $O(\lambda n \cdot \mu(n))$ (for a statistical error of $2^{-\lambda}$). GIMPS relies on the Lucas-Lehmer-Riesel [35] test, which is a generalization of the Lucas-Lehmer test for numbers of the form $k2^n - 1$. PrimeGrid performs a variety of primality tests including Proth's theorem [33] for Proth numbers. They were first to realize that (Pietrzak's) PoE can be used to certify the results of Proth's primality test [32]. They also noticed that low-order elements can affect the soundness of the protocol and, therefore, included some checks on the order of the result [3]. For Proth number $P_{k,n}$, *given* a quadratic non-residue modulo $P_{k,n}$, the complexity of Proth's test [33] is $O(\log(k) \cdot n\mu(n))$; otherwise it is a Las Vegas test (since we currently know how to generate a quadratic non-residue only in expected polynomial-time). An alternative is to use the deterministic Brillhart-Lehmer-Selfridge test [10].

More Related Work on PoE. PoE was introduced in the context of another cryptographic primitive called Verifiable Delay Function (VDF) [7]. The VDFs of Pietrzak [28] and Wesolowski [39], both, implicitly involve the construction of a

---

[10] In fact, Miller's test [27] runs in strict polynomial time assuming the Generalised Riemann Hypothesis.

[11] Since these numbers have a succinct representation, the complexity of these tests is, strictly-speaking, exponential in the size of the input (which is n for M_n).

PoE: an overview and comparison of these PoE protocols can be found in [8]. The soundness of these PoEs relies on new hardness assumptions called *low-order assumption* and, the stronger, *adaptive root assumption*, respectively [8], i.e., strictly-speaking, these are *arguments* of exponentiation. Pietrzak's PoE [28] is, however, statistically-sound in groups with the syntactic guarantee that *no* elements of low order exist, e.g., a subgroup of quadratic residues of RSA group. In addition, there are two more statistically-sound PoE constructions currently known: [6,20]. [6] can be seen as a elaborate parallel repetition of [28] that is statistically sound in *any* group. However, this repetition increases the complexity of the protocol by a multiplicative factor λ, where λ is a statistical security parameter. [20] improves on the construction in [6] and reduces the complexity by almost one order of magnitude *whenever* one can freely choose the exponent in the exponentiation. Finally, PoEs have recently been used as a crucial building block in constructing space-efficient general-purpose succinct non-interactive arguments of knowledge (SNARKs) [6,12], thus establishing a converse relationship with SNARGs (since SNARGs trivially imply PoEs). Recently, Rotem studied the problem of batching PoEs in his work on batching VDFs [37].

2 Preliminaries

Interactive protocols. Let Σ be an alphabet. For $\ell \in \mathbb{N}$, an interactive protocol consists of a pair $(\mathcal{P}, \mathcal{V})$ of interactive Turing machines called prover and verifier, respectively. In an ℓ-round (i.e., $(2\ell - 1)$-message) interactive protocol, $\mathcal{P}$ and $\mathcal{V}$ run on a common input x and proceed as follows: in each round $i \in [1, \ell]$, first $\mathcal{P}$ sends a message $\alpha_i \in \Sigma^a$ to $\mathcal{V}$ and then $\mathcal{V}$ sends a message $\beta_i \in \Sigma^b$ to $\mathcal{P}$, where Σ is a finite alphabet. At the end of the interaction, $\mathcal{V}$ runs a (deterministic) Turing machine on input $\{x, (\beta_1 1 = , \dots 1 = , \beta_\ell), (\alpha_1 1 = , \dots 1 = , \alpha_\ell)\}$. The interactive protocol is *public-coin* if β_i is a uniformly distributed random string in Σ^b.

Interactive proofs. The notion of an interactive proof for a language L is due to Goldwasser, Micali and Rackoff [19].

Definition 1. *An interactive protocol $(\mathcal{P}, \mathcal{V})$ is an ϵ-sound interactive proof system for L if:*

- **Completeness:** *For every $x \in L$, if $\mathcal{V}$ interacts with $\mathcal{P}$ on common input x, then $\mathcal{V}$ accepts with probability 1.*
- **Soundness:** *For every $x \notin L$ and every cheating prover strategy $\widetilde{\mathcal{P}}$, the verifier $\mathcal{V}$ accepts when interacting with $\widetilde{\mathcal{P}}$ with probability at most $\epsilon(|x|)$, where $\epsilon = \epsilon(n)$ is called the* soundness error *of the proof system.*

In particular, the interactive protocol is a statistically-sound *proof if the soundness holds against computationally-unbounded cheating prover strategies and the soundness error is negligible (in the input-length).*

Non-interactive proofs in the random-oracle model. A non-interactive protocol involves the prover sending a single message to the verifier. We are interested in non-interactive proofs in the random-oracle model instead of the more standard non-interactive arguments in the common reference string (CRS) model. Therefore, we now have to consider oracle interactive Turing machines $\mathcal{P}^{(\cdot)}$ and $\mathcal{V}^{(\cdot)}$ for the prover and verifier.

Definition 2. *A pair of oracle machines* $(\mathcal{P}^{(\cdot)}, \mathcal{V}^{(\cdot)})$ *is an ϵ-sound non-interactive proof system for a language L in the random-oracle model if the following properties hold:*

- **Completeness:** *For every $x \in L$,*

$$\Pr_{O \leftarrow \mathcal{O}} \left[\mathcal{V}^O(x, \mathcal{P}^O(x)) = 1 \right] = 1,$$

  where the probability is over the random choice of the oracle $O \in \mathcal{O}$.
- **Soundness:** *For every (computationally-unbounded) cheating prover strategy $\widetilde{\mathcal{P}}$,*

$$\Pr_{\substack{O \leftarrow \mathcal{O} \\ (x, \widetilde{\pi}) \leftarrow \widetilde{\mathcal{P}}^O}} \left[\mathcal{V}^O(x, \widetilde{\pi}) = 1 \wedge x \notin L \right] \leq \epsilon(|x|).$$

Remark 1 (On the complexity of the honest prover and verifier). In standard definitions, the prover is either unbounded and deterministic, or given additional information (e.g., the witness when the language is in **NP**), whereas the verifier is polynomially-bounded and randomised. We prefer a more fine-grained definition where the (deterministic) prover is stronger than the (randomised) verifier, but both parties can be polynomially-bounded.

Remark 2. The definition of interactive PoEs and non-interactive PoEs in the random-oracle model can be recovered by restricting Definitions 1 and 2 to the language $L_{\mathbb{G}}$ from Equation (2).

3   Pietrzak's PoE in Groups of Known Order

In this section, we recall Pietrzak's PoE (PPoE) [28] and some of its properties. The protocol is presented in Fig. 2. By inspection of the protocol we see that it has perfect completeness. Pietrzak proved the following complexity results in [28]:

Proposition 1 ([28, Sect. 6.2]). *On instance $(x, y, T, \mathbb{G})$ PPoE has the following efficiency properties:*

1. *$\mathcal{V}$ performs $3\lambda \log T$ multiplications in $\mathbb{G}$.*
2. *$\mathcal{P}$ performs $2\sqrt{T}$ multiplications in $\mathbb{G}$ and stores $\sqrt{T}$ group elements to compute the proof.*
3. *The size of the proof is $\log T$ elements of $\mathbb{G}$.*

Instance: $(x, y, T, \mathbb{G})$, where $x, y \in \mathbb{G}$ and $T \in \mathbb{N}$ is even

Parameters: statistical security parameter λ

Statement: $x^{2^T} = y$ in $\mathbb{G}$

Protocol:

1. For $T = 1$:
   – If $x^2 = y$, output `accept`.
   – Else, output `reject`.
2. For $T > 1$:
   (a) $\mathcal{P}$ sends $v = x^{2^{T/2}}$ to $\mathcal{V}$.
   (b) If $v \notin \mathbb{G}$, $\mathcal{V}$ outputs `reject`. Otherwise, $\mathcal{V}$ samples $r \leftarrow \{0, 1, \ldots, 2^\lambda - 1\}$ uniformly at random and sends it to $\mathcal{P}$.
   (c) $\mathcal{P}$ and $\mathcal{V}$ compute $x' := x^r v$ and $y' := v^r y$ in $\mathbb{G}$.
   (d) If $T/2$ is even, $\mathcal{P}$ and $\mathcal{V}$ run the protocol on instance $(x', y', T/2, \mathbb{G})$. If $T/2$ is odd, $\mathcal{P}$ and $\mathcal{V}$ run the protocol on instance $(x', y'^2, (T+1)/2, \mathbb{G})$.

Fig. 2. PPoE.

Furthermore, Pietrzak proved that the PoE is statistically sound in groups without low-order elements, in particular safe prime RSA groups. Boneh et al. later proved computational soundness in groups where it is hard to find low-order elements (the low-order assumption) [8]. Ideally, we would like to use PPoE in a group of known order, where an adversary can find low-order elements in polynomial time. However, Boneh et al. showed that this is not sound by presenting an attack with low-order elements in [8]. In the following section, we analyze in what way these low-order elements affect the soundness of PPoE.

3.1   (Non-)Soundness

We analyze the soundness of PPoE in groups of known order. Assume that the correct result of an exponentiation is $x^{2^T} = y \mod N$ but $\tilde{\mathcal{P}}$ claims that for some $\alpha \neq 1 \mod N$ it is $x^{2^T} = y\alpha \mod N$. We sometimes call α the "bad" element and say that the second statement is α-*false*. Note that the prover's statement is of this form without loss of generality because every element has an inverse in a group. This means that if the prover claims that the result is some group element β, we can always find a group element α such that $\beta = y\alpha$. Soundess of PPoE only depends on the order of this bad element α. If its order only has small prime divisors with small exponents, the probability that repeated exponentiation of this element with a random exponent decreases its order to one, and thus the verifier's check for $T = 1$ passes, is not negligible.

The following lemma bounds the probability that the order of the bad element "drops" by a factor p^ℓ in one round of PPoE. It will be the main tool in proving soundness of our non-primality certificate later on.

Lemma 1. *Let $(x, y\alpha, T, \mathbb{G})$ be an α-false statement for some $\alpha \in \mathbb{G}$, $\mu \in \mathbb{G}$ an arbitrary group element, p^e any prime power that divides the order of α and let $r \leftarrow \{0, 1, \ldots, 2^\lambda - 1\}$ be sampled uniformly at random. Assume that the statement $(x^r\mu, \mu^r y\alpha, T/2, \mathbb{G})$ is β-false for some $\beta \in \mathbb{G}$. For any $\ell \leq e$, the probability that $p^{e-\ell+1}$ does not divide the order of β is at most $1/p^\ell$.*

Proof. If the statement $(x^r\mu, \mu^r y\alpha, T/2)$ is β-false, we have $\mu = \gamma x^{2^{T/2}}$ such that $\beta = \alpha\gamma^{r-2^{T/2}}$. We want to bound the following probability

$$\Pr_r[\beta^{p^{e-\ell}s} = \alpha^{p^{e-\ell}s}\gamma^{(r-2^{T/2})p^{e-\ell}s} = 1] = \Pr_r[\gamma^{(r-2^{T/2})p^{e-\ell}s} = \alpha^{-p^{e-\ell}s}]$$

$$\leq \frac{1}{\mathrm{ord}(\gamma^{p^{e-\ell}s})} + \frac{1}{2^\lambda}$$

$$= \frac{\gcd(d, p^{e-\ell}s)}{d} + \frac{1}{2^\lambda}, \tag{5}$$

where d denotes the order of γ and s is any positive integer not divisible by p. The inequality follows from the fact that the size of the randomness space is 2^λ. Now assume that the above event holds. Then we have $\gamma^{p^{e-\ell}sm} = \alpha^{-p^{e-\ell}s}$ for some integer m, hence

$$\mathrm{ord}(\alpha^{-p^{e-\ell}s}) = \mathrm{ord}(\gamma^{p^{e-\ell}sm}) = \frac{d}{\gcd(d, p^{e-\ell}sm)}$$

and equivalently

$$d = \mathrm{ord}(\alpha^{-p^{e-\ell}s})\gcd(d, p^{e-\ell}sm) \geq p^\ell \gcd(d, p^{e-\ell}sm).$$

Plugging into (5) we get

$$\Pr[\alpha^{p^{e-\ell}s}\gamma^{(r-2^{T/2})p^{e-\ell}s} = 1] \leq \frac{\gcd(d, p^{e-\ell}s)}{p^\ell \gcd(d, p^{e-\ell}sm)} + \frac{1}{2^\lambda} \leq \frac{1}{p^\ell} + \frac{1}{2^\lambda}.$$

Remark 3. A lemma of flavour similar to Lemma 1 was proven in [20, Lemma 1] for a parallel-repeated variant of PPoE. However, there are major differences between these: (i) the new statements in the protocol in [20] (and also [6]) are obtained in a slightly different way, using multiple random coins and (ii) [20, Lemma 1] was only proven for restricted choices of numbers p and e. Hence, Lemma 1 does not follow from [20, Lemma 1].

Corollary 2. *Let $(x, y\alpha, T, \mathbb{G})$ be an α-false statement for some $\alpha \in \mathbb{G}$ and 2^e any power of 2 that divides the order of α. The probability that $2^{e-\ell}$ does not divide the order of the bad element after one round of PPoE is at most $1/2^\ell$.*

Proof. By Lemma 1 we know that the probability that $2^{e-\ell+1}$ does not divide the order of the bad element of the instance $(x', y', T/2, \mathbb{G})$ is at most $1/2^\ell$. Now if T is odd, the new instance of the protocol is $(x', y'^2, (T+1)/2, \mathbb{G})$, so the bad element is squared once. This reduces its order by a factor of 2, which yields the claim.

4 Certifying Non-Primality of Proth Primes

In this section, we present the interactive protocol for verifying that a Proth number $N = k2^n + 1$ is *not* prime, i.e., that $x^{k2^{n-1}} = -\mu \mod N$ for some $\mu \neq 1$ and x a small prime number that is a quadratic non-residue modulo N. This means that from now on all group operations will be performed in the group $\mathbb{Z}_N^*$.

The protocol presented in Fig. 3 consists of four steps in which $\mathcal{V}$ performs different checks on the order of the element μ and then chooses the best method for verification accordingly. An overview can be found in Fig. 1.

In the first step, $\mathcal{V}$ checks if x has Jacobi symbol -1 modulo N since the primality test is only conclusive if x is a quadratic non-residue. To this end, $\mathcal{V}$ first computes $a := N \mod x$ and, if $a \neq 0$, checks if the Jacobi symbol $(\frac{x}{N}) = (\frac{a}{x})$ is -1. If $a = 0$ we know that x is a divisor of N and hence N is composite, so $\mathcal{V}$ can already accept in Step 1. If the Jacobi symbol is 1, it is unclear if x is a quadratic residue mod N so $\mathcal{V}$ rejects the proof. If the Jacobi symbol is -1, the protocol moves on to the next step.

In the second step, $\mathcal{V}$ checks if the element μ has small *odd* order dividing $k2^n$, i.e., order dividing k, by computing $\tilde{\mu} := \mu^k \mod N$. If $\tilde{\mu} \neq 1$, the order of μ does not divide k and $\mathcal{V}$ goes on to the next step. If $\tilde{\mu} = 1$, $\mathcal{V}$ can easily find the order d of μ by factoring the (small) integer k. Then $\mathcal{V}$ can verify the statement without any message from $\mathcal{P}$. In fact, $\mathcal{V}$ only verifies the statement $x^{k2^n} = \mu^2$ by computing the 2^n-th root of μ^2. Unfortunately we can not compute the 2^{n-1}-th root of $-\mu$ because $-\mu$ has order $2d$ and the inverse of 2^{n-1} modulo $2d$ does not exist. This additional squaring step eliminates potential "bad" elements of order 2, so this check only proves that $x^{k2^{n-1}} = -\mu \cdot \alpha \mod N$, for some element α of order 2 or $\alpha = 1$. Luckily, this is enough information for $\mathcal{V}$ since we only want to rule out the possibility that the result of the exponentiation is -1 and $\mu^{-1} \neq \alpha$ since μ has odd order.

If $\mathcal{V}$ gets to the third step, we know that the order of μ does not divide k. To make sure that it does not divide k times a small power of 2 either, $\mathcal{V}$ checks if $\mu^{k2^{\lambda \log n}} \neq 1 \mod N$. If this holds, we know that $\mathcal{V}$ can accept a PPoE for the statement $x^{k2^{n-1}} = -\mu \mod N$ because a malicious prover will only be successful in convincing $\mathcal{V}$ with negligible probability. If $\mu^{k2^{\lambda \log n}} = 1$, such a PoE is not sound, so $\mathcal{V}$ goes on to the next step.

If $\mathcal{V}$ gets to the last step, we know that the order of μ is too small to soundly accept a PPoE. However, we now know that the order of μ is even, so we can use the following trick: Instead of sending a PPoE for the statement $x^{k2^{n-1}} = -\mu \mod N$, $\mathcal{P}$ sends a PPoE for the statement $x^{k2^{n-1-\lambda \log n}} = y \mod N$ for some element $y \in \mathbb{Z}_N^*$. Then $\mathcal{V}$ checks if $y^{2^{\lambda \log n}} = -\mu$. If this holds and the PoE is correct, $\mathcal{V}$ outputs accept. Else, $\mathcal{V}$ outputs reject.

Remark 4. The complexity of Steps 3 and 4 of our protocol could be slightly improved with the following changes:

– Instead of $\mathcal{V}$ computing the exponentiation $\tilde{\mu}_1^{2^{\lambda \log n}}$ in Step 3, $\mathcal{P}$ could send a proof for the statement $\tilde{\mu}_1^{2^{\lambda \log n}} \neq 1$. This can be done in a sound manner since again $\mathcal{V}$ only wants to rule out *one* result, so $\mathcal{P}$ and $\mathcal{V}$ can execute Steps 2-4 recursively. This reduces the work for $\mathcal{V}$ but increases the work for $\mathcal{P}$. However, the PoEs can be batched together similarly to the batching protocol in [20] so the proof size only grows by one group element.

- If $\mathcal{V}$ and $\mathcal{P}$ find out in Step 3 that $\tilde{\mu}_1^{2^{\lambda \log n}} = 1$, they also know the smallest integer i such that $\tilde{\mu}_1^{2^{\lambda \log n - i}} \neq 1$. This means that, in Step 4, $\mathcal{P}$ can send a PoE for the statement

$$(x^k)^{2^{n-1-\lambda \log n + i}} = y \quad \mod N,$$

and $\mathcal{V}$ only needs to check if $y^{2^{\lambda \log n - i}} = -\mu \mod N$. This reduces the work for $\mathcal{V}$ by i multiplications.

For simplicity of the analysis and because the improvements are minor, we omit these changes and analyze the protocol as it is stated in Fig. 3.

Instance: (n, k, x, μ), where $n \in \mathbb{N}$, $0 < k < 2^{n-1}$ an odd integer, $\mu \in \mathbb{Z}_N^*$ with $\mu \neq 1$ and $x \in \mathbb{Z}_N^*$ a small prime number with Jacobi symbol -1 modulo $N := k2^n + 1$

Parameters: statistical security parameter λ

Statement: $x^{k2^{n-1}} = -\mu \mod N$

Protocol:

1. $\mathcal{V}$ computes $a := N \mod x$ and if $a \neq 0$ the Jacobi symbol $\left(\frac{a}{x}\right)$.
   - If $a = 0$, output accept.
   - If $a \neq 0$ and $\left(\frac{a}{x}\right) = -1$, go to Step 2.
   - Else, output reject.
2. $\mathcal{P}$ and $\mathcal{V}$ compute $\tilde{\mu}_1 := \mu^k \mod N$
   - If $\tilde{\mu}_1 \neq 1$, go to Step 3.
   - Else, $\mathcal{V}$ computes $d := \mathrm{ord}(\mu)$ and $a := 2^{-n} \mod d$. If $x^k = \mu^{2a} \mod N$ output accept. Else, output reject.
3. $\mathcal{P}$ and $\mathcal{V}$ compute $\tilde{\mu}_2 := \tilde{\mu}_1^{2^{\lambda \log n}} \mod N$.
   - If $\tilde{\mu}_2 = 1$, go to Step 4.
   - Else, $\mathcal{P}$ sends $\mathrm{PPoE}(x^k, -\mu, n-1, N)$. If the PPoE verifier accepts, output accept. Else, output reject.
4. (a) $\mathcal{P}$ sends a group element y and a PPoE $(x^k, y, n-1-\lambda \log n, N)$ for some $y \in \mathbb{Z}_N^*$. If the PPoE verifier rejects, output reject. Else, go to Step 4b.
   (b) $\mathcal{V}$ computes $\tilde{y} := y^{2^{\lambda \log n}} \mod N$. If $\tilde{y} = -\mu$ output accept. Else, output reject.

Fig. 3. The non-primality certificate.

4.1   Completeness

In this section, we show that $\mathcal{V}$ always outputs `accept` if $\mathcal{P}$ is honest.

Theorem 2. *The protocol in Fig. 3 has perfect completeness.*

Proof. We show that if $\mathcal{P}$ is honest, $\mathcal{V}$ does not output `reject` in any step and outputs `accept` in one of the steps.

Step 1. Assume that x does not divide N since otherwise $\mathcal{V}$ accepts in the first step and completeness holds trivially. If $\mathcal{P}$ is honest, x has Jacobi symbol $\left(\frac{x}{N}\right) = -1$. Furthermore, since x is prime and does not divide N, we have

$$\left(\frac{x}{N}\right) = (-1)^{(x-1)k2^n/4}\left(\frac{N}{x}\right) = \left(\frac{N}{x}\right) = \left(\frac{N \mod x}{x}\right),$$

where the first equality follows from the law of quadratic reciprocity. Hence, $\mathcal{V}$ does not reject in this step and goes on to the next one.

Step 2. If $\tilde{\mu}_1 \neq 1$, $\mathcal{V}$ does not output anything in this step and goes on to the next one. Assume $\tilde{\mu}_1 = 1$ and let $a := 2^{-n} \mod d$, where d is the order of μ. Then we have

$$\mu^{2a} = (\mu^2)^{2^{-n}} = ((x^k)^{2^n})^{2^{-n}} = x^k \mod N$$

so $\mathcal{V}$ accepts if $\mathcal{P}$ is honest.

Step 3. If $\tilde{\mu}_2 = 1$, $\mathcal{V}$ does not output anything in this step and goes on to the next one. If $\tilde{\mu}_2 \neq 1$, completeness follows immediately from the completeness property of PPoE.

Step 4. If $\mathcal{P}$ is honest, the verifier does not reject in Step 4a by the completeness property of PPoE. In Step 4b, the verifier checks if

$$y^{2^{\lambda \log n}} = (x^{k2^{n-1-\lambda \log n}})^{2^{\lambda \log n}} = -\mu \mod N,$$

which holds if $\mathcal{P}$ is honest.

4.2   Soundness

For our purposes, it is sufficient to consider a relaxed definition of soundness. We only want to rule out the event that a malicious prover $\tilde{\mathcal{P}}$ can convince $\mathcal{V}$ that a Proth number is not prime even though it is. This means we do not need to care about a cheating prover that convinces $\mathcal{V}$ of a wrong result of the exponentiation $x^{k2^{n-1}} \mod N$ as long as the correct result is not -1.

Definition 3. *We call a non-primality certificate* sound *if the probability that $\mathcal{V}$ outputs* `accept` *on a statement (n, k, x, μ) for some $\mu \neq 1$ but $x^{k2^{n-1}} = -1 \mod N$ is negligible. We call that probability the* soundness error.

Theorem 3. *The protocol in Fig. 3 has soundness error at most $2^{-\lambda+2} \log n$.*

Proof. We bound the probability that $\mathcal{V}$ falsely accepts an incorrect statement in each step individually.

Step 1. If $\mathcal{V}$ accepts in Step 1, x is a divisor of N so N must be composite. Assume that this does not hold and x has Jacobi symbol 1 modulo N, i.e., $\left(\frac{x}{N}\right) = 1$. Then,

$$\left(\frac{a}{x}\right) = \left(\frac{N}{x}\right) = (-1)^{(x-1)k2^n/4}\left(\frac{x}{N}\right) = 1,$$

so $\mathcal{V}$ rejects in Step 1.

Step 2. Recall that we consider a relaxed definition of soundness (see Definition 3). This means that we only need $\mathcal{V}$ to reject, when the correct result of the exponentiation is -1. We show that if this is the case and $\tilde{\mu}_1 = 1$, $\mathcal{V}$ always rejects in Step 2(b). Assume that N is prime. If $\mathcal{V}$ gets to Step 2(b), we know that d is a divisor of k and hence odd. This means that μ^2 has order d. $\mathcal{V}$ computes $a := 2^{-n} \mod d$ and checks if $x^k = (-\mu)^{2a} = \mu^{2a} \mod d$.

1. Since N is prime it holds that $(x^k)^{2^{n-1}} = -1 \mod N$ so the order of x is $2^n k$. This means that the order of x^k is 2^n.
2. On the other hand, we know that the order of μ^2 is d so the order of μ^{2a} is a divisor of d and hence odd.

1. and 2. together yield that $x^k \neq \mu^{2a} \mod N$ so the verifier rejects.

Step 3. If $\mathcal{V}$ gets to Step 3 and $\tilde{\mu}_2 \neq 1$, we know that the order of the bad element μ is divisible by $2^{\lambda \log T}$. This means that a malicious prover convinces $\mathcal{V}$ to falsely accept if the execution of the PoE reduces the order of the bad element on average by 2^λ per round. In particular, there must be at least one round where the order drops by at least 2^λ. By Corollary 2, this happens with probability at most $2^{-\lambda+2}$ for a fixed round. Applying a union bound, we conclude that, in this case, $\mathcal{V}$ accepts with probability at most $2^{-\lambda+2} \log n$.[12]

Step 4. If $\mathcal{V}$ gets to Step 4, a malicious prover needs to cheat in Step 4 (a) since otherwise the check in Step 4 (b) will not go through. This means that the prover needs to multiply the claim in Step 4 (a) by a bad element α. What can we say about the order of α? We know that it needs to pass the following check:

$$(y\alpha)^{2^{\lambda \log T}} = -\mu,$$

where $y^{2^{\lambda \log T}} = -1$. This means that α is of the following form:

$$\alpha^{2^{\lambda \log T}} = \mu.$$

It is well known that

$$\text{ord}(\alpha^{2^i}) = \frac{\text{ord}(\alpha)}{\gcd(2^i, \text{ord}(\alpha))} = \text{ord}(\mu).$$

---

[12] PrimeGrid has already implemented a check $\mu^{k \cdot 2^{64}} = 1$? [3]. Our analysis shows that an exponent of 64 is not sufficient for cryptographic soundness as this only gives $64/\log(n)$ bits of security "per round"; once we apply the Fiat-Shamir methodology to make the proof non-interactive, each round can be attacked individually.

Table 1. Complexity of the protocol in Fig. 3 depending on the step in which it outputs the result. Prover's and Verifier's complexity are measured in the number of multiplications and proof-size in the number of group elements. We denote by λ the statistical security parameter.

Output in	Prover's complexity	Verifier's complexity	Proof size
Step 1	0	$\log n$	0
Step 2	$1.5 \log k$	$2.5 \log k + 2 \log n$	0
Step 3	$1.5 \log k + \lambda \log n + 2\sqrt{n}$	$1.5 \log k + (4\lambda + 1) \log n$	$\log n$
Step 4	$1.5 \log k + \lambda \log n + 2\sqrt{n}$	$1.5 \log k + (5\lambda + 1) \log n$	$\log n + 1$

(A proof can be found in any standard textbook on group theory, e.g., [13, Proposition 5]). Now the order of μ is even so we know that $\mathrm{ord}(\alpha) = 2^i \,\mathrm{ord}(\mu)$ for $i = \lambda \log T$. In particular, we have that $2^{\lambda \log T}$ is a divisor of the order of α. We can apply Corollary 2 and a union bound by the same argument as above and conclude that $\mathcal{V}$ accepts with probability at most $2^{-\lambda+2} \log n$ in this case.

All the cases together show that $\mathcal{V}$ outputs accept with probability at most $2^{-\lambda+2} \log n$ whenever N is prime.

Corollary 3. *The Fiat-Shamir transform of the protocol in Fig. 3 yields a statistically sound non-interactive protocol in the random oracle model: The probability that $\mathcal{P}$ finds a non-primality certificate for a prime number with up to Q random oracle queries is at most $Q2^{-\lambda+2}$.*

Proof. As we have seen in the proof of Theorem 3, a cheating prover $\tilde{\mathcal{P}}$ can convince $\mathcal{V}$ to accept a proof of non-primality of a prime number only if $\tilde{\mathcal{P}}$ manages to decrease the order of the bad element by at least 2^λ in one of the rounds of a PPoE. By Corollary 2, this happens with probability at most $2^{-\lambda+2}$, where the probability depends only on the random coins. Assume that $\tilde{\mathcal{P}}$ makes up to Q queries to the random oracle. By the union bound, the probability that $\tilde{\mathcal{P}}$ finds a query that triggers the above event is at most $Q2^{-\lambda+2}$.

4.3   Efficiency

In this section, we analyze the complexity of the Fiat-Shamir transform of the protocol presented in Fig. 3. Note that this complexity depends on the step in which the protocol returns the output. We summarize the results of this section in Table 1.

Prover's Complexity. We compute the number of multiplications the prover has to perform additionally to finding a quadratic non-residue modulo N and computing the initial exponentiation.

Step 1. If the protocol returns the output in Step 1, $\mathcal{P}$ does not perform any additional computations.

Step 2. $\mathcal{P}$ checks if $\mu^k = 1$ via "square and multiply", which is approximately $1.5 \log k$ multiplications. If this holds, $\mathcal{P}$ does not perform any other computations.

Step 3. If the protocol runs until Step 3, $\mathcal{P}$ has checked if $\mu^k = 1$, which did not hold and now checks if $(\mu^k)^{2^{\lambda \log n}}$, which is $\lambda \log n$ additional multiplications. If this holds, $\mathcal{P}$ computes the proof of $\mathsf{PPoE}(x^k, -\mu, n-1, N)$ which, by Proposition 1, can be done with $2\sqrt{n}$ multiplications and storage of $\sqrt{n}$ group elements.

Step 4. If the protocol runs until Step 4, $\mathcal{P}$ has checked if $\mu^k = 1$ and $(\mu^k)^{2^{\lambda \log n}}$, which did not hold. Now $\mathcal{P}$ computes the proof of $\mathsf{PPoE}\ (x^k, y, n-1-\lambda \log n, N)$, which, by Proposition 1, can be done with $2\sqrt{n - \lambda \log n}$ multiplications and storage of $\sqrt{n - \lambda \log n}$ group elements.

Verifier's Complexity.

Step 1. Computing $a := k2^n + 1 \mod x$ takes approximately $\log n$ multiplications. Computing the Jacobi symbol $(\frac{a}{x})$ takes approximately $\log^2 x$ multiplications. Since x is a very small prime number in practice, we will ignore the $\log^2 x$ multiplications from now on.

Step 2. $\mathcal{V}$ checks if $\mu^k = 1$ via "square and multiply", which is approximately $1.5 \log k$ multiplications. If this holds, $\mathcal{V}$ computes $2^{-n} \mod d$, where d is the order of μ. This is another $\log n + \log k$ multiplications.

Step 3. If the protocol runs until Step 3, $\mathcal{V}$ has checked if $\mu^k = 1$, which did not hold and now checks if $(\mu^k)^{2^{\lambda \log n}}$, which is $\lambda \log n$ additional multiplications. If this holds, $\mathcal{V}$ verifies the proof of $\mathsf{PPoE}(x^k, -\mu, n - 1, N)$ which is $3\lambda \log n$ multiplications by Proposition 1.

Step 4. If the protocol runs until Step 4, $\mathcal{V}$ has checked if $\mu^k = 1$ and $(\mu^k)^{2^{\lambda \log n}}$, which did not hold. Now $\mathcal{V}$ verifies the proof of $\mathsf{PPoE}\ (x^k, y, n - 1 - \lambda \log n, N)$, which is $3\lambda \log(n - \lambda \log n)$ multiplications (by Proposition 1) and then performs an exponentiation with exponent $2^{\lambda \log n}$, which is another $\lambda \log n$ multiplications.

Proof Size.

Step 1. If $\mathcal{V}$ already accepts or rejects in Step 1, there is no proof needed.

Step 2. If $\mu^k = 1$, $\mathcal{V}$ can check the result themselves so there is no proof needed.

Step 3. If $\mathcal{P}$ sends a proof in this step, the proof size is equal to the size of the proof of $\mathsf{PPoE}(x^k, -\mu, n - 1, N)$, which is $\log(n - 1)$ by Proposition 1.

Step 4. If $\mathcal{P}$ sends a proof in this step, it consists of a group element y and the proof of $\mathsf{PPoE}\ (x^k, y, n - 1 - \lambda \log n, N)$, which is $\log(n - 1 - \lambda \log n)$ by Proposition 1.

Example. We give a numerical example of the complexity of the protocol when it outputs the result in Step 4 (the most expensive case) using the largest Proth prime known to date: $10223 \cdot 2^{31172165} + 1$ [31]. For $k = 10223$ and $n = 31172165$ we have $\lceil \log k \rceil = 14$ and $\lceil \log n \rceil = 25$. If we choose the security parameter as $\lambda = 80$, we get that the prover stores $\lceil \sqrt{31172165} \rceil = 5584$ group elements, performs 13188 multiplications, the verifier performs 10046 multiplications and the proof size is 26 elements of size 31172179, i.e., around 102 MB. Note that recomputing the result of the primality test would take $n = 31172165$ multiplications in the same group, so our protocol reduces the number of multiplications by a multiplicative factor of $\lfloor 31172165/(13188 + 10046) \rfloor = 1341$.

Our protocol also achieves significant savings compared to [6]: To compute the PoE of [6], the prover needs to perform $2\lambda\sqrt{n} = 893312$ multiplications and the verifier does $2\lambda^2 \log n + 2\lambda = 318800$ multiplications to verify the proof consisting of $\lambda \log n = 2080$ group elements (i.e. 8160 MB). This means that our protocol reduces the number of multiplications of [6] by a factor of 52 and the proof size by a factor of 80.

4.4 Comparison with Pietrzak's PoE

We saw in Sect. 4.3 that the complexity of the protocol is the highest, when it outputs the result in Step 4. Even in this case the additional cost compared to the naive implementation of PPoE is moderate: Instead of performing $2\sqrt{n}$ multiplications, $\mathcal{P}$ needs $1.5 \log k + \lambda \log n + 2\sqrt{n}$ multiplications to compute the proof. Using the numbers from the example in Sect. 4.3 this is 2021 extra multiplications on top of the 11168 multiplications that are performed in the naive implementation. Instead of performing $3\lambda \log n$ multiplications, $\mathcal{V}$ needs $1.5 \log k + (5\lambda + 1) \log n$ multiplications to verify the result. This is 4046 additional multiplications to the 6000 multiplications of the naive implementation in our example. The proof size grows by one group element from $\log n$ to $\log n + 1$. In our example, this corresponds to a proof size of 102 MB instead of 98 MB. If the protocol outputs the result in Step 1 or Step 2 it is even more efficient than PPoE. Recall that the implementation of PPoE in groups of known order does not have any soundness guarantees and for the groups that we are using, there are known attacks that break soundness. In contrast, we showed in Sect. 4.2 that our protocol is statistically sound in these groups. We conclude that our protocol yields a major soundness improvement at moderate additional costs.

5 Open Problems

In this work, we presented an efficient protocol that gives a certificate of non-primality for Proth numbers. While we believe that a certificate of non-primality is more useful than a certificate of primality in the context of search for giant primes, constructing the latter is certainly an intriguing problem. Though, our techniques are not directly applicable to prove *primality* of Proth numbers because our protocol only rules out that the correct result is *one specific number* (namely -1). Conversely, when proving primality one has to rule out *all results except for one* (again -1). Constructing a cryptographic certificate of primality therefore remains an open problem.

Another open problem is to demonstrate the applicability of PoEs towards certifying (non-)primality of other types of numbers such as, for example, Mersenne numbers. The primality of Mersenne numbers is tested via Lucas Lehmer test amounting to computation of long modular recursive sequences. Equivalently, the test can be performed via exponentiation in a suitable extension ring and, thus, one could hope to employ PoEs also in the context of Mersenne number. However, there are some major differences to the case of Proth numbers. In particular, the order of the corresponding group is not necessarily efficiently computable even when the candidate is a prime, which is one of the issues preventing the use of our protocol.

Finally, can our interactive protocol be made non-interactive under assumptions other than random oracles? Several recent works [5,24] have aimed to derandomise Pietrzak's protocol and its closely-related variant from [6] using more standard cryptographic assumptions. It would be interesting to explore whether these techniques are applicable here.

Acknowledgements. We are grateful to Pavel Atnashev for clarifying via e-mail several aspects of the primality tests implementated in the PrimeGrid project. Pavel Hubáček is supported by the Czech Academy of Sciences (RVO 67985840), the Grant Agency of the Czech Republic under the grant agreement no. 19-27871X, and by the Charles University project UNCE/SCI/004. Chethan Kamath is supported by Azrieli International Postdoctoral Fellowship, ISF grants 484/18 and 1789/19, and ERC StG project SPP: Secrecy Preserving Proofs.

A   Attacking Pietrzak's Protocol in Proth Number Groups

In this section we show how a malicious prover $\mathcal{P}^*$ can falsely convince the verifier $\mathcal{V}$ that a Proth *prime* is composite when using Pietrzak's PoE. This attack was first described in [8]. Let $N = k2^n + 1$ be prime and x be any quadratic nonresidue modulo N. Since N is prime, it holds that $x^{k2^{n-1}} = -1 \mod N$. The easiest way for $\mathcal{P}^*$ to cheat is claiming that the result of this exponentiation is 1 instead of -1 and then multiplying the honest messages by -1 until the recombination step (Step 2d of PPoE) yields a correct instance. The probability that $\mathcal{V}$ accepts this false "proof" of non-primality is $1 - 1/2^{\log(n-1)} = 1 - (n-1)^{-1}$. To see this, consider the first round of the protocol. $\mathcal{P}^*$ multiplies the correct midpoint $v = (x^k)^{2^{(n-1)/2}}$ by -1 and sends the message $-v$ to $\mathcal{V}$. $\mathcal{V}$ samples a random coin r and they both compute $x' = -x^{kr}v$ and $y' = (-v)^r$ to create the new statement $x'^{2^{(n-1)/2}} = y'$. Plugging in the values for x', y' and v, we see that the new statement is correct whenever r is an odd integer:

Instance: $(x, y, T, \mathbb{G})$, where $x, y \in \mathbb{G}$, $T \in \mathbb{N}$ is even and $x^{2^T} = y$ in $\mathbb{G}$

Input to $\mathcal{P}^*$: $\alpha \in \mathbb{G}$

Parameters: statistical security parameter λ

Statement: $x^{2^T} = y\alpha$ in $\mathbb{G}$

Protocol:

1. For $T = 1$:
   - If $x^2 = y$, $\mathcal{V}$ outputs accept.
   - Else, $\mathcal{V}$ outputs reject.
2. For $T > 1$:
   (a) $\mathcal{P}^*$ sends $v = \alpha^{-1} x^{2^{T/2}}$ to $\mathcal{V}$.
   (b) If $v \notin \mathbb{G}$, $\mathcal{V}$ outputs reject. Otherwise, $\mathcal{V}$ samples $r \leftarrow \{0, 1, \ldots, 2^\lambda - 1\}$ uniformly at random and sends it to $\mathcal{P}^*$.
   (c) $\mathcal{P}^*$ and $\mathcal{V}$ compute $x' := x^r v$ and $y' := v^r y$ in $\mathbb{G}$.
   (d) If $T/2$ is even, $\mathcal{P}^*$ and $\mathcal{V}$ run the protocol on instance $(x', y', T/2, \mathbb{G})$ with input $\alpha^{2^{T/2} - r - 1}$ to $\mathcal{P}^*$. If $T/2$ is odd, $\mathcal{P}^*$ and $\mathcal{V}$ run the protocol on instance $(x', y'^2, (T+1)/2, \mathbb{G})$ with input $\alpha^{2(2^{T/2} - r - 1)}$ to $\mathcal{P}^*$.

Fig. 4. An attack with success probability at least $1 - (1 - 1/\operatorname{ord}(\alpha))^{\log T}$.

$$x'^{2^{(n-1)/2}} = y'$$
$$\Leftrightarrow (-x^{kr}v)^{2^{(n-1)/2}} = (-v)^r$$
$$\Leftrightarrow v^{2^{(n-1)/2}} = (-1)^r$$
$$\Leftrightarrow (x^k)^{2^{n-1}} = (-1)^r.$$

If r is even, the statement remains false and $\mathcal{P}^*$ does the same in the next round. $\mathcal{V}$ only outputs reject if all of the random coins are even which happens with probability $1/2^{\log(n-1)} = (n-1)^{-1}$ since $\log(n-1)$ is the number of rounds. Otherwise $\mathcal{V}$ outputs accept on a false statement. A generalization of this attack is shown in Fig. 4. Instead of multiplying the correct statement by -1, $\mathcal{P}^*$ multiplies the correct statement by an arbitrary group element α and adapts its messages accordingly. The success probability can be lower bounded by $1 - (1 - 1/\operatorname{ord}(\alpha))^{\log(n-1)}$ which is the probability that in at least one round the bad element is raised to a multiple of the order of α. If $\operatorname{ord}(\alpha)$ is not a prime number, this bound is not tight since the order of the bad element can decrease during the execution of the rounds, making the success probability even higher. In the case where N is prime, the prover knows the group order $N - 1 = k2^n$ and its factorization and can therefore construct elements of sufficiently low order.

References

1. Agrawal, M., Kayal, N., Saxena, N.: PRIMES is in P. Ann. Math. **160**(2), 781–793 (2004)
2. Atkin, A.O.L., Morain, F.: Elliptic curves and primality proving. Math. Comput. **61**(203), 29–68 (1993)
3. Atnashev, P.: Personal communication, February (2022)
4. Baillie, R., Wagstaff, S.S.: Lucas pseudoprimes. Math. Comput. **35**(152), 1391–1417 (1980)
5. Bitansky, N., et al.: PPAD is as hard as LWE and iterated squaring. TCC 2022, to appear (2022)
6. Block, A.R., Holmgren, J., Rosen, A., Rothblum, R.D., Soni, P.. Time- and space-efficient arguments from groups of unknown order. In: Malkin, T., Peikert, C., eds., Advances in Cryptology – CRYPTO 2021, Part IV, volume 12828 of Lecture Notes in Computer Science, pp. 123–152, Virtual Event, August 16–20, 2021. Springer, Cham (2021). https://doi.org/10.1007/978-3-030-84259-8_5
7. Boneh, D., Bonneau, J., Bünz, B., Fisch, B.: Verifiable delay functions. In: Shacham, H., Boldyreva, A., editors, Advances in Cryptology – CRYPTO 2018, Part I, volume 10991 of Lecture Notes in Computer Science, pp. 757–788, Santa Barbara, CA, USA, August 19–23, 2018. Springer, Heidelberg, Germany. https://doi.org/10.1007/978-3-319-96884-1_25
8. Boneh, D., Bünz, B., Fisch, B.: A survey of two verifiable delay functions. Cryptology ePrint Archive, Report 2018/712, (2018). http://eprint.iacr.org/2018/712
9. Borsos, B., Kovács, A., Tihanyi, N.: Tight upper and lower bounds for the reciprocal sum of proth primes. Ramanujan J. **59**, 181–198 (2022)
10. Brillhart, J., Lehmer, D.H., Selfridge, J.L.: New primality criteria and factorizations of $2^m \pm 1$. Math. Comput. **29**(130), 620–647 (1975)
11. Buchmann, J., Williams, H.C.: A key-exchange system based on imaginary quadratic fields. J. Cryptol. **1**(2), 107–118 (1988)
12. Bünz, B., Fisch, B., Szepieniec, A.: Transparent SNARKs from DARK compilers. In: Canteaut, A., Ishai, Y. (eds.) EUROCRYPT 2020. LNCS, vol. 12105, pp. 677–706. Springer, Cham (2020). https://doi.org/10.1007/978-3-030-45721-1_24
13. Dummit, D.S., Foote, R.M.: Abstract Algebra, 3rd edn. John Wiley and Sons, USA (2003)
14. Fiat, A., Shamir, A.: How to prove yourself: practical solutions to identification and signature problems. In: Odlyzko, A.M. (ed.) CRYPTO 1986. LNCS, vol. 263, pp. 186–194. Springer, Heidelberg (1987). https://doi.org/10.1007/3-540-47721-7_12
15. Fischlin, R., Schnorr, C.-P.: Stronger security proofs for RSA and Rabin bits. J. Cryptol. **13**(2), 221–244 (2000)
16. Great Internet Mersenne Prime Search GIMPS. GIMPS discovers largest known prime number: $2^{82,589,933} - 1$. https://www.mersenne.org/primes/press/M82589933.html, (2018). Accessed 18 May 2022
17. Great Internet Mersenne Prime Search GIMPS. Prime95 v30.3. https://www.mersenneforum.org/showthread.php?t=25823, (2020). Accessed 19 May 2022
18. Goldwasser, S., Kilian, J.: Almost all primes can be quickly certified. In: 18th Annual ACM Symposium on Theory of Computing, pp. 316–329, Berkeley, CA, USA, May 28–30. ACM Press (1986)
19. Goldwasser, S., Micali, S., Rackoff, C.: The knowledge complexity of interactive proof systems. SIAM J. Comput. **18**(1), 186–208 (1989)

20. Hoffmann, C., Hubácek, P., Kamath, C., Klein, K., Pietrzak, K.: Practical statistically-sound proofs of exponentiation in any group. In: Dodis, Y., Shrimpton, T., editors, Advances in Cryptology - CRYPTO 2022, Part II, volume 13508 of Lecture Notes in Computer Science, pp. 370–399, Santa Barbara, CA, USA, August 15–18. Springer, Heidelberg, Germany (2022). https://doi.org/10.1007/978-3-031-15979-4_13

21. Hofheinz, D., Kiltz, E.: The group of signed quadratic residues and applications. In: Halevi, S. (ed.) CRYPTO 2009. LNCS, vol. 5677, pp. 637–653. Springer, Heidelberg (2009). https://doi.org/10.1007/978-3-642-03356-8_37

22. Kilian, J.: A note on efficient zero-knowledge proofs and arguments (extended abstract). In: 24th Annual ACM Symposium on Theory of Computing, pp. 723–732, Victoria, BC, Canada, May 4–6. ACM Press (1992)

23. Lehmer, D.H.: Tests for primality by the converse of Fermat's theorem. Bull. Am. Math. Soc. **33**(3), 327–340 (1927)

24. Lombardi, A., Vaikuntanathan, V.: Fiat-Shamir for repeated squaring with applications to PPAD-hardness and VDFs. In: Micciancio, D., Ristenpart, T. (eds.) CRYPTO 2020. LNCS, vol. 12172, pp. 632–651. Springer, Cham (2020). https://doi.org/10.1007/978-3-030-56877-1_22

25. Lucas, E.: Théorie des fonctions numériques simplement périodiques. Am. J. Math. **1**(4), 289–321 (1878)

26. Micali, S.: CS proofs (extended abstracts). In: 35th Annual Symposium on Foundations of Computer Science, pp. 436–453, Santa Fe, NM, USA, November 20–22. IEEE Computer Society Press (1994)

27. Miller, G.L.: Riemann's hypothesis and tests for primality. J. Comput. Syst. Sci. **13**(3), 300–317 (1976)

28. Pietrzak, K.: Simple verifiable delay functions. In: Blum, A., editor, ITCS 2019: 10th Innovations in Theoretical Computer Science Conference, vol. 124, pp. 60:1–60:15, San Diego, CA, USA, January 10–12. LIPIcs (2019)

29. Pomerance, C., Selfridge, J.L., Wagstaff, S.S.: The pseudoprimes to $25 \cdot 10^9$. Math. Comput. **35**(151), 1003–1026 (1980)

30. Pratt, V.R.: Every prime has a succinct certificate. SIAM J. Comput. **4**(3), 214–220 (1975)

31. PrimeGrid. World record Colbert number discovered! http://www.primegrid.com/forum_thread.php?id=7116, (2016). Accessed 18 May 2022

32. PrimeGrid. Proposal: a new sierpiński problem. https://www.primegrid.com/forum_thread.php?id=9107, (2020). Accessed 19 May 2022

33. Proth, F.: Theoremes sur les nombres premiers. Comptes rendus de l'Académie des Sciences de Paris, 87(926), (1878)

34. Rabin, M.O.: Probabilistic algorithm for testing primality. J. Number Theory **12**(1), 128–138 (1980)

35. Riesel, H.: Lucasian criteria for the primality of $N = h \cdot 2^n - 1$. Math. Comput. **23**(108), 869–875 (1969)

36. Rivest, R.L., Shamir, A., Adleman, L.M.: A method for obtaining digital signatures and public-key cryptosystems (reprint). Commun. ACM **26**(1), 96–99 (1983)

37. Rotem, L.: Simple and efficient batch verification techniques for verifiable delay functions. In: Nissim, K., Waters, B. (eds.) TCC 2021. LNCS, vol. 13044, pp. 382–414. Springer, Cham (2021). https://doi.org/10.1007/978-3-030-90456-2_13

38. Solovay, R., Strassen, V.: A fast Monte-Carlo test for primality. SIAM J. Comput. **6**(1), 84–85 (1977)

39. Wesolowski, B.: Efficient verifiable delay functions. J. Cryptol. **33**(4), 2113–2147 (2020)

Transparent Batchable Time-lock Puzzles and Applications to Byzantine Consensus

Shravan Srinivasan[1]([⊠]), Julian Loss[2], Giulio Malavolta[3], Kartik Nayak[4], Charalampos Papamanthou[5], and Sri AravindaKrishnan Thyagarajan[6]

[1] University of Maryland, College Park, USA
`sshravan@cs.umd.edu`
[2] CISPA Helmholtz Center for Information Security, Saarbrücken, Germany
[3] Max Planck Institute for Security and Privacy, Bochum, Germany
[4] Duke University, Durham, USA
[5] Yale University, New Haven, USA
[6] NTT Research, Sunnyvale, USA
`t.srikrishnan@gmail.com`

Abstract. Time-lock puzzles (TLP) are a fascinating type of cryptographic problem that is easy to generate, but takes a certain time to solve, even when arbitrary parallel speedup is allowed. TLPs have wide-ranging applications including fairness, round efficient computation, and more. To reduce the effort needed to solve large numbers of TLPs, prior work has proposed batching techniques to reduce the cost of solving. However, these proposals either require: (1) a trusted setup or (2) the puzzle size be linear in the maximum batch size, which implies setting an a priori bound on the maximum size of the batch. Any of these limitations restrict the utility of TLPs in decentralized and dynamic settings like permissionless blockchains. In this work, we demonstrate the feasibility and usefulness of a TLP that overcomes all the above limitations using *indistinguishability obfuscation* to show that there are no fundamental barriers to achieving such a TLP construction.

As a main application of our TLP, we show how to improve the resilience of consensus protocols toward network-level adversaries in the following settings: (1) We show a generic compiler that boosts the resilience of a Byzantine broadcast protocol Π as follows: if Π is secure against $t < n$ weakly adaptive corruptions, then the compiled protocol is secure against $t < n$ strongly adaptive corruptions. Here, 'strong' refers to adaptively corrupting a party and deleting messages that it sent while still honest. Our compiler is round and communication preserving, and gives the *first* expected constant-round Byzantine broadcast protocol against a *strongly adaptive* adversary for the *dishonest majority* setting. (2) We adapt the Nakamoto consensus protocol to a *weak model* of synchrony where the adversary can adaptively create minority partitions in the network. Unlike prior works, we do not assume that *all* honest messages are delivered within a known upper bound on the message delay. This is the *first* work to show that it is possible to achieve consensus in the permissionless setting even after relaxing the standard synchrony assumption.

© International Association for Cryptologic Research 2023
A. Boldyreva and V. Kolesnikov (Eds.): PKC 2023, LNCS 13940, pp. 554–584, 2023.
https://doi.org/10.1007/978-3-031-31368-4_20

Keywords: Time-lock puzzles · Batch solving · Distributed consensus · Byzantine broadcast · Mobile-sluggish faults

1   Introduction

A *Time-Lock Puzzle* (TLP) is a cryptographic primitive that allows a sender to lock a message as a computational puzzle in a manner where the receiver will be able to solve the puzzle after a stipulated time $\mathbf{T}$. In terms of efficiency, a sender should be able to generate a puzzle substantially faster than the time required to solve it, and in terms of security, an adversary should not be able to solve the puzzle faster than the stipulated time, even with parallel computation. Rivest, Shamir, and Wagner (RSW) [39] proposed the first TLP construction based on the sequentiality of repeated modular squaring in the RSA group. Many other TLP constructions [8,33,44] have followed suit in different settings but require the same flavor of sequential operations during solving. TLPs have found a wide variety of applications including sealed-bid auctions [33,39], timed-commitments [28,44], e-voting [15,33], fair contract signing [9,33], zero-knowledge proofs [18], cryptocurrency payments [43], distributed consensus [45], blockchain front-running prevention [1], and more applications continue to emerge.

In many TLP applications involving multiple users, it is often the case that a user is required to solve the puzzles of all other users, and record all of the solutions. Say an auction house has to open all the time-locked bids and declare them publicly before announcing the winner. Batching and solving the puzzles is essential for scalability in such TLP applications that have large number of participating users. Intuitively, batch solving of TLPs allows a receiver to solve multiple puzzles simultaneously (at the price of solving one puzzle) without needing to solve each puzzle separately. Specifically, the total running time of the batch-solve operation is bounded by some $p(\lambda, \mathbf{T}) + \tilde{p}(\lambda, n)$ for some fixed polynomials p and $\tilde{p}$, where λ is the security parameter, n is the number of puzzles to be batched, and $\mathbf{T}$ is the timing hardness of a single puzzle.

Modern TLP constructions achieve the seemingly impossible batch-solve property under various settings and assumptions [33,43,44]. However, *all* existing batch solving TLP schemes suffer from the following limitations: (1) requires a trusted setup to generate structured reference string, and/or (2) individual puzzle size scales linearly in the maximum number of puzzles that can be batched, which further implies that there is an a priori upper bound on the number of puzzles that can be batched (which is set upfront during puzzle generation).

Yet emerging blockchain applications like Miner Extractable Value (MEV) prevention [1], cryptocurrency payments [43], distributed consensus [45], etc., either for security or performance, require the TLP scheme to have a *transparent setup*, the puzzle size *independent* of the number of puzzles batched and support batching an *unbounded* number of puzzles. These requirements arise in blockchain systems especially in the permissionless setting for the following reasons:

– First, it is often impossible or impractical to rely on a trusted party to generate the public parameters. Moreover, a compromised setup with trapdoors can violate the security of the system. Precisely for these reasons, such trusted parties are not assumed to exist and usage of cryptosystems requiring such trusted setups are actively discouraged in permissionless blockchain systems.

– Second, in permissionless systems (like Bitcoin), nodes can join and leave the network at will, and there are no mechanisms to authenticate any participant. So the exact number of participants n is unknown at any point in time. However, existing TLP schemes require the bound on the number of users at the time of puzzle generation. Thus, restricting the ability to accommodate more participants on demand after the puzzle generation phase.

– Third, large puzzle size increases the total communication costs. For instance, in a setting where all participants have to exchange puzzles with each other, a linear-sized puzzle of the prior constructions blows up the total communication overhead to $O(n^3)$.

Motivated by these open problems and applications, we ask the following question: *Is it possible to build a TLP scheme with batch solving that has a transparent setup, puzzle size independent of the batch size, and therefore allows unbounded batching?* In this work, we affirmatively answer this question and use our new TLP scheme to solve two elusive problems in distributed consensus:

1. The problem of expected *constant round* Byzantine broadcast under *corrupt majority* and *strongly adaptive model*.
2. The problem of permissionless consensus in a *generalization of synchronous* model of communication called the *mobile sluggish model*.

Below, we motivate how our TLP with the above properties can enhance security and reduce communication costs in the two applications we consider.

At a high level, in both applications, TLPs help to defend against a powerful network adversary that has the ability to delay or delete messages from the network. For instance, a powerful network adversary can simply learn the contents of the message sent by any honest party before deciding to corrupt or deliver the message. However, by time-lock encrypting the message, the adversary cannot learn the contents of the message before time **T** without doing sequential work. In the meantime, all the honest messages would have been delivered. Thus, the adversary is forced to corrupt an honest node without inspecting the contents of the message. Prior works [16,45] showed the feasibility of the distributed consensus in the presence of a network level adversary using TLPs (without batching property) at the cost of polylogarithmic blowup in round complexity. However, batch solving and compact puzzles aid in improving the round complexity and communication costs, respectively, in these applications.

Round-Efficient Byzantine Broadcast. Byzantine broadcast (BB) is a well-studied problem in distributed consensus, and, in recent times, BB has emerged as a fundamental building block in blockchains [23]. Despite decades of study in improving the round efficiency, no prior BB protocol has expected constant round-complexity under strongly adaptive and dishonest majority setting. In the strongly adaptive model, an adversary can observe all the honest messages, corrupt honest nodes on the fly, and perform *after-the-fact* removal, that is, the adversary can delete any honest message *in-flight* before it reaches any other honest nodes.

Current success in constant round BB is in the weakly adaptive model where the adversary's power is severely limited [46]. Wan et al. proposed the first sublinear BB protocol under strongly adaptive and dishonest majority setting [45]. Their work used TLPs to prevent the adversary from inspecting the contents of the message before corrupting a node. Since their TLP construction did not support batching, they proposed a sub-protocol with polylogarithmic round complexity to distribute the task of opening all puzzles to honest nodes, rather than solving the puzzles individually. We observe that by using a TLP with batching property and puzzle size independent of the batch size as a building block, it is possible to achieve expected constant round Byzantine broadcast under strongly adaptive and dishonest majority setting.

Permissionless Protocol in the Mobile Sluggish Model. Guo et al. introduced a relaxation of the synchronous model, which was subsequently called the *mobile sluggish model* [3,25]. In the mobile sluggish model, a fraction of honest nodes, called *sluggish* nodes, can arbitrarily lose synchrony, but they faithfully follow the rest of the protocol. The remaining honest nodes, called *prompt* nodes, are synchronous and faithfully follow the protocol. Additionally, sluggishness can be *mobile*, that is, any honest node can become sluggish over the protocol execution, and if a sluggish node becomes prompt by regaining synchrony, it will receive all the backlogged messages. This model is stronger than the partially synchronous and asynchronous model but weaker than the synchronous model. Pass and Shi showed that it is *impossible to achieve permissionless consensus* in a partially synchronous or asynchronous network [37]. Unfortunately, Nakamoto consensus is vulnerable to consistency violations even in the mobile sluggish model, as we show in this work. Specifically, even a *single* mobile sluggish fault can effectively reduce the collective mining rate of honest nodes by half!

One way to defend against a mobile sluggish adversary is to let an honest block winner simply time-lock encrypt the message before sending it, and other honest nodes time-lock encrypt a *decoy* to distract the adversary from spotting the block winner. Since the adversary cannot learn the contents of the puzzle without spending sufficient time, by setting the TLP duration slightly greater than the round duration, the adversary is now forced to corrupt or deliver the message randomly. At the end of the round, honest nodes can batch solve the TLPs they received and update their chains. Unfortunately, *no* prior TLP with batch solving works in this application, due to the requirements and challenges in the permissionless setting: we cannot rely on a trusted setup [33,39,43], we do not know the number of users in the network a priori, and we do not want to blowup the round [39] and communication complexity [33,43,44].

1.1   Our Contributions

We give the first TLP construction (Sect. 4) that *simultaneously* achieves:

- *Transparent Setup*: Requires a one-time *transparent (public-coin)* setup.

- *Batch Solving*: Supports batch solving of *any* polynomial number of puzzles even after puzzle generation, and the size of individual puzzles is *independent* of the number of puzzles to be batched.

Our construction is based on *Indistinguishability Obfuscation (IO)* [21] where users' puzzles are obfuscated programs. We employ new techniques to achieve compactness in the puzzle size while supporting unbounded batch sizes. Even though our construction is far from being practically efficient, our construction crucially shows that there are no fundamental barriers from achieving a TLP with the above properties and lays a blueprint for future work to instantiate our new techniques with more efficient tools. In Sect. 2, we briefly explain why existing techniques for TLP fail to achieve the desired properties, along with giving a brief overview of the key techniques used in our TLP scheme.

We use our TLP construction as a fundamental building block and overcome other challenges to solve two longstanding open problems in consensus:

1. **Round-efficient Byzantine broadcast:** In the years of distributed consensus research, we present (Sect. 5) the first *expected constant round* Byzantine broadcast under strongly adaptive and corrupt majority setting. To realize our result, we develop a generic compiler that uses *any* batch solving TLP construction to *convert any* broadcast protocol secure against a *weakly* adaptive adversary [46] into a broadcast protocol secure against a *strongly* adaptive adversary in a *round preserving* way, which could also be of independent interest. With our TLP, this compiler is additionally *communication* preserving. We formally prove the security (Thm. 3) of our compiler in the *programmable random oracle* (RO) model.

2. **Permissionless protocol in the mobile sluggish model:** We first show an attack to illustrate that Nakamoto consensus is not secure *even* in the mobile sluggish model (Sect. 6.1). We then present a proof-of-work based permissionless protocol (Sect. 6.3) which does not assume that the network is synchronous or all honest messages arrive on time. To the best of our knowledge, this is the *first* work to show that it is possible to achieve consensus in the permissionless setting even after *relaxing the standard synchrony assumption!* To do this, we develop a novel proof-of-work based *decoy* mechanism that uses TLPs to defend against a mobile sluggish adversary that can arbitrarily delay a fraction of honest messages. We formally analyze our protocol to prove that it achieves *consistency* and *liveness* in the extended version of our paper [42]. Specifically, we show that our protocol realizes the standard properties namely, *chain growth*, *chain quality*, and *common prefix* [42].

1.2   Related Work

Time-lock Puzzles. Bitanski et al. [8] proposed a different approach to construct TLPs, assuming the existence of succinct randomized encodings [7] and non-parallelizable languages. Similar to RSW puzzles, during solving each puzzle has to be *solved individually* to obtain their solutions. Liu et al. [32] combine (extractable) witness encryption [22] and a public reference clock like the Bitcoin blockchain. In their construction, one can batch open many puzzles as the blockchain reaches a certain height as the computational effort is shared by the entire blockchain network in mining new blocks. Their construction relies on Succinct Non-Interactive Argument of Knowledge (SNARKs) [6] and thus non-falsifiable assumptions. Our construction on the other hand does not require such assumptions and does not rely on a global reference clock like a blockchain. Malavolta and Thyagarajan introduced Homomorphic TLPs [33]. Their constructions allowed homomorphic function evaluations to be performed on puzzles to obtain a single puzzle that embeds the function of all the original solutions. However, all constructions from [33] (including their fully homomorphic TLP) and [43] do not support unbounded batching of puzzles and require structured reference string generated using a trusted setup. Thyagarajan et al. [44] proposed a Class group based construction that gets rid of the trusted setup and only requires a transparent public-coin setup. In Table 1, we compare with prior constructions.

Table 1. Comparison with other batch TLP schemes. λ is the security parameter and **T** is time hardness parameter. Compactness of puzzles here refers to the size of puzzles being independent of the batch size.

Scheme	Transparent setup	Unbounded batching	Compact puzzles	One-time Setup time	Practical efficiency
RSA-based [33,43]	✗	✗	✗	$O(\log(\mathbf{T}), \lambda)$	✓
Class-groups based [44]	✓	✗	✗	$O(\mathbf{T}, \lambda)$	✓
IO-based (**This work**)	✓	✓	✓	$O(\mathbf{T}, \lambda)$	✗

Recently, Burdges and Feo [11] proposed a related but a new notion called *delay encryption*. On a high level, users encrypt their messages to some common previously unpredictable identity ID using an Identity-Based Encryption (IBE) scheme. The decryption key for the identity ID can be derived by anyone but the derivation is a delayed operation, meaning that it takes time **T** to derive the key. We can batch decrypt several encryptions provided they are w.r.t. to the same ID. The drawback of their construction is the requirement of a trusted setup which is considered a strong assumption in the applications of our interest. Encryption-to-the-future is a closely related primitive, however, unlike our construction prior works either use a public bulletin (like a blockchain) or a committee of users with an honest majority [12,19].

Strongly Adaptive Byzantine Broadcast. Wan et al. proposed the first expected sub-linear round protocol in the strongly adaptive setting using Public-Key Infrastructure (PKI) and TLPs [45]. Subsequently, Cohen et al. [16] explored the feasibility of *fair* broadcast in the strongly adaptive setting for both property-based and simulation-based definitions. However, our focus is on achieving expected constant-round BB under strongly adaptive and dishonest majority setting. We relate to other works in the extended version our paper [42].

Protocols in the Mobile Sluggish Model. Guo et al. [25] first introduced the mobile sluggish model as "weakly synchronous" model and showed that it is impossible for a Byzantine broadcast protocol to tolerate majority faults (Byzantine or sluggish). Subsequently, Abraham et al. presented a Byzantine

Fault Tolerant blockchain protocol that can tolerate minority corruptions in the mobile sluggish model [3]. Kim et al. [30] observed that many proof-of-stake protocols, such as Dfinity [26], Streamlet [14], OptSync [41], can support mobile sluggish faults. These prior techniques heavily relied on using messages (votes) from a majority of the nodes (certificates) to establish communication with sluggish nodes and ensure safety of the protocol. Since Nakamoto consensus does not rely on such certificates, their techniques do not apply in our setting.

Nakamoto Style Protocols. Prior works can be categorized based on the flavor of synchrony used to analyze Nakamoto consensus. In the lock-step model of synchrony, Garay et al. formally analyzed Nakamoto consensus [20]. Subsequently, Pass et al. and Kiffer et al. showed that the Nakamoto consensus is secure even in the non-lock-step synchrony model where the message delay is bounded and the time proceeds in discrete rounds [20,29,35,48]. Ren discarded the notion of discrete rounds and proved the security of Nakamoto consensus in the continuous model [38]. Even parallelly composed Nakamoto protocols are also in the lock-step model of synchrony [4,47]. Unfortunately, all these analyses assume that *any* honest message reaches other honest nodes in Δ time units regardless of the flavor of synchrony. Our analysis is in the mobile sluggish model, which assumes that a fraction of honest nodes can violate the Δ-assumption. However, the prompt nodes in our setting are assumed to be in lock-step synchrony model.

Network-adversary Lower Bounds and Impossibilities. Abraham et al. showed that a sub-quadratic protocol could not be resilient against a strongly adaptive adversary that can perform *after-the-fact* removal [2]. In Nakamoto consensus, delaying an honest block has the same effects as deleting the block. For example, if a newly mined block is delayed for a sufficiently long time, it could end up as an orphan block, which eventually gets pruned after the main chain stabilizes. Moreover, sluggishness can be mobile, thus making the sluggish adversary more powerful than the strongly adaptive adversary. Pass and Shi showed that it is impossible to achieve permissionless consensus in the partially synchronous/asynchronous network [37]. In these network models, the adversary can *arbitrarily* partition the honest nodes. However, in our setting, the adversary can create only *minority* partitions. Thus, this impossibility does not apply.

2   Technical Overview

We give an overview of our TLP construction that supports batch-solving an unbounded number of puzzles and protocols that use our TLP construction to tolerate network-level adversaries in the BB and Nakamoto consensus.

2.1   Time-Lock Puzzles with Batch Solving

Bounded Batching of TLPs. Before delving into the specific of our construction, we show how standard techniques [33,44] readily give a construction of TLP with *bounded* batched solving, i.e., where the number n of batched solutions is fixed at puzzle generation time. Given a Linearly Homomorphic TLP scheme

LHP with homomorphism over $\mathbb{Z}_q$ and a large enough q, we can homomorphically evaluate the packing algorithm. In more detail, we are given n puzzles $Z_1, \ldots, Z_n$ (of the LHP scheme) each encoding λ-bit values with timing hardness of each puzzle being $\mathbf{T}$. To batch solve these puzzles, we first homomorphically evaluate the linear function: $f(x_1, \ldots, x_n) = \sum_{i=1}^{n} 2^{(i-1)\cdot\lambda} \cdot x_i$.

The resultant evaluated puzzle Z^* is then solved in time $\mathbf{T}$ to obtain all the n values where each of these values were originally encoded as λ-bit values. Importantly, this means that the bit-representation of the plaintext space must be large enough to accommodate all n-secrets, i.e., $\log(q) \approx n \cdot \lambda$. Since the domain has to be fixed at the time of puzzle generation, this means that each puzzle scales linearly with n. In settings with n parties, where each party generates a puzzle and broadcasts it to the other parties, the total communication is $O(n^3)$, assuming a total of $O(n^2)$ communication for a broadcast of a single bit and ignoring factors that depend on λ.

Unbounded Batching? The question that we set out to answer is whether it is possible to construct a TLP that supports *unbounded* batch-solving. One approach to do that is to "defer" the choice of the plaintext space at the solving time, so that the solver can select the appropriate domain, depending on how many puzzles need to be batched. A naive idea is to define a program $\mathbf{P}$ that, on input the batch size n, outputs a LHP puzzle Z embedding the user's message m and where the message space is sufficiently large to accommodate packing of n puzzles. This solution is clearly insecure as it reveals m in the plain, so to amend this we *obfuscate* the program $\tilde{\mathbf{P}} := i\mathcal{O}(\mathbf{P})$, using indistinguishability obfuscation (IO) [21,27]. Setting a super-polynomial upper bound on $n \approx 2^{\omega(\log(\lambda))}$ allows one to batch any polynomial number of puzzles.

Unfortunately, this simple construction runs into issues when proving security. A natural strategy when proving security would be to hybrid over all possible n, hardwire the corresponding puzzle in the description of the circuit and the swap it with a puzzle encoding a fixed string (say 0) appealing to the security of the TLP. However it is not hard to see that this would quickly run into issues: As n grows to super-polynomial, the size of the corresponding puzzle, and consequently of the obfuscated circuit, would also be super-polynomial. This is not only an issue of the security proof, since the actual obfuscated circuit must be padded to the maximum size of the circuits that is defined in the analysis. To get this strategy to work, our construction would yield a super-polynomial size puzzle!

Our Solution. To understand our solution, we first discuss a way to circumvent the above issue. We change the output of the obfuscated circuit to output the n dimensional vector $(0, \ldots, m, \ldots, 0)$, where m is inserted in the i-th slot, masked by the output of a puncturable pseudorandom function (PRF) F and a LHP puzzle Z encoding the PRF key k.

$$\begin{bmatrix} 0 \\ \vdots \\ m \\ \vdots \\ 0 \end{bmatrix} + \begin{bmatrix} \mathsf{F}(k,1) \\ \vdots \\ \mathsf{F}(k,i) \\ \vdots \\ \mathsf{F}(k,n) \end{bmatrix} = \begin{bmatrix} \mathsf{F}(k,1) \\ \vdots \\ \mathsf{F}(k,i) + m \\ \vdots \\ \mathsf{F}(k,n) \end{bmatrix}$$

This structured solution allows us to solve the proof problem by puncturing each position individually, thereby avoiding an exponential blow-up in the size of the obfuscated circuit. To solve this puzzle, the solver can arrange the various masked plaintexts (from other obfuscated circuits of other users) diagonally, and sum up all the results, to obtain

$$
\begin{bmatrix} \mathsf{F}(k_1,1) + m_1 \\ \mathsf{F}(k_1,2) \\ \vdots \\ \mathsf{F}(k_1,n) \end{bmatrix} + \begin{bmatrix} \mathsf{F}(k_2,1) \\ \mathsf{F}(k_2,2) + m_2 \\ \vdots \\ \mathsf{F}(k_2,n) \end{bmatrix} + \ldots + \begin{bmatrix} \mathsf{F}(k_n,1) \\ \mathsf{F}(k_n,2) \\ \vdots \\ \mathsf{F}(k_n,n) + m_n \end{bmatrix}
$$

Here k_i and m_i are the PRF key and message, respectively, of the i-th obfuscated program. However at this point it is not clear how to batch solve the resulting puzzles, since each party will use an independent PRF key k_i. This means that we shifted the problem from recovering the n messages to recovering n PRF keys, bringing us back to square one. Our last idea is to use instead a *key-homomorphic* PRF $\overline{\mathsf{F}}$. Assuming a suitable instantiation [10], we have the above expression evaluate to

$$
= \begin{bmatrix} \sum_i \overline{\mathsf{F}}(k_i,1) + m_1 \\ \sum_i \overline{\mathsf{F}}(k_i,2) + m_2 \\ \vdots \\ \sum_i \overline{\mathsf{F}}(k_i,n) + m_n \end{bmatrix} \approx \begin{bmatrix} \overline{\mathsf{F}}\left(\sum_i k_i, 1\right) + m_1 \\ \overline{\mathsf{F}}\left(\sum_i k_i, 2\right) + m_2 \\ \vdots \\ \overline{\mathsf{F}}\left(\sum_i k_i, n\right) + m_n \end{bmatrix}
$$

We also have a LHP puzzle from each party encoding k_i. The solver can now add all keys homomorphically and solve the resulting LHP puzzle in time $\mathbf{T}$ to obtain $\sum_i k_i$. Once the key is known, the solver can simply unmask all the values in the above vector by evaluating the PRF at points $(1, \ldots, n)$ using the key $\sum_i k_i$. Subtracting the output yields the vector of n plaintexts. Note that in the full construction, the index i for the puzzle of a user is not chosen during puzzle generation, but is assigned during puzzle solving through some deterministic rule.

This gives an outline of our construction. In the actual scheme, extra care is needed to match the modulus of the TLPs with the key space of the PRF, to set the parameters to account for the imperfect homomorphism, and deal with the lack of imperfect correctness of punctured keys in the proof (see Sect. 4 for more details). Notice that the size of each puzzle is dominated by the obfuscated program $\widetilde{\mathbf{P}}$, which can be implemented to be of size logarithmic in n (the batch size). Therefore, in a multi-party setting, we get a total communication of $\tilde{O}(n^2)$ assuming $O(n^2)$ communication for single bit broadcast and ignoring factors that depend on λ.

2.2   Application 1: Efficient Byzantine Broadcast

Byzantine broadcast is a classical problem in distributed consensus, where a *designated sender* holds a bit b and wants to transmit b to all n nodes in the presence of t faults. A BB protocol is secure if it can guarantee *consistency* (all honest nodes output the same bit) and *validity* (if the designated sender is honest, all honest nodes output the designated sender's input b).

With increasing applications for BB (cryptography, blockchains, etc.), we study the round-efficiency of BB under the dishonest majority setting. Prior BB protocols in the dishonest majority setting can broadly tolerate: (1) weakly adaptive or (2) strongly adaptive adversary. Both strongly and weakly adaptive adversary can corrupt honest nodes *on the fly*. But, a weakly adaptive adversary cannot perform *after-the-fact* removal.

Despite decades of study, the state-of-art round-efficient BB in the dishonest majority is in the weakly adaptive setting [46]. Thus, it raises the question:

Is it possible to achieve an expected constant-round Byzantine broadcast under strongly adaptive and corrupt majority?

We affirmatively answer this using PKI, RO, and *any* batch solvable TLP construction. Our solution is a *generic round preserving compiler* that can convert any weakly adaptive BB protocol into a strongly adaptive one. Thus, our compiler can be **efficiently realized** using the batch solvable TLP constructions based on RSA or Class-groups [43,44]. With our batch solvable TLP (Sect. 4.3), our compiler is additionally *communication* preserving as well!

The key ingredient in our compiler is that we use TLPs to hide the contents of the messages sent by the underlying protocol so that the strongly adaptive adversary cannot learn the contents of any message before honest nodes receives it. Prior works use the RSW puzzles to defend against a strongly adaptive adversary [16,45]. But, due to the inability to batch solve RSW proofs, opening all puzzles collectively adds an overhead of polylogarithmic rounds to any protocol [45]. An alternate approach is to use batch solvable TLPs defined in [43,44] to remove the polylogarithmic communication overhead incurred by RSW puzzles. But this increases communication complexity by a linear factor since prior batch solvable TLPs are not compact. Since our TLP is compact and batchable, we can solve all puzzles in one round without increasing the communication complexity.

Even though TLPs can prevent the adversary from inspecting the contents of the message, the primary challenge is in proving that the compiled protocol is secure against an adversary that can perform *after-the-fact* removal. This is because TLPs, apart from hiding the message contents for $\mathbf{T}$ time units, also serve as a commitment to the message inside the puzzle, which prevents the simulator from simulating the honest nodes without knowing the actual contents of the puzzle! Cohen et al. encountered a similar problem in the context of *fair* BB and proposed a non-committing TLP to overcome this challenge [16, Theorem 5].

Non-committing TLPs. Informally, it allows the simulator to equivocate a TLP. That is, the simulator first generates and sends a "fake" TLP to the network, which can be later "opened" be to *any* message. Thus, when the simulator is asked to explain the contents, it programs the RO to open the desired message. In Sect. 4.3, we show how to achieve this property with our TLP construction.

Compiler Overview. Abstractly, in a weakly adaptive protocol $\Pi_{\mathsf{bb-wa}}$, a node performs three *basic steps*: In every round, (1) receives the messages sent by other nodes, (2) performs the state transition based on the messages received and computes the messages to send, and (3) sends the messages to other nodes. Our compiler interleaves each step of $\Pi_{\text{bb-wa}}$ with TLP operations to obtain a strongly adaptive protocol, $\Pi_{\text{bb-sa}}$.

In a bit more detail, before sending a message in the compiled $\Pi_{\text{bb-sa}}$, a node uses non-committing TLPs to encrypt the message it wants to send and computes the puzzle with proof of well-formedness of the puzzle. Thus, instead of sending the plaintext in $\Pi_{\text{bb-wa}}$, a node in $\Pi_{\text{bb-sa}}$ sends the puzzle, ciphertext, and the proof of well-formedness to other nodes. When a node receives puzzles, ciphertexts, proofs of well-formedness from the network, instead of opening one puzzle at time, $\Pi_{\text{bb-sa}}$ uses the batchable TLP proposed in this work to obtain all the solutions simultaneously without incurring additional round complexity or communication complexity to open all the puzzles. Thus, after opening all the puzzles, a node in $\Pi_{\text{bb-sa}}$ invokes the state transition function just like a node in $\Pi_{\text{bb-wa}}$. This process is repeated for every round. We defer the details to Sect. 5.2.

2.3   Application 2: Permissionless Consensus in the Mobile Sluggish Model

Nakamoto's protocol, used in Bitcoin, achieves consensus over the Internet in a *permissionless* setting, where: any node can join and leave the system at any time, the exact number of participating nodes is unknown, and the nodes have to communicate over unauthenticated channels. However, for security, the protocol assumes that the network is synchronous – all honest messages get delivered to one another within a known upper bound on time, Δ units.

Unfortunately, assuming that an Internet scale protocol is synchronous is excessively optimistic. Moreover, Pass and Shi [37] showed that it is *impossible* to achieve permissionless consensus in an asynchronous or even in a partially synchronous network [5], which are relaxations of the synchronous model. Thus, to deploy the protocol in the real-world, the protocol designers are compelled to choose a loose upper bound Δ as the network delay to accommodate nodes with slow network.

In this work, we relax the standard synchrony assumption and study Nakamoto consensus under the mobile sluggish model [3,25]. For Internet scale protocols, the sluggish model is a pragmatic trade-off between the synchronous model and partially synchronous/asynchronous model. Thus, we ask the following question:

Is it possible to achieve consensus in a permissionless setting
in the presence of mobile sluggish faults?

We affirmatively answer this question by proposing a protocol that uses our TLP construction from Sect. 4 as a fundamental building block to show that it is possible to achieve *consistency* (any two prompt chains can differ only in the last few blocks) and *liveness* (every prompt node eventually commits all transactions) even in the presence of mobile sluggish faults.

In this subsection, we show how to adapt the Nakamoto consensus to defend against a mobile sluggish adversary using the our TLP. In our protocol, we use the following ideas: (1) All honest nodes time-lock encrypt any message they transmit, (2) all honest nodes send *decoys* to protect the block winner from getting caught by the adversary, (3) restrict the adversary from flooding with decoys, and (4) ignore malformed puzzles sent by the adversary.

Formally, we define a round, a super-round, and duration of a round in Sects. 6.2 and 6.3. However, as a warm-up, we present strawman solutions to illustrate the inadequacies of the well-known approaches.

Strawman Solutions. The first straightforward solution is to use RSW puzzles to time-lock encrypt any message with a duration equal to the network delay before transmitting across the network [39]. Unfortunately, this approach does not work for the following reasons:

- Recall that in a protocol like the Nakamoto consensus, only the block winner sends a message to the network. Thus, the adversary can easily stop the one message transmitted, whether or not the message is encrypted.
- Say the other honest nodes send out time-lock encrypted dummy messages, which act as a *decoys* to protect an honest block winner from getting caught. Unfortunately, the honest parties have to open all the puzzles to find the winning block. Thus, the honest parties either have to open all the puzzles individually or open them using the *distributed-solve* primitive proposed by Wan et al. [45, Section 4.2]. Both these approaches increase the round complexity of the protocol by linear and polylogarithmic rounds, respectively.

An alternate approach is to use TLPs with batch solving property defined in [43, 44], but we would suffer from large communication costs and fixed batch size problem as explained before. Instead, we can now use our TLP that gets rid of the these issues. Below we give an overview of other challenges we encounter in designing our permissionless consensus protocol.

Decoys, Spam Prevention, and Malformed Puzzles. Since the Nakamoto consensus is in the permissionless setting, there are no identities to tackle Sybil attacks. This setting raises an important question: how to stop the adversary from spawning multiple identities to send decoys? We resort to proof-of-work to tackle the Sybil attack!

Say the difficulty threshold to mine a block is T, then we set the threshold to mine a decoy as T_c, such that $T < T_c$. Each RO query made by a node simultaneously tries to mine a block and a *decoy*. That is, say h is the output of the hash function. If $h < T$, then *a block* is mined, else if $T \leq h < T_c$, then *a decoy* is mined. This is the "2-for-1 POW" trick introduced by Garay et al. [4,20,36]. The parameter T_c presents an interesting trade-off: T_c should be sufficiently high so that honest nodes mine enough decoys whereas the adversary should not be able to overwhelm the honest nodes with many decoy puzzles.

One of the challenges is that nodes do not know the exact number of decoys mined at a given time. However, since our TLP construction can batch a variable number of puzzles, nodes can flexibly batch puzzles on demand. Observe that T_c restricts the number of decoys that the adversary (and the honest nodes) can mine. But, this does not stop the adversary from flooding the honest nodes with malformed puzzles. Batching malformed puzzles along with honest puzzles prevents a node from obtaining the solutions to honest puzzles. To circumvent this problem we equip our TLP with a verifiability property that allows an honest node to reject a puzzle that is not *well-formed* according to the puzzle generation algorithm. Thus, a valid proof guarantees that the plaintext can be obtained by solving the puzzle.

Mine Phase and Solve Phase. Since the mining process is stochastic, the arrival times of a decoy and a block are random. Say if an honest node sends the puzzle as soon as it finds the block, it is unlikely that the rest of the honest nodes will also be sending the decoy puzzles at the same time. If enough honest nodes do not provide "cover" to the block winner, then the probability of the adversary guessing the block winner is high. However, if all honest nodes wait until a pre-determined time to send the respective puzzles, then block winner will have the best chance of not being detected by the adversary.

In order to capture this intuition, we have two phases in our protocol:

- *Mine phase*: All nodes spend a sequence of m rounds mining a block or decoy without sending or receiving any messages.
- *Solve phase*: This phase begins as soon as the mine phase ends and consists of *two* rounds. In the first round, nodes send and receive the puzzles they have mined in the *mine phase*, and check the well-formedness of the received puzzles. In the second round, nodes will batch solve the TLPs to find the block, if any, and update the longest chain.
  We generically denote the duration of the solve phase as D rounds. If one employs RSW puzzles and the *distributed-solve* primitive from Wan et al. [45] instead of our TLP construction, then D can be thought of as the number of rounds required to perform *distributed-solve* procedure. However, when our protocol is instantiated with our TLP construction we have $D = 2$.

Thus, the duration of a super-round is $(m + D)$ rounds.

Putting it all Together. In summary, by using our TLP, the decoy mechanism, and super-rounds, our protocol works as follows: Every honest node performs the following steps in every super-round: (1) Receive transactions from the environment, (2) choose the longest chain it has seen so far and break ties arbitrarily, (3) mine for m rounds (mine phase), and (4) solve for D rounds (solve phase) and update the longest chain. We defer the details of the protocol to Sect. 6.3.

3   Cryptographic Background

We denote by $\lambda \in \mathbb{N}$ the security parameter. We say that a function μ is negligible if it vanishes faster than any polynomial. The notation $[n]$ denotes a set $\{1, \ldots, n\}$. Background and notations relevant to the two applications are deferred to Sects. 6.2 and 5.1, respectively.

3.1   Time-Lock Puzzles

In the following we give a definition for the main object of interest of this work, namely time-lock puzzles (TLPs) [39]. The syntax follows the standard notation for TLPs except that we consider an additional setup phase that depends on the hardness parameter but not on the secret.

Definition 1 (Time-Lock Puzzles). *Let S be a finite domain. A time-lock puzzle (TLP) with solution space S is tuple of four algorithms* (PSetup, PGen, PSol) *defined as follows.*

- pp $\leftarrow$ PSetup($1^\lambda, \mathbf{T}$) *a probabilistic algorithm that takes as input a security parameter 1^λ and a time hardness parameter $\mathbf{T}$, and outputs public parameters* pp.
- $Z \leftarrow$ PGen(pp, s) *a probabilistic algorithm that takes as input public parameters* pp, *and a solution $s \in S$, and outputs a puzzle Z.*
- $s \leftarrow$ PSol(pp, Z) *a deterministic algorithm that takes as input public parameters* pp *and a puzzle Z and outputs a solution s.*

Definition 2 (Correctness). *A TLP scheme* (PSetup, PGen, PSol) *is correct if for all $\lambda \in \mathbb{N}$, all polynomials $\mathbf{T}$ in λ, all secrets $s \in S$, and all* pp *in the support of* PSetup($1^\lambda, \mathbf{T}$), *it holds that:* $\Pr[\mathsf{PSol}(\mathsf{pp}, \mathsf{PGen}(\mathsf{pp}, s)) = s] = 1$.

Security requires that the solution of the puzzles is hidden for all adversaries that run in (parallel) time less than $\mathbf{T}$.

Definition 3 (Security). *A TLP scheme* (PSetup, PGen, PSol) *is secure with gap $\varepsilon < 1$ if there exists a polynomial $\tilde{\mathbf{T}}(\cdot)$ such that for all polynomials $\mathbf{T}(\cdot) \geq \tilde{\mathbf{T}}(\cdot)$ and every polynomial-size adversary $(\mathcal{A}_1, \mathcal{A}_2) = \{(\mathcal{A}_1, \mathcal{A}_2)_\lambda\}_{\lambda \in \mathbb{N}}$ where the depth of $\mathcal{A}_2$ is bounded from above by $\mathbf{T}^\varepsilon(\lambda)$, there exists a negligible function $\mu(\cdot)$, such that for all $\lambda \in \mathbb{N}$ it holds that*

$$\Pr\left[\begin{array}{c} b \leftarrow \mathcal{A}_2(\mathsf{pp}, Z, \mathsf{st}) \\ \wedge \, (s_0, s_1) \in \mathcal{S}^2 \end{array} : \begin{array}{c} \mathsf{pp} \leftarrow \mathsf{PSetup}(1^\lambda, \mathbf{T}(\lambda)) \\ (\mathsf{st}, s_0, s_1) \leftarrow \mathcal{A}_1(1^\lambda, \mathsf{pp}) \\ b \leftarrow \{0, 1\}, Z \leftarrow \mathsf{PGen}(\mathsf{pp}, s_b) \end{array}\right] \leq \frac{1}{2} + \mu(\lambda)$$

Homomorphic Time-Lock Puzzles. We also recall the definition of homomorphic TLPs [33], which allows one to compute functions on secrets homomorphically, without solving the puzzles first.

Definition 4 (Homomorphic TLPs). *Let $\mathcal{C} = \{\mathcal{C}_\lambda\}_{\lambda \in \mathbb{N}}$ be a family of circuits (together with their respective representations). A TLP scheme* (PSetup, PGen, PSol) *is homomorphic if the syntax is augmented with the following interface:*

- $Z' \leftarrow$ PEval(C, pp, $Z_1, \ldots, Z_n$) *a probabilistic algorithm that takes as input a circuit $C \in \mathcal{C}_\lambda$, public parameters* pp *and a set of n puzzles $(Z_1, \ldots, Z_n)$ and outputs a puzzle Z'.*

Homomorphic TLPs must satisfy the following notion of evaluation correctness.

Definition 5 (Evaluation Correctness). *Let* $\mathcal{C} = \{\mathcal{C}_\lambda\}_{\lambda \in \mathbb{N}}$ *be a family of circuits (together with their respective representations). An homomorphic TLP scheme* (PSetup, PGen, PSol, PEval) *is correct (for the class* $\mathcal{C}$ *) if for all* $\lambda \in \mathbb{N}$*, all polynomials* $\mathbf{T}$ *in* λ*, all circuits* $C \in \mathcal{C}_\lambda$ *and respective inputs* $(s_1, \ldots, s_n) \in \mathcal{S}^n$*, all* pp *in the support of* $\mathsf{PSetup}(1^\lambda, \mathbf{T})$*, and all* Z_i *in the support of* $\mathsf{PGen}(\mathsf{pp}, s_i)$*, the following conditions are satisfied:*

- *It holds that*

$$\Pr\left[\mathsf{PSol}(\mathsf{pp}, \mathsf{PEval}(C, \mathsf{pp}, Z_1, \ldots, Z_n)) = C(s_1, \ldots, s_n)\right] = 1.$$

- *There exists a fixed polynomial* $p(\cdot)$ *such that the runtime of* PSol *is bounded by* $p(\lambda, \mathbf{T})$ *and the runtime of* PEval *is bounded by* $p(\lambda)$*.*

We require homomorphic TLPs specifically that support homomorphic evaluations of linear functions over the puzzles, that are secure against depth bounded but sub-exponential size adversaries. We have such constructions from RSA groups [33] and Class groups with imaginary quadratic order [44]. These constructions are proven secure against such adversaries by conjecturing the hardness of the *sequential squaring assumption* [31,33] against depth bounded but sub-exponential size adversaries.

3.2   Puncturable Pseudorandom Functions

A puncturable pseudorandom function (PRF) is an augmented PRF that has an additional puncturing algorithm. Such an algorithm produces a punctured version of the key that can evaluate the PRF at all points except for the punctured one. It is required that the PRF value at that specific point is pseudorandom even given the punctured key. A puncturable PRF can be constructed from any one-way function [24].

Definition 6 (Puncturable PRFs). *A puncturable family of PRFs is a tuple of polynomial-time algorithms* (Setup, KGen, Punc, F) *defined as follows.*

- pp $\leftarrow$ Setup(1^λ) *a probabilistic algorithm that takes as input the security parameter* 1^λ *and outputs public parameters* pp*. Public parameters* pp *are taken as input in all other algorithms.*
- $K \leftarrow$ KGen(pp) *a probabilistic algorithm that takes as input the public parameters* pp *and outputs a key* K*.*
- $K_i \leftarrow$ Punc(K, i) *a deterministic algorithm that takes as input a key* $K \in \mathcal{K}$ *and a position* $i \in \mathcal{X}$ *and returns a punctured key* K_i*.*
- $y \leftarrow$ F(K, i) *a deterministic algorithm that takes as input a key* K *and a string* $i \in \mathcal{X}$ *and returns a string* $y \in \mathcal{Y}$*.*

Definition 7 (Correctness). *For all* $\lambda \in \mathbb{N}$*, for all outputs* $K \leftarrow$ KGen(1^λ)*, for all points* $i \in \mathcal{X}$ *and* $x \in \mathcal{X} \setminus i$*, and for all* $K_{-i} \leftarrow$ Punc(K, i)*, we have that* $\mathsf{F}(K_{-i}, x) = \mathsf{F}(K, x)$*.*

We require that punctured points are pseudorandom to the eyes of any efficient distinguisher.

Definition 8 (Pseudorandomness at Punctured Points). *For all $\lambda \in \mathbb{N}$ and for every PPT adversaries $(\mathcal{A}_1, \mathcal{A}_2)$ there is a negligible function $\mu(\cdot)$, such that*

$$\Pr\left[b \leftarrow \mathcal{A}_2(\tau, K_i, i, y) : \begin{array}{c} \mathsf{pp} \leftarrow \mathsf{Setup}(1^\lambda), (i, \tau) \leftarrow \mathcal{A}_1(\mathsf{pp}) \\ K \leftarrow \mathsf{KGen}(\mathsf{pp}), K_i \leftarrow \mathsf{Punc}(K, i), b \leftarrow \{0, 1\} \\ \text{if } b = 0 \text{ then } y \leftarrow \mathcal{Y}, \text{else } y \leftarrow \mathsf{F}(K, i) \end{array}\right] \leq \frac{1}{2} + \mu(\lambda).$$

Key Homomorphism. We also assume the existence of constructions of puncturable PRFs that satisfy key homomorphism [10].

Definition 9 (γ-Almost Key-Homomorphic PRF). *Let function $\mathsf{F} : \mathcal{K} \times \mathcal{X} \rightarrow \mathbb{Z}_p^m$ be such that $(\mathcal{K}, +)$ is a group. Then the tuple $(\mathsf{F}, +)$ is said to be γ-almost key-homomorphic PRF if the following two conditions hold:*

– *F is a (puncturable) pseudorandom function.*
– *For all $k_1, k_2 \in \mathcal{K}$ and all $x \in \mathcal{X}$, there exists a vector $\mathbf{e} \in [0, \gamma]^m$ such that*

$$\mathsf{F}(k_1, x) + \mathsf{F}(k_2, x) = \mathsf{F}(k_1 + k_2, x) + \mathbf{e} \pmod{p}.$$

The scheme presented in [10] satisfies (additive) key-homomorphism over $\mathbb{Z}_q^n$, which we also use in this work. Their scheme satisfies a weaker notion of correctness, which we state below.

Definition 10 (Computational Functionality Preservation). *For all $\lambda \in \mathbb{N}$ and all PPT adversaries $(\mathcal{A}_1, \mathcal{A}_2)$, there exists a negligible function $\mu(\cdot)$, such that*

$$\Pr\left[\begin{array}{c} x^* \leftarrow \mathcal{A}_2^{\mathsf{F}(K, \cdot)}(1^\lambda, K_{i^*}, \tau) \wedge \\ x^* \neq i^* \wedge \\ \mathsf{F}(K, x^*) \neq \mathsf{F}(K_{i^*}, x^*) \end{array} : \begin{array}{c} \mathsf{pp} \leftarrow \mathsf{Setup}(1^\lambda), K \leftarrow \mathsf{KGen}(\mathsf{pp}) \\ (i^*, \tau) \leftarrow \mathcal{A}_1(\mathsf{pp}) \\ K_{i^*} \leftarrow \mathsf{Punc}(K, i^*) \end{array}\right] \leq \mu(\lambda).$$

For our purposes, we require the above property of the key-homomorphic puncturable PRF from [10] to hold against super-polynomial adversaries, which is possible assuming the hardness of LWE against super-polynomial adversaries.

3.3 Indistinguishability Obfuscation

We recall the definition of indistinguishability obfuscation (iO) for circuits from [21].

Definition 11 (iO for Circuits [21]). *A uniform PPT machine $i\mathcal{O}$ is an indistinguishable obfuscator for circuit class $\{\mathcal{C}_\lambda\}$, if the following are satisfied:*

– *For all $\lambda \in \mathbb{N}$, or all $C \in \mathcal{C}_\lambda$, for all inputs x, we have*

$$\Pr[C'(x) = C(x) : C' \leftarrow i\mathcal{O}(\lambda, C)] = 1$$

– *For all $\lambda \in \mathbb{N}$, all pairs of circuit $(C_0, C_1) \in \mathcal{C}_\lambda$ such that $|C_0| = |C_1|$ and $C_0(x) = C_1(x)$ on all inputs x, it holds that the distributions $\{i\mathcal{O}(\lambda, C_0)\}$ and $\{i\mathcal{O}(\lambda, C_1)\}$ are computationally indistinguishable.*

4   Time-Lock Puzzles with Batch Solving

In this section we formally present the notion and constructions for time-lock puzzles with batched solving.

4.1   Definition

We define the notion of TLPs with batched solving. We borrow the standard interfaces of a TLP from Sect. 3.1 and append it with an interface to allow for batched solving of n puzzles.

Definition 12 (Batch Solving). *A TLP scheme* (PSetup, PGen, PSol) *supports* batch solving *with the aid of an additional interface defined below*

- $(s_1, \ldots, s_n) \leftarrow$ BatchPSol$(\mathsf{pp}, Z_1, \ldots, Z_n)$ *a deterministic algorithm that takes as input public parameters* pp *and puzzles* $Z_1, \ldots, Z_n$, *and outputs solutions* $s_1, \ldots, s_n$.

Definition 13 (Batch Solving Correctness). *An TLP scheme* (PSetup, PGen, PSol) *with batch solving interface* BatchPSol *is correct if for all* $\lambda \in \mathbb{N}$, *all polynomials* $\mathbf{T}$ *in* λ, *all polynomials* n *in* λ, *all solutions* $(s_1, \ldots, s_n) \in \mathcal{S}^n$, *all* pp *in the support of* PSetup$(1^\lambda, \mathbf{T})$, *and all* Z_i *in the support of* PGen(pp, s_i), *the following conditions are satisfied:*

- *There exists a negligible function* $\mu(\cdot)$ *such that*

$$\Pr\left[\mathsf{BatchPSol}(\mathsf{pp}, Z_1, \ldots, Z_n) \neq (s_1, \ldots, s_n)\right] \leq \mu(\lambda).$$

- *There exist fixed polynomials* $p(\cdot), \tilde{p}(\cdot)$ *such that the size complexity of the circuit evaluating* BatchPSol$(\mathsf{pp}, Z_1, \ldots, Z_n)$ *is bounded by* $p(\lambda, \mathbf{T}) + \tilde{p}(\lambda, n)$.

Notice that the above definition rules out trivial solutions, where you solve the n puzzles individually and output the solutions. This is because, in this solution the size scales with $n \cdot \mathbf{T}$, while the definition above only permits the scale to be $n + \mathbf{T}$. One can view $\tilde{p}(\lambda, n)$ as capturing the time taken to read and process the n puzzles, and returning the n solutions. The factor $p(\lambda, \mathbf{T})$ captures the solving of a single puzzle and itself is independent of n.

4.2   Bounded Batching of TLPs

As hinted to in Sect. 2.1, given a linearly homomorphic TLP with homomorphism over $\mathbb{Z}_q$, that has a large enough message space, it was shown in [43,44] that we can homomorphically pack several puzzles into a single puzzle using standard techniques. Solving the single puzzle reveals the solutions to all the n puzzles that we started out with. A crucial requirement for the above batch solving to work is that the message space of the homomorphic time-lock puzzle must be large enough to accommodate all the n λ-bit values. It was shown [43] that this is indeed possible by instantiating the Paillier-based linearly homomorphic time-lock puzzle construction from [33] in the same way Damgård-Jurik [17] extended the Paillier cryptosystem [34]. That is, instantiate the Paillier-based linearly homomorphic TLP from [33] with a modulus N^s instead of modulus N^2, for a large enough value s. A similar domain extension was also shown in the settings of class groups of imaginary quadratic orders [44] that only require a public-coin (transparent) setup.

More formally, the LHP scheme from [33] has the LHP.PSetup algorithm output $\mathsf{pp}_{\mathsf{LHP}} = (\mathbf{T}, N, g, h)$, where $N = pq$ for some λ-bit primes p and q, g is the generator of $\mathbb{J}_N^*$, and $h := g^{2^{\mathbf{T}}} \bmod N$. Here $\mathbb{J}_N^*$ denotes the elements in $\mathbb{Z}_N^*$ with Jacobi symbol $+1$. The puzzle Z embedding message m is of the form (u, v) where

$$u := g^r \bmod N \quad \text{and} \quad v := h^{r \cdot N}(1 + N)^m \bmod N^2,$$

with randomness $r \leftarrow [N^2]$. The security of the scheme follows from the *sequential squaring assumption* [33,39]. The Damgård-Jurik extension from [33,43] lets the puzzle generation algorithm additionally choose $s \in \mathbb{Z}$, and set the puzzle $Z := (u, v)$ where

$$u := g^r \bmod N \quad \text{and} \quad v := h^{r \cdot N^{s-1}}(1 + N)^m \bmod N^s.$$

Here, the message space is $\mathbb{Z}_{N^{s-1}}$ while the puzzle component v is in $\mathbb{Z}_{N^s}$.

Consider n puzzles $Z_1, \ldots, Z_n$ each encoding λ-bit values with timing hardness $\mathbf{T}$, and each of these puzzles are of the Damgård-Jurik extended form. The LHP.BatchPSol algorithm internally evaluates the following linear function

$$f(x_1, \ldots, x_n) = \sum_{i=1}^{n} 2^{(i-1) \cdot \lambda} \cdot x_i$$

homomorphically over the puzzles using the LHP.PEval algorithm. The effect of this evaluation is that the resultant puzzle Z^* embeds the λ-bit values of $(x_1, x_2, \ldots, x_n)$. The LHP.BatchPSol algorithm proceeds to solve the resultant puzzle Z^* in time $\mathbf{T}$ to obtain the n values encoded as λ-bit values.

However, both of the above constructions only support bounded batching as they require the size of each puzzle Z_i (the v component) to scale linearly with the maximum batch size. Also, since the domain extension factor s has to be fixed at puzzle generation time, it determines an upper bound on the input size of the function f and therefore the number of puzzles we can batch solve later.

4.3   Unbounded Batching of TLPs

In this section, we present a new TLP scheme with batched solving which overcome both drawbacks of the scheme above. Namely, our new construction allows for batching where the size of the TLPs output by puzzle generation algorithm is independent of the number of puzzles to be batched. As a consequence, we have unbounded batching (bounded above by a super polynomial $2^{\omega(\log \lambda)}$) meaning that any polynomial number of puzzles can be batched with an one-time setup.

- PSetup(1^λ, **T**):
  - Run $pp_{LHP} \leftarrow$ LHP.PSetup(1^λ, **T**).
  - Run $pp_F \leftarrow$ Setup(1^λ) and $pp_{\overline{F}} \leftarrow \overline{Setup}(1^\lambda)$.
  - Return $pp := (pp_{LHP}, pp_F, pp_{\overline{F}})$.
- PGen(pp, m):
  - Generate $k \leftarrow$ KGen(pp_F).
  - Define $\mathbf{P}_{m,k,pp}(n, i, j)$ as the following circuit:[a]
    * Ensure $i, j \in [n]$.
    * Compute $(\overline{r}, r) \leftarrow F(k, (n, i))$.
    * Compute $\overline{k} \leftarrow \overline{KGen}(pp_{\overline{F}}; \overline{r})$.
    * Compute $Z \leftarrow$ LHP.PGen($pp_{LHP}, \overline{k}; r$).
    * If $j = i$ set $c = \overline{F}(\overline{k}, j) + m \cdot \lceil p/2 \rceil \pmod p$.
    * Else if $j \leq n \leq N$ set $c = \overline{F}(\overline{k}, j)$.
    * Return (Z, c).
  - Return $\widetilde{\mathbf{P}} := i\mathcal{O}(1^\lambda, \mathbf{P}_{m,k,pp})$.
- BatchPSol($pp, Z_1, \ldots, Z_n$):
  - For each $i \in [n]$,
    * Parse $Z_i := \widetilde{\mathbf{P}}_i$.
    * For each $j \in [n]$, compute $(Z_i^*, c_{i,j}) \leftarrow \widetilde{\mathbf{P}}_i(n, i, j)$.
    * Define $\mathbf{c}_i = (c_{i,1}, \ldots, c_{i,n}) \in \mathbb{Z}_p^n$.
  - Set $Z^* \leftarrow$ LHP.PEval($+, pp, Z_1^*, \ldots, Z_n^*$).
  - Compute $k^* \leftarrow$ LHP.PSol(pp, Z^*).
  - Compute $\mathbf{f}^* = \left(\overline{F}(k^*, 1), \ldots, \overline{F}(k^*, n)\right)$
  - Compute $\mathbf{c}^* = \sum_{i=1}^n \mathbf{c}_i$.
  - Return $\mathbf{c}^* - \mathbf{f}^*$ rounded component-wise.

[a] The circuit is padded to the maximum size of the circuits among those defined in the security proof. We refer the reader to the end of this Section for a discussion on the size of this circuit.

Fig. 1. Our construction for TLP with unbounded batch solving.

Our construction uses the following ingredients:

- A linearly homomorphic TLP scheme LHP := (LHP.PSetup, LHP.PGen, LHP.PSol, LHP.PEval) where the homomorphism is over $\mathbb{Z}_q$.
- A puncturable PRF (Setup, KGen, Punc, F) denoted in short by F.
- An indistinguishable obfuscator $i\mathcal{O}$ for circuits.
- A γ-almost key-homomorphic puncturable PRF $(\overline{Setup}, \overline{KGen}, \overline{Punc}, \overline{F})$ (denoted in short by $\overline{F}i$) with key space $\mathbb{Z}_q^n$ and where the noise bound is γ such that $p = 2^{\omega(\log \lambda)} \cdot \gamma$.

Let $N = 2^{\omega(\log \lambda)}$ denote an upper bound on the number of participants. Our construction (PSetup, PGen, BatchPSol) is shown in Fig. 1. For simplicity we consider the messages encoded to be in $\{0, 1\}$, and argue that its straightforward to extend the construction for multiple bits.

A puzzle in our case is an obfuscation of the program **P** which has the message m, a PRF F key k, and the public parameters pp hardwired in it. The program **P** takes as input three values: n indicating number of puzzles to be batched, i "index" of the current puzzle and j "index" of other puzzles. It is important to note that the exact indices for each puzzle are only set later during batch solving. Let i be the symbolic index of the puzzle being generated now (whose concrete value will be set during batch solving). The program internally generates the

PRF key $\overline{k}$ for the key-homomorphic puncturable PRF which then is embedded inside the LHP puzzle Z. In case the indices i and j are the same, a ciphertext c is set to encrypt the message m using the value $\overline{\mathsf{F}}(\overline{k}, j)$ as the masking factor. In any other case, c encrypts 0 with $\overline{\mathsf{F}}(\overline{k}, j)$ as the masking factor. The program returns the puzzle Z and the ciphertext c.

The batch solving algorithm in the beginning, locally indexes the n puzzles in some order based on some rule (e.g., lexicographic ordering). We have them now ordered $(Z_1, \ldots, Z_n)$ where the i-th puzzle is an obfuscated program denoted by $Z_i := \widetilde{\mathbf{P}}_i$. Then, for all $i \in [n]$, we execute the program $\widetilde{\mathbf{P}}_i$ on values (n, i, j) for all $j \in [n]$. In the end we obtain a LHP time-lock puzzle Z_i^* and ciphertexts $c_{i,j}$ for each $j \in [n]$. Recall that when $i = j$ the program $\widetilde{\mathbf{P}}_i$ sets $c_{i,j}$ to encrypt the message m_i (where m_i is the message inside puzzle Z_i), and for all $i \neq j$, the ciphertext $c_{i,j}$ encrypts 0. We then obtain a LHP puzzle Z^* by homomorphically adding the puzzles Z_i^* for all $i \in [n]$ and solving Z^* returns a PRF key k^* of the key-homomorphic puncturable PRF. We retrieve the message m_j (for all $j \in [n]$) by doing the following: (1) compute $c_j^* = \sum_{i=1}^n c_{i,j}$, (2) evaluate $\overline{\mathsf{F}}(k^*, j)$, (3) set m_j as the rounding of $\left(c_j^* - \overline{\mathsf{F}}(k^*, j) \right)$. The correctness and security of our construction is formalized in the theorems below and the formal proofs are deferred to the extended version our paper [42].

Theorem 1. *Let* LHP *be a linearly homomorphic TLP scheme where the homomorphism is over $\mathbb{Z}_q$, let* F *be a puncturable PRF, let* $i\mathcal{O}$ *be an indistinguishable obfuscator for circuits and let* $\overline{\mathsf{F}}$ *be a γ-almost key-homomorphic puncturable PRF with key space $\mathbb{Z}_q^n$ and where the noise bound is γ such that $p = 2^{\omega(\log \lambda)} \cdot \gamma$. If all the above primitives are perfectly correct, then the TLP scheme with batch solving from Fig. 1 is perfectly correct.*

Theorem 2. *Let* LHP *be secure against depth $\mathbf{T}^\varepsilon(\lambda)$-bounded adversaries with sub-exponential advantage,* F *be a sub-exponentially secure puncturable PRF,* $\overline{\mathsf{F}}$ *be a sub-exponentially secure γ-almost key-homomorphic puncturable PRF and* $i\mathcal{O}$ *be a sub-exponentially secure indistinguishable obfuscator. Then, the construction from Fig. 1 is a secure time-lock puzzle with batch solving against all depth $\mathbf{T}^\varepsilon(\lambda)$-bounded adversaries.*

Size of the Obfuscated Circuit. Observe that at any point in the proof, we only hardwire information of size bounded by a fixed polynomial in λ, and in particular independent of the number of parties. Since the size of the obfuscated circuit must be padded to the maximum size of the circuit at any point in the security proof, the size overhead is also independent of the number of parties.

Instantiations and Setup Assumptions. We can instantiate: the linearly homomorphic TLP, LHP, with the Class group based scheme from [44]. We can instantiate the puncturable PRF F with the GGM based PRF [24,40], the $i\mathcal{O}$ scheme with the scheme from [27], and the γ-almost key-homomorphic puncturable PRF with the scheme from [10]. Notice that the above instantiations do not require trusted setups, thus our TLP scheme does not require a trusted setup. However, requires a one-time transparent public-coin setup (for LHP from [44]).

TLP Runtime. The runtime of PGen is dominated by the obfuscation of the circuit **P** which is polynomial in λ and size of **P**. Moreover, the size of **P** is independent of the batch size n or the number of users. Thus, the total runtime is polynomial in λ and size of the time-locked message. The BatchPSol involves executing n obfuscated circuits, combining their outputs homomorphically using LHP.PEval, and solving the resulting TLP using LHP.PSol. The runtime of the first two operations is $poly(\lambda, n)$, whereas the last operation is $poly(\lambda, T)$.

Verifiable TLPs. We can support verifiability for our puzzles where the puzzle generator along with the puzzle also outputs a proof, that convinces a verifier that the puzzle is well-formed. In applications of our TLP scheme (including the ones in later sections), verifying whether a puzzle is in the support of the PGen is paramount for the correctness (Def. 13) of batched solving to hold. To provide such verifiability, we can add two new interfaces: PProve(Z, m, r) run by the puzzle generator that outputs a proof π to ascertain a puzzle Z is well-formed (with message m and randomness r), and PVer(Z, π) run by a verifier that validates the proof w.r.t. the puzzle. In terms properties we want that a verifier shouldn't be convinced of a malformed puzzle and that the proof does not help in solving the puzzle any faster. For a formal definition and a discussion on concrete instantiations, see the extended version of our paper [42].

Non-committing TLPs. A non-committing TLP lets a simulator generate a puzzle first and later "explain" the puzzle as committing to a message m by opening it to reveal m. Note that a TLP is committing to the message once the puzzle is generated. Cohen et al. [16] showed a generic approach to build such non-committing TLPs in the programmable random oracle model (PROM) and we can transform our TLP scheme into one that is non-committing in the same way. The idea is to run $Z' \leftarrow$ PGen(pp, x) for some random r, and the final puzzle Z is set as $Z := (Z', c)$ where $c := H(r) \oplus m$. The simulator when required to equivocate Z as a puzzle embedding the message m, sets the value $H(r) := c \oplus m$ on the fly, as $H()$ is modeled as a PROM. We can modify the construction from Sect. 4.3 by having letting PGen run as before, but output $(\widetilde{\mathbf{P}}, H(r) \oplus m)$ as the final puzzle, where $\widetilde{\mathbf{P}} := i\mathcal{O}(\lambda, \mathbf{P}_{r,k,pp})$. Specifically this means that the PROM computation is outside the $i\mathcal{O}$.

5   Application 1: Byzantine Broadcast

In this section, we present our generic compiler to transform any BB protocol secure against weakly adaptive adversaries to one that is secure against strongly adaptive adversaries.

5.1   Model and Definitions

In our setting, there are n nodes, numbered 1 to n, running a distributed protocol where the identity of each node is known to one another through a PKI.

Communication Model. We assume that each node has access to a shared global clock and all parties are connected by a pairwise reliable channel. We consider the standard synchronous model of communication where there is a known upper bound on the message delay (Δ). The protocols are executed in a round-based fashion, where the duration of each round is Δ time units. Any message sent by an honest node in a round reaches all other honest nodes by the beginning of the next round. Also, each node has access to the functionalities: RECEIVE and SEND. When a node u invokes SEND(m, recipients) in round $r-1$, then m is delivered to recipients using the pairwise reliable channels from u by round r. When a node u invokes RECEIVE in round r, then all messages that were sent to u using the pairwise reliable channels by round $r-1$ are returned. The adversary can read, rearrange, insert, and drop messages between any two nodes (if strongly adaptive). But, cannot forge signatures. Moreover, we also assume that each round is sufficiently long to perform standard cryptographic operations except BatchPSol and PSol.

Let $\mathcal{P}$ be the set of possible internal states of a node and $\mathcal{M}$ be the set of possible messages that can be sent and received by a node.

Definition 14 (Δ-secure Synchronous protocol). *Let $\mathcal{F}_n$ denote the family of transition functions such that:*

$$\mathcal{F}_n = \{f_{r,u} : \mathcal{P} \times \mathcal{M}^n \to \mathcal{P} \times \mathcal{M}^n : u \in [n], r \in \mathbb{Z}\}$$

A synchronous protocol Π_{sync} is executed by n nodes and proceeds in rounds. In every round r, every node $u \in [n]$, reads the messages addressed to it using the RECEIVE *functionality, updates its state and computes the messages to be sent using $f_{r,u}$, and sends the messages to intended recipients using the* SEND *functionality.*

Protocol $\Pi_{\mathsf{sync}}(\lambda, \Delta)$

Setup.
 – Let $S_{0,u}$ be the initial state of node $u \in [n]$
 – Generate and publish public parameters

Protocol. A node $u \in [n]$, for each round r:
 – Fetch messages from each sender: $m := (m_1, \ldots, m_n) \leftarrow$ RECEIVE()
 – Compute next state and messages: $(S_{r+1,u}, m' := (m'_1, \ldots, m'_n)) \leftarrow f_{r,u}(S_{r,u}, m)$
 – Send messages: SEND(m', recipients)

Adversary Model. The adversary can make at most t out of n nodes to arbitrarily deviate from the protocol execution, where $t < n$. Moreover, we assume that the adversary controls the delivery of all the messages in the network.

– We consider a *strongly adaptive adversary* that can corrupt nodes on the fly and perform *after-the-fact* removal.
– Whereas, a *weakly adaptive adversary* can *only* corrupt nodes on the fly, but cannot prevent the delivery of any message that was already sent.

Additionally, we consider a *rushing* adversary that can inspect the messages sent by any honest node before delivering it to other nodes. Moreover, we assume that honest nodes can irrecoverably erase (part of) its state and memory at any time.

Computational Model. All honest nodes are sequential, random access PPT, but the adversary is a non-uniform probabilistic parallel machine with polynomially bounded parallelism running in polynomially bounded parallel steps.

5.2   Protocol

For an n node protocol Π, we define a deterministic function called *output derivation function* for each node $u \in [n]$. This function allows a node to compute its output bit for Π based on the transcript of public messages exchanged by the participants and public parameters.

Definition 15 (Output derivation function) *Let Π be an n node protocol and $\mathcal{Y}$ denote the **public** transcript space of the protocol Π, then $\mathcal{G}_n$ denote the family of **output derivation** functions such that:*

$$\mathcal{G}_n = \{g_u : \mathcal{Y} \to \{0,1\} : u \in [n]\}$$

Functions in $\mathcal{G}_n$, despite being deterministic, may not be efficiently computable without a party's keys.

We recall the definition of a secure Byzantine broadcast protocol below.

Definition 16 ((Δ, t)-secure Byzantine broadcast). *Let λ be the security parameter, Δ be the known upper-bound on the network delay, and node $d \in [n]$ be the* designated sender. *A protocol Π executed by n nodes with specified family of functions $\mathcal{G}_n$, where the* designated sender *holds an input bit $b \in \{0,1\}$, is a (Δ, t)-secure broadcast protocol tolerating at most t corruptions if it satisfies the following properties with probability $1 - negl(\lambda)$:*

- *Consistency: If two honest nodes output bit b_i and b_j respectively, then $b_i = b_j$.*
- *Validity: If the designated sender is honest, then every honest node outputs the designated sender's input bit b.*
- *Termination: Every honest node u outputs a bit from $g_u(\mathsf{transcript})$, where* transcript *is the transcript from running Π.*

*If the protocol can tolerate corruptions by a strongly adaptive and a weakly adaptive adversary, then it is **strongly adaptive** (Δ, t)-secure and **weakly adaptive** (Δ, t)-secure, respectively.*

Let $\Pi_{\mathsf{bb-wa}}$ be a weakly adaptive protocol, we formally describe $\Pi_{\mathsf{bb-sa}}$ below:

Protocol $\Pi_{\mathsf{bb-sa}}(\lambda, \Delta, \Pi_{\mathsf{bb-wa}}, \mathcal{G}_n)$

Text in gray indicates the instructions from $\Pi_{\mathsf{bb-wa}}$.

Setup.
- Let $S_{0,u}$ be the initial state of node $u \in [n]$
- For each round r, pp $\leftarrow$ PSetup($1^\lambda, \Delta$)
- Generate and publish public parameters

Input.
- Let $b \in \{0,1\}$
- If designated sender, d, then $S_{0,d} := S_{0,d} \cup b$

Protocol. A node $u \in [n]$, for each round r:
- Fetch messages from each sender: $m := (m_1, \ldots, m_n) \leftarrow$ RECEIVED
- Parse message m_v as puzzle Z_v, ciphertext C_v, proof of well-formed π_v for all $v \in [n]$

- Check π_v's to verify if Z_v's are well-formed by $\mathsf{PVer}(\mathsf{pp}, Z_v, \pi_v)$
- Extract the individual solutions $(s_1, \ldots, s_n) \leftarrow \mathsf{BatchPSol}(\mathsf{pp}, Z_1, \ldots, Z_n)$
- Decrypt C_v's, set $m_v := C_v \oplus H(s_v)$ for all $v \in [n]$, and $m := (m_1, \ldots, m_n)$
- Set internal state for round r as $S_{r,u} := m_u$
- Compute next state and messages: $(S_{r+1,u}, m' := (m'_1, \ldots, m'_u, \cdot) \leftarrow f_{r,u}(S_{r,u}, m)$
- Pick $s \in \mathcal{S}$, $Z \leftarrow \mathsf{PGen}(\mathsf{pp}, s)$, and compute π to prove that Z is well-formed.
- Reassign $m'_u := (Z, S_{r+1,u} \oplus H(s), \pi)$ and $m'_v := (Z, m'_v \oplus H(s), \pi)$ for all $v \in [n] \setminus \{u\}$
- Set output messages as $m' := (m'_1, \ldots, m'_n)$ and erase $S_{r+1,u}, s, \pi$
- Send messages: $\mathsf{SEND}(m', \text{recipients})$

Output.
- Let transcript be the public transcript of the protocol execution
- Return $b \leftarrow g_u(\text{transcript})$

Theorem 3. *Let $\Pi_{\mathsf{bb-wa}}$ be a weakly adaptive (Δ, t)-secure Byzantine broadcast protocol with output derivation functions $\mathcal{G}_n$ and $\Pi_{\mathsf{bb-sa}}$ be the compiled strongly adaptive (δ, t)-secure protocol with output derivation functions $\mathcal{G}_n$, such that $\Delta = 2\delta$. If an $\mathcal{A}$ violates $\Pi_{\mathsf{bb-sa}}$ with probability at least p, then there exists an adversary $\mathcal{B}$ that violates $\Pi_{\mathsf{bb-wa}}$ with probability at least p.*

Analysis. Suppose $\exists$ an $\mathcal{A}$ that can break $\Pi_{\mathsf{bb-sa}}$, then we build another adversary $\mathcal{B}$ that breaks $\Pi_{\mathsf{bb-wa}}$. At a high level, we show that every attack by $\mathcal{A}$ on $\Pi_{\mathsf{bb-sa}}$ can be translated to an attack on $\Pi_{\mathsf{bb-wa}}$. Observe that $\mathcal{B}$ is as powerful as $\mathcal{A}$, except $\mathcal{B}$ cannot perform *after-the-fact* removal. Thus, to translate the *after-the-fact* removal, $\mathcal{B}$ must know whether $\mathcal{A}$ delivers or removes messages in $\Pi_{\mathsf{bb-sa}}$. $\mathcal{B}$ can know this only by waiting for δ steps to see $\mathcal{A}$'s actions! Hence, $\mathcal{B}$ starts the simulation δ steps ahead of $\Pi_{\mathsf{bb-wa}}$. But, when the simulation begins, $\mathcal{B}$ doesn't yet have the real-world messages from $\Pi_{\mathsf{bb-wa}}$ that *can be copied* to $\Pi_{\mathsf{bb-sa}}$. So $\mathcal{B}$ sends non-committing TLPs to equivocate the contents of the puzzle (possible because of PROM). When $\mathcal{A}$ solves the TLP and queries the RO, actual messages from $\Pi_{\mathsf{bb-wa}}$ will be available, and $\mathcal{B}$ programs the RO to open the corresponding message from $\Pi_{\mathsf{bb-wa}}$. Since the duration between when the messages are sent and the contents learned by the honest nodes should be the same in the simulation and the real-world, we set $\Delta = 2\delta$. Thus, asymptotically, $\Pi_{\mathsf{bb-sa}}$ is round preserving (as $\Delta = 2\delta$) and communication preserving (due to compactness of our TLP). We present the detailed analysis in the extended version of our paper [42].

Expected Constant-round Byzantine Broadcast. Wan et al. [46] proposed an expected constant round BB protocol under a weakly adaptive and dishonest majority setting. Thus, using the compiler (Sect. 5.2), we can obtain resilience in the strongly adaptive setting!

6   Application 2: Nakamoto Consensus Secure Against a Mobile Sluggish Adversary

In this section, we show an attack against the Nakamoto consensus in the mobile sluggish model and how to secure the Nakamoto consensus using our TLP.

6.1   Attack on Nakamoto Consensus in the Mobile Sluggish Model

In Nakamoto consensus, a chain forks when two distinct blocks extend the same parent block. Forks are inherently bad for security as it splits the honest mining efforts across the two branches of the tree. A benign example is when two blocks are mined less than Δ time units apart. Since the messages take Δ to reach others, the winner of the second block would not have been aware of the previous block. Nakamoto consensus is parameterized in a way that the inter-arrival time between two blocks is much longer than the time to transmit between any two farthest nodes in the system. The security threat posed by forks is the exact reason the Nakamoto consensus is secure only in the synchronous model.

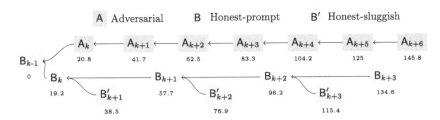

Fig. 2. Double spend attack: This plot depicts average block arrival times. Assuming 52 honest nodes (51 prompt + 1 sluggish) and 48 adversarial nodes, the average inter-arrival time of honest blocks and adversarial blocks in Bitcoin is 19.2 and 20.8 min, respectively. Observe that over 19.2×2 min, even though the honest nodes have mined two blocks, due to sluggishness, the honest chain has grown only by one block.

The mobile sluggish adversary, whenever an honest node mines a block, can simply delay the block propagation until another block extends the same header (see Fig. 2). At this point, the adversary can release both the blocks simultaneously to split the honest mining efforts. The adversary can sustain the forks as long as it has sufficient sluggish budget. Since the adversary is responsible for message delivery and sluggishness can be mobile, it could perform this attack repeatedly. In the meantime, adversarial nodes will continue to extend their chain in private. Using this strategy, even a single mobile sluggish fault has the ability to reduce the honest mining rate by *half*! Thus, an honest majority assumption may not be sufficient to guarantee security in this model. We elaborate this attack in the extended version of our paper [42].

6.2   Model

Let n be the total number of nodes, d be the maximum number of sluggish nodes, and t be the maximum number of adversarial nodes. Thus, there are at least $n-t$ honest nodes and at least $n-d-t$ prompt nodes. We adopt the formal framework from Garay et al. [20], a model inspired by the prior formulations of secure multiparty computation [13].

Sluggish Network Model. We assume that the time proceeds in rounds. Moreover, we assume that the adaptivity of the adversary is static. That is before the protocol execution, the adversary picks the set of nodes to corrupt. Moreover, we also assume that every node has access to a *shared global clock* and a pairwise reliable channel between any two parties.

The standard (lock-step) model of synchrony assumes that any message sent in round r reaches other nodes by $r+1$. We consider a generalization of this model called the *mobile sluggish* model. In this model, if a node is prompt at round r, then any message sent by the node in round $\leq r$ reaches all the nodes that are prompt in round $r + 1$ by round $\leq r + 1$. Due to mobility of the sluggishness, set of prompt nodes in any two adjacent rounds need not be the same.

The adversary is responsible for message delivery. Thus, an adversary can reorder or delay messages (according to prompt and sluggish delay requirement), but *cannot* delete messages. Moreover, any message sent to a prompt node *by a prompt or an adversarial node* reaches all prompt nodes. We can relax this assumption by assuming that nodes gossip/echo any message they receive [35, Footnote 4]. The adversary inspects all messages (including puzzles and blocks) first before delivering to any node.

Round Duration. We assume that the duration of a round is $O(\Delta)$. Specifically, we assume that a round is sufficiently long to send/receive messages and perform cryptographic operations (such as verifying a hash of a message, generating and verifying a zero-knowledge proof of well-formedness of a TLP, computing PGen/PEval, and signing and verifying a signature), *except* PSol, BatchPSol, and RO invocations to mine a block or a decoy.

Computational Model. We adopt the *flat* model of computation introduced by Garay et al. [20]. In this model, all nodes are assumed to have the same computational power. Moreover, any node can make at most q proofs-of-work invocations to the RO in a round. Thus, the adversary can perform $t \cdot q$ RO queries in each round. We remark that each node has an unlimited number of proof-of-work verification queries to the RO [20].

Additionally, we assume that all honest nodes are sequential, random access PPT, but the adversary is a non-uniform probabilistic parallel machine with polynomially bounded parallelism running in polynomially bounded parallel steps.

Environment. The entity *environment* handles the external aspects of the protocol execution such as spawning the nodes and the adversary, injecting transactions, writing inputs and reading outputs of each node, etc. However, the environment *cannot* make queries to RO. This is to prevent the adversary from outsourcing the RO queries to an external entity.

6.3 Protocol

Super-round. Since our protocol proceeds in two phases: (1) Mine phase (m rounds) and (2) Solve phase (D rounds), a super-round consists of a mine phase followed by a solve phase. Thus, the duration is $(m + D)$ rounds.

Mobile Sluggish Nakamoto Protocol

Input.
  - pp, TLP public parameters with $\mathbf{T}$ as one round
  - m, duration of mine phase
  - D, duration of solve phase
  - q, maximum number of RO queries per round
  - T, difficulty threshold to mine a block
  - T_c, difficulty threshold to mine a decoy where $T < T_c$

Initialize. Chain C containing agreed-upon genesis block C[0]

Protocol. Every super-round R (which consists of $(m + D)$ rounds)
  - Get the payload from the environment
  - Let $h_{-1} := \mathsf{H}(\mathsf{C}[-1])$ be the hash of the last block on the longest chain C
  - Let $B = \bot$ be an empty block
  - For m rounds of **mine phase**:
    - For q RO queries:
      * Pick random $\eta \in \{0,1\}^{\lambda}$ and compute $h := \mathsf{H}(h_{-1}, \mathsf{payload}, \eta)$
      * If $h < T_c$ (mined a decoy)
        · Overwrite $B := (h_{-1}, \mathsf{payload}, \eta)$
      * If $h < T$ (mined a block)
        · Overwrite $B := (h_{-1}, \mathsf{payload}, \eta)$
        · Set $\mathsf{C} := \mathsf{C}||B$
        · Break out of the q and m loop
  - If $B \neq \bot$
    - Compute the TLP $Z := \mathsf{PGen}(\mathsf{pp}, B)$
    - Compute proof of well-formed $\pi := \mathsf{PProve}(\mathsf{pp}, Z, B)$
  - **Solve phase** for $D = 2$ rounds:
    - First round, multicast (Z, π) (if one exists), receive all the w puzzles from the network $Z_1, \ldots, Z_w$, and check their well-formedness.
    - Second round, batch solve $(s_1, \ldots, s_w) := \mathsf{BatchPSol}(Z_1, \ldots, Z_w)$.
  - Update the chain C based on output from the solve phase

Assumptions. Let a block mined in a super-round R be a *prompt block*, if mined by an honest node and the node was prompt *at the beginning* of solving phase of *both* $R - 1$ and R. Moreover, let f be the probability of one or more prompt blocks were mined in a super-round, c be the probability of every honest node mining at least one decoy in a super-round, $\varepsilon, \delta \in (0,1)$ be parameters, and p be the probability of a RO query mining a block. Our analysis assumes that:

$$\frac{(m+D)t + md}{cm(n - 2d - t)} \leq (1 - \delta) \quad (1)$$

$$\varepsilon + f < \delta/3 \quad (2)$$

$$pqm(n - 2d - t) < 1/2 \quad (3)$$

$$\frac{2\varepsilon}{1 - \varepsilon} < \delta^2 \quad (4)$$

Analysis. At a high level, our analysis extends the formal tools proposed by Garay et al. [20]. But there are several differences due to mobile sluggish faults and the use of TLPs:

1. The adversary can deviate from the protocol and invoke RO queries even during the solve phase. Intuitively, Eq. 1 quantifies the required advantage of the prompt nodes over sluggish and adversarial nodes for our protocol to be secure. Specifically, the numerator captures the computational advantage enjoyed by the adversarial nodes due to additional RO queries during the solve phase (the term $(m + D)t$) and the loss in honest mining efforts due to sluggish nodes (the term md). Large values of D decreases t (assuming other

values can remain the same). But, due to the batch solving property of our TLP, $D = 2$ in our protocol. Thus, the impact of D is minimal.

2. The mobility of the sluggishness provides the adversary timing based opportunities to reduce the contributions to the "prompt" chain. The adversary with d sluggish budget can toggle the sluggishness of $2d$ nodes. If the adversary toggles the sluggishness when the honest nodes release TLPs at the end of the mining phase, it can reduce the number of nodes contributing to the prompt chain to $(n - 2d - t)$. This is because the d nodes that are sluggish through the mining phase of a super-round may not be mining on the longest chain, and at the end of the mining phase, the adversary can use its mobility to make d prompt node sluggish (See [42, Remark 1]).

3. The sluggish nodes can inadvertently contribute to the adversarial chain. This is because the sluggish nodes may only have access to the view provided to them by the adversary.

4. Coordinated release of TLPs: Observe that from Eq. 3, large values of m decreases p, thus reducing the block arrival frequency. But, a bounded p ensures that the honest nodes do not fork one another and there are sufficient "convergence opportunities" to resolve forks [20,35]. Moreover, no prior permissionless protocol is secure under mobile-sluggish faults even under reduced performance.

5. Impact of decoys: In Eq. 1, the security impact of mining decoys by honest nodes is captured by c. We set the probability of mining a decoy such that honest nodes can mine sufficiently many decoys while simultaneously bounding the total number of decoys mined. Recall that our batch solvable TLP allows simultaneously opening a polynomial number of puzzles.

Notice that our analysis is a generalization of [20], thus by substituting $m = 1, c = 1, d = 0$, and $D = 0$, our analysis, in principle, collapses to [20]'s analysis. We prove liveness and consistency by assuming that the mining-hardness parameter is appropriately set in Eqs. 1 to 4. We present the complete analysis of the protocol in the extended version of the paper [42].

Acknowledgments. This research was partially funded by the German Federal Ministry of Education and Research (BMBF) in the course of the 6GEM research hub under grant number 16KISK038 and by the Deutsche Forschungsgemeinschaft (DFG, German Research Foundation) under Germany's Excellence Strategy - EXC 2092 CASA - 390781972. This work was also supported in part by Novi and VMware gift research grant. Charalampos Papamanthou was supported in part by the National Science Foundation, the Algorand Foundation through the ACE program, VMware, and Protocol Labs.

References

1. Time-lock: Block producer extractable value - tezos (2022). https://tezos.gitlab.io/alpha/timelock.html. Accessed 01 Sept 2022

2. Abraham, I., et al.: Communication complexity of byzantine agreement, revisited. In: Proceedings of the 2019 ACM Symposium on Principles of Distributed Computing (2019)

3. Abraham, I., Malkhi, D., Nayak, K., Ren, L., Yin, M.: Sync HotStuff: simple and practical synchronous state machine replication. In: 2020 IEEE Symposium on Security and Privacy (SP) (2020)

4. Bagaria, V., Kannan, S., Tse, D., Fanti, G., Viswanath, P.: Prism: Deconstructing the blockchain to approach physical limits. In: Proceedings of the 2019 ACM SIGSAC Conference on Computer and Communications Security (2019)

5. Barak, B., Canetti, R., Lindell, Y., Pass, R., Rabin, T.: Secure computation without authentication. In: Shoup, V. (ed.) CRYPTO 2005. LNCS, vol. 3621, pp. 361–377. Springer, Heidelberg (2005). https://doi.org/10.1007/11535218_22

6. Ben-Sasson, E., Chiesa, A., Genkin, D., Tromer, E., Virza, M.: SNARKs for C: verifying program executions succinctly and in zero knowledge. In: Canetti, R., Garay, J.A. (eds.) CRYPTO 2013. LNCS, vol. 8043, pp. 90–108. Springer, Heidelberg (2013). https://doi.org/10.1007/978-3-642-40084-1_6

7. Bitansky, N., Garg, S., Lin, H., Pass, R., Telang, S.: Succinct randomized encodings and their applications. In: Proceedings of the Forty-Seventh Annual ACM Symposium on Theory of Computing, pp. 439–448 (2015)

8. Bitansky, N., Goldwasser, S., Jain, A., Paneth, O., Vaikuntanathan, V., Waters, B.: Time-lock puzzles from randomized encodings. In: Proceedings of the 2016 ACM Conference on Innovations in Theoretical Computer Science, pp. 345–356 (2016)

9. Boneh, D., Naor, M.: Timed commitments. In: Bellare, M. (ed.) CRYPTO 2000. LNCS, vol. 1880, pp. 236–254. Springer, Heidelberg (2000). https://doi.org/10.1007/3-540-44598-6_15

10. Brakerski, Z., Vaikuntanathan, V.: Constrained key-homomorphic PRFs from standard lattice assumptions. In: Theory of Cryptography Conference, pp. 1–30 (2015)

11. Burdges, J., Feo, L.D.: Delay encryption. In: Annual International Conference on the Theory and Applications of Cryptographic Techniques, pp. 302–326 (2021)

12. Campanelli, M., David, B., Khoshakhlagh, H., Konring, A., Nielsen, J.B.: Encryption to the Future. In: Advances in Cryptology - ASIACRYPT 2022 (2022)

13. Canetti, R.: Security and Composition of Multiparty Cryptographic Protocols. J. Cryptol. 13(1), 143–202 (2000). https://doi.org/10.1007/s001459910006

14. Chan, B.Y., Shi, E.: Streamlet: textbook streamlined blockchains. In: Proceedings of the 2nd ACM Conference on Advances in Financial Technologies (2020)

15. Chen, H.C., Deviani, R.: A secure e-voting system based on RSA time-lock puzzle mechanism. In: 2012 Seventh International Conference on Broadband, Wireless Computing, Communication and Applications (2012)

16. Cohen, R., Garay, J., Zikas, V.: Adaptively secure broadcast in resource-restricted cryptography. Cryptology ePrint Archive, Report 2021/775 (2021)

17. Damgård, I., Jurik, M.: A generalisation, a simplification and some applications of paillier's probabilistic public-key system. In: International workshop on public key cryptography, pp. 119–136 (2001)

18. Dwork, C., Naor, M.: Zaps and their applications. In: Proceedings 41st Annual Symposium on Foundations of Computer Science (2000)

19. Döttling, N., Hanzlik, L., Magri, B., Wohnig, S.: McFly: verifiable encryption to the future made practical. Cryptology ePrint Archive, Paper 2022/433 (2022)

20. Garay, J., Kiayias, A., Leonardos, N.: The bitcoin backbone protocol: analysis and applications. In: Advances in Cryptology - EUROCRYPT 2015 (2015)

21. Garg, S., Gentry, C., Halevi, S., Raykova, M., Sahai, A., Waters, B.: Candidate indistinguishability obfuscation and functional encryption for all circuits. In: 2013 IEEE 54th Annual Symposium on Foundations of Computer Science (2013)

22. Garg, S., Gentry, C., Sahai, A., Waters, B.: Witness encryption and its applications. In: Proceedings of the ACM symposium on Theory of computing (2013)

23. Gilad, Y., Hemo, R., Micali, S., Vlachos, G., Zeldovich, N.: Algorand: scaling byzantine agreements for cryptocurrencies. In: Proceedings of the 26th Symposium on Operating Systems Principles (2017)

24. Goldreich, O., Goldwasser, S., Micali, S.: How to construct randolli functions. In: 25th Annual Symposium on Foundations of Computer Science, pp. 464–479 (1984)

25. Guo, Y., Pass, R., Shi, E.: Synchronous, with a chance of partition tolerance. In: Boldyreva, A., Micciancio, D. (eds.) CRYPTO 2019. LNCS, vol. 11692, pp. 499–529. Springer, Cham (2019). https://doi.org/10.1007/978-3-030-26948-7_18

26. Hanke, T., Movahedi, M., Williams, D.: DFINITY Technology overview series, consensus system (2018)

27. Jain, A., Lin, H., Sahai, A.: Indistinguishability obfuscation from well-founded assumptions. In: Proceedings of the 53rd Annual ACM SIGACT Symposium on Theory of Computing, pp. 60–73 (2021)

28. Katz, J., Loss, J., Xu, J.: On the security of time-lock puzzles and timed commitments. In: Theory of Cryptography (2020)

29. Kiffer, L., Rajaraman, R., shelat, a.: A better method to analyze blockchain consistency. In: Proceedings of the 2018 ACM SIGSAC Conference on Computer and Communications Security (2018)

30. Kim, J., Mehta, V., Nayak, K., Shrestha, N.: Making synchronous BFT protocols secure in the presence of mobile sluggish faults. Cryptology ePrint Archive, Report 2021/603 (2021)

31. Lin, H., Pass, R., Soni, P.: Two-round and non-interactive concurrent non-malleable commitments from time-lock puzzles. In: 2017 IEEE 58th Annual Symposium on Foundations of Computer Science (FOCS) (2017)

32. Liu, J., Jager, T., Kakvi, S.A., Warinschi, B.: How to build time-lock encryption. Des. Codes Crypt. **86**(11), 2549–2586 (2018). https://doi.org/10.1007/s10623-018-0461-x

33. Malavolta, G., Thyagarajan, S.A.K.: Homomorphic time-lock puzzles and applications. In: Boldyreva, A., Micciancio, D. (eds.) CRYPTO 2019. LNCS, vol. 11692, pp. 620–649. Springer, Cham (2019). https://doi.org/10.1007/978-3-030-26948-7_22

34. Paillier, P.: Public-key cryptosystems based on composite degree residuosity classes. In: International Conference on the Theory and Applications of Cryptographic Techniques, pp. 223–238 (1999)

35. Pass, R., Seeman, L., Shelat, A.: Analysis of the blockchain protocol in asynchronous networks. In: Coron, J.-S., Nielsen, J.B. (eds.) EUROCRYPT 2017. LNCS, vol. 10211, pp. 643–673. Springer, Cham (2017). https://doi.org/10.1007/978-3-319-56614-6_22

36. Pass, R., Shi, E.: FruitChains: a fair blockchain. In: Proceedings of the ACM Symposium on Principles of Distributed Computing (2017)

37. Pass, R., Shi, E.: Rethinking large-scale consensus. In: 2017 IEEE 30th Computer Security Foundations Symposium (CSF) (2017)

38. Ren, L.: Analysis of nakamoto consensus. Cryptology ePrint Archive, Report 2019/943 (2019)

39. Rivest, R.L., Shamir, A., Wagner, D.A.: Time-lock puzzles and timed-release crypto. Tech. rep. (1996)

40. Sahai, A., Waters, B.: How to use indistinguishability obfuscation: deniable encryption, and more. SIAM J. Comput. 50, 15M1030108 (2021)

41. Shrestha, N., Abraham, I., Ren, L., Nayak, K.: On the optimality of optimistic responsiveness. In: Proceedings of the 2020 ACM SIGSAC Conference on Computer and Communications Security (2020)

42. Srinivasan, S., Loss, J., Malavolta, G., Nayak, K., Papamanthou, C., Thyagarajan, S.A.: Transparent batchable time-lock puzzles and applications to byzantine consensus. Cryptology ePrint Archive, Paper 2022/1421 (2022). https://eprint.iacr.org/2022/1421
43. Thyagarajan, S.A.K., Bhat, A., Malavolta, G., Döttling, N., Kate, A., Schröder, D.: Verifiable timed signatures made practical. In: Proceedings of the 2020 ACM SIGSAC Conference on Computer and Communications Security (2020)
44. Thyagarajan, S.A.K., Castagnos, G., Laguillaumie, F., Malavolta, G.: Efficient CCA timed commitments in class groups. In: Proceedings of the 2021 ACM SIGSAC Conference on Computer and Communications Security (2021)
45. Wan, J., Xiao, H., Devadas, S., Shi, E.: Round-efficient byzantine broadcast under strongly adaptive and majority corruptions. In: Theory of Cryptography (2020)
46. Wan, J., Xiao, H., Shi, E., Devadas, S.: Expected constant round byzantine broadcast under dishonest majority. In: Theory of Cryptography (2020)
47. Yu, H., Nikolic, I., Hou, R., Saxena, P.: OHIE: blockchain scaling made simple. In: 2020 IEEE Symposium on Security and Privacy (SP) (2020)
48. Zhao, J., Tang, J., Li, Z., Wang, H., Lam, K.Y., Xue, K.: An analysis of blockchain consistency in asynchronous networks: deriving a neat bound. In: 2020 IEEE 40th International Conference on Distributed Computing Systems (ICDCS) (2020)

Pairings

Decentralized Multi-Authority Attribute-Based Inner-Product FE: Large Universe and Unbounded

Pratish Datta[1] and Tapas Pal[2(✉)]

[1] NTT Research, Inc., Sunnyvale, CA 94085, USA
pratish.datta@ntt-research.com
[2] NTT Social Informatics Laboratories, Musashino-shi, Tokyo 180-8585, Japan
tapas.pal.wh@hco.ntt.co.jp, tapas.real@gmail.com

Abstract. This paper presents the *first* decentralized multi-authority attribute-based inner product functional encryption (MA-ABIPFE) schemes supporting vectors of a priori unbounded lengths. The notion of AB-IPFE, introduced by Abdalla et al. [ASIACRYPT 2020], combines the access control functionality of attribute-based encryption (ABE) with the possibility of evaluating linear functions on encrypted data. A decentralized MA-ABIPFE defined by Agrawal et al. [TCC 2021] essentially enhances the ABE component of AB-IPFE to the decentralized multi-authority setting where several authorities can independently issue user keys involving attributes under their control. In MA-ABIPFE for unbounded vectors (MA-ABUIPFE), encryptors can encrypt vectors of arbitrary length under access policies of their choice whereas authorities can issue secret keys to users involving attributes under their control and vectors of arbitrary lengths. Decryption works in the same way as for MA-ABIPFE provided the lengths of the vectors within the ciphertext and secret keys match.

We present two MA-ABUIPFE schemes supporting access policies realizable by linear secret sharing schemes (LSSS), in the significantly faster prime-order bilinear groups under decisional assumptions based on the target groups which are known to be weaker compared to their counterparts based in the source groups. The proposed schemes demonstrate different trade-offs between versatility and underlying assumptions. The first scheme allows each authority to control a bounded number of attributes and is proven secure under the well-studied decisional bilinear Diffie-Hellman (DBDH) assumption. On the other hand, the second scheme allows authorities to control exponentially many attributes and attributes are not required to be enumerated at the setup, that is, supports large attribute universe, and is proven secure under a non-interactive q-type variant of the DBDH assumption called L-DBDH, similar to what was used in prior large-universe multi-authority ABE (MA-ABE) construction.

When compared with the only known MA-ABIPFE scheme due to Agrawal et al. [TCC 2021], our schemes offer significantly higher efficiency while offering greater flexibility and security under weaker assumptions at the same time. Moreover, unlike Agrawal et al., our schemes can support the appearance of the same attributes within an access policy arbitrarily many times. Since efficiency and practicality are the prime focus of this work, we prove the security of our constructions in the random oracle model against static adversaries similar to prior works on MA-ABE with similar motivations and assumptions. On

© International Association for Cryptologic Research 2023
A. Boldyreva and V. Kolesnikov (Eds.): PKC 2023, LNCS 13940, pp. 587–621, 2023.
https://doi.org/10.1007/978-3-031-31368-4_21

the technical side, we extend the unbounded IPFE techniques of Dufour-Sans and Pointcheval [ACNS 2019] to the context of MA-ABUIPFE by introducing a novel *hash-decomposition* technique.

Keywords: multi-authority · attribute-based · unbounded · inner product · functional encryption · large universe · static model

1   Introduction

Functional encryption (FE), introduced by Boneh, Sahai and Waters [15] and O'Neill [34] is an advanced form of public key encryption (PKE) designed for computing on encrypted data while maintaining its confidentiality beyond the computed results. FE delivers cryptographic solutions to a wide variety of privacy-enhancing technologies from enabling finer access control to outsourcing computations on sensitive data to the cloud. Starting with the work of Abdalla et al. [3], a long sequence of works [2,4,10,18,40] studied FE schemes for the class of linear functions, also known as inner product FE (IPFE). In IPFE, the ciphertexts and functional secret keys are associated with vectors x and y respectively while a decrypter only learns the inner product $x \cdot y$ and nothing else about x. Although the functionality is simple, IPFE has found a great amount of applications in both theory, for example, designing more expressive FE schemes for quadratic [23,27] and general functions [26,28] and in practice, for example, performing statistical studies on encrypted data, evaluating polynomials, computing conjunctions and disjunctions [3], or calculating hamming weights in biometric authentications [29,45], constructing trace and revoke schemes [6]. However, any IPFE system suffers from an inherent leakage of data due to it's linear functionality. In fact, releasing a set of secret keys for vectors forming a basis of the underlying vector space would result in a complete break of the system since it enables the recovery of the master secret key of the IPFE system and hence uncover all the encrypted data in the system.

One natural way to control such leakage of data in IPFE is to combine it with attribute-based encryption (ABE), that is, to additionally associate access policies/attributes within the ciphertexts/secret keys (or the other way around) in the same spirit as attribute-based encryption (ABE) such that the eligibility for computing on the encrypted data requires a prior validation of the attributes by the policy. Such access control mechanism in IPFE was introduced by Abdalla et al. [5] where they termed this upgraded notion as *attribute-based* IPFE (AB-IPFE). The notion of AB-IPFE [5,8,35] has been mostly explored in the setting where a single authority is responsible for managing all the attributes in the system and issuing secret keys to users. This not only is a limitation from the point of view of trust, but also it is problematic for practical applications. In fact, in reality, different attributes are governed by different authorities, for example, academic degrees are handled by universities, medical attributes are managed by hospitals while driving licenses are controlled by transportation or automobile agencies.

Multi Authority AB-IPFE: Inspired by the notion of *multi-authority* ABE (MA-ABE) [19–21,30,33,36,43] which deals with the decentralization of attribute management in the context of ABE, Agrawal et al. [9] initiated the study of *multi-authority* AB-IPFE (MA-ABIPFE) which enhances the ABE segment of AB-IPFE to the multi-authority setting. That is, just like MA-ABE, in MA-ABIPFE individual authorities are allowed to generate their own master key pairs and provide secret keys for attributes *only* under their control without interacting with the other authorities. A user learns $x \cdot y$ by decrypting a ciphertext generated with respect to a policy P and a vector x using various secret keys associated to a vector y and the different attributes it possesses that are obtained from the authorities controlling those attributes. Some potential practical application of MA-ABIPFE could be computing average salary of employees in an organization possessing a driving license and holding a Ph.D, statistics determining mental health of students of different departments in a university, etc.

Despite its countless potential applications, so far the only candidate MA-ABIPFE scheme, is due to Agrawal et al. [9] which supports access policies realizable by linear secret sharing schemes (LSSS) and is designed in a composite-order group and the security is based on variants of the subgroup decision assumptions which are source group assumptions, that is, assumptions made about the source groups of the underlying bilinear pairing. It is a well-known fact that composite-order bilinear groups are very expensive both in terms of computation and communication/storage. This is reflected in the MA-ABIPFE of [9], especially the decryption takes an unacceptable time of around five days (as shown in Table 2) when run using reasonable parameters, which clearly makes the scheme impractical. In order to address this efficiency bottleneck, a possible way to avoid this heavy efficiency bottleneck is to look for a construction in the prime-order bilinear groups which are way better in terms of the above parameters compared to their composite-order counterparts [22,25,31].

Another significant drawback of the MA-ABIPFE is that the vector lengths are fixed and the number of authorities or attributes are bounded in the setup. Consequently, the system must provision for a vector length bound that captures all possible plaintext vectors that would be encrypted during the lifetime of the system. Further, the size of ciphertexts and the encryption time, however small the length of the plaintext vector x is, scale with the worst-case vector length bound. Also, in the [9] construction, each authority can control at most a bounded number of attributes. This could be a bottleneck in certain applications, for instance, a university may introduce a new academic degree program over time which would require its potential to freely expand the attribute list under its control. Moreover, in the MA-ABIPFE system of [9], new authorities/attributes could not join beyond the upper limit set in the setup. This is clearly a disadvantage for several applications from the point of view of sustainability since it is often impossible to visualize all possible attributes/authorities that can ever come into existence at the time of setting up the system. For instance, new universities may be included in the survey of analyzing mental health of their students, which amplifies the number of authorities/attributes as well as the length of data. Additionally, the MA-ABIPFE scheme of [9] suffer from the so-called "one-use" restriction, that is, an attribute can appear within an access policy at most a bounded number of times, which clearly limits the class of access policies and negatively impacts efficiency. Lastly, in order to gain confidence in a new cryptographic primitive such as MA-ABIPFE, it is always important to have more and more candidates for that primitive under qualitatively weaker computational assumptions. We thus consider the following open problem:

Open Problem: Is it possible to construct efficient MA-ABIPFE schemes for any expressive class of policies, e.g., LSSS, and avoiding the one-use restriction in prime-order bilinear groups under any (possibly qualitatively weaker) computational assumption such that an arbitrary number of authorities (possibly having an unbounded number of attributes under their control) can join at any point of time and an unbounded length data can be processed?

Our Results: In this paper, we answer the above open problem affirmatively. More precisely, we start by formulating the notion of (decentralized) multi-authority attribute-based *unbounded* IPFE (MA-ABUIPFE) which has all the features discussed above, namely, (a) several independent authorities can control different attributes in the system, (b) authorities can join the system at any time and there is no upper bound on the number of authorities that can ever exist in the system, and (c) unbounded length message and key vectors can be processed, that is, each authority can generate their public and master secret keys without fixing the length of vectors that can be processed with their keys. Next, we construct MA-ABUIPFE supporting LSSS access structures in the significantly faster prime-order bilinear group setting under computational assumptions based in the target group which are known to be qualitatively weaker compared to those based in the source group [11,21]. The efficiency improvements achieved by our scheme as compared to the only known MA-ABIPFE scheme [9] is quite significant (see Tables 1 and 2 for a concrete comparison of the schemes). On a more positive note, we are able to overcome the "one-use restriction", that is, support the appearance of attributes within access policies arbitrarily many times.

We present two MA-ABUIPFE schemes with varying trade-offs between versatility and underlying assumptions.

- **Small-Universe MA-ABUIPFE Scheme:** We construct an MA-ABUIPFE scheme where an authority is allowed to control a single (or a bounded number of) attribute(s), but the number of authorities that could be added to the system is still arbitrary. The construction is proven secure under the decisional bilinear Diffie-Hellman (DBDH) assumption [13,38] which is a very well-studied computational assumption based in the target groups. Note that the DBDH assumption underlies the security of classical ABE schemes [24,37,42] and has recently been shown to realize MA-ABE [21]. Our MA-ABUIPFE scheme demonstrates that it is possible to base the security of an even richer functionality on DBDH as well.
- **Large-Universe MA-ABUIPFE Scheme:** We further upgrade our small-universe MA-ABUIPFE scheme to support large attribute universe, that is, where each authority can control exponentially many attributes and attributes need not be enumerated at the setup. We present the security of this construction under a parameterized version of the DBDH assumption which we call the L-DBDH assumption. We justify the validity of this new computational assumption in the generic bilinear group model [12,39] as is done for nearly if not all bilinear group-based computational assumptions used today. Note that, so far, there is no known

MA-ABE scheme supporting large universe in the literature that is proven secure without parameterized assumption. The efficiency of the proposed large-universe scheme is well comparable to the small-universe one. Thus, our large-universe MA-ABUIPFE (LMA-ABUIPFE) scheme addresses several efficiency and practicality issues towards deploying this primitive in practice.

Since our focus on this paper is on efficiency and practicality, we content with proving the security of our schemes in the static model where the adversary has to declare all its ciphertext, secret key, and authority corruption queries upfront following prior work on MA-ABE with similar motivations [36]. However, we would like to mention that while we could not prove our schemes secure against selective adversaries under DBDH or similar target-group-based assumptions, that is, adversaries who must send the challenge ciphertext and authority corruption queries upfront but are allowed to make user secret key queries adaptively afterwards, as considered in [9], we could not identify any vulnerability in our proposed schemes against such adversaries. Also, just like prior MA-ABE schemes proven secure under standard computational assumptions, we make use of the random oracle model[1].

In order to design our small-universe MA-ABUIPFE, we build on the techniques used in the MA-ABE construction from DBDH by [21] and the unbounded IPFE construction from DBDH by [38]. However, as explained in Sect. 2 below, a straightforward combination of those techniques does not work. We devise a novel hash-decomposition technique to decompose the evaluation of the hash values, used as randomizers for tying together the different secret keys for the same user, between the encryption and key generation/decryption algorithms and also for handling satisfying and non-satisfying secret key queries of the adversary during the security proof differently. (Please see Sect. 2 for more details on the hash-decomposition technique.)

Along the way to our small universe MA-ABUIPFE scheme, we also present a single authority ABUIPFE for LSSS access policies in prime-order bilinear groups under the DBDH assumption. Prior to this work, there was no known AB-IPFE scheme even for bounded length vectors that was proven secure under a target group assumption. Thus, the proposed ABUIPFE expands the portfolio of computational assumptions on which this useful primitive can be based on and thereby increasing the confidence in the existence of this primitive in turn. Further, our construction also demonstrates that despite of being a more expressive functionality, MA-ABIPFE is still possible under the same assumption as ABE or MA-ABE. In fact, our AB-IPFE is the first target-group assumption-based FE scheme that goes beyond the "all-or-nothing" paradigm.

---

[1] Very recently, Waters, Wee, and Wu [43] presented a lattice-based MA-ABE scheme that does not make use of random oracles. However, the scheme relies on a recently introduced complexity assumption called evasive LWE [44] which is a strong knowledge type assumption and is not yet cryptanalyzed in detail.

Table 1. Efficiency Comparison of [9] and Our Scheme with 128-bit Security

Scheme	Group order length (in bits)	$\lvert PK_t\rvert$/ $\lvert PK_\theta\rvert$	$\lvert SK_{GID,t,u}\rvert$ $T(t)=\theta$	$\lvert CT\rvert$	Encrypt Time	Decrypt Time
Agrawal et al. [9]	3072	$6054n$	3072	$(n+\ell+2n\ell)3072$	$(n+n\ell)E_{N,T}+(\ell+n\ell)E_{N,S}$	$(\ell+1)P_N+(n+n\ell^2)E_{N,T}+(\ell+n\ell^2)E_{N,S}$
MA-ABUIPFE (Sect. 5)	256	$\lvert PK_t\rvert=256s_{\max}$	256	$[n+\ell s_{\max}(n+1)]256$	$(n+n\ell)E_{q,T}+[\ell s_{\max}(n+2)-\ell(n+1)]E_{q,S}+(2\ell n(s_{\max}-1))P_q$	$[\ell+n(s_{\max}-1)](P_q+E_{q,T})+nE_{q,S}$
LMA-ABUIPFE (Sect. 6)	256	$\lvert PK_\theta\rvert=256s_{\max}$	$256(s_{\max}+1)$	$[n+\ell s_{\max}(n+2)]256$	$(n+n\ell)E_{q,T}+[\ell s_{\max}(n+3)-\ell(n+1)]E_{q,S}+(2\ell n(s_{\max}-1))P_q$	$[\ell+n(s_{\max}-1)](P_q+E_{q,T})+\ell s_{\max}P_q+nE_{q,S}$

The notations from Table 1 are described below:

- $\lvert PK_t\rvert/\lvert PK_\theta\rvert$: size of the public key associated to the attribute t or authority θ
- $\lvert SK_{GID,t,u}\rvert$: size of the secret key associated to the tuple (GID, t, u)
- $\lvert CT\rvert$: size of the ciphertext
- n: length of vectors; $\ell, s_{\max}$: number of rows and columns in LSSS matrix respectively
- $E_{N,S}, E_{q,S}$: exponentiation time in composite and prime order source groups respectively
- $E_{N,T}, E_{q,T}$: exponentiation time in composite and prime order target groups respectively
- P_N, P_q: time to compute a pairing in composite and prime order groups respectively

Table 2. Concrete Efficiency Comparison for 128-bit Security, $n = 200, \ell = 50, s_{\max} = 20$.

Scheme	$\lvert PK_\theta\rvert$	$\lvert CT\rvert$	Encrypt Time	Decrypt Time
Agrawal et al. [9]	≈ 147.8 KB	≈ 7.78 MB	≈ 143.7 mins	≈ 4.9 days
MA-ABUIPFE (Sect. 5)	≈ 0.64 KB	≈ 6.44 MB	≈ 63.14 mins	≈ 7.27 mins
LMA-ABUIPFE (Sect. 6)	≈ 0.64 KB	≈ 6.47 MB	≈ 63.2 mins	≈ 7.35 mins

Advantages of Our Schemes Over Agrawal et al. [9] Beyond Unboundedness: Our MA-ABUIPFE schemes have notable advantages in terms of versatility and performance over the MA-ABIPFE of [9], named as AGT-FE hereafter beyond the unboundedness property that we achieve in this work. Firstly, the composite-order group-based AGT-FE is significantly slower than our prime-order constructions [22,25] because of the inherent efficiency gains offered by prime-order bilinear groups. Especially, the size of group elements of a composite-order group $\mathbb{G}_N$ is much larger than that of a prime-order group $\mathbb{G}_q$ for the same security level: 3072-bit length of $\mathbb{G}_N$ compared to 256-bit length of $\mathbb{G}_q$ for the 128-bit security level. Moreover, one pairing operation is more than 250 times slower in $\mathbb{G}_N$ compared to its prime-order counterpart. A concrete comparison of efficiency is depicted in Tables 1 and 2. As we can see, at 128-bit security level, while AGT-FE takes nearly 5 days for a decryption, our scheme only takes several minutes. We also bring down the public key size (which is constant for any arbitrary length vector) by around 99% and at the same time the ciphertext size is comparable to that of AGT-FE. Thus our constructions mark a significant progress towards the practical deployment of this primitive. Secondly, the security of AGT-FE is based on source-group-assumptions, precisely, various types of subgroup decision assumptions, which are known to be qualitatively stronger than the target-group-based assumptions [11] such as the DBDH assumption considered in this work. The existing transformations from composite-order group-based systems to analogous prime-order group-based systems [16,22,31] that could be applied to AGT-FE, technically replaces the subgroup structures by some vector space structures. Consequently, it incurs additional overheads and potential loss in the efficiency to the resulting prime-order system. Further, the translated scheme would still depend on source group assumptions, e.g. the k-linear or its variants.

Thus, our MA-ABUIPFE exhibits a substantial boost with respect to the performance and at the same time it is secure under a weaker assumption. Furthermore, we extend our MA-ABUIPFE to the large universe setting which has the flexibility to include an unbounded number of attributes under different authorities to the system at any point of time.

Static Security: Our Motivation: The static security may not be the dream security model for MA-ABUIPFE. However, in this work, our main motivation is on performance and versatility. Moreover, as we already mentioned above, we could not find any vulnerability of our schemes against stronger adversaries, e.g., selective adversaries as considered in [9], even though we could not prove it based on the computational assumptions we considered in this paper. Schemes with greater performance and weaker provable security have often found to suit better in practical deployments. Further, weaker security notions have often been a major stepping stone to obtain more advanced security, e.g., adaptive security, for the same primitive. Please note that many primitives like ABE [24,37,42], MA-ABE [19,21,36,43], IPFE [3], and MC-IPFE [1,17], were first built only with selective/static security before being upgraded to adaptive security [10,20,32] based on the same assumptions. Moreover, from a sustainability point of view, it is always important to have a portfolio of candidates for a primitive under various computational assumptions so that if one of the assumptions gets broken, candidates under a different assumption can be deployed. Another motivation for designing a DBDH or related assumption-based scheme is to innovate new techniques that could possibly be translated to the LWE setting, as has previously been done for other FE primitives, e.g., [7,13,19,21].

Paper Organization: The paper is organized as follows. We provide technical overview of our small and large universe MA-ABUIPFE schemes in Sect. 2. Important notations and computational assumptions are given in Sect. 3. The other prerequisites such as definitions of bilinear groups, access structures, LSSS and justification of our newly introduced L-DBDH assumption are given in the full version. We formalize the notion of small and large universe MA-ABUIPFEs for LSSS in Sect. 4. In Sect. 5, we present the construction of small universe MA-ABUIPFE and formally discuss its correctness and security analysis. Next, our LMA-ABUIPFE scheme is described in Sect. 6 whereas its correctness and the security analysis are shifted to the full version. The small universe single authority ABUIPFE scheme along with its correctness and security analysis are provided in the full version.

2 Technical Overview

In this technical overview, we focus on discussing the high level technical details of constructing small universe MA-ABUIPFE since this is where most of our technical ideas lie. For extending it to large universe setting, we depend on the technique of Rouselakis and Waters [36] which we discuss later in this section. Since our goal is to construct the schemes under target-group-based assumptions, we start with the only existing UIPFE scheme of [38] whose security relies on the DBDH assumption. In fact, their UIPFE is designed from the selectively secure (bounded) IPFE of Abdalla et al. [3] using a hash and pairing mechanism.

2.1 Constructing the Small Universe MA-ABUIPFE

In this overview, we denote by q a prime number and by $[\![x]\!]_i$ an element in a group $\mathbb{G}_i$ for $i \in \{1, 2, T\}$. At a high level, given a public key $[\![\alpha]\!]_1$, the encryption algorithm of [38] amplifies entropy by pairing the public key with the outputs of a hash function applied on the indices of the message vectors. More precisely, the ciphertext and secret keys in the [38] UIPFE (DP-UIPFE) takes the following forms.

$$\mathsf{CT}_v : \quad C_0 = [\![r]\!]_1, \quad \{C_i = [\![v_i]\!]_T \cdot e([\![\alpha]\!]_1, r[\![\mathsf{H}(i)]\!]_2)\}_{i \in \mathcal{I}_v}; \quad r \leftarrow \mathbb{Z}_q$$
$$\mathsf{SK}_u : \quad -\alpha \prod_{j \in \mathcal{I}_u} \mathsf{H}(j)^{u_j}$$

where $\mathcal{I}_u, \mathcal{I}_v \subset \mathbb{N}$ are the index sets of u, v respectively, the hash function H maps the indices to elements in $\mathbb{G}_2$ and $(q, \mathbb{G}_1, \mathbb{G}_2, \mathbb{G}_T, e)$ is a prime-order bilinear group. If the index sets are equal, i.e. $\mathcal{I}_u = \mathcal{I}_v = \mathcal{I}$ then one can use the key vector u to extract $[\![u \cdot v]\!]_T$ from the product $\prod_{j \in \mathcal{I}} C_j^{u_j}$ and a single pairing $e(C_0, \mathsf{SK}_u)$. As a natural first step, we seek to utilize the DP-UIPFE to upgrade an existing MA-ABE to a small universe MA-ABUIPFE scheme.

As the aim is to rely on the target-group-based assumption, we consider the DBDH-based MA-ABE of Datta, Komargodski and Waters (DKW-MA-ABE) [21] for this upgrade. As a simpler first step, we investigate the primitive in the bounded and small universe setting, that is, the number of authorities and vector lengths are bounded and each authority controls a single attribute.

2.1.1 The First Step: A Bounded MA-ABIPFE Scheme

Let us start by adding the functionality of IPFE on top of DKW-MA-ABE. For each authority t, the public key and master secret key in the DKW-MA-ABE construction are given by $\mathsf{PK}_t = ([\![\alpha_t]\!]_T, [\![y_{t,2}]\!]_1, \ldots, [\![y_{t,s_{\max}}]\!]_1)$ and $\mathsf{MSK}_t = (\alpha_t, y_{t,2}, \ldots, y_{t,s_{\max}})$ where $s_{\max}$ is a bound on the maximum number of columns in the LSSS access structure and $\alpha_t, y_{t,2}, \ldots, y_{t,s_{\max}} \leftarrow \mathbb{Z}_q$. In order to construct an MA-ABIPFE scheme from the DKW-MA-ABE, we convert the components of MSK_t from scalars to vectors whose lengths are fixed according to the vector length bound of the system. All the other components are similarly upgraded to either vectors or matrices of *fixed* dimensions. In particular, the resulting MA-ABIPFE derived from DKW-MA-ABE can be described in the following way where $P = (\mathbf{M} = (M_{i,j})_{\ell \times s_{\max}}, \rho : [\ell] \to \mathcal{AU})$ is the LSSS access policy associated with the ciphertexts, $\mathcal{AU}$ is the set of all authorities, and $\mathbf{M}_i$ denotes the i-th row of $\mathbf{M}$.

$$
\begin{aligned}
\mathsf{PK}_t : \quad & (\llbracket \boldsymbol{\alpha}_t \rrbracket_T, \llbracket \boldsymbol{y}_{t,2} \rrbracket_1, \ldots, \llbracket \boldsymbol{y}_{t,s_{\max}} \rrbracket_1) \\
\mathsf{MSK}_t : \quad & (\boldsymbol{\alpha}_t, \boldsymbol{y}_{t,2}, \ldots, \boldsymbol{y}_{t,s_{\max}}) \\
\mathsf{CT}_{v,P} : \quad & C_0 = \llbracket \boldsymbol{v} + \boldsymbol{z} \rrbracket_T, \quad C_{1,i} = \llbracket \boldsymbol{M}_i \mathbf{B} + r_i \boldsymbol{\alpha}_{\rho(i)} \rrbracket_T, \\
& C_{2,i} = \llbracket r_i \rrbracket_1, \qquad C_{3,i,j} = \llbracket M_{i,j} \boldsymbol{x}_j + r_i \boldsymbol{y}_{\rho(i),j} \rrbracket_1 \ \forall i \in [\ell], j \in [2, s_{\max}] \\
\mathsf{SK}_{\mathsf{GID},t,u} : \quad & \llbracket \boldsymbol{\alpha}_t \cdot \boldsymbol{u} \rrbracket_2 \cdot \prod_{j=2}^{s_{\max}} \mathsf{H}(\mathsf{GID} \parallel \boldsymbol{u} \parallel j)^{\boldsymbol{y}_{t,j} \cdot \boldsymbol{u}}
\end{aligned}
$$

where $\boldsymbol{z} \leftarrow \mathbb{Z}_q^n, r_i \leftarrow \mathbb{Z}_q$ and n represents the length of $\boldsymbol{u}, \boldsymbol{v}$. Further, $\mathbf{B} \in \mathbb{Z}_q^{s_{\max} \times n}$ and $\{\boldsymbol{x}_j \leftarrow \mathbb{Z}_q^n\}_{j \in [2, s_{\max}]}$ are the secret shares of $\boldsymbol{z}$ and $\mathbf{0}$ respectively. Recall that the decryption algorithm of MA-ABIPFE requires a set of secret keys $\{\mathsf{SK}_{\mathsf{GID},t,u}\}_{t \in S}$ for the same user identifier GID and an authorized subset S of attributes featuring in the LSSS access policy associated with the ciphertext in order to decrypt it. Given such a collection of keys , the decryption algorithm gets rid of the masking term from $C_0 \cdot \boldsymbol{u}$ by computing

$$
\llbracket \boldsymbol{u} \cdot \boldsymbol{z} \rrbracket_T = \prod_{i \in I} \left[\frac{C_{1,i} \cdot \boldsymbol{u} \cdot \prod_{j=2}^{s_{\max}} e\left(\mathsf{H}(\mathsf{GID} \parallel \boldsymbol{u} \parallel j), C_{3,i,j} \cdot \boldsymbol{u}\right)}{e\left(\mathsf{SK}_{\mathsf{GID},\rho(i),u}, C_{2,i}\right)} \right]^{w_i} \tag{2.1}
$$

where I represents the rows of $\mathbf{M}$ associated to S. Note that the Eq. (2.1) holds as the decryption algorithm can efficiently find a coefficients $\{w_i \in \mathbb{Z}_q\}_{i \in I}$ satisfying $(1, 0, \ldots, 0) = \sum_{i \in I} w_i \mathbf{M}_i$ whenever the attributes linked to the rows in I satisfies the policy $(\mathbf{M}, \rho)$.

The role of the public hash function H is to tie together a set of independently generated secret keys under the same user identifier GID while decrypting. In the security proof, H is treated as a random oracle to ensure that a fresh randomness is produced for each user identity GID that links together the different secret keys generated for it and it is infeasible for an adversary to mix and match secret keys generated with respect to different global identifiers even if the attributes associated with those secret keys satisfy the access policy associated with the ciphertext.

In fact, the above bounded MA-ABIPFE scheme can be proven secure in the static model under the DBDH assumption. Let us now proceed to transform the bounded scheme into an unbounded one using the idea of DP-UIPFE sketched above. Unfortunately, a straightforward approach does not work. In particular, we face a few difficulties while incorporating the hash and pairing mechanism of [38] with the DKW-MA-ABE as we describe below.

2.1.2   Challenges in Expanding Authority Keys on the Fly and Our Approach

The foremost problem arises in vectorizing the components of the authority master secret keys MSK_t. This is because there being no upper bound on the length of vectors, we cannot simply use random vectors of predetermined sizes in the vectorization process. Rather, we must provision for generating the components of the vectors on the fly as needed during encryption/key generation. Similar to the idea of [38], we use hash functions modeled as random oracles in order to resolve this issue. More precisely, we proceed as follows: An authority t generates the public/master secret keys as $(\text{PK}_t = (\llbracket \alpha_t \rrbracket_T, \llbracket y_{t,2} \rrbracket_1, \ldots, \llbracket y_{t,s_{max}} \rrbracket_1), \text{MSK}_t = (\alpha_t, y_{t,2}, \ldots, y_{t,s_{max}}))$ without knowing the vector lengths where $\alpha, y_{t,2}, \ldots, y_{t,smx}$ are still scalars. To maintain the simplicity of this overview, we assume that the vectors $\boldsymbol{u} = (u_k)_{k \in \mathcal{I}_u}$ and $\boldsymbol{v} = (v_k)_{k \in \mathcal{I}_v}$ are both associated with the index set $\mathcal{I}_u = \mathcal{I}_v = \mathcal{I} = [n]$ which is unknown to the authority setup. Then the scalar α_t could be vectorized using a hash function H_1 as follows.

$$\text{during encryption :}\quad C_{1,i} = \llbracket M_i \mathbf{B} + \vartheta_i \rrbracket_T$$
$$\text{where } \llbracket \vartheta_{i,k} \rrbracket_T = e(r_i \llbracket \alpha_{\rho(i)} \rrbracket_1, \mathsf{H}_1(\rho(i) \parallel k \parallel \mathcal{I}))$$

$$\text{during key generation :}\quad \alpha_t \cdot \boldsymbol{u} = \prod_{k=1}^{n} \mathsf{H}_1(t \parallel k \parallel \mathcal{I})^{\alpha_t \cdot u_k}$$

The next step is to vectorize the authority master secret key components $y_{t,j}$ according to the vector lengths. One may hope to apply [38] idea to extend $y_{t,j}$ to the same length of the vectors on the fly in a similar way. To see whether it works, let us assume that the hash function H used in the key generation in the above bounded MA-ABIPFE additionally takes an index position and an index set as inputs. That is, let us do the following modification for the key generation of the bounded MA-ABIPFE scheme

$$\mathsf{H}(\text{GID} \parallel \boldsymbol{u} \parallel j)^{y_{t,j} \cdot \boldsymbol{u}} \longrightarrow \prod_{k=1}^{n} \mathsf{H}(\text{GID} \parallel \boldsymbol{u} \parallel j \parallel k \parallel \mathcal{I})^{y_{t,j} \cdot u_k}$$

Thus, using this idea, it is possible to expand $y_{t,j}$ to a vector $\boldsymbol{y}_{t,j}$ of the same length as the key vector $\boldsymbol{u}$ and eventually enabling an authority to compute the term $\mathsf{H}(\text{GID} \parallel \boldsymbol{u} \parallel j \parallel k \parallel \mathcal{I})^{y_{t,j} \cdot \boldsymbol{u}}$ while generating keys for an unbounded length vector. Note that, the hash value $\mathsf{H}(\text{GID} \parallel \boldsymbol{u} \parallel j \parallel k \parallel \mathcal{I})$ has GID and $\boldsymbol{u}$ as inputs. Therefore, this would call for the following modification in the ciphertext computation.

$$C_{3,i,j} = \llbracket M_{i,j} x_j + \varsigma_{i,j} \rrbracket_T$$
$$\text{where } \llbracket \varsigma_{i,j,k} \rrbracket_T = e(r_i \llbracket y_{\rho(i),j} \rrbracket_1, \mathsf{H}(\boxed{\text{GID}} \parallel \boxed{\boldsymbol{u}} \parallel j \parallel k \parallel \mathcal{I}))$$

However, such a vector $\llbracket \boldsymbol{y}_{t,j} \rrbracket_1$ is not known or rather the k-th element $e(\llbracket y_{t,j} \rrbracket_1, \mathsf{H}(\text{GID} \parallel \boldsymbol{u} \parallel j \parallel k \parallel \mathcal{I}))$ can not be computed during encryption. The main reason is that the global identity GID and the vector $\boldsymbol{u}$ are available when an authority generates a secret key, but the encryption algorithm is oblivious of which GID or $\boldsymbol{u}$ will be used to decrypt the ciphertext. In fact, it is natural that the same ciphertext would be decrypted by several users with different GID and $\boldsymbol{u}$ vectors. Hence, a simple hash and pairing technique similar to DP-UIPFE is not sufficient for a data owner to encrypt unbounded length vectors.

At this point, we devise a correlated "hash-decomposition" mechanism which enables us to compute the value of a hash function by combining the outputs of several hash functions applied on different segments of the input to the original hash function. More precisely, our idea is to define the hash value $\mathsf{H}(\mathsf{GID} \parallel \boldsymbol{u} \parallel j \parallel k \parallel \mathcal{I})$ by grouping two independently generated hash values as

$$\mathsf{H}(\mathsf{GID} \parallel \boldsymbol{u} \parallel j \parallel k \parallel \mathcal{I}) = \mathsf{H}_2(j \parallel k \parallel \mathcal{I}) \cdot \mathsf{H}_3(\mathsf{GID} \parallel \boldsymbol{u} \parallel j \parallel k) \tag{2.2}$$

where H_2 and H_3 are two new public hash functions generated during global setup. Now, we observe that the first hash value $\mathsf{H}_2(j \parallel k \parallel \mathcal{I})$ in the product can be computed without knowing GID, which in turn enable the encryptor to expand an authority public key component $[\![y_{t,j}]\!]_1$ into a vector $[\![\boldsymbol{y}_{t,j}^{(2)}]\!]_T$ as $[\![\boldsymbol{y}_{t,j,k}^{(2)}]\!]_T = e([\![y_{t,j}]\!]_1, \mathsf{H}_2(j \parallel k \parallel \mathcal{I}))$. Similarly, an authority expands the master secret key component $y_{t,j}$ into vectors $[\![\boldsymbol{y}_{t,j}^{(2)}]\!]_2$ and $[\![\boldsymbol{y}_{t,j}^{(3)}]\!]_2$ as $[\![\boldsymbol{y}_{t,j,k}^{(2)}]\!]_2 = \mathsf{H}_2(j \parallel k \parallel \mathcal{I}))^{y_{t,j}}$ and $[\![\boldsymbol{y}_{t,j,k}^{(3)}]\!]_2 = \mathsf{H}_3(\mathsf{GID} \parallel \boldsymbol{u} \parallel j \parallel k)^{y_{t,j}}$ respectively while generating a secret key for a vector $\boldsymbol{u}$. However, at this point, it is not immediate how would the vector $[\![\boldsymbol{y}_{t,j}^{(2)}]\!]_T$ be useful for the encryption algorithm.

Next, we carefully look into the decryption equation of the bounded MA-ABIPFE scheme described above (Eq. (2.1)) and try to adapt it for the MA-ABUIPFE setting with the modifications we did so far. We note that the pairing operation in the numerator can be rearranged with the hash function H replaced by H_2 as

$$e\left(\mathsf{H}_2(j \parallel k \parallel \mathcal{I}), C_{3,i,j} \cdot \boldsymbol{u}\right) = e(\mathsf{H}_2(j \parallel k \parallel \mathcal{I}), (M_{i,j}\boldsymbol{x}_j + r_i \boldsymbol{y}_{\rho(i),j}) \cdot \boldsymbol{u})$$
$$= e(\mathsf{H}_2(j \parallel k \parallel \mathcal{I}), M_{i,j}\boldsymbol{x}_j \cdot \boldsymbol{u}) \cdot [\![r_i \boldsymbol{y}_{\rho(i),j}^{(2)} \cdot \boldsymbol{u}]\!]_T$$

Since $\boldsymbol{u}$ is not available during encryption, we only compute the above term without multiplying by $\boldsymbol{u}$ and represent it as a single element

$$C_{3,i,j,k} = e([\![M_{i,j}x_{j,k}]\!]_1, \mathsf{H}_2(j \parallel k \parallel \mathcal{I})) \cdot [\![r_i y_{\rho(i),j,k}^{(2)}]\!]_T.$$

Therefore, the hash-decomposition mechanism allows the encryptor to simulate the *first* part of the hash value $\mathsf{H}(\mathsf{GID} \parallel \boldsymbol{u} \parallel j \parallel k \parallel \mathcal{I})$ from Eq. (2.2) using the hash function H_2. The second part of the hash value still remains to be handled. For this, we generate an additional layer of secret share of zero by sampling $f_2, \ldots, f_{s_{\max}} \in \mathbb{Z}_q$ and introduce the encodings $C_{4,i,j} = [\![M_{i,j}f_j + r_i y_{\rho(i),j}]\!]_1$ for all $i \in [\ell], j \in [2, s_{\max}]$ within the ciphertext. At the time of decryption, $C_{1,i,j}$ will be paired with the term $\mathsf{H}_3(\mathsf{GID} \parallel \boldsymbol{u} \parallel j \parallel k)^{u_k}$. Thus, combining $C_{3,i,j,k}$ and $C_{4,i,j}$ via the hash-decomposition mechanism we are able to distribute the execution of the pairing operation from (Eq. (2.1)) among the encryption and decryption algorithms as follows:

$$e\left(\mathsf{H}(\mathsf{GID} \parallel \boldsymbol{u} \parallel j), C_{3,i,j} \cdot \boldsymbol{u}\right) \qquad\qquad \begin{array}{l} \text{as in MA-ABIPFE} \\ \text{decryption (ref: Eq. (2.1))} \end{array}$$

$$\longrightarrow \prod_{k=1}^{n} C_{3,i,j,k} \cdot u_k \cdot e(C_{4,i,j}, \mathsf{H}_3(\mathsf{GID} \parallel \boldsymbol{u} \parallel j \parallel k)^{u_k}) \qquad \begin{array}{l} \text{new decryption} \\ \text{strategy for MA-ABUIPFE} \end{array}$$

$$= C_{i,j}^{(3,4)}(\boldsymbol{u}) \qquad\qquad\qquad\qquad\qquad\qquad\qquad\qquad\qquad \text{(say)}$$

Equipped with these concepts, we state our final MA-ABUIPFE scheme below by assuming $\mathcal{I}_u = \mathcal{I}_v = \mathcal{I} = [n]$.

$$
\begin{aligned}
\mathsf{PK}_t : &\ ([\![\alpha_t]\!]_T, [\![y_{t,2}]\!]_1, \dots, [\![y_{t,s_{\max}}]\!]_1) \\
\mathsf{MSK}_t : &\ (\alpha_t, y_{t,2}, \dots, y_{t,s_{\max}}) \\
& \quad C_0 = [\![\boldsymbol{v} + \boldsymbol{z}]\!]_T, \quad C_{1,i} = [\![\boldsymbol{M}_i \mathbf{B} + \boldsymbol{\vartheta}_i]\!]_T, \quad C_{2,i} = [\![r_i]\!]_1, \\
\mathsf{CT}_{v,P} : &\ C_{3,i,j,k} = e([\![M_{i,j} x_{j,k}]\!]_1, \mathsf{H}_2(j \parallel k \parallel \mathcal{I})) \cdot [\![r_i y_{\rho(i),j,k}^{(2)}]\!]_T, \\
& \quad C_{4,i,j} = [\![M_{i,j} f_j + r_i y_{\rho(i),j}]\!]_1, \quad \forall i \in [\ell], \ j \in [2, s_{\max}], \ k \in [n] \\
\mathsf{SK}_{\mathsf{GID},t,u} : &\ \prod_{k=1}^{n} \mathsf{H}_1(t \parallel k \parallel \mathcal{I})^{\alpha_t \cdot u_k} \cdot \prod_{j=2}^{s_{\max}} \prod_{k=1}^{n} ([\![y_{t,j,k}^{(2)}]\!]_2 \cdot [\![y_{t,j,k}^{(3)}]\!]_2)^{u_k}
\end{aligned}
$$

The components $\boldsymbol{\vartheta}_i, y_{t,j,k}^{(2)}, y_{t,j,k}^{(3)}$ are defined as above. The decryption follows by canceling the masking term from $C_0 \cdot \boldsymbol{u}$ using a similar computation like in Eq. (2.1) executed as

$$[\![\boldsymbol{u} \cdot \boldsymbol{z}]\!]_T = \prod_{i \in I} \left[\frac{C_{1,i} \cdot \boldsymbol{u} \cdot \prod_{j=2}^{s_{\max}} C_{i,j}^{(3,4)}(\boldsymbol{u})}{e\left(\mathsf{SK}_{\mathsf{GID},\rho(i),u}, C_{2,i}\right)} \right]^{w_i} \qquad (2.3)$$

We next look into the security of the proposed construction. Here again, we face several challenges while adapting the security proof of [21, 38] into our setting.

2.1.3   Challenges in the Security Analysis and Our Approach

The main difference between the MA-ABE and MA-ABUIPFE security model is in the secret key queries made by the adversary. This is because MA-ABUIPFE is more like an FE scheme and the adversary is entitled to ask for secret keys that would decrypt the challenge ciphertext which is in contrast to any MA-ABE scheme where only non-authorized keys are released. On the other hand, proving security of MA-ABUIPFE is more technically challenging compared to the (bounded) MA-ABIPFE (like AGT-FE [9]) as an authorized key which always leads to a successful decryption in case of MA-ABIPFE, may not be eligible for decrypting a ciphertext of MA-ABUIPFE. The index set associated with the authorized key must match to the index set of the encrypted vector for successful decryption in MA-ABUIPFE. In other words, the adversary should be restricted to infer any information about the encrypted message vector from the authorized keys whose index sets are not equal to the index set of the message vector. Moreover, AGT-FE is proven secure under subgroup decision assumptions which are source group assumptions while our target is to prove security under DBDH which is a target group assumption, thus the dual system encryption technique [41] used for the security proof of AGT-FE does not work in our case. Hence, we design a different proof strategy that works coherently with the hash-decomposition mechanism and for target group assumptions in the prime-order bilinear group.

We prove the security of our MA-ABUIPFE in the static model similar to the DKW-MA-ABE. The adversary is asked to submit all it's queries including the challenge message vectors v_0, v_1 with a common index set $\mathcal{I}^*$ and an associated challenge access structure $(\mathbf{M}, \rho)$. Recall that the adversary can also corrupt or even maliciously generate some of the authorities indicated by a set $\mathcal{C}$ of corrupted authorities or attributes. Let us consider a DBDH instance $([\![a]\!]_1, [\![b]\!]_2, [\![c]\!]_1, [\![\tau]\!]_T)$ where τ is either abc or random. In the first step, we use the information-theoretic *partitioning* lemma, the so-called "zero-out" lemma [36, Lemma 1], to isolate and ignore the set of rows of $\mathbf{M}$ that correspond to the corrupted authorities throughout the analysis. In particular, the lemma allows us to replace the LSSS matrix $\mathbf{M}$ with an updated simpler matrix $\mathbf{M}'$ such that a subset of columns, say $C_{\mathbf{M}'}$, of $\mathbf{M}'$ can be set to zero that are related to the corrupted authorities. Next, we follow the proof techniques of [3,38] and sample a basis $\tilde{S} = \{(v_0 - v_1), b_2, \ldots, b_n\}$ of $\mathbb{Z}_q^n$ where n denotes the size of $\mathcal{I}^*$ to represent key vectors u whose lengths are equal to n. However, answering the hash and secret key queries require a careful treatment while embedding the DBDH challenge instance. The role of the hash function of DKW-MA-ABE was limited to simulating the non-authorized keys of a fixed length. However, in our case, we need to deal with both authorized and unauthorized keys and here again, our hash-decomposition mechanism plays a crucial role. Moreover, a key can be non-authorized with respect to the index set or the associated policy, or both.

Let S be the set of attributes queried under a user identifier GID as a part of secret key queries such that S contains at least an attribute involved in the challenge policy. The main idea of simulating secret keys of DKW-MA-ABE was to sample a special vector $d \in \mathbb{Z}_q^{s_{max}}$ such that the inner product of d with M_i' is zero for all $i \in \rho^{-1}(S \cup \mathcal{C})$ and to set the hash values as

$$\mathsf{H}(\mathsf{GID} \parallel j) = (g_2^b)^{d_j} \cdot g_2^{h_j}, \ \forall j \in C_{\mathbf{M}'}, \ \text{and uniform otherwise.} \tag{2.4}$$

This, in fact, enables in simulating the secret keys using the properties of d and by embedding the matrix $\mathbf{M}'$ into the public keys of authorities linked to the challenge policy. Unfortunately, we observe that such encoding of hash values is not compatible with our hash-decomposition mechanism. Firstly, the hash function H_2 does not take a GID as input and hence it is not possible to encode the hash values depending on a vector like d which is sampled according to an unauthorized set of attributes ($S \cup \mathcal{C}$) under a given global identity. In our case, H_2 should generate a good amount of entropy for indices of key vectors irrespective of any global identity. This would restrict an adversary to gain any illegitimate information about the encrypted message from any secret key where the associated index set does not match with $\mathcal{I}^*$ even though the attributes associated to the key satisfy the challenge policy. Secondly, H_3 takes a GID as it's input along with a key vector, a column number and an index set. The role of H_3

is to make a secret key generated under a given GID useless to the adversary whenever the associated attributes does not satisfy the challenge policy.

In the static security model the simulator knows all the secret key queries in advance. We exploit this fact to prepare encodings for the hash values keeping in mind their roles in the security experiment. Our idea is to sample all possible $\{d_\phi\}_\phi$ vectors corresponding to the sets $\{S_\phi \cup C\}_\phi$ such that $S_\phi \cup C$ constitutes an unauthorized subset of row of M and use the information of $\{d_\phi\}_\phi$ in the encodings of the hash functions. More precisely, we use an *add and subtract* technique to set the hash values as follows

$$H_2(j \parallel k \parallel \mathcal{I}^*) = (g_2^b)^{\sum_\phi d_{\phi,j}} \cdot g_2^{h_{2,j}}, \; \forall j \in C_{M'}, \text{ and uniform otherwise.}$$

$$H_3(\text{GID} \parallel \boldsymbol{u}_{\phi'} \parallel j \parallel k) = (g_2^b)^{\sum_{\phi \neq \phi'} -d_{\phi,j}} \cdot g_2^{h_{3,j}}, \; \forall j \in C_{M'}, \text{ and uniform otherwise.}$$

Now, we multiply the above hash encodings while simulating non-authorized secret key queries and obtain a hash encoding similar to Eq. (2.4).

$$H_2(j \parallel k \parallel \mathcal{I}^*) \cdot H_3(\text{GID} \parallel \boldsymbol{u}_{\phi'} \parallel j \parallel k) = (g_2^b)^{d_{\phi',j}} \cdot g_2^{h_{2,j}+h_{3,j}} \; \forall j \in C_{M'}.$$

For simplicity of this section, we have ignored a few additional elements in the above encodings that connect the hash values with the H_1 encodings which actually facilitates in using the fact that $\boldsymbol{d}_\phi \cdot M'_i = 0$ for all $i \in \rho^{-1}(S_\phi \cup C)$ for non-authorized keys such that $\mathcal{I}_{\boldsymbol{u}_\phi} = \mathcal{I}^*$. Lastly, when simulating authorized secret keys we use the basis $\widetilde{S}$ to obtain a vector η satisfying $\eta \cdot \boldsymbol{u}_\phi = 0$ with the help of the admissibility condition $\boldsymbol{u}_\phi \cdot (\boldsymbol{v}_0 - \boldsymbol{v}_1) = 0$ for all keys leading to a successful decryption of the challenge ciphertext. The full security analysis can be found in Sect. 5.3.

2.2   Constructing the Large Universe MA-ABUIPFE

We recall that in the large universe setting each authority is allowed to control exponentially many attributes. We upgrade our small universe scheme to a large universe MA-ABUIPFE (LMA-ABUIPFE) by extending the techniques presented in [36] from encrypting a fixed length message to encrypting an unbounded length vector in the context of MA-ABUIPFE. To support exponentially many attributes, we use an additional hash function R which maps arbitrary attributes to elements of $\mathbb{G}_2$. We replace the map ρ of the LSSS access structure (M, ρ) by decomposition of two mappings T and δ, that is $\rho(i) = T(\delta(i)) = \theta$ where δ labels row numbers i of the LSSS access matrix to some attributes $\delta(i)$ and T assigns the attributes $\delta(i)$ to its respective authorities denoted by θ. Our LMA-ABUIPFE is described as follows.

$$\mathsf{PK}_\theta : ([\![\alpha_\theta]\!]_T, [\![y_{\theta,2}]\!]_1, \ldots, [\![y_{\theta,s_{\max}}]\!]_1)$$
$$\mathsf{MSK}_\theta : (\alpha_\theta, y_{\theta,2}, \ldots, y_{\theta,s_{\max}})$$

$$\mathsf{CT}_{v,P} : \begin{array}{c} C_0 = [\![\boldsymbol{v} + \boldsymbol{z}]\!]_T, \quad C_{1,i} = [\![\boldsymbol{M}_i \mathbf{B} + \boldsymbol{\vartheta}_i]\!]_T, \quad C_{2,i} = [\![r_i]\!], \\ C_{3,i,j,k} = e([\![M_{i,j} x_{j,k}]\!]_1, \mathsf{H}_2(j \parallel k \parallel \mathcal{I})) \cdot [\![r_i y^{(2)}_{\rho(i),j,k}]\!]_T, \\ C_{4,i,j} = [\![M_{i,j} f_j + r_i y_{\rho(i),j}]\!]_1, \quad C_{5,i,j} = \mathsf{R}(\delta(i) \parallel j \parallel \mathcal{I}) \\ \forall i \in [\ell], \; j \in [2, s_{\max}], \; k \in [n] \end{array}$$

$$\mathsf{SK}_{\mathsf{GID},t,u} : \begin{array}{c} \displaystyle\prod_{k=1}^{n} \mathsf{H}_1(t \parallel k \parallel \mathcal{I})^{\alpha_\theta \cdot u_k} \cdot \displaystyle\prod_{j=2}^{s_{\max}} \prod_{k=1}^{n} ([\![y^{(2)}_{\theta,j,k}]\!]_2 \cdot [\![y^{(3)}_{\theta,j,k}]\!]_2)^{u_k} \cdot \displaystyle\prod_{j=1}^{s_{\max}} \mathsf{R}(t \parallel j \parallel \mathcal{I})^{\tau_j}, \\ \mathbf{Z}_{t,j} = [\![\tau_j]\!]_1, \; \forall j \in [s_{\max}] \end{array}$$

The components $\boldsymbol{\vartheta}_i, \boldsymbol{y}^{(2)}_{\theta,j}, \boldsymbol{y}^{(3)}_{\theta,j}$ are defined similarly as in our MA-ABUIPFE scheme.

$$[\![\vartheta_{i,k}]\!]_T = e(r_i [\![\alpha_{\rho(i)}]\!]_1, \mathsf{H}_1(\rho(i) \parallel k \parallel \mathcal{I}_v)),$$
$$[\![y^{(2)}_{\theta,j,k}]\!]_T = e([\![y_{\theta,j}]\!]_1, \mathsf{H}_2(j \parallel k \parallel \mathcal{I})), \quad [\![y^{(2)}_{\theta,j,k}]\!]_2 = \mathsf{H}_2(j \parallel k \parallel \mathcal{I})^{y_{\theta,j}},$$
$$[\![y^{(3)}_{\theta,j,k}]\!]_2 = \mathsf{H}_3(\mathsf{GID} \parallel \boldsymbol{u} \parallel j \parallel k)^{y_{\theta,j}}, \; \forall k \in [n].$$

The decryption procedure is similar to our MA-ABUIPFE scheme. We consider static security of LMA-ABUIPFE and model the hash functions as random oracles. However, it may not be possible to base security on the plain DBDH assumption. Following the same notations that we used to sketch the proof technique of our MA-ABUIPFE, we discuss the main reason which prevent using the DBDH assumption as before. The R-values related to the authorities in the challenge policy in our proposed LMA-ABUIPFE scheme described above are roughly set as $\mathsf{R}(t \parallel j \parallel \mathcal{I}^*) = g_2^{\zeta_{t,j}} g_2^{a M'_{i,j}}$, where $\zeta_{t,j}$ is a random $\mathbb{Z}_q$-element and $M'_{i,j}$ is the (i,j)-th entry of the updated LSSS matrix $\mathbf{M}'$ in the challenge policy. On the other hand, the randomness r_i used in the encryption[2] are set as $r_i = c$. Hence, the reduction requires the group element g_2^{ac} in order to simulate the components $C_{5,i,j}$ of the challenge ciphertext. However, the DBDH assumption does not make it possible to make g^{ac} available to an adversary.

Thus, for basing the security, we look into the parameterized versions of the DBDH assumptions. Unlike [36] where they consider a much more complex parameterized assumption, a primary motivation of our security reduction is to depend on a simpler parameterized assumption that is as close as possible to the plain DBDH assumption. More specifically, [36] consider an *exponent* type assumption where each instance consists of at least $O(L_{\max}^3)$ group elements and $L_{\max} \geq \max\{\ell, s_{\max}\}$, where $\ell, s_{\max}$ is the number of rows and columns of the challenge LSSS access matrix respectively. Consequently, the reduction becomes more involved and complex. In contrast, we prove the security of LMA-ABUIPFE based on the newly introduced L-DBDH assumption where each instance has $O(L^2)$ group elements with $L \geq \ell$. We show that the L-DBDH assumption is generically secure using the techniques of [12,36]. Although incomparable with the assumption used in [36], it seems that our L-DBDH assumption is weaker as it contains fewer elements. Therefore, our LMA-ABUIPFE improves upon the previous results of [36] even without considering the enhanced functionality of UIPFE.

---

[2] The ciphertext is re-randomized to ensure the distribution of its components is unharmed.

There are some other technical hurdles in the security reduction that does not directly allow using the *program and cancel* technique similar to [36] while simulating secret key queries. This is due to the fact that we are handling unbounded length messages and using a hash-decomposition mechanism on top of large universe paradigm. In contrast to the small universe scheme, an authority in a queried secret key of LMA-ABUIPFE may be present in the challenge policy but none of their attributes are linked to it. We use our *add and subtract* technique which enables the reduction to combine the decomposed hash values into a single hash value that eventually produces an adequate amount of randomness preventing the leakage of unwanted information about the underlying message vector from such secret keys.

On the other hand, if the authorities as well as some of their controlled attributes are present in the challenge policy but the associated secret key is unauthorized then we observe that the program and cancel technique of [36] is not sufficient to handle an adversary of LMA-ABUIPFE given the fact that it can query for secret keys corresponding to vectors of arbitrary lengths. In order to make these secret keys useless for an adversary irrespective of the associated lengths of vectors, we delicately program the hash queries that enables the reduction to procreate additional entropy via an interplay between the *program and cancel* technique of [36] and *add and subtract* mechanism of ours at the time of simulating such unauthorized secret keys. Although the high-level proof technique is inspired from [36], the technical obstacles mentioned above prevent applying their approach straightforwardly into our setting. As a whole, we carefully embed the L-DBDH instance into the adversary's queries by extending the [36] technique in the context of amplifying entropy for supporting computation over unbounded length vectors and at the same time making it compatible for hash-decomposition mechanism used in our scheme. We present a detailed security analysis in the full version.

3   Preliminaries

In this section, we present the notations used in this paper and the new L-DBDH assumption we introduce.

3.1   Notations

We will denote the underlying security parameter by λ throughout the paper. A function $\text{negl} : \mathbb{N} \to \mathbb{R}$ is said to be a negligible function of λ, if for every $c \in \mathbb{N}$, there exists a $\lambda_c \in \mathbb{N}$ such that $\forall \lambda > \lambda_c$, $\text{negl}(\lambda) < \lambda^{-c}$. We denote the set of positive integers $\{1, \ldots, n\}$ as $[n]$. We denote $\emptyset$ as the empty set. We use the abbreviation PPT for probabilistic polynomial-time. For a set X, we write $x \leftarrow X$ to denote that x is sampled according to the uniform distribution over the elements of X. Also for any set X, we denote by $|X|$ and 2^X the cardinality and the power set of the set X respectively. We use bold lower case letters, such as v, to denote vectors and upper-case, such as $\mathbf{M}$, for matrices. We assume all vectors, by default, are row vectors. The ith row of a matrix is denoted by $\mathbf{M}_i$ and analogously for a set of row indices I, we denote $\mathbf{M}_I$ for the sub-matrix of $\mathbf{M}$ that consists of the rows $\mathbf{M}_i, \forall i \in I$. By rowspan($\mathbf{M}$), we denote the linear span of the rows of a matrix $\mathbf{M}$.

For an integer $q \geq 2$, we let $\mathbb{Z}_q$ denote the ring of integers modulo q. We represent $\mathbb{Z}_q$ as integers in the range $(-q/2, q/2]$. The set of matrices of size $m \times n$ with elements in $\mathbb{Z}_q$ is denoted by $\mathbb{Z}_q^{m \times n}$. The operation $(\cdot)^\top$ denotes the transpose of vectors/matrices. Let $\boldsymbol{u} = (u_i)_{i \in \mathcal{I}_u} \in \mathbb{Z}_q^{|\mathcal{I}_u|}, \boldsymbol{v} = (v_i)_{i \in \mathcal{I}_v} \in \mathbb{Z}_q^{|\mathcal{I}_v|}$ where $\mathcal{I}_u$ and $\mathcal{I}_v$ are the associated index sets, then the inner product between the vectors is denoted as $\boldsymbol{v} \cdot \boldsymbol{u} = \boldsymbol{u}^\top \boldsymbol{u} = \sum_{i \in \mathcal{I}} u_i v_i \in \mathbb{Z}_q$ whenever $\mathcal{I}_u = \mathcal{I}_v = \mathcal{I}$.

3.2 Complexity Assumptions

We use bilinear groups of prime order to build our MA-ABUIPFE schemes.

Here, we formally define the DBDH assumption and a parameterized version of it, we call L-DBDH which would underlie of security of our small and large universe MA-ABUIPFE schemes respectively.

Assumption 3.1 (Decisional Bilinear Diffie-Hellman (DBDH). [14,38]) *For a security parameter* $\lambda \in \mathbb{N}$, *let* $\mathsf{G} = (q, \mathbb{G}_1, \mathbb{G}_2, \mathbb{G}_T, g, e) \leftarrow \mathcal{G}(1^\lambda)$ *be a bilinear group and let* $a, b, c \leftarrow \mathbb{Z}_q$. *The* DBDH *assumption states that for any* PPT *adversary* $\mathcal{A}$, *there exists a negligible function* negl *such that for any security parameter* $\lambda \in \mathbb{N}$, *given the distribution* $(\mathsf{G}, [\![a]\!]_1, [\![c]\!]_1, [\![a]\!]_2, [\![b]\!]_2, [\![\tau]\!]_T)$, $\mathcal{A}$ *has advantage*

$$\mathsf{Adv}_{\mathcal{A}}^{\mathsf{DBDH}}(\lambda) = \left| \Pr\left[1 \leftarrow \mathcal{A}\left(1^\lambda, \mathcal{D}, [\![abc]\!]_T\right)\right] - \Pr\left[1 \leftarrow \mathcal{A}\left(1^\lambda, \mathcal{D}, [\![\tau]\!]_T\right)\right] \right| \leq \mathsf{negl}(\lambda),$$

Assumption 3.2 (L-Decisional Bilinear Diffie-Hellman (L-DBDH)). *Let* $\mathsf{G} = (q, \mathbb{G}_1, \mathbb{G}_2, \mathbb{G}_T, g, e) \leftarrow \mathcal{G}(1^\lambda)$ *be a bilinear group and let* $a, b, c, \mu_1, \ldots, \mu_L \leftarrow \mathbb{Z}_q$. *The* L-DBDH *assumption states that for any* PPT *adversary* $\mathcal{A}$, *there exists a negligible function* negl *such that for any security parameter* $\lambda \in \mathbb{N}$, *given the distribution*

$$\left(\mathsf{G}, \begin{pmatrix} [\![b]\!]_1, [\![c]\!]_1, \\ [\![a]\!]_2, [\![b]\!]_2 \end{pmatrix}, \left\{ \begin{matrix} [\![a\mu_i]\!]_1, [\![c/\mu_i]\!]_1, \\ [\![a\mu_i]\!]_2 \end{matrix} \right\}_{i \in [L]}, \left\{ \begin{matrix} [\![c\mu_\iota/\mu_i]\!]_1, [\![ac\mu_\iota/\mu_i]\!]_1, \\ [\![ac\mu_\iota/\mu_i]\!]_2 \end{matrix} \right\}_{\substack{i, \iota \in [L], \\ i \neq \iota}}, [\![\tau]\!]_T \right)$$

$\mathcal{A}$ *has advantage*

$$\mathsf{Adv}_{\mathcal{A}}^{L\text{-}\mathsf{DBDH}}(\lambda) = \left| \Pr\left[1 \leftarrow \mathcal{A}\left(1^\lambda, \mathcal{D}, [\![abc]\!]_T\right)\right] - \Pr\left[1 \leftarrow \mathcal{A}\left(1^\lambda, \mathcal{D}, [\![\tau]\!]_T\right)\right] \right| \leq \mathsf{negl}(\lambda),$$

4 Decentralized (Large Universe) MA-ABUIPFE for LSSS

A large universe decentralized multi-authority attribute-based inner-product functional encryption (LMA-ABUIPFE) scheme LMA-ABUIPFE = (GlobalSetup, LocalSetup, KeyGen, Encrypt, Decrypt) for access structures captured by linear secret sharing schemes (LSSS) over some finite field $\mathbb{Z}_q$ with $q = q(\lambda)$ and inner product value space $\mathcal{U}$ consists of five algorithms with the following syntax. We denote by $\mathcal{AU}$ the authority universe and by $\mathcal{GID}$ the universe of users' global identifiers in the system. The attribute universe is denoted as $\mathsf{U}_{\mathsf{att}}$ which may be arbitrary. Further, an authority $\theta \in \mathcal{AU}$ may have any arbitrary number of attributes from $\mathsf{U}_{\mathsf{att}}$ under its control. Following [36], we assume a publicly computable function $\mathsf{T} : \mathsf{U}_{\mathsf{att}} \to \mathcal{AU}$ that maps each attribute $t \in \mathsf{U}_{\mathsf{att}}$ to a unique authority $\theta = \mathsf{T}(t)$. The algorithms proceed as follows:

GlobalSetup(1^λ, s_{max}): It is the global setup algorithm which on input the security parameter λ and a maximum width s_{max} of the LSSS matrix, and outputs the global public parameters GP. We assume that GP includes the descriptions of $\mathcal{AU}$ and $\mathcal{GID}$.

LocalSetup(GP, θ): The authority $\theta \in \mathcal{AU}$ runs the local setup algorithm during its initialization with the global parameters GP and generates its public parameters and a master secret key pair $(\text{PK}_\theta, \text{MSK}_\theta)$.

KeyGen(GP, GID, MSK$_\theta$, t, u, $\mathcal{I}_u$): The key generation algorithm takes input the global parameter GP, a user's global identifier GID $\in \mathcal{GID}$, a master secret key MSK$_\theta$ for authority θ controlling an attribute $t \in U_{\text{att}}$, and a vector $u \in \mathbb{Z}_q^{|\mathcal{I}_u|}$ with an associated index set $\mathcal{I}_u$. It outputs a secret key $\text{SK}_{\text{GID},t,u}$ which contains $(u, \mathcal{I}_u)$.

Encrypt(GP, $(\mathbf{M}, \delta)$, $\{\text{PK}_\theta\}_\theta$, v, $\mathcal{I}_v$): The encryption algorithm takes input the global parameter GP, an LSSS access structure $(\mathbf{M}, \delta)$ where $\mathbf{M}$ is a matrix over $\mathbb{Z}_q$ and δ is a row-labeling function that assigns to each row of $\mathbf{M}$ an attribute in U_{att}. We define the function $\rho : [\ell] \to \mathcal{AU}$ as $\rho(\cdot) := \mathsf{T}(\delta(\cdot))$ which maps row indices of $\mathbf{M}$ to authorities $\theta \in \mathcal{AU}$. Accordingly, the encryption algorithm further takes a set $\{\text{PK}_\theta\}_\theta$ of public keys for all the authorities in the range of ρ, and a message vector $v \in \mathbb{Z}_q^{|\mathcal{I}_v|}$ with an associated index set $\mathcal{I}_v$. It outputs a ciphertext CT. We assume that CT implicitly contains the description of $(\mathbf{M}, \delta)$ and $\mathcal{I}_v$.

Decrypt(GP, GID, CT, $\{\text{SK}_{\text{GID},t,u}\}_t$): The decryption algorithm takes in the global parameters GP, a ciphertext CT generated with respect to some LSSS access policy $(\mathbf{M}, \delta)$ and an index set $\mathcal{I}$ associated to the message, and a collection of keys $\{\text{SK}_{\text{GID},t,u}\}_t$ corresponding to user ID-attribute pairs (GID, $S \subseteq U_{\text{att}}$) and a key vector $(u, \mathcal{I}_u)$ possessed by a user with global identifier GID. It outputs a message ζ when the collection of attributes associated with the secret keys $\{\text{SK}_{\text{GID},t,u}\}_t$ satisfies the LSSS access policy $(\mathbf{M}, \delta)$, i.e., when the vector $(1, 0, \ldots, 0)$ belongs to the linear span of those rows of $\mathbf{M}$ which are mapped by δ to the set of attributes in S that corresponds to the secret keys $\{\text{SK}_{\text{GID},t,u}\}_{t \in S}$ possessed by the user with global identifier GID. Otherwise, decryption returns $\bot$.

Correctness: An LMA-ABUIPFE scheme for LSSS-realizable access structures and inner product message space $\mathcal{U}$ is said to be correct if for every $\lambda \in \mathbb{N}$, every message vector $v \in \mathbb{Z}_q^{|\mathcal{I}_v|}$, key vector $u \in \mathbb{Z}_q^{|\mathcal{I}_u|}$ such that $\mathcal{I} = \mathcal{I}_v = \mathcal{I}_u$, and GID $\in \mathcal{GID}$, every LSSS access policy $(\mathbf{M}, \delta)$, and every subset of authorities $S \subseteq U_{\text{att}}$ controlling attributes which satisfy the access structure it holds that

$$\Pr\left[\Gamma = v \cdot u \; \middle| \; \begin{array}{l} \text{GP} \leftarrow \text{GlobalSetup}(1^\lambda, 1^n), \\ (\text{PK}_\theta, \text{MSK}_\theta) \leftarrow \text{LocalSetup}(\text{GP}, \theta), \\ \text{SK}_{\text{GID},t,u} \leftarrow \text{KeyGen}(\text{GP}, \text{GID}, \text{MSK}_\theta, t, u), \\ \text{CT} \leftarrow \text{Encrypt}(\text{GP}, (\mathbf{M}, \delta), \{\text{PK}_\theta\}_\theta, v), \\ \Gamma = \text{Decrypt}(\text{GP}, \text{CT}, \{\text{SK}_{\text{GID},t,u}\}_{t \in S}) \end{array} \right] = 1.$$

Static Security: In this paper, we consider static security for LMA-ABUIPFE formalized by the following game between a challenger and an adversary. The static security model is adapted from [36], defined for MA-ABE, to the context of LMA-ABUIPFE. We emphasize that unlike MA-ABE, our static security model allows the adversary to ask for secret keys which are capable of decrypting the challenge ciphertext.

Global Setup: The challenger runs $\mathsf{GlobalSetup}(1^\lambda, s_{\max})$ to get and send the global public parameters GP to the attacker.

Adversary's Queries: The adversary sends the following queries:

1. A list $\mathcal{C} \subset \mathcal{AU}$ of corrupt authorities and their respective public parameters $\{\mathsf{PK}_\theta\}_{\theta \in \mathcal{C}}$, which it might have created in a malicious way.

2. A set $\mathcal{N} \subset \mathcal{AU}$ of non-corrupt authorities, i.e., $\mathcal{C} \cap \mathcal{N} = \emptyset$, for which the adversary requests the public keys.

3. A set $\mathcal{Q} = \{(\mathsf{GID}, S, \boldsymbol{u}, \mathcal{I}_u)\}$ of secret key queries with $\mathsf{GID} \in \mathcal{GID}$, $S \subseteq \mathsf{U}_{\mathrm{att}}$ such that $\mathsf{T}(S) \cap \mathcal{C} = \emptyset$, $\boldsymbol{u} \in \mathbb{Z}^{|\mathcal{I}_u|}$ and $\mathcal{I}_u \subset \mathbb{Z}$ where GIDs are distinct in each of these tuples.

4. Two message vectors $\boldsymbol{v}_0, \boldsymbol{v}_1 \in \mathbb{Z}_q^{|\mathcal{I}^*|}$ having the same index set $\mathcal{I}^*$, and a challenge LSSS access policy $(\mathbf{M}, \delta)$ with $\mathbf{M} = (M_{i,j})_{\ell \times s_{\max}} = (\mathbf{M}_1, \ldots, \mathbf{M}_\ell)^\top \in \mathbb{Z}_q^{\ell \times s_{\max}}$, $\delta : [\ell] \to \mathsf{U}_{\mathrm{att}}$ and satisfying the constraint that for each $(\mathsf{GID}, S, \boldsymbol{u}, \mathcal{I}_u) \in \mathcal{Q}$, either $S \cup \bigcup_{\theta \in \mathcal{C}} \mathsf{T}^{-1}(\theta) \subseteq [\ell]$ constitutes an unauthorized subset of rows of the access matrix $\mathbf{M}$ or the secret key vector $\boldsymbol{u}$ satisfies the relation $(\boldsymbol{v}_0 - \boldsymbol{v}_1) \cdot \boldsymbol{u} = 0$ whenever $\mathcal{I}_u = \mathcal{I}^*$. Note that the set $\bigcup_{\theta \in \mathcal{C}} \mathsf{T}^{-1}(\theta)$ contains the attributes belonging to the corrupt authorities.

Challenger's Replies: The challenger flips a random coin $\beta \leftarrow \{0, 1\}$ and replies with the following:

1. The public keys $\mathsf{PK}_\theta \leftarrow \mathsf{LocalSetup}(\mathsf{GP}, \theta)$ for all $\theta \in \mathcal{N}$.

2. The secret keys $\mathsf{SK}_{\mathsf{GID},t,\boldsymbol{u}} \leftarrow \mathsf{KeyGen}(\mathsf{GP}, \mathsf{GID}, \mathsf{MSK}_\theta, t, \boldsymbol{u})$ for all $(\mathsf{GID}, S, \boldsymbol{u}) \in \mathcal{Q}, t \in S$.

3. The challenge ciphertext $\mathsf{CT} \leftarrow \mathsf{Encrypt}(\mathsf{GP}, (\mathbf{M}, \delta), \{\mathsf{PK}_\theta\}_{\theta \in \mathcal{C} \cup \mathcal{N}}, \boldsymbol{v}_\beta)$.

Guess: The adversary outputs a guess β' for β.

The advantage of the adversary $\mathcal{A}$ is $\mathsf{Adv}_{\mathcal{A},\mathrm{SS\text{-}CPA}}^{\mathsf{LMA\text{-}ABUIPFE}}(\lambda) \triangleq |\Pr[\beta = \beta'] - 1/2|$.

Definition 4.1 (Static Security for LMA-ABUIPFE for LSSS) *An* LMA-ABUIPFE *scheme for* LSSS-*realizable access structures satisfies static security if for any* PPT *adversary* $\mathcal{A}$ *there exists* $\mathsf{negl}(\cdot)$ *such that for all* $\lambda \in \mathbb{N}$, *we have* $\mathsf{Adv}_{\mathcal{A},\mathrm{SS\text{-}CPA}}^{\mathsf{LMA\text{-}ABUIPFE}}(\lambda)$ $\leq \mathsf{negl}(\lambda)$.

Remark 4.1 (Static Security in the Random Oracle Model.) *Similar to [19, 21, 36], we additionally consider the aforementioned notion of selective security with static corruption in the ROM. In this context, we assume a global hash function* H *published as part of the global public parameters and accessible by all the parties in the system. In the security proof, we will model* H *as a random oracle programmed by the challenger. In the security game, therefore, we let the adversary* $\mathcal{A}$ *submit a collection of* H-*oracle queries to the challenger immediately after seeing the global public parameters, along with all the other queries it makes in the static security game as described above.*

Remark 4.2 (Small Universe MA-ABUIPFE.) *The above definition of* LMA-ABUIPFE *captures the large universe scenario where one authority can control multiple attributes. We can similarly define a small universe* MA-ABUIPFE *or simply* MA-ABUIPFE *by restricting each authority to control only a single attribute [36]. Hence, we would use the words "authority" and "attribute" interchangeably in the case of* MA-ABUIPFE. *There are a few syntactic and semantic changes in the above definition when adapted for the small universe setting:*

1. *There is a bijection between the attribute universe* $\mathsf{U}_{\mathsf{att}}$ *and the authority universe* $\mathcal{AU}$.
2. $\mathsf{LocalSetup}(\mathsf{GP}, t)$ *outputs* $(\mathsf{PK}_t, \mathsf{MSK}_t)$ *for an authority/attribute* $t \in \mathcal{AU}$.
3. $\mathsf{KeyGen}(\mathsf{GP}, \mathsf{GID}, \mathsf{MSK}_t, \boldsymbol{u}, \mathcal{I}_u)$ *outputs* $\mathsf{SK}_{\mathsf{GID}, t, u}$.
4. *For an LSSS access structure* (M, δ), *we have* $\rho(\cdot) = \delta(\cdot)$ *is an injective map*.
5. *The changes in the security definition follow accordingly. Due to space constraints, we state them directly in the proof of our small universe scheme in Sect. 5.3.*

5   The Proposed Small Universe **MA-ABUIPFE** from **DBDH**

In this section, we describe the formal construction and proof for our MA-ABUIPFE scheme. The construction is in prime-order groups and uses a hash functions that will be modeled as a random oracle in the security proof.

5.1   The Construction

GlobalSetup(1^λ, s_{max}): The global setup algorithm takes input the security parameter λ, the maximum width of an LSSS matrix supported by the scheme $s_{\mathsf{max}} = s_{\mathsf{max}}(\lambda)$ and the vector length n in unary. It generates $\mathsf{G} = (q, \mathbb{G}_1, \mathbb{G}_2, \mathbb{G}_T, g, e)$. Consider the hash functions $\mathsf{H}_1 : \mathsf{U}_{\mathsf{att}} \times \mathbb{Z} \times \mathbb{Z}^* \to \mathbb{G}_2$, $\mathsf{H}_2 : [s_{\mathsf{max}}] \times \mathbb{Z} \times \mathbb{Z}^* \to \mathbb{G}_2$, $\mathsf{H}_3 : \mathcal{GID} \times \mathbb{Z}^* \times [s_{\mathsf{max}}] \to \mathbb{G}_2$. It outputs a global parameter $\mathsf{GP} = (\mathsf{G}, \mathsf{H}_1, \mathsf{H}_2, \mathsf{H}_3)$.

LocalSetup(GP, t): The authority setup algorithm takes as input GP and an authority index/attribute $t \in \mathcal{AU}$. It samples vectors $\alpha_t, y_{t,2}, \ldots, y_{t,s_{\mathsf{max}}} \leftarrow \mathbb{Z}_q$ and outputs

$$\mathsf{PK} = \left(\{ [\![\alpha_t]\!]_1, \{ [\![y_{t,j}]\!]_1 \}_{j \in \{2, \ldots, s_{\mathsf{max}}\}} \}_{t \in \mathsf{U}_{\mathsf{att}}} \right), \quad \mathsf{MSK} = \{ \{ \alpha_t, \{ y_{t,j} \}_{j \in \{2, \ldots, s_{\mathsf{max}}\}} \}_{t \in \mathsf{U}_{\mathsf{att}}} \}$$

KeyGen($\mathsf{GP}, \mathsf{GID}, \mathsf{MSK}_t, \boldsymbol{u}, \mathcal{I}_u$): The key generation algorithm takes input GP, the user's global identifier GID, the authority's secret key MSK_t and a vector $\boldsymbol{u} \in \mathbb{Z}_q^{|\mathcal{I}_u|}$. It proceeds as follows

1. Parse $\mathcal{I}_u = \{\iota_1, \ldots, \iota_n\}$ and $\boldsymbol{u} = (u_{\iota_1}, \ldots, u_{\iota_n})$.
2. Compute

$$\mathsf{SK}_{t,u} = \prod_{k=1}^{n} \mathsf{H}_1(t \parallel \iota_k \parallel \mathcal{I}_u)^{\alpha_t u_{\iota_k}} \cdot \prod_{j=2}^{s_{\mathsf{max}}} \prod_{k=1}^{n} (\mathsf{H}_2(j \parallel \iota_k \parallel \mathcal{I}_u) \cdot \mathsf{H}_3(\mathsf{GID} \parallel \boldsymbol{u} \parallel j \parallel \iota_k))^{y_{t,j} u_{\iota_k}}.$$

3. Output $\mathsf{SK}_{\mathsf{GID}, t, u} = (\mathsf{GID}, \boldsymbol{u}, \mathsf{SK}_{t,u}, \mathcal{I}_u)$ as the secret key.

Encrypt($\mathsf{GP}, (M, \rho), \{\mathsf{PK}_t\}, v, \mathcal{I}_v$): The encryption algorithm takes input the global parameter GP, an LSSS access structure (M, ρ) where $M = (M_1, \ldots, M_\ell)^\top \in \mathbb{Z}_q^{\ell \times s_{\mathsf{max}}}$ and $\rho : [\ell] \to \mathcal{AU}$, a set $\{\mathsf{PK}_t\}$ of public keys for all the authorities in the range of ρ, and a message vector $v \in \mathbb{Z}_q^m$. The function maps the row indices of M to authorities or attributes. We assume ρ is an injective function, that is, an authority/attribute is associated with at most one row of M. The algorithm proceeds as follows:

1. Parse $\mathcal{I}_v = \{\iota_1, \ldots, \iota_m\}$ and $v = (v_{\iota_1}, \ldots, v_{\iota_m})$.

2. Sample $\{r_i \leftarrow \mathbb{Z}_q\}_{i \in [\ell]}$ and $\boldsymbol{f} = (f_2, \ldots, f_{s_{\max}}) \leftarrow \mathbb{Z}_q^{s_{\max}-1}$.

3. Sample $z, \boldsymbol{b}_2, \ldots, \boldsymbol{b}_{s_{\max}}, \boldsymbol{x}_2, \ldots, \boldsymbol{x}_{s_{\max}} \leftarrow \mathbb{Z}_q^m$.

4. Set the matrix $\mathbf{B} = \left[z, \boldsymbol{b}_2, \ldots, \boldsymbol{b}_{s_{\max}} \right]^{\top}_{s_{\max} \times m}$.

5. Compute $\vartheta_{i,k} = e(r_i[\![\alpha_{\rho(i)}]\!]_1, \mathsf{H}_1(\rho(i) \parallel \iota_k \parallel \mathcal{I}_v))$ and set $\vartheta_i := (\vartheta_{i,1}, \ldots, \vartheta_{i,m})$.

6. Compute the following terms:

$$C_0 = [\![\boldsymbol{v} + \boldsymbol{z}]\!]_T, \quad C_{1,i} = [\![\boldsymbol{M}_i \mathbf{B} + \vartheta_i]\!]_T, \quad C_{2,i} = [\![r_i]\!]_1,$$
$$C_{3,i,j,k} = e([\![M_{i,j}x_{j,k}]\!]_1, \mathsf{H}_2(j \parallel \iota_k \parallel \mathcal{I}_v)) \cdot e(r_i[\![y_{\rho(i),j}]\!]_1, \mathsf{H}_2(j \parallel \iota_k \parallel \mathcal{I}_v)),$$
$$C_{4,i,j} = [\![M_{i,j}f_j + y_{\rho(i),j}r_i]\!]_1$$

for all $i \in [\ell], j \in \{2, \ldots, s_{\max}\}, k \in [m]$.

7. Output the ciphertext

$$\mathsf{CT} = \left((\mathbf{M}, \rho), C_0, \{C_{1,i}, C_{2,i}, C_{3,i,j,k}, C_{4,i,j}\}_{i \in [\ell], j \in \{2, \ldots, s_{\max}\}, k \in [m]}, \mathcal{I}_v \right).$$

Decrypt(GP, GID, CT, $\{\mathsf{SK}_{\mathsf{GID},t,u}\}$): The decryption algorithm takes input the public key PK, a secret key $\mathsf{SK}_{S,u}$ for an attribute set $S \subseteq \mathsf{U}_{\mathsf{att}}$ and a vector $\boldsymbol{u} \in \mathbb{Z}_q^n$ and a ciphertext CT for an access structure $(\mathbf{M}, \rho)$ with $\mathbf{M} \in \mathbb{Z}_q^{\ell \times s_{\max}}$ and an injective map $\rho : [\ell] \rightarrow \mathsf{U}_{\mathsf{att}}$.

Parse $\mathsf{SK}_{\mathsf{GID},S,u} = \left(\mathsf{GID}, \boldsymbol{u}, \{\mathsf{SK}_{\rho(i),u}\}_{\rho(i) \in S}, \mathcal{I}_u \right)$, where $i \in [\ell]$ and $\mathsf{CT} = ((\mathbf{M}, \rho), C_0, \{C_{1,i}, C_{2,i}, C_{3,i,j,k}, C_{4,i,j}\}_{i \in [\ell], j \in \{2, \ldots, s_{\max}\}, k \in [m]}, \mathcal{I}_v)$. Denote $I = \{i | \rho(i) \in S\} \subseteq [\ell]$. If $(1, 0, \ldots, 0)$ is not in the span of $\mathbf{M}_I$ (i.e., $\mathbf{M}$ restricted to the set of rows from I) or $\mathcal{I}_u \neq \mathcal{I}_v$ decryption returns $\bot$. Else, when S satisfies $(\mathbf{M}, \rho)$, the algorithm finds $\{w_i \in \mathbb{Z}_q\}_{i \in I}$ such that $(1, 0, \ldots, 0) = \sum_{i \in I} w_i \mathbf{M}_i$. It then computes $[\![\Gamma]\!]_T = C_0 \cdot \boldsymbol{u} \cdot [\![\mu]\!]_T$ where $[\![\mu]\!]_T$ is given by

$$\left(\prod_{i \in I} \left[\frac{C_{1,i} \cdot \boldsymbol{u} \cdot \prod_{j=2}^{s_{\max}} \prod_{k=1}^{n} u_{\iota_k} \cdot C_{3,i,j,k} \cdot e(C_{4,i,j}, \mathsf{H}_3(\mathsf{GID} \parallel \boldsymbol{u} \parallel j \parallel \iota_k)^{u_{\iota_k}})}{e\left(\mathsf{SK}_{\rho(i),u}, C_{2,i}\right)} \right]^{w_i} \right)^{-1}$$

and outputs $\log_{g_T}([\![\Gamma]\!]_T)$.

5.2 Correctness

Consider a secret key $\mathsf{SK}_{\mathsf{GID},S,u} = (\mathsf{GID}, \boldsymbol{u}, \{\mathsf{SK}_{t,u}\}_{t \in S}, \mathcal{I}_u)$ consisting of a set of attributes satisfying the LSSS access structure $(\mathbf{M}, \rho)$ associated with a ciphertext $\mathsf{CT} = ((\mathbf{M}, \rho), C_0, \{C_{1,i}, C_{2,i}, C_{3,i,j,k}, C_{4,i,j}\}_{i \in [\ell], j \in \{2, \ldots, s_{\max}\}, k \in [m]}, \mathcal{I}_v)$ such that $\mathcal{I}_u = \mathcal{I}_v = \mathcal{I}$. In particular, the vector $(1, 0, \ldots, 0) \in \mathsf{rowspan}(\mathbf{M}_I)$ corresponding to the set of indices $I = \{i \in I | \rho(i) = t \in S\}$.

For each $i \in I$, we have the following:

$$e(\mathsf{SK}_{\rho(i),u}, C_{2,i}) = \prod_{k=1}^{n} e(g_1, \mathsf{H}_1(\rho(i) \parallel \iota_k \parallel \mathcal{I}))^{r_i \alpha_{\rho(i)} u_{\iota_k}} \cdot$$

$$\prod_{j=2}^{s_{\max}} \prod_{k=1}^{n} (e(g_1, \mathsf{H}_2(j \parallel \iota_k \parallel \mathcal{I})) \cdot e(g_1, \mathsf{H}_3(\mathsf{GID} \parallel \boldsymbol{u} \parallel j \parallel \iota_k)))^{r_i y_{\rho(i),j} u_{\iota_k}}$$

For $i \in I, j \in \{2, \ldots, s_{\max}\}, k \in [n]$,

$$u_{\iota_k} C_{3,i,j,k} = e([\![M_{i,j} x_{j,k}]\!]_1, \mathsf{H}_2(j \parallel \iota_k \parallel \mathcal{I}))^{u_{\iota_k}} \cdot e(g_1, \mathsf{H}_2(j \parallel \iota_k \parallel \mathcal{I}))^{r_i y_{\rho(i),j} u_{\iota_k}}$$

For $i \in I, j \in \{2, \ldots, s_{\max}\}, k \in [n]$,

$$e(C_{4,i,j}, \mathsf{H}_3(\mathsf{GID} \parallel \boldsymbol{u} \parallel j \parallel \iota_k)^{u_{\iota_k}})$$
$$= e([\![M_{i,j} f_j]\!]_1, \mathsf{H}_3(\mathsf{GID} \parallel \boldsymbol{u} \parallel j \parallel \iota_k))^{u_{\iota_k}} \cdot e(g_1, \mathsf{H}_3(\mathsf{GID} \parallel \boldsymbol{u} \parallel j \parallel \iota_k))^{r_i y_{\rho(i),j} u_{\iota_k}}$$

Finally, for each $i \in I$, we have $C_{1,i} = [\![M_i \mathbf{B} + \boldsymbol{\vartheta}_i]\!]_T$ and so

$$\frac{C_{1,i} \cdot \boldsymbol{u} \cdot \prod_{j=2}^{s_{\max}} \prod_{k=1}^{n} (u_{\iota_k} \cdot C_{3,i,j,k} \cdot e(C_{4,i,j}, \mathsf{H}_3(\mathsf{GID} \parallel \boldsymbol{u} \parallel j \parallel \iota_k)^{u_{\iota_k}}))}{e\left(\mathsf{SK}_{\rho(i),\boldsymbol{u}}, C_{2,i}\right)}$$

$$= [\![M_i \mathbf{B} \cdot \boldsymbol{u}]\!]_T \prod_{k=1}^{n} e(g_1, \mathsf{H}_1(\rho(i) \parallel \iota_k \parallel \mathcal{I}))^{r_i \alpha_{\rho(i)} u_{\iota_k}} \cdot$$

$$\frac{\prod_{j=2}^{s_{\max}} \prod_{k=1}^{n} (u_{\iota_k} \cdot C_{3,i,j,k} \cdot e(C_{4,i,j}, \mathsf{H}_3(\mathsf{GID} \parallel \boldsymbol{u} \parallel j \parallel \iota_k)^{u_{\iota_k}}))}{e\left(\mathsf{SK}_{\rho(i),\boldsymbol{u}}, C_{2,i}\right)}$$

$$= [\![M_i \mathbf{B} \cdot \boldsymbol{u}]\!]_T \cdot \prod_{j=2}^{s_{\max}} \prod_{k=1}^{n} e([\![M_{i,j} x_{j,k}]\!]_1, \mathsf{H}_2(j \parallel \iota_k \parallel \mathcal{I}))^{u_{\iota_k}} \cdot$$

$$\prod_{j=2}^{s_{\max}} \prod_{k=1}^{n} e([\![M_{i,j} f_j]\!]_1, \mathsf{H}_3(\mathsf{GID} \parallel \boldsymbol{u} \parallel j \parallel \iota_k))^{u_{\iota_k}}$$

Since $\mathsf{SK}_{S,\boldsymbol{u}}$ corresponds to a set of qualified authorities, $\exists \{w_i \in \mathbb{Z}_q\}_{i \in I}$ such that $\sum_{i \in I} w_i M_i \mathbf{B} \cdot \boldsymbol{u} = (1, 0, \ldots, 0) \mathbf{B} \cdot \boldsymbol{u} = \boldsymbol{z} \cdot \boldsymbol{u}$ and it holds that $\sum_{i \in I} w_i M_{i,j} = 0, \forall j \in \{2, \ldots, s_{\max}\}$. Hence, we have

$$\prod_{i \in I} \left[\frac{C_{1,i} \cdot \boldsymbol{u} \cdot \prod_{j=2}^{s_{\max}} \prod_{k=1}^{n} (u_{\iota_k} \cdot C_{3,i,j,k} \cdot e(C_{4,i,j}, \mathsf{H}_3(\mathsf{GID} \parallel \boldsymbol{u} \parallel j \parallel \iota_k)^{u_{\iota_k}}))}{e\left(\mathsf{SK}_{\rho(i),\boldsymbol{u}}, C_{2,i}\right)} \right]^{w_i}$$

$$= [\![\sum_{i \in I} w_i M_i \mathbf{B} \cdot \boldsymbol{u}]\!]_T = [\![\boldsymbol{z} \cdot \boldsymbol{u}]\!]_T$$

Finally, the message is recovered as $\log_{g_T}([\![\Gamma]\!]_T)$ where

$$[\![\Gamma]\!]_T = (C_0 \cdot \boldsymbol{u}) / [\![\boldsymbol{z} \cdot \boldsymbol{u}]\!]_T = [\![\boldsymbol{v} \cdot \boldsymbol{u} + \boldsymbol{z} \cdot \boldsymbol{u}]\!]_T / [\![\boldsymbol{z} \cdot \boldsymbol{u}]\!]_T = [\![\boldsymbol{v} \cdot \boldsymbol{u}]\!]_T$$

5.3 Security Analysis

Theorem 5.1. *If the* DBDH *assumption holds, then all* PPT *adversaries have a negligible advantage in breaking the static security of the proposed small universe* MA-ABUIPFE *scheme in the random oracle model.*

Proof. We prove this theorem by showing that if there is any PPT adversary $\mathcal{A}$ who breaks the static security of MA-ABUIPFE then there is a PPT adversary $\mathcal{B}$ who solves the DBDH problem with a non-negligible advantage. Suppose, $\mathcal{B}$ gets an instance $(G, [\![a]\!]_1, [\![c]\!]_1, [\![a]\!]_2, [\![b]\!]_2, [\![\tau]\!]_T)$ of the DBDH problem where $G = (q, \mathbb{G}_1, \mathbb{G}_2, \mathbb{G}_T, g, e) \leftarrow \mathcal{G}(1^\lambda)$ is a group description, the elements $a, b, c \leftarrow \mathbb{Z}_q$ are random integers, and the element $\tau \in \mathbb{Z}_q$ is either abc or a random element of $\mathbb{Z}_q$. The algorithm $\mathcal{B}$ works as follows: On input λ, $\mathcal{A}$ outputs $s_{\max}, \mathsf{U}_{\mathsf{att}}$ and queries the following.

Attacker's Queries: Upon initialization, the adversary $\mathcal{A}$ sends the following to $\mathcal{B}$:

(a) A list $\mathcal{C} \subset \mathcal{AU}$ of corrupt authorities and their respective public keys

$$\{\mathsf{PK}_t = (\mathrm{Y}_{t,1}, \mathrm{Y}_{t,2}, \dots, \mathrm{Y}_{t,s_{\max}})\}_{t \in \mathcal{C}},$$

where $\mathrm{Y}_{t,1}, \mathrm{Y}_{t,2}, \dots, \mathrm{Y}_{t,s_{\max}} \in \mathbb{G}_1$ for all $t \in \mathcal{C}$.

(b) A set $\mathcal{N} \subset \mathcal{AU}$ of non-corrupt authorities, i.e., $\mathcal{C} \cap \mathcal{N} = \emptyset$, for which $\mathcal{A}$ requests the public keys.

(c) A collection of hash queries $\mathcal{H}_1 = \{(t, \iota_k, \mathcal{I}) : t \in \mathsf{U}_{\mathsf{att}}, \iota_k \in \mathbb{Z}, \mathcal{I} \subset \mathbb{N}\}, \mathcal{H}_2 = \{(j, \iota_k, \mathcal{I}) : j \in \{2, \dots, s_{\max}\}, \iota_k \in \mathbb{Z}, \mathcal{I} \subset \mathbb{N}\}$ and $\mathcal{H}_3 = \{(\mathsf{GID}, \boldsymbol{u}, j, \iota_k) : \mathsf{GID} \in \mathcal{GID}, \boldsymbol{u} \in \mathbb{Z}^*, j \in \{2, \dots, s_{\max}\}, \iota_k \in \mathbb{Z}\}$.

(d) A set $\mathcal{Q} = \{(\mathsf{GID}, S, \boldsymbol{u}, \mathcal{I}_u)\}$ of secret key queries with $\mathsf{GID} \in \mathcal{GID}, S \subseteq \mathsf{U}_{\mathsf{att}}, \boldsymbol{u} \in \mathbb{Z}^{|\mathcal{I}_u|}$ and $\mathcal{I}_u \subset \mathbb{Z}$.

(e) Two message vectors $\boldsymbol{v}_0, \boldsymbol{v}_1 \in \mathbb{Z}_q^n$ having the same index set $\mathcal{I}^*$, and a challenge LSSS access policy $(\mathbf{M}, \rho)$ with $\mathbf{M} = (M_{i,j})_{\ell \times s_{\max}} = (\mathbf{M}_1, \dots, \mathbf{M}_\ell)^\top \in \mathbb{Z}_q^{\ell \times s_{\max}}$ and $\rho : [\ell] \to \mathcal{C} \cup \mathcal{N}$ injective and satisfying the constraint that for each $(S, \boldsymbol{u}, \mathcal{I}_u) \in \mathcal{Q}_u$, either $\rho^{-1}(\mathcal{C} \cup S) \subseteq [\ell]$ constitutes an unauthorized subset of rows of the access matrix $\mathbf{M}$ or the secret key vector $\boldsymbol{u}$ satisfies the relation $(\boldsymbol{v}_0 - \boldsymbol{v}_1) \cdot \boldsymbol{u} = 0$ whenever $\mathcal{I}_u = \mathcal{I}^*$.

Before answering $\mathcal{A}$'s queries, the adversary $\mathcal{B}$ substitute the secret sharing matrix $\mathbf{M}$ with the matrix $\mathbf{M}'$ from Lemma 3.1 of [36] computed using $\rho^{-1}(\mathcal{C})$ as the unauthorized subset of rows. Lemma 3.1 of [36] guarantees the fact that if $\mathcal{B}$ uses $\mathbf{M}'$ instead of $\mathbf{M}$ in the simulation, the view of $\mathcal{A}$ in the simulated game is information theoretically the same as if $\mathcal{B}$ would have used the original matrix $\mathbf{M}$. Furthermore, Lemma 3.1 of [36] implies that if we assume the subspace spanned by $\mathbf{M}_{\rho^{-1}(\mathcal{C})}$ has dimension $\widetilde{c}$, then so is the dimension of the subspace spanned by $\mathbf{M}'_{\rho^{-1}(\mathcal{C})}$ and $M'_{i,j} = 0$ for all $(i, j) \in \rho^{-1}(\mathcal{C}) \times [s_{\max} - \widetilde{c}]$. $\mathcal{B}$ now proceeds to answer the queries of $\mathcal{A}$. Denote $\widehat{s_{\max}} = s_{\max} - \widetilde{c}$, where $\widetilde{c}$ is the dimension of the sequence spanned by the rows of $\mathbf{M}_{\rho^{-1}(\mathcal{C})}$, the latter being the rows of $\mathbf{M}$ controlled by corrupted authorities, $\mathcal{C}$.

Note that $\mathcal{I}^*$ can be any subset of $\mathbb{Z}$ and w.l.o.g one can consider $\mathcal{I}^* = [n]^3$ for some $n \in \mathbb{N}$. Inspired by the proof techniques of prior works [3,38], the reduction first computes a basis of $(\boldsymbol{v}_0 - \boldsymbol{v}_1)^\perp$ as $\{\widetilde{\boldsymbol{b}}_1, \ldots, \widetilde{\boldsymbol{b}}_{n-1}\}$. Then the set $\widetilde{\mathcal{S}} = \{\boldsymbol{v}_0 - \boldsymbol{v}_1, \widetilde{\boldsymbol{b}}_1, \ldots, \widetilde{\boldsymbol{b}}_{n-1}\}$ form a basis of $\mathbb{Z}_q^n$. For any vector $\boldsymbol{u} \in \mathbb{Z}_q^n$, if we represent it as the linear combination of the vectors in $\widetilde{\mathcal{S}}$ as

$$\boldsymbol{u} = \zeta \cdot (\boldsymbol{v}_0 - \boldsymbol{v}_1) + \sum_{k=1}^{n-1} \zeta_k \widetilde{\boldsymbol{b}}_k, \quad \text{for some } \zeta, \zeta_k \in \mathbb{Z}_q$$

then $\zeta = 0$ whenever it holds that $(\boldsymbol{v}_0 - \boldsymbol{v}_1) \cdot \boldsymbol{u} = 0$. Let $\boldsymbol{e}_k$ be the k-th vector in the standard basis of $\mathbb{Z}_q^n$. We write $\boldsymbol{e}_i$ for each $i \in [n]$ as

$$\boldsymbol{e}_i = \eta_i \cdot (\boldsymbol{v}_0 - \boldsymbol{v}_1) + \sum_{k=1}^{n-1} \lambda_{i,k} \widetilde{\boldsymbol{b}}_k \quad \text{for some } \eta, \lambda_{i,k} \in \mathbb{Z}_q.$$

Generating Public Key: There are two cases to consider:

1. **Case 1** — $t \in \mathcal{N} \setminus \rho([\ell])$ (i.e., attribute t is absent in the challenge policy $(\mathbf{M}, \rho)$ but it belongs to a non-corrupt authority) — In this case, $\mathcal{B}$ executes the Setup algorithm according to the real experiment. It samples $\alpha_t, y_{t,2}, \ldots, y_{t,s_{\max}} \leftarrow \mathbb{Z}_q$ by itself, and computes the public key component corresponding to attribute t as $(\llbracket \alpha_t \rrbracket_1, \llbracket y_{t,2} \rrbracket_1, \ldots, \llbracket y_{t,s_{\max}} \rrbracket_1)$.

2. **Case 2**—$t \in \rho([\ell]) \setminus \mathcal{C}$ (i.e., attribute t appears in the challenge policy $(\mathbf{M}, \rho)$ and it does not belong to a corrupt authority) — In this case, $\mathcal{B}$ samples $\alpha_t', y_{t,2}', \ldots, y_{t,s_{\max}}' \leftarrow \mathbb{Z}_q$ and implicitly sets $\alpha_t = \alpha_t' + a \cdot M_{\rho^{-1}(t),1}'$ and $y_{t,j} = y_{t,j}' + a M_{\rho^{-1}(t),j}'$ for $j \in \{2, \ldots, \widehat{s_{\max}}\}$ and $y_{t,j} = y_{t,j}'$ for $j \in \{\widehat{s_{\max}} + 1, \ldots, s_{\max}\}$(these are well-defined as ρ is injective), and sets the public key elements w.r.t. attribute t as $(\llbracket \alpha_t \rrbracket_1, \llbracket y_{t,2} \rrbracket_1, \ldots, \llbracket y_{t,s_{\max}} \rrbracket_1)$ where the elements $\llbracket \alpha_t \rrbracket_1$ and $\llbracket y_{t,j} \rrbracket_1$ for $j \in \{2, \ldots, \widehat{s_{\max}}\}$ are computed as follows:

$$\llbracket \alpha_t \rrbracket_1 = \llbracket \alpha_t' \rrbracket_1 \cdot M_{\rho^{-1}(t),1}' \llbracket a \rrbracket_1, \quad \llbracket y_{t,j} \rrbracket_1 = \llbracket y_{t,j}' \rrbracket_1 \cdot M_{\rho^{-1}(t),j}' \llbracket a \rrbracket_1 \tag{5.1}$$

for all $j \in [2, \widehat{s_{\max}}]$. Note that, α_t and $\{y_{t,j}\}_{j \in \{2, \ldots, s_{\max}\}}$ are distributed uniformly over $\mathbb{Z}_q$ and hence each of these elements of the public key is properly distributed.

Answering Hash Queries:

1. H_1 **queries.** If $(\iota_k \in \mathcal{I}^* \wedge \mathcal{I} = \mathcal{I}^*)$, then sample uniformly random elements $h_{1,\widehat{k}}, h_{1,t,\iota_k}$ from $\mathbb{Z}_q$ and set

---

[3] In particular, we consider a map $\gamma : \mathcal{I}^* \to [n]$ and use $\gamma(k) = \iota_k$ throughout the security analysis.

$$H_1(t \parallel \iota_k \parallel \mathcal{I}) = (g_2^b)^{\eta_k} \cdot \prod_{\widehat{k}=1}^{n-1} g_2^{h_{1,\widehat{k}} \lambda_{k,\widehat{k}}} \cdot g_2^{h_{1,t,\iota_k}}. \tag{5.2}$$

Otherwise, if $(\iota_k \notin \mathcal{I}^* \vee \mathcal{I} \neq \mathcal{I}^*)$, then output a random $\mathbb{G}_2$ element, i.e., sample uniformly random element h'_{1,t,ι_k} from $\mathbb{Z}_q$ and set $H_1(t \parallel \iota_k \parallel \mathcal{I}) = g_2^{h'_{1,t,\iota_k}}$. The reduction stores the hash queries for future use.

2. H_2 **queries.** If $(\iota_k \in \mathcal{I}^* \wedge \mathcal{I} = \mathcal{I}^*)$, then sample uniformly random elements $h_{2,\widehat{k}}, h_{2,j,\iota_k}$ for $j \in \{2, \ldots, \widehat{s_{\max}}\}$ (in Eq. 5.3) and elements h'_{2,j,ι_k} for $j \in \{\widehat{s_{\max}} + 1, \ldots, s_{\max}\}$ from $\mathbb{Z}_q$ (in Eq. 5.4) and set

$$H_2(j \parallel \iota_k \parallel \mathcal{I}) = (g_2^b)^{\eta_k \sum_{\phi=1}^{Q} d_{\phi,j}} \cdot \prod_{\widehat{k}=1}^{n-1} g_2^{h_{2,\widehat{k}} \lambda_{k,\widehat{k}}} \cdot g_2^{h_{2,j,\iota_k}} \tag{5.3}$$

$$H_2(j \parallel \iota_k \parallel \mathcal{I}) = g_2^{h'_{2,j,\iota_k}} \tag{5.4}$$

where Q denotes the total number of *non-accepting* key queries $\{(S_\phi, \boldsymbol{u}_\phi, \mathcal{I}_{\boldsymbol{u}_\phi})\}_{\phi \in [Q]}$ made by the adversary in the case where $\mathcal{I}_{\boldsymbol{u}_\phi} = \mathcal{I}^*$ but the attributes in S_ϕ does not satisfy the challenge policy $(\mathbf{M}, \rho)$. Note that, for such secret key queries, there exists a vector $\boldsymbol{d}_\phi = (d_{\phi,1}, \ldots, d_{\phi,s_{\max}}) \in \mathbb{Z}_q^{s_{\max}}$ such that $d_{\phi,1} = 1$ and the inner product $\boldsymbol{M}'_i \cdot \boldsymbol{d}_\phi = 0$ for all $i \in \rho^{-1}(\mathcal{C} \cup S_\phi)$, where $\boldsymbol{M}'_i$ denotes the i-th row of $\mathbf{M}'$. Additionally, the set of rows $\mathcal{R} = \{\boldsymbol{M}'_i \in \mathbb{Z}_q^{s_{\max}} : i \in \rho^{-1}(\mathcal{C})\}$ has dimension c and $M'_{i,j} = 0$ for all $(i,j) \in \rho^{-1}(\mathcal{C}) \times [\widehat{s_{\max}}]$. Therefore, $\mathcal{R}$ spans the entire subspace $\mathbb{V} = \left\{(\overbrace{0, \ldots, 0}^{\widehat{s_{\max}}}, \boldsymbol{\nu}) : \boldsymbol{\nu} \in \mathbb{Z}_q^c\right\}$. Thus, it follows that $\boldsymbol{d}_\phi$ is orthogonal to any of the vectors

$$\left\{(\overbrace{0, \ldots, 0}^{\widehat{s_{\max}}}, \overbrace{0, \ldots, 0}^{j-1}, 1, \overbrace{0, \ldots, 0}^{c-j})\right\}_{j \in \{\widehat{s_{\max}}+1, \ldots, s_{\max}\}}.$$

In other words, $d_{\phi,j} = 0$ for all $j \in \{\widehat{s_{\max}} + 1, \ldots, s_{\max}\}$. Combining the above two facts, we have $(\boldsymbol{M}'_i|_{[\widehat{s_{\max}}]}) \cdot (\boldsymbol{d}_\phi|_{[\widehat{s_{\max}}]}) = 0$ for all $i \in \rho^{-1}(S_\phi)$, where for a vector $\boldsymbol{x}$, $\boldsymbol{x}|_X$ denotes a vector formed by taking the entries of $\boldsymbol{x}$ having indices in the set $X \in \mathbb{N}$. For simplicity of notation, let us denote $\boldsymbol{M}'_i \star \boldsymbol{d}_\phi = (\boldsymbol{M}'_i|_{[\widehat{s_{\max}}]}) \cdot (\boldsymbol{d}_\phi|_{[\widehat{s_{\max}}]})$ for $i \in \rho^{-1}(S_\phi)$.

Otherwise, if $(\iota_k \notin \mathcal{I}^* \vee \mathcal{I} \neq \mathcal{I}^*)$, then output a random $\mathbb{G}_2$ element, i.e., sample uniformly random element h''_{2,t,ι_k} from $\mathbb{Z}_q$ and set $H_2(j \parallel \iota_k \parallel \mathcal{I}) = g_2^{h''_{2,t,\iota_k}}$. The reduction stores the hash queries for future use.

3. H_3 **queries.** If $(\mathsf{GID}, S_\phi, \boldsymbol{u}_\phi, \mathcal{I}_{\boldsymbol{u}_\phi}) \in \mathcal{Q}$ and $S_\phi \cap \rho([\ell]) \neq \emptyset$ and $\rho^{-1}(S_\phi \cup \mathcal{C})$ constitutes an unauthorized subset of the rows of $\mathbf{M}$ then sample h_{3,j,ι_k} for

$j \in \{2, \ldots, \widehat{s_{\max}}\}$ (in Eq. 5.5) and elements h'_{3,j,ι_k} for $j \in \{\widehat{s_{\max}} + 1, \ldots, s_{\max}\}$ from $\mathbb{Z}_q$ (in Eq. 5.6) and set

$$H_3(\mathsf{GID} \parallel \boldsymbol{u}_\phi \parallel j \parallel \iota_k) = (g_2^b)^{\eta_k \sum_{\phi' \in [Q] \setminus \{\phi\}} -d_{\phi',j}} \cdot g_2^{h_{3,j,\iota_k}} \tag{5.5}$$

$$H_3(\mathsf{GID} \parallel \boldsymbol{u}_\phi \parallel j \parallel \iota_k) = g_2^{h'_{3,j,\iota_k}} \tag{5.6}$$

for all $\iota_k \in \mathcal{I}_{\boldsymbol{u}_\phi}$ such that $\mathcal{I}_{\boldsymbol{u}_\phi} = \mathcal{I}^*$ and d_ϕ is as defined above.
If $(\mathsf{GID}, S_\phi, \boldsymbol{u}_\phi, \mathcal{I}_{\boldsymbol{u}_\phi}) \in \mathcal{Q}$ and $S_\phi \cap \rho([\ell]) \neq \emptyset$ and $\mathcal{I}_{\boldsymbol{u}_\phi} \neq \mathcal{I}^*$ then sample h''_{3,j,ι_k}
uniformly at random from $\mathbb{Z}_q$ and set $H_3(\mathsf{GID} \parallel \boldsymbol{u}_\phi \parallel j \parallel \iota_k) = g_2^{h''_{3,j,\iota_k}}$.
On the other hand, if $(\mathsf{GID}, S_\phi, \boldsymbol{u}_\phi, \mathcal{I}_{\boldsymbol{u}_\phi}) \in \mathcal{Q}$ and $S_\phi \cap \rho([\ell]) \neq \emptyset$ and $\rho^{-1}(S_\phi \cup \mathcal{C})$
constitutes an authorized subset of the rows of $\mathbf{M}$ then sample $h'''_{3,j,\iota_k} \leftarrow \mathbb{Z}_q$ and set
$H_3(\mathsf{GID} \parallel \boldsymbol{u}_\phi \parallel j \parallel \iota_k) = g_2^{h'''_{3,j,\iota_k}}$. The reduction stores the hash queries for future
use. For all other cases, the reduction simple outputs a uniformly random element
from $\mathbb{G}_2$ to answer the hash query $H_3(\mathsf{GID} \parallel \boldsymbol{u}_\phi \parallel j \parallel \iota_k)$.

Generating Secret Keys: For any $(\mathsf{GID}, S_\phi, \boldsymbol{u}_\phi, \mathcal{I}_{\boldsymbol{u}_\phi}) \in \mathcal{Q}$, $\mathcal{B}$ returns a secret key
$\mathsf{SK}_{\mathsf{GID}, S_\phi, \boldsymbol{u}_\phi} = (\mathsf{GID}, \boldsymbol{u}_\phi, \{\mathsf{SK}_{t, \boldsymbol{u}_\phi}\}_{t \in S_\phi}, \mathcal{I}_{\boldsymbol{u}_\phi})$, where it computes each of its components as follows. We denote

$$H_{2 \cdot 3}(\mathsf{GID}, \boldsymbol{u}_\phi, j, k) = H_2(j \parallel \iota_k \parallel \mathcal{I}_{\boldsymbol{u}_\phi}) \cdot H_3(\mathsf{GID} \parallel \boldsymbol{u}_\phi \parallel j \parallel \iota_k)$$

for simplifying the representation of equations. For each $t \in S_\phi$ and $\mathcal{I}_{\boldsymbol{u}_\phi}$, it has four
different cases to consider:

1. **Case 1**—$(t \in S_\phi \setminus \rho([\ell]))$ (i.e., the attribute is absent in the challenge policy
   (M, ρ))—In this case, $\mathcal{B}$ simulates the secret keys according to the real experiment.
   It knows $\alpha_t, y_{t,j}$ for all $j \in \{2, \ldots, s_{\max}\}$ in clear and hence can compute

$$\mathsf{SK}_{\phi, t, \boldsymbol{u}_\phi} = (\prod_{k=1}^{n} H_1(t \parallel \iota_k \parallel \mathcal{I}_{\boldsymbol{u}_\phi})^{\alpha_t u_{\iota_k}}) \cdot \prod_{j=2}^{s_{\max}} \prod_{k=1}^{n} H_{2 \cdot 3}(\mathsf{GID}, \boldsymbol{u}_\phi, j, k)^{y_{t,j} u_{\iota_k}}$$

   where $H_3(\mathsf{GID} \parallel \boldsymbol{u}_\phi \parallel j \parallel \iota_k)$ were sampled uniformly.
2. **Case 2**—$(t \in S_\phi \cap \rho([\ell]) \wedge \mathcal{I}_{\boldsymbol{u}_\phi} \neq \mathcal{I}^*)$ (i.e., the attribute is present in the challenge
   policy, but the associated index set does not match with the challenge index set) In
   this case, $\mathcal{B}$ extracts the corresponding exponents of the hash values from the list of
   hash queries and computes

$$\mathsf{SK}_{\phi, t, \boldsymbol{u}_\phi} = (\prod_{k=1}^{n} H_1(t \parallel \iota_k \parallel \mathcal{I}_{\boldsymbol{u}_\phi})^{\alpha_t u_{\iota_k}}) \cdot \prod_{j=2}^{s_{\max}} \prod_{k=1}^{n} H_{2 \cdot 3}(\mathsf{GID}, \boldsymbol{u}_\phi, j, k)^{y_{t,j} u_{\iota_k}}$$

   where $H_3(\mathsf{GID} \parallel \boldsymbol{u}_\phi \parallel j \parallel \iota_k) = g_2^{h''_{3,j,\iota_k}}$ were sampled uniformly from $\mathbb{Z}_q$.
3. **Case 3**—$(t \in S_\phi \cap \rho([\ell]) \wedge \mathcal{I}_{\boldsymbol{u}_\phi} = \mathcal{I}^*)$ and $\rho^{-1}(\mathcal{C} \cup S_\phi)$ constitutes an unauthorized
   subset of the rows of $\mathbf{M}$ (i.e., S_ϕ does not satisfy the challenge policy $(\mathbf{M}, \rho)$).
   Note that the inner product value $(\boldsymbol{v}_0 - \boldsymbol{v}_1) \cdot \boldsymbol{u}_\phi$ can be either zero or non-zero

in this case. Since S_ϕ does not satisfy the challenge policy $(\mathbf{M}, \rho)$, there exists a vector $\boldsymbol{d}_\phi = (d_{\phi,1}, \dots, d_{\phi,s_{\max}}) \in \mathbb{Z}_q^{s_{\max}}$ such that $d_{\phi,1} = 1$ and the inner product $\boldsymbol{M}_i' \star \boldsymbol{d}_\phi = 0$ for all $i \in \rho^{-1}(S_\phi)$, where $\boldsymbol{M}_i'$ denotes the i-th row of $\mathbf{M}'$. $\mathcal{B}$ computes the secret key $\mathsf{SK}_{t,u}$ as follows.

$$
\begin{aligned}
\mathsf{SK}_{\phi,t,\boldsymbol{u}_\phi} &= \Big(\prod_{k=1}^{n} \mathsf{H}_1(t \parallel \iota_k \parallel \mathcal{I}_{\boldsymbol{u}_\phi})^{\alpha_t u_{\iota_k}}\Big) \cdot \prod_{j=2}^{s_{\max}} \prod_{k=1}^{n} \mathsf{H}_{2\cdot3}(\mathsf{GID}, \boldsymbol{u}_\phi, j, k)^{y_{t,j} u_{\iota_k}} \\
&= \Big(\prod_{k=1}^{n} (g_2^{ab})^{\eta_k M'_{\rho^{-1}(t),1} u_{\iota_k}}\Big) \cdot \prod_{j=2}^{\widehat{s_{\max}}} \prod_{k=1}^{n} (g_2^{ab})^{\eta_k d_{\phi,j} M'_{\rho^{-1}(t),j} u_{\iota_k}} \cdot g_2^{L_\phi(a,b)} \\
&= \prod_{j=1}^{\widehat{s_{\max}}} \prod_{k=1}^{n} (g_2^{ab})^{\eta_k d_{\phi,j} M'_{\rho^{-1}(t),j} u_{\iota_k}} \cdot g_2^{L_\phi(a,b)} \\
&= \prod_{k=1}^{n} (g_2^{ab})^{\eta_k u_{\iota_k} (M'_{\rho^{-1}(t)} \star \boldsymbol{d}_\phi)} \cdot g_2^{L_\phi(a,b)} = g_2^{L_\phi(a,b)}
\end{aligned}
$$

where $L_\phi(a,b)$ represents a linear function in a, b and hence $g_2^{L_\phi(a,b)}$ can be efficiently computable by $\mathcal{B}$. The first equality follows from the definition of $\alpha_t, y_{t,j}$ (Eq. (5.1)) and the hash functions H_1 (Eq. (5.2)) and H_2 (Eqs. (5.3) and (5.4)) and H_3 (Eqs. (5.5) and (5.6)). The last equality holds since $\boldsymbol{M}'_{\rho^{-1}(t)} \star \boldsymbol{d}_\phi = 0$ and the second last equality holds since $d_{\phi,1} = 1$.

4. **Case 4**—$(t \in S_\phi \cap \rho([\ell]) \wedge \mathcal{I}_{\boldsymbol{u}_\phi} = \mathcal{I}^*)$ and $\rho^{-1}(S_\phi)$ constitutes an authorized subset of rows of $\mathbf{M}$ (i.e., S_ϕ satisfies the challenge policy $(\mathbf{M}, \rho)$) – In this case, $\mathcal{B}$ computes the secret key $\mathsf{SK}_{\phi,t,\boldsymbol{u}_\phi}$ as follows.

$$
\begin{aligned}
\mathsf{SK}_{\phi,t,\boldsymbol{u}_\phi} &= \Big(\prod_{k=1}^{n} \mathsf{H}_1(t \parallel \iota_k \parallel \mathcal{I}_{\boldsymbol{u}_\phi})^{\alpha_t u_{\iota_k}}\Big) \cdot \prod_{j=2}^{s_{\max}} \prod_{k=1}^{n} \mathsf{H}_{2\cdot3}(\mathsf{GID}, \boldsymbol{u}_\phi, j, k)^{y_{t,j} u_{\iota_k}} \\
&= \Big(\prod_{k=1}^{n} (g_2^{ab})^{\eta_k M'_{\rho^{-1}(t),1} u_{\iota_k}}\Big) \cdot \prod_{j=2}^{\widehat{s_{\max}}} \prod_{k=1}^{n} \Big((g_2^{ab})^{\eta_k \sum_{\phi=1}^{Q} d_{\phi,j}} \Big)^{M'_{\rho^{-1}(t),j} u_{\iota_k}} \cdot g_2^{L_\phi(a,b)} \\
&= \Bigg[(g_2^{ab})^{\eta_k M'_{\rho^{-1}(t),1}} \cdot \prod_{j=2}^{\widehat{s_{\max}}} (g_2^{ab})^{\eta_k \sum_{\phi=1}^{Q} d_{\phi,j} M'_{\rho^{-1}(t),j}}\Bigg]^{\boldsymbol{\eta} \cdot \boldsymbol{u}_\phi} \cdot g_2^{L_\phi(a,b)} = g_2^{L_\phi(a,b)}
\end{aligned}
$$

where the last equality follows from the fact that $\boldsymbol{\eta} \cdot \boldsymbol{u}_\phi = 0$ if the secret key query satisfies the condition $(\boldsymbol{v}_0 - \boldsymbol{v}_1) \cdot \boldsymbol{u}_\phi = 0$ as S_ϕ is authorized. Hence, in this case, $\mathcal{B}$ can efficiently simulates the secret key as $L_\phi(a,b)$ is linear in a, b.

Generating the Challenge Ciphertext: $\mathcal{B}$ implicitly sets the vectors

$$
\begin{aligned}
\boldsymbol{z} &= -abc \cdot \boldsymbol{\eta} = -abc(\eta_1, \dots, \eta_n) \in \mathbb{Z}_q^n, \\
\boldsymbol{x}_j &= -(ac, \dots, ac) \in \mathbb{Z}_q^n, \quad f_j = -ac \in \mathbb{Z}_q, \quad \forall j \in \{2, \dots, \widehat{s_{\max}}\}, \\
\boldsymbol{x}_j &= \boldsymbol{0} \in \mathbb{Z}_q^n, \quad f_j = 0 \in \mathbb{Z}_q, \quad \forall j \in \{\widehat{s_{\max}} + 1, \dots, s_{\max}\}
\end{aligned}
$$

There are two cases to consider according to the authority whether it is corrupted or non-corrupted.

1. **Case 1**—$\rho(i) \in \mathcal{C}$ (meaning that the authority associated with this row is corrupted)—In this case, it holds that $M'_i B = 0$ and $M'_{i,j} x_j = 0$ for all $(i,j) \in \rho^{-1}(\mathcal{C}) \times [\widehat{s_{\max}}]$ since $M'_i|_{[\widehat{s_{\max}}]} = \overbrace{\{0,\ldots,0\}}^{\widehat{s_{\max}}}$ and due to the above implicit setting of B, x_j. Thus, for each such row, $\mathcal{B}$ picks $r_i \leftarrow \mathbb{Z}_q$, and using the authority public key $\mathsf{PK}_{\rho(i)} = (\mathrm{Y}_{\rho(i),1}, \mathrm{Y}_{\rho(i),2}, \ldots, \mathrm{Y}_{\rho(i),s_{\max}})$ obtained from $\mathcal{A}$, it computes

$$C_0 = [\![v_\beta + z]\!]_T, \quad C_{1,i} = [\![M'_i B + \vartheta_i]\!]_T = [\![\vartheta_i]\!]_T, \quad C_{2,i} = [\![r_i]\!]_1,$$

$$C_{3,i,j,k} = e([\![M'_{i,j} x_{j,k}]\!]_1, \mathsf{H}_2(j \parallel \iota_k \parallel \mathcal{I}^*)) \cdot e(r_i [\![\mathrm{Y}_{\rho(i),j}]\!]_1, \mathsf{H}_2(j \parallel \iota_k \parallel \mathcal{I}^*))$$

$$= e(r_i [\![\mathrm{Y}_{\rho(i),j}]\!]_1, \mathsf{H}_2(j \parallel \iota_k \parallel \mathcal{I}^*))$$

$$C_{4,i,j} = [\![M'_{i,j} f_j + \mathrm{Y}_{\rho(i),j} r_i]\!]_1 = [\![\mathrm{Y}_{\rho(i),j} r_i]\!]_1$$

for all $i \in [\ell], j \in \{2, \ldots, s_{\max}\}$ and $k \in [n]$, where $\vartheta_i = (\vartheta_{i,1}, \ldots, \vartheta_{i,m})$ and

$$\vartheta_{i,k} = e(r_i [\![\mathrm{Y}_{\rho(i)}]\!]_1, \mathsf{H}_1(\rho(i) \parallel \iota_k \parallel \mathcal{I}^*)).$$

2. **Case 2**—$\rho(i) \in \mathcal{N}$ (meaning that the authority associated with this row is uncorrupted)—Firstly, $\mathcal{B}$ sets $C_0 = [\![v_\beta + z]\!]_T$ where β is the challenge bit for $\mathcal{A}$. It also implicitly sets $r_i = c$ and the matrix $B = (z, 0, \cdots, 0)^\top \in \mathbb{Z}_q^{s_{\max} \times n}$. This implies $M'_i B = M'_{i,1} z = -M'_{i,1} \cdot abc \cdot \eta$ and the k-th element of the vector is $(M'_i B)_k = -M'_{i,1} abc\eta_k$. Recall that, for each $i \in [\ell]$, we have $\alpha_{\rho(i)} = \alpha'_{\rho(i)} + a \cdot M'_{i,1}$ and $y_{\rho(i),j} = y'_{\rho(i),j} + aM'_{i,j}$. Now, $\mathcal{B}$ implicitly computes the vector $\vartheta_i := (\vartheta_{i,1}, \ldots, \vartheta_{i,m})$ as

$$\vartheta_{i,k} = e(r_i [\![\alpha_{\rho(i)}]\!]_1, \mathsf{H}_1(\rho(i) \parallel \iota_k \parallel \mathcal{I}^*))$$

$$= e([\![c\alpha'_{\rho(i)} + ac \cdot M'_{i,1}]\!]_1, [\![b\eta_k + \sum_{\widehat{k}=1}^{n-1} h_{1,\widehat{k}} \lambda_{k,\widehat{k}} + h_{1,\rho(i),\iota_k}]\!]_2)$$

$$= [\![bc\alpha'_{\rho(i)} \eta_k + M'_{i,1} abc\eta_k + (c\alpha'_{\rho(i)} + ac \cdot M'_{i,1})\mathfrak{h}_{1,i,k}]\!]_T$$

where $\mathfrak{h}_{1,i,k} = \sum_{\widehat{k}=1}^{n-1} h_{1,\widehat{k}} \lambda_{k,\widehat{k}} + h_{1,\rho(i),\iota_k}$. We write $\mathfrak{h}_{1,i} = (h_{1,\rho(i),\iota_k})_{k=1}^n$. Thus, for each $i \in [\ell]$, $\mathcal{B}$ sets $C_{2,i} = [\![c]\!]_1$ and computes

$$C_{1,i} = [\![M_i B + \vartheta_i]\!]_T = [\![bc\alpha'_{\rho(i)} \eta + (c\alpha'_{\rho(i)} + ac \cdot M'_{i,1})\mathfrak{h}_{1,i}]\!]_T$$

$$= e(g_1^c, g_2^b)^{\alpha'_{\rho(i)} \eta} \cdot e(g_1^c, g_2)^{\alpha'_{\rho(i)} \mathfrak{h}_i} \cdot e(g_1^c, g_2^a)^{M'_{i,1} \mathfrak{h}_{1,i}}$$

Next, $\mathcal{B}$ computes $C_{3,i,j,k}$ as follows. Recall that $C_{3,i,j,k}$ is a product of two pairing operations. Note that, $M'_{i,j} x_{j,k} = 0$ if $j \in \{\widehat{s_{\max}} + 1, \ldots, s_{\max}\}$. Thus, for $j \in \{2, \ldots, \widehat{s_{\max}}\}$, the first pairing is computed as

$$e([\![M'_{i,j} x_{j,k}]\!]_1, \mathsf{H}_2(j \parallel \iota_k \parallel \mathcal{I}^*))$$

$$= e([\![M'_{i,j} x_{j,k}]\!]_1, (g_2^b)^{\eta_k \sum_{\phi=1}^Q d_{\phi,j}} \cdot \prod_{\widehat{k}=1}^{n-1} g_2^{h_{2,\widehat{k}} \lambda_{k,\widehat{k}}} \cdot g_2^{h_{2,\rho(i),\iota_k}})$$

$$= [\![M'_{i,j} x_{j,k} b\eta_k d_j^+ + M'_{i,j} x_{j,k} \mathfrak{h}_{2,i,k}]\!]_T$$

where $d_j^+ = \sum_{\phi=1}^Q d_{\phi,j}$ and $\mathfrak{h}_{2,i,k} = \sum_{\widehat{k}=1}^{n-1} h_{2,\widehat{k}}\lambda_{k,\widehat{k}} + h_{2,\rho(i),\iota_k}$. If $j \in \{2, \ldots, \widehat{s_{\max}}\}$, the second pairing is computed as

$$e(r_i[\![y_{\rho(i),j}]\!]_1, \mathsf{H}_2(j \parallel \iota_k \parallel \mathcal{I}^*))$$

$$= e([\![cy'_{\rho(i),j} + acM'_{i,j}]\!]_1, (g_2^b)^{\eta_k \sum_{\phi=1}^Q d_{\phi,j}} \cdot \prod_{\widehat{k}=1}^{n-1} g_2^{h_{2,\widehat{k}}\lambda_{k,\widehat{k}}} \cdot g_2^{h_{2,\rho(i),\iota_k}})$$

$$= [\![bc(y'_{\rho(i),j} + aM'_{i,j})\eta_k d_j^+ + c(y'_{\rho(i),j} + aM'_{i,j})\mathfrak{h}_{2,i,k}]\!]_T$$

Finally, for each $i \in [\ell], j \in \{2, \ldots, \widehat{s_{\max}}\}, k \in [n]$, the ciphertext component $C_{3,i,j,k}$ is obtained as

$$C_{3,i,j,k} = e([\![M'_{i,j}x_{j,k}]\!]_1, \mathsf{H}_2(j \parallel \iota_k \parallel \mathcal{I}^*)) \cdot e(r_i[\![y_{\rho(i),j}]\!]_1, \mathsf{H}_2(j \parallel \iota_k \parallel \mathcal{I}^*))$$

$$= [\![bcy'_{\rho(i),j}\eta_k d_j^+ + cy'_{\rho(i),j}\mathfrak{h}_{2,i,k}]\!]_T$$

$$= e(g_1^c, g_2^b)^{y'_{\rho(i),j}\eta_k d_j^+} \cdot e(g_1^c, g_2)^{y'_{\rho(i),j}\mathfrak{h}_{2,i,k}}$$

which $\mathcal{B}$ can compute as a part of the challenge ciphertext. Now, if $j \in \{\widehat{s_{\max}} + 1, \ldots, s_{\max}\}$, recall that $y_{\rho(i),j}$ are known is clear and hence $\mathcal{B}$ computes $C_{3,i,j,k}$ as

$$C_{3,i,j,k} = e([\![M'_{i,j}x_{j,k}]\!]_1, \mathsf{H}_2(j \parallel \iota_k \parallel \mathcal{I}^*)) \cdot e(r_i[\![y_{\rho(i),j}]\!]_1, \mathsf{H}_2(j \parallel \iota_k \parallel \mathcal{I}^*))$$

$$= e(r_i[\![y_{\rho(i),j}]\!]_1, [\![h'_{2,j,\iota_k}]\!]_2) = e(g_1^c, g_2)^{y_{\rho(i),j}h'_{2,j,\iota_k}}$$

for all $i \in [\ell], k \in [n]$. The last remaining part $C_{4,i,j}$ is given by

$$C_{4,i,j} = [\![M'_{i,j}f_j + y_{\rho(i),j}r_i]\!]_1 = [\![-acM'_{i,j} + cy'_{\rho(i),j} + acM'_{i,j}]\!]_1 = (g_1^c)^{y'_{\rho(i),j}}$$

if $i \in [\ell], j \in \{2, \ldots, \widehat{s_{\max}}\}$. Note that, $M'_{i,j}f_j = 0$ and $y_{\rho(i),j}$ are known in clear for $j \in \{\widehat{s_{\max}} + 1, \ldots, s_{\max}\}$. Hence, $\mathcal{B}$ computes $C_{4,i,j}$ as

$$C_{4,i,j} = [\![M'_{i,j}f_j + y_{\rho(i),j}r_i]\!]_1 = [\![cy_{\rho(i),j}]\!]_1 = (g_1^c)^{y_{\rho(i),j}}$$

for each $i \in [\ell], j \in \{2, \ldots, s_{\max}\}$. Observe that, the elements $\mathbf{B}, \boldsymbol{x}_j, f_j$ and r_i are not properly distributed. Thus, $\mathcal{B}$ re-randomizes the ciphertext components using the algorithm CTRand described below before it sends to $\mathcal{A}$.

Ciphertext Re-randomization Algorithm: The algorithm described below provides properly distributed ciphertexts even if the randomness used within the ciphertexts inputted into the algorithm are not uniform. The algorithm uses only publicly available information to perform the re-randomization and hence rectify the distribution of the challenge ciphertext in the reduction.

CTRand$((\mathbf{M}, \rho), \mathsf{CT}, \mathsf{PK})$: The algorithm takes input an LSSS access policy $(\mathbf{M}, \rho)$, where $\mathbf{M} = (M_{i,j})_{\ell \times s_{\max}} = (\boldsymbol{M}_1, \ldots, \boldsymbol{M}_\ell)^\top \in \mathbb{Z}_q^{\ell \times s_{\max}}$ and $\rho : [\ell] \to \mathsf{U}_{\mathrm{att}}$, a ciphertext $\mathsf{CT} = ((\mathbf{M}, \rho), C_0, \{C_{1,i}, C_{2,i}, C_{3,i,j,k}, C_{4,i,j}\}_{i \in [\ell], j \in \{2,\ldots,s_{\max}\}, k \in [m]}, \mathcal{I}_v)$, and the public key components PK such that $\rho([\ell]) \subseteq \mathsf{U}_{\mathrm{att}}$.

1. Sample

(a) $r'_1, \ldots, r'_\ell \leftarrow \mathbb{Z}_q; x'_2, \ldots, x'_{s_{\max}} \in \mathbb{Z}_q^n; f'_2, \ldots, f'_{s_{\max}} \in \mathbb{Z}_q,$

(b) $\mathbf{B}' = (z', b'_2, \ldots, b'_{s_{\max}})^\top \in \mathbb{Z}_q^{s_{\max} \times n},$

2. Compute $C'_0 = C_0 \cdot [\![z']\!]_T.$

3. For all $i \in [\ell], j \in \{2, \ldots, s_{\max}\}$ and $k \in [n]$, compute

$$C'_{1,i} = C_{1,i} \cdot [\![M_i \mathbf{B}' + \vartheta'_i]\!]_T, \ \ C'_{2,i} = C_{2,i} \cdot [\![r'_i]\!]_1,$$

$$C'_{3,i,j,k} = C_{3,i,j,k} \cdot e([\![M_{i,j} x'_{j,k}]\!]_1, \mathsf{H}_2(j \parallel \iota_k \parallel \mathcal{I}^*)) \cdot e(r'_i [\![y_{\rho(i),j}]\!]_1, \mathsf{H}_2(j \parallel \iota_k \parallel \mathcal{I}^*))$$

$$C'_{4,i,j} = C_{4,i,j} \cdot [\![M_{i,j} f'_j + y_{\rho(i),j} r'_i]\!]_1$$

where $\vartheta'_i = (\vartheta'_{i,1}, \ldots, \vartheta'_{i,n})$ and $\vartheta'_{i,k} = e(r'_i [\![\alpha_{\rho(i)}]\!]_1, \mathsf{H}_1(\rho(i) \parallel \iota_k \parallel \mathcal{I}^*)).$

4. Output the ciphertext

$$\mathsf{CT} = \Big((\mathbf{M}, \rho), C'_0, \{C'_{1,i}, C'_{2,i}, C'_{3,i,j,k}, C'_{4,i,j}\}_{i \in [\ell], j \in \{2, \ldots, s_{\max}\}, k \in [m]}, \mathcal{I}_v \Big).$$

Guess: If $\mathcal{A}$ guesses the challenge bit $\beta \in \{0, 1\}$ correctly, $\mathcal{B}$ returns 1; Otherwise $\mathcal{B}$ outputs 0. Now, observe that $z = -\tau \cdot \eta$ where $[\![\tau]\!]_T$ is the DBDH challenge element. If $\tau = abc$, then all the secret keys and the challenge ciphertext are distributed properly, in particular, the challenge ciphertext is an encryption of the message vector v_β for $\beta \leftarrow \{0, 1\}$. Therefore, in this case, $\mathcal{A}$ outputs $\beta' = \beta$ with probability $1/2 + \epsilon(\lambda)$ where $\epsilon(\lambda)$ is the advantage of $\mathcal{A}$ in the static security game of the MA-ABUIPFE scheme. On the other hand, if τ is a random element of $\mathbb{Z}_q$ then the ciphertext element C_0 is uniformly random in $\mathbb{G}_T$, and hence from $\mathcal{A}$'s point of view there is no information of the challenge bit β in the challenge ciphertext. So, the probability of $\mathcal{A}$ outputting $\beta' = \beta$ is exactly $1/2$. Hence, by the guarantee of DBDH assumption, $\mathcal{A}$ has a non-negligible advantage against the proposed MA-ABUIPFE scheme in the static security game. This completes the proof. □

6 The Proposed Large Universe MA-ABUIPFE from L-DBDH

In this section, we describe the construction of our LMA-ABUIPFE scheme. The construction is in prime-order groups and additionally uses hash functions that are modelled as random oracles in the security proof just like our small universe construction.

GlobalSetup$(1^\lambda, s_{\max})$: The global setup algorithm takes input the security parameter λ and a vector length n both in unary, and the maximum width of an LSSS matrix supported by the scheme $s_{\max} = s_{\max}(\lambda)$. It generates $\mathsf{G} = (q, \mathbb{G}_1, \mathbb{G}_2, \mathbb{G}_T, g, e)$ and specify hash functions $\mathsf{H}_1 : \mathsf{U}_{\mathsf{att}} \times \mathbb{Z} \times \mathbb{Z}^* \to \mathbb{G}_2$, $\mathsf{H}_2 : [s_{\max}] \times \mathbb{Z} \times \mathbb{Z}^* \to \mathbb{G}_2$, $\mathsf{H}_3 : \mathcal{GID} \times \mathbb{Z}^* \times [s_{\max}] \times \mathbb{Z} \to \mathbb{G}_2$ and $\mathsf{R} : \mathsf{U}_{\mathsf{att}} \times [s_{\max}] \times \mathbb{Z}^* \to \mathbb{G}_2$ mapping strings $(t, j) \in \mathsf{U}_{\mathsf{att}} \times [s_{\max}]$ to elements in $\mathbb{G}_2$. It outputs a global parameter $\mathsf{GP} = (\mathsf{G}, \mathsf{H}_1, \mathsf{H}_2, \mathsf{H}_3, \mathsf{R})$.

LocalSetup(GP, θ): The authority setup algorithm takes input the global parameter GP and an authority index $\theta \in \mathcal{AU}$. It samples $\alpha_\theta, y_{\theta,2}, \ldots, y_{\theta,s_{\max}} \leftarrow \mathbb{Z}_q$ and outputs $\mathsf{PK}_\theta = ([\![\alpha_\theta]\!]_1, [\![y_{\theta,2}]\!]_1, \ldots, [\![y_{\theta,s_{\max}}]\!]_1)$ and $\mathsf{MSK}_\theta = (\alpha_\theta, y_{\theta,2}, \ldots, y_{\theta,s_{\max}})$.

KeyGen$(\mathsf{GP}, \mathsf{GID}, \mathsf{MSK}_\theta, t, u, \mathcal{I}_u)$: The key generation algorithm takes input GP, the user's global identifier GID, the authority's secret key MSK_θ, an attribute t controlled by the authority and a vector $u \in \mathbb{Z}_q^{|\mathcal{I}_u|}$. It samples $\tau_j \leftarrow \mathbb{Z}_p$ for $j \in [s_{\max}]$ and proceeds as follows:

1. Parse $\mathcal{I}_u = \{\iota_1, \ldots, \iota_n\}$ and $\boldsymbol{u} = (u_{\iota_1}, \ldots, u_{\iota_n})$.
2. Compute

$$\mathsf{K}_{t,u} = \left(\prod_{k=1}^n \mathsf{H}_1(t \parallel \iota_k \parallel \mathcal{I}_u)^{\alpha_\theta u_{\iota_k}}\right) \cdot \prod_{j=2}^{s_{\max}} \prod_{k=1}^n (\mathsf{H}_2(j \parallel \iota_k \parallel \mathcal{I}_u) \cdot \mathsf{H}_3(\mathsf{GID} \parallel \boldsymbol{u} \parallel j \parallel \iota_k))^{y_{\theta,j} u_{\iota_k}}.$$

3. Compute $\mathsf{SK}_{t,u} = \mathsf{K}_{t,u} \cdot \prod_{j=1}^{s_{\max}} \mathsf{R}(t \parallel j \parallel \mathcal{I}_u)^{\tau_j}$ and $\mathsf{Z}_t^{(j)} = [\![\tau_j]\!]_1 \; \forall \; j \in [s_{\max}]$.

Output $\mathsf{SK}_{\mathsf{GID},t,u} = (\mathsf{GID}, \boldsymbol{u}, \mathsf{SK}_{t,u}, \mathsf{Z}_t^{(j)}, \mathcal{I}_u)$.

Encrypt(GP, $(\mathbf{M}, \delta), \{\mathsf{PK}_\theta\}, \boldsymbol{v}, \mathcal{I}_v$): The encryption algorithm takes input the global parameter GP, an LSSS access structure $(\mathbf{M}, \delta)$ where $\mathbf{M} = (\boldsymbol{M}_1, \ldots, \boldsymbol{M}_\ell)^\top \in \mathbb{Z}_q^{\ell \times s_{\max}}$ and $\delta : [\ell] \to \mathsf{U}_{\mathsf{att}}$, a set $\{\mathsf{PK}_\theta\}$ of public keys for all the relevant authorities, and a message vector $\boldsymbol{v} \in \mathbb{Z}_q^m$. The function δ maps the row indices of $\mathbf{M}$ to attributes. We define the function $\rho : [\ell] \to \mathcal{AU}$ as $\rho(\cdot) = \mathsf{T}(\delta(\cdot))$ which maps row indices of $\mathbf{M}$ to authorities. The algorithm proceeds as follows:

1. Parse $\mathcal{I}_v = \{\iota_1, \ldots, \iota_m\}$ and $\boldsymbol{v} = (v_{\iota_1}, \ldots, v_{\iota_m})$.
2. Sample $\{r_i \leftarrow \mathbb{Z}_q\}_{i \in [\ell]}$ and $\boldsymbol{f} = (f_2, \ldots, f_{s_{\max}}) \leftarrow \mathbb{Z}_q^{s_{\max}-1}$.
3. Sample $z, \boldsymbol{b}_2, \ldots, \boldsymbol{b}_{s_{\max}}, \boldsymbol{x}_2, \ldots, \boldsymbol{x}_{s_{\max}} \leftarrow \mathbb{Z}_q^m$.
4. Set the matrix $\mathbf{B} = [z, \boldsymbol{b}_2, \ldots, \boldsymbol{b}_{s_{\max}}]_{s_{\max} \times m}^\top$.
5. Compute $\vartheta_{i,k} = e(r_i [\![\alpha_{\rho(i)}]\!]_1, \mathsf{H}_1(\rho(i) \parallel \iota_k \parallel \mathcal{I}_v))$ and set $\boldsymbol{\vartheta}_i := (\vartheta_{i,1}, \ldots, \vartheta_{i,m})$.
6. Compute the following terms:

$$C_0 = [\![\boldsymbol{v} + z]\!]_T, \quad C_{1,i} = [\![\boldsymbol{M}_i \mathbf{B} + \boldsymbol{\vartheta}_i]\!]_T, \quad C_{2,i} = [\![r_i]\!]_1,$$
$$C_{3,i,j,k} = e([\![M_{i,j} x_{j,k}]\!]_1, \mathsf{H}_2(j \parallel \iota_k \parallel \mathcal{I}_v)) \cdot e(r_i [\![y_{\rho(i),j}]\!]_1, \mathsf{H}_2(j \parallel \iota_k \parallel \mathcal{I}_v)),$$
$$C_{4,i,j} = [\![M_{i,j} f_j + y_{\rho(i),j} r_i]\!]_1,$$

for all $i \in [\ell], j \in \{2, \ldots, s_{\max}\}, k \in [m]$.
7. Compute $C_{5,i,j} = \mathsf{R}(\delta(i) \parallel j \parallel \mathcal{I}_v)^{r_i}$ for all $i \in [\ell], j \in [s_{\max}]$.
8. Output the ciphertext

$$\mathsf{CT} = \left((\mathbf{M}, \delta), C_0, \{C_{1,i}, C_{2,i}, C_{3,i,j,k}, C_{4,i,j}, C_{5,i,1}, C_{5,i,j}\}_{\substack{j \in \{2, \ldots, s_{\max}\}, \\ i \in [\ell], k \in [m]}}, \mathcal{I}_v \right).$$

Decrypt(GP, GID, CT, $\{\mathsf{SK}_{\mathsf{GID},t,u}\}$): It takes input the public key PK, a secret key $\mathsf{SK}_{S,u}$ for an attribute set $S \subseteq \mathsf{U}_{\mathsf{att}}$ and a vector $\boldsymbol{u} \in \mathbb{Z}_q^n$ and a ciphertext CT for an access structure $(\mathbf{M}, \delta)$ with $\mathbf{M} \in \mathbb{Z}_q^{\ell \times s_{\max}}$ and a map $\delta : [\ell] \to \mathsf{U}_{\mathsf{att}}$.

Parse $\mathsf{SK}_{\mathsf{GID},t,u} = (\mathsf{GID}, \boldsymbol{u}, \mathsf{SK}_{t,u}, \mathsf{Z}_t^{(j)}, \mathcal{I}_u)$, where $i \in [\ell]$ and $\mathsf{CT} = ((\mathbf{M}, \delta), C_0, \{C_{1,i}, C_{2,i}, C_{3,i,j,k}, C_{4,i,j}, C_{5,i,1}, C_{5,i,j}\}_{i \in [\ell], j \in \{2, \ldots, s_{\max}\}, k \in [m]}, \mathcal{I}_v)$. Denote a set $I = \{i | \delta(i) \in S\} \subseteq [\ell]$. If $(1, 0, \ldots, 0)$ is not in the span of $\mathbf{M}_I$ (i.e., $\mathbf{M}$ restricted to the set of rows from I) or $\mathcal{I}_u \neq \mathcal{I}_v$ decryption returns $\perp$. Else, when S satisfies $(\mathbf{M}, \rho)$, the algorithm finds $\{w_i \in \mathbb{Z}_q\}_{i \in I}$ such that $(1, 0, \ldots, 0) = \sum_{i \in I} w_i \mathbf{M}_i$. It first computes

$$[\![\Lambda_i]\!]_T = \prod_{j=2}^{s_{\max}} \prod_{k=1}^n u_{\iota_k} \cdot C_{3,i,j,k} \cdot e(C_{4,i,j}, \mathsf{H}_3(\mathsf{GID} \parallel \boldsymbol{u} \parallel j \parallel \iota_k)^{u_{\iota_k}})$$

and outputs $\log_{g_T}\left([\![\Gamma]\!]_T\right)$ where $[\![\Gamma]\!]_T = C_0 \cdot \boldsymbol{u} \cdot [\![\mu]\!]_T$ and

$$
[\![\mu]\!]_T = \left(\prod_{i \in I} \left[\frac{C_{1,i} \cdot \boldsymbol{u} \cdot [\![\Lambda_i]\!]_T \cdot \prod_{j=1}^{s_{\max}} e(\mathsf{Z}_{\delta(i)}^{(j)}, C_{5,i,j})}{e\left(\mathsf{SK}_{\rho(i),\boldsymbol{u}}, C_{2,i}\right)} \right]^{w_i} \right)^{-1}.
$$

Theorem 6.1. *If the* L-DBDH *assumption holds, then all* PPT *adversaries have a negligible advantage in breaking the static security of the proposed* LMA-ABUIPFE *scheme in the random oracle model.*

References

1. Abdalla, M., Benhamouda, F., Gay, R.: From single-input to multi-client inner-product functional encryption. In: Galbraith, S.D., Moriai, S. (eds.) ASIACRYPT 2019. LNCS, vol. 11923, pp. 552–582. Springer, Cham (2019). https://doi.org/10.1007/978-3-030-34618-8_19
2. Abdalla, M., Benhamouda, F., Kohlweiss, M., Waldner, H.: Decentralizing inner-product functional encryption. In: Lin, D., Sako, K. (eds.) PKC 2019. LNCS, vol. 11443, pp. 128–157. Springer, Cham (2019). https://doi.org/10.1007/978-3-030-17259-6_5
3. Abdalla, M., Bourse, F., De Caro, A., Pointcheval, D.: Simple functional encryption schemes for inner products. In: Katz, J. (ed.) PKC 2015. LNCS, vol. 9020, pp. 733–751. Springer, Heidelberg (2015). https://doi.org/10.1007/978-3-662-46447-2_33
4. Abdalla, M., Bourse, F., Caro, A.D., Pointcheval, D.: Better security for functional encryption for inner product evaluations. Cryptology ePrint Archive, Paper 2016/011 (2016). https://eprint.iacr.org/2016/011
5. Abdalla, M., Catalano, D., Gay, R., Ursu, B.: Inner-product functional encryption with fine-grained access control. In: Moriai, S., Wang, H. (eds.) ASIACRYPT 2020. LNCS, vol. 12493, pp. 467–497. Springer, Cham (2020). https://doi.org/10.1007/978-3-030-64840-4_16
6. Agrawal, S., Bhattacherjee, S., Phan, D.H., Stehlé, D., Yamada, S.: Efficient public trace and revoke from standard assumptions: Extended abstract. CCS 2017, pp. 2277–2293, New York, NY, USA (2017). Association for Computing Machinery
7. Agrawal, S., Boneh, D., Boyen, X.: Efficient lattice (H)IBE in the standard model. In: Gilbert, H. (ed.) EUROCRYPT 2010. LNCS, vol. 6110, pp. 553–572. Springer, Heidelberg (2010). https://doi.org/10.1007/978-3-642-13190-5_28
8. Agrawal, S., Goyal, R., Tomida, J.: Multi-input quadratic functional encryption from pairings. In: Malkin, T., Peikert, C. (eds.) CRYPTO 2021. LNCS, vol. 12828, pp. 208–238. Springer, Cham (2021). https://doi.org/10.1007/978-3-030-84259-8_8
9. Agrawal, S., Goyal, R., Tomida, J.: Multi-party functional encryption. In: Nissim, K., Waters, B. (eds.) TCC 2021. LNCS, vol. 13043, pp. 224–255. Springer, Cham (2021). https://doi.org/10.1007/978-3-030-90453-1_8
10. Agrawal, S., Libert, B., Stehlé, D.: Fully secure functional encryption for inner products, from standard assumptions. In: Robshaw, M., Katz, J. (eds.) CRYPTO 2016. LNCS, vol. 9816, pp. 333–362. Springer, Heidelberg (2016). https://doi.org/10.1007/978-3-662-53015-3_12
11. Benson, K., Shacham, H., Waters, B.: The k-BDH assumption family: bilinear map cryptography from progressively weaker assumptions. In: Dawson, E. (ed.) CT-RSA 2013. LNCS, vol. 7779, pp. 310–325. Springer, Heidelberg (2013). https://doi.org/10.1007/978-3-642-36095-4_20

12. Boneh, D., Boyen, X., Goh, E.-J.: Hierarchical identity based encryption with constant size ciphertext. In: Cramer, R. (ed.) EUROCRYPT 2005. LNCS, vol. 3494, pp. 440–456. Springer, Heidelberg (2005). https://doi.org/10.1007/11426639_26

13. Boneh, D., Franklin, M.: Identity-based encryption from the weil pairing. In: Kilian, J. (ed.) CRYPTO 2001. LNCS, vol. 2139, pp. 213–229. Springer, Heidelberg (2001). https://doi.org/10.1007/3-540-44647-8_13

14. Boneh, D., Lynn, B., Shacham, H.: Short signatures from the weil pairing. In: Boyd, C. (ed.) ASIACRYPT 2001. LNCS, vol. 2248, pp. 514–532. Springer, Heidelberg (2001). https://doi.org/10.1007/3-540-45682-1_30

15. Boneh, D., Sahai, A., Waters, B.: Functional encryption: definitions and challenges. In: Ishai, Y. (ed.) TCC 2011. LNCS, vol. 6597, pp. 253–273. Springer, Heidelberg (2011). https://doi.org/10.1007/978-3-642-19571-6_16

16. Chen, J., Gong, J., Kowalczyk, L., Wee, H.: Unbounded ABE via bilinear entropy expansion, revisited. In: Nielsen, J.B., Rijmen, V. (eds.) EUROCRYPT 2018. LNCS, vol. 10820, pp. 503–534. Springer, Cham (2018). https://doi.org/10.1007/978-3-319-78381-9_19

17. Chotard, J., Dufour Sans, E., Gay, R., Phan, D.H., Pointcheval, D.: Decentralized multi-client functional encryption for inner product. In: Peyrin, T., Galbraith, S. (eds.) ASIACRYPT 2018. LNCS, vol. 11273, pp. 703–732. Springer, Cham (2018). https://doi.org/10.1007/978-3-030-03329-3_24

18. Datta, P., Dutta, R., Mukhopadhyay, S.: Functional encryption for inner product with full function privacy. In: Cheng, C.-M., Chung, K.-M., Persiano, G., Yang, B.-Y. (eds.) PKC 2016. LNCS, vol. 9614, pp. 164–195. Springer, Heidelberg (2016). https://doi.org/10.1007/978-3-662-49384-7_7

19. Datta, P., Komargodski, I., Waters, B.: Decentralized multi-authority ABE for DNFs from LWE. In: Canteaut, A., Standaert, F.-X. (eds.) EUROCRYPT 2021. LNCS, vol. 12696, pp. 177–209. Springer, Cham (2021). https://doi.org/10.1007/978-3-030-77870-5_7

20. Datta, P., Komargodski, I., Waters, B.: Fully adaptive decentralized multi-authority ABE. Cryptology ePrint Archive, Paper 2022/1311 (2022)

21. Datta, P., Komargodski, I., Waters, B.: Decentralized multi-authority ABE from NC^1 from computational-BDH. Cryptology ePrint Archive, Paper 2021/1325, ePrint (2021)

22. Freeman, D.M.: Converting pairing-based cryptosystems from composite-order groups to prime-order groups. In: Gilbert, H. (ed.) EUROCRYPT 2010. LNCS, vol. 6110, pp. 44–61. Springer, Heidelberg (2010). https://doi.org/10.1007/978-3-642-13190-5_3

23. Gay, R.: A new paradigm for public-key functional encryption for degree-2 polynomials. In: Kiayias, A., Kohlweiss, M., Wallden, P., Zikas, V. (eds.) PKC 2020. LNCS, vol. 12110, pp. 95–120. Springer, Cham (2020). https://doi.org/10.1007/978-3-030-45374-9_4

24. Goyal, V., Pandey, O., Sahai, A., Waters, B.: Attribute-based encryption for fine-grained access control of encrypted data. In Proceedings of the 13th ACM conference on Computer and communications security, pp. 89–98 (2006)

25. Guillevic, A.: Comparing the pairing efficiency over composite-order and prime-order elliptic curves. In: Jacobson, M., Locasto, M., Mohassel, P., Safavi-Naini, R. (eds.) ACNS 2013. LNCS, vol. 7954, pp. 357–372. Springer, Heidelberg (2013). https://doi.org/10.1007/978-3-642-38980-1_22

26. Jain, A., Lin, H., Matt, C., Sahai, A.: How to leverage hardness of constant-degree expanding polynomials over $\mathbb{R}$ to build $i\mathcal{O}$. In: Ishai, Y., Rijmen, V. (eds.) EUROCRYPT 2019. LNCS, vol. 11476, pp. 251–281. Springer, Cham (2019). https://doi.org/10.1007/978-3-030-17653-2_9

27. Jain, A., Lin, H., Sahai, A.: Simplifying constructions and assumptions for $i\mathcal{O}$. Cryptology ePrint Archive, Paper 2019/1252 (2019)

28. Jain, A., Lin, H., Sahai, A.: Indistinguishability obfuscation from well-founded assumptions. In: Khuller, S., Williams, V.V. (eds.) STOC 2021: 53rd Annual ACM SIGACT Symposium on Theory of Computing, Virtual Event, Italy, 21–25 June 2021, pp. 60–73. ACM (2021)

29. Lee, J., Kim, D., Kim, D., Song, Y., Shin, J., Cheon, J.H.: Instant privacy-preserving biometric authentication for hamming distance. Cryptology ePrint Archive, Paper 2018/1214 (2018). https://eprint.iacr.org/2018/1214

30. Lewko, A., Waters, B.: Decentralizing attribute-based encryption. In: Paterson, K.G. (ed.) EUROCRYPT 2011. LNCS, vol. 6632, pp. 568–588. Springer, Heidelberg (2011). https://doi.org/10.1007/978-3-642-20465-4_31

31. Lewko, A.: Tools for simulating features of composite order bilinear groups in the prime order setting. In: Pointcheval, D., Johansson, T. (eds.) EUROCRYPT 2012. LNCS, vol. 7237, pp. 318–335. Springer, Heidelberg (2012). https://doi.org/10.1007/978-3-642-29011-4_20

32. Nguyen, K., Phan, D.H., Pointcheval, D.: Multi-client functional encryption with fine-grained access control. In: Agrawal, S., Lin, D. (eds.) Advances in Cryptology–ASIACRYPT 2022. ASIACRYPT 2022. LNCS, vol 13791, pp. 95–125. Springer, Cham (2022). https://doi.org/10.1007/978-3-031-22963-3_4

33. Okamoto, T., Takashima, K.: Decentralized attribute-based encryption and signatures. IEICE Trans. Fundam. Electron. Commun. Comput. Sci. **103**-A(1), 41–73 (2020)

34. O'Neill, A.: Definitional issues in functional encryption. Cryptology ePrint Archive, Paper 2010/556, ePrint (2010)

35. Pal, T., Dutta, R.: Attribute-based access control for inner product functional encryption from LWE. In: Longa, P., Ràfols, C. (eds.) LATINCRYPT 2021. LNCS, vol. 12912, pp. 127–148. Springer, Cham (2021). https://doi.org/10.1007/978-3-030-88238-9_7

36. Rouselakis, Y., Waters, B.: Efficient statically-secure large-universe multi-authority attribute-based encryption. In: Böhme, R., Okamoto, T. (eds.) FC 2015. LNCS, vol. 8975, pp. 315–332. Springer, Heidelberg (2015). https://doi.org/10.1007/978-3-662-47854-7_19

37. Sahai, A., Waters, B.: Fuzzy identity-based encryption. In: Cramer, R. (ed.) EUROCRYPT 2005. LNCS, vol. 3494, pp. 457–473. Springer, Heidelberg (2005). https://doi.org/10.1007/11426639_27

38. Dufour-Sans, E., Pointcheval, D.: Unbounded inner-product functional encryption with succinct keys. In: Deng, R.H., Gauthier-Umaña, V., Ochoa, M., Yung, M. (eds.) ACNS 2019. LNCS, vol. 11464, pp. 426–441. Springer, Cham (2019). https://doi.org/10.1007/978-3-030-21568-2_21

39. Shoup, V.: Lower bounds for discrete logarithms and related problems. In: Fumy, W. (ed.) EUROCRYPT 1997. LNCS, vol. 1233, pp. 256–266. Springer, Heidelberg (1997). https://doi.org/10.1007/3-540-69053-0_18

40. Tomida, J.: Tightly secure inner product functional encryption: multi-input and function-hiding constructions. In: Galbraith, S.D., Moriai, S. (eds.) ASIACRYPT 2019. LNCS, vol. 11923, pp. 459–488. Springer, Cham (2019). https://doi.org/10.1007/978-3-030-34618-8_16

41. Waters, B.: Dual system encryption: realizing fully secure IBE and HIBE under simple assumptions. In: Halevi, S. (ed.) CRYPTO 2009. LNCS, vol. 5677, pp. 619–636. Springer, Heidelberg (2009). https://doi.org/10.1007/978-3-642-03356-8_36

42. Waters, B.: Ciphertext-policy attribute-based encryption: an expressive, efficient, and provably secure realization. In: Catalano, D., Fazio, N., Gennaro, R., Nicolosi, A. (eds.) PKC 2011. LNCS, vol. 6571, pp. 53–70. Springer, Heidelberg (2011). https://doi.org/10.1007/978-3-642-19379-8_4

43. Waters, B., Wee, H., Wu, D.J.: Multi-authority ABE from lattices without random oracles. In: Kiltz, E., Vaikuntanathan, V. (eds.) Theory of Cryptography. TCC 2022. LNCS, vol. 13747, pp. 651–679. Springer, Cham (2022). https://doi.org/10.1007/978-3-031-22318-1_23

44. Wee, H.: Optimal broadcast encryption and CP-ABE from evasive lattice assumptions. In: Dunkelman, O., Dziembowski, S. (eds.) Advances in Cryptology–EUROCRYPT 2022. EUROCRYPT 2022. LNCS, vol. 13276, pp. 217–241. Springer, Cham (2022). https://doi. org/10.1007/978-3-031-07085-3_8

45. Zhou, K., Ren, J.: PassBio: privacy-preserving user-centric biometric authentication. IEEE Trans. Inf. Forensics Secur. **13**(12), 3050–3063 (2018)

Multi-Client Inner Product Encryption: Function-Hiding Instantiations Without Random Oracles

Elaine Shi and Nikhil Vanjani$^{(\boxtimes)}$

Carnegie Mellon University, Pittsburgh, USA
nvanjani@cmu.edu

Abstract. In a Multi-Client Functional Encryption (MCFE) scheme, n clients each obtain a secret encryption key from a trusted authority. During each time step t, each client i can encrypt its data using its secret key. The authority can use its master secret key to compute a functional key given a function f, and the functional key can be applied to a collection of n clients' ciphertexts encrypted to the same time step, resulting in the outcome of f on the clients' data. In this paper, we focus on MCFE for *inner-product* computations.

If an MCFE scheme hides not only the clients' data, but also the function f, we say it is *function hiding*. Although MCFE for inner-product computation has been extensively studied, how to achieve function privacy is still poorly understood. The very recent work of Agrawal et al. showed how to construct a *function-hiding* MCFE scheme for inner-product assuming standard bilinear group assumptions; however, they assume the existence of a random oracle and prove only a relaxed, selective security notion. An intriguing open question is whether we can achieve function-hiding MCFE for inner-product *without* random oracles.

In this work, we are the first to show a function-hiding MCFE scheme for inner products, relying on standard bilinear group assumptions. Further, we prove *adaptive* security without the use of a random oracle. Our scheme also achieves succinct ciphertexts, that is, each coordinate in the plaintext vector encrypts to only $O(1)$ group elements.

Our main technical contribution is a new upgrade from single-input functional encryption for inner-products to a multi-client one. Our upgrade preserves function privacy, that is, if the original single-input scheme is function-hiding, so is the resulting multi-client construction. Further, this new upgrade allows us to obtain a conceptually simple construction.

Keywords: multi-client functional encryption · adaptive security · bilinear group

1 Introduction

Multi-Input Functional Encryption (MIFE), first proposed by Goldwasser et al. [19], allows us to evaluate certain functions on multiple users' encrypted

N. Vanjani—Author ordering is randomized.

A. Boldyreva and V. Kolesnikov (Eds.): PKC 2023, LNCS 13940, pp. 622–651, 2023.
https://doi.org/10.1007/978-3-031-31368-4_22

data. In MIFE, a trusted setup gives an encryption key to each of n users, and then each user i can use its encryption key to encrypt some value x_i. A data analyst can ask the trusted setup for a cryptographic token to evaluate a specific function f. Equipped with the token, the data analyst can evaluate the outcome $f(x_1, \ldots, x_n)$ when presented with n ciphertexts each encoding $x_1, \ldots, x_n$, respectively.

It is also well-understood that the MIFE formulation suffers from some limitations. For instance, it does not make any attempt to limit the mix-and-match of ciphertexts. The evaluator can take any combination of users' ciphertexts, one from each user, to evaluate the function f. As a simple example, imagine that two users each encrypted two values, x_0, x_1 and y_0, y_1, respectively. Then, the evaluator can learn the outcome of $f(x_{b_0}, y_{b_1})$ for any combination of $b_0, b_1 \in \{0, 1\}$. In some applications, this may be too much leakage, and we want to limit the extent of mix-and-match. As a result, a related notion called Multi-Client Functional Encryption (MCFE) was introduced [19,26]. One way to understand the MCFE abstraction is to think of a "streaming" setting [26]: imagine that in every time step t, each user i encrypts a value $x_{i,t}$. Given the ciphertexts, the evaluator can evaluate $f(x_{1,t}, \ldots, x_{n,t})$ for each time step t, but it cannot mix-and-match the ciphertexts across different time steps and combine them in the evaluation. This greatly restricts the inherent leakage of the scheme. More generally, MCFE schemes allow users to encrypt to a label t, and only ciphertexts encrypted to the same label t can be used together during the functional evaluation. MCFE has numerous applications. For example, it has been applied to privacy-preserving, time-series data aggregation [26]. It is also useful in federated learning [14,24] where a server may wish to (incrementally) train some machine learning model based on data collected from users' mobile devices for each period of time. Very recent work also showed that function-hiding MCFE schemes can be used to construct a non-interactive anonymous routing scheme [27].

In vanilla MCFE schemes, our goal is to hide the plaintexts. However, in some applications [10,27], we also want an additional privacy property: not only should the ciphertexts hide the underlying messages, we also want the tokens to hide the function f being evaluated. An MCFE scheme that achieves this extra property is said to be *function-hiding* or *function-private* [10].

Status quo of Our Knowledge. The holy grail is to be able to construct MCFE for general functions from standard assumptions. However, it is believed that supporting general functions may be no easier than achieving indistinguishability obfuscation [11,13,21]. On the other hand, assuming the existence of indistinguishability obfuscation and the existence of a random oracle, we can indeed construct (function-revealing) MCFE for general functions [19].

Given that indistinguishability obfuscation will unlikely become practical in the near term, a natural question is for which functions can we construct efficient MCFE schemes, and ideally from standard assumptions? Along this direction, a line of work has explored how to construct (function-revealing) MCFE schemes for inner product computation, also called Multi-Client Inner-Product

Encryption (MCIPE)[1]. This exploration culminated in the work of Libert and Titiu [22], who showed how to construct an adaptively secure, function-revealing MCFE from standard lattice assumptions; and moreover, their scheme achieves succinct ciphertexts (i.e., each client's ciphertext size does not grow w.r.t. the number of parties). An independent work of Abdalla et al. [1] also achieved almost the same result as Libert and Titiu [22], except that 1) they can instantiate their constructions from DDH, LWE, or DCR assumptions; and 2) their ciphertexts are not succinct and grow linearly in the number of clients. Besides the work of Libert and Titiu [22] and that of Abdalla et al. [1], all other MCIPE constructions, even in the function-revealing setting, rely on random oracles for proving security [4,15,16].

When it comes to function privacy, however, our knowledge is relatively little. So far, the only known function-hiding MCIPE construction is the elegant work by Agrawal et al. [10], who constructed such a scheme from standard bilinear group assumptions, and additionally, assuming the existence of a random oracle; moreover, their construction is only *selectively* secure. To date, it remains elusive how to construct a function-hiding MCIPE scheme without random oracles.

Therefore, the status quo of MCIPE begs the following natural questions:

1. Can we construct an MCIPE scheme with *succinct ciphertexts* from *non-lattice* assumptions and *without random oracles*? This question is open *even for selective security and without requiring function privacy*.
2. Can we construct a *function-hiding* MCIPE scheme from *any standard* assumptions, *without random oracles*? This question is open *even for selective security, and even without caring about efficiency*.

Recall that the recent lower bound result Ünal [29] suggests that one cannot hope to achieve function-private (even single-input) inner-product encryption from lattices using a class of natural approaches. Therefore, being able to answer the first question above could open up more avenues towards eventually getting function privacy (i.e., the second question).

1.1   Our Results and Contributions

In this paper, we present a new MCIPE scheme from standard bilinear groups assumptions (against polynomial-time adversaries), and we prove the scheme to satisfy adaptive, function-hiding security. Our scheme is concretely efficient in the sense that every coordinate in the plaintext vector encrypts to only $O(1)$ group elements, and every coordinate in a key vector will result in $O(1)$ group elements in the functional key.

Therefore, we not only provide an affirmative answer to the above open questions, we also achieve all the desirable properties in a single unifying construction. More specifically, we prove the following theorem.

---

[1] Throughout this paper, the term "inner-product encryption" always means "inner-product *functional* encryption". This terminology is standard in this space.

Table 1. Comparison with prior MCIPE schemes where $O_\lambda(\cdot)$ hides terms related to the security parameter λ.

Scheme	Assumptions	Func privacy	Adaptive	per-coordinate CT
[15]	DDH + RO	✗	✔	$O_\lambda(1)$
[1]	DDH or DCR or LWE	✗	✔	$O_\lambda(n)$
[22]	LWE	✗	✔	$O_\lambda(1)$
[4]	(bilinear or DCR or LWE) + RO	✗	✔	$O_\lambda(1)$
[10]	bilinear + RO	✔	✗	$O_\lambda(1)$
Our work	bilinear	✔	✔	$O_\lambda(1)$

Theorem 1. *Suppose that the Decisional Linear (DLin) and Decisional Bilinear Diffie-Hellman (DBDH) assumptions hold in suitable bilinear groups. There exists an MCIPE scheme that satisfies adaptive, function-hiding, indistinguishability-based security. Moreover, the scheme achieves succinct ciphertext.*

Techniques: A Function-Privacy-Preserving Upgrade from Single-input to Multi-client. Notably, our MCIPE construction is conceptually simpler than some prior (even function-revealing) constructions. Since the *conceptual simplicity* could make it easier for future work to further extend and improve our framework, we believe it yet another contribution made by our work.

To get our result, we describe a new upgrade from a single-input inner-product encryption (IPE) to MCIPE. Further, if the underlying IPE scheme satisfies adaptive function-hiding security, so does the resulting MCIPE scheme. We believe our upgrade technique can be of independent interest. Previously, a couple works [1,10] also take the approach of upgrading from a single-input IPE scheme; however, previous techniques suffer from several drawbacks. Abdalla et al. [1] showed how to upgrade a single-input IPE scheme to a multi-client one. Their technique suffers from a couple drawbacks: 1) even if the original IPE scheme is function-private, their upgrade does not preserve function privacy; and 2) their upgrade incurs a $\Theta(n)$ blowup in the per-client ciphertext size. The recent work of Agrawal et al. [10] can also be viewed as an upgrade from a function-hiding IPE to a function-hiding MCIPE scheme—however, as mentioned, their construction critically relies on a random oracle and is only selectively secure.

We compare our contributions with prior work in Table 1 where n denotes the total number of clients.

1.2 Additional Related Work

We now review related work, and explain why some of those ideas do not easily extend to our new result.

Multi-input Functional Encryption. As mentioned, multi-input functional encryption (MIFE), originally proposed by Goldwasser et al. [19], can be viewed as a weakening of MCFE where all ciphertexts are encrypted to the same label. This relaxation often makes constructing MIFE easier. For example, for general functions, we know how to construct MIFE assuming indistinguishability obfuscation and other standard cryptographic assumptions. However, when it comes to MCFE for general functions, we not only need indistinguishability obfuscation but also the random oracle model (unless we can publish separate public parameters for each different label that will ever be encountered).

A line of work explored how to construct MIFE for inner-product from standard assumptions. This line culminated in the work of Abdalla et al. [5], who showed a construction that satisfies adaptive function-hiding security, assuming standard bilinear group assumptions, and achieving succinct ciphertexts. Again, their technique does not easily give rise to a multi-*client* counterpart. In fact, without the use of a random oracle, we do not even know how to construct a *function-revealing* non-lattice-based MCIPE scheme with succinct ciphertexts, let alone a function-hiding one; and for getting function privacy, it is believed that there may be potential barriers using lattice techniques [29].

Recently, Agrawal et al. [9] showed how to construct MIFE for *quadratic functions*—however, their scheme does not allow corruption of a subset of the clients and therefore does not directly extend to the multi-client setting; moreover, their scheme is not function hiding. Abdalla et al. [7] showed how to construct a 2-round MCFE scheme for *quadratic functions*. In their construction, encryption involves a 2-round interaction between a client and a set of authorities. Moreover, their scheme is not function hiding.

Throughout our paper (including Table 1), we assume static corruption. Besides our notion of adaptive security where encryption and key queries can be chosen adaptively by the adversary, Abdalla et al. [1,2], Libert and Titiu [22] and Nguyen et al. [25] also considered a different, adaptive corruption notion, where the clients are corrupted in an adaptive fashion—however, their constructions are non-function-hiding. Abdalla et al. [2] constructed an MIFE scheme for adaptive corruptions but the scheme is not function-hiding. Abdalla et al. [1] and Libert and Titiu [22] obtained similar results in the stronger multi-client setting from pairings and lattice assumptions respectively. Nguyen et al. [25] constructed MCFE with fine-grained access control from pairings in the RO model. Our work can also secure against adaptive corruption if we make sub-exponential assumptions and use standard complexity leveraging techniques. To the best of our knowledge, *no known technique can achieve adaptive corruption for the function-hiding setting* without relying on complexity leveraging, even for multi-input inner-product encryption, and even for selective-query security. How to achieve security against adaptive corruption in the function-private setting is an open question. Our current proof techniques adopt a sequence of hybrids that are incompatible with adaptive corruption—this also applies to other known constructions with function privacy [10,27]: since we must answer the queries differently for corrupt coordinates and honest coordinates, the current proof framework will not work if the challenger does not have know this upfront.

The main challenge for adaptive corruption is that in our hybrid sequence, we make use of a multiple-slot trick tailored for the function-hiding setting—for example, switching from $(\mathbf{x}_i^{(1)}, 0^m, \ldots)$ and $(\mathbf{y}_i^{*(1)}, 0^m, \ldots)$ to $(\mathbf{x}_i^{(1)}, \mathbf{x}_i^{(0)})$ and $(\mathbf{y}_i^{*(1)}, 0^m, \ldots)$ for an honest coordinate i (see Hybrid Real_1 to Hyb_0 transition in Table 2). For adaptive corruption, if i is not corrupt yet but will eventually become corrupt, we should not make this switch for coordinate i—but we cannot predict whether i will be eventually corrupt. In the function-revealing schemes [1, 2, 22, 25], their proofs do not rely on this type of multiple-slot trick making it much easier to prove adaptive corruption.

Comparison with Shi and Wu [27]. Recently, the work of Shi and Wu [27] considered a simple special case of inner-product, that is, "selection". Selection is the task of selecting one coordinate from the plaintext vector, i.e., inner product with a special vector where one coordinate is set to 1, and all other coordinates are set to 0. They showed how to achieve a *selective*, function-hiding MCFE scheme for selection. Shi and Wu's framework cannot be easily extended to get our result. First, their proof technique only works for proving *selective* security, whereas we want to prove *adaptive* security. Second, their framework is tailored for selection and does not easily extend to general inner product computation. Specifically, to construct a *function-hiding* MCFE scheme for selection, they first construct a *function-revealing* MCFE scheme for selection without RO, and then perform a function-privacy upgrade. We are not able to follow the same paradigm, since Previously, it was not even known how to construct a non-lattice-based, *function-revealing* MCIPE scheme without RO and with *succinct ciphertexts*. The only known non-lattice-based, function-revealing MCIPE scheme without RO is the elegant work by Abdalla et al. [1]. Unfortunately, their scheme has an $\Theta(n)$ blowup in the ciphertext size that we want to avoid. Although it is known how to construct a *function-revealing* MCIPE scheme without RO using lattices [22], the recent lower bound result Ünal [29] suggests that one cannot hope to achieve function-private IPE from lattices using a class of natural approaches.

Decentralizing MIFE and MCFE Schemes. An elegant line of work [8, 10, 15, 17] considers how to decentralize the key generation in multi-input and multi-client functional encryption schemes. The resulting schemes are typically referred to as ad-hoc MIFE [8] or as dynamic decentralized functional encryption (DDFE) [10, 17]. Roughly speaking, ad-hoc MIFE can be viewed as a generalization of MIFE, and DDFE can be viewed as a generalization of MCFE, where the key generation can be performed in a decentralized fashion without relying on a trusted party. This line of work culminated in the recent work of Agrawal et al. [10] who constructed a function-hiding DDFE scheme from bilinear groups in the random oracle model. Therefore, an interesting question left open by our work is whether there exists a function-hiding DDFE scheme from standard assumptions, without relying on a random oracle. This question is open even for selective security and even without caring about efficiency.

2 Overview of Our Constructions and Techniques

We now give an informal overview of our construction and proof techniques. In our subsequent technical sections, we will present formal definitions, detailed scheme description, and formal proofs.

Notations. Throughout, we will use boldface letters such as $\mathbf{x}$ to denote vectors. Given a bilinear group $\mathbb{G} \times \mathbb{G} \to \mathbb{G}_T$ of prime order q, we use the notation $[\![x]\!]$ and $[\![x]\!]_T$ to denote the group encoding of $x \in \mathbb{Z}_q$ in the source and target groups; and a similar notation is used for vectors too.

2.1 Why Prior Work Needed a Random Oracle

The recent work of Agrawal et al. [10] suggested the following elegant idea for constructing a function-hiding MCFE scheme for inner-product (also called MCIPE). Let IPE be a *function-hiding* inner-product encryption scheme (i.e., a single-input FE scheme for inner-product). We assume that IPE is built from suitable bilinear groups. We additionally assume the following nice property about IPE: the encryption algorithm (denoted **Enc**) and the functional key generation algorithm (denoted **KGen**) should work even when taking in the group encoding of the plaintext or key vector rather than the vector itself.

Let $\mathbf{x} = (\mathbf{x}_1, \ldots, \mathbf{x}_n)$ denote the plaintext vector where $\mathbf{x}_i$ is the component corresponding to client $i \in [n]$. let $\mathbf{y} = (\mathbf{y}_1, \ldots, \mathbf{y}_n)$ be the key vector where $\mathbf{y}$ is the component corresponding to client $i \in [n]$. Agrawal et al. [10]'s construction works as follows. Henceforth let $H(\cdot)$ be a random oracle and let $[\![\rho_t]\!] = H(t)$ which is a hash of the time step t (also called label).

<table>
<tr><td>Ciphertext:</td><td></td><td>Functional key:</td></tr>
<tr><td>$\mathsf{ct}_1 = \mathsf{IPE.Enc}(\mathsf{imsk}_1, [\![\mathbf{x}_1, \rho_t]\!])$</td><td>$\Leftrightarrow$</td><td>$\mathsf{isk}_1 = \mathsf{IPE.KGen}(\mathsf{imsk}_1, [\![\mathbf{y}_1, z_1]\!])$</td></tr>
<tr><td>$\vdots$</td><td></td><td>$\vdots$</td></tr>
<tr><td>$\mathsf{ct}_n = \mathsf{IPE.Enc}(\mathsf{imsk}_n, [\![\mathbf{x}_n, \rho_t]\!])$</td><td>$\Leftrightarrow$</td><td>$\mathsf{isk}_n = \mathsf{IPE.KGen}(\mathsf{imsk}_n, [\![\mathbf{y}_n, z_n]\!])$</td></tr>
</table>

In the above, each client $i \in [n]$ has an independent IPE instance whose master secret key is imsk_i also chosen by the trusted setup; the terms $z_1, \ldots, z_n$ are chosen freshly at random for each client respectively during each **KGen** query, such that their summation is 0, that is, $z_1 + z_2 + \ldots + z_n = 0$.

Henceforth, suppose $H(t) = [\![\rho_t]\!]$. To decrypt, we can $\mathsf{IPE.Dec}(\mathsf{ct}_i, \mathsf{isk}_i)$ to obtain the partial decryption $\langle \mathbf{x}_i, \mathbf{y}_i \rangle + \rho_t \cdot z_i$ encoded as the exponent of some group element. When we sum up all the partial decryptions, the part $\rho_t \cdot z_1 + \rho_t \cdot z_2 + \ldots + \rho_t \cdot z_n$ cancel out, and we are left with $\langle \mathbf{x}, \mathbf{y} \rangle$.

Intuitively, the ciphertext terms $H(t)$ and key terms z_i's serve to re-randomize each partial decryption. In this way, the adversary is forced to use all n clients' ciphertext components from the same time step to yield a meaningful decryption result. If the adversary mixes and matches ciphertext components from different time steps, decryption gives garbage and no information is leaked. If the adversary uses a proper subset of the clients' ciphertext components but not all n of them, decryption also gives garbage. Agrawal et al. [10]'s scheme critically relies on a random oracle $H(\cdot)$ due to a combination of following reasons:

1. For functionality, the multiple clients must coordinate and put in a *common term* that is multiplied with the z_i's during the decryption. Only in this way, can the randomizing terms cancel out when all partial decryptions are summed up;

2. For security, the aforementioned common term must be *random*, and not only so, must be fresh for each time step t. Henceforth let $\mathcal{H}$ denote the set of honest clients. Without going into full details about their proof, basically, in some critical step in their hybrid sequence, they want to argue the following computational indistinguishability statement for some "challenge key" which involves the terms $z_1^*, \ldots, z_n^*$:

$$\{[\![\rho_t \cdot z_i^*]\!]\}_{i \in \mathcal{H}, t=1,2,3,\ldots} \overset{c}{\equiv} \{R_{i,t}\}_{i \in \mathcal{H}, t=1,2,3,\ldots} \tag{1}$$

where $\{R_{i,t}\}_{i \in \mathcal{H}, t=1,2,3,\ldots}$ are randomly chosen group elements such that the product is preserved in every time step, that is:

$$\forall t : \prod_{i \in \mathcal{H}} R_{i,t} = \prod_{i \in \mathcal{H}} [\![\rho_t \cdot z_i^*]\!] \tag{2}$$

Agrawal et al. [10] argue that the above holds under the SXDH assumption as long as each $H(t) = [\![\rho_t]\!]$ is a random group element.

In summary, in the scheme by Agrawal et al., the random oracle $H(\cdot)$ allows the clients to coordinate without communication, and adopt the same random term that is refreshed for each t in their respective ciphertexts. One naïve way to avoid the RO is for the trusted step to publish all random $\{[\![\rho_t]\!]\}_{t=1,2,3\ldots}$ terms in the sky upfront, but then the scheme would not be able to support an unbounded number of time steps.

2.2 Removing the RO: A Strawman Idea

In Agrawal et al.'s scheme, the coordinated randomness $z_1, \ldots, z_n$ is part of the functional key; therefore, in the ciphertext, all clients must put in shared common randomness to pair with these terms. To remove the RO, a strawman idea is move the coordinated randomness to the ciphertext. To this end, we will employ a *correlated pseudorandom function*, denoted CPRF. In a CPRF scheme, each client $i \in [n]$ obtains a secret key K_i from a trusted setup. Then, given a message t, the user can compute CPRF.Eval(K_i, t) to obtain an outcome that is computationally indistinguishable from random, subject to the constraint that

$$\sum_{i \in [n]} \mathsf{CPRF.Eval}(K_i, t) = 0 \tag{3}$$

Further, even when a subset of the clients may be corrupted, the outcomes of the honest clients' evaluations are nonetheless pseudorandom subject to the constraint in Eq. (3)—see Sect. 4.2 for the formal definition. Earlier works have shown how to construct such a CPRF assuming the existence of pseudorandom functions [1,14]. With such a CPRF, we can construct the following strawman scheme where we use the shorthand notation $\mathsf{CPRF}(K_i, t) = \mathsf{CPRF}.\mathbf{Eval}(K_i, t)$, and z denotes a term shared across the different clients $1, \ldots, n$ for the same functional key, but *freshly chosen for every functional key*:

Ciphertext:

$$\mathsf{ct}_1 = \mathsf{IPE}.\mathbf{Enc}(\mathsf{imsk}_1, (\mathbf{x}_1, \mathsf{CPRF}(K_1, t))) \quad \Leftrightarrow$$

$\vdots$

$$\mathsf{ct}_n = \mathsf{IPE}.\mathbf{Enc}(\mathsf{imsk}_n, (\mathbf{x}_n, \mathsf{CPRF}(K_n, t))) \quad \Leftrightarrow$$

Functional key:

$$\mathsf{isk}_1 = \mathsf{IPE}.\mathbf{KGen}(\mathsf{imsk}_1, (\mathbf{y}_1, z))$$

$\vdots$

$$\mathsf{isk}_n = \mathsf{IPE}.\mathbf{KGen}(\mathsf{imsk}_n, (\mathbf{y}_n, z))$$

The use of the CPRF in the above allows the distributed clients to adopt correlated randomness that is refreshed for each t at encryption time, and thus avoids the RO. However, the strawman scheme does not work since the security proof fails to go through. Let $\mathcal{H}$ denote the set of honest clients. In a critical step Agrawal et al.'s proof, they rely on the security of the IPE scheme to hide the $\{z_i^*\}_{i \in \mathcal{H}}$ terms in some "challenge key", and instead move information about $[\![\rho_t \cdot z_i^*]\!]_{i \in \mathcal{H}, t=1,2,3,\ldots}$ into the ciphertext components—recall that in their scheme, the term $\rho_t \cdot z_i^*$ is the randomizing term that protects client i's message in the i-th partial decryption. They argue that the terms $[\![\rho_t \cdot z_i^*]\!]_{i \in \mathcal{H}, t=1,2,3,\ldots}$ are computationally indistinguishable from random except their product is conserved for every time step t—see Eqs. (1) and (2).

Unfortunately, this strategy no longer works, as now all the key components share the same randomness z. When the adversary corrupts a subset of the clients, it will learn info about the randomness $[\![z^*]\!]$ in the challenge key. Additionally, the adversary can gain info about $[\![\mathsf{CPRF}(K_i, t)]\!]_{i \in \mathcal{H}, t=1,2,3,\ldots}$ from the ciphertexts. Hence, the adversary can easily distinguish $\{[\![\mathsf{CPRF}(K_i, t) \cdot z^*]\!]\}_{i \in \mathcal{H}, t=1,2,3,\ldots}$ from random terms through a DDH-style attack. We stress that using asymmetric group and SXDH does not fix this attack, as the ciphertext and the key must come from opposite source groups to be paired with each other[2].

2.3 Our Selectively Secure Construction

We start with the goal of achieving selective security (i.e., assuming that the adversary must submit all **KGen** queries ahead of encryption queries), and

---

[2] In Appendix E of the online full version, we show that a variant of the strawman scheme can indeed be proven secure in a different selective model, i.e., the adversary must submit all encryption queries ahead of **KGen** queries. However, we do not know any easy way to build from this selective scheme and get adaptive security eventually.

later describe additional techniques for achieving adaptive security. We sketch our selectively secure construction below—a more formal presentation can be found in subsequent technical sections. Recall that IPE denotes a function-hiding (single-input) inner-product encryption scheme. In our scheme the public parameters are just the public parameters of the underlying function-hiding secure IPE scheme.

- **Setup**: we run n independent instances of IPE.**Setup** to sample n secret keys denoted $\mathsf{imsk}_1, \ldots, \mathsf{imsk}_n$, respectively. We also run the setup algorithm of the CPRF, and obtain $K_1, \ldots, K_n$. Finally, we generate a random $a_i \stackrel{\$}{\leftarrow} \mathbb{Z}_q$ for each client $i \in [n]$. In summary, each client's secret key is composed of the terms $(\mathsf{imsk}_i, K_i, a_i)$, and the master secret key is simply the union of all clients' secret keys.

- **KGen**: an authority with the master secret key can compute a functional key for the vector $\mathbf{y} = (\mathbf{y}_1, \ldots, \mathbf{y}_n) \in \mathbb{Z}_q^{m \cdot n}$ as follows where $\rho \stackrel{\$}{\leftarrow} \mathbb{Z}_q$ is fresh randomness:

$$\{\mathsf{isk}_i := \mathsf{IPE}.\mathbf{KGen}(\mathsf{imsk}_i, \widetilde{\mathbf{y}}_i)\}_{i \in [n]} \text{ where } \widetilde{\mathbf{y}}_i = (\mathbf{y}_i, 0^m, \rho, -\rho a_i, 0)$$

- **Enc**: for client $i \in [n]$ to encrypt $\mathbf{x}_i \in \mathbb{Z}_q^m$ to some label t, it samples $\mu_{i,t} \stackrel{\$}{\leftarrow} \mathbb{Z}_q$ if it has not been sampled before, and outputs the following ciphertext:

$$\mathsf{IPE}.\mathbf{Enc}\,(\mathsf{imsk}_i, \widetilde{\mathbf{x}}_i) \text{ where } \widetilde{\mathbf{x}}_i = (\mathbf{x}_i, 0^m, \mathsf{CPRF}.\mathbf{Eval}(K_i, t) + a_i \mu_{i,t}, \mu_{i,t}, 0)$$

- **Dec**: to decrypt, simply use each isk_i to decrypt the ciphertext ct_i from the i-th client and obtain a partial decryption p_i; then, output the discrete log of $\prod_{i \in [n]} p_i$. Since decryption requires computing discrete logarithm, the outcome of the inner-product computation must lie within a polynomially-bounded space for the decryption to be efficient.

We now show correctness. Suppose that $\mathsf{ct}_1, \ldots, \mathsf{ct}_n$ are n honestly generated ciphertexts all for the same label t, and for plaintext vectors $\mathbf{x}_1, \ldots, \mathbf{x}_n$, respectively. Further, suppose that $(\mathsf{isk}_1, \ldots, \mathsf{isk}_n)$ is the functional key for the vector $\mathbf{y} = (\mathbf{y}_1, \ldots, \mathbf{y}_n)$. Then, applying isk_i to ct_i gives the partial decryption result

$$p_i = [\![\langle \mathbf{x}_i, \mathbf{y}_i \rangle + \rho \cdot \mathsf{CPRF}.\mathbf{Eval}(K_i, t) + \rho \cdot a_i \mu_{i,t} - \rho a_i \cdot \mu_{i,t}]\!]_T$$
$$= [\![\langle \mathbf{x}_i, \mathbf{y}_i \rangle + \rho \cdot \mathsf{CPRF}.\mathbf{Eval}(K_i, t)]\!]_T$$

Therefore, when we compute the product $\prod_{i \in [n]} p_i$, the part related to the CPRF all cancel out, leaving us the term $[\![\mathbf{x}, \mathbf{y}]\!]_T$ where $\mathbf{x} := (\mathbf{x}_1, \ldots, \mathbf{x}_n)$.

Intuition. In comparison with the strawman scheme in Sect. 2.2, here we introduce the additional term $a_i \mu_{i,t}$ to protect the randomizing term $\mathsf{CPRF}.\mathbf{Eval}(K_i, t)$ in the ciphertext, where a_i is part of the master secret key for client i. We also introduce the extra term $[\![\mu_{i,t}]\!]$ to client i's ciphertext component, and the extra term $[\![-\rho a_i]\!]$ to client i's key component, where ρ shared across all clients' key vectors but fresh for each key. These terms make sure that the newly introduced

Table 2. Sequence of hybrids, where $\star$ denotes the most technical step to be elaborate later. Here we show the vectors passed to the underlying IPE's **Enc** and **KGen** functions in each hybrid. Q_{kgen} denotes the maximum number of **KGen** queries made by the adversary. For conciseness, we write $\mathsf{CPRF}(K_i, t)$ as a shorthand for $\mathsf{CPRF}.\mathbf{Eval}(K_i, t)$. Note that the ρ term is sampled fresh at random for each **KGen** query.

Hybrid	Enc	KGen	Assumption
Real_1	$\left(\mathbf{x}_i^{(1)}, \mathbf{0}, \mathsf{CPRF}(K_i,t) + a_i\mu_{i,t}, \mu_{i,t}, 0\right)$	$\left(\mathbf{y}_i^{(1)}, \mathbf{0}, \rho, -\rho a_i, 0\right)$	
Hyb_0	$\left(\mathbf{x}_i^{(1)}, \mathbf{x}_i^{(0)}, \mathsf{CPRF}(K_i,t) + a_i\mu_{i,t}, \mu_{i,t}, 0\right)$	$\left(\mathbf{y}_i^{(1)}, \mathbf{0}, \rho, -\rho a_i, 0\right)$	FH-IND of IPE
Hyb_ℓ $\ell \in [Q_{\mathrm{kgen}}]$	same as Hyb_0	first ℓ: $\left(\mathbf{0}, \mathbf{y}_i^{(0)}, \rho, -\rho a_i, 0\right)$ remaining: $\left(\mathbf{y}_i^{(1)}, \mathbf{0}, \rho, -\rho a_i, 0\right)$	explained below $\star$
Hyb^*	$\left(\mathbf{0}, \mathbf{x}_i^{(0)}, \mathsf{CPRF}(K_i,t) + a_i\mu_{i,t}, \mu_{i,t}, 0\right)$	$\left(\mathbf{0}, \mathbf{y}_i^{(0)}, \rho, -\rho a_i, 0\right)$	FH-IND of IPE
Real_0	$\left(\mathbf{x}_i^{(0)}, \mathbf{0}, \mathsf{CPRF}(K_i,t) + a_i\mu_{i,t}, \mu_{i,t}, 0\right)$	$\left(\mathbf{y}_i^{(0)}, \mathbf{0}, \rho, -\rho a_i, 0\right)$	FH-IND of IPE

$a_i\mu_{i,t}$ term would cancel out during decryption, such that each client's partial decryption result is preserved as in the strawman scheme.

In our security proof, we will rely on the security of IPE to hide the $[\![-\rho^* \cdot a_i]\!]_{i \in \mathcal{H}}$ terms pertaining to honest clients $\mathcal{H}$ from some "challenge key" whose shared randomness is ρ^*, and instead move information about $\{[\![\rho^* \cdot \mathsf{CPRF}.\mathbf{Eval}(K_i,t)]\!]\}_{i \in \mathcal{H}, t=1,2,3,\ldots}$ to the honest clients' ciphertext components (see hybrid $\mathsf{H}_{\ell-1,1}$ in Sect. 2.4). We then argue that under the Decisional Linear assumption, the terms $\{[\![\rho^* \cdot \mathsf{CPRF}.\mathbf{Eval}(K_i,t)]\!]\}_{i \in \mathcal{H}, t=1,2,3,\ldots}$ are computationally indistinguishable from random terms such that for each t their product is conserved (see hybrid $\mathsf{H}_{\ell-1,3}$ of Sect. 2.4). Moreover, the above should hold even when the adversary may have information about $[\![\rho^*]\!]$ (from knowledge of the challenge key and corrupt clients' master secret keys), $\{[\![\mathsf{CPRF}.\mathbf{Eval}(K_i,t)]\!]\}_{i \in \mathcal{H}, t=1,2,3,\ldots}$ (from honest clients' ciphertexts), and $\{[\![\rho \cdot a_i]\!]\}_{i \in \mathcal{H}}$ for any ρ contained in a non-challenge key (from knowledge of non-challenge keys).

2.4   Proving Selective Function-Hiding Security

We first describe how to prove *selective*, function hiding security, assuming that the underlying IPE scheme satisfies *selective*, function-hiding, indistinguishability-based security, the CPRF scheme is secure, and that the Decisional Linear problem is computationally hard. Later in Sect. 2.5, we discuss the additional techniques needed for proving adaptive security.

To prove that our scheme satisfies selective function-hiding indistinguishability-based security, we need to go through a sequence of hybrids as shown in Table 2. Note that Table 2 shows only how the challenger generates ciphertext

Table 3. Selective security: inner hybrids to go from $\mathsf{Hyb}_{\ell-1}$ to Hyb_ℓ. $\mathbf{y}^{*(b)} := (\mathbf{y}_1^{*(b)}, \dots, \mathbf{y}_n^{*(b)})$ for $b \in \{0, 1\}$ denote the key vectors submitted in the ℓ-th **KGen** query, and ρ^* is the randomness used in the ℓ-th **KGen** query.

Hybrid		Assumption
$\mathsf{Hyb}_{\ell-1}$	see Table 2	
$H_{\ell-1,1}$	**Enc** : $\left(\mathbf{x}_i^{(1)}, \mathbf{x}_i^{(0)}, \mathsf{CPRF}(K_i, t) + a_i\mu_{i,t}, \mu_{i,t}, \mathsf{CPRF}(K_i, t) \cdot \rho^* + \langle \mathbf{x}_i^{(1)}, \mathbf{y}_i^{*(1)} \rangle\right)$ **KGen** : first $\ell - 1$: $\left(0^m, \mathbf{y}_i^{(0)}, \rho, -\rho a_i, 0\right)$ ℓ-th: $(0^m, 0^m, 0, 0, 1)$ remaining: $\left(\mathbf{y}_i^{(1)}, 0^m, \rho, -\rho a_i, 0\right)$	FH-IND of IPE
$H_{\ell-1,2}$	**Enc** : $\left(\mathbf{x}_i^{(1)}, \mathbf{x}_i^{(0)}, R_{i,t} + a_i\mu_{i,t}, \mu_{i,t}, R_{i,t} \cdot \rho^* + \langle \mathbf{x}_i^{(1)}, \mathbf{y}_i^{*(1)} \rangle\right)$ where $\sum_{i \in \mathcal{H}} R_{i,t} = -\sum_{i \in \mathcal{K}} \mathsf{CPRF}(K_i, t)$ **KGen** : same as $H_{\ell-1,1}$	correlated pseudorand. of CPRF
$H_{\ell-1,3}$	**Enc** : $\left(\mathbf{x}_i^{(1)}, \mathbf{x}_i^{(0)}, R_{i,t} + a_i\mu_{i,t}, \mu_{i,t}, T_{i,t} + \langle \mathbf{x}_i^{(1)}, \mathbf{y}_i^{*(1)} \rangle\right)$ where $\sum_{i \in \mathcal{H}} T_{i,t} = -\rho^* \cdot \sum_{i \in \mathcal{K}} \mathsf{CPRF}(K_i, t)$ **KGen** : same as $H_{\ell-1,1}$	DLin
$H'_{\ell-1,3}$	**Enc** : $\left(\mathbf{x}_i^{(1)}, \mathbf{x}_i^{(0)}, R_{i,t} + a_i\mu_{i,t}, \mu_{i,t}, T_{i,t} + \langle \mathbf{x}_i^{(0)}, \mathbf{y}_i^{*(0)} \rangle\right)$ where $\sum_{i \in \mathcal{H}} T_{i,t} = -\rho^* \cdot \sum_{i \in \mathcal{K}} \mathsf{CPRF}(K_i, t)$ **KGen** : same as $H_{\ell-1,1}$	identically distributed
$H'_{\ell-1,2}$	**Enc** : $\left(\mathbf{x}_i^{(1)}, \mathbf{x}_i^{(0)}, R_{i,t} + a_i\mu_{i,t}, \mu_{i,t}, R_{i,t} \cdot \rho^* + \langle \mathbf{x}_i^{(0)}, \mathbf{y}_i^{*(0)} \rangle\right)$ where $\sum_{i \in \mathcal{H}} R_{i,t} = -\sum_{i \in \mathcal{K}} \mathsf{CPRF}(K_i, t)$ **KGen** : same as $H_{\ell-1,1}$	DLin
$H'_{\ell-1,1}$	**Enc** : $\left(\mathbf{x}_i^{(1)}, \mathbf{x}_i^{(0)}, \mathsf{CPRF}(K_i, t) + a_i\mu_{i,t}, \mu_{i,t}, \mathsf{CPRF}(K_i, t) \cdot \rho^* + \langle \mathbf{x}_i^{(0)}, \mathbf{y}_i^{*(0)} \rangle\right)$ **KGen** : same as $H_{\ell-1,1}$	correlated pseudorand. of CPRF
Hyb_ℓ	see Table 2	FH-IND of IPE

and key components for an *honest* client $i \in [n]$. For a *corrupted* client i, the security game stipulates that $\mathbf{x}_i^{(0)} = \mathbf{x}_i^{(1)}$ and $\mathbf{y}_i^{(0)} = \mathbf{y}_i^{(1)}$, and thus the challenger simply runs the honest **Enc** or **KGen** algorithm as in the real world.

The steps where we apply the function-hiding indistinguishability security (denoted FH-IND in Table 2) of the underlying IPE are relatively straightforward. The most technical part in the proof is to argue that $\mathsf{Hyb}_{\ell-1}$ is computationally indistinguishable from Hyb_ℓ for $\ell \in [Q_{\mathsf{kgen}}]$, where we are switching the keys queries one by one from world 1 to world 0. In $\mathsf{Hyb}_{\ell-1}$, the first $\ell - 1$ key queries are answered using $\mathbf{y}^{*(0)}$, whereas the remaining are answered using $\mathbf{y}^{*(1)}$. We want to switch the ℓ-th key query to using $\mathbf{y}^{*(0)}$ instead which will lead to Hyb_ℓ.

To this end, we carry out another sequence of inner hybrids as shown in Table 3. We first rely on the security of the IPE scheme to accomplish the following (see the experiment $H_{\ell-1,1}$):

1. move information about $[\![CPRF(K_i,t)\rho^* + \langle \mathbf{x}_i^{(1)}, \mathbf{y}_i^{*(1)} \rangle]\!]_{i\in\mathcal{H},t=1,2,3,...}$ from the key to the honest ciphertexts, where ρ^* denotes the shared randomness in the challenge key query; and
2. remove information about $[\![\rho^* a_i]\!]_{i\in\mathcal{H}}$ from the challenge key.

At this moment, we can switch the $[\![CPRF(K_i,t)\rho^*]\!]_{i\in\mathcal{H},t=1,2,3,...}$ terms in the honest ciphertexts to random denoted $[\![T_{i,t}]\!]_{i\in\mathcal{H},t=1,2,3,...}$ (subject to the constraint that their product is preserved in each time step t), and uncorrelate these terms with the other ciphertext terms containing information about $CPRF(K_i,t)$. This can be accomplished through a reduction to the security of the CPRF and the Decisional Linear assumption (hybrids $H_{\ell-1,2}$ and $H_{\ell-1,3}$). The Decisional Linear step is arguably the most technical step in our selective security proof, and we provide the detailed proof in Claim 4 in the subsequent formal sections (see also the intuition in Sect. 2.3).

At this moment, we can switch the terms $[\![T_{i,t} + \langle \mathbf{x}_i^{(1)}, \mathbf{y}_i^{*(1)} \rangle]\!]_{i\in\mathcal{H},t=1,2,3,...}$ contained in the honest ciphertexts to $[\![T_{i,t} + \langle \mathbf{x}_i^{(0)}, \mathbf{y}_i^{*(0)} \rangle]\!]_{i\in\mathcal{H},t=1,2,3,...}$ through an information theoretic step. For this step to hold, we rely on the admissibility rule imposed on the adversary, that is, for any honest plaintexts $\left\{ \left(\mathbf{x}_i^{(0)}, \mathbf{x}_i^{(1)} \right) \right\}_{i\in\mathcal{H}}$ queried for the same label t, and for any pair of key vectors queried $(\mathbf{y}^{(0)}, \mathbf{y}^{(1)})$,

$$\left\langle \{\mathbf{x}_i^{(0)}\}_{i\in\mathcal{H}}, \{\mathbf{y}_i^{(0)}\}_{i\in\mathcal{H}} \right\rangle = \left\langle \{\mathbf{x}_i^{(1)}\}_{i\in\mathcal{H}}, \{\mathbf{y}_i^{(1)}\}_{i\in\mathcal{H}} \right\rangle \tag{4}$$

This admissibility rule implies that if for some $i \in \mathcal{H}$, the pair $(\mathbf{x}_i^{(0)}, \mathbf{x}_i^{(1)})$ and the pair $(\widetilde{\mathbf{x}}_i^{(0)}, \widetilde{\mathbf{x}}_i^{(1)})$ were queried on the same label t, then the following must hold for any key pair $(\mathbf{y}^{(0)}, \mathbf{y}^{(1)})$ queried:

$$\left\langle \mathbf{x}_i^{(0)}, \mathbf{y}_i^{(0)} \right\rangle - \left\langle \widetilde{\mathbf{x}}_i^{(0)}, \mathbf{y}_i^{(0)} \right\rangle = \left\langle \mathbf{x}_i^{(1)}, \mathbf{y}_i^{(1)} \right\rangle - \left\langle \widetilde{\mathbf{x}}_i^{(1)}, \mathbf{y}_i^{(1)} \right\rangle \tag{5}$$

Finally, we can go through symmetric steps mirroring the first half of proof, and eventually arrive at Hyb_ℓ.

2.5   Achieving Adaptive Function-Hiding Security

We need additional techniques for proving adaptive security. To aid understanding, it helps to first observe why our previous proof is inherently selective. In a critical step (i.e., from $Hyb_{\ell-1}$ to Hyb_ℓ) where we switched the challenge key (i.e., the ℓ-th key query) from $(\mathbf{y}_i^{*(1)}, \mathbf{0}, \rho^*, -\rho^* a_i, 0)$ to $(\mathbf{0}, \mathbf{y}_i^{*(0)}, \rho^*, -\rho^* a_i, 0)$, we need to go through an inner hybrid experiment where we remove information about $\{\rho^* a_i\}_{i\in\mathcal{H}}$ from the honest clients' key components, and instead encode information about $\{\mathsf{CPRF}(K_i, t) \cdot \rho^* + \langle \mathbf{x}_i^{(1)}, \mathbf{y}_i^{*(1)} \rangle\}_{i \in \mathcal{H}}$ into the ciphertexts (see the experiment $\mathsf{H}_{\ell-1,1}$). In this step, we made use of the fact that the challenger knows the challenge key vector $\mathbf{y}^*$ upfront.

In adaptive security, the adversary need not commit to all the key queries upfront. A naïve approach to prove adaptive security is via complexity leveraging, i.e., the challenger guesses the challenge key query upfront, and abort the experiment if the guess turns out to be wrong later. The problem with this approach is that it incurs exponential loss in the security failure, and therefore we would have to make the underlying computationally assumptions secure against sub-exponential time adversaries to absorb this security loss. By contrast, our approach does not incur such a loss in security, and we can thus reduce the adaptive function-hiding security of our MCIPE scheme to standard assumptions against polynomial-time adversaries.

Specifically, we show that the scheme described in Sect. 2.3, when instantiated with a *particular* IPE scheme that satisfies adaptive, function-hiding indistinguishable security, the resulting MCIPE scheme would indeed satisfy function-hiding, adaptive security. To prove this, we can no longer treat the underlying IPE as a blackbox as in our selective security proof. We need to completely unwrap the construction and rely on properties of the specific IPE employed to prove adaptive security. Our proof techniques are inspired by those of Abdalla et al. [5], who constructed an adaptively secure, *multi-input* inner-product encryption (MIIPE). MIIPE can be considered as a special case of MCIPE where *all ciphertexts have the same label* (or time step). This relaxation makes it easier to construct MIIPE. Therefore, the adaptive function-hiding MIIPE scheme by Abdalla et al. [5] does not easily imply a multi-client counterpart. In particular, for MCIPE, unless we are willing to tolerate linear in n ciphertext size per client, all known *non-lattice-based* constructions require RO, *even for function-revealing* constructions [4,10,15].

Our adaptively Secure Scheme. Concretely, we first apply the function-privacy upgrade of Lin [23] to an adaptively secure, function-revealing IPE scheme of Abdalla et al. [5], resulting in an adaptively secure, weak-function-hiding IPE scheme. We then use the resulting IPE scheme to instantiate our MCIPE scheme described in Sect. 2.3. The resulting MCIPE scheme, when unwrapped, is as follows—it turns out that we will not need the last slot in the ciphertexts and keys for each client in our adaptive proof, so we remove it from this construction:

- **Setup**: we generate $a_i \xleftarrow{\$} \mathbb{Z}_q$ and random matrices $\mathbf{A}_i, \mathbf{B}_i \xleftarrow{\$} \mathbb{Z}_q^{(k+1) \times k}$ of full rank k, $\mathbf{U}_i \xleftarrow{\$} \mathbb{Z}_q^{(2m+2) \times (k+1)}$, $\mathbf{V}_i \xleftarrow{\$} \mathbb{Z}_q^{(2m+k+3) \times (k+1)}$ for each client $i \in [n]$. We also run the setup algorithm of the CPRF, and obtain $K_1, \ldots, K_n$. In summary, each client's secret key is composed of the terms $(\mathbf{A}_i, \mathbf{B}_i, \mathbf{U}_i, \mathbf{V}_i, K_i, a_i)$, and the master secret key is simply the union of all clients' secret keys.
- **KGen**: an authority with the master secret key can compute a functional key for the vector $\mathbf{y} = (\mathbf{y}_1, \ldots, \mathbf{y}_n) \in \mathbb{Z}_q^{m \cdot n}$ as follows where $\widetilde{\mathbf{y}}_i = (\mathbf{y}_i, 0^m, \rho, -\rho a_i)$

for some fresh random $\rho \xleftarrow{\$} \mathbb{Z}_q, \mathbf{t}_i \xleftarrow{\$} \mathbb{Z}_q^k$:

$$\left\{ \llbracket \mathbf{d}_i \rrbracket = \llbracket (\mathbf{I}, \mathbf{U}_i)^T \, \widetilde{\mathbf{y}}_i + \mathbf{V}_i \mathbf{B}_i \mathbf{t}_i \rrbracket, \llbracket \mathbf{d}_i' \rrbracket = \llbracket -\mathbf{B}_i \mathbf{t}_i \rrbracket \right\}_{i \in [n]}$$

- **Enc:** for client $i \in [n]$ to encrypt a vector $\mathbf{x}_i \in \mathbb{Z}_q^m$ to some label t, it samples $\mu_{i,t} \xleftarrow{\$} \mathbb{Z}_q$ if it has not been sampled before, and outputs the following:

$$\left(\llbracket \mathbf{c}_i \rrbracket = \llbracket ((\widetilde{\mathbf{x}}_i + \mathbf{U}_i \mathbf{A}_i \mathbf{s}_i)^T, (-\mathbf{A}_i \mathbf{s}_i)^T)^T \rrbracket, \llbracket \mathbf{c}_i' \rrbracket = \llbracket \mathbf{V}_i^T \mathbf{c}_i \rrbracket \right)$$
$$\text{where } \widetilde{\mathbf{x}}_i = (\mathbf{x}_i, 0^m, \mathsf{CPRF}.\mathbf{Eval}(K_i, t) + a_i \mu_{i,t}, \mu_{i,t})$$

- **Dec:** to decrypt, simply compute $e \left(\llbracket \mathbf{c}_i^T \rrbracket, \llbracket \mathbf{d}_i \rrbracket \right) \cdot e \left(\llbracket \mathbf{c}_i'^T \rrbracket, \llbracket \mathbf{d}_i' \rrbracket \right)$ for the i-th client and obtain a partial decryption p_i; then, output the discrete log of $\prod_{i \in [n]} p_i$. Since decryption requires computing discrete logarithm, the outcome of the inner-product computation must lie within a polynomially-bounded space for the decryption to be efficient.

Proof Roadmap for Adaptive Security. In our adaptive proof, the outer hybrids remain the same as in Table 2 except that we now need the underlying IPE scheme to have adaptive function-hiding security for make the switches. To switch from $\mathsf{Hyb}_{\ell-1}$ to Hyb_ℓ, we can no longer rely on the previous sequence of inner hybrids (Table 3). Instead, we provide a new sequence of inner hybrids outlined in Table 4.

As shown in Table 4, there are a couple important differences between the previous selective proof and our new adaptive proof. In the selective proof, we switch the challenge key query to IPE functional keys of the vector $(0^m, 0^m, 0, 0, 1)$. This allowed us to erase not just information about $\{\rho^* a_i\}_{i \in \mathcal{H}}$, but also information about the challenge vector $\{\mathbf{y}_i^{*(1)}\}_{i \in \mathcal{H}}$ from the challenge key. Instead, this information is moved to the honest ciphertexts reflected in the terms $\llbracket \mathsf{CPRF}(K_i, t) \cdot \rho^* + \langle \mathbf{x}_i^{(1)}, \mathbf{y}_i^{*(1)} \rangle \rrbracket_{i \in \mathcal{H}, t=1,2,3,\dots}$. But this would require the challenger to know the challenge vector in advance, which we now want to avoid.

In our adaptive proof, we instead switch the challenge key query to IPE functional keys of the vector $(\mathbf{y}_i^{*(1)}, 0^m, 0, 0)$. Here we only remove information about $\{\rho^* a_i\}_{i \in \mathcal{H}}$ from the challenge key, but we retain information about the challenge vector $\{\mathbf{y}_i^{*(1)}\}_{i \in \mathcal{H}}$. Therefore, we only move the terms $\llbracket \mathsf{CPRF}(K_i, t) \cdot \rho^* \rrbracket_{i \in \mathcal{H}, t=1,2,3,\dots}$ to the honest ciphertexts, and the challenger need not know the challenge key vector in advance to do so. Not only so, here, to make this switch, we rely on the structure of the underlying IPE in a non-blackbox fashion (see hybrids $\mathsf{H}_{\ell-1,1}$ and $\mathsf{H}_{\ell-1,2}$). At this moment, we switch the challenge key from using $(\mathbf{y}_i^{*(1)}, 0^m, 0, 0)$ to $(0^m, \mathbf{y}_i^{*(0)}, 0, 0)$ for all $i \in \mathcal{H}$. To make this switch, we make non-blackbox usage of the structure of the underlying IPE, and argue that this switch can be made without affecting the distribution at all, i.e., $\mathsf{H}_{\ell-1,4}$ and $\mathsf{H}_{\ell-1,4}'$ are *identically distributed*, as long as the adversary satisfies the admissibility rule stated in Eq. (4) which also implies Eq. (5). The rest of the proof takes mirroring steps as the first half to eventually reach hybrid Hyb_ℓ.

The formal proof of adaptive, function-hiding security will be presented in Appendix B.4 of the online full version.

Why We Use IPE in a Non-blackbox Way. In our hybrid sequence for both selective and adaptive proofs, at some point of time we need to switch the inner products from $\langle \mathbf{x}_i^{(1)}, \mathbf{y}_i^{*(1)} \rangle$ to $\langle \mathbf{x}_i^{(0)}, \mathbf{y}_i^{*(0)} \rangle$. This step cannot rely on the function-hiding security of IPE because it is possible that $\langle \mathbf{x}_i^{(1)}, \mathbf{y}_i^{*(1)} \rangle \neq \langle \mathbf{x}_i^{(0)}, \mathbf{y}_i^{*(0)} \rangle$ for some honest user $i \in \mathcal{H}$. So, our idea is to make this switch in a way that the two resulting distributions are identically distributed ($\mathsf{H}_{\ell-1,3}$ to $\mathsf{H}'_{\ell-1,3}$ in the selective proof in Table 3 and $\mathsf{H}_{\ell-1,4}$ to $\mathsf{H}'_{\ell-1,4}$ in the adaptive proof in Table 4). To make this switch in the selective proof, we first switch to a hybrid ($\mathsf{H}_{\ell-1,3}$ in Table 3) in which $\langle \mathbf{x}_i^{(1)}, \mathbf{y}_i^{*(1)} \rangle$ is in the ciphertext, where we rely on the external randomizing terms $T_{i,t}$ to mask $\langle \mathbf{x}_i^{(1)}, \mathbf{y}_i^{*(1)} \rangle$. However, using this technique means we have to know the key queries upfront.

In our adaptive proof, we need to find another way for the proof to go through without knowledge of the key queries. The key step is going from $\mathsf{H}_{\ell-1,4}$ to $\mathsf{H}'_{\ell-1,4}$ in Table 4, where we switch the key from $(\mathbf{y}_i^{*(1)}, 0^m, \ldots)$ to $(0^m, \mathbf{y}_i^{*(0)}, \ldots)$. Here, we argue that making the switch does not affect the distribution if the admissibility rule holds—to do so, we rely on the internal randomness inside the (single-input) IPE scheme, since we no longer can leverage the external random masks $T_{i,t}$ as before.

Why Tomida's Techniques do Not Work. We compare with Tomida [28] and explain why their techniques do not work in the online full version.

2.6   Removing the "All-or-Nothing" Admissibility Rule

So far, our scheme is proven secure in an "all-or-nothing" query setting, that is, for every label t, the adversary must either make at least one ciphertext query on behalf of every honest client, or make none such queries at all. Although it is known that one can remove this restriction on the adversary by wrapping the MCIPE ciphertexts inside a layer of "all-or-nothing encryption" [10,16,17], we cannot use the existing techniques as is to get adaptive security and succinct ciphertext at the same time. Recall that in an all-or-nothing encryption (AoNE) scheme [10,16,17], if one collects n clients' ciphertexts encrypted to the same label t, then all of them can be decrypted. Otherwise if the collection is not complete for some label t, then no ciphertext encrypted to t can be decrypted and all the plaintexts are kept secret.

Unfortunately, previous AoNE constructions [16,17] are either not efficient in the sense that the per-client ciphertext size grows linearly with respect to the number of parties [17]; or rely on a random oracle [16,17]. Moreover, it is also not clear how to extend the existing proof techniques (for removing the "all-or-nothing" query restriction) to the *adaptive function-hiding* setting while retaining succinct ciphertext size [1,16,17].

Table 4. Adaptive security: inner hybrids to go from $\mathsf{Hyb}_{\ell-1}$ to Hyb_ℓ. $\mathbf{y}^{*(b)} := (\mathbf{y}_1^{*(b)}, \dots, \mathbf{y}_n^{*(b)})$ for $b \in \{0,1\}$ denote the key vectors submitted in the ℓ-th **KGen** query, and ρ^* is the randomness used in the ℓ-th **KGen** query. Values $\mathbf{u}_i$ in $\mathsf{H}_{\ell-1,1}, \dots, \mathsf{H}'_{\ell-1,1}$ and $\mathbf{b}_i^\perp$ in $\mathsf{H}_{\ell-1,2}, \dots, \mathsf{H}'_{\ell-1,2}$ are sampled once $\forall i \in [n]$ at **Setup**.

Hybrid		assumption
$\mathsf{Hyb}_{\ell-1}$	**Enc** : $\mathbf{c}_i = \left((\widetilde{\mathbf{x}}_i + \mathbf{U}_i\mathbf{A}_i\mathbf{s}_i)^T, (-\mathbf{A}_i\mathbf{s}_i)^T\right)^T$, $\mathbf{c}_i' = \mathbf{V}_i^T\mathbf{c}_i$ where $\widetilde{\mathbf{x}}_i = \left(\mathbf{x}_i^{(1)}, \mathbf{x}_i^{(0)}, \mathsf{CPRF}(K_i, t) + a_i\mu_{i,t}, \mu_{i,t}\right)$ **KGen** : $\mathbf{d}_i = \left(\mathbf{I}, \mathbf{U}_i\right)^T \widetilde{\mathbf{y}}_i + \mathbf{V}_i\mathbf{B}_i\mathbf{t}_i$, $\mathbf{d}_i' = -\mathbf{B}_i\mathbf{t}_i$, where $\widetilde{\mathbf{y}}_i$ is as follows based on which **KGen** query it is: first $\ell-1$: $\left(\mathbf{0}^m, \mathbf{y}_i^{(0)}, \rho, -\rho a_i\right)$, else: $\left(\mathbf{y}_i^{(1)}, \mathbf{0}^m, \rho, -\rho a_i\right)$	
$\mathsf{H}_{\ell-1,1}$	**Enc** : same as $\mathsf{Hyb}_{\ell-1}$ **KGen** : $\mathbf{d}_i = \left(\mathbf{I}, \mathbf{U}_i\right)^T \widetilde{\mathbf{y}}_i + \mathbf{V}_i(\mathbf{B}_i\mathbf{t}_i + \mathbf{u}_i)$, $\mathbf{d}_i' = -(\mathbf{B}_i\mathbf{t}_i + \mathbf{u}_i)$, where $\mathbf{u}_i \leftarrow \mathbb{Z}_q^{k+1} \setminus span(\mathbf{B}_i)$ and $\widetilde{\mathbf{y}}_i$ is same as $\mathsf{Hyb}_{\ell-1}$	k-MDDH
$\mathsf{H}_{\ell-1,2}$	**Enc** : $\mathbf{c}_i, \widetilde{\mathbf{x}}_i$: same as $\mathsf{H}_{\ell-1,1}$, $\mathbf{c}_i' = \mathbf{V}_i^T\mathbf{c}_i - (\mathbf{b}_i^\perp)\rho^*\mathsf{CPRF}(K_i, t)$ where $\mathbf{b}_i^\perp \leftarrow orth(\mathbf{B}_i)$ s.t. $\langle \mathbf{u}_i, \mathbf{b}_i^\perp \rangle = 1$ **KGen** : $\mathbf{d}_i, \mathbf{d}_i'$: same as $\mathsf{H}_{\ell-1,1}$ except $\widetilde{\mathbf{y}}_i$ is as follows based on which **KGen** query it is: ℓ-th: $\left(\mathbf{y}_i^{*(1)}, \mathbf{0}^m, 0, 0\right)$, else: same as $\mathsf{H}_{\ell-1,1}$	identically distributed
$\mathsf{H}_{\ell-1,3}$	**Enc** : $\mathbf{c}_i$: same as $\mathsf{H}_{\ell-1,1}$ except $\widetilde{\mathbf{x}}_i = \left(\mathbf{x}_i^{(1)}, \mathbf{x}_i^{(0)}, R_{i,t} + a_i\mu_{i,t}, \mu_{i,t}\right)$ $\mathbf{c}_i' = \mathbf{V}_i^T\mathbf{c}_i - (\mathbf{b}_i^\perp)\rho^* R_{i,t}$ where $\sum_{i\in\mathcal{H}} R_{i,t} = -\sum_{i\in\mathcal{K}} \mathsf{CPRF}(K_i, t)$ **KGen** : same as $\mathsf{H}_{\ell-1,2}$	correlated pseudorand. of CPRF
$\mathsf{H}_{\ell-1,4}$	**Enc** : $\mathbf{c}_i, \widetilde{\mathbf{x}}_i$: same as $\mathsf{H}_{\ell-1,1}$, $\mathbf{c}_i' = \mathbf{V}_i^T\mathbf{c}_i - (\mathbf{b}_i^\perp)T_{i,t}$ where $\sum_{i\in\mathcal{H}} T_{i,t} = -\rho^* \sum_{i\in\mathcal{K}} \mathsf{CPRF}(K_i, t)$ **KGen** : same as $\mathsf{H}_{\ell-1,2}$	DLin
$\mathsf{H}'_{\ell-1,4}$	**Enc** : same as $\mathsf{H}_{\ell-1,4}$ **KGen** : $\mathbf{d}_i, \mathbf{d}_i'$: same as $\mathsf{H}_{\ell-1,4}$ except $\widetilde{\mathbf{y}}_i$ is as follows based on which **KGen** query it is: ℓ-th: $\left(\mathbf{0}^m, \mathbf{y}_i^{*(0)}, 0, 0\right)$, else: same as $\mathsf{H}_{\ell-1,1}$	identically distributed
$\mathsf{H}'_{\ell-1,3}$	**Enc** : $\mathbf{c}_i, \widetilde{\mathbf{x}}_i$: same as $\mathsf{H}_{\ell-1,1}$, $\mathbf{c}_i' = \mathbf{V}_i^T\mathbf{c}_i - (\mathbf{b}_i^\perp)\rho^* R_{i,t}$ where $\sum_{i\in\mathcal{H}} R_{i,t} = -\sum_{i\in\mathcal{K}} \mathsf{CPRF}(K_i, t)$ **KGen** : same as $\mathsf{H}'_{\ell-1,4}$	DLin
$\mathsf{H}'_{\ell-1,2}$	**Enc** : $\mathbf{c}_i$: same as $\mathsf{H}_{\ell-1,1}$, $\mathbf{c}_i' = \mathbf{V}_i^T\mathbf{c}_i - (\mathbf{b}_i^\perp)\rho^*\mathsf{CPRF}(K_i, t)$ $\widetilde{\mathbf{x}}_i = \left(\mathbf{x}_i^{(1)}, \mathbf{x}_i^{(0)}, \mathsf{CPRF}(K_i, t) + a_i\mu_{i,t}, \mu_{i,t}\right)$ **KGen** : same as $\mathsf{H}'_{\ell-1,4}$	correlated pseudorand. of CPRF
$\mathsf{H}'_{\ell-1,1}$	**Enc** : $\mathbf{c}_i, \widetilde{\mathbf{x}}_i$: same as $\mathsf{H}_{\ell-1,1}$, $\mathbf{c}_i' = \mathbf{V}_i^T\mathbf{c}_i$ **KGen** : $\mathbf{d}_i, \mathbf{d}_i'$: same as $\mathsf{H}'_{\ell-1,2}$ except $\widetilde{\mathbf{y}}_i$ is as follows based on which **KGen** query it is: ℓ-th: $\left(\mathbf{0}^m, \mathbf{y}_i^{*(0)}, \rho^*, -\rho^* a_i\right)$, else: same as $\mathsf{H}_{\ell-1,1}$	identically distributed
Hyb_ℓ	see Table 2	k-MDDH

We propose new techniques for performing this upgrade without asymptotically blowing up the ciphertext size, without random oracles, while retaining the adaptive function-hiding security. To make this work, we additionally make the following contributions:

- In Appendix C of the online full version, we construct a new, adaptively secure AoNE scheme that achieves succinct ciphertexts, and reduce its security to Decisional Bilinear Diffie-Hellman assumption.
- Even with an adaptively secure AoNE scheme, it turns out to be difficult to directly prove the security of the upgraded scheme in the adaptive function-hiding setting. We overcome this challenge by introducing a stepping stone: we first prove that the upgraded construction satisfies a relaxed notion called adaptive *weak*-function-hiding security. We then rely on standard techniques [23,27] to upgrade the resulting adaptive *weak*-function-hiding MCIPE scheme to one that satisfies full adaptive function-hiding security.

We defer the detailed exposition of these new techniques to Appendices C and D of the online full version.

3   Definitions: Multi-Client Inner Product Encryption

Henceforth, we use m to denote the number of coordinates encrypted by each client, and use n to denote the number of clients. In a Multi-Client Inner-Product Functional Encryption (MCIPE) scheme, in every time step, each client $i \in [n]$ encrypts a vector $\mathbf{x}_i \in \mathbb{Z}_q^m$ using its private key ek_i. An authority holding a master secret key msk can generate a functional key $\mathsf{sk_y}$ for a vector $\mathbf{y} \in \mathbb{Z}_q^{mn} = (\mathbf{y}_1, \mathbf{y}_2, \ldots, \mathbf{y}_n)$ where each $\mathbf{y}_i \in \mathbb{Z}_q^m$. One can now apply the functional key $\mathsf{sk_y}$ to the collection of all n clients' ciphertexts belonging to the same time step, and an evaluation procedure gives the result $\langle \mathbf{x}, \mathbf{y} \rangle$ where $\mathbf{x} := (\mathbf{x}_1, \ldots, \mathbf{x}_n)$.

We use a standard notion of selective indistinguishability for multi-client inner-product encryption [10]. In this standard definition, the time step t is generalized and encoded as an arbitrary label, and only ciphertexts encrypted to the same label can be combined during the decryption process. Mix-and-match among ciphertexts encrypted to different labels should be prevented; however, mix-and-match among the same label is allowed. Formally, an MCIPE scheme consists of the following possibly randomized algorithms:

- $\mathsf{pp} \leftarrow \mathbf{Gen}(1^\lambda)$: the parameter generation algorithm $\mathbf{Gen}$ takes in a security parameter λ and chooses parameters pp—we will assume that pp contains a λ-bit long prime number $q \in \mathbb{N}$ and the description of a suitable cyclic group $\mathbb{G}$ of prime order q.
- $(\mathsf{mpk}, \mathsf{msk}, \{\mathsf{ek}_i\}_{i \in [n]}) \leftarrow \mathbf{Setup}(\mathsf{pp}, m, n)$: takes in the parameters q, $\mathbb{G}$, m, and n, and outputs a public key mpk, a master secret key msk, and n user secret keys needed for encryption, denoted $\mathsf{ek}_1, \ldots, \mathsf{ek}_n$, respectively. Without loss of generality, henceforth we may assume that mpk encodes pp so we need not write the parameters pp explicitly below.

- $\mathsf{sk_y} \leftarrow \mathbf{KGen}(\mathsf{mpk}, \mathsf{msk}, \mathbf{y})$: takes in the public key mpk, the master secret key msk, and a vector $\mathbf{y} \in \mathbb{Z}_q^{mn}$, and outputs a functional secret key $\mathsf{sk_y}$.
- $\mathsf{ct}_{i,t} \leftarrow \mathbf{Enc}(\mathsf{mpk}, \mathsf{ek}_i, \mathbf{x}_i, t)$: takes in the public key mpk, a user secret key ek_i, a plaintext $\mathbf{x}_i \in \mathbb{Z}_q^m$, and a label $t \in \{0,1\}^*$, outputs a ciphertext $\mathsf{ct}_{i,t}$.
- $v \leftarrow \mathbf{Dec}(\mathsf{mpk}, \mathsf{sk_y}, \{\mathsf{ct}_{i,t}\}_{i\in[n]})$: takes in the public key mpk, the functional secret key $\mathsf{sk_y}$, and a collection of ciphertexts $\{\mathsf{ct}_{i,t}\}_{i\in[n]}$, outputs a decrypted outcome $v \in \mathbb{Z}_q$.

Correctness. For correctness, we require that for any $\lambda \in \mathbb{N}$, for any $\mathsf{pp} := (q, \ldots)$ in the support of $\mathbf{Gen}(1^\lambda)$, the following holds with probability 1 for any $m, n \in \mathbb{N}$: for any $\mathbf{y} \in \mathbb{Z}_q^{mn}$, and any $\mathbf{x} := (\mathbf{x}_1, \ldots, \mathbf{x}_n) \in \mathbb{Z}_q^n$, and any $t \in \{0,1\}^*$: let $(\mathsf{mpk}, \mathsf{msk}, \{\mathsf{ek}_i\}_{i\in[n]}) \leftarrow \mathbf{Setup}(\mathsf{pp}, m, n)$, let $\mathsf{sk_y} \leftarrow \mathbf{KGen}(\mathsf{mpk}, \mathsf{msk}, \mathbf{y})$, let $\mathsf{ct}_{i,t} \leftarrow \mathbf{Enc}(\mathsf{mpk}, \mathsf{ek}_i, \mathbf{x}_i, t)$ for $i \in [n]$, and let $v \leftarrow \mathbf{Dec}(\mathsf{mpk}, \mathsf{sk_y}, \{\mathsf{ct}_{i,t}\}_{i\in[n]})$, it must be that $v = \langle \mathbf{x}, \mathbf{y} \rangle$.

Function-hiding IND-security for MCIPE . Consider the following experiment between an adversary $\mathcal{A}$ and a challenger $\mathcal{C}$.

Experiment MCIPE-Expt$^b(1^\lambda)$:
- **Setup.** $\mathcal{A}(1^\lambda)$ outputs a set of corrupted parties $\mathcal{K} \subset [n]$, as well as the parameters m and n to the challenger $\mathcal{C}$. The challenger $\mathcal{C}$ runs $\mathsf{pp} \leftarrow \mathbf{Gen}(1^\lambda)$, and $(\mathsf{mpk}, \mathsf{msk}, \{\mathsf{ek}_i\}_{i\in[n]}) \leftarrow \mathbf{Setup}(\mathsf{pp}, m, n)$; it gives mpk and $\{\mathsf{ek}_i\}_{i\in\mathcal{K}}$ to $\mathcal{A}$.
- **Query.** The adversary can make the following types of queries:
  - **KGen queries.** Whenever the adversary $\mathcal{A}$ makes a **KGen** query with two vectors $\mathbf{y}^{(0)} \in \mathbb{Z}_q^{mn}$ and $\mathbf{y}^{(1)} \in \mathbb{Z}_q^{mn}$: $\mathcal{C}$ calls $\mathsf{sk}_{\mathbf{y}^{(b)}} := \mathbf{KGen}(\mathsf{mpk}, \mathsf{msk}, \mathbf{y}^{(b)})$ and returns $\mathsf{sk}_{\mathbf{y}^{(b)}}$ to $\mathcal{A}$;
  - **Enc queries.** Whenever $\mathcal{A}$ makes an **Enc** query with the tuple $(i, t, \mathbf{x}_{i,t}^{(0)}, \mathbf{x}_{i,t}^{(1)})$, the challenger $\mathcal{C}$ calls $\mathsf{ct}_{i,t} := \mathbf{Enc}(\mathsf{mpk}, \mathsf{ek}_i, \mathbf{x}_{i,t}^{(b)}, t)$ and returns $\mathsf{ct}_{i,t}$ to $\mathcal{A}$;

An adversary $\mathcal{A}$ is said to be *admissible* iff the following hold with probability 1 where $\mathcal{H} := [n]\backslash\mathcal{K}$ denotes the set of honest clients:

1. for every label $t \in \{0,1\}^*$, either for every $i \in \mathcal{H}$, $\mathcal{A}$ has made at least one **Enc** query of the form $(i, t, \_, \_)$, or $\mathcal{A}$ made no **Enc** query of the form $(i, t, \_, \_)$ for any $i \in \mathcal{H}$.

2. if $\mathcal{A}$ ever makes an **Enc** query with the tuple $(i, t, \mathbf{x}_{i,t}^{(0)}, \mathbf{x}_{i,t}^{(1)})$ for some corrupt $i \in \mathcal{K}$, it must be that $\mathbf{x}_{i,t}^{(0)} = \mathbf{x}_{i,t}^{(1)}$;

3. for any pair $(\mathbf{y}^{(0)}, \mathbf{y}^{(1)})$ submitted in a **KGen** query where for $b \in \{0,1\}$, $\mathbf{y}^{(b)} := (\mathbf{y}_1^{(b)}, \ldots, \mathbf{y}_n^{(b)}) \in \{0,1\}^{mn}$, it must be that
   (a) for $i \in \mathcal{K}$, $\mathbf{y}_i^{(0)} = \mathbf{y}_i^{(1)}$.
   (b) for any collection $\{\mathbf{x}_{i,t}^{(0)}, \mathbf{x}_{i,t}^{(1)}\}_{i\in\mathcal{H}}$ pertaining to the same t where each pair $(\mathbf{x}_{i,t}^{(0)}, \mathbf{x}_{i,t}^{(1)})$ for $i \in \mathcal{H}$ has been submitted in an **Enc** query of the form

$$(i, t, \mathbf{x}_{i,t}^{(0)}, \mathbf{x}_{i,t}^{(1)}),$$

$$\left\langle (\mathbf{x}_{i,t}^{(0)})_{i \in \mathcal{H}}, (\mathbf{y}_i^{(0)})_{i \in \mathcal{H}} \right\rangle = \left\langle (\mathbf{x}_{i,t}^{(1)})_{i \in \mathcal{H}}, (\mathbf{y}_i^{(1)})_{i \in \mathcal{H}} \right\rangle \tag{6}$$

Definition 1 (Adaptive, function-hiding IND-security of MCIPE). *We say that an* MCIPE *scheme is adaptive, function-hiding IND-secure iff for any non-uniform probabilistic polynomial-time admissible adversary $\mathcal{A}$, its views in* MCIPE-Expt$^0(1^\lambda)$ *and* MCIPE-Expt$^1(1^\lambda)$ *are computationally indistinguishable.*

Definition 2 (Selective, function-hiding IND-security of MCIPE). *We say that an* MCIPE *scheme is selective, function-hiding IND-secure iff for any non-uniform probabilistic polynomial-time (PPT) admissible adversary $\mathcal{A}$ also satisfying an additional constraint that $\mathcal{A}$ always makes all* **KGen** *queries ahead of any* **Enc** *query, its views in* MCIPE-Expt$^0(1^\lambda)$ *and* MCIPE-Expt$^1(1^\lambda)$ *are computationally indistinguishable.*

Remark 1 (The all-or-nothing admissibility rule). We also call the first admissibility rule the "all-or-nothing" admissibility rule. Jumping ahead, this rule is necessary later to show that the hybrids $\mathsf{H}_{\ell,3}$ and $\mathsf{H}'_{\ell,3}$ are identically distributed. In Appendices C and D.2 of the online full version, we present new techniques for eventually *removing the all-or-nothing admissibility rule*, thus strengthening the security of the scheme.

4   Preliminaries

We review bilinear groups and relevant hardness assumptions in Appendix A of the online full version.

4.1   Function-Hiding (Single-Input) Inner Product Encryption

We will need a single-input inner-product encryption scheme—henceforth we call this building block Inner Production Encryption (IPE). IPE can be viewed as a special case of multi-client inner product encryption when $n = 1$. However, we will need our underlying IPE to satisfy a few nice properties, including the fact that **Enc** and **KGen** should still work when taking in the group encoding of the plaintext or key vector; moreover, we want that the scheme computes the "inner-product in the exponent". Formally, the special IPE scheme we need consists of the following possibly randomized algorithms:

- pp $\leftarrow$ **Gen**(1^λ): takes in a security parameter λ and samples public parameters pp. We will assume that pp contains the description of a bilinear group $(\mathbb{G}, \mathbb{G}_T)$ of prime order q, a random generator $g \in \mathbb{G}$, and the description of the pairing operator $e : \mathbb{G} \times \mathbb{G} \to \mathbb{G}_T$.
- imsk $\leftarrow$ **Setup**(pp, m): takes in the public parameters pp and the dimension m of the plaintext vector, outputs a secret key imsk.

- $\mathsf{sk_y} \leftarrow \mathbf{KGen}(\mathsf{imsk}, [\![\mathbf{y}]\!])$: takes in the secret key imsk, and a vector of group elements $[\![\mathbf{y}]\!] \in \mathbb{G}^m$ which represents the group encoding of the vector $\mathbf{y} \in \mathbb{Z}_q^m$, outputs a functional (secret) key $\mathsf{sk_y}$.
- $\mathsf{ct} \leftarrow \mathbf{Enc}(\mathsf{imsk}, [\![\mathbf{x}]\!])$: takes in the secret key imsk, a plaintext vector $[\![\mathbf{x}]\!] \in \mathbb{G}^m$ represented in group encoding, and outputs a ciphertext ct.
- $[\![v]\!]_T \leftarrow \mathbf{Dec}(\mathsf{sk_y}, \mathsf{ct})$: takes in the functional key $\mathsf{sk_y}$ and a ciphertext ct, and outputs a decrypted outcome $[\![v]\!]_T$.

Correctness. Correctness requires that for any $\lambda, m \in \mathbb{N}, \mathbf{x}, \mathbf{y} \in \mathbb{Z}_q^m$, the following holds with probability 1: let $\mathsf{pp} \leftarrow \mathbf{Gen}(1^\lambda)$, $\mathsf{imsk} \leftarrow \mathbf{Setup}(\mathsf{pp}, m)$, $\mathsf{sk_y} \leftarrow \mathbf{KGen}(\mathsf{imsk}, [\![\mathbf{y}]\!])$, $\mathsf{ct} \leftarrow \mathbf{Enc}(\mathsf{imsk}, [\![\mathbf{x}]\!])$, $[\![v]\!]_T \leftarrow \mathbf{Dec}(\mathsf{sk_y}, \mathsf{ct})$, then, it must be that $v := \langle \mathbf{x}, \mathbf{y} \rangle$.

Function-hiding Security. Consider the following experiment $\mathsf{IPE\text{-}Expt}^b(1^\lambda)$ between an adversary $\mathcal{A}$ and a challenger $\mathcal{C}$:

Experiment $\mathsf{IPE\text{-}Expt}^b(1^\lambda)$:
- **Setup.** The challenger $\mathcal{C}$ runs $\mathsf{pp} \leftarrow \mathbf{Gen}(1^\lambda)$, and $\mathsf{imsk} \leftarrow \mathbf{Setup}(\mathsf{pp}, m)$, and gives pp to $\mathcal{A}$.
- **Query.** $\mathcal{A}$ makes the following types of queries to $\mathcal{C}$:
  - **KGen** queries: the adversary $\mathcal{A}$ submits $(\mathbf{y}^{(0)}, \mathbf{y}^{(1)})$; the challenger $\mathcal{C}$ computes $\mathsf{sk}_{\mathbf{y}^{(b)}} \leftarrow \mathbf{KGen}(\mathsf{msk}, [\![\mathbf{y}^{(b)}]\!])$ and returns to $\mathcal{A}$ the resulting $\mathsf{sk}_{\mathbf{y}^{(b)}}$.
  - **Enc** queries: the adversary $\mathcal{A}$ submits $(\mathbf{x}^{(0)}, \mathbf{x}^{(1)})$; the challenger $\mathcal{C}$ computes $\mathsf{ct} \leftarrow \mathbf{Enc}(\mathsf{mpk}, [\![\mathbf{x}^{(b)}]\!])$, and returns ct to $\mathcal{A}$.

An adversary $\mathcal{A}$ is said to be *admissible* iff the following holds with probability 1: for any $(\mathbf{x}^{(0)}, \mathbf{x}^{(1)})$ tuple submitted in an **Enc** query, for any $(\mathbf{y}^{(0)}, \mathbf{y}^{(1)})$ tuple submitted in a **KGen** query, it must be that $\langle \mathbf{x}^{(0)}, \mathbf{y}^{(0)} \rangle = \langle \mathbf{x}^{(1)}, \mathbf{y}^{(1)} \rangle$.

Definition 3 (Adaptive, Function-hiding IND-security of *IPE*). *We say that the IPE scheme satisfies adaptive, function-hiding IND-security, iff for any non-uniform probabilistic polynomial-time (*PPT*) admissible adversary, its views in $\mathsf{IPE\text{-}Expt}^0$ and $\mathsf{IPE\text{-}Expt}^1$ are computationally indistinguishable.*

Definition 4 (Selective, Function-hiding IND-security of *IPE*). *We say that the IPE scheme satisfies selective, function-hiding IND-security, iff for any non-uniform PPT admissible adversary also satisfying an additional constraint that all **KGen** queries must be made before any **Enc** query, its views in $\mathsf{IPE\text{-}Expt}^0$ and $\mathsf{IPE\text{-}Expt}^1$ are computationally indistinguishable.*

Prior works [5,27,31] showed how to construct a function-hiding IPE scheme from the Decisional Linear assumption in bilinear groups. The idea is to first construct an IPE scheme without function privacy from Decisional Linear [5, 27,31] and then apply a function privacy upgrade [5,23,27,31]. The resulting constructions indeed satisfy the aforementioned nice properties that we need.

4.2   Correlated Pseudorandom Function

A correlated pseudorandom function family consists of the following randomized algorithms:

– $(K_1, \ldots, K_n) \leftarrow \mathbf{Gen}(1^\lambda, n, q)$: takes a security parameter 1^λ and the number of users n, some prime q, and outputs the user secret key K_i for each $i \in [n]$.
– $v \leftarrow \mathbf{Eval}(K_i, x)$: given a user secret key K_i and an input $x \in \{0, 1\}^\lambda$, output an evaluation result $v \in \mathbb{Z}_q$.

Correctness. For correctness, we require that for any $\lambda \in \mathbb{N}$, any $(K_1, \ldots, K_n)$ in the support of $\mathbf{Gen}(1^\lambda)$, any input $x \in \{0, 1\}^\lambda$, the following holds:

$$\sum_{i \in [n]} \mathsf{CPRF}.\mathbf{Eval}(K_i, x) = 0 \mod q$$

Correlated Pseudorandomness. We require that for any non-uniform PPT adversary $\mathcal{A}$ who is allowed corrupt $f \leq n - 2$ users and obtain their user secret keys, for any subset U of at most $n - f - 1$ honest users, for any input x, the evaluations $\{\mathsf{CPRF}.\mathbf{Eval}(K_i, x)\}_{i \in U}$ are computationally indistinguishable from random values, as long as the adversary has not made a query on the input x.

More formally, correlated pseudorandomness is defined as below. Consider a game denoted $\mathsf{CPRF\text{-}Expt}^b (1^\lambda, n, q)$ between $\mathcal{A}$ and a challenger $\mathcal{C}$, parameterized by a bit $b \in \{0, 1\}$.

– **Setup.** $\mathcal{A}$ submits a set of corrupt nodes $\mathcal{K} \subset [n]$ of size at most $n - 2$. Henceforth, let $\mathcal{H} := [n]\backslash\mathcal{K}$. Now, $\mathcal{C}$ runs the honest $(K_1, \ldots, K_n) := \mathsf{CPRF}.\mathbf{Gen}(1^\lambda, n, q)$ algorithm, and gives $\{K_i\}_{i \in \mathcal{K}}$ to $\mathcal{A}$.
– **Queries.** $\mathcal{A}$ can adaptively make queries: for each query, $\mathcal{A}$ submits an input x. If $b = 0$, the challenger $\mathcal{C}$ chooses random $\{v_i\}_{i \in \mathcal{H}} \xleftarrow{\$} \mathbb{Z}_q^{|\mathcal{H}|}$ subject to the condition that $\sum_{i \in \mathcal{H}} v_i + \sum_{j \in \mathcal{K}} \mathsf{CPRF}.\mathbf{Eval}(K_j, x) = 0$, and returns $\{v_i\}_{i \in \mathcal{H}}$ to $\mathcal{A}$. Else if $b = 1$, the challenger gives $\{\mathsf{CPRF}.\mathbf{Eval}(K_i, x)\}_{i \in \mathcal{H}}$ to $\mathcal{A}$.

We say that CPRF satisfies correlated pseudorandomness, iff for any n and q, any non-uniform PPT adversary $\mathcal{A}$'s views in $\mathsf{CPRF\text{-}Expt}^0(1^\lambda, n, q)$ and $\mathsf{CPRF\text{-}Expt}^1 (1^\lambda, n, q)$ are computationally indistinguishable.

Construction. Several prior works [1,14] showed how to construct a correlated pseudorandom function from a standard pseudorandom function (PRF). Without loss of generality, we may assume that PRF's output range is $[0, q-1]$. During the setup phase denoted by **Gen**, sample random PRF keys $k_{i,j}$ for all $i < j$, and let $k_{j,i} = k_{i,j}$. Party i's secret key K_i is defined to be the set $\{k_{i,j}\}_{j \in [n], j \neq i}$. The evaluation function $\mathbf{Eval}(K_i, x)$ is defined as follows:

$$\mathbf{Eval}(K_i, x) = \sum_{j \in [n], j \neq i} (-1)^{j < i} \cdot \mathsf{PRF}(k_{i,j}, x) \mod q$$

Prior works [1,14,27] proved that this CPRF satisfies correctness and correlated pseudorandomness, assuming the underlying PRF is secure.

5   Function-Hiding MCIPE

In this section, we give our detailed constructions of function-hiding multi-client inner-product encryption schemes and their formal proofs. In Sect. 5.1 we present the selective function-hiding secure variant and in Appendix B of the online full version we present the adaptive function-hiding secure variant.

5.1   Selective Function-Hiding MCIPE

Detailed Construction. Let IPE := (**Gen, Setup, KGen, Enc, Dec**) denote a function-hiding inner-product encryption scheme, and let CPRF := (**Gen, Eval**) denote a correlated pseudorandom function.

Selective Function-hiding, multi-client inner-product encryption

- **Gen**(1^λ): let $\mathsf{pp} \leftarrow \mathsf{IPE.Gen}(1^\lambda)$, and output pp.
- **Setup**(pp, m, n):
  - let $(K_1, \ldots, K_n) := \mathsf{CPRF.Gen}(1^\lambda, n, q)$;
  - for $i \in [n]$: let $\mathsf{imsk}_i \leftarrow \mathsf{IPE.Setup}(\mathsf{pp}, 2m+3)$, and $a_i \xleftarrow{\$} \mathbb{Z}_q$;
  - output $\mathsf{mpk} := \mathsf{pp}$, $\mathsf{msk} := \{\mathsf{imsk}_i, a_i\}_{i \in [n]}$, and $\{\mathsf{ek}_i := (\mathsf{imsk}_i, K_i, a_i)\}_{i \in [n]}$.
- **KGen**$(\mathsf{mpk}, \mathsf{msk}, \mathbf{y})$:
  - sample $\rho \xleftarrow{\$} \mathbb{Z}_q$;
  - let $\widetilde{\mathbf{y}}_i = (\mathbf{y}_i, 0^m, \rho, -\rho a_i, 0)$;
  - let $\mathsf{isk}_i \leftarrow \mathsf{IPE.KGen}(\mathsf{imsk}_i, [\![\widetilde{\mathbf{y}}_i]\!])$, and output $\mathsf{sk}_\mathbf{y} := \{\mathsf{isk}_i\}_{i \in [n]}$.
- **Enc**$(\mathsf{mpk}, \mathsf{ek}_i, \mathbf{x}_i, t)$:
  - sample $\mu_{i,t} \xleftarrow{\$} \mathbb{Z}_q$ if $\mu_{i,t}$ has not been sampled before;
  - let $\widetilde{\mathbf{x}}_i = (\mathbf{x}_i, 0^m, \mathsf{CPRF.Eval}(K_i, t) + a_i \mu_{i,t}, \mu_{i,t}, 0)$;
  - call $\mathsf{ct} \leftarrow \mathsf{IPE.Enc}(\mathsf{imsk}_i, [\![\widetilde{\mathbf{x}}_i]\!])$, and output ct.
- **Dec**$(\mathsf{mpk}, \mathsf{sk}_\mathbf{y}, \{\mathsf{ct}_{i,t}\}_{i \in [n]})$: let $[\![v]\!]_T := \prod_{i \in [n]} \mathsf{IPE.Dec}(\mathsf{isk}_i, \mathsf{ct}_i)$, and output $v := \log([\![v]\!]_T)$.

Asymptotic Efficiency. We can instantiate the function-hiding IPE using the scheme described in earlier works [5,27,31], based on the Decisional Linear assumption. For the underlying IPE scheme, the ciphertext contains $O(m)$ group elements where m is the length of the vector being encrypted. Similarly, each functional key has only $O(m)$ group elements too. The public parameters contain only the group description.

In our MCIPE construction, to encrypt a length-m vector, each client's ciphertext has only $O(m)$ group elements. A functional key for a length $(n \cdot m)$-vector has size $O(n \cdot m)$ group elements. Each client's secret key has size $O(n)$ where the big-O hides terms related to the security parameter. The public parameters contain only the group description.

Theorem 2. *Suppose that the Decisional Linear assumption holds in $\mathbb{G}$, IPE satisfies selective, function-hiding IND-security (see Definition 4), and* *moreover, CPRF satisfies correlated pseudorandomness. Then, the above* MCIPE *scheme satisfies selective function-hiding IND-security.*

We next present the proof of Theorem 2.

Proof of Theorem 2 We consider a sequence of outer hybrid experiments summarized as follows:

$$\text{MCIPE-Expt}^1 \approx_c \text{Hyb}_0 \approx_c \ldots \approx_c \text{Hyb}_\ell \approx_c \ldots \approx_c \text{Hyb}_{Q_{\text{kgen}}} \approx_c \text{Hyb}^* \approx_c \text{MCIPE-Expt}^0$$

Further, in Lemma 1 to prove $\text{Hyb}_{\ell-1} \approx_c \text{Hyb}_\ell$, we consider a sequence of inner hybrid experiments summarized as follows:

$$\text{Hyb}_{\ell-1} \approx_c \text{H}_{\ell-1,1} \approx_c \text{H}_{\ell-1,2} \approx_c \text{H}_{\ell-1,3} \approx_c \text{H}'_{\ell-1,3} \approx_c \text{H}'_{\ell-1,2} \approx_c \text{H}'_{\ell-1,1} \approx_c \text{Hyb}_\ell$$

Looking ahead, the proof falls short of showing adaptive security and only shows selective security because in the inner hybrids, the challenger embeds the challenge key $y^{*(b)}$ for $b \in \{0,1\}$ inside the ciphertexts and doing this requires the adversary to make all **KGen** queries before any **Enc** query is made.

Experiment MCIPE-Expt^1. This is the real-world experiment, parameterized by $b = 1$. In this experiment, the challenger $\mathcal{C}$ answers **Enc** and **KGen** queries using the following vectors where ρ is freshly chosen for every **KGen** query:

$$\widetilde{\mathbf{x}}_i = \left(\mathbf{x}_i^{(1)}, 0^m, \text{CPRF.}\mathbf{Eval}(K_i, t) + a_i \mu_{i,t}, \mu_{i,t}, 0 \right), \quad \widetilde{\mathbf{y}}_i = \left(\mathbf{y}_i^{(1)}, 0^m, \rho, -\rho a_i, 0 \right)$$

Experiment Hyb_0. Same as MCIPE-Expt^1 except that for any honest $i \in \mathcal{H}$, the challenger $\mathcal{C}$ answers **Enc** queries using

$$\widetilde{\mathbf{x}}_i = \left(\mathbf{x}_i^{(1)}, \mathbf{x}_i^{(0)}, \text{CPRF.}\mathbf{Eval}(K_i, t) + a_i \mu_{i,t}, \mu_{i,t}, 0 \right)$$

Claim 1. *If the* IPE *scheme is function-hiding IND-secure, then,* MCIPE-Expt^1 *and* Hyb_0 *are computationally indistinguishable.*

Proof. Since this modification preserves the inner products $\langle \widetilde{\mathbf{x}}_i, \widetilde{\mathbf{y}}_i \rangle$ for any pair of encryption and key vectors queried, and for any $i \in \mathcal{H}$, Hyb_0 is indistinguishable from MCIPE-Expt^1 due to the function-hiding IND-security of the IPE scheme.

Experiment Hyb_ℓ. We next define a sequence of hybrid experiments Hyb_ℓ where $\ell \in [Q_{\text{kgen}}]$ where Q_{kgen} denotes an upper bound the number of **KGen** queries made by $\mathcal{A}$. In Hyb_ℓ, for the first ℓ **KGen** queries, the challenger $\mathcal{C}$ uses $\widetilde{\mathbf{y}}_i = \left(0^m, \mathbf{y}_i^{(0)}, \rho, -\rho a_i, 0 \right)$ for any honest $i \in \mathcal{H}$, and uses $\widetilde{\mathbf{y}}_i = \left(\mathbf{y}_i^{(1)}, 0^m, \rho, -\rho a_i, 0 \right)$ for any corrupt $i \in \mathcal{K}$. For the remaining $Q_{\text{kgen}} - \ell$ number of **KGen** queries, $\mathcal{C}$ uses $\widetilde{\mathbf{y}}_i = \left(\mathbf{y}_i^{(1)}, 0^m, \rho, -\rho a_i, 0 \right)$ for all $i \in [n]$.

In Lemma 1, we prove that $\text{Hyb}_{\ell-1} \approx_c \text{Hyb}_\ell$ for $\ell \in [Q_{\text{kgen}}]$.

Experiment Hyb*. The challenger $\mathcal{C}$ answers **Enc** and **KGen** queries using the following vectors for any honest $i \in \mathcal{H}$:

$$\widetilde{\mathbf{x}}_i = \left(0^m, \mathbf{x}_i^{(0)}, \mathsf{CPRF}.\mathbf{Eval}(K_i, t) + a_i\mu_{i,t}, \mu_{i,t}, 0\right), \quad \widetilde{\mathbf{y}}_i = \left(0^m, \mathbf{y}_i^{(0)}, \rho, -\rho a_i, 0\right)$$

For corrupt $i \in \mathcal{K}$, the challenger $\mathcal{C}$ still uses:

$$\widetilde{\mathbf{x}}_i = \left(\mathbf{x}_i^{(1)}, 0^m, \mathsf{CPRF}.\mathbf{Eval}(K_i, t) + a_i\mu_{i,t}, \mu_{i,t}, 0\right), \quad \widetilde{\mathbf{y}}_i = \left(\mathbf{y}_i^{(1)}, 0^m, \rho, -\rho a_i, 0\right)$$

Claim 2. *If the IPE scheme is function-hiding IND-secure, then,* $\mathsf{Hyb}_{Q_{\mathrm{kgen}}}$ *and* Hyb* *are computationally indistinguishable.*

Proof. Observe that $\mathsf{Hyb}_{Q_{\mathrm{kgen}}}$ and Hyb* are almost identical except that the first m coordinates in $\widetilde{\mathbf{x}}_i$ are replaced with 0^m for $i \in \mathcal{H}$. Since this modification preserves the inner products $\langle \widetilde{\mathbf{x}}_i, \widetilde{\mathbf{y}}_i \rangle$ for any pair of encryption and key vectors queried, and for any $i \in \mathcal{H}$, Hyb* is computationally indistinguishable from $\mathsf{Hyb}_{Q_{\mathrm{kgen}}}$ due to the function-hiding IND-security of the IPE scheme.

Experiment MCIPE-Expt⁰. This is the real-world experiment, parameterized by $b = 0$. In the experiment MCIPE-Expt⁰, the challenger $\mathcal{C}$ answers **Enc** and **KGen** queries using the following vectors:

$$\widetilde{\mathbf{x}}_i = \left(\mathbf{x}_i^{(0)}, 0^m, \mathsf{CPRF}.\mathbf{Eval}(K_i, t) + a_i\mu_{i,t}, \mu_{i,t}, 0\right), \quad \widetilde{\mathbf{y}}_i = \left(\mathbf{y}_i^{(0)}, 0^m, \rho, -\rho a_i, 0\right)$$

where ρ is freshly chosen for every **KGen** query.

Claim 3. *If the IPE scheme is function-hiding IND-secure, then,* Hyb* *and* MCIPE -Expt⁰ *are computationally indistinguishable.*

Proof. Observe that Hyb* is computationally indistinguishable from MCIPE-Expt⁰ since for honest $i \in \mathcal{H}$, the inner-product $\langle \widetilde{\mathbf{x}}_i, \widetilde{\mathbf{y}}_i \rangle$ is preserved for any pair of encryption and key vectors queried; and for corrupt $i \in \mathcal{K}$, recall that our admissibility stipulates that $\mathbf{x}_i^{(0)} = \mathbf{x}_i^{(1)}$ and $\mathbf{y}_i^{(0)} = \mathbf{y}_i^{(1)}$, and thus it makes no difference whether $\mathbf{x}_i^{(0)}, \mathbf{y}_i^{(0)}$ is used or whether $\mathbf{x}_i^{(1)}, \mathbf{y}_i^{(1)}$ is used by $\mathcal{C}$.

Therefore, to complete the proof of Theorem 2, it suffices to prove the following lemma, i.e., the computational indistinguishability of $\mathsf{Hyb}_{\ell-1}$ and Hyb_{ℓ}.

Lemma 1. *Suppose that the Decisional Linear assumption holds in* $\mathbb{G}$, *IPE satisfies selective function-hiding IND-security, and moreover, CPRF satisfies correlated pseudorandomness. Then,* $\mathsf{Hyb}_{\ell-1}$ *is computationally indistinguishable from* Hyb_{ℓ} *for any* $\ell \in [Q_{\mathrm{kgen}}]$.

Proof. We consider a sequence of hybrid experiments.

Experiment $\mathsf{H}_{\ell-1,1}$. In $\mathsf{H}_{\ell-1,1}$, for any honest $i \in \mathcal{H}$, the challenger $\mathcal{C}$ uses the following vectors to answer **Enc** and **KGen** queries where $\rho^* \xleftarrow{\$} \mathbb{Z}_q$, and we use $\mathbf{y}^{*(0)}$, $\mathbf{y}^{*(1)}$ to denote the key vectors submitted during the ℓ-th **KGen** query:

$$\widetilde{\mathbf{x}}_i = \left(\mathbf{x}_i^{(1)}, \mathbf{x}_i^{(0)}, \mathsf{CPRF.Eval}(K_i, t) + a_i \mu_{i,t}, \mu_{i,t}, \mathsf{CPRF.Eval}(K_i, t) \cdot \rho^* + \langle \mathbf{x}_i^{(1)}, \mathbf{y}_i^{*(1)} \rangle \right),$$

$$\widetilde{\mathbf{y}}_i = \begin{cases} \left(0^m, \mathbf{y}_i^{(0)}, \rho, -\rho a_i, 0 \right) & \text{first } \ell - 1 \textbf{ KGen} \text{ queries} \\ (0^m, 0^m, 0, 0, 1) & \ell\text{-th } \textbf{KGen} \text{ query} \\ \left(\mathbf{y}_i^{(1)}, 0^m, \rho, -\rho a_i, 0 \right) & \text{remaining } Q_{\mathrm{kgen}} - \ell \textbf{ KGen} \text{ queries} \end{cases}$$

Above, ρ is freshly chosen for every **KGen** query, and ρ^* corresponds to the randomness chosen for the challenge **KGen** query, i.e., the ℓ-th **KGen** query.

Observe that $\mathsf{H}_{\ell-1,1}$ is almost identical to $\mathsf{Hyb}_{\ell-1}$ except for the above modifications highlighted in blue. Since these modification preserves the inner products $\langle \widetilde{\mathbf{x}}_i, \widetilde{\mathbf{y}}_i \rangle$ for any pair of encryption and key vectors queried, and for any $i \in \mathcal{H}$, $\mathsf{H}_{\ell-1,1}$ and $\mathsf{Hyb}_{\ell-1}$ are computationally indistinguishable due to the function-hiding IND-security of the IPE scheme.

Observe that in this hybrid, the challenger needs to know challenge key $\mathbf{y}^{*(1)}$ when answering **Enc** queries and hence $\mathcal{A}$ must make all **KGen** queries ahead of any **Enc** query. This is why our proof technique works only for selective security.

Experiment $\mathsf{H}_{\ell-1,2}$. Almost identical to $\mathsf{H}_{\ell-1,1}$, except that for each t label that appears first in an **Enc** query, the challenger $\mathcal{C}$ chooses $\{R_{i,t}\}_{i \in \mathcal{H}}$ at random from $\mathbb{Z}_q$ subject to $\sum_{i \in \mathcal{H}} R_{i,t} = -\sum_{i \in \mathcal{K}} \mathsf{CPRF.Eval}(K_i, t)$. For honest $i \in \mathcal{H}$, the challenger $\mathcal{C}$ uses the following vector to answer **Enc** queries:

$$\widetilde{\mathbf{x}}_i = \left(\mathbf{x}_i^{(1)}, \mathbf{x}_i^{(0)}, R_{i,t} + a_i \mu_{i,t}, \mu_{i,t}, R_{i,t} \cdot \rho^* + \langle \mathbf{x}_i^{(1)}, \mathbf{y}_i^{*(1)} \rangle \right)$$

Experiment $\mathsf{H}_{\ell-1,2}$ is computationally indistinguishable from $\mathsf{H}_{\ell-1,1}$ due to the correlated pseudorandomness of CPRF.

Experiment $\mathsf{H}_{\ell-1,3}$. Almost identical to $\mathsf{H}_{\ell-1,2}$, except that the challenger $\mathcal{C}$ chooses random $\{T_{i,t}\}_{i \in \mathcal{H}}$ subject to $\sum_{i \in \mathcal{H}} T_{i,t} = -\rho^* \cdot \sum_{i \in \mathcal{K}} \mathsf{CPRF}(K_i, t)$, and uses the following vector in any **Enc** query for an honest $i \in \mathcal{H}$:

$$\widetilde{\mathbf{x}}_i = \left(\mathbf{x}_i^{(1)}, \mathbf{x}_i^{(0)}, R_{i,t} + a_i \mu_{i,t}, \mu_{i,t}, T_{i,t} + \langle \mathbf{x}_i^{(1)}, \mathbf{y}_i^{*(1)} \rangle \right)$$

Claim 4. *Suppose that the Decisional Linear assumption holds in* $\mathbb{G}$. *Then,* $\mathsf{H}_{\ell-1,3}$ *is computationally indistinguishable from* $\mathsf{H}_{\ell-1,2}$.

Proof. We will consider a sequence of hybrid experiments over the set of honest clients. Henceforth let d be the number of honest clients, and let $\mathcal{H} := \{i_1, i_2, \ldots, i_d\} \subseteq [n]$ denote the set of honest clients. We define the hybrid G_j as follows where $j \in [d-1] \cup \{0\}$:

- If i is among the first j honest clients, then $\mathcal{C}$ chooses $\widetilde{T}_{i,t}$ at random;
- If i is not among the first j honest clients and $i \neq i_d$, then, the challenger $\mathcal{C}$ chooses $\widetilde{T}_{i,t} = R_{i,t} \cdot \rho^*$;
- For the last honest client $i = i_d$, the challenger $\mathcal{C}$ chooses $\widetilde{T}_{i,t}$ such that

$$\sum_{i \in \mathcal{H}} \widetilde{T}_{i,t} = -\rho^* \sum_{i \in \mathcal{K}} \mathsf{CPRF.Eval}(K_i, t)$$

$\mathcal{C}$ uses the following vector when answering **Enc** queries for any honest $i \in \mathcal{H}$:

$$\widetilde{\mathbf{x}}_i = \left(\mathbf{x}_i^{(1)}, \mathbf{x}_i^{(0)}, R_{i,t} + a_i \mu_{i,t}, \mu_{i,t}, \widetilde{T}_{i,t} + \langle \mathbf{x}_i^{(1)}, \mathbf{y}_i^{*(1)} \rangle \right) \tag{7}$$

Observe that G_0 is the same as $\mathsf{H}_{\ell-1,2}$, and G_{d-1} is the same as $\mathsf{H}_{\ell-1,3}$. Therefore, to prove Claim 4, it suffices to prove that any two adjacent hybrids G_j and G_{j+1} are computationally indistinguishable for $j \in \{0, 1, \ldots, d-2\}$. Below, we prove that if the Decisional Linear assumption holds in $\mathbb{G}$, then indeed G_j and G_{j+1} are computationally indistinguishable for $j \in \{0, 1, \ldots, d-2\}$.

Suppose there is an efficient adversary $\mathcal{A}$ that can distinguish G_j and G_{j+1} with non-negligible probability, we show how to construct an efficient reduction $\mathcal{B}$ that can break the Decisional Linear assumption. Let Q_{enc} denote the maximum number of labels t submitted during **Enc** queries. $\mathcal{B}$ obtains an instance $(\llbracket 1 \rrbracket, \llbracket \beta \rrbracket, \llbracket \gamma \rrbracket, \llbracket \mathbf{u} \rrbracket, \llbracket \beta \mathbf{v} \rrbracket, \llbracket \mathbf{z} \rrbracket)$ from a Vector Decisional Linear challenger (see Appendix A.1 of the online full version), where $\mathbf{u}, \mathbf{v}, \mathbf{z} \in \mathbb{Z}_q^{Q_{\mathrm{enc}}}$ and $\beta, \gamma \in \mathbb{Z}_q$. $\mathcal{B}$'s task is to distinguish whether $\llbracket \mathbf{z} \rrbracket = \llbracket \gamma(\mathbf{u} + \mathbf{v}) \rrbracket$ or random. $\mathcal{B}$ will now interact with $\mathcal{A}$ and embed this Decisional Linear instance in its answers.

Let $i^* = i_{j+1} \in \mathcal{H}$ be the index of the $(j+1)$-th honest client.

- **Setup.** $\mathcal{B}$ chooses $\xi \in \mathbb{Z}_q$ at random, and implicitly sets $a_{i^*} = \beta^{-1}$ and $a_{i_d} = \xi \cdot \beta^{-1}$, without actually computing them. $\mathcal{B}$ chooses all other terms in the **Setup** algorithm honestly, and gives mpk and $\{\mathsf{ek}_i\}_{i \in \mathcal{K}}$ to $\mathcal{A}$.
- **KGen queries.**
  1. For the first $\ell - 1$ **KGen** queries:
     - for any honest $i \in \mathcal{H}$, $i \neq i^*$ and $i \neq i_d$, $\mathcal{B}$ knows all the terms necessary to compute isk_i.
     - for $i = i^*$, the reduction $\mathcal{B}$ does not know a_{i^*}, but it can replace the terms $\llbracket \rho, -\rho a_{i^*} \rrbracket$ with $\llbracket \beta \rho', -\rho' \rrbracket$ instead where $\rho' \xleftarrow{\$} \mathbb{Z}_q$. It can compute $\llbracket \beta \rho \rrbracket$ because it knows $\llbracket \beta \rrbracket$ and ρ'. $\mathcal{B}$ can now continue computing $\mathsf{isk}_{i^*} \leftarrow \mathsf{IPE.KGen}(\mathsf{imsk}_i, \llbracket 0^m, \mathbf{y}_i^{(0)}, \beta \rho', -\rho', 0 \rrbracket)$ normally.
     - for $i = i_d$, $\mathcal{B}$ can compute isk_{i_d} in a similar fashion as above, even if it does not know $a_{i_d} = \xi \cdot \beta^{-1}$.
     - for any corrupt $i \in \mathcal{K}$, $\mathcal{B}$ computes isk_i using the original honest algorithm, since it knows all the necessary terms.
  2. For any **KGen** query after the first ℓ queries, the reduction $\mathcal{B}$ can compute functional key just like for the first $\ell - 1$ queries.
  3. For the ℓ-th **KGen** query, $\mathcal{B}$ wants to embed the γ term from the Decisional Linear challenge into the ρ term for this specific functional key. Recall that $\mathcal{B}$ knows only $\llbracket \gamma \rrbracket$ but not γ itself.

- For any corrupt $i \in \mathcal{K}$, observe that $\mathcal{B}$ can compute their respective key component isk_i knowing only $[\![\gamma]\!]$ but not γ itself.
- For any honest $i \in \mathcal{H}$, $\mathcal{B}$ computes $\mathsf{isk}_i \leftarrow \mathsf{IPE.KGen}(\mathsf{imsk}_i, [\![0^m, 0^m, 0, 0, 1]\!])$.

- **Enc queries.** The adversary $\mathcal{A}$ submits $(i, t, \mathbf{x}_{i,t}^{(0)}, \mathbf{x}_{i,t}^{(1)})$. If $i \in \mathcal{K}$, $\mathcal{B}$ can compute the ciphertext normally since it knows all the necessary terms. Below we focus on the case when $i \in \mathcal{H}$. The first time the label t appears in an **Enc** query for some honest $i \in \mathcal{H}$, the reduction $\mathcal{B}$ picks $\{\widetilde{T}_{i,t}\}_{i \in \mathcal{H}}$ as follows, where u_t, v_t, and z_t denote the t-th component of the vector $\mathbf{u}$, $\mathbf{v}$, and $\mathbf{z}$ from the Decisional Linear challenge[3].

(a) If $i \in \mathcal{H}$, $i \neq i^*$, and $i \neq i_d$: $\mathcal{B}$ chooses $\widetilde{T}_{i,t}$ at random if i is among the first j honest clients, else it implicitly lets $\widetilde{T}_{i,t} := R_{i,t} \cdot \gamma$.

(b) If $i = i^*$: $\mathcal{B}$ implicitly chooses

$$R_{i^*,t} + a_{i^*}\mu_{i^*,t} = u_t, \quad \mu_{i^*,t} = -\beta v_t, \quad \widetilde{T}_{i^*,t} = z_t$$

(c) If $i = i_d$: $\mathcal{B}$ samples $\phi \xleftarrow{\$} \mathbb{Z}_q$, and implicitly chooses

$$\mu_{i_d,t} = -\mu_{i^*,t} \cdot \xi^{-1} + a_{i^*}^{-1} \cdot \phi, \ R_{i_d,t} = -\left(\sum_{i \in \mathcal{H}, i \neq i_d} R_{i,t} + \sum_{i \in \mathcal{K}} \mathsf{CPRF.Eval}(K_i, t)\right),$$

$$\widetilde{T}_{i_d,t} = -\left(\sum_{i \in \mathcal{K}} \mathsf{CPRF.Eval}(K_i, t) + \sum_{i \in \mathcal{H}, i \neq i^*, i \neq i_d} \widetilde{T}_i + z_t\right)$$

For case (a), computing the ciphertext (see Eq. 7) is straightforward. For case (b), it is also easy to see that given $\mathcal{B}$'s knowledge of $[\![u_t]\!]$, $[\![\beta v_t]\!]$, and $[\![z_t]\!]$, one can compute the ciphertext in a straightforward way. For case (c), observe the following. Let

$$\nu = -\left(\sum_{i \in \mathcal{H}, i \neq i_d, i \neq i^*} R_{i,t} + \sum_{i \in \mathcal{K}} \mathsf{CPRF.Eval}(K_i, t)\right);$$

and thus $R_{i_d,t} = \nu - R_{i^*,t}$.

$$\begin{aligned}
[\![R_{i_d,t} + a_{i_d}\mu_{i_d,t}]\!] &= [\![\nu - R_{i^*,t} + \xi a_{i^*} \cdot (-\mu_{i^*,t} \cdot \xi^{-1} + a_{i^*}^{-1} \cdot \phi)]\!] \\
&= [\![\nu - R_{i^*,t} - a_{i^*}\mu_{i^*,t} + \xi \cdot \phi]\!] \\
&= [\![\nu - u_t + \xi \cdot \phi]\!]
\end{aligned}$$

Further, $[\![\mu_{i_d,t}]\!] = [\![\beta v_t \cdot \xi^{-1} + \beta \cdot \phi]\!]$. Therefore, both $[\![R_{i_d,t} + a_{i_d}\mu_{i_d,t}]\!]$ and $[\![\mu_{i_d,t}]\!]$ can be computed knowing ν, $[\![u_t]\!]$, ξ, ϕ, $[\![\beta v_t]\!]$, and $[\![\beta]\!]$.

---

[3] For convenience, we may imagine that the labels t have been renamed to be the integers $\{1, 2, \ldots, Q_{\mathsf{enc}}\}$.

Observe that $R_{i^*,t} \cdot \gamma = (u_t - a_{i^*}\mu_{i^*,t})\gamma = (u_t + \beta^{-1} \cdot \beta v_t)\gamma = (u_t + v_t)\gamma$. Therefore, in the Decisional Linear challenge $([\![1]\!], [\![\beta]\!], [\![\gamma]\!], [\![\mathbf{u}]\!], [\![\beta\mathbf{v}]\!], [\![\mathbf{z}]\!])$ obtained by $\mathcal{B}$, if $\mathbf{z} = \gamma(\mathbf{u} + \mathbf{v})$, then $\mathcal{A}$'s view is identically distributed as in G_j. Else $\mathcal{A}$'s view is identically distributed as in G_{j+1}.

We now continue with the proof of Lemma 1.

Experiment $\mathsf{H}'_{\ell-1,3}$. Almost identical to $\mathsf{H}_{\ell-1,3}$, except that the challenger $\mathcal{C}$ uses the following vector in any **Enc** query for an honest $i \in \mathcal{H}$:

$$\widetilde{\mathbf{x}}_i = \left(\mathbf{x}_i^{(1)}, \mathbf{x}_i^{(0)}, R_{i,t} + a_i\mu_{i,t}, \mu_{i,t}, T_{i,t} + \langle \mathbf{x}_i^{(0)}, \mathbf{y}_i^{*(0)} \rangle \right)$$

where the terms $\{T_{i,t}\}_{i\in\mathcal{H}}$ are chosen at random subject to $\sum_{i\in\mathcal{H}} T_{i,t} = -\rho^* \cdot \sum_{i\in\mathcal{K}} \mathsf{CPRF}(K_i, t)$.
As long as $\mathcal{A}$ respects the admissibility rule defined in Sect. 3, $\mathsf{H}_{\ell-1,3}$ and $\mathsf{H}'_{\ell-1,3}$ are identically distributed.

Experiment $\mathsf{H}'_{\ell-1,2}$. Almost identical to $\mathsf{H}_{\ell-1,2}$, except that the challenger $\mathcal{C}$ chooses uses the following vector to answer **Enc** queries:

$$\widetilde{\mathbf{x}}_i = \left(\mathbf{x}_i^{(1)}, \mathbf{x}_i^{(0)}, R_{i,t} + a_i\mu_{i,t}, \mu_{i,t}, R_{i,t} \cdot \rho^* + \langle \mathbf{x}_i^{(0)}, \mathbf{y}_i^{*(0)} \rangle \right)$$

Experiment $\mathsf{H}'_{\ell-1,1}$. Almost identical to $\mathsf{H}_{\ell-1,1}$, except that the challenger $\mathcal{C}$ chooses uses the following vector to answer **Enc** queries:

$$\widetilde{\mathbf{x}}_i = \left(\mathbf{x}_i^{(1)}, \mathbf{x}_i^{(0)}, \mathsf{CPRF.Eval}(K_i, t) + a_i\mu_{i,t}, \mu_{i,t}, \mathsf{CPRF.Eval}(K_i, t) \cdot \rho^* + \langle \mathbf{x}_i^{(0)}, \mathbf{y}_i^{*(0)} \rangle \right)$$

Using a symmetric argument as before, we can prove the computational indistinguishability between $\mathsf{H}'_{\ell-1,3}$ and $\mathsf{H}'_{\ell-1,2}$, and between $\mathsf{H}'_{\ell-1,2}$ and $\mathsf{H}'_{\ell-1,1}$.

Finally, $\mathsf{H}'_{\ell-1,1}$ and Hyb_ℓ are computationally indistinguishable due to the function-hiding IND-security of the IPE scheme, since the inner-product $\langle \widetilde{\mathbf{x}}_i, \widetilde{\mathbf{y}}_i \rangle$ is preserved for any pair of encryption and key vectors queried and for $i \in \mathcal{H}$. This concludes the proof of Lemma 1.

References

1. Abdalla, M., Benhamouda, F., Gay, R.: From single-input to multi-client inner-product functional encryption. In: Asiacrypt (2019)
2. Abdalla, M., Benhamouda, F., Kohlweiss, M., Waldner, H.: Decentralizing inner-product functional encryption. In: PKC, vol. 11443, pp. 128–157 (2019)
3. Abdalla, M., Bourse, F., De Caro, A., Pointcheval, D.: Simple functional encryption schemes for inner products. In: PKC (2015)
4. Abdalla, M., Bourse, F., Marival, H., Pointcheval, D., Soleimanian, A., Waldner, H.: Multi-client inner-product functional encryption in the random-oracle model. In: SCN (2020)
5. Abdalla, M., Catalano, D., Fiore, D., Gay, R., Ursu, B.: Multi-input functional encryption for inner products: Function-hiding realizations and constructions without pairings. In: CRYPTO (2018)

6. Abdalla, M., Gay, R., Raykova, M., Wee, H.: Multi-input inner-product functional encryption from pairings. In: EUROCRYPT (2017)
7. Abdalla, M., Pointcheval, D., Soleimanian, A.: 2-step multi-client quadratic functional encryption from decentralized function-hiding inner-product. Cryptology ePrint Archive (2021)
8. Agrawal, S., Clear, M., Frieder, O., Garg, S., O'Neill, A., Thaler, J.: Ad hoc multi-input functional encryption. In: ITCS (2020)
9. Agrawal, S., Goyal, R., Tomida, J.: Multi-input quadratic functional encryption from pairings. In: CRYPTO (2021)
10. Agrawal, S., Goyal, R., Tomida, J.: Multi-party functional encryption. In: TCC (2021)
11. Ananth, P., Jain, A., Sahai, A.: Indistinguishability obfuscation from functional encryption for simple functions. Cryptology ePrint Archive (2015)
12. Bellare, M., Ristenpart, T.: Simulation without the artificial abort: Simplified proof and improved concrete security for waters' IBE scheme. In: Eurocrypt (2009)
13. Bitansky, N., Vaikuntanathan, V.: Indistinguishability obfuscation from functional encryption. J. ACM **65**(6), 1–37 (2018)
14. Bonawitz, K., et al.: Practical secure aggregation for privacy-preserving machine learning. In: CCS (2017)
15. Chotard, J., Dufour Sans, E., Gay, R., Phan, D.H., Pointcheval, D.: Decentralized multi-client functional encryption for inner product. In: ASIACRYPT (2018)
16. Chotard, J., Dufour Sans, E., Gay, R., Phan, D.H., Pointcheval, D.: Multi-client functional encryption with repetition for inner product. Cryptology ePrint (2018)
17. Chotard, J., Dufour Sans, E., Gay, R., Phan, D.H., Pointcheval, D.: Dynamic decentralized functional encryption. In: CRYPTO (2020)
18. Escala, A., Herold, G., Kiltz, E., Rafols, C., Villar, J.L.: An algebraic framework for Diffie-Hellman assumptions. In: CRYPTO (2013)
19. Goldwasser, S., et al.: Multi-input functional encryption. In: Eurocrypt (2014)
20. Jager, T.: Verifiable random functions from weaker assumptions. In: TCC (2015)
21. Kitagawa, F., Nishimaki, R., Tanaka, K.: Obfustopia built on secret-key functional encryption. In: EUROCRYPT (2018)
22. Libert. B., Titiu, R.: Multi-client functional encryption for linear functions in the standard model from LWE. In: ASIACRYPT (2019)
23. Lin, H.: Indistinguishability obfuscation from SXDH on 5-linear maps and locality-5 PRGs. In: CRYPTO (2017)
24. McMahan, B., Ramage, D.: Federated learning: collaborative machine learning without centralized training data (2017)
25. Nguyen, K., Phan, D.H., Pointcheval, D.: Multi-client functional encryption with fine-grained access control. In: ASIACRYPT (2023)
26. Shi, E., Chan, T.-H.H., Rieffel, E., Chow, R., Song, D.: Privacy-preserving aggregation of time-series data. In: NDSS (2011)
27. Shi, E., Wu, K.: Non-interactive anonymous router. In: Eurocrypt (2021)
28. Tomida, J.: Tightly secure inner product functional encryption: multi-input and function-hiding constructions. Theoret. Comput. Sci. **833**, 56–86 (2020)
29. Ünal, A.: Impossibility results for lattice-based functional encryption schemes. In: Eurocrypt, pp. 169–199 (2020)
30. Waters, B.: Efficient identity-based encryption without random oracles. In: Eurocrypt (2005)
31. Wee, H.: New techniques for attribute-hiding in prime-order bilinear groups. Manuscript (2016)

GLUE: Generalizing Unbounded Attribute-Based Encryption for Flexible Efficiency Trade-Offs

Marloes Venema[1,2(✉)] and Greg Alpár[2,3]

[1] University of Wuppertal, Wuppertal, Germany
Marloes.Venema@ru.nl
[2] Radboud University, Nijmegen, The Netherlands
g.alpar@cs.ru.nl
[3] Open University of the Netherlands, Heerlen, The Netherlands

Abstract. Ciphertext-policy attribute-based encryption is a versatile primitive that has been considered extensively to securely manage data in practice. Especially completely unbounded schemes are attractive, because they do not restrict the sets of attributes and policies. So far, any such schemes that support negations in the access policy or that have online/offline extensions have an inefficient decryption algorithm.

In this work, we propose GLUE (Generalized, Large-universe, Unbounded and Expressive), which is a novel scheme that allows for the efficient implementation of the decryption while allowing the support of both negations and online/offline extensions. We achieve these properties simultaneously by uncovering an underlying dependency between encryption and decryption, which allows for a flexible trade-off in their efficiency. For the security proof, we devise a new technique that enables us to generalize multiple existing schemes. As a result, we obtain a completely unbounded scheme supporting negations that, to the best of our knowledge, outperforms all existing such schemes in the decryption algorithm.

Keywords: attribute-based encryption · unbounded attribute-based encryption · online/offline attribute-based encryption · non-monotone attribute-based encryption

1 Introduction

Attribute-based encryption (ABE) is an advanced type of public-key encryption in which the key pairs are associated with attributes [47]. In ciphertext-policy (CP) ABE, messages are encrypted under an access policy [17]. The resulting ciphertexts can then be decrypted by a secret key associated with a set of attributes[1] that satisfies the policy. Conversely, in key-policy (KP) ABE, the keys

---

[1] In this paper, we will use the terms "sets of attributes" and "(attribute) sets" to refer to the attributes associated with the secret keys. We use the term "universe of attributes" to refer to the total set of attributes that can be used in the system.

© International Association for Cryptologic Research 2023
A. Boldyreva and V. Kolesnikov (Eds.): PKC 2023, LNCS 13940, pp. 652–682, 2023.
https://doi.org/10.1007/978-3-031-31368-4_23

are associated with access policies and the ciphertexts with sets of attributes [26]. To securely and efficiently implement access control on data, especially pairing-based CP-ABE proves to be an attractive primitive [17,34,36,48,53]. In 2018, the European Telecommunications Standards Institute (ETSI) published two technical reports on ABE [24,25], which include detailed descriptions of use cases, varying from cloud settings to mobile networks. In such settings, the computational resources of the encryption and decryption devices may vary. Thus, different use cases may require schemes with different efficiency trade-offs.

According to ETSI, ABE schemes should be efficient and secure. Interestingly, while ETSI proposes ABE to be used to enforce attribute-based access control [32] on data, it explicitly notes that ABE cannot satisfactorily support it, because ABE cannot support negations efficiently [25]. Indeed, the decryption algorithm of most ABE schemes supporting negations is incredibly expensive [11,37,43,57]. Recently, some interesting progress was made, yielding significant speed-ups in decryption time [14,49]. However, those schemes still have a costly decryption [14] or restrict the attribute sets [49].

In this work, we introduce GLUE, which is a new scheme that enables the realization of the following properties:

(1) Large-universe: any string can be used as an attribute;
(2) Unbounded: no restrictions on e.g., the sizes of the policies or attributes sets, or the number of times that an attribute may occur in the policy;
(3) Expressive: support of monotone span programs, ensuring that policies represented as Boolean formulas consisting of conjunctions and disjunctions can be supported;
(4) Non-monotone: support of non-monotone span programs, ensuring that the policies can use negations;
(5) Compact: the number of key and ciphertext components depends at most linearly on the set size or the policy length, and in particular does not depend on other parameters (implicit or explicit)[2].

GLUE is designed to offer a flexible choice in the encryption/decryption efficiency trade-off during the setup of the parameters. More specifically, it is parametrized in variables n_k and n_c, where the encryption costs increase in $n_k + n_c$ and the decryption costs decrease in n_k and n_c, e.g., in the factor n_k if $n_k = n_c$ holds. In this way, the scheme can be fine-tuned to take into account the computational resources of the encryption and decryption devices. In particular, this feature allows for significant speed-ups in the decryption algorithm compared to other schemes that also satisfy the listed properties.

Large-Universe and Unbounded ABE. The universe of attributes, i.e., the attributes that can be used in the scheme, can be small or large [47]. In small-universe constructions, the number of attributes is bounded after the setup, e.g.,

---

[2] For example, parameters such as those in schemes with a flexible efficiency trade-off (e.g., [12,52]) or the number of re-uses of the same attribute in the policy (e.g., [35]).

because a public key needs to be generated for each attribute. In large-universe constructions, the universe of attributes is effectively unbounded. Moreover, the public keys do not depend on the attributes in the system, and a user can directly encrypt messages using the master public key and the attribute string. Large-universe ABE is thus more scalable than small-universe ABE, as the encrypting users do not need to first locate the necessary public keys before encrypting. Some large-universe schemes [13,47,56] are however undesirably restrictive [39], as they are bounded in the sizes of the policies or attribute sets, or the number of times that an attribute may occur in the policy. Oftentimes, the scheme's efficiency depends on such bounds, e.g., the encryption costs grow linearly in the bounds on the policies or sets [55]. Hence, choosing high bounds is not a suitable solution either. Preferably, a scheme is unbounded in all parameters.

Expressivity and Non-monotonicity. Most state-of-the-art ABE schemes are expressive in that their policies support monotone span programs (MSPs) [2,11,40,49]. An important subclass of MSPs are Boolean formulas consisting of conjunctions and disjunctions. As mentioned, popular access control models such as attribute-based access control [32] allow the policies to be any Boolean formula, including negations. ABE schemes that support negations are called non-monotone [11,14,43,49,57]. In addition to being more expressive, such schemes readily support revocation systems [37], which is crucial in practice as well.

Different Types of Non-monotonicity. For large-universe constructions, three types of non-monotonicity exist: OSW-type [43], OT-type [42], and OSWOT-type [14]. In OSW-type negations, e.g., "NOT user: Alice", the entire attribute set, e.g., "{user: Bob, course: linear algebra, course: calculus}", is compared with the negated attribute to establish that the set does not contain it. In ABE implementations, this translates in a decryption cost that grows in not only the size of the policy, but also in size of the attribute sets. Such negations may thus not be efficient if the sets are large. In OT-type negations, e.g., "user: NOT Alice", the attribute labels, e.g., "user", play a role. In particular, the set must contain an attribute with label "user" and its value, e.g., "Bob", must differ from the negated attribute. While this is more efficient than OSW-type negations, the set of attributes is allowed to contain only one attribute for each label, e.g., such negations are not supported for the label "course" in our first example. Thus, schemes supporting this type of negations are bounded in the number of label re-uses, which is not always desirable. For instance, like in our example, users may have multiple attributes for labels such as "departments at a hospital", "courses followed at a university" or "mail addresses". As a solution, Attrapadung and Tomida [14] introduced OSWOT-type negations, e.g., "course: NOT cryptography", to extend OT-type negations, such that the negated attribute is compared with all attributes in the set that share the same label, e.g., "{course: linear algebra, course: calculus}". In this way, the flexibility of OSW-type negations and the efficiency of OT-type negations can be combined.

Table 1. Comparison of large-universe schemes supporting (non-)monotone span programs. For each scheme, we list whether it is unbounded (in the sets $\mathcal{S}$ and policies $\mathbb{A}$, and the number of attribute and label re-uses), whether it supports negations or has a provably secure extension that supports negations, whether it is compact and supports a flexible efficiency trade-off (FET). Note that we have only listed schemes that are structurally different "in the exponent", i.e., their associated pair encodings [9] are different. For instance, the unbounded schemes in [35,39] have a similar structure and therefore only [39] is listed.

Scheme	KP/CP	Unbounded				Negations			Compact	FET
		$|\mathcal{S}|$	$|\mathbb{A}|$	ARU	LRU	OSW	OT	OSWOT		
GPSW06-LU [26]	KP	✗	✓	✓	✓	✓ [43]	✗	✗	✓	✗
BSW07 [17]	CP	✓	✓	✓	✓	✗	✗	✗	✓	✗
ALP11 [13]	KP	✗	✓	✓	✓	✓	✗	✗	✗	✗
W11-LU I [56]	CP	✓	✓	✓	✓	✗	✗	✗	✓	✗
W11b-LU [55]	CP	✗	✗	✗	✗	✗	✗	✗	✓	✗
LW11b [39,45]	KP	✓	✓	✓	✓	✓ [37]	✓ [11]	✓ [14]	✓	✗
OT12 [42]	CP	✓	✓	✗	✗	✗	✓	✗	✗	✗
RW13 [45]	CP	✓	✓	✓	✓	✓ [57]	✓ [11]	✓ [14]	✓	✗
AHM+16 [12]	KP	✓	✓	✓	✓	✓ [13]	✗	✗	✗	✓
AC16 [1]	CP	✗	✗	✓	✓	✓ [6,11]	✓ [6,14]	✓ [6,14]	✗	✗
AC17b [2]	CP(/KP)	✓	✓	✗	✗	✗	✗	✗	✓	✗
ABGW17 [7]	KP/CP	✓	✓	✓	✓	✗	✗	✗	✓	✗
Att19-I-CP [11]	CP(/KP)	✓	✓	✓	✓	✓	✓ [14]	✓ [14]	✓	✗
Att19-II-CP [11]	CP(/KP)	✗	✓	✓	✓	✓	✗	✗	✗	✗
Att19-III-CP [11]	CP(/KP)	✓	✗	✓	✓	✓	✗	✗	✗	✗
TKN20 [49]	KP/CP	✓	✓	✓	✗	✗	✓	✗	✓	✗
VA22 [52]	CP	✓	✓	✓	✓	✓ [6]	✗	✗	✗	✓
GLUE	CP(/KP)	✓	✓	✓	✓	✓	✓	✓ [14]	✓	✓

Note: $\mathcal{S}$ = attribute set; $\mathbb{A}$ = access policy;
ARU = attribute re-use in the policies; LRU = label re-use in the sets and policies

Achieving Properties (1)-(5) Simultaneously. Only a limited number of existing schemes support properties (1)-(5) simultaneously [53]. In fact, all pairing-based schemes that provide non-monotonicity and large-universeness use a polynomial-based hash—also known as a "Boneh-Boyen (BB) hash" [18]—that maps arbitrary attribute strings into the scheme [43,47]. Of those schemes, the only ones that are completely unbounded [11,14,37,57] are based on the schemes by Lewko and Waters (the KP-ABE version) [39] and Rouselakis and Waters (the CP-ABE version) [45] (Table 1). However, all those schemes have an inefficient decryption algorithm compared to other ABE schemes [44], which use a full-domain hash (FDH) to achieve large-universeness. For this reason, such schemes are often favored in practice, despite their inability to support negations [24,25]. Nevertheless, since supporting negations fosters the expressivity of ABE, we aim at improving the decryption efficiency of schemes using a BB hash.

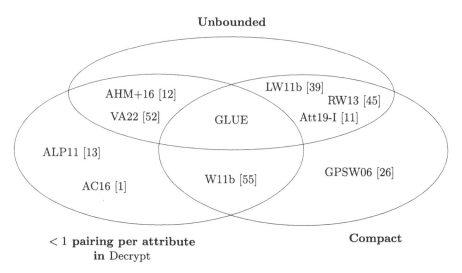

Fig. 1. Overview of large-universe schemes using a BB hash.

Improving Decryption Efficiency of Schemes Using a BB Hash. To determine whether we can improve on the decryption efficiency of the existing schemes satisfying properties (1)-(5), we investigate *all* schemes using a BB hash to achieve large-universeness. In particular, if we consider all such schemes, then we see that a scheme that is unbounded, compact and costs less than one pairing operation per attribute during decryption does not exist yet (Fig. 1). Because pairing operations are the most expensive operations in pairing-based ABE, it is therefore important to minimize the use of those. In this work, we aim to achieve this: we provide a scheme that satisfies properties (1)-(5), while requiring less than one pairing operation per attribute during decryption.

1.1 Our Contributions

We first give a high-level overview of our contributions. Then, we provide more (technical) details about these contributions.

- **New construction:** We present a new unbounded large-universe scheme using a BB hash (thus avoiding random oracles). Its encryption/decryption efficiency trade-off can be fine-tuned by taking into account the computational resources of the devices.
- **Generalizations:** Concretely, the scheme can be considered a generalization of two large-universe schemes: the Rouselakis-Waters (RW13) scheme [45] and the bounded large-universe scheme without random oracles by Waters (W11b) [55]. This generalization also illustrates a deeper connection among various designs.
- **Security proof:** We develop new proof techniques to ensure that the randomness provided by a BB hash can be simultaneously used for the keys and

ciphertexts. To the best of our knowledge, we are the first to achieve this in the unbounded setting, and in the full-security setting.

- **Extensions:** We provide three extensions to the basic scheme: one online/offline [31] and two non-monotone extensions supporting OT-type and OSW-type negations, respectively. Notably, we obtain an online/offline ABE scheme and a scheme supporting OSW-type negations with the most efficient decryption algorithms. This enables us to support OSWOT-type negations more efficiently, which is the most desirable in practice.

1.2   New Construction: GLUE

We focus on three schemes that satisfy at least two out of the three depicted properties (see Fig. 1): W11b [55], RW13 [45] and AHM+16 [12]. Those three schemes provide a good starting point for GLUE, our new scheme which satisfies all required properties. Intuitively, we apply the partitioning techniques of AHM+16 to combine the unbounded RW13 and the bounded W11b that allows for efficient decryption. However, as we show later, for the secure combination of these techniques, GLUE requires a more intricate approach.

We give a high-level description of the partitioning approach as introduced by AHM+16. First, we partition the attribute sets into smaller subsets. Then, we apply a (bounded) scheme with efficient decryption (in their case, ALP11 [13]) to each subset. Lastly, we use the unbounded techniques of e.g., RW13 or LW11b [39] to securely connect the subsets. In this way, the decryption costs of the scheme can be decreased. Unfortunately, this comes at a cost. Because bounded schemes typically have a more expensive encryption, the encryption costs are increased. From a broader perspective, this approach creates a scheme with a (flexibly) efficiency trade-off feature. As we will show later, this trade-off is determined by some parameter n. The encryption costs are higher by a factor n than those of unbounded schemes such as RW13, whereas the decryption costs are lower by this factor. Because this parameter n can be chosen during setup, it can be fine-tuned for the given practical context. If decryption needs to be efficient (which is often the case), one can choose larger n than in cases in which encryption needs to be efficient.

The main reason why we achieve the compactness property, in contrast to AHM+16, is due to the bounded scheme that is used. Because AHM+16 uses ALP11 [13], a scheme with constant-size ciphertexts and large keys whose sizes depend on the parameter n, its keys are large and its key generation is very expensive. Moreover, although the number of pairing operations required during decryption decreases, the number of exponentiations grows by a factor n for each matching attribute. As we will show, this means that AHM+16 decryption is not much more efficient than unbounded schemes such as RW13. As a solution, we use the W11b scheme, whose decryption costs consist of a constant number of pairing operations and no additional exponentiations. In this way, we achieve a much better speed-up in decryption, and since W11b is compact, the key sizes and key generation costs are not affected.

1.3   Generalizing RW13 by Generalizing the Hash

The main difference between the partitioning approach as applied by AHM+16 and us is that we have to partition both the key sets and the ciphertext policies. The reason for this is that AHM+16 uses ALP11, which is bounded in only the ciphertexts, whereas we use W11b, which is bounded in both the keys and ciphertexts. By extension, we need to apply some technique to connect the resulting key and ciphertext "parts". However, we will show that the security proof of W11b does not generalize to the unbounded setting, meaning that we have to devise a new proof technique for W11b that does generalize. Furthermore, it is not possible to apply the exact same approach as that of AHM+16. In particular, to prove security, they embed the scheme in the fully secure key-policy doubly-spatial encryption [30] scheme in [9], and then, they apply the embedding lemma [12]. We cannot use this approach, because, to the best of our knowledge, the W11b scheme cannot be similarly embedded in an existing scheme.

Hence, we take a slightly different approach: we generalize RW13 by generalizing its specific instantiation of the BB hash. A BB hash first takes as input a unique representation x_{att} of an attribute att in the integer set $\mathbb{Z}_p$, where p is the prime order of group $\mathbb{G}$ with generator $g \in \mathbb{G}$. Then, it computes the hash as $F_n(x_{att}) = \prod_{i=0}^{n} B_i^{x_{att}^i}$, where the generators $B_i = g^{b_i}$ implicitly embed the coefficients of the polynomial $f_n(x_{att}) = \sum_{i=0}^{n} b_i x_{att}^i$. Where RW13 (and its unbounded derivatives [11,31]) uses an implicit 1-degree polynomial, we use an implicit n-degree polynomial, like W11b [55]. However, as we will show, simply replacing the 1-degree polynomial by some n-degree polynomial does not immediately yield a secure scheme. To solve this, we replace another public-key variable used in the scheme by a polynomial.

1.4   Security Proof

The AC17 Framework. To benefit from the strong security guarantees as well as the generic transformations [6,11] within the Agrawal-Chase (AC17) [3] framework, we prove security within it. In general, the AC17 framework considers the pair encoding schemes (PESs) associated with an ABE scheme [9]. Intuitively, PESs are an abstraction of ABE schemes to what happens in the exponent space. If a PES is secure, the AC17 framework transforms it into a fully (also known as adaptively) secure scheme. The security notion for PES is called symbolic security, which consists of two parts: the selective and co-selective symbolic property. These properties hold for any scheme that is not trivially broken, so the AC17 framework simplifies the effort of proving full security considerably by giving such transformations. A small drawback is that the resulting schemes are provably secure under q-type assumptions [19], which are less well-understood than static security assumptions. Regardless, the assumptions used in the AC17 framework are implied by commonly-used q-type assumptions [9]. These have not been shown to yield less secure schemes in practice yet. Another advantage of the AC17 framework is that any symbolically secure PES can be transformed in a PES that supports negations [6]. It is notoriously difficult to achieve this in the full-security model in combination with the large-universe property [11].

Proving the Symbolic Property. Proving the (co-)selective symbolic property is similar to proving selective security. In the selective-security model, the attacker commits to the challenge access policy (resp. set of attributes) before seeing the public keys. Many schemes proven security in this model use the "program-and-cancel" strategy [45, 56], in which the challenger embeds the policy (resp. set) in the public keys. In the simulation of the secret keys and challenge ciphertext, the components are programmed in a specific way, using that the set does not satisfy the policy (resp. policy is not satisfied by the set). Typically, the components that cannot be programmed are canceled by other non-programmable components. In the AC17 framework, this "programming" is replaced by "substitution", and the "canceling" is replaced by "evaluating to 0".

Security Proof. One of the main difficulties of our scheme is proving the symbolic property. In the first place, proving security is difficult due to the lack of provably secure schemes that use the randomness provided by the BB hash for *both the keys and ciphertexts*. To the best of our knowledge, previously, only W11b [55] used the hash for both the keys and ciphertexts, but only in the bounded setting and in the selective-security model. However, the proof does not seem to readily generalize to the unbounded setting (see the full version [54]). Hence, we develop a novel technique to prove security. We do this, in part, by combining several techniques.

- **Proof techniques using the hash for the keys:** We generalize the proof techniques used by Agrawal and Chase in [3] to prove full security of their scheme in [1]: the AC16 [1] scheme. AC16 is a CP-ABE scheme with constant-size ciphertexts, in which the randomness provided by the Boneh-Boyen hash is used for the *keys*. In the selective proof, the polynomial embedded in the public keys needs to be used by the secret keys after the public keys are generated. The proof does this by embedding a "reprogrammable" polynomial in the public keys. We call these polynomials to be reprogrammable in the sense that the randomizers of the secret keys can later program it to a suitable target polynomial. We use this general strategy for the keys.
- **Proof techniques using the hash for the ciphertext:** Even though the W11b [55] proof does not generalize to the unbounded setting, we are able to use a part of the proof strategy. In the selective proof, the implicit polynomial embedded in the public key is "programmed" to take into account the attributes that will be used in the challenge ciphertext. We use this general strategy for the ciphertexts.
- **Unbounded proof techniques:** One of the bottlenecks of the two aforementioned strategies is that they are bounded approaches: they use only one randomizer for the keys and one for the ciphertexts. To make them unbounded, we use the general approach of the RW13 [45] proof. This proof gives us a

rough idea of how the implicit polynomial and the randomizers should be programmed. Furthermore, it shows us how to use the polynomial an unbounded number of times: using layering and individual randomness techniques allows us to select the required instance of the polynomial.

Another bottleneck is that the "programmed" and "reprogrammable" approaches are orthogonal, and can therefore not be used simultaneously in the same polynomial without applying a trick. Presumably, this is also the reason why the W11b proof uses the programmed approach for both the keys and the ciphertexts, and applies an algebraic argument to ensure that everything can be simulated as required. We eliminate this bottleneck and combine all these proof techniques, by splitting the polynomial in the product of two smaller polynomials: one "programmed" polynomial and one "reprogrammable" polynomial. For the selective proof, we use the programmed polynomial for the ciphertexts and the reprogrammable polynomial for the keys. For the co-selective proof, the roles of the polynomials are reversed.

1.5   Practical Extensions

We provide several extensions to our scheme, most of which can be found in the full version [54]. Because we prove security in the AC17 [3] framework, some of these extensions are automatically provably secure.

- **The key-policy and dual-policy versions**, by applying [11];
- **Online/offline extensions**, by generalizing HW14 [31]. Owing to its generality, these extensions also apply to the following extensions;
- **Non-monotone versions**, by applying [6,11,49]. We give versions supporting OT-type and OSW-type negations in the full version [54].

Online/offline Extension. The algebraic structure of large-universe schemes using a BB hash can also be exploited to increase the efficiency. Hohenberger and Waters [31] show how the key generation and encryption of RW13 [45] can be split in an online and offline phase. In this way, most of the computations required by these algorithms can be performed in an offline phase. During the online phase, little computational power is required. This is especially useful in practice when secret keys need to be generated frequently, e.g., in revocation systems [46]. The key generation authority then does not need to have computationally powerful resources to do this in an acceptable time frame. Similarly, the online/offline encryption variant can be used to minimize the encryption costs. This comes however at a cost: the decryption costs increase. Thus, reducing the decryption costs of the basic scheme also helps reducing the decryption costs of the online/offline version. With the online/offline version of GLUE, we can not only improve on the decryption efficiency of existing such schemes, but we can also mitigate the impact of the increase of n on the encryption efficiency.

Table 2. Theoretical efficiency comparison of all compact unbounded large-universe CP-ABE schemes supporting MSPs (that (can) support OSW(OT)-type negations), by analyzing the key generation, encryption and decryption costs with respect to the number of exponentiations $c_{\exp}$ and pairings c_{pair}.

Scheme	Key generation $c_{\exp}$	Encryption $c_{\exp}$	Decryption $c_{\exp}$	Decryption c_{pair}
RW13 [45]	$4+4\lvert\mathcal{S}\rvert$	$4+10\lvert\mathbb{A}\rvert$	$4\lvert\varUpsilon\rvert$	$4+4\lvert\varUpsilon\rvert$
Att19-I-CP [11]	$12+12\lvert\mathcal{S}\rvert$	$4+16\lvert\mathbb{A}\rvert$	$4\lvert\varUpsilon\rvert$	$8+4\lvert\varUpsilon\rvert$
GLUE	$4+2\lvert\mathcal{S}\rvert+2\left\lceil\frac{\lvert\mathcal{S}\rvert}{n_k}\right\rceil$	$4+2\lvert\mathbb{A}\rvert(n_k+2n_c+1)+2\left\lceil\frac{\lvert\mathbb{A}\rvert}{n_c}\right\rceil$	$2\lvert\varUpsilon\rvert$	$4+2\left\lceil\frac{\lvert\varUpsilon\rvert}{n_k}\right\rceil+2\left\lceil\frac{\lvert\varUpsilon\rvert}{n_c}\right\rceil$
GLUE-N	$12+8\lvert\mathcal{S}\rvert+4\left\lceil\frac{\lvert\mathcal{S}\rvert}{n_k}\right\rceil$	$4+2\lvert\mathbb{A}\rvert(n_k+2n_c+4)+2\left\lceil\frac{\lvert\mathbb{A}\rvert}{n_c}\right\rceil$	$4\lvert\varUpsilon\rvert$	$8+2\left\lceil\frac{\lvert\varUpsilon\rvert}{n_k}\right\rceil+2\left\lceil\frac{\lvert\varUpsilon\rvert}{n_c}\right\rceil$

(a) Costs for non-negated policies

Scheme	$c_{\exp}$	c_{pair}
Att19-I-CP [11]	$4\lvert\varUpsilon\rvert\cdot\lvert\mathcal{S}\rvert$	$8+2\lvert\varUpsilon\rvert+2\min(\lvert\varUpsilon\rvert,\lvert\mathcal{S}\rvert)$
GLUE-N (worst case)	$4\lvert\varUpsilon\rvert\cdot\lvert\mathcal{S}\rvert+2\left\lceil\frac{\lvert\mathcal{S}\rvert}{n_k}\right\rceil\cdot\lvert\varUpsilon\rvert$	$8+2\lvert\varUpsilon\rvert+2\left\lceil\frac{\lvert\mathcal{S}\rvert}{n_k}\right\rceil$
GLUE-N (best case)	$4\left\lceil\frac{\lvert\varUpsilon\rvert}{n_c}\right\rceil\cdot\lvert\mathcal{S}\rvert+2\left\lceil\frac{\lvert\mathcal{S}\rvert}{n_k}\right\rceil\cdot\lvert\varUpsilon\rvert$	$8+2\left\lceil\frac{\lvert\varUpsilon\rvert}{n_c}\right\rceil+2\left\lceil\frac{\lvert\mathcal{S}\rvert}{n_k}\right\rceil$

(b) Decryption costs for negated policies

Note: $\mathcal{S}$ = attribute set; $\mathbb{A}$ = access policy; $\varUpsilon$ = matching attributes; n_k, n_c = parameters chosen during setup

1.6 Efficiency Comparison with Existing Schemes Supporting (1)-(5)

We generalize RW13 to achieve a scheme that supports or can support properties (1)-(5) whilst being able to achieve a more efficient decryption algorithm. In Table 2, we compare the efficiency of RW13 and its OSW-type non-monotone variant Att19-I-CP with GLUE (which supports MSPs only) and GLUE-N (which additionally supports OSW-type negations). The table shows that, if $n_k = n_c$, the number of pairing operations required during decryption is reduced by roughly a factor of $n_k = n_c$. In Sect. 6, we give more concrete estimates for the timings in practice and how they compare to existing schemes.

2 Preliminaries

Notation. A negligible function parametrized by λ is denoted as $\mathrm{negl}(\lambda)$. We use $x \in_R S$ to indicate that an element x is chosen uniformly at random from a finite set S. For integers $a < b$, we denote $[a, b] = \{a, a+1, ..., b-1, b\}$, $[b] = [1, b]$ and $\overline{[b]} = [0, b]$. We denote $a : \mathbf{A}$ to substitute variable a by a matrix or vector $\mathbf{A}$. We define $\mathbf{1}_{i,j}^{d_1 \times d_2} \in \mathbb{Z}_p^{d_1 \times d_2}$ as the matrix with 1 in the i-th row and j-th column, and 0 everywhere else, and $\mathbf{1}_i^{d_1}$ and $\overline{\mathbf{1}}_i^{d_2}$ as the row and column vectors with 1 in the i-th entry and 0 everywhere else.

2.1 Access Structures

Definition 1 (Access structures represented by LSSS matrices *[27]).*
We represent an access structure as a pair $\mathbb{A} = (\mathbf{A}, \rho)$ *such that* $\mathbf{A} \in \mathbb{Z}_p^{n_1 \times n_2}$
is an LSSS matrix, where $n_1, n_2 \in \mathbb{N}$*, and* ρ *is a function that maps its rows
to attributes in the universe. Then, for some vector* $\mathbf{v} = (s, v_2, ..., v_{n_2}) \in_R \mathbb{Z}_p^{n_2}$*,
the i-th share of secret s generated by this matrix is* $\lambda_i = \mathbf{A}_i \mathbf{v}^\mathsf{T}$*, where* $\mathbf{A}_i$
denotes the i-th row of $\mathbf{A}$*. In particular, if* $\mathcal{S}$ *satisfies* $\mathbb{A}$*, there exist a set of
rows* $\Upsilon = \{i \in [n_1] \mid \rho(i) \in \mathcal{S}\}$ *and coefficients* $\varepsilon_i \in \mathbb{Z}_p$ *for all* $i \in \Upsilon$ *such that*
$\sum_{i \in \Upsilon} \varepsilon_i \mathbf{A}_i = (1, 0, ..., 0)$*, and by extension* $\sum_{i \in \Upsilon} \varepsilon_i \lambda_i = s$*, holds. Otherwise,
there exists* $\mathbf{w} = (1, w_2, ..., w_{n_2}) \in \mathbb{Z}_p^{n_2}$ *such that* $\mathbf{A}_i \mathbf{w}^\mathsf{T} = 0$ *for all* $i \in \Upsilon$ *[16].*

2.2 Attribute-based Encryption

Predicate Family. A predicate family [9] is a set $P = \{P_\kappa\}_{\kappa \in \mathbb{N}^c}$ for some
constant c, where $P_\kappa \colon \mathcal{X}_\kappa \times \mathcal{Y}_\kappa \to \{0, 1\}$. For κ, it holds that $\kappa = (p, \mathrm{par})$, where
p is a natural number and par denote the rest of the entries.

Definition 2 (Attribute-based encryption (ABE) *[3]). An attribute-based
encryption scheme for a predicate family* $P = \{P_\kappa\}_{\kappa \in \mathbb{N}^c}$ *over a message space*
$\mathcal{M} = \{M_\lambda\}_{\lambda \in \mathbb{N}}$ *consists of four algorithms:*

- *Setup*$(\lambda, \mathrm{par}) \to (MPK, MSK)$*: On input the security parameter* λ *and parameters* par*, this probabilistic algorithm generates the domain parameters, the
  master public key MPK and the master secret key MSK. In addition,* κ *is set
  to* $\kappa = (p, \mathrm{par})$*, where p denotes a natural number.*
- *KeyGen*$(MSK, y) \to SK_y$*: On input the master secret key MSK and* $y \in \mathcal{Y}_\kappa$*,
  this probabilistic algorithm generates a secret key* SK_y*.*
- *Encrypt*$(MPK, x, M) \to CT_x$*: On input the master public key MPK,* $x \in \mathcal{X}_\kappa$
  and message M, this probabilistic algorithm generates a ciphertext CT_x*.*
- *Decrypt*$(MPK, SK_y, CT_x) \to M$*: On input the master public key MPK, the
  secret key* SK_y*, and the ciphertext* CT_x*, if* $P_\kappa(x, y) = 1$*, then it returns M.
  Otherwise, it returns an error message* $\perp$*.*

Correctness. For all par, $M \in \mathcal{M}_\lambda$, $x \in \mathcal{X}_\kappa$, and $y \in \mathcal{Y}_\kappa$ such that $P_\kappa(x, y) = 1$,

$$\Pr[(MPK, MSK) \leftarrow \mathrm{Setup}(1^\lambda);$$
$$\mathrm{Decrypt}(MPK, \mathrm{KeyGen}(MSK, y)), \mathrm{Encrypt}(MPK, x, M)) \neq M] \leq \mathrm{negl}(\lambda).$$

Unbounded Large-Universe Ciphertext-Policy ABE. A specific instance
of ABE is ciphertext-policy ABE. In this type of ABE, the key predicate y is
a set of attributes $\mathcal{S}$ over some universe of attributes $\mathcal{U}$, and the ciphertext
predicate x is an access policy $\mathbb{A} = (\mathbf{A}, \rho)$, in this work represented as LSSS
matrices (Definition 1). We consider a scheme to be large-universe if it does not
impose bounds on the size of the universe. We call it unbounded, if it does not

impose bounds on the sizes of the universe, sets of attributes and access policies, or on the number of times that an attribute occurs in an access policy. The term "unbounded ABE" is more prominently used for schemes that achieve this without requiring random oracles in the proof.

2.3   Full Security Against Chosen-Plaintext Attacks

Definition 3 (Full security against chosen-plaintext attacks (CPA) *[3]). We define the security game IND-CPA between challenger and attacker as:*

- **Setup phase:** *The challenger runs Setup(λ) to obtain MPK and MSK, and sends the master public key MPK to the attacker.*
- **First query phase:** *The attacker queries secret keys for $y \in \mathcal{Y}_\kappa$, and obtains $SK_y \leftarrow KeyGen(MSK, y)$ in response.*
- **Challenge phase:** *The attacker specifies some $x^* \in \mathcal{X}_\kappa$ such that for all y in the first key query phase, we have $P_\kappa(x^*, y) = 0$, and generates two messages M_0 and M_1 of equal length in $\mathcal{M}_\lambda$, and sends these to the challenger. The challenger flips a coin, i.e., $\beta \in_R \{0, 1\}$, encrypts M_β under x^*, i.e., $CT_{x^*} \leftarrow Encrypt(MPK, x^*, M_\beta)$, and sends the resulting ciphertext CT_{x^*} to the attacker.*
- **Second query phase:** *This phase is identical to the first query phase, with the additional restriction that the attacker can only query $y \in \mathcal{Y}_\kappa$ such that $P_\kappa(x^*, y) = 0$.*
- **Decision phase:** *The attacker outputs a guess β' for β.*

The attacker's advantage is defined as $\mathsf{Adv}_{PE,IND\text{-}CPA} = |\Pr[\beta' = \beta] - \frac{1}{2}|$. A scheme is fully secure if all polynomial-time attackers have at most a negligible advantage in this security game, i.e., $\mathsf{Adv}_{PE,IND\text{-}CPA} \leq negl(\lambda)$. In the selective security model, the attacker commits to the predicate $x^* \in \mathcal{X}_\kappa$ before the Setup.

2.4   Pairings (or Bilinear Maps)

We define a pairing to be an efficiently computable map e on three groups $\mathbb{G}, \mathbb{H}$ and $\mathbb{G}_T$ of prime order p, such that $e \colon \mathbb{G} \times \mathbb{H} \to \mathbb{G}_T$, with generators $g \in \mathbb{G}, h \in \mathbb{H}$ such that for all $a, b \in \mathbb{Z}_p$, it holds that $e(g^a, h^b) = e(g, h)^{ab}$ (bilinearity), and for $g^a \neq 1_\mathbb{G}, h^b \neq 1_\mathbb{H}$, it holds that $e(g^a, h^b) \neq 1_{\mathbb{G}_T}$, where $1_{\mathbb{G}'}$ denotes the unique identity element of the associated group $\mathbb{G}'$ (non-degeneracy). We refer to $\mathbb{G}$ and $\mathbb{H}$ as the two source groups, and $\mathbb{G}_T$ as the target group.

2.5   Pair Encoding Schemes

Definition 4 (Pair encoding schemes (PES) *[3]). A pair encoding scheme for a predicate family $P_\kappa \colon \mathcal{X}_\kappa \times \mathcal{Y}_\kappa \to \{0, 1\}$, indexed by $\kappa = (p, \text{par})$, where par specifies some parameters, is given by four deterministic polynomial-time algorithms as described below.*

- *Param*(par) → *n*: *On input* par, *the algorithm outputs* $n \in \mathbb{N}$ *that specifies the number of common variables, which are denoted as* $\mathbf{b} = (b_1, ..., b_n)$.
- *EncKey*(y, p) → $(m_1, m_2, \mathbf{k}(\mathbf{r}, \hat{\mathbf{r}}, \mathbf{b}))$: *On input* $p \in \mathbb{N}$ *and* $y \in \mathcal{Y}_\kappa$, *this algorithm outputs a vector of polynomials* $\mathbf{k} = (k_1, ..., k_{m_3})$ *defined over non-lone variables* $\mathbf{r} = (r_1, ..., r_{m_1})$ *and lone variables* $\hat{\mathbf{r}} = (\hat{r}_1, ..., \hat{r}_{m_2})$. *Specifically, the polynomial* k_i *is expressed as*

$$k_i = \delta_i \alpha + \sum_{j \in [m_2]} \delta_{i,j} \hat{r}_j + \sum_{j \in [m_1], k \in [n]} \delta_{i,j,k} r_j b_k,$$

for all $i \in [m_3]$, *where* $\delta_i, \delta_{i,j}, \delta_{i,j,k} \in \mathbb{Z}_p$.
- *EncCt*(x, p) → $(w_1, w_2, \mathbf{c}(\mathbf{s}, \hat{\mathbf{s}}, \mathbf{b}))$: *On input* $p \in \mathbb{N}$ *and* $x \in \mathcal{X}_\kappa$, *this algorithm outputs a vector of polynomials* $\mathbf{c} = (c_1, ..., c_{w_3})$ *defined over non-lone variables* $\mathbf{s} = (s, s_2, ..., s_{w_1})$ *and lone variables* $\hat{\mathbf{s}} = (\hat{s}_1, ..., \hat{s}_{w_2})$. *Specifically, the polynomial* c_i *is expressed as*

$$c_i = \sum_{j \in [w_2]} \eta_{i,j} \hat{s}_j + \sum_{j \in [w_1], k \in [n]} \eta_{i,j,k} s_j b_k,$$

for all $i \in [w_3]$, *where* $\eta_{i,j}, \eta_{i,j,k} \in \mathbb{Z}_p$.
- *Pair*(x, y, p) → $(\mathbf{E}, \overline{\mathbf{E}})$: *On input* p, x, *and* y, *this algorithm outputs two matrices* $\mathbf{E}$ *and* $\overline{\mathbf{E}}$ *of sizes* $(w_1 + 1) \times m_3$ *and* $w_3 \times m_1$, *respectively.*

A PES is correct for every $\kappa = (p, \text{par})$, $x \in \mathcal{X}_\kappa$ and $y \in \mathcal{Y}_\kappa$ such that $P_\kappa(x, y) = 1$, it holds that $\mathbf{s}\mathbf{E}\mathbf{k}^\mathsf{T} + \mathbf{c}\overline{\mathbf{E}}\mathbf{r}^\mathsf{T} = \alpha s$.

Definition 5 (Symbolic property *[3]*). *A pair encoding scheme* $\Gamma = (Param, EncKey, EncCt, Pair)$ *for a predicate family* $P_\kappa : \mathcal{X}_\kappa \times \mathcal{Y}_\kappa \rightarrow \{0, 1\}$ *satisfies the* (d_1, d_2)-*selective symbolic property for positive integers* d_1 *and* d_2 *if there exist deterministic polynomial-time algorithms EncB, EncS, and EncR such that for all* $\kappa = (p, \text{par})$, $x \in \mathcal{X}_\kappa$ *and* $y \in \mathcal{Y}_\kappa$ *with* $P_\kappa(x, y) = 0$, *we have that*

- *EncB*(x) → $\mathbf{B}_1, ..., \mathbf{B}_n \in \mathbb{Z}_p^{d_1 \times d_2}$;
- *EncR*(x, y) → $\mathbf{r}_1, ..., \mathbf{r}_{m_1} \in \mathbb{Z}_p^{d_1}, \mathbf{a}, \hat{\mathbf{r}}_1, ..., \hat{\mathbf{r}}_{m_2} \in \mathbb{Z}_p^{d_2}$;
- *EncS*(x) → $\mathbf{s}_0, ..., \mathbf{s}_{w_1} \in \mathbb{Z}_p^{d_2}, \hat{\mathbf{s}}_1, ..., \hat{\mathbf{s}}_{w_2} \in \mathbb{Z}_p^{d_1}$;

such that $\langle \mathbf{s}_0, \mathbf{a} \rangle \neq 0$, *and if we substitute*

$$\hat{s}_{i'} : \hat{\mathbf{s}}_{i'}^\mathsf{T} \qquad s_i b_j : \mathbf{B}_j \mathbf{s}_i^\mathsf{T} \qquad \alpha : \mathbf{a} \qquad \hat{r}_{k'} : \hat{\mathbf{r}}_{k'} \qquad r_k b_j : \mathbf{r}_k \mathbf{B}_j,$$

for $i \in [w_1], i' \in [w_2], j \in [n], k \in [m_1], k' \in [m_2]$ *in all the polynomials of* $\mathbf{k}$ *and* $\mathbf{c}$ *(output by EncKey and EncCt, respectively), they evaluate to* $\mathbf{0}$.

Similarly, a pair encoding scheme satisfies the (d_1, d_2)-*co-selective symbolic security property if there exist EncB, EncR, EncS that satisfy the above properties but where EncB and EncR only take* y *as input, and EncS takes* x *and* y *as input.*

A scheme satisfies the (d_1, d_2)-*symbolic property if it satisfies the* (d_1', d_2')-*selective and* (d_1'', d_2'')-*co-selective properties for* $d_1', d_1'' \leq d_1$ *and* $d_2', d_2'' \leq d_2$.

Agrawal and Chase [3] prove that any PES satisfying the (d_1, d_2)-symbolic property can be transformed in a fully secure ABE scheme.

3 Generalizing Rouselakis-Waters

We first show how RW13 [45] can be generalized. On a high level, we do this by substituting the implicit 1-degree polynomial in the RW13 keys and ciphertexts with an n-degree polynomial. Like W11b [55], the randomness provided by this n-degree polynomial will be shared between the keys and ciphertexts. That is, suppose that n_k and n_c are positive integers such that $n = n_k + n_c - 1$, then the n-degree polynomial provides enough randomness for $n_k - 1$ attributes in the keys, and n_c attributes in the ciphertext. To optimally use this randomness, we therefore split the keys and ciphertexts in partitions of at most n_k and n_c attributes, respectively. For instance, if $\mathcal{S}$ denotes the set of attributes for which a key is requested, then $\mathcal{S}$ is split in partitions of maximum size n_k, i.e., $\mathcal{S} = \mathcal{S}_1 \cup ... \cup \mathcal{S}_m$ such that $|\mathcal{S}_l| \leq n_k$ for each $l \in [m]$. Then, to avoid boundedness, we apply the RW13 trick by introducing one "randomizer" for each partition (both in the keys and ciphertexts).

3.1 The Rouselakis-Waters Scheme

First, we briefly review the RW13 scheme [45]. Specifically, the secret keys and ciphertexts are of the form

$$\mathrm{SK} = (K = h^{\alpha - rb}, K' = h^r, \{K_{1,\mathrm{att}} = h^{rb' + r_{\mathrm{att}}(x_{\mathrm{att}} b_1 + b_0)}, K_{2,\mathrm{att}} = h^{r_{\mathrm{att}}}\}_{\mathrm{att} \in \mathcal{S}}),$$
$$\mathrm{CT} = (C = M \cdot e(g,h)^{\alpha s}, C' = g^s, \{C_{1,j} = B^{\lambda_j} \cdot (B')^{s_j},$$
$$C_{2,j} = (B_1^{x_{\mathrm{att}_j}} B_0)^{s_j}, C_{3,j} = g^{s_j}\}_{j \in [n_1]}),$$

where $B = g^b, B_1 = g^{b_1}, B_0 = g^{b_0}$ and $B' = g^{b'}$ denote public keys, $r, r_{\mathrm{att}} \in_R \mathbb{Z}_p$ are randomly chosen integers during the key generation for set $\mathcal{S}$, s, s_j are randomly chosen integers during encryption under access policy $\mathbb{A} = (\mathbf{A}, \rho)$ with $\mathbf{A} \in \mathbb{Z}_p^{n_1 \times n_2}$, and x_{att} is the representation of attribute att in $\mathbb{Z}_p$. We have also denoted $x_{\mathrm{att}_j} = \rho(j)$ to clearly indicate the attributes in the ciphertext.

3.2 First Attempt: A Naive Approach

Our first attempt is to directly replace the 1-degree polynomial, $x_{\mathrm{att}} b_1 + b_0$, by an n-degree polynomial, i.e., $f_n(x_{\mathrm{att}}) = \sum_{i=0}^{n} b_i x_{\mathrm{att}}^i$ (where $n = n_k + n_c - 1$):

$$\mathrm{SK} = (K = h^{\alpha - rb}, K' = h^r, \{K_{1,\mathrm{att}} = h^{rb' + \boxed{r_{\mathrm{att}} f_n(x_{\mathrm{att}})}}, K_{2,\mathrm{att}} = h^{r_{\mathrm{att}}}\}_{\mathrm{att} \in \mathcal{S}}),$$
$$\mathrm{CT} = (C = M \cdot e(g,g)^{\alpha s}, C' = g^s, \{C_{1,j} = B^{\lambda_j} \cdot (B')^{s_j},$$
$$C_{2,j} = \boxed{F_n(x_{\mathrm{att}_j})^{s_j}} = \left(\prod_{i=0}^{n} B_i^{x_{\mathrm{att}_j}^i}\right)^{s_j}, C_{3,j} = g^{s_j}\}_{j \in [n_1]}),$$

where $B_i = g^{b_i}$ for all $i \in [0, n]$. We split $\mathcal{S}$ in partitions of maximum size n_k, and the rows of $\mathbb{A}$ in partitions of size n_c. We ensure that the same randomizer is used for all attributes in the same partition, i.e., set $r_{\mathrm{att}} = r_{\mathrm{att}'}$ and $s_j = s_{j'}$, if att and att', and att_j and $\mathrm{att}_{j'}$ are in the same partitions, respectively.

Unfortunately, the resulting scheme is insecure (see the full version [54] for a concrete attack). Roughly, the reason is that $C_{1,j} = g^{\lambda_j b + s_j b'}$ does not sufficiently hide $\lambda_j b$, because the same s_j is used for all attributes in the same partition. Therefore, we need to introduce more randomness.

3.3 Second (Successful) Attempt

We show how to use another polynomial to introduce enough randomness. Because we only need enough randomness for the ciphertext partitions, we require an $(n_c - 1)$-degree polynomial. This polynomial, $f'_{n_c-1}(x_{\text{att}}) = \sum_{i=0}^{n_c-1} b'_i x^i_{\text{att}}$, will replace the "0-degree polynomial" b'. Because s_j provides randomness for one attribute, and f'_{n_c-1} provides randomness for $n_c - 1$ attributes in the partition, this sufficiently hides λ_j. The resulting scheme is then

$$SK = (K = h^{\alpha-rb}, K' = h^r, \{K_{1,\text{att}} = h^{\boxed{rf'_{n_c-1}(x_{\text{att}})} + \boxed{r_{\text{att}} f_n(x_{\text{att}})}},$$
$$K_{2,\text{att}} = h^{r_{\text{att}}}\}_{\text{att}\in\mathcal{S}}),$$
$$CT = (C = M \cdot e(g,h)^{\alpha s}, C' = g^s, \{C_{1,j} = B^{\lambda_j} \cdot \boxed{F'_{n_c-1}(x_{\text{att}_j})^{s_j}},$$
$$C_{2,j} = \boxed{F_n(x_{\text{att}_j})^{s_j}}, C_{3,j} = g^{s_j}\}_{j\in[n_1]}),$$

where $F'_{n_c-1}(x_{\text{att}}) = \prod_{i=0}^{n_c-1}(B'_i)^{x^i_{\text{att}}} = g^{f'_{n_c-1}(x_{\text{att}})}$, and $B'_i = g^{b'_i}$ for all $i \in [0, n_c - 1]$. Note that this scheme is a generalization of RW13, because setting $n = n_c = n_k = 1$ yields RW13.

3.4 More Efficient Decryption

Generalizing the polynomial allows for an improved decryption efficiency. To understand why this yields a significant improvement, we briefly review the W11b scheme. We consider the keys and ciphertexts, which are of the form:

$$SK = (K = h^{\alpha-rb}, K' = h^r, \{K_{\text{att}} = h^{rf_n(x_{\text{att}})}\}_{\text{att}\in\mathcal{S}}),$$
$$CT = (C = M \cdot e(g,h)^{\alpha s}, C' = g^s, \{C_j = B^{\lambda_j} F_n(\rho(j))^s\}_{j\in[n_1]}),$$

where $r, s \in \mathbb{Z}_p$ are randomly chosen integers, $B = g^b$ is a public key, α is the master key, and $\rho(j)$ is the j-th attribute of the policy of length n_1, and λ_j is a sharing of s with respect to the policy. To decrypt, one computes

$$C/e(C', K) \cdot \prod_{j\in\Upsilon} e(C_j, K')^{\varepsilon_j} / \prod_{j\in\Upsilon} e(C', K_{\rho(j)})^{\varepsilon_j},$$

where ε_j for $j \in \Upsilon \subseteq [n_1]$ are integers that allow us to reconstruct the secret s. Each such product of pairings can be computed more efficiently by using the bilinearity property on the shared arguments, e.g., $\prod_j e(K', C_j)^{\varepsilon_j}$ can be computed more efficiently by first multiplying C_j and then taking a pairing:

$$C/e\left(C', K \cdot \prod_{j \in \Upsilon} K_{\rho(j)}^{\varepsilon_j}\right) \cdot e\left(\prod_{j \in \Upsilon} C_j^{\varepsilon_j}, K'\right).$$

This requires only two pairing operations instead of $2|\Upsilon|+1$. While decryption is very efficient, the drawback of W11b is that it is bounded in both the keys and ciphertexts. Because F_n embeds an n-degree polynomial, its randomized variant only provides sufficient randomness for $n+1$ attributes shared between the keys and ciphertexts. In contrast, RW13 uses an implicit 1-degree polynomial for the hash. To provide unboundedness, each instance of the hash—which in itself only provides sufficient randomness for one attribute—is randomized. As a result, both the keys and ciphertexts consist of components of the form $(g^{t_i}, F_1(x_{att})^{t_i})$, such that each randomizer part g^{t_i} needs to be paired with the part involving the hash during decryption. Hence, a linear number of pairing operations is required during decryption instead of a constant. By generalizing the 1-degree polynomial, we can use the same randomizer for multiple attributes. Thus, we can achieve a similar speed-up in decryption efficiency as W11b, whilst benefiting from the unboundedness of RW13.

Note that this also illustrates why it is important that the BB hash is used for both the keys and the ciphertexts. For example, in the GPSW06 large-universe scheme [26, §5], the randomness provided by the hash is used only for the ciphertexts. As a result, the keys require a fresh randomizer for each attribute, and therefore, decryption costs at least one pairing operation per attribute.

4   Our Construction

We now present the complete description of our scheme in the selective security setting obtained by using [50] (see the full version [54] for a fully secure version). In this scheme, we also introduce the mappings ι and τ, which map the attributes of the keys and ciphertexts, respectively, into arbitrary partitions of maximum sizes n_k and n_c.

Definition 6 (GLUE). *GLUE is defined as follows.*

– *Setup(λ): On input the security parameter λ, the setup generates three groups $\mathbb{G}, \mathbb{H}, \mathbb{G}_T$ of prime order p with generators $g \in \mathbb{G}, h \in \mathbb{H}$, and chooses a pairing $e\colon \mathbb{G} \times \mathbb{H} \to \mathbb{G}_T$. It also defines the universe of attributes $\mathcal{U} = \mathbb{Z}_p$, chooses $n_k \in \mathbb{N}$ and $n_c \in \mathbb{N}$ as the maximum partition sizes of the keys and ciphertexts, respectively, and sets $n = n_k + n_c - 1$. It then generates random $\alpha, b, b_i, b'_{i'} \in_R \mathbb{Z}_p$ for all $i \in [0, n], i' \in [0, n_c - 1]$. It outputs $MSK = (\alpha, b, \{b_i, b'_{i'}\}_{i \in [0,n], i' \in [0, n_c - 1]})$ as its master secret key and publishes the master public key as*

$$MPK = (g, h, A = e(g,h)^{\alpha}, B = g^b, \{B_i = g^{b_i}, B'_{i'} = g^{b'_{i'}}\}_{i \in \overline{[n]}, i' \in \overline{[n_c - 1]}}).$$

– $KeyGen(MSK, \mathcal{S})$: *On input set of attributes* $\mathcal{S}$, *the key generation computes* $m = \left\lceil \frac{|\mathcal{S}|}{n_k} \right\rceil$, *defines* $\iota\colon \mathcal{S} \to [m]$ *such that* $|\iota^{-1}(l)| \leq n_k$ *for each* $l \in [m]$, *generates random integers* $r, r_1, ..., r_m \in_R \mathbb{Z}_p$, *and outputs the secret key as*

$$SK_\mathcal{S} = (K = h^{\alpha - rb}, K' = h^r, \iota,$$

$$\{K_{1,att} = h^{r_{\iota(att)}(\sum_{i=0}^n b_i x_{att}^i) + r(\sum_{i=0}^{n_c - 1} b_i' x_{att}^i)}\}_{att \in \mathcal{S}}, \{K_{2,l} = h^{r_l}\}_{l \in [m]}).$$

– $Encrypt(MPK, \mathbb{A}, M)$: *A message* $M \in \mathbb{G}_T$ *is encrypted under policy* $\mathbb{A} = (\mathbf{A}, \rho)$ *with* $\mathbf{A} \in \mathbb{Z}_p^{n_1 \times n_2}$ *and* $\rho\colon [n_1] \to \mathcal{U}$ *by computing* $m' = \max\left(\left\lceil \frac{n_1}{n_c} \right\rceil, \max_{j \in [n_1]} |\rho^{-1}(\rho(j))| \right)$ *and defining* $\tau\colon [n_1] \to [m']$ *such that* $|\tau^{-1}(l')| \leq n_c$ *for each* $l' \in [m']$ *and if* $j, j' \in [n_1]$ *with* $j \neq j'$ *such that* $\rho(j) = \rho(j')$, *then* $\tau(j) \neq \tau(j')$, *i.e., multiple occurrences of the same attribute are mapped to different partitions.* (Note that this works because m' is defined to be at least as large as the maximum number of occurrences of each attribute.) *It then generates random integers* $s, s_1, ..., s_{m'}, v_2, ..., v_{n_2} \in_R \mathbb{Z}_p$ *and outputs the ciphertext as*

$$CT_\mathbb{A} = (C = M \cdot A^s, C' = g^s, \tau, \{C_{1,j} = B^{\lambda_j} \cdot \prod_{i=0}^{n_c - 1} (B_i')^{s_{\tau(j)} x_{\rho(j)}^i},$$

$$C_{2,j} = \prod_{i=0}^n B_i^{s_{\tau(j)} x_{\rho(j)}^i}\}_{j \in [n_1]}, \{C_{3,l'} = g^{s_{l'}}\}_{l' \in [m']}),$$

such that λ_j *denotes the* j-*th entry of* $\mathbf{A} \cdot (s, v_2, ..., v_{n_2})^\intercal$.

– $Decrypt(SK_\mathcal{S}, CT_\mathbb{A})$: *Suppose that* $\mathcal{S}$ *satisfies* $\mathbb{A}$, *and let* $\Upsilon = \{j \in [n_1] \mid \rho(j) \in \mathcal{S}\}$, *such that* $\{\varepsilon_j \in \mathbb{Z}_p\}_{j \in \Upsilon}$ *exist with* $\sum_{i \in \Upsilon} \varepsilon_j \mathbf{A}_j = (1, 0, ..., 0)$ *(Definition 1). Then, the plaintext* M *is retrieved by computing*

$$C / \left(e(C', K) \cdot \prod_{j \in \Upsilon} \left(e(C_{1,j}, K') / e(C_{3,\tau(j)}, K_{1,\rho(j)}) \cdot e(C_{2,j}, K_{2,\iota(\rho(j))}) \right)^{\varepsilon_j} \right).$$

This can be computed more efficiently as

$$C / \left(e(C', K) \cdot e(\prod_{j \in \Upsilon} C_{1,j}^{\varepsilon_j}, K') \cdot \left(\prod_{l' \in [m']} e(C_{3,l'}, \prod_{j \in \Upsilon \cap \tau^{-1}(l')} K_{1,\rho(j)}^{-\varepsilon_j}) \right. \right.$$

$$\left. \left. \cdot \prod_{l \in [m]} e(\prod_{j \in \Upsilon \cap \rho^{-1}(\iota^{-1}(l))} C_{2,j}^{-\varepsilon_j}, K_{2,l}) \right) \right),$$

which costs, on average, $2 + \left\lceil \frac{|\Upsilon|}{n_k} \right\rceil + \left\lceil \frac{|\Upsilon|}{n_c} \right\rceil$ *pairing operations.*

The scheme is correct, i.e., we have $C / e(C', K) = M \cdot e(g, h)^{\alpha s} \cdot e(g, h)^{-\alpha s + rsb} = M \cdot e(g, h)^{rsb}$ *and*

$$\prod_{j \in \Upsilon} \left(e(C_{1,j}, K') / e(C_{3,\tau(j)}, K_{1,\rho(j)}) \cdot e(C_{2,j}, K_{2,\iota(j)}) \right)^{\varepsilon_j}$$

$$= \prod_{j \in \Upsilon} (e(g, h)^{r\lambda_j b + rs_{\tau(j)} \sum_{i=0}^{n_c - 1} b_i' \rho(j)^i}$$

$$\cdot e(g,h)^{-r_{\iota(\rho(j))}s_{\tau(j)}(\sum_{i=0}^n b_i\rho(j)^i)-rs_{\tau(j)}\sum_{i=0}^{n_c-1}b_i'\rho(j)^i}$$

$$\cdot e(g,h)^{r_{\iota(\rho(j))}s_{\tau(j)}\sum_{i=0}^n b_i\rho(j)^i)^{\varepsilon_j}}$$

$$=\prod_{j\in\varUpsilon}e(g,h)^{r\varepsilon_j\lambda_j b}=e(g,h)^{rb\sum_{j\in\varUpsilon}\varepsilon_j\lambda_j}=e(g,h)^{rsb},$$

which yields the plaintext, i.e., $M\cdot e(g,h)^{rsb}/e(g,h)^{rsb}=M.$

Unique Representation of Attributes. In the scheme, we assume that any attribute string att $\in\{0,1\}^*$ can be uniquely represented in $\mathbb{Z}_p$. In practice, this can be done by using a collision-resistant hash function $\mathcal{H}\colon\{0,1\}^*\to\mathbb{Z}_p$ [47].

4.1 The Associated Pair Encoding Scheme

To prove security, we define the pair encoding scheme associated with our scheme in Definition 6, for which we use the variables $n_c, n_k, n, \mathcal{S}, \iota, \rho, \tau,\ n_1, n_2, \lambda_i, m, m'$ from Definition 6, as follows.

Definition 7 (PES for GLUE).

- Param(par) $\to 2n_c + n_k + 3$. Let $\mathbf{b} = (b, b_0, ..., b_n, b_0', ..., b_{n_c-1}')$, *where* $n = n_k + n_c - 1$.
- EncKey($\mathcal{S}$) $\to (\mathbf{r}, k', \{k_{1,att}\}_{att\in\mathcal{S}})$. *Let* $\mathbf{r} = (r, \{r_l\}_{l\in[m]})$, $k' = \alpha - rb$ *and* $k_{1,att} = r_{\iota(att)}(\sum_{i=0}^n b_i x_{att}^i) + r(\sum_{i=0}^{n_c-1} b_i' x_{att}^i).$
- EncCt($(\mathbf{A}, \rho)$) $\to (\mathbf{s}, \hat{\mathbf{s}}, \{c_{1,j}, c_{2,j}\}_{j\in[n_1]})$. *Let* $\mathbf{s} = (s, \{s_{l'}\}_{l'\in[m']})$ *and* $\hat{\mathbf{s}} = (\hat{v}_2, ..., \hat{v}_{n_2})$, *and* $c_{1,j} = \mathbf{A}_j(sb, \hat{\mathbf{s}})^\mathsf{T} + s_{\tau(j)}\sum_{i=0}^{n_c-1} b_i'\rho(j)^i$ *and* $c_{2,j} = s_{\tau(j)}\sum_{i=0}^n b_i\rho(j)^i.$

In Sect. 5, we prove security of the PES.

Theorem 1. *The PES for GLUE in Definition 7 satisfies the symbolic property (Definition 5).*

Therefore, instantiating the PES in the AC17 framework yields a fully secure scheme, and instantiating the PES with [50] yields a selectively secure scheme.

5 The Security Proof

While the construction of the scheme already provides some idea on why it may be secure, the proof requires some additional insights. First, we briefly review some important aspects in the Rouselakis-Waters proof, to gain some deeper understanding of the structure of the selective property proof. Then, we show how existing techniques can be combined to generalize the selective proof.

On a high level, the selective proof consists of the splitting of the n-degree polynomial, which provides randomness for the keys *and* ciphertexts, into a product of three polynomials f_1, f_{n_c-1}' and g_{n_k-1}. We use g_{n_k-1} for the keys,

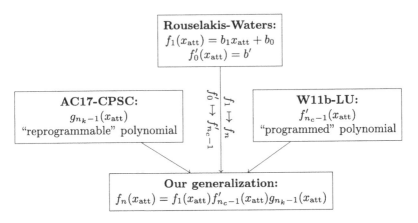

Fig. 2. A high-level overview of the polynomials used in the combined proofs and our generalized selective proof.

and $f_1 f'_{n_c-1}$ for the challenge ciphertext. For the key polynomial g_{n_k-1}, we use Agrawal and Chase's [4] techniques. In their selective proof of the CP-ABE scheme with short ciphertexts, they embed a polynomial in the public keys such that this polynomial can be reprogrammed to some polynomial associated with the set of attributes of the key. We call such polynomials "reprogrammable". For the ciphertext polynomials f_1, f'_{n_c-1}, we use a combination of the proofs of RW13 [45] and W11b [55]. Roughly, in these proofs, they embed polynomials in the public keys, such that these polynomials are associated with the attributes that occur in the challenge access policy. We call such polynomials "programmed". These techniques ensure that the polynomials evaluate to the right values when the set and policy attributes are evaluated. Figure 2 depicts the relationship between the existing proofs and ours. A similar approach can be taken in the co-selective proof, by swapping the roles of the two polynomials.

5.1   The Rouselakis-Waters Proof

We briefly review the Rouselakis-Waters selective security proof. They use the commonly used "program-and-cancel" technique [26,56], in which the challenge access policy $\mathbb{A} = (\mathbf{A}, \rho)$ is split in two disjoint subsets with respect to the set of attributes S associated with the queried key. One subset $\Upsilon = \{j \in [n_1] \mid \rho(j) \in S\}$ contains all the rows of matrix $\mathbf{A}$ for which the corresponding attribute is in the set, while the other set $\overline{\Upsilon} = S \setminus \Upsilon$ contains the rest of the rows. In the simulation of the key, it then uses the property that if S does not satisfy $\mathbb{A}$, there exists a vector $\mathbf{w} = (1, w_2, ..., w_{n_2}) \in \mathbb{Z}_p^{n_2}$ such that $\mathbf{A}_j \mathbf{w}^\intercal = 0$ for all $j \in \Upsilon$. Furthermore, they introduce the layering and individual randomness technique to ensure that the challenge ciphertext can be simulated. Roughly, they embed the attributes that occur in the policy in the public keys as well as their corresponding row in the matrix in a layered fashion, using an individual randomness for each layer. During the key query and challenge phases, the randomizer embeds a single individual randomness to select the correct attribute layer, such that the key and ciphertext components can be simulated.

The selective symbolic security proof can be analogously structured, such that the substitutions ensure that all polynomials $k_{1,\text{att}}$, $c_{1,j}$ and $c_{2,j}$ evaluate to $\mathbf{0}$. In general, an attribute layer in the public keys is represented as a matrix $\mathbf{1}_{i,j}^{d_1 \times d_2} \in \mathbb{Z}_p^{d_1 \times d_2}$. Then, the appropriate attribute layer can be selected by the vector that represents the associated individual randomness, i.e., $\mathbf{1}_i^{d_1} \in \mathbb{Z}_p^{d_1}$. Multiplying this vector with the matrix yields $\overline{\mathbf{1}}_j^{d_2} \in \mathbb{Z}_p^{d_2}$. Effectively, only one remaining entry needs to evaluate to $\mathbf{0}$. This is done by embedding the policy in the public keys in a certain way. Specifically, in $c_{1,j} = \mathbf{A}_j(sb,\hat{\mathbf{s}})^\mathsf{T} + s_j b'$, where $\mathbf{A}_j(sb,\hat{\mathbf{s}})^\mathsf{T} = \sum_{k \in [n_2]} A_{j,k} v_k$ (where $v_1 = sb$) and $s_j b'$ are supposed to cancel out one another. This can be ensured by embedding all rows $\mathbf{A}_j$ of the policy in b', and using individual randomness (represented as a vector) to select the appropriate row. More concretely, b' could be substituted by $-\sum_{j \in [n_1], k \in [n_2]} A_{j,k} \mathbf{1}_{j,k}^{d_1 \times d_2}$ and s_j by $\mathbf{1}_j^{d_1}$ such that $s_j b' = -\sum_{k \in [n_2]} A_{j,k} \overline{\mathbf{1}}_k^{d_2}$. Then, if v_k is substituted by $\overline{\mathbf{1}}_{(0,k)}^{d_2}$, s by $\mathbf{1}_0^{d_1}$ and b by $\mathbf{1}_{0,(0,1)}^{d_1 \times d_2}$, then $\mathbf{A}_j(sb,\hat{\mathbf{s}})^\mathsf{T} = \sum_{k \in [n_2]} A_{j,k} \overline{\mathbf{1}}_{(0,k)}^{d_2}$. Similarly, $c_{2,j}$ evaluates to $\mathbf{0}$ by defining b_0 and b_1 such that for each attribute layer associated with row j, the 1-degree polynomial $F_{1,j}(x) = x - \rho(j)$ is embedded. The individual randomness ensures that this polynomial is selected with s_j. To ensure that the key $k_{1,\text{att}} = r_{\text{att}} f_1(x_{\text{att}}) + r b'$ evaluates to $\mathbf{0}$, we embed the vector $\mathbf{w}$ in r and r_{att}, which ensures that all attribute layers that are also in the set $\mathcal{S}$ go to $\mathbf{0}$. For those attribute layers that are not in the set $\mathcal{S}$, i.e., $\overline{\Upsilon}$, we ensure that layers $F_{1,j}(x_{\text{att}})\mathbf{A}_j\mathbf{w}^\mathsf{T}$ in $r_{\text{att}} f_1(x_{\text{att}})$ cancel out layers $\mathbf{A}_j\mathbf{w}^\mathsf{T}$ in $r b'$. Roughly, this is done by embedding $\frac{1}{F_{1,j}(x_{\text{att}})}$ in r_{att} for all $j \in \overline{\Upsilon}$, such that the $\mathbf{A}_j\mathbf{w}^\mathsf{T}$ in the two summands cancel out one another.

5.2   Generalizing the Rouselakis-Waters Proof

We generalize the Rouselakis-Waters proof by layering the policy embedded in the public keys in a partition-wise fashion instead of attribute-wise. In this way, the ciphertext-specific variable $s_{l'}$, which is used for all attributes in the same partition, can select all attributes associated within the l'-th partition. As such, in the computation of $c_{1,j}$ and $c_{2,j}$, $s_{\tau(j)}f'_{n_c-1}(\rho(j))$ needs to cancel out $\mathbf{A}_j(sb,\hat{\mathbf{s}})^\mathsf{T}$ and $s_{\tau(j)}f_n(\rho(j))$ needs to go to $\mathbf{0}$. To this end, we need to substitute f'_{n_c-1} in such a way that it outputs exactly $-\sum_{k \in [n_2]} A_{j,k} \overline{\mathbf{1}}_{(0,k)}^{d_2}$ when $s_{\tau(j)}f'_{n_c-1}(\rho(j))$ is computed. Similarly, the key-specific variable r_l needs to be constructed such that $k_{1,\text{att}}$ goes to $\mathbf{0}$, which happens when $r_{\iota(\text{att})}f_n(x_{\text{att}})$ cancels out $r f'_{n_c-1}(x_{\text{att}})$.

To accomplish this, we define f_n and f'_{n_c-1} as mentioned before, i.e., $f_n(x_{\text{att}}) = f_1(x_{\text{att}})f'_{n_c-1}(x_{\text{att}})g_{n_k-1}(x_{\text{att}})$. Roughly, we substitute f_1 in the same way as in the Rouselakis-Waters proof, while we use the polynomials f'_{n_c-1} and g_{n_k-1} to ensure that $c_{1,j}$ and $c_{2,j}$, and $k_{1,\text{att}}$ evaluate to $\mathbf{0}$, respectively. Because we are given the challenge access structure a priori, i.e., as input to EncB, we can program these as required in the substitutions of the polynomials f_1 and f'_{n_c-1} in the public keys. Concretely, we substitute $b_0, ..., b_n$ such that

$$f_n(x_{\text{att}}) \;:\; \sum_{j \in [n_1], k \in [n_2]} A_{j,k} F_{n,j,k}(x_{\text{att}})$$

$$= \sum_{j \in [n_1], k \in [n_2]} A_{j,k} \underbrace{F_{1,j}(x_{\text{att}}) F'_{n_c-1,j}(x_{\text{att}}) \hat{G}_{n_k-1,j,k}(x_{\text{att}})}_{F_{n,j,k}(x_{\text{att}})},$$

where $F_{1,j}(x_{\text{att}}) = (x_{\text{att}} - \rho(j))$ and

$$F'_{n_c-1,j}(x_{\text{att}}) = \sum_{i=0}^{n_c-1} d'_{i,j} x^i_{\text{att}} = \prod_{j' \in \chi_j \setminus \{j\}} \frac{x_{\text{att}} - \rho(j')}{\rho(j) - \rho(j')},$$

with $\chi_j = \{j' \in [n_1] \mid \tau(j') = \tau(j)\}$. We refer to these polynomials as the "programmed" polynomials. These ensure that $F_{n,j}(\rho(j')) = 0$ for all $j' \in \chi_j$, $F'_{n_c-1,j}(\rho(j)) = 1$ and $F'_{n_c-1,j'}(\rho(j)) = 0$ for all $j' \in \chi_j \setminus \{j\}$. Then, $c_{1,j}$ and $c_{2,j}$ evaluate to $\mathbf{0}$, if we substitute

$$f'_{n_c-1}(x_{\text{att}}) \;:\; \sum_{j \in [n_1], k \in [n_2]} A_{j,k} F'_{n_c-1,j}(x_{\text{att}}) \mathbf{1}^{d_1 \times d_2}_{(1,\tau(j)),(0,k)}.$$

In contrast, the set of attributes associated with a key is given after the public keys have been established, i.e., as input to EncR, so we need to somehow achieve that we can program the polynomial $\hat{G}_{n_k-1,j}$ after the public keys are generated. We do this by setting

$$\hat{G}_{n_k-1,j,k}(x_{\text{att}}) = \sum_{i=0}^{n_k-1} \mathbf{1}^{d_1 \times d_2}_{(1,\tau(j)),(1,i,j,k)} x^i_{\text{att}},$$

such that $\hat{G}_{n_k-1,j,k}$ constitutes a "reprogrammable" polynomial. It can be reprogrammed by ensuring that r_l consists of the coefficients $u_{i,j,l}$ of some target polynomial(s), i.e., by multiplying

$$\left(\sum_{i=0}^{n_k-1} \mathbf{1}^{d_1 \times d_2}_{(1,\tau(j)),(1,i,j,k)} x^i_{\text{att}} \right) \left(\sum_{i=0}^{n_k-1} u_{i,j,l} \overline{\mathbf{1}}^{d_2}_{(1,i,j,k)} \right) = \sum_{i=0}^{n_k-1} u_{i,j,l} \mathbf{1}^{d_1}_{(1,\tau(j))} x^i_{\text{att}}.$$

We use this to "reprogram" polynomial $\hat{G}_{n_k-1,j,k}(x_{\text{att}})$ for all $j \in \overline{\Upsilon}$, which is well-defined, because $\rho(j) \notin S$. This then yields $F'_{n_c-1,j}(x_{\text{att}})$ and cancels out the $F'_{n_c-1,j}(x_{\text{att}})$ in $r f'_{n_c-1}(x_{\text{att}})$ part in $k_{1,\text{att}}$ for all $j \in \overline{\Upsilon}$. Note that, like in Rouselakis-Waters, we have $\mathbf{A}_j \mathbf{w}^\intercal = 0$ for all $j \in \Upsilon$, so those layers automatically go to $\mathbf{0}$ in the computation of $k_{1,\text{att}}$. Hence, for each partition $\Psi_l = \{\text{att} \in S \mid \iota(\text{att}) = l\}$ with $l \in [m]$, we define the polynomial

$$G_{n_k-1,j,l}(x_{\text{att}}) = \sum_{i=0}^{n_k-1} u_{i,j,l} x^i_{\text{att}} = \sum_{\text{att}' \in \Psi_l} \frac{1}{F_{1,j}(x_{\text{att}'})} \prod_{\text{att}'' \in \Psi_l \setminus \{\text{att}'\}} \frac{x_{\text{att}} - x_{\text{att}''}}{x_{\text{att}'} - x_{\text{att}''}},$$

for each $j \in \overline{\Upsilon}$, such that $G_{n_k-1,j,l}(x_{\text{att}}) = \frac{1}{F_{1,j}(x_{\text{att}})}$ for all $\text{att} \in \Psi_l$.

Putting it all together, we substitute $b_0,...,b_n$ with coefficients such that the polynomial f_n is substituted by

$$\sum_{j\in[n_1],k\in[n_2]} A_{j,k}F_{n,j,k}(x_{\text{att}}) = \sum_{j\in[n_1],k\in[n_2]} A_{j,k}\sum_{i=0}^{n} d_{i,j,k}x_{\text{att}}^i,$$

where

$$d_{i,j,k} = \sum_{i'\in\overline{[n_k-1]},i''\in\overline{[n_c-1]}:i'+i''=i} d'_{i',j}\mathbf{1}^{d_1\times d_2}_{(1,\tau(j)),(1,i'',j,k)}.$$

5.3   The Selective Symbolic Property

We prove the selective symbolic property, using m,m',τ,ι as in Sect. 4 and $F_{n,j,k},d_{i,j,k},F'_{n_c-1,j},d'_{i,j},G_{n_k-1,j,l},u_{i,j,l}$ and χ_j as in Sect. 5.2. For simplicity of notation, we write the second index of $\mathbf{1}^{d_1\times d_2}$ and the index of $\overline{\mathbf{1}}^{d_2}$ as a tuple $(1,i,j,k)$ (with $i\in\overline{[n_k]},j\in[n_1],k\in[n_2]$) such that it represents a unique integer in $[n_2+1,(((n_k+1)n_1+1)n_2)]$. Note that we use $(0,k)$ to indicate the first n_2 columns, which are associated with only k and not (i,j). For the first index of $\mathbf{1}^{d_1\times d_2}$ and the index of $\mathbf{1}^{d_1}$, we start counting at 0. Note that, therefore, $d_1=n_2+1$ and $d_2=((n_k+1)n_1+1)n_2$. The substitutions are, for all $i\in\overline{[n]},i'\in\overline{[n_k]},l\in[m],l'\in[m'],k\in[2,n_2]$:

$$b \ : \ \mathbf{1}^{d_1\times d_2}_{0,(0,1)}, \quad b_i \ : \ \sum_{j\in[n_1],k\in[n_2]} A_{j,k}d_{i,j,k}$$

$$b'_{i'} \ : \ \sum_{j\in[n_1],k\in[n_2]} A_{j,k}d'_{i',j}\mathbf{1}^{d_1\times d_2}_{(1,\tau(j)),(0,k)}, \quad s \ : \ \mathbf{1}^{d_1}_0$$

$$s_{l'} \ : \ -\mathbf{1}^{d_1}_{(1,l')}, \quad \alpha \ : \ \mathbf{1}^{d_1}_0, \quad \hat{v}_k \ : \ \overline{\mathbf{1}}^{d_2}_{(0,k)}, \quad r \ : \ \sum_{k'\in[n_2]} w_{k'}\overline{\mathbf{1}}^{d_2}_{(0,k')}$$

$$r_l \ : \ -\sum_{i'\in\overline{[n_k-1]},j'\in\overline{\Upsilon},k'\in[n_2]} w_{k'}u_{i',j',l}\overline{\mathbf{1}}^{d_2}_{(1,i',j',k')}.$$

Then, $c_{1,j},c_{2,j},k'$ and $k_{1,\text{att}}$ indeed go to $\mathbf{0}$ (see the full version [54]).

5.4   Co-selective Symbolic Property

We prove that the co-selective symbolic property also holds. For this proof, the roles of the reprogrammable and the programmed polynomial are reversed, because we are allowed to use an attribute set $\mathcal{S}$ in the programming of the public keys and secret keys, and the policy $\mathbb{A}$ only for the ciphertext. Similarly as in the selective case, we use the Rouselakis-Waters proof as inspiration for the structure of the proof. In particular, we use the selective security proof of the KP-ABE variant of the Rouselakis-Waters scheme (which is analogous to the co-selective proof of the CP-ABE variant).

In this proof, we substitute the polynomials with:

$$f_n(x_{\text{att}}) \; : \; \sum_{l\in[m]} \left(\underbrace{\hat{F}_{n_c-1,1,l}(x_{\text{att}})G_{n_k,l}(x_{\text{att}})}_{G_{n,l}(x_{\text{att}})} - \hat{F}_{n_c-1,2,l}(x_{\text{att}}) \right),$$

$$f'_{n_c-1}(x_{\text{att}}) \; : \; \hat{F}_{n_c-1,2,0}(x_{\text{att}}),$$

where we define $G_{n,l}(x_{\text{att}}) = \sum_{i=0}^{n} \tilde{u}_{i,l}x_{\text{att}}^i$, and

$$G_{n_k,l}(x_{\text{att}}) = \sum_{i=0}^{n_k} u_{i,l}x_{\text{att}}^i = \prod_{\text{att}'\in\Psi_l}(x_{\text{att}} - x_{\text{att}'})$$

is a programmed polynomial with $G_{n_k,l}(x_{\text{att}}) = 0$ for att $\in \Psi_l$, and

$$\hat{F}_{n_c-1,1,l}(x_{\text{att}}) = \sum_{i=0}^{n_c-1} 1_{(1,i,l),l}^{d_1\times d_2} \text{ and } \hat{F}_{n_c-1,2,l}(x_{\text{att}}) = \sum_{i=0}^{n_c-1} 1_{(2,i),l}^{d_1\times d_2}$$

are the reprogrammable polynomials, to be reprogrammed to

$$F_{n_c-1,1,j,l}(x_{\text{att}}) = \sum_{i=0}^{n_c-1} \tilde{d}_{i,j,l}x_{\text{att}}^i = \frac{1}{G_{n_k,l}(\rho(j))}F'_{n_c-1,j}(x_{\text{att}}),$$

$$F'_{n_c-1,j}(x_{\text{att}}) = \sum_{i=0}^{n_c-1} d'_{i,j}x_{\text{att}}^i,$$

respectively, for $j \in \overline{\Upsilon}$. Note that $F_{n_c-1,1,j,l}(\rho(j)) = \frac{1}{G_{n_k,l}(\rho(j))}$ if $j \in \overline{\Upsilon}$ and $F_{n_c-1,1,j',l}(\rho(j)) = 0$ for $j' \in \chi_j$. Concretely, we have

$$\tilde{u}_{i,l} = \sum_{i'\in\overline{[n_c-1]},i''\in\overline{[n_k]}:i'+i''=i} u_{i'',l}1_{(1,i',l),l}^{d_1\times d_2}.$$

Then, for $i \in \overline{[n_c-1]}, i' \in [n_c,n], l \in [m], l' \in [m'], k \in [n_2]$ we make the following substitutions:

$$b \; : \; 1_{0,0}^{d_1\times d_2}, \quad b_i \; : \; \sum_{l\in[m]} \left(\tilde{u}_{i,l} - 1_{(2,i),l}^{d_1\times d_2} \right), \quad b_{i'} \; : \; \sum_{l\in[m]} \tilde{u}_{i,l}$$

$$b'_i \; : \; 1_{(2,i),0}^{d_1\times d_2}, \quad \alpha \; : \; 1_0^{d_1}, \quad \hat{v}_k \; : \; w_k\overline{1}_0^{d_2}, \quad r \; : \; \overline{1}_0^{d_2}, \quad r_l \; : \; \overline{1}_l^{d_2}$$

$$s \; : \; 1_0^{d_1}, \quad s_{l'} \; : \; - \sum_{i\in\overline{[n_c-1]},j\in\hat{\chi}_{l'}\cap\overline{\Upsilon},k\in[n_2]} A_{j,k}w_k \left(d'_{i,j}1_{(2,i)}^{d_1} + \tilde{d}_{i,j} \right),$$

where $\tilde{d}_{i,j} = \sum_{l\in[m]} \tilde{d}_{i,j,l}1_{(1,i,l)}^{d_1}$, $d_1 = n_c(m+1)+1$ and $d_2 = m+1$. For simplicity, we use tuple notations $(1,i,l)$ and $(2,i)$ for the first index of $1^{d_1\times d_2}$ and the index of 1^{d_1} for all $i \in \overline{[n_c-1]}, l \in [m]$, which map injectively into the intervals $[2, n_cm+1]$ and $[n_cm+2, d_1]$, respectively, and index 0 maps to the first row. Then, $c_{1,j}, c_{2,j}, k'$ and $k_{1,\text{att}}$ indeed go to $\mathbf{0}$ (see the full version [54]).

6 Performance Analysis

We analyze the efficiency of our schemes. An important aspect in this analysis are the parameters n_k and n_c, which are chosen during the setup (e.g., by a practitioner). On a high level, the key generation, encryption and decryption of the selectively secure version of GLUE (via [50]) incur the following costs:

- KeyGen: $2 + |\mathcal{S}| + \left\lceil \frac{|\mathcal{S}|}{n_k} \right\rceil$ exponentiations in $\mathbb{H}$;

- Encrypt: 1 exponentiation in $\mathbb{G}_T$, $1 + \left\lceil \frac{n_1}{n_c} \right\rceil$ exponentiations, n_1 multi-exponentiations with $n_c + 1$ bases and n_1 multi-exponentiations with $n_k + n_c$ bases in $\mathbb{G}$;

- Decrypt: roughly $2 + \left\lceil \frac{|\Upsilon|}{n_k} \right\rceil + \left\lceil \frac{|\Upsilon|}{n_c} \right\rceil$ pairing operations.

The efficiency of these algorithms depends on the one hand on the efficiency of these operations, and on the other hand on the choices of n_k and n_c. By analyzing these rough costs from a mathematical point of view, the trade-off between the encryption and decryption efficiency is optimal when $n_k = n_c$ (which follows from the arithmetic mean-harmonic mean inequality). However, when the set of attributes $\mathcal{S}$ is large, and n_k is small, it may occur that all matching attributes are in different partitions. As such, choosing n_k to be larger, e.g., $n_k = 10$, ensures that the matching attributes are in the same key partitions with a large probability, and therefore the actual number of pairing operations is higher. In general, it holds that, the larger the partition sizes, the fewer pairing operations are needed during decryption. Unfortunately, the drawback is that encryption becomes more expensive, meaning that we may want to use the online/offline version of the scheme in practice. In the full version [54], we give more details on how a suitable partition size may be chosen. For our analysis, we consider three parameter settings: $(n_k, n_c) \in \{(3, 3), (5, 5), (10, 5)\}$. Furthermore, for the variant that supports OSW-type negations, we consider $|\mathcal{S}| \in \{1, 5\}$.

On the Comparability of the Schemes. For a fair comparison, we optimize all the schemes in the same way when instantiating the schemes in the asymmetric setting [44]. Specifically, we optimize the decryption and encryption efficiency. For the analysis of the RW13 [45], HW14 [31], Att19-I-CP and Att19-I-CP-OO [11] schemes, we have used the performance analysis of our associated schemes for $n_k = n_c = 1$ (which have the same encodings). We also compare our monotone schemes with AHM+16 [12] and ABGW17 [7] (see the full version [54] for the compared instantiations). To place the costs based on our theoretical analyses of the selectively secure instantiations (via [50]) in the full-security setting, we multiply the costs for each element and operation in $\mathbb{G}$ and $\mathbb{H}$ by a factor 2. This overhead corresponds to the most efficient instantiation of the schemes in the AC17 framework [3]. For all schemes, we also assume that the access policies are Boolean formulas, so that for decryption, it is ensured that $\varepsilon_j \in \{0, 1\}$ [38].

Estimates Based on Benchmarks in RELIC. We estimate the computational costs of the schemes by obtaining benchmarks of various algorithms and extrapolating the results by analyzing the descriptions of the schemes. We analyze the efficiency in this way for two reasons. First, it allows us to analyze the efficiency of many scheme configurations without having to implement each one, which is a cumbersome and error-prone effort. Second, it allows us to compare the schemes more accurately and more fairly. Currently, the simplest and most popular way [2,45,53] to benchmark schemes is by using Charm [5]. However, Charm only supports curves that do not provide sufficient security anymore, and de la Piedra et al. [44] show that benchmarking the schemes on these curves yields inaccurate and unfair comparisons. To compare the schemes more accurately and fairly, we estimate[3] the costs of the schemes by applying their approaches [44]. In particular, we have run benchmarks in RELIC [8], a cryptographic library for efficient implementations of pairing-based cryptography on state-of-the-art elliptic curves. This library has implementations for exponentiations, including fixed-base and multi-base variants. In fixed-base exponentiation, the base g in g^x is fixed after setup, and as such, a precomputation table can be made to speed up the computation [20]. In a multi-base exponentiation, the product of multiple exponentiations, e.g., $g_1^{x_1} g_2^{x_2}$, is computed more efficiently [41]. We have run these benchmarks on a 1.6 GHz Intel i5-8250U processor for the BLS12-446 curve [15], which provides approximately 132-134 bits of security [28,29]. These benchmarks can be found in the full version [54] and are used in our analysis.

Comparison. Tables 3a and 3b show the performances of all unbounded schemes using a BB hash that support MSPs and NMSPs. The tables illustrate that the decryption algorithms of our regular schemes are significantly faster than the established schemes. While the encryption costs increase compared to the other schemes, our online/offline versions also provide a solution in this regard, incurring minimal online costs. This comes with a slight trade-off in the ciphertext size and the decryption efficiency compared to the regular version, but overall, our online/offline schemes outperform the established schemes in all algorithms. Importantly, the decryption of our schemes supporting negations with parameters $n_k = n_c = 5$ outperforms the only other unbounded OSW-type non-monotone scheme. Importantly, decryption is faster by a factor 4 for non-negated attributes, and faster by a factor 4-5 for negated attributes and $|\mathcal{S}| = 5$, bringing down the costs from almost two seconds to 382 ms. As a result, our schemes could provide a more attractive building block for OSWOT-type non-monotone schemes, as they support more efficient decryption algorithms for negated and non-negated attributes, and for small and large sets of attributes for each label. Furthermore, owing to the online/offline extensions, the key generation and encryption algorithms do not need to suffer from heavy online computations. Instead, encrypting users need to store only 3.17-10.17 kilobytes per one intermediate ciphertext of the first type and sufficient of the second type

---

[3] Although approximated theoretically, we expect our estimates to be close to the costs of actual implementations [54].

Table 3. Rough estimates of the storage costs of the secret keys and the ciphertexts in kilobytes (KB), where 1 KB = 1024 bytes, and the (online) computational costs incurred by the key generation, encryption and decryption algorithms of $GLUE_{(n_k,n_c)}$ (and its online/offline (suffixed with "OO") and OSW-non-monotone (suffixed with "N") variants) and the other unbounded CP-ABE schemes, expressed in milliseconds (ms), for 10 and 100 attributes. Note that the offline key generation and encryption costs of each online/offline scheme are equal to the key generation and encryption costs of its regular version. The code used to generate these benchmarks is available at [51].

	Scheme	|MPK|	SK 10	SK 100	CT 10	CT 100	KeyGen 10	KeyGen 100	Encrypt 10	Encrypt 100	Decrypt 10	Decrypt 100
Regular	RW13 [45]	1.42	4.86	44.58	4.05	33.58	26.0	238.7	32.9	305.9	46.2	375.2
	AHM+16 [12] ($n_k = 2$)	1.75	5.3	45.02	6.45	55.67	16.5	122.9	40.8	368.3	43.7	317.4
	ABGW17 [7]	1.42	2.65	22.51	3.94	33.47	14.2	120.5	32.3	305.2	27.9	192.4
	$GLUE_{(3,3)}$	2.08	3.53	30.02	3.39	26.36	18.9	160.7	59.8	571.4	24.3	133.9
	$GLUE_{(5,5)}$	2.74	3.09	26.93	3.17	24.83	16.5	144.2	82.3	800.4	17.0	82.8
	$GLUE_{(10,5)}$	3.28	2.87	24.72	3.17	24.83	15.4	132.3	102.1	998.5	15.1	64.5
O/O	HW14 [31]	1.42	5.23	48.29	4.79	41.0	0	0	0	0	51.5	416.2
	$GLUE_{(3,3)}$	2.08	3.9	33.73	5.62	48.62	0	0	0	0	33.6	202.6
	$GLUE_{(5,5)}$	2.74	3.46	30.64	6.88	61.94	0	0	0	0	27.6	157.5
	$GLUE_{(10,5)}$	3.28	3.24	28.43	8.74	80.49	0	0	0	0	24.2	123.4

(a) Schemes supporting MSPs only.

	Scheme	|MPK|	SK 10	SK 100	CT 10	CT 100	KeyGen 10	KeyGen 100	Encrypt 10	Encrypt 100	Decrypt 10	Decrypt 100	Decrypt 10	Decrypt 100	Decrypt 10	Decrypt 100
Regular	Att19-I-CP [11]	1.42	10.89	100.01	6.37	55.76	59.0	541.8	66.6	637.5	51.7	380.7	55.3	367.9	216.2	1779.0
	GLUE-N$_{(3,3)}$	2.08	7.59	63.66	5.04	41.19	44.8	385.9	90.0	865.1	29.8	139.4	62.3	374.9	109.5	745.5
	GLUE-N$_{(5,5)}$	2.74	6.49	55.95	4.6	38.1	40.1	352.8	111.4	1086.0	22.4	88.3	55.3	367.9	55.3	382.5
	GLUE-N$_{(10,5)}$	3.28	5.94	50.44	4.6	38.1	37.7	329.2	131.2	1284.0	20.6	70.0	78.5	599.4	78.5	614.1
O/O	Att19-I-CP-OO	1.42	12.01	111.15	7.11	63.18	0	0	0	0	61.0	461.3	64.6	448.5	225.5	1859.6
	GLUE-N$_{(3,3)}$	2.08	8.7	74.79	7.27	63.46	0	0	0	0	46.7	275.2	79.3	510.6	126.4	881.3
	GLUE-N$_{(5,5)}$	2.74	7.6	67.08	8.31	75.21	0	0	0	0	41.8	235.9	74.7	515.5	74.7	530.1
	GLUE-N$_{(10,5)}$	3.28	7.05	61.58	10.17	93.77	0	0	0	0	36.8	185.9	94.7	715.4	94.7	730.0

(b) Schemes supporting OSW-type negations. The decryption costs are for non-negated, and negated policies with $|S| \in \{1,5\}$, respectively.

for ten attributes (depending on the instantiation). This means that, with just a megabyte of space, a user can store at least 100 intermediate ciphertexts for a total of 1000 attributes. For computing devices such as computers and smartphones, which have an abundance of storage space nowadays, this is a more than acceptable trade-off. Similarly, key generation authorities can store intermediate keys for at least 286 users and 2860 attributes with just a megabyte of space. Thus, with gigabytes, an authority can precompute keys for hundreds of thousands of users and millions of attributes.

7   Applying Multiple Instantiations of GLUE in Practice

The flexible efficiency trade-offs that GLUE provides can be exploited in practice. In particular, practitioners can choose one suitable instantiation of GLUE, or choose multiple instantiations of GLUE to support different computational devices. Interestingly, by using the direct sum with parameter reuse transformation of Attrapadung [11], GLUE would be able to support multiple instances of itself simultaneously, such that the size of the master public key is upper-bounded in the maximum size of the public keys of all instances. This may be useful in settings in which the devices have varying computational resources. For instance, in the WLAN use case considered by ETSI [24], the decryption devices may be any mobile device in a network, including more constrained devices such as smartwatches. For those devices, it is more beneficial to use a scheme with fast decryption, e.g., $\text{GLUE}_{(5,5)}$, while for faster devices, it is sufficient to employ a scheme with slower decryption, e.g., RW13. In WLAN systems, the access point sends, for instance, an encrypted WPA2-PSK key to the connecting device, which can decrypt it if is satisfies the policy. Because this exchange is interactive, the connecting device and access point could first negotiate on the particular instance of GLUE for which the connecting device has a secret key before encrypting the WPA2-PSK key. In non-interactive systems, e.g., cloud settings [24], it may be more desirable to use multiple instances in parallel. Powerful devices could, for example, use multiple instances to support less powerful devices that only use the more efficient instances. For example, powerful decryption devices could have keys for both $\text{GLUE}_{(5,5)}$ and RW13, while less powerful encryption devices use RW13 or an online/offline variant of GLUE to encrypt.

8   Future Work

For future work, it would be interesting to investigate the following. First, we have proven our scheme secure in the AC17 framework, which yields full security under a q-type assumption. Although frameworks exist that prove security generically under static assumptions [9,10,21], these use a strong security notion called the master-key hiding property. Like other unbounded ABE using a BB hash, ours does not satisfy this property [9]. To achieve such strong notions of security, more intricate proof techniques need to be devised, such as [22]. Second, we have analyzed the efficiency of the schemes on the BLS12-446 curve. Presumably, the encryption and decryption costs can improve if curves such as KSS16-339 [33] are used, which provide faster arithmetic in $\mathbb{G}$ and provide more efficient products of pairing operations [23]. GLUE (and RW13) may also benefit from fixed-base multi-base exponentiations [41], which RELIC does not support. Finally, while we have given the first steps towards realizing more efficient schemes supporting OSWOT-type negations, we have not explicitly specified these schemes. Our analysis in Sect. 6 indicates that any such schemes would benefit from the efficiency of our schemes, including those supporting OSW-type negations (see the full version [54] for more details).

9   Conclusion

We have proposed GLUE, a new unbounded large-universe scheme with flexible efficiency trade-off. This scheme is a generalization of RW13 [45] and W11b [55], in that it supports polynomials of any degree for the Boneh-Boyen hash. To optimally use the randomness provided by the hash, we use the partitioning approach (previously also used by AHM+16 [12]), splitting the sets of attributes and the policies in partitions of maximum sizes n_k and n_c, respectively. This allows for a decreased number of pairing operations required during decryption compared to RW13 (and related variants). Roughly, the pairing costs decrease by a factor $n_k = n_c$ (if chosen to be equal). Along the way, we have also introduced new proof techniques. These ensure that the randomness provided by the BB hash can be used for both the keys and ciphertexts in the unbounded setting. Finally, we have shown that our schemes indeed outperform existing schemes using a BB hash in the decryption, and notably, all schemes supporting OSW-type negations. Because our non-monotone schemes are unbounded and faster than 1.2 s in all algorithms on a laptop, even for large policies and sets, they are more suitable for practice than existing non-monotone schemes.

References

1. Agrawal, S., Chase, M.: A study of pair encodings: predicate encryption in prime order groups. In: Kushilevitz, E., Malkin, T. (eds.) TCC 2016. LNCS, vol. 9563, pp. 259–288. Springer, Heidelberg (2016). https://doi.org/10.1007/978-3-662-49099-0_10

2. Agrawal, S., Chase, M.: FAME: fast attribute-based message encryption. In: CCS, pp. 665–682. ACM (2017)

3. Agrawal, S., Chase, M.: Simplifying design and analysis of complex predicate encryption schemes. In: Coron, J.-S., Nielsen, J.B. (eds.) EUROCRYPT 2017. LNCS, vol. 10210, pp. 627–656. Springer, Cham (2017). https://doi.org/10.1007/978-3-319-56620-7_22

4. Agrawal, S., Chase, M.: Simplifying design and analysis of complex predicate encryption schemes. Cryptology ePrint Archive, Report 2017/233 (2017)

5. Akinyele, J.A., et al.: Charm: a framework for rapidly prototyping cryptosystems. J. Cryptogr. Eng. **3**(2), 111–128 (2013)

6. Ambrona, M.: Generic negation of pair encodings. In: Garay, J.A. (ed.) PKC 2021. LNCS, vol. 12711, pp. 120–146. Springer, Cham (2021). https://doi.org/10.1007/978-3-030-75248-4_5

7. Ambrona, M., Barthe, G., Gay, R., Wee, H.: Attribute-based encryption in the generic group model: Automated proofs and new constructions. In: CCS, pp. 647–664. ACM (2017)

8. Aranha, D.F., Gouvêa, C.P.L., Markmann, T., Wahby, R.S., Liao, K.: RELIC is an Efficient LIbrary for Cryptography. https://github.com/relic-toolkit/relic (2020)

9. Attrapadung, N.: Dual system encryption via doubly selective security: framework, fully secure functional encryption for regular languages, and more. In: Nguyen, P.Q., Oswald, E. (eds.) EUROCRYPT 2014. LNCS, vol. 8441, pp. 557–577. Springer, Heidelberg (2014). https://doi.org/10.1007/978-3-642-55220-5_31

10. Attrapadung, N.: Dual system encryption framework in prime-order groups via computational pair encodings. In: Cheon, J.H., Takagi, T. (eds.) ASIACRYPT 2016. LNCS, vol. 10032, pp. 591–623. Springer, Heidelberg (2016). https://doi.org/10.1007/978-3-662-53890-6_20

11. Attrapadung, N.: Unbounded dynamic predicate compositions in attribute-based encryption. In: Ishai, Y., Rijmen, V. (eds.) EUROCRYPT 2019. LNCS, vol. 11476, pp. 34–67. Springer, Cham (2019). https://doi.org/10.1007/978-3-030-17653-2_2

12. Attrapadung, N., Hanaoka, G., Matsumoto, T., Teruya, T., Yamada, S.: Attribute based encryption with direct efficiency tradeoff. In: Manulis, M., Sadeghi, A.-R., Schneider, S. (eds.) ACNS 2016. LNCS, vol. 9696, pp. 249–266. Springer, Cham (2016). https://doi.org/10.1007/978-3-319-39555-5_14

13. Attrapadung, N., Libert, B., de Panafieu, E.: Expressive key-policy attribute-based encryption with constant-size ciphertexts. In: Catalano, D., Fazio, N., Gennaro, R., Nicolosi, A. (eds.) PKC 2011. LNCS, vol. 6571, pp. 90–108. Springer, Heidelberg (2011). https://doi.org/10.1007/978-3-642-19379-8_6

14. Attrapadung, N., Tomida, J.: Unbounded dynamic predicate compositions in ABE from standard assumptions. In: Moriai, S., Wang, H. (eds.) ASIACRYPT 2020. LNCS, vol. 12493, pp. 405–436. Springer, Cham (2020). https://doi.org/10.1007/978-3-030-64840-4_14

15. Barreto, P.S.L.M., Lynn, B., Scott, M.: Constructing elliptic curves with prescribed embedding degrees. In: Cimato, S., Persiano, G., Galdi, C. (eds.) SCN 2002. LNCS, vol. 2576, pp. 257–267. Springer, Heidelberg (2003). https://doi.org/10.1007/3-540-36413-7_19

16. Beimel, A.: Secure schemes for secret sharing and key distribution, Ph. D. thesis, Ben Gurion University (1996)

17. Bethencourt, J., Sahai, A., Waters, B.: Ciphertext-policy attribute-based encryption. In: S&P, pp. 321–334. IEEE (2007)

18. Boneh, D., Boyen, X.: Efficient selective-ID secure identity-based encryption without random oracles. In: Cachin, C., Camenisch, J.L. (eds.) EUROCRYPT 2004. LNCS, vol. 3027, pp. 223–238. Springer, Heidelberg (2004). https://doi.org/10.1007/978-3-540-24676-3_14

19. Boneh, D., Boyen, X., Goh, E.-J.: Hierarchical identity based encryption with constant size ciphertext. In: Cramer, R. (ed.) EUROCRYPT 2005. LNCS, vol. 3494, pp. 440–456. Springer, Heidelberg (2005). https://doi.org/10.1007/11426639_26

20. Brickell, E.F., Gordon, D.M., McCurley, K.S., Wilson, D.B.: Fast exponentiation with precomputation. In: Rueppel, R.A. (ed.) EUROCRYPT 1992. LNCS, vol. 658, pp. 200–207. Springer, Heidelberg (1993). https://doi.org/10.1007/3-540-47555-9_18

21. Chen, J., Gay, R., Wee, H.: Improved dual system ABE in prime-order groups via predicate encodings. In: Oswald, E., Fischlin, M. (eds.) EUROCRYPT 2015. LNCS, vol. 9057, pp. 595–624. Springer, Heidelberg (2015). https://doi.org/10.1007/978-3-662-46803-6_20

22. Chen, J., Gong, J., Kowalczyk, L., Wee, H.: Unbounded ABE via bilinear entropy expansion, revisited. In: Nielsen, J.B., Rijmen, V. (eds.) EUROCRYPT 2018. LNCS, vol. 10820, pp. 503–534. Springer, Cham (2018). https://doi.org/10.1007/978-3-319-78381-9_19

23. Clarisse, R., Duquesne, S., Sanders, O.: Curves with fast computations in the first pairing group. In: Krenn, S., Shulman, H., Vaudenay, S. (eds.) CANS 2020. LNCS, vol. 12579, pp. 280–298. Springer, Cham (2020). https://doi.org/10.1007/978-3-030-65411-5_14

24. ETSI: ETSI TS 103 458 (V1.1.1). Technical specification, European Telecommunications Standards Institute (ETSI) (2018)

25. ETSI: ETSI TS 103 532 (V1.1.1). Technical specification, European Telecommunications Standards Institute (ETSI) (2018)

26. Goyal, V., Pandey, O., Sahai, A., Waters, B.: Attribute-based encryption for fine-grained access control of encrypted data. In: CCS. ACM (2006)

27. Goyal, V., Pandey, O., Sahai, A., Waters, B.: Attribute-based encryption for fine-grained access control of encrypted data. Cryptology ePrint Archive, Report 2006/309 (2006)

28. Guillevic, A.: A short-list of pairing-friendly curves resistant to special TNFS at the 128-Bit security level. In: Kiayias, A., Kohlweiss, M., Wallden, P., Zikas, V. (eds.) PKC 2020. LNCS, vol. 12111, pp. 535–564. Springer, Cham (2020). https://doi.org/10.1007/978-3-030-45388-6_19

29. Guillevic, A., Singh, S.: On the alpha value of polynomials in the tower number field sieve algorithm. Cryptology ePrint Archive, Report 2019/885 (2019)

30. Hamburg, M.: Spatial encryption. Cryptology ePrint Archive, Report 2011/389 (2011)

31. Hohenberger, S., Waters, B.: Online/offline attribute-based encryption. In: Krawczyk, H. (ed.) PKC 2014. LNCS, vol. 8383, pp. 293–310. Springer, Heidelberg (2014). https://doi.org/10.1007/978-3-642-54631-0_17

32. Hu, C.T., et al.: Guide to attribute based access control (ABAC) definition and considerations (2019). https://tsapps.nist.gov/publication/get_pdf.cfm?pub_id=927500

33. Kachisa, E.J., Schaefer, E.F., Scott, M.: Constructing brezing-weng pairing-friendly elliptic curves using elements in the cyclotomic field. In: Galbraith, S.D., Paterson, K.G. (eds.) Pairing 2008. LNCS, vol. 5209, pp. 126–135. Springer, Heidelberg (2008). https://doi.org/10.1007/978-3-540-85538-5_9

34. Kamara, S., Lauter, K.: Cryptographic cloud storage. In: Sion, R., et al. (eds.) FC 2010. LNCS, vol. 6054, pp. 136–149. Springer, Heidelberg (2010). https://doi.org/10.1007/978-3-642-14992-4_13

35. Kowalczyk, L., Wee, H.: Compact adaptively secure ABE for NC^1 from k-Lin. In: Ishai, Y., Rijmen, V. (eds.) EUROCRYPT 2019. LNCS, vol. 11476, pp. 3–33. Springer, Cham (2019). https://doi.org/10.1007/978-3-030-17653-2_1

36. Ladd, W., Venema, M., Verma, T.: Portunus: Re-imagining access control in distributed systems. Cryptology ePrint Archive, Paper 2023/094 (2023)

37. Lewko, A., Sahai, A., Waters, B.: Revocation systems with very small private keys. In: IEEE S & P, pp. 273–285 (2010)

38. Lewko, A., Waters, B.: Decentralizing attribute-based encryption. In: Paterson, K.G. (ed.) EUROCRYPT 2011. LNCS, vol. 6632, pp. 568–588. Springer, Heidelberg (2011). https://doi.org/10.1007/978-3-642-20465-4_31

39. Lewko, A., Waters, B.: Unbounded HIBE and attribute-based encryption. In: Paterson, K.G. (ed.) EUROCRYPT 2011. LNCS, vol. 6632, pp. 547–567. Springer, Heidelberg (2011). https://doi.org/10.1007/978-3-642-20465-4_30

40. Lin, H., Luo, J.: Compact adaptively secure ABE from k-lin: Beyond nc^1 and towards NL. Cryptology ePrint Archive, Paper 2020/318 (2020)

41. Möller, B.: Algorithms for multi-exponentiation. In: Vaudenay, S., Youssef, A.M. (eds.) SAC 2001. LNCS, vol. 2259, pp. 165–180. Springer, Heidelberg (2001). https://doi.org/10.1007/3-540-45537-X_13

42. Okamoto, T., Takashima, K.: Fully secure unbounded inner-product and attribute-based encryption. In: Wang, X., Sako, K. (eds.) ASIACRYPT 2012. LNCS, vol. 7658, pp. 349–366. Springer, Heidelberg (2012). https://doi.org/10.1007/978-3-642-34961-4_22

43. Ostrovsky, R., Sahai, A., Waters, B.: Attribute-based encryption with non-monotonic access structures. In: CCS, pp. 195–203. ACM (2007)

44. de la Piedra, A., Venema, M., Alpár, G.: ABE squared: Accurately benchmarking efficiency of attribute-based encryption. TCHES **2022**(2), 192–239 (2022)

45. Rouselakis, Y., Waters, B.: Practical constructions and new proof methods for large universe attribute-based encryption. In: CCS, pp. 463–474. ACM (2013)
46. Sahai, A., Seyalioglu, H., Waters, B.: Dynamic credentials and ciphertext delegation for attribute-based encryption. In: Safavi-Naini, R., Canetti, R. (eds.) CRYPTO 2012. LNCS, vol. 7417, pp. 199–217. Springer, Heidelberg (2012). https://doi.org/10.1007/978-3-642-32009-5_13
47. Sahai, A., Waters, B.: Fuzzy identity-based encryption. In: Cramer, R. (ed.) EUROCRYPT 2005. LNCS, vol. 3494, pp. 457–473. Springer, Heidelberg (2005). https://doi.org/10.1007/11426639_27
48. Santos, N., Rodrigues, R., Gummadi, K.P., Saroiu, S.: Policy-sealed data: a new abstraction for building trusted cloud services. In: USENIX Security Symposium, pp. 175–188. USENIX Association (2012)
49. Tomida, J., Kawahara, Y., Nishimaki, R.: Fast, compact, and expressive attribute-based encryption. In: Kiayias, A., Kohlweiss, M., Wallden, P., Zikas, V. (eds.) PKC 2020. LNCS, vol. 12110, pp. 3–33. Springer, Cham (2020). https://doi.org/10.1007/978-3-030-45374-9_1
50. Venema, M.: A practical compiler for attribute-based encryption: new decentralized constructions and more. In: To appear at CT-RSA 2023. Springer (2023). Cryptology ePrint Archive, Paper 2023/143
51. Venema, M., Alpár, G.: Performance estimates for the GLUE paper. https://github.com/mtcvenema/glue
52. Venema, M., Alpár, G.: TinyABE: Unrestricted ciphertext-policy attribute-based encryption for embedded devices and low-quality networks. In: Batina, L., Daemen, J. (eds.) Progress in Cryptology - AFRICACRYPT 2022. AFRICACRYPT 2022. Lecture Notes in Computer Science, vol. 13503, pp. 103–129. Springer (2022). https://doi.org/10.1007/978-3-031-17433-9_5
53. Venema, M., Alpár, G., Hoepman, J.: Systematizing core properties of pairing-based attribute-based encryption to uncover remaining challenges in enforcing access control in practice. Des. Codes Cryptogr. **91**(1), 165–220 (2023)
54. Venema, M., Alpàr, G.: Glue: Generalizing unbounded attribute-based encryption for flexible efficiency trade-offs. Cryptology ePrint Archive, Paper 2022/613 (2022)
55. Waters, B.: Ciphertext-policy attribute-based encryption: An expressive, efficient, and provably secure realization. Cryptology ePrint Archive, Report 2008/290 (2008)
56. Waters, B.: Ciphertext-policy attribute-based encryption: an expressive, efficient, and provably secure realization. In: Catalano, D., Fazio, N., Gennaro, R., Nicolosi, A. (eds.) PKC 2011. LNCS, vol. 6571, pp. 53–70. Springer, Heidelberg (2011). https://doi.org/10.1007/978-3-642-19379-8_4
57. Yamada, S., Attrapadung, N., Hanaoka, G., Kunihiro, N.: A framework and compact constructions for non-monotonic attribute-based encryption. In: Krawczyk, H. (ed.) PKC 2014. LNCS, vol. 8383, pp. 275–292. Springer, Heidelberg (2014). https://doi.org/10.1007/978-3-642-54631-0_16

Key Exchange and Messaging

EKE Meets Tight Security in the Universally Composable Framework

Xiangyu Liu[1,2], Shengli Liu[1,2,3]($\boxtimes$), Shuai Han[1,2], and Dawu Gu[1]

[1] School of Electronic Information and Electrical Engineering,
Shanghai Jiao Tong University, Shanghai 200240, China
{xiangyu_liu,slliu,dalen17,dwgu}@sjtu.edu.cn
[2] State Key Laboratory of Cryptology, P.O. Box 5159, Beijing 100878, China
[3] Westone Cryptologic Research Center, Beijing 100070, China

Abstract. (Asymmetric) Password-based Authenticated Key Exchange ((a)PAKE) protocols allow two parties establish a session key with a pre-shared low-entropy password. In this paper, we show how Encrypted Key Exchange (EKE) compiler [Bellovin and Merritt, S&P 1992] meets tight security in the Universally Composable (UC) framework. We propose a strong 2DH variant of EKE, denoted by 2DH-EKE, and prove its tight security in the UC framework based on the CDH assumption. The efficiency of 2DH-EKE is comparable to the original EKE, with only $O(\lambda)$ bits growth in communication (λ the security parameter), and two (resp., one) extra exponentiation in computation for client (resp., server).

We also develop an asymmetric PAKE scheme 2DH-aEKE from 2DH-EKE. The security reduction loss of 2DH-aEKE is N, the total number of client-server pairs. With a meta-reduction, we formally prove that such a factor N is inevitable in aPAKE. Namely, our 2DH-aEKE meets the optimal security loss. As a byproduct, we further apply our technique to PAKE protocols like SPAKE2 and PPK in the relaxed UC framework, resulting in their 2DH variants with tight security from the CDH assumption.

Keywords: (Asymmetric) PAKE · UC Framework · Tight Security

1 Introduction

Password-based Authenticated Key Exchange (PAKE) [8] allows two parties (client and server) who share a low-entropy password pw to agree on a session key via public networks. Such session keys can later be used to establish secure channels. Different from authenticated key exchange (AKE) which needs a PKI to authenticate the validity of public keys, PAKE takes short human-memorizable passwords rather than long cryptographic keys. Therefore, PAKE is more convenient for deployments and applications.

For PAKE, the server has to store all clients' passwords and once compromised, all clients are in high risk. Asymmetric PAKE (aPAKE) [9,19] is a variant

© International Association for Cryptologic Research 2023
A. Boldyreva and V. Kolesnikov (Eds.): PKC 2023, LNCS 13940, pp. 685–713, 2023.
https://doi.org/10.1007/978-3-031-31368-4_24

of PAKE that considers security against server compromise. In the scenario of aPAKE, the server stores a password file (usually a hash value $H(\mathsf{pw})$) for the client, rather than a plain password. A client can establish a session key with a server if it holds a pre-image of the password file.

Started from the pioneering works by Belloven and Merritt [8,9], (a)PAKE has been studied extensively, and a variety of protocols have been proposed over the past decades. For example, SPEKE [28], PPK/PAK [35], SPAKE2 [4], Dragonfly [24], J-PAKE [23], KOY [31], KV [32] for PAKE, and VB-PAKE [33], OPAQUE [30], KC-SPAKE2+ [41], KHAPE [21], YLZT [44], aEKE and OKAPE [39] for aPAKE. Among these protocols, SPAKE2, J-PAKE, OPAQUE are under the process of standardization [5,27,38,40]. (a)PAKE protocols have also been increasingly applied to numerous settings, including TLS [30,37], ad hoc networks [43], and the Internet of Things [42].

Since passwords have limited entropy, an adversary $\mathcal{A}$ can always try a password guess and actively engage in a session, and hence break the security with a noticeable probability. Such online attacks are inherit to (a)PAKE, but we can still fence these attacks via engineering methods, e.g., by limiting the number of online password guesses. Another type of attacks is offline dictionary attacks, i.e., the adversary eavesdrops on executions of the protocol and tries to break the security via a brute-force attack with all possible passwords in a given dictionary. Intuitively, a PAKE protocol is secure, if offline dictionary attacks help nothing to the adversary, and the only feasible way to break the security, is to engage in an online attack. In aPAKE, we further consider security when the server is compromised. That is, the password files help nothing for the adversary in impersonating a client, as long as $\mathcal{A}$ does not obtain the correct password from the compromised password file via brute-force search.

Security Models for (a)PAKE. There are two types of security notions for (a)PAKE, namely, the game-based security in the Indistinguishability (IND) model (see [7] for PAKE and [10,11,33] for aPAKE) and the simulation-based security in the Universally Composable (UC) framework (see [15] for PAKE and [19] for aPAKE). The IND model is formalized as an experiment between a challenger $\mathcal{C}$ and an adversary $\mathcal{A}$. We say an (a)PAKE protocol is secure in this model, if $\mathcal{A}$ cannot distinguish a real session key from a random session key, after it implements a variety of attacks.

The UC framework/model is another popular approach to formalize the security of (a)PAKE. In the UC framework, an ideal function $\mathcal{F}$ is defined to capture the essential functionality of an (a)PAKE protocol in the ideal world. We say that an (a)PAKE protocol is secure in the UC framework, if it securely emulates $\mathcal{F}$, i.e., no PPT environment can distinguish the real world execution from the ideal world execution (involving $\mathcal{F}$ and an ideal world simulator).

The UC framework is preferable to the IND model in a number of important aspects.

– The UC framework allows an arbitrary correlation and distribution for passwords. But in the IND model, passwords are required to be uniformly distributed over the password set (or at least have a min-entropy) for the sake of security proofs, e.g., [7,31].

- UC security is preserved even if the protocol is running in arbitrary networks, where multiple different protocols may run concurrently. This is guaranteed by the universal composition theorem [14] in the UC framework.
- PAKE with UC security implies simulation-based security of secure-channel protocols built on PAKE [15]. In contrast, it is not sure for the IND security [41].

Tight Security. The security of (a)PAKE (in both the IND and UC models) is achieved by a security reduction under proper assumptions. The security reduction transforms the ability of a successful adversary $\mathcal{A}$ to an algorithm $\mathcal{B}$ solving some well-known hard problem in about the same running time. If $\mathcal{A}$'s attack succeeds with probability ϵ, then $\mathcal{B}$ solves the problem with probability ϵ/L. Here L is defined as the security loss factor. We say that the reduction is tight if L is a constant. Otherwise the reduction is loose. A loose factor L is generally a polynomial of Q, where Q is the total number of queries involved by $\mathcal{A}$, and it can be of arbitrary polynomial. PAKE and aPAKE are generally implemented in the multi-user and multi-challenge setting. With a loose security reduction, the deployment of (a)PAKE has to choose a larger security parameter to compensate the loss factor L, resulting in larger elements and slower computations in the execution of (a)PAKE. Therefore, pursuing tight security of (a)PAKE is not only of theoretical value but also of practical significance.

There are very few works considering tight security of (a)PAKE. Becerra et al. [6] proved that the security of the PAK protocol [35] can be tightly reduced to the Gap DH assumption in the IND model. Under the same assumption, Abdalla et al. [1] proved that SPAKE2 [4] is tightly secure in the relaxed UC framework. However, both of the works used the non-standard Gap DH assumption, which states that it is hard to compute g^{xy}, given g^x, g^y, and an oracle deciding whether the input (g^a, g^b, g^c) is a DDH tuple. Besides, their securities are proved in the IND or relaxed UC model [1], rather than the (regular) UC framework. Up to now, there is no research on (a)PAKE with tight security in the UC framework.

Therefore, a challenging question is:

Can we construct a tightly secure (a)PAKE protocol in the UC framework, preferably from the standard assumption?

Our Contributions. In this paper, we aim to answer the above question. For PAKE, we propose a tightly secure PAKE protocol based on the CDH assumption in the UC framework, and hence answer the question for PAKE in affirmative. For aPAKE, we prove a negative result via a meta-reduction, showing that a loss factor $L = N$ (the number of client-server pairs) is inevitable in aPAKE. Nevertheless, we still come up with an aPAKE protocol that meets this optimal security loss. In more detail, we revisit the EKE compiler/protocol in [8], and make the following contributions.

1. We propose a strong 2DH variant of EKE, denoted by 2DH-EKE, and prove that it is a tightly secure PAKE from the CDH assumption in the UC framework. The efficiency of 2DH-EKE is comparable to the original EKE, with

only $O(\lambda)$ bits growth in communication (λ the security parameter) and two (resp., one) extra exponentiation in computation for client (resp., server).

2. We show a negative result for aPAKE, indicating that it is impossible for aPAKE to be tightly secure. With a meta-reduction, we prove that the security loss of aPAKE is lower bounded by N, the number of client-server pairs.

3. We develop our 2DH-EKE to an aPAKE protocol, denoted by 2DH-aEKE, that meets the optimal security loss N based on the CDH assumption. Compared with 2DH-EKE, the 2DH-aEKE protocol adds one extra round for message authentications.

4. As a byproduct, we further apply our technique to PAKE protocols like SPAKE2 [4] and PPK [35] in the relaxed UC framework [1], resulting in their 2DH variants with tight security from the CDH assumption.

Related Works. Bellovin and Merritt started the research of PAKE in [8], and proposed the well-known EKE compiler/protocol. The security of EKE was formally proved later by Bellare et al. [7] in the IND model, and by Dupont et al. [17] in the UC framework. Most of the efficient PAKE constructions ([4,12,13,35,36], to name a few) rely on <u>R</u>andom <u>O</u>racles (RO), and they can be viewed as different variants of the classical EKE compiler [8]. There are some works [18,20,31,32] that consider PAKE in the standard model (i.e., without any ideal functions), but the constructions usually rely on heavy building blocks like CCA2-secure PKE [20] or NIZK [32], and hence are less efficient.

Given the advantages of the UC framework over the IND model, a large amount of (a)PAKE protocols [21,30,39,41] are proposed and proved in the UC framework recently. There are some other works [2,3] focusing on the existing IND-secure (a)PAKE schemes and aiming to prove their security in the stronger UC framework. In [1], Abdalla et al. relaxed the UC framework by introducing a modified lazy-extraction PAKE functionality, which allows the adversary in the ideal world to postpone its password guess until *after* the session is completed. Under this relaxed model, they proved that SPEKE [29], SPAKE2 [4], and TBPEKE [36] are UC-secure.

The only two works considering tight security of PAKE are [6] by Becerra et al., and [3] by Abdalla et al. (both of them are in the RO model). However, their securities are proved in the IND model or the relaxed UC framework [3], based on the non-standard Gap DH assumption. As far as we know, there exists no tightly secure (a)PAKE schemes in the regular UC framework up to now.

1.1 Technical Overview

In this subsection we briefly overview the technique used in this paper.

The main challenge to achieve tight security for (a)PAKE, is to embed the hard problem into *multiple* sessions, while keeping the ability to output their session keys in case the adversary $\mathcal{A}$ has the power to compute them (e.g., $\mathcal{A}$ correctly guesses the password). Furthermore, the reduction algorithm should extract (possibly from a set) the correct solution for the hard problem, if $\mathcal{A}$ wins the security experiment non-trivially.

Now let us consider the EKE compiler/protocol [8]. The client samples x and sends $E(pw, g^x)$, where $E(\cdot)$ is a symmetric encryption under key pw. Similarly, the server samples y and sends $E(pw, g^y)$. The session key is computed as $key = H(aux, Z = g^{xy}, pw)$ with aux some public information. Now we explain why it is difficult for EKE to achieve tight security based on the CDH assumption.

In the reduction, given a CDH problem instance $(g^{\bar{x}}, g^{\bar{y}})$, the reduction algorithm $\mathcal{B}$ may use the random self-reducibility of the DH problem to generate multiple (g^{x_i}, g^{y_j}), and embed them into multiple protocol sessions. Since $H(\cdot)$ works as a random oracle, $\mathcal{A}$ has no advantage in distinguishing a real session key from a random key, unless it queries $H(\cdot)$ on the right CDH value $g^{x_i y_j}$. Now suppose that $\mathcal{A}$ does query $H(\cdot)$ on the right CDH value, here come two problems for $\mathcal{B}$.

(1) $\mathcal{A}$ may ask hash queries on (aux, Z_i, pw) with different Z_i, but $\mathcal{B}$ cannot identify/compute the right CDH value $g^{\bar{x}\bar{y}}$ from all Z_i. Therefore, $\mathcal{B}$ has to guess one for the CDH problem, leading to a loose security factor Q_h (maximum number of hash queries).
(2) $\mathcal{A}$ may correctly guess the password and send g^y out after seeing some g^{x_i}, i.e., $\mathcal{A}$ has the power to compute $g^{x_i y}$ and hence the session key. However, without the knowledge of x_i, $\mathcal{B}$ is unable to compute $g^{x_i y}$.

To solve these two problems, a natural idea is resorting to a decision oracle, and that is exactly what [1,6] did. However, [1,6] rely on the non-standard Gap DH assumption. In this paper, we solve these two problems with the twin DH decision oracle and the standard CDH assumption.

Twin DH Decision Oracle. In [16], Cash et al. proposed the strong twin-DH (st2DH) assumption and proved its equivalence to the (standard) CDH assumption. Here the strong 2DH problem is to compute $(g^{\bar{x}_1 \bar{y}}, g^{\bar{x}_2 \bar{y}})$, given $g^{\bar{x}_1}, g^{\bar{x}_2}, g^{\bar{y}}$, as well as a decision oracle $2DH(\cdot, \cdot, \cdot)$ that inputs (Y, Z_1, Z_2) and outputs whether $(\bar{X}_1, Y, Z_1)$ and $(\bar{X}_2, Y, Z_2)$ are both DDH tuples. Inspired by [16], we propose our 2DH variant protocol for EKE, named 2DH-EKE. Now the client sends $E(pw, g^{x_1}||g^{x_2})$ and the server sends $E(pw, g^y)$, and the session key is computed as $key = H(aux, Z_1 = g^{x_1 y}, Z_2 = g^{x_2 y}, pw)$ with aux some public information. Next, we show how the twin DH decision oracle can be used to solve the above two problems.

(1) With the decision oracle $2DH(\cdot, \cdot, \cdot)$, the reduction algorithm $\mathcal{B}$ can easily locate the correct Z_1, Z_2 among all possible candidates, by checking whether $2DH(Y, Z_1, Z_2) = 1$. In this way, $\mathcal{B}$ succeeds in solving the strong 2DH problem, and avoiding the loose factor Q_h.
(2) In the reduction $\mathcal{B}$ may need to simulate the session key $key = H(aux, g^{x_1 y}, g^{x_1 y}, pw)$ for some adversarially generated g^y, and the exponents $x_1||x_2$ are unknown to $\mathcal{B}$ due to the embedded hard problem. In this case, $\mathcal{B}$ randomly samples a key and implicitly sets it as the "right" key. Since $H(\cdot)$ works as a random oracle, $\mathcal{A}$ will not obverse this difference unless it asks a hash query on the right 2DH values Z_1, Z_2 later. If this happens, $\mathcal{B}$ can detect

it with the decision oracle, and reprogram the random oracle such that $H(\mathsf{aux}, Z_1, Z_2, \mathsf{pw}) = \mathsf{key}$, and the view of $\mathcal{A}$ is consistent.

Towards UC Security. To achieve UC security, we need to construct a PPT simulator to simulate the interactions with the environment in the real world, with the help of the ideal functionality $\mathcal{F}$. In our 2DH-EKE protocol, the symmetric encryption (E, D) is modeled as an Ideal Cipher (IC), and hence the transcripts $(e_1 = \mathsf{E}(\mathsf{pw}, X_1 || X_2)$ and $e_2 = \mathsf{E}(\mathsf{pw}, Y))$ are perfect hiding. Consequently, the simulator can perfectly simulate the transcripts with random messages.

To deal with the adversarially generated message (say e'_1), we can always look up the IC list to extract the password $\mathcal{A}$ guesses "in mind". Then the simulator can resort to the TestPW interface provided by $\mathcal{F}$, to check whether $\mathcal{A}$ succeeds in guessing the password. If yes, the simulator can compute the "real" session key, with the help of the twin DH decision oracle, as discussed above. Otherwise, the session key is simulated as a random key, and this is indistinguishable to the adversary due to the CDH assumption.

Asymmetric PAKE. Generally in the scenario of aPAKE, the server stores a password file (usually a hash of the password) rather than the password in plain. The resistance to server compromise requires that getting the password file helps nothing for the adversary in impersonating a client, unless it implements a brute-force attack and successfully recovers the pre-image pw. In this paper, we develop our 2DH-EKE to an aPAKE protocol 2DH-aEKE, with only one extra round to transmit a confirming message.

2DH-aEKE inherits the idea of the generic CDH-based compiler in [26], and it works as follows. Let $\mathsf{H}_0(\cdot)$ be a hash function, $\mathsf{H}_0(\mathsf{pw}) = (\mathsf{h}, v_1, v_2)$ and $V_1 := g^{v_1}, V_2 := g^{v_2}$. Now the password file stored in the server is (h, V_1, V_2). In the execution of 2DH-aEKE, the client and the server first run the symmetric 2DH-EKE protocol using h as the key of symmetric encryption. Recall that the client and the server's unencrypted messages are $(X_1 || X_2) = (g^{x_1} || g^{x_2})$ and $Y = g^y$, respectively. Let $H(\mathsf{aux}, g^{x_1 y}, g^{x_2 y}, g^{v_1 y}, g^{v_2 y}, \mathsf{h}) = (\mathsf{key}, \sigma)$, where aux is the public information, key is the session key, and σ is the key confirmation message. Then the client sends σ to the server as an extra round message. From the strong 2DH assumption we know that it is hard to compute $g^{v_1 y} || g^{v_2 y}$, even with the password file (h, V_1, V_2) and Y. That is how the security of 2DH-aEKE is guaranteed even after the server compromise. Note that the security reduction has a loss factor of N, the number of total client-server pairs, due to the commitment of client's password in the password file.

With a meta-reduction, we prove that the security loss of aPAKE is lower bounded by N. Hence, our 2DH-aEKE meets the optimal reduction loss. Now we give an intuition why the loss factor N is inevitable in aPAKE. In the reduction, the hard problem $(\bar{X}_1, \bar{X}_2, \bar{Y})$ is embedded into the password file $V_1 || V_2$ and the server's message Y, respectively. Meanwhile, if $\mathcal{A}$ asks the value of $\mathsf{H}_0(\mathsf{pw})$ with the correct password, then the discrete log of $V_1 || V_2$ should be returned. However, the reduction algorithm does not know whether and when $\mathcal{A}$ will issue such a query. Hence, it has to choose a particular client-server pair among all N

pairs, embed the hard problem into this password file, and hope $\mathcal{A}$ breaks the security of one session involving this password file but does not query $H_0(\mathsf{pw})$ at the time being.

Recall that almost all previous aPAKE schemes [21, 26, 41] have a loose reduction loss at least $Q_h N\theta$, where Q_h, N, θ denote the maximum numbers of hash queries, client-server pairs, and protocol executions per client-server pair, respectively. We stress that the decision oracle 2DH helps us improving the loss factor from $Q_h N\theta$ to the optimal bound N (note that $Q_h N\theta \gg N$ in general).

Extend to the Relaxed UC Framework. Our method can also apply to some IC-free protocols like SPAKE2 [4] and PPK [35], to get their 2DH variants. And the tight security can be proved based on the CDH assumption in the relaxed UC framework [1]. We take the SPAKE2 protocol as an example. In SPAKE2, the transcript messages are $X \cdot M^{\mathsf{pw}}$ and $Y \cdot N^{\mathsf{pw}}$ with M, N public parameters. In our 2DH-SPAKE2, X is replaced by $(X_1||X_2) = (g^{x_1}||g^{x_2})$, Y is replaced by $(Y_1||Y_2) = (g^{y_1}||g^{y_2})$, and the session key is computed as $\mathsf{key} = H(\mathsf{aux}, g^{x_1 y_1}, g^{x_1 y_2}, g^{x_2 y_1} g^{x_2 y_2}, \mathsf{pw})$. Similar to the proof of 2DH-EKE, the decision oracle 2DH is essential to make a tight reduction in the relaxed UC framework.

Forward Security. Both 2DH-EKE and 2DH-aEKE achieve Perfect Forward Security [22] (PFS, a.k.a. perfect forward secrecy). PFS means that once a party is corrupted at some moment, then all session keys completed before the corruption remain hidden from the adversary. Let us take 2DH-EKE as an example. Note that a completed session has already uniquely determined e_1 and e_2, even if one of them is adversarially generated. If $\mathcal{A}$ later gets pw via a corruption, the information it obtains from the corruption is limited by $X_1||X_2 = \mathsf{D}(\mathsf{pw}, e_1)$ and $Y = \mathsf{D}(\mathsf{pw}, e_2)$. However, given $X_1||X_2$ and Y, computing the session key is as hard as solving the 2DH problem, and PFS is guaranteed as a result. The analysis of PFS for SPAKE2 (2DH-SPAKE2) can be found in [1].

1.2   Roadmap

This paper is organised as follows. In Sect. 2 we present preliminaries, including notations and some hardness assumptions. In Sect. 3 we describe the UC framework for PAKE, propose the 2DH-EKE protocol, and prove its security. In Sect. 4 we describe the UC framework for aPAKE, and propose the asymmetric variant 2DH-aEKE protocol. The optimal reduction loss in aPAKE is shown in Sect. 5. Consequently, we extend our technique to SPAKE2 to obtain 2DH-SPAKE2 in Sect. 6. We refer the full version [34] for details of the proofs, and the functionalities of ideal ciphers, random oracles, and lazy-extraction PAKE.

2   Preliminaries

We use $\lambda \in \mathbb{N}$ to denote the security parameter throughout the paper. Denote by $x := y$ the operation of assigning y to x. Denote by $x \xleftarrow{\$} \mathcal{X}$ the operation of sampling x uniformly at random from a set $\mathcal{X}$. For an algorithm $\mathcal{A}$, denote by $y \leftarrow \mathcal{A}(x; r)$, or simply $y \leftarrow \mathcal{A}(x)$, the operation of running $\mathcal{A}$ with input x and randomness r and assigning the output to y. "PPT" is short for probabilistic polynomial-time.

The the functionalities of ideal ciphers and random oracles are given in the full version [34].

2.1   Hardness Assumptions

Let GGen be a group generation algorithm such that $(\mathbb{G}, q, g) \leftarrow \mathsf{GGen}(1^\lambda)$, where $\mathbb{G}$ is a cyclic group of prime order q with generator g.

Definition 1. *For any adversary $\mathcal{A}$, its advantage in solving the Computational Diffie-Hellman (CDH) problem is defined as*

$$\mathsf{Adv}^{\mathsf{CDH}}_{\mathbb{G},\mathcal{A}}(\lambda) := \Pr[x, y \xleftarrow{\$} \mathbb{Z}_q : \mathcal{A}(g, g^x, g^y) = g^{xy}].$$

In [16], Cash et al. proposed the Strong Twin Diffie-Hellman (strong 2DH or st2DH) problem, and proved that it is as hard as the CDH problem.

Definition 2. *[16] For any adversary $\mathcal{A}$, its advantage in solving the st2DH problem is defined as*

$$\mathsf{Adv}^{\mathsf{st2DH}}_{\mathbb{G},\mathcal{A}}(\lambda) := \Pr[\bar{x}_1, \bar{x}_2, \bar{y} \xleftarrow{\$} \mathbb{Z}_q : \mathcal{A}^{\mathsf{2DH}(\cdot,\cdot,\cdot)}(g, g^{\bar{x}_1}, g^{\bar{x}_2}, g^{\bar{y}}) = (g^{\bar{x}_1\bar{y}}, g^{\bar{x}_2\bar{y}})],$$

where the decision oracle $\mathsf{2DH}(\cdot,\cdot,\cdot)$ inputs (g^y, g^{z_1}, g^{z_2}) and outputs 1 if $(\bar{x}_1 y = z_1) \wedge (\bar{x}_2 y = z_2)$ and 0 otherwise.

The st2DH assumption was proven equivalent to the CDH assumption [16].

Theorem 1. *[16] For any PPT adversary $\mathcal{A}$ against the st2DH problem, there exists a PPT algorithm $\mathcal{B}$ against the CDH problem such that $\mathsf{Adv}^{\mathsf{st2DH}}_{\mathbb{G},\mathcal{A}}(\lambda) \leq \mathsf{Adv}^{\mathsf{CDH}}_{\mathbb{G},\mathcal{B}}(\lambda) + Q/q$, where Q is the maximum number of decision oracle queries.*

In the following sessions, we also use the notations $\mathsf{CDH}(g^x, g^y) = g^{xy}$, and $\mathsf{2DH}(g^{x_1}, g^{x_2}, g^y) = (g^{x_1 y}, g^{x_2 y})$ for arbitrary elements $g^x, g^y, g^{x_1}, g^{x_2}$ in $\mathbb{G}$.

3   PAKE with Tight Security in the UC Framework

3.1   UC Framework for PAKE

We assume basic familiarity with the Universally Composable framework (UC framework, a.k.a. UC model) for PAKE. The ideal functionality $\mathcal{F}_{\mathsf{pake}}$ is shown in Fig. 1. We mainly follow the definition by Shoup in [41], which is a modified version of [15] by Canetti et al. For a full understanding of UC framework, we refer [15,41] for details.

Overview of the UC Framework. The ideal functionality $\mathcal{F}_{\mathsf{pake}}$ plays the role of a trusted authority in the ideal world. A client and a server first share the same password when registration, after which $\mathcal{F}_{\mathsf{pake}}$ records the password privately. When initializing a new PAKE session, both the two parties send a query to $\mathcal{F}_{\mathsf{pake}}$, and the client additionally sends a password (since it is very possible for a client to mistype the password, see the description below). Then $\mathcal{F}_{\mathsf{pake}}$ verifies whether the password from the client matches the (correct) password stored by the server. If yes, these two parties are "matched" and they will get the same random session key from $\mathcal{F}_{\mathsf{pake}}$. Otherwise, they are "dismatched" and the execution of PAKE fails (the output may be arbitrary in this case). Security in this ideal model holds inherently, since nothing except the identities of involved parties is leaked to the simulator/adversary Sim in the ideal world, and the only attack Sim can apply, is an online attack.

The security target of a PAKE protocol Π, is to emulates the ideal functionality $\mathcal{F}_{\mathsf{pake}}$ in the real world. More precisely, consider an environment $\mathcal{Z}$ that controls passwords for all parties[1], and it aims to distinguish the real world from the ideal world, i.e., distinguish the case where outputs including session keys are produced via executions of Π compelled by an adversary $\mathcal{A}$, from the case where outputs are obtained from $\mathcal{F}_{\mathsf{pake}}$ and an simulator Sim interacting with $\mathcal{F}_{\mathsf{pake}}$. If for any PPT environment $\mathcal{Z}$, the distinguishing advantage is negligible, we say PAKE protocol Π securely emulates $\mathcal{F}_{\mathsf{pake}}$.

Now we describe $\mathcal{F}_{\mathsf{pake}}$ in more detail.

Password Storage and Sessions. We require two parties involved in a PAKE execution have different roles (client or server), and each party has a unique identity, namely, $\mathsf{C}^{(i)}$ or $\mathsf{S}^{(j)}$. In the registration stage, the environment $\mathcal{Z}$ allocates a password $\hat{\mathsf{pw}}$ for each client-server pair $(\mathsf{C}^{(i)}, \mathsf{S}^{(j)})$. The functionality $\mathcal{F}_{\mathsf{pake}}$ then records this password after a StorePWFile query from $\mathsf{C}^{(i)}$ or $\mathsf{S}^{(j)}$. Without loss of generality, we assume each pair of $(\mathsf{C}^{(i)}, \mathsf{S}^{(j)})$ has only one password.

For a party P, we call an execution of protocol a (session) instance, and index it with an instance identity iid. After registration, P can initialize a new session instance via a NewClient or NewServer query to $\mathcal{F}_{\mathsf{pake}}$. For a server $\mathsf{S}^{(j)}$, the password pw used in this instance is set to be the correct password $\hat{\mathsf{pw}}$ pre-shared between $\mathsf{C}^{(i)}$ and $\mathsf{S}^{(j)}$. For a client $\mathsf{C}^{(i)}$, it is possible that $\mathsf{pw} \neq \hat{\mathsf{pw}}$ due to a mistyped/misremembered password.

Following the definition in [41], we explicitly model mistyped or misremembered passwords in $\mathcal{F}_{\mathsf{pake}}$, instead of absorbing it into an active attack by the adversary $\mathcal{A}$ (though this is enough from the perspective of PAKE security, i.e., preventing a bad client from logging into the server). Actually, a mistyped password is very close to the correct password, and an accidental mismatch would not compromise this nearly-identical password to $\mathcal{A}$.

---

[1] Let the environment deciding passwords captures the security in case users' passwords are arbitrarily distributed and correlated. This is one aspect in which the UC framework is superior to the IND model.

Functionality $\mathcal{F}_{\mathsf{pake}}$

The functionality $\mathcal{F}_{\mathsf{pake}}$ is parameterized by a security parameter λ. It interacts with a simulator Sim and a set of parties via the following queries:

Password Storage

Upon receiving a query $(\mathsf{StorePWFile}, C^{(i)}, S^{(j)}, \hat{\mathsf{pw}})$ from a client $C^{(i)}$ or a server $S^{(j)}$:

If there exists a record $\langle\mathsf{file}, C^{(i)}, S^{(j)}, \cdot\rangle$, ignore this query.

Otherwise, record $\langle\mathsf{file}, C^{(i)}, S^{(j)}, \hat{\mathsf{pw}}\rangle$, and send $(\mathsf{StorePWFile}, C^{(i)}, S^{(j)})$ to Sim.

Sessions

Upon receiving a query $(\mathsf{NewClient}, iid^{(i)}, S^{(j)}, \mathsf{pw})$ from a client $C^{(i)}$:

Retrieve the record $\langle\mathsf{file}, C^{(i)}, S^{(j)}, \hat{\mathsf{pw}}\rangle$. Send $(\mathsf{NewClient}, C^{(i)}, iid^{(i)}, S^{(j)}, \mathsf{pw} = \hat{\mathsf{pw}}?)$ to Sim. Record $(C^{(i)}, iid^{(i)}, S^{(j)}, \mathsf{pw})$ and mark it as fresh.

In this case, $S^{(j)}$ is called the intended partner of $(C^{(i)}, iid^{(i)})$.

Upon receiving a query $(\mathsf{NewServer}, iid^{(j)}, C^{(i)})$ from a server $S^{(j)}$:

Retrieve the record $\langle\mathsf{file}, C^{(i)}, S^{(j)}, \hat{\mathsf{pw}}\rangle$. Send $(\mathsf{NewServer}, S^{(j)}, iid^{(j)}, C^{(i)})$ to Sim. Set $\mathsf{pw} := \hat{\mathsf{pw}}$, record $(S^{(j)}, iid^{(j)}, C^{(i)}, \mathsf{pw})$ and mark it as fresh.

In this case, $C^{(i)}$ is called the intended partner of $(S^{(j)}, iid^{(j)})$.

Two instances $(C^{(i)}, iid^{(i)})$ and $(S^{(j)}, iid^{(j)})$ are said to be partnered, if there are two fresh records $(C^{(i)}, iid^{(i)}, S^{(j)}, \mathsf{pw})$ and $(S^{(j)}, iid^{(j)}, C^{(i)}, \mathsf{pw})$ sharing the same pw.

Active Session Attacks

Upon receiving a query $(\mathsf{TestPW}, P, iid, \mathsf{pw}')$ from Sim:

If there is a fresh record $(P, iid, \cdot, \mathsf{pw})$:

– If $\mathsf{pw}' = \mathsf{pw}$, mark the record compromised and reply to Sim with "correct guess".
– If $\mathsf{pw}' \neq \mathsf{pw}$, mark the record interrupted and replay with "wrong guess".

Key Generation

Upon receiving a query $(\mathsf{FreshKey}, P, iid, sid)$ from Sim:

If 1) there is a fresh or interrupted record (P, iid, Q, pw); and 2) sid has never been assigned to P's any other instance (P, iid'):

Pick a new random key k, mark the record (P, iid, Q, pw) as completed, assign it with sid, send (iid, sid, k) to P, and record (P, Q, sid, k).

Upon receiving a query $(\mathsf{CopyKey}, P, iid, sid)$ from Sim:

If 1) there is a fresh record (P, iid, Q, pw) and a completed record $(Q, iid^*, P, \mathsf{pw})$ s.t. (P, iid) and (Q, iid^*) are partnered; and 3) there is a unique (Q, iid^*) that has been assigned with sid:

Retrieve the record (Q, P, sid, k), mark the record (P, iid, Q, pw) as completed, assign it with sid, and send (iid, sid, k) to P.

Upon receiving a query $(\mathsf{CorruptKey}, P, iid, sid, k)$ from Sim:

If 1) there is a compromised record (P, iid, Q, pw); and 2) sid has never been assigned to P's any other instance (P, iid'):

Mark the record (P, iid, Q, pw) as completed, assign it with sid, and send (iid, sid, k) to P.

Fig. 1. The PAKE functionality $\mathcal{F}_{\mathsf{pake}}$ [41].

Active Attacks. To capture online attacks in the real world, $\mathcal{F}_{\mathsf{pake}}$ allows the simulator Sim in the ideal world to make a password guess per instance via the interface TestPW. If the guess is correct, then the session instance is marked as compromised, which means that the adversary succeeds in attacking this instance and can affect the generation of the session key. If the guess is wrong, then the instance is marked as interrupted, indicating a failed online attack, and the session key is chosen at random.

Via (static) corruptions, a real world adversary can learn the password hold by a party and control its behaviour completely. To make the view of the environment consistent, the simulator Sim in the ideal world also obtains the password of that party, and simulates what it outputs in an indistinguishable way. Note that the corruption process is not explicitly presented in $\mathcal{F}_{\text{pake}}$ in Fig 1.

Key Generation. For an instance (P, iid), when the protocol execution is completed, $\mathcal{F}_{\text{pake}}$ will assign to the instance a key and a session identity sid which is determined by Sim. And sid is required to uniquely index this completed instance (the two parties in a session would share the same sid if there is no active attack). Furthermore, $\mathcal{F}_{\text{pake}}$ provides three types of interfaces for key generation.

- FreshKey. When a successful protocol execution finishes and one instance needs to output a session key first, or the passwords do not match (including the case of a failed password guess), the instance is assigned with an independent and random key.
- CopyKey. If there are two instances that match with each other, and a fresh key has been assigned to one instance before, then a copy of the session key is passed to the other instance.
- CorruptKey. If one of the participating parties is corrupted, or the adversary successfully guesses the password, then the session key is totally determined by Sim.

Remark 1 (Session identities). $\mathcal{F}_{\text{pake}}$ implicitly assumes that sid allocated by the simulator differs for each instance (even for two different instances of the same party) except for the two partnered instances. As we will see, this is indeed the case in 2DH-EKE, since sid connects the identities of the client, the server, and the session transcripts, and each instance contributes its own randomness to transcripts. So once an instance is completed and has been assigned with (sid, k), the information of sid is sufficient to locate the unique and partnered pair (P, iid, Q, pw) and (Q, iid^*, P, pw), when dealing with CopyKey queries.

Remark 2 (Corruptions). Our PAKE framework deals with static corruptions, i.e., the adversary can corrupt some parties and get their passwords prior to the protocol execution. Note that there is a stronger model that supports adaptive corruptions, where the adversary can corrupt parties adaptively throughout the execution, and obtain not only the passwords but also the internal states. Almost all UC frameworks [15,41] for PAKE are defined in the way of static corruptions.

3.2 The 2DH-EKE Protocol

The EKE compiler/protocol was proposed by Bellovin and Merritt in [8], and formally proved later by Bellare et al. in the IND model [7], and by Dupont et al. in the UC framework [17]. The security proof is based on the CDH assumption in the IC and RO model, and has a security loss $L = Q_h \cdot N \cdot \theta$, with Q_h, N, θ the maximum numbers of hash queries, client-server pairs, and protocol executions per client-server pair, respectively.

In this subsection, we present a variant of EKE, named 2DH-EKE protocol, and prove its tight security based on the strong 2DH assumption (equivalently, the CDH assumption) in the UC framework.

The 2DH-EKE protocol is shown in Fig. 2. Here (E_1, D_1) is a symmetric encryption with key space $\mathcal{PW}$, plaintext space $\mathbb{G}^2$ and ciphertext space $\mathcal{E}_1$, and (E_2, D_2) is a symmetric encryption with key space $\mathcal{PW}$, plaintext space $\mathbb{G}$ and ciphertext space $\mathcal{E}_2$. Hash function H is defined as $H : \{0,1\}^* \mapsto \mathcal{K}$ with $\mathcal{K}$ the space of session keys. C, S are identities of Client and Server.

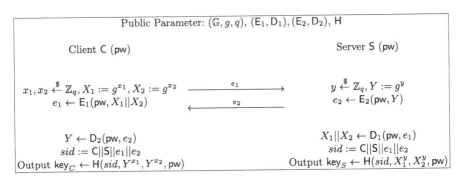

Fig. 2. The 2DH-EKE protocol.

Remark 3. The 2DH-EKE protocol can be modified to a variant protocol by interchanging the operations of Client and Server: the client sends $e_1 = E_1(pw, X)$ and the server sends $e_2 = E_2(pw, Y_1 || Y_2)$. In this way, the computational cost of Client is reduced, but Server has to initiate the session. In this paper we do not take this variant, since Client will start a session in general cases.

Remark 4 (Ideal ciphers on group elements). The ideal cipher in the 2DH-EKE protocol can be accomplished with a block cipher like AES. Take $e_1 = E_1(pw, X)$ as an example. First, the group element X is mapped to an n-bit string through a quasi bijection [21], and then the encryption algorithm encrypts the n-bit string with the password. The decryption algorithm D_1 can be similarly defined. For more details on implementations of IC, see [21].

Remark 5 (Comparisons with the Twin DH Protocol [16]). and KC-SPAKE2 [41]] Note that Cash et al. [16] extended the DH key exchange protocol to a twin DH version and proved its tight security. In the twin DH protocol, one party publishes (X_1, X_2) and the other party publishes (Y_1, Y_2), and the session key is the hash value $H(g^{x_1 y_1}, g^{x_1 y_2}, g^{x_2 y_1}, g^{x_2 y_2})$. In contrast, the server's (plain) message in our 2DH-EKE protocol consists of only one element Y, which greatly decreases the computation/communication cost.

In [41], Shoup showed the (non-tight) security of KC-SPAKE2 based on the CDH assumption, and argued that the reduction is tight under the Gap DH assumption. In contrast, our tight reduction of 2DH-EKE is based on the standard CDH assumption.

3.3 Security Analysis

Theorem 2 (Security of 2DH-EKE). *If the st2DH assumption (equivalently, the CDH assumption) holds in* $\mathbb{G}$, $(\mathsf{E}_1, \mathsf{D}_1)$ *and* $(\mathsf{E}_2, \mathsf{D}_2)$ *work as ideal ciphers, and* H *works as a random oracle, then the 2DH-EKE protocol in Fig. 2 securely emulates* $\mathcal{F}_{\mathsf{pake}}$. *More precisely, for any PPT environment* $\mathcal{Z}$ *and real world adversary* $\mathcal{A}$ *which has access to ideal ciphers* $(\mathsf{E}_1, \mathsf{D}_1), (\mathsf{E}_2, \mathsf{D}_2)$ *and random oracle* H, *there exist a PPT simulator* Sim, *which has access to the ideal functionality* $\mathcal{F}_{\mathsf{pake}}$, *and algorithms* $\mathcal{B}, \mathcal{B}'$, *s.t. the advantage of* $\mathcal{Z}$ *in distinguishing the real world running with* $\mathcal{A}$ *and the ideal world running with* Sim *is bounded by*

$$\mathsf{Adv}_{\mathsf{2DH\text{-}EKE}, \mathcal{Z}}(\lambda) \leq 2\mathsf{Adv}_{\mathbb{G}, \mathcal{B}}^{\mathsf{st2DH}}(\lambda) + \frac{Q_{ic}^2}{|\mathcal{E}_1|} + \frac{Q_{ic}^2}{|\mathcal{E}_2|} + 2^{-\Omega(\lambda)}$$
$$\leq 2\mathsf{Adv}_{\mathbb{G}, \mathcal{B}'}^{\mathsf{CDH}}(\lambda) + 2^{-\Omega(\lambda)}.$$

where Q_{ic} *denotes the maximum number of IC queries.*

Proof. The main task of the proof, is to construct a PPT simulator Sim, which has access to the ideal functionality $\mathcal{F}_{\mathsf{pake}}$ and interactions with the environment $\mathcal{Z}$, and simulates the real world 2DH-EKE protocol interactions among the adversary $\mathcal{A}$, parties, and the environment $\mathcal{Z}$. To this end, Sim needs to simulate honestly generated messages from real parties, respond adversarial messages approximately, and simulate ideal functions $(\mathsf{E}_1, \mathsf{D}_1), (\mathsf{E}_2, \mathsf{D}_2)$, and H, as shown in Fig. 3. The functionality $\mathcal{F}_{\mathsf{pake}}$ provides information to Sim through interfaces including TestPW, NewClient, NewServer, FreshKey, CopyKey, and CorruptKey, as defined in Fig. 1. Recall that Sim has no secret inputs (i.e., passwords).

The full description of the simulator Sim is given in Fig. 4. Let $\mathbf{Real}_{\mathcal{Z}, \mathcal{A}}$ be the real experiment where environment $\mathcal{Z}$ interacts with real parties and adversary $\mathcal{A}$, and $\mathbf{Ideal}_{\mathcal{Z}, \mathsf{Sim}}$ be the ideal experiment where $\mathcal{Z}$ interacts with simulator Sim. We prove that $|\Pr[\mathbf{Real}_{\mathcal{Z}, \mathcal{A}} \Rightarrow 1] - \Pr[\mathbf{Ideal}_{\mathcal{Z}, \mathsf{Sim}} \Rightarrow 1]|$ is negligible via a series of games **Game 0 − 5**, where **Game 0** is $\mathbf{Real}_{\mathcal{Z}, \mathcal{A}}$, **Game 5** is $\mathbf{Ideal}_{\mathcal{Z}, \mathsf{Sim}}$, and argue that the adjacent two games are indistinguishable from $\mathcal{Z}$'s prospective of view.

We consider the scenario of multi-users and multi instances. Let $\mathsf{C}^{(i)}$ (resp., $\mathsf{S}^{(j)}$) denote clients (resp., servers) with superscript (i) (resp., (j)) indexing different clients (resp., servers). Let $(\mathsf{C}^{(i)}, iid^{(i)})$ denote client instances of $\mathsf{C}^{(i)}$ with $iid^{(i)}$ indexing its different instances. Similarly, let $(\mathsf{S}^{(j)}, iid^{(j)})$ denote server instances of $\mathsf{S}^{(j)}$ with $iid^{(j)}$ indexing its different instances. For better presentation of the proof, we give some definitions as follows.

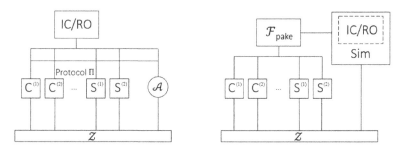

Fig. 3. The real world execution (left) and the ideal world execution (right).

Good/Bad Client Instance. We call a client instance $(C^{(i)}, iid^{(i)})$ a *good* (resp., *bad*) one, if the password pw used in this instance equals (resp., differs from) the correct password p̂w shared between $C^{(i)}$ and its intended partner $S^{(j)}$. Note that a bad client instance indicates the case that the client mistypes its password.

Linked Instances. We say that a server instance $(S^{(j)}, iid^{(j)})$ is linked to a client instance $(C^{(i)}, iid^{(i)})$ (no matter good or bad), if e_1 generated by $(C^{(i)}, iid^{(i)})$ is received by one instance $(S^{(j)}, iid^{(j)})$ of its intended partner $S^{(j)}$. Similarly, we say a client instance $(C^{(i)}, iid^{(i)})$ is linked to a server instance $(S^{(j)}, iid^{(j)})$, if e_2 generated by $(S^{(j)}, iid^{(j)})$ is received by one instance $(C^{(i)}, iid^{(i)})$ of its intended partner $C^{(i)}$. If the two instances are linked to each other, then they are called linked instances.

Game 0. This is the real experiment $\mathbf{Real}_{\mathcal{Z}, \mathcal{A}}$. In this experiment, $\mathcal{Z}$ initializes a password for each client-server pair, sees the interactions among clients, servers and adversary $\mathcal{A}$, and also obtains the corresponding session keys of protocol instances. Here $\mathcal{A}$ may implement attacks like view, modify, insert, or drop messages over the network. We have

$$\Pr[\mathbf{Real}_{\mathcal{Z}, \mathcal{A}} \Rightarrow 1] = \Pr[\mathbf{Game\ 0} \Rightarrow 1].$$

Game 1. (Add an ideal layout.) From this game on, we add an ideal layout Sim^2, which is only a toy construction in **Game 1**, but will be complete with games going on and arrive at the final Sim defined in Fig. 4. In **Game 1**, Sim still needs to take passwords as inputs. With the help of passwords, it perfectly simulates the executions in $\mathbf{Real}_{\mathcal{Z}, \mathcal{A}}$, except that the encryption of IC is simulated in a collision-free way. Meanwhile, Sim also necessarily keeps the exponent values of the decrypted group elements from D_1 and D_2. More precisely, it maintains lists $\mathcal{L}_{\mathsf{IC}_1}, \mathcal{L}_{\mathsf{IC}_2}, \mathcal{T}_{\mathsf{IC}_1}, \mathcal{T}_{\mathsf{IC}_2}, \mathcal{L}_{\mathsf{H}}, \mathcal{DL}$ (all initialized to be empty sets) and works as follows.

---

[2] The simulators in **Game 1 − 4** are semi-manufactured, which help us to analyze the differences between the real world and the ideal world step by step. For simplicity, we still use the same notation Sim in **Game 1 − 4**.

Sim maintains lists $\mathcal{L}_{\mathsf{IC}_1}, \mathcal{L}_{\mathsf{IC}_2}, \mathcal{T}_{\mathsf{IC}_1}, \mathcal{T}_{\mathsf{IC}_2}, \mathcal{L}_{\mathsf{H}}, \mathcal{T}, \mathcal{DL}$ (all initialized to be empty) in the simulation.

- $\mathcal{L}_{\mathsf{IC}_1}, \mathcal{L}_{\mathsf{IC}_2}, \mathcal{T}_{\mathsf{IC}_1}, \mathcal{T}_{\mathsf{IC}_2}$: store records w.r.t. ideal ciphers $(\mathsf{E}_1, \mathsf{D}_1)$ and $(\mathsf{E}_2, \mathsf{D}_2)$.
- $\mathcal{L}_{\mathsf{H}}$: store records w.r.t. random oracle H.
- $\mathcal{T}$: store messages sent by client/server instances.
- $\mathcal{DL}$: store discrete logarithms.

PAKE Sessions
on $(\mathsf{NewClient}, \mathsf{C}^{(i)}, iid^{(i)}, \mathsf{S}^{(j)}, b)$ from $\mathcal{F}_{\mathsf{pake}}$:

$\quad e_1 \xleftarrow{\$} \mathcal{E}_1 \backslash \mathcal{T}_{\mathsf{IC}_1}$, $\mathcal{T}_{\mathsf{IC}_1} := \mathcal{T}_{\mathsf{IC}_1} \cup \{e_1\}$, $\mathcal{T} := \mathcal{T} \cup \{(\mathsf{C}^{(i)}, iid^{(i)}, e_1)\}$, send e_1 from $\mathsf{C}^{(i)}$ to $\mathcal{A}$.
$\quad$ If $b = 1$: mark $(\mathsf{C}^{(i)}, iid^{(i)})$ as correct-pw. // client $\mathsf{C}^{(i)}$ correctly inputs the password
on $(\mathsf{NewServer}, \mathsf{S}^{(j)}, iid^{(j)}, \mathsf{C}^{(i)})$ from $\mathcal{F}_{\mathsf{pake}}$ and e_1 from $\mathcal{A}$ as a client message from $\mathsf{C}^{(i)}$ to $(\mathsf{S}^{(j)}, iid^{(j)})$:

$\quad e_2 \xleftarrow{\$} \mathcal{E}_2 \backslash \mathcal{T}_{\mathsf{IC}_2}$, $\mathcal{T}_{\mathsf{IC}_2} := \mathcal{T}_{\mathsf{IC}_2} \cup \{e_2\}$, $\mathcal{T} := \mathcal{T} \cup \{(\mathsf{S}^{(j)}, iid^{(j)}, e_2)\}$, send e_2 from $\mathsf{S}^{(j)}$ to $\mathcal{A}$.
$\quad sid := \mathsf{C}^{(i)} \| \mathsf{S}^{(j)} \| e_1 \| e_2$.
$\quad$ If $\exists (\mathsf{pw}', X_1 \| X_2, e_1, enc) \in \mathcal{L}_{\mathsf{IC}_1}$: ask $(\mathsf{TestPW}, \mathsf{S}^{(j)}, iid^{(j)}, \mathsf{pw}')$ to $\mathcal{F}_{\mathsf{pake}}$, and if $\mathcal{F}_{\mathsf{pake}}$ returns "correct guess":
$\quad\quad$ Let $X_1 \| X_2 \leftarrow \mathsf{D}_1(\mathsf{pw}', e_1)$ and $Y \leftarrow \mathsf{D}_2(\mathsf{pw}', e_2)$, retrieve item $(Y, y) \in \mathcal{DL}$, $Z_1 := X_1^y$, $Z_2 := X_2^y$, key $\leftarrow \mathsf{H}(sid, Z_1, Z_2, \mathsf{pw}')$, send $(\mathsf{CorruptKey}, \mathsf{S}^{(j)}, iid^{(j)}, sid, \mathsf{key})$ to $\mathcal{F}_{\mathsf{pake}}$.
$\quad$ In other cases: send $(\mathsf{FreshKey}, \mathsf{S}^{(j)}, iid^{(j)}, sid)$ to $\mathcal{F}_{\mathsf{pake}}$.
on e_2 from $\mathcal{A}$ as a server message from $\mathsf{S}^{(j)}$ to $(\mathsf{C}^{(i)}, iid^{(i)})$:

$\quad$ Retrieve $(\mathsf{C}^{(i)}, iid^{(i)}, e_1) \in \mathcal{T}$, $sid := \mathsf{C}^{(i)} \| \mathsf{S}^{(j)} \| e_1 \| e_2$.
$\quad$ If $(\mathsf{C}^{(i)}, iid^{(i)})$ is correct-pw, $\exists (\mathsf{S}^{(j)}, \cdot, e_2) \in \mathcal{T}$, and Sim has queried $(\mathsf{FreshKey}, \mathsf{S}^{(j)}, \cdot, sid)$:
$\quad\quad$ Send $(\mathsf{CopyKey}, \mathsf{C}^{(i)}, iid^{(i)}, sid)$ to $\mathcal{F}_{\mathsf{pake}}$.
$\quad$ If $\exists (\mathsf{pw}', Y, e_2, enc) \in \mathcal{L}_{\mathsf{IC}_2}$: ask $(\mathsf{TestPW}, \mathsf{C}^{(i)}, iid^{(i)}, \mathsf{pw}')$ to $\mathcal{F}_{\mathsf{pake}}$, and if $\mathcal{F}_{\mathsf{pake}}$ returns "correct guess":
$\quad\quad$ Let $X_1 \| X_2 \leftarrow \mathsf{D}_1(\mathsf{pw}', e_1)$ and $Y \leftarrow \mathsf{D}_2(\mathsf{pw}', e_2)$, retrieve item $(X_1 \| X_2, x_1 \| x_2) \in \mathcal{DL}$, $Z_1 := Y^{x_1}$, $Z_2 := Y^{x_2}$, key $\leftarrow \mathsf{H}(sid, Z_1, Z_2, \mathsf{pw}')$, send $(\mathsf{CorruptKey}, \mathsf{C}^{(i)}, iid^{(i)}, sid, \mathsf{key})$ to $\mathcal{F}_{\mathsf{pake}}$.
$\quad$ In other cases: send $(\mathsf{FreshKey}, \mathsf{C}^{(i)}, iid^{(i)}, sid)$ to $\mathcal{F}_{\mathsf{pake}}$.

On Ideal Ciphers and Random Oracles
on $\mathsf{E}_1(\mathsf{pw}, X_1 \| X_2)$ from $\mathcal{A}$:

$\quad$ If $\exists (\mathsf{pw}, X_1 \| X_2, e_1, \cdot) \in \mathcal{L}_{\mathsf{IC}_1}$: return e_1.
$\quad$ Otherwise: $e_1 \xleftarrow{\$} \mathcal{E}_1 \backslash \mathcal{T}_{\mathsf{IC}_1}$, $\mathcal{L}_{\mathsf{IC}_1} := \mathcal{L}_{\mathsf{IC}_1} \cup \{(\mathsf{pw}, X_1 \| X_2, e_1, enc)\}$, $\mathcal{T}_{\mathsf{IC}_1} := \mathcal{T}_{\mathsf{IC}_1} \cup \{e_1\}$, return e_1.
on $\mathsf{D}_1(\mathsf{pw}, e_1)$ from $\mathcal{A}$:

$\quad$ If $\exists (\mathsf{pw}, X_1 \| X_2, e_1, \cdot) \in \mathcal{L}_{\mathsf{IC}_1}$: return $X_1 \| X_2$.
$\quad$ Otherwise: $x_1, x_2 \xleftarrow{\$} \mathbb{Z}_q$, $X_1 := g^{x_1}$, $X_2 := g^{x_2}$, $\mathcal{L}_{\mathsf{IC}_1} := \mathcal{L}_{\mathsf{IC}_1} \cup \{(\mathsf{pw}, X_1 \| X_2, e_1, dec)\}$, $\mathcal{DL} := \mathcal{DL} \cup \{(X_1 \| X_2, x_1 \| x_2)\}$, return $X_1 \| X_2$.
on $\mathsf{E}_2(\mathsf{pw}, Y)$ from $\mathcal{A}$:

$\quad$ If $\exists (\mathsf{pw}, Y, e_2, \cdot) \in \mathcal{L}_{\mathsf{IC}_1}$: return e_2.
$\quad$ Otherwise: $e_2 \xleftarrow{\$} \mathcal{E}_2 \backslash \mathcal{T}_{\mathsf{IC}_2}$, $\mathcal{L}_{\mathsf{IC}_2} := \mathcal{L}_{\mathsf{IC}_2} \cup \{(\mathsf{pw}, Y, e_2, enc)\}$, $\mathcal{T}_{\mathsf{IC}_2} := \mathcal{T}_{\mathsf{IC}_2} \cup \{e_2\}$, return e_2.
on $\mathsf{D}_2(\mathsf{pw}, e_2)$ from $\mathcal{A}$:

$\quad$ If $\exists (\mathsf{pw}, Y, e_2, \cdot) \in \mathcal{L}_{\mathsf{IC}_2}$: return Y.
$\quad$ Otherwise: $y \xleftarrow{\$} \mathbb{Z}_q$, $Y := g^y$, $\mathcal{L}_{\mathsf{IC}_2} := \mathcal{L}_{\mathsf{IC}_2} \cup \{(\mathsf{pw}, Y, e_2, dec)\}$, $\mathcal{DL} := \mathcal{DL} \cup \{(Y, y)\}$, return Y.
on $\mathsf{H}(\mathsf{C}, \mathsf{S}, e_1, e_2, Z_1, Z_2, \mathsf{pw})$ from $\mathcal{A}$:

$\quad sid := \mathsf{C} \| \mathsf{S} \| e_1 \| e_2$.
$\quad$ If $\exists (sid, Z_1, Z_2, \mathsf{pw}, \mathsf{key}) \in \mathcal{L}_{\mathsf{H}}$ for some key: return key.
$\quad$ Otherwise: key $\xleftarrow{\$} \mathcal{K}$, record $(sid, Z_1, Z_2, \mathsf{pw}, \mathsf{key})$ in $\mathcal{L}_{\mathsf{H}}$, and return key.

Fig. 4. Simulator Sim for 2DH-EKE in the proof of Theorem 2.

- On $\mathsf{E}_1(\mathsf{pw}, X_1 \| X_2)$: If there exists $(\mathsf{pw}, X_1 \| X_2, e_1, \cdot) \in \mathcal{L}_{\mathsf{IC}_1}$, return e_1. Otherwise, $e_1 \xleftarrow{\$} \mathcal{E}_1 \backslash \mathcal{T}_{\mathsf{IC}_1}$, add $(\mathsf{pw}, X_1 \| X_2, e_1, enc)$ in $\mathcal{L}_{\mathsf{IC}_1}$, add e_1 in $\mathcal{T}_{\mathsf{IC}_1}$, and return e_1. Here "enc" indicates that the record is created in encryption.

- On $D_1(pw, e_1)$: If there exists $(pw, X_1 || X_2, e_1, \cdot) \in \mathcal{L}_{IC_1}$, return $X_1 || X_2$. Otherwise, $x_1, x_2 \xleftarrow{\$} \mathbb{Z}_q$, $X_1 := g^{x_1}$, $X_2 := g^{x_2}$, add $(pw, X_1 || X_2, e_1, dec)$ in $\mathcal{L}_{IC_1}$, add $(X_1 || X_2, x_1 || x_2)$ in $\mathcal{DL}$, and return $X_1 || X_2$. Here "dec" indicates that the record is created in decryption.
- On $E_2(pw, Y)$: If there exists $(pw, Y, e_2, \cdot) \in \mathcal{L}_{IC_2}$, return e_2. Otherwise, $e_2 \xleftarrow{\$} \mathcal{E}_2 \backslash \mathcal{T}_{IC_2}$, add (pw, Y, e_2, enc) in $\mathcal{L}_{IC_2}$, add e_2 in $\mathcal{T}_{IC_2}$, and return e_2.
- On $D_2(pw, e_2)$: If there exists $(pw, Y, e_2, \cdot) \in \mathcal{L}_{IC_2}$, return Y. Otherwise, $y \xleftarrow{\$} \mathbb{Z}_q$, $Y := g^y$, add (pw, Y, e_2, dec) in $\mathcal{L}_{IC_2}$, add (Y, y) in $\mathcal{DL}$, and return Y.
- On $H(C, S, e_1, e_2, Z_1, Z_2, pw)$: Let $sid := C || S || e_1 || e_2$. If there exists $(sid, Z_1, Z_2, pw, key) \in \mathcal{L}_H$, return key. Otherwise, key $\xleftarrow{\$} \mathcal{K}$, add (sid, Z_1, Z_2, pw, key) in $\mathcal{L}_H$ and return key.

According to the ideal functionality of ideal ciphers, we know that distinct inputs of E_1 (and E_2) collide to the same ciphertext with probability $1/|\mathcal{E}_1|$ (and $1/|\mathcal{E}_2|$). By union bound, we have

$$|\Pr[\textbf{Game 1} \Rightarrow 1] - \Pr[\textbf{Game 0} \Rightarrow 1]| \leq \frac{Q_{ic}^2}{|\mathcal{E}_1|} + \frac{Q_{ic}^2}{|\mathcal{E}_2|},$$

where Q_{ic} denotes the maximum number of IC queries.

Game 2. (Randomize keys for passively attacked instances.) In this game, for any session, if $\mathcal{A}$ only eavesdrops on the protocol instance, then Sim returns a random key instead of the real session key (the hash value of H). More precisely, **Game 2** is changed as follows.

(1) If server instance $(S^{(j)}, iid^{(j)})$ is linked to a good client instance $(C^{(i)}, iid^{(i)})$, then Sim generates a random session key for $(S^{(j)}, iid^{(j)})$.

(2) If a good client instance $(C^{(i)}, iid^{(i)})$ and a server instance $(S^{(j)}, iid^{(j)})$ are linked to each other, and $(S^{(j)}, iid^{(j)})$ has already been assigned with a random key, then Sim copies the key as the session key for $(C^{(i)}, iid^{(i)})$.

Define bad_1 as the event that there exists a passively attacked session w.r.t. a good client instance $(C^{(i)}, iid^{(i)})$ and a server instance $(S^{(j)}, iid^{(j)})$, and $\mathcal{A}$ ever asks a hash query on $H(C^{(i)}, S^{(j)}, e_1, e_2, \hat{Z}_1, \hat{Z}_2, \hat{pw})$ such that

$$(\hat{Z}_1, \hat{Z}_2) = 2DH(D_1(\hat{pw}, e_1), D_2(\hat{pw}, e_2)),$$

where e_1 and e_2 are the transcripts, and $\hat{pw}$ is the correct password pre-shared between them.

Obviously $\mathcal{A}$ will not detect the change in **Game 2** unless bad_1 happens. We show that if bad_1 happens, then we can construct an algorithm $\mathcal{B}_1$ to solve the strong 2DH problem. Due to the page limitation, we provide the reduction in our full version [34]. Consequently we have

$$|\Pr[\textbf{Game 2} \Rightarrow 1] - \Pr[\textbf{Game 1} \Rightarrow 1]| \leq \mathsf{Adv}_{G, \mathcal{B}_1}^{st2DH}(\lambda).$$

Game 3. (Randomize simulated messages.) In this game, Sim directly samples random messages to simulate the transcripts e_1 and e_2, and postpones the usage of ideal ciphers (E_1, D_1) and (E_2, D_2) until necessary (like the generation of session keys). More precisely, **Game 3** is now simulated by Sim as follows.

- For the simulation of a client instance $(C^{(i)}, iid^{(i)})$ generating the first message e_1, Sim chooses a random $e_1 \xleftarrow{\$} \mathcal{E}_1 \backslash \mathcal{T}_{\mathsf{IC}_1}$ (without any encryption) as the output message and adds e_1 in $\mathcal{T}_{\mathsf{IC}_1}$.
- For the simulation of a server instance $(S^{(j)}, iid^{(j)})$ generating the second message e_2 and the session key, Sim chooses a random $e_2 \xleftarrow{\$} \mathcal{E}_2 \backslash \mathcal{T}_{\mathsf{IC}_2}$ (without any encryption) as the output message and adds e_2 in $\mathcal{T}_{\mathsf{IC}_2}$. Let e_1 be the message that $S^{(j)}$ has received .
  - If $(S^{(j)}, iid^{(j)})$ is linked to some good client instance, then the session key is set to be random, just like **Game 2**.
  - If $(S^{(j)}, iid^{(j)})$ is not linked to any good client instance, then Sim invokes $Y \leftarrow D_2(\hat{\mathsf{pw}}, e_2)$ by sampling $y \xleftarrow{\$} \mathbb{Z}_q$, computing $Y := g^y$ and adding $(\hat{\mathsf{pw}}, Y, e_2, dec)$ to $\mathcal{L}_{\mathsf{IC}_2}$. The session key is generated by $\mathsf{key} \leftarrow H(C^{(i)}, S^{(j)}, e_1, e_2, 2\mathsf{DH}(D_1(\hat{\mathsf{pw}}, e_1), Y), \hat{\mathsf{pw}})$ with the knowledge of y, where $C^{(i)}$ is the intended partner of $(S^{(j)}, iid^{(j)})$ and $\hat{\mathsf{pw}}$ is the (correct) password. In this way, the session key is the same hash value as that in **Game 2**.
- For the simulation of a client instance $(C^{(i)}, iid^{(i)})$ that sends e_1 out and receives e_2, if $(C^{(i)}, iid^{(i)})$ is bad or e_2 was adversarially generated, then Sim invokes $(X_1, X_2) \leftarrow D_1(\mathsf{pw}, e_1)$ by sampling $x_1, x_1, \xleftarrow{\$} \mathbb{Z}_q$, computing $X_1 := g^{x_1}$, $X_2 := g^{x_2}$ and adding $(\mathsf{pw}, X_1 \| X_2, e_1, dec)$ to $\mathcal{L}_{\mathsf{IC}_1}$. The session key is generated as $\mathsf{key} \leftarrow H(C^{(i)}, S^{(j)}, e_1, e_2, 2\mathsf{DH}(X_1, X_2, D_2(\mathsf{pw}, e_2)), \mathsf{pw})$ with the knowledge of x_1, x_2, where $S^{(j)}$ is the intended partner of $(C^{(i)}, iid^{(i)})$ and pw is the (possible incorrect) password used in this instance. In this way, the session key is the same hash value as that in **Game 2**.

Recall that in **Game 2**, the transcripts e_1 and e_2 are randomly distributed via the simulation of E_1 and E_2, so they have the same distribution as that in **Game 3**. As shown above, the generation of all session keys in **Game 3** is also the same as that in **Game 2**. Therefore, we have

$$\Pr[\textbf{Game 3} \Rightarrow 1] = \Pr[\textbf{Game 2} \Rightarrow 1].$$

Game 4. (Randomize keys for actively attacked server/client instances in case of incorrect password guesses.) In **Game 4**, the simulator further changes the session key generation of server/client instances.

For any server instance $(S^{(j)}, iid^{(j)})$ that receives e_1, let $C^{(i)}$ be its intended partner and $\mathsf{pw}(= \hat{\mathsf{pw}})$ be the (correct) password used in this instance. Sim generates the session key for it in the following way.

Case (S.1). If $(S^{(j)}, iid^{(j)})$ is linked to some good client instance $(C^{(i)}, iid^{(i)})$, then Sim generates a random key for $(S^{(j)}, iid^{(j)})$, just as that in **Game 3**.

Case (S.2). $(\mathsf{S}^{(j)}, iid^{(j)})$ is not linked to any good client instance $(\mathsf{C}^{(i)}, iid^{(i)})$. We further divide it into the following two subcases.

> **Case (S.2.1).** If there exists a record $(\mathsf{pw}' = \mathsf{pw}, X_1 \| X_2, e_1, enc) \in \mathcal{L}_{\mathsf{IC}_1}$, then Sim sets key $\leftarrow \mathsf{H}(\mathsf{C}^{(i)}, \mathsf{S}^{(j)}, e_1, e_2, 2\mathsf{DH}(X_1, X_2, \mathsf{D}_2(\mathsf{pw}, e_2)), \mathsf{pw})$ as the session key, just like that in **Game 3**. Note that there exists at most one such record in $\mathcal{L}_{\mathsf{IC}_1}$, since E_1 is simulated in a collision-free way.
>
> **Case (S.2.2).** If there does not exist a record $(\mathsf{pw}' = \mathsf{pw}, X_1 \| X_2, e_1, enc) \in \mathcal{L}_{\mathsf{IC}_1}$, then Sim generates a random key for $(\mathsf{S}^{(j)}, iid^{(j)})$.

For any client instance $(\mathsf{C}^{(i)}, iid^{(i)})$ that sends e_1 out and receives e_2, let $\mathsf{S}^{(j)}$ be the intended partner and pw be the (possibly incorrect) password used in this instance. Sim generates the session key for it in the following way.

Case (C.1). If $(\mathsf{C}^{(i)}, iid^{(i)})$ and some server instance $(\mathsf{S}^{(j)}, iid^{(j)})$ are linked to each other, and $(\mathsf{C}^{(i)}, iid^{(i)})$ is good, then Sim assigns the same random session key of $(\mathsf{S}^{(j)}, iid^{(j)})$ to $(\mathsf{C}^{(i)}, iid^{(i)})$, just as that in **Game 3**.

Case (C.2). If $(\mathsf{C}^{(i)}, iid^{(i)})$ is not linked to any server instance, or $(\mathsf{C}^{(i)}, iid^{(i)})$ is bad. We further divide it into the following two subcases.

> **Case (C.2.1).** If there exists a record $(\mathsf{pw}' = \mathsf{pw}, Y, e_2, enc) \in \mathcal{L}_{\mathsf{IC}_2}$, then Sim sets key $\leftarrow \mathsf{H}(\mathsf{C}^{(i)}, \mathsf{S}^{(j)}, e_1, e_2, 2\mathsf{DH}(\mathsf{D}_1(\mathsf{pw}, e_1), Y), \mathsf{pw})$ as the session key, just like that in **Game 3**. Note that there exists at most one such record in $\mathcal{L}_{\mathsf{IC}_2}$, since E_2 is simulated in a collision-free way.
>
> **Case (C.2.2).** If there does not exist a record $(\mathsf{pw}' = \mathsf{pw}, Y, e_2, enc) \in \mathcal{L}_{\mathsf{IC}_2}$, then Sim generates a random key for $(\mathsf{C}^{(i)}, iid^{(i)})$.

Note that the differences between **Game 3** and **Game 4** lie in Cases (S.2.2) and (C.2.2), since in **Game 3** the session keys are the hash values (rather than random elements) in Cases (S.2.2) and (C.2.2.).

We define bad_2 as the event that there exists a server instance $(\mathsf{S}^{(j)}, iid^{(j)})$ in Case (S.2.2), or a client instance $(\mathsf{C}^{(i)}, iid^{(i)})$ in Case (C.2.2), and $\mathcal{A}$ ever asks a hash query on $\mathsf{H}(\mathsf{C}^{(i)}, \mathsf{S}^{(j)}, e_1, e_2, \hat{Z}_1, \hat{Z}_2, \mathsf{pw})$ such that

$$(\hat{Z}_1, \hat{Z}_2) = 2\mathsf{DH}(\mathsf{D}_1(\mathsf{pw}, e_1), \mathsf{D}_2(\mathsf{pw}, e_2)),$$

where e_1 and e_2 are the transcripts w.r.t. $(\mathsf{S}^{(j)}, iid^{(j)})$ or $(\mathsf{C}^{(i)}, iid^{(i)})$, and pw is the password used in this instance.

Obviously **Game 4** and **Game 3** are the same unless bad_2 happens. We show that if bad_2 happens, then we can construct a reduction algorithm $\mathcal{B}_2$ to solve the strong 2DH problem. Due to the page limitation, we provide the reduction in our full version [34].

$$|\Pr[\textbf{Game 4} \Rightarrow 1] - \Pr[\textbf{Game 3} \Rightarrow 1]| \leq \mathsf{Adv}_{\mathbb{G}, \mathcal{B}_2}^{\mathsf{st2DH}}(\lambda) + 2^{-\Omega(\lambda)}.$$

Now in **Game 4**, Sim does not use pw any more, except the case of session key generation when the adversary $\mathcal{A}$ correctly guesses the password pw and actively engages into a client/server instance, i.e., there exists a record

$(\mathsf{pw}, X_1 \| X_2, e_1, enc) \in \mathcal{L}_{\mathsf{IC}_1}$ or $(\mathsf{pw}, Y, e_2, enc) \in \mathcal{L}_{\mathsf{IC}_2}$. Now we are ready to introduce the complete simulator in Fig. 4, which helps us stepping to the ideal experiment $\mathbf{Ideal}_{\mathcal{Z}, \mathsf{Sim}}$.

Game 5. (Use $\mathcal{F}_{\mathsf{pake}}$ interfaces.) In the final game we introduce the ideal functionality $\mathcal{F}_{\mathsf{pake}}$. By using interfaces to interact with $\mathcal{F}_{\mathsf{pake}}$, the simulator Sim can perfectly simulates **Game 4** as follows.

- It simulates $(\mathsf{E}_1, \mathsf{D}_1), (\mathsf{E}_2, \mathsf{D}_2)$, and H as described in **Game 4**.
- When Sim receives $(\mathsf{NewClient}, \mathsf{C}^{(i)}, iid^{(i)}, \mathsf{S}^{(j)}, b)$ from $\mathcal{F}_{\mathsf{pake}}$, it marks this instance as correct-pw if $b = 1$, indicating that $\mathsf{C}^{(i)}$ inputs the correct password in this client instance. Meanwhile, Sim chooses a random $e_1 \xleftarrow{\$} \mathcal{E}_1 \backslash \mathcal{T}_{\mathsf{IC}_1}$ as the output message and adds e_1 in $\mathcal{T}_{\mathsf{IC}_1}$.
- When server instance $(\mathsf{S}^{(j)}, iid^{(j)})$ receives e_1 and $(\mathsf{NewServer}, \mathsf{S}^{(j)}, iid^{(j)}, \mathsf{C}^{(i)})$ from $\mathcal{F}_{\mathsf{pake}}$, Sim chooses a random $e_2 \xleftarrow{\$} \mathcal{E}_2 \backslash \mathcal{T}_{\mathsf{IC}_2}$ as the output message and adds e_2 in $\mathcal{T}_{\mathsf{IC}_2}$. Meanwhile, it sets the session identity to be $sid := \mathsf{C}^{(i)} \| \mathsf{S}^{(j)} \| e_1 \| e_2$ and checks whether $(\mathsf{S}^{(j)}, iid^{(j)})$ is linked to a good client instance $(\mathsf{C}^{(i)}, iid^{(i)})$.
  - If it is the case, Sim allocates a random key to $(\mathsf{S}^{(j)}, iid^{(j)})$ by directly asking a query $(\mathsf{FreshKey}, \mathsf{S}^{(j)}, iid^{(j)}, sid)$ to $\mathcal{F}_{\mathsf{pake}}$. According to the definition of FreshKey interface, this performs identically as that in **Game 4**.
  - Otherwise, Sim checks whether there exists a record $(\mathsf{pw}', \cdot, e_1, enc) \in \mathcal{L}_{\mathsf{IC}_1}$. If such a record exists, Sim issues a TestPW query $(\mathsf{TestPW}, \mathsf{S}^{(j)}, iid^{(j)}, \mathsf{pw}')$ to ask $\mathcal{F}_{\mathsf{pake}}$ whether $\mathsf{pw}' = \mathsf{pw}$, where pw is the (correct) password used in $(\mathsf{S}^{(j)}, iid^{(j)})$.
    * If the record exists and $\mathcal{F}_{\mathsf{pake}}$ returns "correct guess" (i.e., $\mathsf{pw}' = \mathsf{pw}$), then Sim computes the session key as $\mathsf{key} \leftarrow \mathsf{H}(sid, 2\mathsf{DH}(\mathsf{D}_1(\mathsf{pw}, e_1), \mathsf{D}_2(\mathsf{pw}, e_2)), \mathsf{pw})$, and allocates sid and key to $(\mathsf{S}^{(j)}, iid^{(j)})$ via a query $(\mathsf{CorruptKey}, \mathsf{S}^{(j)}, iid^{(j)}, sid, \mathsf{key})$ to $\mathcal{F}_{\mathsf{pake}}$. According to the definition of CorruptKey interface, the environment $\mathcal{Z}$ has the same view as that in **Game 4**.
    * If the record does not exist, or $\mathcal{F}_{\mathsf{pake}}$ returns "wrong guess" (i.e., $\mathsf{pw}' \neq \mathsf{pw}$), then Sim allocates sid and a random key to $(\mathsf{S}^{(j)}, iid^{(j)})$ by asking a query $(\mathsf{FreshKey}, \mathsf{S}^{(j)}, iid^{(j)}, sid)$ to $\mathcal{F}_{\mathsf{pake}}$. According to the definition of FreshKey, this results in the same view to the environment $\mathcal{Z}$ as that in **Game 4**.
- When client instance $(\mathsf{C}^{(i)}, iid^{(i)})$ receives e_2, let e_1 be the message sent out and $\mathsf{S}^{(j)}$ be its intended partner. Sim sets the session identity to be $sid := \mathsf{C}^{(i)} \| \mathsf{S}^{(j)} \| e_1 \| e_2$ and checks whether $(\mathsf{C}^{(i)}, iid^{(i)})$ and a server instance $(\mathsf{S}^{(j)}, iid^{(j)})$ are linked to each other, and $(\mathsf{C}^{(i)}, iid^{(i)})$ is marked as correct-pw.
  - If it is the case, then sid and a random key key must have been assigned to $(\mathsf{S}^{(j)}, iid^{(j)})$. Sim assigns the same sid and key to $(\mathsf{C}^{(i)}, iid^{(i)})$ via a query $(\mathsf{CopyKey}, \mathsf{C}^{(i)}, iid^{(i)}, sid)$ to $\mathcal{F}_{\mathsf{pake}}$. According to the definition of CopyKey, this performs identically as that in **Game 4**.

- Otherwise, Sim retrieves the record $(\mathsf{pw}', Y, e_2, enc) \in \mathcal{L}_{\mathsf{IC}_2}$ if it exists, and uses the TestPW interface provided by $\mathcal{F}_{\mathsf{pake}}$ to check whether $\mathsf{pw}' = \mathsf{pw}$, where pw is the (possible incorrect) password used in $(\mathsf{C}^{(i)}, iid^{(i)})$.

  • If the record exists and $\mathcal{F}_{\mathsf{pake}}$ returns "correct guess" (i.e., $\mathsf{pw}' = \mathsf{pw}$), then Sim computes the session key as $\mathsf{key} \leftarrow \mathsf{H}(sid, 2\mathsf{DH}(\mathsf{D}_1(\mathsf{pw}, e_1), \mathsf{D}_2(\mathsf{pw}, e_2)), \mathsf{pw})$, and allocates sid and key to $(\mathsf{C}^{(i)}, iid^{(i)})$ via a query $(\mathsf{CorruptKey}, \mathsf{C}^{(i)}, iid^{(i)}, sid, \mathsf{key})$ to $\mathcal{F}_{\mathsf{pake}}$. According to the definition of CorruptKey interface, the environment $\mathcal{Z}$ has the same view as that in **Game 4**.

  • If the record does not exist, or $\mathcal{F}_{\mathsf{pake}}$ returns "wrong guess" (i.e., $\mathsf{pw}' \neq \mathsf{pw}$), then Sim allocates sid and a random key to $(\mathsf{C}^{(i)}, iid^{(i)})$ by asking a query $(\mathsf{FreshKey}, \mathsf{C}^{(i)}, iid^{(i)}, sid)$ to $\mathcal{F}_{\mathsf{pake}}$. According to the definition of FreshKey, this results in the same view to the environment $\mathcal{Z}$ as that in **Game 4**.

The full description of Sim is shown in Fig. 4. From the analysis above we know **Game 4** and **Game 5** are conceptually identical. Furthermore, one can easily see that **Game 5** is just the experiment in the ideal world. Therefore, we have

$$\mathsf{Ideal}_{\mathcal{Z}, \mathsf{Sim}} = \textbf{Game 5} = \textbf{Game 4}.$$

Theorem 2 follows immediately from **Game 0** to **Game 5**, and Theorem 1.

4 Asymmetric PAKE with Optimal Tightness in the UC Framework

4.1 UC Framework for aPAKE

In aPAKE, the server stores a password file (usually a hash of the password) rather than the password in plain. This somehow protects the password even if the server is compromised. If the server's password file is obtained by the adversary due to compromise, the adversary can implement offline attacks to guess the password, or impersonate the server to run the aPAKE protocol with the client. However, it is still infeasible for the adversary to impersonate the client to log in the server, if it fails to find the correct password and actively engage into one protocol execution.

To capture the attacks due to server compromise[3] in the asymmetric setting, the ideal functionality $\mathcal{F}_{\mathsf{apake}}$ is augmented with more interfaces like StealPWFile and OfflineTestPW, compared with $\mathcal{F}_{\mathsf{pake}}$. Meanwhile, the CorruptKey interface also takes into consideration the case of server compromise. Furthermore, we add a new interface Abort to deal with the case that the explicit authentication fails. The augments of $\mathcal{F}_{\mathsf{apake}}$ are shown below.

---

[3] In the real world, the server continues to faithfully execute protocols as normal after a compromise of password files.

Functionality $\mathcal{F}_{\mathsf{apake}}$

The functionality $\mathcal{F}_{\mathsf{apake}}$ is parameterized by a security parameter λ. It interacts with an adversary Sim and a set of parties (clients and servers) via the following queries:

Password Storage

  Upon receiving a query $(\mathsf{StorePWFile}, \mathsf{C}^{(i)}, \mathsf{S}^{(j)}, \mathsf{p\hat{w}})$ **from a client** $\mathsf{C}^{(i)}$ **or a server** $\mathsf{S}^{(j)}$:

    If there exists a record $\langle \mathsf{file}, \mathsf{C}^{(i)}, \mathsf{S}^{(j)}, \cdot \rangle$, ignore this query.

    Otherwise, record $\langle \mathsf{file}, \mathsf{C}^{(i)}, \mathsf{S}^{(j)}, \mathsf{p\hat{w}} \rangle$, mark it as fresh, and send $(\mathsf{StorePWFile}, \mathsf{C}^{(i)}, \mathsf{S}^{(j)})$ to Sim.

Stealing Password File

  Upon receiving a query $(\mathsf{StealPWFile}, \mathsf{C}^{(i)}, \mathsf{S}^{(j)})$ **from server** $\mathsf{S}^{(j)}$:

    Mark the password data record $\langle \mathsf{file}, \mathsf{C}^{(i)}, \mathsf{S}^{(j)}, \mathsf{p\hat{w}} \rangle$ as compromised, and send $(\mathsf{StealPWFile}, \mathsf{C}^{(i)}, \mathsf{S}^{(j)})$ to Sim.

    If there is a record $\langle \mathsf{offline}, \mathsf{C}^{(i)}, \mathsf{S}^{(j)}, \mathsf{p\hat{w}} \rangle$, then send $\mathsf{p\hat{w}}$ to Sim.

  Upon receiving a query $(\mathsf{OfflineTestPW}, \mathsf{C}^{(i)}, \mathsf{S}^{(j)}, \mathsf{pw}')$ **from Sim**:

    If there exists a record $\langle \mathsf{file}, \mathsf{C}^{(i)}, \mathsf{S}^{(j)}, \mathsf{p\hat{w}} \rangle$ marked compromised, check whether $\mathsf{pw}' = \mathsf{p\hat{w}}$: return "correct guess" if yes, and "wrong guess" otherwise.

    Else, store $\langle \mathsf{offline}, \mathsf{C}^{(i)}, \mathsf{S}^{(j)}, \mathsf{pw}' \rangle$.

Sessions

  Upon receiving a query $(\mathsf{NewClient}, iid^{(i)}, \mathsf{S}^{(j)}, \mathsf{pw})$ **from a client** $\mathsf{C}^{(i)}$:

    Retrieve the record $\langle \mathsf{file}, \mathsf{C}^{(i)}, \mathsf{S}^{(j)}, \mathsf{p\hat{w}} \rangle$. Send $(\mathsf{NewClient}, \mathsf{C}^{(i)}, iid^{(i)}, \mathsf{S}^{(j)}, \mathsf{pw} = \mathsf{p\hat{w}}?)$ to Sim. Record $(\mathsf{C}^{(i)}, iid^{(i)}, \mathsf{S}^{(j)}, \mathsf{pw})$ and mark it as fresh.

    In this case, $\mathsf{S}^{(j)}$ is called the intended partner of $(\mathsf{C}^{(i)}, iid^{(i)})$.

  Upon receiving a query $(\mathsf{NewServer}, iid^{(j)}, \mathsf{C}^{(i)})$ **from a server** $\mathsf{S}^{(j)}$:

    Retrieve the record $\langle \mathsf{file}, \mathsf{C}^{(i)}, \mathsf{S}^{(j)}, \mathsf{p\hat{w}} \rangle$. Send $(\mathsf{NewServer}, \mathsf{S}^{(j)}, iid^{(j)}, \mathsf{C}^{(i)})$ to Sim. Set $\mathsf{pw} = \mathsf{p\hat{w}}$, record $(\mathsf{S}^{(j)}, iid^{(j)}, \mathsf{C}^{(i)}, \mathsf{pw})$ and mark it as fresh.

    In this case, $\mathsf{C}^{(i)}$ is called the intended partner of $(\mathsf{S}^{(j)}, iid^{(j)})$.

  Two instances $(\mathsf{C}^{(i)}, iid^{(i)})$ and $(\mathsf{S}^{(j)}, iid^{(j)})$ are said to be partnered, if there are two fresh records $(\mathsf{C}^{(i)}, iid^{(i)}, \mathsf{S}^{(j)}, \mathsf{pw})$ and $(\mathsf{S}^{(j)}, iid^{(j)}, \mathsf{C}^{(i)}, \mathsf{pw})$ sharing the same pw.

Active Session Attacks

  Upon receiving a query $(\mathsf{TestPW}, P, iid, \mathsf{pw}')$ **from Sim**:

    If there is a fresh record $(P, iid, \cdot, \mathsf{pw})$:

      – If $\mathsf{pw}' = \mathsf{pw}$, mark the record compromised and reply to Sim with "correct guess".

      – If $\mathsf{pw}' \neq \mathsf{pw}$, mark the record interrupted and replay with "wrong guess".

Key Generation

  Upon receiving a query $(\mathsf{FreshKey}, P, iid, sid)$ **from Sim**:

    If 1) there is a fresh or interrupted record (P, iid, Q, pw); and 2) sid has never been assigned to P's any other instance (P, iid'):

      Pick a new random key k, mark the record (P, iid, Q, pw) as completed, assign it with sid, send (iid, sid, k) to P, and record (P, Q, sid, k).

  Upon receiving a query $(\mathsf{CopyKey}, P, iid, sid)$ **from Sim**:

    If 1) there is a fresh record (P, iid, Q, pw) and a completed record $(Q, iid^*, P, \mathsf{pw})$ s.t. (P, iid) and (Q, iid^*) are partnered; and 2) sid has never been assigned to P's any other instance (P, iid'); and 3) there is a unique (Q, iid^*) that has been assigned with sid:

      Retrieve the record (Q, P, sid, k), mark the record (P, iid, Q, pw) as completed, assign it with sid, and send (iid, sid, k) to P.

  Upon receiving a query $(\mathsf{CorruptKey}, P, iid, sid, k)$ **from Sim**:

    If 1) sid has never been assigned to some record (P, iid'); and 2) either: 2.1) there is a compromised record (P, iid, Q, pw), or 2.2) there is a fresh record (P, iid, Q, pw) with P a client, and there is a compromised record $\langle \mathsf{file}, P, Q, \mathsf{p\hat{w}} \rangle$ such that $\mathsf{pw} = \mathsf{p\hat{w}}$:

      Mark the record $(P, iid, \cdot, \mathsf{pw})$ as completed, assign it with sid, and send (iid, sid, k) to P.

  Upon receiving a query (Abort, P, iid) **from Sim**:

    If P is a server: mark the record $(P, iid, \cdot, \mathsf{pw})$ as completed, and send $(iid, \perp)$ to P.

Fig. 5. The aPAKE functionality $\mathcal{F}_{\mathsf{apake}}$ [41].

– The StealPWFile interface. The server may send a StealPWFile query to $\mathcal{F}_{\mathsf{apake}}$, indicating that the password file stored in it has been compromised by the adversary. Then $\mathcal{F}_{\mathsf{apake}}$ will pass this query message to the simulator Sim (so that Sim "simulates" a password file for the adversary).

– The OfflineTestPW interface. Sim issues OfflineTestPW together with a password guess, and $\mathcal{F}_{\mathsf{apake}}$ tests whether the guess is the pre-image of the password file and returns the test result to Sim.[4]

– The CorruptKey interface. Beyond the cases considered in $\mathcal{F}_{\mathsf{pake}}$, if the password file has been compromised by the adversary, Sim also assigns a key to a client instance by issuing a CorruptKey query[5].

– The Abort interface. If the explicit authentication from the client to the server fails, Sim assigns the session key $k = \perp$ to the server instance via an Abort query, indicating that the execution of aPAKE fails.

The functionality of $\mathcal{F}_{\mathsf{apake}}$ is shown in Fig. 5. We mainly follow the definition by Shoup in [41], which is a modified version of [19] by Gentry et al. and [25] by Hesse.

Remark 6. $\underline{P}$erfect $\underline{F}$orward $\underline{S}$ecurity [22] (PFS, a.k.a. perfect forward secrecy) requires that once a party has been corrupted at some moment, the session keys completed before the corruption remain hidden from the adversary. An aPAKE protocol with implicit authentication cannot achieve PFS due to the following reason. For the adversary who steals the password file and actively engages into one session as the client, it can always stage a (successful) offline dictionary attack, to find out the correct password, and hence obtain the "completed" session key. A canonical approach to PFS is to add an explicit authentication from the client to the server. And the server will output a specific key $k = \perp$ to terminate the session, once the authentication fails.

4.2   The 2DH-aEKE Protocol

In this section, we provide an asymmetric variant of 2DH-EKE, named 2DH-aEKE. The 2DH-aEKE protocol meets the optimal reduction loss factor $L = N$, the maximum number of client-server pairs. A formal proof for the optimality is shown in Sect. 5.

The 2DH-aEKE protocol is shown in Fig. 6. Here $(\mathsf{E}_1, \mathsf{D}_1)$ is a symmetric encryption with key space $\mathcal{H}$, plaintext space $\mathbb{G}^2$ and ciphertext space $\mathcal{E}_1$, and $(\mathsf{E}_2, \mathsf{D}_2)$ is a symmetric encryption with key space $\mathcal{H}$, plaintext space $\mathbb{G}$ and ciphertext space $\mathcal{E}_2$. Two hash functions are defined as: $\mathsf{H} : \{0,1\}^* \mapsto \mathcal{K}$ with $\mathcal{K}$ the space of session keys, and $\mathsf{H}_0 : \{0,1\}^* \times \mathcal{PW} \mapsto \mathcal{H} \times \mathbb{Z}_q^2$. And C, S are identities of Client and Server.

---

[4] Such definitions seem reasonable only in a hybrid world where random oracles or ideal ciphers exist. See further discussions in [21,25,41].

[5] More precisely, a (corrupted) session key is assigned via CorruptKey, if $\langle \mathsf{file}, P, Q, \hat{pw} \rangle$ is compromised and the password pw used in the client instance is correct. If pw is incorrect, then Sim would assign a random key for this client instance via FreshKey.

In the registration stage, Server stores the password file $\mathsf{S.file}[\mathsf{C}] := (\mathsf{h}, V_1, V_2)$, where $(\mathsf{h}, v_1, v_2) \leftarrow \mathsf{H}_0(\mathsf{C}, \mathsf{S}, \mathsf{pw})$, and $V_1 := g^{v_1}$, $V_2 := g^{v_2}$.

Public Parameter: $(\mathbb{G}, g, q)$, $(\mathsf{E}_1, \mathsf{D}_1)$, $(\mathsf{E}_2, \mathsf{D}_2)$, H, H_0

Client C (pw)		Server S (h, V_1, V_2)
$(\mathsf{h}, v_1, v_2) \leftarrow \mathsf{H}_0(\mathsf{C}, \mathsf{S}, \mathsf{pw})$ $x_1, x_2 \xleftarrow{\$} \mathbb{Z}_q, X_1 := g^{x_1}, X_2 := g^{x_2}$ $e_1 \leftarrow \mathsf{E}_1(\mathsf{h}, X_1 \Vert X_2)$	$\xrightarrow{e_1}$	
	$\xleftarrow{e_2}$	$y \xleftarrow{\$} \mathbb{Z}_q, Y := g^y$ $e_2 \leftarrow \mathsf{E}_2(\mathsf{h}, Y)$
$Y \leftarrow \mathsf{D}_2(\mathsf{h}, e_2)$ $sid := \mathsf{C} \Vert \mathsf{S} \Vert e_1 \Vert e_2$ $(\mathsf{key}_C, \sigma_C) \leftarrow \mathsf{H}(sid, Y^{x_1}, Y^{x_2}, Y^{v_1}, Y^{v_2}, \mathsf{h})$	$\xrightarrow{\sigma_C}$	$X_1 \Vert X_2 \leftarrow \mathsf{D}_1(\mathsf{h}, e_1)$ $sid := \mathsf{C} \Vert \mathsf{S} \Vert e_1 \Vert e_2$ $(\mathsf{key}_S, \sigma_S) \leftarrow \mathsf{H}(sid, X_1^y, X_2^y, V_1^y, V_2^y, \mathsf{h})$
Output key_C		If $\sigma_S = \sigma_C$: output key_S Otherwise : output $\perp$

Fig. 6. The 2DH-aEKE protocol.

4.3 Security Analysis

Theorem 3 (Security of 2DH-aEKE). *If the st2DH assumption (equivalently, the CDH assumption) holds in* $\mathbb{G}$, $(\mathsf{E}_1, \mathsf{D}_1), (\mathsf{E}_2, \mathsf{D}_2)$ *work as ideal ciphers, and* H, H_0 *work as random oracles, then the 2DH-aEKE protocol in Fig. 6 securely emulates* $\mathcal{F}_{\mathsf{apake}}$. *More precisely, for any PPT environment* $\mathcal{Z}$ *and real world adversary* $\mathcal{A}$ *which has access to ideal ciphers* $(\mathsf{E}_1, \mathsf{D}_1), (\mathsf{E}_2, \mathsf{D}_2)$ *and random oracles* H, H_0, *there exist a PPT simulator* Sim, *which has access to the ideal functionality* $\mathcal{F}_{\mathsf{apake}}$, *and algorithms* $\mathcal{B}, \mathcal{B}'$, *s.t. that advantage of* $\mathcal{Z}$ *in distinguishing the real world running with* $\mathcal{A}$ *and the ideal world running with* Sim *is bounded by*

$$\begin{aligned}\mathsf{Adv}_{\mathsf{2DH\text{-}aEKE},\mathcal{Z}}(\lambda) \leq& (N+3) \cdot \mathsf{Adv}_{\mathbb{G},\mathcal{B}}^{\mathsf{st2DH}}(\lambda) + \frac{Q_{ic}^2}{|\mathcal{E}_1|} + \frac{Q_{ic}^2}{|\mathcal{E}_2|} + \frac{Q_{\mathsf{H}_0}^2}{|\mathcal{H}|} + 2^{-\Omega(\lambda)} \\ \leq& (N+3) \cdot \mathsf{Adv}_{\mathbb{G},\mathcal{B}'}^{\mathsf{CDH}}(\lambda) + 2^{-\Omega(\lambda)},\end{aligned}$$

where Q_{ic} *and* Q_{H_0} *denote the maximum numbers of IC and* H_0 *queries, and* N *denotes the number of client-server pairs.*

The proof is shown in the full version [34].

Remark 7 (On the optimal tightness of 2DH-aEKE). As we can see, the security reduction in Theorem 3 has a loss factor of N. Actually, such a loose factor is unavoidable in the scenario of aPAKE, since the correct password is committed by the hash value to the adversary in the form of password file, and it can be adaptively revealed via offline dictionary attacks (i.e., password hash queries). In Sect. 5 we give a formal proof to show that, the loss factor $L = N$ is essentially optimal—at least for "simple" reductions.

Nevertheless, the optimal factor N is superior to a loose factor $(Q_h \cdot N \cdot \theta)$ (the maximum numbers of hash queries, client-server pairs, and protocol executions per client-server pair, respectively). Usually there are thousands of protocol executions per user (especially for the server), and $Q_h N \theta \gg N$ in general.

5 Optimal Reduction Loss in aPAKE

In this section we show that the security loss of $L = N$ in Theorem 3 is essentially optimal, at least for "simple" reductions. Here "simple" means that the reduction algorithm runs a single copy of the adversary only once. Almost all known security reductions (for PAKE and aPAKE) are either of this type, or use the forking lemma (e.g., KHAPE-HMQV [21]).

We consider the class of DH-type aPAKE protocols defined as follows.

Definition 3 (DH-Type aPAKE Protocol). *An asymmetric PAKE protocol Π is DH-type, if it satisfies the following properties.*

1. *In the phase of password storage (registration), the server stores a password file* file *based on the pre-shared password* pw *(and some salts, perhaps).*
2. *In an execution of Π, the honest client first obtains a secret input* si *from the identities of the two parties, the password* pw *(and the first message by the server, perhaps). In this case, we say* si *is matched with the password file* file *(stored in the server).*
3. *For each* file*, there exists only one matching secret input* si*. And there exists an efficiently comutable function* R(file, si)*, to check whether* si *is matched with* file*.*
4. *There exists an efficiently computable function* F *that inputs the identities of the two parties, the password* pw*, and the password file* file *(stored in the server), and outputs the matching secret input* si*.*
5. *With secret input* si*, an adversary can impersonate the client to communicate with the server and compute the session key.*

We take 2DH-aEKE protocol in Fig. 6 as an example, to show how it satisfies the definition of DH-type aPAKE protocol.

1. Let pw be the password shared between C and S. The password file stored in S is file $= (h, V_1, V_2)$.
2. In the execution, C first obtains the secret input $(h, v_1, v_2) \leftarrow H_0(C, S, pw)$.
3. For each file $= (h, V_1, V_2)$, there exists only one matching si $= (h, v_1, v_2)$. And the matching relation can be efficiently verified.
4. Given identities C, S, pw, and file $= (h, V_1, V_2)$, the secret input si can be efficiently obtained by computing $H_0(C, S, pw)$.
5. The last property is self-evident.

Apart from 2DH-aEKE, a large number of existing aPAKE protocols, including KC-SPAKE2+ [41], KHAPE-HMQV [21], aEKE-HMQV and OKAPE-HMQV [39], fall into the DH-type class.

Definition 4 (Simple Reduction). *A simple reduction $\mathcal{R}$ to a problem class $\mathcal{P}$ interacts with an adversary/environment $\mathcal{Z}$ as follows.*

1. *$\mathcal{R}$ receives a problem instance $P \in \mathcal{P}$ from its own challenger, it also has access to an oracle $\mathcal{O}$ provided by the challenger.*
2. *$\mathcal{R}$ randomly samples a bit $\beta \xleftarrow{\$} \{0,1\}$. If $\beta = 0$, then $\mathcal{R}$ simulates the real world running for $\mathcal{Z}$. And if $\beta = 1$, then $\mathcal{R}$ simulates the ideal world running for $\mathcal{Z}$.*
3. *$\mathcal{R}$ outputs its solution s.*

We say $\mathcal{R}$ is a simple $(t_{\mathcal{R}}, \epsilon_{\mathcal{R}}, \epsilon_{\mathcal{Z}})$-reduction, if it runs in time at most $t_{\mathcal{R}}$, and for any adversary/environment $\mathcal{Z}$ with distinguishing advantage $\epsilon_{\mathcal{Z}}$, the output s is a solution to P with probability at least $\epsilon_{\mathcal{R}}$.

The specification of oracle $\mathcal{O}$ depends on the problem class $\mathcal{P}$ (and of cause $\mathcal{O}$ can be defined as NULL). In this paper we consider the strong twin DH problem, where a problem instance is $P = (\bar{X}_1, \bar{X}_2, \bar{Y})$, and $\mathcal{O}$ takes (Y, Z_1, Z_2) as inputs and outputs whether $(Z_1, Z_2) = 2\mathsf{DH}(\bar{X}_1, \bar{X}_2, Y)$.

Theorem 4. *Let Π be a DH-type aPAKE protocol, and $\mathcal{K}$ be the session key space of Π. For any simple $(t_{\mathcal{R}}, \epsilon_{\mathcal{R}}, 1 - 1/|\mathcal{K}|)$-reduction $\mathcal{R}$ from the security of Π defined in Subsect. 4.1 to the hardness of $\mathcal{P}$, there exists a meta-reduction algorithm $\mathcal{M}$ that solves $\mathcal{P}$ in time $t_{\mathcal{M}}$ and with success probability $\epsilon_{\mathcal{M}}$, such that $t_{\mathcal{M}} \approx N \cdot t_{\mathcal{R}}$, and*

$$|\epsilon_{\mathcal{R}} - \epsilon_{\mathcal{M}}| \leq 1/N,$$

where N denotes the total number of client-server pairs.

The proof is shown in the full version [34] due to the page limitation.

From the inequality $|\epsilon_{\mathcal{R}} - \epsilon_{\mathcal{M}}| \leq 1/N$ we know $\epsilon_{\mathcal{M}} \geq \epsilon_{\mathcal{R}} - 1/N$. Namely, even with a "perfect" adversary $\mathcal{Z}$ whose advantage is overwhelming, the success probability $\epsilon_{\mathcal{R}}$ of $\mathcal{R}$ cannot significantly exceed $1/N$, as otherwise there exists an efficient algorithm $\mathcal{M}$ against the hard problem $\mathcal{P}$ (e.g., the strong 2DH problem). This implies that the reduction of $\mathcal{R}$ leads to a loss factor at least N.

6 Tight Security for 2DH-SPAKE2 in the Relaxed UC Framework

In [1], Abdalla et al. relaxed the definition of PAKE functionality to a so-called lazy-extraction PAKE (lePAKE), and proved some widely used PAKE protocols, like SPEKE [29], SPAKE2 [4], and TBPEKE [36], are secure under this relaxed model. We provide the definition of lazy-extraction UC PAKE functionality $\mathcal{F}_{\mathsf{le\text{-}pake}}$ in our full version [34]. Informally, $\mathcal{F}_{\mathsf{le\text{-}pake}}$ allows the adversary/simulator in the ideal world to postpone its password guess until *after* the session is completed.

In this section, we show how our technique can be extended to get tightly secure and ideal cipher-free protocols in the relaxed UC framework. We take

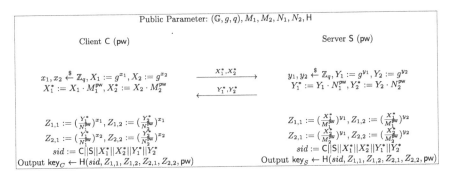

Fig. 7. The 2DH-SPAKE2 Protocol.

2DH-SPAKE2 (Fig. 7) as an example. Here randomly sampled (M_1, M_2, N_1, M_2) servers as the common reference string (CRS), and hash function H is defined as: $H : \{0,1\}^* \mapsto \mathcal{K}$ with $\mathcal{K}$ the space of session keys. C, S are identities of Client and Server.

Theorem 5 (Security of 2DH-SPAKE2). *If the CDH assumption holds in* $\mathbb{G}$, H *works as a random oracle, then the 2DH-SPAKE2 protocol in Fig. 7 securely emulates* $\mathcal{F}_{\mathsf{le\text{-}pake}}$. *More precisely, for any PPT environment* $\mathcal{Z}$ *and real world adversary* $\mathcal{A}$ *which has access to random oracle* H, *there exist a PPT simulator* Sim, *which has access to the ideal functionality* $\mathcal{F}_{\mathsf{le\text{-}pake}}$, *and an algorithm* $\mathcal{B}$, *s.t. that advantage of* $\mathcal{Z}$ *in distinguishing the real world running with* $\mathcal{A}$ *and the ideal world running with* Sim *is bounded by*

$$\mathsf{Adv}_{\mathsf{2DH\text{-}SPAKE2}, \mathcal{Z}}(\lambda) \leq 3\mathsf{Adv}_{\mathbb{G}, \mathcal{B}}^{\mathsf{CDH}}(\lambda) + 2^{-\Omega(\lambda)}.$$

The proof is shown in the full version [34].

Note that the technique can be further used to extend PAKE protocol PPK [35] to 2DH-PPK, that achieves tight security in the relaxed UC framework. We omit the details due to the similarity.

Acknowledgments. We would like to thank the anonymous reviewers for their constructive comments, especially on the perfect forward security of 2DH-aEKE.

Shengli Liu and Xiangyu Liu were partially supported by National Natural Science Foundation of China (NSFC No. 61925207), Guangdong Major Project of Basic and Applied Basic Research (2019B030302008), and the National Key R&D Program of China under Grant 2022YFB2701500. Shuai Han was partially supported by National Natural Science Foundation of China (Grant No. 62002223), Shanghai Sailing Program (20YF1421100), Young Elite Scientists Sponsorship Program by China Association for Science and Technology (YESS20200185), and Ant Group through CCF-Ant Research Fund (CCF-AFSG RF20220224). Dawu Gu is partially supported by the National Key Research and Development Project (Grant No. 2020YFA0712302).

References

1. Abdalla, M., Barbosa, M., Bradley, T., Jarecki, S., Katz, J., Xu, J.: Universally composable relaxed password authenticated key exchange. In: Micciancio, D., Ristenpart, T. (eds.) CRYPTO 2020. LNCS, vol. 12170, pp. 278–307. Springer, Cham (2020). https://doi.org/10.1007/978-3-030-56784-2_10

2. Abdalla, M., Barbosa, M., Rønne, P.B., Ryan, P.Y.A., Sala, P.: Security characterization of J-PAKE and its variants. IACR Cryptology ePrint Archive, Paper 2021/824 (2021)

3. Abdalla, M., Haase, B., Hesse, J.: Security analysis of CPace. In: Tibouchi, M., Wang, H. (eds.) ASIACRYPT 2021. LNCS, vol. 13093, pp. 711–741. Springer, Cham (2021). https://doi.org/10.1007/978-3-030-92068-5_24

4. Abdalla, M., Pointcheval, D.: Simple password-based encrypted key exchange protocols. In: Menezes, A. (ed.) CT-RSA 2005. LNCS, vol. 3376, pp. 191–208. Springer, Heidelberg (2005). https://doi.org/10.1007/978-3-540-30574-3_14

5. Anderson, T.: Local-use ipv4/ipv6 translation prefix. RFC **8215**, 1–7 (2017)

6. Becerra, J., Iovino, V., Ostrev, D., Šala, P., Škrobot, M.: Tightly-secure PAK(E). In: Capkun, S., Chow, S.S.M. (eds.) CANS 2017. LNCS, vol. 11261, pp. 27–48. Springer, Cham (2018). https://doi.org/10.1007/978-3-030-02641-7_2

7. Bellare, M., Pointcheval, D., Rogaway, P.: Authenticated key exchange secure against dictionary attacks. In: Preneel, B. (ed.) EUROCRYPT 2000. LNCS, vol. 1807, pp. 139–155. Springer, Heidelberg (2000). https://doi.org/10.1007/3-540-45539-6_11

8. Bellovin, S.M., Merritt, M.: Encrypted key exchange: password-based protocols secure against dictionary attacks. In: 1992 IEEE Computer Society Symposium on Research in Security and Privacy, pp. 72–84. IEEE Computer Society (1992)

9. Bellovin, S.M., Merritt, M.: Augmented encrypted key exchange: a password-based protocol secure against dictionary attacks and password file compromise. In: CCS 1993. pp. 244–250. ACM (1993)

10. Benhamouda, F., Blazy, O., Chevalier, C., Pointcheval, D., Vergnaud, D.: New techniques for SPHFs and efficient one-round PAKE protocols. In: Canetti, R., Garay, J.A. (eds.) CRYPTO 2013. LNCS, vol. 8042, pp. 449–475. Springer, Heidelberg (2013). https://doi.org/10.1007/978-3-642-40041-4_25

11. Benhamouda, F., Pointcheval, D.: Verifier-based password-authenticated key exchange: New models and constructions. IACR Cryptology ePrint Archive, p. 833 (2013)

12. Bresson, E., Chevassut, O., Pointcheval, D.: Security proofs for an efficient password-based key exchange. In: CCS 2003, pp. 241–250. ACM (2003)

13. Bresson, E., Chevassut, O., Pointcheval, D.: New security results on encrypted key exchange. In: Bao, F., Deng, R., Zhou, J. (eds.) PKC 2004. LNCS, vol. 2947, pp. 145–158. Springer, Heidelberg (2004). https://doi.org/10.1007/978-3-540-24632-9_11

14. Canetti, R.: Universally composable security: a new paradigm for cryptographic protocols. In: FOCS 2001, 14–17 October 2001, Las Vegas, Nevada, USA, pp. 136–145. IEEE Computer Society (2001)

15. Canetti, R., Halevi, S., Katz, J., Lindell, Y., MacKenzie, P.: Universally composable password-based key exchange. In: Cramer, R. (ed.) EUROCRYPT 2005. LNCS, vol. 3494, pp. 404–421. Springer, Heidelberg (2005). https://doi.org/10.1007/11426639_24

16. Cash, D., Kiltz, E., Shoup, V.: The twin Diffie-Hellman problem and applications. In: Smart, N. (ed.) EUROCRYPT 2008. LNCS, vol. 4965, pp. 127–145. Springer, Heidelberg (2008). https://doi.org/10.1007/978-3-540-78967-3_8

17. Dupont, P.-A., Hesse, J., Pointcheval, D., Reyzin, L., Yakoubov, S.: Fuzzy password-authenticated key exchange. In: Nielsen, J.B., Rijmen, V. (eds.) EURO-CRYPT 2018. LNCS, vol. 10822, pp. 393–424. Springer, Cham (2018). https://doi.org/10.1007/978-3-319-78372-7_13

18. Gennaro, R., Lindell, Y.: A framework for password-based authenticated key exchange. In: Biham, E. (ed.) EUROCRYPT 2003. LNCS, vol. 2656, pp. 524–543. Springer, Heidelberg (2003). https://doi.org/10.1007/3-540-39200-9_33

19. Gentry, C., MacKenzie, P., Ramzan, Z.: A method for making password-based key exchange resilient to server compromise. In: Dwork, C. (ed.) CRYPTO 2006. LNCS, vol. 4117, pp. 142–159. Springer, Heidelberg (2006). https://doi.org/10.1007/11818175_9

20. Groce, A., Katz, J.: A new framework for efficient password-based authenticated key exchange. In: CCS 2010, pp. 516–525. ACM (2010)

21. Gu, Y., Jarecki, S., Krawczyk, H.: KHAPE: asymmetric PAKE from key-hiding key exchange. In: Malkin, T., Peikert, C. (eds.) CRYPTO 2021. LNCS, vol. 12828, pp. 701–730. Springer, Cham (2021). https://doi.org/10.1007/978-3-030-84259-8_24

22. Günther, C.G.: An identity-based key-exchange protocol. In: Quisquater, J.-J., Vandewalle, J. (eds.) EUROCRYPT 1989. LNCS, vol. 434, pp. 29–37. Springer, Heidelberg (1990). https://doi.org/10.1007/3-540-46885-4_5

23. Hao, F., Ryan, P.Y.A.: J-PAKE: authenticated key exchange without PKI. Trans. Comput. Sci. 11, 192–206 (2010)

24. Harkins, D.: Dragonfly key exchange. RFC 7664, 1–18 (2015)

25. Hesse, J.: Separating symmetric and asymmetric password-authenticated key exchange. In: Galdi, C., Kolesnikov, V. (eds.) SCN 2020. LNCS, vol. 12238, pp. 579–599. Springer, Cham (2020). https://doi.org/10.1007/978-3-030-57990-6_29

26. Hwang, J.Y., Jarecki, S., Kwon, T., Lee, J., Shin, J.S., Xu, J.: Round-reduced modular construction of asymmetric password-authenticated key exchange. In: Catalano, D., De Prisco, R. (eds.) SCN 2018. LNCS, vol. 11035, pp. 485–504. Springer, Cham (2018). https://doi.org/10.1007/978-3-319-98113-0_26

27. ISO/IEC: ISO/IEC 11770–4:2017 information technology - security techniques - key management - part 4: Mechanisms based on weak secrets. https://www.iso.org/standard/67933.html

28. Jablon, D.P.: Strong password-only authenticated key exchange. Comput. Commun. Rev. 26(5), 5–26 (1996)

29. Jablon, D.P.: Extended password key exchange protocols immune to dictionary attacks. In: 6th Workshop on Enabling Technologies (WET-ICE 1997), pp. 248–255. IEEE Computer Society (1997)

30. Jarecki, S., Krawczyk, H., Xu, J.: OPAQUE: an asymmetric PAKE protocol secure against pre-computation attacks. In: Nielsen, J.B., Rijmen, V. (eds.) EURO-CRYPT 2018. LNCS, vol. 10822, pp. 456–486. Springer, Cham (2018). https://doi.org/10.1007/978-3-319-78372-7_15

31. Katz, J., Ostrovsky, R., Yung, M.: Efficient password-authenticated key exchange using human-memorable passwords. In: Pfitzmann, B. (ed.) EUROCRYPT 2001. LNCS, vol. 2045, pp. 475–494. Springer, Heidelberg (2001). https://doi.org/10.1007/3-540-44987-6_29

32. Katz, J., Vaikuntanathan, V.: Round-optimal password-based authenticated key exchange. In: Ishai, Y. (ed.) TCC 2011. LNCS, vol. 6597, pp. 293–310. Springer, Heidelberg (2011). https://doi.org/10.1007/978-3-642-19571-6_18

33. Kwon, J.O., Sakurai, K., Lee, D.H.: One-round protocol for two-party verifier-based password-authenticated key exchange. In: Leitold, H., Markatos, E.P. (eds.) CMS 2006. LNCS, vol. 4237, pp. 87–96. Springer, Heidelberg (2006). https://doi.org/10.1007/11909033_8

34. Liu, X., Liu, S., Han, S., Gu, D.: Eke meets tight security in the universally composable framework. Cryptology ePrint Archive, Paper 2023/170 (2023). https://eprint.iacr.org/2023/170

35. Mackenzie, P.: The PAK suite: protocols for password-authenticated key exchange (2002)

36. Pointcheval, D., Wang, G.: VTBPEKE: verifier-based two-basis password exponential key exchange. In: AsiaCCS 2017, pp. 301–312. ACM (2017)

37. Rescorla, E.: The transport layer security (TLS) protocol version 1.3. RFC **8446**, 1–160 (2018)

38. RFC: Crypto forum (cfrg). https://datatracker.ietf.org/rg/cfrg/documents/

39. Santos, B.F.D., Gu, Y., Jarecki, S., Krawczyk, H.: Asymmetric PAKE with low computation and communication. In: Dunkelman, O., Dziembowski, S. (eds.) Advances in Cryptology – EUROCRYPT 2022. EUROCRYPT 2022. Lecture Notes in Computer Science, vol. 13276, pp. 127–156. Springer, Cham (2022). https://doi.org/10.1007/978-3-031-07085-3_5

40. Shin, S., Kobara, K.: Efficient augmented password-only authentication and key exchange for ikev2. RFC **6628**, 1–20 (2012)

41. Shoup, V.: Security analysis of SPAKE2+. IACR Cryptology ePrint Archive, p. 313 (2020)

42. Tanwar, S., et al.: Human arthritis analysis in fog computing environment using Bayesian network classifier and thread protocol. IEEE Consumer Electron. Mag. **9**(1), 88–94 (2020)

43. Williams, M., et al.: Magic Wormhole, pp. 253–284. Apress, Berkeley, CA (2019)

44. Yu, J., Lian, H., Zhao, Z., Tang, Y., Wang, X.: Provably secure verifier-based password authenticated key exchange based on lattices. Adv. Comput. **120**, 121–156 (2021)

A Universally Composable PAKE
with Zero Communication Cost
(And Why It Shouldn't Be Considered UC-Secure)

Lawrence Roy[1]([✉]) and Jiayu Xu[2]

[1] Aarhus University, Aarhus, Denmark
ldr709@gmail.com
[2] Oregon State University, Corvallis, USA
xujiay@oregonstate.edu

Abstract. A Password-Authenticated Key Exchange (PAKE) protocol allows two parties to agree upon a cryptographic key, when the only information shared in advance is a low-entropy password. The standard security notion for PAKE (Canetti et al., Eurocrypt 2005) is in the Universally Composable (UC) framework. We show that unlike most UC security notions, UC PAKE does not imply correctness. While Canetti et al. has briefly noticed this issue, we present the first comprehensive study of correctness in UC PAKE:

1. We show that TrivialPAKE, a no-message protocol that does not satisfy correctness, is a UC PAKE;
2. We propose nine approaches to guaranteeing correctness in the UC security notion of PAKE, and show that seven of them are equivalent, whereas the other two are unachievable;
3. We prove that a direct solution, namely changing the UC PAKE functionality to incorporate correctness, is impossible;
4. Finally, we show how to naturally incorporate correctness by changing the model—we view PAKE as a three-party protocol, with the man-in-the-middle adversary as the third party.

In this way, we hope to shed some light on the very nature of UC-security in the man-in-the-middle setting.

1 Introduction

A *password-authenticated key exchange (PAKE)* protocol allows two parties to jointly establish a cryptographically strong key, where the only information shared in advance is a low-entropy password. Crucially, such protocols must remain secure in the presence of a man-in-the-middle adversary. Since its first proposal in 1992 [5], PAKE protocols have been extensively studied in various security models and under various assumptions; a very incomplete list of works includes [1,3,4,7,10,18,22,23]. Interest in the deployment of PAKE protocols in practice—especially their integration with TLS—has been on the rise in recent years, culminating in the standardization process by the IRTF in 2019–20 [13,26]. Several classes of extensions, such as asymmetric PAKE [6,20] and fuzzy PAKE [14], have also been considered.

A. Boldyreva and V. Kolesnikov (Eds.): PKC 2023, LNCS 13940, pp. 714–743, 2023.
https://doi.org/10.1007/978-3-031-31368-4_25

Security Definitions for PAKE. Since passwords have low entropy, any security definition of PAKE has to take into account the fact that an adversary has non-negligible probability of guessing it correctly. Roughly speaking, the basic security property of PAKE is that the only feasible attack is via online guessing, whose probability of success is $1/|\mathsf{Dict}|$ per session (where Dict is the password dictionary, i.e., the set of all possible passwords). In particular, offline dictionary attacks, where the adversary performs a brute-force search over the dictionary upon seeing protocol messages, must be prevented.

There are two major paradigms of PAKE security definitions: game-based [4] and Universally Composable (UC) [10]. In multi-party computation, the UC definition is generally preferable since it supports arbitrary composition, namely the security of PAKE is preserved when composed with itself or other protocols, sequentially or in parallel. In the context of PAKE, the UC definition has the additional advantage that it naturally takes reused password or correlated passwords into consideration, which is difficult to model in the game-based setting since the latter is stand-alone in nature. The UC definition has become the de facto standard of PAKE security; in particular, all candidates in the second round of the IRTF standardization competition have a UC security analysis [1,2,18,20].

UC PAKE and Correctness. A cryptographic protocol usually needs to satisfy some notion of correctness (sometimes called completeness), namely the parties' outputs meet some desired requirements when there is no attack. For a PAKE protocol, correctness means that the two parties should output the same key as long as their passwords are equal. In the game-based definitions, correctness and security are usually defined separately. By contrast, in the UC setting, correctness is often a trivial implication of UC-security; that is, if we remove the ideal adversary and let all protocol parties be honest in the UC functionality and observe their outputs, then correctness can be seen immediately from the functionality's code. This the case for e.g., universally composable commitment schemes [9] and oblivious transfer protocols [12].

Somewhat surprisingly, we show that for PAKE protocols, UC-security does not imply correctness. In particular, in Sect. 3 we show protocol TrivialPAKE, where the two parties independently output random keys, is a UC PAKE. At a high level, this is because the UC PAKE functionality allows the ideal adversary to cause the two protocol parties to output independent keys, even if both parties are honest; therefore, a simulator can leverage such mechanism to complete the simulation for TrivialPAKE. Of course, the same argument also goes for protocols in which the two parties communicate in some arbitrary manner, and then output independent random keys.

We note that the original UC PAKE paper [10] has already noticed that UC PAKE does not imply correctness (called non-triviality therein). In [10, Section 7], the authors wrote:

A protocol is non-trivial if two honest parties are ensured to agree on matching session keys at the conclusion of a protocol execution (except *perhaps with negligible probability), provided that (1) both parties use the same password, and (2) the adversary passes all messages between the parties without modifying them or inserting any messages of its own. The non-triviality requirement is needed since the "empty" protocol where parties do nothing securely realizes $\mathcal{F}_{\mathsf{pwKE}}$ (the ideal-model simulator simply never issues a* NewKey *query to the functionality and so the parties never actually obtain keys).*

However, the "empty" protocol realizes *any* two-party UC functionality, and can be easily ruled out by requiring both parties to output *something*. (Indeed, this is the approach suggested by [11, Section 2] in the context of generic two-party computation.) By contrast, the issue with our TrivialPAKE is unique to PAKE. We will see in Sect. 4.1 that the underlying mechanisms of these two counterexamples are different: one is because the simulator might send some commands while it should not (in TrivialPAKE), the other is because the simulator might not send some commands while it should (in the "empty" protocol).

Furthermore, the fact that correctness needs to be checked separately from UC-security appears under-appreciated: some works on UC PAKE do not perform this correctness check [15,17,20,25], which is sometimes not completely trivial.[1]

Guaranteeing Correctness. At first glance, it seems trivial to fix the definition of a UC PAKE: just require that the protocol satisfy correctness as well as realize the PAKE ideal functionality. However, we believe a deeper understanding of this issue is warranted, to learn *why* the PAKE functionality fails to guarantee correctness (as opposed to most UC functionalities that do imply correctness) and *how* to best address the issue. In Sect. 4, we study several approaches to enforcing the correctness requirement in UC PAKE, finding that some are impossible to achieve, while the rest are equivalent.

These definitions come from two different styles. First, as mentioned above, we could enforce correctness separately from UC-security; namely, we require that two honest parties using the same password, without any adversary interference, must get the same key at the end. However, while UC definitions are based on a correspondence between a real world and an ideal world, the aforementioned definition of correctness only involves the real world; as a result, it

---

[1] The cases of [17,25] are especially problematic, since their (asymmetric) PAKE protocols use a UC-secure authenticated key exchange (AKE) protocol as a building block, and their modelings of UC AKE also do not guarantee correctness. Therefore, a proof of PAKE correctness would need a separate correctness notion for AKE: roughly, that there exists an efficient algorithm Gen such that if we run it twice and obtain two key pairs (pk, sk) and (pk', sk'), then two AKE parties with inputs (pk, pk', sk) and (pk', pk, sk') should output the same key (assuming there is no adversarial interference). Such structural requirement is not mentioned in any of the aforementioned works (and in particular, the Key.Gen algorithm in [25, Fig. 6] is undefined; a similar problem appears in [20]). The exact requirement of AKE correctness used in [17,20,25] is out of the scope of this work.

fails to provide any kind of composability, which makes it harder to either prove that a protocol is a valid PAKE (such as for [17, 20, 25](see footnote 1)), or to make use of this proof in a higher level protocol—that is, the correctness of the higher level protocol always needs to be proved separately.

Next, we consider placing constraints on the UC simulator for PAKE. The basic observation here is that the simulator for TrivialPAKE always interrupts the protocol sessions, causing the two protocol parties to output independent random keys, even though such "interruption" mechanism in the PAKE functionality is meant only to model a man-in-the-middle adversary that modifies protocol messages. In other words, the underlying reason why TrivialPAKE is UC-secure is that the simulator is given too much power. We consider two slightly different ways to disallow such "rogue" interruptions of protocol sessions: requiring either a so-called *reasonable simulator* or a *strong reasonable simulator*. That is, we show that the existence of a (strong) reasonable simulator is equivalent to the PAKE protocol being correct. We further prove that a seemingly stronger notion, namely *all* successful simulators must be (strong) reasonable simulators, is also equivalent to the PAKE protocol being correct. Finally, we consider the question of whether the simulator can perform a "rogue" interruption with negligible or zero probability; we call the latter kind a *(strong) perfectly reasonable simulator*, and show that PAKE correctness is equivalent to the existence of a (strong) perfectly reasonable simulator. However, for any correct PAKE there always exist simulators that fail to be perfectly reasonable. In sum, we present eight approaches to placing requirements on the simulator, and show that six of them are equivalent to directly enforcing PAKE correctness, whereas the other two are unachievable. Finally, we note that this definition style has been used to address a separate issue in the context of *asymmetric* PAKE [15, 20]; however, the necessity of similar constraints on simulators for (regular) PAKE protocols went unnoticed.

Placing constraints on the simulator has the advantage that they often compose easily (a similar observation is made in [15] in the context of asymmetric PAKE). Still, such solutions are ad-hoc and we might ask whether we can just modify the PAKE ideal functionality so that it implies correctness. Unfortunately, in Sect. 5 we show that this is impossible. The problem is that the ideal functionality has no clue whether the adversary is tampering with the PAKE messages; therefore, it must allow the simulator to interrupt the session in case the adversary interferes with the PAKE protocol in the real world, but then the simulator can always use this interface to stop the keys from matching.

Finally, in Sect. 6 we show how a more sophisticated model bypasses the impossibility result and allows correctness to be included in the UC PAKE functionality, making it fully composable. We add a third party called the *router*, which is connected to both protocol parties via an authenticated channel; when the router is honest, it simply forwards messages between the two protocol parties. (Of course, a corrupted router is free to deviate from its description arbitrarily, namely it can modify the messages sent between the two protocol parties.)

Correspondingly, in our modified PAKE ideal functionality we require that session interruption must be done by a *corrupted party*, who must be one of the three participants (including the router), rather than the UC simulator. We prove that our notion of UC three-party PAKE is equivalent to the definition of UC PAKE plus correctness.

2   Preliminaries

Notations. For any $q \in \mathbb{N}^+$, define $[q]$ as the set $\{1, \ldots, q\}$. We let λ denote the security parameter. For a set X, let $x \leftarrow X$ denote the process of sampling an element x uniformly at random from X. We use "efficient" as a shorthand for "probabilistic polynomial time".

2.1   Overview of the UC Framework

In this section, we briefly review the Universally Composable framework by Canetti [8], and introduce necessary notations to be used in later sections. For simplicity's sake, we only cover two-party protocols, and it extends to the case of multi-party protocols (used in Sect. 6 only) naturally.

A *protocol* Π involves two parties (modeled as efficient interactive Turing machines), P and P', sending messages to each other. In an *execution* of protocol Π, there are two additional parties, the *environment* $\mathcal{Z}$ and the *adversary* $\mathcal{A}$, where $\mathcal{Z}$ sends inputs to P and P' and receives outputs from them; furthermore, $\mathcal{Z}$ and $\mathcal{A}$ may communicate with each other at any time during protocol execution. Multiple sessions may run in parallel during protocol execution, distinguished by a *session id* denoted *sid* (which is agreed upon before protocol execution and is not part of the protocol description). For a PAKE protocol, we consider the man-in-the-middle setting, where all messages sent between P and P' pass the adversary $\mathcal{A}$, which can arbitrarily modify these messages or simply drop them. In the special case where $\mathcal{A}$ merely transmits all messages between P and P' without modifying or dropping any of them, we say $\mathcal{A}$ is an *eavesdropper*.

The above describes the *real world*. In the *ideal world*, there is an uncorruptable *ideal functionality* $\mathcal{F}$ whose code is public, and the adversary $\mathcal{A}$'s role is replaced by an *ideal adversary* (a.k.a. *simulator*) $\mathcal{S}$. $\mathcal{F}$ communicates with protocol parties P and P', as well as the ideal adversary $\mathcal{S}$; P and P' are "dummy" parties that merely transmit messages between $\mathcal{F}$ and $\mathcal{Z}$ without any modifications. Importantly, $\mathcal{F}$ and $\mathcal{Z}$ do not communicate with each other directly.

In both the real world and the ideal world, the view of the environment $\mathcal{Z}$ consists of its input to/output from protocol parties P and P', as well as its communications with either the (real) adversary $\mathcal{A}$ or the ideal adversary $\mathcal{S}$. In a nutshell, UC-security says that any efficient environment's view can be successfully simulated by an efficient simulator, meaning that $\mathcal{Z}$ cannot distinguish whether it is in the real world or the ideal world:

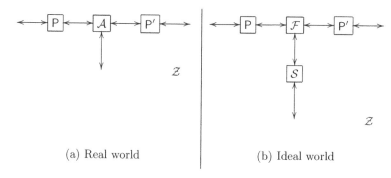

(a) Real world   (b) Ideal world

Fig. 1. Real world and ideal world in the UC framework

Definition 1. *For a protocol* Π, *an ideal functionality* $\mathcal{F}$, *and a (real) adversary* $\mathcal{A}$, *we say a simulator* $\mathcal{S}$ *is* successful *w.r.t.* $\mathcal{A}$ *if (1)* $\mathcal{S}$ *is efficient, and (2) for any efficient environment* $\mathcal{Z}$,

$$\mathbf{Dist}_{\Pi,\mathcal{F}}(\mathcal{A},\mathcal{S},\mathcal{Z}) \triangleq |\Pr[\mathcal{Z} \text{ outputs } 1 \text{ in the real world with } \Pi, \mathcal{A}]$$
$$- \Pr[\mathcal{Z} \text{ outputs } 1 \text{ in the ideal world with } \mathcal{F}, \mathcal{S}]|$$

is negligible, where the probability is taken over the randomness generated in the execution of Π, *as well as the random tapes of* $\mathcal{F}$, $\mathcal{A}$, $\mathcal{S}$, *and* $\mathcal{Z}$.

Definition 2. *We say protocol* Π UC-realizes *functionality* $\mathcal{F}$ *if for any efficient adversary* $\mathcal{A}$, *there exists a successful simulator w.r.t.* $\mathcal{A}$.

A standard result [8, Claim 11] states that only the dummy adversary, i.e., the adversary that merely transmits all messages between the environment and the protocol parties, needs to be considered. (We may intuitively say that $\mathcal{A}$ follows $\mathcal{Z}$'s "instructions", e.g., $\mathcal{Z}$ "instructs" $\mathcal{A}$ to send message (sid, m) to protocol party P.) That is, Definition 2 is equivalent to the following:

Definition 3. *We say protocol* Π UC-realizes *functionality* $\mathcal{F}$ *if there exists a successful simulator w.r.t. the dummy adversary.*

Definition 3 is what we will use in subsequent sections. Since the adversary $\mathcal{A}$ is now fixed, we may simply say "the simulator $\mathcal{S}$ is successful" and write $\mathbf{Dist}_{\Pi,\mathcal{F}}(\mathcal{S},\mathcal{Z})$. Furthermore, when Π and $\mathcal{F}$ are clear from context, we may drop them and write $\mathbf{Dist}(\mathcal{S},\mathcal{Z})$.

2.2 Overview of PAKE

A *password-authenticated key exchange (PAKE)* is a two-party protocol where each party inputs a supposedly low-entropy string (called the *password*) and outputs a cryptographic *session key*. Let Dict be the set of all candidate passwords; we place no restrictions on |Dict| except that |Dict| ≥ 2. Correctness requires that if the two parties' passwords match, and there is no man-in-the-middle attack, then they output a shared key with overwhelming probability:

- On input (NewSession, sid, P, P', pw, role) from P, send (NewSession, sid, P, P', role) to $\mathcal{S}$. Furthermore, if this is the first NewSession message for sid, or this is the second NewSession message for sid and there is a record $\langle$P', P, $\cdot\rangle$, then record $\langle$P, P', pw$\rangle$ and mark it fresh.
- On (TestPwd, sid, P, pw*) from $\mathcal{S}$, if there is a record $\langle$P, P', pw$\rangle$ marked fresh, then do:
  - If pw* = pw, then mark the record compromised and send "correct guess" to $\mathcal{S}$.
  - If pw* $\neq$ pw, then mark the record interrupted and send "wrong guess" to $\mathcal{S}$.
- On (NewKey, sid, P, $K^* \in \{0,1\}^\lambda$) from $\mathcal{S}$, if there is a record $\langle$P, P', pw$\rangle$, and this is the first NewKey message for sid and P, then output (sid, K) to P, where K is defined as follows:
  - If the record is compromised, or either P or P' is corrupted, then set $K := K^*$.
  - If the record is fresh, a key (sid, K') has been output to P', at which time there was a record $\langle$P', P, pw$\rangle$ marked fresh, then set $K := K'$.
  - Otherwise sample $K \leftarrow \{0,1\}^\lambda$.
  Finally, mark the record completed.

Fig. 2. UC PAKE functionality $\mathcal{F}_{\text{PAKE}}$

Definition 4. *We say a PAKE protocol Π is* correct *if the following holds: for any* pw $\in$ Dict, *in an execution of Π, if both protocol parties P and P' input (sid, pw) (with appropriate additional fields for UC-compatibility; see Fig. 2 below), both P and P' are honest, and the adversary $\mathcal{A}$ is an eavesdropper, then*

$$\Pr[\text{Correct(pw)}] \triangleq \Pr[\text{P } outputs\ (sid, K) \wedge \text{P' } outputs\ (sid, K') \wedge K = K' \in \{0,1\}^\lambda]$$

is overwhelming, where the probability is taken over the randomness generated in the execution of Π.

Note that our notion of correctness requires that P and P' must output *something* at the end of the session. This is a trivial requirement since the parties can always output a random key.

The UC PAKE Functionality. We recall in Fig. 2 the standard UC PAKE functionality $\mathcal{F}_{\text{PAKE}}$ from [10] (with minor notational changes).

The functionality allows for three types of commands:

- A NewSession command, sent from a protocol party P, indicates that P (whose password is pw) wants to jointly establish a key with another party P'.[2] This initiates a session from P to P'; for each session id *sid*, only one session from P to P' and one session from P' to P is allowed. The NewSession command is transmitted to the ideal adversary $\mathcal{S}$ (without the password pw), which corresponds to the real-world scenario where the adversary sees the first message from P to P' and thus learns that the P → P' session has started.

– A TestPwd command models the inevitable attack in which the adversary chooses a password guess pw* and communicates with P by running the algorithm of P' on pw*. If pw* happens to be the password of P (i.e., the adversary's password guess is correct), then the adversary learns the session key of P when the session ends; otherwise the adversary should not learn anything about the session key of P.[3] Thus, $\mathcal{F}_{\mathrm{PAKE}}$ marks the P → P' session record compromised (for a correct guess) or interrupted (for a wrong guess) accordingly. Importantly, once the session record becomes compromised or interrupted, all further TestPwd commands for the same session will be ignored; this implies that the adversary can test at most one password for the P → P' session and at most one password for the P' → P session.

– Finally, a NewKey command models the end of a session where the party outputs a session key. How the session key is determined depends on the status of the session:

• If *both* the P → P' session and the P' → P session are fresh, i.e., the adversary did not interrupt the communication between P and P', then the two parties should output the same key as long as their passwords match; furthermore, the key should be random to the adversary. This is formally modeled as follows: assume w.l.o.g. that P receives its session key before P' does. Then P should output a random session key (modeled in the third case under NewKey), and when P' outputs its session key, the key should be equal to what was previously output by P (modeled in the second case under NewKey).

• If the session is compromised, i.e., the adversary successfully guessed the password during an online attack, then as noted above, the adversary learns the session key. In this case, we consider all security guarantees to be lost, so we might as well let the ideal adversary $\mathcal{S}$ choose the session key. This is modeled in the first case under NewKey.

• If the session is interrupted, i.e., the adversary performed an online attack using a wrong password guess, then as noted above, the session key should be independent of the adversary's view. The same goes for the case where

---

[2] The role field might be necessary for the description of the protocol when the algorithms of the two parties are not identical (especially when one party must wait for the other party's message before starting its own session; see [10, Figure 5] for an example), but it has nothing to do with the security of the protocol.

[3] The functionality in Fig. 2 lets the ideal adversary $\mathcal{S}$ learn whether its password guess is correct or not. This is necessary for the simulation of some PAKE protocols but not for others. The variant where $\mathcal{S}$ does not learn this information is called *implicitly-only PAKE*; see [14] for further discussion. We follow the standard PAKE functionality, but note that all theorems below apply to implicitly-only PAKE as well.

the session P $\to$ P′ is fresh but its counter-session P′ $\to$ P has been attacked (either compromised or interrupted); as well as the case where both the P $\to$ P′ session and the P′ $\to$ P session are fresh, yet the passwords of P and P′ are different. This is modeled in the third case under NewKey.
After outputting the session key, the session record is marked completed to prevent TestPwd from being sent after the session ends.

The functionality above only achieves *implicit authentication*, namely if a session is interrupted by the adversary (or the passwords do not match), then the two parties do not learn this fact and merely output independent random keys. In a PAKE with *explicit authentication*, the two parties output an "abort" symbol instead. Explicit authentication can be achieved by adding one round to an implicit-authentication PAKE [16].

3   A No-Message UC PAKE

In this section, we consider protocol TrivialPAKE, where each party simply outputs a random string as the key. For a formal presentation in the UC framework, see Fig. 3.

---

1. On input (NewSession, sid, P, P′, pw, role), if this is the first NewSession message for sid, party P samples $K \leftarrow \{0,1\}^\lambda$ and outputs (sid, K).

Fig. 3. Protocol TrivialPAKE

Obviously TrivialPAKE does not satisfy correctness. On the other hand:

Proposition 1. *Protocol TrivialPAKE (Fig. 3) realizes* $\mathcal{F}_{PAKE}$.

Proof. For the dummy adversary $\mathcal{A}$, construct simulator $\mathcal{S}$ as follows:

Simulator $\mathcal{S}$:

1. On (NewSession, sid, P, P′, role) from $\mathcal{F}_{PAKE}$, send (TestPwd, sid, P, $\bot$) to $\mathcal{F}_{PAKE}$ followed by (NewKey, sid, P, 0^λ).

We claim that $\mathcal{S}$'s simulation is perfect, i.e., any environment $\mathcal{Z}$'s views in the real world and the ideal world are identical. Suppose $\mathcal{Z}$ inputs

(NewSession, sid, P, P', pw, role) to party P.[4] In the ideal world, $\mathcal{F}_{\mathrm{PAKE}}$ stores a record $\langle$P, P', pw$\rangle$ and marks it fresh. When $\mathcal{F}_{\mathrm{PAKE}}$ receives (TestPwd, sid, P, $\perp$), since pw $\neq \perp$, the status of the record is changed to interrupted. Finally, when $\mathcal{F}_{\mathrm{PAKE}}$ receives (NewKey, sid, P, 0^λ), it enters the third case, so P receives a random string $K \leftarrow \{0,1\}^\lambda$ (independent of everything else) and outputs (sid, K). We conclude that in the ideal world, each party independently outputs a random key in $\{0,1\}^\lambda$ together with the session id—which is exactly the case in the real world. (Note that there are no protocol messages, so the only strings $\mathcal{Z}$ receives are parties' outputs.) This completes the proof. ∎

Remark 1. One might hope to prevent TrivialPAKE from being a UC PAKE by simply disallowing the simulator from sending (TestPwd, sid, $\cdot$, $\perp$) to $\mathcal{F}_{\mathrm{PAKE}}$, i.e., $\mathcal{F}_{\mathrm{PAKE}}$ would ignore a (TestPwd, sid, $\cdot$, x) message if $x \notin$ Dict. Assuming |Dict| is polynomial and the password is chosen uniformly at random from Dict, the simulator always has non-negligible probability of guessing the password correctly (hence setting the session record compromised). However, a simulator that sends (TestPwd, sid, P, x) for any $x \in$ Dict followed by (NewKey, sid, P, K) for $K \leftarrow \{0,1\}^\lambda$, still ensures that each party independently outputs a random key (if $x = $ pw, P outputs K; if $x \neq $ pw, P outputs a random key freshly sampled by $\mathcal{F}_{\mathrm{PAKE}}$), thus its simulation is perfect.

4 Seven Equivalent Ways to Guarantee Correctness

4.1 Three Equivalent Ways to Guarantee Correctness

While TrivialPAKE is indeed trivial and the issue appears minor, closer scrutiny shows that there are a number of natural ways to guarantee correctness, resulting from different insights on the essence of the issue. In this section, we propose three such approaches, and show that they are equivalent.

First of all, a straightforward approach would be explicitly requiring correctness:

Proposal 1. Only consider PAKE protocols that both realize $\mathcal{F}_{\mathrm{PAKE}}$ and are correct.

It is instructive, however, to understand why $\mathcal{F}_{\mathrm{PAKE}}$ fails to guarantee correctness. Correctness is meant to be enforced in the second case under NewKey, where two parties output the same key if their passwords match and both of their session records are fresh—the latter of which in turn models an eavesdropping adversary. However, as we have seen in the proof of Proposition 1, there is a gap in the modeling, namely *the ideal adversary can interrupt the protocol sessions (causing the two parties to output independent keys) even if the real adversary*

---

[4] We can assume w.l.o.g. that $\mathcal{Z}$ never reuses a session id, i.e., it never sends (NewSession, sid, P, $\cdot$, $\cdot$, $\cdot$) to P twice (otherwise the second message will be ignored in both the real world and the ideal world).

merely eavedrops. In other words, the ideal adversary is too strong, resulting in an unreasonably weak functionality.

To bridge this gap, we could limit the ideal adversary's power (thus making the power of the ideal adversary and the real adversary "equal") by enforcing the following rule: the ideal adversary is forbidden from sending TestPwd, if the real adversary merely eavesdrops. To formalize this, we borrow some notations from [10]. Consider any PAKE protocol Π, and fix a simulator $\mathcal{S}$ for the dummy adversary $\mathcal{A}$. For any environment $\mathcal{Z}$, define SpuriousGuess$(\mathcal{S}, \mathcal{Z})$ as the following event: both P and P′ are honest, there exists a session sid in which $\mathcal{A}$ is an eavesdropper, yet $\mathcal{S}$ sends a (TestPwd, $sid, \cdot, \cdot$) message to $\mathcal{F}_{\text{PAKE}}$. As a separate condition, define NoOutput$(\mathcal{S}, \mathcal{Z})$ as the following event: both P and P′ are honest, there exists a session sid in which $\mathcal{S}$ receives (NewSession, sid, P, $\cdot, \cdot$) from $\mathcal{F}_{\text{PAKE}}$, yet $\mathcal{S}$ does not send (NewKey, sid, P, $K \in \{0,1\}^\lambda$) to $\mathcal{F}_{\text{PAKE}}$ before it halts.

Definition 5. *We say a simulator $\mathcal{S}$ is* reasonable *if for any efficient environment $\mathcal{Z}$,* Pr[SpuriousGuess$(\mathcal{S}, \mathcal{Z})$] *and* Pr[NoOutput$(\mathcal{S}, \mathcal{Z})$] *are both negligible, where the probability is taken over the randomness generated in the execution of Π, as well as the random tapes of $\mathcal{S}$, $\mathcal{Z}$, and $\mathcal{F}_{\text{PAKE}}$.*[5]

We can now consider a proposal where only reasonable simulators "count", and unreasonable simulators (such as the one in the proof of Proposition 1) are considered invalid:

Proposal 2. Only consider PAKE protocols for which a successful reasonable simulator exists.

The above proposal does not rule out the possibility that for some protocols, there are some reasonable simulators and some unreasonable simulators. We could strengthen it to:

Proposal 3. Only consider PAKE protocols for which **all** successful simulators are reasonable.

Which, then, is the "right" proposal to guarantee correctness? We now show that all three are the "right" approach, since they are equivalent:

Lemma 1. *Let Π be any PAKE protocol. Then the followings are equivalent:*

(1) Π is correct and realizes $\mathcal{F}_{PAKE}$;
(2) There exists a successful reasonable simulator for Π;
(3) Π realizes $\mathcal{F}_{PAKE}$, and all successful simulators for Π are reasonable.

---

[5] The purpose of considering NoOutput is to rule out the "empty" protocol mentioned in Sect. 1, where P and P′ simply don't do anything (and $\mathcal{S}$ also doesn't do anything). Although our primary focus is to rule out protocols like TrivialPAKE, with the requirement on NoOutput in place and with how we define correctness (Definition 4), we can formally rule out the "empty" protocol as well.

Proof. *(1)⇒(3):* This is [10, Lemma A.1], except that [10] requires correctness to be perfect. See the full version of this work for a complete proof.

(3)⇒(2): This is immediate.

(2)⇒(1): The intuition is that, a reasonable simulator cannot send TestPwd in a session where the adversary merely eavesdrops, so in the ideal world this session must remain fresh, hence $\mathcal{F}_{\mathrm{PAKE}}$ will let the two parties output the same key. This must happen in the real world as well (since the simulator is successful), which implies correctness.

Formally, let $\mathcal{S}$ be a successful reasonable simulator as in the statement of (2). Since $\mathcal{S}$ is successful, Π realizes $\mathcal{F}_{\mathrm{PAKE}}$. We now show that Π is correct.

For any pw $\in$ Dict, consider the following environment $\mathcal{Z}$:

Environment $\mathcal{Z}$:

1. Initialize a single session between P and P' on pw. That is, pick any sid, and input (NewSession, sid, P, P', pw, role) to P and (NewSession, sid, P', P, pw, role') to P'.
2. Instruct $\mathcal{A}$ to be an eavesdropper in session sid.
3. When P outputs (sid, K) and P' outputs (sid, K'), output 1 if $K = K' \in \{0,1\}^\lambda$ and output 0 otherwise. If P or P' does not output anything when it halts, then output 0.

Since $\mathcal{S}$ is reasonable, we know that

$$\Pr[\mathsf{SpuriousGuess}(\mathcal{S}, \mathcal{Z})] = \Pr[\mathcal{S} \text{ sends } (\mathsf{TestPwd}, sid, \cdot, \cdot) \text{ to } \mathcal{F}_{\mathrm{PAKE}}]$$

is negligible (where the equation is due to the fact that there is only one session, and $\mathcal{A}$ is an eavesdropper in this session). Suppose $\mathsf{SpuriousGuess}(\mathcal{S}, \mathcal{Z})$ does not occur. Then in the ideal world, when $\mathcal{S}$ sends (NewKey, sid, P, $\cdot$) and (NewKey, sid, P', $\cdot$) to $\mathcal{F}_{\mathrm{PAKE}}$ (note that $\mathcal{S}$ must send such commands except with negligible probability $\Pr[\mathsf{NoOutput}(\mathcal{S}, \mathcal{Z})]$), $\mathcal{F}_{\mathrm{PAKE}}$'s records $\langle$P, P', pw$\rangle$ and $\langle$P', P, pw$\rangle$ are both fresh, resulting in P and P' outputting the same key $K = K'$ (together with sid), as can be seen from the second case of $\mathcal{F}_{\mathrm{PAKE}}$.[6] This causes $\mathcal{Z}$ to output 1. Therefore,

$$\Pr[\mathcal{Z} \text{ outputs 1 in the ideal world}] \geq 1 - \Pr[\mathsf{SpuriousGuess}(\mathcal{S}, \mathcal{Z})]$$
$$- \Pr[\mathsf{NoOutput}(\mathcal{S}, \mathcal{Z})].$$

It follows that

$$\Pr[\mathcal{Z} \text{ outputs 1 in the real world}] \geq 1 - \Pr[\mathsf{SpuriousGuess}(\mathcal{S}, \mathcal{Z})]$$
$$- \Pr[\mathsf{NoOutput}(\mathcal{S}, \mathcal{Z})] - \mathbf{Dist}(\mathcal{S}, \mathcal{Z}),$$

---

[6] More precisely, assume w.l.o.g. that $\mathcal{S}$ sends (NewKey, sid, P, $\cdot$) first and (NewKey, sid, P', $\cdot$) next. Then when $\mathcal{S}$ sends (NewKey, sid, P, $\cdot$), $\mathcal{F}_{\mathrm{PAKE}}$ enters the third case, so P receives and outputs (sid, K) for $K \leftarrow \{0,1\}^\lambda$; when $\mathcal{S}$ sends (NewKey, sid, P, $\cdot$), $\mathcal{F}_{\mathrm{PAKE}}$ enters the second case, so P receives and outputs (sid, K') for $K' := K$.

i.e., in the real world P outputs K, P' outputs K', and $K = K'$ with overwhelming probability ($\mathbf{Dist}(\mathcal{S}, \mathcal{Z})$ is negligible since $\mathcal{S}$ is successful). This implies that Π is correct.   ∎

Discussion. In traditional game-based definitions, correctness and security are usually defined separately. In the UC framework, by contrast, there is usually one functionality achieving various desired properties, including correctness. However, as TrivialPAKE shows, correctness cannot be taken "for granted"; apart from the standard "sanity check" that UC-security implies game-based *security*, one should also try to prove (or disprove) that UC-security implies *correctness*.

Proposal 1 above can be viewed as simply "conceding" that in the context of PAKE, UC-security only implies a notion of security, and correctness needs to be separately defined—just as in game-based notions. On the other hand, Proposals 2 and 3 attempt to address the underlying reason that causes the issue, namely $\mathcal{F}_{\mathrm{PAKE}}$ gives the ideal adversary too much power. Intuitively, TestPwd corresponds to an adversary incorporating a password guess pw^* in a message m^*, and replacing an honest party's message m with m^*. (The adversary sending random garbage is modeled as $\mathsf{pw}^* = \bot$.) Therefore, *any ideal adversary sending* TestPwd *should be viewed as modifying protocol messages, which disqualifies it from being a valid simulator for an eavesdropper*. Essentially, Proposals 2 and 3 are a formalization of this intuition.

4.2   Three Sets of Variants

In this section, we consider some variants of reasonable simulators (Definition 5).

Strong Reasonable Simulators. Requiring a simulator to be reasonable only implies that it cannot send TestPwd if the (real) adversary is an eavesdropper; this does not prevent the simulator from sending TestPwd *before* the adversary modifies a protocol message (if the adversary does modify one eventually). For example, suppose the adversary passes the first two protocol messages without modification, and modifies the third; a reasonable simulator may send TestPwd when the first message is sent. Intuitively, sending TestPwd "in advance" should not be considered reasonable, since this would again cause a discrepancy between the simulator's power and the adversary's power: the simulator modifies protocol messages even when the adversary does not.

We now consider the notion of *strong* reasonable simulators, which essentially says that the simulator is not allowed to send TestPwd unless *and until* the adversary modifies a protocol message. It turns out that formalizing this notion is not as straightforward as formalizing reasonable simulators: in the latter case we can consider the adversary and the simulator separately, whereas here we need to consider the *order* of the two parties' actions, namely the adversary modifying a protocol message and the simulator sending TestPwd. Furthermore, these two events occur in two different worlds, so we cannot compare their timing directly.

We overcome this difficulty by requiring that the simulator send TestPwd only *with permission from the environment*, which bridges the real world and the ideal world since the environment participates in both worlds. Formally, assume w.l.o.g. that for each session sid, the environment always sends a (Modify, sid) message while instructing the adversary to modify a protocol message for the first time in this session, and does not send such messages anywhere else (so $\mathcal{Z}$ sends at most one Modify message for each session).[7] For any environment $\mathcal{Z}$, define GeneralSpuriousGuess($\mathcal{S}, \mathcal{Z}$) as the following event: both P and P' are honest, and there exists a session sid in which $\mathcal{S}$ sends a (TestPwd, $sid, \cdot, \cdot$) message to $\mathcal{F}_{\text{PAKE}}$ without receiving (Modify, sid) from $\mathcal{Z}$.

Definition 6. *We say a simulator $\mathcal{S}$ is* strong reasonable *if for any efficient environment $\mathcal{Z}$,* $\Pr[\text{GeneralSpuriousGuess}(\mathcal{S}, \mathcal{Z})]$ *and* $\Pr[\text{NoOutput}(\mathcal{S}, \mathcal{Z})]$ *are both negligible, where the probability is taken over the randomness generated in the execution of Π, as well as the random tapes of $\mathcal{S}$, $\mathcal{Z}$, and $\mathcal{F}_{\text{PAKE}}$.*

The following straightforward lemma states that the strong reasonability requirement is indeed stronger than the ordinary reasonability requirement:

Lemma 2. *Any strong reasonable simulator is also a reasonable simulator.*

Proof. Suppose $\mathcal{S}$ is a strong reasonable simulator. For any efficient environment $\mathcal{Z}$, let SID be the set of sessions in which $\mathcal{Z}$ instructs the adversary to be an eavesdropper. If SpuriousGuess($\mathcal{S}, \mathcal{Z}$) occurs, there exists a $sid \in SID$ such that $\mathcal{S}$ sends (TestPwd, $sid, \cdot, \cdot$) to $\mathcal{F}_{\text{PAKE}}$. However, since the adversary never modifies a protocol message in sid, $\mathcal{Z}$ never sends a (Modify, sid) message, so GeneralSpuriousGuess($\mathcal{S}, \mathcal{Z}$) occurs. It follows that

$$\Pr[\text{SpuriousGuess}(\mathcal{S}, \mathcal{Z})] \leq \Pr[\text{GeneralSpuriousGuess}(\mathcal{S}, \mathcal{Z})],$$

which is negligible. So $\mathcal{S}$ is a reasonable simulator. ∎

We now show that the notion of "reasonably realizing $\mathcal{F}_{\text{PAKE}}$" remains equivalent if we replace reasonable simulators with strong reasonable simulators:

Lemma 3. *Let Π be any PAKE protocol. Then the followings are equivalent:*

(2$^+$) *There exists a successful strong reasonable simulator for Π;*
(3) *Π realizes $\mathcal{F}_{\text{PAKE}}$, and all successful simulators for Π are reasonable;*
(3$^+$) *Π realizes $\mathcal{F}_{\text{PAKE}}$, and all successful simulators for Π are strong reasonable.*

Proof. *(2$^+$)$\Rightarrow$(3):* This is because (2$^+$) implies (2) by Lemma 2, and (2) implies (3) by Lemma 1.

---

[7] This is w.l.o.g. because any environment $\mathcal{Z}$ can be converted into another environment $\mathcal{Z}'$ that behaves exactly like $\mathcal{Z}$, except that $\mathcal{Z}'$ additionally sends (Modify, sid) when $\mathcal{Z}$ instructs the adversary to modify a protocol message for the first time in session sid. Obviously the distinguishing advantages of $\mathcal{Z}$ and $\mathcal{Z}'$ are equal.

$(3) \Rightarrow (3^+)$: The high-level idea is that, before the adversary modifies a protocol message, a reasonable simulator does not know whether the adversary will eventually be an eavesdropper or not, so it "dare not" send TestPwd to $\mathcal{F}_{\text{PAKE}}$ (in case the adversary turns out to be an eavesdropper).

Let $\mathcal{S}$ be a successful simulator for Π; then $\mathcal{S}$ is reasonable, and we need to show that $\mathcal{S}$ is strong reasonable. Let $\mathcal{Z}$ be an efficient environment. As a warm-up, we first prove the lemma in the case that $\mathcal{Z}$ only initiates a single session sid. If $\mathcal{Z}$ instructs its adversary $\mathcal{A}$ to be an eavesdropper, then $\text{SpuriousGuess}(\mathcal{S}, \mathcal{Z})$ and $\text{GeneralSpuriousGuess}(\mathcal{S}, \mathcal{Z})$ are equivalent, so the lemma is immediate. Otherwise consider the following environment $\mathcal{Z}'$, which inputs the passwords that $\mathcal{Z}$ inputs, and instructs its adversary $\mathcal{A}'$ to be an eavesdropper:

Environment $\mathcal{Z}'$:

1. Run $\mathcal{Z}$. When $\mathcal{Z}$ sends (NewSession, sid, P, P', pw, role) (resp. (NewSession, sid, P', P, pw', role')) to P (resp. P'), send the same message to P (resp. P').
2. Instruct $\mathcal{A}'$ to be an eavesdropper in session sid.
3. When session is completed, output $b \leftarrow \{0, 1\}$.[8]

Since $\mathcal{A}$ (the adversary corresponding to $\mathcal{Z}$) is not an eavesdropper, there exists an $r \in \mathbb{N}^+$ such that $\mathcal{A}$ does not modify the first $r - 1$ protocol messages, but modifies the r-th protocol message.[9] The key observation is that $\mathcal{Z}$ and $\mathcal{Z}'$ behave identically up to the r-th protocol message, since both use password pw for P and password pw' for P', and both instruct the adversary to pass the first $r - 1$ messages without modification. Therefore, we have (below we abbreviate (TestPwd, sid, $\cdot$, $\cdot$) as TestPwd):

$\Pr[\mathcal{S}$ sends TestPwd before receiving the r-th protocol message in the world of $\mathcal{Z}]$
$= \Pr[\mathcal{S}$ sends TestPwd before receiving the r-th protocol message in the world of $\mathcal{Z}']$
$\leq \Pr[\mathcal{S}$ sends TestPwd in the world of $\mathcal{Z}']$
$= \Pr[\text{SpuriousGuess}(\mathcal{S}, \mathcal{Z}')]$.

However, since the r-th protocol message is the first time when $\mathcal{Z}$ instructs $\mathcal{A}$ to modify a protocol message, this is also when $\mathcal{Z}$ sends (Modify, sid). Therefore, (in the world of $\mathcal{Z}$) $\mathcal{S}$ receives (Modify, sid) together with the r-th protocol message from $\mathcal{Z}$. GeneralSpuriousGuess$(\mathcal{S}, \mathcal{Z})$ is defined as $\mathcal{S}$ sends TestPwd before this, i.e., $\mathcal{S}$ sends TestPwd before receiving the r-th protocol message. So,

$\Pr[\mathcal{S}$ sends TestPwd before receiving the r-th protocol message in the world of $\mathcal{Z}]$
$= \Pr[\text{GeneralSpuriousGuess}(\mathcal{S}, \mathcal{Z})]$.

---

[8] In fact $\mathcal{Z}'$ does not need to output anything, since we rely on the fact that $\Pr[\text{SpuriousGuess}(\mathcal{S}, \mathcal{Z}')]$ is negligible, rather than the distinguishing advantage of $\mathcal{Z}'$ is negligible; whether SpuriousGuess$(\mathcal{S}, \mathcal{Z}')$ happens or not is already determined before $\mathcal{Z}'$ finally outputs a bit.

[9] Formally, r is a random variable depending on the random tape of $\mathcal{Z}$, and all probabilities below are also taken over the random tape of $\mathcal{Z}$.

Combining the above, we obtain

$$\Pr[\mathsf{GeneralSpuriousGuess}(\mathcal{S}, \mathcal{Z})] \leq \Pr[\mathsf{SpuriousGuess}(\mathcal{S}, \mathcal{Z}')],$$

which is negligible. This shows that $\mathcal{S}$ is strong reasonable.

In the general case, assume $\mathcal{Z}$ initiates q sessions $sid_1, \ldots, sid_q$. $\mathcal{Z}$ may instruct $\mathcal{A}$ to be an eavesdropper in some of them, and to modify messages in others. For $\ell \in [q]$, if $\mathcal{A}$ is not an eavesdropper, then there exist an $r_\ell \in \mathbb{N}^+$ such that $\mathcal{A}$ does not modify the first $r_\ell - 1$ protocol messages, but modifies the r_ℓ-th protocol message; if $\mathcal{A}$ is an eavesdropper, then let $r_\ell = \infty$. Environment $\mathcal{Z}'$ works exactly as in the simple-session case, except that it does not output the bit b until all sessions are completed. Just as the single-session argument above, we observe that *in session sid_ℓ, $\mathcal{Z}$ and $\mathcal{Z}'$ behave identically up to the r_ℓ-th protocol message*, so

$$\Pr[\mathsf{GeneralSpuriousGuess}(\mathcal{S}, \mathcal{Z})]$$
$$= \Pr[\text{There exists } \ell \in [q] \text{ such that } \mathcal{S} \text{ sends } (\mathsf{TestPwd}, sid_\ell, \cdot, \cdot)$$
$$\text{before receiving the } r_\ell\text{-th protocol message in the world of } \mathcal{Z}]$$
$$\leq \Pr[\mathsf{SpuriousGuess}(\mathcal{S}, \mathcal{Z}')],$$

which is negligible. So $\mathcal{S}$ is strong reasonable.

(3^+)$\Rightarrow$(2^+): This is immediate.   ∎

(Strong) Perfectly Reasonable Simulators. If we require that a simulator never make a spurious guess (rather than making it with negligible probability), we get:

Definition 7. *We say a simulator $\mathcal{S}$ is* perfectly reasonable *if for any efficient environment $\mathcal{Z}$, $\Pr[\mathsf{SpuriousGuess}(\mathcal{S}, \mathcal{Z})] = 0$ and $\Pr[\mathsf{NoOutput}(\mathcal{S}, \mathcal{Z})] = 0$, where the probability is taken over the randomness generated in the execution of Π, as well as the random tapes of $\mathcal{S}$, $\mathcal{Z}$, and $\mathcal{F}_{PAKE}$.*

Similarly, for general spurious guesses,

Definition 8. *We say a simulator $\mathcal{S}$ is* strong perfectly reasonable *if for any efficient environment $\mathcal{Z}$, $\Pr[\mathsf{GeneralSpuriousGuess}(\mathcal{S}, \mathcal{Z})] = 0$ and $\Pr[\mathsf{NoOutput}(\mathcal{S}, \mathcal{Z})] = 0$, where the probability is taken over the randomness generated in the execution of Π, as well as the random tapes of $\mathcal{S}$, $\mathcal{Z}$, and $\mathcal{F}_{PAKE}$.*

Remark 2. Interestingly, strong perfectly reasonable simulators have been studied while addressing a separate definitional issue in the context of *asymmetric* PAKE (aPAKE), where one party (called the user) holds the plain password and another party (called the server) holds a *password file* file, namely a one-way mapping of the password. For the purpose of our discussion, it suffices to let file $= H(\mathsf{pw})$, where H is a random oracle. We want to ensure that after compromising the server and learning file, the adversary needs $\Theta(|\mathsf{Dict}|)$ time to recover pw.

Formally, this is modeled as follows: after compromising the server, the ideal adversary can send an $(\mathsf{OfflineTestPwd}, sid, \mathsf{pw}^*)$ command to the functionality, which returns "correct guess" (if pw^* is the correct password) or "wrong guess". Here an issue analogous to our "general spurious guess" emerges: what prevents the simulator from sending $\mathsf{OfflineTestPwd}$ for all $x \in \mathsf{Dict}$ and learning the password, before the real adversary makes any H queries?

This issue has been discussed in [15,20], where the proposed solution is similar to requiring the simulator to be strong perfectly reasonable; that is, the simulator is not allowed to send $(\mathsf{OfflineTestPwd}, sid, x)$, unless and until the real adversary queries $H(x)$. Both of the aforementioned works require $\mathsf{OfflineTestPwd}$ messages to be "accounted for by the environment" (yet neither of them formally defines what "accounted for by the environment" means).

However, it was later pointed out [19] that such a solution is insufficient for aPAKE. In a nutshell, this is because the random oracle H can be queried by the *environment* directly (rather than the environment instructing the real-world adversary to do so); therefore, an environment can learn H input/output pairs without sending any permission to the adversary, causing the simulator not being able to send any $\mathsf{OfflineTestPwd}$ messages (even when the environment already learns the password). (For a formal treatment of the discussion above, see [19, Appendix D].) We do not suffer from this issue, because in our setting all protocol messages must be passed by the real adversary, rather than the environment itself—in contrast to the environment being able to query the random oracle on its own.

It is not hard to see that for (2) and (2^+), the analogous conditions—where the simulator is required to be perfect—are equivalent to (2^+), whereas for (3) and (3^+), the analogous conditions cannot be satisfied:

Lemma 4. *Let* Π *be any PAKE protocol. Then the followings are equivalent:*

(2^+) There exists a successful strong reasonable simulator for Π*;*
(2^*) There exists a successful perfectly reasonable simulator for Π*;*
(2^{*+}) There exists a successful strong perfectly reasonable simulator for Π*.*

Furthermore, the following do not hold:

(3^*) Π realizes $\mathcal{F}_{PAKE}$, and all successful simulators for Π are perfectly reasonable;
(3^{*+}) Π realizes $\mathcal{F}_{PAKE}$, and all successful simulators for Π are strong perfectly reasonable.

The proof is straightforward and is deferred to the full version of this work.

4.3   Putting It Together

By Lemmas 1, 3 and 4, we get:

Theorem 1. *Let* Π *be any PAKE protocol. Then the followings are equivalent:*

(1) Π *is correct and realizes* $\mathcal{F}_{PAKE}$;
(2) *There exists a successful reasonable simulator for* Π;
(2*) *There exists a successful perfectly reasonable simulator for* Π;
(2$^+$) *There exists a successful strong reasonable simulator for* Π;
(2*$^+$) *There exists a successful strong perfectly reasonable simulator for* Π;
(3) Π *realizes* $\mathcal{F}_{PAKE}$, *and all successful simulators for* Π *are reasonable;*
(3$^+$) Π *realizes* $\mathcal{F}_{PAKE}$, *and all successful simulators for* Π *are strong reasonable.*

Furthermore, the followings do not hold:

(3*) Π *realizes* $\mathcal{F}_{PAKE}$, *and all successful simulators for* Π *are perfectly reasonable;*
(3*$^+$) Π *realizes* $\mathcal{F}_{PAKE}$, *and all successful simulators for* Π *are strong perfectly reasonable.*

Since all seven conditions in the first part of Theorem 1 are equivalent, we can now define the notion of *reasonably realizing* the PAKE functionality:

Definition 9. *We say a PAKE protocol* Π reasonably realizes $\mathcal{F}_{PAKE}$ *if* Π *is correct and realizes* $\mathcal{F}_{PAKE}$, *i.e.,* Π *satisfies condition (1) in Theorem 1 (equivalently,* Π *satisfies any of conditions (2), (2*), (2$^+$), (2*$^+$), (3), and (3$^+$) in Theorem 1).*

5   Impossibility of a Direct Solution

All proposals in Sect. 4 are somewhat unsatisfactory, in that they either require correctness to be separate from security (Proposal 1) or place additional requirements on the UC simulator, hence changing the very definition of UC-security (all other proposals). Is it possible to have a direct solution, i.e., to incorporate correctness directly into the UC *functionality*, without changing the definition of UC-security? In this section, we give a negative answer.

Theorem 2. *There does not exist a UC functionality* $\mathcal{F}$ *such that a PAKE protocol* Π *reasonably realizes* $\mathcal{F}_{PAKE}$ *if and only if it realizes* $\mathcal{F}$.

Proof. The high-level idea is as follows: in a PAKE protocol, if the protocol messages are $\perp$, then the two parties output independent random keys. This means that there must be some mechanism in $\mathcal{F}$ that allows the two parties to output independent random keys. But then a simulator can use the same mechanism to complete the simulation for TrivialPAKE. The formal proof follows.

Assume towards contradiction that there exists such a UC functionality $\mathcal{F}$. Take any "natural" PAKE protocol that reasonably realizes $\mathcal{F}_{\mathsf{PAKE}}$; for concreteness, here we use Diffie-Hellman-based Encrypted Key Exchange (DH-EKE, Fig. 4). Correctness can be checked as follows: assuming both parties P and P' hold the same password pw, and the adversary is an eavesdropper, then party P outputs

$$H((\mathcal{D}_{\mathsf{pw}}(Y))^x) = H((\mathcal{D}_{\mathsf{pw}}(\mathcal{E}_{\mathsf{pw}}(g^y)))^x) = H((g^y)^x) = H(g^{xy})$$

together with sid, and so does P'. Furthermore, it has been proven that DH-EKE realizes $\mathcal{F}_{\mathsf{PAKE}}$ in the ideal cipher model and the random oracle model, under the computational Diffie-Hellman assumption in the group $(\mathbb{G}, g, q)$ [14, 24]. Therefore, DH-EKE reasonably realizes $\mathcal{F}_{\mathsf{PAKE}}$ and thus realizes $\mathcal{F}$.

The protocol uses a group $(\mathbb{G}, g, q)$, an ideal cipher $(\mathcal{E}, \mathcal{D})$ where $\mathcal{E}$: Dict $\times\, \mathbb{G} \to \{0,1\}^\lambda$ and $\mathcal{D}$: Dict $\times \{0,1\}^\lambda \to \mathbb{G}$, and a random oracle $H : \mathbb{G} \to \{0,1\}^\lambda$. The protocol is completely symmetric, so we only describe the behavior of party P.

1. On input (NewSession, sid, P, P', pw, role), if this is the first NewSession message for sid, party P samples $x \leftarrow \mathbb{Z}_q$, computes $X := \mathcal{E}_{\mathsf{pw}}(g^x)$, and sends (sid, X) to P'.
2. On (sid, Y) from party P', if $Y \notin \{0,1\}^\lambda$, then party P samples $K \leftarrow \{0,1\}^\lambda$ and outputs (sid, K). Otherwise P computes $K := H(\mathcal{D}_{\mathsf{pw}}(Y))$ and outputs (sid, K).

Fig. 4. Protocol DH-EKE

Let $\mathcal{S}$ be the simulator for DH-EKE realizing $\mathcal{F}$. We now use $\mathcal{S}$ to show that TrivialPAKE also realizes $\mathcal{F}$. The simulator $\mathcal{S}'$ works as follows:

Simulator $\mathcal{S}'$:

1. Upon receiving the first message from $\mathcal{F}$, activate $\mathcal{S}$ using the same message. After that, pass messages between $\mathcal{S}$ and $\mathcal{F}$ without any modifications. That is, upon receiving a message from $\mathcal{S}$ (aimed at $\mathcal{F}$), send the same message to $\mathcal{F}$; upon receiving a message from $\mathcal{F}$, send the same message to $\mathcal{S}$ (as a message from $\mathcal{F}$).
2. Upon receiving a message (sid, X) from $\mathcal{S}$ as a message from P to P', send $(sid, \perp)$ to $\mathcal{S}$ as a message from P' to P. The same goes for P'.
3. Continue passing messages between $\mathcal{S}$ and $\mathcal{F}$.

We now prove that $\mathcal{S}'$ is successful. As warm-up, we first show that if $\mathcal{F} = \mathcal{F}_{\mathsf{PAKE}}$, then $\mathcal{S}'$ is exactly the simulator for TrivialPAKE in the proof of Proposition 1. The first message $\mathcal{S}'$ receives from $\mathcal{F}_{\mathsf{PAKE}}$ is (NewSession, sid, P, P', role), and $\mathcal{S}'$ passes this message to $\mathcal{S}$. Then $\mathcal{S}$ begins to simulate protocol messages, i.e., $\mathcal{S}$ sends (sid, X) aimed at P'. $\mathcal{S}'$ then behaves like an environment that instructs the adversary to respond with $(sid, \bot)$. Upon receiving $(sid, \bot)$, $\mathcal{S}$ needs to simulate P's behavior of outputting a random key; it does so by sending $(\mathsf{TestPwd}, sid, \mathsf{P}, \bot)$ followed by $(\mathsf{NewKey}, sid, \mathsf{P}, 0^\lambda)$ to $\mathcal{F}_{\mathrm{PAKE}}$ (whose role is played by $\mathcal{S}'$).[10] This means that $\mathcal{S}'$ also sends these two messages to its own $\mathcal{F}_{\mathrm{PAKE}}$. At this point we recover the simulator in the proof of Proposition 1.

In general, the crucial point is that $\mathcal{S}'$, while communicating with $\mathcal{S}$, behaves like an environment that instructs the real adversary to send $(sid, \bot)$ to protocol parties (causing them to output independent random keys). To see this formally, for any environment $\mathcal{Z}'$ in the world of $\mathcal{S}'$ and attacking TrivialPAKE, consider the following environment $\mathcal{Z}$ in the world of $\mathcal{S}$ and attacking DH-EKE:

Environment $\mathcal{Z}$:

1. When $\mathcal{Z}'$ activates a new session for $\langle \mathsf{P}, \mathsf{P}' \rangle$ on password pw, do the same thing.
2. Instruct the adversary to send $(sid, \bot)$ as protocol messages.

Recall that $\mathcal{S}$ communicates with two parties: $\mathcal{F}$ to which it sends UC commands, and $\mathcal{Z}$ to which it sends protocol messages (as messages from P aimed at P', or vice versa). $\mathcal{S}'$ plays the roles of both $\mathcal{F}$ and $\mathcal{Z}$ to $\mathcal{S}$. For the former interface, $\mathcal{S}'$ merely passes all messages from $\mathcal{F}$ to $\mathcal{S}$, and from $\mathcal{S}$ to $\mathcal{F}$; furthermore, $\mathcal{Z}'$ behaves exactly like $\mathcal{Z}$ when sending messages to $\mathcal{F}$ via P. Therefore, the view of $\langle \mathcal{S}' \rightleftarrows \mathcal{F} \rightleftarrows \mathsf{P} \rightleftarrows \mathcal{Z}' \rangle$ is identical to the view of $\langle \mathcal{S} \rightleftarrows \mathcal{F} \rightleftarrows \mathsf{P} \rightleftarrows \mathcal{Z} \rangle$. On the other hand, $\mathcal{S}'$ replaces all protocol messages with $(sid, \bot)$, which is exactly what $\mathcal{Z}$ does. We conclude that $\mathcal{S}'$ perfectly simulates $\mathcal{Z}$ to $\mathcal{S}$.

Since $\mathcal{Z}$ sends $(sid, \bot)$ as protocol messages, in a real execution, this causes P and P' to output independent random keys in $\{0,1\}^\lambda$ (together with sid). Thus, in the ideal world simulated by $\mathcal{S}$, the output distribution of parties is indistinguishable with each party independently outputting a random string in $\{0,1\}^\lambda$ (together with sid) per session. Recall again that the messages sent between $\mathcal{S}'$ and $\mathcal{F}$ (whose role is played by $\mathcal{S}$) are exactly the same with the messages sent between $\mathcal{S}$ and $\mathcal{F}$; it follows that the parties' output distribution in the world of $\mathcal{Z}$ and $\mathcal{S}$ is also indistinguishable with the above, i.e., each party independently outputting a random string in $\{0,1\}^\lambda$ (together with sid) per session. But TrivialPAKE has no protocol messages, and the only strings $\mathcal{Z}$ receives are parties' outputs (also see the proof of Proposition 1). This shows that the view of $\mathcal{Z}$ simulated by $\mathcal{S}$ is indistinguishable from the real view—i.e., $\mathcal{S}$ is "as successful as" $\mathcal{S}'$. Therefore, TrivialPAKE realizes $\mathcal{F}$.

Since TrivialPAKE does not satisfy correctness, it does not reasonably realize $\mathcal{F}_{\mathrm{PAKE}}$. So we have a PAKE protocol that does not reasonably realize $\mathcal{F}_{\mathrm{PAKE}}$ but realizes $\mathcal{F}$, which contradicts the hypothesis about $\mathcal{F}$. ∎

---

[10] 0^λ can be replaced by any string in $\{0,1\}^\lambda$.

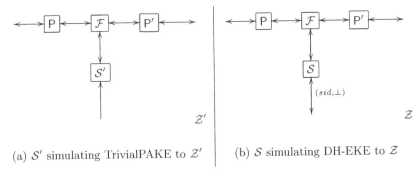

(a) $\mathcal{S}'$ simulating TrivialPAKE to $\mathcal{Z}'$ | (b) $\mathcal{S}$ simulating DH-EKE to $\mathcal{Z}$

Fig. 5. Comparison of $\mathcal{S}'$ simulating TrivialPAKE to $\mathcal{Z}'$ and $\mathcal{S}$ simulating EKE to $\mathcal{Z}$. The messages in the upper halves of (a) and (b) are identical. However, in (b), $\mathcal{Z}$ (whose role is played by $\mathcal{S}'$ in (a)) sends $(sid, \bot)$ as protocol messages to $\mathcal{S}$. Since $\mathcal{S}$ is successful, P and P$'$ must output independent random keys in (b), which in turn implies that P and P$'$ output independent random keys in (a), so $\mathcal{S}'$ is also successful. Note that $\mathcal{S}'$ never sends any messages to $\mathcal{Z}'$, as there are no protocol messages to simulate.

Fig. 6. Changes to the real-world model used by PAKE. The left is for the usual PAKE definition with a man-in-the-middle adversary, while the right shows the router model (where the router R is corrupted). The unauthenticated channel becomes two authenticated channels, with an extra router party passing messages back and forth.

6 PAKE as a Three-Party Protocol

In this section, we show how to bypass the impossibility result in the previous section and directly incorporating correctness into the PAKE functionality, by changing the execution model of the PAKE to add a third party called the *router* R. Such a definition allows a UC PAKE to compose with other protocols in the normal sense of UC composition, allowing the higher level protocols to use the fact that the PAKE is correct in a natural way.

Concretely, any protocol in the router model is required to have a distinguished party R, and authenticated channels (Fig. 7) connecting every party to R; parties other than R do not communicate with each other directly. The protocol's code for R must tell it to simply route messages between the parties—where each message sent to R is prefixed with the desired destination, while each message sent by R is prefixed with the original source. However, R is a corruptible party like any other, and when corrupted the adversary can have it modify the

> – On input (sid, R, m) from S, send $(sid, \mathsf{S}, \mathsf{R}, m)$ to $\mathcal{A}$. Wait for (Ok, sid) from
> $\mathcal{A}$. Then send (sid, S, m) to R.

Fig. 7. The authenticated channel functionality, $\mathcal{F}_{\text{AUTH}}$ (includes highlighted), together with its guaranteed delivery variant $\mathcal{F}'_{\text{AUTH}}$ (excludes highlighted). Note that we do not allow corrupted parties to modify their own messages – this feature is unimportant for our purposes. $\mathcal{F}'_{\text{AUTH}}$ is modified from $\mathcal{F}_{\text{AUTH}}$ to guarantee that every message is delivered eventually. This is needed in Section 6.2, as otherwise the protocol might not complete even when both parties are honest.

messages arbitrarily. Intuitively, R represents the man-in-the-middle adversary, and an honest R corresponds to the adversary being an eavesdropper. The modified structure for PAKE protocols in the router model is illustrated in Fig. 6.

6.1   Correctness

In this section, we first deal with the case that both protocol parties must output a key. This covers TrivialPAKE but not the "empty" protocol. In Fig. 8, we present a modified PAKE ideal functionality that works in the router model. Below we show that it is equivalent to a UC PAKE that satisfies correctness.

Definition 10. *A PAKE protocol* Π *has* guaranteed output when all parties are honest, *or simply* guaranteed output, *if in any session where all parties are honest (including the router* R*), the protocol parties both output a string in* $\{0,1\}^\lambda$ *(together with sid) with overwhelming probability before they halt.*

Theorem 3. *For any PAKE protocol* Π *that is based on an unauthenticated channel and has guaranteed output, there is a corresponding router model PAKE protocol* $\widetilde{\Pi}$ *that is based on an authenticated channel and has guaranteed output, and vice versa, such that the following conditions are equivalent:*

(a) Π *reasonably realizes* $\mathcal{F}_{PAKE}$ *(Definition 9);*
(b) $\widetilde{\Pi}$ *realizes* $\mathcal{F}_{PAKE\text{-}3}$ *(Fig. 8), where* R *follows the* **static** *corruption model;*
(c) $\widetilde{\Pi}$ *realizes* $\mathcal{F}_{PAKE\text{-}3}$*, where* R *follows the* **adaptive** *corruption model.*

Proof. The correspondence between Π and $\widetilde{\Pi}$ is already completely specified by the router model. Below we prove equivalence of the three conditions.

$(a)\Rightarrow(c)$: Let $\mathcal{S}$ be a successful strong perfectly reasonable simulator for Π, which must exist by Theorem 1. We now construct a simulator $\widetilde{\mathcal{S}}$ for $\widetilde{\Pi}$. Essentially, $\widetilde{\mathcal{S}}$ does whatever $\mathcal{S}$ does, except that $\widetilde{\mathcal{S}}$ treats the corrupted R as the man-in-the-middle adversary while simulating protocol messages and sending TestPwd commands:

– On input (NewSession, sid, P, P', pw, role) from P, create a record $\langle$P, P', pw$\rangle$ and mark it fresh if either: (a) this is the first NewSession message for sid, or (b) this is the second NewSession message for sid and there is a record $\langle$P', P, $\cdot\rangle$. Send (NewSession, sid, P, P', role) to S.

After sending NewSession, check if case (b) happened and P, P' and R are all honest. If so, run the NewKey handler below for P and then P', i.e., behave as if the messages (NewKey, sid, P, 0^λ) and (NewKey, sid, P', 0^λ) were sent by S.

– On (TestPwd, sid, P, pw*) from R or P', if it is corrupted and there is a record $\langle$P, P', pw$\rangle$ marked fresh, then do:
  • If pw* = pw, mark the record compromised and send "correct guess" to R.
  • If pw* $\neq$ pw, mark the record interrupted and send "wrong guess" to R.
– On (NewKey, sid, P, $K^* \in \{0,1\}^\lambda$) from S, if there is a record $\langle$P, P', pw$\rangle$, and this is the first NewKey message for sid and P, then output (sid, K) to P, where K is defined as follows:
  • If the record is compromised, or either P or P' is corrupted, then set $K := K^*$.
  • If the record is fresh, and a key (sid, K') has been output to P', at which time there was a record $\langle$P', P, pw$\rangle$ marked fresh, then set $K := K'$.
  • Otherwise sample $K \leftarrow \{0,1\}^\lambda$.
Finally, mark the record completed.

Fig. 8. Three-party model UC functionality $\mathcal{F}_{\text{PAKE-3}}$ for PAKE. Differences with the standard PAKE functionality (Figure 2) are highlighted in light grey. $\mathcal{F}'_{\text{PAKE-3}}$ adds the lines highlighted in dark grey to guarantee output.

Simulator $\widetilde{S}$:

1. Upon receiving the first message from $\mathcal{F}_{\text{PAKE-3}}$ (which must be NewSession), activate S using the same message. After that, forward $\mathcal{F}_{\text{PAKE-3}}$'s other NewSession messages to S (as messages from $\mathcal{F}_{\text{PAKE}}$).

2. On (sid, m) from S as the simulation of a protocol message from P to P', if R is honest, then send $(sid, \text{P}, \text{R}, m)$ and $(sid, \text{R}, \text{P}', m)$ to $\widetilde{Z}$ (as messages from $\mathcal{F}_{\text{AUTH}}$ to the adversary; same below), and (sid, m) to S (as a message from S's environment; same below). If R is corrupted, then send $(sid, \text{P}, \text{R}, m)$ to $\widetilde{Z}$ and (sid, m) to R; on (sid, m') from R, send $(sid, \text{R}, \text{P}', m')$ to $\widetilde{Z}$ and (sid, m') to S.

3. On (TestPwd, sid, P, pw*) from S, if either R or P' is corrupted, then forward this message to $\mathcal{F}_{\text{PAKE-3}}$ (as a message from the corrupted party), and forward $\mathcal{F}_{\text{PAKE-3}}$'s response ("correct/wrong guess") back to S.
   On the other hand, if both R and P' are honest but P is corrupted, note that $\mathcal{F}_{\text{PAKE-3}}$ does not allow a party to attack itself—that is, P cannot trigger

(TestPwd, sid, P, pw*). Instead, simply check if pw* matches the password of P, which can be seen from the NewSession message.

4. On (NewKey, $sid, \cdot, \cdot$) from $\mathcal{S}$, forward this message to $\mathcal{F}_{\text{PAKE-3}}$.

We now prove that $\widetilde{\mathcal{S}}$ is successful; that is, for any efficient environment $\widetilde{\mathcal{Z}}$ attacking $\widetilde{\Pi}$, $\widetilde{\mathcal{S}}$ generates a view indistinguishable from the real view of $\widetilde{\mathcal{Z}}$. The key point is that $\widetilde{\mathcal{S}}$ acts like an environment—whose behavior corresponds to $\widetilde{\mathcal{Z}}$'s behavior—in the view of $\mathcal{S}$. To formalize this argument, define an environment $\mathcal{Z}$ in the world of $\mathcal{S}$ and attacking Π:

Environment $\mathcal{Z}$:

1. When $\widetilde{\mathcal{Z}}$ activates a new session for $\langle$P, P$'\rangle$ on password pw, do the same thing.
2. As long as R is honest, instruct the adversary to transmit messages between P and P$'$ without any modifications.
3. When R is corrupted, $\widetilde{\mathcal{Z}}$ may let R modify the protocol messages arbitrarily, and $\mathcal{Z}$ matches this by instructing its own adversary modify the unauthenticated channel messages in the same way. That is, when R receives (sid, m) from P and sends (sid, m') to P$'$, instruct the adversary to send (sid, m') to P$'$.
4. When $\widetilde{\mathcal{Z}}$ outputs a bit b, output the same bit b.

In the real world, the only difference between an execution of $\widetilde{\Pi}$ by $\widetilde{\mathcal{Z}}$ and the corresponding execution of Π by $\mathcal{Z}$ is how the messages are passed and modified: in $\widetilde{\Pi}$, the protocol messages are passed through $\mathcal{F}_{\text{AUTH}}$ to the router, which may modify them when corrupted; while in Π, the protocol messages are passed and modified directly by the man-in-the-middle adversary. However, we made $\mathcal{Z}$ instruct the man-in-middle adversary to apply the same message modifications as would be made by the router (as can be seen in step 3 above). Therefore, the view of $\widetilde{\mathcal{Z}}$ in the execution of $\widetilde{\Pi}$ is identical to the view of $\mathcal{Z}$ in the corresponding execution of Π. We have that

$$\Pr[\widetilde{\mathcal{Z}} \text{ outputs 1 in the real world}] = \Pr[\mathcal{Z} \text{ outputs 1 in the real world}].$$

In the ideal world, we first claim that the view of $\mathcal{S}$ when run by $\widetilde{\mathcal{S}}$, is identical to the view of $\mathcal{S}$ in the world of $\mathcal{Z}$. Indeed, the behavior of $\widetilde{\mathcal{S}}$ when communicating with $\mathcal{S}$ is exactly the same as $\mathcal{Z}$ and $\mathcal{F}_{\text{PAKE}}$ combined, except that when P, P$'$ and R are all honest, $\widetilde{\mathcal{S}}$ ignores TestPwd commands from $\mathcal{S}$. However, notice that as long as all parties are honest, $\mathcal{Z}$ instructs the adversary to transmit messages between P and P$'$ without any modifications, so $\mathcal{S}$ sending TestPwd to $\mathcal{F}_{\text{PAKE}}$ means that GeneralSpuriousGuess($\mathcal{S}, \mathcal{Z}$) occurs—which violates the assumption that $\mathcal{S}$ is a strong perfectly reasonable simulator for Π. That is, it is impossible for $\mathcal{S}$ to send TestPwd when all parties are honest, so $\widetilde{\mathcal{S}}$ does not need to consider such an event.

We now argue that the view of $\widetilde{\mathcal{Z}}$ simulated by $\widetilde{\mathcal{S}}$ is identical to the view of $\mathcal{Z}$ simulated by $\mathcal{S}$. For protocol messages, $\widetilde{\mathcal{S}}$ simply sends whatever messages simulated by $\mathcal{S}$ to $\widetilde{\mathcal{Z}}$ (as from $\mathcal{F}_{\text{AUTH}}$). For the outputs from P and P', they are triggered by a NewKey command from $\widetilde{\mathcal{S}}$. $\widetilde{\mathcal{S}}$ sends TestPwd to $\mathcal{F}_{\text{PAKE-3}}$ whenever $\mathcal{S}$ sends such a message to $\mathcal{F}_{\text{PAKE}}$, and sends NewKey to $\mathcal{F}_{\text{PAKE-3}}$ whenever $\mathcal{S}$ sends such a message to $\mathcal{F}_{\text{PAKE}}$. Finally, note that $\mathcal{F}_{\text{PAKE-3}}$ processes NewKey messages in the same way as $\mathcal{F}_{\text{PAKE}}$ does. We conclude that

$$\Pr[\widetilde{\mathcal{Z}} \text{ outputs 1 in the ideal world with } \widetilde{\mathcal{S}}] = \Pr[\mathcal{Z} \text{ outputs 1 in the ideal world with } \mathcal{S}].$$

Combining the above, we get that $\mathbf{Dist}_{\widetilde{\Pi}, \mathcal{F}_{\text{PAKE-3}}}(\widetilde{\mathcal{S}}, \widetilde{\mathcal{Z}}) = \mathbf{Dist}_{\Pi, \mathcal{F}_{\text{PAKE}}}(\mathcal{S}, \mathcal{Z})$, which is negligible since $\mathcal{S}$ is successful. This shows that $\widetilde{\mathcal{S}}$ is successful, i.e., $\widetilde{\Pi}$ realizes $\mathcal{F}_{\text{PAKE-3}}$.

(c)⇒(b): This implication is trivial, because the adaptive corruption model is stronger than the static corruption model.

(b)⇒(a): We first prove that Π realizes $\mathcal{F}_{\text{PAKE}}$. Let $\widetilde{\mathcal{S}}$ be a successful simulator for $\widetilde{\Pi}$. The simulator $\mathcal{S}$ for Π is relatively simple so we only provide a sketch: $\mathcal{S}$ runs $\widetilde{\mathcal{S}}$, passing its inputs and outputs to the appropriate parties and functionalities. While simulating the environment for $\widetilde{\mathcal{S}}$, since R does not exist for Π, $\mathcal{S}$ runs a fake party itself, treating R as always corrupted. Any communication between $\mathcal{S}$ and $\mathcal{F}_{\text{PAKE-3}}$ is passed through directly by $\widetilde{\mathcal{S}}$ (using $\mathcal{F}_{\text{PAKE}}$ instead of $\mathcal{F}_{\text{PAKE-3}}$). For protocol messages, $\mathcal{S}$ needs to translate between protocol message tampering by $\mathcal{A}$ and tampering by R—that is, when $\widetilde{\mathcal{S}}$ sends e.g., $(sid, \mathsf{P}, \mathsf{R}, m)$ as a message from $\mathcal{F}_{\text{AUTH}}$ to the adversary, $\mathcal{S}$ sends (sid, m) as a message from P to P'; when $\mathcal{S}$ receives (sid, m') aimed at P', it sends the same message to $\widetilde{\mathcal{S}}$ as a message from R.

To show that $\mathcal{S}$ is successful, for any environment $\mathcal{Z}$ attacking Π, let $\widetilde{\mathcal{Z}}$ be an environment attacking $\widetilde{\Pi}$ that corrupts R at the beginning of the protocol. Whenever $\mathcal{Z}$ instructs its adversary to tamper with protocol messages in Π, $\widetilde{\mathcal{Z}}$ translates this into tampering by R in $\widetilde{\Pi}$. With this change to the environment, the real and ideal worlds of Π exactly match the real and ideal worlds of $\widetilde{\Pi}$, and following the same structure as the proof of (a)⇒(c), we can see that $\mathcal{S}$ is successful.

Finally, we must prove that Π is correct. To see this, consider an environment $\widetilde{\mathcal{Z}}$ attacking $\widetilde{\Pi}$, which activates a session between P and P' with the two parties using the same password pw, and outputs 1 if P and P' output the same key when they halt. ($\widetilde{\mathcal{Z}}$ does not corrupt R.) In the ideal world of $\widetilde{\mathcal{Z}}$, TestPwd cannot be used so session records must remain fresh, guaranteeing that P and P' output the same key. This means that in a real execution of $\widetilde{\Pi}$, when P and P' are honest using the same password pw, and R is honest, P and P' must eventually output the same key with overwhelming probability. (The argument above relies on the fact that $\widetilde{\Pi}$ has guaranteed output, i.e., P and P' must output *some* key in $\widetilde{\Pi}$.) By the definition of $\widetilde{\Pi}$, this immediately implies the correctness of Π, where the condition "R is honest" is replaced by "the adversary is an eavesdropper". ∎

6.2   PAKE Guaranteeing Output

Figure 6 also presents $\mathcal{F}'_{\text{PAKE-3}}$, another PAKE ideal functionality in the router model, this time designed to guarantee output as well as correctness. The idea is to have the ideal functionality itself trigger the NewKey interface if the simulator does not do it.

Unfortunately, two complications come with this change to the router model PAKE functionality. First, we need to guarantee delivery of all messages sent through the authenticated channel, as otherwise this functionality is impossible to realize. We use a modified authenticated channel functionality $\mathcal{F}'_{\text{AUTH}}$ (see Fig. 7), where the message is both sent to the adversary and delivered directly.

Parallel Execution. More importantly, these modified ideal functionalities now send more than one message per activation, which is unusual for UC. Normally ideal functionalities (as well as adversaries and simulators) are supposed to send just one message and halt, not send other messages that might be processed in parallel—in which case there might a "race condition".

To see why this is problematic, consider the following example: let the environment start a PAKE session with P, P′, and R all honest. The corresponding protocol messages must then be simulated. If the ideal functionality were to "run faster" than the simulator, i.e., if it triggers the NewKey handlers before the simulator finishes generating the protocol messages, then the key will be delivered too early. This would let the real world and ideal world be easily distinguished.

We clarify the execution order by specifying that if program is of the form "Send message m to party X, then do y", the action y waits until after m is sent and every action that occurs as a result of send m completes.[11] For example, with adaptive corruption, if the adversary receives $(sid, \text{P}, \text{R}, m)$ from $\mathcal{F}'_{\text{AUTH}}$ it could decide to corrupt R; this corruption would take place *before* (sid, S, m) is sent to R. This ensures that there is still only one thread of execution occurring at a time, and the ideal functionality merely writes down some action for later (when there is nothing left to do).

While this is not a usual description of UC functionalities, it can be made rigorous using the techniques from [21]. In their model, the environment is given the power to slowly advance the protocol through the honest party's interfaces, by repeatedly triggering an Output interface in the functionality. On every Output message[12], let the ideal functionality start performing whatever action was saved for later. As long as these queries are made by the environment, the functionality will work as described above.

---

[11] This can be viewed as a priority system. In programs of this form, we assign the action y a lower priority than sending m to X, all processing done by X, all messages sent by X as a result, and so on.

[12] Technically, Output must be sent by every honest party. Additionally, it must be sent some polynomial number of times, not just once, to allow protocols with multiple rounds. See [21] for details.

Theorem 4. *A router model PAKE protocol $\widetilde{\Pi}$ realizes $\mathcal{F}_{PAKE\text{-}3}$ with guaranteed output if and only if $\widetilde{\Pi}$ realizes $\mathcal{F}'_{PAKE\text{-}3}$ (in the guaranteed delivery router model, i.e., all protocol messages are sent via $\mathcal{F}'_{AUTH}$). This holds whether the router is modeled with static or adaptive corruption.*

Proof. $\mathcal{F}'_{PAKE\text{-}3} \Rightarrow \mathcal{F}_{PAKE\text{-}3}$ *with guaranteed output:* It is trivial that $\widetilde{\Pi}$ realizes $\mathcal{F}_{PAKE\text{-}3}$, because removing the extra NewKey trigger in NewSession only strengthens the simulator's power, as does adding the ability to not deliver messages sent through $\mathcal{F}_{AUTH}$. That is, the simulator can send (NewKey, sid, P, 0^λ) and (NewKey, sid, P', 0^λ) to $\mathcal{F}_{PAKE\text{-}3}$ at the end, like $\mathcal{F}'_{PAKE\text{-}3}$ would have done, and can always choose to have all messages delivered eventually, like in $\mathcal{F}'_{AUTH}$.

We now show that $\widetilde{\Pi}$ has guaranteed output. Consider the following environment in the world of $\mathcal{F}'_{PAKE\text{-}3}$:

Environment $\widetilde{\mathcal{Z}}$:

1. Initialize a single session between P and P' on pw. That is, pick any sid, and input (NewSession, sid, P, P', pw, role) to P and (NewSession, sid, P', P, pw, role') to P'.
2. Instruct $\mathcal{A}$ to be an eavesdropper in session sid.
3. Output 1 if P outputs $(sid, K \in \{0,1\}^\lambda)$ and P' outputs $(sid, K' \in \{0,1\}^\lambda)$ before they halt, and output 0 otherwise.

Let $\mathcal{S}$ be a successful simulator for $\widetilde{\mathcal{Z}}$. In the ideal world, note that the extra clause in $\mathcal{F}'_{PAKE\text{-}3}$ (under the NewSession command) guarantees that (NewKey, sid, P, $\cdot$) and (NewKey, sid, P', $\cdot$) will be called at least once, causing P and P' to output a key in $\{0,1\}^\lambda$ (together with sid). Thus, $\widetilde{\mathcal{Z}}$ always outputs 1. This means that in the real world,

$$\Pr[\text{P outputs } (sid, K \in \{0,1\}^\lambda) \wedge \text{P' outputs } (sid, K' \in \{0,1\}^\lambda)] \geq 1 - \mathbf{Dist}(\mathcal{S}, \mathcal{Z}),$$

which is overwhelming. This shows that $\widetilde{\Pi}$ has guaranteed output.

$\mathcal{F}_{PAKE\text{-}3}$ *with guaranteed output* $\Rightarrow \mathcal{F}'_{PAKE\text{-}3}$: Given a successful simulator $\widetilde{\mathcal{S}}$ for $\widetilde{\Pi}$ realizing $\mathcal{F}_{PAKE\text{-}3}$ using $\mathcal{F}_{AUTH}$, we define a simulator $\widetilde{\mathcal{S}}'$ for $\widetilde{\Pi}$ realizing $\mathcal{F}'_{PAKE\text{-}3}$ using $\mathcal{F}'_{AUTH}$:

Simulator $\widetilde{\mathcal{S}}'$:

1. Run $\widetilde{\mathcal{S}}$, and processing each message as if $\widetilde{\mathcal{S}}'$ had received it.
2. Whenever $\widetilde{\mathcal{S}}$ sends $(sid, \mathsf{S}, \mathsf{R}, m)$ to $\mathcal{A}$, instruct $\widetilde{\mathcal{S}}$ to deliver (sid, S, m) to the recipient R.

Let $\widetilde{\mathcal{Z}}'$ be an efficient environment against $\widetilde{\Pi}$ realizing $\mathcal{F}'_{PAKE\text{-}3}$. Consider the following environment $\widetilde{\mathcal{Z}}$ against $\widetilde{\Pi}$ realizing $\mathcal{F}'_{PAKE\text{-}3}$:

Environment $\widetilde{\mathcal{Z}}$:

1. Run $\widetilde{\mathcal{Z}}'$, and pass messages between $\widetilde{\mathcal{Z}}'$ and P, P' and $\mathcal{F}'_{\text{AUTH}}$ without any modifications (when a message is sent from $\mathcal{F}_{\text{AUTH}}$, pass this message to $\widetilde{\mathcal{Z}}'$ as if it is from $\mathcal{F}'_{\text{AUTH}}$).
2. Whenever a message $(sid, \mathsf{S}, \mathsf{R}, m)$ is sent from $\mathcal{F}_{\text{AUTH}}$ to $\widetilde{\mathcal{Z}}'$, wait until $\widetilde{\mathcal{Z}}'$ finishes processing the message and all actions it triggers complete. Then let $\mathcal{F}_{\text{AUTH}}$ deliver the message to its destination R.
3. When $\widetilde{\mathcal{Z}}'$ outputs a bit b, output the same bit b.

In the real world, $\widetilde{\mathcal{Z}}$ behaves identically to $\widetilde{\mathcal{Z}}'$. Indeed, waiting for $\widetilde{\mathcal{Z}}'$'s processing (and whatever $\widetilde{\mathcal{Z}}'$ triggers) to finish before delivering the message is exactly the semantics given above for the execution splitting in $\mathcal{F}'_{\text{AUTH}}$ (see discussion at the start of this section).

In the ideal world, this same feature of $\widetilde{\mathcal{Z}}$ matches with $\widetilde{\mathcal{S}}'$ always instructing $\widetilde{\mathcal{S}}$ to simulate delivering its messages. This makes the ideal world with $\mathcal{F}'_{\text{PAKE-3}}$, $\widetilde{\mathcal{S}}'$ and $\widetilde{\mathcal{Z}}'$, and the ideal world with $\mathcal{F}_{\text{PAKE-3}}$, $\widetilde{\mathcal{S}}$ and $\widetilde{\mathcal{Z}}$, differ only in the extra clause in $\mathcal{F}'_{\text{PAKE-3}}$. However, this clause only matters when all three parties are honest, and no NewKey message has been sent for both P and P'—in which case in the ideal world with $\mathcal{F}_{\text{PAKE-3}}$, $\widetilde{\mathcal{S}}$ and $\widetilde{\mathcal{Z}}$, $\widetilde{\mathcal{Z}}$ might halt without the key sent to P and P'. We have that

$$\mathbf{Dist}_{\widetilde{\Pi}, \mathcal{F}'_{\text{PAKE-3}}}(\widetilde{\mathcal{S}}', \widetilde{\mathcal{Z}}')$$

$$= \Pr[\mathsf{P}, \mathsf{P}' \text{ output nothing in some session in the ideal world with } \mathcal{F}_{\text{PAKE-3}}, \widetilde{\mathcal{S}} \text{ and } \widetilde{\mathcal{Z}}]$$

$$\leq \Pr[\mathsf{P}, \mathsf{P}' \text{ output nothing in some session in the real world with } \widetilde{\Pi} \text{ and } \widetilde{\mathcal{Z}}]+$$

$$\mathbf{Dist}_{\widetilde{\Pi}, \mathcal{F}_{\text{PAKE-3}}}(\widetilde{\mathcal{S}}, \widetilde{\mathcal{Z}}),$$

which is negligible since $\widetilde{\Pi}$ has guaranteed output and $\widetilde{\mathcal{S}}$ is successful. So $\widetilde{\mathcal{S}}'$ is successful and we conclude that $\widetilde{\Pi}$ realizes $\mathcal{F}'_{\text{PAKE-3}}$. ∎

7   Conclusion

In this work, we presented a comprehensive study of correctness in universally composable symmetric PAKE. Our contributions are four-fold:

1. We showed that TrivialPAKE, a protocol where the two parties simply output independent random keys, realizes the standard UC PAKE functionality;
2. We showed nine possible ways to address the issue, including adding a separate notion of correctness and placing "reasonability" constraints on the UC simulator. We proved that seven of the approaches above are equivalent, while the other two are unachievable;
3. We proved that it is impossibly to modify the UC PAKE functionality to include correctness;
4. We showed how to bypass the impossibility result by modeling PAKE as a three-party protocol, including a third party called the router. We presented a three-party PAKE functionality that is equivalent to normal PAKE with correctness.

While this work is in the context of PAKE, it seems that similar issues about correctness appear in *any* protocol in the man-in-the-middle setting. For example, the UC authenticated key exchange (AKE) functionalities in [17,25] also do not guarantee correctness: the functionalities include an Interfere command which causes the corresponding party to output a random key, just like TestPwd in $\mathcal{F}_{\mathrm{PAKE}}$ (when the password guess is incorrect); thus, an incorrect protocol where the two parties output independent random keys still has a successful simulator, just as with TrivialPAKE. We conjecture that results similar to ours—including the natural fix by switching to the router model—hold for other UC functionalities in the man-in-the-middle setting.

Finally, as pointed out in Remark 2, reasonable simulators have been (informally) discussed while addressing another definitional issue in *asymmetric* PAKE (aPAKE), although not in the context of correctness (hence the underlying reason why this constraint on the UC simulator is needed is different from ours). It would be interesting to explore whether a similar impossibility result holds for aPAKE, and whether the requirement that a simulator be reasonable can be removed by adding another party to the modeling of aPAKE.

References

1. Abdalla, M., Barbosa, M., Bradley, T., Jarecki, S., Katz, J., Xu, J.: Universally composable relaxed password authenticated key exchange. In: Micciancio, D., Ristenpart, T. (eds.) CRYPTO 2020. LNCS, vol. 12170, pp. 278–307. Springer, Cham (2020). https://doi.org/10.1007/978-3-030-56784-2_10
2. Abdalla, M., Haase, B., Hesse, J.: Security analysis of CPace. In: ASIACRYPT 2021, Part IV, Dec. (2021)
3. Abdalla, M., Pointcheval, D.: Simple password-based encrypted key exchange protocols. In: Menezes, A. (ed.) CT-RSA 2005. LNCS, vol. 3376, pp. 191–208. Springer, Heidelberg (2005). https://doi.org/10.1007/978-3-540-30574-3_14
4. Bellare, M., Pointcheval, D., Rogaway, P.: Authenticated key exchange secure against dictionary attacks. In: Preneel, B. (ed.) EUROCRYPT 2000. LNCS, vol. 1807, pp. 139–155. Springer, Heidelberg (2000). https://doi.org/10.1007/3-540-45539-6_11
5. Bellovin, S.M., Merritt, M.: Encrypted key exchange: password-based protocols secure against dictionary attacks. In: 1992 IEEE Symposium on Security and Privacy, May (1992)
6. Bellovin, S.M., Merritt, M.: Augmented encrypted key exchange: a password-based protocol secure against dictionary attacks and password file compromise. In: ACM CCS 93, Nov. (1993)
7. Boyko, V., MacKenzie, P., Patel, S.: Provably secure password-authenticated key exchange using diffie-hellman. In: Preneel, B. (ed.) EUROCRYPT 2000. LNCS, vol. 1807, pp. 156–171. Springer, Heidelberg (2000). https://doi.org/10.1007/3-540-45539-6_12
8. Canetti, R.: Universally composable security: a new paradigm for cryptographic protocols. In: 42nd FOCS, Oct. (2001)
9. Canetti, R., Fischlin, M.: Universally composable commitments. In: Kilian, J. (ed.) CRYPTO 2001. LNCS, vol. 2139, pp. 19–40. Springer, Heidelberg (2001). https://doi.org/10.1007/3-540-44647-8_2

10. Canetti, R., Halevi, S., Katz, J., Lindell, Y., MacKenzie, P.: Universally composable password-based key exchange. In: Cramer, R. (ed.) EUROCRYPT 2005. LNCS, vol. 3494, pp. 404–421. Springer, Heidelberg (2005). https://doi.org/10.1007/11426639_24

11. Canetti, R., Kushilevitz, E., Lindell, Y.: On the limitations of universally composable two-party computation without set-up assumptions. In: Biham, E. (ed.) EUROCRYPT 2003. LNCS, vol. 2656, pp. 68–86. Springer, Heidelberg (2003). https://doi.org/10.1007/3-540-39200-9_5

12. Canetti, R., Lindell, Y., Ostrovsky, R., Sahai, A.: Universally composable two-party and multi-party secure computation. In: 34th ACM STOC, May (2002)

13. Crypto Forum Research Group. PAKE selection (2020). https://github.com/cfrg/pake-selection

14. Dupont, P.-A., Hesse, J., Pointcheval, D., Reyzin, L., Yakoubov, S.: Fuzzy password-authenticated key exchange. In: Nielsen, J.B., Rijmen, V. (eds.) EUROCRYPT 2018. LNCS, vol. 10822, pp. 393–424. Springer, Cham (2018). https://doi.org/10.1007/978-3-319-78372-7_13

15. Gentry, C., MacKenzie, P., Ramzan, Z.: A method for making password-based key exchange resilient to server compromise. In: Dwork, C. (ed.) CRYPTO 2006. LNCS, vol. 4117, pp. 142–159. Springer, Heidelberg (2006). https://doi.org/10.1007/11818175_9

16. Groce, A., Katz, J.: A new framework for efficient password-based authenticated key exchange. In: ACM CCS 2010, Oct. (2010)

17. Gu, Y., Jarecki, S., Krawczyk, H.: KHAPE: asymmetric PAKE from key-hiding key exchange. In: CRYPTO 2021, Part IV, Aug. (2021)

18. Haase, B., Labrique, B.: AuCPace: efficient verifier-based PAKE protocol tailored for the IIoT. Cryptology ePrint Archive, Report 2018/286, (2018). https://eprint.iacr.org/2018/286

19. Hesse, J.: Separating symmetric and asymmetric password-authenticated key exchange. In: SCN 20, Sept. (2020)

20. Jarecki, S., Krawczyk, H., Xu, J.: OPAQUE: an asymmetric PAKE protocol secure against pre-computation attacks. In: Nielsen, J.B., Rijmen, V. (eds.) EUROCRYPT 2018. LNCS, vol. 10822, pp. 456–486. Springer, Cham (2018). https://doi.org/10.1007/978-3-319-78372-7_15

21. Katz, J., Maurer, U., Tackmann, B., Zikas, V.: Universally composable synchronous computation. In: Sahai, A. (ed.) TCC 2013. LNCS, vol. 7785, pp. 477–498. Springer, Heidelberg (2013). https://doi.org/10.1007/978-3-642-36594-2_27

22. Katz, J., Ostrovsky, R., Yung, M.: Efficient password-authenticated key exchange using human-memorable passwords. In: Pfitzmann, B. (ed.) EUROCRYPT 2001. LNCS, vol. 2045, pp. 475–494. Springer, Heidelberg (2001). https://doi.org/10.1007/3-540-44987-6_29

23. Katz, J., Vaikuntanathan, V.: Smooth projective hashing and password-based authenticated key exchange from lattices. In: Matsui, M. (ed.) ASIACRYPT 2009. LNCS, vol. 5912, pp. 636–652. Springer, Heidelberg (2009). https://doi.org/10.1007/978-3-642-10366-7_37

24. McQuoid, I., Rosulek, M., Roy, L.: Minimal symmetric PAKE and 1-out-of-N OT from programmable-once public functions. In: ACM CCS 2020, Nov. (2020)

25. Santos, B.F.D., Gu, Y., Jarecki, S., Krawczyk, H.: Asymmetric PAKE with low computation and communication. In: EUROCRYPT 2022, Part II, May/June (2022)

26. Smyshlyaev, S.V.: Results of the PAKE selection process (2020). https://mailarchive.ietf.org/arch/msg/cfrg/LKbwodpa5yXo6VuNDU66vt_Aca8

Sender-binding Key Encapsulation

Laurin Benz[1,2], Wasilij Beskorovajnov[3], Sarai Eilebrecht[3],
Jörn Müller-Quade[1,2,3], Astrid Ottenhues[1,2], and Rebecca Schwerdt[1,2(✉)]

[1] Karlsruhe Institute of Technology (KIT), Karlsruhe, Germany
{laurin.benz,mueller-quade,ottenhues,schwerdt}@kit.edu
[2] KASTEL Security Research Labs, Karlsruhe, Germany
[3] FZI Research Center for Information Technology, Karlsruhe, Germany
{beskorovajnov,eilebrecht}@fzi.de

Abstract. Secure communication is gained by combining encryption
with authentication. In real-world applications encryption commonly
takes the form of KEM-DEM hybrid encryption, which is combined with
ideal authentication. The pivotal question is how weak the employed
key encapsulation mechanism (KEM) is allowed to be to still yield universally composable (UC) secure communication when paired with symmetric encryption and ideal authentication. This question has so far been
addressed for public-key encryption (PKE) only, showing that encryption does not need to be stronger than sender-binding CPA, which binds
the CPA secure ciphertext non-malleably to the sender ID. For hybrid
encryption, prior research unanimously reaches for CCA2 secure encryption which is unnecessarily strong. Answering this research question is
vital to develop more efficient and feasible protocols for real-world secure
communication and thus enable more communication to be conducted
securely.

In this paper we use ideas from the PKE setting to develop new
answers for hybrid encryption. We develop a new and significantly
weaker security notion—sender-binding CPA for KEMs—which is still
strong enough for secure communication. By using game-based notions
as building blocks, we attain secure communication in the form of ideal
functionalities with proofs in the UC-framework. Secure communication is reached in both the classic as well as session context by adding
authentication and one-time/replayable CCA secure symmetric encryption respectively. We furthermore provide an efficient post-quantum
secure LWE-based construction in the standard model giving an indication of the real-world benefit resulting from our new security notion.
Overall we manage to make significant progress on discovering the minimal security requirements for hybrid encryption components to facilitate
secure communication.

Keywords: IND-SB-CPA · Key Encapsulation · Secure
Communication · Authenticated Channels · UC

1 Introduction

Secure communication has always been the first and foremost goal of cryptography. The common way to reach this goal is to combine encryption with

© International Association for Cryptologic Research 2023
A. Boldyreva and V. Kolesnikov (Eds.): PKC 2023, LNCS 13940, pp. 744–773, 2023.
https://doi.org/10.1007/978-3-031-31368-4_26

authentication. Development on the encryption side has come a long way from the roots of symmetric encryption schemes via public-key encryption (PKE) [1] to modern hybrid encryption [2], where keys are exchanged via a public-key key encapsulation mechanism (KEM) and subsequently used to symmetrically encrypt messages.

For secure communication via PKE it has long been known that CCA2 secure encryption is unnecessarily strong if authentication is already provided [3]. A recent breakthrough in this setting [4] showed that sender-binding encryption (SBE) and IND-SB-CPA security are the right concepts to realize secure message transfer from authenticated channels in the universal composability (UC) model. SBE is a PKE adaption which binds the ciphertext to the sender ID. The authors of [4], however, only consider PKE while real world applications have moved on to hybrid encryption.

In the field of hybrid encryption, on the other hand, the question of how strong (or weak) encryption should be for secure communication has been completely ignored. Constructing indistinguishability under adaptive chosen ciphertext attack (IND-CCA2) secure PKE is seen as the only significant goal, regardless of the fact that in practice encryption schemes are then usually paired with authentication via digital signatures to gain secure communication.

We bridge the gap between these two worlds by bringing sender-binding ideas to real world efficient KEM-DEM hybrid encryption [2,5]:

Our Contribution. Our contribution includes an adaptation of the concept of SBE from the PKE to the KEM setting, yielding the notion of sender-binding key encapsulation mechanism (SB-KEM) with corresponding IND-SB-CPA security. We prove IND-SB-CPA$_{\text{SB-KEM}}$[1] security to be the weakest so far—other than plain CPA security—by investigating its relation to previously proposed (tag-)KEM security notions. Furthermore we show that IND-SB-CPA$_{\text{SB-KEM}}$ security is in fact the KEM equivalent of IND-SB-CPA$_{\text{SBE}}$. This directly leads us to the proof that IND-SB-CPA$_{\text{SB-KEM}}$ is still strong enough to facilitate secure communication via the KEM-DEM principle over authenticated channels. We present the security proofs both for the single-message setting as well as for session communication, resulting in the ideal functionalities of secure message transfer and secure channels respectively. Lastly we indicate the potential practical benefit of our theoretic advancements by giving a concrete IND-SB-CPA secure SB-KEM construction. Our construction is a simplified version of the recently proposed and, as far as we know, currently most efficient KEM construction in the standard model [6]. Overall we manage to provide a new and weaker–but still sufficiently strong–security notion for the public-key encryption part of secure communication which could lead to efficiency gains. The different parts of our contribution can be viewed in Fig. 1. They are distributed throughout this paper as follows:

---

[1] When not obvious, the type of scheme a security notion pertains to is given in subscript.

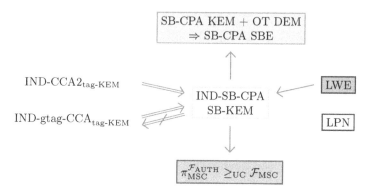

Fig. 1. Overview of Our Contribution. (Duck or rabbit?)

- In Section 4 we adapt the concept of SBE and IND-SB-CPA$_{SBE}$ to the KEM setting, developing SB-KEM and IND-SB-CPA$_{SB\text{-}KEM}$. We furthermore highlight some relations to other KEM security notions in Section 4 .

  In Appendix A of the full version of this paper [7] we furthermore provide a generic transformation from dual receiver key encapsulation mechanism (DR-KEM) which is analogous to the SBE construction from receiver encryption (DRE). This aids us in separating IND-SB-CPA$_{SB\text{-}KEM}$ from IND-gtag-CCA$_{tag\text{-}KEM}$.

- In Section 5 we prove that IND-SB-CPA secure KEM can be combined with a one-time (OT) secure data encapsulation mechanism (DEM) to gain IND-SB-CPA$_{SBE}$. This in turn UC-realizes secure message transfer when authenticated channels are added.

- For Section 6 we switch from the classic setting to the setting of session communication and prove that IND-SB-CPA$_{SB\text{-}KEM}$ in conjunction with IND-CCA2$_{DEM}$ (or IND-RCCA$_{DEM}$) and authenticated channels UC-realize secure channels. This is an improvement over the results of [8] which needed CCA2 security from both the KEM and DEM component.

- In Section 7 we present an efficient post-quantum secure SB-KEM construction based on the standard learning with errors (LWE) assumption in the standard model and prove it to be IND-SB-CPA$_{SB\text{-}KEM}$ secure. In Appendix B of the full version of this paper [7] we furthermore propose an efficient learning parity with noise (LPN) based construction.

2 Preliminaries

We start by providing some basic knowledge needed to understand our research. This includes an introduction to the KEM-DEM- as well as UC-framework and definitions of various game-based and ideal functionality security notions. Readers who are already familiar with these topics might want to skip this section and only come back to it later if they want to look something up.

2.1   The KEM-DEM Framework

First, we briefly recap the KEM-DEM framework which was introduced in [5] and subsequently included in the encryption ISO standard in 2006 [2,9]. The KEM-DEM framework is a special form of hybrid encryption which combines the advantages of both public-key and symmetric encryption: The symmetric encryption of messages makes encryption more efficient while the KEM public key infrastructure alleviates the need for a key exchange protocol. In particular, the KEM-DEM framework consists of two modular components. The first component is a public-key key encapsulation mechanism (KEM) which generates a symmetric key and encrypts it, while the second component is a symmetric data encapsulation mechanism (DEM) which uses this symmetric key to encrypt a message:

Definition (KEM): A *key encapsulation mechanism (KEM)* is given by a set of three probabilistic polynomial time (PPT) algorithms $(\mathsf{gen}, \mathsf{enc}, \mathsf{dec})$ with

$$\mathsf{gen} : 1^\lambda \mapsto (sk, pk), \qquad \mathsf{enc} : pk \mapsto (K, C), \qquad \mathsf{dec} : (sk, C) \mapsto K$$

such that the correctness property holds, i.e. $K = \mathsf{dec}(sk, C)$ whenever $(sk, pk) \leftarrow \mathsf{gen}(1^\lambda)$ and $(K, C) \leftarrow \mathsf{enc}(pk)$.

Definition (DEM): A *data encapsulation mechanism (DEM)* is given by a set of two PPT algorithms $(\mathsf{DEM.enc}, \mathsf{DEM.dec})$ with $\mathsf{DEM.enc} : (K, m) \mapsto c$ and $\mathsf{DEM.dec} : (K, c) \mapsto m$ such that $m = \mathsf{DEM.dec}(K, c)$ whenever $c \leftarrow \mathsf{DEM.enc}(K, m)$ (correctness).

The KEM-DEM framework comes in two flavors which slightly differ in the combination of the KEM and DEM. One construction–which we call *single-message* communication– generates a fresh symmetric key for each encryption of a message. This is the original definition of the KEM-DEM framework and intuitively yields a PKE scheme $(\mathsf{Gen}, \mathsf{Enc}, \mathsf{Dec})$ where $\mathsf{Gen} \equiv \mathsf{gen}$ and

$\mathsf{Enc}(pk, m)$:
- $(K, C) \leftarrow \mathsf{enc}(pk)$.
- $c \leftarrow \mathsf{DEM.enc}(K, m)$.
$\hookrightarrow$ Return (C, c).

$\mathsf{Dec}(sk, (C, c))$:
- $K \leftarrow \mathsf{dec}(sk, C)$.
- $m \leftarrow \mathsf{DEM.dec}(K, c)$.
$\hookrightarrow$ Return m.

For *Session* communication on the other hand, one party (who does not need a KEM key pair themselves) generates a persistent symmetric key via the KEM and sends it to the communication partner once. This symmetric session key is then used for many messages between the two involved parties.

Tag-KEMs. A slight variation of classical KEMs are tag-key encapsulation mechanisms (tag-KEMs) [10] which additionally use tag to encapsulate and decapsulate the symmetric key. The encapsulation phase of the tag-KEM is split in two separate phases: A first phase that generates the symmetric key and a second phase that encapsulates the given symmetric key using the tag. The split is made to allow for the tag to depend on the symmetric key itself.

Definition (Tag-KEM): A *tag-KEM* is given by a set of four PPT algorithms $(\mathsf{gen}, \mathsf{key}, \mathsf{enc}, \mathsf{dec})$ with

$$\mathsf{gen}: \qquad 1^\lambda \mapsto (sk, pk) \qquad\qquad \mathsf{key}: \qquad pk \mapsto (K, aux)$$
$$\mathsf{enc}: \quad (\tau, aux) \mapsto C \qquad\qquad\quad \mathsf{dec}: \quad (sk, \tau, C) \mapsto K$$

such that the correctness property holds, i.e. $K = \mathsf{dec}(sk, \tau, C)$ whenever $(sk, pk) \leftarrow \mathsf{gen}(1^\lambda)$, $(K, aux) \leftarrow \mathsf{key}(pk)$ and $C \leftarrow \mathsf{enc}(\tau, aux)$.

When introducing tag-KEMs, Abe et al. [10] use them in a slightly modified tag-KEM-DEM framework where the symmetrically encrypted message is used as the tag for encapsulation which allows for a weaker DEM to be used.

2.2 Game-based Security Notions

In this section we recap previously defined game-based security notions used in this paper. First we give definitions for PKE schemes, then KEM and finally DEM schemes. Whenever it is not immediately obvious for which type of scheme a security notion is intended, we denote it in its index, e.g. IND-CCA2$_{\mathrm{PKE}}$.

IND-SB-CPA$_{\mathrm{SBE}}$. The PKE security notion which inspired this whole paper is called IND-SB-CPA and was recently introduced by Beskorovajnov et al. [4]. We use this notion as a basis for the new KEM security definition we introduce in Sect. 4. IND-SB-CPA$_{\mathrm{SBE}}$ security pertains to the special PKE case of SBE where both encryption and decryption take the ID S of the encrypting (or sending) party as additional input, binding a ciphertext not only to the receiver (via their public key) but to the sender as well. The intuition behind IND-SB-CPA$_{\mathrm{SBE}}$ security is that an adversary may be able to modify the message content of ciphertexts arbitrarily but is not able to change a ciphertext such that it is bound to a party ID other than that of the sender or receiver. More formally:

Definition (IND-SB-CPA$_{\mathrm{SBE}}$): An SBE scheme $(\mathsf{gen}, \mathsf{enc}, \mathsf{dec})$ with set of party IDs **P** satisfies *indistinguishability under sender-binding chosen plaintext attack (IND-SB-CPA)* (cf. [4]), iff for any PPT adversary $\mathcal{A}_{\mathrm{SB-CPA}}$ the advantage to win the IND-SB-CPA game in Fig. 2 is negligible in security parameter λ.

IND-gtag-CCA$_{\mathrm{TBE}}$ Tag-based encryption (TBE) [11] is closely related to SBE. Instead of party IDs the tags given to both encryption and decryption are taken from a dedicated tag space **T**. For our paper we only need the weakest notion so far proposed for TBE–IND-gtag-CCA–which we later on adapt to KEMs to develop a better understanding of how strong (or rather weak) IND-SB-CPA$_{\mathrm{SB-KEM}}$ is in comparison to other notions. The following definition is taken from [4].

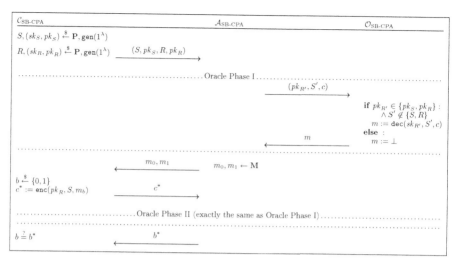

Fig. 2. The IND-SB-CPA$_{\mathrm{SBE}}$ Game for SBE from [4].

Definition (IND-gtag-CCA$_{\mathbf{TBE}}$): A TBE scheme $\Sigma = (\mathsf{gen}, \mathsf{enc}, \mathsf{dec})$ with tag space $\mathbf{T}$ satisfies *indistinguishability under given-tag weakly chosen ciphertext attack (IND-gtag-CCA)*, iff for any PPT adversary $\mathcal{A} = (\mathcal{A}_1, \mathcal{A}_2)$ the advantage

$$\mathsf{Adv}_{\mathcal{A},\Sigma}^{\mathrm{gtag\text{-}CCA}}(\lambda) := \left| \mathbb{P}\left[b \leftarrow \mathcal{A}_2^{\mathcal{O}^*}(c^*, aux) \,\middle|\, \tau^* \xleftarrow{\$} \mathbf{T}; (sk, pk) \leftarrow \mathsf{gen}(1^\lambda); \right.\right.$$

$$(aux, m_0, m_1) \leftarrow \mathcal{A}_1^{\mathcal{O}^*}(pk, \tau^*); b \xleftarrow{\$} \{0,1\};$$

$$\left.\left. c^* \leftarrow \mathsf{enc}(pk, \tau^*, m_b) \right] - \tfrac{1}{2} \right|$$

is negligible in λ, where $\mathcal{O}^*(\tau, c)$ returns $\bot$ for $\tau = \tau^*$ and $\mathsf{dec}(sk, \tau, c)$ otherwise.

IND-CCA2$_{\mathbf{tag\text{-}KEM}}$. The following definition was taken from [10]. Note that in [10] there is a first oracle phase where the adversary only has pk as prior input. Since the adversary has equal oracle access for the second phase and only gains additional input inbetween (rather than making any output themselves), the first oracle phase is redundant and we choose to present the notion without it.

Definition (IND-CCA2$_{\mathbf{tag\text{-}KEM}}$): A tag-KEM $\Sigma = (\mathsf{gen}, \mathsf{key}, \mathsf{enc}, \mathsf{dec})$ satisfies *IND-CCA2*, iff for any PPT adversary $\mathcal{A} = (\mathcal{A}_1, \mathcal{A}_2)$ the advantage

$$\mathsf{Adv}_{\mathcal{A},\Sigma}^{\mathrm{CCA2}}(\lambda) := \left| \mathbb{P}\left[b \leftarrow \mathcal{A}_2^{\mathcal{O}^*}(C^*, aux_{\mathcal{A}}) \,\middle|\, (sk, pk) \leftarrow \mathsf{gen}(1^\lambda); \right.\right.$$

$$(aux, K_0) \leftarrow \mathsf{key}(pk); K_1 \xleftarrow{\$} \{0,1\}^{|K_0|}; b \xleftarrow{\$} \{0,1\};$$

$$\left.\left. (\tau^*, aux_{\mathcal{A}}) \leftarrow \mathcal{A}_1^{\mathcal{O}}(pk, K_b); C^* \leftarrow \mathsf{enc}(aux, \tau^*) \right] - \tfrac{1}{2} \right|$$

is negligible in λ, where $\mathcal{O}$ denotes $\mathsf{dec}(sk, \cdot, \cdot)$ and $\mathcal{O}^*(\tau, C)$ returns $\bot$ for $(\tau, C) = (\tau^*, C^*)$ and $\mathsf{dec}(sk, \tau, C)$ otherwise.

For symmetric private-key security notions we follow the more descriptive notation of [12]. With the also commonly used PX-CY notation of [13], one-time attack (OT) corresponds to P0-C0, while CCA2 corresponds to P2-C2.

IND-OT$_{\text{DEM}}$. The OT notion for DEMs is an even weaker security notion than classic CPA, as it does not even provide the adversary with an encryption oracle. We use this notion later on in Sect. 5 in combination with an IND-SB-CPA$_{\text{SB-KEM}}$ secure KEM to realize secure message transfer.

Definition (IND-OT$_{\text{DEM}}$): A DEM $\Sigma = (\text{DEM.enc}, \text{DEM.dec})$ satisfies *indistinguishability under one-time attack (IND-OT)*, iff for any PPT adversary $\mathcal{A} = (\mathcal{A}_1, \mathcal{A}_2)$ the following advantage is negligible in λ:

$$\text{Adv}_{\mathcal{A},\Sigma}^{\text{OT}}(\lambda) := \left| \mathbb{P}\left[b \leftarrow \mathcal{A}_2(c^*, aux) \,\middle|\, K \xleftarrow{\$} \{0,1\}^{n(\lambda)}; (m_0, m_1, aux) \leftarrow \mathcal{A}_1(1^\lambda); \right.\right.$$
$$\left.\left. b \xleftarrow{\$} \{0,1\}; c^* \leftarrow \text{enc}(K, m_b) \right] - \tfrac{1}{2} \right|.$$

IND-CCA2$_{\text{DEM}}$ and IND-RCCA$_{\text{DEM}}$. Session communication–where each symmetric key may be used more than once–requires stronger DEMs. We therefore recap the private key CCA2 security notion as well and formulate a replayable chosen ciphertext attack (RCCA) DEM notion corresponding to the respective PKE notion [3]. The intuition behind RCCA lies in replayability. This means an adversary is allowed to be able to modify ciphertexts to other valid ciphertexts as long as the message content is not changed, e.g. via rerandomization.

Definition (IND-CCA2$_{\text{DEM}}$, IND-RCCA$_{\text{DEM}}$): A DEM $\Sigma = (\text{DEM.enc}, \text{DEM.dec})$ satisfies *IND-CCA2*, iff for any PPT adversary $\mathcal{A} = (\mathcal{A}_1, \mathcal{A}_2)$ the advantage

$$\text{Adv}_{\mathcal{A},\Sigma}^{\text{CCA2}}(\lambda) := \left| \mathbb{P}\left[b \leftarrow \mathcal{A}_2^{\mathcal{O}_{\text{enc}}, \mathcal{O}_{\text{dec}}^*}(c^*, aux) \,\middle|\, K \xleftarrow{\$} \{0,1\}^{n(\lambda)}; \right.\right.$$
$$(m_0, m_1, aux) \leftarrow \mathcal{A}_1^{\mathcal{O}_{\text{enc}}, \mathcal{O}_{\text{dec}}}(1^\lambda);$$
$$\left.\left. b \xleftarrow{\$} \{0,1\}; c^* \leftarrow \text{enc}(K, m_b) \right] - \tfrac{1}{2} \right|$$

is negligible in λ, where $\mathcal{O}_{\text{enc}}$ denotes the oracle $\text{DEM.enc}(K, \cdot)$, $\mathcal{O}_{\text{dec}}$ denotes $\text{DEM.dec}(K, \cdot)$ and $\mathcal{O}_{\text{dec}}^*(c)$ returns $\perp$ for $c = c^*$ and $\text{DEM.dec}(K, c)$ otherwise.

The notion of *IND-RCCA* for DEMs differs only in the definition of $\mathcal{O}_{\text{dec}}^*$, which returns $\perp$ whenever $\mathcal{O}_{\text{dec}}(c) \in \{m_0, m_1\}$.

Now that we are familiar with all these game-based definitions let us jump to the parallel world of simulation-based and in particular UC security.

2.3   Simulation-based Security and UC

As we have seen in Sect. 2.2, game-based security notions are attack-centered. A scheme fulfills a game-based security notion if and only if one specific attack (e.g., distinguishing which message is contained in a ciphertext) can never be successful in specific circumstances (e.g., without oracle access). While this is a nice way to model simple and isolated properties, it is not easy to comprehensively define the security of real-world scenarios which usually require multiple interrelated properties and are conducted concurrent with other protocols. For this purpose simulation-based security and in particular universal composability (UC) were developed. We briefly introduce both concepts in this section, more details can be found in [14] and [15] respectively.

With simulation-based security, properties are not captured in individual games but the whole scenario is modeled as an ideal process which inherently captures all properties at once. This ideal process is called an *ideal functionality* $\mathcal{F}$ and can be thought of as a trusted third party which is handed all inputs of all parties via ideal secure channels, honestly conducts the actual protocol and distributes outputs again in an ideally secure way. Any adversarial powers to influence this process are specified within the ideal functionality and therefore explicitly known. Functionalities for different purposes are distinguished by name, while different instances of the same functionality are distinguished via session IDs *sid*. Security with respect to an ideal functionality $\mathcal{F}$ means that a protocol π solves the given problem *at least as securely* as the ideal functionality does. More concretely: Any real adversary $\mathcal{A}$ attacking an execution of the protocol can be simulated by some simulator $\mathcal{S}$ in an interaction with the ideal functionality such that the two are computationally indistinguishable. In this case the protocol π is said to *securely realize* the functionality $\mathcal{F}$.

UC security is a form of simulation-based security which is even stricter. Not only do transcripts of $\mathrm{EXEC}_{\pi,\mathcal{A}}$ and $\mathrm{IDEAL}_{\mathcal{F},\mathcal{S}}$ of the protocol and ideal experiment have to be computationally indistinguishable, but the distinguisher–called environment $\mathcal{Z}$–adaptively provides inputs to and receives outputs from the protocol parties trying to make protocol and ideal functionality diverge. The adaptivity of $\mathcal{Z}$ also means that standard techniques like rewinding are not feasible in the UC setting. The bright sight of this additional work is that UC secure protocols remain secure under arbitrary and concurrent composition (hence the name) while the same is not true in the classic stand-alone simulation-based security. The following definition stems from [15] with the exact formulation taken from [4]. It captures UC security more formally:

Definition (UC Security): Let $\mathcal{F}$ be an ideal functionality and π a protocol. We say that π *UC-realizes* the ideal functionality $\mathcal{F}$, iff for any PPT adversary $\mathcal{A}$ there is a PPT simulator $\mathcal{S}$ such that no PPT environment $\mathcal{Z}$ can distinguish $\mathrm{EXEC}_{\pi,\mathcal{A},\mathcal{Z}}$ from $\mathrm{IDEAL}_{\mathcal{F},\mathcal{S},\mathcal{Z}}$ with non-negligible probability. In this case we write $\pi \geq_{\mathrm{UC}} \mathcal{F}$.

Having two adversarial entities $\mathcal{Z}$ and $\mathcal{A}$ can be slightly hard to follow, but as Canetti showed in [15] we can equivalently consider an adversarial environment $\mathcal{Z}$ while reducing the adversary $\mathcal{A}$ to a mere dummy $\mathcal{D}$.

With this general knowledge of UC security we can go on to recap some specific ideal functionalities.

2.4   Ideal Functionalities

In this section we formally define the authenticated and secure channel functionalities $\mathcal{F}_{\mathrm{AUTH}}$ and $\mathcal{F}_{\mathrm{MSC}}$ we use in this paper. Although the secure message transfer (SMT) functionality $\mathcal{F}_{\mathrm{MSMT}}$ is somewhat central to Sect. 5, it is sufficient to know that it does capture SMT. The detailed inner workings (see [4]) are not necessary to understand this paper. Furthermore we briefly encounter functionalities $\mathcal{F}_{\mathrm{KEM}}$, $\mathcal{F}_{\mathrm{KEM\text{-}DEM}}$, $\mathcal{F}_{\mathrm{SIG}}$, $\mathcal{F}_{\mathrm{CA}}$ and $\mathcal{F}_{\mathrm{CERT}}$ in Sect. 3 but again do not require further details. Interested readers can find them in [8] and [16].

For PKE schemes, SMT functionalities are commonly used to model secure communication [3,4,15]. But for session communication we follow the lead of [8,17] and use a secure channel functionality instead. This yields the same level of message security but is specifically designed for communication in sessions. The classic definition of $\mathcal{F}_{\mathrm{SC}}$ can be found in [17]. For our proof in Sect. 6 we instead use an (equivalent) multi-session version $\mathcal{F}_{\mathrm{MSC}}$, where some abort possibilities of the adversary (implicitly present in $\mathcal{F}_{\mathrm{SC}}$) are made explicit as well.

$\mathcal{F}_{\mathrm{MSC}}$

Provides:
Multiple secure two-party communication sessions.

State:

- Active function $f_{\mathrm{act}} \colon \mathbf{SID} \times \{\{A, B\} \mid A, B \in \mathbf{P}\} \to \{\mathsf{true}, \mathsf{false}, \mathsf{init}\}$ initialized to $f_{\mathrm{act}} \equiv \mathsf{false}$.
- Function $p_{\mathrm{Msg}} \colon \mathbf{SID} \times \mathbf{MID} \to \mathbf{M} \times \mathbf{P}^2$ of pending messages.

Behaviour:

- Upon receiving $(\mathtt{init}, sid, B)$ from some party A, set $f_{\mathrm{act}}(sid, \{A, B\}) := \mathtt{init}$ and send $(\mathtt{inited}, sid, A, B)$ to the adversary $\mathcal{A}$.
- Upon receiving $(\mathtt{establish}, sid, A)$ from party B, check $f_{\mathrm{act}}(sid, \{A, B\}) = \mathtt{init}$, set $f_{\mathrm{act}}(sid, \{A, B\}) := \mathtt{true}$ and send $(\mathtt{established}, sid, A, B)$ to $\mathcal{A}$.
- Upon receiving $(\mathtt{send}, sid, R, m)$ from some party S, check $f_{\mathrm{act}}(sid, \{S, R\}) = \mathtt{true}$, draw fresh mid, send $(\mathtt{send}, sid, mid, S, R)$ to the adversary $\mathcal{A}$ and append $(sid, mid) \mapsto (m, S, R)$ to p_{Msg}.
- Upon receiving $(\mathtt{send\ ok}, sid, mid)$ from the adversary look up $(m, S, R) := p_{\mathrm{Msg}}(sid, mid)$. If it exists, and if $f_{\mathrm{act}}(sid, \{S, R\}) = \mathtt{true}$, output $(\mathtt{sent}, sid, S, m)$ to R.
- Upon receiving $(\mathtt{expire}, sid, B)$ from some party A, set $f_{\mathrm{act}}(sid, \{A, B\}) := \mathtt{false}$.

Once the notational differences are ignored there is only one distinction between $\mathcal{F}_{\mathrm{SC}}$ and $\mathcal{F}_{\mathrm{MSC}}$: $\mathcal{F}_{\mathrm{MSC}}$ allows for multiple communication sessions between different pairs of communication partners within one instance (i.e. with the same sid) while a new $\mathcal{F}_{\mathrm{SC}}$ instance (sid) is needed for each communication session. Everything else is identical. For normal settings, where arbitrarily many sessions between arbitrary communication partners are allowed, multiple instances (or their multi-session extensions) are needed of both $\mathcal{F}_{\mathrm{SC}}$ and $\mathcal{F}_{\mathrm{MSC}}$ and the sole difference lies in whether or not a new *sid* is used for a new session.

$$\mathcal{F}_{\mathbf{AUTH}}$$

Provides:

Single-receiver single-message single-sender authenticated message transfer with constant message size.

Behaviour:

- Upon invocation with input (**send**, sid, R, m) from some party S, send backdoor message (**send**, sid, S, R, m) to the adversary $\mathcal{A}$.
- Upon receiving (**send ok**, sid) from adversary $\mathcal{A}$: If output not yet generated, then output (**sent**, sid, S, R, m) to R.
- Ignore all further inputs.

With these previously known definitions fresh in our minds we go on to give some more context to our paper in the next section by discussing prior works.

3 Related Work

While there are lots of papers pertaining to the general topic of hybrid encryption via the KEM-DEM framework, most of the works focus on more efficient constructions of KEMs, such as the hybrid encryption scheme by Cramer and Shoup [5], the Kurosawa-Desmedt-KEM [18] or the newly standardized Kyber-KEM [19]. For this section, however, we stay with the main contribution of our paper and instead consider those papers which give proofs on what levels of secure communication can be reached with various KEM and DEM security notions.

As mentioned in Sect. 2.1, there are two branches of KEM-DEM-based hybrid encryption: Single-message and session communication. We start in the more common single-message setting. With one symmetric key per message IND-CCA2$_{\mathrm{PKE}}$ has always been seen as the goal to construct secure communication. Hence the main security analysis is usually conducted by constructing an IND-CCA2$_{\mathrm{PKE}}$ secure PKE scheme from successively weaker (and more efficient) KEM and DEM notions. When originally introducing the KEM-DEM framework, Shoup showed that combining a KEM and DEM which satisfy the respective notions of IND-CCA2 security yields an IND-CCA2$_{\mathrm{PKE}}$ secure PKE as a result [2,5]. Also in [5] it was shown that if one relaxes the security of the DEM to one-time-IND-CCA2$_{\mathrm{DEM}}$ security (sometimes called IND-OTCCA [12]), the construction still suffices for an IND-CCA2 secure PKE as each symmetric key will only be used once. In [12], Herranz, Hofheinz, and Kiltz give an overview of all previously proposed game-based KEM and DEM security notions and comprehensively identify which combinations lead to which security notions for the resulting PKE. One main finding was that CCA2 security could so far *only* be reached via a CCA2 secure KEM in conjunction with (one-time-)CCA2 DEM. All other combinations result in less secure PKE schemes. Kurosawa and Desmedt managed to present a KEM-DEM construction for an IND-CCA2$_{PKE}$ scheme in [18] where the employed KEM scheme is not IND-CCA2 secure [20]. However, it was shown in [21] that the Kurosawa-Desmedt-KEM is not far off, as it becomes IND-CCA2$_{KEM}$ secure with a slight twist. Abe et al. modify the KEM-DEM framework to a new tag-KEM-DEM framework [10] (cf. Section 2.1). They show that for this type of hybrid encryption an IND-CCA2 secure KEM together with an only IND-OT secure DEM yields an IND-CCA2 PKE as well. They also show that the aforementioned Kurosawa-Desmedt-KEM can be considered a tag-KEM in which case it actually satisfies IND-CCA2$_{tag-KEM}$ security. A similar not quite IND-CCA2 secure KEM construction was used in [6] as well.

In contrast to these works we employ the results of [3,4] which state that IND-CCA2$_{PKE}$ is unnecessarily strong to realize secure communication and hence do not try to construct an IND-CCA2 secure PKE in this paper. Aiming for the weaker but sufficient notion of IND-SB-CPA$_{SBE}$ security [4], we develop the corresponding KEM notion of IND-SB-CPA$_{SB-KEM}$. We show that in combination with the weakest possible DEM–satisfying only IND-OT security–our new notion still provides IND-SB-CPA$_{SBE}$ security for the SBE scheme constructed via the classic KEM-DEM framework. Using such a weak DEM scheme was previously only possible via the more complex tag-KEM-DEM framework. Furthermore we show that if our SB-KEM is viewed as a (simpler) version of a tag-KEM, the KEM security notion IND-SB-CPA, which we introduce in this work, is strictly weaker than the IND-CCA2$_{tag-KEM}$ notion employed in the tag-KEM-DEM framework.

Although Canetti and Krawczyk consider various UC and non-UC security notions for key exchange and session key security in [17,22], Nagao, Manabe, and Okamoto were the first to take the KEM-DEM framework into the world of UC security [8]. They also make the switch to session communication where each symmetric key is used not only for multiple messages but bi-directional communication as well. Nagao, Manabe, and Okamoto firstly introduce an ideal functionality $\mathcal{F}_{KEM}$ capturing the security intuitively expected from a KEM and prove a generic protocol to UC-realize $\mathcal{F}_{KEM}$ if and only if the KEM used in the protocol is IND-CCA2$_{KEM}$ secure. In a second step a complete KEM-DEM functionality $\mathcal{F}_{KEM-DEM}$ is defined and similarly shown that it is realized by a generic DEM-protocol in the $\mathcal{F}_{KEM}$-hybrid model if and only if the DEM satisfies IND-CCA2$_{DEM}$ security. Lastly it is shown that using $\mathcal{F}_{KEM-DEM}$ in conjunction with the signature and certification functionalities $\mathcal{F}_{SIG}$ and $\mathcal{F}_{CA}$ suffices without any other cryptographic building blocks to realize a single-session bi-directional secure channel $\mathcal{F}_{SC}$. An overview of this process is shown in Fig. 3.

The additional functionalities $\mathcal{F}_{SIG}$ and $\mathcal{F}_{CA}$ are used for authentication during the key exchange and could equally be substituted by $\mathcal{F}_{AUTH}$, as it was shown in [16] that such a use of signatures combined with certification already UC-realizes $\mathcal{F}_{AUTH}$. The two equivalences between respective CCA2 security

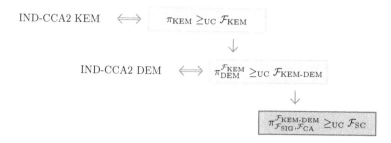

Fig. 3. Overview of Secure Channel Realization from [8].

notions and ideal KEM and KEM-DEM functionalities from [8] could be taken to indicate that CCA2 is a necessary condition for achieving secure channels via the session KEM-DEM framework. In this paper we show that this is not actually true. The main factor to realize here is that authentication in the form of $\mathcal{F}_{\mathrm{SIG}}$ and $\mathcal{F}_{\mathrm{CA}}$ is only used for the key exchange and added after the fact to the KEM-DEM functionality to realize $\mathcal{F}_{\mathrm{SC}}$. Directly using the KEM on an authenticated channel and binding the key ciphertext to the sender lets us achieve the same level of security with significantly less security requirements on the KEM. For our proof in Sect. 6 we skip the detour via $\mathcal{F}_{\mathrm{KEM}}$ and $\mathcal{F}_{\mathrm{KEM\text{-}DEM}}$ and directly show that an IND-SB-CPA$_{\mathrm{SB\text{-}KEM}}$ secure KEM combined with $\mathcal{F}_{\mathrm{AUTH}}$ and an IND-CCA2$_{\mathrm{DEM}}$ secure DEM UC-realize a secure channel.

4   Sender-binding Key Encapsulation

In this section we develop the security notion of IND-SB-CPA$_{\mathrm{KEM}}$ and give some transformations to show its relation to other KEM security notions. Before doing so, we first introduce what it means for a KEM to be called sender-binding.

Definition (SB-KEM): A *sender-binding key encapsulation mechanism (SBKEM)* is given by a set of three PPT algorithms (gen, enc, dec) with

$$\mathsf{gen} : 1^\lambda \mapsto (sk, pk), \qquad \mathsf{enc} : (pk, S) \mapsto (K, C), \qquad \mathsf{dec} : (sk, S, C) \mapsto K$$

such that the correctness property holds, i.e. $K = \mathsf{dec}(sk, S, C)$ whenever $(sk, pk) \leftarrow \mathsf{gen}(1^\lambda)$ and $(K, C) \leftarrow \mathsf{enc}(pk, S)$.

Note that so far, this is only the traditional KEM interface enhanced by a party ID as input for encapsulation and decryption. Although the denomination suggests this, the "sender" and "binding" part only become meaningful with the respective security notion. Any classic KEM instantly satisfies this definition when its input is adjusted to incorporate a party ID, regardless of whether this ID specifies some sender, receiver or just a random party, regardless of whether there is any binding property or the ID can be easily exchanged, even regardless of whether this ID is used at all in the protocol. The intended use, however, is that the sending or encapsulating party inserts its *own* ID upon encapsulation, this ID is then non-malleably bound to an otherwise malleable ciphertext and decryption is only successful if the *same* ID is used. These properties are expressed in the following IND-SB-CPA$_{KEM}$ notion. The idea for this notion comes from the corresponding SBE notion introduced in [4], which we adapt to fit the KEM setting.

Definition (IND-SB-CPA$_{SB-KEM}$): An SB-KEM (gen, enc, dec) satisfies *indistinguishability under sender-binding chosen plaintext attack (IND-SB-CPA)* security, iff for any PPT adversary $\mathcal{A}_{SB-CPA}$ the probability to win the IND-SB-CPA game shown in Fig. 4 is negligible in λ.

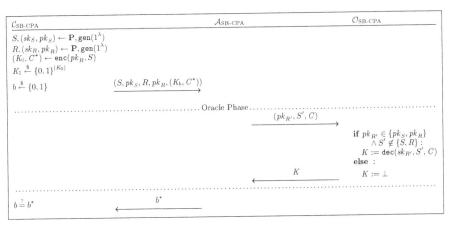

Fig. 4. The IND-SB-CPA$_{SB-KEM}$ Game for SB-CPA$_{SB-KEM}$

We would like to remark several things about this definition.

Firstly, IND-SB-CPA$_{KEM}$ looks very different from other KEM notions at first glance because it has only one oracle phase instead of two. This is not due to less oracle access but because this way is simpler but equivalent: For IND-SB-CPA, the first and second oracle phase permit exactly the same oracle queries (in constrast to CCA2 for instance). Furthermore in the KEM setting the adversary does not generate any outputs between oracle phases I and II. Hence with IND-SB-CPA$_{KEM}$ the adversary can save all oracle queries it would make in the first oracle phase and ask them in the second oracle phase instead. We therefore decided to simplify the definition by only including the second oracle phase.

Secondly, note that although the IND-SB-CPA$_{KEM}$ security notion contains a key pair (sk_S, pk_S) for party S, no such keys need to exist in any protocol. Especially in the session communication setting—but also if communication is one-directional in the single-message setting—only one party needs to have a key pair for the SB-KEM to set up a symmetrically encrypted session. The reason behind the existence of these keys in our security notion is that it makes the notion strictly weaker than if (sk_S, pk_S) were not picked by the challenger.

Intuitively, an IND-SB-CPA$_{\mathrm{KEM}}$ secure KEM does not need to guarantee anything if S's keys may be adversarially chosen rather than honestly (and secretly) generated. This can clearly be seen when considering the generic DRE construction of an SB-KEM in Appendix A of the full version of this paper [7]: For this construction each encapsulated key is decryptable by both the receiver *and* sender. Hence the adversary choosing or knowing sk_S would completely break the encapsulation.

Before we discuss in which ways IND-SB-CPA$_{\mathrm{SB\text{-}KEM}}$ fits into the landscape of other security notions for KEMs, notice that IND-SB-CPA$_{\mathrm{SBE}}$ obviously implies IND-SB-CPA$_{\mathrm{SB\text{-}KEM}}$ by the standard PKE to KEM construction of randomly drawing and then encrypting a symmetric key. For KEM security notions, classifying IND-SB-CPA$_{\mathrm{SB\text{-}KEM}}$ with respect to classic KEM security is unfortunately rather infeasible. While a classic KEM takes no input and requires secrecy and various forms of integrity about the internally determined key, IND-SB-CPA$_{\mathrm{SB\text{-}KEM}}$ asserts only secrecy (no integrity) of the key but additionally provides integrity (without secrecy) of some user input–the identity S. Since those two settings are even more incompatible than comparing SBE to classic PKE notions, we will only consider IND-SB-CPA$_{\mathrm{SB\text{-}KEM}}$ in relation to the similar setting of tag-KEMs.

Relation to tag-KEM Security Notions. Let $(\mathsf{gen}, \mathsf{key}, \mathsf{enc}, \mathsf{dec})$ be a tag-KEM. We construct an SB-KEM $(\mathsf{Gen}, \mathsf{Enc}, \mathsf{Dec})$ in the natural way by using sender IDs as tags, and combining key and enc into a single encryption algorithm. I.e. $\mathsf{Gen} \equiv \mathsf{gen}$, $\mathsf{Enc}(pk_R, S) = (K, C)$ where $(aux, K) \leftarrow \mathsf{key}(pk_R)$ and $C \leftarrow \mathsf{enc}(aux, S)$, and $\mathsf{Dec} \equiv \mathsf{dec}$.

Lemma 1: *If $(\mathsf{gen}, \mathsf{key}, \mathsf{enc}, \mathsf{dec})$ is an IND-CCA2 secure tag-KEM then $(\mathsf{Gen}, \mathsf{Enc}, \mathsf{Dec})$ is an IND-SB-CPA secure SB-KEM.*

Proof. Assume on the contrary that $\mathcal{A}_{\mathrm{SB}}$ is an adversary with non-negligible success probability in winning the IND-SB-CPA$_{\mathrm{SB\text{-}KEM}}$ game. We use $\mathcal{A}_{\mathrm{SB}}$ to construct an equally successful adversary $\mathcal{A}_{\mathrm{tag\text{-}KEM}}$. This adversary mainly forwards messages between $\mathcal{A}_{\mathrm{SB}}$ and the challenger and oracle. Additionally it creates credentials for S and uses them to decrypt respective oracle queries. The detailed reduction can be found in Fig. 5.   □

It is easy to see from the reduction that the CCA2 game grants a lot more oracle access than we need which indicates that IND-SB-CPA$_{\mathrm{SB\text{-}KEM}}$ is a lot weaker than IND-CCA2$_{\mathrm{tag\text{-}KEM}}$. To further substantiate this claim we take the weakest security notion proposed for TBE, adapt it to the KEM setting and show that it still implies IND-SB-CPA$_{\mathrm{SB\text{-}KEM}}$ via the above construction. Note that as far as we know, no weaker security notions than IND-CCA2$_{\mathrm{tag\text{-}KEM}}$ have been proposed for tag-KEM so far, which is why we take the detour over a TBE notion. The TBE notion in question is IND-gtag-CCA$_{\mathrm{TBE}}$ which was recapitulated in Sect. 2.2. The difference to IND-CCA2$_{\mathrm{tag\text{-}KEM}}$ lies in the oracle access as well as when and by whom the challenge tag τ^* is chosen: Both oracle phases grant

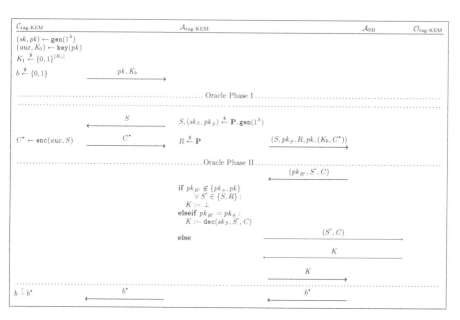

Fig. 5. Reduction for IND-CCA2$_{\text{tag-KEM}}$ Construction

access to a decryption oracle punctuated at $\tau = \tau^*$, i.e. the complete challenge tag is excluded from decryption rather than just the challenge tuple (τ^*, C^*). The challenge tag itself is not chosen adaptively and not even by the adversary at all anymore, but randomly drawn by the challenger. The adaptive interface of a tag-KEM—where encapsulation is divided into key and enc so that the tag may depend on the output of key—does not seem quite fitting anymore when in the security game the tag is drawn at random and hence independent of the output of key. Nevertheless we cannot rule out that such a security notion may still be meaningful for a tag-KEM with separate key and enc and therefore keep the division.

Definition (IND-gtag-CCA$_{\text{tag-KEM}}$): A tag-KEM $\Sigma = (\text{gen}, \text{key}, \text{enc}, \text{dec})$ satisfies *IND-gtag-CCA*, iff for any PPT adversary $\mathcal{A} = (\mathcal{A}_1, \mathcal{A}_2)$ the advantage

$$\mathsf{Adv}_{\mathcal{A},\Sigma}^{\text{gtag}}(\lambda) := \Big| \mathbb{P}\Big[b \leftarrow \mathcal{A}_2^{\mathcal{O}^*}(K_b, C^*) \,\big|\, \tau^* \xleftarrow{\$} \mathbf{T}; (sk, pk) \leftarrow \text{gen}(1^\lambda);$$

$$(aux_{\mathcal{A}}) \leftarrow \mathcal{A}_1^{\mathcal{O}^*}(pk, \tau^*); (aux, K_0) \leftarrow \text{key}(pk);$$

$$C^* \leftarrow \text{enc}(aux, \tau^*); K_1 \xleftarrow{\$} \{0,1\}^{|K_0|}; b \xleftarrow{\$} \{0,1\} \Big] - \tfrac{1}{2} \Big|$$

is negligible in λ, where $\mathcal{O}^*$ returns $\bot$ for $\tau = \tau^*$ and $\text{dec}(sk, \tau, C)$ otherwise.

We go on to show that this weaker notion is still sufficient to imply IND-SB-CPA$_{\text{SB-KEM}}$.

Lemma 2: *If* $(\text{gen}, \text{key}, \text{enc}, \text{dec})$ *is an IND-gtag-CCA secure tag-KEM then* $(\text{Gen}, \text{Enc}, \text{Dec})$ *is an IND-SB-CPA secure SB-KEM.*

Proof. The proof of Lemma 2 works almost exactly the same as the proof of Lemma 1. The sole difference is that the identity S is randomly provided by the challenger $C_{\text{tag-KEM}}$ rather than randomly drawn by $A_{\text{tag-KEM}}$. Note that the provision $S' \notin \{S, R\}$ guarantees that oracle queries forwarded to $O_{\text{tag-KEM}}$ get decrypted correctly. $\qquad\square$

In Appendix A of the full version of this paper [7] we furthermore show that the transformation from Lemma 2 is just an implication and no equivalence, proving IND-SB-CPA$_{\text{SB-KEM}}$ to be strictly weaker than IND-gtag-CCA$_{\text{tag-KEM}}$.

5   Realizing Secure Message Transfer

In this section we show that IND-SB-CPA$_{\text{SB-KEM}}$ is—in conjunction with IND-OT secure DEM and authenticated channels—strong enough to facilitate the realization of secure message transfer. Since Beskorovajnov et al. [4] already showed the same for IND-SB-CPA secure SBE with authenticated channels, we can build on their work and only fill in the gap: We show that IND-SB-CPA$_{\text{SB-KEM}}$ combined with IND-OT$_{\text{DEM}}$ via the KEM-DEM-framework yields an IND-SB-CPA secure SBE scheme.

Hence let $(\text{gen}, \text{enc}, \text{dec})$ be an IND-SB-CPA$_{\text{SB-KEM}}$ secure SB-KEM and $(\text{DEM.enc}, \text{DEM.dec})$ be a compatible IND-OT secure DEM. We construct an SBE scheme via the KEM-DEM principle by setting $\text{Gen} \equiv \text{gen}$ and:

$\text{Enc}(pk_R, S, m)$:
- $(K, C) \leftarrow \text{enc}(pk_R, S)$.
- $c \leftarrow \text{DEM.enc}(K, m)$.
$\hookrightarrow$ Return (C, c).

$\text{Dec}(sk_R, S, (C, c))$:
- $K := \text{dec}(sk_R, S, C)$.
- $m := \text{DEM.dec}(K, c)$.
$\hookrightarrow$ Return m.

Theorem 1: *The SBE scheme* $(\text{Gen}, \text{Enc}, \text{Dec})$ *is IND-SB-CPA secure.*

Proof. Assume there is an adversary A_{SBE} for the IND-SB-CPA game with success probability $\mathbb{P}[A_{\text{SBE}} \text{ successful}] = \frac{1}{2} + \rho$, where ρ is non-negligible in λ. We use this to construct an adversary $A_{\text{SB-KEM}}$ for the IND-SB-CPA$_{\text{SB-KEM}}$ game as follows: $A_{\text{SB-KEM}}$ is started with input $(S, pk_S, R, pk_R, (K_b, C^*))$ by the KEM challenger $C_{\text{SB-KEM}}$ and hands (S, pk_S, R, pk_R) on to A_{SBE}. For any valid oracle query $(pk_{R'}, S', (C, c))$ from A_{SBE} the DEM key is decrypted via the SB-KEM oracle $O_{\text{SB-KEM}}$ and subsequently used for DEM decryption of c. When $A_{\text{SB-KEM}}$ receives challenge messages m_0, m_1 the adversary $A_{\text{SB-KEM}}$ draws a random challenge bit $b' \xleftarrow{\$} \{0, 1\}$ and determines the challenge as $c^* \leftarrow \text{DEM.enc}(K_b, m_{b'})$. The following second oracle phase is conducted exactly as the first one was. Finally, in case A_{SBE} correctly answers with b', $A_{\text{SB-KEM}}$ chooses to answer the challenger with $b^* = 0$, else it answers with $b^* = 1$. The detailed reduction is shown in Fig. 6.

Let us briefly analyse the success probability of $A_{\text{SB-KEM}}$. If $b = 0$, $A_{\text{SB-KEM}}$ has the same success probability that A_{SBE} has. If $b = 1$ we claim that the success probability can only negligibly differ from $\frac{1}{2}$. We show this again by

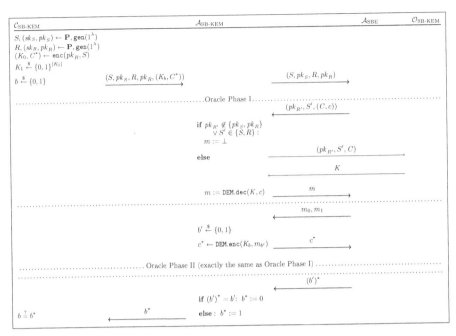

Fig. 6. Reduction from SBE to SB-KEM.

contradiction with a reduction to the IND-OT secure DEM scheme: Assume that when the game is conducted with $b = 1$, $\mathcal{A}_{SBE}$ has a success probability non-negligibly different from guessing—w.l.o.g. better (rather than worse) than one half. We use $\mathcal{A}_{SBE}$ to construct an adversary $\mathcal{A}_{DEM}$ against the DEM IND-OT game: $\mathcal{A}_{DEM}$ does not get any input from the challenger. It firstly draws S and R, generates $(sk_S, pk_S), (sk_R, pk_R)$, and hands (S, pk_S, R, pk_R) to $\mathcal{A}_{SBE}$. Every valid oracle query $(pk_{R'}, S', (C, c))$ is answered by using the corresponding secret key with $m := \mathsf{Dec}(sk_{R'}, S', (C, c))$. When $\mathcal{A}_{SBE}$ chooses challenge messages m_0, m_1 they are handed through to the DEM challenger $\mathcal{C}_{DEM}$ who responds with a corresponding challenge c^*. This challenge is paired with an output C^* from $\mathsf{enc}(pk_R, S)$ and handed to $\mathcal{A}_{SBE}$. The second oracle phase, again, is handled exactly as the first one was. Finally the answer b^* from $\mathcal{A}_{SBE}$ is passed on to the challenger. The detailed reduction is shown in Fig. 7.

This reduction to the underlying IND-OT secure DEM shows that for $b = 1$ in the first reduction, the adversary $\mathcal{A}_{SBE}$ cannot perform non-negligibly better or worse than guessing. Hence, paired with the case $b = 0$, the adversary $\mathcal{A}_{SB\text{-}KEM}$ has success probability $\mathbb{P}[\mathcal{A}_{SB\text{-}KEM} \text{ successful}] = \frac{1}{2} + \frac{1}{2}\rho$. □

Corollary 1: *Combining the KEM-DEM framework from [2] with the encrypt-then-authenticate protocol from [4], an IND-SB-CPA$_{SB\text{-}KEM}$ secure KEM and IND-OT secure DEM suffice to UC-realize secure message transfer functionality $\mathcal{F}_{MSMT}$ in the $\mathcal{F}_{AUTH}$-hybrid model.*

The proof of this corollary follows directly from Theorem 1 and [4, Thm. 3].

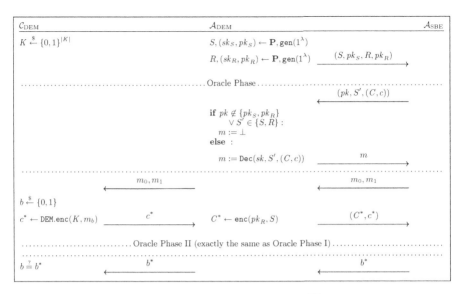

Fig. 7. Reduction from SBE to DEM.

6   Realizing Secure Channels

At this point we make the switch from single-message to session communication. This means symmetric keys are exchanged via the KEM and subsequently used by both parties to send messages encrypted with the corresponding DEM. The benefits are that only one communication partner needs credentials for the KEM and that secure communication can be achieved even if the authenticated channel is only used for the key exchange and not the actual messages. The employed DEM, on the other hand, needs to be stronger than for single-message KEM-DEM.[2] In this section we show how IND-SB-CPA$_\mathrm{KEM}$ in conjuction with IND-CCA2$_\mathrm{DEM}$ or just IND-RCCA$_\mathrm{DEM}$ suffices to UC-realize secure channels $\mathcal{F}_\mathrm{MSC}$ in the $\mathcal{F}_\mathrm{AUTH}$-hybrid model. We do so by first providing a protocol π_MSC and corresponding simulator $\mathcal{S}_\mathrm{MSC}$ before giving the actual theorem and proof.

Protocol π_MSC. Let $(\mathsf{gen}, \mathsf{enc}, \mathsf{dec})$ be an SB-KEM and $(\mathsf{DEM.enc}, \mathsf{DEM.dec})$ a compatible DEM. The idea behind π_MSC is the following: To establish a session between parties P and P', a new symmetric key is generated and encapsulated via $\mathsf{enc}(pk_{P'}, P)$ by P. The resulting ciphertext C is sent to P' via authenticated channel. When decryption $\mathsf{dec}(sk_{P'}, P, C)$ is successful, both parties can encrypt messages to the other party via $\mathsf{DEM.enc}$ and send them on a plain channel. All details can be found in the formal definition:

---

[2] Note that the security of the DEM can be significantly extenuated if we are willing to use authenticated channels for all messages.

π_{MSC}

Realizes:

Multiple secure two-party communication sessions.

Parameters:

- Functionality $\mathcal{F}_{\mathrm{AUTH}}$.
- KEM $(\mathsf{gen}, \mathsf{enc}, \mathsf{dec})$.
- DEM $(\mathsf{DEM.enc}, \mathsf{DEM.dec})$.

State of party P:

- A personal KEM key function $f_{\mathrm{KEM}} \colon sid \mapsto (pk, sk)$.
- A partial KEM key function $f_{\mathrm{PK}} \colon (sid, P') \mapsto pk_{P'}$.
- A partial DEM session key function $f_{\mathrm{SK}} \colon (sid, P') \mapsto K$.
- An (almost) boolean function $f_{\mathrm{act}} \colon \mathbf{SID} \times \mathbf{P} \to \{\mathsf{true}, \mathsf{false}, \mathtt{init}\}$ initialized to $f_{\mathrm{act}} \equiv \mathsf{false}$.

Behaviour of Party P:

\\ Initialization

- Upon input $(\mathsf{sent}, sid_{\mathrm{AUTH}}, P', P, (sid, pk))$ from $\mathcal{F}_{\mathrm{AUTH}}$, append $(sid, P') \mapsto pk_{P'}$ to f_{PK} if this entry does not yet exist.
- Upon input $(\mathtt{init}, sid, P')$ from the environment:
  (1) If no entry $f_{\mathrm{KEM}}(sid)$ exists set $f_{\mathrm{KEM}}(sid) := (pk, sk) \leftarrow \mathsf{gen}(1^{\lambda})$.
  (2) Check that $f_{\mathrm{act}}(sid, P') = \mathsf{false}$ and set $f_{\mathrm{act}}(sid, P') := \mathtt{init}$.
  (3) Draw fresh sid_{AUTH} and call $\mathcal{F}_{\mathrm{AUTH}}$ with input $(\mathsf{send}, sid_{\mathrm{AUTH}}, P', (sid, pk))$.
- Upon input $(\mathsf{establish}, sid, P')$ from the environment:
  (1) Look up $pk_{P'} := f_{\mathrm{PK}}(sid, P')$.
  (2) $(K, C) \leftarrow \mathsf{enc}(pk_{P'}, P)$.
  (3) Check that $f_{\mathrm{act}}(sid, P') = \mathsf{false}$, set $f_{\mathrm{act}}(sid, P') = \mathsf{true}$ and append $(sid, P') \mapsto K$ to f_{SK}.
  (4) Draw fresh sid_{AUTH} and call $\mathcal{F}_{\mathrm{AUTH}}$ with input $(\mathsf{send}, sid_{\mathrm{AUTH}}, P', (sid, C))$.
- Upon input $(\mathsf{sent}, sid_{\mathrm{AUTH}}, P', P, (sid, C))$ from $\mathcal{F}_{\mathrm{AUTH}}$:
  (1) Look up $(pk, sk) := f_{\mathrm{KEM}}(sid)$.
  (2) $K := \mathsf{dec}(sk, P', C)$.
  (3) Check that $f_{\mathrm{act}}(sid, P') = \mathtt{init}$, set $f_{\mathrm{act}}(sid, P') = \mathsf{true}$ and append $(sid, P') \mapsto K$ to f_{SK}.

\\ Data Exchange

- Upon input $(\mathsf{send}, sid, P', m)$ with $m \in \{0, 1\}^{l}$ from environment $\mathcal{Z}$:
  (1) Check $f_{\mathrm{act}}(sid, P') = \mathsf{true}$, look up $K := f_{\mathrm{SK}}(sid, P')$ and set $c \leftarrow \mathsf{DEM.enc}(K, m)$.
  (2) Send (sid, P, c) to P'
- Upon receiving message (sid, P', c):
  (1) Check $f_{\mathrm{act}}(sid, P') = \mathsf{true}$, look up $K := f_{\mathrm{SK}}(sid, P')$ and set $m \leftarrow \mathsf{DEM.dec}(K, c)$.
  (2) Output $(\mathsf{sent}, sid, P', m)$ to the environment.

\\ Session Expiration

- Upon input $(\mathsf{expire}, sid, P')$ from the environment:
  (1) Check $f_{\mathrm{act}} = \mathsf{true}$ and send $(\mathsf{expire}, sid, P)$ to P'.
  (2) Erase $f_{\mathrm{SK}}(sid, P')$ and set $f_{\mathrm{act}}(sid, P') := \mathsf{false}$.
- Upon receiving message $(\mathsf{expire}, sid, P')$ erase $f_{\mathrm{SK}}(sid, P')$ and set $f_{\mathrm{act}}(sid, P') := \mathsf{false}$.

Simulator $\mathcal{S}_{\mathrm{MSC}}$. To show that protocol π_{MSC} realizes $\mathcal{F}_{\mathrm{MSC}}$ we need to construct a simulator which interacts with $\mathcal{F}_{\mathrm{MSC}}$ in such a way that no environment $\mathcal{Z}$ can distinguish this ideal world from an interaction with the real protocol and (dummy) adversary $\mathcal{A}$. The idea behind our simulator $\mathcal{S}_{\mathrm{MSC}}$ is striving for near perfect simulation: It plays all honest parties (conducting protocol π_{MSC}) as well as the functionality $\mathcal{F}_{\mathrm{AUTH}}$ in its head, using $\mathcal{F}_{\mathrm{MSC}}$'s outputs to give them mock inputs from $\mathcal{Z}$ and using their outputs in turn to determine inputs to $\mathcal{F}_{\mathrm{MSC}}$. An overview can be found in Fig. 8. For proof simplicity purposes—that become apparent later on—the simulator swaps symmetric keys for random values if the two involved parties are both honest. The only situations in which $\mathcal{S}_{\mathrm{MSC}}$ is unable to provide perfect simulation due to lack of knowledge are actual messages between two honest parties. In this case it sends encryptions of zeros instead. The formal definition of $\mathcal{S}_{\mathrm{MSC}}$ looks as follows:

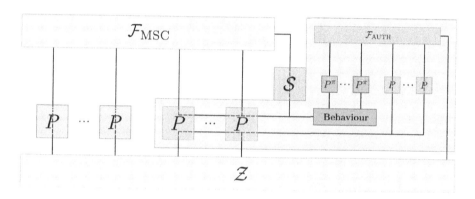

Fig. 8. Overview of Simulator $\mathcal{S}_{\mathrm{MSC}}$ adapted from [4].

$$\mathcal{S}_{\mathrm{MSC}}$$

Realizes:
Multiple secure two-party communication sessions.

Parameters:

- Security parameter λ.
- KEM $(\mathtt{gen}, \mathtt{enc}, \mathtt{dec})$.
- DEM $(\mathtt{DEM.enc}, \mathtt{DEM.dec})$.

In-the-head Parties:

- Functionality $\mathcal{F}_{\mathrm{AUTH}}$. This functionality communicates in-the-head with all honest in-the-head parties as well as with the environment $\mathcal{Z}$ as adversary.

- Copies of honest parties running a modified version of the protocol π_{MSC}, which we will denote as P^π. These parties communicate in-the-head with the in-the-head functionality $\mathcal{F}_{\mathrm{AUTH}}$. Their interface to the environment is played by the simulator (defined in "Behaviour" below). The modification from π_{MSC} looks as follows:
  - Upon input (establish, sid, P') from the environment:
    (3) Check that $f_{\mathrm{act}}(sid, P') = \mathsf{false}$, set $f_{\mathrm{act}}(sid, P') = \mathsf{true}$, ask $\mathcal{S}$ for freshly drawn random key $K_1 \overset{\$}{\leftarrow} \{0,1\}^{|K|}$ for parties $\{P, P'\}$ and append $(sid, P') \mapsto K_1$ to f_{SK}.
  - Upon input (sent, sid_{AUTH}, P', P, (sid, C)) from $\mathcal{F}_{\mathrm{AUTH}}$:
    (3) Check that $f_{\mathrm{act}}(sid, P') = \mathsf{init}$, set $f_{\mathrm{act}}(sid, P') = \mathsf{true}$, ask $\mathcal{S}$ for key K_1 corresponding to parties $\{P, P'\}$ and append $(sid, P') \mapsto K_1$ to f_{SK}.
- Dummy corrupted parties. Whenever the simulator is asked by the environment to call functionality $\mathcal{F}_{\mathrm{AUTH}}$ in the name of a corrupted party, this in-the-head dummy calls the in-the-head functionality correspondingly and reports all outputs back to the environment $\mathcal{Z}$.

State:

- Everything the in-the-head parties and functionalities store in their states.
- Partial key function $\{\{P, P'\} \mid P, P' \text{ honest}\} \to \{0,1\}^{n(\lambda)}, \{P, P'\} \mapsto K_1$.

Behaviour:

Initialization by honest party

- Upon receiving (inited, sid, A, B) from $\mathcal{F}_{\mathrm{MSC}}$ for honest party A, start in-the-head party A^π with input (init, sid, B) from the environment $\mathcal{Z}$.
- Upon receiving (established, sid, A, B) from $\mathcal{F}_{\mathrm{MSC}}$ for honest party B, start in-the-head party B^π with input (establish, sid, A) from the environment $\mathcal{Z}$.

Initialization by corrupted party

- Upon in-the-head party B^π receiving output (sent, sid_{AUTH}, A, B, (sid, pk)) from $\mathcal{F}_{\mathrm{AUTH}}$ for corrupted A, call $\mathcal{F}_{\mathrm{SC}}$ with input (init, sid, B) in the name of A.
- Upon in-the-head party A^π setting $f_{\mathrm{act}}(sid, B)$ from init to true, call $\mathcal{F}_{\mathrm{MSC}}$ with input (establish, sid, A) in the name of B.

Message from honest to honest party

- Upon receiving (send, sid, mid, S, R) from $\mathcal{F}_{\mathrm{MSC}}$ to $\mathcal{A}$ for honest parties S and R:
  (1) Start in-the-head party S^π with input (send, sid, R, 0) from the environment $\mathcal{Z}$.
  (2) If in-the-head party R^π at some point reports output (sent, sid, S, 0), call $\mathcal{F}_{\mathrm{MSC}}$ with input (send ok, sid, mid).

Message from honest to corrupted party

- Upon receiving (send, sid, mid, S, R) from $\mathcal{F}_{\mathrm{MSC}}$ to $\mathcal{A}$ for honest party S and corrupted party R:
  (1) Call $\mathcal{F}_{\mathrm{MSC}}$ with input (send ok, sid, mid).

(2) Receive output (**sent**, sid, S, m) from $\mathcal{F}_{\mathrm{MSC}}$ to R.

(3) Start in-the-head party S^π with input (**send**, sid, R, m) from the environment $\mathcal{Z}$.

V. Message from corrupted to honest party

- Upon in-the-head honest party R^π reporting output (**sent**, sid, S, m):
  (1) Call $\mathcal{F}_{\mathrm{MSC}}$ with input (**send**, sid, R, m) in the name of S.
  (2) Receive output (**send**, sid, mid, S, R) from $\mathcal{F}_{\mathrm{MSC}}$ to $\mathcal{A}$.
  (3) Call $\mathcal{F}_{\mathrm{MSC}}$ with input (**send ok**, sid, mid).

Security Theorem and Proof. Now that we have constructed both protocol and simulator it remains to show that together they make the real and ideal world indistinguishable for any environment. We do so by first explicitly stating the differences between the simulators efforts and perfect simulation. Then we go on to define several hybrid experiments which help us conduct the proof of our security theorem.[3]

Remark 1: It is easy to see that the simulator $\mathcal{S}_{\mathrm{MSC}}$ provides nearly perfect simulation. The two notable exceptions are:

(1) Symmetric keys of sessions between two honest parties: The modification of protocol π_{MSC} for the in-the-head honest parties P^π changes the session keys for each session between two honest parties. While a session key K is generated and the corresponding ciphertext C is sent via $\mathcal{F}_{\mathrm{AUTH}}$—just like in the real protocol—all messages of the session are encrypted with a randomly drawn and unrelated key $K_1 \xleftarrow{\$} \{0,1\}^{|K|}$.

(2) Message content between two honest parties: Let S, R and m be the honest partys and message in question. In this case a message $(sid, S, \mathrm{DEM.enc}(K_1, 0))$ will be sent from S to R in the ideal experiment while the protocol execution contains message $(sid, S, \mathrm{DEM.enc}(K, m))$ instead.

Hence any environment $\mathcal{Z}$ which distinguishes experiments $\mathrm{EXEC}^{\pi_{\mathrm{MSC}}}_{\mathcal{D}, \mathcal{Z}}$ and $\mathrm{IDEAL}^{\mathcal{F}_{\mathrm{MSC}}}_{\mathcal{S}_{\mathrm{MSC}}, \mathcal{Z}}$ can only do so by session keys or messages between honest parties.

Before we proceed to our security theorem and proof we need several hybrid experiments and also prove an auxiliary lemma which lets us deal with infinite chains of hybrids.

Definition (Hybrids H^-, $H_k^\vdash$, $H_{k,m}^\dashv$):

- We use a "middle" hybrid H^- where all honest parties swap encapsulated session keys K for randomly drawn K_1's, while still using ciphertexts C corresponding to K. I.e. parties conduct the same modified protocol as the simulator's in-the-head honest parties P^π which means that session keys of two

---

[3] We assume the simulator to internally track the protocol executions to know which mid to use.

honest parties are handled exactly as in the ideal experiment. Note that in contrast to the ideal experiment for every message m between two honest parties in H^- there is a message $(sid, S, \text{DEM.enc}(K_1, m))$ which contains an encryption of m and *not* an encryption of 0.

- Let $k \in \mathbb{N}_0$ be a natural number or zero. We define $H_k^{\vdash}$ to be almost identical to the real-world execution of π_{MSC} with the sole difference that for the first k sessions between two honest parties, the encapsulated key K is swapped for a randomly drawn K_1. Hence we have $H_0^{\vdash} = \text{EXEC}_{\mathcal{D},\mathcal{Z}}^{\pi_{\text{MSC}}}$ and $\lim_{k \to \infty} H_k^{\vdash} = H^-$.

- Let $k \in \mathbb{N}$, $m \in \mathbb{N}_0$ again be natural numbers with m possibly zero. We define $H_{k,m}^{\dashv}$ to be almost identical to H^- with the exception that for all messages in the first $k-1$ sessions between two honest parties and the first m messages sent in the k-th session between two honest parties, encryptions of zeros are sent over the channel instead of encryptions containing the real messages. Hence we have $H_{1,0}^{\dashv} = H^-$, individual limits $\lim_{m \to \infty} H_{k,m}^{\dashv} = H_{k+1,0}^{\dashv}$ for all $k \in \mathbb{N}$ and overall limit $\lim_{k \to \infty} H_{k,m}^{\dashv} = \text{IDEAL}_{\mathcal{S}_{\text{MSC}},\mathcal{Z}}^{\mathcal{F}_{\text{MSC}}}$.

These hybrid definitions give us the following double-chain of hybrids connecting the real-world execution of π_{MSC} and the ideal experiment with $\mathcal{F}_{\text{MSC}}$:

$$\text{EXEC}_{\mathcal{D},\mathcal{Z}}^{\pi_{\text{MSC}}} = H_0^{\vdash}, H_1^{\vdash}, \ldots \to H^- = H_{1,0}^{\dashv}, H_{2,0}^{\dashv}, \ldots \to \text{IDEAL}_{\mathcal{S}_{\text{MSC}},\mathcal{Z}}^{\mathcal{F}_{\text{MSC}}}$$

where each $H_{k,0}^{\dashv}$ is again connected to $H_{k+1,0}^{\dashv}$ by a chain of hybrids $\{H_{k,m}^{\dashv}\}_m$. The following lemma will help us deal with this infinite series of infinite hybrid series:

Lemma 3 *Let $\{H_k\}_{k \in \mathbb{N}_0}$ be series of PPT experiments where executions of H_{k-1} and H_k do not differ before their k-th activation. Let furthermore limit $H_\infty := \lim_{k \to \infty} H_k$ exist and $\mathcal{Z}$ be a PPT environment which distinguishes experiments H_0 and H_∞. Then there is a $\kappa \in \mathbb{N}$ such that a PPT environment $\mathcal{Z}_\kappa$ exists which distinguishes consecutive experiments $H_{\kappa-1}$ and H_κ.*

Proof. Let $p_{\mathcal{Z}}$ be a polynomial which bounds the runtime of the distinguishing PPT environment $\mathcal{Z}$. Since $\mathcal{Z}(\lambda)$ takes at most $p_{\mathcal{Z}(\lambda)}$ steps for the execution of any experiment, all experiments $\{H_k\}_{k > p_{\mathcal{Z}(\lambda)}}$ are necessarily indistinguishable for $\mathcal{Z}$, since they do not differ before their $p_{\mathcal{Z}(\lambda)}$-th activation. Hence $\mathcal{Z}$ is a distinguisher for H_0 and $H_{p_{\mathcal{Z}}}$. We now use the fact that computational indistinguishability is an equivalence relation and in particular transitive. This yields the existence of a $\kappa < p_{\mathcal{Z}}$ and distinguisher $\mathcal{Z}_\kappa$ for experiments $H_{\kappa-1}$ and H_κ. $\square$

Now we are finally ready to formally state and prove that π_{MSC} realizes secure channels:

Theorem 2: *Under static corruption the protocol π_{MSC} with IND-SB-CPA secure SB-KEM and IND-CCA2$_{DEM}$ secure DEM realizes $\mathcal{F}_{MSC}$ in the $\mathcal{F}_{AUTH}$-hybrid model. I.e.*

$$\pi_{MSC}^{\mathcal{F}_{AUTH}} \geq_{UC} \mathcal{F}_{MSC}.$$

Proof. We conduct the proof in two steps, we separately show that (1) $\text{EXEC}_{\mathcal{D},\mathcal{Z}}^{\pi_{\text{MSC}}}$ is indistinguishable from H^-, and (2) H^- is indistinguishable from $\text{IDEAL}_{\mathcal{S}_{\text{MSC}},\mathcal{Z}}^{\mathcal{F}_{\text{MSC}}}$. We reduce the first step to the IND-SB-CPA security of the underlying SB-KEM scheme and the second step to the IND-CCA2$_{\text{DEM}}$ security of the DEM scheme. For both parts we employ Lemma 3 to go from the corresponding infinite hybrid chain to two consecutive hybrids.

(1) Assume that $\text{EXEC}_{\mathcal{D},\mathcal{Z}}^{\pi_{\text{MSC}}}$ and H^- are computationally distinguishable. Then by Lemma 3 there is a $\kappa_1 \in \mathbb{N}$ and environment $\mathcal{Z}_1$ which can distinguish consecutive hybrids $H_{\kappa_1-1}^\vdash$ and $H_{\kappa_1}^\vdash$, i.e. $H_{\kappa_1-1}^\vdash \not\approx_{\mathcal{Z}_1} H_{\kappa_1}^\vdash$. We use this to construct a non-negligibly successful adversary $\mathcal{A}_1 = \mathcal{A}_{\text{SB-KEM}}$ in the following way: The adversary $\mathcal{A}_1$ is started by $\mathcal{C}_{\text{SB-KEM}}$ with input $(S, pk_S, R, pk_R, (K_b, C^*))$ and in turn starts $\mathcal{Z}_1$ in its head, playing all other parties just like they would conduct hybrid $H_{\kappa_1-1}^\vdash$ or $H_{\kappa_1}^\vdash$. If $\mathcal{Z}_1$ corrupts either S or R, the adversary aborts. Since S and R were randomly drawn by the challenger and since by Remark 1 $\mathcal{Z}_1$ needs a message between honest parties to distinguish anything, $\mathcal{A}_1$ has a polynomial chance to not abort at this point.

When $\mathcal{Z}_1$ asks honest party S or R to initialize for the first time, $\mathcal{A}_1$ inserts pk_S/pk_R as S/R's public key respectively for the KEM scheme. Every time in-the-head party S or R send a cipher C encrypted under pk_S/pk_R by some corrupted party P, $\mathcal{A}_1$ decrypts it via the IND-SB-CPA$_{\text{SB-KEM}}$ oracle. This is possible since S and R are honest and hence $P \notin \{S, R\}$. Since honest parties only get interface inputs from $\mathcal{Z}_1$, $\mathcal{A}_1$ already knows the content of all ciphertexts C sent from honest parties to S and R and does not need the oracle to decrypt them.

If the κ_1-th request of $(\texttt{establish}, sid, P)$ by $\mathcal{Z}$ to establish a session between two honest parties is not made to S with $P = R$, abort. This again gives $\mathcal{A}_1$ a polynomial chance not to abort at this stage. Otherwise insert the challenge cipher C^* into the message $(\texttt{send}, sid_{\text{AUTH}}, P', (sid, C^*))$ from S to R via $\mathcal{F}_{\text{AUTH}}$ and have S and R use challenge key K_b as the DEM key throughout this session. For all following sessions use the encapsulated session keys K just as $H_{\kappa_1-1}^\vdash$ and $H_{\kappa_1}^\vdash$ both specify. When $\mathcal{Z}_1$ halts, $\mathcal{A}_1$ outputs $b = 0$ if $\mathcal{Z}_1$ outputs $H_{\kappa_1-1}^\vdash$, and $b = 1$ if $\mathcal{Z}_1$ outputs $H_{\kappa_1}^\vdash$. This way $\mathcal{A}_1$ wins the IND-SB-CPA$_{\text{SB-KEM}}$ game whenever it did not abort and $\mathcal{Z}_1$ successfully distinguished $H_{\kappa_1-1}^\vdash$ and $H_{\kappa_1}^\vdash$, i.e. with non-negligible probability. This contradicts the IND-SB-CPA$_{\text{SB-KEM}}$ security of the underlying KEM scheme and shows that $\text{EXEC}_{\mathcal{D},\mathcal{Z}}^{\pi_{\text{MSC}}}$ must be indistinguishable from H^-.

(2) Assume that H^- and $\text{IDEAL}_{\mathcal{S}_{\text{MSC}},\mathcal{Z}}^{\mathcal{F}_{\text{MSC}}}$ are computationally distinguishable. Then by Lemma 3 there is a $\kappa_2 \in \mathbb{N}$ such that consecutive hybrids $H_{\kappa_2,0}^\dashv$ and $H_{\kappa_2+1,0}^\dashv$ are computationally distinguishable as well. Again by Lemma 3 there is a $\mu \in \mathbb{N}$ and environment $\mathcal{Z}_2$ which can distinguish consecutive hybrids $H_{\kappa_2,\mu-1}^\dashv$ and $H_{\kappa_2,\mu}^\dashv$, i.e. $H_{\kappa_2,\mu-1}^\dashv \not\approx_{\mathcal{Z}_2} H_{\kappa_2,\mu}^\dashv$. We use this to construct a non-negligibly successful adversary $\mathcal{A}_2 = \mathcal{A}_{\text{CCA2-DEM}}$ in the following way: After the challenger $\mathcal{C}_{\text{CCA2-DEM}}$ has randomly drawn the challenge key, the adversary $\mathcal{A}$ is started without input and in turn starts $\mathcal{Z}_2$ in its head,

playing all other parties just like they would conduct hybrid $H_{\kappa_2,\mu-1}^{\dashv}$ or $H_{\kappa_2,\mu}^{\dashv}$. When $\mathcal{Z}_2$ asks for the κ-th session between two honest parties—call them S and R—to be established, $\mathcal{A}$ does not draw a fresh random session key K_1 but rather inserts the (unknown) challenge key instead. This is no problem as all necessary encryptions and decryptions can be obtained via the IND-CCA2$_{\mathrm{DEM}}$ oracle.[4] For the μ-th message m_μ of this session—which by Remark 1 has to be send by an honest party and hence S or R—$\mathcal{A}$ hands m_μ and 0 to the challenger and in return obtains ciphertext c^* which it uses as the channel content reported to $\mathcal{Z}_2$. Now continue to use encryptions of zeros for all further messages of this session, just as $H_{\kappa_2,\mu-1}^{\dashv}$ and $H_{\kappa_2,\mu}^{\dashv}$ require. Whenever the challenge ciphertext c^* is sent to S or R within this session again, act as if the decryption oracle had yielded message m_μ. When $\mathcal{Z}_2$ halts, $\mathcal{A}_2$ outputs $b = 0$ if $\mathcal{Z}_2$ outputs $H_{\kappa_2,\mu-1}^{\dashv}$, and $b = 1$ if $\mathcal{Z}_2$ outputs $H_{\kappa_2,\mu}^{\dashv}$. This way $\mathcal{A}_2$ wins the IND-CCA2$_{\mathrm{DEM}}$ game whenever $\mathcal{Z}_2$ successfully distinguished $H_{\kappa_2,\mu-1}^{\dashv}$ and $H_{\kappa_2,\mu}^{\dashv}$, i.e. with non-negligible probability. This contradicts the IND-CCA2$_{\mathrm{DEM}}$ security of the underlying DEM scheme and shows that H^- must be indistinguishable from IDEAL$_{\mathcal{S}_{\mathrm{MSC}},\mathcal{Z}}^{\mathcal{F}_{\mathrm{MSC}}}$.

With these two steps transitivity of computational indistinguishability concludes our proof.   □

Just as with many other applications of CCA2 security, the building block can be swapped for one satisfying the strictly weaker RCCA security if the message space is super-polynomial in size.

Theorem 3: *Under static corruption the protocol π_{MSC} with IND-SB-CPA secure SB-KEM and IND-RCCA secure DEM with super-polynomial message size realizes $\mathcal{F}_{MSC}$ in the $\mathcal{F}_{AUTH}$-hybrid model as well.*

Proofsketch. Because the proof largely follows the proof of Theorem 2, we will only sketch the differences. Instead of sending encryptions of 0 for messages between honest parties, the simulator draws a uniformly random value r from the message space **M** at the start of the execution and uses this value throughout the protocol. This is vital for when in proof step (2)—after the insertion of c^* as the ciphertext of the μ-th message—other ciphertexts are sent within the same session which the IND-RCCA$_{\mathrm{DEM}}$ oracle refuses to decrypt. Whenever this happens, let $\mathcal{A}_2$ act as if decryption yielded message m_μ. By definition of the oracle the ciphertext may also contain r instead of m_μ which would lead to a simulation error and hence we have no guarantees on the output of $\mathcal{Z}_2$ in this case. But since r was randomly drawn from a super-polynomial message space, the probability that $\mathcal{Z}_2$ tries to send a ciphertext containing it is negligible and the error does not impede our construction of a non-negligibly successful adversary $\mathcal{A}_2$.   ▽

---

[4] Note that although $\mathcal{A}$ knows the content of any message that $\mathcal{Z}_2$ asks S or R to send, this communication is not handled via $\mathcal{F}_{\mathrm{AUTH}}$ and hence every corrupted party may send ciphertexts to S or R expecting them to decrypt as if they were from the other party.

7   Efficient LWE-based Construction

After the very theoretic definitions and transformation from Sects. 4 and 5 we now go on to show the real-world benefit of the new IND-SB-CPA$_{\text{SB-KEM}}$ notion. We do so by giving an LWE based SB-KEM construction in the standard model which is even simpler than the, as far as we know, most efficient standard model construction previously used to construct IND-CCA2$_{\text{PKE}}$ security [6] and show that it still satisfies our IND-SB-CPA$_{\text{SB-KEM}}$ notion. Our construction is a tweaked version of the KEM part from [6,23], where we use sender IDs instead of a hash and remove the employed MAC entirely.

Building blocks needed for this construction are the trapdoor function and gadget matrix G from [23] as well as the corresponding `invert` function, a full-rank difference encoding function `FRD` from [24] translating sender IDs to suitable matrices, a key derivation function (KDF) `KDF` and gaussian distributions $\mathcal{D}$. Using these building blocks we define an SB-KEM $\Sigma := (\text{gen}, \text{enc}, \text{dec})$ as follows:

$\text{gen}(1^\lambda)$:
- $A \xleftarrow{\$} \mathbb{Z}_q^{n \times m}$
- $R \leftarrow \mathcal{D}^{m \times o}_{\omega(\sqrt{\log(n)})}$
- $A_1 := A \cdot R$
- $\hookrightarrow$ Return $(sk, pk) := \big(R, (A, A_1)\big)$.

$\text{enc}(pk, S) = \text{enc}\big((A, A_1), S\big)$:
- $e \leftarrow \mathcal{D}^n_{\alpha \cdot q}$; $e_0 \leftarrow \mathcal{D}^m_{\alpha \cdot q}$; $e_1 \leftarrow \mathcal{D}^o_\sigma$,
  where $\sigma^2 = \big(\|e_0\|^2 + m(\alpha q)^2\big) \cdot \omega\big(\sqrt{\log(n)}\big)^2$.
- $k \xleftarrow{\$} \{0, 1\}^n$
- $s = k \cdot \lfloor \frac{q}{2} \rfloor + e$
- $c_0 = s^\top A + e_0$
- $c_1 = s^\top (A_1 + \text{FRD}(S)G) + e_1$
- $\hookrightarrow$ Return $(K, C) := \big(\text{KDF}(k), (c_0, c_1)\big)$.

$\text{dec}(sk, S, C) = \text{dec}\big(R, S, (c_0, c_1)\big)$:
- $(s, e_0, e_1) \leftarrow \text{invert}\big(R, [A | A_1 + \text{FRD}(S)G], [c_0^\top, c_1^\top]\big)$
- Check $\|e_0\| \leq \alpha q \sqrt{m}$ and $\|e_1\| \leq \alpha q \sqrt{2mo} \cdot \omega\big(\sqrt{\log(n)}\big)$.[5]
- For $i \in \{0, \ldots, n-1\}$: $k[i] := \begin{cases} 0, & \text{if } s[i] \text{ closer to } 0 \\ 1, & \text{if } s[i] \text{ closer to } \frac{q}{2} \end{cases}$.
- Check $\|s - k\| \leq \alpha q \sqrt{n}$. (See footnote 5)
- $\hookrightarrow$ Return $K = \text{KDF}(k)$.

The correctness of the scheme directly carries over from the similar scheme in [6] which is why we concentrate on its security properties in this work. The security of Σ is based on the hardness of the normal form LWE (NLWE) problem.

---

[5] If any check fails, abort with output $\bot$.

NLWE is an equivalent version of the standard LWE problem where the secret vector is drawn from an error distribution as well [6]. From the straightline reduction to LWE follows the post-quantum security of our construction.

Theorem 4: *The SB-KEM* $\Sigma = (\text{gen}, \text{enc}, \text{dec})$ *is IND-SB-CPA secure, given that the LWE assumption holds. In particular, let* $\mathcal{A}$ *be an IND-SB-CPA$_{\text{SB-KEM}}$ adversary against the SB-KEM. Then there are distinguishers* $\mathcal{A}_{\text{LWE}}$ *for NLWE and* $\mathcal{A}_{\text{KDF}}$ *for KDF* KDF, *such that for all* $\lambda \in \mathbb{N}$

$$\text{Adv}^{\text{SB-CPA}}_{\mathcal{A},\Sigma}(\lambda) \leq \text{Adv}^{\text{LWE}}_{\mathcal{A}_{\text{LWE}}}(\lambda) + \text{Adv}^{\text{KDF}}_{\mathcal{A}_{\text{KDF}}}(\lambda) + \varepsilon,$$

where ε *is negligible in* λ.

Proof. We roughly follow the proof idea of [6], constructing a series of games which slowly transform the original IND-SB-CPA$_{\text{SB-KEM}}$ game into a one which is obviously unwinnable. At each definition of a new game we show how the adversary's view changes from the last one.

Game 0: This is the IND-SB-CPA$_{\text{SB-KEM}}$ game.

Game 1: At this point $A_1 = AR$ is swapped for $(AR - \text{FRD}(S)G)$ in the generation of $pk_R = (A, A_1)$. Since the distributions of AR and $(AR - \text{FRD}(S)G)$ are both statistically close to uniform randomness over $\mathbb{Z}_q^{n \times o}$ they are by transitivity statistically close to each other. Since FRD is a full-rank difference encoding $\text{FRD}(S') - \text{FRD}(S)$ is invertible if and only if $S' \neq S$. I.e. with the new definition of pk_R decryption of ciphertexts is still possible for any sender ID other than S. As oracle queries with $S' = S$ are not permitted for IND-SB-CPA$_{\text{SB-KEM}}$ anyway, this does not change the oracle at all. Hence the adversary's view in Game 1 is statistically close to the view in Game 0.

Game 2: This game is identical to Game 1, other than the definition of the challenge (c_0^*, c_1^*). Instead of using r we draw a new vector $\bar{c} \xleftarrow{\$} \mathbb{Z}_q^m$ uniformly at random and set $c_0^* := (\bar{c} + (k^* \cdot \lfloor \frac{q}{2} \rfloor)^\top A)$. For the construction of c_1^* a new random error $\bar{e} \leftarrow \mathcal{D}_{\bar{\sigma}}^\omega$ with $\bar{\sigma}^2 = m(\alpha q)^2 \cdot \omega(\sqrt{\log(n)})^2$ is drawn and c_1^* set to $c_1^* := ((c_0^*)^\top R + \bar{e})$. We reduce this change to the hardness of NLWE by showing that from an adversary $\mathcal{A}_{1|2}$ distinguishing Game 1 and Game 2 with non-negligible success probability we can construct an adversary $\mathcal{A}_{\text{LWE}}$ with the same success probability in breaking the NLWE assumption: After getting input (B, b) from the challenger $\mathcal{C}_{\text{LWE}}$, $\mathcal{A}_{\text{LWE}}$ follows Game 1 apart from two definitions. In R's public key $pk_R = (A, A_1)$ the first value is taken to be $A := B$ which also results in $A_1 = BR$. The value $\bar{c}$ is not drawn randomly but set to b. The rest–including oracle queries–is handled as in Game 1 (which is the same as in Game 2). When $\mathcal{A}_{1|2}$ outputs bit b, which indicates that $\mathcal{A}_{1|2}$ thinks it interacts with Game $(b+1)$, $\mathcal{A}_{\text{LWE}}$ outputs the same b to $\mathcal{C}_{\text{LWE}}$.

For the analysis of the reduction firstly note that the distribution of the public key A has not changed at all. In case b is of the form $b = x^\top B + y$, we have

$$c_0^* = \left(b + (k^* \cdot \lfloor \tfrac{q}{2} \rfloor)^\top A\right) = (k^* \cdot \lfloor \tfrac{q}{2} \rfloor + x)^\top A + y \sim s^\top A + e_0 \tag{1}$$

$$c_1^* = (c_0^*)^\top R + \bar{e} \overset{(1)}{\sim} (s^\top A + e_0)^\top R + \bar{e} \overset{(*)}{\sim} s^\top \left(A_1 + \mathrm{FRD}(S)G\right) + e_1,$$

where the second statistic closeness $(*)$ is gained by adapting Theorem 3.1 of [25] and Corollary 3.10 of [26]. This means the view of $\mathcal{A}_{1|2}$ is statistically close to Game 1 if b is an NLWE sample. If, on the other hand, $b \overset{\$}{\leftarrow} \mathbb{Z}_q^m$ is random, $\bar{c}$ and hence (c_0^*, c_1^*) is obviously distributed the same as in Game 2.

Game 3: Instead of the construction via $\bar{c}$ from Game 2, c_0^* is drawn uniformly at random from $\mathbb{Z}_q^m$. This means the challenge ciphertext C^* is now completely independent of the key K_0. As the value $\bar{c}$ acted as a one-time-pad on $\left((k^* \cdot \lfloor \tfrac{q}{2} \rfloor)^\top A\right)$ to define c_0^* in Game 2, the statistical view of the adversary does not change by this modification.

Game 4: As the last step, the key K_0 is drawn uniformly at random rather than generated via the KDF as $\mathrm{KDF}(k)$. It is obvious that with this change, an adversary distinguishing Game 3 and Game 4 can be used to directly construct a KDF distinguisher with the same success probability.

In Game 4 we see that the adversary is tasked to decide which of two randomly drawn keys K_0 and K_1 it was sent while the rest of its view is completely independent of these keys. This gives the adversary an even one half chance to win Game 4 and overall provides us with the inequality claimed in Theorem 4. $\qquad \square$

8   Conclusion

In this paper we have introduced the new notion of a sender-binding key encapsulation mechanism (SB-KEM) with corresponding IND-SB-CPA security, building on the works of Beskorovajnov et al. [4]. Although slightly stronger than plain CPA, IND-SB-CPA security is weaker than all other previously proposed (tag-)KEM notions, giving CPA security only for the encapsulated key and non-malleability for the sender ID. Despite its weakness we showed that the sender-binding property makes up for the lack of key non-malleability: It is still possible to realize secure communication via authenticated channels from an IND-SB-CPA secure SB-KEM. This is true both for single-message and session communication, where the SB-KEM needs to be paired with IND-OT$_{\mathrm{DEM}}$ and IND-RCCA$_{\mathrm{DEM}}$ respectively. This means it is now possible to get secure communication from weaker assumptions. We show the real world merit of this advancement by providing a post-quantum secure SB-KEM construction based on the standard assumption of LWE. The efficiency of our construction is directly derived from the previous KEMs construction [6] ours is based on.

An interesting theoretic problem for future work is whether IND-SB-CPA security is in fact the weakest possible KEM notion to allow for UC-secure communication via hybrid encryption and authenticated channels.

Acknowledgements. We thank the PKC 2023 anonymous reviewers for their valuable feedback. The work presented in this paper has been funded by the German Federal Ministry of Education and Research (BMBF) under the project "PQC4MED" (ID 16KIS1044) and by KASTEL Security Research Labs.

References

1. Diffie, W., Hellman, M.: New directions in cryptography. IEEE Trans. Inf. Theory **22**(6), 644–654 (1976)
2. Shoup, V.: A Proposal for an ISO Standard for Public Key Encryption. Cryptology ePrint Archive, Paper 2001/112 (2001). https://eprint.iacr.org/2001/112
3. Canetti, R., Krawczyk, H., Nielsen, J.B.: Relaxing chosen-ciphertext security. In: Boneh, D. (ed.) CRYPTO 2003. LNCS, vol. 2729, pp. 565–582. Springer, Heidelberg (2003). https://doi.org/10.1007/978-3-540-45146-4_33
4. Beskorovajnov, W., Gröll, R., Müller-Quade, J., Ottenhues, A., Schwerdt, R.: A new security notion for PKC in the standard model: weaker, simpler, and still realizing secure channels. In: Hanaoka, G., Shikata, J., Watanabe, Y. (eds.) Public-Key Cryptography - PKC 2022. Lecture Notes in Computer Science, vol. 13178, pp. 316–344. Springer, Cham (2022). https://doi.org/10.1007/978-3-030-97131-1_11
5. Cramer, R., Shoup, V.: Design and analysis of practical public-key encryption schemes secure against adaptive chosen ciphertext attack. SIAM Journal on Computing **33**, 167–226 (2002). https://doi.org/10.1137/S0097539702403773
6. Boyen, X., Izabachène, M., Li, Q.: Secure hybrid encryption in the standard model from hard learning problems. In: Cheon, J.H., Tillich, J.-P. (eds.) PQCrypto 2021 2021. LNCS, vol. 12841, pp. 399–418. Springer, Cham (2021). https://doi.org/10.1007/978-3-030-81293-5_21
7. Schwerdt, R., Benz, L., Beskorovajnov, W., Eilebrecht, S., Müller-Quade, J., Ottenhues, A.: Sender-binding key encapsulation, Cryptology ePrint Archive, Paper 2023/127 (2023). https://eprint.iacr.org/2023/127. https://eprint.iacr.org/2023/127. 2023
8. Nagao, W., Manabe, Y., Okamoto, T.: A Universally composable secure channel based on the KEM-DEM framework. In: Kilian, J. (eds.) Theory of Cryptography. TCC 2005. Lecture Notes in Computer Science, vol. 3378, pp. 28–38. Springer, Heidelberg (2006). https://doi.org/10.1007/978-3-540-30576-7_23
9. Information technology – Security techniques – Encryption algorithms – Part 2: Asymmetric ciphers. Standard, Geneva, CH: International Organization for Standardization (2006)
10. Abe, M., Gennaro, R., Kurosawa, K., Shoup, V.: Tag-KEM/DEM: a new framework for hybrid encryption and a new analysis of Kurosawa-Desmedt KEM. In: Cramer, R. (ed.) EUROCRYPT 2005. LNCS, vol. 3494, pp. 128–146. Springer, Heidelberg (2005). https://doi.org/10.1007/11426639_8
11. MacKenzie, P., Reiter, M.K., Yang, K.: Alternatives to non-malleability: definitions, constructions, and applications. In: Naor, M. (ed.) TCC 2004. LNCS, vol. 2951, pp. 171–190. Springer, Heidelberg (2004). https://doi.org/10.1007/978-3-540-24638-1_10
12. Herranz, J., Hofheinz, D., Kiltz, E.: Some (in)sufficient conditions for secure hybrid encryption. Inf. Comput. **208**, 1243–1257 (2010). https://doi.org/10.1016/j.ic.2010.07.002

13. Katz, J., Yung, M.: Characterization of security notions for probabilistic private-key encryption. J. Cryptol. **19**, 67–95 (2006). https://doi.org/10.1007/s00145-005-0310-8

14. Canetti, R.: Security and composition of multiparty cryptographic protocols. J. Cryptol. **13**(1), 143–202 (2000)

15. Canetti, R.: Universally composable security: a new paradigm for cryptographic protocols. In: Proceedings 42nd IEEE Symposium on Foundations of Computer Science, pp. 136–145 (2001)

16. Canetti, R.: Universally composable signature, certification, and authentication. In: Proceedings 17th IEEE Computer Security Foundations Workshop, pp. 219–233 (2004)

17. Canetti, R., Krawczyk, H.: Universally composable notions of key exchange and secure channels. In: International Conference on the Theory and Applications of Cryptographic Techniques, pp. 337–351 (2002)

18. Kurosawa, K., Desmedt, Y.: A new paradigm of hybrid encryption scheme. In: Franklin, M. (ed.) CRYPTO 2004. LNCS, vol. 3152, pp. 426–442. Springer, Heidelberg (2004). https://doi.org/10.1007/978-3-540-28628-8_26

19. Bos, J., et al.: CRYSTALS - Kyber: A CCA-secure module-lattice- based KEM. In: 2018 IEEE European Symposium on Security and Privacy, pp. 353–367 (2018). https://doi.org/10.1109/EuroSP.2018.00032

20. Choi, S.G., et al.: The Kurosawa-Desmedt key encapsulation is not chosen-ciphertext secure. Inf. Process. Lett. **109**(16), 897–901 (2009)

21. Kurosawa, K., Trieu Phong, L.: Kurosawa-Desmedt key encapsulation mechanism, revisited. In: Pointcheval, D., Vergnaud, D. (eds.) AFRICACRYPT 2014. LNCS, vol. 8469, pp. 51–68. Springer, Cham (2014). https://doi.org/10.1007/978-3-319-06734-6_4

22. Canetti, R., Krawczyk, H.: Analysis of key-exchange protocols and their use for building secure channels. In: International Conference on the Theory and Applications Of Cryptographic Techniques, pp. 453–474 (2001)

23. Micciancio, D., Peikert, C.: TRapdoors for lattices: simpler, tighter, faster, smaller. In: Pointcheval, D., Johansson, T. (eds.) EUROCRYPT 2012. LNCS, vol. 7237, pp. 700–718. Springer, Heidelberg (2012). https://doi.org/10.1007/978-3-642-29011-4_41

24. Agrawal, S., Boneh, D., Boyen, X.: Efficient lattice (H)IBE in the standard model. In: Gilbert, H. (ed.) EUROCRYPT 2010. LNCS, vol. 6110, pp. 553–572. Springer, Heidelberg (2010). https://doi.org/10.1007/978-3-642-13190-5_28

25. Peikert, C.: An efficient and parallel gaussian sampler for lattices. In: Rabin, T. (ed.) CRYPTO 2010. LNCS, vol. 6223, pp. 80–97. Springer, Heidelberg (2010). https://doi.org/10.1007/978-3-642-14623-7_5

26. Regev, O.: On lattices, learning with errors, random linear codes, and cryptography. J. ACM **56**(6), 84–93 (2009). https://doi.org/10.1145/1568318.1568324

Pattern Matching in Encrypted Stream from Inner Product Encryption

Élie Bouscatié[1,2]([✉]), Guilhem Castagnos[2], and Olivier Sanders[1]

[1] Orange Labs, Applied Crypto Group, Cesson-Sévigné, France
elie.bouscatie@orange.com
[2] Université de Bordeaux, INRIA, CNRS, IMB UMR 5251, 33405 Talence, France

Abstract. Functional encryption features secret keys, each associated with a key function f, which allow to directly recover $f(x)$ from an encryption of x, without learning anything more about x. This property is particularly useful when delegating data processing to a third party as it allows the latter to perform its task while ensuring minimum data leakage. However, this generic term conceals a great diversity in the cryptographic constructions that strongly differ according to the functions f they support.

A recent series of works has focused on the ability to search a pattern within a data stream, which can be expressed as a function f. One of the conclusions of these works was that this function f was not supported by the current state-of-the-art, which incited their authors to propose a new primitive called Stream Encryption supporting Pattern Matching (SEPM). Some concrete constructions were proposed but with some limitations such as selective security or reliance on non-standard assumptions.

In this paper, we revisit the relations between this primitive and two major subclasses of functional encryption, namely Hidden Vector Encryption (HVE) and Inner Product Encryption (IPE). We indeed first exhibit a generic transformation from HVE to SEPM, which immediately yields new efficient SEPM constructions with better features than existing ones. We then revisit the relations between HVE and IPE and show that we can actually do better than the transformation proposed by Katz, Sahai and Waters in their seminal paper on predicate encryption. This allows to fully leverage the vast state-of-the-art on IPE which contains adaptively secure constructions proven under standard assumptions. This results in countless new SEPM constructions, with all the features one can wish for. Beyond that, we believe that our work sheds a new light on the relations between IPE schemes and HVE schemes and in particular shows that some of the former are more suitable to construct the latter.

Keywords: Pattern Matching · Functional Encryption · Hidden Vector Encryption · Inner Product Encryption

A. Boldyreva and V. Kolesnikov (Eds.): PKC 2023, LNCS 13940, pp. 774–801, 2023.
https://doi.org/10.1007/978-3-031-31368-4_27

1   Introduction

Outsourcing IT services has become very common worldwide[1] for multiple reasons ranging from costs reduction to improved services. Whatever the actual reason is, the concrete consequence for the company that delegates such services is that a third party ends up with its data in clear because of the well-known limitations of standard encryption.

Ideally, this third party should only learn the minimal information necessary for performing the requested processing, which has motivated the design of countless encryption schemes compatible with specific processing. Such schemes belong to the realm of functional encryption [6], where the third party recovers a function $f(x)$ from an encryption of x without learning anything else about x, with minimal interaction. Of course, the function f, and hence the encryption scheme, strongly depends on the considered application, which explains the profusion of papers related to this topic.

1.1   Related Works

As functional encryption schemes supporting a large set of functions (e.g. [2,15]) tend to be quite complex, a variety of schemes have been tailored to a specific function and therefore to the requirements of specific use-cases. In this paper, we will focus on the ability to detect specific patterns within an encrypted string (also called *pattern matching*), which is very useful for many scenarios such as Intrusion Detection Systems (IDS) or search on genomic data.

At first glance, this problem seems to be directly related to the area of *searchable* encryption (e.g. [4,12]) where one can decide if a ciphertext C encrypts some data x provided that it has received a trapdoor T_x specific to x. Unfortunately, as noted in [13], this does not solve the problem of pattern matching because there is a huge difference between deciding whether C encrypts x or whether C encrypts a string y that contains x as a substring. One could try to follow the tokenization approach of [24], which consists in splitting the encrypted string into many overlapping substrings that will be individually encrypted using searchable encryption. However, this only works if all searched patterns are strings of a unique same length, which is not true in practice[2]. Adaptations of this approach are possible but lead to other problems, as also discussed in [13]. We also note that techniques tailored to use-cases related to external storage (*e.g.* [9,17]) do not work in our context as, in the latter, the entity performing the test is the data owner which allows to reveal more information. In our case, the test is performed by a third entity which should only learn the result of the pattern matching.

Similarly, previous papers on pattern matching (*e.g.* [13,24], [3,8]) dismissed so-called predicate encryption [16], a sub-class of functional encryption where f is essentially a boolean function, as they noticed, here again, that this primitive

---

[1] https://sumatosoft.com/blog/it-outsourcing-2019-overview-trends.
[2] See e.g. the length distribution of Snort rules https://snort.org/downloads#rules.

does not exactly answer our problem. More specifically, they considered two related primitives, namely Inner Product Encryption (IPE) [16] and Hidden Vector Encryption (HVE) [7] that seem to provide the kind of features one needs for pattern matching. The former allows to test if the inner product of some vector associated with the ciphertext and some other vector associated with the secret key is zero whereas the latter allows to test if a ciphertext is associated with a vector of attributes, potentially with wildcards. However, they noted that using such schemes for pattern matching on data streams require to provide, for each searched pattern, a secret key linear in the size of the stream, which quickly becomes cumbersome. This is truly unfortunate as this area of cryptography has been extensively studied, with very impressive results. For example, if we focus on the specific case of Inner Product Encryption (e.g. [10,16,20–23]), one can find schemes with remarkable features such as adaptive security, proofs under standard assumptions, etc.

This state of affairs led very recent papers [3,8,13] to define a new primitive called Stream Encryption supporting Pattern Matching (SEPM), directly tailored to the pattern matching use-case. Conceptually, this primitive is close to predicate encryption but aims at providing constant size secret keys that yet allow to search the patterns anywhere in the stream. As this feature seemed incompatible with IPE or HVE, the authors of these papers started from scratch with constructions only achieving selective security and, for most of them, under very strong interactive assumptions.

1.2   Our Contributions

In this paper we completely revisit SEPM by identifying generic and efficient transformations linking IPE and SEPM through HVE. The direct consequence of our work is that it allows to leverage all the state-of-the art related to IPE and HVE to directly build SEPM with new features. More specifically, we proceed in two main steps, as follows.

Our natural starting point is HVE for two reasons. Firstly, by identifying the characters of our data streams with the attributes of HVE, one gets the ability to search patterns while ensuring data privacy. Secondly, HVE supports wildcards, that is, a special character ⋆ that matches all characters. This allows to detect more advanced patterns such as ab ⋆ ⋆ cd, meaning ab followed by cd with an offset of 2. This kind of patterns is necessary in many applications such as IDS, as illustrated by the Snort data rules mentioned above. Moreover, when it comes to data stream, this allows to test the presence of some pattern abc at any position within the stream by providing secret keys for the patterns abc ⋆ ⋆ . . ., ⋆ abc ⋆ . . ., etc. Obviously, the natural downside of this approach is that one must issue secret keys for any possible position of the pattern, which quickly becomes cumbersome. This is actually the reason why [13] dismissed HVE as a potential solution. The latter paper managed to have constant-size secret keys allowing to search a pattern *everywhere* in the data stream but at the cost of a very large public key.

In a follow-up work, [3] addressed the problem of the large public key through a technique called fragmentation which consists in splitting the stream into overlapping and redundant substrings. The same technique was used in [8] to construct a scheme with better complexity and security.

In this work we show that this fragmentation technique is actually much more powerful than initially thought because, intuitively, it allows to reduce the problem of finding a pattern anywhere in a stream to the one of searching this pattern within fixed-length substrings, called fragments, which limits the consequences of the problem mentioned above. This allows us to propose a generic transformation from HVE to SEPM which automatically improves the state-of-the-art of SEPM.

Once this is done, we try to further improve our result by trying to connect SEPM to IPE, which has been much more studied than HVE.

Here, we do not start from scratch as Katz, Sahai and Waters [16] already showed a relation between IPE and HVE. More specifically, they noted that if one encrypts a vector $(\mathbf{xr}, -\mathbf{r}) \in \mathbf{F}_p^{2n}$ with an IPE scheme, where $\mathbf{xr}$ denotes the element-wise product of the vector $\mathbf{x}$ and some random vector $\mathbf{r}$, then one can test if $\mathbf{x} = \mathbf{k}$ (and thus get an HVE scheme) given an IPE secret key for $(1, \ldots, 1, \mathbf{k}) \in \mathbf{F}_p^{2n}$. Indeed, one can note that the scalar product between these two vectors is 0. Obviously, the opposite must be true and this is the purpose of the vector $\mathbf{r}$. Without this randomness $\mathbf{r}$ in the ciphertext, one could indeed easily construct another secret key that would cancel $\mathbf{x}$ without being equal to $\mathbf{x}$. This, combined with the way it handles wildcards, described in the body of this paper, explains why this transformation doubles the size of the original vectors. We stress the importance of $\mathbf{r}$ being hidden in the ciphertext by the security of the IPE scheme. Surprisingly, this fact is not mentioned by [16] to prove the security of their transformation. Actually, the arguments they provide still apply to our next transformation but we show a counterexample in this case, *i.e.* an secure IPE scheme whose conversion is not secure. As a warm-up, we provide a complete proof of security for their transformation, which allows to identify the subtleties that arise in the process.

As the KSW transformation entails a doubling of the ciphertext size, we propose in this paper a new conversion with a ratio very close to 1. Our core idea, which allows us to handle wildcards with fewer coordinates, is to move the randomness $\mathbf{r}$ to the secret key in the following way. We set our ciphertext as $(\mathbf{x}, -1) \in \mathbf{F}_p^{n+1}$ whereas the secret key is $(\mathbf{r}, \langle \mathbf{k}, \mathbf{r} \rangle)$. Here again, we get an HVE scheme that allows to test whether $\mathbf{k} = \mathbf{x}$, but with a better efficiency. However, proving security of the resulting transformation is much more complex. Intuitively, the problem stems from the fact that security inherently depends on the secrecy of $\mathbf{r}$. When $\mathbf{r}$ is embedded in the ciphertext, as in the KSW transformation, one can rely on the security of the encryption scheme itself. In our case, this is no longer possible as there is no equivalent property for the secret key itself. Theoretically, one could learn $\mathbf{r}$ from the secret key and thus break security of the conversion. We study this problem more thoroughly and show that it actually depends on the exact model we consider.

In the case of selective security, we show that an adversary is unable to exploit this problem and so that our conversion IPE to HVE remains secure for all schemes.

In the adaptive case, we cannot prove such a result in general, and actually show a counterexample with an IPE scheme from the literature. Fortunately, we show that we can circumvent this problem if the underlying IPE scheme satisfies a new property that we formalize. This property concerns the secret keys of the IPE schemes and we show that many such constructions naturally achieve it under the discrete logarithm assumption. With this additional property, we are at last able to prove adaptive security of the HVE schemes resulting from this conversion. This allows to leverage the whole state-of-the-art of IPE schemes with a better efficiency than with the KSW conversion. Besides that, this shows that some IPE schemes are more suitable to design HVE schemes, which clarifies the relation between these two primitives.

In a last section, we draw the consequences of our generic conversions. Whereas all known SEPM proposals only achieved selective security under strong assumptions, we show that it is possible to achieve adaptive security under DLIN by loosing only a constant factor on efficiency.

2   Definitions

In this section, we first give useful notations for the context of pattern matching and then review notions of functional encryption still in this context. In particular, we consider Hidden Vector Encryption and Inner Product Encryption, two primitives that we will use to construct Stream Encryption supporting Pattern Matching. As we shall see, we will consider predicate only versions of these two primitives, viewing attributes as messages.

Notations and Vocabulary. We denote by $\mathbf{N}$ the set of positive integers and for any $n \in \mathbf{N}$, we note $[\![n]\!] := \{1, \ldots, n\}$. For any set A, we write $x \xleftarrow{\$} A$ to say that x is chosen uniformly at random in A, we note $A^* := \bigcup_{i \geq 1} A^i$ where A^i is the usual Cartesian product $A \times \cdots \times A$ and for an element $\mathbf{a} \in A^*$, we note $\mathsf{len}(\mathbf{a})$ the non negative integer such that $\mathbf{a} \in A^{\mathsf{len}(\mathbf{a})}$ and call the *length* of $\mathbf{a}$. Let $\star$ be the wildcard symbol and Σ a finite alphabet that does not contain $\star$. An element $\mathbf{x} \in \Sigma^*$ is called a *string*, an element $\mathbf{k} \in (\Sigma \cup \{\star\})^*$ a *pattern* and the set $\mathsf{supp}(\mathbf{k}) := \{1 \leq i \leq \mathsf{len}(\mathbf{k}) : k_i \neq \star\}$ is called the *support* of $\mathbf{k}$. We say that the pattern $\mathbf{k}$ *matches* the string $\mathbf{x}$ if $\mathsf{len}(\mathbf{k}) = \mathsf{len}(\mathbf{x})$, and

$$\forall i \in \mathsf{supp}(\mathbf{k}), k_i = x_i.$$

More generally, if $\mathsf{len}(\mathbf{k}) \leq \mathsf{len}(\mathbf{x})$, then for any $1 \leq i \leq \mathsf{len}(\mathbf{x}) - \mathsf{len}(\mathbf{k}) + 1$, we say that the pattern $\mathbf{k}$ *matches* the string $\mathbf{x}$ at *position* i if

$$\forall j \in \mathsf{supp}(\mathbf{k}), k_j = x_{i+j-1}.$$

Other notations are deferred to the beginning of Sect. 4 where the choice of Σ becomes more specific.

2.1   Functional Encryption

Syntax. We recall the general definition of functional encryption as introduced in [6]. A functionality F defined over (K, X) is a function $F : K \times X \to \{0, 1\}^*$ described as a (deterministic) Turing Machine. The set K is called the key space and the set X is called the plaintext space.

A functional encryption scheme for the functionality F enables one to evaluate $F(\mathbf{k}, \mathbf{x})$ given the encryption of $\mathbf{x}$ and a secret key $\mathsf{sk}_\mathbf{k}$ for $\mathbf{k}$. The algorithm for evaluation $F(\mathbf{k}, \mathbf{x})$ using $\mathsf{sk}_\mathbf{k}$ is called decrypt. More precisely, a functional encryption scheme is defined as a tuple of four PPT algorithms (setup, keygen, enc, dec) as follows:

- $(pp, \mathsf{pk}, \mathsf{mk}) \leftarrow \mathsf{setup}(1^\lambda)$, generates public parameters that are implicit inputs of the other algorithms, a public key and a master secret key;
- $\mathsf{sk}_\mathbf{k} \leftarrow \mathsf{keygen}(\mathsf{mk}, \mathbf{k})$, generates a secret key for $\mathbf{k}$;
- $\mathbf{c} \leftarrow \mathsf{enc}(\mathsf{pk}, \mathbf{x})$, encrypts the message $\mathbf{x}$;
- $y \leftarrow \mathsf{dec}(\mathsf{sk}_\mathbf{k}, \mathbf{k}, \mathbf{c})$, uses sk to compute $y \in \{0, 1\}^*$ from $\mathbf{c}$.

Correctness. As we are essentially interested in pattern matching applications, the definition of correctness that we give will be associated with the notion of *false positive* (a pattern is mistakenly detected). However, for all the schemes that we consider there is no false negative, patterns that are present, will always be detected. Moreover, although we could provide a generic definition of correctness, we choose to distinguish two relevant cases in our context, the one where the output of F is 0 or 1 and the one where this output can be parsed as some finite subset of $\mathbf{N}$. It will lead to more intuitive definitions. These definitions are similar to those in [1] but we consider a slightly weaker notion of false positive. A functional encryption scheme with functionality F such that $F(\mathbf{k}, \mathbf{x}) \in \{0, 1\}$ is correct if for all $\mathbf{k} \in K, \mathbf{x} \in X$,

- $F(\mathbf{k}, \mathbf{x}) = 1 \implies \mathsf{dec}(\mathsf{keygen}(\mathsf{mk}, \mathbf{k}), \mathbf{k}, \mathsf{enc}(\mathsf{pk}, \mathbf{x})) = 1$.
- $F(\mathbf{k}, \mathbf{x}) = 0$ and $\mathsf{dec}(\mathsf{keygen}(\mathsf{mk}, \mathbf{k}), \mathbf{k}, \mathsf{enc}(\mathsf{pk}, \mathbf{x})) = 1$ (*i.e.* a false positive) occurs with negligible probability $\mu(\lambda)$ over the coins of all the algorithms.

A functional encryption scheme with functionality F such that $F(\mathbf{k}, \mathbf{x})$ is a finite subset of $\mathbf{N}$ is correct if for all $\mathbf{k} \in K, \mathbf{x} \in X, i \in \mathbf{N}$,

- $i \in F(\mathbf{k}, \mathbf{x}) \implies i \in \mathsf{dec}(\mathsf{keygen}(\mathsf{mk}, \mathbf{k}), \mathbf{k}, \mathsf{enc}(\mathsf{pk}, \mathbf{x}))$.
- $i \notin F(\mathbf{k}, \mathbf{x})$ and $i \in \mathsf{dec}(\mathsf{keygen}(\mathsf{mk}, \mathbf{k}), \mathbf{k}, \mathsf{enc}(\mathsf{pk}, \mathbf{x}))$ (*i.e.* a false positive) occurs with negligible probability $\mu(\lambda)$ over the coins of all the algorithms.

Security. We here recall the classical $\mathsf{IND-CPA}$ security for functional encryption schemes.

Definition 1 ($\mathsf{IND-CPA}$ for functional encryption). *A Functional Encryption scheme is* $\mathsf{IND-CPA}$ *secure if no probabilistic polynomial time adversary* $\mathcal{A}$ *has a non-negligible advantage in the following game,* $\mathsf{Exp}_{\mathcal{A}}^{\mathsf{IND-CPA}}$:

> *Setup: run* $(pp, \mathsf{pk}, \mathsf{mk}) \leftarrow \mathsf{setup}(1^{\lambda})$ *and give* pp, pk *to* $\mathcal{A}$.
> *Query Phase 1:* $\mathcal{A}$ *submits queries* $\mathbf{k} \in K$ *and gets* $\mathsf{sk}_{\mathbf{k}} \leftarrow \mathsf{keygen}(\mathsf{mk}, \mathbf{k})$
> *Challenge:* $\mathcal{A}$ *submits two messages* $\mathbf{m}^{(0)}, \mathbf{m}^{(1)} \in X$ *such that every queried pattern* $\mathbf{k}$ *follows the natural restriction:*
>
> $$F(\mathbf{k}, \mathbf{m}^{(0)}) = F(\mathbf{k}, \mathbf{m}^{(1)}). \tag{1}$$
>
> *The challenger chooses* $\beta \xleftarrow{\$} \{0, 1\}$ *and gives* $\mathbf{c} \leftarrow \mathsf{enc}(\mathsf{pk}, \mathbf{m}^{(\beta)})$ *to* $\mathcal{A}$.
> *Query Phase 2:* $\mathcal{A}$ *can issue key queries as before but subject to restriction (1).*
> *Guess:* $\mathcal{A}$ *eventually outputs a bit* β' *in* $\{0, 1\}$.
>
> *The advantage of* $\mathcal{A}$ *is defined as* $\left| \Pr[\beta = \beta'] - \dfrac{1}{2} \right|$.

This definition is sometimes called *adaptive* $\mathsf{IND-CPA}$ *security*. In a weaker model, *selective security*, the adversary $\mathcal{A}$ has to choose $\mathbf{m}^{(0)}, \mathbf{m}^{(1)}$ at the beginning of the game, before seeing the public key and public parameters and before Query Phase 1.

2.2   Some Classes of Functional Encryption

Hidden Vector Encryption. This primitive, HVE for short, was introduced in [7]. The original definition follows the paradigm of predicate encryption. A secret key encapsulates a key pattern (a string with possible wildcards) while a ciphertext encrypts both an attribute string and a payload message. A first security notion, called *payload hiding*, ensures that a ciphertext hides all information about the payload message unless one has a secret key for a key pattern that matches the attribute string, in this case, he recovers the payload message. An additional security notion, called *attribute hiding* (cf. [16]), ensures that a ciphertext hides all information about the attribute string and decryption does not reveal any information about the attribute string other than the fact that it matches the key pattern or not.

It was noted in [13] that an attribute hiding HVE can be used for pattern matching on the attribute without revealing extra information about it but with the strong limitations recalled in our introduction. While other applications may not consider attribute hiding or weaker versions of it, this notion is crucial to achieve this purpose.

In many works on HVE (*e.g.* [11,16]) a first building block is presented, called a *predicate-only* HVE. This focuses on the attribute, not considering the payload message. The reason behind this is that attribute hiding is the hardest part to achieve (especially when adaptive security is targeted as in [19]) and the full-fledged HVE is then obtained using a key encapsulation mechanism. In the following, we will abuse the terminology of [16], as in [11], and simply refer to *predicate-only* HVE as HVE. Thus what we called an attribute will be seen as the message and the attribute hiding security notion will coincide with the classical IND − CPA security notion for functional encryption.

This gives the following definition.

Definition 2 ((Predicate-Only) Hidden Vector Encryption). *An n-HVE scheme for some integer n is formally described as a functional encryption scheme where:*

1. *The key space K is $(\Sigma \cup \{\star\})^n$.*
2. *The plaintext space X is Σ^n.*
3. *The functionality is $F_{\text{HVE}} \colon K \times X \longrightarrow \{0,1\}$*

$$(\mathbf{k}, \mathbf{x}) \longmapsto F_{\text{HVE}}(\mathbf{k}, \mathbf{x}) = \begin{cases} 1 & \text{if } \mathbf{k} \text{ matches } \mathbf{x}, \\ 0 & \text{otherwise.} \end{cases}$$

Inner Product Encryption. We will also consider Inner Product Encryption (IPE), a primitive introduced by [16] who additionally noted a relation to HVE (we will review and improve this result in Sects. 4 and 5). Here keys and attributes are vectors and one tests whether their inner product is zero, instead of testing matching. Again we consider a predicate-only version of this primitive which is sufficient for our purposes. We adapt the definition from [6] that uses the vector space $\mathbf{F}_p^n$ to define an IPE.

Definition 3 ((Predicate-Only) Inner product Encryption). *An n-IPE scheme for some integer n is formally described as a functional encryption scheme where:*

1. *The setup algorithm defines a randomly chosen prime p of length λ, where λ is the security parameter.*
2. *The key space K and plaintext space X are $\mathbf{F}_p^n$.*
3. *The functionality is $F_{\text{IPE}} \colon K \times X \longrightarrow \{0,1\}$*

$$(\mathbf{u}, \mathbf{v}) \longmapsto F_{\text{IPE}}(\mathbf{u}, \mathbf{v}) = \begin{cases} 1 & \text{if } \langle \mathbf{u}, \mathbf{v} \rangle = 0, \\ 0 & \text{otherwise.} \end{cases}$$

Stream Encryption Supporting Pattern Matching. This primitive has been recently considered in [3,8]. It can be formalized as a functional encryption scheme as follows. A plaintext x is a stream, an element of Σ^*. Given a pattern $\mathbf{k}$ of length upper bounded by n, the functionality returns all the integers i such that $\mathbf{k}$ matches $\mathbf{x}$ at position i.

Definition 4 (Stream Encryption supporting Pattern Matching). *An* n-*SEPM scheme for some integer* n *is formally described as a functional encryption scheme where:*

1. *The key space* K *is* $\bigcup_{i=1}^{n} (\Sigma \cup \{\star\})^i$ *completed by the empty key* ϵ.
2. *The plaintext space* X *is* Σ^*.
3. *The functionality is defined as*

$$F_{\text{SEPM}} : (K \setminus \{\epsilon\}) \times X \longrightarrow \{S \subset \mathbf{N} : S \text{ is finite}\}$$
$$(\mathbf{k}, \mathbf{x}) \longmapsto F_{\text{SEPM}}(\mathbf{k}, \mathbf{x}) = \{i : \mathbf{k} \text{ matches } \mathbf{x} \text{ at position } i\}.$$

And we let $F_{\text{SEPM}}(\epsilon, \mathbf{x}) = \text{len}(\mathbf{x})$ *to leak the length of the message intentionally.*

3   From HVE to SEPM Through Fragmentation

There are several ways of designing a public key encryption scheme supporting pattern matching but, as explained in [13], they usually lead to systems suffering from very concrete limitations, such as the restriction of the set of possible patterns to strings of a unique same length, secret keys (called trapdoors in [13]) whose size is linear in the maximum size of the encryption stream, etc. The authors of [13] proposed an alternative primitive that theoretically addresses these issues but with rather poor performance. Two follow-up works [3] and [8] improved this by introducing SEPM schemes. They both extensively rely on a technique called *fragmentation* that enables to circumvent the need for shiftable trapdoors identified in [13] by splitting the stream into fragments with some redundancy.

We first recall this technique and then show, as a first contribution, that fragmentation creates a strong relation between SEPM and HVE: we expose a generic conversion from a 2d-HVE scheme to a n-SEPM with $n = d + 1$ and its security.

3.1   Fragmentation

Let n be an upper bound on the length of the patterns supported by the SEPM scheme. To enable pattern matching for string $\mathbf{x}$ of any length, the fragmentation technique splits the latter into overlapping substrings $\mathbf{x}_i$ of size $2d$, where $d :=$ $n - 1$, as follows

$$\mathbf{x}_i = (x_{(i-1)d+1}, \ldots, x_{(i+1)d}) \qquad \text{for } i = 1, \ldots, \left\lceil \frac{\text{len}(\mathbf{x})}{d} \right\rceil.$$

This leads to this decomposition of $\mathbf{x}$:

$$\mathbf{x} = \overbrace{x_1, \ldots, x_d, \underbrace{x_{d+1}, \ldots, x_{2d}}_{\mathbf{x}_2}, \overbrace{x_{2d+1}, \ldots, x_{3d}}^{\mathbf{x}_3}, \underbrace{x_{3d+1}, \ldots, x_{4d}}_{\mathbf{x}_4}, x_{4d+1}, \ldots, x_{5d}, \cdots}^{\mathbf{x}_1}$$

Our first contribution in this paper is to revisit this notion of fragmentation to show that it actually creates a strong relation between SEPM and HVE. More specifically, we show that once a string has been fragmented in this way, one can divert the use of any 2d-HVE scheme to build an SEPM scheme. This observation allows to leverage the work that has already been done on Hidden Vector Encryption and even on Inner Product Encryption as we will explain in Sect. 4. In particular, it avoids the need to build a new system from scratch, as was done in [3] and [8]. Actually, one can show that the constructions of these works implicitly define a 2d-HVE scheme.

Remark 1. Note that if d does not divide len($\mathbf{x}$), the last fragment is not completely defined. A generic solution is to complete it with padding but this could create a problem if the streaming resumes. However, in the latter case, one can simply retransmit this last fragment, completed with the new data. Alternatively, several HVE schemes, such as the ones implicitly used in [8], allow to produce the encryption of an incomplete message that may later be completed consistently. Our point here is that incomplete fragments can easily be handled and so that we can, from now on, assume that d divides len($\mathbf{x}$).

3.2   Conversion

We first remark that fragmentation reduces the problem of encrypting a string of arbitrary length into the one of encrypting several substrings of fixed length. We can therefore run the encryption algorithm of any fixed-length primitive such as a 2d-HVE scheme. However, this is true for any splitting of $\mathbf{x}$. The specificity of fragmentation is that it avoids the problem of patterns straddling fragments by ensuring that any searchable pattern will always be entirely contained in at least one fragment. Thanks to this feature, and by appropriately generating the secret keys of the underlying HVE system, one can ensure that any pattern will be detected.

We depict in Fig. 1 our generic conversion from a 2d-HVE scheme to a n-SEPM with $n = d + 1$.

Correctness of the SEPM scheme of Fig. 1. Suppose that a pattern $\mathbf{k}$ matches $\mathbf{x}$ at some position ℓ, meaning that $\ell \in F_{\text{SEPM}}(\mathbf{k}, \mathbf{x})$ where F_{SEPM} is defined in Definition 4. Let $i = \lceil \frac{\ell}{d} \rceil$. By construction, $\mathbf{k}$ is fully contained inside $\mathbf{x}_i = (x_{(i-1)d+1}, \ldots, x_{(i+1)d})$. We indeed have both:

1. $(i-1)d + 1 \leq \ell$
2. $\ell + \text{len}(\mathbf{k}) - 1 \leq \ell + n - 1 = \ell + d \leq (i+1)d$

where the last inequality stands as $\ell \leq i \cdot d$, by definition of i. Therefore, within the fragment $\mathbf{x}_i$, $\mathbf{k}$ starts at some position $1 \leq j \leq d$ and will be detected by sk_j with probability 1 by correctness of $\mathcal{E}_{\text{HVE}}$. We thus have that $\ell \in S$ with probability 1 where S is the output of $\text{dec}_{\text{SEPM}}(\text{sk}, \mathbf{c})$.

Conversely suppose that $\ell \notin F_{\text{SEPM}}(\mathbf{k}, \mathbf{x})$, but $\ell \in S$. This means that $\text{dec}_{\text{HVE}}(\text{sk}_j, \mathbf{c}_i)$ has returned 1. By correctness of $\mathcal{E}_{\text{HVE}}$, this can occur only with negligible probability as the pattern is not present in the fragment $\mathbf{x}_i$. Consequently, the probability of false positives of $\mathcal{E}_{\text{SEPM}}$ is the same as the one of $\mathcal{E}_{\text{HVE}}$. $\qquad\square$

- Let $n \in \mathbf{N}$, $n \geq 2$, $d = n - 1$.
- Let $\mathcal{E}_{\text{HVE}} := (\text{setup}_{\text{HVE}}, \text{keygen}_{\text{HVE}}, \text{enc}_{\text{HVE}}, \text{dec}_{\text{HVE}})$ be a $2d$-HVE scheme.
- $\text{setup}_{\text{SEPM}}$ is $\text{setup}_{\text{HVE}}$.
- $\text{keygen}_{\text{SEPM}}(\text{mk}, \mathbf{k})$ takes as input a pattern $\mathbf{k}$ with $\text{len}(\mathbf{k}) \leq n$ and computes

$$\text{sk}_j \leftarrow \text{keygen}_{\text{HVE}}(\text{mk}, \mathbf{k}_j)$$

for all $j \in [\![d]\!]$, where $\mathbf{k}_j$ is the $2d$ long pattern $(\overbrace{\star, \ldots, \star}^{j-1}, \mathbf{k}, \star, \ldots, \star)$. It then returns $\text{sk} := (\text{sk}_1, \ldots, \text{sk}_d)$.
- $\text{enc}_{\text{SEPM}}(\text{pk}, \mathbf{x})$ takes a string $\mathbf{x}$ of length $f \cdot d$ for some $f \in \mathbf{N}$ (see Remark 1) and computes

$$\mathbf{c}_i \leftarrow \text{enc}_{\text{HVE}}(\text{pk}, (x_{(i-1)d+1}, \ldots, x_{(i+1)d}))$$

for all $i \in [\![f]\!]$, to return $\mathbf{c} := (\mathbf{c}_1, \ldots, \mathbf{c}_f)$.
- $\text{dec}_{\text{SEPM}}(\text{sk}, \mathbf{c})$ parses sk as $(\text{sk}_1, \ldots, \text{sk}_d)$ and $\mathbf{c}$ as $(\mathbf{c}_1, \ldots, \mathbf{c}_f)$ for some $f \in \mathbf{N}$. Then it sets $S = \varnothing$ and, for every $i \in [\![f]\!]$ and $j \in [\![d]\!]$, it tests whether $1 = \text{dec}_{\text{HVE}}(\text{sk}_j, \mathbf{c}_i)$, in which case it updates $S \leftarrow S \cup \{(i-1)d + j\}$. Finally, it outputs S.

Fig. 1. Generic construction of an n-SEPM scheme $\mathcal{E}_{\text{SEPM}}$ from a $2d$-HVE scheme

Remark 2. Our conversion described in Fig. 1 leads to secret keys sk whose size is *independent* of the length of $\mathbf{x}$. Technically, our conversion would also work for symmetric HVE schemes but in such a case we would have to change the encryption key, and therefore the secret keys, for each fragment, which would be rather cumbersome.

3.3   Security

Theorem 1. *The conversion in Fig. 1 transforms an* $\mathsf{IND-CPA}$ *secure* $2(n-1)$-*HVE scheme* $\mathcal{E}_{\text{HVE}}$ *into an* $\mathsf{IND-CPA}$ *secure* n-*SEPM* $\mathcal{E}_{\text{SEPM}}$ *scheme.*

Proof. For the sake of clarity, we slightly adapt $\text{Exp}_{\mathcal{A}}^{\mathsf{IND-CPA}}(\mathcal{E}_{\text{SEPM}})$ for SEPM by defining $\text{Exp}_{\mathcal{A}}^{\mathsf{IND-CPA-0}}(\mathcal{E}_{\text{SEPM}})$ (resp. $\text{Exp}_{\mathcal{A}}^{\mathsf{IND-CPA-1}}(\mathcal{E}_{\text{SEPM}})$) as the original experiment where the challenger always choose $\beta = 0$ (resp. $\beta = 1$). We must then show that

$$\left| \Pr[\text{Exp}_{\mathcal{A}}^{\mathsf{IND-CPA-0}} \rightarrow 0] - \Pr[\text{Exp}_{\mathcal{A}}^{\mathsf{IND-CPA-1}} \rightarrow 0] \right| \text{ is negligible.}$$

In other words, the behavior of $\mathcal{A}$ must be the same in both games.

Let $\mathbf{x}^0$ and $\mathbf{x}^1$ be the challenge messages submitted by the adversary $\mathcal{A}$ and $\mathbf{x}_1^0, \ldots, \mathbf{x}_f^0$ and $\mathbf{x}_1^1, \ldots, \mathbf{x}_f^1$ their respective fragments. In this proof we will proceed through a sequence of games where we will progressively replace $\mathbf{x}_i^0$ by $\mathbf{x}_i^1$ in the challenge ciphertext. Any discrepancy in the behavior of $\mathcal{A}$ would then imply that it has been able to distinguish two HVE ciphertexts, and so an attack against the $\mathsf{IND} - \mathsf{CPA}$ security of the HVE scheme.

More formally, we define the following sequence of games:

- $\mathbf{game}_0$ is $\mathsf{Exp}_{\mathcal{A}}^{\mathsf{IND}-\mathsf{CPA}-0}(\mathcal{E}_{\mathrm{SEPM}})$,
- for $i = 1, \ldots, f$, $\mathbf{game}_i$ is the same game as $\mathbf{game}_{i-1}$ except that,

$$\mathbf{c} = \big(\mathsf{enc}_{\mathrm{HVE}}(\mathsf{pk}, \mathbf{x}_1^1), \ldots, \mathsf{enc}_{\mathrm{HVE}}(\mathsf{pk}, \mathbf{x}_i^1),$$
$$\mathsf{enc}_{\mathrm{HVE}}(\mathsf{pk}, \mathbf{x}_{i+1}^0), \ldots, \mathsf{enc}_{\mathrm{HVE}}(\mathsf{pk}, \mathbf{x}_f^0)\big),$$

so $\mathbf{game}_f$ is exactly $\mathsf{Exp}_{\mathcal{A}}^{\mathsf{IND}-\mathsf{CPA}-1}(\mathcal{E}_{\mathrm{SEPM}})$.

For $i = 0, \ldots, f$, let Z_i be the event that the adversary outputs 0 in $\mathbf{game}_i$. We thus have,

$$\big|\Pr[\mathsf{Exp}_{\mathcal{A}}^{\mathsf{IND}-\mathsf{CPA}-0}(\mathcal{E}_{\mathrm{SEPM}}) \to 0] - \Pr[\mathsf{Exp}_{\mathcal{A}}^{\mathsf{IND}-\mathsf{CPA}-1}(\mathcal{E}_{\mathrm{SEPM}}) \to 0]\big|$$
$$\leq \sum_{i=1}^{f} \big|\Pr[Z_i] - \Pr[Z_{i-1}]\big|.$$

Let us assume that there exists $i^* \in [\![f]\!]$ such that $\big|\Pr[Z_{i^*}] - \Pr[Z_{i^*-1}]\big|$ is not negligible. We describe an adversary $\mathcal{B}$ that uses $\mathcal{A}$ against the $\mathsf{IND} - \mathsf{CPA}$ security of $\mathcal{E}_{\mathrm{HVE}}$. Let $\mathcal{C}(\mathcal{E}_{\mathrm{HVE}})$ be the challenger of $\mathsf{Exp}^{\mathsf{IND}-\mathsf{CPA}}(\mathcal{E}_{\mathrm{HVE}})$.

Setup. $\mathcal{B}$ runs $\mathcal{C}(\mathcal{E}_{\mathrm{HVE}})$ to get the public parameters and keys of the system and forwards them to $\mathcal{A}$.

Query Phase 1. When $\mathcal{A}$ makes a query for a pattern $\mathbf{k}$, $\mathcal{B}$ proceeds as in Fig. 1 and then queries d times $\mathcal{C}(\mathcal{E}_{\mathrm{HVE}})$ to build the associated secret key sk.

Challenge. The algorithm $\mathcal{B}$ uses the public key to set the ciphertext elements

$$\mathbf{c}_i \leftarrow \mathsf{enc}_{\mathrm{HVE}}(\mathsf{pk}, \mathbf{x}_i^1) \qquad \text{for } i = 1, \ldots, i^* - 1,$$
$$\text{and } \mathbf{c}_i \leftarrow \mathsf{enc}_{\mathrm{HVE}}(\mathsf{pk}, \mathbf{x}_i^0) \qquad \text{for } i = i^* + 1, \ldots, f.$$

It then submits $\mathbf{x}_{i^*}^0$ and $\mathbf{x}_{i^*}^1$ to $\mathcal{C}(\mathcal{E}_{\mathrm{HVE}})$ as challenge messages which returns a ciphertext element used by $\mathcal{B}$ as $\mathbf{c}_{i^*}$. The algorithm $\mathcal{B}$ can then send $(\mathbf{c}_1, \ldots, \mathbf{c}_f)$ to $\mathcal{A}$ as the challenge ciphertext.

Query phase 2. The algorithm $\mathcal{B}$ proceeds as in the first phase.

Guess. $\mathcal{B}$ finally forwards the bit β' issued by the adversary to $\mathcal{C}(\mathcal{E}_{\mathrm{HVE}})$.

First note that the restrictions placed on pattern queries in the SEPM experiment implies that all key queries to $\mathcal{C}(\mathcal{E}_{\mathrm{HVE}})$ are valid. In other words, if a pattern $\mathbf{k}$ matched $\mathbf{x}_{i^*}^0$ but not $\mathbf{x}_{i^*}^1$ in the HVE game, then the same would be true for $\mathbf{x}^0$ and $\mathbf{x}^1$ in the SEPM game, which is not possible.

Finally, the challenge ciphertext returned by $\mathcal{C}(\mathcal{E}_{\mathrm{HVE}})$ is either an encryption of $\mathbf{x}_{i^*}^0$ or $\mathbf{x}_{i^*}^1$. In the first case, we are playing $\mathbf{game}_{i^*-1}$. In the second case, this is exactly $\mathbf{game}_{i^*}$. Any adversary such that $\left|\Pr[Z_{i^*}] - \Pr[Z_{i^*-1}]\right|$ is non-negligible can then be used against the $\mathsf{IND} - \mathsf{CPA}$ experiment of HVE.   □

Remark 3. This proof readily adapts to the case of selective security.

4   Hidden Vector Encryption from Inner Product Encryption

In the previous section, we have shown that any HVE scheme could be used to construct an SEPM scheme. However, we note that there is not many HVE schemes in the literature, in particular when one wants specific properties such as adaptive security. This stands in sharp contrast with a related primitive, Inner Product Encryption, for which countless constructions exist. Actually, the relatively low number of publications on HVE can perhaps be explained by a subsection of [16] where the authors explain how one can generically build a n-HVE scheme from a $2n$-IPE scheme (referred as KSW conversion in the following). To our knowledge, this result has not been formally proven and [16] seems to only consider selective security. In this section, we first show, as a warm-up that this conversion is secure, even in the adaptive case, although the proof is not that straightforward. In particular, we will see that subtleties appear in the proof, concerning the conversions of valid key queries made by an HVE adversary to valid key queries for an IPE adversary.

As this conversion doubles ciphertext size, we then revisit the links between these two primitives to show that one can achieve a much better ratio (almost 1) through a new conversion that we introduce. We then show that one can prove that this construction is secure in the selective case, using similar information theoretic arguments than in the proof of the KSW conversion. We defer the case of adaptive security to Sect. 5.

Notations. In the following conversions, we suppose $\Sigma = \mathbf{F}_p^{\times}$ and $\star = 0$ which implies $\Sigma \cup \{\star\} = \mathbf{F}_p$. For two vectors of same length $\mathbf{u} = (u_1, \ldots, u_n)$ and $\mathbf{v} = (v_1, \ldots, v_n)$, we denote by $\mathbf{uv}$ the vector of same length obtained by element-wise product

$$\mathbf{uv} := (u_1 v_1, \ldots, u_n v_n)$$

For a vector $\mathbf{k} \in \mathbf{F}_p^n$, we denote by $\mathbb{1}_{\mathbf{k}}$ the vector $(s_1, \ldots, s_n)$ where for all $i \in [\![n]\!]$, $s_i = 1$ if $i \in \mathsf{supp}(\mathbf{k})$ and $s_i = 0$ if $i \notin \mathsf{supp}(\mathbf{k})$.

4.1   KSW Conversion

In [16, Subsection 5.2], Katz, Sahai and Waters give the following conversion from a $2n$-IPE scheme to an n-HVE scheme. We define the applications

$$f\colon\ \Sigma^n \times \mathbf{F}_p^n\ \longrightarrow\ \mathbf{F}_p^{2n}$$
$$(\ \mathbf{x}\ ,\ \mathbf{r}\ )\longmapsto(\ \mathbf{xr}\ ,\ -\mathbf{r}\ )$$

$$g\colon\quad \mathbf{F}_p^n\ \longrightarrow\ \mathbf{F}_p^{2n}$$
$$\mathbf{k}\quad\longmapsto(\ \mathbb{1}_{\mathbf{k}}\ ,\ \mathbf{k}\ )$$

where we have put the coordinates in a different order than [16], simplifying our notations without fundamentally changing the original conversion. The construction of Katz, Sahai and Waters is depicted in Fig. 2.

- Let $\mathcal{E}_{\mathrm{IPE}} := (\mathsf{setup}_{\mathrm{IPE}}, \mathsf{keygen}_{\mathrm{IPE}}, \mathsf{enc}_{\mathrm{IPE}}, \mathsf{dec}_{\mathrm{IPE}})$ be a $(2n)$-IPE scheme.
- $\mathsf{setup}_{\mathrm{HVE}}(1^\lambda, n)$ is $\mathsf{setup}_{\mathrm{IPE}}(1^\lambda, 2n)$.
- $\mathsf{keygen}_{\mathrm{HVE}}(\mathsf{mk}, \mathbf{k})$ returns $\mathsf{sk}_{\mathbf{k}} \leftarrow \mathsf{keygen}_{\mathrm{IPE}}(\mathsf{mk}, g(\mathbf{k}))$.
- $\mathsf{enc}_{\mathrm{HVE}}(\mathsf{pk}, \mathbf{x})$ chooses $\mathbf{r} \xleftarrow{\$} \mathbf{F}_p^n$ and returns $\mathbf{c} \leftarrow \mathsf{enc}_{\mathrm{IPE}}(\mathsf{pk}, f(\mathbf{x}, \mathbf{r}))$.
- $\mathsf{dec}_{\mathrm{HVE}}(\mathsf{sk}_{\mathbf{k}}, \mathbf{c})$ is $\mathsf{dec}_{\mathrm{IPE}}(\mathsf{sk}_{\mathbf{k}}, \mathbf{c})$.

Fig. 2. KSW construction of an n-HVE scheme $\mathcal{E}_{\mathrm{HVE}}$ from a $2n$-IPE scheme

Correctness. Let us remark that $\langle f(\mathbf{x}, \mathbf{r}), g(\mathbf{k})\rangle = \langle(\mathbf{xr}, -\mathbf{r}), (\mathbb{1}_{\mathbf{k}}, \mathbf{k})\rangle = \langle\mathbf{xr}, \mathbb{1}_{\mathbf{k}}\rangle - \langle\mathbf{r}, \mathbf{k}\rangle = \langle\mathbb{1}_{\mathbf{k}}\mathbf{x}, \mathbf{r}\rangle - \langle\mathbf{k}, \mathbf{r}\rangle = \langle\mathbb{1}_{\mathbf{k}}\mathbf{x} - \mathbf{k}, \mathbf{r}\rangle$. Moreover, if a pattern $\mathbf{k}$ matches $\mathbf{x}$, then with the notations that we have just introduced, we have $\mathbb{1}_{\mathbf{k}}\mathbf{x} - \mathbf{k} = \mathbf{0}$.

As a result, if $\mathbf{k}$ matches $\mathbf{x}$, this inner product is 0 for all choices of r. By correctness of $\mathcal{E}_{\mathrm{IPE}}$, with probability 1 decryption of a ciphertext for $\mathbf{x}$ with $\mathsf{sk}_{\mathbf{k}}$ will return 1.

Conversely, if $\mathbf{k}$ does not match $\mathbf{x}$, then $\mathbb{1}_{\mathbf{k}}\mathbf{x} - \mathbf{k} \neq \mathbf{0}$. The probability for a random vector $\mathbf{r}$ in $\mathbf{F}_p^n$ of being orthogonal to a non-zero vector is $1/p$. So decryption will return 1 with negligible probability $1/p + (1 - 1/p) \cdot \mu(\lambda)$ where $\mu(\lambda)$ is the probability of false positive for $\mathcal{E}_{\mathrm{IPE}}$. This proves the correctness of the conversion.   □

As we explain above, the authors of [16] do not prove the security of this conversion but only provide a very informal argument to support this claim from correctness and seem to consider only selective security. Below, we show that this conversion indeed results in an adaptively (resp. selectively) secure HVE scheme if the IPE scheme is adaptively (resp. selectively) secure but also that this result is not that straightforward. Intuitively, the problem stems from the fact that there is some discrepancy between the restriction on key queries in an HVE experiment and the one in the IPE experiment. More concretely, an adversary in the HVE experiment may submit a key query for a vector $\mathbf{k}$

that does not match any of the challenge messages of the HVE experiment (this is thus a valid query) but that yet results, through this conversion, in an illicit query for the IPE experiment. The status of a query (illicit or not) will depend on the randomness **r** that is included in the challenge ciphertext. Before the challenge ciphertext is revealed, this randomness is still unknown and, as suggested in [16], one can use the same argument that we saw when we proved correctness, for stating that false positives are unlikely. However, this argument does not hold in phase 2. Once the challenge ciphertext has been revealed, the randomness is no longer perfectly hidden. Fortunately, we can rely on another information theoretic argument as we explain in the proof.

4.2 Security Analysis of KSW Conversion

We prove in this section the following theorem.

Theorem 2. *The KSW conversion transforms a selective (resp. adaptive)* IND− CPA *secure 2n-IPE scheme* $\mathcal{E}_{\mathrm{IPE}}$ *into a selective (resp. adaptive)* IND − CPA *secure n-HVE* $\mathcal{E}_{\mathrm{HVE}}$ *scheme.*

Proof. Consider an adversary $\mathcal{A}$ against the IND − CPA security of $\mathcal{E}_{\mathrm{HVE}}$. Let $\mathcal{C}(\mathcal{E}_{\mathrm{IPE}})$ be the challenger of the IND − CPA experiment for $\mathcal{E}_{\mathrm{IPE}}$. We build an adversary $\mathcal{B}$ against the IND − CPA security of $\mathcal{E}_{\mathrm{IPE}}$, using $\mathcal{A}$. An overview of the adversary $\mathcal{B}$ is given in Fig. 3.

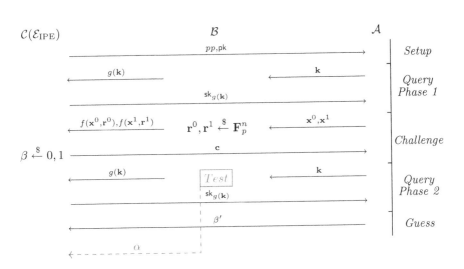

$\boxed{Test}$ checks if conditions (2) and (3) are met in which case it returns the value α of condition (3) and stops the simulation.

Fig. 3. Overview of the adversary $\mathcal{B}$ in the proof of Theorem 2.

Setup. The adversary $\mathcal{B}$ simply forwards the public parameters and public key from $\mathcal{C}(\mathcal{E}_{\text{IPE}})$ to the adversary $\mathcal{A}$.

Query Phase 1. As there is no restriction on the possible queries in this phase in either security game, $\mathcal{B}$ simply answers a query $\mathbf{k}$ of $\mathcal{A}$ by submitting $g(\mathbf{k})$ as a query to $\mathcal{C}(\mathcal{E}_{\text{IPE}})$ and forwards the secret key to $\mathcal{A}$.

Challenge. In this phase, $\mathcal{A}$ submits two messages $\mathbf{x}^0$ and $\mathbf{x}^1$. We only have to handle the case where this pair satisfies the restriction of the HVE game. In this case, $\mathcal{B}$ chooses $\mathbf{r}^0, \mathbf{r}^1 \in \mathbf{F}_p^n$, submits the messages $f(\mathbf{x}^0, \mathbf{r}^0)$ and $f(\mathbf{x}^1, \mathbf{r}^1)$ and forwards the resulting challenge ciphertext to $\mathcal{A}$.

However a problem can occur if $f(\mathbf{x}^0, \mathbf{r}^0)$ and $f(\mathbf{x}^1, \mathbf{r}^1)$ do not satisfy the restriction of the IPE game. Let $\mathbf{k}$ be a pattern queried by $\mathcal{A}$. From the restriction of the HVE game, there are two cases.

First, $\mathbf{k}$ matches both x^0 and x^1. In this case, as we have seen for correctness, $\forall \alpha \in \{0,1\}, \langle f(\mathbf{x}^\alpha, \mathbf{r}^\alpha), g(\mathbf{k}) \rangle = 0$, for all choices of randomness. As a result the messages $f(\mathbf{x}^0, \mathbf{r}^0)$ and $f(\mathbf{x}^1, \mathbf{r}^1)$ always satisfy the restriction of the IPE game.

The second case is a little more complex. The problematic conditions are

$$\forall \alpha \in \{0,1\}, \mathbf{k} \text{ does not match } \mathbf{x}^\alpha, \text{ and,}$$

$$\exists \alpha \in \{0,1\}, \langle f(\mathbf{x}^\alpha, \mathbf{r}^\alpha), g(\mathbf{k}) \rangle = 0 \text{ and } \langle f(\mathbf{x}^{1-\alpha}, \mathbf{r}^{1-\alpha}), g(\mathbf{k}) \rangle \neq 0.$$

As seen before, this can be rewritten as follows:

$$\forall \alpha \in \{0,1\}, \mathbb{1}_\mathbf{k} \mathbf{x}^\alpha - \mathbf{k} \neq \mathbf{0} \tag{2}$$

$$\exists \alpha \in \{0,1\}, \langle \mathbb{1}_\mathbf{k} \mathbf{x}^\alpha - \mathbf{k}, \mathbf{r}^\alpha \rangle = 0 \text{ and } \langle \mathbb{1}_\mathbf{k} \mathbf{x}^{1-\alpha} - \mathbf{k}, \mathbf{r}^{1-\alpha} \rangle \neq 0 \tag{3}$$

At this stage, we can still rely on the correctness argument as in [16] because $\mathbf{r}^0$ and $\mathbf{r}^1$ were still unknown at the time of the queries. As a result, if equation (2) holds, equation (3) holds with negligible probability $2 \cdot \left(\frac{1}{p} \cdot \left(1 - \frac{1}{p}\right)\right) = \frac{2}{p} - \frac{2}{p^2} < \frac{2}{p}$.

Query Phase 2. Unlike in phase 1, we can no longer argue that $\mathbf{r}^0$ and $\mathbf{r}^1$ are unknown to the adversary and this is where we cannot rely only on the arguments developed for correctness as suggested in [16]. Concretely, the HVE adversary $\mathcal{A}$ could get information on one of these random values from the challenge ciphertext and so submit a query $\mathbf{k}$ satisfying conditions (2) and (3). It might perhaps be possible to exclude such cases by assuming some appropriate computational assumption but this could only be done on a case-by-case basis and so would be irrelevant for this generic conversion.

Fortunately we can proceed differently: if the adversary $\mathcal{A}$ submits a query $\mathbf{k}$ that does not match either challenge message but such that $\langle \mathbb{1}_\mathbf{k} \mathbf{x}^\alpha - \mathbf{k}, \mathbf{r}^\alpha \rangle = 0$ for some $\alpha \in \{0,1\}$, and $\langle \mathbb{1}_\mathbf{k} \mathbf{x}^{1-\alpha} - \mathbf{k}, \mathbf{r}^{1-\alpha} \rangle \neq 0$, then $\mathcal{B}$ returns α to $\mathcal{C}(\mathcal{E}_{\text{IPE}})$ and stops. The intuition here is that the probability that $\mathcal{A}$ submits such a query with $\alpha = 1 - \beta$ is negligible because it has no information about $\mathbf{r}^{1-\beta}$. Formally, for any query $\mathbf{k}$ that does not match either challenge message, $\langle \mathbb{1}_\mathbf{k} \mathbf{x}^{1-\beta} - \mathbf{k}, \mathbf{r}^{1-\beta} \rangle = 0$ happens with probability $\frac{1}{p}$ and in the other case, $\mathcal{B}$ wins the security game.

Guess. Finally, $\mathcal{B}$ forwards the guess of $\mathcal{A}$ to $\mathcal{C}(\mathcal{E}_{\mathrm{IPE}})$.   □

4.3   Our Conversion

A clear downside of the previous approach is that it requires a $2n$-IPE scheme to build a n-HVE scheme, which does not seem optimal. In this section, we propose a new generic transformation that halves this cost. We keep the same overall idea, of testing if a pattern $\mathbf{k}$ matches $\mathbf{x}$ by testing if the inner product $\langle \mathbb{1}_\mathbf{k}\mathbf{x} - \mathbf{k}, \mathbf{r} \rangle$ is 0 for a random $\mathbf{r}$, but we add this randomness during key generation instead of encryption which allows us to handle the wildcards of $\mathbf{k}$ without doubling the coordinates. However, as we will see, this change has profound consequences on the security proofs.

$$f: \quad \Sigma^n \quad \longrightarrow \quad \mathbf{F}_p^{n+1}$$
$$\mathbf{x} \quad \longmapsto (\quad \mathbf{x} \quad , \quad -1 \quad)$$

$$g: \quad \mathbf{F}_p^n \times \mathbf{F}_p^n \quad \longrightarrow \quad \mathbf{F}_p^{n+1}$$
$$(\quad \mathbf{k} \quad , \quad \mathbf{r} \quad) \longmapsto (\mathbb{1}_\mathbf{k}\mathbf{r} \, , \, \langle \mathbf{k}, \mathbf{r} \rangle)$$

We depict in Fig. 4 our generic conversion from an $(n+1)$-IPE scheme to a n-HVE scheme.

- Let $\mathcal{E}_{\mathrm{IPE}} := (\mathsf{setup}_{\mathrm{IPE}}, \mathsf{keygen}_{\mathrm{IPE}}, \mathsf{enc}_{\mathrm{IPE}}, \mathsf{dec}_{\mathrm{IPE}})$ be a $(n+1)$-IPE scheme.
- $\mathsf{setup}_{\mathrm{HVE}}(1^\lambda, n)$ is $\mathsf{setup}_{\mathrm{IPE}}(1^\lambda, n+1)$.
- $\mathsf{keygen}_{\mathrm{HVE}}(\mathsf{mk}, \mathbf{k})$ chooses $\mathbf{r} \xleftarrow{\$} \mathbf{F}_p^n$ and returns $\mathsf{sk}_\mathbf{k} \leftarrow \mathsf{keygen}_{\mathrm{IPE}}(\mathsf{mk}, g(\mathbf{k}, \mathbf{r}))$.
- $\mathsf{enc}_{\mathrm{HVE}}(\mathsf{pk}, \mathbf{x})$ returns $\mathbf{c} \leftarrow \mathsf{enc}_{\mathrm{IPE}}(\mathsf{pk}, f(\mathbf{x}))$.
- $\mathsf{dec}_{\mathrm{HVE}}(\mathsf{sk}_\mathbf{k}, \mathbf{c})$ is $\mathsf{dec}_{\mathrm{IPE}}(\mathsf{sk}_\mathbf{k}, \mathbf{c})$.

Fig. 4. Our construction of an n-HVE scheme $\mathcal{E}_{\mathrm{HVE}}$ from a $(n+1)$-IPE scheme

Correctness. Let $\mathbf{x} = (x_1, \ldots, x_n) \in \Sigma^n$ be a message and $\mathbf{c}$ be an encryption of $\mathbf{x}$. Let $\mathbf{k} = (k_1, \ldots, k_n) \in (\Sigma \cup \{\star\})^n$ be a pattern and $\mathsf{sk}_\mathbf{k}$ be the secret key of $\mathbf{k}$ generated as $\mathsf{keygen}_{\mathrm{IPE}}(\mathsf{mk}, g(\mathbf{k}, \mathbf{r}))$ for some vector $\mathbf{r} \in \mathbf{F}_p^n$. A calculation similar to the one we did before gives $\langle f(\mathbf{x}), g(\mathbf{k}, \mathbf{r}) \rangle = \langle \mathbb{1}_\mathbf{k}\mathbf{x} - \mathbf{k}, \mathbf{r} \rangle$. This leads to one the following two cases:

- If $\mathbf{k}$ matches $\mathbf{x}$, then $\mathbb{1}_\mathbf{k}\mathbf{x} - \mathbf{k} = \mathbf{0}$, and $\langle f(\mathbf{x}), g(\mathbf{k}, \mathbf{r}) \rangle = 0$ for all choices of r. By correctness of the IPE scheme, with probability 1, $\mathsf{dec}_{\mathrm{HVE}}(\mathsf{sk}_\mathbf{k}, \mathbf{c})$ will return 1.
- If $\mathbf{k}$ does not match $\mathbf{x}$, then $\mathbb{1}_\mathbf{k}\mathbf{x} - \mathbf{k} \neq \mathbf{0}$ and we only have $\langle \mathbb{1}_\mathbf{k}\mathbf{x} - \mathbf{k}, \mathbf{r} \rangle = 0$ with probability $1/p$ from the uniformity of $\mathbf{r}$. As the probability of a false positive for $\mathcal{E}_{\mathrm{IPE}}$ is some negligible function $\mu(\lambda)$, the probability of a false positive for the HVE scheme is less than $1/p + \mu(\lambda)$ which is negligible.   □

4.4   Selective Security

We now make a first assessment of the security of our new conversion. Unlike the KSW conversion, we need to distinguish the case of selective security from the case of adaptive security. Indeed, as we shall see, in the selective case, there is no problem of conversion of key queries from the HVE scheme to the IPE scheme: as the adversary chooses the challenge message at the beginning of the security game, the choice of the randomness will be always made *after* the choice of these messages and the choice of the query $\mathbf{k}$. As a result, the randomness is independent of the choices of the HVE adversary and we can still rely on an information theoretic argument. However for full adaptive security, this will no longer be the case. In the next section, we will show that we can rely on a computational argument related to the IPE scheme in order to go through the proof.

Theorem 3. *The conversion in Fig. 4 transforms a selective* IND − CPA *secure* $(n+1)$-*IPE scheme* $\mathcal{E}_{\mathrm{IPE}}$ *into a selective* IND−CPA *secure n-HVE scheme* $\mathcal{E}_{\mathrm{HVE}}$.

Remark 4. This theorem could actually be slightly extended in the sense that the result still holds if the adversary has access to the public key at the beginning of the security game but is not allowed to make key queries before committing to the challenge messages (*i.e.*, there is no Query Phase 1).

Proof. We denote by $\mathcal{C}_{\mathrm{sel}}(\mathcal{E}_{\mathrm{IPE}})$ the challenger of the selective IND−CPA security game for $\mathcal{E}_{\mathrm{IPE}}$. Again we build an adversary $\mathcal{B}$ that interacts with this challenger, using an adversary $\mathcal{A}$ against the selective security of $\mathcal{E}_{\mathrm{HVE}}$.

Setup. The adversary $\mathcal{B}$ receives the challenge messages $\mathbf{x}^0, \mathbf{x}^1 \in \Sigma^n$ from $\mathcal{A}$ and then forwards $f(\mathbf{x}^0), f(\mathbf{x}^1)$ to $\mathcal{C}_{\mathrm{sel}}(\mathcal{E}_{\mathrm{IPE}})$. Then $\mathcal{B}$ forwards the public key received from $\mathcal{C}_{\mathrm{sel}}(\mathcal{E}_{\mathrm{IPE}})$ to $\mathcal{A}$.

Query Phase 1. On key query $\mathbf{k} \in \mathbf{F}_p^n$, $\mathcal{B}$ chooses $\mathbf{r}$ at random in $\mathbf{F}_p^n$ and submits the key query $g(\mathbf{k}, \mathbf{r})$ to $\mathcal{C}_{\mathrm{sel}}(\mathcal{E}_{\mathrm{IPE}})$ and forwards the secret key to $\mathcal{A}$.

Challenge. The challenger $\mathcal{C}_{\mathrm{sel}}(\mathcal{E}_{\mathrm{IPE}})$ sends a ciphertext $\mathbf{c}$, encrypting either $f(\mathbf{x}^0)$ of $f(\mathbf{x}^1)$, which is forwarded to $\mathcal{A}$.

Query Phase 2. The adversary $\mathcal{B}$ proceeds as in the first query phase.

Guess. Finally, $\mathcal{B}$ forwards the guess of $\mathcal{A}$ to $\mathcal{C}_{\mathrm{sel}}(\mathcal{E}_{\mathrm{IPE}})$.

By construction, the guess of the adversary $\mathcal{A}$ can be used straightforwardly against the selective IND−CPA security of $\mathcal{E}_{\mathrm{IPE}}$ if $\mathcal{B}$ is a valid adversary. The only issue we need to consider here is the validity of the key queries. We actually face a situation rather similar to the one of the proof of Theorem 2. The problematic case is a query by $\mathcal{A}$ for a pattern $\mathbf{k}$ such that

$$\forall \alpha \in \{0,1\}, \mathbb{1}_{\mathbf{k}} \mathbf{x}^\alpha - \mathbf{k} \neq \mathbf{0}$$

$$\exists \alpha \in \{0,1\}, \langle \mathbb{1}_{\mathbf{k}} \mathbf{x}^{\alpha} - \mathbf{k}, \mathbf{r}^{\alpha} \rangle = 0 \text{ and } \langle \mathbb{1}_{\mathbf{k}} \mathbf{x}^{1-\alpha} - \mathbf{k}, \mathbf{r}^{1-\alpha} \rangle \neq 0.$$

This corresponds to a valid query for the HVE security experiment but not from the IPE security experiment. Fortunately, in the case of selective security, we can easily rule out this scenario. Indeed, in this case, the randomness $\mathbf{r}$ is selected by $\mathcal{B}$ *after* the choice of $\mathbf{x}^{\alpha}$ and $\mathbf{k}$ by $\mathcal{A}$. We can then rely on the same argument as in phase 1 of the proof of Theorem 2 to bound the probability of this event by $\frac{2}{p}$, which concludes the proof. $\qquad\square$

5 Adaptive Security

A natural question at this stage is how one can extend the previous result regarding our conversion to the case of adaptive security. Clearly, the approach of the selective security proof above cannot be generalized to this setting as we strongly relied on the fact that the adversary committed to the challenge messages *before* requesting any secret keys. Fortunately, we show in this section that we can prove the adaptive security of this generic conversion at the cost of imposing an additional requirement on the IPE scheme. We formalize this requirement as a property that we call *key privacy*. This notion is related to function privacy but implies weaker requirements on the secret key itself. This allows us to circumvent well-known limitations (see *e.g.* [5]) of function-privacy for public key encryption, in particular the reliance on the entropy of the key space. As a consequence, one can decide once and for all if a given IPE scheme achieves this property, regardless of the distribution of the secret keys (and so of the context). We then consider some of the most popular constructions of IPE schemes and show that some of them achieve this property under very reasonable assumption (*e.g.* the Discrete Logarithm (DL) assumption) whereas some others do not. This highlights the fact that all IPE schemes are not equally suitable to construct HVE schemes.

5.1 Key Privacy

Definition 5 (Key privacy for IPE). *An IPE scheme has key privacy if no probabilistic polynomial time adversary $\mathcal{A}$ has a non-negligible success in the following game, $\mathrm{Exp}_{\mathcal{A}}^{\mathsf{sk}-priv}$:*

> *Setup: Run $(pp, \mathsf{pk}, \mathsf{mk}) \leftarrow \mathsf{setup}(1^{\lambda})$ and give pp, pk to $\mathcal{A}$.*
> *Query Phase 1: $\mathcal{A}$ submits queries $\mathbf{k} \in \mathbf{F}_p^n$ and gets $sk_{\mathbf{k}} \leftarrow \mathsf{keygen}(\mathsf{mk}, \mathbf{k})$*
> *Challenge: $\mathcal{A}$ submits a vector $\mathbf{y} \in \mathbf{F}_p^n$. The challenger chooses uniformly at random $\mathbf{u} \xleftarrow{\$} \{\mathbf{v} \in \mathrm{Vect}(\mathbf{y})^{\perp} : \mathsf{supp}(\mathbf{v}) \subset \mathsf{supp}(\mathbf{y})\}$ and gives $sk_{\mathbf{u}} \leftarrow \mathsf{keygen}(\mathsf{mk}, \mathbf{u})$ to $\mathcal{A}$.*
> *Query Phase 2: This phase is identical to Query Phase 1.*
> *Guess: $\mathcal{A}$ eventually outputs a vector $\mathbf{z} \in \mathbf{F}_p^n \setminus \mathrm{Vect}(\mathbf{y})$ such that $\mathsf{supp}(\mathbf{z}) \subset \mathsf{supp}(\mathbf{y})$ and wins if $\langle \mathbf{z}, \mathbf{u} \rangle = 0$.*

Intuitively, this notion states the hardness of finding a non-trivial vector $\mathbf{z}$ that is orthogonal to a vector $\mathbf{u}$, given only $\mathsf{sk_u}$. Obviously, we cannot reveal $\mathbf{u}$ to the adversary but we allow it to take part in the choice of $\mathbf{u}$ by submitting a vector $\mathbf{y}$ such that $\langle \mathbf{y}, \mathbf{u} \rangle = 0$. Very concretely, this models the fact that, in practice, the adversary may have some information about $\mathbf{u}$ since it knows (and may even choose) the pattern $\mathbf{y}$ that $\mathsf{sk_u}$ allows to detect. However, for some schemes, this should essentially be the only information leaking about $\mathbf{u}$ from $\mathsf{sk_u}$. As we do not want to reason in terms of entropy, we choose to define a computational goal (output $\mathbf{z} \in \mathbf{F}_p^n \setminus \mathrm{Vect}(\mathbf{y})$) which is much more convenient and yet sufficient to prove the adaptive security of our generic conversion. In particular, this allows us to evaluate this property for a given scheme independently of any application, as illustrated below.

5.2   Examples of Key Private IPE Schemes

Before showing how this new security notion can be used to prove adaptive security of our generic conversion, we show in this subsection that it is naturally satisfied by some of the most popular IPE schemes, namely those from [16] and [21]. More generally, the technique we use below to prove this fact tends to show that IPE schemes where the components of the vector $\mathbf{u}$ associated with $\mathsf{sk_u}$ appear as exponents in the latter key should satisfy this property. Intuitively, this stems from the fact that the vector $\mathbf{z}$ returned by the adversary provides a non-trivial relation between secret exponents, which can be used to solve a DL problem.

In the following, we use the same notations as in the original papers to facilitate verification of our claims without having to recall all the description of these schemes.

Katz-Sahai-Waters IPE Scheme. Our proof does not require the full knowledge of the IPE scheme of [16] but will only use the fact that a secret key $\mathsf{sk_u}$ associated with $\mathbf{u}$ contains two elements $K_{1,i} = g_p^{r_{1,i}} g_q^{f_1 u_i}$ and $K_{2,i} = g_p^{r_{2,i}} g_q^{f_2 u_i}$ where $r_{1,i}, r_{2,i}, f_1, f_2$ are random scalars. In our proof, the reduction will insert the DL challenge g_q^a in $g_q^{u_i}$, for $i \in \{i_1, i_2\}$, and generate all the other elements as in the regular use of the scheme. As $g_q^{u_i}$ is only involved in the elements $K_{1,i}$ and $K_{2,i}$ above we just have to explain how the reduction can proceed to construct them without knowing a. Actually, we only explain it for $K_{1,i}$ as $K_{2,i}$ has exactly the same structure.

More formally, our reduction is given a DL challenge $A = g_q^a$ in $\mathbb{G}_q$ and will interact with an adversary $\mathcal{A}$ against the key privacy of the IPE scheme to extract a.

In the security experiment, our reduction generates the secret key as usual and so is perfectly able to answer any query. The adversary will then eventually output a challenge $\mathbf{y}$ that will be managed as explained below.

But first we need to state some facts about $\mathbf{y}$. The goal of the adversary is to output $\mathbf{z}$ such that (1) $\mathsf{supp}(\mathbf{z}) \subset \mathsf{supp}(\mathbf{y})$ and (2) $\mathbf{y}$ and $\mathbf{z}$ are not colinear. There are therefore at least two indices $1 < i_1 < i_2 < n$ such that $y_{i_1} z_{i_2} \neq y_{i_2} z_{i_1}$, which implies that $\mathsf{supp}(y)$ contains at least one element. Actually, the latter set must contain at least two elements, otherwise z could not satisfy both (1) and (2). If y has only two non-zero components then a simple computation shows that the only possibility to meet (1) and (2) is when $u = 0$, which does not occur with probability greater than $\frac{1}{q}$.

So, any adversary succeeding with non-negligible probability must output a vector y with at least three non-zero components. Let i_3 be the index of one of them, different from i_1 and i_2 defined above.

Upon receiving y, our reduction chooses $s_{i_1}, s_{i_2} \in \mathbf{F}_q$ and implicitly sets

$$u_{i_1} = s_{i_1} + y_{i_2} a$$
$$u_{i_2} = s_{i_2} - y_{i_1} a.$$

For all $i \in [\![n]\!] \setminus \{i_1, i_2, i_3\}$, the reduction explicitly sets $u_i \overset{\$}{\leftarrow} \mathbf{F}_q$ if $i \in \mathsf{supp}(y)$ and $u_i = 0$ otherwise. Finally it defines

$$u_{i_3} = -\left(y_{i_1} s_{i_1} + y_{i_2} s_{i_2} + \sum_{\substack{i=1 \\ i \neq i_1, i_2, i_3}}^{n} y_i u_i\right).$$

Thus, we have $\langle y, u \rangle = 0$ and the distribution of u generated this way is exactly the uniform distribution over $\{v \in \mathsf{Vect}(y)^{\perp} : \mathsf{supp}(v) \subset \mathsf{supp}(y)\}$.

The reduction can then compute K_{1,i_1} as

$$K_{1,i_1} = g_p^{r_{i_1,1}} (g_q^{s_{i_1}} A^{y_{i_2}})^{f_1}$$

and proceeds similarly for K_{1,i_2}. All the other elements $K_{1,i}$ can be computed directly as the reduction knows all the involved exponents.

At some stage, the adversary returns a guess z. If the latter is valid, then we must have:

$$\sum_{i=1}^{n} (y_i - z_i) u_i = 0.$$

If we group the components in i_1 and i_2 together, we get

$$(y_{i_1} - z_{i_1}) u_{i_1} + (y_{i_2} - z_{i_2}) u_{i_2} = scal_1$$

where $scal_1$ is a *known* scalar. As $y_{i_1} u_{i_1} + y_{i_2} u_{i_2} = s_{i_1} + s_{i_2}$, we can actually write the previous equation as

$$z_{i_1} u_{i_1} + z_{i_2} u_{i_2} = scal_2$$

where $scal_2 = scal_1 - (s_{i_1} + s_{i_2})$ is still a known scalar. We thus have

$$z_{i_1}(s_{i_1} + y_{i_2} a) + z_{i_2}(s_{i_2} - y_{i_1} a) = scal_2.$$

which can be written as

$$z_{i_1} y_{i_2} a - z_{i_2} y_{i_1} a = scal_3$$

for a known scalar $scal_3$. This gives

$$a(z_{i_1} y_{i_2} - z_{i_2} y_{i_1}) = scal_3.$$

As the factor $(z_{i_1} y_{i_2} - z_{i_2} y_{i_1})$ is assumed to be different from zero, we can recover a as $scal_3(z_{i_1} y_{i_2} - z_{i_2} y_{i_1})^{-1}$, which concludes the proof. $\qquad\square$

Okamoto-Takashima IPE Scheme. We show that the previous proof adapts very well to the construction of Sect. 4 of [21]. Here, we use the additive notation of this paper. The setup of this scheme chooses a group $\mathbf{G}$ of order p and a generator $G \in \mathbf{G}$, so we use a DL challenge $A \in \mathbf{G}$ where implicitly $A = aG$ for some $a \in \mathbf{F}_p$ and the reduction sets the vector $\mathbf{u}$ as in the previous proof with respect to this challenge. This setup also generates a dual orthonormal basis among which the vectors $\mathbf{b}_{i_1}^*$ and $\mathbf{b}_{i_2}^*$ should be used to encode the positions i_1 and i_2 of the vector $\mathbf{u}$. These vectors are set as

$$\mathbf{b}_i^* = \sum_{j=1}^{4n+2} \vartheta_{i,j} (\overbrace{0, \ldots, 0}^{j-1}, G, \overbrace{0, \ldots, 0}^{4n+2-j}) \qquad \text{for } i = i_1, i_2$$

where $\vartheta_{i,j}$ are chosen by the reduction. The vector $\mathsf{sk_u}$ generated by KeyGen is a sum of vectors that can all be computed regularly by the reduction except the two vectors $\sigma u_{i_1} \mathbf{b}_{i_1}^*$ and $\sigma u_{i_2} \mathbf{b}_{i_2}^*$ where σ is chosen regularly by the reduction. Instead, the reduction computes these two vectors as

$$\sigma[s_{i_1} \mathbf{b}_{i_1}^* + y_{i_2} \sum_{j=1}^{4n+2} \vartheta_{i_1,j} (\overbrace{0, \ldots, 0}^{j-1}, A, \overbrace{0, \ldots, 0}^{4n+2-j})]$$

$$\text{and } \sigma[s_{i_2} \mathbf{b}_{i_2}^* + y_{i_1} \sum_{j=1}^{4n+2} \vartheta_{i_2,j} (\overbrace{0, \ldots, 0}^{j-1}, A, \overbrace{0, \ldots, 0}^{4n+2-j})]$$

and sums them together with the other ones to generate the secret key. The rest of the proof is identical to the previous one. $\qquad\square$

5.3   Examples of Non Key Private IPE Schemes

Here we show that some techniques used to build IPE with constant secret keys size in [10,20] do not allow key privacy, and in fact do not allow adaptive security using our conversion. In this case, one must use the KSW conversion. More specifically, this incompatibility stems from the fact that these constructions necessitate sharing the coordinates of the key vector inside its secret key *as scalars*.

We first show that such a scheme is not key private. In the key privacy game with $n \geq 3$, this allows for a winning strategy which consists in submitting $\mathbf{y} = (1, \ldots, 1)$, learning $\mathbf{u}$ from $\mathsf{sk_u}$ and solving the linear equation $u_1 z_1, \ldots, u_n z_n =$

0 whose space of solutions has at least dimension $3 - 1 = 2$ and allows to successfully return $\mathbf{z}$.   □

We now show that using our conversion on such IPE schemes can actually not give adaptively secure HVE schemes. Indeed, an adversary against the adaptive security game of the resulting HVE has the following strategy. It first issues a query with key $\mathbf{k} = (1, \ldots, 1)$ and receives a secret key $\mathsf{sk}_{\mathbf{k}}$ which is also a secret key for the vector $g(\mathbf{k}, \mathbf{r}) = (\mathbf{r}, \langle \mathbf{k}, \mathbf{r} \rangle)$ in the underlying IPE scheme and contains the coordinates of this vector as scalars. With overwhelming probability, r_1 and r_2 are distinct from each other and from 0. Thus an adversary can build the n long vectors $\mathbf{x}^1 = (\frac{r_2}{r_1}, \frac{r_1}{r_2}, 1, \ldots, 1)$ and $\mathbf{x}^0 = (2, \ldots, 2)$. As $\mathbf{k}$ does not match either of these vectors, our adversary can submit them as challenge vectors and receives $\mathbf{c} \leftarrow \mathsf{enc}_{\mathrm{IPE}}(\mathsf{pk}, f(\mathbf{x}^\beta))$ for some unknown $\beta \in \{0, 1\}$. However we have $\langle f(\mathbf{x}^1), g(\mathbf{k}, \mathbf{r}) \rangle = 0 \neq \langle f(\mathbf{x}^0), g(\mathbf{k}, \mathbf{r}) \rangle$ with overwhelming probability and running $\mathsf{dec}_{\mathrm{HVE}}(\mathsf{sk}_{\mathbf{k}}, \mathbf{c})$ which is the same as $\mathsf{dec}_{\mathrm{IPE}}(\mathsf{sk}_{\mathbf{k}}, \mathbf{c})$ returns β.   □

5.4   Security Result

We now have all we need to state the adaptive security of a HVE scheme resulting from our conversion applied to an adaptive IPE scheme.

Theorem 4. *The conversion in Fig. 4 transforms an adaptive* $\mathsf{IND} - \mathsf{CPA}$ *secure* $(n+1)$*-IPE scheme* $\mathcal{E}_{\mathrm{IPE}}$ *achieving key privacy into an adaptive* $\mathsf{IND} - \mathsf{CPA}$ *secure* n*-HVE scheme* $\mathcal{E}_{\mathrm{HVE}}$.

Proof. We use the same reduction as in the proof of selective security of Theorem 3, using an adversary $\mathcal{A}$ against the HVE scheme to attack the security of the IPE scheme. The core issue is still the discrepancy between the key queries restrictions of these two primitives. Concretely, compared to the selective proof, a problem occurs in the reduction if $\mathcal{A}$ submits challenge messages $\mathbf{x}^0, \mathbf{x}^1 \in \Sigma$ such that there exists a query for a pattern $\mathbf{k}$ in Query Phase 1 satisfying the two following equations:

$$\forall \alpha \in \{0, 1\}, \mathbb{1}_{\mathbf{k}} \mathbf{x}^\alpha - \mathbf{k} \neq \mathbf{0} \tag{4}$$

$$\exists \alpha \in \{0, 1\}, \langle \mathbb{1}_{\mathbf{k}} \mathbf{x}^\alpha - \mathbf{k}, \mathbf{r}^\alpha \rangle = 0 \text{ and } \langle \mathbb{1}_{\mathbf{k}} \mathbf{x}^{1-\alpha} - \mathbf{k}, \mathbf{r}^{1-\alpha} \rangle \neq 0 \tag{5}$$

For Query Phase 2, as the challenge messages have been committed, the arguments of the selective proof hold again and the reduction can always use $\mathcal{C}(\mathcal{E}_{\mathrm{IPE}})$ to obtain the appropriate secret keys except with negligible probability.

Our strategy will then be to consider two types of adversary $\mathcal{A}$. Type 1 adversaries are those that *do not* output challenge messages satisfying conditions (4) and (5) for a queried $\mathbf{k}$ in phase 1. The selective proof of Theorem 3 readily adapts in this case. Conversely, Type 2 adversaries output challenge messages satisfying those conditions and we show in the following that they can be used to attack the key privacy notion of the IPE scheme contradicting the hypothesis that the IPE scheme has key privacy.

We denote by q a bound on the number of key queries that the adversary $\mathcal{A}$ may submit before the challenge phase. Let $\mathcal{C}_{\mathsf{sk}}(\mathcal{E}_{\mathrm{IPE}})$ be the challenger of the key privacy game of $\mathcal{E}_{\mathrm{IPE}}$. We now explicit a reduction that uses $\mathcal{A}$ to solve the key privacy experiment.

Setup. The reduction simply forwards the public parameters and public key from $\mathcal{C}_{\mathsf{sk}}(\mathcal{E}_{\mathrm{IPE}})$ to the Type 2 adversary $\mathcal{A}$ of the $\mathcal{E}_{\mathrm{HVE}}$ security game. The reduction chooses uniformly at random an integer $m \in [\![q]\!]$.

Query phases 1 and 2. The reduction handles any key query $\mathbf{k}$ other than the mth one by choosing $\mathbf{r} \xleftarrow{\$} \mathbf{F}_p^n$ and submitting $g(\mathbf{k}, \mathbf{r})$ to $\mathcal{C}_{\mathsf{sk}}(\mathcal{E}_{\mathrm{IPE}})$ and forwarding the received secret key.

For the mth key query $\mathbf{k} \in \mathbf{F}_p^n$, the reduction chooses the vector $\mathbf{y} = (\mathbf{k}, -1)$ as the challenge vector for $\mathcal{C}_{\mathsf{sk}}(\mathcal{E}_{\mathrm{IPE}})$ and forwards the received secret key sk for some implicit vector $\mathbf{u} \in \mathbf{F}_p^{n+1}$ to the adversary. We show that this secret key is well distributed as there exists a well distributed vector $\mathbf{r}^{(\mathbf{u})}$ such that $u = g(\mathbf{k}, \mathbf{r}^{(\mathbf{u})})$.

By definition, $\mathbf{u}$ is a vector from $\mathrm{Vect}(\mathbf{y})^{\perp}$ with $\mathsf{supp}(\mathbf{u}) \subset \mathsf{supp}(\mathbf{y})$. Let us consider a vector $\mathbf{r}^{(\mathbf{u})} \in \mathbb{F}_p^n$ such that $r_i^{(\mathbf{u})} = u_i$ for all $i \in \mathsf{supp}(\mathbf{k})$, and random values elsewhere. As $\langle \mathbf{y}, \mathbf{u} \rangle = 0$ and $y_{n+1} = -1$, this means that $u_{n+1} = \langle \mathbf{k}, \mathbf{r}^{(\mathbf{u})} \rangle$ and we have indeed $u = g(\mathbf{k}, \mathbf{r}^{(\mathbf{u})})$. Finally, the distribution of $\mathbf{u}$ as defined in the key privacy experiment implies that $\mathbf{r}^{(\mathbf{u})}$ (and so the associate secret key) is well distributed.

Challenge. When the adversary submits the challenge messages $\mathbf{x}^0, \mathbf{x}^1 \in \Sigma^n$, the reduction checks if the mth key query satisfies (4) and (5) for an $\alpha \in \{0, 1\}$. If this is the case, the reduction returns $\mathbf{z} = (\mathbb{1}_{\mathbf{k}} \mathbf{x}^\alpha, -1)$ otherwise, it returns $\perp$.

For a Type 2 adversary, this vector $\mathbf{z}$ is indeed a valid answer in the key privacy security game because:

- $\mathsf{supp}(\mathbf{z}) \subset \mathsf{supp}(\mathbf{y})$ by construction.
- $z_{n+1} = y_{n+1} = -1$ but $\mathbf{z} \neq \mathbf{y}$ because of (4), which means that these two vectors are not colinear.
- $\langle \mathbf{z}, \mathbf{u} \rangle = \langle f(\mathbf{x}^\alpha), g(\mathbf{k}, \mathbf{r}^{\mathbf{u}}) \rangle = 0$ because of (5).

Therefore, any type 2 adversary against the adaptive $\mathsf{IND} - \mathsf{CPA}$ security of the HVE scheme can be converted into an adversary against the key privacy of the IPE scheme provided that the guess on m is valid, which occurs with probability at least $\frac{1}{q}$. $\qquad\qquad\qquad\qquad\qquad\qquad\qquad\qquad\qquad\qquad\square$

6   Consequences

In this section we draw the practical consequences of our generic conversions which allows to leverage the remarkable results obtained for Inner Product Encryption. The most significant results regarding complexity and security are presented in Fig. 5. Among other things, the latter shows that our conversions lead to the first SEPM schemes with adaptive security under standard assumptions, without significant performance loss compared to the underlying IPE scheme. In particular, starting from the IPE scheme of [10, Subsection 3.4], we obtain, under the DLIN assumption, an adaptively secure SEPM scheme whose test complexity does not depend on the length of the fragment or the pattern.

As a first example illustrating our conversion, we choose to start from [11] which is, to our knowledge, the only adaptively secure HVE scheme in the literature. At first glance, it seems to yield the SEPM scheme with the lowest number of elements in the ciphertext but we stress that one cannot directly compare this scheme with others as it is defined over bilinear groups of composite orders which are larger and lead to slow implementations compared to prime order bilinear groups. Conversion from one setting to another is possible (see e.g. [14,18]) but has a great impact on the number of group elements.

We showed in Subsect. 5.2 that the IPE scheme from [21] satisfies our key privacy property and can therefore be converted using either the KSW conversion (Fig. 2) or our shorter conversion (Fig. 4). We highlight the differences between the schemes resulting from these conversions in the next two columns of Fig. 5 and show that our conversion gives the adaptively secure SEPM scheme with the most succinct ciphertext in prime order groups. Moreover, it shows that our new IPE to HVE conversion decreases complexity by a factor up to 4 compared to the KSW conversion.

Our last example uses the IPE scheme from [10]. We use the KSW conversion of Fig. 2 to get an HVE as the scheme does not have the key privacy property. This yields the adaptively secure SEPM scheme with the most compact public key. Moreover, decryption time in one position is constant.

For completeness, Fig. 5 also recalls the features of the three most recent SEPM schemes. We stress that the comparison is not very meaningful as those schemes only achieved selective security under non-standard assumptions, something that we wanted to avoid with our conversions.

Notations. In Fig. 5, we assume fragments of size $2d$ (allowing to handle patterns of length up to $d+1$) and plaintexts are arbitrary long strings of characters from an alphabet of size $|\Sigma|$. To retain legibility of the table, we only keep the terms of highest order in d and thus make some minor approximations in our complexity evaluation.

- Our first two rows indicate the generic transformations we apply.
- PK indicates the number of group elements in the public key to support fragments of size $2d$.
- CT is the number of group elements to encrypt one element from Σ. Ciphertext size is linear in the size of the encrypted string: to obtain the cost for a string of n elements, one must multiply the CT line by n.
- SK_k is the number of group elements in the secret key allowing to search a pattern k at a given position within any fragment.

	Existing SEPM schemes			New SEPM schemes built by conversions			
	[3, sec. 3]	[8, sec. 4.3]	[8, sec. 4.4]	[11]	[21, sec. 4.2]	[21, sec. 4.2]	[10, sec. 3.4]
IPE→HVE					KSW (Fig. 2)	Ours (Fig. 4)	KSW (Fig. 2)
HVE→SEPM				Ours (Fig. 1)	Ours (Fig. 1)	Ours (Fig. 1)	Ours (Fig. 1)
PK	$2d \cdot |\Sigma|$	$4d$	$6d$	$2d \cdot |\Sigma|$	$64d^2$	$16d^2$	$40d$
CT	4	2	4	2	16	8	20
SK$_\mathbf{k}$	2	2	3	len($\mathbf{k}$)	$16d$	$8d$	8
TEST	2	2	3	len($\mathbf{k}$)	$16d$	$8d$	8
Group Order	Prime	Prime	Prime	Composite	Prime	Prime	Prime
Security	Selective	Selective	Selective	**Adaptive**	**Adaptive**	**Adaptive**	**Adaptive**
Assumption	i-GDH	i-GDH	EXDH	CSD, CDDH	**DLIN**	**DLIN**	**DLIN**

Fig. 5. Comparison table of SEPM schemes (*see Notations above*)

- TEST refers to the number of pairings necessary to test the presence of a pattern **k** at a given position.

We refer to the original papers for a definition of the computational assumptions underlying their security.

Acknowledgments. The work of the second author was supported by the French ANR SANGRIA project (ANR-21-CE39-0006) and the French PEPR Cybersécurité SecureCompute project (ANR-22-PECY-0003). The third author is grateful for the support of the ANR through project ANR-19-CE39-0011-04 PRESTO and project ANR-18-CE-39-0019-02 MobiS5.

References

1. Abdalla, M., et al.: Searchable encryption revisited: consistency properties, relation to anonymous IBE, and extensions. J. Cryptol. **21**(3), 350–391 (2008)
2. Agrawal, S., Maitra, M., Vempati, N.S., Yamada, S.: Functional encryption for Turing machines with dynamic bounded collusion from LWE. In: Malkin, T., Peikert, C. (eds.) CRYPTO 2021. LNCS, vol. 12828, pp. 239–269. Springer, Cham (2021). https://doi.org/10.1007/978-3-030-84259-8_9
3. Bkakria, A., Cuppens, N., Cuppens, F.: Privacy-preserving pattern matching on encrypted data. In: Moriai, S., Wang, H. (eds.) ASIACRYPT 2020, Part II. LNCS, vol. 12492, pp. 191–220. Springer, Cham (2020). https://doi.org/10.1007/978-3-030-64834-3_7
4. Boneh, D., Di Crescenzo, G., Ostrovsky, R., Persiano, G.: Public key encryption with keyword search. In: Cachin, C., Camenisch, J.L. (eds.) EUROCRYPT 2004. LNCS, vol. 3027, pp. 506–522. Springer, Heidelberg (2004). https://doi.org/10.1007/978-3-540-24676-3_30
5. Boneh, D., Raghunathan, A., Segev, G.: Function-private identity-based encryption: hiding the function in functional encryption. In: Canetti, R., Garay, J.A. (eds.) CRYPTO 2013, Part II. LNCS, vol. 8043, pp. 461–478. Springer, Heidelberg (2013). https://doi.org/10.1007/978-3-642-40084-1_26

6. Boneh, D., Sahai, A., Waters, B.: Functional encryption: definitions and challenges. In: Ishai, Y. (ed.) TCC 2011. LNCS, vol. 6597, pp. 253–273. Springer, Heidelberg (2011). https://doi.org/10.1007/978-3-642-19571-6_16

7. Boneh, D., Waters, B.: Conjunctive, subset, and range queries on encrypted data. In: Vadhan, S.P. (ed.) TCC 2007. LNCS, vol. 4392, pp. 535–554. Springer, Heidelberg (2007). https://doi.org/10.1007/978-3-540-70936-7_29

8. Bouscatié, É., Castagnos, G., Sanders, O.: Public key encryption with flexible pattern matching. In: Tibouchi, M., Wang, H. (eds.) ASIACRYPT 2021. LNCS, vol. 13093, pp. 342–370. Springer, Cham (2021). https://doi.org/10.1007/978-3-030-92068-5_12

9. Chase, M., Shen, E.: Substring-searchable symmetric encryption. PoPETs **2015**(2), 263–281 (2015)

10. Chen, J., Gong, J., Wee, H.: Improved inner-product encryption with adaptive security and full attribute-hiding. In: Peyrin, T., Galbraith, S. (eds.) ASIACRYPT 2018, Part II. LNCS, vol. 11273, pp. 673–702. Springer, Cham (2018). https://doi.org/10.1007/978-3-030-03329-3_23

11. De Caro, A., Iovino, V., Persiano, G.: Fully secure hidden vector encryption. In: Abdalla, M., Lange, T. (eds.) Pairing 2012. LNCS, vol. 7708, pp. 102–121. Springer, Heidelberg (2013). https://doi.org/10.1007/978-3-642-36334-4_7

12. Demertzis, I., Papadopoulos, D., Papamanthou, C.: Searchable encryption with optimal locality: achieving sublogarithmic read efficiency. In: Shacham, H., Boldyreva, A. (eds.) CRYPTO 2018, Part I. LNCS, vol. 10991, pp. 371–406. Springer, Cham (2018). https://doi.org/10.1007/978-3-319-96884-1_13

13. Desmoulins, N., Fouque, P.-A., Onete, C., Sanders, O.: Pattern matching on encrypted streams. In: Peyrin, T., Galbraith, S. (eds.) ASIACRYPT 2018, Part I. LNCS, vol. 11272, pp. 121–148. Springer, Cham (2018). https://doi.org/10.1007/978-3-030-03326-2_5

14. Freeman, D.M.: Converting pairing-based cryptosystems from composite-order groups to prime-order groups. In: Gilbert, H. (ed.) EUROCRYPT 2010. LNCS, vol. 6110, pp. 44–61. Springer, Heidelberg (2010). https://doi.org/10.1007/978-3-642-13190-5_3

15. Jain, A., Lin, H., Sahai, A.: Indistinguishability obfuscation from well-founded assumptions. In: Proceedings of the 53rd Annual ACM SIGACT Symposium on Theory of Computing, STOC 2021, pp. 60–73. Association for Computing Machinery, New York (2021)

16. Katz, J., Sahai, A., Waters, B.: Predicate encryption supporting disjunctions, polynomial equations, and inner products. In: Smart, N. (ed.) EUROCRYPT 2008. LNCS, vol. 4965, pp. 146–162. Springer, Heidelberg (2008). https://doi.org/10.1007/978-3-540-78967-3_9

17. Leontiadis, I., Li, M.: Storage efficient substring searchable symmetric encryption. In: Proceedings of the 6th International Workshop on Security in Cloud Computing, SCC '18, pp. 3–13. Association for Computing Machinery (2018)

18. Lewko, A.: Tools for simulating features of composite order bilinear groups in the prime order setting. In: Pointcheval, D., Johansson, T. (eds.) EUROCRYPT 2012. LNCS, vol. 7237, pp. 318–335. Springer, Heidelberg (2012). https://doi.org/10.1007/978-3-642-29011-4_20

19. Okamoto, T., Takashima, K.: Fully secure functional encryption with general relations from the decisional linear assumption. In: Rabin, T. (ed.) CRYPTO 2010. LNCS, vol. 6223, pp. 191–208. Springer, Heidelberg (2010). https://doi.org/10.1007/978-3-642-14623-7_11

20. Okamoto, T., Takashima, K.: Achieving short ciphertexts or short secret-keys for adaptively secure general inner-product encryption. In: Lin, D., Tsudik, G., Wang, X. (eds.) CANS 2011. LNCS, vol. 7092, pp. 138–159. Springer, Heidelberg (2011). https://doi.org/10.1007/978-3-642-25513-7_11

21. Okamoto, T., Takashima, K.: Adaptively attribute-hiding (hierarchical) inner product encryption. In: Pointcheval, D., Johansson, T. (eds.) EUROCRYPT 2012. LNCS, vol. 7237, pp. 591–608. Springer, Heidelberg (2012). https://doi.org/10.1007/978-3-642-29011-4_35

22. Okamoto, T., Takashima, K.: Fully secure unbounded inner-product and attribute-based encryption. In: Wang, X., Sako, K. (eds.) ASIACRYPT 2012. LNCS, vol. 7658, pp. 349–366. Springer, Heidelberg (2012). https://doi.org/10.1007/978-3-642-34961-4_22

23. Ramanna, S.C.: More efficient constructions for inner-product encryption. In: Manulis, M., Sadeghi, A.-R., Schneider, S. (eds.) ACNS 2016. LNCS, vol. 9696, pp. 231–248. Springer, Cham (2016). https://doi.org/10.1007/978-3-319-39555-5_13

24. Sherry, J., Lan, C., Popa, R.A., Ratnasamy, S.: Blindbox: deep packet inspection over encrypted traffic. In: Uhlig, S., Maennel, O., Karp, B., Padhye, J. (eds.) SIGCOMM 2015, pp. 213–226 (2015)

Author Index

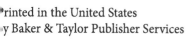
Printed in the United States
by Baker & Taylor Publisher Services